THE WORLD'S LEADING AUTOGRAPH PRICING AUTHORITY

THE SANDERS AUTOGRAPH PRICE GUIDE

7th edition

D1548071

Visit us online
at www.SandersPriceGuide.com
or through our publisher at
www.AutographMagazine.com

THE WORLD'S LEADING AUTOGRAPH PRICING AUTHORITY

THE SANDERS AUTOGRAPH PRICE GUIDE

7th edition

DR. RICHARD SAFFRO

Published by
Autograph Magazine
Autograph Media

The Sanders Autograph Price Guide
7th Edition

Author: Dr. Richard Saffro

Editors: Steven Cyrkin, Tamara Berger, Nicole LeMaster & Carina Calhoun

Publisher:
Autograph Magazine imprint/Autograph Media Inc.
P.O. Box 25559
Santa Ana, CA 92799
Ph: 800.996.3977 or 714.263.3560 Intl.
www.autographmagazine.com
email: sanders@autographmagazine.com

Cover Design: Kenny Boyer & Steven Cyrkin

Interior Design & Layout: Type-F

Printed & Bound in the United States

10 9 8 7 6 5 4 3 2 1
7th Edition
Editions 1 through 6 published by Alexander Books as *The Sanders Price Guide to Autographs*

ISBN: 978-0-615-26462-2

Bibliography:
Author: Saffro, Richard, 1950-

We'd like to thank the following companies for the autographs they allowed us to use on the front cover:
1.   Profiles in History: Abraham Lincoln photograph
2.   Julien's Auctions: Thomas Edison signature
3.   Heritage Auctions: Babe Ruth baseball
4.   Markus Brandes: Michael Schumacher photo
5.   RRAUCTION: Neil Armstrong & John Wayne
6.   Sotheby's & SCP: Mickey Mantle 1958 World Series bat
7.   Signed, Sealed, Delivered: Elvis Presley photo

Table of Contents

Autograph Prices, Non-Sports

Sports Autograph Prices

Introduction

Welcome to the 7th Edition of *The Sanders Autograph Price Guide*. This edition represents over two years of intense work, meant to provide you with the most accurate and reliable autograph pricing information. Whether you're a sophisticated autograph dealer or a novice collector, the *Sanders Guide* will be the autograph reference book you use the most.

The prices are derived by averaging the prices of autographed items that have been listed or sold by reputable dealers and auction houses. A few prices were obtained from eBay auctions, but only when I was certain that the items were authentic, or were sold by reputable autograph dealers.

Creating the *Sanders Guide* required the compilation of autograph pricing from multiple sources. To acknowledge every source would be impossible, but I'd like to acknowledge some of our valuable contributors:

Alexander Autographs
Dr. Richard Bagdasarian
David M. Beach
Markus Brandes Autographs
Gary Combs Autographs
Dr. James T. Currie
Christie's
EAC Gallery
Early American History Auctions
Roger Epperson: Signed, Sealed, Delivered
Gil Griggs, Signature House
Roger Gross Ltd.
Heritage Auction Galleries
Ronald B. Keurajian
Stuart Lutz, Stuart Lutz Historical Documents
Mastro Auctions
Matthew Bennett Auctions
Brandon Mysinger
Professional Sports Authenticator's *Sports Market Report*
R&R Enterprises Autograph Auctions
Steven Raab, The Raab Collection
John Reznikoff, University Archives
Brad Shafran, Shafran Collectibles
RM Smythe & Company, Inc.

Sotheby's
Scott J. Winslow Associates, Inc.

I'd also like to thank the innumerable smaller auction houses, and the many *Sanders Guide* readers who sent me names we missed in prior editions, prices and corrections. Please keep letting me know how to make the *Sanders Guide* better at the email address below.

I am indebted to each and every one of you. Without your contributions, creating the 7th Edition of *The Sanders Autograph Price Guide* would have been impossible.

Dr. Richard Saffro

Email: sandersguide@gmail.com

Chapter 1

Authentication

By John Reznikoff and Herman Darvick

"How do you know it's real?"

That's the question you often hear when you show a friend an autograph you just bought. If it's a movie star or baseball player's penmanship you're displaying, the inquiry is based on the common knowledge that celebrities usually have people who handle their mail, and it can be difficult to get a celebrity to sign in person, unless they're at a signing event. On the other hand, if you're holding a document bearing the signature "G. Washington," the question of authenticity is based on common belief, though incorrect, that those kinds of documents are all in museums or the National Archives, so you couldn't possibly have one. One collector was dumbfounded when he showed a framed Napoleon document to his new neighbor, who commented, "Can you imagine what it would be worth if it were real?"

Few autographs can only be found in museums, libraries or archives; Columbus and Shakespeare are two examples. There's even a document in Berlin's Egyptian Museum supposedly signed by Cleopatra. The autograph of almost every famous person of the past 500 years can be obtained for a price. But how *do* you know it is real?

The most important rule is to *know the seller*. Up until the 1990s, if collectors wanted to buy an autographed item, they would have to purchase it at a major auction house such as Christie's or Sotheby's, from an autograph dealer's printed catalog, or at the dealer's place of business or an autograph show. The Universal Autograph Collectors Club (U.A.C.C.) has held shows across the U.S.A., as well as England and Holland, since the late 1960s. Forty years ago there were less than two dozen full-time autograph dealers worldwide. Mary Benjamin and Charles Hamilton were the leaders of the autograph industry at that time. Miss Benjamin's father had established Walter R. Benjamin Autographs in 1887. Hamilton opened a store in Manhattan in 1953 and began issuing price lists. 10 years later,

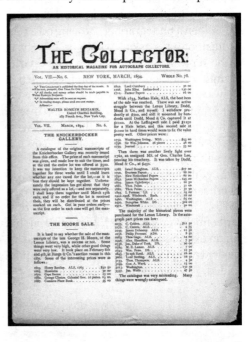

he founded the world's first autograph auction house "that will handle only material it can expertize [sic] and unconditionally guarantee," wrote Hamilton in his first auction catalog, "instead of asking the purchaser to gamble on an 'as is' hodgepodge of books and autographs." Amazing as it may seem, auction houses selling autographs on a regular basis at the time were offering them as-is. In Hamilton's Terms of Sale, term one was "All autographs listed in this catalog are unconditionally guaranteed to be genuine."

Hamilton invented the word philography, meaning autograph collecting, from the Greek words philos (loving) and graphos (something drawn or written). He felt that since a stamp collector was a philatelist and a coin collector was a numismatist, there ought to be a term for an autograph collector. He chose philographer, because philographist might be confused with philatelist. Philography and philographer are now in the dictionary.

When a philographer showing off a new acquisition was asked where he bought it, if the reply was Mary Benjamin or Charles Hamilton, authenticity was unquestioned. If they said it was real, it was real. There were other autograph dealers in the 1960s with indisputable reputations. But there were also a few unscrupulous dealers. "You can have this Richard Nixon for $85 as is, or for $125 with a guarantee of authenticity," was overheard at a dealer's booth at show in the 1970s. The dealer was either not sure of the authenticity or suspected it wasn't real, but for an extra $40, he'd guarantee it. The same dealer trying to seal the deal on another item added, "If it turns out it's not real, you can

*White House letter signed
"Richard Nixon" by a secretary*

return it and I'll refund your money." A money-back guarantee of authenticity is an absolute necessity in all sales, but saying those words to a collector revealed the dealer's uncertainty of authenticity. Isn't he sure? In each case, the prospective customer wasn't offended by the dealer's terms. But he should have been.

It is of the utmost importance to know the dealer you are buying an autograph from. With the arrival of the Internet and eBay, buying and selling autographs has become much easier. But the downside is, it's become just as easy to sell forgeries, facsimiles and secretarially and Autopen signed autographs represented as authentic.

During the 1990s the FBI initiated an investigation into the sports memorabilia market, where forgeries flourished. Aptly called Operation Foul Ball, 14 people in five states either forging or distributing forgeries were convicted. A follow-up FBI investigation, Operation Bullpen, resulted in another 62 convictions. Major League Baseball then began its own memorabilia authentication program, affixing uniquely numbered holograms to each item they sold. Companies which witness athlete signings have similar programs. But what about non-athlete autographs?

Forged Mother Teresa signed baseball uncovered by the FBI

The FBI reported that "the subjects convicted in this investigation had all used the story line that their celebrity signed pictures and posters were obtained by 'runners'. Runners are people who happen to catch a celebrity at an event and obtain a signed picture there. Most of the convicted subjects obtained one or two signatures that way and then forged many more, claiming they were from the meeting. All of the convicted subjects noted that it was impossible to make a living as a runner. The amount of time needed to get the couple of signatures a person needs does not generate an adequate income. The overwhelming number of celebrity signed photographs and posters being sold throughout the world are sold under this pretense; this investigation would suggest they are almost all forged." What a frightening conclusion. Even if a photograph of the signing accompanied the signed item, how do you know it was the item you purchased that was being signed? How can a collector be sure of authenticity?

Autograph dealer Thomas F. Madigan (1890-1936) grew up in his father's New York

A CATALOGUE OF
Autographs

With a Few Brief Extracts from
"WORD SHADOWS OF THE GREAT"

☙

THOMAS F. MADIGAN
2 East 54th St., corner Fifth Ave.
NEW YORK, N. Y.
Telephone: Wickersham 1912-3

bookshop and learned the trade from him. In his 1930 book, *Word Shadows of the Great/The Lure of Autograph Collecting,* Madigan wrote, "The collector who deals with a competent and responsible dealer need have no fear. He is assured of adequate protection; and nowadays, with a rising autograph market, this is a very important kind of insurance."

How do you know which dealers are competent and responsible? Founded in 1965, the U.A.C.C. established a Registered Dealers program in the late 1990s. Each dealer applying must fill out a lengthy application, with customer and dealer references, providing a mailing as well as a physical address, and other information a prospective buyer of an autograph would consider important in determining competency and responsibility. This does not mean that someone selling autographs who is not a U.A.C.C. Registered Dealer should be avoided. There are reputable dealers who choose not to join the U.A.C.C., which is a requirement of the Registered Dealer program. And there are honest collectors who sell autographs from their personal collections.

Caveat emptor: let the buyer beware. Every autograph you buy must come with a clearly written money-back guarantee of authenticity. What if it is proven that the autograph is not real? If you do not have that written guarantee, you are out of luck. The independent authentication service that issued the Letter or Certificate of Authenticity that may have accompanied the autograph does not guarantee its authenticity; it simply renders an opinion. If you researched the dealer before buying the autograph, you would have the seller's written and signed statement guaranteeing the authenticity of the autograph, based on years of experience, with an impeccable reputation for selling authentic autographs. Even the most experienced dealer can occasionally make a mistake but they stand behind their guarantee 100-percent and will refund your purchase price if they do. Dealers know that a good reputation is difficult to earn, but easy to lose. If a dealer refuses to give you a written, money-back guarantee, it is proof-positive that the dealer is not sure of its authenticity. Nothing the dealer can tell you should result in your buying the autograph. Producer Samuel Goldwyn said it best: "An oral guarantee isn't worth the paper it's written on." It's the same with autograph sales.

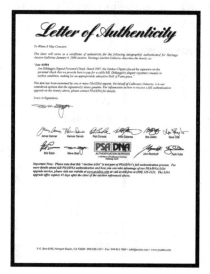 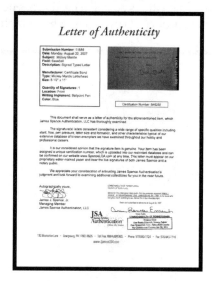

In 1991 a Honus Wagner baseball card sold at auction for $451,000 — a record back then. This kicked off the boom market of sports collectibles and autographs. Collectors of sports cards became concerned. Couldn't someone using the right printing press and ink counterfeit an old baseball card? Professional Sports Authenticator (PSA) was established in 1991 to authenticate and grade sports cards; a market where condition is of the utmost importance in determining value. Autograph prices saw tremendous increases in the 1990s, leading to a commensurate increase in forgeries in all areas of the autograph market. In 1998, PSA initiated PSA/DNA, the first major third-party autograph authentication company. Today PSA/DNA and JSA (James Spence Authentication) are the leading third-party sports authentication services (Spence was one of the original experts at PSA/DNA). Each authenticates sports and non-sports autographs and have experts in all autograph collecting areas, but their websites, www.psadna.com and www.spenceloa.com, only have images of sports autographs, their specialty. Each company has representatives at major sports shows. The need for a third-party autograph authentication company not specializing in sports resulted in the formation in 2006 of PASS-CO, the Professional Authentication Services & Standards Co., which provides authentications for historical autographs and does not authenticate modern material in the areas of sports and movie stars.

So, all forgeries are worthless, right? Wrong. Believe it or not, it depends on the forger. Robert Spring (1813-1876) was an expert forger. He was selling books in Philadelphia when he realized that he did very well at selling the few American historical autographs that he would come across. He first began forging signatures, then checks and letters, using contemporary paper, sometimes from the blank leaves of 18th century books and pamphlets. He was an expert at forging George Washington and other colonial autographs. During the Civil War, Spring expanded his market to England and Canada where there was less familiarity with American autographs. When requests came for autographs of Confederate leaders, Spring obliged. He was successful because collectors did not have authentic examples with which to compare his forgeries. Joseph Cosey (1887-1950) also forged American historical documents. Lincoln legal briefs and Benjamin Franklin pay warrants were his specialty. The Library of Congress was one of his many unsuspecting customers. Both Spring and Cosey used the correct paper and ink color, making it difficult for 19th and 20th century collectors to spot their forgeries. Documents forged by Spring and Cosey are collected and have sold for in excess of $500.

Most autograph collectors are not autograph experts. They have to rely on the expertise of the seller, the reputable autograph dealer. But once in a while, maybe in a used bookstore or at a flea market, you have the chance to add an item to your collection. What if you're offered an autograph album signed by members of the 37th Congress (1861-1863)? The first page is signed "Abraham Lincoln" in dark brown fountain pen ink. Over 50 Senators and Representatives have signed pages in the album; many of them included the state they represented. It looks real. It is. The autograph album is authentic. It was signed during the Civil War — but it was not signed by Lincoln. It looks like Lincoln's signature, but it was not signed by

Forgery of a George Washington check by Robert Spring

him. President Lincoln, with very few exceptions, only signed his name in full on documents. On letters and in notes and in autograph albums, Lincoln always signed "A. Lincoln." And Waterman didn't introduce the fountain pen until 1884. The other signatures in the album were signed with metal nibbed pens, which had replaced the quill in the early 19th century and were still being used in the 1860s. The Lincoln signature was forged. Knowledge of writing instruments, ink and paper, plus characteristics of an authentic autograph is just part of a reputable dealer's background.

The popularity of the autograph album brings up another problem for collectors. No one has ever seen an album without blank pages, whether it is signed by politicians, movie stars, or baseball players. A forger can easily add a signature to a blank page. Autographs of Robert F. Kennedy, Clark Gable or Lou Gehrig would greatly increase the value of an autograph album. Knowledge of the type of paper used in these albums would be of no help because the album itself is authentic. What may help you is knowledge of the instrument used to sign the autograph. Kennedy died before roller ball pens were used, Gable before flair pens, and Gehrig before ballpoint pens were introduced. Sometimes the paper written upon can uncover a forger. In the 1980s, a JFK handwritten and signed "Ask not..." quote penned on official White House stationery looked authentic and the person offering it for sale was a Kennedy family friend. The "1977" watermark was the forger's downfall.

Then there are multi-signed letters and documents. Members of committees of the Continental Congress would frequently sign letters concerning information desired or reports requested. They would also sign documents. It was not unusual for a forger to add a signature to a letter or document already signed by three or four statesmen. The added signature, probably penned a century later, resembles an authentic example. The key to spotting an added forgery is usually the ink used. Spreading of modern ink on old paper is clearly seen, especially with a microscope. Forgers tend to sign slowly with more of the ink seeping into the old paper. Signatures have also been forged on previously unsigned documents, such as 18th and 19th century receipts and account pages.

Not only are signatures added, but dates are as well. An undated "J. A. Garfield" signed card would be worth much more if it were dated during his presidential term. It would be easy to add "March 10, 1881," seemingly in Garfield's hand. While it is true that Garfield usually signed autographs "J. A. Garfield," almost all his presidential autographs for collectors were signed as "James A. Garfield." Or how about adding "8/9/74" to a White House card signed by Gerald R. Ford? That was the day Nixon resigned and Ford was sworn in. This signed card exists. While the formation of the numbers resembled Ford's handwriting, doubt arose about the date's authenticity when it was noticed that the slant of the two slashes in the date differed from the slant of Ford's signature.

Several forensic devices have recently been introduced into the world of authenticating. They are perfect additions to the arsenal of tools used by reputable dealers in their quest for proper identification of forgeries. One tool is the ProScope. Anyone who watches the *CSI* TV series will recognize this device used to gather evidence at crime scenes. It is a handheld microscope capable of up to a 200X magnification that can be viewed and manipulated on a computer screen. It's very effective for identifying ink

and paper types, as well as exposing characteristics associated with forgery, such as hesitation, feathering of ink, and puddling of ink. Another modern machine which has revolutionized certain types of authentication is the Video Spectral Comparator (VSC4). It costs about $30,000 and is not available to the general public for fear that it would fall into the wrong hands. Right now only three exist in the trade, at PSA/DNA, JSA, and one here, at University Archives. This machine has the ability to do many of the things the ProScope can, and more. You can superimpose questioned signatures on top of or next to known examples and place it on a computer screen for further study or manipulation. It also has the ability to properly enlarge and photograph watermarks and paper characteristics with a special underlighting technique. Perhaps most impressive is the ability to separate ink types by breaking down their spectral range. No two inks are exactly alike. If one ink that looks just like another to the naked eye is applied to a document, the VSC4 can identify the different inks. If words are completely obliterated by over-crossing, the VSC4 can read what lies beneath. It can also electrostatically read the impressions left by what was written on a page above a questioned document. But while the machine is very useful, it does not replace the talent of a trained eye and a good set of known genuine examples. The applications here are many fold, but again never replace the talent of a trained eye and a good set of known examples. When the Gerald R. Ford "dated' White House card was placed under the VSC4, it was easy to see that different inks were used to sign the autograph and date. There was no doubt as to the authenticity of the signature. However, the added date, which would have greatly increased the value of the signed White House card, was forged.

Another problem autograph collectors face is an authentic "wrong" signature. One James Madison (1749-1812) was a Bishop in Virginia. His cousin, also a Virginian, was the fourth U.S. President (1751-1836). A letter written by James Madison from Virginia in 1800 could have been written by either man. New Jerseyian John Hart was a Signer of the Declaration of Independence, but there were at least five John Harts in New Jersey in the 1770s. In fact, John De Hart, who wasn't a Signer, and John Hart each represented New Jersey in the Continental Congress in 1776. Their signatures are often confused by collectors.

Autographs and letters signed by Theodore

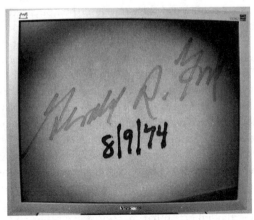

Video Spectral Comparator 4

Roosevelt are frequently offered for sale on eBay. A 1922 typed letter signed by "ex-President Theodore Roosevelt" was offered on eBay a few years ago. Familiarity with the appearance of an authentic President Theodore Roosevelt signature made it easy to tell that the signature was signed by someone else. Even if the potential buyer had never seen an authentic signature, the 1922 date revealed that it could not have been signed by the 26th President, since he died in 1919. It wasn't a forgery. It was signed by his son and namesake. You'd assume that the seller would have done the basic research, but in many cases they don't. It's never a good practice to make assumptions.

Perhaps the most common mistaken identity autograph collectors must face is that of Winston Churchill. If you bought an autograph of Churchill with a money-back guarantee that it was authentic, unless you bought it from a reputable dealer, you may have a problem. Which Winston Churchill did you buy? The British Prime Minister (1874-1965) or the American novelist (1871-1947)? The two knew of each other's existence. Since the American Churchill was already well-known for his novels before his British namesake became famous, the future British Prime Minister wrote to the American author and informed him that he would always use his middle name Spencer or initial S when writing, so as not to confuse prospective readers of their works. It also helps autograph collectors. The novelist didn't have a middle name. The statesman always signed "W.S. Churchill" or "Winston S. Churchill," the author simply signed as, "Winston Churchill." And, of course, their handwriting was different.

American Author Winston Churchill

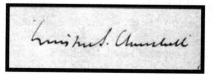

British Prime Minister Winston S. Churchill

At times, facsimiles of authentic documents and letters fool collectors. You would be surprised how many people think they own an authentic Declaration of Independence when they actually own one of the souvenirs on brown parchment sold at National Historic Sites. After Harry S. Truman left the White House, he received many letters wishing him well. He replied by handwriting a letter and making facsimile copies, which he sent out to well-wishers. Truman did the same after he appeared on the *Person to Person* TV show in 1955. Herbert Hoover sent facsimile handwritten letters of thanks for birthday wishes. Sir Winston Churchill also replied to letters with facsimile handwritten thank you notes. The easiest way to recognize these facsimiles is that they are not addressed to anyone.

Two facsimiles frequently thought to be authentic by their owners are the King George V handwritten letter welcoming U.S. soldiers in April 1918, and the handwritten dedication to U.S. soldiers in Ulysses S. Grant's autobiography. In 1918, every soldier, upon landing in England, was given an envelope with these words on it, "A Message to You from His Majesty King George." Inside was a facsimile handwritten letter on red crested Windsor Castle stationery beginning "Soldiers of the United States, the people of the British Isles welcome you." A few years ago, an elderly gentleman offered one to an autograph dealer, saying that it was given to him by his father, who was next to King George V when he gave it to General Pershing, who, in turn, gave it to his father saying, "You can keep this, kid." The dealer didn't have the heart to tell him the true story, and simply said, "It's worth more to you than it is to me."

A facsimile dedication by the author appears on a front flyleaf of every Volume I of *The*

Personal Memoirs of U.S. Grant. Dated "New York City/May 23d 1885," Grant wrote "These volumes are dedicated to the American soldier and sailor." Although the original dedication was penned in May, Gen. Grant finished his manuscript on July 19, 1885, four days before his death. He never even saw his memoirs in print.

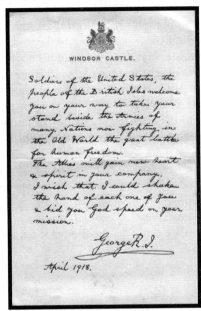
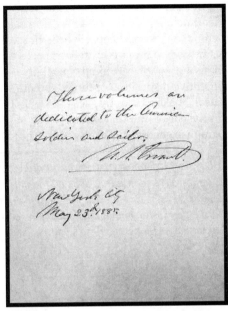

In 1833, an Act of Congress allowed the President of the United States to select an individual who would be authorized to sign his name to land grants. Tens of thousands of land grants signed after 1833 were signed with the president's name by a secretary who also signed the document in the blank space beneath the president's name, "By____Secretary." Some secretaries, such as John Hill Wheeler who worked for Franklin Pierce, tried to imitate the president's signature; most didn't. John Tyler was known to have personally signed a few land grants.

Letters and photographs signed by secretaries are also common in the hobby. The first U.S. president to use the Autopen signature machine was Dwight D. Eisenhower when he was president of Columbia University. John F. Kennedy, who made frequent use of the Autopen in the U.S. Senate, installed the machine in The White House. The Autopen company's website states that "Autopen machines provide high quality signature replication with any common pen, pencil, or marker... If desired, they can be special ordered to sign items such as books or athletic equipment." A person supplies signatures, which are replicated on matrices. Signatures signed with the same Autopen matrix can differ slightly depending upon how tightly the pen or marker is attached to the holder. In addition, the curved surface of a baseball or football would result in each signature differing from each other. This can make determining authenticity a real problem.

There are so many types of autographs that are not real. With all of the forgeries, facsimiles, secretarials and Autopens on the market, what can a collector to do to be certain of authenticity? The answer is simple. The sound advice Thomas F. Madigan gave to autograph collectors over 75 years ago is still as wise today as it was then: "The detection of forgeries, the determination of the genuineness or falsity of an autograph, are subjects over which the collector need lose no sleep. He need but salt his enthusiasm with a grain or two of common sense, he need but place his reliance on a reputable dealer and the chances of his acquiring spurious autographs are almost negligible. The success of an imposture depends more upon the receptive disposition of those who are selected as its victims than upon the chicanery of the cheat. Shakespeare supplies the key to the mystery of such a success: 'A jest's prosperity lies in the ear of him that hears it.' The best answer to the question, 'how do you know an autograph is genuine?' will always be the knowledge that it came from a reliable source."

John Reznikoff is founder and President of University Archives. Formed in 1979, University is one of the largest dealers in autographs and historical documents. John is also an autograph and document authenticator. He consults for PSA/DNA, James Spence Authentication, and authenticates and provides expert testimony for auction houses, dealers, non-profit organizations and governments. For more information, see University's advertisement on the back cover of this guide or go to www.universityarchives.com.

Chapter 2

What Really Matters: The Place of Quality & Content in Autograph Values

By Steven S. Raab

An Introduction to the Concept

We recently had two Franklin D. Roosevelt letters in our catalog and on our website; one for $1,000 and the other for $10,000. A new collector emailed who found our name in the price guide and then visited our website. He observed that the $1,000 letter was consistent with the price guide value, and asked how I could possibly justify the higher price of the other letter. His question was an important one, going to the very heart of understanding what matters most in collecting autographs and manuscripts.

I got into in this field back in 1986. I was like a kid in a candy store, buying without much discrimination whatever caught my eye. Over lunch a respected dealer gave me some unsolicited advice: Buy fewer things but make them the highest quality you can afford. I was impressed, and so began my search for the true meaning of quality that has defined my relationship with autographs ever since. It has led me to analyze dealer and auction catalogs by the thousands, to make uncountable purchases at both private and public venues, and innumerable conversations with knowledgeable enthusiasts. In the end, it would take me many years to fully understand the enormous value of the advice. This chapter contains the lessons I've learned.

Defining Quality in Letters, Manuscripts & Documents

An autograph's quality is based on its content or intrinsic importance. By this I mean that it has importance in and of itself. Understand these two concepts and you will have the tools you need to navigate successfully in autograph waters. And considering the price of autographs today, these are tools you can't afford to be without. Can you measure something as seemingly subjective as quality? Absolutely. Here are the rules we use.

Let's begin with three key terms, letters, manuscripts and documents, and how they're commonly used in the autograph field. Letters are communications between people, whether handwritten or typed. They will usually address someone by name, such as "Dear Mrs. Jones." Manuscripts are descriptive narratives, creative materials or other original handwritten or typed papers not intended as interpersonal communications. Classroom notes and diaries would be good examples. Documents are signed forms or official papers, such as your driver's license. I do not deal with signatures alone here, as even if valuable, they lack content or intrinsic importance.

Assessing Content and Importance

The content of a letter or manuscript, put simply, is what it says. But it is more; it is the creative product of the human mind. It can be illuminating, dramatic, incisive, artistic or comic. It can carry any emotion or message. Content is the most important facet of an autograph's value, so determining the quality of the content is crucial. Content is divided into three grades of quality: good, medium and low.

A good content piece is one in which the writer either tells you something of great interest or significance about himself or a primary field of his endeavor, or provides valuable descriptions or information about an important event.

A medium content piece is one that says something of moderate interest or significance, or relates to matters or events outside of the writer's primary field of endeavor. It offers nothing especially valuable or creative.

A low content piece is merely a sample of the person's writing. It has no real interest, is not creative and says nothing significant or valuable.

A letter by George Washington simply saying he is too busy to accept a dinner invitation says nothing anyone benefits by knowing, so it has low content. A Washington letter about farming would be more interesting because it is germane to running his plantation at Mount Vernon, but since he is best remembered for his leadership as general and president, it would be considered medium quality. But a Revolutionary War Washington letter ordering his chief spy, Benjamin Tallmadge, to obtain information on enemy troop dispositions has good content: it is historically significant and directly relates to his performance as commander of the Continental Army.

An Albert Einstein letter about what compelled him to a life in science is good content. A letter he wrote to try to help a refugee get a teaching position in the U.S. is medium content. An Einstein thank you note for a birthday greetings is low content.

A Grover Cleveland-penned letter describing the nature of the presidency is good content. One about his oral surgery is medium content. A note about going fishing is low content.

Not all good content letters are expensive. Robert Ballard relating his emotions on first seeing the Titanic is just as good content in that sphere as Washington's war date letter was in his.

Good content is equally key in manuscripts. The original handwritten notes John Quincy Adams used for his first case before the U.S. Supreme Court may safely be said to have good content. Some of his poems, often written to ladies, would have medium content. His docket on the verso of a letter would have low content. Orville Wright notes on his early aviation experiments is good content. George Gershwin composing a musical manuscript is the most creative content imaginable.

As with letters, good content manuscripts may not be expensive. A Mozart signature would be very expensive but have no content, while a diary from Woodstock could have great content and be very affordable.

Although they may recite crucial facts, like the ultimate document, the Declaration of Independence, documents do not strictly speaking have content. Some, however, have significant importance. Such documents are often mementos of a key moment in history or were the cause or result of a memorable event. Meriwether Lewis' signed pay receipt for the

Lewis and Clark expedition is intrinsically important, as is Lincoln's appointment of George Meade to command the Union Army and Thomas Edison's patent papers for his invention of the phonograph. As with content, intrinsic importance and expensive are not synonymous. A receipt signed by Benjamin Franklin may be expensive but lack any claim to importance, while Calvin Coolidge's appointment of Dwight Morrow to head the first Aviation Board would be important yet inexpensive.

The prices in the *Sanders Guide* are for autographs of typical content unless otherwise noted, and based on typical or average prices asked or paid. Autographs of medium and good content can be worth from a little more to many times these prices. Knowing the rarity and value of the autographs you want to acquire is critical.

Gradations of Autograph Values

To illustrate the difference in autograph values, let's assess four letters by British Prime Minister Winston Churchill. A TLS concerning a minor business transaction has low content and is worth $2,000; it is not interesting and says little about Churchill. A Churchill letter thanking someone for their help in his successful 1951 election campaign has medium content, because it relates to his public service but makes no important statements. It's worth about $4,000. A TLS we saw defending his controversial role in World War I had good content and dealt with a subject that mattered. It fetched over $10,000. Now to introduce the fourth price gradation, for an autograph of outstanding importance. We have a Churchill TLS as World War II Prime Minister thanking the American people for their support. It sells for $25,000. Imagine how inclusion of this latter letter would skew the average (and thus the price guide value) for a Churchill TLS!

It is the same for manuscripts. A low content Theodore Roosevelt typescript with a few handwritten notes would be worth $500. A similar example with some interesting holograph content about his opposition to corruption would have medium content and sell for $3,000. A handwritten magazine article about conservation would have good content and be worth about $10,000. In the outstanding category, we had a portion of the original typed manuscript of the speech he gave to his Bull Moose loyalists in June 1912, where he told them "We stand at Armageddon, and we battle for the Lord." It contained his copious handwritten revisions but was not signed. Even in this incomplete state, it brought over $20,000 years ago. Another example, a Civil War soldier's low content diary, would be worth $1,000. If there were some decent descriptions of activity, it would become medium content and rise to $3,500. We recently sold a diary with fine battle content for $9,000, and have an important, outstanding five-volume war date journal that served as the basis of a published book that might well bring many times that amount.

The same principle holds true for documents. A business receipt signed by John Hancock would be lower grade and might bring $4,000. An appointment of a militia officer, signed by him as governor of Massachusetts, is more interesting (thus medium grade) and might fetch $5,000. Military appointments Hancock signed as president of the Continental Congress, many dated in the magic year of 1776, are a definite step up to good grade and should sell for about $13,000. However, if the document commissions an officer who made a notable contribution to the Revolutionary War effort, it may have some intrinsic importance as well, and begin to climb towards the outstanding category. Hancock's appointment of Benedict Arnold as major general came on the market in 2002, and at the top of the outstanding grade, sold for $75,000. The importance of the document thus accounts for the spread between $3,000 and $75,000.

Signed Photographs

Many people collect signed photographs, and even here our concepts of content and intrinsic importance hold true. We always start with the perhaps surprising proposition that photographs inscribed to a named individual are best. One reason this is preferable is that the more handwriting there is on the photograph, the more certain the determination of authenticity. However, the added writing is also laden with possibilities for content. Perhaps the inscription will reveal something important about the writer, as when Harry Truman signs the famous photograph showing him holding the Chicago Tribune with its premature headline "Dewey Defeats Truman," saying that this was the most memorable day of his life. It may also illustrate something interesting about the relationship between the signer and the recipient, as in a photograph we owned inscribed by Warren Harding to his corrupt Veteran's Bureau administrator, Charles Forbes. It was filled to the brim with expressions of trust and praise, emotions that showed Harding's view of the men's relationship, but were repaid by Forbes with betrayal. Signed photographs with such inscriptions have good content and may even rise to the level of important. They are two to four times more valuable than similar uninscribed pictures.

With signed photographs, what they show can be as important as what they say, as that is a form of content. A signed portrait photograph of Franklin D. Roosevelt as Governor of New York would be worth $1,500 or so, while one as President might sell for $3,500. However, if the photograph pictures FDR with his cabinet (and if the other cabinet members have also signed), the value would rise to at least $6,000. A signed photograph of him delivering his first inaugural address or war message to Congress would easily jump to $10,000 or even $15,000, if you could find one. The collector of signed photographs must be equipped to make these kinds of distinctions.

These same rules apply to signed books, the analogous criteria in the case of a book being the importance of the book within the context of the author's work. Thus, a copy of *The White Company* signed by Arthur Conan Doyle would be lucky to fetch $800, but one of *The Adventures of Sherlock Holmes* should sell for at least $6,000. A signed copy of F. Scott Fitzgerald's still-read *The Great Gatsby* might be worth $15,000, while one of the seldom-read *All the Sad Young Men* could bring $3,500. Here, too, the inscribee can be important. If the latter book was inscribed "To my astonishing wife Zelda", the value would rise by many times.

The Impact of Condition on Prices

Another important factor affecting the value of autographs, even those of high quality, is condition. This requires an item-by-item analysis and does not lend itself to categorization, but here are some illustrative examples. A good content letter of George Washington written during the Revolutionary War in fine condition might be worth $50,000. If it has faded a little, that number might be $40,000. Now add a pervasive water stain and it may drop to $20,000. With a small piece missing that causes the loss of a few key words or the signature, it might fetch $15,000. As the bard said, "What a falling off was there?" And not even content could prevent the fall.

It must be noted that there are three exceptions to this analysis on the role of condition, and they are often related: uniqueness, extraordinary importance and true rarity. If the Washington letter in our example was addressed to the Continental Congress and accepted its offer of the supreme command of the American army, then it would be both unique and extraordinarily important (to say the least), and be desirable regardless of condition. A somewhat faded letter of Robert E. Lee to George Meade that crossed the battle lines at Gettysburg, in which he asked about the safety of a Mississippi colonel wounded in Pickett's Charge, would be an example of uniqueness (as no other such letter exists in private hands) without extraordinary importance. It would generate excitement despite condition. An example of extraordinary importance without uniqueness would be a stained document of Franklin D. Roosevelt appointing a Supreme Court justice (he appointed eight). As for true rarity, I am not referring to autographs that are merely uncommon and nice to find, like Civil War date ALsS of Stonewall Jackson. I mean autographs like those of Columbus or Shakespeare, where just finding one would be a news-making event. Condition simply would not matter then.

Learning What to Avoid

Here's something else you need to know. Sadly, it is not uncommon to find sellers of autographs who are not satisfied with the lily they have and try to gild it. They will praise the most routine letter as having good (if not great) content, label as important the most mundane manuscript, and say a stained document is in super fine condition. Logically, we know that a letter simply turning down a speaking invitation cannot be considered interesting, no less have good content. Presidents signed untold thousands of documents appointing postmasters, and one naming John Doe the postmaster of Peoria cannot be made important simply by labeling it important. And a manuscript that is torn and stained is simply not in choice condition. Some sellers utterly lack self-restraint, and slant or mischaracterize almost everything they offer in this way. Skepticism must therefore be the starting point in assessing seller representations.

You should also take care to avoid fads or temporary bumps in the market. When Princess Diana died, her autographs (mainly signed Christmas cards) increased in value from about $800 to as much as $10,000. Interest in her was no fad, yet the price was clearly being influenced by the tragedy and intense emotion that followed it. The market ultimately stabilized the value at about $2,000.

The Autograph Marketplace Today

The last dozen years have seen substantial growth in interest in autographs, and at the same time more and more good content and important autographs have disappeared from the private marketplace into institutions or major collections. These factors alone cause scarcity and affect price. And unlike in years past, when letters and manuscripts of recent notables provided a constant source of new material, there is no longer a reliable, corresponding replenishment of supply. This is because, as I mentioned in a *Wall Street Journal* piece, emails, text messages, faxes, cell phones and the like have reduced the volume of postally-mailed letters to a trickle, and of this pittance, a growing number are signed mechanically by Autopen or printer. When to this dismal picture is added the fact that manuscripts are usually created today in computers, and more and more forms have preprinted signatures, it seems clear that there will be precious few authentic personally-signed autographs to collect that were created from the year 2000 forward. This is putting pressure on the supply of remaining autographs of the past, and finding quality autographs has become more difficult. In fact, the difference between the substantial number of important items readily available when I started as a dealer in 1989 and the reduced number on the market today is striking.

Yet I do not want to leave the impression that it is hard for collectors today to build superb collections. If quality is what motivates you, fine things are still out there waiting to be found. You simply need to hunt to ferret them out and be patient, careful and persistent.

If price is a factor, remember there is one very inexpensive commodity that is often directly exchangeable for cash: knowledge. The more you know about an autograph, the greater the chance you will discover a true bargain.

Have fun building your collection.

Steven S. Raab is President of The Raab Collection, a dealer in historical letters, documents and manuscripts since 1989. He is a founding member of the Professional Autograph Dealer Association (PADA) and a member of the Manuscript Society and UACC. You can reach Steven Raab through his website at www.raabcollection.com.

Chapter 3

Vintage Hollywood

By Joe Maddalena

Let's talk about vintage Hollywood autographs. First, I'll give you an overview of the history of these autographs, and then we'll talk about collecting: How to authenticate and how to assess the value of an item.

The History of Vintage Hollywood Autographs

In the 1920s and 1930s, the Hollywood studio system created a method of marketing and merchandising each studio star independently. So, if you were under contract, say at Paramount and you were Louise Brooks, the studio would actually employ a team of photographers and public relations people to decide what your look would be, how your hair would be cut, what restaurants you would be seen at and who you dated! They literally marketed you, as a person, to the world.

In order to keep up with the fan base, the studios would employ legions of secretaries to sign photographs and mail them out to people. So, not through any devious intentions on anyone's part, tens of thousands of autographs were turned out by the studios to give to the fans who would write in for an autograph. Because of this, it's very difficult to assess how many secretarial vintage Hollywood autographs exist.

Guidelines for Authentication

1. Quality Photographs

I've been collecting these autographs for 30 years. And 30 years ago, when Hollywood autographs were pretty much worthless, there was a very limited number of them. When a Marilyn Monroe signed photograph would surface, nine times out of ten it was a double-weight, high-quality photograph, not a flimsy, single-weight, glossy photograph. Marilyn Monroe, in particular, did not sign fan mail. She would sign photographs to friends and intimates and people who worked with her. There may be a few dozen or so authentically signed Marilyn Monroe photographs in the world. Unfortunately, with the arrival of the mass-produced forgeries that have broken into our field now, there are thousands of them. But, what you'll see when you start to collect these autographs is that the great stars primarily had access to the best quality photographs.

For instance, when you see an oversize Carole Lombard it's a double-weight, and Otto Dyer is usually the photographer, or Eugene Robert Richee. They're exceptional photographs. They are what Lombard would have had personal access to. So if a friend, colleague or a fellow star requested an autograph, she would generally take one of these photographs, inscribe it to whoever this person was and present it to them — much different than something you would receive in the mail from the autograph area, the publicity department of the studio.

You have to be extremely cautious when you're buying vintage Hollywood autographs. Boris Karloff signed photographs of himself as Frankenstein's Monster are extremely rare. There can't be but a handful in the world. I've seen less than five, and the ones that I've seen were always double-weight studio photographs. For instance, I had one once where Boris Karloff inscribed it to Jack Pierce, the *Frankenstein* makeup artist. These stars just didn't sign these "character" images for fans at the time, as it took years before these roles would reach iconic stature in film history.

2. Authenticity of the Inscription

As you start to collect vintage Hollywood, there's so much you have to ask yourself. Where did this piece come from? Let's say you're looking at a photograph signed by James Dean. Is it inscribed to somebody? He had a very short life. Who was it inscribed to? Did this person really exist? Did this person know James Dean? What type of photograph is it? Is it some flimsy, single-stock photograph, or is it a high-quality, studio photograph, something Dean would have had access to? The secret to collecting these vintage, classic Hollywood autographs of Bogart, Gable and Flynn, and the other great stars is to really ask yourself the above questions. Not a day goes by that somebody doesn't walk in my office and hand me a pile of glossy, single-weight photographs that are either secretarial or plain out forgeries.

3. Analyze the Photograph

The arrival of forgeries in this field is astronomical, so let's talk about how a collector can independently analyze a photograph. To break it down really simply, I'm going to take a couple of stars and just talk about them in general. I'll use Carole Lombard as an example — one of the greatest stars, pre-World War II, who died tragically in an airplane crash. Carole Lombard was also part of the star system. So, you'll see 5x7 head shots of her just usually signed "Cordially, Carole Lombard" that nine times out of ten are secretarial. They were pumped out by the studios to keep fans watching her films.

Now let's go to the 8x10's and 11x14's. Usually, when you see them, they have lengthy inscriptions. They're gorgeous photographs, mostly double-weight in composition, and they're beautiful. There may be 100 to 200 8x10 inscribed photographs of Lombard in existence and they are generally priced in the $1,500 range. The 11x14 photographs of Carole Lombard are much more rare – there are maybe 20 or 30 of them in the world. And the price for an 11x14 photograph might be $2,000 to $15,000. At first glance, an 8x10 at $1,500 seems like a better value than a $5,000 11x14. But the real long-term values for a collector are the oversize signed photographs because they are the rarest. They usually bear personal inscriptions and they are the highest form of collecting Hollywood signed photographs.

That said, let's look at Marilyn Monroe. This classic Hollywood star is a different animal altogether and assessing value is a very subjective matter. Let's just take a simple album page that Marilyn Monroe would have had thrust into her hand when she was walking down the street or entering a restaurant. That simple autograph will bring a few thousand dollars in today's market. A signed check, of which there are quite a few, is worth $2,000 to $3,000. At one time, there were over 1,000 of them that I knew of, so they're definitely out there.

But now we go to the signed photograph category. Again, a day rarely goes by that somebody doesn't tell me, "I have a Marilyn Monroe signed photograph signed in red ink. She loved red ink because it was the color of her lipstick." It's just not true. There's no such thing as a real Marilyn Monroe signed photograph in red ink. That's just folklore. There's never been one that I know of. So, when you hear those kind of things, again use common sense. If it sounds too good to be true, it is too good to be true. An authentic Marilyn Monroe signed photograph is going to cost you $15,000 to $25,000. There's no such thing as a $2,000 or $3,000 one. But go to eBay and there are a gazillion of them for sale. *They're all fake.*

Marilyn Monroe took tremendous pride in presenting her intimate circle of friends with signed photographs. She just didn't sign them for the fans. So to get one, you were somebody in her circle: her hairdresser, a close friend, a fellow celebrity. And again, she only gave them double-weight, high quality, beautiful studio photographs. What you see on the market now are just gobs and gobs of single-weight, poor quality scene stills and later printed photographs that just are not real.

Always look for the very best quality. Try to find signed photographs that are beautiful, that are studio produced, that are double-weight, that are really exceptional photographs, and start with that as your criteria. And, believe it or not, it's better to have an inscription. I know there are lots of collectors who just want something signed "Marilyn Monroe," but nine times out ten they're not going to be real. It's better to have them inscribed. There's more handwriting to authenticate, there's a better story and you have a better shot of getting something genuine.

Valuations

It's really important to talk about values and how values are determined. The most important thing you should ask yourself is, "*What* is the object I'm interested in buying?" No matter *who* it is, what is it signed on? Is it signed on an album page? Is the album page in nice condition? Is it signed in pencil or pen? Does it have something affixed to the album page that's going to make it less attractive? A lot of it is visual appeal. All of those things are going to influence price. Is the photograph creased? Is it solarized? Is it stained? Is the ink faded? Is it signed in an attractive place on the image? Is it signed in a dark area which makes it hard to see? Is it inscribed in an area that obscures the person's face? All of these little distinctions go into determining the value of what an autograph is worth.

Next, evaluate the quality of the photograph itself. Is it a stamped studio photograph or is it a commercially-made inexpensive photograph? Then you can start to evaluate this information and say to yourself, "Gee, now I understand why this photograph is $250 and that photograph is $750." Why is a Roy Rogers still, signed in the last 25 years, worth $25 and one signed in the 1950s of him on Trigger worth $250? It's vintage. And that is also a key element to determining value. When were these things signed? The price is higher when the stars signed them during their heyday, as opposed to things that were signed 20 and 30 years later. If you have photographs in the 1930s that were signed in the 1930s, they're worth one price. If you have the same photographs from the 1930s signed by the celebrity years later, in the '60s or '70s, they're worth a fraction of that price.

These are all the things you have to look at when determining value. So often now I hear people saying they want a bargain. Frankly, they want something that is too good to be true. You're not going to get a Marilyn Monroe signed photograph for $2,000. Okay, maybe you could luck out. Somebody had it hidden or found it among their grandfather's collectibles. But in general, you're not going to get it. Ask yourself: Is this too good to be true?

Pricing can vary dramatically. I may say something's worth $10,000, somebody else might say $5,000 and somebody else may say $15,000. How do you take those wide swings in value and try to stipulate some type of standardization? Really and truly, it's aesthetics.

It's what the item is signed upon. It's when the item was signed. It's to whom it was signed.

For instance, I have this amazing William Randolph Hearst inscribed photograph. Let's say it's just a William Randolph Hearst inscribed photograph to anyone. It's worth $1,000. But this one is oversized and it's inscribed to none other than Marion Davies, his mistress, on Valentine's Day, where he writes, "To Marion, your Valentine's present. Love, W.R.H." And, then, he writes a poem, a love poem, on this photograph. I value this photograph at $25,000 because it's the ultimate William Randolph Hearst piece you could ever possibly get. It's to Marion Davies. It would be like having that Boris Karloff photograph as Frankenstein's Monster signed, "To Jack Pierce, I enjoyed working with you on the movie. Thanks for all your help. Boris Karloff 'The Monster.'" It would be worth $50,000 while a routine vintage Karloff signed image might be worth $1,500.

That's the thing collectors have to understand. You can look at each individual photograph and say, "Gee, I want a Marlon Brando and I want something from the 1950s." Well, do you want him on a photograph from the 1950s signed in the 1950s, or do you want a photograph from the 1950s signed in the 1980s? It makes a big difference in the value today and it will make an even bigger difference over the long-term. If you want a Marlon Brando signed photograph from the period of *A Streetcar Named Desire* or *The Wild One*, it may be worth $2,000 or $3,000. That same photograph signed in the 1990s may be worth $400 or $500.

Again, ask yourself, when was it signed? Where was it signed? Am I buying something that was signed at the time, or am I buying a piece that was signed 20 years later? Is the Orson Welles signed photograph signed in 1941 during *Citizen Kane*, or is it signed in 1981 when he was old and retired? The same photograph — totally different values.

No matter the celebrity or era of vintage Hollywood that you are interested in collecting, you should realize that most celebrity-signed photographs, signed in the '20s, '30s and '40s that are *not* personalized (a photograph with a signature only, a photograph signed "Cordially, Clarke Gable." or "Best wishes, Jean Harlow") are going to be secretarial nine times out of ten. That's just the way it worked back then. It's the opposite for inscribed 11x14's. Nine times out of ten, *those* are real, not secretarial. The 5x7's are usually always secretarial. The 8x10's are a mixed lot. I would say at least 30 percent are secretarial. Look for inscriptions. Look for quality photographs. Research the inscription. Don't jump at the to good to be true. All these pointers will guide the collector of vintage Hollywood towards authenticity. And the single most important thing is to buy from a well known dealer who offers an unconditional money back guarantee of authenticity. Happy collecting.

Joe Maddelena is President and CEO of Profiles in History, located in Calabasas Hills, Calif. Founded in 1985, Profiles in History is one of the top auction houses for entertainment and historic collectibles. For more information, see their advertisement on page 545 or go to www.profilesinhistory.com.

Chapter 4

Collecting U.S. Presidents

By Brad Shafran

When I meet potential autograph collectors, the first question they ask is invariably, "What kinds of autographs can I obtain?" My answer always starts with "The presidents" and before I can answer further, I see the excitement in the collector's eyes. The ability to purchase, possess and proudly display holographic material from the United States' great leaders has spawned many new autograph collectors who previously thought such material was unobtainable.

Presidential autographs are readily available in many forms and price ranges. While you can spend less than $100 for an authentically signed presidential piece, you will be quite limited by the items you can collect on such a budget. But with a slight increase in your presidential autograph expenditures, your collection can contain many of our country's most storied names.

The most important step before purchasing an autograph is to verify its authenticity and research the source from which the autograph comes. Provenance, the evidence of the history of the piece, can help in many ways. Putting authenticity aside just for sake of this article, the next step is to judge the item on these factors:

Content and Association: What does the letter or document say? Who is it written to? Is the letter from an important date in history?

For example, a senatorial typed letter signed (TLS) from John F. Kennedy wishing a constituent a happy birthday may be priced at $1,500. A White House TLS with the same greetings may fetch $2,500. However, a White House TLS dated November 21, 1963 discussing his upcoming trip to Dallas could easily top $100,000.

Condition: Although quite subjective, what is the condition of the item?

Rarity and content will outweigh condition in most instances, as even a tattered and faded Abraham Lincoln letter discussing a Civil War battle or the subject of slavery will far outweigh the value of a pristine letter where Lincoln simply forwards his autograph.

Once you choose to embark on a collection of presidential autographs, the journey can take many twists and turns. Some collectors choose only to collect autograph material dated while the president was in office, whether it's an Autograph Letter Signed (ALS), a letter entirely in the correspondent's handwriting and signed by them; a Typed Letter Signed (TLS), a letter with typed text but authentically signed; a Document Signed (DS), various documents such as military appointments and land grants; or signed photographs (SP), Executive Mansion/The White House cards, free franks, or signed books or cut signatures. There are many opportunities to obtain autograph material. Each is discussed briefly below.

Autograph Letter Signed (ALS)

An autograph letter signed is a letter written entirely in the hand of, and signed by, the president. Most collectors consider an ALS as president to be the greatest of all presidential autographs. Surprising to most collectors, a presidential ALS from recent presidents can be priced above a George Washington ALS! As shocking as that is, it is based on the readily available technology now present. From the advent of the typewriter to the current age of computers, and from adept secretaries to the invention of the Autopen, today's presidents are far less inclined to take the time to handwrite a letter than their predecessors. The marketplace is filled with many letters from early presidents who took the time to handwrite a full page in response to an autograph request. A similar request today would almost certainly result in a machine-signed response. One current development is the sale of the papers of many prominent politicians and statesmen, which adds a great wealth of new material not previously available to collectors. In recent years, presidential material from the archives of Daniel Patrick Moynihan, Paul Simon, Pat Brown, George Murphy and several others have come to public auction and into the catalogs of prominent dealers, helping to increase the supply of 20th century presidential material.

After presidential-dated ALsS, many collectors seek quality pre- and post-presidential ALsS. Dwight Eisenhower, according to his presidential library, wrote over 300 letters to his wife Mamie while stationed overseas during World War II. Many of these letters have battle content and personal details that many covet more than a presidential dated letter. William Howard Taft served as Chief Justice of the Supreme Court, a position he cherished greater than the presidency, and his ALsS as Chief Justice can be found for less than his White House ALsS. Conversely, the war material of several presidents who served in the military, such as Andrew Jackson, U.S. Grant and Dwight Eisenhower may be priced higher than in their presidential material because their battle exploits may have overshadowed their presidential accomplishments.

Regardless of the time period, ALsS from presidents will always be coveted by collectors and among the finest pieces available.

Typed Letter Signed (TLS)

Letters typed by a secretary but authentically signed by a president are usually less expensive than a fully handwritten letter, but a desirable content TLS can sell for many times the price of a mundane ALS. The patent for the typewriter was issued in June 1868 and the first president to regularly send TLsS from the President's house was William McKinley. The term "President's house" is used because at one time it was called the Executive Mansion, which would become White House under Theodore Roosevelt and eventually The White House. More on this when Executive Mansion/White House cards are discussed.

TLsS as president offer the collector the opportunity to obtain a presidential signature on a dated piece of history. I often suggest that new clients start their collection with a variety of 20th century presidential TLsS. Theodore Roosevelt and Franklin D. Roosevelt letters can be obtained for $1,500 or less. William Taft, Woodrow Wilson, Warren Harding, Calvin Coolidge and Herbert Hoover for about half that. Of historical note, Wilson actually took the time to type many of his own White House letters, which adds a nice touch to an already valuable manuscript. The most expensive 20th century president, without regard to content, would be John F. Kennedy. His routine letters can be found in the $2,000-3,000 range. One of the more common presidents in TLS form as president is Harry Truman, with letters found in the $400-$600 range. Truman often took the time to add a holographic postscript to his letters, which is coveted by collectors. All material after Truman should be closely examined, as secretarials were prevalent in the Eisenhower Administration and the Autopen was widely used from JFK forward.

The TLS is the most common form of autograph material for almost all 20th century presidents. Truman continued to send letters to autograph seekers up until his death in 1972. While many were simply fulfilling requests, some were historically significant, including a form letter he sent out in 1960 to all Democratic Congressmen supporting JFK for president, which would garner a higher price than many Truman White House TLsS.

Collecting TLsS also allows you to capture moments in time throughout a politician's career. A fan of Teddy Roosevelt can obtain a TLS with a variety of letterheads starting with his service on the U.S. Civil Service Commission, as president of the Board of NYC Police Commissioners, Assistant Secretary of the Navy, New York Governor, vice president, president and as editor of *Outlook Magazine*!

Documents Signed (DS)

At many times in the U.S.'s history, presidents were required, by law, to authentically sign documents. These offer wonderful opportunities for collectors, as military appointments are beautiful for presentation, with grand lithography and vignettes. Land grants are the more common form of presidential document. These were all authentically signed prior to and during Andrew Jackson's first term in office. Anything signed after this period should be closely examined as, with very few exceptions, they are secretarially signed. Some forms available are the aforementioned military appointments, land grants, seal authorizations (many times these are to affix the Presidential Seal to a warrant for a pardon and should not be mistaken for an actual pardon which are many times rarer), postmaster appointments (these should be scrutinized closely, especially after Teddy Roosevelt, as many are facsimile signed), four-language ship's papers (among the scarcest and most impressive), Mediterranean ships passports and political appointments (should be examined closely from all recent administrations).

Another fascinating aspect of collecting presidential documents is the combinations of signatures they sometimes offer, since future presidents often served in the cabinets of their predecessors. Some famous duos represented on documents are Washington and Jefferson, Jefferson and Madison, Madison and Monroe, Monroe and John Quincy Adams, Andrew Jackson and Van Buren, Polk and Buchanan, Franklin Pierce and Jefferson Davis, Theodore Roosevelt and Taft, Wilson and Franklin D. Roosevelt, and Coolidge and Hoover.

Signed Photographs (SP)

Photographs signed by presidents are among the most visually-impressive items available. Nearly every president starting with Grant is available in this form. John Quincy Adams was the first president to be photographed, but it was well after he left office. He, as well as his predecessors, were portrayed by the greatest artist's of their days, but not with photographic images. The first president photographed in office was William Henry Harrison but the whereabouts of this image is unknown.

While signed photographs of Abraham Lincoln can be found, they are of the utmost in scarcity, with prices far exceeding $50,000. Signed photographs of Millard Fillmore and James Buchanan can be found in the $5,000 to $7,000 range but are rarely offered. The more common signed images are of the turn of the century presidents, many of whom were photographed by Harris & Ewing, a prominent studio in Washington D.C. known for their portraits of government officials. These images are generally half-bust length stoic portraits. Many times these photos were generously signed, inscribed and dated in the lower white border, making them ideal for prominent display.

Another uncommon form of a signed photograph is a Cabinet photograph showing, and signed by, the president and his entire cabinet. These images, usually oversized, command a premium, as the combination of signatures offers several prominent men on the same item; such as Taft as secretary of war under Theodore Roosevelt, Coolidge as vice president, Hoover as secretary of commerce under Harding, and Nixon as vice president under Eisenhower. Although these types of photos rarely come to the marketplace, I suggest acquiring one if ever offered.

Executive Mansion and White House Cards

Executive Mansion and White House Cards, small, generally 4¼-inch by 2¾-inch cards, have become increasing popular among collectors. The first president to issue such one was U.S. Grant, although signed Grant cards may not still exist. These cards feature "Executive Mansion, Washington," "White House, Washington" or "The White House, Washington" in the upper right corner. Cards prior to Teddy Roosevelt were from the "Executive Mansion" but Roosevelt changed it to "White House" and then ultimately "The White House." They have increased in value considerably over the last few years and although not truly rare, they are becoming more difficult to find. Another form of White House card is the slightly larger Bureau of Engraving and Printing card showing a vignette of the White House signed by the president below the image. These are most commonly found for Chester Arthur, William McKinley and Grover Cleveland and are highly displayable.

Rutherford B. Hayes often used his Executive Mansion cards to pen short notes to cabinet officers. Grover Cleveland signed most cards during his first term with his name only but added the date during his second term. Woodrow Wilson always signed his White House cards at the top left so nobody could add any text above his signature. Cards signed after Harry Truman should be closely examined as many are facsimile signed—Dwight Eisenhower cards usually have a notation that the signature is a facsimile on the reverse. Be aware that some collectors have printed their own mock White House cards in recent years. In nearly every instance, White House cards signed by Ford through Bush are souvenir cards and not authentic.

Free Franks

Franking is the privilege afforded to government officials to send official business through the postal system free of charge. The practice dates back to the 17th century British House of Commons, but its first appearance in the U.S. dates to 1775, when the Continental Congress decided to give members the privilege of sending mail to constituents free of charge. Generally, a frank will appear in the upper-right corner usually reserved for a postage stamp. Presidents Washington through Grant were afforded this privilege, but the right to frank was rescinded in 1873 due to abuses of the system, as many of the otherwise virtuous early presidents and congressmen would attach their name to letters for their wives or for other non-governmental affairs. The right was reinstituted in 1895 for Congress but not for the president.

There are varieties in presidential franks, as Washington would many times simply write "The President of the U.S." in the lower left of the address leaf. John Adams would sign his name to the left of the addressee's information. Several presidents, including Jefferson and

John Quincy Adams would add "Pr. Of the U.S." or some variation. Franks of early presidents are an attractive and affordable way to collect, as many had the privilege before their term in their capacities as cabinet officials and congressmen.

Most 20th century presidential franks should be closely examined. No more than a handful are known to exist and all would be considered illegal. Many envelopes will bear a printed franking signature. Also, some collectors were able to procure presidential signatures on envelopes and added a postmark, but these are souvenirs and not true franks and should not be treated the same in terms of value.

Signed Books

Autographed books are an increasingly popular format for presidential collectors. Although difficult to find, many books from the libraries of our earliest presidents come to market, generally with the ownership signature of the president on the first free end page. The most popular presidential books are limited edition books signed by presidents. Woodrow Wilson and Herbert Hoover each issued such a book, as did Franklin D. Roosevelt, who signed 2,500 copies of *The Democratic Book 1936*, which always commands a strong price. Dwight D. Eisenhower signed a facsimile of his D-Day Order Of The Day in his limited edition book *Crusade in Europe*. All presidents from Richard Nixon through George W. Bush have issued signed limited edition books.

Jimmy Carter, who has authored more than 20 books since leaving office, routinely travels the country appearing at bookstores to promote and sign copies of his newest book. These events offer collectors the opportunity to obtain an authentic signed book, as well as the enjoyment of meeting a former president. Bill Clinton embarked on two national tours for his best-sellers, signing tens of thousands of books in the process.

The Good, the Bad and the Ugly

When collecting autographs, the first and most important aspect is that you *enjoy* the item. Whether the autograph is bound for display on your wall or for storage in a vault, the item should bring you joy — that is why we collect. I can rack up hours of telephone time talking to clients about new acquisitions. The postman and I have an interesting relationship, as I usually meet him halfway to the door because I want to see what new items he has brought me. Some presidential signatures are so nice that we can sometimes overlook the mediocrity of the signer's presidency. The best example is James Buchanan. He had gorgeous, flowing handwriting and a wonderful way of using words to always relate to his correspondent. Other presidents with attractive writing and signatures are Washington, Adams, John Quincy Adams, Taft, Reagan and Clinton.

Several presidents wrote in a nearly indecipherable hand. Cleveland and Kennedy top that list, with Hayes and Van Buren close behind.

Several presidents show a distinct variation in their signature over time. These differences are generally due to age or stress but do not tend to affect pricing.

Cut Signatures

Signatures removed from documents or letters are referred to as "cuts," as only the signature remains from the original manuscript. As a rule, cut signatures should be heavily scrutinized for authenticity. I strongly urge clients to invest in a full letter or document as opposed to a cut. The additional funds spent will, in the long run, offer a better investment and more peace of mind.

Suggestions

Do your own research: Dealers can only provide a certain amount of detail about an item. An astute buyer's research can lead to additional information that enhances its value. Presidential libraries are wonderful sources of information and are easily accessible via the Internet or telephone.

Maintain want lists: Let dealers know what you are looking for and let them help you find the quality material you seek. These are free services with no commitment.

Be disciplined: Don't chase autographs at prices higher than you are willing to spend. If you miss out on something today, there will be another fantastic item offered to you tomorrow. However, do keep in mind that most of these items are unique.

Enjoy the hobby: Collectors often lose sight of the pure joy that autographs bring. We are holding pieces of our country's history in our hands and the power of this should always be respected and cherished.

Brad Shafran was a longtime collector before becoming the proprietor of Shafran Collectibles, a New York dealer in guaranteed authentic autographic material, from history to entertainment. For more information, see Brad Shafran's advertisement on page 553 or go to www.shafrancollectibles.com.

Chapter 5

Buying Autographs and Manuscripts on eBay: The Double Edged Sword

By Stuart Lutz

Dr. Saffro, the author of the *Sanders Autograph Price Guide*, and I have a game we play. It is unofficially entitled "Who Can Find the Worst eBay Autograph Forgery This Week?" A typical contest starts when Dr. Saffro emails me an eBay listing with a Neil Armstrong signature that is so shaky that it looks like he signed it from Tranquility Base. I'll counter with a John Kennedy letter with a well-known Autopen signature and an opening price of $1,500 and a certificate of authenticity (of course!). Then my friendly competitor replies with a fine listing from a Louisiana peddler offering a "genuine" John Wilkes Booth signature with a starting price of $1. At that point, I admit defeat to Dr. Saffro and hope that I can beat him next week by finding an even more outrageous eBay forgery before he does.

eBay is the greatest change to the autograph field in decades, perhaps since the rise of dealer catalogs a century ago. In just 13 years, eBay has displaced the traditional auction houses like Christie's and Sotheby's to become the largest auctioneer of autograph material in the world in terms of sales.

As with all change, there have been positive and negative developments with the rise of eBay, and the adjustment has not always been smooth. In this article, I examine the good and bad changes wrought by eBay, review some of the improvements eBay has made, and suggest ways for you to protect yourself from autograph forgeries and fraud.

The Good

eBay has been a terrific buying and selling tool for me, a full-time historic document and manuscript dealer, and I think that many of my fellow autograph dealers would agree. I have purchased tremendous pieces on eBay, including Dwight Eisenhower's handwritten bridge tallies, a fine Charles Lindbergh archive about the New Jersey house where his son was kidnapped, a Felix Frankfurter book inscribed to Harpo Marx and a Bob Hope archive about entertaining troops in Vietnam. Before eBay, my chances of finding these gems, many of which came from other parts of the country, were remote. I have also discovered that people looking to sell autographs see that I sell on eBay, and have contacted me to sell their material for them.

Similarly, I have sold letters and manuscripts to new clients around the world. Before eBay, dealers could display their wares at regional fairs, but if a dealer had a booth at a San Francisco exhibition, the chances of someone from Cincinnati purchasing an autograph there was small. With eBay, the whole world is my marketplace. Many of these eBay collectors have never joined autograph collector organizations like The Manuscript Society or the Universal Autograph Collectors Club (U.A.C.C.), so the chances of me reaching them through a traditional dealer catalog are small.

For the autograph buying public, eBay has continually upgraded itself to make purchasing easier. The company has the Buy It Now feature and also emails "Saved Searches" daily, telling buyers when something they're looking for is available.

The mere existence of eBay has created many new collectors. Before eBay, few people realized that they could, with the click of a mouse own something signed by Babe Ruth, John F. Kennedy or Thomas Edison. Growing the collector pool is an asset for the business.

The Bad

The obvious downside of eBay is the enormous influx of non-genuine pieces, mainly intentional but also including some unintentional forgeries. .

Unintentional forgeries are secretarial, facsimile and Autopen material offered as genuine because the seller lacks the expertise to distinguish genuine from unauthentic pieces. 15 years ago, if Mrs. Jones cleaned out Aunt Gertie's house and found a letter from John Kennedy with Autopen pattern No. 3 on it, she would probably have called an autograph dealer to sell it. The dealer would have seen it was a mechanical signature, and declined to purchase it. That would have marked the end of the Kennedy letter. Today, if Mrs. Jones finds that same Kennedy letter to dear Aunt Gertie she can sell it on eBay. Not knowing it's an Autopen, she sees that similar but genuine, Kennedy, Presidential letters sell for over $1,000 on eBay, and asks a similar price for her nearly worthless letter. (When I inform casual autograph sellers that they are selling an Autopen letter, and propose to email them the identical pattern from a reference book, almost all decline my offer).

Unintentional forgeries come in a variety of types in addition to Autopens. I am shocked at the number of worthless Certificates of Authenticity (COAs) that accompany Autopen, secretarial or facsimile materials. There are pre-printed facsimiles, like Lincoln's Gettysburg Address or his letter to Mrs. Bixby concerning the death of her five sons in the Civil War. Facsimiles are not limited to letters. Mark Twain printed the blurb "This is the authorized Uniform Edition of all my books" in some of his volumes. Likewise, President Ulysses S. Grant's *Memoirs* were published after his death, and the deceptive inscription "These volumes are dedicated to the American soldier and sailor is part of the printing." There are also secretarial signatures, such as presidential land grants. Andrew Jackson was the last president to sign land grants and he quit halfway through his term, meaning not all Jackson land grants are genuine. All the land grants "signed" by presidents Polk, Lincoln, Grant and later *were not* autographed by a president at all.

I have seen some very creative marketing of genuine material by casual autograph sellers. I once saw a genuine presidential military commission advertised as triple signed. The naïve or sleazy seller thought that the handwritten engrossment of the commission, in which the secretary also handwrote the president's name twice at the top of the document, counted as genuine autographs. A simple comparison of the genuine signature at the bottom and the engrossment of the names should have informed him that there was only one authentic autograph on it. Another time, I saw a Richard Nixon secretarial letter offered as "guaranteed old," even though the warranty did not guarantee the letter was genuinely signed by Nixon. Finally, I have seen exaggerations of the rarity of pieces. Harry Truman, as ex-president, mailed out hundreds of letters a year. Yet some sellers list routine Harry Truman typed letters signed (TLS) from the 1960s as very rare, when they are plentiful. (Harry Truman handwritten letters as president *are* rare.) Turning our attention to deliberate forgeries, autographs are the easiest field to create spurious pieces for eBay, and many crooks have taken advantage of this simplicity. All it takes to create a fake is a pen, a desirable item to sign, and three to four seconds. A good forger can crank out tens of thousands of dollars in forgeries a day. As a result, eBay the perfect forum for forgers. The counterfeits come in all sizes and shapes, from Washington and Lincoln to modern athletes.

Beware of false provenance. Dr. Saffro tracked down an eBay seller who claimed that a grouping of World War II autographs came from his father and the money was being used to send him and his brother to college (the World War II vet must have been pretty old when he had his sons). The autographs included a bad Joe Rosenthal signed photograph of the Iwo Jima flag raising and a fake Ronald Reagan signed image. When Dr. Saffro pressed the sellers about the provenance, they suddenly changed their story. It became the vet's grandchildren who were being put through college.

The same personal computers used to connect to eBay have created a new class of forgeries: high quality color copies. An unscrupulous person can purchase a genuine Abraham Lincoln or Charles Lindbergh letter, use his scanner and color printer to duplicate it, and sell it on eBay as genuine. To a person seeing it on the Internet, the handwriting would appear authentic. Once the collector receives it, there may be no way to determine it is a color copy except by using a magnifying glass, but if you do, the odds of getting your money back are slim at best.

No one would sell a genuine Lincoln for cents of the dollar. A legitimate dealer has to pay thousands for one, and if you inherited an autograph collection, there's no reason to sell Lincoln material for far less than it is worth. Never forget: If the price is too good to be true...

The Improved

On the positive side, eBay has made solid efforts to prevent sales of autograph forgeries over the past few years. It no longer takes its former easy going approach, but has taken steps to kick known forgers off the site and they cooperate with law enforcement in the investigation of forgeries.

eBay has improved itself by disallowing certificates of authenticity from authenticators known to be certifying fakes as genuine.

eBay reserves the right to remove any autographed item listed on its site if it feels that it is not genuine.

FBI's well-publicized Operation Bullpen shut down a number of sports memorabilia forgers who were peddling forgeries on eBay. The government seized over $10 million in fraudulent material.

eBay has improved its bidding policies, including eliminating shill bidding, stopping bidders who put in ridiculously high bids to scare off other bidders before revoking the high bid just before the auction ends, and improving feedback .

The Suggestions

Despite the improvements, eBay is still an autograph minefield. You must always be wary of bad material. Educate yourself so you can spot questionable autographs.

Points to Remember

1. A high feedback rating is no sign that material is genuine. The seller offering the John Wilkes Booth signature for a dollar had a rating over 98-percent. Feedback means that the deal was completed to the satisfaction of both parties, not that the material was authentic.

2. There is a difference between a full-time autograph dealer, who knows what he or she is selling and guarantees it in writing, and a casual autograph seller or general antiques dealer, who occasionally brokers autographs and manuscripts and may not have the reference library and expertise to determine authenticity.

3. Certificates of Authenticity (COAs) mean nothing unless they're from a dealer with a good reputation and backed up by lifetime guarantee for a full refund of the purchase price in writing if the autograph is found to be unauthentic.

4. Letters that begin "Dear Friend" or have no specific greeting are almost always facsimiles.

5. Don't bid on pieces that don't have a scan that is large enough and sharp enough to easily examine the autograph.

6. Beware of dealers who constantly have very rare pieces, especially at low prices. If a dealer has a Button Gwinnett signature, an Edgar Allan Poe letter or a Christy Mathewson single-signed baseball, on a monthly basis, be suspicious.

7. I am cautious about sellers who opt to use the "Private Auction" feature on eBay. I've seen many forged pieces sold that way, since there is no way for an expert to alert a winning bidder about authenticity problems.

8. If a dealer claims a piece is rare, do a search on eBay for similar pieces. If the before mentioned Harry Truman TLS from the 1960s is advertised by the dealer as "rare" and you find eight similar ones on eBay at the same time, how rare can it really be?

9. I am wary of clipped signatures and signed album pages, because they can skillfully forged by the hundreds.

10. If you want to buy a genuine presidential piece, try a presidential commission with the attractive engravings. Presidents were required to sign each one, and there are thousands of them. For example, it is probably the safest way to buy an Abraham Lincoln. Do not, however, purchase presidential land grants signed by the Commander In Chief after Andrew Jackson, as they are secretarial. Likewise, cancelled checks are generally safer than clipped signatures. Recently, the check archives of Thomas Edison and Lucille Ball have been located, and a collector can feel confident when purchasing one of their checks.

Protect Yourself

Many of the most prestigious autograph and manuscript organizations list their members of their websites. Some unscrupulous dealers falsely claim they are members of these groups. Feel free to research dealers by using these sites:

The Professional Autograph Dealer's Association (PADA): www.padaweb.org

The Manuscript Society: www.manuscript.org/dealers.html

Universal Autograph Collector's Club (U.A.C.C.) Registered Dealers: www.uacc. org and then you will see a link for Registered Dealers on the left side of the page

The Antiquarian Booksellers Association of America (ABAA): www.abaa.org

The Ephemera Society: www.ephemerasociety.org

Attaining membership in the UACC Registered Dealer program, PADA and the ABAA is difficult. New dealers often need to find three sponsors to support their membership; they have to fill out an application stating their qualifications, education, years in business, size of their reference library and other credentials which are carefully verified. Then they have to be voted in.

If you suspect something on eBay may be Autopen, use the Internet to help you find out. One good Autopen site I use is www.geocities.com/~sbeck/

Educate Yourself

Purchase autograph reference books. Many of the out-of-print ones can be bought on eBay. Some of the best ones I use on a regular basis include:

Charles Hamilton: *Collecting Autographs and Manuscripts* (the best and most comprehensive basic autograph reference book), *The Signature of America*, *American Autographs* (but good luck finding a copy), and *Great Forgers and Famous Fakes* (proving that counterfeits started long before eBay).

Ken Rendell: *History Comes to Life* and *Forging History*.

Ray Rawlins: *The Stein and Day Book Of World Autographs*.

Mark Allen Baker: *Collecting Autographs* and *Advanced Autograph Collecting*.

Mary Benjamin: *Autographs: A Key to Collecting*

Larry Vrzalik and Michael Minor: *From the President's Pen*.

John M. Taylor – *From The White House Inkwell*. Also, Taylor edited the infinitely useful *Autograph Collector's Checklist*, published by the Manuscript Society.

Go to autograph shows and book fairs held around the country. One fine calendar for this is www.bookfairs.com. Hold material in your hand, meet dealers and pick up some catalogs. Notice how the iron gall ink used two hundred years ago "rusts" to an auburn color, so if you see a Thomas Jefferson or George Washington signature in jet black ink, you know it is likely a forgery. See that Babe Ruth and Humphrey Bogart never signed with a Sharpie or ballpoint pen. Examining autographs and manuscripts in person is a three dimensional experience. Looking at them on a computer screen cannot compare to seeing them live.

Don't be fooled by eBay spam in your inbox. Any email that states something like "Bid cancelled" or a generic "What is your best price for this item?" and asks you to sign into eBay is a scam. This is called phishing and you should report it to eBay. The email senders insert a fake link that, when you click on it, looks like you are logging into eBay, but you are not. What they are after is your eBay user name and password so they can go on a buying spree.

The bottom line on purchasing autographs on eBay is authenticity and responsibility. Just as you buy clothes or electronics from a store where you can take it back if find them inadequate, buy autographs from a responsible and knowledgeable party. With this said, I confess that 90-percent of the manuscripts I purchase on eBay are from other dealers, because I know the material is genuine and, in the very rare case it turns out to not be authentic, I can return it to the dealer for a full refund. Only on rare occasions do I purchase letters from people who claim to have uncovered correspondence in their attic.

Happy hunting on eBay!

Stuart Lutz, a full-time historic document and manuscript dealer, owns Stuart Lutz Historic Documents, Inc. He can be reached at (877) I-BUY-DOCS [428-9362], or at Stuart@HistoryDocs.com. For more information, see his advertisement on page 543 or go to www.historydocs.com.

Chapter 6

Buying Autographs at Auction

By Gil Griggs

Auctions are hot, hot, hot. The world of autograph collecting has evolved from a somewhat secretive hobby closely guarded by an elite few to anyone who wants to own an autograph by their favorite entertainer or sports star.

Auctions make sense for owners and buyers alike. The owner consigns his collection to an autograph house, comes to an agreement with the auctioneer on the estimated value, and sometimes places a reserve to protect his investment. This can be a simple process in return for the agreed commission. The bidder knows what they want to pay for a particular autograph and makes an offer. They can adjust the bid to the amount they're willing to pay and can drop out of the process at their discretion—unless they get caught up in competitive bidding and refuse to let the autograph go to someone else. They may kick themselves afterwards, but at least they won it.

Collecting autographs is a time-honored hobby. One of the first recorded autograph collectors was the Roman philosopher, Cicero. The signatures and scrawls of the famous and not-so-famous have been hoarded by collectors for centuries. Some ancient rarities find their way into museum vaults. Other treasures await discovery in someone's dusty attic or private collections. I wonder what the signature of Jesus Christ would bring — to a lesser degree, Julius Caesar. The signatures, sometimes questionable, of Christopher Columbus and William Shakespeare have appeared on the auction block, but these remain unobtainable, but to a few very wealthy collectors.

Auctions can be traced to ancient times. As early as 500 BC, children were known to be sold to the wife of the highest bidder. There were estate auctions as early as the Roman Empire, some to satisfy debts, that included household furnishings and stolen items from local disputes or even war. In 191 the entire Roman Empire went under the hammer by the Praetorian Guard. Much later, when the Pilgrims arrived in America, auctions were the quickest way to turn crops and livestock into cash. However, catalog auctions of rare collectibles that we might recognize today did not come into vogue until 18th century Europe, especially in France where they were held in taverns. Stockholm boasts the world's oldest auction house. The rarest autographs and manuscripts are housed in museums and academic or state archives. They are seldom found in private collections and even less on the open market.

Until the 1980s, the autograph market in the United States was, for the most part, controlled by six or seven New England dealers. One of those dealers was the great collector and authenticator of his day, Charles Hamilton, who also held his own auctions. His books and the knowledge he shared with the collecting community were invaluable. He was one of the most interesting men I have ever met. Autographs and letters penned by historical notables were his treasures. Important and interesting content make them all the more valuable. There was a story he liked to tell from the 1970s, in which he attended a housewarming on Cape Cod with a friend. It was a lovely old house, and the proud owner provided a tour along with the wine and cheese. When Hamilton was introduced to the host, he recognized his name and asked if he was the author of a book on autographs of famous people he'd heard of. The host replied yes and smugly continued to tell Hamilton that when he bought the house he had found a trunk full of letters by George Washington, John Adams, Thomas Jefferson and more. Hamilton's eyes lit up and he asked "Where are they now?" The young host, seeking to impress his guest, informed him that they were burned in the fireplace of the old mansion. Hamilton grew red with anger. Turning his wineglass over, he requested his friend to leave with him immediately. Before departing, he turned and said to the host: "You sir, are a fool. You would have been better off burning this old house down and keeping the letters."

With the 1980s came a rise in the economy. Two things caused an explosion in autograph collecting; it went from being a hobby with relatively few dealers who set the prices, and it took a new direction with new players entering the business aided by the growing economy.

George and Helen Sanders of Ashville, N.C., were avid lifetime collectors. They recognized a need for a reference that would help them determine the value of autographs and what they should pay for them. Thus the *Sanders Price Guide* was born. It provided a new generation of collectors with comparative pricing for signatures, signed photographs, handwritten or typed letters and documents. It became the benchmark of autograph price guides.

Around the same time, some of the old stalwarts in the hobby were going out of business. A new auction house in Maine, Remember When Auctions, took the business to the next level. They provided a free catalog with illustrations and descriptions. In order to expand the autograph marketplace, they generously sponsored five new auction houses. Our business, Signature House, was one. This opened the door for today's abundance of auction houses.

Sotheby's and Christie's, friendly rivals since the 18th century, have handled some of the most notable autograph collections though they are primarily known for their art auctions. In my humble opinion, when it comes to autograph auction houses, R&R of New Hampshire, with its large monthly auctions, is a stand-out. Bob Eaton gave me a tour a few years ago and it still amazes me how he does it. It is one incredible job to publish a catalog the magnitude of theirs every month.

Because of the rapid growth of auction houses and the tremendous popularity of eBay auctions, bidding and consigning in today's market can be both confusing and treacherous to the uninformed. When dealing with an auction house, the most important thing is trust, either as a bidder or consignor. If you are buying, your trust must extend beyond the initial transaction. An auction house that does not offer a lifetime guarantee on your purchase is not worthy of your business. Some provide a 30 day or limited period guarantee. The authenticity of an autograph does not expire in 30 days. If an auction house sells their autograph collectibles as is, it doesn't know or doesn't care about its merchandise and does not deserve your business. There are many reputable houses that guarantee what they sell.

Consignor commission rates and buyer's premiums have risen to as high as 25-percent. The expense of publishing a catalog is quite costly. From the time a consignment comes through the door, it is subject to cataloging, illustration, layouts, printing, publishing and shipping. Many have the extra cost of hosting a live auction. Add a large staff and a large office, and the costs can be mind-boggling. Someone has to pay for all of this, and you can guess who that is. It becomes your job to make your purchase worthwhile.

With that in mind, when bidding at auction, follow the same rules you would when purchasing from a flea market or a dealer. Bid on things you like and have some knowledge about. It is a rule worth repeating. Bid on things you like and know about, setting a limit on what you are willing to pay, and always keep in mind the premium that will be added. If you are successful and get it for less than you had in mind, you've made a good buy. There are some buyers with enough savvy to be able to buy from one auction, pay the premium and consign the same item to another auction house, pay their commission and still make a handsome profit. It takes a lot of knowledge and experience to do that. Their reward is well earned.

Buying at auction can be very rewarding for the knowledgeable bidder. There are three different market prices, somewhat similar to the Kelly Blue Book used to price used cars. The first is the retail price you would pay if you walk into an autograph dealer with his beautifully displayed inventory. His price is set, but he has a good reputation and you are confident of the purchase. You establish a relationship with him and he will inform you if an item you're interested in becomes available. The other option is to buy at auctions on your own. Some homework is required on your part. Finding auctioneers you can trust and building a working relationship with may take some time, but you will have the satisfaction of buying what you want at the price you want. Then there is the dealer price, should you want to sell your autograph or collection. It will always be less than retail and sometimes less than auction prices. The advantage is that you are paid immediately and the transaction is simple. However, if you place it in auction and pay a small commission, you will typically get significantly more—the same price a dealer would get when selling at auction.

One question I've been asked several times by potential consignors, especially for valuable autographs or collections, is if they should donate their treasure to a museum. I have found the opinion famously expressed in the will of Edmund de Goncourt helpful in answering that question. He wrote: "My wish is that my Drawings, my Prints, my Curiosities, my Books—in a word, these things of art which have been the joy of my life—shall not be consigned to the cold tomb of a museum, and subjected to the stupid glance of the careless passer-by; but I require that they shall all be dispersed under the hammer of the Auctioneer, so that the pleasure which the acquiring of each one of them has given me shall be given again, in each case to some inheritor of my own tastes."

These are my observations on current trends in autograph auctions, by category:

United States Presidents are the leader at most autograph auction houses. The most sought after are Washington, Lincoln and Jefferson. John Adams' desirability is on the rise. John Kennedy is at the top of modern presidents. The rarest is William H. Harrison as president, who died after only a month in office and always commands premium prices; as well as James Garfield, mortally wounded a little over a month in office; and Zachary Taylor who served only one year.

Americana spans a broad range of American cultural history. Western autographs of lawmen and outlaws to Native and African Americans are popular. Also desirable are other autographs and collectibles peculiar to our national heritage, whether they are letters from the California Gold Rush, survivors of the great San Francisco fire, or daguerreotypes, tintypes or albumen photos of our ancestors. The carte-de-visite, or CDV was something between a trading card and a business card. It was an economical commercial image, often used as a calling card in the 19th century. They reached their peak popularity during the Civil War when soldiers sought to send their likeness to loved ones as keepsakes. One signed by a general is very desirable as a collectible.

War and political items are always highly sought after. A letter or document penned by Napoleon is in high demand. His signatures on documents are much more common. He was known to dictate five or six letters at a time, but to find one entirely written in his hand is rare. Recently, sales of WWII notables have taken a jump in the market, causing renewed interest in many collectors.

Colonial autographs remain a staple and are becoming scarcer. The Signers of the Declaration of Independence remain among the most desirable and some can be had without breaking the bank. But if you desire a complete set, finding Button Gwinnett, Thomas Lynch Jr., or Arthur Middleton will cost you a pretty penny.

The Civil War continues to be popular even though interest peaked in the 1990s. That market has declined somewhat since then, but it seems to be making a comeback. Confederate autographs are approximately three times more expensive than Union ones, especially if the writer was killed in action. Letters from ordinary soldiers are more valuable with content describing their battle experiences.

Popular entertainment remains trendy because there is plethora of these collectibles on the market. As the population ages, interest in the silent film stars and even autographs of mid-twentieth century film and music stars has waned among younger, newer collectors. Marilyn Monroe has replaced Jean Harlow in popularity, as James Dean replaced Errol Flynn who replaced Douglas Fairbanks. The Beatles are more popular than Glenn Miller.

Sports remains strong, but buyers are increasingly wary due to the growing number of forgeries online. Baseball stars are what most people go after, and those "Damn Yankees" are at the top of their wish list. No collection can be complete without Babe Ruth and Lou Gehrig, who endure as the most sought after. If a collector has been buying only Hall of Fame legends he would be doing well.

Heads of State and royalty show increasing interest due to the massive global influence of the Internet and the ability of bidders to find those world political leaders or royals of special interest. As mentioned before, Napoleon is hot as well as Russia's Peter the Great and his offspring.

Literature. There is wide interest, not only in letters and photos but also among collectors of first printing books, particularly if they meet the bibliophile's strict requirements. It is a category in which condition is of paramount importance. Authors Hemingway, Steinbeck and F. Scott Fitzgerald always do well.

Classical music & opera: Fewer collectors are interested but we have had good success and are making efforts to build this category. The true classical composers have never lost their luster and a rare Autograph Musical Quote Signed can stimulate spirited bidding.

Space & aviation: Astronauts are becoming more desirable, especially as the pioneers have aged or died. Neil Armstrong remains the most desirable because of his special place in space history and the fact he quit signing for the general public some years ago. Still, aviation pioneers Lindbergh and Amelia Earhart continue to fascinate collectors.

Science: All branches continue to be popular, from inventors such as Edison to Nobel Laureates, particularly manuscripts or letters having to do with their area of expertise.

Law: Although jurists and cabinet members continue to sell, they are not in high demand because they are more common, with the possible exception of Supreme Court justices, again depending on content.

Judeo-Christian. There is strong demand in this category. From Popes to old-time preachers and other clerics, we were surprised at first by the demand for the autographs and related artifacts of such notables. While many auctioneers have assigned these a lower priority, this category keeps growing in popularity for us. C.S. Lewis, Spurgeon and Catholic Popes are popular; but the rarer Calvin, Luther or Wesley are particularly desirable.

Besides rarity, the one constant determinant of value is content. Letters and documents with desirable content will continue to command the highest prices at auction, as discriminating collectors consider this above all else. We sold a burned Lincoln ALS once that contained only a few words to his Secretary of the Navy, but it hammered down at $12,000, well over the signature value, because enough of its content revealed its significance in war preparations.

Many collectors use auctions as a way to raise cash in order to upgrade their collections. Perhaps a collector might have started with clipped signatures, which can make an attractive and affordable matted and framed display. As ones collection grows and their funds allow it, they may wish to enhance the value and the desirability of their collection by continuously upgrading their collection in small intervals. They can start by selling a signature at auction in order to buy a letter signed by the same person. Later, they can sell that to buy a letter entirely handwritten and signed. Or they may find one with much better content, so they auction an item they already have in order to purchase the more desirable one. Auctions are a particularly useful tool in gauging the market value of your autographs and determining when it is a good time to divest some of your collection or increase your investment.

In summary, whether buying or selling at auction, get to know the companies and people you are doing business with and their reputation in the industry. Only buy from those that offer lifetime guarantees and who have known, honest reputations to back them up. In other words, know the value of their certificate of authenticity (COA) — it is only as good as their reputation. Bid on collectibles you like and with which you are familiar. If you are selling, make sure it is something you are willing to part with and that you have reasonable expectations of market value.

Auctions are here to stay. Learn to make wise use of them to get the best return on your collectibles investment and have a little fun in the process. Happy auction bidding.

Gil Griggs and his wife, Karen Griggs, own Signature House, which has conducted auctions since the 1980s. Signature House publishes a catalog for their mail, phone, email and fax auctions every four months or so, offering a broad range of autograph material including Presidents, Civil War, Entertainment, Sports, Literature, Science & Technology, Colonial, Military, Aviators and Explorers as well as Judeo-Christian and Antiquities and collectibles related to each genre. For more information, see their advertisement on page 546 or go to www.signaturehouse.com.

Chapter 7

Signed Books, Autographed History in Your Hands

By Tim Miller

The phenomenon of autograph collecting stems from the 16th century when German students kept albums of their correspondence with family, friends and noblemen. By the 18th century, autograph collecting had evolved into our present concept of the hobby and had become a favorite pastime of millions of people around the globe.

Perhaps you're already an autograph collector, carefully archiving those signatures of your favorite personalities. Maybe you want to begin a collection, or you've come across an autograph that you think could be quite valuable. If any of these instances apply, you've come to the right place.

For many years, *The Sanders Autograph Price Guide* has been a valuable resource for autograph collectors, helping them evaluate, enhance and market the investment they've made in their collections. Even the most seasoned collectors refer to this helpful tool. In my own journey, I have gone from collector to proprietor of a thriving autograph-related business, and I still find this guide especially useful.

Flatsigned

Signed books are one of the fastest-growing segments of autographed collectibles. I've noticed an interesting trend over the years. In any economy, strong or weak, the value of signed books continued to rise. The reason is simple: when the stock market is up, people have extra money to spend on items and pastimes they enjoy. When it is down and the cost of living goes up, people don't want to spend their money unwisely on luxuries that have no real value. Instead, they seek investment opportunities. Mainly, they invest in what interests them most. Those that love collecting signed books will continue to do so in any market.

While no investment comes with a guarantee, some collectors have seen the market value of their first edition, signed books skyrocket over time. In some cases, a signed book originally valued at $2000 has increased in value to $25,000 in just a decade. Similarly, an already valuable first edition copy of *To Kill a Mockingbird* worth $1000 may instantly be worth $20,000 if you can to get the author, Harper Lee, to sign it.

The most widely desirable signed books are those that are flatsigned, meaning that the author has signed the book directly on the title page as opposed to on a bookplate or sticker and has not written a personalized inscription like "To Sue Jack" or "To Danny."

There are exceptions to this. Let's say the author has inscribed the book with an unusual message. An inscription from John Grisham reading, "Judy, thanks for the hot date last night," could gain a lot of collector interest and bring a strong premium. Books personalized by the author to a celebrity or well-known person or noting a special date or occasion in the inscription would also be an exception. A copy of *To Kill a Mockingbird* signed by Harper Lee with a message to her friend Truman Capote would be a highly desirable collectible.

In most cases, though, a flatsigned book has the most market value. I'd like to add that a book is still considered flatsigned if the autograph contains the date and place of the signing. And a flatsigned book doesn't necessarily have to be signed in black ink. A signature doesn't need to be simple in order to be flatsigned.

Through my work and experience collecting signed documents and memorabilia, I have seen flatsigned, first printing books become one of the most highly prized and regarded autograph collectibles of the 21st century. The demand and value of flatsigned books has increased accordingly.

Being First

How does one define a true *first printing*? Literally, a first printing (referred to as an "impression" in the United Kingdom) is any book from the initial print run of the title. Each copy is considered a "first edition." A printing refers to a single run on a printing press. If a publisher orders a first print run of 10,000 copies, then later orders a run of another 5000 copies to be printed with no changes, the result is a *second printing of a first edition*, which is much less collectable.

In collecting, it is the first printing that is most desirable. If an expert refers to a first edition without qualification, they are referring to the first printing of the first edition.

How can you tell if a book is a first edition? Many people believe that all the information that they need to know about the printing of the book can be found in the "number line" of the book's copyright page. However, it's not as easy as just looking at that line of numbers or searching for the words "first edition" following the copyright. Correctly deciphering if a book is truly a first edition comes from years of research and reference books.

Often the industry learns information about a book decades after it was printed. Still, if we use the number line as our standard and if the "1" on the number line is present, it is almost always a first printing, but not always. Some publishers handle the number line in different ways or include unique information on the copyright page. For example, Random House books have to include the words "first edition" to be a first printing. Scholastic, the U.S. publishers of the Harry Potter books, made it more complicated because they put the printing line on the same line as the year. This has caused some confusion. For example, with the Potter books published in 2001, buyers would see the "1" in the number line and think that the book was a first printing when it simply meant that it was printed in 2001.

The State of Things

Now that I've explained the meaning of a true first printing, I should mention that sometimes it is possible for copies of a book from a single printing to differ from one another. This occurrence is called a "state" or "issue."

A separate state of a printing occurs when a change is made to book during the press run. Say that while a 10,000 copy first printing was on the press, a typographical error was noticed after 2,000 were printed. The press would be stopped, the error would be corrected in the source file and the remaining 8,000 copies of the first printing would be printed. When completed, all 10,000 books would be sent to the publisher for distribution. In this instance, the publisher would be distributing both a first and second state of the first edition/first printing with the second state referring to those 8,000 books that were printed with the typographical error corrected.

A famous example of a first and second state of a book occurred with John Steinbeck's *Of Mice and Men* when, after the book had been sent to press, the word "pendula" on page seven was changed to "loosely." Only a few thousand books had been printed with the word "pendula" before the change was made. In the world of collecting, those few thousand books (the first state) are vastly more desirable. Had twenty thousand books been printed with the word "pendula" and only five thousand printed with the word "loosely," the "pendula" books would still be more valuable because a collector will always seek out the earliest version of the book even if it is not the rarest.

A similar example can be found with a printing of Hemingway's *The Sun Also Rises*, in which "stop" is spelled "stoppp." It's the triple "p" that has caused that particular first issue, first printing book to become a $10,000 book—even when it is not in a dust jacket. If you find that first issue, first printing in a dust jacket even without a signature, it could bring $100,000. With a signature, you're looking at potentially a $250,000 book, whether or not it's in the best of condition.

Condition is Critical

Collectors need to be careful when purchasing a signed book. You should always be mindful of the condition. Books in excellent, undamaged condition—called MINT or NEAR MINT—bring the highest prices.

Condition is most important when dealing with "hyper-modern" books: books printed during the last 20 years or so. During this period, people have been more careful about preserving their books. When looking at a flatsigned, hyper-modern book, the greatest value will be given to those in the best condition.

Keep in mind that even VERY GOOD copies of books (not MINT OR NEAR MINT, but still quite good) that are highly prized will still command a good price. For example: a J.D. Salinger book labeled VERY GOOD is still considered a fine investment.

In book collecting the word GOOD translates to "bad." Unless it's rare or exceptional in other ways, don't be fooled by someone offering to sell you a book in GOOD condition.

Future Collectibles

Your local bookstore is holding a book signing for a new author that has gathered considerable interest. Perhaps you've read some good reviews of this author's first novel. Maybe you've gotten the sense that one day this fresh writer will be the next big thing. What does it hurt to buy a copy and stand in line for a signature?

Keep an eye open for those new authors. If you spend $30 on a MINT, hardcover, signed first printing of a new book, you could have a future fortune in your hands. At the very least, you'll have another book to read and another autograph for your collection. With any luck, you may find that you've added the signature of the next Hemingway.

Another good idea is to stay abreast of the latest literary awards. One of the first signs that an autographed book will go up in value is if the author or the title itself wins a prominent award.

Other good investments are those books signed by established authors with consistent track-records. These signed books often make the best investments. Hemingway, Steinbeck, Faulkner, Fitzgerald and even Steven King and Anne Rice, are going to remain popular.

Always collect what you enjoy. The real thrill of collecting is being able to hold a part of something that excites you, something that you value. Chances are, if you value it, someone else will, too.

Collecting autographs and autographed books is an exciting adventure. It allows you to be a part of living history. To this day, I still get a thrill from holding the signature of a famous author, politician, artist or celebrity in my hands. For a brief moment, it's as if we're in the same room. I've been most fortunate to not only have this exciting hobby, but to also make my living from it. My wish for other collectibles enthusiasts is that they experience the same fortune and enjoyment I've had.

Tim Miller is president and CEO of FlatSigned, Inc., a retail, rare book and publishing company specializing in sales and publishing of rare and collectible books, first-edition signed books, manuscripts, historical documents, art, and autographs. FlatSigned has worked with many of the world's most famous authors and other notables, including the late former U.S. President Gerald Ford, Senator Hilary Clinton, Astronaut Buzz Aldrin and others. See their ad on page 549.

Chapter 8

Selling your Collection

By Sandra Palomino

Deciding how to sell your collection will be one of the most important decisions you ever have to make as a collector. Perhaps you've inherited items that you know little about, or have reached a point in your life when you must part with a collection carefully selected and treasured over the years. Regardless, when the time comes to sell there is only one objective: to maximize your return. Selling at auction is a great option, and to get the most out of your collection be prepared to do your homework before making any commitments. Remember, these are your treasured possessions; there are no "do-overs" once the final hammer falls.

Auction houses generate profit from seller's commissions and buyer's premiums, which will vary by company. A seller's commission is what the auction house charges the person who is selling the item and is usually based on a percentage of the hammer price. This commission is always deducted at time of settlement. Conversely, the buyer pays a premium added to the selling price. Be sure to know up front what the seller's commission will be. Ask specifically if there are any administrative fees that apply. Some auction houses will charge for incidentals such as photography, insurance, handling, and cataloguing. There may even be fees applied if items are not successful in selling. Individually, the fees may be nominal but they can add up very quickly. Best to know ahead of time what your true net return will be; receiving an impressive estimate on an autograph initially doesn't prepare you for the final net after all the fees have been deducted.

Payment is generally issued from 30 to 60 days after the date of the auction. It may seem like a long time, but collecting funds from every buyer in any auction can sometimes be as arduous a task as preparing the initial auction. Be sure to ask when settlement checks are mailed, and if they are always mailed promptly. If timing is an issue, most auction houses can offer advances. These factors help to tell the financial stability of an auction house, as well as indicating sound business practices which will have a direct impact on the management of your collection.

Seller's commissions can vary greatly, but be cautious to not be taken in by a low seller's commission. A low commission rate may seem like a good deal, but if your items perform poorly at auction your take-home will be greatly reduced. A company offering a bargain fee often cannot deliver a strong selling price, in which case your overall net return will be disappointing. The difference in performance can vary dramatically, and many factors contribute to selling prices.

The more tangible factors are easy to research. Ask for past catalogs and prices realized. How is the quality of illustration and writing? What is the discrepancy between the estimates listed and the prices realized? What percentage of the material is sold at any given auction?

These are all basic assessments that you can make for yourself.

The potential size of a bidding audience is critical to the successful sale of your collection. The number of catalogs mailed and the existing number of clients will provide only a part of the answer. A less measurable factor is the amount of publicity an auction house can muster. Of course, the participating bidders determine how high the selling price will be; however attention received in mainstream media outlets can bring new bidders from unlikely places. Be sure that the company you choose has an experienced media relations teams. Even if your particular collection will not receive the direct spotlight, it will benefit from the associative value of being in a high profile auction.

The age of the internet has changed the auction world forever. Technological advances have made it possible to have a worldwide audience bidding on your material. However, not all auction houses have the same tools and features available. So be sure to visit their website to determine how much of an advantage their website can be to the selling of your collection. Be sure to compare all of your prospective auctioneers' web traffic against each other by using www.Compete.com. Also register at each site you are researching and compare how that website functions as an auction tool. For example, can absentee bids be left, and until what time prior to the auction? Can it accept live bids during the floor session? As you navigate a company's website ask yourself how valuable a resource can it be. Can you easily search their past prices conveniently online? Chances are potential bidders for your collection will form a similar opinion.

One of the biggest apprehensions in turning your collection over for auction is the fear of not knowing what will happen once it is out of your hands. You must have confidence in the company you have chosen; make certain that you will have access to information during the various stages of the consignment process. The consignment process should be an enjoyable one. Ideally bringing your collection to auction is a celebration of your work, the end result being that the individual items will find new homes where they will be equally treasured.

Sandra Palomino is Director of Historical Manuscripts for Heritage Auctions, the world's largest auctioneer of collectibles. For more information, see their advertisement on the inside front cover of this guide or go to www.ha.com.

Chapter 9

How to Use the Sanders Guide

In the 1980s George and Helen Sanders published the first edition of *The Sanders Price Guide to Autographs,* now *The Sanders Autograph Price Guide.* They compiled their data using autograph dealer catalogs and retail price lists as a reference. Today, we have access to infinite amount of data regarding pricing and as the author of this price guide, I have spent the last two years reviewing, revising and updating every price and category that we chose to include in the 7th edition.

Our stated prices were compiled, with permission, from trusted autograph dealer websites and autograph catalogs. The most important source for autograph pricing still remains the realized prices attained at autograph auctions. In some instances, prices realized by reliable dealers selling on eBay were also averaged into the database.

It is important to remember that the prices in Sander's reflect average prices derived from these multiple sources. Every autograph is unique, with variations of presentation and condition that determine its market value. The value of autographs is based on content, the date the autograph was signed and the condition of the autograph, in that order. For example, a magnificent Abraham Lincoln signed autographed letter (ALS) as President, sold this past summer for over $3,000,000. The average price of an Abraham Lincoln ALS as President is listed in the 7th edition of Sander's for $22,369. Why the differential? The $3,000,000 Lincoln ALS had sensational content, date, and condition. The *Sanders Guide* cannot replace your need to become educated in the areas you collect, nor the importance of building relationships with respected autograph professionals.

Listings in the *Sanders Guide* are separated into two sections; the main section with everything but sports, and the sports section following it, because many sports have unique autograph price categories that can't be accommodated in the main section. We think you'll like how it's organized and appreciate the extra prices it allows us to include.

Begin your research and use of this guide by becoming familiar with the format as well as the common abbreviations used in the autograph industry. I have chosen to break down each non-sport price category into columns: SIG, LS/DS, ALS, SP. Since sports prices may require unique pricing categories, I have given them separate abbreviations that will be covered in that section.

SIG: This is the price of just a signature. The signature could be on a card, the back of an envelope or a scrap of paper. If additional writing accompanies the signature, such as a date or rank, the price would be higher. Signatures on certain items, such as presidential signatures on Executive Mansion or White House cards, can be worth many times the price listed.

LS/DS: Letter Signed or Document Signed. This is the trickiest category. This could represent a manuscript letter (a letter written by a secretary or aid) that is authentically signed, a typed letter authentically signed, or any document authentically signed, including signed checks and contracts.

ALS: Autograph Letter, Signed. This is usually the most desirable form of autograph for collectors of presidential and historical letters. An ALS is a letter, written and signed, by the same individual.

SP: Signed Photograph. These are immensely popular. Prices are primarily for 8x10s and the metric equivalent, although in certain categories, and around the turn of the 20th century and before, prices may reflect smaller photos. The SP is often inscribed to the recipient of the picture. This is especially true in the case of signed vintage Hollywood or music photos. Inscriptions can either increase or decrease the value of the SP.

Please refer to the abbreviation key on the following pages to aid your navigation through the _The Sanders Autograph Price Guide._

Autograph Category Abbreviations

The autograph category abbreviations below are used throughout the main Sanders pricing section that starts on page 59. Most of the abbreviations are easy to determine without using this key, but take a quick read just in case. Autograph collecting terms and abbreviations, and country abbreviations, are on page 57.

1st Fmly	First Family
1st Lady	First Lady
2nd Lady	Vice President's Wife
Abolit	Abolitionist
Adven	Adventurer
Aero	Aeronautics
Afr-Am Ldr	African-American Leader
Am Ind	American Indian
Archaeol	Archaeologist
Archtct	Architect
Assass	Assassin
Band	Big Bandleader, member
Bus	Business
Cab	Cabinet
Celeb	Celebrity
Civ Engr	Civil Engineer
Civ Rts	Civil Rights
Civ War	Civil War
Clmnst	Columnist
Cntry Mus	Country Music
Comics	Cartoonist
Comp	Composer
Crime	Criminal
Diplo	Diplomat
Econ	Economist
Educ	Education
Engr	Engineer
Ent	Entertainment
Expl	Explorer
Fash	Fashion
Fem	Feminist/Women's Rights
Finan	Finance

Autograph Terms & Abbreviations

AA .... Academy Award
Ace .... Aviation Ace w/5 or more kills
ADS .... Autographed Document Signed
Afr-Am .... African-American
ALS .... Autographed Letter Signed
AManS .... Autographed Manuscript Signed
AMusQS .... Autographed Musical
Quotation Signed
AMusMS .... Autographed Musical
Manuscript Signed
ANS .... Autographed Note Signed
AQS .... Autographed Quotation Signed
CDV .... Carte de Visite
Chk .... Check
Cont .... Content
CSA .... Confederate States of America
CW .... Civil War
D .... Died
Dir .... Director
DoI .... Declaration of Independence
DS .... Document Signed
FDC .... First Day Cover
FF .... Free Frank
Gen .... General

GG .... Golden Globe
GLAC .... Goal Line Art Card
GWTW .... Gone With the Wind
HOF .... Hall of Fame
Intl. .... International
ISP .... Inscribed Signed Photo
KIA .... Killed in Action
LS .... Letter Signed
MOC .... Member of Congress
MOH .... Medal of Honor
Off .... Official
Pc .... Postcard
PM .... Prime Minister or Postmaster
S .... Signed
SB .... Signed Book
Sig .... Signature
Sopr. .... Soprano
SP .... Signed Picture
Sp .... Special
Stk .... Stock
TLS .... Typed Letter Signed
TMS .... Typed Manuscript Signed
WD .... War Date
WOZ .... Wizard of Oz

Country Abbreviations

Afr .... Africa
Am .... America
Aus .... Austria
Aust .... Australia
Belg .... Belgium
Br .... Britain
Can .... Canada
Chin .... China
Czech .... Czechoslovakia
Fin .... Finland
Fr .... France

Ger .... Germany
Hung .... Hungary
Ir .... Ireland
It .... Italy
Lux .... Luxembourg
Jap .... Japan
NZ .... New Zealand
Pol .... Poland
Rus .... Russia
Sp .... Spain
Swe .... Sweden

Autograph Prices

Main Section

See Page 478 for Sports

NAME	DATES	CATEGORY	SIG	LS/DS	ALS	SP	COMMENTS
Aaliyah	1979-2001	Music	46	90	118	194	Singer. S Album 120
Aalto, Hugo Alvar	1899-1976	Archtct	62	138		125	Finnish Architect-Designer
Abagnale, Frank		Celeb	10	15	20	28	
Abba		Music	234			602	S Album 400
Abbado, Claudio		Ent	15			50	Symph. & Opera Conductor
Abbe, Cleveland	1838-1916	Sci	15		50	35	Co-Fndr. US Weather Service 1869
Abbett, Leon	1836-1894	Gov	10	30	40		
Abbey, Edwin Austin		Artist	15	30	50		Am. Portraitist, Illust.
Abbot, Charles Greeley	1873-1973	Sci	12	42		29	Am. Astrophysicist
Abbott & Costello		Ent	670	840		1113	S Album 2400
Abbott, Bessie		Ent	25			45	Opera
Abbott, Bud	1895-1974	Ent	218	348	265	338	Radio, Film, TV Comedian
Abbott, George	1887-1995	Ent	25	45	60	92	Prod./Dir./Plays
Abbott, Henry Larcom	1831-1927	Civ War	30	45	82		Union Gen. Sig/Rank 45
Abbott, Henry Livermore	1842-1864	Civ War	120	302			Union Gen. Sig/Rank 125. Killed at Wilderness
Abbott, John		Ent	10			12	
Abbott, John S. C.	1805-1877	Author	12		40		
Abbott, Lyman	1835-1922	Clergy	23	38	50	75	Congregational Min. -Author
Abdnor, James		Congr	10	15		10	Sen. SD
Abdul, Paula		Ent	21	28	40	50	Singer-Dancer; Am. Idol judge
Abdullah II, King		Royal				75	4th ruler of Jordan. Son of King Hussein
Abeken, Heinrich	1809-1872	Clergy			40		Ger. Theologian
Abel, I. W.		Labor	10	25	40	25	Pres. United Steel Workers
Abel, Rudolph Ivanovich		Mil		252			Soviet spy
Abel, Walter	1898-1987	Ent	15	32	30	65	Vint. Char. Actor-Leading Man
Abercrombie, John Joseph	1798-1877	Civ War	46	65	96		Union Gen.
Abercrombie, John Joseph (WD)	1798-1877	Civ War	65	102	188		Union Gen. ALS '64 525
Abercrombie, Leslie P.	1879-1957	Archtct		35			Specialist in town planning
Abercrombie, Neil A		Congr	10				Member US Congress
Aberdeen, Lord, 4th Earl	1784-1860	HOS	35	45	78		Br. Prime Min.
Abernathy, Ralph D.	1926-1990	Clergy	38	70	112	74	Civ. Rights. Martin Luther King deputy
Abernathy, Robert		Celeb	10				Pol. celebrity
Abernathy, Thomas Gerstle		Congr	10	10		10	Congressman MS
Abernethy, John	1764-1831	Sci	85	108	280		Devised External Iliac Artery Surgery
Abraham, F. Murray		Ent	11	22	35	43	AA Winner. 'Amadeus'
Abrahams, Jon		Ent	13			38	
Abrams, Creighton W.	1912-1974	Mil	23	30	45	72	Gen. WWII Tank Cmdr.
Abrams, Elliott		Diplo	10	20		25	State Dept.
Abril, Victoria		Ent	10				Actress
Abruzzo, Ben A.	1930-1985	Aero	26			70	Am. hot air balloonist & businessman
Abt, Franz	1819-1885	Comp	100		183		Ger. Comp.
Abzug, Bella	1920-1998	Pol	22	30	46	58	Lawyer, Rep, NY; women's movement leader.
AC/DC		Music	103	100		166	Color Poster 150; S Album 400
Acevedo-Vila, Anibal		Congr	10				Member US Congress
Acheson, Dean	1893-1971	Cab	35	82	95	95	Truman Sec. of State. Executed Marshall Plan
Acheson, George R.		Mil	10		20	15	
Ackerman, Gary L. A		Congr	10				Member US Congress
Ackland, Joss		Ent	10				Actor
Ackles, Jensen		Ent	17			50	
Ackte, Aino	1876-1944	Opera	15			40	Finnish born Sopr.
Acland, Arthur Wm.	1805-1877	Mil					SEE Hood, Arthur W.
Acosta, Bert		Aero	40	55	118	88	
Acquanetta, Burna		Ent	10			40	Actress
Acton, Loren		Space	10		35	25	

NAME	DATES	CATEGORY	SIG	LS/DS	ALS	SP	COMMENTS
Acuff, Roy		Cntry Mus	16		35	54	Grand Ole Opry Star.
Adair, Allen		Mil	32	25	55	80	Br. Gen. Operation Mkt. Garden
Adair, John		Gov	40	125	185		Early Gov. KY
Adair, Red		Celeb	20	35	55	30	Oil Well Fires
Adam 12 (cast)		Ent	20			55	Kent McCord, Martin Milner
Adam, Adolphe-Charles	1803-1856	Comp	40	125	410	108	Fr. Opera & Ballet (Giselle). "O Holy Night"
Adam, Juliette	1836-1936	Author		30	45		
Adam, Paul	1862-1920	Author	15		40		Fr. historical novels
Adamic, Louis	1899-1951	Author	15	58	110	45	Am. Novels. Born Yugoslavia
Adamowski, Timothee		Comp	15			35	AMusQS 45
Adams, Abigail	1744-1818	1st Lady	641	2162	5615		
Adams, Alva		Gov	10		15	10	Gov. CO
Adams, Alvin	1804-1877	Bus	20		50		Formed Adams Express Co.
Adams, Amy		Ent	13			40	
Adams, Andrew	1736-1797	Rev War	132	284	558		Continental Congress
Adams, Andy	1859-1935	Author			30		Am. cowboy & author
Adams, Ansel	1902-1984	Artist	171	370	513	226	Photographer
Adams, Brooke		Ent	10		16	20	Actress.
Adams, Bryan		Music	20			62	Rock
Adams, Charles F.	1866-1954	Cab	15	30	55		Sec. of Navy
Adams, Charles Follen	1842-1918	Author			40		Am. poet
Adams, Charles Francis	1807-1886	Diplo	51	170	229		Son of John Q. Adams, Civil War Amb. To Eng.
Adams, Charles Francis	1835-1915	Civ War	15	40	75		Union Brevet Brig. Gen.
Adams, Charles R.	1834-1900	Opera	20		60		Am. 'sgreatest tenor
Adams, Clara		Aero	50	65		84	Pioneer Zeppelin Flyer. 1st
Adams, Daniel W.	1821-1872	Civ War	191	324	1117		CSA Gen. Sig/Rank 250, War Dte. DS 400
Adams, Dawnn		Ent	10			15	Actress
Adams, Don	1923-2005	Ent	12	14	23	52	Actor. 'Get Smart'. Voice Artist
Adams, Edie	1927-2008	Ent	10	12	20	40	Singer-Actress/Ernie Kovac's Widow
Adams, Edwin	1834-1877	Ent	25			70	Vintage Stage Actor
Adams, Fletcher E.	KIA 1944	WWII	250				WWII ace w/9 kills
Adams, Gerry		HOS	60	75		125	Leader Sinn Fein, IRA
Adams, Hannah	1755-1831	Author	200		350		Historian. May be 1st Fem. Am. Prof. Writer
Adams, Harriet		Author	35	45	65		
Adams, Helen		Celeb	10				
Adams, Henry Brooks	1838-1918	Author	152	445	522		Am. Hist., Philosopher, Critic. ALS/cont 2800
Adams, Herbert	1858-1945	Artist	15	25	40		Busts in the Am. Hall of Fame
Adams, J. Q. & J. Monroe		Pres	2000	3367			Signed by Both
Adams, James S.		Bus	10	35	45	25	
Adams, James Truslow	1878-1949	Author	20		45		Historian, 1922 Pulitzer Pr.
Adams, Joey		Ent	10			18	Comedian
Adams, Joey Lauren		Ent	10			38	Actress.
Adams, John	1825-1864	Civ War	289	609	895		CSA Gen. KIA (WD) DS 2350, S 400-495
Adams, John	1735-1826	Pres	2138	7594	18958		FF 2500, Significant LS 38,000
Adams, John	1778-1854	Congr	25		40		Early MOC. NY
Adams, John & Marshall		Pres		7968			Pres. & Secretary of State
Adams, John (as Pres.)		Pres	3000	11575	21577		LS/Cont $39500, FF 3500, ALS/Cont $30000; 4 LSP w/ Marshall $10000; w/Pickering $8000
Adams, John Couch	1812-1892	Sci	32	50	126		Astronomer. Discovered Neptune
Adams, John Quincy	1767-1848	Pres	353	1413	2689	6030	Engr. S 2990-12500. ALS/Cont 25000. FF 345-450
Adams, John Quincy (as Pres.)		Pres	375	1066	4230		6th Pres. ALS/Cont 11950, Land Grants 400-600
Adams, Julie		Ent	10	18	20	22	Actress. Westerns, Horror Sci-Fi SP 30
Adams, Louisa Catherine	1775-1852	1st Lady	356	677	2082		Wife of J. Q. Adams. Only Foreign Born 1st Lady
Adams, Mason	1919-2005	Ent	10			18	Char. Actor. Films, TV, Radio. Familiar Voice

NAME	DATES	CATEGORY	SIG	LS/DS	ALS	SP	COMMENTS
Adams, Maud		Ent	15			45	
Adams, Maude	1872-1953	Ent	42	50	85	125	Am. Stage Actress. 'Peter Pan'
Adams, Nate		Ent	12			35	
Adams, Nick	1932-1968	Ent	128	285	293	328	Actor. 'The Rebel'
Adams, Patch		Med	15			30	Theraputic clowning
Adams, Samuel	1722-1803	Rev War	1036	2030	4208		Signer Dec. of Indepen. AManS 9500
Adams, Sherman	1899-1986	Gov	20	75	110	45	Eisenhower Asst., Gov. NH
Adams, Stanley		Comp	15	25	45	25	Lyricist
Adams, Stephen	1807-1857	Congr	10		35		US Sen. Mississippi
Adams, Suzanne		Ent	60			295	Opera. Great Coloratura Sopr. SP Pc S 150
Adams, William T. (Oliver Optic)	1822-1897	Author	20	25	60	55	Various Popular Series Books For Boys
Adams, William Wirt	1819-1888	Civ War	285	602	662		CSA Gen.
Adams, William Wirt (WD)		Civ War	408		1368		CSA Gen.
Adamson, James C.		Space	10	15		20	
Adamson, William C.		Congr	10	20		30	19th C. Congressman GA
Addams, Charles		Comics	77	110	127	357	Addams Family, S drawing 248
Addams, Dawn		Ent	10			15	Actress
Addams, Jane	1860-1935	Reformer	77	211	241	380	Social Reformer, Nobel Peace
Adderley, Julian 'Cannonball'		Music	144	145		315	Blues-Jazz; S Album 225
Addington, Henry	1757-1844	HOS	40	85	100	63	Sidmouth, 1st Viscount. Prime Min. Eng.
Addinsell, Richard	1940-1977	Comp	20	30	150	45	Br. ' Warsaw Concerto'
Addis, Don		Comics	10			35	
Addison, Chris		Celeb	10				Comedian
Addison, Joseph	1672-1719	Author	93	200	340		Br. Poet, Essayist, Plays
Addy, Mark		Ent	14			43	
Ade, George	1866-1944	Author	25	75	150	65	Am. Humorist, Dramatist. AQS 50
Ade, Jerry		Ent	10			20	Actor
Adelaide, Queen England	1792-1849	Royal	65	152	231		Queen of Wm. IV. Adelaide, Australia Namesake
Adelman, Ken		Celeb	10			15	Pol. celebrity
Adenauer, Konrad (der Alte)	1876-1967	HOS	37	50	75	90	1st Chan. Fed. Rep. of Ger.
Ader, Rose		Ent	28			85	Opera
Aderholt, Robert B. A		Congr	10				Member US Congress
Ades, Thomas		Comp	15				English Comp. AMusQS 65
Adjani, Isabelle		Ent	20			75	Opera
Adler, Alfred	1870-1937	Sci	143	588	1114	295	Psychiatrist. ALS/Cont 2,000
Adler, Buddy		Ent	10			25	Film Prod.
Adler, Cyrus	1863-1940	Celeb	25	40	100		Am. Jewish Leader
Adler, Felix B.		Ent	15			30	Professional Clown
Adler, Hermann	1839-1911	Clergy	20		75		Br. Chief Rabbi
Adler, Jerry		Ent	15			45	Hesh Rabkin, Sopranos
Adler, Kurt A.	1905-1997	Sci	20		45		Psychiatrist, son of Alfrred Adler
Adler, Larry	1914-2001	Ent	20			35	Harmonica Virtuoso. AMusQS 75
Adler, Luther	1903-1984	Ent	10	20	25	35	Vintage Actor-Stage & Film
Adler, Max		Bus	15	26	40	35	Pres. Sears, Roebuck. Philanthropy
Adler, Richard		Comp	20	30	55	35	AMusQS 35-135
Adler, Stella		Ent	20	15	20	25	Drama Teacher & Coach
Adolph I	1817-1905	Royal	50	200			Ruler of Luxembourg
Adonis, Joe		Crime	180	589			Orig. name: Guiseppe A. D. Adonis; S Chk 500
Adoree, Renee		Ent	30	45		70	Vintage Film Star. Early Talkies.
Adrian, Edgar Lord	1889-1977	Sci	32	45	135	65	Nobel Physiology
Adrian, Iris		Ent	10	15	15	22	Char. Actress. 30s-40's
Aerosmith (All)		Music	92	250		181	Rock Superstars. S Album 350
Afanasyev, Viktor		Space	20			40	Soyuz TM-11 & 18
Affleck, Ben		Ent	20			45	Actor 'Good Will Hunting'

NAME	DATES	CATEGORY	SIG	LS/DS	ALS	SP	COMMENTS
Affleck, Casey		Ent	15			45	
Affre, Auguste	1858-1931	Opera	15		50		Fr. opera singer
Aga Khan III, Sultan	1877-1957	Royal	77	199	275	184	Sultan Sir Mohammed Shah.
Aga Khan IV		Royal	25	40	85	55	
Agar, John		Ent	20	30	33	30	Actor. Westerns. Shirley Temple's 1st husband
Agassiz, Alexander	1835-1910	Sci	20		95		Son of Louis. Naturalist
Agassiz, Jean Louis	1807-1873	Sci	65	110	289	591	Swiss-Am. Zoologist, Biologist
Agena, Keiko		Ent	15			45	
Agerich, Martha		Music				150	Pianist
Aghdashloo, Shohreh		Ent	13			40	
Agnew, Spiro	1918-1996	VP	54	130	242	87	VP-Resigned. Special Bumper Sticker S. 150
Agnus, Felix	1839-1925	Civ War	30	55	85		165th NY. Union Gen. War Date ALS 250
Aguilera, Christina		Music	25			50	
Aguinaldo, Emilio		HOS	75	112	146	140	Filipino Leader Against Spain
Agutter, Jenny		Ent	10	14	18	25	Br. Emmy Winner.
Aherne, Brian	1902-1986	Ent	15	15	23	57	Br. Leading Man. Films from 1924
Aherne, Caroline		Celeb	10			15	Comedienne
Ahidjo, Ahmadou	1924-1989	HOS	15		40	45	Cameroon
Ahlfors, Lars V., Dr.		Sci	10	25		25	
Ahtisaari, Martii		Pol	20			50	Pres. of Finland
Aiello, Danny		Ent	13	16	25	39	Pleasant Char. Actor. Stage-Films-TV
Aiken, Alfred L.	1870-1946	Banker	10		25		Bank pres. Helped Organize Fed. Reserve
Aiken, Conrad	1889-1973	Author	25	96	98	60	Am. Novels, Poet. Pulitzer
Aiken, George D.		Congr	20	25		30	Sen. & Gov. VT
Aiken, John W.		Pol	20			30	Socialist Pres. Cand. 1936
Aiken, William	1806-1887	Gov	10	15	30	75	Gov. & Congressman SC
Ailey, Alvin	1931-1990	Ent	100	150	200	172	Am. Dancer, Choreogr. Fndr. Am. Dance Theatre
Ainger, Alfred		Clergy	10	15	30	25	
Air, Donna		Celeb	10			15	Celebrity model
Airy, George B.	1801-1892	Sci	42	130	265		Br. Royal Astronomer
Aitken, Robert	1734-1802	Pub	87	180	360		1st English Bible Printed in Am
Aitken, Robert Grant		Sci	12	20	45		Astronomer
Aitken, Robert Ingersoll		Artist	35	75	170	45	Am. Sculptor Mil. Statues
Akaka, Daniel		Congr	10				US Senate (D-HI)
Akbar, Taufik		Space	10			25	Indonesia
Akerman, Amos T.	1821-1880	Cab	20	40	65		US Attorney Gen.
Akerman, Malin		Ent	18			55	
Akers Peter		Clergy	35	45	60		
Akers, Elizabeth		Author	10		20	15	
Akers, Tom		Space	10			24	
Akhmatova, Anna	1888-1966	Author	295	575			Russian Lyric Poet. Russia's Greatest. AMS 2800
Akihito & Machiko (Both)		Royal	440				Emperor & Empress of Japan
Akihito, Emperor of Japan		Royal	475	580	650	668	
Akin, Susan		Ent	10			18	Miss America
Akin, W. Todd A		Congr	10				Member US Congress
Akin, Warren	1811-1877	Civ War	62	81	116	95	CSA Congress. Whig Cand. for Gov. GA
Akins, Claude		Ent	10	12	18	35	Char. Actor.
Akins, Zoe		Author	10	25	50	20	Poet, Plays. Pulitzer
Akroyd, Dan		Ent	15	55	35	48	Comedian-Actor
Aksyonov, Vladimir		Space	20			40	Soyuz T-2 mission
Al Fayed, Mohammed		Bus	25	95		30	Billionaire Owner of Harrod's. Father of Dodi
Al Sharpton, Rev.		Clergy	10			25	
Alabama (signed by all 4)		Cntry Mus	30			59	
Alagna, Roberta		Opera				75	Tenor

NAME	DATES	CATEGORY	SIG	LS/DS	ALS	SP	COMMENTS
Alard, Nelly		Ent	10			10	
Alaskey, Joe		Ent	16			48	
Alazraqui, Carlos		Ent	13			40	
Alba, Jessica		Ent	20			40	
Albanese, Licia		Ent	35	45	60	48	It. Sopr. Opera, Concert
Albani, Emma, Dame	1847-1930	Ent	55	60	118	190	Canadian Sopr. Opera. AMusQS 40, SP Pc 85
Albee, Edward	1928-	Author	15	110	133	55	Am. Dramatist. Pulitzer. 'Virginia Wolfe'
Alberghetti, Anna Maria		Ent	10			40	Singer-Actress.
Albert (Eng)	1819-1861	Royal	150	350	342	600	Husband of Queen Victoria; Prince Albert
Albert I (Belgium)		Royal	25	166	260	150	
Albert III (Rainier-Monaco)		Royal	95	200	435	155	
Albert Russell Wynn		Congr	10				Member US Congress
Albert Victor, Duke of Athlone		Royal	150		1250	550	Eldest Son Edward VII
Albert, Carl		Congr	10	15	20	20	Spkr. of the House. OK
Albert, Don		Ent	25			50	Trumpet & Bandleader
Albert, Eddie	1906-2005	Ent	16	35	38	37	Actor. 'Green Acres'. 100's Versatile Roles
Albert, Edward		Ent	10			20	Actor Son of Eddie
Albert, Ernest	1857-1946	Artist	20		55		Am. painter & designer
Albert, Marv		Ent	10	12	16	21	TV Host. Sports Ann'cer
Albert, Prince	1819-1861	Royal	188	406	407		Consort of Queen Victoria
Albert, Stephen		Ent	20			35	Pulitzer, AMusQS 75
Albertson, Frank		Ent	15	20		30	
Albertson, Jack	1910-1981	Ent	25	30	46	51	Actor. Oscar Winner
Albertson, Joseph A.		Bus	10	10	20	25	Fndr. Large Am. Grocery Chain
Albom, Mitch		Author	10	13	19	22	'Tuesdays w/Morrie'
Alboni, Marietta	1823-1894	Opera	25		75		Italian Operatic Contralto
Albright, Charles (C. W.)		Congr	15	20	35		Union Col. CW, Congressman PA
Albright, Lola		Ent	10	10	20	22	Early TV Series Star
Albright, Madeleine		Statsmn	25			50	1st woman Secretary of State
Albright, William F.	1891-1971	Sci	15	35	60		Am. Archaeologist
Albritton, Louise		Ent	20	22	30	45	Promising Actress. Early Death
Albury, Charles Donald, Capt.		Aero	20	45	60	55	
Alcock, J. & Brown A. W.		Aero	558			985	Signed by Both Pioneer Aviators
Alcock, John William	1892-1919	Aero	310	495	685	600	Pioneer Aviator/A. W. Brown
Alcorn, James Lusk	1816-1894	Civ War	78	216	315		CSA Gen. US Sen. & Postwar Gov. MS
Alcott, Amos Bronson	1799-1888	Author	40	85	135		Social, Civil, Education Reform
Alcott, Louisa May	1832-1888	Author	225	342	800		1 pg AM01nS 3500
Alda, Alan		Ent	12	15	30	35	TV-Film Star. 'M*A*S*H' SP 40
Alda, Frances	1883-1952	Ent	65			85	Opera. New Zealand Born Sopr.
Alda, Robert	1914-1986	Ent	10	15	15	30	Stage-TV-Film Actor. Father of Alan
Aldasoro, Eduardo		Aero	15		55	40	
Aldasoro, J. Pablo		Aero	15		55	55	
Alden, James	1810-1877	Civ War	70	100	142		Am. Rear Adm.
Alderton, Terry		Celeb	10			15	Comedian
Aldington, Richard	1892-1962	Author	25	125	170	35	Br. Poet, Novels, Biographer
Aldred, Joel		WWII	18	38	50	65	Canadian ACE WWII
Aldred, Norman		Ent	12	25	48	55	Radio Personality
Aldred, Stephanie		Ent	10			20	Actress
Aldrich, Bess Streeter	1881-1954	Author	10	15	35	40	Am. Novels, Short Story Writer
Aldrich, Louis	1843-1901	Ent	15			50	Vintage Actor
Aldrich, Nelson W.		Congr	10	15		20	Sen. NY
Aldrich, Richard	1902-1986	Ent	10	30	45		Broadway Prod.
Aldrich, Thomas Bailey	1836-1907	Author	33	30	70	225	Novels, Poetry, Editor
Aldridge, Kay	1917-1995	Ent	10			35	40's Serial Star. Perils of Nyoka

NAME	DATES	CATEGORY	SIG	LS/DS	ALS	SP	COMMENTS
Aldrin, Edwin 'Buzz'		Space	85	276	350	254	2nd Moonwalker. LS/Cont 1000-2000, ALS/Cont 4500; SP w/Lovell 400
Aleichem, Shalom	1859-1916	Author			2757		Rus. Born Jewish Writer-Humorist
Aleizandre, Vincent	1898-1984	Author	25		80		Spanish Poet, Nobel Pr.
Alekan, Henry		Celeb	10			15	Film industry
Aler, John		Ent	10			32	
Alexander I	1777-1825	Royal	254	861	895		Czar or Russia. Helped defeat Napoleon
Alexander I	1876-1903	Royal	75	250			King of Serbia, murdered
Alexander II	1818-1888	Royal	195	978	1239		Assass.
Alexander III	1845-1894	Royal	300	782	468	280	Czar of Russia. Cabinet SP/Czarina 2500
Alexander III (Pope)		Clergy		45000			Very Rare
Alexander VII	1599-1667	Clergy		437			Pope from 1659-1667
Alexander, Albert, Sir		Statsmn	20	85			Br. M. P
Alexander, Barton S.	1819-1878	Civ War	56	80	115		Union Gen. War Dte. S 90, DS 125
Alexander, Ben	1911-1969	Ent	55	50		108	Jack Webb Sidekick 'Dragnet'. SP w/Jack Webb 314
Alexander, Cecil Frances		Clergy	10	20	25	35	
Alexander, Clifford, Jr.	1933-	Cab	10		25	25	Sec. Army under Carter. Chmn. EEOC
Alexander, Edward Porter	1835-1910	Civ War	252	700	1062		CSA Gen.
Alexander, Edward Porter (WD)		Civ War	550	925	3075		CSA Gen. War Dte. ALS/Cont 6500
Alexander, George		Ent	10		15	15	
Alexander, Harold R. L., Sir	1891-1969	Mil	75	90	163	110	Alexander of Tunis, WWII
Alexander, Henry		Bus	10		15	10	
Alexander, J. B.		Gov	10	25		20	Guam
Alexander, Jamie		Ent	15			45	
Alexander, Jane		Ent	10	10	14	20	Actress, Stage-Film-TV. Arts Activist
Alexander, Jason		Ent	25	50		60	Multi-Talented Actor-Singer. 'Seinfeld'. Emmy
Alexander, Jay Dr.	1952-	Med	12			20	Famous cardiologist
Alexander, John		Ent	20			40	Played T. Roosevelt. 'Arsenic & Old Lace'
Alexander, John	1856-1915	Artist	25		80		Am. painter, portraitist
Alexander, John		Congr			35		FF 53
Alexander, Joshua Wallis	1853-1936	Cab	15	40		25	Sec. Commerce, Congress MO
Alexander, Lamar		Congr	10			15	US Senate (R-TN)
Alexander, Robert		Rev War	30	65			
Alexander, Rodney A		Congr	10				Member US Congress
Alexander, Sasha		Ent				35	
Alexander, William, Arch.		Clergy	20	30	40	35	
Alexander, Wm. (Lord Stirling)		Rev War	250	725	1388		Gen. in Continental Army
Alexanderson, Ernst F. W.	1878-1975	Sci	60	115	195	85	Father of TV
Alexandra	1872-1918	Royal	150	235	1286	675	Assass. Czarina. ALS/Cont 5000; SP w/Nicholas 878
Alexandra	1844-1925	Royal	133		302	715	Dan. Queen of Edw. VII (Eng.) Coronation SP 1500
Alexis, Kim		Ent	12			30	Actress.
Alfano, Franco		Comp	50				AMusQS 285, AMusQS 120 (3 bars mus.)
Alfieri, Carlo		Ent	10		35	35	Opera
Alfono, Heradio		Aero	15			35	
Alfonso II	1533-1597	Royal		2750			Alfonso d'Este, Duke Ferrara.
Alfonso V	1396-1458	Royal		3250			Aragon, Naples & Sicily. 'Magnanimo'
Alfonso XII	1857-1885	Royal	150	450	850		King of Spain 1874-85
Alfonso XIII	1886-1941	Royal	140	500	625	500	King of Spain, desposed by Franco
Alfonso, Kristian		Ent	10			15	
Alford, Henry		Clergy	10	20	30	25	
Alfred, Prince		Royal	25	35	75		2nd Son of Queen Victoria
Alfven, Hannes		Sci	20	30	45	30	Nobel Physics
Alger, Horatio	1832-1899	Author	144	215	400	245	Popular Books For Boys
Alger, Russell Alexander	1836-1907	Civ War	50	60	85	92	Union Gen., Gov. MI, Sec. War

NAME	DATES	CATEGORY	SIG	LS/DS	ALS	SP	COMMENTS
Algren, Nelson		Author	30	60	185	185	Am. Novels. Naturalistic Novels
Ali Khan, R. (Prince)		Royal	15		90	45	
Ali, Mahershalalhashbaz		Ent	13			40	
Alice in Chains		Music	45			104	Music. 4 Member Rock Group
Alice, Mary		Ent	10			26	Afr-Am Actress. 'Sparkle'
Alice, Princess		Royal	15		65		2nd Daughter of Queen Victoria
Alicia, Ana		Ent	10		15	15	
Alieu, Geydar		HOS	30	110			Pres. of Azerbaijan
Alito, Samuel		Sup Crt	165				
All in the Family (Cast)		Ent	139			252	4 Leading Chars.
All My Children		Ent					Signed script 200
Allan, Brent Dr.	1952-	Sci	10			15	Physician, author, scientist, businessman
Allan, Buddy		Cntry Mus	10	10		10	Singer. Buck Owens' son
Allan, Robert		Bus	17				
Allard, Gen. Jean-Victor	1913-1996	Mil	24			30	WWII Canadian Gen.
Allard, Wayne		Congr	10				US Senate (R-CO)
Allen, Adrienne		Ent	10	10	20	25	
Allen, Amos L.	1837-1911	Congr	10			40	Repr. ME
Allen, Andrew		Space	10	10		25	
Allen, Barbara Jo (Vera Vague)		Ent	22			38	Comedienne AKA Vera Vague. Radio-Films-Early TV
Allen, Betty		Ent	10			25	Afr-Am Dancer, Teacher, Choreographer
Allen, Charles L.		Clergy	10	35	50	35	
Allen, Debbie		Ent	10		20	28	Actress-Dancer-Singer-Choreographer-Dir. -Prod.
Allen, Deborah		Cntry Mus	10			15	Singer-Songwriter
Allen, Elizabeth	1908-1990	Ent	20		15	35	Br. Actress. Leading Lady. 'Berkely Square'
Allen, Ethan	1738-1789	Rev War	1050	3050	9400		Col. Green Mounain Boys. ALS/Cont 21,000
Allen, Florence E.	1884-1966	Fem	30	75	125		Am. Jurist & Feminist
Allen, Frank A., Jr.		Mil	10	25	45		
Allen, Fred	1894-1956	Ent	50	65	110	100	Popular Radio Comedian/Portland Hoffa
Allen, George		Congr	10			15	US Senate (R-VA)
Allen, Ginger Lynn		Model	10			20	
Allen, Gracie	1902-1964	Ent	88	73	75	189	SP w/husband George Burns 350
Allen, Grant		Author	10	15	30	10	
Allen, Henry J.	1868-1950	Congr	10	20			Sen., Kansas
Allen, Henry T.		Mil	25	70	125	50	Gen. WWI
Allen, Henry Watkins	1820-1866	Civ War	186	685			CSA Gen.
Allen, Henry Watkins (WD)	1820-1866	Civ War	250	540	1055		CSA Gen. 1820-66
Allen, Horatio	1802-1890	Bus	65		115		Designed & Ran 1st Locomotive on Am. RR.
Allen, Ira (Brother of Ethan)		Rev War		1367	3811		Rev. War Date LS 15,000
Allen, Irwin	1916-1991	Ent	20			45	Dir. Disaster Films.
Allen, Joan		Ent	10			38	Actress. Oscar Nominee. 'Pleasantville'
Allen, Joseph P.		Space	10			30	
Allen, Karen		Ent	10	10	14	26	Actress, 'Raiders of Lost Ark' SP 35
Allen, Macon B.	1816-1894	Law	195	865			Paved Way for Blacks To Become Lawyers
Allen, Marty	1922-	Ent	10	10	12	20	Bushy Haired Comedian
Allen, Nancy		Ent	12			35	
Allen, Paul		Bus	10			30	Microsoft Co-Fndr.
Allen, Peter		Comp	40			125	
Allen, Rex		Ent	10	10	15	28	Singer-Actor. Western Star
Allen, Robert	1811-1886	Civ War	37	60	91		Union Gen.
Allen, Robert (WD)		Civ War	50	60	95		Union Gen. (1811-86)
Allen, Robert F.		Bus	10			10	Pres., CEO Carrier Corp.
Allen, Rosalie		Cntry Mus	10			45	Singer. 'The Prairie Star'
Allen, Steve	1921-2000	Ent	22	40	42	56	Comp., Pianist, TV-Radio Host

NAME	DATES	CATEGORY	SIG	LS/DS	ALS	SP	COMMENTS
Allen, Thomas H. A.		Congr	10				Member US Congress
Allen, Thomas S.	1825-1905	Civ War	40	70	110		Union Brevet Brig. Gen.
Allen, Tim		Ent	17			59	Comic Star of 'Home Improvement'
Allen, Valerie		Ent	10			10	Actress. 2nd Leads, 50s Films
Allen, Viola		Ent	15	20	35	35	Vintage Stage Star 1898
Allen, William	1790–1856	Congr	15				Jurist; FF 45
Allen, William M.		Bus	15	40	55	30	
Allen, William Wirt	1835-1894	Civ War	194	519	712		CSA Gen., War Dte DS 510, ALS 1, 275, LS 775
Allen, Willis		Congr	10				FF 28
Allen, Woody	1935-	Ent	34	53	65	55	Actor, Comedian, Plays, AA Dir.
Allenby, Edmund	1861-1936	Mil	74	130	423	368	1st Viscount. Br. Fld Marshal, ALS/Cont 750
Allende Gossens, Salvador		HOS	35	113	285	70	1st Marxist Pres. Chile
Allers, Franz		Music				100	Czech conductor & musical Dir.
Alley, Kirstie		Ent	10	10	12	30	Actress-Comedian.
Allgood, Sara		Ent	15		35	55	Vintage Screen Char. Actress
Allingham, Margery	1904-1966	Author	40	65	155	70	Br. Mystery Writer
Allingham, William		Author	50		100		Irish Poet
Allison, Alexander		Civ War	218	352			Artist, publisher
Allison, Fran		Ent	25	30	45	85	Early TV kid's Show. 'Kukla, Fran & Ollie'
Allison, May	1890-1989	Ent	15			40	
Allison, Mose		Comp	15			30	Jazz Pianist-Vocalist
Allison, William B.	1829-1908	Congr	10	15	25	15	Sen. IA
Allizard, Adolphe		Ent	12		35	45	Opera. Bass
Allman Brothers		Music	2246				Original Rock Band
Allman, Duane	1946-1971	Music		1668			
Allman, Greg		Music	35	150		70	Rock Star. 'Allman Brothers'
Allred, Gloria		Lawyer	10			30	Feminist Atty. Brown vs O. J. Simpson
Allred, James V.	1899-1959	Gov	15	30	45		Gov. of TX 1935-39
Allston, Washington	1779-1843	Artist	275	400	862		Pioneered Romantic Landscapes. Author
Allyson, June	1917-2007	Ent	11	14	19	31	MGM Star. 2nd Career in TV Commercials
Alma-Tadema, Lawrence	1836-1912	Artist	20	65	135		Br. Painter of Roman Scenes
Almodovar, Pedro		Celeb	10			15	Film industry
Almond, Lt. -Gen. Edward M.	1892-1979	Mil	30		50	35	WWII US Gen.
Almonte, Juan Nepomuceno	1804-1869	Mil	50	200	305		Mex. Gen., Pol.
Almy, John J.	1815-1895	Civ War			1900		Union Adm. ALS/Cont 1900
Alonso, Alicia		Ballet				150	Cuban prima ballerina
Alonso, Maria		Ent	13			38	
Alonzo, Maria Conchita		Ent	10	15	25	23	Actress.
Alpert, Herb		Music	13	15	16	35	Big Band Leader-Trumpet. 'Tijuana Brass'
Alphand, Nicole H.		Celeb	10			10	
Alred, Gloria		Law	10			20	Noted Trial Attorney
Al-Said, Sultan		Space	15			35	Saudi Arabia
Alsop, Joseph		Author	10	15	25	10	Journalist, Synd. Columnist
Alsop, Stewart		Author	10	25	35	15	Journalist, Synd. Columnist
Alt, Carol		Ent	11	12	18	38	Actress.
Altchewsky, Ivan		Ent	100			250	Opera (Rare)
Altgeld, John P.		Gov	10	40			Gov. IL
Altice, Summer	1979-	Ent				55	Actress
Altieri, Albert (Johnny)		Celeb	10			10	Philip Morris Trademark
Altman, Benjamin	1840-1913	Bus	45	125			Altman's' NY Dry-Goods Co. Philan. Art
Altman, Robert	1925-2006	Ent	15	19	29	40	Movie Dir.
Alva, Tony		Ent	23			70	
Alvarado, Angela		Ent	10			30	
Alvarez, Albert R.	1861-1933	Opera	20		60		Fr. Operatic tenor

NAME	DATES	CATEGORY	SIG	LS/DS	ALS	SP	COMMENTS
Alvarez, Luis W., Dr.		Sci	20	35	85	40	Nobel Physics
Alvarez, Roma		Ent	10			10	
Alvary, Lorenzo		Ent	10	12	25	25	
Alvord, Benjamin	1813-1884	Civ War	25	54	75		Union Gen. Mex. War Vet., Civ. War in OR Terr.
Aly Khan, Prince		Royal	75				
Alyn, Kirk	1910-1999	Ent	18	24	30	42	Original Superman in Movie Serials
Ama, Shola		Music	10			20	Performing musical artist
Amandes, Tom		Ent	13			40	
Amara, Lucine		Ent	15		55	45	Opera
Amato, Pasquale		Ent	25			125	It. Baritone. Opera
Ambler, Eric Clifford		Author	50	150			Br. Novels
Ambrose, Bert	1896-1971	Ent	15			45	Notable Br. Bandleader
Ambrose, Lauren		Ent	15			35	Claire Fisher, Six Feet Under
Ambrose, Stephen	1936-2002	Author	20	40	50	40	Band of Brothers
Ameche, Don	1908-1993	Ent	22	35	45	55	Versatile Oscar Winner.
Ameche, Jim	1914-1983	Ent	10	25		30	Look-alike brother. Radio's 'Jack Armstrong. '
Ameling, Elly		Mus	15			70	Singer
Ament, Jeff		Mus	13			45	Music. Guitar 'Pearl Jam'
American Beauty (cast)		Ent				85	Spacey/ Bening
American Graffiti		Ent				250	Signed poster 200; Entire cast SP 1010
American Pie (cast)		Ent				175	Cast of 5
American Pres., The (cast)		Ent				135	Bening, Douglas
Ames, Adelbert	1835-1933	Civ War	60	75	116		Union Gen., MOH Bull Run. Last Surviving Gen.
Ames, Ed	1927-	Ent	10	16		22	Singer-Actor of Ames Bros. Group
Ames, Fisher	1758-1808	Statsmn	130		500		Organized Federalist Party
Ames, Joseph S. (1864-1943)		Sci	15		30		Pres. of Johns Hopkins, Physicist
Ames, Leon		Ent	10	12	15	45	Life w/Father' Star. TV-Films.
Ames, Nancy		Ent	10			12	Singer-Actress
Ames, Oakes	1804-1873	Finan	150	410	1900		Fndr. Union Pac. RR. Rare RR DS 2250; FF 65
Ames, Oliver		Bus	180	1350	2500		Union Pacific RR. Rare RR DS 2550
Amherst, Jeffrey Lord (1717-97)		Rev War	455	1051	1433		Gov. Gen. Br. No. Br. Gen.
Amick, Madchin		Ent	10			18	Actress
Amin Dada, Idi		HOS	150	642		723	Dictator of Uganda
Amis, Kingsley		Author	15	30	65	25	
Amis, Suzy		Ent	10			18	
Ammen, Daniel	1820-1898	Civ War	41	75	107	175	Union Gen.
Ammen, Jacob	1806-1894	Civ War	25	40	75		Union Gen.
Ammons, John		Author	10			12	Baptist history
Amos & Andy (Corell & Gosden)		Ent	177	242		278	Signed by Both
Amos, John		Ent				35	Actor
Amos, Tori		Ent	15			46	Actress
Amos, Wally 'Famous'		Bus	10	10	20	20	Cookie King
Amoute, John		Ent	10			20	Actor
Amparan, Belen		Ent	10			35	Opera
Ampere, Andre Marie	1775-1836	Sci	212	420	1502		Fr. Physicist, Mathematician
Amsden, Ben		WWII	16	22	38	40	Navy ACE WWII
Amsterdam, Morey	1908-1996	Ent	20			45	Comedian-Actor. 'Dick Van Dyke Show'
Amundsen, Roald	1872-1928	Expl	126	210	450	453	Norwegian Polar Explr.
Anabuki, Satoshi		WWII				120	Leading Jap. ace w/51 kills
Analyze This (cast)		Ent				95	DeNrio/Crystal
Anastasio, Trey	1964-	Music					Phish'; Actor; S Guitar 300
Anastos, Ernie		Celeb	10			15	Media/TV personality
Anaya, Pedro Maria		Pol	200	518			19th C. Pres. of Mexico
Ancona, Mario		Ent			65	150	Singer. London Premiere 'Pagliacci' 1893

NAME	DATES	CATEGORY	SIG	LS/DS	ALS	SP	COMMENTS
Ancona, Sydenham E.	1824-1913	Congr	20	25	45		Civil War Congressman PA
Anders, Allison	1954-	Celeb	14			20	Am. film & TV Dir.
Anders, David		Ent	13			40	
Anders, Luana	1938-1996	Ent	17	20		35	Actress. 'Song of the South'
Anders, Pamela		Ent	20			35	
Anders, Peter		Ent	25			75	Opera
Anders, William A.	1933-	Space	89	468	950	366	Apollo 8 lunar module pilot; Ambassador
Andersen, Hans Christian	1805-1875	Author	1482	1598	1726	2484	AQS on CDV 1450-3200, AQS 1725-3500
Anderson, Anthony		Ent	13			40	
Anderson, Barbara	1945-	Ent	10	15		32	Actress. TV on 'Ironside'
Anderson, Bill		Cntry Mus	10			15	'Whisperin' Bill'
Anderson, 'Bloody' Bill		Civ War				2500	Lt. Quantrill's Raiders. Rare CDV 'in death' 2500
Anderson, Brad		Comics	20		35	35	'Marmaduke'
Anderson, 'Bronco Billy'		Ent	119	175	200	375	
Anderson, C. E. Bud		WWII	20	28	45	42	WWII ACE. 16. 5 kills
Anderson, Carl David		Sci	25	35		70	Nobel Physics 1936
Anderson, Carl T.		Comics	20	45		60	'Henry'
Anderson, Carol Grace		Author	10			12	Motivatinal, gift books
Anderson, Clifford		Civ War	83	130	95		CSA Congress
Anderson, Clinton		Cab	15	20		25	Sec. Agriculture. Sen. NM
Anderson, Dr. Wayne Scott		Med	10			10	Diet expert, 'Take Shape for Life'
Anderson, Dusty		Ent	15			35	Actress, Artist. Top 40s Model.
Anderson, Eddie Rochester	1905-1977	Ent	77		210	295	Jack Benny's Rochester. GWTW
Anderson, Elizabeth G., Dr.	1836-1917	Sci	75	242	238		1st Eng. Hospital for Women
Anderson, George Burgwyn	1831-1862	Civ War	309	528			CSA Gen. War Dte DS 625. D. at Antietam
Anderson, George T. Tige	1824-1901	Civ War	104	162	349	295	CSA Gen. War Dte. Sig/Rank 395
Anderson, George W.		Mil	22	40	62	72	
Anderson, Gillian		Ent	16			101	X Files. SP w/Duchovny 50; script 200
Anderson, Harry		Ent	15	28	20	31	Actor-Comed. -Magician. 'Night Court' SP 30
Anderson, Henry James		Educ	12				
Anderson, Jack	1922-	Author	10	15	20	20	Outspoken Newspaper Columnist
Anderson, James Patton	1822-1872 .	Civ War	100	243	506		CSA Gen.
Anderson, James Patton (WD)	1822-1872	Civ War	311	690			CSA Gen.
Anderson, John		Cntry Mus	10			15	Black Sheep #1
Anderson, John B.		Mil	10	10	20		
Anderson, John Jr.		Gov	12	15		15	Governor KS
Anderson, Joseph	1757-1837	Rev War	77	235	390		Early Sen. TN
Anderson, Joseph R. (WD)		Civ War	260	705	1140		CSA Gen.
Anderson, Joseph Reid	1813-1892	Civ War	82	260	828		CSA Gen.
Anderson, Judith, Dame		Ent	30	35	45	63	Powerful Legitimate Theater & Film Actress
Anderson, June		Ent	10			25	Opera
Anderson, Ken	1909-1993	Ent	10			35	Disney Animator, Art Dir., Architect
Anderson, Kevin		Ent	10			20	Actor
Anderson, Laurie		Ent	10	15		20	
Anderson, Leroy		Comp	38	75	195	162	AMusMS 325
Anderson, Les 'Carrot-top'		Cntry Mus	15	18		25	Top Instrumentalist w/Spade Cooley
Anderson, Loni	1946-	Ent	10	12	18	28	Actress.
Anderson, Louie		Ent	10			25	Stand-up & TV Comic
Anderson, Lynn	1947-	Cntry Mus	10			32	Country Singer Superstar
Anderson, Marian	1902-1993	Ent	104	151	238	283	1st Afro-Am Singer to Perform at Met. '58
Anderson, Martin B.		Clergy	10	15	25		
Anderson, Mary (American)	1859-1942	Ent	15	40	50	100	Actress
Anderson, Mary (English)		Ent	10	20	30	30	
Anderson, Maxwell	1888-1959	Author	30	70	135	62	Am. Dramatist. Pulitzer. 'Winterset'.

NAME	DATES	CATEGORY	SIG	LS/DS	ALS	SP	COMMENTS
Anderson, May		Ent	15			45	
Anderson, Melissa Sue		Ent	10	22		26	Actress. 'Little House on the Prairie' SP 35
Anderson, Michael P.		Space	50	75		225	Perished on Space Shuttle Columbia re-entry 2003
Anderson, Michael, Jr.		Ent	10			20	Prod.
Anderson, O. A.		Aero	10	25	40	30	Gen.
Anderson, Pamela		Ent	28			85	
Anderson, Pamela Lee		Ent	15			41	Actress. SP Nude 75
Anderson, Philip W.		Sci	45	55	95	50	Nobel Physics
Anderson, Poul		Author	10	35	45		Science fiction, Hugo & Nebula award winner
Anderson, Richard	1926-	Ent	10		15	15	Actor. 2nd Leads. Versatile Supporting Player
Anderson, Richard Dean		Ent	10	12	18	27	Actor. 'McGyver' Star
Anderson, Richard Heron	1821-1879	Civ War	89	145	293		CSA Gen., Present at Ft. Sumter Bombardment
Anderson, Richard Heron (WD)		Civ War	290	508			CSA Gen. Ft. Sumter Vet.
Anderson, Robert	1805-1871	Civ War	190	314	723	1555	Cmdr. Ft. Sumter, War dte ALS 3500-17, 250
Anderson, Robert	1917-	Author	10	20	45	25	Plays, Screenwriter. 'Tea & Sympathy'
Anderson, Robert B.		Cab	10	17	35	20	Sec. Treasury
Anderson, Robert Houstoun	1835-1888	Civ War	125	400	462		CSA Gen.
Anderson, Robert Houstoun (WD)	1835-1888	Civ War	242	561			CSA Gen.
Anderson, Roy A.		Bus	10	15	20	10	
Anderson, Samuel		Mil	40	130	220		Early Congressman PA 1827
Anderson, Samuel Read	1804-1883	Civ War	162	362	865		CSA Gen. Sig/Rank 200, War Dte. ALS 1500
Anderson, Sherwood	1876-1941	Author	35	95	153	45	Novels, Journalist, Poet
Anderson, Stephen		Ent	12			35	
Anderson, Terry	1947-	Jrnalist	12			25	Radio Host. Longest held Am. Hostage Lebanon
Anderson, Tim		Ent	10			20	Actor
Anderson, Warner	1911-1976	Ent				110	Actor
Anderson, William B.		Mil	15	35		50	Cmdr. N/S Nautilus
Anderson, Willie Y.		WWII	10	25	35	30	WWII ACE; 7 kills
Anderson-Gunter, Jeffrey		Ent	10			20	Actor
Andes, Keith	1920-2005	Ent	10	10		28	Actor. Radio-Stage-Films.
Andino, Tiburcio C.	1876-1943	HOS	30	70			Pres. of Honduras 1933-49
Andre, John	1750-1780	Rev War	1350	3500	13938		Br. Off. Hanged as Spy
Andreissen, Frans		Celeb	10			15	Pol. celebrity
Andreotti, Guilio		HOS	10	20	35	20	It. Journalist, Prime Min.
Andress, Ursula		Ent	12	16	22	36	Actress.
Andrew, A. Piatt		Congr	10	10		10	MOC MA
Andrew, Duke of York		Royal				400	
Andrew, John A.	1818-1883	Gov	45	65	120		Civil War Gov. MA
Andrews Sisters (All 3)		Music	150			473	40's Close Harmony Trio. Radio, Records, Films
Andrews, Arkansas Slim		Ent	10		10	10	
Andrews, Chris. C.	1829-1922	Civ War	33	70	195		Union Gen. ALS '64 265
Andrews, Dana	1909-1992	Ent	24	35		56	Actor. Popular 40s Leading Man. 'Laura'
Andrews, Edward	1914-1985	Ent	20			50	Char. Actor of Stage, Film, TV
Andrews, George Leonard	1828-1899	Civ War	38	58	86		Union Gen.
Andrews, George Leonard (WD)	1828-1899	Civ War	160				Union Brig. Gen.
Andrews, Giuseppe		Ent	13			40	
Andrews, Harry	1911-1989	Ent	10			30	Br. Char. Actor. Key Supporting Part.
Andrews, Julie	1935-	Ent	21	24	25	80	Actress
Andrews, Landaff W.	1803-1887	Congr	10		20		MOC KY
Andrews, Maxine	1918-1995	Ent	15	20	20	35	Singer. (One of Andrews Sisters)
Andrews, Patti		Ent	10			25	Lead Singer of Andrews Sisters
Andrews, Robert E. A		Congr	10				Member US Congress
Andrews, Roy Chapman	1884-1960	Sci	75		135	125	Naturalist, Explr., Author
Andrews, Stanley O.		WWII	15	30		40	WWII Ace; 6 kills.

NAME	DATES	CATEGORY	SIG	LS/DS	ALS	SP	COMMENTS
Andrews, V. C.		Author	10			10	Novels
Andrews, William Frederick		Bus	10			10	CEO Scoville, Inc.
Andric, Ivo (1892-1975)		Author	35		120	50	Yugoslav Poet, 1961 Nobel Pr.
Andrieux, Francois	1759-1833	Author	25		65		Fr. poet & Plays
Andriola, Alfred		Comics	10			30	Kerry Drake
Andropov, Yuri	1914-1984	Pol		500			Sov. Premier for 15 mo. Brezhnev died
Andros, Edmund, Sir		Rev War			7500		Only Reported Amount Shown
Andrus, Cecil D.		Cab	10	10	35	15	Sec. Interior
Anduran, Lucienne		Ent	10			35	Fr. Operatic Mezzo-Sopr.
Anfinsen, Christian		Sci	18	25	45	45	Nobel Chemistry
Angel, Heather		Ent	10	12	18	50	Br. Leading Lady of 30s-40's
Angel, Jonathan		Ent	10			20	Actor
Angel, Vanessa		Ent	10			15	Actress TV's Wierd Science
Angeli, Pier	1932-1971	Ent	86	159	195	266	Actress. D. Young. Rare Autograph
Angelici, Marthe		Ent	20			75	Corsican Lyric Sopr.
Angell, Norman, Sir		Author	30	60	95	95	Nobel Peace Pr.
Angelou, Maya		Author	44	55	60	68	Black Am. Poet
Anglesea, Marquis of		Mil	15	35	60		
Angus, Joseph		Clergy	10	20	25		
Animals, The (5)		Music	178			802	Rock HOF
Aniston, Jennifer		Ent	26			65	Actress. 'Friends'
Anitua, Fanny		Opera				175	Mexican contralto
Anka, Paul		Comp	18	20	28	40	Music Comp.
Ankers, Evelyn		Ent	15	30	60	40	
Ankin, Michael Dr.	1949-	Med	11			25	Famous Pulmonologist; Fndr. Ultimate Health
Ann Geyer, Georgie		Celeb	10			15	Media/TV personality
Anna Ivanovna (Rus)	1693-1740	Royal	269	448	1750		Czarina of Russia. Niece of Peter the Great
Annabella	1909-1997	Ent	18	17	28	37	Fr. Actress. Maj Euro Star. M. Tyrone Power
Annaloro, Antonio		Ent	10		35	40	It. Tenor, Opera
Annan, Kofi		Pol	28			50	Head of UN
Anne of Austria	1601-1666	Royal	150	231			Queen of France
Anne of Denmark	1574-1671	Royal		600			Queen of King James I
Anne Worley, Jo		Ent	10			25	Actress
Anne, Queen	1665-1714	Royal	365	600	2200		Queen of GB & Ireland; AMS 24,000
Annenberg, Walter H.		Bus	15	25	40	40	Publisher
Annesley, H. N.		Lawman	10	10		15	Northern Ireland
Annigoni, Pietro		Artist	95	150			Portrait painter
Ann-Margret	1941-	Ent	15			88	Actress. AA.
Annseau, Fernand		Ent	20			75	Opera
Anouilh, Jean		Author	35	87	157	223	Fr. Dramatist, Screenwriter
Ansara, Michael		Ent	10	12	15	26	Actor
Anselmi, Giuseppe	1876-1929	Ent	52			162	Opera. Idolized Handsome Tenor Star
Anselmo, Tony		Ent	10			25	Actor-Animator. Voice of Donald Duck 1980+
Ansermet, Ernest	1883-1969	Ent	100			200	Swiss Conductor. SPc 75
Anson, George		Mil	50		150		English Gen. Waterloo
Ant, Adam		Music	30			58	Punk Rock
Anthony, Henry B.		Congr	10	15	35		Editor, Gov., Sen. RI
Anthony, HRH		Royal	35	100			King of Saxony
Anthony, Lysette		Ent	10			20	Actress.
Anthony, Marc		Music	15			50	Latin-rock music
Anthony, Ray		Music	10	13	16	21	Big Band Leader
Anthony, Robert N.		Sci	20			35	Nobel
Anthony, Susan B.	1820-1906	Fem	322	975	2198	1800	Reformer, Women's Rights. ALS/Cont 3500
Antokolski, Mark Matveyevich		Artist	30	65	155		Russ. Sculp. 1843-1902

NAME	DATES	CATEGORY	SIG	LS/DS	ALS	SP	COMMENTS
Anton, Susan		Ent	10	11	13	29	Actress
Antonelli, Giacomo	1806-1876	Clergy	50	120			Roman Catholic Cardinal
Antonelli, Laura		Ent	16	18	45	132	Actress
Antonioni, Michelangelo	1912-2007	Ent	25			108	Film Dir.
Antrup, Wilhelm		WWII	25			75	Ger. WWII Ace
Anwar, Gabrielle	1969-	Ent	15			42	Br. Actress.
Aoki, Devon		Ent	12			35	
Aoki, Rocky	1939-2008	Bus	10	15	30	20	Benihana Jap. Resaurants
Apgar, Virginia	1909-1974	Sci	25	50			Physician, Blue baby test
Apollinaire, Guillaume	1880-1918	Author	168	400	1575		Avant Garde Poet, Art Critic
Apollo 1		Space	2750			9500	Chaffee, White, Grissom
Apollo 10		Space		450		696	Young, Cernan, Stafford
Apollo 11		Space	859	1250		6985	Armstrong, Aldrin, Collins
Apollo 12		Space	275	120		372	Bean, Conrad, Gordon; Ins Cvr. 500-700
Apollo 13		Space				1603	Lovell, Swigert, Haise
Apollo 13 (cast Movie)		Ent				75	Bacon, Hanks, Paxton
Apollo 14		Space		460		578	Mitchell, Shepard Roosa; S Cvr. 600
Apollo 15		Space		450		902	Scott, Worden, Irwin. Insurance Cvr. 200-350
Apollo 16		Space				1012	Young, Mattingly, Duke. S Cvr. reCvr. y 900
Apollo 17		Space		350		648	Schmidt, Cernan, Evans; S Cvr. 180
Apollo 7		Space		350		593	1st US 3 Man Flight. Eisele, Cunningham, Schirra; Postal Cvr. 568
Apollo 8		Space				594	
Apollo 9		Space	225			497	McDivitt, Scott, Schweickart
Apollo/Soyuz Mission		Space	175			400	All 5
Apollonia		Music	20			42	Purple Rain
Appell, Paul	1855-1930	Sci	30	60			Fr. mathematician
Apple, Fiona		Music	20			47	Rock Star
Applegate, Christina		Ent	20	32		53	Actress-Model.
Appleton, Daniel	1785-1849	Pub	15				Appleton's Cyclopaedia
Appleton, Edward, Sir		Sci	25	35			Nobel Physics
Appleton, John F.	1839-1870	Civ War	40		70		Union Brevet Brig. Gen.
Appleton, Nathan	1779-1861	Bus	40		95		Am. Textile Manufacturer
Apt, Jay		Space	10	15		30	
Aquino, Corazon		HOS	20			45	Pres. Philippines
Arafat, Yassir	1929-2004	HOS	90	195		164	PLO Leader. Nobel Peace Pr.
Aragones, Sergio		Comics	10			35	Mad Magazine. S drawing 265
Araiza, Francesco		Ent	10			30	Opera, Concert, Mexican Tenor
Arambula, Roman		Comics	40			60	Mickey Mouse
Arangi-Lombardi, Giannina		Opera	100			200	Opera.
Arau, Alfonso		Celeb	10			15	Film industry
Araujo, Arturo		HOS	15	40		30	Salvador
Arber, Werner		Sci	20	35		35	Nobel Med.
Arbos, E. Fernandez		Comp	40			45	AMusQS 350
Arbour, Louise		Celeb	15			25	Chief Prosecutor UN Intl War Crimes Tribunal
Arbuckle, Maclyn		Ent	15	15	30	25	
Arbuckle, Roscoe 'Fatty'	1887-1933	Ent	364	786	880	953	Comic-Actor. Involved In Major Scandal
Archbold, John	1848-1916	Finan	650	1900	2000		Standard Oil. TLS Std. Oil Ltrhd 4400
Archer, Anne		Ent	14	14	15	35	Actress.
Archer, James J.		Civ War	244	578	735		CSA Gen.
Archer, Jeffrey		Author	10	15		35	Novels
Archer, Jules		Author	10			10	
Archer, William S.	1789-1855	Congr	12				Sen. & Repr. VA
Archi, Attila		Opera	10	15	40	45	Opera

NAME	DATES	CATEGORY	SIG	LS/DS	ALS	SP	COMMENTS
Archipenko, Alexander	1887-1964	Artist	90		246		Rus. Painter-Sculptor
Arden, Elizabeth		Bus	40	80	145	110	Fndr. & Owner Eliz. Arden Co.
Arden, Eve	1908-1990	Ent	20	25	40	55	Actress. 'Our Miss Brooks'
Arditi, Luigi	1822-1903	Music	30		80		Italian Violinist
Arena, Angelina		Opera	10		30	25	Australian Sopr.
Arens, Moshe		Diplo	20	80			Israeli author
Argentia, Imperia	1889-1962	Ent	25			45	Argentine Dancer-Actress. 30s Spanish film star
Argento, Asia		Ent	15			30	
Argento, Dominick		Comp	15	30	65	65	Pulitzer, AMusQS 135-175
Argyll, 8th Duke.	1823-1900	Statsmn	20	45			Geo. D. Campbell. P. M. Gen, Sec State India
Argyll, 9th Duke	1845-1914	HOS	30	40	55		John D. Campbell. Gov-Gen. Canada
Arias Sanchez, Oscar		HOS	35		65	50	Nobel Peace, Pres. Costa Rica
Arias, Harmodio		HOS	25	50		30	
Arias, Yancey		Ent	15			45	
Arie, Raffaele		Opera	10			25	Bulgarian Basso
Ariyoshi, George R.		Gov	15			25	Governor Hawaii
Arkell, Bartlett		Bus	10	27	45	15	
Arkell, W. J. (Judge Publ)		Bus	10	15	30	10	
Arkin, Adam		Ent	10	12		26	Actor. 'Chicago Hope'SP 22
Arkin, Alan		Ent	15	22	30	40	Char. Actor, AA winner
Arledge. John		Ent	10			25	2nd Leads 40s
Arlen, Harold	1905-1986	Comp	132	152	288	668	Over the Rainbow'. AMusQS up to 1, 600
Arlen, Michael	1895-1956	Author	20				English Novels, SB 100
Arlen, Richard	1900-1976	Ent	25	30	70	60	Early Talkies Star of 'Wings'
Arletty		Ent	25			75	Fr. Actress
Arliss, Florence		Ent	15	30	40	35	
Arliss, George	1868-1946	Ent	56	45	112	86	Br. Actor. Early Academy Award for 'Disraeli'
Arlosoroff, Chaim	1899-1933	Celeb	150				Assass. Zionist leader
Armand, Charles	1762-1822	Artist			2185		Fr. Painter
Armand, Elizabeth		Celeb			150		Mistress of Lenin
Armani, Giorgio		Design	15			45	
Armapour, Kristiana		Celeb	10			20	Media/TV personality
Armendariz, Pedro		Ent	30	35	45	65	
Armetta, Henry		Ent	25	30	50	29	
Armey, Dick		Congr	10	20		20	Majority Leader
Armiliato, Marco		Cond				65	Italian
Armistead, Lewis Addison	1817-1863	Civ War	8531	19000	22500		CSA Gen. (rare)
Armour, Philip D.	1832-1901	Bus	173	1238	1750	619	Meat Packing. Armour & Co.
Arms, Russ(ell)		Ent	10			25	Singer-Actor. Radio's 'Your Hit Parade'
Armstead, Henry Hugh		Artist	10	20	35		Br. Sculptor. Albert Memorial
Armstrong, Charlotte	1905-1969	Author	20	55			Am. mystery writer
Armstrong, Edw. R., Dr.		Sci	30	75	150		Inventor Seadrome
Armstrong, Edwin H.	1890-1954	Sci	100	250			Invented FM Broadcasting. TLS/cont 2000
Armstrong, Frank Crawford	1835-1909	Civ War	330	400	1035		CSA Gen.
Armstrong, Harry	1879-1951	Comp	85	184	195		Sweet Adeline' AMusQS 365-650
Armstrong, John	1758-1843	Cab	60	181	872		Sec. War. Cont. Congr., War of 1812
Armstrong, John	1725-1795	Rev War	100	200	325		Am. Brig. Gen.
Armstrong, Louis	1900-1971	Ent	145	340	701	570	Satchmo'. Immortal. Jazz Trumpet. SP p/c 350
Armstrong, Martin		Author	10			15	
Armstrong, Neil & Aldrin, Buzz		Space				10350	Apollo XI, both S
Armstrong, Neil A.	1930-	Space	849	1954	4740	3305	1st Moonwalker. ALS/Cont 9500, LS/Cont 2500-7500; ISP 1850-3500; SP 4300-19700
Armstrong, Robert		Mil	200	725			Gen. TN Vols, Indian Fighter. Jackson aide-de-camp
Armstrong, Robert		Ent	55	60	75	70	Actor King Kong

A

NAME	DATES	CATEGORY	SIG	LS/DS	ALS	SP	COMMENTS
Armstrong, Samaire		Ent	11			34	
Armstrong, Samuel Chapman		Civ War	75	120	350		Union Off. Cmdr. Black Regiment
Armstrong, William, Dr.		Sci	22	50	110	70	Inventor
Arnaud, Yvonne	1892-1958	Ent	15			40	Fr. Film, Stage actress & pianist.
Arnaz, Desi	1917-1986	Ent	58	234	280	317	Actor/Singer/Prod. DS (Will) 750; SP w/Lucy 500-1000; S Chk 125
Arnaz, Desi, Jr.		Ent	10			20	Rock Group. Dino, Desi, Billy
Arnaz, Luci		Ent	10		10	19	Actress Daughter of Lucy & Desi
Arnberg, Lee		Ent	13			40	
Arness, James		Ent	20	24	27	61	Actor. 'Gunsmoke'
Arnett, Peter		TV News	10			25	CNN News
Arnett, Will		Ent	15			45	
Arngrim, Alison		Ent	10			10	
Arnheim, Gus		Band				45	
Arnim, Achim von	1781-1831	Poet			1200		Ger. Romantic Poet/Novels 1781-1831
Arno, Peter		Comics	15	30	75	25	The New Yorker
Arnold, Abraham	1837-1901	Civ War	40		90		Union Off., MOH
Arnold, Archibald		Mil	20	62	102		
Arnold, Benedict	1741-1801	Rev War	1648	4347	5276		Am. Army Off., Traitor
Arnold, Eddy		Cntry Mus	12	48		30	Country Music Hall of Fame
Arnold, Edward	1890-1956	Ent	30	40		85	Longtime Versatile Char. Actor
Arnold, Edwin, Sir	1832-1904	Author	50	90	150	80	Br. Poet, Journalist
Arnold, Ernst		Comp		125			Austrain Comp., AMusQ 125
Arnold, Fredric		WWII	20	35		50	ACE, WWII P-38
Arnold, Henry 'Hap'	1886-1950	Mil	82	341	475	356	USAF Gen. WWII; S pass to Quebec Conf. 1943 3000
Arnold, Jonathan	1741-1793	Rev War	75	125			Am. patriot
Arnold, Lemuel	1792-1852	Gov	20		50		Gov. RI
Arnold, Leslie P.		Aero	10	295		48	Pioneer Pilot. '24 Round the World Flight
Arnold, Lewis Golding	1817-1871	Civ War	50	97	205		Union Gen.
Arnold, Matthew	1822-1888	Author	112	190	433		Br. Poet, Critic
Arnold, Richard	1828-1882	Civ War	45	113			Union Gen.
Arnold, Tom		Ent	10			33	Comic Actor
Arnoldson, Sigrid	1861-1943	Ent	30			100	Swedish Operatic Sopr.
Arnot, Bob Dr.		Celeb	10			15	Media/TV personality
Arnot, William		Clergy	10	20	25		
Arnt, Charles		Ent	10			25	
Arntzen, Heinrich		Aero	25	60			Br. Ace WWI
Aronson, Judi		Ent	10			20	Actress.
Arp, Jean		Artist	75		275		Fr. DaDa Artist, Sculptor
Arquette, Alexis		Ent	15				
Arquette, Cliff		Ent	21	20		118	'Charlie Weaver'
Arquette, David		Ent	15			30	Actor. 'Scream' SP 35
Arquette, Patricia		Ent	16			33	Actress.
Arquette, Rosanna		Ent	15	15		42	Actress
Arrau, Claudio	1903-1991	Ent		45		155	Chilean Pianist. 3x5 SP 120
Arrhenuis, Svante A.	1859-1927	Sci	95	295	725		Nobel Chemistry 1903
Arrington, A. H.		Civ War	92	130			CSA Congress
Arriola, Gus		Comics	10			25	Gordo
Arrow, Kenneth J.		Econ	35	55			Nobel Economics
Artbuthnot, Marriott		Rev War			483		Vice-Adm. of the White
Arthur, Beatrice	1926-	Ent	12	12	22	30	Actress. 'Maude', 'Golden Girls'
Arthur, Chester & Lincoln, Robert		Pres		1360			DS by both
Arthur, Chester A.	1829-1886	Pres	341	771	1151	872	ALS as Actg Pres 3000. CW Dte LS 650-1500, SB 1265
Arthur, Chester A. & Ellen		Pres		2500			Rare as Pair

NAME	DATES	CATEGORY	SIG	LS/DS	ALS	SP	COMMENTS
Arthur, Chester A. (As Pres.)		Pres	372	1031	4304		WH Card S 500-650
Arthur, Duke of Connought	1850-1942	HOS	10	18	25		Governor Gen. of Canada
Arthur, Ellen Lewis		1st Lady	600	1000	1200		
Arthur, George K.		Ent	10		15	10	Comedian, Prod.
Arthur, Jean	1905-1991	Ent	154	238	325	404	Reclusive. Retired Early. 'Shane' Last
Arthur, Julia		Ent	15			35	Pioneer Film Star
Arthur, Timothy Shay	1809-1885	Author	20	45			Ten Nights In A Barroom
Artot, Desiree		Opera	35		150	70	Opera, Concert
Artsebarsky, Anatoly		Space	20			60	Soyuz TM-14
Artyukhin, Yuri		Space	25			65	Soyuz 14
Arundell of Wardour		Mil			225		Henry 3rd Baron. Fought for Charles I in Civ. War
Arvin, Newton		Author	18	40	85		
Asaphiev, Boris	1884-1949	Comp	40		240		Russian Comp.
Asboth, Alexander S.	1811-1868	Civ War	49	219	178		Union Gen. ALS '64 330
Asbury, Francis, Bish.		Clergy	175	290	625		
Asbury, Richard		WWII	20			40	WWII Ace; 5 kills
Asch, Sholem	1880-1957	Author	15	45			Polish Novels & Plays
Aschenbrener, Robert		WWII	20			50	WWII Ace; 10 kills
Asgeirsson, Asgeir	1894-	HOS	25				4x Premier of Iceland
Ash, Mary Kay		Bus					SEE Kay, Mary
Ash, Roy L.		Bus	10	20	50	35	
Ashanti		Music	15			50	Singer
Ashby, Hal		Ent	10		15	15	
Ashby, Turner	1828-1862	Civ War	397	716	1250	1250	CSA Gen.
Ashby, Turner (WD)		Civ War	497	1969	2069		CSA Gen.
Ashcroft, Dame Peggy	1907-1991	Ent	75	25	35	65	
Ashcroft, Richard		Ent	10			40	Music. Lead Singer 'The Verve'
Ashe, John		Rev War	100	225	450		NC Gen.
Ashe, Thomas	1812-1887	Civ War	72	144			Member Conf. Congress
Ashe, William Shepperd		Congr	35	90			CW Blockade Runner
Ashford & Simpson		Music	15			45	
Ashley, Alfred	1835-1913	Author	25				Br. Poet Laureate after Tennyson
Ashley, Edward		Ent	15			35	
Ashley, Elizabeth		Ent	10		15	18	Actress.
Ashley, John		Ent	10			15	
Ashley, William		Celeb	200	750			Pioneer. Route for Oregon Trail
Ashman, Howard	1950-1991	Comp	25	75		100	Am. Plays & movie music lyricist; AA
Ashmun, George	1804-1870	Congr	15	35	60		Advisor to A. Lincoln
Ashton, Frederick	1904-1988	Ent	20		60		English Ballet Dancer
Ashurst, Henry	1874-1962	Congr	30				1st Arizona Sen.
Ashworth, Ernie		Cntry Mus	10			25	'Talk Back Trembling Lips'
Ashworth, Frederick	1912-2005	Aero	40			60	Weaponeer on Bock's Car(Nagasaki)
Asimov, Isaac	1920-1992	Author	55	160		100	Rus-Am Biochemist. Sci-Fi Writer
Askew, Reubin		Gov	12			15	Governor FL
Asner, Ed		Ent	10	20	12	35	Actor. 'Lou Grant'
Asner, Jules		Ent	22			65	
Aspin, Les		Cab	10				Clinton Sec. Defense
Asquith, Herbert H.	1852-1928	HOS	35	75	135	150	Prime Min. Earl of Oxford
Assad, Bashar	1965-	Pol	25			100	Syrian Pres.
Assad, Hafez	1930-2000	HOS	25	40	105	115	Syria
Assante, Armand		Ent	10	16	20	30	Actor. Leading Man
Association		Music	200	1310			Rock group; S Guitar 300
Astaire, Adele		Ent	25			62	Dancer Sister of Fred Astaire
Astaire, Fred	1899-1987	Ent	80	148	300	230	Dancing actor/singer. SP/G. Rogers 775-1750

NAME	DATES	CATEGORY	SIG	LS/DS	ALS	SP	COMMENTS
Astaire, Fred & Rogers, Ginger		Ent	125			522	Signed sheet music 400
Asther, Nils	1897-1981	Ent	25	35	65	160	
Astin, John		Ent	11	14	16	28	
Astin, Sean		Ent	17			50	
Astley, Rick		Music	10			20	Singer
Aston, Francis W.		Sci	35	80	155		Nobel Chemistry 1922
Astor, Brooke		Author	10	15			
Astor, John J.	1886-1971	Pub	15	40	65	35	1st US multimillionaire. Owned 'The Times'
Astor, John Jacob	1763-1848	Bus	462	1401	2700		Fur Trader-Financier. LS/Cont 9500
Astor, John Jacob III		Bus	210	850	671		Grandson of Fndr.
Astor, John Jacob IV	1864-1912	Bus	600	1900	2400		D. On the Titanic. RARE
Astor, John Jacob Jr.		Bus	300	750	950	325	Union Gen., Financier
Astor, John Jacob Mrs.		Bus	35	100	195		
Astor, Mary	1906-1987	Ent	35	70		135	AA
Astor, Nancy (Visc.)	1879-1964	Celeb	40	120	95	60	1st Woman To Sit As Br. M. P. Am. -Born
Astor, Vincent		Bus	10	20	45	20	
Astor, Waldorf	1879-1952	Pol	15	35	80	55	Br. M. P., Publisher Observer
Astor, William Backhouse	1792-1875	Bus	375	838	1500		Administered Astor Estate. Son of Fndr.
Astor, William Waldorf	1848-1919	Bus	65	200	350		Journalist-Capitalist-Financier
Astruc, Gabriel		Ballet			125		Fr. Impresario
Asturias, Miquel Angel	1899-1974	Author	50	135	285		Guatamala. Nobel Literature
Ataneli, Lado		Opera				50	Georgian baritone
Ataturk, Kemel	1881-1938	HOS		150			Pres. of Turkey
Atcher, Bob	1914-1993	Cntry Mus	10			25	'National Barn Dance' Star
Atchison, David Rice	1807-1866	Pres	407	749	916		Pres. for one day; ALS/Cont 4500
A-Team, The		Ent				410	Cast S; Peppard, Schultz, Benedict
Ates, Roscoe		Ent	25	30	60	65	
Athenagoras, Arch.		Clergy	25	40	55	50	
Atherton, Chas. G.	1804-1853	Congr	20	30			Sen. NH
Atherton, Gertrude	1857-1948	Author	30	55	150	150	Am. Novels
Athlone, Earl, Prin. Alex. of Teck		HOS	15	25	40		Governor-Gen. of Canada
Atholl, Katharine, Duch. of	1874-1960	Pol	65				Br. Anti-Nazi. 1st Woman Cabinet Member
Atkins, Chet		Cntry Mus	15	17		31	Guitar Legend
Atkins, Christopher		Ent	10		15	20	Actor. 'Blue Lagoon'.
Atkins, Essence		Ent	13			40	
Atkins, Gaius Glenn		Clergy	15	30	45		
Atkins, John DeWitt	1825-1908	Civ War	57	162			Member Conf. Congress
Atkins, Robert	1930-2003	Sci	15	25	50	30	Cardiologist, Atkins diet
Atkins, Smith D.	1835-1913	Civ War	35		150		Union Gen. 2nd Illinois. ALS Chickamauga 750
Atkins, Tom		Ent	10			20	Actor
Atkinson, Brooks	1894-1984	Author	15	35		30	Theater Drama Critic, Columnist N. Y. Times
Atkinson, Joseph H.		Mil	10	25	30		
Atkinson, Rowan		Ent	10			22	Br. Actor-Comic
Atkinson-Wood, Helen		Ent	10			20	Actress
Atlantov, Vladimir		Opera	25		75	55	Opera. Rus. Tenor
Atlas, Charles		Bus	52	294	325	423	Mail Order Phys. Culture
Attenborough, David, Sir		Celeb	20			25	Naturalist
Attenborough, Richard		Ent	24	30	30	44	AA Br. Actor-Dir.
Attenborough, Sir David		Sci	20	70			
Atterbury, William W.	1866-1935	Mil	15	50			Gen. WWI, Pres. Penn. RR
Attlee, Clement	1883-1967	HOS	52	140	225	75	Prime Min. 1st Earl
Atwill, Lionel	1885-1946	Ent	100				
Auber, Daniel Francois	1782-1871	Comp	110		136		Father of Fr. Opera, AMusQS 350
Auberjonos, Rene		Ent	30			90	Char. Actor; 'Star Trek', 'Deep Space Nine'

NAME	DATES	CATEGORY	SIG	LS/DS	ALS	SP	COMMENTS
Aubert, Lenore		Ent	10		15	15	
Aubrey, M. E.		Clergy	10	15	20		
Aubry, Cecile		Ent	15				Fr. Actress
Auchincloss, Janet L.		Bus	10		10	10	
Auchincloss, Louis		Author	15	35	75	75	US Novels, Short Story
Auchinleck, Claude J. E., Sir		Mil	45	75	100	125	Br. Fld. Marshal WWII
Auckland, Baron (Geo. Eden)		HOS	40	50	100		Gov-Gen India
Audemars, Edmund	1882-1970	Aero	62			200	1st Aviator to fly from Paris to Berlin
Auden, W(ystan) H(ugh)	1907-1993	Author	135	388	372	700	Br. -Am. Poet, Pulitzer
Audran, Edmond		Comp	45	85	175		Fr. Operettas
Audran, Marius		Opera	12		75		Opera. Tenor
Audubon, John J.	1785-1851	Artist	1290	1742	3321		Ornithologist. 'Birds of America'; ALS/LS/Cont 5000
Auel, Jean M.		Author	10	10	25	25	Novels
Auer, Leopold		Music	25	200			Hungarian Violinist
Auer, Mischa	1905-1967	Ent	30	30	45	40	
Auf Der Maur, Melissa		Ent	13			40	
Auger, Arleen		Opera	25				Opera. Am Sopr.
Auger, Christopher C.		Civ War	40	112	174		Union Gen.
Augereau, PFC de Castiglione		Mil	100	218	525		Marshal of Napoleon
Augsburg, Alex. S., Prince	1663-1737	Royal		328			Prince Bishop of Augsburg. Count Palatine of Rhine
Augusta, Queen of Prussia	1811-1890	Royal		135			Consort William I. Empress of Ger.
Augustus I, Duke of Saxony		Royal	2000				1526-1586
Augustus II	1670-1733	Royal		650			King of Poland 1697-1733
Augustus III		Royal	145	425	345		King Poland
Auld, Georgie		Ent	10		15	15	
Aumont, Jean Pierre	1909-	Ent	40	45	20	95	
Auric, Georges	1899-1983	Comp	85		400		Fr. Member 'The Six'. AMusQS 250-395
Auriol, Jacqueline	1917-2000	Aero	30	35	70	70	Early female test pilot; broke sound barrier.
Auriol, Vincent	1884-1966	HOS	45	60	85		1st Pres. 4th Republ. France
Ausensi, Maurel		Opera	15				Opera, Sp. Baritone
Auslander, Joseph		Author	25	125			Poet. Harvard Lecturer Poetry
Aust, Abner		Aero	10			35	US Ace; 5 kills
Austen, Jane	1717-1817	Author	625	2250	7500		Br. Novels. 'Pride & Prejud. ' Adr. Panel 1995
Austin, Bobby		Cntry Mus	10			15	
Austin, Horace		Gov	10				Governor MN
Austin, Karen		Ent	10		12	15	
Austin, Moses	1761-1821	Pioneer	588	1950	3748		Founded TX. Mine Owner, Merchant
Austin, Stephen F.	1793-1836	Tex	1000	3293	7500		Historical DS 6500-7500
Austin, Teri		Ent	10		10	10	
Austin, Warren R.		Congr	10	10			Sen. VT
Autry, Gene	1907-1998	Ent	63	91	125	190	Singing Cowboy, Businessman.
Avallone, Michael		Author	10	15			
Avalon, Al		Ent	10				TV & film
Avalon, Frankie		Ent	20	25	35	42	Singer-Actor
Avalov-Bermondt Col.		Mil				300	Hussar of Convoy
Avebury, John Lubbock	1834-1913	Sci	28		150		Naturalist. Paleolithic
Avedon, Richard		Artist	50	180	213	210	Photographer. Book S 375
Average White Band		Music	20			50	Rock
Averell, William Woods	1832-1900	Civ War	60	80	115		Union Gen. ALS '62 360
Avery, James		Ent	10			15	
Avery, John, Jr.		Rev War	50	86			
Avery, Milton	1893-1965	Artist	35	225		45	Am. Figure Painter 30-40's. Later Landscapes
Avery, Sewell L.		Bus	35	55	105	40	CEO Montgomery Ward
Avery, Tex		Comics	25			400	Animator.

NAME	DATES	CATEGORY	SIG	LS/DS	ALS	SP	COMMENTS
Avery, William W.		Civ War	93	157			CSA Congress
Avildsen, John G.		Ent	10			20	Film Dir.
Avril, Anson Dr		Celeb	10			15	Edwardian Country Mansion
Awdry, Wilbert, Rev.		Author	50		175		Railway Series of kid's Books
Ax, Emanuel		Music				75	Pianist
Axelrod, Julius		Sci	35	60	95	35	Nobel Med.
Axmann, Arthur		WWII				200	Nazi leader
Axtell, George		Aero	12	25	45	35	Marine ACE; 6 kills.
Axton, Hoyt		Cntry Mus	10	12		22	Singer-Songwriter
Ayckbourn, Alan		Author	10	15	35	65	Br. Prolific Plays
Ayer, Lewis Malone	1821-1895	Civ War	54	130			Member Conf. Congress
Aykroyd, Dan		Ent	14	24	30	33	Actor. 'Saturday Night Live'. 'Ghostbusters'
Ayres, Agnes		Ent	60	75	150	125	Silent Film Star
Ayres, Lew		Ent	14	28	36	32	Actor. Oscar Winner. Original 'Dr. Kildare'
Ayres, Pam		Celeb	10			15	Comedienne
Ayres, Romeyn B. (WD)		Civ War	70	135	440		Union Gen.
Ayres, Romeyn Beck	1825-1888	Civ War	38	68	104		Union Gen.
Ayub Khan, Gen.		HOS	20	35	75	100	Afghan Prince. Gen.
Azaria, Hank		Ent	10			40	Actor
Azenberg, Emanuel		Ent	10			20	Actor
Aznavour, Charles		Ent	10			35	
B Jazzie		Music	10				DJ
B52's		Music	38			100	Rock Group
Babbage, Charles	1792-1871	Invent	288	370	605		Br. Pioneer of Mdrn. Computers. Inventor
Babbitt, Bruce		Cab	10	20		15	Gov. AZ
Babbitt, Harry		Ent	10			20	Band Vocalist, Radio
Babbitt, Milton		Comp	25		70	30	AMusQS 85-150
Babcock, Alfred, Dr.	1805-1871	Congr	20	25			Repr. NY
Babcock, Joseph W.		Congr	10		30		Congressman WI
Babcock, Orville E.	1845-1884	Civ War	30	103	162		Union Gen.
Babcock, Orville E. (WD)		Civ War	45	104	117		Union Gen. LS as Grant ADC 385
Babcock, Tim	1919-	Gov	12	20	25	15	Governor MT
Babcock, Verne C.		Aero	20			52	Early Bird of Aviation
Babilee, Jean		Ent	30	45			Ballet
Babson, Roger	1875-1967	Econ	75			121	Predicted 1919 Crash. Founded Babson Coll.
Baby Peggy		Ent	10		15	15	
Babyface		Music	20			51	Young Singer-Songwriter
Baca, Joe B		Congr	10				Member US Congress
Bacall, Lauren	1924-	Ent	22	55	60	41	Stage & Film
Bacardi Maso, Facundo	1815-1886	Bus		625			Fndr. Bacardi Rum & Emilio B. 2 DS 1250
Baccaloni, Salvatore		Ent	20	25	40	45	Opera, Concert, Films
Bach, Barbara		Ent	15	18	25	25	Married to Ringo Starr
Bach, Catherine		Ent	10	15	15	20	
Bach, Johann Sebastian		Comp	2500	6760	11000		
Bach, Richard		Author	25	100	175		
Bach, Sebastian		Music	20			50	Rock
Bacharach, Burt		Comp	20	25	40	40	
Bacharach, Fabian		Artist	50	100	150	75	
Bachauer, Gina		Music				75	Greek Pianist
Bache, Alexander D.		Sci	30	50	110	40	1st Pres. Nat'l Acad. Science
Bache, Harold L.		Bus	15	45	110	65	US Stockbroker. J. S. Bache & Co.
Bache, Jules S.		Finan	350	1100	1400		Fndr. J. S. Bache & Co.
Bachelder, John B.		Civ War		360			US Gen.
Bacheller, Irving		Author	25	60	65	75	Am. Novels, Editor

NAME	DATES	CATEGORY	SIG	LS/DS	ALS	SP	COMMENTS
Bachman, Nathan L.		Congr	10				Sen., TN
Bachus, Spencer B		Congr	10				Member US Congress
Back, George, Sir	1796-1878	Expl	45	105	175		Arctic Navigator
Backhaus, Wilhelm	1884-1969	Music	46		65	300	Ger. Concert Pianist
Backhouse, James		Clergy	20	35	50		
Backstreet Boys (5)		Music	50			104	Rock Group (5)
Backus, Jim	1913-1989	Ent	32	45	50	62	Actor, Mr. Magoo. SP/Nat. Schafer 138
Baclanova, Olga		Ent	10			25	
Bacon, Augustus Octavius	1839-1914	Congr	12		48		Sen GA; FF 48
Bacon, Francis, Sir		Author	1500	3650	6500		Br. Philosopher, Statesman
Bacon, Frank		Ent	10	12	20	15	
Bacon, Kevin		Ent	15	17	20	40	Actor
Bacon, Leonard		Clergy	10	15	20	25	
Bacon, Lloyd		Ent	12			20	Film Dir.
Bacon, Peggy		Artist	35	50	150		
Bacon, Robert		Congr	15	25		30	Congressman NY. Mil.
Bacon, Walter W.		Gov	10		25	25	Governor DE
Badal, Adam J.		Music	10			16	Drummer; 'AduB'
Badalucco, Michael		Ent	15		45		
Baddeley, Hermione		Ent	12	15	22	30	
Baddiel, David		Celeb	10			15	Comedian
Badeau, Adam	1831-1895	Civ War	44	96	147		Union Gen.
Badeau, Adam (WD)		Civ War	58	125	275		Union Gen.
Baden-Powell, Robert, Sir,	1857-1941	Mil	157	441	466	786	Br. Gen., Defender Mafeking, Founded Boy Scouts
Bader, Diedrich		Ent	16		48		
Bader, Douglas, Sir		Aero	55	183	250	100	Br. Ace
Badger, Charles J.	1853-1932	Mil	20	45	70	40	US Navy Adm.
Badger, George E.	1795-1866	Cab	15	62	80		Sec. Navy, Sen. NC. Jurist
Badger, Oscar C.	1890-1958	Mil	30	45		50	Adm. USN WWII
Badgley, Penn		Ent	15		45		
Badham, John		Ent	10			20	Film Dir.
Badham, W. L.		Aero	35	50	75	55	Bi-plane, WWI
Badler, Jane		Ent	10		20	25	
Badoglio, Pietro		HOS	40	95	135	65	It. Gen., succeeded Mussolini
Badura-Skoda, Paul		Music	10			65	Pianist. SP Pc 25: AMusQS 50
Baekeland, L. H. Dr.	1863-1944	Invent	35	60	140		Invented Bakelite, 1st Plastic
Baer, Arthur Bugs	1886-1959	Jrnalist	10			40	Syndicated Columnist, Cartoonist
Baer, George F.		Bus	14	25	45	30	Pres. Reading RR
Baer, John		Ent	10			20	Actor.
Baer, Max, Jr.		Ent	28	45	52	40	Son of boxer. Jethro on 'Beverly Hillbillies'
Baer, Parley		Ent	10	15	22		50s familiar Char. actor. 'Young Lions'
Baez, Joan	1941-	Music	15	20	20	40	Folksinger, Pol. Activist
Bagby, Arthur	1833-1921	Civ War	146		483		Conf. Gen.
Bagian, James P.		Space	10	10	20		
Baglioni, Bruna		Opera	10		45	35	Opera
Bagnold, Enid	1889-1981	Author		75	185	75	Novels, Plays. 'National Velvet', 'Chalk Garden'
Bagot, Charles, Sir	1781-1843	Statsmn		45	125		Br. Diplomat. Gov. -Gen. Canada
Bailey Hutchison, Kay		Pol	10			15	Pol. celebrity
Bailey, Bill		Celeb	10			15	Comedian
Bailey, Buster		Music	30			75	Jazz Clarinet, Sax
Bailey, Carl E.		Gov	10	15			Governor AR
Bailey, Damion 'DaDa'		Author	10			12	Afr. -Am. poet
Bailey, David		Celeb	10			15	Photographer
Bailey, F. Lee		Law	20	25	65	30	Noted Trial Attorney

NAME	DATES	CATEGORY	SIG	LS/DS	ALS	SP	COMMENTS
Bailey, G. W.		Ent	10			20	Actor
Bailey, Goldsmith Fox		Congr	10				FF 27
Bailey, Jack		Ent	10	12	16	20	Early Radio-TV M. C. 'Breakfast Club'
Bailey, James Anthony	1847-1906	Ent	275	812	1050		Barnum & Bailey Circus
Bailey, Jim		Ent	10			20	Actor
Bailey, Joseph	1825-1867	Civ War	98	232	245		Union Gen. ALS '64 1265
Bailey, Louise H		Author	10			12	Regional history
Bailey, Mildred		Music				188	Blues-Jazz artist
Bailey, Mildred C.		Mil	25			268	Brigadier Gen.
Bailey, Pearl	1918-1990	Music	30	32	50	100	Singer-Actress
Bailey, Raymond	1904-1990	Ent	40			80	Milburn Drysdale on the Beverly Hillbillies
Bailey, Razzie		Cntry Mus	10			20	
Bailey, Temple		Author	30	45	110		
Bailey, Theodorus	1805-1877	Civ War	44	100	142		Union Naval Off. Sig/Rank 70, DS 160
Bailey, Walter R.		Bus	10	35	45	20	
Baillie, David		Ent	13			40	
Baillie, Joanna	1762-1851	Author	45	65	120		Successful Scottish Dramatist, Poet
Baillie, John		Clergy	35	75	110	50	
Bailly, Jean-Sylvain	1736-1793	Sci	60	95	160		Astronomer. Fr. Pol. Guillotined
Bain, Barbara		Ent	18	32	15	37	Actress. TV's 'Mission Impossible'
Bain, Conrad		Ent	10			10	Actor. 'Mork & Mindy' TV Series
Bainbridge, William	1774-1833	Mil	172	290	725		US Naval Off. War 1812
Bainter, Fay	1892-1968	Ent	64	85	130	190	Actress. Vintage. Stage, Films. AA Winner
Baio, Scott	1961-	Ent	10	17	15	25	Actor. Juvenile 'Happy Days', 'Chachi'
Bair, Hilbert L.		Aero	20			55	US Ace. WWI
Baird, Absalom	1824-1905	Civ War	40	74	115		Union Gen. ALS '64 200. S/Rank 70
Baird, Brian B		Congr	10				Member US Congress
Baird, John Logie		Sci	150	295	150	600	1st TV Picture of Moving Object
Baird, Robert		Author	10		52		
Bairnsfather, Bruce	1888-1959	Comics	20	30	110	35	Br. WWI 'Old Bill' Cartoons
Bakaleinikoff, Constantin	1898-1966	Comp	225				Russion Music Dir. RKO Studios
Baker, Alpheus	1828-1891	Civ War	175	375	717		CSA Gen. Sig/Rank 310
Baker, Anita		Ent	20			35	Singer
Baker, Art	1898-1966	Ent	10	15		20	Early Radio-TV M. C. Master of The Art!
Baker, Benny	1907-1994	Ent	10			25	Chubby, Baby-faced comedian, actor
Baker, Blanche	1956-	Ent	10		15	20	Actress-Daughter of Carroll Baker.
Baker, Bob		Ent	50	70		90	Singing Cowboy 1930's
Baker, Bonnie Wee		Music	10		15	20	Big Band Vocalist w/Wee Small Voice
Baker, Carroll	1931-	Ent	10	25	40	55	Actress. AAN 'Baby Doll'.
Baker, Charles S.		Congr	10	10		10	Congressman NY.
Baker, Chauncey		Mil	18		25	20	Gen. WWI
Baker, Chet		Music	272	460	1408	395	Blues-Jazz musician; S Album 350
Baker, Diane	1938-	Ent	10			25	Actress. Leading Lady, mature leads
Baker, Edward D.	1811-1861	Civ War	198	572	850		Union Gen. RARE. 2nd Gen. Killed. Sig/Rank 465
Baker, Ellen		Space	10			30	
Baker, George	1915-1975	Comics	43	250		244	'Sad Sack'. Orig. Sketch S 350
Baker, Howard Henry, Jr.		Congr	10		25	25	Sen. TN. WH Chief of Staff
Baker, James A., III		Cab	15	25		35	Bush Sec. State
Baker, James McNair		Civ War	52	117			Member Conf. Congress
Baker, Janet, Dame		Opera	10	15		35	Opera. Br. Mezzo Sopr.
Baker, Jehu	1822-1903	Congr	10		25		Repr. IL
Baker, Josephine	1906-1975	Ent	155	242	410	529	Highest Paid Ent in Eur. '20s.
Baker, Kenny	1912-1985	Ent	15	15	25	50	Singer-Actor. Jack Benny Show Vocalist. Films
Baker, Kenny		Ent	26			48	Actor. 'R2D2'

NAME	DATES	CATEGORY	SIG	LS/DS	ALS	SP	COMMENTS
Baker, La Fayette Curry	1826-1868	Civ War	139	185	316		Interesting Union Gen. Sig/Rank 325
Baker, Laurence S.	1830-1907	Civ War	126	216	450		CSA Gen. Sig/Rank 205, War Dte. DS 400+
Baker, LaVerne		Ent	28			55	Jazz Vocalist
Baker, Lucien		Congr	10		30		Sen. KS
Baker, Mark		Ent	10	10		30	Opera
Baker, Michael		Space	10	10		32	
Baker, Newton D.	1837-1937	Cab	20	84	93	78	Wilson Sec. War
Baker, Phil	1896-1963	Ent	16			30	Early radio comic. Few Films
Baker, Richard H. B		Congr	10				Member US Congress
Baker, Royal N.		WWII	20		90	45	Air Ace Korea, WWII
Baker, Samuel W., Sir	1821-1893	Expl	68	92	188		Br. Located Sources of Nile
Baker, Tom		Ent	10			20	Actor
Bakewell, William		Ent	20			52	'Gone w/The Wind' (Cast Member)
Bakker, Jim		Clergy	17	25	35	30	Built TV Ministry Empire. Served time in prison.
Bako, Brigitte		Ent	10			20	Actress. Movies
Bakshi, Ralph		Celeb		230			Prod. Lord of the Rings
Bakst, Leon	1866-1924	Artist	95		650		Rus. Painter, Scenic Designer
Bakula, Scott		Ent	20			33	'Quantum Leap' etc
Bakunin, Mikhail	1814-1876	Revol	305		1625		Russian Revolutionist
Balaban Bob		Ent	20			30	Actor
Balakirev, Mily	1837-1910	Comp	295		865		Russian
Balanchine, George	1904-1983	Ballet	168		250	287	Ballet-Choreographer
Balbo, Italo	1896-1940	Aero	135	160	200	195	Lt. Air Marshal-Pioneer. Valuable Postals Avail.
Balch, Emily Greene	1867-1961	Econ	35	35	60	75	Nobel Economist, Reformer, Pacifist
Balchen, Bernt		Aero	35	45	75	57	
Balck, Hermann		Mil	25			148	Ger. Panzer Gen.
Baldridge, Howard Malcolm		Congr	10	15		15	MOC NE
Baldridge, Malcolm	1922-1987	Cab	25	145		45	Sec Commerce Reagan.
Baldwin, Abraham	1754-1807	Statsmn	1150	3375			Signer Constitution, Rare
Baldwin, Adam		Ent	15			45	
Baldwin, Alec	1958-	Ent	25	75		48	Actor.
Baldwin, Faith	1893-1978	Author	35	25	60	45	Popular Novels & Screenwriter
Baldwin, Frank D.		Author		115			
Baldwin, Henry	1780-1844	Sup Crt	80	132	203		
Baldwin, James	1924-1987	Author	76	298	394	216	Afr-Am. Novels, Essayist. ALS/Cont 975
Baldwin, John Brown		Civ War	57	117			Member Conf. Congress
Baldwin, Judy		Ent	10			20	
Baldwin, Loammi	b 1744	Rev War		253			
Baldwin, Raymond E.		Gov	10	20		20	Governor, Sen. CT
Baldwin, Roger		Pol	30	35	45		Civil Libertarian. Fndr. ACLU
Baldwin, Roger Sherman		Congr	35		50		Early Gov. 1844, Sen. CT 1847
Baldwin, Stanley	1867-1947	HOS	67	182	162	150	3 Term Br. PM. Edw. VIII Abdication
Baldwin, Stephen		Ent	20			40	Actor
Baldwin, Tammy B		Congr	10				Member US Congress
Baldwin, William		Ent	20			40	Actor
Baldwin, William Edwin	1827-1864	Civ War	305	710	2975		CSA Gen. Sig/Rank 420, War Dte. ALS 2975
Bale, Christian		Ent	20			35	Actor
Balewa, A. T., Sir		HOS	20	35	85	38	Nigeria
Balfe, Michael William		Comp	35	55	125		AMusQS 750
Balfour, Arthur J.	1848-1930	HOS	95	209	281	800	Br. PM. 1st Earl. 'Balfour Declaration'
Balfour, Eric		Ent	15			46	
Balfour, Howard		Aero	25		75	45	Br. Ace WWI
Balistier, Elliot		Editor	10	15			Liberty Magazine
Balk, Fairuza		Ent				35	

NAME	DATES	CATEGORY	SIG	LS/DS	ALS	SP	COMMENTS
Ball, Alan		Ent	20			40	Dir./Writer Six Feet Under
Ball, Albert	1896-1917	Aero	175	225	330	275	Brit. RAF ACE WWI. Downed 43 Enemy Planes
Ball, Harvey	1921-2001	Celeb	25	32	40	50	Creator of Smiley face., Illustrated face 50
Ball, Joseph H.		Congr	12			75	Sen.
Ball, Lucille & Arnaz, Desi		Ent	314	486		802	
Ball, Lucille (Lucy)	1911-1989	Ent	103	270	295	392	Comedianne
Ballace, Elaine		Ent	12			35	
Ballance Jr., Frank W. B		Congr	10				Member US Congress
Ballantine, Carl		Ent	15			45	
Ballard, Hank		Music	25			60	Rock Pioneer; H. Ballard Midnighters sigs 60
Ballard, Kaye		Ent	10			22	Actress
Ballard, Robert, Dr.	1942-	Sci	20	40	85	30	Oceanographer. Found Titanic
Ballenger, Cass B		Congr	10				Member US Congress
Ballew, Smith		Ent	15	20		40	Actor
Ballinger, Richard A.		Cab	10	25	50	25	Sec Interior 1909
Ballmer, Steven A.		Bus	15			20	CEO Microsoft
Ballou, Charles		Mil	30	110		40	Gen. WWI
Balsam, Martin	1919-1996	Ent	26	30	20	51	Actor. AA Winner. Supporting Actor
Balsmeyer, Jeff		Ent	13			40	
Baltimore, David, Dr.		Sci	20	25	40	35	Nobel Med. Controversial Scientist
Balzac, Honoré de	1799-1850	Author	550	1338	1594		Fr. Novels
Bampton, Rose	1909-1997	Opera	20	35	45	40	Opera, Concert. Metropolitan
Bana, Eric		Ent	15			35	
Bananarama		Music	30			48	(4)
Bancroft, Anne	1931-2005	Ent	20	22	30	50	Actress. Stage-Films. AA. 'Miracle Worker'
Bancroft, Cameron		Ent	10			20	Actor
Bancroft, Edward	1744-1821	Rev War			4900		Inventor & Spy for Br. During Am. Rev.
Bancroft, Edward W.	1837-1920	Civ War	30		85		MOH during CW. Later promoted to Brig. Gen.
Bancroft, George	1800-1891	Cab	35	85	125	135	Polk Sec Navy, Historian, Diplomat
Bancroft, George	1882-1956	Ent	30	60	85	120	Vintage Actor
Band, The		Music	401			650	Rock HOF. DS 400
Banda, Hastings		Pol				60	Malawi statesman, PM 1963-66. 1st Pres 1966-94
Bandaranike, S. W. R. D		HOS	10	25	45	30	Prime Min. Sri Lanka
Banderas, Antonia		Ent	25			75	
Banderas, Antonio		Ent	20			46	Latin Actor
Bandy, Moe		Cntry Mus	10			15	Honky Tonk Artist
Bangles, The (All)		Ent	40			72	Rock
Bangs, John Kedrick		Author	10	45		20	Humor Editor Harper's Magazine
Banisadr, A.		HOS	35	45	80	65	Iran. Exiled
Bank, C. D.		Cab	10	25			
Bank, Frank	1942-	Ent	20			40	Lumpy Rutherford on Leave it to Beaver
Bankhead, Tallulah	1902-1968	Ent	108	145	200	244	Deep Voiced Actress. Orig. Wilding Photo. SP 600
Bankhead, Wm. B.	1874-1940	Congr	10	40			Spkr. of the House
Banks, Billy		Music	80			250	Jazz
Banks, Jeff		Celeb	10			15	Designer
Banks, Joseph, Sir	1743-1820	Expl	40	130	533		Br. Naturalist, Botanist. Sailed/Capt. Cook
Banks, Leslie	1890-1952	Ent	25			48	Distinguished Br. Stage-Screen Actor
Banks, Michael A.		Author	10	10	25	10	Science fiction, computer book author
Banks, Morwenna		Celeb	10			15	Comedienne
Banks, Nathaniel P.	1816-1894	Civ War	53	101	165		Gov. MA, MOC, Union Gen. FF 28
Banks, Nathaniel P. (WD)		Civ War	165	432	487		Union Gen.
Banks, Tyra		Ent	15			35	Model/actress
Banky, Vilma	1902-1991	Ent	65	112	200	163	Silent Star. Valentino costar. Early Vamp
Banner, John	1910-1973	Ent	75	145		217	Actor. 'Hogan's Heroes' as 'Sgt. Schultz'

NAME	DATES	CATEGORY	SIG	LS/DS	ALS	SP	COMMENTS
Banning, Henry Blackstone		Civ War	30	65			Union Gen., Congressman OH
Banning, Margaret C.		Author	10	12	25	10	
Banting, Frederick G.	1891-1941	Sci	378	908	1650	943	disc. Insulin w/Best. Nobel 1923
Bantock, Granville		Comp	40			125	Br. Comp.
Bara, Theda	1890-1955	Ent	135		300	256	The Vamp'. Silent Screen Star.
Barak, Ehud		Pol	30	40	50	65	Former PM of Israel
Baraka, Imamu A. (LeRoi Jones)		Author	35	90	85	65	Afr-Am Plays, Poet, Novels, Essayist
Baranski, Christine		Ent	12			35	
Barazza, Adriana		Ent	15			45	
Barbara, Agatha		HOS	10			20	Pres. of Malta
Barbarigo, St. Gregorio L.	1625-1697	Clergy		3500			Saint. Canonized 1960
Barbarin, Paul		Music	25		65		Bandleader, Drummer
Barbeau, Adrienne	1945-	Ent	10	15	15	25	Actress
Barbee, John Henry		Music	35			65	Blues Vocalist
Barbejacque, Prince		Ent	10			20	
Barbe-Marbois, Francois de	1745-1837	Pol	45	75	250		As Napoleon's Min. Finance-Louisiana Purchase
Barber, Charles E.	1842-1917	Artist			2300		
Barber, Noyes		Congr	10		50		FF 50
Barber, Rex T.	1917-2001	WWII	30	42	88	72	Am. ACE WWII, Downed Yamamoto
Barber, Samuel	1910-1981	Comp	65	651	312	131	Opera, Songs, Strings. AMusQS/SP 1250-2500
Barber, William		Mil	25			65	Marine MOH Korea
Barbera, Joe		Comics	50			160	Hanna-Barbera. Flintstones, Yogi Bear. SP w/Hanna 250
Barberie, Jillian		Ent	15			45	
Barbier, George	1865-1945	Ent	15	15	25	42	Vintage Char. Actor
Barbieri, Fedora		Opera	25			75	Opera, Concert
Barbieri, Paula		Celeb	10			15	Model
Barbirolli, John, Sir	1899-1970	Cond	38	42	60	150	Br. Conductor
Barbour, Dave		Comp	15			40	Jazz Guitar
Barbour, James	1775-1842	Cab	50		155		Sec War, Gov. & Sen. VA. US Min. GB
Barbour, John Strode		Congr	12		45		FF 46
Barbour, Philip	1783-1841	Sup Crt					MOC, Spkr., Pres. VA Consti. Con. No prices known
Barbour, William Warren		Congr	10	35		15	Sen. NJ
Barclay, Thomas		Rev War	45	55			Adj. -Gen Nova Scotia
Barclay, William		Clergy	40	75	95	75	
Barcroft, Roy		Ent	60			150	
Bard, Ralph A.		Cab	15	25		25	FDR. Sec. Navy
Bardeen, John		Sci	30	50	105	69	Nobel. S Bio Card 55, Invented transistor, U of I; Sketch of trans. 150
Bardem, Javier	1969-	Ent				50	Actor; AA
Bardot, Brigitte		Ent	115	120	120	156	Fr. actress. Intl. Sex Symbol
Bardshar, F. A.		WWII	15	25	45	40	Navy ACE, WWII; 7. 5 kills.
Barere de Vieuzac, Bertrand	1755-1841	Fr Rev	40	120	150		The Anacreon of the Guillotine'. Exiled
Baretti, Giuseppe	1719-1789	Author	35	80	155		Friend of Burke, Johnson. Italian Critic
Bari, Lynn		Ent	10		15	20	Actress. Deep Voiced 'Other Woman' Roles
Baring, Alexander	1774-1848	Banker	130		750		Formalized Webster-Ashburton Treaty
Baring, Francis, Sir	1796-1866	Bus	35	50	110		1st Lord of Adm. ty. ALS/Cont 1975
Baring, Thomas G.	1826-1904	HOS	15	25	55		English Earl. Viceroy of India
Baring-Gould, Sabine	1834-1929	Author	50	120	165	80	'Onward Christian Soldiers' AMS 2400
Barinholtz, Ike		Ent	13			40	
Barker, Bob		Ent	14	30	36	30	Hosted TV's 'The Price is Right'
Barker, Clive		Author	20	25		42	Br. Horror Novels
Barker, Lex	1919-1973	Ent	92	138	160	161	Actor. Ex-Husb Lana Turner. 'Tarzan'
Barker, William George		Aero	125	225	350	295	Canadian ACE, WWI
Barkey, Robert Merrill		WWII	15			35	WWII Ace; 5 kills.

NAME	DATES	CATEGORY	SIG	LS/DS	ALS	SP	COMMENTS
Barkhorn, Gerhard		WWII	130	185		298	Ger. ACE, #2 Worldwide
Barkin, Ellen	1955-	Ent	15			40	Actress
Barkley, Alben W.	1877-1956	VP	29	70	175	78	Truman. Oldest, Only VP To Marry In Office.
Barks, Carl		Comics	35			210	Donald Duck, Scrooge
Barksdale, Ethelbert		Civ War	38	60	89		CSA Congress
Barksdale, William	1821-1863	Civ War	608		1220		CSA Gen. KIA Gettysburg '63
Barksdale, William (WD)	1821-1863	Civ War	908				CSA Gen. KIA Gettysburg '63
Bar-Lev, Chaim		Mil	20	65		50	Israeli Mil. Leader
Barlow, Francis C.	1834-1896	Civ War	79	90	301	825	Union Gen.
Barlow, Gary		Music	10			15	Performing musical artist
Barlow, Howard		Cond	40			50	Popular Radio/TV Conductor
Barlow, Jane		Author	10	15	25		
Barlow, Joel		Diplo	40	120	245		Author, Chaplain Rev. War
Barlow, Thelma		Ent	10			20	Actress
Barnabee, Henry Clay		Opera	10	15	25	15	Operatic Comedian
Barnaby, Ralph S.		Aero	82			350	Aviation pioneer
Barnard, Christian, Dr.		Sci	40	95	85	78	Heart Specialist
Barnard, Daniel D.	1797-1861	Congr	12		85		MOC. NY, Min. Prussia
Barnard, Frederick A. P.	1809-1889	Educ	75	165	275		Barnard Coll. For Women's Ed. Pres. Columbia
Barnard, George Grey	1863-1938	Artist	25		85		Sculptor. Works in Met. Mus. Art, The Cloisters
Barnard, John Gross	1815-1882	Civ War	32	90	143		Union Gen. Sig/Rank 45, War Dte. ALS 165
Barnes, Binnie	1903-1998	Ent	18	12	15	33	Br. Actress. Leading Lady & Light Comedy
Barnes, Demus		Congr	10		20		Congressman NY. Writer
Barnes, Djuna		Author	45	110	260	85	Am. Novels-Short Story Writer
Barnes, James	1801-1869	Civ War	177	186	248		Union Gen. Very Scarce
Barnes, Joanna		Ent	10		15	15	Actress
Barnes, Joseph K.	1817-1883	Civ War	188	410	550		Union Surgeon Gen. Lincoln's Deathbed Dr.
Barnes, Julius H.	1873-1939	Bus	10	20		20	Corp Off. Pres. US Chamber of Commerce
Barnes, Priscilla		Ent	10	10	20	26	Actress.
Barnet, Charlie		Music	15			30	Big Band Leader-Tenor Sax
Barnet, Isaac		Pol	10	20			Mayor Cincinnati
Barnet, Will		Artist				104	
Barnett, Ross R.		Gov	10		25	15	Governor MS
Barnette, Vince		Ent	20	20	35	56	Vintage Char. Actor
Barneveld, Jan Van Olden		Statsmn		2000			Father of Dutch Independence
Barney, Natalie	1876-1972	Author	110	315	412		Am. Poet, Translator, Parisian Hostess
Barnhart, George 'Eddié		Aero	20	35		50	
Barnum, Henry Alanson	1833-1892	Civ War	49	106	132		Union Gen. ALS '64 190, Sig/Rank 70
Barnum, Malvern H.		Mil	10		35	30	Gen. WWI
Barnum, Phineas T.	1810-1891	Bus	168	601	836	1196	ALS/Cont 1, 100-1, 500-2,000-3800
Barnwell, Robert Woodward		Civ War	64	117			CSA Congress
Baron Cohen, Sasha		Ent	17			50	
Baronova, Irina		Ballet	20			58	Rus. -Br. Ballerina
Barr, Candy		Ent	17			37	Stripper. Prison for Shooting Husband
Barr, Doug		Ent	10			15	
Barr, Joseph Walker		Cab	10	15	30	15	Sec. Treasury, Congressman IN
Barr, Roseanne		Ent	20	20	40	35	
Barranco, Maria		Ent	10			20	Actress
Barras, Paul-Francois-Jean		Fr Rev	85	250			Jacobin Club. Exiled From Paris
Barrault, Jean-Louis		Ent	40			125	
Barrett, J. Gresham B		Congr	10				Member US Congress
Barrett, John		Mil	20		50		WWI Victoria Cross
Barrett, Lawrence	1838-1891	Civ War	20				Union Off., Actor
Barrett, Majel		Ent	10			35	Star Trek

NAME	DATES	CATEGORY	SIG	LS/DS	ALS	SP	COMMENTS
Barrett, Rona		Ent	10	12	15	20	
Barrett, S. M.		Author	10			12	Journalist, interviewed Geronimo
Barrett, Wilson	1847-1904	Ent	15		90	65	Br. Plays, Actor, Manager
Barrie, Barbara		Ent	10	13	16	25	Successful Broadway & Film Actress
Barrie, Chris		Ent	10				Actor
Barrie, James M., Sir	1860-1937	Author	100	295	378	438	Plays, Novels. 'Peter Pan'
Barrie, Mona		Ent	15	15	35	30	
Barrie, Wendy		Ent	20	25	30	45	
Barrier, Edgar		Ent	10		10	15	
Barringer, Daniel M.	1806-1873	Congr	12				Repr. NC, Min. Spain
Barringer, Rufus	1821-1895	Civ War	118	322	380		CSA Gen.
Barrington, Shute		Clergy	10	15	25	25	
Barrios, Justo R.	1835-1885	HOS	50	112			Pres. Guatemala. Killed in Battle
Barron, Blue		Band	18			18	
Barron, Clarence		Bus	25	45		40	Editor, Publisher Barron's
Barrow, Clyde	1909-1934	Crime	2500		5688	12650	Bonnie & Clyde
Barrow, Edward G.		Bus	100	147		125	Gen Mgr. NY Yankees
Barrow, John, Sir	1764-1848	Statsmn	50	170	325		Explr., Traveller, Author
Barrow, Robert H.		Mil	10	30	50	50	
Barrows, Lewis O.		Gov	12		25	15	Governor ME
Barrows, Sydney Biddle		Celeb	10			30	Mayflower Madame
Barry, Charles, Sir	1795-1860	Archtct	45	55	138		Br. Houses of Parliament, Westminster Palace
Barry, Dan		Comics	25			100	Flash Gordon
Barry, Dan		Space	10			22	
Barry, Dave		Author	20			30	Creator Dave's World
Barry, Don 'Red'		Ent	22	45	35	58	
Barry, Gene		Ent	15	18	22	35	Actor. Westerns, Straight Leads. Films-TV
Barry, John		Rev War	799	1083			Ir. Born US Naval Off.
Barry, John Decatur	1839-1867	Civ War	186	334	445		CSA Gen.
Barry, John Wolfe, Sir		Celeb	10	15	35	20	
Barry, Marion		Pol	10	14	18	20	Mayor Washington, D. C.
Barry, Sy		Comics	20			50	'Phantom'
Barry, Thomas		Mil	35		150	40	Gen. WWI
Barry, Wesley		Ent	10	12	25	20	
Barry, William Taylor		Civ War	87				CSA Cong.
Barry, Wm. Farquhar	1818-1879	Civ War	54	141	151		Union Gen. War Dte. S 85
Barrymore, Diana		Ent	30	35	45	42	
Barrymore, Drew	1975-	Ent	20			42	Actress
Barrymore, Ethel	1898-1954	Ent	102	190		233	Stage Star before films. 'The Corn is Green'
Barrymore, John	1882-1942	Ent	149	368	425	592	The Great Profile'. Academy Award.
Barrymore, Lionel	1878-1954	Ent	85	233		173	Member 1st Family of Am. Theatre. Oscar 1931
Barrymore, Maurice	1847-1905	Ent	35			90	Founding Member of Am. Family of Actors
Bartato, Elisabeth		Crime	15			40	Opera
Bartel, Jean	1925-	Ent	20			65	Miss Am. '43, Actress. Set new image.
Barth, John		Author	30	40	85	35	Am. Novels
Barth, Karl		Clergy	40	95	125	75	
Barthelmess, Richard		Ent	25	30	75	82	Vintage Actor.
Bartholdi, Fred. Auguste,	1834-1904	Artist	222	520	421	978	Statue of Liberty Print S 700-1395
Bartholomew, Freddie		Ent	30	35	45	73	Brit. Child Actor of 30s-40's
Bartilson, Lynsey		Ent	13			40	
Bartle, Joyce		Ent	10			10	
Bartlett, Bonnie		Ent	10			10	
Bartlett, Joseph J.	1729-1795	Rev War	225	390			Signer of DI; Rev War Off.
Bartlett, Joseph Jackson	1834-1893	Civ War	65	114			Union Gen.

NAME	DATES	CATEGORY	SIG	LS/DS	ALS	SP	COMMENTS
Bartlett, Josiah	1729-1795	Rev War	220	611	1185		Signer. ALS/Cont 3250-8000, FF 950-1050
Bartlett, Paul Wayland		Artist	10	15	30		US Sculptor
Bartlett, Robert Abram		Expl	50	175	125		Cmdr. Ship on Peary Arctic Exp.
Bartlett, Roscoe G. B		Congr	10				Member US Congress
Bartlett, Thomas		Clergy	15	20	35		
Bartlett, William F.		Civ War	48	89	147		Union Gen.
Bartoe, John David		Space	10	20		35	
Bartok, Bela	1881-1945	Comp	362	1102	1312	2408	Hung. Pianist-Comp. AMusQS 1800-2750
Bartok, Eva		Ent	10			15	Actress
Bartoli, Cecilia		Opera	15			60	It. Mezzo. Opera
Bartolotta, Vince Jr.		Law	10	15	20	20	Prominent lawyer
Barton, Bruce	1886-1967	Bus	10	35	40	30	Advertising Exec. BBD&O. Writer, Rep. NY
Barton, Clara	1821-1912	Humanit	175	472	507	734	Fndr. -1st Pres. Am. Red Cross. ALS/Cont 1250
Barton, Derek H. R., Sir		Sci	20	30	40	25	Nobel Chemistry
Barton, Diana		Ent	10			20	Actress
Barton, James		Ent	40			70	
Barton, Joe B		Congr	10				Member US Congress
Barton, Mischa		Ent	15			35	
Barton, Seth Maxwell	1829-1900	Civ War	104	281	308		CSA Gen.
Barton, Seth Maxwell (WD)	1829-1900	Civ War	252		935		CSA Gen.
Bartow, Francis Stebbins	1816-1861	Civ War	91	236	360		CSA Congress
Barty, Billy		Ent	10	18	20	25	Diminuative Char. Actor
Baruch, Bernard M.	1870-1965	Statsmn	37	127	235	159	Financier, Pres. Advisor
Baryshnikov, Mikail		Ballet	62	85	130	161	Rus-Born Ballet Star
Barzun, Jacques		Author	10	12	25	15	
Basch, Peter		Ent	10			20	Actor
Basehart, Richard		Ent	10	10	20	20	
Basie, William 'Count'	1904-1984	Comp	100	225	292	257	Big Band Leader-Pianist
Basile, Frank M.		Celeb	10			15	
Basinger, Kim		Ent	13	25	30	38	Actress; AA
Baskett, James	1904-1948	Ent	225			650	Afr Am actor. Uncle Remus
Baskin, Leonard	1922-2000	Artist	35			50	Sculptor & Graphic Artist
Basov, Nickolay		Sci	20	45		30	Rus. Nobel Physicist
Basquette, Lina		Ent	15			50	1920's Star
Basquiat, Jean-Michel	1960-1988	Artist	500				
Bass, Charles F. B		Congr	10				Member US Congress
Bass, Lance		Music	15			50	Rock
Basset, Henry		Rev War	195	320			Br. Mil. Off. who headed Ft. Detroit
Bassett, Angela		Ent	16			44	Singer
Bassett, Charles A.	1931-1966	Space	250			1800	D. w/Elliott See in T-38 training flight
Bassett, Leslie		Comp	15	30	65		Pulitzer, AMusQS 100
Bassett, Richard		Rev War	375	800			Signer Constitution
Bassey, Shirley		Ent	10			35	Actress
Bassi, Amedeo		Opera	35			150	Favorite Tenor of Toscanini
Bate, William B. (WD)		Civ War	150	208	1045		CSA Gen., Sen, Gov. TN (Listed ALS/Cont)
Bate, William Brimage	1826-1905	Civ War	85	132	175		CSA Gen., Also Gov. Tenn.
Bateman, Jason		Ent	15			30	
Bateman, Justine		Ent	15	15	25	25	
Bates, Alan		Ent	10			32	Br. Actor
Bates, Arthur Laban		Congr	10	10		20	Congressman PA
Bates, Blanche	1873-1941	Ent	20	25	40	50	
Bates, Clayton 'Peg-Leg'	1907-1998	Ent	20			50	One-Legged Tap Dancer. Vaud. -TV-Films
Bates, Edward	1793-1869	Cab	50	135	365	450	Lincoln Atty Gen. War Dte ALS/Cont 895
Bates, Florence		Ent	10				

NAME	DATES	CATEGORY	SIG	LS/DS	ALS	SP	COMMENTS
Bates, John C.		Mil	25		110	40	Am. Gen.
Bates, Joshua H.	1817-1908	Civ War	50		184		Union Gen.
Bates, Katharine Lee	1859-1929	Author	131	232	369	308	AManS 'Am. The Beautiful' 51750, Printed 2000-2500
Bates, Kathy		Ent	25			57	Actress; AA
Bates, Sanford		Lawman	10	35			Commissioner of Prisons
Bathazar, Getty		Ent	15			35	'The Young Riders' SP 80
Bathori, Jane	1876-1970	Ent	25		75	75	Opera. Legendary Fr. Sopr.
Bathurst, Henry		Clergy	15	25	40	30	
Batista, Fulgencio	1901-1973	HOS	136	334	475	204	Cuban Pres. 1940-44, 1952-59. Dictator
Batiuk, Tom		Comics	10			25	Funky Winkerbean
Batman (original cast)		Ent	50			115	West/ Ward
Battaglia, Franco		Opera	15			50	Opera, Concert
Bataille, Charles	1822-1872	Opera	10		50		Opera
Batten, Hugh		WWII	10	25	40	30	Navy ACE, WWII
Batten, Jean	1909-1982	Aero	45	85		90	Pioneer NZ Aviatrix
Battenberg, Louis	1854-1921	Mil	10		50	95	Br. Adm of the Fleet 1919
Battle, Cullen Andrews	1829-1905	Civ War	295	405	595		CSA Gen.
Battle, Kathleen		Opera	20	40		52	Opera, Concert
Battu, Marie	1838-1888	Opera	15		75		Opera. Sang in World Premiere of L'Africaine
Batz, Willhelm		WWII	40			110	Ger. ACE, #7 Worldwide
Baucus, Bob		Aero	10	20	35	25	
Baucus, Max		Congr	10				US Senate (D-MT)
Baudelaire, Charles-Pierre	1821-1867	Author	335	2250	2370		Fr. Mdrn. ist Poet, Symbolist, Critic
Baudouin, King (Belg)		Royal	35	100	250	125	King of Belgium
Baudry, Patrick		Space	12	25		25	
Bauduc, Ray		Music	10			25	Big Band Bassist
Bauer, Harold		Music	38	80	125	70	Br. Piano Virtuoso
Bauer, Jaime Lyn		Ent	10			28	
Bauer, Michelle		Ent	20			125	B-Film Star. S Lip Print. 15.
Bauer, Steven		Ent	10			20	
Baulieu, Etienne		Sci	20		45	40	Inventor RU486 Abortion Pill
Baum, Kurt		Opera				40	Operatic Tenor
Baum, L. Frank		Author	1924	2947	6528		The Wizard of Oz books
Baum, Vicki	1888-1960	Author	20				Novels. Grand Hotel
Baum, William W., Card.		Clergy	35	55	70	50	
Baumer, Steven		Ent	10	15	20	25	
Baur, Hans		WWII	30	45	90	100	Hitler's Personal Pilot
Baur, Harry		Ent	52			175	Fr. Star Executed by Nazis
Bauvais, Garcelle		Ent				40	Models, Inc.
Bavier, Frances	1902-1989	Ent	125	128	148	192	Aunt Bee on the Andy Griffith Show
Bax, Arnold		Comp	70				AMusQS 200
Bax, Kylie		Ent	21			64	
Baxley, Barbara		Ent	10			15	
Baxter, Anne	1923-1985	Ent	30	38	40	125	AA
Baxter, Henry	1821-1873	Civ War	53	150	314		Union Gen.
Baxter, James P. III		Author	10	15	30	10	
Baxter, Keith		Ent	10			15	
Baxter, Les		Band	26		40		Arranger, Comp.
Baxter, Percival P.		Gov	12		25		Governor ME
Baxter, Warner	1892-1951	Ent	88	50	155	165	Early Leading Man & Oscar Winner
Baxter-Birney, Meredith		Ent	10	16	20	30	
Bay, Michael		Ent	16			49	
Bayard, George Dashiell	1835-1862	Civ War	155	170	694		Union Gen., KIA Fredericksburg
Bayard, George Dashiell (WD)	1835-1862	Civ War	395		1222		Union Gen.

NAME	DATES	CATEGORY	SIG	LS/DS	ALS	SP	COMMENTS
Bayard, John B.	1738-1807	Rev War	40	132	168		Continental Congress, Rev. War Col.
Bayard, Richard Henry		Congr	20	40	85		Sen. DE
Bayard, Thomas F., Sr.		Cab	25	35	80		Sec. State, Sen. DE
Bayard, William		Rev War	100	220	450		
Bayh, Birch		Congr	10	25		20	Sen. IN
Bayh, Evan		Congr	10				US Senate (D-IN)
Bayne, Barbara		Ent	20			55	
Bayne, Beverly		Ent	10	10	20	20	
Baywatch (cast)		Ent	65			188	Original cast of 6
Beach Boys (4)		Ent	376			402	Album S by 5 w/Johnston 500; Orig. Band SP 2500.
Beach, Amy M.	1867-1944	Comp	45		462	200	1st Am. Woman Comp. of Note. AMusQS 175
Beach, Michael		Ent	10			20	Actor
Beach, Rex	1877-1949	Author	20	35	95	35	Am. Novels
Beacham, Stephanie		Ent	10		15	20	Actress
Beadle, George Wells, Dr.		Sci	20	30	45	40	Nobel Med.
Beakley, Wallace M.		Mil	10	15	25		
Beal, George Lafayette	1825-1896	Civ War	50	123	156	150	Union Gen. ALS '64 440
Beal, John		Ent	15	15	25	25	
Beale, Richard Lee Turberville	1819-1893	Civ War	83	105	251		CSA Gen.
Beale, Richard Turberville (WD)		Civ War	175		550		CSA Gen.
Beall, Lloyd J.		Civ War	100	1093	2415		
Beall, William N. R. (WD)		Civ War	200	350	772	883	CSA Gen.
Beals, Jennifer		Ent	20	20	40	30	
Bean, Alan L.		Space	25	183	110	101	Moonwalker Astro. ADS re Apollo 12 975
Bean, L. L.	1872-1967	Bus	50	72	95	300	Unique Business Empire
Bean, Orson	1928-	Ent	10			22	Actor-Comed; 2nd cousin Calvin Coolidge.
Bean, Roy, Judge	1825-1903	West	3950	4500			The Law West of the Pecos, "Hanging Judge"
Bean, Sean		Ent	10			20	Actor
Beane, Hilary		Ent	10	10	15	10	
Beard, Charles A.	1874-1948	Author	10	28	65	85	Am. Historian, Teacher, Pol. Scientist
Beard, Daniel C.	1850-1941	Author	110	253	335	175	Fndr. Boy Scouts of Am. Author, Teacher
Beard, James	1903-1985	Celeb	20			45	Father of Am. Cooking
Beard, Matthew "Stymie"	1925-1981	Ent	144			192	Little Rascals
Bearden, Romare	1914-1988	Artist	45	225	475	200	Artist. Principally Blk. -Am. Life Collage
Beardslee, Lester Anthony		Mil	30		100	95	Adm. Spanish Am. War
Beardsley, Aubrey	1872-1898	Artist	175	375	1712	2300	Br. Illust. Art Nouveau
Beardsley, Samuel	1790-1860	Congr	10				Repr. NY, Assoc. Judge NY Supr. Ct.
Beart, Emmanuelle		Ent	10			20	Actress
Beasley, John		Ent	15			45	
Beastie Boys (3)		Music	50			98	Rock Group (3)
Beatles (all four) on one piece		Music	5998	11246		11473	SP w/S 1st names 4933
Beatles with Pete Best		Music				18683	Beatle's drummer prior to Ringo Starr
Beaton, Cecil	1904-1980	Photog	40	155	202	375	Br. Portraitist. Theatrical Designer
Beatrice, Princess		Royal	50	125	142	135	Youngest Daughter Q. Victoria
Beatrix, Queen		Royal	100		450		Netherlands
Beatty, Clyde	1903-1965	Bus	60	122	175	200	Animal Trainer. Circus Performer-Owner
Beatty, David, Adm.	1871-1936	Mil	32	75	90	150	Br. Adm. WWI
Beatty, John (WD)	1828-1914	Civ War		60			Union Brig. Gen.
Beatty, Ned		Ent	15	18	20	40	Actor
Beatty, Samuel	1820-1885	Civ War	50	59	79		Union Gen.
Beatty, Warren	1937-	Ent	30	119		72	Actor, Oscar 1981 for 'Reds' Dir.
Beatty. John		Civ War	46	69	100		Union Gen.
Beauharnais, Eugene de	1781-1824	Royal	72	250	265		Son of Josephine, Adopted by Napoleon
Beauharnais, Hortense de	1783-1837	Royal	70		435		Wife of Louis Bonaparte

NAME	DATES	CATEGORY	SIG	LS/DS	ALS	SP	COMMENTS
Beauman, Maj. Gen. Archibald B.	1888-1977	Mil	252				WWII Br. Gen.
Beaumarchais, Caron de	1732-1799	Author	200	1413			Fr. Plays. Aided Am. Colonies In Rev. War
Beaumont, Hugh		Ent	450	1200		645	Dad on "Leave it to Beaver"
Beaumont, Kathryn		Ent	25			65	Voice of Alice in Wonderland, Peter Pan
Beauprez, Bob B		Congr	10				Member US Congress
Beauregard, Pierre G. T.	1818-1893	Civ War	266	733	635	1360	CSA Gen. Stock Cert. S 3950
Beauregard, Pierre G. T. (WD)	1818-1893	Civ War	484	1810	1805	2650	CSA Gen. Fired on Fort Sumter
Beauvais, Garcelle		Ent	10			40	Actress, Models, Inc.
Beauvoir, Simone de	1908-1986	Author	115	178	512		Fr. Novels. Philosopher. Existentialist
Beaux, Cecilia	1863-1942	Artist	55	58	65		Am. Portrait Painter
Beaver, James A.		Civ War	35	55	110		Union Gen., Gov. PA
Beaver, Jim		Ent	10			30	
Beaverbrook, Max, Lord		Pub					SEE Maxwell, William
Beavers, Louise		Ent	59			226	Popular Afr. -Am. Film Actress; vintage SP 625
Becerra, Xavier B		Congr	10				Member US Congress
Bechet, Sidney	1897-1959	Music	130	328	422	350	Jazz Clarinetist-Saxaphonist
Bechi, Gino		Opera	25			55	Opera
Beck		Music	20			55	Rock
Beck, C. C		Comics	30			100	Captain Marvel
Beck, Dave	1894-1993	Labor	20	50	50	50	Union Exec. Sent to Prison for Union Fraud
Beck, James M.	1861-1936	Congr		25			Repr. PA
Beck, Jeff		Music	50			177	Rock Guitarist
Beck, John		Ent	10			15	
Beck, Ken		Author	10			12	Trivia books
Becker, Barbara		Ent	10			10	
Beckett, Samuel	1906-1989	Author	139	315	367	520	Ir. Plays. Nobel Lit. 'Waiting for Godot'. S Man. 4500
Beckett, Scotty		Ent	175				Child Actor; 'Our Gang'
Beckham, Victoria		Ent				160	
Beckinsale, Kate		Ent	15			65	
Beckman, Arnold	1900-	Invent	18			30	Beckman Instruments. pH testing meter
Beckwith, Edward G.		Civ War	45	65	80		Union Gen.
Beckwith, Geo. Sir	1753-1823	Rev War	200	390			Br. Gen. in the Am. War
Beckwith, J. Carroll		Artist	35	80	145		
Becquerel, Edmond	1820-1891	Sci	250		1450		Fr. Physicist MsS 3500
Becquerel, Henri	1852-1908	Sci	200	450	520		Nobel Curies' Radioactivity., AMS 10,000
Bedard, Irene		Ent	10			20	Actress
Beddoe, Don		Ent	10			20	
Bedelia, Bonnie		Ent	10		10	18	
Bedell, Grace	1849-1936	Pres	1250	3500	13200		Wrote Lincoln recommending that he grow a beard
Bedford, Brian		Ent	10			20	Actor
Bedford, Gunning, Jr.		Rev War	300	700			Signer of Constitution. Scarce
Bedford, Gunning, Sr.		Rev War	200	325			Cousin of above, Scarce
Bedinger, George M.		Mil		6500			Major; Northwest Indian War
Bedwell, Randall		Author	10			12	Regional histories/publisher
Bee Gees (3)		Music	190	375		300	Barry, Robin, Maurice Gibb. 'Stayin' Alive'
Bee, Barnard E.	1824-1861	Civ War	1189	867	2515	1238	CSA Gen., Sec. War Rep. TX
Bee, Carlos		Congr	10	20		20	Congressman TX
Bee, Hamilton Prioleau	1822-1897	Civ War	100	153	425		CSA Gen.
Bee, Hamilton Prioleau (WD)	1822-1897	Civ War	322	295			CSA Gen.
Bee, Molly		Cntry Mus	10			20	
Beebe, Charles William	1877-1962	Expl	40	60	212	95	Bathysphere. Naturalist. Author, Scientist
Beebe, Marshall		WWII	20	35	55	42	ACE, WWII
Beech, Olive Ann		Aero	20	45		50	Beechcraft Airplane Mfg.
Beecham, Stephanie		Ent	10			20	Actress

NAME	DATES	CATEGORY	SIG	LS/DS	ALS	SP	COMMENTS
Beecham, Thomas, Sir	1879-1961	Cond	68	195		262	Flamboyant Br. Conductor. 3x5 Half-Tone SP 120
Beecher, Henry Ward	1813-1887	Clergy	52	98	140	321	Abolition, Temperance Activist, Orator
Beecher, Lyman		Clergy	40	55	65	45	Early Anti Slavery
Beecher, Philemon		Congr	10				FF 35
Beehner, John F.		Author	10			12	Biblical principles of business
Beems, Patricia		Ent	10			12	
Beene, Geoffrey		Bus	20	25		35	Fashion Designer
Beerbohm, Max, Sir Henry	1872-1956	Author	55	135	162	75	Humorist, Caricaturist
Beerbohm-Tree, Herbert		Ent	20			65	Classical Actor
Beery, Noah	1884-1946	Ent	100		250	275	
Beery, Noah Jr.		Ent	15	20	25	35	
Beery, Wallace	1885-1949	Ent	155	195	350	317	Vintage Oscar Winner. 'The Champ'
Beeson, Jack	1921-	Comp	15	30	63	25	AMusQS 35
Beethoven, Ludwig van		Comp	7800	17500	40475		
Beggs, James		Space	10			30	
Begin, Menachem	1914-1992	HOS	65	272	320	150	P. M. Israel. Nobel Peace Pr. ALS/Cont 1295
Begley, Ed, Jr.		Ent	15	16	17	38	Actor
Begley, Ed, Sr.		Ent	25	45	70	70	Actor
Behan, Brendan F.		Author	160	400	645		Ir. Author-Plays
Behr, Henrich von, Baron		Mil	10			30	
Behr, Jason		Ent	14			43	
Behrman, S. N.		Author	15	25	60	25	Am. Plays, Screenplays
Beichel, Rudolph		Sci	25			55	Rocket Pioneer/von Braun
Beiderbecke, Bix		Music	3822				Jazz Musician
Beinhorn, Elly		Aero	20	28	45	52	Ger. Aviation Pioneer
Beisswenger, Hans		WWII	50			200	Luftwaffe Ace
Beith, Ian Hay (John)		Author	10	30	60	35	Br. Novels, Plays
Beke, Charles Tilstone		Expl	35	50	125		Br. Geographer. Nile Source
Bekhterev, Vladimir	1857-1927	Sci		1750	2500		Russ. Neuropathologist/Pavlov
Bekins, Milo		Bus	35	45	160	160	Bekins Van & Storage Co.
Bel Geddes, Barbara		Ent	10			25	Dallas. NY Drama Critic Award
Bel Geddes, Norman		Artist	20	50	155	35	Scenic Designer Theater
Bela, Magyar		Space	10			25	Hungary
Belafonte, Harry		Ent	20	25		45	
Belafonte, Shari		Ent	10	16	20	25	
Belasco, David		Ent	35	30	70	272	Theatrical Prod.
Belaunde, Fernando T.		HOS	10	20	50	25	
Belcher, Edward, Sir	1799-1877	Mil	15	35	60		Br. Royal Navy
Belcher, Jonathan	1681-1757	Colonial	210	362	650		Gov. MA, NH, NJ. Instrumental as Fndr. Princeton
Belita		Ent	15	25	45	45	
Belknap, George		Civ War	45	50	60		Union Naval Off. C. W. Cabinet
Belknap, Reginald R.	1871-1959	Mil	50	150			US Adm. Invented Collapsable Sub Net
Belknap, William W.		Civ War	50	121	112	350	Union Gen., Sec. War (Grant) Impeached
Bell, Alexander Graham	1847-1922	Sci	855	1552	3456	5379	Invented Telephone, ALS/TLS cont 1500-10000
Bell, Camilla		Ent	15			45	
Bell, Caspar Wistar	1819-1898	Civ War	64				Member of the CSA Congress
Bell, Catherine		Ent	15			40	Actress.
Bell, Charles H.	1798-1875	Civ War	50	100	145		Union Naval Captain, Adm.
Bell, Charles, Sir	1774-1842	Sci	150		475		Scot Surgeon-Anatomist. Nervous System Authority
Bell, Chris B		Congr	10				Member US Congress
Bell, Digby		Ent	12			30	Vintage Actor
Bell, Eric Temple (John Taine)		Author	30		130	55	Scot., Math Books, Sci-Fi
Bell, Griffin		Cab	10			20	Atty Gen.
Bell, Henry H.	1808-1868	Civ War	60	250			Rear Adm under Farragut

NAME	DATES	CATEGORY	SIG	LS/DS	ALS	SP	COMMENTS
Bell, Herbert A.		Bus	15	20	75	50	
Bell, Hiram Parks	1827-1907	Civ War	60	117			Member of the CSA Congress
Bell, John		Cab	46	145			W. H. Harrison, Tyler Sec War
Bell, Kristen		Ent	17			50	
Bell, Lauralee		Ent	10	16		20	Soaps Actress
Bell, Peter Hansborough		Gov	75	195			Gov. TX 1849-53
Bell, Rex		Ent	50			125	
Bell, Terrel H.		Cab	10	15	26	15	Sec. Education
Bell, Tyree Harris	1815-1902	Civ War	78	165	239		CSA Gen.
Bell, Vanessa		Artist	100				Br. Artist-Sister of Virginia Woolf
Bellamy Bros.		Cntry Mus	10			20	Howard & David
Bellamy, David, Prof.		Celeb	10				Naturalist
Bellamy, Edward	1850-1898	Author	25	75	150		Novels
Bellamy, Elizabeth W.		Author	10		18		
Bellamy, Madge		Ent	10	15	40	35	
Bellamy, Ralph	1904-1991	Ent	18	20	28	45	Actor-Leading Man & Char. -Films, Stage
Bellanca, Giuseppe M.		Aero	40	85	160	125	Bellanca Aircraft Designer-Mfg.
Belle, Lulu		Cntry Mus	10			20	
Beller, Kathleen		Ent	10			15	
Belleri, Marguerite		Opera	10		30	25	Metropolitan Opera 1917-20
Bellew, John Chippendall		Clergy	10	20	25	20	
Belli, Melvin		Law	10	15	35	20	Trial Attorney
Belliard, A. D. (Count)	1769-1832	Mil	30	55	175		Fr. Gen. under Napoleon
Bellincioni, Gemma		Opera	118		195	175	It. Sopr. Sang Premiere of 'Cavalleria Rusticana'
Bellini, Vincenzo	1801-1835	Comp	478		3330		It. Opera. 'Norma', 'La Sonnambula'
Bellmer, Hans	1902-1975	Artist	65	160	500		Ger. Surrealist Painter, Engraver, Photographer
Bellmon, Henry Louis		Congr	15	20			Sen. OK, Gov. OK
Bello, Don Andres	1781-1865	Educ	350				Simon Bolivar's Teacher; Chile University Fndr.
Bello, Maria		Ent	13			40	
Belloc, Hilaire	1870-1953	Author	40	85	128	50	Versatile Novels, Poet, Critic
Belloc-Lowndes, Marie		Author	20	40	110	30	Br. Author of Historical Works
Bellon, Leoncadia		Opera	16			45	Opera, Film
Bellonte, Maurice		Aero	100	155	270	370	
Bellow, Saul	1915-	Author	42	106	267	84	Nobel Literature 1976. Novels
Bellows, George	1882-1925	Artist	147	300	450	495	Urban Scenes, Sports, Landscape
Bellows, Henry W.	1814-1882	Clergy	20	40	55		Fndr. Antioch College. Unitariarn Clergyman
Bellson, Louis		Music	30		55	65	Jazz Drummer
Belluccii, Monica		Ent				75	Actress
Bellwood, Pamela		Ent	10	12	15	26	
Belmont, August	1816-1890	Bus	183	396	888	683	Banker, Diplomat, Belmont Park Stk. Cert. S 2500
Belmont, August, Jr.		Bus	45	120			
Belmont, August, Mrs.		Celeb	15	25	40		Socialite
Belsham, Thomas		Clergy	15	20	35	30	
Beltran, Robert		Ent	15			45	
Belushi, James		Ent	15	20	25	40	
Belushi, Jim		Ent	16			48	
Belushi, John	1949-1982	Ent	365	377		751	Comed. 'Second City', 'Sat. Nite Live'; S Chk 925
Bemelmans, Ludwig	1898-1962	Author	45	182	255	50	Writer-Illust. Novels
Benacerraf, Baruj		Sci	30	55		40	Nobel Med. -Physiology
Benaderet, Bea	1906-1968	Ent		128		145	Actress; Cousin Pearl on The Beverly Hillbillies
Benatar, Pat		Ent	25			60	
Benavidez, Roy		Mil	10	25	40	40	
Benchley, Peter		Author	20	25	50	40	Sketch of Jaws S 15-35
Benchley, Robert		Author	35	80	195	195	Am. Drama Critic, Humorist

NAME	DATES	CATEGORY	SIG	LS/DS	ALS	SP	COMMENTS
Bendix, William	1906-1964	Ent	77	93	60	170	
Benederet, Bea		Ent	40			100	
Benedict XV, Pope		HOS	280	1119	450	550	
Benedict, Dick		Ent	15	20	25	30	
Benedict, Julius, Sir		Comp	15			25	Br. Pianist
Benedict, Pope XVI		Clergy	456			650	Joseph Card. Ratzinger
Benedict, William		Ent	25			60	
Beneke, Tex		Music	30			87	Sax for Glenn Miller. Big Band
Benes, Eduard	1884-1948	HOS	85	90	145	200	P. M. & Pres. Czech.
Benet, Stephen Vincent	1898-1943	Author	70	154	168	150	Poet, Novels. Pulitzer (2)
Ben-Gurion, David	1886-1973	HOS	168	1025	1498	420	Israel's 1st PM. LS-ANS/Cont 5500; S Israel DOI 90,000-120,000
Benham, George W. (WD)		Civ War	120	225	389		Union Gen.
Benham, Henry W.	1813-1884	Civ War	50	368	150		Union Gen.
Benighi, Roberto		Ent	15			40	Actor. Films
Bening, Annette		Ent	20	25	45	50	Actress
Benjamin, Judah P.	1811-1884	Civ War	340	640	876		CSA Gen. & Sec. of State
Benjamin, Judah P. (WD)		Civ War	497	1871	2750		CSA Sec. of State
Benjamin, Park	1809-1864	Author		40			Am. Journalist
Benjamin, Richard		Ent	10			35	Actor-Dir.
Bennett, Arnold		Author	40	175			Br. Novels
Bennett, Bruce (Herman Brix)		Ent	15	24	30	50	Early Tarzan. Athlete as Herman Brix
Bennett, Constance		Ent	30	60	120	81	Glamour Leading Lady of 30s-40's
Bennett, Floyd		Aero	115	370	750	750	Pilot w/Byrd over North Pole
Bennett, James Gordon	1841-1918	Pub	45	138	150		Financed Stanley-Livingstone Afr. Exped.
Bennett, Joan	1910-1990	Ent	16	18	35	66	Actress. Leading Lady Sister of Constance
Bennett, Johnstone		Ent	15			35	Actress w/Mansfield
Bennett, Jonathan		Ent	15			45	
Bennett, Julie		Ent	10			10	
Bennett, Richard		Ent	20			50	Stage & Silent Films
Bennett, Robert		Law	15			35	Power Atty for Pres. Clinton vs Paula Jones
Bennett, Robert		Congr	10				US Senate (R-UT)
Bennett, Robert Russell		Comp	50		250	95	Great Broadway Comp. Academy Award
Bennett, Samuel F.		Comp	35	75	150		In the Sweet Bye & Bye., AQS 920
Bennett, Tony	1926-	Music	20	31	35	60	Top Recording & Club Singer
Bennett, Wallace F.		Congr	10			15	Sen. UT
Bennett, William J.		Cab	20	60	75	75	Book of Virtues. Sec. Ed.
Bennett, Wm. Andrew		HOS	10	10	15	10	
Benning, Henry Lewis	1814-1875	Civ War	205	317	472		CSA Gen., Statesman. Fort Benning, GA So Named
Benny, Jack	1894-1974	Ent	74	209		208	Great Radio-TV Comedian
Benois, Alexander		Artist	45	195	425		Rus. Designed Sets, Costumes
Benoit, Francois		Bus		500			18th C. Fur Trader
Benson, Amber		Ent	16			48	
Benson, Arthur Christopher	1862-1925	Celeb			75		'Man of Letters'
Benson, Edward Frederic	1867-1940	Author	20	40	112		Satirical, Macabre Novels. Scholar
Benson, Edward W., Arch.		Clergy	20	35	55	35	
Benson, Egbert	1746-1833	Rev War	58	75	170		Rep NY in Cont. Congress & the HOR
Benson, Elmer A.		Gov	10	12	20	15	Governor & Sen. MN
Benson, Ezra Taft	1899-1994	Relig	50	100	250	75	Pres. Mormon Church; Secc AG under Eisenhower
Benson, Frank Robert, Sir		Ent	15	20	35	30	Vintage Br. Actor
Benson, George		Music	15			30	Music
Benson, Jodi		Ent	10			30	Actress. Disney Voice
Benson, Richard Meux		Clergy	35	55	65	75	
Benson, Robbie		Ent	15	16	20	25	Juvenile & Adult Actor. Disney Voice Over

NAME	DATES	CATEGORY	SIG	LS/DS	ALS	SP	COMMENTS
Benson, William S.		Mil	10	20	35	25	Adm. USN WWI
Bent, James Theodore	1852-1897	Expl	10	10	35	25	Br. Archaeologist. Greece, Asia Minor, Abyssinia
Benteen, Frederick W.		Mil		2057	2846	3167	Involved in the Battle of Big Horn 1876
Bentham, Jeremy	1748-1832	Jurist	120		1300		Br. Writer ; Philosopher
Bentley, Jay		Ent	10			30	
Benton, Barbi		Model	18	25	30	70	Playboy Playmate of the Month, Actress
Benton, Robert		Ent	10			20	AA Dir. 'Kramer vs Kramer', 'Bonnie & Clyde'
Benton, Samuel	1820-1864	Civ War	412	675			CSA Gen. D. Battle of Atlanta 1864
Benton, Thomas Hart	1782-1858	Congr	84	110	137		30-Year Sen. From Missouri
Benton, Thomas Hart	1889-1975	Artist	101	244	710		ALS/Cont 1350
Benton, William	1900-1973	Congr	10	30	65	20	Publisher, Statesman, Businessman, Sen. CT
Benton, William Plummer	1828-1867	Civ War	110	166			Union Gen. Rare
Bentsen, Lloyd	1921-2006	Sen/Cab	10	30		20	Sen. TX, Sec. Treas.
Ben-Ur, Aviva		Author	10			12	Sephardic history
Ben-Yehuda, Eliezer		Author	50	175	425		Jewish Scholar
Benz, Julie		Ent	15			45	
Benzali, Daniel		Ent	10			20	Actor
Benzell, Mimi		Opera	15			35	Opera
Ben-Zvi, Itzhak	1884-1963	HOS	74	191	250	160	2nd Pres. Israel
Ben-Zvi, Yitzhak		Pol	35	80	125	100	Pres. of Israel
Beradino, John	1917-1996	Ent	25			50	Actor 'Our Gang' comedies, Baseball Player
Berdan, Hiram	1824-1893	Civ War	150	506	646		Union Gen.
Berdyaev, Nikolai	1874-1948	Phil	75	100	145	175	Russ. Orth. Layman, Marxist. Critic of Both
Berenger, Tom		Ent	10			48	Actor
Berenson, Marisa		Ent	10	20	15	25	Model-Actress. Willowy Member Intl Jet Set
Berenstain, Stan		Comics	20			75	'Berenstain Bear'
Beresford, Bruce		Celeb	10			15	Film industry
Beresford, Charles, Lord	1846-1919	Mil	20	35	100	80	Br. Adm. Bombardment AlexAndria. Khartoum Exped
Bereuter, Doug B		Congr	10				Member US Congress
Berfield, Justin		Ent	13			40	
Berfson, Henri-Louis		Author	30	80	155		
Berg, Alban	1885-1935	Comp	135	660	1502		Austrian. Atonal Music. Orchestral, Songs
Berg, Carmen		Ent	15			45	
Berg, Gertrude		Ent	18	15	25	50	Vintage Actress. Stage & Radio
Berg, Moe	1902-1972	Celeb	225				Lawyer, Mathematician, Spy
Berg, Paul		Sci	27	35	65	40	Nobel Chemistry
Berg, Peter		Ent	10			30	Actor-Dir.
Berganza, Teresa		Opera	10			48	Opera
Bergdorf, Gary		Ent	10			30	Radar'. Mash
Bergen, Bob		Ent	15			45	
Bergen, Candice		Ent	20	45	25	50	Actress. Films. Emmys
Bergen, Edgar	1903-1978	Ent	50	80	125	155	Am. Ventriloquist-Comed. -Actor. Special AA
Bergen, Frances		Ent	10			10	
Bergen, Polly	1930-	Ent	10	10	18	26	Actress, Singer, Films, TV. Cosmetics Mfg.
Berger, Erna		Opera	10			30	Opera
Berger, Gottlob		WWII	50	236	246	200	WWII Gen. of the Waffen SS
Berger, Senta		Ent	10	15	35	30	Actress. Leading Lady of Am. & Intl Films
Bergere, Lee		Ent	10			15	
Bergeron, Marion		Celeb	45			133	Miss Am. 1933. Crowned at age 15 1/2
Berggrav, Eivind Josef		Clergy		50			Bishop Norway. World Council of Churches
Bergh, Henry	1811-1888	Reform	85		400		Fndr. ASPCA
Bergin, Patrick		Ent	10			20	Actor
Bergland, Bob		Cab	10		20	15	Sec. Agriculture, Congress MN
Bergman, Ingmar	1918-2007	Ent	97	109	150	200	Swe. Film Dir.

NAME	DATES	CATEGORY	SIG	LS/DS	ALS	SP	COMMENTS
Bergman, Ingrid	1913-1982	Ent	124	207	242	503	3x Academy Award Winner. SPc 250-325
Bergman, Jaime		Ent	23			68	
Bergman, Sandahl		Ent	10		15	20	
Bergner, Elizabeth	1898-1968	Ent	20	35	60	30	Pol-Born Actress. Max Reinhardt
Bergonzi, Carlo		Opera	30			65	Opera
Bergson, Henri	1859-1941	Author	40	125			Philosopher. Nobel Literature 1928. Educator
Beria, Lavrenty Pavlovich	1899-1953	Mil		563	2645		Head of Soviet Secret police
Berigan, Bunny		Music	160	285		340	One of greatest trumpet players in jazz history
Berio, Luciano		Comp	20	30	75		
Beriot, Charles Auguste de		Comp	40		175		Violinist Virtuoso. Visual Artist
Berjerac, Jacques		Ent	15			40	Fr. Actor of Am. Films. 40s-50'2
Berkeley, Busby		Ent	64	155	275	295	Dance Choreographer-Dir.
Berkley, Elizabeth		Ent	15			32	Showgirls', actress
Berkley, Shelley B		Congr	10				Member US Congress
Berkoff, Steven		Ent	10			20	Actor
Berkowitz, David		Crime	85	90	250		Son of Sam, Serial Murderer
Berle, Adolph	1895-1971	Econ	15	35			Am. Member of FDR's Original 'Brain Trust'
Berle, Milton	1908-2002	Ent	50	118	145	237	Comed. Vaude., Radio, 'MR. TV'
Berlier, Jean Baptiste	1843-1911	Sci	45	62	70		Fr. Engineer. Paris Underground RR System
Berlier, Theophile, Count		Fr Rev	100	150	295		
Berlik, Jan		Opera	25			50	Czech. Operatic Tenor
Berlin, Irving	1888-1990	Comp	226	641	957	939	AMusQS 1500-2500. Many TLSsS & ALsS S Irving
Berlioz, Hector	1803-1869	Comp	245	1225	1688		Dist. Fr. Comp. AMusQS 3, 900-8, 500
Berlitz, Charles		Bus	20	35		40	Language Educator
Berlitz, Maximilian		Bus		425			Fndr. of the Berlitz Language Schools in 1878
Berman, Eugene	1899-1972	Artist	40	105	195		Rus. -Born Painter-Designer
Berman, Howard L. B		Congr	10				Member US Congress
Berman, Pandro S.	1905-1996	Ent	20	40		50	Prod. 1977 Irving Thalberg Award
Berman, Shelley	1926-	Ent	20	25	35	35	Comedian; Curb Your Enthusiasm
Bernacchi, Antonio		Music			2500		Classical Singer (Castrato) for Handel
Bernadotte, Jean-Baptiste		Royal	120	296	650		Charles XIV John. Marshal of Nap.
Bernard, Carlos		Ent	14			43	
Bernard, Claude	1813-1878	Sci	145		602		Fr. Fndr. Experimental Med.
Bernard, Crystal		Ent	13			41	Actress. 'Wings'
Bernard, Francis, Sir	1712-1779	Colonial	200	522	750		Col. Gov. Mass. Bay Colony
Bernard, John Henry, Arch.		Clergy	95	45	50	40	
Bernard, Rueben F. (WD)		Civ War			200		Col. US Cavalry
Bernard, Simon	1779-1839	Mil	50	125			Fr. Eng'r. Nap. At Waterloo. US Gen. 1816
Bernardin, Joseph Cardinal	1928-1996	Clergy	35	50	75	75	Cardinal
Berndt, Walter		Comics	10			50	'Smitty'
Berners-Lee, Tim		Sci	20			30	Creator of the worldwide web
Bernhard, Sandra		Ent	10	15		20	Comedienne.
Bernhardt, Sarah	1844-1923	Ent	100	233	260	585	The Divine Sarah'. Great Fr. Actress
Bernie, Ben		Ent	20		25	25	Big Band Leader-M. C. -Comedian.
Bernsen, Corbin		Ent	15	20	40	40	Actor. 'L. A. Law'
Bernstein, Carl		Author	10			38	Journalist
Bernstein, Elmer		Comp	25	40	125	50	Am. Comp. -Conductor. ALS/Cont 600
Bernstein, Leonard	1918-1990	Comp	103	287	645	374	AMusMS 500-2500
Berosini, Josephine		Ent	10	10	25	30	
Berrien, J. Macpherson	1781-1856	Cab	30	55	105		Jackson Atty Gen.
Berrigan, Daniel, Fr.		Clergy	30	30	65	40	Controversial Pol. Priest
Berry, Chuck		Music	126	294		198	Rock. Alb. S 115
Berry, Halle		Ent	15			45	Actress, AA
Berry, Hiram G.	1824-1863	Civ War	388	783			Union Gen. Killed in Action

NAME	DATES	CATEGORY	SIG	LS/DS	ALS	SP	COMMENTS
Berry, Hiram G. (WD)	1824-1863	Civ War	500	909			Killed in Action
Berry, Jim		Comics	10			35	'Berry's World'
Berry, Ken		Ent	10	10	15	30	Actor. 'F Troop', 'Mama's Family'
Berry, Lucien		Mil	20	50		55	Gen. WWI
Berry, Marion B		Congr	10				Member US Congress
Berry, Nick		Ent	10			20	Actor
Berry, Richard	1936-1997	Comp	30	45		60	Comp. 'Louie, Louie'
Berry, Sidney M.		Clergy	10	15	25		
Berry, Tom		Gov	10			25	Gov. SD
Berry, William H.		Civ War	20				6th Missouri Survivor
Berryman, Clifford		Artist	55	75	95	150	'Created The 'Teddy Bear'
Berryman, John	1914-1972	Author	75	300			64 Pulitzer for Poetry. Short Stories
Bertelson, Richard L.		WWII	10		25	38	30	Navy ACE, WWII; 5 kills.
Berthier, L. Alexandre	1753-1815	Napol	75	143	258		Marshal of Napoleon
Berthold, Rudolf		Aero	200	350	650	475	ACE, WWI, The Iron Knight
Berthollet, Claude-Louis, Count	1748-1822	Sci	60	150	330		Fr. Chemist. Sen. of Napoleon
Bertinelli, Valerie		Ent	10	12	25	25	Actress. TV-Films
Bertolucci, Bernardo	1940-	Ent	15	70		60	Film Dir. 'Last Tango in Paris'
Bertram, Laura		Ent	10			20	Actress
Bertrand, Henri G.	1773-1844	Mil	70	120	305		Count Bertrand. Gen. Chamberlain to Napoleon
Berwick, Duke (J. Fitzjames)	1670-1734	Fr Mil	150	400			Gen. of Louis XIV, Marshal Fr.
Berzelius, Jons Jacob	1779-1848	Sci	75	165	475		Swe. Chemist. Chemical Symbols
Besant, Annie Wood	1847-1933	Clergy	50	245	398		Br. Radical Free-Thinker.
Besant, Walter	1836-1901	Author	35	125	130	125	Br. Novels. AMans 9000
Besch, Bibi		Ent	10			20	
Beser, Jacob		Aero	45	100		60	Both Atomic Bomb Missions
Besnard, Albert	1849-1934	Artist	30	65			Fr. post-impressionist artist
Bess, Gordon		Comics	10			25	'Redeye'
Bessell, Ted		Ent	10	20		25	Boyfriend in 'That Girl'
Bessemer, Henry, Sir	1813-1898	Invent	35	60	200	95	Invented Blast Furnace to make Steel; Metallurgist
Besser, Joe		Ent	36	40	75	80	One of 'The Three Stooges'
Bessieres, Bertrand		Fr Rev	55	100			
Bessieres, Jean-Baptiste	1766-1813	Fr Mil	175	337			Marshal of France under Napoleon
Besson, Luc		Author				100	Fr. writer, Dir.
Best, Charles H.	1899-1978	Sci	86	183	277	130	Discovered Insulin/Banting
Best, Edna	1900-1974	Ent	35	42	32	55	Brit. Char. Actress. Films & Stage
Best, Erna		Ent				50	Actress
Best, James	1926-	Ent	10			20	Actor 'Dukes of Hazzard'
Best, Pete		Music	38			107	Pre Ringo. Beatles Drummer
Best, Willie	1916-1962	Ent	67			172	Vintage Film Actor
Bestor, Don		Band	15			30	Jack Benny's 1st Bandleader
Beswick, Martine		Ent	10			15	
Betham-Edwards, Matilda		Author	10		20		
Bethe, Hans, Dr.		Sci	35	55		45	Nobel Physics
Bethune, Mary McLeod	1875-1955	Educ	160	318	500	175	Black Teacher, Activist. TLS/Cont 895
Betjeman, John, Sir	1906-1984	Author	43	111	135	75	Br. Poet Laureate
Bett, William Rose	1886-1956	Author	20	35	65	65	Poet, Editor. Pulitzer
Bettelheim, Bruno		Sci	35	65	85	150	Psychiatrist researched Autism
Bettger, Lyle	1915-	Ent	10			32	Actor. Films. 50s. Western Heavy
Betty, Henry		Ent			125		Br. Juvenile actor of the 19th C.
Betz, Carl	1920-1978	Ent	57			125	Actor; Husband 'Donna Reed Show'
Beugnot, J. C., Count		Fr Mil	85	160			
Beverage, John		Civ War	35	85			Union Gen., Gov. IL
Beveridge, Albert J.	1862-1927	Congr	10	20	35		US Sen., Historian. Organizer Progressive Party

NAME	DATES	CATEGORY	SIG	LS/DS	ALS	SP	COMMENTS
Bevin, Ernest	1881-1951	Statsmn	25	55	125	45	Br. Powerful Union Leader. NATO Treaty
Bewick, Thomas	1753-1828	Artist	105	275	625		Br. Illust., Wood Engraver
Bexley, Don 'Bubba'		Ent	10	15	30	35	Actor-Comed. 'Sanford & Son'
Bey, Turhan	1920-	Ent	15	20	35	40	Actor. Exotic & Mysterious Roles in 40s Films
Bhutto, Benazir	1953-2007	Pol	20	50	75	100	Ex-Pres. Pakistan; Father Z. A. Bhutto; Killed.
Bhutto, Zulfikar Ali	1928-1979	HOS	50	102	175	225	Pakistan, Pres. & PM. Coup. Executed
Biaggi, Mario		Congr	10	15		15	Congressman NY. NY Police MOH
Bialik, Chaim N.	1873-1934	Author	65	225	425	115	Jewish Poet
Bialik, Mayim		Ent	20			30	Blossom
Biasini, Piero		Opera	10			35	Opera
Bibb, George M.	1776-1859	Cab	30	45	80		Early Sec. Treas., Sen. KY
Bibb, Wm. Wyatt	1781-1820	Gov	25	45			Gov. GA
Bickersteth, Edward H., Bish.		Clergy	15	25	35	35	
Bickford, Charles	1889-1967	Ent	30	45	65	100	Actor. Burlesque 1914-Broadway 1919-Films 1929
Biddle, Clement	1740-1814	Rev War	179	481	871		Revolutionary Off., Merchant, War Hero
Biddle, Clement Carroll	1784-1855	Mil	25	40	75		Col. of 1st Inf. PA. 1812. Pol. Science
Biddle, Francis	1886-1968	Cab	20	35	75		Atty Gen. Judge Intern'l Tribunal-Nurnberg
Biddle, George		Artist	25	85	210		
Biddle, Nicholas	1786-1844	Bus	131	254	329		Pres. US Bank, Financier
Biden, Joseph		Congr	25			75	Sen. (D-DE); Dem. VP Cand. 2008
Bidwell, Daniel Davidson	1819-1864	Civ War	298	595	1128		Union Gen. ALS '63 1595, KIA 1864
Bidwell, John	1819-1900	West	55	275	86		Cal. Pioneer, Pres. Cand. -Prohibition Ticket
Biehn, Michael		Ent	10	10	20	35	Actor
Biel, Jessica		Ent	20			45	Actress
Bierbauer, Charles		Celeb	10			15	Media/TV personality
Bierce, Ambrose	1842-1914	Author	170	532	696		Journalist, Short Stories. Literary ALS 1250-2750
Bieri, Ramon		Ent	10			35	
Bierstadt, Albert	1830-1902	Artist	140	220	512		Of the Hudson River School. Landscapes
Biery, James S.		Congr	10	15		25	Congressman PA
Big Bopper		Music	842			4608	Rock. Rarest of 3 Killed In Plane Crash
Big Man, Chief Max		Am Ind	30			60	Chief
Bigard, Barney		Music	70			150	Jazz Clarinet, Ten. Sax
Bigelow, Erastus B.	1814-1879	Bus	100	290	595		Power Looms for Carpet Weaving
Bigelow, John	1817-1911	Pub	10	20	55	25	Editor& Co-Owner NY Evening Post. Diplomat
Bigelow, Poultney	1855-1954	Jrnalist	10		22		Traveller, Author. Son of John
Bigge, Arthur, Sir		Mil	10	30	65		
Bigger, Margaret		Author	10			12	Humor books
Biggers, Earl Derr		Author	150	210	382	350	Am. Novels, Mystery Writer. 'Charlie Chan'
Biggert, Judy B		Congr	10				Member US Congress
Biggs, Asa		Civ War	35	70			CSA Judge, US Sen. NC
Biggs, Jason		Ent	15			45	
Biggs, Ronnie		Crime	25			95	Train Robber. His Book S 100
Bikel, Theodore	1924-	Ent	10			35	Vienna-Born Char. Actor-Singer
Bilbo, Theodore G.	1877-1947	Congr	20	27		25	Sen. MS, Gov. MS. Demagogue, Racist
Bilirakis, Michael B		Congr	10				Member US Congress
Bill, Max	1908-1994	Artist	10	25	40	35	Swiss Painter-Sculptor. Pc Repro Sculpture S 60
Bill, Tony		Ent	10			20	Actor, Film Dir., Prod. -'The Sting'
Billings, John		Civ War	45	117	250		Union Surgeon
Billings, Josh	1818-1885	Author	25	80	165	73	Am. Humorist. (H. W. Shaw)
Billingsley, Barbara		Ent	15	18	18	35	Actress. 'Leave It To Beaver'
Billingsley, John		Ent	14			42	
Billingsley, Peter		Ent	10			12	'Xmas Story' SP 30
Billington, E.		Opera	55		250		Opera. Intl. Famous Prima Donna.
Billo, James D.		WWII	10	25	40	30	Navy ACE, WWII

NAME	DATES	CATEGORY	SIG	LS/DS	ALS	SP	COMMENTS
Billroth, Theodor	1829-1894	Sci	55	260	295		Ger. Surgeon. Use of Antisepsis
Bilson, Rachel		Ent	15			45	
Binci, Mario		Opera	15			45	Opera
Bing, Herman	1889-1947	Ent	20			40	Actor. Ger. Born. Circus Clown, Vaudevilian
Bing, Rudolph	1903-1997	Opera	15	35	46	35	Longtime Met. Opera Dir.
Bingaman, Jeff		Congr	10				Senate (D-NM)
Bingham, Amelia		Ent	10	10	15	25	
Bingham, Henry		Civ War	50		110		Union Gen., MOH Wilderness
Bingham, John A.		Congr	30	35	90		MOC. OH, Lincoln Judge Adv.
Bingham, Judson David	1831-1909	Civ War	40	130	185		Union Gen.
Bingham, Traci		Ent	10			34	Actress.
Bingham, William	1752-1804	Rev War	120	260	340		Cont. Congr. Sen. PA. Fndr. 1st Bank in Am.
Binney, Thomas		Clergy	20	30	45	35	
Binnig, Gerd, Dr.		Sci	20	60		45	Nobel Physics
Binns, Edward		Ent	10			20	Actor. Familiar Face in Supporting Roles
Binoche, Juliette		Ent	17			53	Actress. 'English Patient'
Biot, Jean Baptiste	1774-1862	Sci	100		575		Fr. Mathematician, Physicist, Astronomer
Birch, Thora		Ent	16			35	Actress
Bird & John Fortune, John		Celeb	10				Comedian
Bird, Billie		Ent	10			15	Char. actress
Birdsall, Jesse		Ent	10			20	Actor
Birdseye, Clarence	1886-1956	Bus	82	295	432	262	Frozen Foods. Prolific Inventor. 300+ Patents
Birdwood, William R., Sir	1865-1951	Mil	45	145			Br. Fld. Marshal, WWI
Birendra, Bir B.		HOS	10	15		25	Prime Min. Nepal
Birge, Henry Warner	1825-1888	Civ War	45	124	230		Union Gen.
Birney, David		Ent	10			25	Actor
Birney, David Bell	1825-1864	Civ War	243	383	572		Union Gen. ANS '63 990. Sig/Rank 365
Birney, William	1819-1907	Civ War	40	89	110		Union Gen. Sig/Rank 80
Bisbee, Horatio, Jr.		Civ War	25	45	105		Union Off. & MOC
Bishop Jr., Sanford D. B		Congr	10				Member US Congress
Bishop, Barry		Celeb	10	14			
Bishop, Elizabeth	1911-1979	Author	35	125			Am. Poet. Pulitzer Pr. '55
Bishop, J. Michael, Dr.		Sci	25	40		35	Nobel Med.
Bishop, Jim		Author	15	35	50	20	Journalist. Best Selling Novels.
Bishop, Joey	1918-2007	Ent	20	22	23	50	Comed member of Sinatra's 'Rat Pack'
Bishop, Julie		Ent	10		15	15	Actress
Bishop, Kelly		Ent	13			38	
Bishop, Rob B		Congr	10				Member US Congress
Bishop, Stephen		Music	10			25	Rock Star
Bishop, Timothy H. B		Congr	10				Member US Congress
Bishop, Wm. 'Billy'	1894-1956	Aero	138	225	325	166	ACE, WWI, 72 Kills
Bismark, Prince Otto von	1815-1898	Royal	250	560	1042	2262	The Iron Chancellor
Bispham, David		Ent	60	80	110	120	Opera
Bissell, Clayton L.		Aero	25	40	100		
Bissell, Emily P.	1861-1948	Humanit	125	150			Introduced U. S Xmas Seals
Bissell, Whit	1919-	Ent	10		15	30	Char. Actor in Films from Mid-40's
Bissell, William H.		Gov	10	28	60		Governor IL, MOC
Bisset, Jacqueline	1944-	Ent	15	20	30	36	Brit. Actress. Leading Roles Since 70s
Bissett, Josie		Ent	12			35	Actress, 'Melrose Place'
Bissit, J. E.		Mil	10	25		20	Cmdr. HMS Queen Eliz.
Bitter, Karl Theodore	1867-1915	Artist	25	75	155	100	Am. Sculptor
Bittrich, Wilhelm		Mil	27	115	135	60	
Bixby, Bill	1934-1993	Ent	35	58	58	164	Actor. My Favorite Martian
Bizet, Georges	1838-1875	Comp	332	790	1527		Fr. Comp. 'Carmen', L'Arlesienne Suite

NAME	DATES	CATEGORY	SIG	LS/DS	ALS	SP	COMMENTS
Bjerknes, Jacob A. B.	1887-1975	Sci	35	50			Discovered Origin of Cyclones
Bjoerling, Jussi	1911-1960	Opera	284	575	950	1046	Great 20th C. Swedish Tenor.
Bjork		Music	15			50	Icelandic Singer/Songwriter/Comp./Prod. & Actress
Bjork, Anita	1923-	Ent				60	Swedish actress
Bjorlin, Nadia		Ent	15			45	
Bjorling, Jussi		Opera	202				
Bjornson, Bjornstjerne	1832-1910	Author	50	65	345		3rd Nobel for Literature
Bjornstad, Alfred		Mil	10	20	35		Gen. WWI
Blacher, Boris		Comp	40				Rus-Ger. Classical & Experimental Music
Black Crowes		Music				100	Rock group; S Guitar 400
Black Eyed Peas		Music		335		125	Rock group; S Album 150
Black Sabbath		Music	100	160		203	Rock group; S Album 120-515; S Guitar 275-1500
Black Sheep Squadron		WWII				138	
Black, Alexander		Author	10			10	
Black, Clint		Cntry Mus	25			52	Country-Western
Black, Eugene R.	1898-1992	Bus	10		30	20	
Black, Frank, Dr.		Cond	10			35	NBC Dir. of Music in '40's
Black, Hugo	1886-1971	Sup Crt	63	103	268	105	Justice 1937-71. Bill of Rights, Consti. Champ
Black, Jack		Ent	15			52	Actor, comedian
Black, Jeremiah		Cab	30	60	115		Atty Gen. (Buchanan)
Black, John Charles	1835-1915	Civ War	50	112	162		Union Gen., MOH
Black, Karen		Ent	15	12	15	35	Actress. 'Easy Rider', '5 Easy Pieces'
Black, Richard B.		Mil	10	25	45		
Black, William		Mil	20			45	Gen. WWI
Blackburn, John T.		WWII	20	24	40	35	ACE, WWII; 11 kills.
Blackburn, Luke P.		Gov	15	35			Governor KY
Blackburn, Marsha B		Congr	10				Member US Congress
Blackett, Patrick M.		Sci	20	35	50	30	Nobel Physics. Cosmic Rays
Blackman, Honor		Ent	15	15	25	62	Br. Actress. 'James Bond'. Leading Lady
Blackmer, Sidney	1895-1973	Ent	20	115		60	Actor. Stage (Tony Award) Films.
Blackmon, Fred L.		Congr	10	20		15	MOC AL
Blackmore, Richard D.		Author	15	40	95		Br. Novels. 'Lorna Doone'
Blackmun, Harry A.	1908-1999	Sup Crt	50	230	248	117	
Blackstone, Harry		Ent	122	350	450	238	Magician. Self Sketch S 375
Blackstone, Harry, Jr		Ent	22	30	35	40	Magician
Blackstone, William Sir	1723-1780	Jurist			4200		GB Jurist: 'Commentaries on the Laws of Eng.'
Blackton, Stuart & Smith, Albert		Ent	20	45			Co-Fndrs Vitagraph Films. Inventor
Blackwell, Alice Stone	1857-1950	Reform	151	250	240		Woman's Suffrage. Editor
Blackwell, Elizabeth		Med	150	222	650		1st Woman to get M. D. Degree in Mdrn. times
Blackwell, Mr.		Bus	10	10		15	Fashion Critic
Blackwell, Otis		Comp	25	85	175		
Blades, Ruben		Ent	10			20	Actor
Blaha, John E.		Space	10	10		25	
Blaine, James G.	1830-1893	Cab	44	83	159	231	US Sen. ME, Garfield Sec. St., Pres. Cand.
Blaine, Vivian	1921-1995	Ent	14	12	15	75	Actress-Singer. 'Guys & Doll', 'State Fair'
Blair, Austin	1814-1894	Civ War	20		55		CW Governor of MI
Blair, Charles		Aero	45			60	
Blair, Eric (See Orwell, George)		Author					Pen-name of George Orwell
Blair, Francis P., Jr.	1821-1875	Civ War	47	91	156		Union Gen., US Sen. MO. Sig/Rank 75
Blair, Frank		Jrnalist	15	15	20	35	Radio-TV News Anchor & Correspondent
Blair, Jacob B.		Civ War	25		70		Virginia MOC Who Remained Loyal to Union
Blair, Janet		Ent	10	10	20	25	Actress-Singer. 'My Sister Eileen'.
Blair, John	1802-1899	Bus	150	750	950		Helped Charter UP RR. Built 1st 100 Mile
Blair, John		Sup Crt	175	918	1200		Signer of Constitution

NAME	DATES	CATEGORY	SIG	LS/DS	ALS	SP	COMMENTS
Blair, Linda		Ent	10	10	20	30	Young Actress in 'The Exorcist'
Blair, Montgomery		Law	95	286	500		Counsel to Dred Scott
Blair, Selma		Ent	16			47	
Blake, Amanda	1927-1989	Ent	65	128	115	158	Veteran 'Gunsmoke' Actress. 'Miss Kitty'
Blake, Bud		Comics	15			55	Tiger'. S Original Three Panel Strip 125
Blake, Eubie	1883-1983	Comp	78	172	260	201	Songwriter & Ragtime Pianist. AMusQS 350-600
Blake, Eugene Carson		Clergy	50	95	150	70	
Blake, Madge		Ent	150			575	Actress. 'Aunt Harriet' on TV's 'Batman' Series
Blake, Robert (Bobby)		Ent	15	15	22	40	'Our Gang' to 'In Cold Blood' & TV's Baretta'
Blake, William		Artist					Cont. ALS 30000
Blakely, Art		Music	120			180	Drummer
Blakely, Colin		Ent				120	Br. Actor
Blakely, Susan		Ent	10		15	20	Actress
Blakely, Troy		Ent	10			20	Actor
Blakerslee, Don		WWII				60	Ace; 14 kills
Blakeslee, Don		WWII	10	25	40	30	ACE, WWII
Blanc, Louis	1811-1882	Author	20	40	100		Fr. Socialist, Journalist, Pol., Historian
Blanc, Mel	1908-1989	Ent	70	136	142	178	Voice of Bugs Bunny
Blanchard, Albert Gallatin	1810-1891	Civ War	142	247			CSA Gen.
Blanchard, Albert Gallatin (WD)	1810-1891	Civ War	245	1595			CSA Gen.
Blanchard, Marjorie		Author	10			15	
Blanchard, Rachel		Ent	10			35	Actress. TV's 'Clueless'.
Blanchett, Cate		Ent	20			55	Actress. Golden Globe Award
Bland, Richard P.	1835-1899	Congr	15				Repr. MO, Defeated by W. J. Bryan for Pres.
Bland, Schuyler Otis		Congr	10	15	25		MOC VA
Bland, William T.		Congr	10	15	20		MOC MO
Blandford, Mark Harden	1826-1902	Civ War	48	100	188		CSA Congress
Blandick, Clara	1880-1962	Ent	913	1350		1050	Auntie Em in Oz. Rarest Oz Signature
Blane, Ralph		Comp	15			40	AMusMS 36
Blane, Sally		Ent	10		15	15	
Blanks, Mary Lynn		Ent	10				
Blanton, Leonard Ray		Gov	10			15	Governor TN, MOC TN
Blanton, Thomas L.		Congr	10	20		20	Sen. TX, MOC TX
Blaschka, Rudolph		Artist	10	35	75		Bohemian Artist in Glass
Blasco-Ibanez, Vicente		Author	100			250	Sp. Novels. Self Exiled
Blaskowitz, Col. -Gen. Johannes	1883-1948	Mil	25			242	WWII Ger. Gen.
Blaslev, Lisabeth		Opera	10			25	Opera
Blass, Bill	1922-2002	Bus	15	22	35	35	Fashion Designer
Blatchford, Samuel		Sup Crt	62	135	190		Supreme Court in 1882
Blatty, William Peter	1928-	Author	15	32	45	25	The Exorcist, AA. TsS 150
Bledsoe, Tempest		Ent	15	20		25	Vanessa Huxtable, 'Cosby Show'
Bleeth, Yasmine		Ent	15			40	'Baywatch'
Blenker, Louis (Ludwig)	1812-1863	Civ War	100	218			Union Gen
Blenker, Louis (WD)	1812-1863	Civ War		538			Union Brig. Gen.
Blennerhassett, Harman		Rev War	115	368	253		Funds, Refuge-Burr Conspiracy
Bleriot, Louis	1872-1936	Aero	225	425	458	750	1st To Fly English Channel
Bless, Frederick		Aero	10	22	38	32	ACE, Korea
Blessed, Brian		Ent	10			20	Actor
Bletcher, Billy	1894-1979	Ent	55			225	Diminutive actor, 'Our Gang', movies, TV
Blethyn, Brenda		Ent	10			42	
Blige, Mary		Ent	13			40	
Bligh, William, Capt.		Mil	1544	7730	11875		Br. Adm. Capt. HMS Bounty
Blind Faith		Music	362			450	Rock group: S Album 450
Blind Melon		Music		40		65	Rock group:

NAME	DATES	CATEGORY	SIG	LS/DS	ALS	SP	COMMENTS
Blind, Karl	1826-1907	Author	30		45		
Bliss, Arthur, Sir		Comp	25	85	109		Brit. Opera, Orch. works
Bliss, Cornelius		Cab	10	25	55	40	Sec. Interior
Bliss, George Jr.		Civ War	10	15	25		MOC OH
Bliss, J. S.		Civ War	10	10	20		
Bliss, Tasker H.		Mil	15	25	50	30	US Gen. 1st Cmdr. War College
Bliss, William Wallace S.		Mil	130	292	500		Pvt. Sec, Chief of Staff to Gen Zachary Taylor
Bliss, Zenas R.		Civ War	42	110	160		Union Off.
Blitstein, Jonathan	1982-	Ent	10			20	Film Prod. 'Let Them Chirp Awhile'
Blitstein, Mark David Dr.	1949-	Sci	10			20	Gastroenterologist, Chief Med. LFH
Blitzer, Wolf		Jrnalist	15		20	30	TV News
Blitzstein, Marc		Comp	122	215	468		Opera. Brilliant US Comp. Mack the Knife.
Blixen, Karen (Isak Dinesen)		Author	110	500		200	Danish Novels Out of Africa
Blizzard of OZZ		Music	625				Heavy Metal. Album S by group incl. Randy Rhodes
Bloch, Ernest	1880-1959	Comp	90		382	288	Swiss-Am. Comp., Teacher; AMusQS 300
Bloch, Ernst		Author	55	140	425	90	Ger. Philosopher.
Bloch, Felix		Sci	25	40	100	75	Nobel Physics
Bloch, Konrad, Dr.		Sci	20	30	45	30	Nobel Med.
Bloch, Raymond		Comp	10	20	35	30	
Bloch, Robert		Author	35	125	332	90	Novels. TMsS 450
Block, Harlan	1924-1945	WWII	500				Iwo Jima flag raiser1945 (rare)
Block, Henry W.		Bus	25	45	50	65	H & R Block. Fndr. w/Brother
Block, Herb		Comics	25			100	Herblock-Pol.
Block, John R.		Cab	10	10	15	10	
Block, Joseph L.		Bus	10				
Block, Martin		Ent	10			15	Early radio deejay
Block, Richard		Bus	20	35	90	30	H & R Block
Blocker, Dan	1928-1972	Ent	180	625		438	'Hoss' On 'Bonanza'
Blodget, Samuel Jr.		Rev War	240	429	1370		Inventor, Soldier, Judge
Bloembergen, Nicolaas Dr.		Sci	20	35	40	30	Nobel Physics
Blomberg, Werner Von		Mil	45	295	165	224	Ger. Fld. Marshal WWII
Blomfield, Ezekial		Clergy	35	45	60		
Blondell, Joan		Ent	40	40	65	98	Oscar Winner
Blondie		Music	30	50		135	Female vocalist
Blondin, Charles	1824-1897	Ent	30	60	175	60	Tightrope walker Niagara Falls
Blonsky, Nikki		Ent	15			45	
Blood, Robert O.		Gov	10		25		Governor NH
Blood, Sweat & Tears		Music	65			208	Rock group
Bloodworth-Thomason, Linda		Celeb	10			15	Film industry
Bloom, Adam		Celeb	10				Comedian
Bloom, Claire		Ent	10			25	
Bloom, David		Ent	20			35	TV News reporter D. Cvr. ing the Iraq War 2003
Bloom, Lindsay		Ent	10			15	
Bloom, Orlando		Ent	20			50	Actor
Bloomer, Amelia		Reform	275	350			Pioneer Dress & Social Reformer
Bloomfield, Joseph		Rev War	45	95	157		Off., Attorney, Gov. NJ
Bloomfield-Zeisler, Fannie		Music	25			75	Concert Pianist
Blore, Eric	1887-1959	Ent	20	25	65	65	Played the part of a gentleman or butler
Blossom Rock		Ent	40			75	
Blough, Roger		Bus	10			15	
Blount, James H.		Civ War	50	68			CSA Off., MOC GA
Blount, William		Congr	260	680			Continental Congr. Sen. TN
Blount, Winton M.		Cab	10	15	25	10	Postmaster Gen.
Blowers, Sean		Ent	10			20	Actor

NAME	DATES	CATEGORY	SIG	LS/DS	ALS	SP	COMMENTS
Blucas, Mark		Ent	15			45	
Blucher, Gebhard L. von		Mil	200	557	2200		Pruss. Fld. Marshal vs Napoleon
Blue Oyster Cult		Music				150	Rock group; S Guitar 260-460; S Album 125
Blue, Ben	1901-1975	Ent	26	30	60	55	
Blue, Callum		Ent	14			43	
Blue, Monte	1880-1963	Ent	25	25	45	85	Griffith Great Silent Star
Bluford, Guion S. Jr.		Space	30			50	!st Afro-Am. Astronaut
Blum, Leon (Fr)		HOS	25	40	110	35	Pres. France WWII
Blum, Norbert		Statsmn	10			10	Ger. Min. & Statesman
Blumberg, Baruch S.		Sci	20	30	55	25	Nobel Med.
Blumenauer, Earl B		Congr	10				Member US Congress
Blumenfeld, Felix		Comp	70	150		300	Russ. Conductor, Teacher
Blumenthal, Heston		Celeb	10			15	Chef
Blumenthal, Jacques		Comp	40		350		Pianist
Blumenthal, W. Michael		Cab	10	10	15	10	
Blunden, Edmund	1896-1974	Poet	55		238		Poet, Critic, Biographer. AManS 200-750
Blunt, Anthony	1907-1983	Mil	45	127			Br. Mil. Intel.
Blunt, Asa P.		Mil	35		200		Gen.
Blunt, James G., Dr.		Civ War	52	75			Union Gen.
Blunt, John Henry		Clergy	15	25	35	25	
Blunt, Roy B		Congr	10				Member US Congress
Bly, Julian		Celeb	10			15	Designer
Blyden, Larry		Ent	10			20	
Blysma, Fred Dr.		Sci	10			20	Neuropsychologist
Blyth, Ann		Ent	10		15	18	Actress-Singer
Blythe, Betty	1893-1972	Ent	35		75	129	Silent Star. Beautiful 'Vamp' of Early Movies
Blyukher, Vasily		Mil	100	285			Russian Gen.
Boardman, Eleanor	1898-1991	Ent	20	20	40	52	Vintage Silent Film Actress. 'The Squaw Man'
Boardman, Russell		Aero	25	55	95	80	
Boardman, Stan		Celeb	10			15	Comedian
Bob & Ray		Ent	30			75	
Bob, Tim		Music	16			38	Music. Bass Guitar 'Rage Against the Machine'
Bobkins, Addie		Ent	10			20	
Bobko, Karol J.		Space	10			25	
Bocelli, Andrea		Opera				175	Tenor
Bochco, Steven		Ent	10	15		25	TV Emmy Prod.
Bochner, Lloyd		Ent	10			20	
Bock, Feodor von	1880-1945	Mil	100	295		470	Ger. Gen. WWII. Failed
Bock, Jerry		Comp	40	50	70	50	Fiddler. AMusQS 250
Bocock, Thomas S.		Civ War	41	95	125		CSA Spkr. of the House
Bodenschatz, Karl		Aero	30	75	150	95	
Bodwell, Joseph R.		Gov	10	12		10	Gov. ME
Boe, Nils A.	1913-1992	Gov	10	15			Governor SD
Boehlert, Sherwood B		Congr	10				Member US Congress
Boehner, John A. B		Congr	10				Member US Congress
Boeing, William E.	1881-1956	Bus	165	2000	2100	400	Signed stock cert. 2850
Boerhaave, Herman	1668-1738	Sci		2188			Dutch Physician, Med. Educator
Boesch, Ruthilde		Opera	10	10		20	Opera
Bogard, Dirk		Ent	80		95	100	
Bogart, Humphrey	1899-1957	Ent	767	1893	1875	2727	Academy Award. 'Afr. Queen'
Bogdonavich, Peter		Ent	10	30		35	Film Dir. actor.
Boggs, Charles		Civ War	54	108	136		Union Adm.
Boggs, Hale		Congr	10	25			MOC LA
Boggs, Lindy (Mrs. H. Boggs)		Congr	10	15		15	MOC LA

NAME	DATES	CATEGORY	SIG	LS/DS	ALS	SP	COMMENTS
Boggs, William R.	1829-1911	Civ War	76	195	315		CSA Gen.
Boggs, William R. (WD)		Civ War	180	345	495		CSA Gen.
Bogguss, Suzy		Cntry Mus	15			30	
Bogosian, Eric		Ent	10			20	Actor
Bohay, Heidi		Ent	10			20	
Bohlen, Henry	1810-1862	Civ War	130				Union Gen.
Bohm, Karl		Music	15		75	75	Conductor. Dir. Vienna State Opera
Bohnen, Carl		Artist	20	35			
Bohr, Aage Niels	1922-	Sci	25			55	Nobel Physics 1975
Bohr, Niels H. D.	1885-1962	Sci	520	1257	3750	1644	Danish Physicist. Nobel 1922. A Bomb
Bohrod, Aaron (Bohrad)	1907-1992	Artist	15	46			Am. Artist
Boht, Jean		Ent	10			20	Actress
Boisrond-Canal	1832-1905	Pol	35	102			Pres. of Haiti 1876-79
Boito, Arrigo		Comp	45	110	325		Verdi Librettist. AMusQS 750
Bok, Edward W.		Bus	30	55	140	95	Editor, Curtis Publishing, Pulitzer
Bokor, Margit		Opera	10			30	Hung. Sopr.
Boland, Frederick		Celeb	10	15	40	10	
Boland, Mary		Ent	40	75		78	
Bolcom, William		Comp	15	25	65		Pulitzer, AMusQS 75
Bolden, Charles F. Jr.		Space	10			30	
Boles, Charles E. (Black Bart)		Crime	469	795			Notorious stagecoach robber
Boles, John		Ent	20	35	45	40	
Bolet, Jorge		Music	20			120	Pianist
Bolger, Emma		Ent	32			95	
Bolger, James		HOS	10			20	P. M. New Zealand
Bolger, Ray	1904-1987	Ent	108	130	515	303	WOZ. SP/Scarecrow 250-500; ALS/Oz Cont 3275
Bolger, Ray & Haley, Jack		Ent		1500		595	SP (OZ) 595
Bolingbroke, Henry (St. John)		Author	35	150	398		1st Viscount, Pol., Writer
Bolivar, Simon	1783-1830	HOS	336	3164	3950		Statesman, Revolutionary Leader
Boll, Heinrich	1917-1985	Author	32	30	95	30	Nobel Lit., Novels, Poet
Bolling, Tiffany		Ent	10	12	15	20	
Bolt, John		WWII	12	30	50	35	ACE, WWII & Korea; 6 kills.
Bolton, Frances Payne		Congr	10	25			MOC OH
Bolton, Guy		Author	15	100			Plays
Bolton, James		Invent	50	100	180		Sewing Machine Inventor
Bolton, Michael		Music	15			35	Singer, Comp.
Bolton-Jones, Hugh		Artist	10	25	45		Am. Landscape Painter
Bombeck, Erma	1927-1996	Author	10	18	40	25	Humorous Columnist; SB 50
Bomford, George		Mil	65	200			Invented Howitzer Bomb Cannon
Bomford, James Voty		Civ War	37	80	116		
Bon Jovi, Jon		Music	22			87	Rock
Bonaduce, Danny		Ent	10			25	
Bonaparte, Caroline		Royal	50	95	275		Marie-Annonciade
Bonaparte, Charles	1851-1921	Cab	40	70			Sec. Navy, Atty Gen. Gr. Nephew Napol.
Bonaparte, Elisa (Maria Ana)		Royal	350		442		Oldest Sister of Napoeon
Bonaparte, Eugene Napoleon		Royal	150	200	435		Adopted by Napoleon
Bonaparte, Jerome Napoleon	1822-1891	Royal	78	256	270		Son of King of Westphalia
Bonaparte, Joseph	1768-1844	Royal	120	288	330		Elder Bro. of Napoleon. King of Two Sicilies
Bonaparte, Josephine	1763-1814	Royal		2167	2312		Empress of France
Bonaparte, Letizia		Royal		1500	2700		Mother of Napoleon
Bonaparte, Louis	1778-1846	HOS	91	276			Bro. of I., King of Holland 1806-1810
Bonaparte, Louis-Napoleon	1914-1997	Royal	70	240			Called 'Le Prince Napoleon' 1926 to Death
Bonaparte, Lucien	1775-1849	Royal	81	342	353		Brother. Opposed Nap., Exiled
Bonaparte, Marie Louise		Royal	195	815	1487		Wife of Napoleon

NAME	DATES	CATEGORY	SIG	LS/DS	ALS	SP	COMMENTS
Bonaparte, Mathilde	1820-1904	Royal	50		150		Daughter of King Jerome
Bonaparte, Napoleon		Royal					SEE Napoleon I
Bonaparte, Pauline	1780-1825	Royal		200	550		Princess Of Italy
Bonar, Horatius		Clergy	15	20	25		
Bonci, Alessandro		Opera	35			115	Opera
Bond, Butch "Tommy"	1926-2005	Ent	20			40	Little Rascals; served in WWII
Bond, Carrie Jacobs		Comp	35	55	70	70	Am. Comp. Art Songs
Bond, Charles		WWII	10	28	40	30	ACE, WWII, Flying Tigers; 7 kills.
Bond, Christopher Kit		Congr	10	10		15	Sen. MO
Bond, Ford		Ent	10			15	Early Network Radio Ann'cer
Bond, Johnny		Cntry Mus	10			20	
Bond, Julian		Pol	15	20	50	25	Civ. Rights Activist. Poet
Bond, Ward	1903-1960	Ent	122	301	395	278	GWTW, Wagon Train. Western Actor
Bond, William C.		Sci	45	190	350		Am. Astronomer. Harvard Observatory
Bondi, Beulah		Ent	15	15	30	30	
Bonds, Gary U. S.		Music	25	100		95	Rock
Bondur, Roberta		Space	10			20	Canadian Astronaut
Boner, Edmond	1500-1569	Clergy	650				Appealed to Pope for Henry VIII
Bonerz, Peter		Ent	10			15	
Bonesteel, Charles H.		Mil	11	35	58		
Bonet, Lisa	1967-	Ent	15			25	Actress
Bong, Richard	1920-1945	WWII	1175	3000	3250	5000	ACE, WWII, Top US Ace
Bongo, Albert B.		HOS	100			425	Pres. of Gabon. Elected '72, '79, '86, '93
Bonham, Joe 'Bonzo'	1948-1980	Ent	150			450	Drummer of Led Zeppelin
Bonham, Milledge L.	1813-1890	Civ War	98	244	262		CSA Gen.
Bonham, Milledge L. (WD)		Civ War	200	332	454		CSA Gen.
Bonham-Carter, Helena		Ent	15			25	Actress
Bonheur, Rosa	1822-1899	Artist	110	155	235		Fr. Horse Fair & Rural Scenes
Bonilla, Henry B		Congr	10				Member US Congress
Boninsegna, Celestina		Opera	150			850	Legendary Sopr. Vintage
Bonnard, Pierre	1867-1947	Artist	126	280	812		Fr. Post-impressionist, Illust., Graphic Artist
Bonnat, Leon		Artist			76		Fr. Academic painter
Bonner, Jo B	1833-1922	Congr	10				Member US Congress
Bonneville, Benj. L. E. de	1795-1878	Mil	225	600	897		Pioneer Explr. NW Territory
Bonney, Barbara		Opera	15			35	Opera
Bono		Music	72	95		171	Lead singer U-2
Bono, Mary B		Congr	10				Member US Congress
Bono, Sonny	1935-1998	Ent	40			75	Mayor Palm Springs, Congress. 'Sonny & Cher'
Bonstelle, Jessie		Ent	25		40		Stage Actress, Prod., Teacher
Bontemps, Arna		Author	25	175			Am. Novels, Non-Fiction, Poetry
Bonvalot, Gabriel		Celeb				155	
Bonynge, Richard		Cond	15			50	Dame Joan Sutherland's Conductor Husband
Book of Love (4)		Music	15			35	Rock Group
Book, Sorrell		Ent	10			20	Actress
Booke, Sorrell	1930-1994	Ent				98	Actor; 'Dukes of Hazzard'
Booker T. & the MG's		Music	95			138	Rock group:
Boone Pickens, T.		Celeb	15			20	Financial expert
Boone, Daniel	1734-1820	Rev War	2568	8123	14847		Am. Pioneer Cumberland Gap, AMS 25,000
Boone, Debbie		Ent	10	15		20	Singer
Boone, Don		Author	10			12	Series of motivational books
Boone, Laura,		Author	10			12	Series of motivational books
Boone, Pat	1934-	Ent	15	20	23	28	Singer-Actor
Boone, Randy		Ent	10			25	Actor. 'The Virginian' Co-Star
Boone, Richard		Ent	179	198	295	632	Actor. 'Palladin'

NAME	DATES	CATEGORY	SIG	LS/DS	ALS	SP	COMMENTS
Boone, Squire		Rev War			1150		NC Farmer. Father of Daniel
Boorda, Jeremy M.		Mil	30		95		Adm. US Navy
Boorman, John		Celeb	10			15	Film industry
Boorstin, Daniel J.		Author	25				The Creators
Boosler, Elayne		Ent	10		30	23	Stand-up Comedienne
Booth, Adrian		Ent	10			50	Vintage Actress
Booth, Ballington		Clergy	50	100	165		Co-Cmdr. Salvation Army
Booth, Bromwell		Clergy	25	50	75		
Booth, Edwin	1833-1893	Ent	122	175	207	275	Great 19th Cen. Actor. Bro. of John Wilkes
Booth, Evangeline	1865-1950	Reform	50	122	345	100	Salvation Army Gen.
Booth, Ewing	1870-1949	Mil	20			50	WWI Gen. Pershing Chief of Staff
Booth, John Wilkes	1838-1865	Civ War	12500	15000	42000	25000	Lincoln assassin. AManS 35,000. Rare all forms
Booth, Junius Brutus, Jr.	1821-1883	Ent	50	105			Actor Brother of John Wilkes
Booth, Maude	1865-1948	Reform	40	100	225	350	Fndr. Volunteers of Am. & PTA, SB 100
Booth, Newell S., Bish.		Clergy	20	35	50	50	
Booth, Newton		Congr	15	25	60		Governor CA, Sen. CA
Booth, Shirley	1907-1992	Ent	27	45		55	Stage, film actress. AA: 'Come Back, Little Sheba'
Booth, William	1829-1912	Clergy	87	298	350	333	Fndr. & Gen. Salvation Army
Booth, William Bramwell		Clergy	40	75	100	100	Eldest Son & Organizer
Boothe, Powers		Ent	10			15	
Boozer, Brenda		Ent	10			15	
Boozman, John B		Congr	10				Member US Congress
Bor, Tadeusz		Mil	15	45	75		
Borah, William E.		Congr	10	20		25	Sen. ID
Borch, F. J.		Bus	10	10		10	Pres. Gen. Electric
Borchers, Adolf		Aero	10	15	30	25	
Bordaberry, Juan M		HOS	10	15	25	10	Uraguay
Bordallo, Madeleine Z. B		Congr	10				Member US Congress
Bordelon, Guy		Aero	10	20	35	25	ACE, Korea
Borden, Lizzy		Celeb			9110		Alleged Ax Murderess
Borden, Olive	1906-1947	Ent	30	35	45	150	Silent movie star
Borden, Robert L.	1854-1937	HOS	35				P. M. Canada 1911-20
Bordogni, Giulio-Marco		Opera			40		Opera. Tenor. Teacher
Bordoni, Irene		Ent	15	15	35	35	
Boreanaz, David		Ent	10			33	Actor 'Buffy'
Boreman, Arthur I.	1823-1896	Pol	50	95			1st Govenor of West Virginia
Borge, Victor	1909-2000	Ent	20	30	35	62	Pianist-Comedian. Concert Stage & Recordings
Borges, Jorge Luis	1899-1986	Author	75	350			Argentinian. Fiction, Poetry
Borghese, Camillo		HOS					SEE Paul V, Pope
Borghese, Pauline Bonaparte		Royal	110		575		Sister of Napoleon
Borgia, Francis, Saint	1510-1572	Clergy	3200	2200			Roman Catholic Saint
Borglum, Gutzon	1867-1941	Artist	200	325	397	489	Creator Mt. Rushmore Sculptures. Sketch S 950
Borglum, Lincoln		Artist	25	60	85		Son of Gutzon. Sculptor
Borglum, Solon		Artist	15		45		
Borgmann, Heinrich	d. 1945	WWII	65				Nazi winner of Knight's Cross w/Oak Leaves
Borgnine, Ernest		Ent	15	38	41	50	Actor. Oscar Winner
Bori, Lucrezia	1887-1960	Opera	40	95		90	Opera. Sp. Lyric Sopr. SP 9x13 (Violetta)200
Boring, Wayne		Comics	30			400	Superman
Boris III		Royal	120			185	King & Dictator Bulgaria
Bork, Robert A.		Jurist	10	20		30	Non-confirmed for the Supreme Court
Borkh, Inge		Opera	10			75	Opera. Salome
Borland, Carol	1914-1997	Ent	30			100	Actress. Vintage Horror Films.
Borlaug, Norman, Dr.		Sci	20	35	80	80	Nobel Peace Pr.
Borman, Frank		Space	30	73	95	94	

NAME	DATES	CATEGORY	SIG	LS/DS	ALS	SP	COMMENTS
Borman, M. & Himmler, H.		WWII		3000			Nazi leaders
Bormann, Martin	1900-1945	Mil	383	774	1500	850	Nazi Private Sec. to Hitler
Born, Max	1882-1970	Sci	145	388	432		Nobel, Ger. -Br. Physicist., Archive 13, 800
Borne, Hermann von Dem		Mil	20	45	90		
Borno, Louis		HOS	15	75			Pres. Haiti
Borodin, Alexander		Comp	250	450	1100		Rus. Comp. & Prof. Chemistry
Borowski, Felix		Comp	15	40	100	50	
Borso, Umberto		Opera	15			45	It. Tenor
Borzage, Frank		Ent	40			150	Film Dir. -Prod.
Bosanquet, Helen D.		Author	10	15	22		
Bose, Jagadis, Sir		Sci	27	40	150		Indian Physicist
Bose, Lucia	1931-	Ent	17			35	Span. Actress. Films from 1950
Boshell, Louise		Ent	10		15	15	
Bosley, Tom		Ent	10	13	20	25	
Bosson, Barbara		Ent	10	10	10	20	
Bostic, Earl		Band	15			25	Jazz Saxaphonist
Bostwick, Barry		Ent	10	12	15	25	
Bostwick, George		WWII	10	25	40	30	ACE, WWII; 8 kills.
Boswell, Connie		Ent	10	10	25	10	
Boswell, James	1740-1795	Author	750		4545		Biographer of Sam'l Johnson
Boswell, Leonard L. B		Congr	10				Member US Congress
Bosworth, Hobart	1867-1970	Ent	25	30	40	60	Films Actor from 1909-43
Boteler, Alexander Robinson	1815-1892	Civ War	84	184	442		Member of CSA Congress
Botha, Louis		HOS	52	142	95		S. Afr. Soldier, Statesman
Botta, Lucca	1882-1917	Music	75			225	Enrico Caruso Protege.
Bottesini, G.		Music	50				Double-Bass Virtuoso, Conductor. AMusQS 200
Bottolfsen, C. A.		Gov	12		25	15	Governor ID
Bottome, Margaret		Author	15	45	100	25	Lecturer
Bottoms, Joseph		Ent	10	10	15	22	
Bottoms, Sam		Ent	10			20	
Bottoms, Timothy		Ent	10			25	
Bouchard, Lucien		Celeb	10			15	Pol. celebrity
Boucher, Rick B		Congr	10				Member US Congress
Boucicault, Dion		Ent	25	35	50	52	19th C. Am. Actor-Plays
Bouck, William C.	1786-1859	Gov	15	25	50		Gov. NY. Supervised Part Constr. of Erie Canal
Boudin, Eugene-Louis		Artist	105	280	431		Fr. Sea & Beach Scenes
Boudinot, Elias	1740-1821	Rev War	200	2245	773		Washington's Atty Gen. & Close Friend
Boudinot, Elias Cornelius	1835-1890	Civ War	68	130	190		Member of CSA Congress
Boughton, Rutland	1878-1960	Comp	25				Opera.AMusQS 125
Bouguereau, Adolphe Wm.	1825-1895	Artist	25		110		Fr. Painter. Mostly Religious & Mythological
Boulanger, Nadia		Comp	35		142	115	Fr. Conductor, Teacher
Boulard, Georges		Aero	15		60	35	
Boulez, Pierre		Comp	40	45	75	100	Fr. Comp. -Conductor-Pianist. AMusQS 325
Boullanger, George	1837-1891	Mil	100				Gen & Pol. 'Man on Horseback'. Suicide
Boulle, Pierre	1912-1994	Author	15	15	40	115	'Bridge Over the River Kwai'
Boult, Adrian, Sir		Cond	20	45	100	75	Esteemed Br. Conductor
Bouquet, Carole		Celeb	10			15	Model
Bourbon-Parma, Zita	1892-1989	Royal				450	Last Austrian Empress
Bourchier, John	1499-1561	Royal			775		3rd Earl of Bath Lady Jane Grey Trial Comm.
Bourguiba, Habib	1903-2000	HOS	15	40	100	25	Pres. Tunisia
Bourke-White, Margaret	1904-1971	Artist	80	217	220		Spec. SP 770. Photo Essays Life Mag. S Chk 125
Bourmont, Louis A. V.	1773-1846	Fr Mil		80	160		Gen. under Napoleon
Bourn, Benjamin	1755-1808	Pol	40		98		US Congressman from RI
Bourne, Francis, Card.		Clergy	35	45	60	40	

NAME	DATES	CATEGORY	SIG	LS/DS	ALS	SP	COMMENTS
Bourrienne, L. A. F. de		Fr Rev	45	60	120		Pvt. Sec. to Napoleon
Bouton, Chas. Marie		Artist	110	165	400		
Boutwell, George S.	1818-1905	Cab	20	45	150	97	Grant Sec. Treasury. Pol. Leader. TLS 250
Bow, Clara	1905-1965	Ent	145	191	330	495	The 'It' Girl. Silent Film Star
Bowden, Dorris		Ent	10			20	
Bowditch, Nathaniel	1773-1838	Sci	100	230	610		Astronomer, Mathematician
Bowdoin, James		Rev War			9500		Rev. War, Gov. Mass. ALS Cont. 9500
Bowe, Rosemarie		Ent	10			15	
Bowen, Andrea		Ent	13			40	
Bowen, Elizabeth		Author	25	75	170	170	Ir. -Br. Psychological Novels
Bowen, George F., Sir		HOS	10	25	35		Governor Australia, New Zealand
Bowen, Ira Sprague		Sci	10	25	35	35	Dir. Mt. Wilson-Palomar Obs.
Bowen, James	1808-1886	Civ War	44	84	133		Union Gen.
Bowen, John Stevens	1830-1863	Civ War	115	248	528		CSA Gen.
Bowen, John Stevens (WD)		Civ War	175	378	1265		CSA Gen. Early Prisoner
Bowen, Louise de Koven		Reformer	12	20	45		Pres. Hull House
Bowen, Otis		Cab	10	10			Sec. Health & Human Services
Bowen, Thomas Meed		Civ War	40				Union Gen., Sen. CO
Bower, Antoinette		Ent	10				
Bowers, George M.		Congr	10	20		10	MOC WV
Bowes, Major Edward	1874-1946	Ent	20	22	24	35	Amateur talent radio show 1934-1952
Bowie, David		Music	70	188		100	Rock
Bowie, George Washington	1835-1882	Civ War	90	525			Union Gen.
Bowie, James (Jim)		Mil		15000			Co-Cmdr. Alamo. Bowie Knife
Bowie, Sydney J.		Congr	10	20	35		MOC AL
Bowker, Judi		Ent	10		15	22	
Bowler, Metcalf		Jurist	75	135	250		Opponent of The Stamp Act 1765
Bowles, Chester		Gov	10	25	85	40	Diplomat, Advertising Exec.
Bowlin, James B.		Congr	15	30	45		MOC MO
Bowman, Lee		Ent	10	20	25	25	
Boxcar Willie	1931-1999	Cntry Mus	15	21		30	Singer
Boxer, Barbara		Congr	15			25	US Senate (D-CA)
Boxleitner, Bruce		Ent	10		19	35	
Boy George		Ent	20	30	45	62	
Boyce, Max		Celeb	10				Comedian
Boyce, William	1711-1779	Comp		633			
Boyce, William Waters	1818-1890	Civ War	45				Member of CSA Congress
Boyd, Alan S.		Cab	10				Sec. Trans., CEO Amtrak
Boyd, Allen B		Congr	10				Member US Congress
Boyd, Belle	1843-1900	Civ War	2010	7061	7475		CSA Spy
Boyd, Billy		Ent	17			50	
Boyd, John Huggins		Congr	10				FF 27
Boyd, Joseph Fulton		Civ War	36	72			Union Gen.
Boyd, Linn	1800-1859	Congr	20	30	55		Repr. KY, Spkr. of House; FF 30
Boyd, Stephen		Ent	42	46	70	106	Actor
Boyd, William 'Bill'	1895-1972	Ent	192	385		266	Silent Screen Matinee Idol. 'Hopalong Cassidy'
Boyer, Charles	1897-1978	Ent	50	80	184	154	Fr. Actor. Hollywood Screen Lover
Boyer, Jean-Pierre		HOS	35	125			Pres. Haiti
Boyer, Richard L.		Author	12			22	Edgar Allen Poe award winner
Boyes, John		Author	20			45	Afr. adventure
Boyesen, Hjalmar H.		Author	15	35	70	20	
Boyington, Gregory 'Pappy'	1912-1988	WWII	107	160	305	174	ACE WWII Marine, #4 US, CMH
Boykin, Edward M.		Author	10			12	Author, Civil War
Boykin, Richard Manning		Author	10			12	Civil War

NAME	DATES	CATEGORY	SIG	LS/DS	ALS	SP	COMMENTS
Boyle, Jeremiah Tilford	1818-1871	Civ War	46	110	150		Union Gen.
Boyle, John J.		Artist	10	10	20		
Boyle, Kay	1903-1993	Author	25	75	175	40	Am. Short Story Writer, Novels. Expatriot
Boyle, Lara Flynn		Ent	20			45	
Boyle, Peter	1935-2006	Ent	20	25	28	60	Favorite Char. Actor
Boynton, Henry Van Ness		Civ War	61	100	169		Union Off. & MOH winner
Boyz II Men		Music	35			50	Rock group:
Boze, Marie		Ent	20			65	Vintage Actress
Braakensiek, Annalise		Celeb	10			15	Celebrity model
Brabazon-Moore, John T.		Aero	40	60	85	75	1st Licensed. WWI Pilot
Bracco, Lorraine		Ent	20	25		46	Dr. Melfi, Sopranos
Bracken, Eddie	1915-2002	Ent	15	20	24	50	SP w/Veronica Lake 400
Brackett, Charles		Ent	20			70	Prod. 2 Oscars as Screenwriter
Bradbury, James Ware		Congr	20	25	40		Sen. ME 1847
Bradbury, Norris E.		Sci	15		25		
Bradbury, Ray		Author	38	149	275	69	Sci-Fi Writer, S draw 241; SB 200-300; S 1st Ed. 'Fah. 451' 15535
Bradford, Alexander Blackburn	1798-1873	Civ War	54	122	190		Member of CSA Congress
Bradford, Augustus W.	1805-1881	Civ War		85			Unionist Gov. MD
Bradford, Barbara P.		Author	10			10	
Bradford, Gamaliel		Author	10			12	Civil War, history
Bradford, William	1755-1856	Cab	108	164			G. Washington Atty Gen
Bradford, William	1729-1808	Congr	125	350	590		Sen. RI 1793
Bradlee, Ben		Editor	18	30		45	Ed. Washington Post
Bradley, Benjamin Franklin	1825-1897	Civ War	45	117			Member of CSA Congress
Bradley, Bill		Congr	12	20		25	Sen. NJ., Pro. Basketball
Bradley, Ed	1941-2006	Ent	15	28	38	38	TV News. '60 Minutes'
Bradley, James		Mil	11	35	58		
Bradley, Jeb B		Congr	10				Member US Congress
Bradley, John H.	1923-1994	WWII	108	185	273	438	Iwo Jima Flag Raiser FDC 200 S. Only Navy Man
Bradley, Joseph P.		Sup Crt	39	175	500		
Bradley, Kathleen		Ent	10			10	Price is Right Model
Bradley, Luther Prentice	1822-1910	Civ War	40	85			Union Gen.
Bradley, Omar N. (Gen.)	1893-1981	Mil	85	140	259	180	5 Star Gen. WWII. ALS/Cont 2000, TLS. 1000
Bradley, Owen	1915-1998	Cntry Mus	20			35	Country Music Record Prod. Musician
Bradley, Tom	1917-1998	Pol	10	27	35	29	Ex Poiceman. Mayor Los Angeles.
Bradna, Olympe		Ent	10	75		25	
Bradshaw, Tiny		Band	10				
Bradstreet, John		Colonial	60	140	354		Br. Soldier. Ticonderoga
Brady Bunch The		Ent				238	
Brady, Alice	1892-1939	Ent	90		95	112	Academy Award Winner
Brady, Charles, Jr.		Space	10			40	
Brady, James B. 'Diamond Jim'		Bus	375	1400	1338	500	Financier. TLS 3800. RR DS 6500
Brady, James S.		Pol	39	65		50	Injured in Reagan assassination attempt
Brady, Kevin B		Congr	10				Member US Congress
Brady, Mathew B.	1823-1896	Photog	486	1275	2600		Pres. & Civil War Photos, SP 15000+
Brady, Pat	1914-1972	Ent	100			250	
Brady, Ray		Celeb	10			15	Media/TV personality
Brady, Robert A. B		Congr	10				Member US Congress
Brady, Scott		Ent	15	15	25	40	Actor. Sometime Western Heavy/John Wayne
Brady, William A.	1863-1950	Ent	35			65	Actor/manager/stage & film prod/sports promoter
Braeden, Eric	1941-	Ent	10			25	Victor Newman on The Young & the Restless.
Braff, Zach		Ent	17			50	
Braga, Gaetano		Comp	85			312	Cello Music. 8 Operas

NAME	DATES	CATEGORY	SIG	LS/DS	ALS	SP	COMMENTS
Braga, Sonia		Ent	10	15	30	33	Brazilian Leading Lady
Bragg, Braxton	1817-1876	Civ War	428	648	960	900	CSA Gen.
Bragg, Braxton (WD)	1817-1876	Civ War	563	1340	2305	3000	CSA Gen.
Bragg, Edward Stuyvesant	1827-1912	Civ War	46	113	140		Union Gen., Statesman, MOC
Bragg, Thomas	1818-1872	Civ War	168	250			CSA Atty Gen.
Bragg, Wm. Henry, Sir	1862-1942	Sci	50	95			Nobel Physics w/son Wm. L. in 1915
Bragg, Wm. Lawrence, Sir	1890-1971	Sci	50	85			Nobel Physics w/father W. H.
Braham, John (Abraham)	1774-1856	Opera	25		100		Supreme Br. Opera, Concert Performer
Brahms, Johannes	1833-1897	Comp	1000	1612	3365	4350	Major 19th C. Comp. AMusQS, 750-12, 500
Brailowsky, Alexander		Music	50			85	Concert Pianist; Chopin Specialist
Brainard, David		Expl	40		125		Arctic Explr./G. B. Grinnell
Braithwaite, Kent		Author	10			12	Mystery Novels
Braithwaite, Wm. Stanley		Author	35	120	235	175	
Bramesfeld, Heinrich		Mil	15		25	40	Ger. Capt. of See. RK Winner
Branagh, Kenneth		Ent	18			40	Br. Actor-Dir. -Dramatist
Branch, Anthoney Martin	1823-1867	Civ War	65		134		Member of CSA Congress
Branch, John	1782-1863	Cab	30	75	148		Sec. Navy, Gov. NC, Gov. FL
Branch, Lawrence O'Brien	1820-1862	Civ War	341	619	1388		CSA Gen.
Branch, Lawrence O'Brien (WD)	1820-1862	Civ War	779	975	1592		CSA Gen. KIA 1862, Antietam
Brand, Christopher Q., Sir		Aero	75	150	300	200	ACE, WWI, Only night Ace
Brand, Harry		Ent	10			20	Motion Picture Prod.
Brand, Jo		Celeb	10			15	Comedienne
Brand, Max	1892-1944	Author	50			100	Novels. 'Destry Rides Again', 'Dr. Kildare'
Brand, Neville	1921-1992	Ent	195	250		150	Dependable Heavy Through Many Years
Brand, Vance D.		Space	20	45		80	Apollo Soyuz; SP w/Lind 150
Brandauer, Klaus Maria	1944-	Ent	20	15	30	45	Austrian Actor-Dir. 'Out of Africa'
Brandegee, Augustus		Congr	15	35	200		MOC. CT. Civil War Member
Brandeis, Louis D.	1856-1941	Sup Crt	122	303	453	1275	1st Jewish Supr. Ct. Judge. Important ALS 2200
Brandenstein, Daniel		Space	10			20	
Brandi, Albrecht		WWII				218	U-Boat ace & Knights Cross w/Diamonds recipient
Brandis, Jonathan	1976-2003	Ent	25			50	Child actor
Brando, Marlon	1924-2004	Ent	270	788	480	859	Reclusive Oscar Winning Actor.
Brandon, Henry	1912-1990	Ent	10			10	Am. Char. Actor. Reliable Menace for 30 Years
Brandon, Michael	1945-	Ent	10			22	Actor. Leading Man
Brandon, William Lindsay	1801-1890	Civ War	113	242	325		CSA Gen.
Brandstrader, Benjamin Palmer	1979-	Ent	10			20	Screenwriter
Brandt, Karl	1899-1975	Mil	161	300			Hitler's personal physician
Brandt, Marianne		Opera	25		80	75	Opera
Brandt, Willy	1913-1992	HOS	25	92	155	80	Germ. Chancellor. Nobel Peace Pr.
Brandy		Ent	20			75	Singer-Actress 'Cinderella'
Brangwyn, Frank	1867-1956	Artist	25		125		Br. Painter-Decorator
Branigan, Laura		Music	15			38	Singer
Branly, Edouard	1844-1940	Sci	105	315	264	475	Fr. Physicist. Inventor Radio Wave Detector
Brann, Louis J.		Gov	10	15		10	Gov. ME
Brannan, Charles F.		Cab	10	15		15	Sec. Agriculture
Brannan, John Milton	1819-1892	Civ War	38	75	110		Union Gen.
Brant, Joseph		Am Ind	888	4150	5900		1742-1807. Mohawk Who Fought w/Br.
Brantley, William Felix	1830-1870	Civ War	117	210	320		CSA Gen.
Branzell, Karin	1891-1974	Opera	40			155	Opera. Celebrated in Wagnerian Roles
Braque, Georges	1882-1963	Artist	707	785	1306		Fr. Developed Cubism w/Picasso. SB 975
Brasselle, Keefe		Ent	25			55	Leading man in the 40s & 50s
Bratt, Benjamin		Ent	20			40	Actor
Brattain, Walter		Sci	35	50	110	55	Nobel Physics. Transistor
Bratton, John, Dr.	1831-1898	Civ War	98	218	412		CSA Gen. Physician. Wounded, Captured

NAME	DATES	CATEGORY	SIG	LS/DS	ALS	SP	COMMENTS
Brauchitsch, Heinrich von	1881-1948	Mil				242	Ger. Gen. WWII
Brauchitsch, Walther von	1881-1948	Mil	75	184	225	250	WWII Ger. Gen.
Brauer, Bruno Oswald		Mil				127	Ger. Gen.
Braugher, Andre		Ent	13			40	Actor
Braun, Eva	1912-1945	WWII	1568	2611	2856		Hitler's Mistress-Wife
Braun, Magnus von		Sci	20			50	Rocket Pioneer/Brother Wernher
Braun, Wernher von	1912-1977	Sci	177	490	1422	408	Ger-Am Rocket Pioneer. Planned Apollo Program
Brautigan, Richard		Author	45	150			Counter-Culture Classic
Braxton, Carter	1736-1797	Rev War	362	1025	2979		Signer Dec. of Indepen.
Braxton, Toni		Music	15			40	Actress. Singer
Brayman, Mason	1813-1895	Civ War	35	101			Union Gen., Gov. Idaho
Brayton, Charles Ray		Civ War	54	65	100		Union Gen.
Brazzi, Rossano	1916-1994	Ent	15	20	25	48	Romantic Italian Actor
Brearley, David	1745-1790	Rev War	375	927	1075		Continental Congress
Breathed, Berke		Comics	20			175	'Bloom County'
Breaux, John		Congr	10				US Senate (D-LA)
Brecht, Bertolt	1898-1956	Author	400	1192	3100		Important 20th C. Ger. -Jewish Plays, Poet
Breckinridge, John Cabell	1821-1875	Civ War	340	659	854	633	Buchanan VP, KY Sen, CSA Gen., CSA Sec War. Sig/Rank 525, ALS 1585
Breckinridge, Robert Jefferson		Civ War	44	81			Member of CSA Congress
Breckinridge, Wm. C.	1837-	Civ War	110	228	275		CSA Off.
Breeding, J. Floyd		Congr	10	15		10	MOC KS
Breen, Bobby		Ent	16	22	30	35	Child Singer. Radio & Films
Breese, Lou		Music	20	40	45	70	Big Band leader
Breese, Vance		Aero	30	115		63	Aviator & Aircraft Designer
Bremer, Lucille		Ent	20			40	Astaire Dancing Partner MGM Musical
Bremner, Rory		Celeb	10			15	Impressionist
Brendel, El	1890-1964	Ent	20	35		48	Stage & Film Comedy Roles
Brendon, Nicholas		Ent	15			45	
Breneman, Tom		Ent	15	15	30	20	Popular Radio Host
Brennan, Eileen		Ent	15	15	25	30	Char. Actress. Accident Slowed Career
Brennan, Francis J., Card.		Clergy	30	45	55	50	
Brennan, Walter	1894-1974	Ent	112	125	262	214	Actor; 3 Time Oscar Winner
Brennan, William J.	1913-1997	Sup Crt	70	92	175	103	Important 20th C. Justice. 1200+ Opinions
Brennecke, Kurt		Mil	15	35	60	35	
Brenneman, Amy		Ent	15			40	Actress
Brenner, Victor D.	1871-1924	Artist	347	355	675		Designer Lincoln Penny-V. D. B.
Brent, Charles H., Bish.		Clergy	25	40	55	40	
Brent, Evelyn		Ent	20	20	25	47	Vintage Leading Lady
Brent, George		Ent	25	35	35	60	Vintage Leading Man.
Brent, George Wm.		Civ War	100	210	300		
Brent, Joseph Lancaster	1826-1905	Civ War	110	163	396		CSA Col. Sig/Rank Brig. Gen. 225
Brent, Robert		Mil	35	100	165		
Brereton, Lewis Hyde	1890-1967	Aero	55	150		300	Am. Cmdr. 1st Allied Airborne Army WWII
Bres, Edward S.		Mil	10	30	50		
Bres, Madeleine	1842-1921	Med			250		1st Fr. female to get MD degree
Breslau, Sophie		Opera	35			90	Opera
Breslin, Abigail		Ent	20			60	
Breslin, Jimmy		Celeb	10	15	40	25	Journalist, Novels
Breslin, Spencer		Ent	17			51	
Bresser-Gianoli, Clotilde		Opera	20			55	Opera
Bressler, Heidi		Ent	13			40	
Breton, Andre	1896-1966	Author	68	175	400		Fr. Poet, Essayist, Critic, Editor. ALS/Cont 1000
Brett, George H.	1886-1963	Mil	45	125		45	Air Corps Gen. WWII

NAME	DATES	CATEGORY	SIG	LS/DS	ALS	SP	COMMENTS
Brett, Jeremy	1935-1995	Ent	35			195	Portrayed Sherlock Holmes. SP Pc 95
Breu, Paul		Aero	10			25	Ger. Bomber Pilot. RK
Breuer, Marcel		Archtct	20	60	125	150	Bauhaus School/Gropius
Brevard, Theodore Washington	1835-1882	Civ War	78	166			CSA Gen.
Brewer, David J.		Sup Crt	88	157	160	100	
Brewer, Teresa		Music	15	19	22	30	Big Band Singer. Recording Artist
Brewerton, Henry		Civ War			125		Union Gen. Corps of Engineers
Brewster, Benjamin		Cab	20	35	50		Chester A. Arthur Atty Gen.
Brewster, David, Sir	1781-1868	Sci	50	75	198		Physicist. Invented Kaleidoscope
Brewster, Jordana		Ent	15			45	
Brewster, Kingman Jr		Educ	10	15	25	15	Diplomat
Brewster, Paget		Ent	13			40	
Brewster, Ralph Owen		Congr	10	25	40	30	Sen., MOC ME
Breyer, Stephen		Sup Crt	35	95	125	100	
Brezhnev, Leonid I.		HOS	350	503		450	Soviet Communist Party Leader
Brian, Mary		Ent	25	37	45	40	Vintage Actress. Ingenue
Brice, Benjamin W.		Civ War	15	45			Union Paymaster Gen.
Brice, Fanny	1891-1951	Ent	126	194	300	391	Vintage Stage, Radio, Films. Comed. -Singer
Brickell, Edie		Ent	10			30	
Bricker, John W.		Congr	15	30		20	Gov. Ohio
Brico, Antonia, Dr.		Cond	15			150	Eccentric Female Conductor
Bridgers, Robert Rufus	1819-1888	Civ War	51		117		Member of CSA Congress
Bridges, Angelica		Ent	10			30	
Bridges, Beau		Ent	20	20	30	40	Actor. Like Lloyd & Jeff--Versatile Parts
Bridges, H. Styles		Congr	10	15		10	Sen. NH
Bridges, Harry		Labor	70	180		140	Pres. Longshoreman Union. Powerful
Bridges, Jeff		Ent	15	28	15	40	Actor. Versatile Leading Man. Variety of Parts
Bridges, Lloyd	1913-1998	Ent	30	40	45	50	Actor. 'Seahunt'
Bridges, Robert	1844-1930	Author	40	95	108		Poet Laureate England
Bridges, Roy D. Jr.		Space	10			25	
Bridges, Todd		Ent	15	20		30	Child actor. 'Different Strokes'
Bridgman, Laura D.	1829-1889	Celeb	61	68	205		1st Blind, Deaf, Systematically Educated
Bridy, Pat		Comics	10		25		'Rose is Rose'
Briggs, Austin		Comics	25			200	'Flash Gordon'
Briggs, Charles F.		Author	15	40	125		Editor NY Times
Briggs, Clare A.	1875-1930	Comics	15			50	Mr. & Mrs.
Briggs, George Nixon		Congr	12		51		FF 51
Briggs, Harlan	1879-1952	Ent				65	Actor
Briggs, Henry Shaw	1824-1887	Civ War	41		190	250	Union Gen. Wounded 'Seven Pines'. War Dte ALS 340
Briggs, James E.		Mil	10	25	50	20	
Briggs, Johnny		Ent	10			20	Actor
Briggs, Le Baron Russell	1855-1934	Educ	10		20		Legendary Harvard Professor
Briggs, Roxanne Dawson		Ent	20			40	Actress, Star Trek
Brigham, Louis S.		Bus	10	35	45	20	
Bright, John	1811-1889	Statsmn	35	50	155		Radical Br. Orator. (Corn Laws)
Bright, Richard	1789-1858	Sci	150		525		Physician
Brightman, Sarah		Ent	20			50	Star of Andrew Lloyd Weber's Musicals. Ex Wife
Brigitte, Simone		Ent	10			20	Model/actress
Brill, Steven		Ent	15			45	
Brillat-Savarin, Jean Anthelme	1755-1826	Author		120			Fr. Lawyer/Pol. Famous Epicure & gastronome
Brimley, Wilford		Ent	15			25	Char. Actor. Films/TV
Brimmer, Andrew F.		Pol	10	15		15	Gov. Fed. Res. Board
Brinegar, Paul		Ent	10	15	20	25	
Brinkley, Christie		Ent	15	25	30	38	Model

NAME	DATES	CATEGORY	SIG	LS/DS	ALS	SP	COMMENTS
Brinkley, David		Jrnalist	25			63	TV News Anchor-Commentator
Brinson, Samuel Mitchell		Congr	10	20	45		MOC NC
Brisbane, Arthur		Author	15	35	100	30	Influential Editorial Writer
Brisbin, James Sanks	1837-1892	Civ War	41	95	129		Cmdr. Afr-Am. Cavalry. Abolitionist. ALS/Cont 775
Brisebois, Danielle		Ent	10			15	Actress
Brissette, Tiffany	1974-	Ent	10			15	Child Actress
Brisson, Carl		Ent	15	15	25	20	Danish Actor. Stage-Screen
Bristol, Henry Platt		Bus	275	850	1075		Fndr. Bristol-Myers
Bristol, Mark		Mil	20	25		30	Adm. WWI
Bristow, Benjamin Helm	1832-1896	Cab	30	65	120		Civil War Commanded 25th KY
Britt, Mai		Ent	10			25	Actress
Britt, Maurice L., Capt.	1912-1984	Mil	25	35		50	WWII Hero CMH & Football Star
Brittain, Delia Tipton		Author	10			12	Southern mountain history
Brittany, Morgan		Ent	10	15	25	25	Actress
Britten, Benjamin	1913-1976	Comp	158	344	554	337	Br. Conductor. 'Peter Grimes'. AMusQS 990-1600
Britton, Barbara		Ent	10	12	15	30	Actress-Model. Leading Lady.
Britton, Pamela		Ent	10			15	Actress
Britton, Sherry		Ent	10		15	10	
Brix, Herman		Ent	10	12	15	15	SEE Bruce Bennett
Broadbent, Jim		Ent	20			45	AA winner
Broadhead, James Overton		Law	30		65		Atty Friend of Lincoln
Broca, Paul	1824-1880	Sci	125		746		Fr. Pathologist, Surgeon, Anthropologist
Broccoli, Cubby	1909-1996	Ent	15	20	20	40	Dir. James Bond series Prod.
Brochler, Jan		Opera	10			35	Opera, Dutch Baritone
Brochtrup, Bill		Ent	15			45	
Brock, Thomas, Sir	1847-1922	Artist	10		35		Br. Sculptor. Statues of Longfellow, Q. Victoria
Brock, William		Clergy	15	25	40	25	
Brock, William G. Sen.		Bus	20	70	125	40	
Brockenbrough, John White	1806-1877	Civ War	64		134		Member of CSA Congress
Brod, Max	1884-1968	Author	90		675		Czech-born Austrian Writer. Biographer. Kafka Ed.
Broder, David	1929-	Celeb	10			15	Media/TV personality
Broderick, Helen		Ent	30			92	Vintage Char. Actress.
Broderick, Matthew		Ent	18	22	25	42	Actor. Films-TV-Stage
Brodhead, Daniel	1736-1809	Rev War	200	650			Legendary Am. Off., Negotiator, Renegade
Brodhead, James E.		Ent	10		15	15	
Brodhead, Richard		Congr	15	35	75		Sen. from PA
Brodie, Benjamin C. Sir	1783-1880	Sci	35	65	138		Br. Orthopedic Surgeon
Brodie, Steve	1856-1901	Ent	125				World Champion. Jumped off Brooklyn Bridge
Brodie, Steve	1919-1992	Ent	15			35	Actor. Major Film Player in Major Prod.
Brodsky, Joseph		Author	10	15	25	30	Poet. Nobel Laureate
Brodsky, Michael Aaron Ed L., MD	1950-	Med	10		10	20	Famous Electrophysiologist. The Flying Shun.
Brody, Adam		Ent	12			35	
Brody, Adrien		Ent	25			50	AA winner, "Pianist"
Brody, Lane		Ent	10			20	
Broglie, Duke A-C-L-V		Statsmn	135	270	540		Fr. Pol. Author
Broglie, Louis Victor de	1892-1987	Sci	73	248	355	595	Nobel Physics. Quantum Mechanics
Broglin, Winnie W.		Author	10			12	Church history
Broke, Sir Philip V. I.		Mil			345		
Brokow, Tom		Jrnalist	15	12	25	40	TV News Anchor-Commentator-Author
Brolin, James		Ent	15	20	30	40	Actor. 'Marcus Welby', 'Hotel' TV Series
Brolin, Josh		Ent	13			45	Actor; 'W'
Bromberg, J. Edward		Ent	30			120	Char. Actor. Major Films
Bromfield, John		Ent	10			30	Actor;.
Bromfield, Louis	1896-1950	Author	35	125	175	65	Am. Novels. Pulitzer. 'Mrs. Parkington'

NAME	DATES	CATEGORY	SIG	LS/DS	ALS	SP	COMMENTS
Bronk, Detlev W.	1897-1975	Sci	15	25	40	25	Pres. Nat. Acad. of Sci. Physiologist, Neurology
Bronson, Betty		Ent	65			258	Vintage Actress
Bronson, Charles	1921-2003	Ent	28	73	60	95	Major Action Star 70s.
Bronson, David	1800-1863	Congr	25				Repr. ME, Collector of Customs
Bronson, Wilfred S.		Artist					Signed drawing 130
Bronte, Charlotte		Author			8250		Br. Novels. Jane Eyre
Brook, Alexander		Artist	25	40	75		
Brook, Clive	1887-1974	Ent	55	75	85	128	Br. Actor. 1st Talky 'Sherlock Holmes'
Brook, Kelly		Celeb	10			15	Celebrity model
Brooke, Alan, Fld Marshal, Sir		Mil	40	110	205	125	Cmdr. Br. II Corps WWII, Dunkirk
Brooke, Charles Sir		Mil		500			Rajah of Sarawak; Englishman who would be King
Brooke, Edward W.		Congr	10	15		25	Afr.-Am. Rep. Sen. MA
Brooke, Hillary		Ent	20	22	25	67	Actress. Blonde-Sophisticated Other Woman
Brooke, John M.	1826-1906	Civ War	95	225	370		Cmdr. CSA Navy
Brooke, John Rutter	1838-1926	Civ War	50	85	282		Union Gen. Sig/Rank. Wounded at Gettysburg
Brooke, Rupert	1887-1915	Author	540	575	1890		Br. Poet. D. in WW at 28
Brooke, Walter	1813-1869	Civ War	45	118			Member of CSA Congress
Brooke-Popham, Robert		Mil	30	65	95	50	Br. Air Chief Marshal WWII
Brookes, Bruno		Music	10			15	DJ
Brookhart, Smith W.		Congr	10	15		15	Sen. IA
Brooks & Dunn		Cntry Mus	20			65	Kic & Ronnie
Brooks, A. Raymond		Aero	35	60	85	75	Bi-Plane ACE, WWI
Brooks, Albert		Ent	20			45	Actor. Comedian.
Brooks, Angie		Statsmn	15	20	25	30	Pres. U. N. Assembly
Brooks, Arthur		Aero	15		30	35	
Brooks, Avery		Ent	20			63	Star Trek
Brooks, Chas. Wm. Shirley	1816-1874	Author	15		55		Humorist, Editor of 'Punch'
Brooks, Clive		Ent	25			120	Actor
Brooks, Dick		Comics	10			35	Jackson Twins
Brooks, Foster		Ent	15	20	20	35	Char. Actor. Everybody's Favorite 'Drunk'
Brooks, Fred Emerson		Author	10	15	35		Poet
Brooks, Garth		Cntry Mus	25		35	86	Singer. Mega Grammy Winner. S guitar 450
Brooks, Golden		Ent	13			40	
Brooks, Gwendolyn	1917-2000	Poet	25		100		Afr.-Am. poet
Brooks, James		Ent	18			55	
Brooks, Jason		Ent	10			20	Actor
Brooks, John		Mil	55	139	275		Am. Revolution Gen., Gov. MA
Brooks, Leslie		Ent	10	12	15	20	Actress-Dancer.
Brooks, Louise	1906-1985	Ent	362	421	452	510	One of the Screen's Great Beauties. Rare
Brooks, Mel		Ent	25	40	50	50	Actor-Comic-Dir. AA
Brooks, Peter H.		Clergy	15	25	35		
Brooks, Phillips	1835-1893	Author	82	120	130	125	Episcopal Bishop. 'O Little Town of Bethlehem'.
Brooks, Rand		Ent	25	25	40	74	GWTW 'Chas. Hamilton'. Scarlett's 1st Husband
Brooks, Randi		Ent	10		15	15	
Brooks, Richard	1912-1992	Ent	20	30		60	AA Film Dir.
Brooks, Wm. Thos. H.	1821-1870	Civ War	50	85	148		Union Gen. ALS '64 245
Broom, Jacob		Rev War	400	900	2000		Continental Congress
Broomall, John M.		Congr	25	28	40		MOC DE 1863. CW Off.
Broonzy, Bill Big		Music	100	200			Blues-Jazz
Brophy, Ed		Ent	25			40	Char. Actor. Rotund. Cigar-Smoking
Brophy, Kevin		Ent	10			20	
Brophy, Theodore F.		Bus	10			10	CEO GTE
Brosnan, Pierce		Ent	25	40	45	55	Newest James Bond. SP 65
Brostoff, Alan		Bus	10			20	

NAME	DATES	CATEGORY	SIG	LS/DS	ALS	SP	COMMENTS
Brothers, Joyce		Sci	10	10	25	25	TV Psychiatrist. Frequent Consulting Guest
Brough, Candi & Randi		Ent	10			25	
Brough, Fanny		Ent	10	10	12	25	Vintage Actress
Brough, Lionel		Ent	10	10	12	20	Vintage Actor
Brougham, Henry, Lord	1778-1868	Statsmn	82	115	250		Designed One Horse Brougham. Author, Scholar
Brougham, John	1814-1880	Ent	20			50	Am. Actor-Plays-Mgr. 'London Assurance:
Broughton, Joseph M.		Congr	10	12		10	Sen./MOC NC
Broun, Heywood	1888-1939	Author	10	35	70	20	Journalist, Novels, Columnist
Brouncker, William	1620-1684	Sci		65			
Browder, Earl	1891-1973	Pol	15	35	65	25	US Communist Party Leader
Brower, Jordan		Celeb	10			20	
Brown, A. Roy		Aero	230				Can. Ace. Downed Richtofen
Brown, Aaron V.	1795-1859	Cab	45	125			PMG, Repr. & Sen. TN
Brown, Albert Gallatin		Gov	69	78	95		CSA Sen., Gov. Miss., Member of CSA Congr.
Brown, Alice		Author	20	75	100	60	Prolific Novels, Poet
Brown, Arthur Whitten	1886-1948	Aero	292	410	575	575	Alcock & Brown 1st Nonstop Flight Over Atlantic
Brown, Benjamin Gratz	1826-1885	Congr	15		25		Sen. MO
Brown, Blair		Ent	10	10	15	25	Actress.
Brown, Bo		Comics	10			20	Magazine Cartoonist
Brown, Bobby		Ent	10			18	
Brown, Bothwell		Ent	10	15	25	45	Vintage Actor
Brown, Bryan		Ent	10			20	Actor
Brown, Catherine		Celeb	10			15	Scottish Chef
Brown, Charles		Music	20			50	Blues Singer. Rock/Roll HOF
Brown, Charles Brockden	1771-1810	Author	975		6500		Father of the Am. Novel
Brown, Clancy		Ent	15			45	
Brown, Clarence		Ent	10			25	
Brown, Corrine B		Congr	10				Member US Congress
Brown, Curtis, Jr.		Space	10			25	
Brown, Danielle		Ent	10			20	Actress
Brown, David		Ent	10			20	Prod. Oscar Winner
Brown, David M.		Space	110			250	D. on Space Shuttle Columbia re-entry 2003
Brown, Down Town Julie		Ent	10			15	TV Host-Singer
Brown, Edmund G. 'Jerry'		Gov	10	25		20	Gov. CA, Pres. Cand. Mayor Oakland, CA
Brown, Edmund G. 'Pat'	1905-1996	Gov	20	25		25	Gov. CA. Liberal Civ. Rights Champion
Brown, Edward N.		Bus	12			15	RR Exec.
Brown, Egbert Benson	1816-1902	Civ War	40	72	128		Union Gen.
Brown, Faith		Celeb	10			15	Comedienne
Brown, Ford Madox	1821-1893	Artist	45		105		Br. Historical Painter
Brown, George Stan		Ent	10			20	Actor
Brown, Harold, Dr.		Cab	10	20		22	Sec. Defense; Scientist
Brown, Harry Joe		Ent	20	40	65	40	Film Prod., Dir.
Brown, Helen Gurley		Author	10	15	20	30	Editor, Publisher
Brown, Henry B.		Sup Crt	62	175	250		
Brown, Henry E. B., Jr.		Congr	10				Member US Congress
Brown, Henry W.		WWII	12	25	45	35	ACE, WWII; 6 kills.
Brown, Herbert C., Dr.		Sci	25	30	45	35	Nobel Chemistry
Brown, Jacob	1775-1828	Mil	65	135	219		Important Gen War of 1812
Brown, James	1933-2006	Music	50			238	The Godfather of Soul. Album S 500-750
Brown, James		Ent	10			25	Actor
Brown, Jim Ed		Cntry Mus	10			15	
Brown, Joe E.	1892-1973	Ent	25	50	72	80	Vintage Film Comedian
Brown, John	1800-1859	Civ War	1142	2033	5267	6910	Fanatical Abolitionist-Hung for treason
Brown, John Calvin	1827-1889	Civ War	126	205	350		CSA Gen. Sig/Rank 240. Gov. TN 1871-75

Sanders Autograph Price Guide

NAME	DATES	CATEGORY	SIG	LS/DS	ALS	SP	COMMENTS
Brown, John George		Artist	10	30	45		
Brown, John Y.		Bus	10	25	35	20	
Brown, Johnny Mack		Ent	50	75		125	Cowboy Actor
Brown, Joseph Emerson		Civ War	48	75	169		Civil War Gov. Georgia
Brown, Julie		Ent	15			35	Actress
Brown, Les		Music	15			35	Big Band Leader. Years w/Bob Hope. Radio
Brown, Lt. John		Rev War	85	175	400		
Brown, Lytle	1872-1951	Mil	50			95	US Army Gen. Sp-Am. War. Battle San Juan Hill
Brown, Mark N.		Space	10			25	
Brown, Marty		Cntry Mus	10			15	Traditional Country Sound
Brown, Moses		Rev War	55		265		Naval Cmdr.
Brown, Nicholas	1729-1791	Rev War	50	110	195		Businessman. Supplied Army. Brown U.
Brown, Norma		Mil	10	20	30	15	
Brown, Norman		Ent	10			10	
Brown, Phil	1916-2006	Ent	25			60	Actor. 'Star Wars'. Uncle Owen
Brown, Phyllis George		Ent	10	12	20	20	
Brown, Prentiss M.		Congr	10	25		15	Sen. MI
Brown, Preston		Mil	32	35		45	Gen. WWI. Chief of Staff
Brown, Reno		Ent	20			55	Actress. Early Westerns
Brown, Rob		Ent	13			40	
Brown, Robert	1773-1858	Sci	150		775		Scot. Botanist. Living Cells Nucleus
Brown, Robert		Mil	30		75	125	Gen. WWI
Brown, Ron		Cab	37	40		68	Sec Comm. Clinton. Tragic Plane Crash
Brown, Ruth		Music	25			55	Rock & Roll HOF
Brown, Sam J.		WWII	20	40	55	45	ACE, WWII
Brown, Sherrod B		Congr	10				Member US Congress
Brown, T. Graham		Cntry Mus	10			20	Country/Soul/Rock Sound
Brown, Tom		Ent	10	15	25	25	Actor. Many Youthful Parts
Brown, William		Celeb	10			15	Pol. celebrity
Brown, William Wallace		Congr	10	15	30		Repr. PA. CW Off.
Brownback, Sam		Congr	10			20	US Senate (R-KS)
Browne, Charles Farrar		Rev War					SEE Ward, Artemus
Browne, Chris		Comics	20			75	'Hagar'
Browne, Coral		Ent	15		135	50	Actress
Browne, Dik		Comics	20			60	Hi & Lois, Hagar
Browne, Hablot Knight		Artist	25	90	150		Watercolor. Illust. of Dickens
Browne, Jackson		Music	20	35		50	Rock
Browne, Leslie		Ent	10			10	
Browne, Maj.-Gen. Beverly Wood	d. 1948	WWII	24			45	WWII Canadian Gen.
Browne, William Montague	1827-1883	Civ War	76	176	295		CSA Gen.
Brownell, Francis E.		Civ War	368				CMOH
Brownell, Herbert Jr.	1904-1996	Cab	15	20	40	40	Eisenhower Atty Gen. Adm. 'Time' Cvr. S 35
Browning, Eliz. Barrett		Author	315	1040	2820	3167	Br. Poet
Browning, George		Bus	195	580			Browning Arms Mfg.
Browning, John B.		Bus	50	160		75	Pres. Browning Arms Co.
Browning, John Moses	1855-1926	Invent	195	310	575	1650	Fire Arms Inventor-Designer. Browning Auto.
Browning, Orville H.	1806-1881	Cab	25	125			Sec. of Interior, Sen. IL
Browning, Ricou		Ent	12			35	Creature, Olympic Swimmer
Browning, Robert	1812-1889	Author	258	385	939	1825	Br. Poet. AManS 3250, 3400. AQS 3500
Browning, Tod	1880-1962	Ent	165			1625	Dir. of Dracula (1931)
Brownlee, John		Opera	10		45	30	Opera, Australian/Am. Baritone
Brownlow, William G.	1848-1902	Jrnalist		242			
Brown-Sequard, Chas. E.	1817-1894	Sci	200	295	482		Fr. MD. Father: Endocrinology. Brown-Sequard Synd.
Brown-Waite, Ginny B		Congr	10				Member US Congress

NAME	DATES	CATEGORY	SIG	LS/DS	ALS	SP	COMMENTS
Brubeck, Dave		Music	30	50	55	200	Jazz Great. Pianist, Comp.
Bruce, Andrew D.		Mil	35	175		90	Gen. 77th Infantry Div. So. Pacific. WWII
Bruce, Blanche K.	1841-1898	Congr	150	367	400		Born a Slave. 1st Afro-Am. Full Term Sen.
Bruce, Carol		Music	10	10	15	40	Blues-Jazz Vocalist, Actress. ALS/Cont 95
Bruce, David		Ent	10			20	
Bruce, Ed		Music	10			15	Singer/Songwriter
Bruce, Eli Metcalfe	1828-1866	Civ War	60	102			Member of CSA Congress
Bruce, Horatio Wasington	1830-1903	Civ War	50		138		Member of CSA Congress
Bruce, Lenny	1926-1966	Ent	443	555	1100	1075	ALS/Typescript Archive 5750; Chk 600-950
Bruce, Nigel	1895-1953	Ent	150	175	300	388	Noted for Dr. Watson. Caricature S 250
Bruce, Thos. (7th Earl Elgin)	1766-1841	Diplo	50	190	340		Conveyed Elgin Marbles. Greece to Br. Museum
Bruce, Virginia		Ent	20			50	Actress. Late 30s-40's Sophis. Leading Lady
Bruce, Wallace		Author	35		120		
Bruce, Wm. Cabell	1860-1946	Congr	10	15	30	10	Sen. MD, Author
Bruch, Max	1838-1920	Comp	92	180	250	256	Ger. Opera, AMusQS 950-1, 100-2, 500
Bruckner, Agnes		Ent	12			35	
Bruckner, Anton	1824-1896	Comp		1875			Austrian
Bruckner, Josef Anton	1824-1896	Comp	1600	2750	5500	2500	Aus. 10 Symphonies.
Brummel, Geo. B. 'Beau'	1778-1840	Celeb	95	220	850		Br. Man of Fashion, Friend of Prince Regent
Brummer, Renate		Space	10			25	Ger.
Bruna Rasa, Lina		Opera	65			300	Opera. Great Verismo Sopr. Mascagni Favorite
Brune, G. M. A.	1763-1815	Napol	100	240	450		Marshal of Nap. Assass.
Brunel, Marc Isambard, Sir	1769-1849	Sci	75	181	323		Fr. -Br. Inventor, Engineer
Bruning, Heinrich	1885-1971	HOS	35		100	425	Ger. Chancellor. Fled to US '34
Brunner, Emil		Clergy	45	75	110	50	
Bruno, Walter	1876-1962	Cond	110	120		150	Ger. conductor & Comp.
Bruscantini, Sesto		Opera	15			45	Opera
Bruson, Renato		Opera	10			30	Opera
Bry, Ellen		Ent	10			20	Actress
Bryan, Charles W.		Gov	12	15			Governor NE
Bryan, George		Rev War	135	350	750		Jurist. Proposed Abolition 1777
Bryan, Goode	1811-1885	Civ War	172		539		CSA Gen. Sig/Rank 300. Poor Health, Resigned '64
Bryan, Jane		Ent	10	10	20	35	Actress. 40s Warner Bros. Leading Lady
Bryan, William E.		WWII	15	22	42	34	ACE, WWII; 7. 5 kills
Bryan, William Jennings	1860-1925	Cab	91	272	364	432	Pres. Nominee 3 Times. Sec State. TLS/Cont 1150
Bryant, Alys McKey		Aero	35	60	140	75	
Bryant, Anita		Ent	10	20	20	20	Singer
Bryant, Ed		Congr	10			15	Tennessee
Bryant, Joy		Ent	13			40	
Bryant, William Cullen	1794-1878	Author	165	275	445	383	Am. Poet, ALS/Cont 1, 750; AQS 300
Brynner, Yul	1915-1985	Ent	45	55	75	179	Academy Award for 'King & I' 1952
Bryson, Ann		Ent	10			25	Actress
Brzezinski, Zbigniew		Pol	10			25	Pol. celebrity
Buber, Martin		Clergy	75	175	289	90	
Buchan, John, Lord	1875-1940	Author	25	236			Gov. Gen. Canada, Novels
Buchanan, Edgar	1902-1979	Ent	52	40	55	75	Jovial-Rugged AM. Char. Actor. 1939-71
Buchanan, Franklin	1800-1874	Civ War	160	348	495		CSA Adm.
Buchanan, Jack		Ent				50	Song & dance
Buchanan, James	1791-1868	Pres	349	1170	1294	2583	Special SP 12500, FF 350-450, ALS/cont 2000-5000
Buchanan, James (as Pres.)		Pres	417	1248	2283		15th Pres. of USA
Buchanan, James M.		Econ	35	45	85	40	Nobel Economics
Buchanan, Patrick		Pol	12	15		30	Pol. Commentator. Pres. Cand.
Buchanan, Robert C. 'Old Buck'	1811-1878	Civ War	50	128	210		Union Gen.
Buchel, August	1813-1864	Civ War		92			1st TX Calvary

NAME	DATES	CATEGORY	SIG	LS/DS	ALS	SP	COMMENTS
Bucher, Lloyd M.	1927-2004	Mil	32	90	150	90	Captured Capt. of USS Pueblo
Buchli, James F.		Space	10	15		25	
Buchman, Franklin	1878-1961	Clergy	20	35	65		
Buchwald, Art	1925-2007	Author	12	15	25	42	Syndicated Humor Columnist
Buck, Clayton Douglass		Congr	11	15	25	20	Sen. -Governor DE
Buck, Dudley	1839-1909	Comp	10				Organist
Buck, Frank	1884-1950	Author	50	80	198	105	Bring 'Em Back Alive'. Author, Lecturer
Buck, Paul H.		Author	10	10	15	15	
Buck, Pearl S.	1892-1973	Author	48	201	251	60	Am. Novels. Nobel, Pulitzer,. AMS 1000
Buckingham, Catharinus P.	1808-1888	Civ War	42	114	138		Union Gen. LS '62 745
Buckingham, George V.	1628-1687	Royal			700		2nd Duke of Buckingham, Pol.
Buckingham, George V.	1592-1628	Royal	100		700		1st Duke of.
Buckingham, William A.		Gov	30	55	83	75	Civil War Gov. CT. & US Sen.
Buckland, Ralph P. (WD)	1812-1892	Civ War	130	150	250		Union Gen.
Buckle, Henry Thomas		Author	10	10	25		
Buckley, Emerson		Cond				125	Am. conductor of Regional Opera
Buckley, James	1923-	Congr	10	15		10	
Buckley, William F., Jr.	1925-2008	Author	10	15	45	40	National Revue, Conservative Journalist
Buckner, Simon Bolivar	1823-1914	Civ War	181	312	468	295	CSA Gen.
Buckner, Simon Bolivar (WD)		Civ War	450	2500	4608		CSA Gen.
Buckstone, John B.	1802-1879	Ent	20		25	50	Br. Actor, Comedian, Plays
Budd, Julie		Ent	10	10	15	20	
Buell, Don Carlos	1818-1898	Civ War	90	105	162	250	Union Gen. ADS '62 400
Buell, Nathaniel		Rev War	50	225			His Reg't Secured Ft Ticonderoga. Lt. Col.
Buffalo Bill Jr.		Ent	25				
Buffalo Springfield		Music	275			375	Rock group; S Album 400; S Guitar 470-2000
Buffett, Jimmy		Music	35	150		150	Rock; AQS 6500; S Album 175
Buffington, Thomas Mitchell		West	350	550			Chief Cherokee Nations; DS/Theo Roosevelt 2500
Buffy the Vampire Slayer (cast)		Ent				367	Cast of 7
Buford, Abraham	1820-1884	Civ War	188	356	1144		CSA Gen.
Buford, John	1826-1863	Civ War	350	1582	3822		Union Gen., S engraving 2415, KIA Gettysburg
Buford, Napoleon Bonaparte	1807-1883	Civ War	58	152	232		Union Gen. ALS '62 320
Bugliosi, Vince		Law	16				Manson Trial Atty
Buhari, Mohammed		HOS	15	50	130	25	
Buick, David D.		Bus	165	750	1250	885	Buick Motor Co.
Bujold, Genevieve	1942-	Ent	10	12	15	35	
Bukowski, Charles	1920-1994	Author	70	150		100	Avant-Garde Writer. BS 750, AManS 95, S drw 550
Bulfinch, Charles		Archtct	130	375	850		Fanueil Hall, Finished construction of Capitol
Bulfinch, Thomas		Author	25	45	100		Bulfinch's Mythology
Bulganin, Nicholai	1895-1975	Mil	50	155			Soviet Mil. & Pol. leader
Bulkley, John D.		Mil	35	65		65	Adm. USN WWII
Bull, Clarence Sinclair		Photog		175			Hollywood & Motion Picture Photographer; AA
Bull, John S.		Space	15			25	
Bull, Ole B.		Comp	25		125	125	Nor. Violin Virtuoso
Bull, William II	1710-1791	Rev War	110	310	750		Colonial Governor SC
Bullard, Joe		Author	10			12	Florida castles
Bullard, Robert Lee		Mil	20	75	130	130	Gen. WWI
Bullard, William		Mil	15	35		65	Adm. WWI
Buller, Redvers, Sir		Mil	40	110	250	175	Cmdr-in-Chief South Africa
Bullet Boys (4)		Ent	10			40	
Bullitt, William P.		Diplo	10	20		25	Ambassador To USSR
Bulloch, Terrence		Aero	20			35	Br. Aviator WWII
Bullock, Robert	1828-1905	Civ War	80	120	195		CSA Gen.
Bullock, Sandra		Ent	15	25		48	Actress. Popular Star.

NAME	DATES	CATEGORY	SIG	LS/DS	ALS	SP	COMMENTS
Bullock, Seth		Lawman	200	500			Stock Cert. S 975
Bulow, Bernhard H. M. K. von		HOS	30	65	195	40	Prussian Imperial Chancellor
Bulow, Claus von		Celeb	15	25		25	Danish Count. Accused Murderer
Bulow, Hans von	1830-1894	Cond	55	120	285	475	Germ. Conductor, Pianist. ALS/Cont 500
Bultmann, Rudolph		Clergy	70	90	165	80	
Bulwer, Elizabeth		Author	10		25		
Bulwer, Wm. Henry Lytton	1801-1872	Diplo	20	40	75		Clayton-Bulwer Treaty. US & Eng
Bulwer-Lytton, Edward		Author	60	220	460		
Bumbry, Grace		Opera	10	20		55	Opera. SP 5x7 30
Bumgarner, Wiley		Author	10			12	Religion
Bumpers, Dale		Gov	12	15		20	Sen. AR
Bunce, Francis M.		Mil	35	55	125	125	Adm. Spanish-Am. War
Bunche, Ralph J.	1904-1971	Diplo	53	100	188	111	Diplomat. Nobel Peace Pr.
Bundy, McGeorge		Lawman	15	35	45	18	Dir. FBI
Bundy, Omar		Mil	35	90		55	Gen. WWI
Bundy, Ted		Crime	125	542	650		Infamous Convicted Mass Murderer
Bunin, Ivan	1870-1953	Poet	95		322		Russian poet
Bunker, Eng & Cheng		Celeb				1500	Siamese twins
Bunner, Henry C.	1855-1896	Jrnalist	70	82	135		Editor Puck Magazine. Story-writer
Bunning, Jim		Pol	15			35	Congress from KY; HOF BB pitcher
Bunny, John		Ent	100	130	160	200	Vintage Film Comedian
Bunsen, Christian K. J., Baron		Diplo	20	45	115		Prussian Theologian, Scholar
Bunsen, Robert W.	1811-1899	Sci	200	485	858	1920	Ger. Chemist, Bunsen Burner
Bunting, William M.		Clergy	45	100	150		
Buntline, Ned (Pseud)	1823-1886	Author	140	185	370	835	(E. Z. C. Judson) Novels, Adventr., Dime Novels.
Bunzel, John		Celeb	10			15	Pol. celebrity
Buono, Victor	1938-1982	Ent	85	150		165	AA-nom. Role, 'Whatever Happened to Baby Jane?'
Burbank, Luther	1849-1926	Sci	89	173	272	140	Pioneer, Exper. Botanist. Original Plants-Veg
Burbridge, Stephen Gano	1831-1894	Civ War	50	91	175		Union Gen.
Burder, George		Clergy	10	15	20	15	
Burdette, Robert J.		Author	20	55	135	80	
Burgdorff, Wilhelm		WWII				190	Ger. Off. who gave Rommel his suicide pill
Burge, V. L.		Aero	18			35	
Burger, Warren E.		Sup Crt	65	132	210	150	Chief Justice
Burges, Tristam		Congr	10		25		
Burgess, Anthony	1917-1993	Author	40	55	125		Br. Novels. Clockwork Orange
Burgess, Michael C. B		Congr	10				Member US Congress
Burgess, Thomas, Bish.	1874-1965	Clergy	15	25	35		
Burgess, Thornton W.		Author	62	233	325		Peter Rabbit; SB 160-240; AQS 100
Burghley, Wm. Cecil, Lord	1520-1593	Statsmn	585	1725			Elizabeth I, Tudor Statesman. LS/Essex 1550
Burghoff, Gary	1940-	Ent	15	35		30	Actor. 'Radar' on 'Mash'
Burgoyne, John	1722-1792	Rev War	1250	3025	3553		Br. Gen. vs Am. Colonies
Burke, Arleigh	1901-1996	Mil	35	55	110	75	Adm. USN WWII
Burke, Billie (Ziegfield)	1885-1970	Ent	143	200	225	353	SP as Glinda the Good Witch in WOZ 5000
Burke, Billy	1966-	Ent	12			35	Actor
Burke, Brooke		Ent	15			35	
Burke, Chris	1965-	Ent	10			25	Actor
Burke, Delta		Ent	15	20	25	31	Actress. 'Designing Women'
Burke, Edmund	1729-1797	Author			2450		Irish Born Br. Statesman, Author, Orator
Burke, Edmund		Congr	10	12	20		US MOC NH
Burke, Edward A.		Pol	35	45		150	Dom. LA Pol. 1880's. Embezzled over 1M
Burke, Paul		Ent	10	13	15	20	
Burke, Selma		Artist	10	20	52	40	
Burke, Yvonne B.		Congr	10				3 Term Repr CA

B

NAME	DATES	CATEGORY	SIG	LS/DS	ALS	SP	COMMENTS
Burleigh, Harry Thacker		Comp	25		150		Singer. AMusQS 200-300
Burleigh, Walter A.	1820-1896	Congr	10				Delegate from Dakota Terr.
Burleson, Albert S.		Cab	10	25	35		P. M. Gen., MOC TX
Burleson, Edward	1798-1851	Tex		1637			Pioneer of TX
Burleson, OmarTruman		Congr	10	15		10	MOC TX
Burmester, Willy		Music	90		275		Ger. Violinist. AMusQS 350
Burne-Jones, Edward	1833-1898	Artist	125	235	452		Pre-Raphaelite Painter, Designer
Burnet, David G.	1788-1870	Tex	300	347	1300		1st Pres. Repub. TX
Burnet, William	1688-1728	Colonial	170	465			Br. Gov. NY & NJ
Burnett, Carol	1933-	Ent	37	81	100	95	Comedienne.
Burnett, Frances Hodgson	1849-1924	Author	100	145	215		Little Lord Fauntleroy' AQS 150
Burnett, Johnny		Ent		200			
Burnett, Leo		Bus	20	30	42	50	Advertising
Burnett, Peter H.		Gov	200		550		California Pioneer & 1st Gov.
Burnette, Michelle		Author	10			12	Civil War book
Burnette, Smiley		Ent	40	50		150	
Burnette, Talmadge L.		Author	10			12	Regional history, nostalgia
Burney, Cecil, Sir		Mil	15	35		50	Br. Adm. WWI
Burnham, Hiram	1814-1864	Civ War	52	195	225		Union Gen.
Burns, Bob		Ent	25	25	45	45	Bazooka
Burns, Brooke		Ent	17			50	
Burns, Conrad		Congr	10				US Senate (R-MT)
Burns, Edmund		Ent	30			65	Silent Screen Star
Burns, Edward		Ent	20			45	Actor. 'Saving Private Ryan'
Burns, Geo. & Gracie Allen		Ent	225	375		421	Comedy team, husband & wife
Burns, George	1896-1996	Ent	30	65	70	80	Vaude. -Radio-TV-Film Comedian
Burns, James MacGregor		Author	20	30			Educator, Pol. Science
Burns, John	1791-1872	Civ War	310			1056	Vet. War 1812. Vol. Gettysburg
Burns, John A.	1909-1975	Gov	12	15		20	Hawaii
Burns, Ken		Ent	15			25	Documentary Film Maker
Burns, Max B		Congr	10				Member US Congress
Burns, Robert	1759-1796	Author	1156	1975	4283		Scottish Poet, Early Poem Draft 13500
Burns, William Chalmers		Clergy	25	40	50	35	
Burns, William J.		Bus	35	58	175		Chief FBI 1921-24, Det. Agency
Burns, William Wallace	1825-1892	Civ War	50	93	126	150	Union Gen.
Burnside, Ambrose E.	1824-1881	Civ War	98	200	237	797	
Burnside, Ambrose E. (WD)	1824-1881	Civ War	150	370	1190	760	Union Gen.
Burpee, David		Bus	25	35	70	35	Burpee Seed Co.
Burpee, Jonathan		Bus	10	25	50	20	Burpee Seed Co.
Burr, Aaron	1756-1836	VP	408	803	1282		ALsS/Cont 7,000-12,000+. Rev. War ALS 5800
Burr, Raymond	1917-1993	Ent	25	38	30	92	Perry Mason
Burr, Richard B		Congr	10				Member US Congress
Burritt, Elihu	1810-1879	Author	20		120		Pacifist. AKA 'Learned Blacksmith'. AQS 150
Burroughs, Edgar Rice	1875-1950	Author	242	451	509	938	Tarzan. TLS/Cont 1900; Chk 125
Burroughs, John	1837-1921	Author	68	122	496	525	Am. Naturalist, Philosopher, AManS 1200
Burroughs, John		Gov	10		25	15	Governor NM
Burroughs, Sherman Everett		Congr	10	15	25	10	MOC NH
Burroughs, William	1914-1997	Author	75	350		450	Am. Influenced 50s Beat Writers. S book 300
Burrows, Abe		Author	10	15	25	25	Plays, Pulitzer
Burrows, J. C.		Congr	10		25		Sen. MI
Burrows, Malandra		Ent	10			20	Actress
Burrows, Saffron		Ent	15			45	
Bursch, Daniel		Space	10			20	
Burstyn, Ellen		Ent	10	12	15	40	Actress

NAME	DATES	CATEGORY	SIG	LS/DS	ALS	SP	COMMENTS
Bursum, Holm Olaf		Congr	10	15	25		Sen. NM
Burton, Charlotte		Ent	10	10	12	15	
Burton, Dan B		Congr	10				Member US Congress
Burton, Harold H.	1888-1964	Sup Crt	36	170	325	90	
Burton, Isabel, Lady		Author	25	85	180		
Burton, LeVar		Ent	15	22	22	35	Actor. 'Roots'
Burton, Richard	1925-1984	Ent	112	188		301	Actor. Important DS 950
Burton, Richard F., Sir	1821-1890	Expl	150	285	1703		Orientalist, Linguist, Author
Burton, Theodore E.		Congr	10	10	15	10	Sen., MOC OH
Burton, Tim		Ent	20			45	Film Dir., Actor
Busby, George Henry		Gov	10	15			Governor GA
Buscalia, Leo	1924+1998	Author	15	25	40	25	Educator, Author, Lecturer
Buscemi, Steve		Ent	15			40	Actor
Busch, Adolphus	1839-1913	Bus	300	3500	4000		Fndr. Anheuser-Busch. TLS 5800
Busch, August A.		Bus	250	1850	2500		Anheuser-Busch Brewery
Busch, Fritz		Cond	45	175	135	250	Ger. Conductor
Busch, Mae		Ent				250	Laurel & Hardy co-star
Busch, Niven		Author	12		25	25	Dramatist, Screenwriter
Busch, Wilhelm	1832-1908	Artist	200		950		Painter & Poet.
Busell, Darcey		Ballet	15			40	Ballet
Busey, Gary	1944-	Ent	12	18	15	35	Actor.
Bush		Music	45			176	Music. 4 Member Rock Group
Bush, Barbara	1925-	1st Lady	53	92	72	88	
Bush, George & Barbara		Pres				200	S Christmas Card as Pres. 600-1920
Bush, George H. W.	1924-	Pres	94	251	650	262	Signed Vice Presidential Card 195
Bush, George H. W. (as Pres.)	1924-	Pres	160	622	986	322	WH Cd. S 500, Pres. Cd. 950. SP Oath 1295
Bush, George W.		Pres	92	308	712	300	Baseball Exec., TX Gov.
Bush, George W. (as Pres.)		Pres	157	658	2500	461	
Bush, Irving T.		Bus	10	25			Owned Largest Shipping Terminal
Bush, Owen	1921-2001	Ent	10			30	Char. Actor
Bush, Prescott		Congr	25	75		90	Sen. CT Father, Grandfather of George & Geo. W.
Bush, Vannevar	1890-1974	Sci	60	180	255	125	Pioneer In Analog Computers. Atom Bomb
Bushkin, Joe		Ent	10			15	
Bushman, Francis X.	1883-1966	Ent	50	65	110	129	Silent Star, Ben Hur. S Chk 65; S passport 325
Bushmiller, Ernie		Comics	20			125	Nancy
Bushnell, David	1742-1824	Sci	250	690	1250		Invented 1st Submarine
Bushnell, Horace	1802-1876	Clergy	25	35	45		New Engl. Congregational Min.
Bushyhead, D. W.		Am Ind	200		1500		Principal Chief, Cherokee Nation, Tahlequah.
Busoni, Ferruccio	1866-1924	Music			210		Classical musician, AMusQS 330
Busse, Henry		Music	20			50	Big Band Leader
Bussey, Cyrus	1833-1915	Civ War	50	80	140		Union Gen.
Bustamante, Jose Luis		Celeb	10	35	60		
Busteed, Richard	1822-1898	Civ War	50	118	210		Union Gen.
Butcher, Susan	1954-	Celeb	10	15		20	Dog Breeder; Iditarod
Bute, John Stuart		Royal	85	130			Earl of Bute
Butenandt, Adolf F. J.		Sci	20	30	45	25	Nobel Chemistry
Buthelezi, Gatsha M.		HOS	20			35	Chief of Zulu Nation
Butler, Benjamin F.	1818-1893	Civ War	60	315	184		Union Gen., LS '62 2750. DS '63 700
Butler, Benjamin F.	1795-1858	Cab	30	75	150		PMG for Jackson; FF 67
Butler, Carl & Pearl		Cntry Mus	15			30	
Butler, Daws	1916-1988	Ent	15	15	20	40	Cartoon voices: Yogi Bear & Huckleberry Hound.
Butler, Dean		Ent	10		12	15	
Butler, Ellis Parker	1869-1937	Author	10	60	92	40	Pigs is Pigs
Butler, Jerry		Music	15			70	Singer & songwriter

NAME	DATES	CATEGORY	SIG	LS/DS	ALS	SP	COMMENTS
Butler, John		Rev War	100	185	375		Am. Loyalist. Butler's Rangers
Butler, John		Clergy	10	15	20	20	
Butler, Matthew C.	1836-1909	Civ War	78	142	285		CSA Gen., US Sen. SC
Butler, Matthew C. (WD)	1836-1909	Civ War	155	345	675		CSA Gen.
Butler, Nicholas Murray		Educ	15	35	90	30	Nobel Peace Pr. Educator
Butler, Pierce	1744-1822	Rev War	62	144	1265		Signer of Constitution
Butler, Pierce	1866-1939	Sup Crt	40	90	200	70	Jurist 1922-39
Butler, Samuel	1835-1902	Author	20	60	125		Br. Author, Artist, Musician
Butler, Smedley D.	1881-1940	Mil	15	35	75	75	Marine Corps Gen/2 CMH
Butler, Thomas S.		Congr	10	15			MOC PA
Butler, Walter	1752-1781	Rev War		550	675		Captured, escaped. Butler's Rangers
Butler, William Orlando		Mil	70	210			Hero Battle of New Orleans
Butler, Yancy		Ent	10			40	Actress. Mann & Machine, Hard Target, Drop Zone
Butler, Zebulon		Mil	80	225			Col. Revolutionary War
Butt, Clara	1873-1936	Opera	35			45	Opera
Buttafuco, Joey		Celeb	10			15	
Butterfield, Billy		Music	25			45	Jazz Trumpet, Bandleader
Butterfield, Daniel	1831-1901	Civ War	77	243	296		Union Gen. Composed 'Taps'
Butterfield, Daniel (WD)		Civ War	145	577	360	745	Union Gen. Composed TAPS
Butterworth, Charles	1896-1946	Ent	35			101	Actor
Buttons, Red	1919-2007	Ent	20	27	45	62	Academy Award in Sayonara
Buttram, Pat		Ent	20	95		62	Gene Autry Movie Sidekick
Buttrick, George A.		Clergy	25	45	75	75	
Buttrick, John		Rev War		1208			Hero of Lexington/Concord
Butts, Alfred M.		Invent	35	62	75		Scrabble
Butz, Earl L.	1909-2008	Cab	10	18	30	20	Sec. Agriculture
Buxton, Sarah		Ent	13			40	
Buyer, Steve B		Congr	10				Member US Congress
Buzzi, Ruth		Ent	10	13	15	25	
Buzzini, Brian		Celeb	10			15	Model
Byers, Samuel Hawkins		Author	25	40	60		Union Soldier-Author
Byington, Spring		Ent	25			76	
Bykovsky, Valeri		Space				40	Russian Cosmonaut
Byner, John		Ent	10	10	16	30	
Bynes, Amanda		Ent	15			45	
Byng, Geo. Visc. Torrington		Mil	75	112			Br. Adm. Destroyed Sp. Fleet 1719
Byrd, Charlie		Music	15			50	Jazz Guitar
Byrd, Harry F. Byrd, Sr.		Gov	25				Gov. VA
Byrd, Harry F., Jr.		Congr	10	25		25	Sen. VA
Byrd, Jerry		Cntry Mus	10			20	
Byrd, Ralph	1909-1952	Ent	70	150		350	Dick Tracey
Byrd, Richard E.	1888-1957	Expl	75	169	304	299	Adm. USN, Polar Expl. TLS/Cont 575
Byrd, Robert C.		Congr	15	30	50	100	Sen. WV
Byrds, The (Entire Group)		Music	649			950	Rock group; S album 950
Byrne, Bobby		Music	20				Big Band leader
Byrne, Gabriel		Ent	15			35	Actor, Films
Byrne, Jane		Pol	10	10	28	10	Mayor
Byrne, Rose		Ent	13			40	
Byrnes, Edd		Ent	10			35	Kookie
Byrnes, James F.		Sup Crt	30	125	235	105	
Byrns, Joseph Wellington		Congr	15	25		20	MOC TN
Byron, Arthur		Ent	15	15	20	35	
Byron, Geo. Gordon, Lord	1788-1824	Author	1239	2750	7125		Inflluential, Romantic Br. Poet
Byron, Jean	1926-2006	Ent	15			40	Patty Duke's Mom on TV

NAME	DATES	CATEGORY	SIG	LS/DS	ALS	SP	COMMENTS
Caan, James		Ent	20	26	30	49	'Godfather' SP 100
Cabana, Robert D.		Space	10			20	
Cabell, Earle		Mayor	10				Dallas JFK Assassination TLS 475
Cabell, James Branch	1879-1958	Author	30	120	165		Novels Attacked for Immorality
Cabell, William L.	1827-1911	Civ War	200	460			CSA Gen.
Cable, George Washington	1844-1925	Author	33	48	101	50	CSA Soldier, Short Story Writer
Cabot, Bruce	1904-1972	Ent	50	55	90	163	John Wayne Sidekick
Cabot, George	1751-1823	Congr	35	45	100		Sen. MA. Ratified US Constitution
Cabot, Sebastian		Ent	65	40	90	100	Actor
Cabot, Susan	d 1986	Celeb				144	Portrayed The Wasp Woman; beaten to death in 1986
Cabrera, Santiago		Ent	15			45	
Cabrini, Saint Francis Xavier		Relig	780				S Chk 1440
Caceres, Andreas A.		HOS	10	25	65	20	Peru
Cadbury, George		Bus	50		170	50	Cadbury Chocolate Mfg.
Cadbury, Richard		Bus	40	45	160	50	Cadbury Chocolate Mfg.
Cade, Robert, Dr.		Bus	15	15		25	Inventor of Gatorade
Cadman, Chas. Wakefield		Comp	50	147	223	181	AMusQS 195
Cadman, S. Parkes		Clergy	20	35	50	35	
Cadmus, Paul		Artist	50	110	120		Repro. S 75
Cadwalader, George	1806-1879	Civ War	50	124	167		Union Gen. LS '63 385
Cadwalader, Lambert		Rev War	65	140	335		Continental Congress
Cady, Daniel		Congr	20	35	50		MOC NY 1815
Caesar, Irving	1895-1996	Comp	42	130	140	59	Lyricist 'Tea for Two' Collaberator: Gershwin
Caesar, Sid	1922-	Ent	25	41	58	65	Comedian. Classic early TV
Cage, John M.	1912-1992	Comp	75	364	195	165	AMusQS 125-250. AManS 3750
Cage, Nicolas	1964-	Ent	24	38		58	AA Actor
Cagney, James	1899-1987	Ent	80	108	138	248	AA Actor. Dancer, Singer
Cagney, Jeanne		Ent	20			30	Jimmy Cagney's Actress Sister
Cahier, Madame Charles		Opera	25			90	Early Opera
Cahn, Sammy	1913-1993	Comp	25	76	125	76	AMusQS 250
Cain, Dean		Ent	15			42	Superman
Cain, James		Author	40	55	90		Novels. Hard Boiled Fiction
Caine, John T.	1829-1911	Congr				50	Dem. Rep. From Utah. Newspaper Editor
Caine, Michael	1933-	Ent	10	12	24	50	Brit. AA winning actor.
Caine, Thos. Hall, Sir	1853-1931	Author	20	45	74	60	Br. Novels, Dramatist
Calandral, Joe		Music	10			25	Music. Bass Guitar 'Monster Magnet'
Calavano, Phil		Music	10			25	Music. 'Monster Magnet'
Calder, A. Stirling	1870-1945	Artist			65		Sculptor. Father of Alexander Calder
Calder, Alexander (Sandy)	1898-1976	Artist	108	225	490	256	Sculptor, Mobiles. ALS/Cont 1000-1500; S Sket 3500
Calder, William M.	1869-1945	Congr		20			Sen. NY
Calderio, Frank		Space	10			20	
Calderon, A. W. Gen.		HOS	10	15	35	10	
Caldicott, Helen		Celeb	10			15	Pol. celebrity
Caldwell, Erskine	1903-1986	Author	38	88	162	81	Tobacco Road', 'God's Little Acre'; S Manu. 325
Caldwell, George A.	1814-1866	Congr	20				Repr. KY, Off. Mexican War
Caldwell, John Curtis	1833-1912	Civ War	64	82		250	Union Gen.
Caldwell, Sarah		Cond	15			55	1st Woman Conductor NY Met.
Caldwell, Taylor		Author	35	150	225	150	Novels
Caldwell, Zoe		Ent	10	25	15	15	
Calhern, Louis		Ent	38	45	45	102	Eminent Stage-Film Actor
Calhoun, Alice		Ent	15	15	35	30	
Calhoun, Eleanor		Ent	10			20	
Calhoun, James	1845-1876	Mil		2300			Custer bro-in-law. Killed, Little Big Horn
Calhoun, John C.	1782-1850	VP	204	558	544	475	Andrew Jackson VP. Statesman, Sec. War

NAME	DATES	CATEGORY	SIG	LS/DS	ALS	SP	COMMENTS
Calhoun, Rory		Ent	20	28	54	64	Actor
Calhoun, William Barron		Congr	10	15	35		Rep. MA 1835
Calhoun, William M.		Congr	10	10			
Caliendo, Frank		Ent	15			45	
Calkin, Dick		Comics	75			500	Buck Rogers; sketch 500
Callaghan, James	1912-2005	HOS	35	75	140	50	Br. Prime Min.
Callahan, Laurence K.		Aero	10	20	45	30	
Callas, Charlie		Ent	10			30	
Callas, Maria Meneghini	1923-1977	Opera	595	873	592	1580	Opera, Concert. Small SP 525-850-950-1075
Callcott, Maria Lady	1785-1842	Author			100		
Calleia, Frank		Ent	19	25	45	45	
Calleia, Joseph		Ent	35			79	
Calley, William Lt.		Mil	30	35	45	130	My Lai, Viet Nam
Calloway, Cab	1907-1995	Ent	45	55	70	146	Big Band Leader. Jazz Musician
Calve, Emma		Opera	55	90	105	217	Opera
Calvert, Ken C		Congr	10				Member US Congress
Calvert, Louis		Ent	10			15	
Calvert, Phyllis		Ent	10			15	
Calvet, Corinne	1925-2001	Ent	10	12	15	21	Fr. Actress. 50s Genre.
Calvin, John		Clergy	5500	7500	10000		
Calvin, Melvin, Dr.		Sci	25	35	55	30	Nobel Chemistry
Camacho, Manuel Avila		HOS	35		80	40	Pres. Mexico
Camargo, Alberto		HOS	10	18	35	20	Columbia
Cambaceres, J. J. R. (Parma)		Napol	115	160			Prince & Duke
Cambell, James		Cab	35	80	120		Pierce P. M. Gen.
Cambern, Donn		Ent	10			25	Actor Mayberry
Cambon, Jules		Diplo	20	25	35		Fr. Ambassador to US
Cambreleng, Churchill Caldom		Congr	10				FF 35
Cambridge, G. O.		Clergy	10	20	25		
Cambridge, Godfrey		Ent	32	35		111	Afr-Am Comedian, Activist
Cameron, Betsy		Author	10	10	20	10	
Cameron, Candace		Ent	10			20	Actress
Cameron, George	1861-1944	Mil	20		45	50	Gen. WWI
Cameron, James		Ent	15	25	50	50	Titanic
Cameron, James D.	1833-1918	Cab	30	35	45		Sen. PA. Sec. War
Cameron, Kenneth		Space	10			15	
Cameron, Kirk		Ent	14	20		48	'Growing Pains' Star
Cameron, Matt		Music	10			25	Music. Drummer 'Soundgarden'
Cameron, Robert Alexander	1828-1894	Civ War	50	92			Union Gen. ALS '62 175
Cameron, Rod	1910-1983	Ent	15			78	Actor. Rugged Star of Westerns & 'B' Films
Cameron, Simon	1800-1889	Cab	67	145	162	295	Lincoln Sec. War, Financier; FF 54
Cameron, Simon (WD)		Cab	130	210	265	350	
Cammaerts, Emile		Author	10	20	40	15	Belgian Poet-Writer
Camp, Colleen		Ent	10			18	
Camp, Dave C		Congr	10				Member US Congress
Campanella, Joseph		Ent	10	10	15	26	
Campanini, Italo		Ent	58	80	175		
Campbell, Alexander William	1828-1893	Civ War	90	175	250		CSA Gen.
Campbell, Archibald		Rev War	110	275			Br. Gen.
Campbell, Archie		Cntry Mus	10			25	
Campbell, Beatrice Stella	1865-1940	Ent	25	40	45	78	Mrs. Patrick Campbell. Actress
Campbell, Ben		Congr	10				US Senate (R-CO)
Campbell, Billy		Ent	28			63	Actor
Campbell, Bruce		Ent	16			48	

NAME	DATES	CATEGORY	SIG	LS/DS	ALS	SP	COMMENTS
Campbell, Charles Thomas	1823-1895	Civ War	47	90	129		Union Gen.
Campbell, Christa		Ent	15			45	
Campbell, Colin, Sir	1792-1863	Mil	30	55	85		Br. Gen. Vs US, War 1812
Campbell, Douglas		Aero	38	65	80	125	ACE, WWI, Bi-plane Ace; SB 125
Campbell, E. Simms		Comics	20			150	1st Black Mag. Cartoonist
Campbell, Ernest T.		Clergy	20	30	40	30	
Campbell, Geo. (8th Duke Argyl)		Statsmn	25	60	130		Author. Br. Cabinet
Campbell, George W.	1769-1848	Cab	65	160	310		Sec. Treas. Sen. TN 1803
Campbell, Glen		Music	15	25	30	48	Singer-Guitarist. 'Wichita Lineman' Alb. S 30
Campbell, Jack M.		Gov	10	20			Governor NM
Campbell, Jacob M.	1821-1888	Civ War			45		Col. Union army
Campbell, James E.		Gov	15	25	30		Governor OH, MOC
Campbell, John		Rev War	78	175	290		Br. Gen.
Campbell, John A.		Sup Crt	100	210	375		
Campbell, John Hull	1800-1868	Congr	10				Repr. PA
Campbell, Josiah Adams	1830-1917	Civ War	54	85			Member of CSA Congress
Campbell, Larry		Ent	15			45	
Campbell, Lewis Davis		Congr	10				FF 32
Campbell, Martin		Ent	15			45	
Campbell, Mary		Ent	35		50	95	Miss Am. 1922-23
Campbell, Naomi		Model	20	22	28	45	
Campbell, Neve		Ent	20			45	Actress. 'Scream', 'Party of Five' SP 65
Campbell, Patrick, Mrs.	1865-1940	Ent	35	60		75	Vintage Stage Actress (Beatrice)
Campbell, Philip P.	1862-1944	Congr	12				Kansas
Campbell, Tisha		Ent	13			40	
Campbell, William (Bill)		Ent	15	25	30	50	SP As Rocketeer 35. Star Trek SP 20
Campbell, William Bowen	1807-1867	Civ War	50	65	103		Union Gen., Congress TN
Campbell-Bannerman, Henry	1836-1908	HOS	40	72	108	85	Br. Prime Min.
Campion, Jane		Celeb	10			15	Film industry
Campora, Giuseppe		Opera	10			40	It. Tenor, Opera
Camus, Albert	1913-1960	Author	75	308	737		Nobel. Poet, Philosopher. AManS (Poem) 595
Canary, David	1938-	Ent	15			25	Actor; Emmy
Canby, Edward R. Sprigg	1817-1873	Civ War	91	260	598		Union Gen. ALS '64 330
Cander, John		Comp	20	40		55	Pop Music
Candler, Asa Griggs		Bus	475	1275		595	Fndr. of Coca Cola
Candler, Warren Akin		Clergy	25	35	50		
Candlish, Robert Smith		Clergy	10	15	25	35	
Candy, John	1950-1994	Ent	54	74	102	112	Comedian.
Canetti, Elia		Author	80	225	350		Bulg. -Br. Nobel Literature
Canfield, Jack		Celeb	10			15	Med. expert
Canham, Erwin		Jrnalist	10	20			Christian Science Monitor
Caniff, Milton	1907-1988	Comics	40	54	138	215	'Terry & the Pirates' & 'Steve Canyon'
Caniglia, Maria		Opera	25			88	Opera. Dramatic Sopr.
Canned Heat		Music	125			560	Rock group
Cannell, Stephen J.		Ent	10	10		10	TV Prod.
Canning, Charles John	1812-1862	HOS	50		65	62	Governor-Gen. & 1st Viceroy of India
Canning, Effie I.		Author	55		300		AManS 5000
Canning, George	1770-1827	HOS	55	155	145		Prime Min. Served only 3 Months.
Cannon, Annie Jump	1863-1941	Sci			100		Great Woman Astronomer
Cannon, Chris C		Congr	10				Member US Congress
Cannon, Dyan		Ent	15	14	24	44	Actress
Cannon, Frank J.		Congr	10			10	Sen. UT
Cannon, George Q.		Congr	50	140	200		Utah's 1st Congressman
Cannon, Howard W.		Congr	10			15	Sen. NV

NAME	DATES	CATEGORY	SIG	LS/DS	ALS	SP	COMMENTS
Cannon, Jos. G. 'Uncle Joe'		Congr	20	40	95	40	Spkr. of the House
Cannon, Martha H., Dr.		Sci	25	30	60	30	
Cannon, Nick		Ent	15			45	
Canova, Antonio	1757-1822	Artist	85	250	612		It. Sculptor. Classical Revival
Canova, Diana		Ent	10	10	15	22	
Canova, Judy		Ent	32	38	41	68	Singer-Comedienne
Cantelli, Guido		Cond		500			
Cantey, James	1818-1874	Civ War	80		196		CSA Gen.
Cantinflas	1911-1995	Ent	33			87	
Canton, Frank (Joe Horner)	1849-1927	West	200	776			Western lawman
Cantor, Eddie	1892-1964	Ent	66	147		177	Early Comed., Singer. Vaude., Films, Radio
Cantor, Eric C		Congr	10				Member US Congress
Cantrell, Blu		Ent	13			40	
Cantrell, Jerry		Music	10			25	Music. Guitar, Vocals 'Alice in Chains'
Cantrell, Lana		Ent	10	10	15	10	
Cantwell, Maria		Congr	10				US Senate (D-WA)
Canutt, Yakima		Ent	34	42	45	66	AA. Legendary Stuntman & Dir.
Capa, Robert	1913-1954	Photog	250	350		650	War Photographer
Capers, Ellison	1837-1903	Civ War	88	166	267		CSA Gen.
Capers, Ellison (WD)	1837-1908	Civ War	130	325	630		CSA Gen.
Capers, Virginia	1925-2004	Ent	20	25	30	45	Tony Award-winning Am. actress.
Caperton, William		Mil	25			50	Adm. WWI
Capito, Shelley Moore C.		Congr	10				Member US Congress
Capka, Carol		Ent	10	10	10	20	
Caplin, Mortimer		Celeb	15	25	30	25	Quotes
Capon, Robert F.		Clergy	10	15	20	15	
Capone, Al		Crime	4227	16917		14600	Gangster
Capote, Truman	1924-1984	Author	132	435	511	288	Novels, Short Story Writer
Capp, Al		Comics	85	160		250	Li'l Abner, S comic strip 500; sketch 450
Capper, Arthur	1865-1951	Congr	12	25		30	Sen. KS
Capps, Lois C		Congr	10				Member US Congress
Capra, Frank	1897-1991	Ent	25	155		98	AA Film Dir. TLS Ltr/Poem 450
Caprice		Ent	17			50	
Capshaw, Jessica		Ent	15			45	
Capshaw, Kate		Ent	20	30	35	50	Actress
Captain & Tennile		Ent	20	25	30	40	
Capuano, Michael E. C		Congr	10				Member US Congress
Capucine	1931-1990	Ent	25	30	70	120	Fr. actress-model; 'Pink Panther'
Caraway, Hattie	1878-1950	Congr	25	55	35	35	1st Woman US Sen., AR
Carberry, John J., Card.		Clergy	50	65	80	80	
Cardigan, 7th Earl Brudenell		Mil	85	175	250	250	Br. Gen. Charge of Light Brigade
Cardin, Benjamin L. C		Congr	10				Member US Congress
Cardinale, Claudia		Ent	20			40	Actress
Cardoza, Dennis A. C		Congr	10				Member US Congress
Cardozo, Benjamin N.	1870-1938	Sup Crt	138	272	424	546	
Carell, Steve		Ent	15			45	
Carere, Christine		Ent	10			20	Actress
Carey, Drew	1958-	Ent	25	40		50	Comedian-Actor
Carey, Harry Jr.	1921-	Ent	20	20	25	55	Cowboy actor
Carey, Harry Sr.	1878-1947	Ent	122	110	175	483	
Carey, Hugh L.		Gov	10	15		15	Governor NY
Carey, MacDonald		Ent	20	25	30	60	Days of Our Lives' Star. 50s-70's Movies
Carey, Mariah		Music	25	65		65	Singer
Carey, Michele		Ent	10			25	

NAME	DATES	CATEGORY	SIG	LS/DS	ALS	SP	COMMENTS
Carey, Ron		Ent	10	15	20	25	Comedianne
Cargill, Henson		Cntry Mus	10			18	Skip a Rope #1
Carias Andino, Tiburcio		HOS	40	125		45	Pres. Honduras
Carl XIV Johan	1763-1844	Royal	150	580			King Sweden
Carl XV	1826-1872	Royal	125	425			King of Sweden & Nor. from 1859
Carl XVI Gustaf	1946-	Royal	55	150			King Sweden
Carl, Marion		WWII	35	50	75	150	ACE, WWII, 1st Marine Ace. 18. 5 kills
Carle, Frankie		Music	15			42	Big Band Leader
Carleton, Guy, Sir (Baron)	1724-1808	Rev War	250	583	800		Br. Cmdr. -in-Chief
Carleton, James H.	1814-1873	Civ War	50	86	110		Union Gen. LS '63 825
Carleton, Will	1845-1912	Author	35	50	75	75	Ir. Novels
Carlin, George	1937-2008	Ent	20	40	45	60	Standup Comedian
Carlin, Lynn	1938-	Ent	10	15	20	35	Oscar Nom. Best Supporting Actress Oscar, 'Faces'
Carlin, William Passmore	1829-1903	Civ War	72	275	192		Union Brig. Gen.
Carlisle, 7th Earl	1802-1864	Pol	25	45	115		George W. F. Howard. Poet, Orator, Viceroy of Ir., BR. Pol. & Statesman
Carlisle, Belinda		Music	15	20	25	42	'Go-Gos Lead Singer
Carlisle, John Griffin		Sen/Cab	15	25	35	30	Spkr. Sen. KY, Sec. Treas.
Carlisle, Kitty	1910-2007	Ent	30	40	40	45	What's My Line' Regular.
Carlisle, Mary	1912-	Ent	25	32	38	77	Actress
Carlo Alberto	1798-1849	Royal	45	150	375		King of Sardinia
Carlos, Juan, King of Spain	1938-	Royal				285	King of Spain
Carlotta (Marie-Charlotte-Amalie)		Royal	340	770	1700		Empress of Mex. Became Insane
Carlsen, Capt. Kurt		Celeb	20	55	125	45	
Carlson, Frank		Congr	10	18	25	15	Governor, Sen. KS
Carlson, Fred		Artist	10			10	'Lunch Box King'
Carlson, Kelly		Ent	15			45	
Carlson, Richard		Ent	15			42	Film Leading Man. 40s-50's
Carlucci, Frank		Celeb	10			15	Pol. celebrity
Carlyle, Robert	1961-	Ent	10			30	Actor
Carlyle, Russ		Band	10			15	Bandleader
Carlyle, Thomas	1795-1881	Author	76	175	337	235	Br. Philo., Social Critic, Essayist. AQS 150-300
Carmack, Chris		Ent	15			45	
Carman, Tex J.		Cntry Mus	10			20	
Carmen, Jean	1913-1993	Ent	15	20	25	45	
Carmer, Carl		Author	20	45	175		
Carmichael, Hoagy	1899-1981	Comp	55	130	425	141	Stardust'. AMusQS 250, 320, 375
Carmichael, Oliver C.		Educ	20	35		25	Pres. U Alabama
Carnarvon, Henry 4th Earl		Statsmn	15	35	80		Created Fed. Dominion Canada
Carne, Judy		Ent	10	12	15	25	Br. Comedienne.
Carnegie, Andrew	1835-1919	Indust	216	582	733	796	TLS/Cont 9800, S Stock Cert. 24000-125000
Carnegie, Dale	1888-1955	Author	45	115		205	'How To Win Friends & Influence People'
Carnes, Kim		Music	15			30	Singer
Carney, Art	1918-2003	Ent	25	106	65	109	Norton on 'The Honeymooners'. Oscar Winner
Carney, Robert B.		Mil	12	20	35	48	Eisenhower CNO
Carnot, Lazare N. M.		Fr Rev	110	250	325		Min. of War. Exiled
Carnot, Marie Francois Sadi	1837-1894	HOS		218	190		Pres. France 1887-1894. Assass.
Carnovsky, Morris		Ent	20		40	60	Char. Actor
Carol I	1839-1914	Royal					King Roumania & Queen Elizabeth. 2 SP's 1250
Carol II		Royal	75	160			
Carol, Cindy	1945-	Ent	10			30	Actress. Played 'Gidget'
Carol, Sue (Ladd)		Ent	10	14	18	40	Silent Screen. Wife & Agent of Alan Ladd
Caroline	1776-1841	Royal		90	175		2nd Queen of Maximilian I (Bavaria)
Caroline	1768-1821	Royal	95	150	342		Estranged Queen George IV England

NAME	DATES	CATEGORY	SIG	LS/DS	ALS	SP	COMMENTS
Caroline of Anspach		Royal	335	450	1000		Queen of George II (Eng.)
Carolla, Adam		Ent	17			50	
Caron, George R.	1919-1995	WWII	33	40	118	75	Enola Gay Tail gunner WWII.
Caron, Leslie	1931-	Ent	15	30		39	Fr. Dancer-Actress
Carosio, Margherita		Opera	15			85	Opera
Carpenter, Edward	1844-1929	Author	25		60		
Carpenter, Francis Bicknell	1830-1890	Artist	50				Emancipation Proclamation Engraving DS 3500
Carpenter, Jennifer		Ent	16			48	
Carpenter, John		Ent	10			25	Film Dir. -Writer
Carpenter, Joseph Estlin		Clergy	40	50	60	75	
Carpenter, Karen	1950-1983	Ent	229	534		280	Singer.
Carpenter, Mary-Chapin		Ent	25			40	Award Winning Country Singer-Comp.
Carpenter, Matthew H.		Congr	10	15	30	35	Sen. WI
Carpenter, Richard		Ent	15	20	25	30	Performer-Songwriter
Carpenter, Scott	1925-	Space	50	113	125	186	Mercury 7. 2nd Am. To orbit Earth & 4th in space
Carpenter, W. Boyd, Bish.		Clergy	10	20	30		
Carpenter, William B.		Expl	10	35	60		Br. Physiologist
Carpenter, William S.		Mil	12	15	40	30	Viet Nam Hero
Carpenters, The		Ent	320	568		795	Richard & Karen
Carper, Thomas		Congr	10				US Senate (D-DE)
Carr, Eugene Asa	1830-1910	Civ War	52	162	200	220	Union Gen. CMH, ALS '63 2200. Indian Fighter
Carr, Gerald P.		Space	20			35	
Carr, Jane	1950-	Ent	10			20	Actress
Carr, Jerry		Space	15			40	
Carr, Joseph Bradford	1828-1895	Civ War	50	116	150		Union Gen.
Carr, Tommy		Ent	20			35	
Carr, Vicki		Ent	10	15	20	30	Singer, Recording Artist. Award Winner
Carradine, David		Ent	10	20		38	Actor. 'Kung Fu'
Carradine, John		Ent	60	125	150	128	Versatile Actor. Many Chars. Many Films
Carradine, Keith		Ent	15			25	Stage, Screen, TV Star
Carradine, Robert		Ent	15			25	14 Page DS 150. 'Revenge of Nerds'
Carranza, Emilio	1905-1928	Aero	500				Mexican "Lone Eagle" (rare)
Carranza, Venustiano		HOS	52	205	400		Revolutionary Pres. Mex. Murdered
Carrel, Dr. Alexis		Sci	75	220	300	210	Nobel Med.
Carrell, Steve		Ent	25			55	
Carreno, Terresa		Comp	25		118	90	Venez. Conductor-Pianist-Singer. Gottschalk Pupil
Carrera, Barbara		Ent	10			36	Actress
Carreras, Jose		Opera	25	40		65	Operatic Tenor
Carrere, Christine		Ent	10			20	Fr. Actress
Carrere, Tia		Ent	15			35	
Carrey, Jim		Ent	32			77	Comedian-Actor
Carrigain, Philip		Law	20	50			Surveyed NH, Named Granite St.
Carrillo, Leo	1880-1961	Ent	42	58	65	120	TLS/Cont 150. 'Pancho'
Carrington, Henry Beebee	1824-1912	Civ War	55	125	140		Union Gen.
Carrol, Eddie		Ent	15			40	Voice of Jimney Cricket
Carroll, Charles	1737-1832	Rev War	325	787	851		Signer. Important Rev. War ALS 8500
Carroll, Daniel	1730-1796	Rev War	208	402	655		Cont. Congress, Constitution Signer/Maryland
Carroll, Diahann	1935-	Ent	15	20	28	35	Singer-Actress
Carroll, Earl		Ent	85	105	210	190	
Carroll, Eddie		Ent	18			53	
Carroll, Georgia		Ent	10			25	
Carroll, Gladys Hasty	1904-1999	Author	15				US Novels
Carroll, John		Ent	10			40	Singing-Strutting Leading Man.
Carroll, John Lee		Gov	10		30		Governor MD

NAME	DATES	CATEGORY	SIG	LS/DS	ALS	SP	COMMENTS
Carroll, Julian M.		Gov	10		35		Governor KY
Carroll, Lee		Celeb	10			15	Comedian
Carroll, Leo G.		Ent	53	120		220	Br. Actor. 'Topper', 'U. N. C. L. E. '
Carroll, Lewis		Author					SEE: Dodgson, Charles L.
Carroll, Lisa Hart		Ent	10	12	15	25	
Carroll, Madeleine		Ent	54	150		138	Beautiful Brit. Star of 30s-40's
Carroll, Mickey		Ent	10			30	Wizard of Oz Munchkin
Carroll, Nancy		Ent	25	35	45	162	
Carroll, Samuel Sprigg	1832-1893	Civ War	62	92	140		Union Gen.
Carroll, William		Mil	35		90		Gen. TN Militia, Gov. TN 1821
Carroll, William H.	1810-1868	Civ War	75	176	302		CSA Gen.
Carrott, Jasper		Celeb	10			15	Comedian
Carryl, Guy Wetmore		Author	10	15	25		
Cars, The		Music	95			350	S Album 350
Carson, Benjamin Dr.		Med	10			15	Pediatric neurosurgeon of world-renown
Carson, Brad C.		Congr	10				Member US Congress
Carson, Christopher Kit	1809-1868	Frontier	2958			4667	Union Gen, Scout, Indian Agt., Trapper, Explr.
Carson, Frank		Celeb	10			15	Comedian
Carson, Jack		Ent	25			185	
Carson, John		Mil	25			40	Gen. WWI
Carson, Johnny	1925-2005	Ent	82	270	250	222	Comedian. Tonight Show Host
Carson, Julia C		Congr	10				Member US Congress
Carson, Leonard 'Kit'		WWII	20	25	42	40	ACE, WWII; 18. 5 kills
Carson, Rachel	1907-1964	Author	75	240	428	275	ALS/Cont 1650. S 1st Ed. 'Silent Spring' 1000. AQS 350-700
Carson, Sunset		Ent	20	25		55	Actor; Westerns
Carstares, William	1649-1715	Clergy			120		Chaplin to William the Third
Carter, Ann S.		Aero	25	40			1st Woman Helicopter Pilot
Carter, Ben		Ent	100			200	Vaude. partner of Mantan Moreland
Carter, Benny	1907-	Music	40	60	100	98	Jazz. Alto Sax, Trumpet. Arranger
Carter, Betty		Music	45			200	Lionel Hampton Vocalist
Carter, Billy		Celeb	15	20	25	25	Pres. Carter's Brother
Carter, Boake		Radio	10	20	35	40	Radio Commentator-Vintage
Carter, Carlene		Cntry Mus	10			35	Grammy Nominee
Carter, Chris		Ent	10		25	30	Creator 'X Files'
Carter, Dixie		Ent	10			25	Actress. TV Star. 'Designing Women'
Carter, Elliott		Comp	32	175	202		Pulitzer Pr. 'The Minotaur'
Carter, Helen		Cntry Mus	10			20	
Carter, Helena Bonham		Ent	17	30		44	Br. Actress.
Carter, Hodding		Pol	10		12	10	White House Aide
Carter, Howard	1874-1939	Archaeol	1295		1600		Found King Tut's Tomb. S 'The Tomb of Tut Ankh Amen' Vol. II. 1st Ed. 9500
Carter, Janis	1913-1994	Ent	15	25	35	52	
Carter, Jimmy	1924-	Pres	82	238	887	90	Books S 65-200. War-dte ALS 3000.
Carter, Jimmy & Rosalyn		Pres	100			295	
Carter, Jimmy (As Pres.)		Pres	125	867	6674	185	TLS(Cont.) 3000
Carter, John Carpenter	1837-1864	Civ War	267				CSA gen, KIA Franklin, TN
Carter, John R. C		Congr	10				Member US Congress
Carter, Leslie, Mrs.	1862-1937	Ent	32	75	90	130	Stage & Films; "The Am. Sarah Bernhardt"
Carter, Lillian		Celeb	12	25		25	Pres. Carter's Mother
Carter, Lynda		Ent	15	25	25	40	Actress. 'Wonder Woman'.
Carter, Manly L. 'Sonny'	1947-1991	Space	50	100		200	Space Shuttle Discovery. Killed '91 in air crash.
Carter, Mother Maybelle		Cntry Mus	40			80	
Carter, Nell	1948-2003	Ent	25			110	Actress; comedianne

NAME	DATES	CATEGORY	SIG	LS/DS	ALS	SP	COMMENTS
Carter, Nick		Music	10			30	
Carter, Robert	1633-1732	Colonial		1400			VA official & Landholder
Carter, Rosalynn		1st Lady	37	90	130	75	
Carter, Rubin		Celeb	10			15	Pol. celebrity
Carter, Samuel Powhatan	1819-1891	Civ War	50	142	210		Union Gen.
Carter, Sarah		Ent	12			35	
Carter, Stephen L.		Law	10			15	Pol. writer
Carter, Thomas H.		Congr	10		35	25	Sen. MT. 1st Repr. from State
Carter, Wilf	1904-1996	Cntry Mus	20			35	Canadian AKA Montana Slim
Carteret, George	1610-1680	Mil		1600			Br. Naval Off. Named New Jersey
Carteri, Rosanna		Music	15			35	Classical musician
Carter-Scott, Cheri		Author	10			15	Motivational training
Cartland, Barbara, Dame		Author	10	25	70	75	Br. Novels. Over 500 Romantic Novels
Cartwright, Angela		Ent	10	15	15	30	'Lost in Space' TV Script S 40
Cartwright, Lionel		Cntry Mus	10			30	Leap of Faith #1
Cartwright, Nancy		Ent	20			38	Voice of Bart Simpson. Signs as 'Bart'
Cartwright, Veronica		Ent	10			22	Child Actress; Older Sister of Angela
Carty, John J.	1861-1932	Sci	60	150	275	150	Telephone Pioneer. AT&T
Caruso, Anthony		Ent	25	29	70	57	
Caruso, David	1958-	Ent	15	35		40	Actor
Caruso, Enrico	1873-1921	Ent	399	385	989	952	Signed Caric. Self-Portr. Sket 650; SP w/Sket 2250
Caruso, Enrico, Jr.	1904-1986	Ent	25			55	Actor Son of Caruso Sr.
Caruthers, Robert L.	1800-1882	Congr	12				Repr. TN, CW Gov. TN
Carvel, Elbert M.		Gov	10	15			Governor DE
Carver, Bill		Author	10			12	Mountain humorist
Carver, Geo. Washington	1864-1943	Sci	174	404	746	3495	HOF, Botanist, Educator. Intl Fame
Carvey, Dana		Ent	15	25		40	Comedian-Actor. 'Sat. Night Live'
Carville, Edward P.		Congr	12	15	40	40	Sen., Governor NV
Carville, James		Celeb	10			20	Pol. celebrity, commentator
Cary, Annie Louise		Opera	35	40	275	150	Opera. 1st Famous Am. Mezzo.
Cary, Jeremiah E.	1803-1888	Congr	10				Repr. NY
Cary, Phoebe		Author	10	15			Am. Poet/Sister Alice
Cary, Samuel Fenton		Congr	10		30	25	MOC OH
Casadesus, Robert, Dr.		Comp	45		100	100	Fr. Concert Pianist-Comp.
Casals, Pablo	1876-1973	Music	96	105	215	338	Spanish Cellist, Cond., Comp. AMusQS 400
Casanovo, Giacomo		Author	500	600	915		Adventurer, Gambler, Spy
Case, A. Ludlow	1813-1888	Civ War	50	95			Adm. North Atlantic Fleet
Case, Clifford P.		Congr	10	15		10	Sen., MOC NJ
Case, Ed C		Congr	10				Member US Congress
Case, Francis H.		Congr	10	25		15	Sen., MOC IA
Case, Jerome I.		Bus	35	60	155		Case Tractors & Farm Implements
Case, Kenny		Music			35		Tenor of 4 Ink Spots
Case, Norman S.		Gov	10	25			Governor RI
Casella, Alfredo		Comp	35	130	250		Pianist, Conductor
Casella, Max	1967-	Ent	10			25	Actor
Casellato, Renzo		Opera	20			50	Opera. Tenor
Caselotti, Adriana		Ent	10	15	35	40	Voice of Snow White
Casement, John S.	1829-1909	Civ War	45	75			Union Gen., 103rd Ohio
Casey, Bernie		Ent	25			140	Movie-TV-Artist
Casey, James S.		Civ War	50	125			1st Lt. Won CMH in Battle vs 'Crazy Horse'
Casey, Silas	1807-1882	Civ War	50	105	160		Union Gen. ALS '63 550
Cash, Johnny		Cntry Mus	50	583	1500	336	CW singer; handwritten lyrics 8500
Cash, Johnny & June Carter		Cntry Mus	100			450	Husband/Wife Legends
Cash, June Carter	d. 2003	Cntry Mus	25	65		65	Singer. Carter Family

NAME	DATES	CATEGORY	SIG	LS/DS	ALS	SP	COMMENTS
Cash, Kellye		Celeb	10		12	20	Miss Am. 1987; actress
Cash, Rosanne		Ent	10	12	15	45	Actress
Cash, Tommy		Cntry Mus	10		10	20	
Casimir-Perier, Jean Paul P.	1847-1907	HOS	50		150		Pres. France 1894-95
Casper (cast)		Ent				100	Four Cast Members
Casper, Billy		Ent	16			47	
Casper, John H.		Space	15		95	40	
Cass, Lewis	1782-1866	Cab	50	110	152		Jackson Sec. War, Sen. MI
Cass, Peggy		Ent	15			40	
Cassatt, Mary		Artist	350	685	1803		ALS/Cont 5,000
Cassavetes, John	1929-1989	Ent	28	240	75	55	Actor, Film Dir.
Cassidy, Bryan		Celeb	10			15	Pol. celebrity
Cassidy, David		Ent	15			30	
Cassidy, Jack	1927-1976	Ent	30	68		100	Actor
Cassidy, Joanna	1944-	Ent	15	25	25	55	Actress.
Cassidy, Shaun		Ent	10			30	
Cassidy, Ted	1932-1979	Ent	222	275	325	441	SP as Lurch 650
Cassin, Jimmy		Comp	10	40			Songwriter
Cassin, Rene		Statsmn	30	75	175	45	Fndr. UNESCO, Nobel Peace
Cassini, Oleg	1913-2006	Bus	20	35	50	55	Fashion Designer
Cassizzi, Vic		Author	10			20	Religious historical Novels
Casson, Mel		Comics	10			20	Redeye
Castagna, Bruna		Opera	20			100	Opera.
Castanzo, Jack		Music	10			28	Jazz Musician
Castelluccio, Federico		Ent	15			60	Furio Giunta, Sopranos
Castelnuovo-Tedesco, M.		Comp	65		300	125	Versatile Comp. All Fields. AMusQS 125-325
Casteneda, Jorge Ubico		HOS	25	75			
Castle, Irene		Ent	90		115	95	
Castle, Irene & Vernon		Ent	125			475	Dance Couple
Castle, Keith- Lee		Ent	10	15	15	20	Br. actor
Castle, Michael N. C		Congr	10				Member US Congress
Castle, Peggy	1927-1973	Ent	25			65	Actress. Often "the other woman" in B-movies
Castle, Vernon		Ent	50			150	
Castle, William		Ent	205			175	Famed B movie Dir., Prod.
Castle-Hughes, Keisha		Ent	13			40	
Castlereagh, R. Stewart, Visc.	1769-1822	Statsmn	25	142	250		Min. War vs Napol. Suicide
Castro, Emilio		Clergy	25	30	35	35	
Castro, Fidel	1927-	HOS	465	1215	2139	1919	Communist Premier of Cuba
Castro, Raul		Mil	25			45	Younger Brother of Fidel
Castro, Raul H.		Gov	10				Governor AZ
Cates, Clifton B.		Mil	10	25	55	20	
Cates, Phoebe		Ent	10			50	Actress
Catesby, Robert	1573-1605	Crime		1065			Involved in Guy Fawkes Gunpowder Conspiracy
Cathcart, Wm. Schaw Sir		Rev War	80	125			Cmdr. Br. Legion in America
Cather, Willa	1873-1947	Author	166	853	1242	550	Novels. ALS/Cont 2, 250
Catherine I (Rus)	1684-1727	Royal	440	1733	3567		
Catherine II ('The Great')	1729-1796	Royal	438	1366	2675		Empress Russia from 1762-96.
Catherine, Marshall		Clergy	25	30	50	50	
Catherwood, Mary		Author	10	15	20		
Catlett, Mary Jo	1938-	Ent	10			20	Actress. Pearl Gallagher on 'Diff'rent Strokes'
Catlett, Walter		Ent	10	15	25	25	
Catlin, George	1796-1872	Artist	200	452	2200		Travel Books. Indian Scenes
Catlin, Isaac		Civ War	50	95	330		Union Gen., CMH
Catron, John	1779-1865	Jurist	175				Supreme Ct. Justice

NAME	DATES	CATEGORY	SIG	LS/DS	ALS	SP	COMMENTS
Catt, Carrie Chapman	1859-1947	Fem	72	390	418	225	Suffragette Leader. Feminist.
Catterson, Robert Francis	1835-1914	Civ War	48	102	190		Union Gen.
Catton, Bruce		Author	30	70	125	75	Historian, Editor. Pulitzer
Cattrall, Kim		Ent	15			45	Samantha Jones, Sex in the City
Caulfield, Emma		Ent	15			45	
Caulfield, Jo		Celeb	10			15	Comedienne
Caulfield, Joan	1922-1991	Ent	20			78	Actress. 40s Ingenue.
Cavalieri Muratore, Lina		Opera	50			220	Opera
Cavallaro, Carmen		Band	15			35	Big Band Leader-Pianist
Cavanagh, Paul		Ent	10			20	
Cavanaugh, Hobart	1886-1950	Ent	15	18	20	62	Film debut in 'San Francisco Nights' (1928)
Cavanaugh, Hobert		Ent				40	Actor
Cavell, Edith	1865-1915	Sci	250	450	750		Br. Nurse. Allied Heroine. Court Martialed. Shot
Cavendish, William	1720-1764	HOS	100	210	355		English Prime Min. Duke of Devonshire.
Cavendish-Bentinck, William H.	1738-1809	HOS	60	108	180		
Cavett, Dick		Ent	15	20	25	25	Late Nite TV Host; Writer
Cavour, Camillo, Count	1810-1818	HOS	125	290			Architect of Italy's Unification. P. M.
Cayce, Edgar		Author	70	193			Am. Rural Healer, Seer
Cayvan, Georgia	1858-1906	Ent	20	25	35	65	Popular 1880s-90s stage actress & vocalist
Ceausecu, Nicolae		HOS	50	335		110	Pres. Romania. Assass.
Cech, Thomas R., Dr.		Sci	20	35		25	Nobel Chemistry
Cecil, Edg. Algernon, Lord	1864-1958	Diplo	35	45	185		Statesman. Pres. League of Nations. Nobel Peace
Cecil, Robert A.	1830-1903	HOS	40	45	72		Br. Prime Min.
Cedric the Entertainer		Ent	18			55	
Celeste		Ent				34	Porn Queen
Celine, Louis Ferd.		Author	175		912		(Destouches) 1894-1961. Fr. Physician, Novels
Celler, Emanuel		Congr	10	20		10	MOC NY
Cellini, Benvenuto		Artist	1000	4800	13500		Florentine Goldsmith, Sculptor
Cenker, Robert		Space	10			20	
Cera, Michael		Ent				40	Actor
Cerf, Bennett	1898-1971	Author	15	20	30	30	Random House Ed., Author, Game Show Guest
Cermak, Anton J.		Pol	25	40	95	125	Assass. Mayor of Chicago
Cernan, Eugene A.		Space	50	82	100	146	Moonwalker
Cervantes, Miguel de		Author	10000	15000			Sp. Novels, Poet. Don Quixote
Cesky, Charles J.		WWII	10	22	38	35	ACE, WWII; 8. 5 kills
Cetywayo, King of Zulu	d. 1884	Royal	375				King of the Zulus
Cezanne, Paul	1839-1906	Artist	1250	2500	8200		Fr. Impressionist to Cubism
Chabas, Paul Emile		Artist	35	60	135		
Chabert, Lacey		Ent	15			48	Child Actress
Chabot, Phillipe de Brion, Comte		Mil	1750				1480-1543. Fr. Cmdr. In Chief
Chabot, Steve C		Congr	10				Member US Congress
Chabrier, Alexis Emmanuel		Comp	70	255	408		Fr. Opera, Orchestral, Piano
Chadwick, George Whitefield	1854-1931	Comp			95		'Tam O'Shanter'
Chadwick, James, Sir		Sci	65	215	450		Nobel Phys. Disc. Neutron,. ALS/Cont 1000
Chadwick, June		Ent	10			25	Brit. Actress. 'Riptide'
Chafee, Lincoln		Congr	10				US Senate (R-RI)
Chaffee, Adna R.	1884-1941	Mil	25	50	80	125	Gen. Boxer Rebellion, Father of Armored Force
Chaffee, Roger		Space	242	380	546	802	D. Aboard Apollol I, 1-27-67
Chagall, Marc	1887-1985	Artist	219	286	684	524	Color Repro S 225-295-395-650-1095; Sketch 1550
Chaka Kahn		Music	10			36	Singer
Chakiris, George		Ent	12	15	25	40	
Chalia, Rosalia		Ent	25	40	65		
Chaliapin, Feodor	1873-1938	Opera	103	174	500	254	Opera. Rus. Basso.
Chalker, Jack		Author	10	20	40	30	

NAME	DATES	CATEGORY	SIG	LS/DS	ALS	SP	COMMENTS
Challenger mission crew		Space				7500	Signed by all 7; all perished 1986
Chalmers, James R.	1831-1898	Civ War	135	452			CSA Gen.
Chalmers, James R. (WD)	1831-1898	Civ War	250				CSA Gen.
Chalmers, Thomas	1780-1847	Clergy	55	69	90	90	Theologian, Philan.
Chalon, Alfred E.	1780-1860	Artist	200		375		Portr. of Q. Victoria Appearing on 1st Stamp
Chamberlain, Austen, Sir	1863-1937	Statsmn	30	85	100	100	Br. Pol. Nobel Peace Pr. 1925
Chamberlain, Daniel		Gov	50	125			Carpetbag Gov. SC
Chamberlain, Joseph A.	1836-1914	Pol	60	85	85	90	Statesman, Nobel Peace Pr. Colonial Sec.
Chamberlain, Joshua L.	1828-1914	Civ War	525	750	1152	15000	ALS/Gettysburg 3500. Union Off, Gov ME, S CW CDV 15000
Chamberlain, Neville	1869-1940	HOS	124	567	625	180	PM England; "Peace in our time"
Chamberlain, Owen, Dr		Sci	25	35	75	30	Nobel Physics
Chamberlain, Richard		Ent	15	15	30	35	Actor. 'Dr. Kildare' & many mini-series
Chamberlain, S. J.		Mil	10	30	50		
Chamberlain, Thomas		Civ War		1380	1093		Brother to Joshua, 20th Maine
Chamberlaine, William		Mil	10		35	35	Gen. WWI
Chamberlin, Clarence		Aero	50	188	222	242	Record Non-Stop Flight NY-Ger.
Chamberlin, Jimmy		Music	10			30	Music. Drummer 'Smashing Pumpkins'
Chambers Brothers (All)		Music	50			225	Rock Group
Chambers, Alexander	1832-1888	Civ War	50	105	180		Union Gen.
Chambers, Henry Cousins	1823-1871	Civ War	50	130			Member of CSA Congress
Chambers, Marilyn		Ent	15	15	22	35	Adult Film Star of 70s.
Chambers, Robert Wm.	1874-1958	Poet	10	15	102		Canadian Poet
Chambers, Whittaker		Jrnalist	25	50	250	25	Charged Alger Hiss as Communist
Chambliss, John Randolph Jr.	1833-1864	Civ War	326				CSA Gen.
Chambliss, Saxby		Congr	10				US Senate (R-GA)
Chaminade, Cecile	1857-1944	Comp	85	195	212	300	AMusQS 125
Champion, Gower		Ent	20	30	60	45	Successful Film-Stage Choreographer-Dancer
Champion, Gower & Marge		Ent	30			85	Dance Partner Legends
Champion, Marge		Ent	10	15	20	25	Dancer-Actress.
Champlin, Stephen Gardner	1827-1864	Civ War	102	162		184	Union Gen.
Champollion, Jean-Francois	1790-1832	Archaeol			2695		Fr. Translator: Egyptian Hieroglyphics 1st Time
Chan, Genie		Comics	10			35	Conan
Chan, Jackie		Ent	20			76	Karate-Judo Films
Chanan, Gerald	1943-	Bus	10			20	Steel Magnet
Chancellor, John	1927-1996	Jrnalist	20	35	50	40	Radio-TV News & Commentator
Chandler, A. B. 'Happy'		Sen/Gov	15	35		50	Sen., Gov. KY. Baseball Comm.
Chandler, Christopher		Celeb	10		40		
Chandler, Dorothy 'Buff'		Bus	10	20	45	25	Buffums Dept. Stores
Chandler, George		Ent	15			58	Char. Actor
Chandler, Helen		Ent	94			200	
Chandler, Jeff	1918-1961	Ent	60	75	150	179	Major Radio-Film Star.
Chandler, Joseph Ripley		Congr	15		35		Repr. PA 1843. Editor US Gazette
Chandler, Kyle		Ent	13		40		
Chandler, Lane		Ent	20		40		
Chandler, Norman		Bus	15	35	75	30	L. A. Times
Chandler, Otis		Bus	20	45	95	40	Fndr. L. A. Times
Chandler, Raymond		Author	260	887	975		Novels. Detective Fiction LS Cont. 2950
Chandler, William E.		Congr	20	38	65		Sen. NH, Sec. Navy
Chandler, Zachariah		Congr	25	35	50		Sen. NH, Sec. Int., Atty Gen
Chandrasekhar, Jay		Ent	13		40		
Chandrasekhar, Subrahmanyan		Sci	30	110	225		Nobel, Astrophysicist
Chandu the Magician		Ent	10		25	20	
Chanel, Coco		Bus	60	110	235	100	Fashion Designer, Perfumer

NAME	DATES	CATEGORY	SIG	LS/DS	ALS	SP	COMMENTS
Chaney, Lon, Jr.	1906-1973	Ent	516	557	500	1114	
Chaney, Lon, Sr.	1881-1930	Ent	1055			2362	Man of a 1000 Faces. SP in Char. 2000 & up
Chaney, Norman	1918-1936	Ent	185			595	Chubby in the Little Rascals
Chang		Ent	15				Chinese Giant
Chang, Franklin R.		Space	10			20	
Chang, Min-Chu	1909-1991	Sci	50		145		discoverer of 'In Vitro' Fertilization
Chang, Sarah		Music				120	Violinist
Channing, Carol		Ent	28	30		46	Unique Broadway Musical Star. 'Hello Dolly'
Channing, Stockard		Ent	10	15	25	38	Actress
Channing, William Ellery	1780-1842	Clergy	40	70	120		'Apostle of Unitarianism'
Channing, William Henry		Clergy	35	45	65	65	
Chantels		Music				210	Music group
Chantrey, Francis Sir	1781-1841	Artist			185		Sculptor
Chaparral, John & Paul		Cntry Mus	20			40	
Chapin, Edward Payson	1831-1863	Civ War	138	567			Union Gen.
Chapin, Harry		Comp	125	213		258	Singer-Songwriter
Chapin, Lauren		Ent	10			25	Child actress
Chaplin, Ben	1970-	Ent	10			25	Br. Actor
Chaplin, Charles, Sir	1889-1977	Ent	394	620	750	926	Legendary Film Comedian. BS (Auto-Bio)550
Chaplin, Geraldine		Ent	10	12	28	25	Actress-Daughter of Charlie.
Chaplin, Lita Grey	1908-1995	Ent	20	25	45	25	
Chaplin, Sydney	1885-1965	Ent	20	25	35	55	Half brother to Charles Chaplin
Chapman, Ben, Jr.		Ent	15			38	Actor. 'Creature From Black Lagoon' SP 75
Chapman, George Henry	1832-1882	Civ War	50	110	180		Union Gen.
Chapman, Graham		Ent	15	20	25	25	
Chapman, Leonard, Jr.		Mil	15	30		40	USMC Gen., WWII
Chapman, Marguerite		Ent	25			90	Vintage actress
Chapman, Mark David		Crime	100	155	230	210	John Lennon's assassin
Chapman, Oscar L.		Cab	20	20	30	35	Sec. Interior 1849
Chapman, Pat		Celeb	10			15	Curry Chef
Chapman, Philip K.		Space	15			25	
Chappell, Clovis G.		Clergy	20	25	30	30	
Chappell, William	1809-1888	Bus	20	45	110	35	Music Publisher
Chappelle, Dave		Ent	25			65	Comedian
Chaptal, Jean Antoine, Count	1756-1832	Napol	135	200			Chemist. Min. Agri., Interior
Charbonneau, Patricia		Ent	10			20	Actress.
Charcot, Jean Martin	1825-1893	Sci	125	288	839		Fr. Neurologist & Prof. of Pathological Anatomy
Charcot, Jean-Baptiste	1867-1936	Expl		100	135		Headed 2 Arctic Exped. s. Drowned/38 of his men
Charendoff, Tara		Ent	13			40	
Charisse, Cyd		Ent	15	20	25	42	Dancing Star
Charlemagne		Royal	75000				Price Estimate Only
Charles & Camilla		Royal				1800	
Charles & Diana		Royal	800	1592		2975	Prince & Princess of Windsor
Charles Albert (Sardinia)		Royal			225		Count of Savoy
Charles Edw. Stuart	1720-1788	Royal	110	362	1440		'The Young Pretender'; Jacobite Claiment
Charles Emmanuel I	1562-1630	Royal	595	900			The Great
Charles I (Eng)	1600-1649	Royal	558	1997	4000		Important DS (1642) 4500
Charles II & Samuel Pepys		Royal		1575			Signed by both
Charles II (Eng)	1630-1685	Royal	440	1377	3512		King Eng & Ireland. 'Merry Monarch'
Charles II (Sp)		Royal	275	395			
Charles in Charge		Ent				150	Cast singed
Charles IV (Sp)	1748-1819	Royal	185	518	762		Don Carlos. King of Sp. Forced to Abdicate
Charles IX (Fr)	1550-1574	Royal	295	1122	1700		King of France 1560-1574
Charles V (Charles I (Spain)		Royal	550	3467	5000		(Charles I & Juana DS 1500)

NAME	DATES	CATEGORY	SIG	LS/DS	ALS	SP	COMMENTS
Charles VI (Charles III {Sp})		Royal	375	1562			Holy Roman Emperor 1711-1740
Charles VIII	1470-1498	Royal		863			King of France
Charles X (Fr)	1757-1836	Royal	150	407	725		King of France.
Charles XIV John (Swe)		Royal	120	296	650		See also Bernadotte
Charles XV (Swe-Nor)		Royal	45	140	320		
Charles, Craig	1964-	Ent	10			20	Br. Comedian
Charles, Ernest		Comp	20	80			
Charles, Josh		Ent	15			30	Actor
Charles, Prince of Wales	1948-	Royal	775	842	1500	862	Philip Arthur George
Charles, Ray		Music	800				Blind Singer-Musician; Ex. Rare, Mostly forgeries
Charles, Suzette		Ent	10		15	20	Miss Am. 1984
Charlie's Angels		Celeb	65			200	Cast SP
Charlotte Sophia	1741-1818	Royal	145	275	452		Queen of George III (Eng)
Charlotte, Grand Duchess		Royal	25	75	180	55	Luxembourg
Charmed		Ent	65			160	Cast S
Charo		Ent	10	15	15	20	
Charpentier, Gustave	1860-1956	Comp	100	250	300	305	AMusQS 150-450-625-750
Charriere, Henri		Author		863			Papillon
Charteris, Leslie		Author	20	55	135	68	The Saint. FDC S 75
Charvet, David		Ent	12			35	Actor 'Baywatch'
Chase, Charley		Ent	104	240		219	Vintage Film Comedian
Chase, Cheryl		Ent	13			40	
Chase, Chevy		Ent	15	20	25	45	Actor-Comedian. SP 'Xmas Vacation' 38
Chase, Ilka		Ent	15	25	40	100	Author
Chase, Mary Ellen	1887-1973	Author	25	70	150	80	Educator, Essayist, Pulitzer Pr. "Harvey"
Chase, Salmon P.	1808-1873	Sup Crt	80	402	413	300	Chief Justice Supr. Ct. Lincoln's Sec. Treas.
Chase, Samuel	1741-1811	Rev War	407	2272	3255		Signer Dec. of Indepen.
Chase, William C.		Mil	10	20	35		
Chase, William Merritt	1849-1916	Artist	95				US Painter of Western Scenes
Chateaubriand, Francois R. de	1768-1848	Author	150	252	408		Fr. Novels, Dipl. Fndr. Fr. Romantic Movement
Chatterton, Ruth		Ent	35			139	
Chatwin, Justin		Ent	15			45	
Chauncey, Isaac	1772-1840	Mil	50	95	105		Am. Naval Off. Tripoli, War 1812
Chausson, Ernest		Comp	50	145	345		Fr. Opera, Symphonies
Chauvel, Henry, Sir		Mil	25	75			Aussie Gen. WWI
Chavez, Anna		Celeb	10			15	Media/TV personality
Chavez, Carlos		Comp	15	35	70	40	Mexican Conductor-Comp.
Chavez, Cesar E.	1927-1993	Labor	70	145		163	Migrant Labor Organizer. Social Activist
Chavez, Dennis		Congr	10	25		25	Sen NM. 1st Hispanic MOC & Sen.
Chavez, George A.		Aero	45	60	175	65	
Chavez, Linda		Celeb	10			25	1st Hispanic woman nom. To the US Cabinet.
Chawla, Kalpana		Space	100	335		275	Columbia Tragedy
Chayefsky, Paddy (Sidney)		Author	55	123	165	120	Plays, TV Dramas, Screenplays
Cheadle, Don		Ent	15			40	Actor
Cheap Trick		Music	50			140	S Album 135
Cheatham, Benj. Franklin	1820-1886	Civ War	253	481			CSA Gen.
Cheatham, Benjamin F. (WD)	1820-1886	Civ War	390	550	652		CSA Gen.
Checker, Chubby		Music	25	147	95	95	Rock
Cheech & Chong		Ent	52	400		195	Comic Duo
Cheek, John		Opera	10			25	Opera
Cheers (Cast) (6)		Ent	100			367	Signed script 350
Cheever, Charles A., Dr.		Sci	40	100		75	
Cheever, George B.	1814-1890	Clergy	10		30		Author
Cheever, John	1912-1981	Author	45	125	220	88	Subtle, Ironic Novels. Pulitzer 1979

C

NAME	DATES	CATEGORY	SIG	LS/DS	ALS	SP	COMMENTS
Chekhov, Anton	1860-1904	Author	560	1815	4156		Rus. Dramatist. Novels, Physician
Chen, Joan		Ent	20			50	Model/actress
Chen, Tina		Comp	10	10		15	
Cheney, Dick		Pol	50			70	Vice Pres. under GW Bush
Cheney, Sherwood		Mil	10		25		Gen. WWI
Cheng, Nien		Author	10			18	"Life & Death in Shanghai"
Chennault, Anna	1925-	Celeb	20	25	50	40	Aviation Exec., Writer, Lecturer. Wife of Gen.
Chennault, Claire L.	1890-1958	WWII	383	622	835	758	WWII Flying Tigers. USAF Gen. War dte LS 1000
Chenowith, Kristin		Ent	15			45	
Cher		Ent	30	40	62	100	AA Winning Actress.
Cherkassky, Shura		Opera	20			60	Opera
Chernenko, Konstantin	1911-1985	Pol	80	407		525	Soviet leader
Chernov, Vladimir		Ent	10			30	Opera, Rus. Baritone
Cherry, Don	1924-1996	Music	60			95	Singer. Popular Decca Recording Artist
Cherry, R. Gregg		Gov	10	15		10	Governor NC
Cherubini, Luigi	1760-1842	Comp	175	352	402		It. 29 Operas, 15 Masses
Chesebrough, Amos	1709-1760	Colonial	125	275			Lt. Col. 8th Reg. Fr. -Ind. War
Chesebrough, George M.		Sci		750			
Chesebrough, Robert		Bus	15	30	50		Vaseline Products. Chesebrough Mfg. Co.
Cheshire, Leonard		Mil	15	50	65	40	Br. RAF
Chesney, Kenny		Cntry Mus	60			75	CW singer
Chesnutt, Mark		Cntry Mus	35	90		65	Consistent Top 10 Artist
Chester, Bob		Band	20			40	Big Band Leader
Chester, Colby M.		Bus	10			55	CEO Gen. Foods
Chester, John		Rev War	50	80			Continental Army. Judge
Chesterfield, Fourth Earl of		Statsmn		375			SEE STANHOPE, P. D.
Chesterton, Gilbert Keith		Author	44	305	325	190	Father Brown, Detective'
Chestnut, James	1815-1885	Civ War	125				CSA Gen.
Cheswell, Wentworth	1746-1817	Rev War	100	295	500		S Assoc. Test, Afr. -Am. Teacher, Patriot, RARE
Chetlain, Augustus Louis	1824-1914	Civ War	50	95	145		Union gen., Recruited a Black Regiment
Chevaerie, Kurt von der		Mil	10			40	
Chevalier, Albert	1861-1923	Comp	10	25	40	25	Br. Actor, Singer, Humorist
Chevalier, Maurice	1888-1972	Ent	55		150	173	Fr. Film & Vaude. Actor-Singer. 'Gigi'
Chevrolet, Louis	1879-1941	Bus	850	3168			Chevrolet Auto Mfg. & Glen Martin Aircraft
Chew, Virginia	1905-1987	Ent	10		25		Char. Actress. Mostly Broadway, some films
Chianese, Dominic		Ent	20			50	Uncle Jr. Sopranos
Chiao, Leroy		Space	10			25	
Chiari, Walter	1924-1992	Ent	20			45	Comic Italian Actor. Intl recognition.
Chicago		Music	50			130	Rock Group
Chicago (cast)		Ent				145	Gere, Zellweger, Zeta-Jones
Chichester, Francis, Sir		Celeb	35	100	165	75	Adventurer, Aviator, Sailed Gypsy Moth IV
Chickering, Thos. E.	1824-1871	Bus	35	77	142		Union Gen., Manufacturer of Chickering Piano
Chiklis, Michael		Ent	15			50	Emmy winner
Child, Julia	1912-2004	Celeb	20	30	55	150	TV Chef. Cookbook Author
Child, Lydia Maria		Author	30	90	155		Abolitionist, Reformer, Editor
Childress, Alvin		Ent	50		75	125	
Childs, George Wm.	1829-1894	Pub	65	145	167		ALS Cont. 925
Chiles, Lawton Mainor, Jr.		Congr	10	15	20	15	Sen. FL
Chiles, Lois	1947-	Ent	10			25	Actress
Chilton, Kevin P.		Space	10			25	
Chilton, Robert Hall	1815-1879	Civ War	185		506		CSA Gen.
Chilton, Robert Hall (WD)	1815-1879	Civ War	395	3125			CSA Gen.
Chilton, Samuel	1804-1867	Congr	50	145			MOC VA. John Brown's Atty
Chirac, Jacques		HOS	30	75	185	58	Pres. of Fr. Repub.

NAME	DATES	CATEGORY	SIG	LS/DS	ALS	SP	COMMENTS
Chirico, Giorgio de	1888-1978	Artist			765		Major Italian Surrealist
Chisholm, Shirley A.	1924-	Congr	30			100	1st Afro-Am. Congresswoman
Chittenden, Thos. C.	1788-1866	Congr	25	75		125	MOC NY
Chittenden, Uncle Russ		Author	10				Cookbooks
Chlumsky, Anna		Ent	15			35	Young Actress
Cho, John		Ent	20			60	
Choate, Joseph H.	1832-1917	Diplo	15	60	125	45	Prosecuted Tweed Ring
Choate, Rufus	1799-1859	Congr	20	35	52		Boston Statesman, Orator, NY Sen; FF 45
Chochaki, David		Ent				36	Actor
Chocola, Chris C		Congr	10				Member US Congress
Choiseul, Leopold C. de, Card.		Clergy	100	165			
Chokachi, David		Ent	10			35	Actor. 'Baywatch'
Chomsky, Noam		Celeb	10			15	Pol. celebrity
Chong, Rae Dawn		Ent	40	65	85	50	Actress
Chong, Tommy		Ent	25			50	Cheech & Chong
Chopin, Frederic	1810-1849	Comp	1800	14175	15167		Polish Comp.
Chou En-Lai		HOS	1155	4000	10000	5000	Chinese Communist Premier
Chouteau, Rene Auguste	1749-1829	Rev War	350	1000	1515		Am. Pioneer. Fur Trader. Fndr. St. Louis
Chow, China		Ent	13			40	
Chretien, Jean-Loup		Space	10			20	France
Chriqui, Emmanuelle		Ent	14			43	
Christensen, Donna M. C		Congr	10				Member US Congress
Christensen, Erika		Ent	13			40	
Christensen, Hayden		Ent	10			40	Actor
Christian IX (Den)	1818-1906	Royal	90	250			King of Denmark 1863-1906
Christian VII (Den & Nor)	1749-1808	Royal	125	325	625		King of Denmark
Christian, Claudia		Ent	15			62	Actress.
Christian, Eric		Ent	13			40	
Christian, George B.		Congr	10	20		10	Sen. OH
Christian, Prince	1831-1917	Royal	45		150		Prince Schleswig-Holstein, Victoria's Son-in-Law
Christian, Spencer		Celeb	10			20	Media/TV personality
Christians, Mady		Ent	25	30	65	52	Star from Golden Years of Am. Theater
Christianson, Helena		Celeb	15			35	Celebrity model
Christie, Agatha	1890-1976	Author	282	470	564	925	Classic Detective Novels, AMS 2300
Christie, Julie	1940-	Ent	28	30	33	50	Brit. Actress Oscar Winner.
Christina, Queen (Swe)		Royal	250	2088	2400		
Christine, Virginia		Ent	10	15	15	45	
Christo		Artist	10	15	20	85	Sculptor in Fabric
Christophe Novelli, Jean		Celeb	10			15	Chef
Christophe, Henry	1767-1820	HOS	1325	1500			Haitian Revolutionary, Sovereign.
Christopher, Dennis	1955-	Ent	10	15	15	30	Actor; ' Breaking Away'
Christopher, Roy		Celeb	10			20	Art Dir.
Christopher, Warren		Cab	15	35		25	Sec. State
Christopher, William	1932-	Ent	15	20	25	35	Father Mulcahy on 'M*A*S*H'
Christy, Eileen	1927-	Ent	10			30	Vintage Actress
Christy, Howard Chandler	1873-1952	Artist	60	82	256	490	Illust., Portraitist. Books
Christy, June		Music	10			25	Stan Kenton Vocalist. Recording Star
Chrysler, Morgan Henry	1822-1890	Civ War	47	110	161		Union Gen.
Chrysler, Walter P.	1875-1940	Bus	288	820	1175	1077	Fndr. Chrysler Motors. TLS 3500
Chrysler, Walter P. Jr.		Bus	75	275	350	150	Walter's Son & Financier
Chuikov, Vasily		Mil		200			Soviet Gen.
Chukovsky, Korney	1882-1969	Author			750		Russian; kid's poetry
Chun Doo-Hwan		HOS	25		50		
Chung, Connie		Ent	10	10	20	30	TV News Anchor

C

NAME	DATES	CATEGORY	SIG	LS/DS	ALS	SP	COMMENTS
Chung, Kyung-Wha		Music	10			65	Contemporary Violin Sensation
Chung, Myung Whun		Cond				75	Controversial Korean Maestro
Church, Benjamin		Rev War	250	530	1010		Am. Physician & Spy
Church, Charlotte		Opera				30	Welsh Sopr.
Church, Frank		Congr	10			25	Sen. ID
Church, Frederick E.	1826-1900	Artist	112	425	1020		Am. Dramatic Landscapes
Church, Frederick S.		Artist	40	65	122		ALS/Sketch 500, ANS/Sketch 225
Church, R. W.		Clergy	20	35	50		
Church, Thomas		Ent	15			45	
Church, Thomas Haydon	1960-	Ent	15			45	Emmy-winning actor. AA nominee 'Sideways'
Churchill, Clementine S.	1885-1977	1st Lady	74	200	252	160	Wife of Winston S. Churchill
Churchill, Jennie(Jerome)	1854-1921	Celeb	15	100	305	95	W. S. Churchill's Am. Born Mother
Churchill, John	1650-1722	Mil	360	785			1st Duke of Marlborough
Churchill, Mary		Celeb	10		25		
Churchill, Randolph, Lord	1849-1895	Statsmn	45	90	225		Father of Winston S.
Churchill, Sarah	1660-1744	Royal	117	275			Powerful Confidante of Queen Anne.
Churchill, Sarah		Ent	20	45	30	35	Actress-Daughter of Winston S.
Churchill, Thomas James	1824-1905	Civ War	75	107	223		CSA Gen., Gov. AR
Churchill, Thomas James (WD)	1824-1905	Civ War	195	460			CSA Gen.
Churchill, Winston	1871-1947	Author	15	35	60	60	Historical Novels
Churchill, Winston S.	1874-1965	HOS	1008	2615	7294	4525	GB PM WWII. 3x5 SP 1500; S Chk 3200; ALS/LS/Cont 7500+
Cialini, Julie		Celeb	10			15	Model
Ciannelli, Eduardo	1889-1969	Ent	20			55	Actor
Ciano, Galeazzo, Conte		Royal	65	295			Son-in-Law of Mussolini
Cibrian, Eddie	1973-	Ent	10			25	Actor
Cicognani, A. G., Card.		Clergy	35	50	75	60	
Cigna, Gina		Opera	50	70		65	Opera
Cilea, Francesco		Comp	100			500	It. Comp. of 'Adriana Lecouvreur'
Cimaro, Pietro		Cond	10	25	50		It. Conductor
Cimino, Michael		Ent	10	15	22	32	Film Dir.
Ciny, Alain		Ent	20			45	Fr. Char. Actor 'La Dolce Vita'
Cisneros, Henry	1947-	Cab	10			20	Sec. HUD. Major Problems w/FBI
Citroen, Andre-Gustave	1878-1935	Bus	85	395		700	Engineer-Industrialist. Citroen Auto Mfg.
Civiletti, Benjamin		Cab	10	10	20	10	
Clack, Mrs. Louise		Author	10			12	Gen. Lee & Santa Claus
Clair, Ren	1898-1981	Ent	115	145	320		Fr. Film Maker, Actor, Writer
Clairborne, Liz	1929-2007	Bus	25			50	Clothing Designer
Claire, Ina		Ent	15	15	35	48	Vintage Leading Lady. Stage-Films
Claire, Marion		Opera	10			25	Am. Sopr.
Clamorgan, Jacques		Expl		750			MO Co. 1795. Precursor of Louis & Clark, Trader
Clancey, Tom		Author	15	25		25	Am. Novels
Clanton, James Holt	1827-1871	Civ War	135	567			CSA Gen.
Clanton, Jimmy		Music	20			25	Rock
Clanton, N. H.		West	1100				Father of Billy, OK Corral
Clapp, Gordon	1948-	Ent	10			25	Actor NYPD
Clapton, Eric		Music	175	650	900	402	Rock HOF. S Album 550-800
Clark & McCullough		Ent				275	Vaude. & burlesque team
Clark, Abraham	1726-1794	Rev War	510	725	4500		Signer Dec. of Indepen.
Clark, Barzilla W.		Gov	10	12	20		Governor ID
Clark, Buddy		Music	10			30	40's Singer
Clark, Candy		Ent	10	10	10	20	
Clark, Carol Higgins		Author	10	15		20	All Around the Town
Clark, Champ	1850-1921	Pol		20		30	Spkr. of the house

NAME	DATES	CATEGORY	SIG	LS/DS	ALS	SP	COMMENTS
Clark, Charles	1811-1877	Civ War	152	331	434		CSA Gen., CW Gov. of Miss.
Clark, Clarence D.		Congr	10		35	15	Sen. WY
Clark, Cottonseed		Cntry Mus	15			30	Singer
Clark, Dan		Celeb	10			15	Member of the Speakers Hall of Fame
Clark, Dane	1913-1998	Ent	18	20	25	55	Actor noted for 'Tough Guy' roles From 1942
Clark, Dick		Ent	20	28	45	69	Am. Bandstand Host
Clark, Edward	1815-1880	Civ War		150			Governor of TX
Clark, Eugene		Ent	15			45	
Clark, Francis E.		Clergy	10	15	25	20	
Clark, Frank		Congr	10	35		10	Congressman FL; FF 35
Clark, Fred	1914-1968	Ent	32			120	Am. Char. -Comed. Actor 1947-68
Clark, Gene		Music	60			245	'Byrds'
Clark, George Rogers	1752-1818	Rev War	712	2150	4250		Gen., Frontier Leader
Clark, James B. (Champ)	1850-1921	Congr	60	40	145	95	Spkr. of the House. MO
Clark, James, Sir		Med	15	35	85		Phys. to Queen Victoria & Albert
Clark, Joe		Celeb	10			15	Keynote Spkr.
Clark, John Bullock, Jr.		Civ War	82				CSA gen.
Clark, John Bullock, Jr. (WD)	1831-1903	Civ War	180	395			CSA Gen. ALS/Cont 8250
Clark, John Chamberlain		Congr	10				FF 26
Clark, Kenneth B.	1914-	Activist	20			55	Psychologist-Writer. Brown vs Board of Ed.
Clark, Laurel		Space	50			225	Perished on Space Shulltle Columbia re-entry 2003
Clark, Louis Gaylord		Author	20	35	122		Editor 'Knickerbocker' Magazine
Clark, Marguerite	1883-1940	Ent	25			76	Stage. Film Rival Mary Pickford
Clark, Mark W.	1896-1984	Mil	40	200	196	120	WWII Gen. 5th Army. S FDC 50; WWII dte TLS/ALS 250-700; Korean War dte TLS 350
Clark, Mary		Mil	10		15	15	
Clark, Mary Higgens		Author		38		20	Suspense Novels
Clark, Myron H.		Gov	10	20	35	15	Governor NY
Clark, Petula		Music	15	25		40	Br. Singer-Actress
Clark, Ramsay		Cab	15	35	60	20	Atty Gen.
Clark, Roy		Cntry Mus	15	30		40	Singer-Guitarist-Comedian. 'Hee Haw'
Clark, Susan		Ent	10		12	25	Actress.
Clark, Terri		Cntry Mus	10			20	Singer-Country
Clark, Tim		Celeb	10			20	Comedian
Clark, Tom C.	1889-1977	Sup Crt	40	103	145	125	US Attorney Gen.
Clark, Walter J.		WWII	10	22	38	30	ACE, WWII; 7 kills
Clark, Wesley Gen.		Mil	20	20	25	52	NATO Supreme Cmdr.
Clark, William	1770-1838	Expl	500	3300	2290		Lewis & Clark Exped. Gov. MO Territory
Clark, William A.		Congr	35	135	195		RR & Mining Magnate
Clark, William Thomas	1831-1905	Civ War	50	64	110		Union Gen.
Clarke, Adam		Clergy	75	145	350		
Clarke, Annie		Ent	15	15	25	25	
Clarke, Arthur C.		Author	15	35	75	55	2001
Clarke, Charles G.		Ent	10			20	Film Dir.
Clarke, Charles Mansfield		Med	20	65	140		Br. Obstetrician
Clarke, George		Colonial	85	350			
Clarke, Henri J. G. Duc de		Napol	75	287	345		Marshal of Napoleon
Clarke, James Freeman		Clergy	40	50	89	75	
Clarke, James McClure		Congr	10			10	MOC NC
Clarke, Mae		Ent	40		75	83	Actress. SP/James Cagney 400-550
Clarke, Maj.-Gen. Sir Edward MC	1885-1971	Mil	25				
Clarke, Melinda		Ent	13			40	
Clarke, Robert	1986-	Ent	10			25	
Clarke, Thomas		Rev War	165	550			

NAME	DATES	CATEGORY	SIG	LS/DS	ALS	SP	COMMENTS
Clarke, Warren	1947-	Ent	10			20	Br. Actor
Clarkson, Kelly		Ent	17			50	
Clarkson, Mathew	1758-1825	Rev War	55	110	200		Rev. Soldier, Philan.
Clarkson, Patrica		Ent	13			40	
Clarkson, Thomas	1760-1846	Reform	45		100		Br. Devoted Entire Life to Abolition of Slavery
Clary, Alice		Author	15	25		15	
Clary, Julian		Celeb	10			15	Comedian
Clary, Robert		Ent	10	15	15	20	Diminuative Fr. Actor. 'Hogan's Heroes'
Clash		Music	242			315	Rock group; S Album 400-2940
Clavell, James		Author	10	25	55	55	Novels
Clay, Brutus Junius		Congr	10				FF 25
Clay, Cassius Marcellus	1810-1903	Civ War	86	269	500		Union Gen., Senate, Abolition.
Clay, Henry	1777-1852	Pol	137	907	1207	350	Sec State, ALS 9300, LS/Cont 1500; FF 105-145
Clay, Lucius D.	1897-1978	Mil	50	173	150	118	Gen. WWII. US Mil. Gov. Berlin Blockade
Clay, William L., Sr.	1931-	Congr	15			25	Congressman MO. Civ. Rights Activist
Clay, Wm. Lacy C		Congr	10				Member US Congress
Clayburgh, Jill	1945-	Ent	10	15	15	40	Actress. Twice Nominated for Oscar.
Clayton, Buck		Music				50	Jazz trumpeter
Clayton, Ethel	1882-1966	Celeb	20			45	Silent Movie star
Clayton, Henry D.		Congr	10	10			MOC AL
Clayton, Henry Delamar	1827-1889	Civ War	125	200	250		CSA Gen.
Clayton, Jan		Ent	15	15	15	30	Actress-Singer. Mother on 'Lassie'
Clayton, John M.		Cab	30	65	140		Taylor Sec. State
Clayton, Joshua	1744-1798	Rev War	220	425			1st Gov. DE. Sen. DE
Clayton, Powell	1833-1914	Civ War	50	84	122		Union Gen.
Clayton, S. J.		Congr	10	10			
Clayton, William	1814-1879	Relig	250	500	900		Mormon hymn writer; author; inventor
Clear Sky, Chief		Am Ind	30			50	Iroquois Chief
Cleave, Mary		Space	10			25	
Cleaveland, Moses	1754-1806	Rev War	200	850			Cleveland, Ohio Namesake
Cleburne, Patrick R.	1828-1864	Civ War	3975	4650			CSA Gen., KIA Franklin, TN
Cleese, John		Ent	20	30		40	Actor
Clem, John L. (Johnny)	1851-1937	Civ War	275	747	323	633	Union Drummer Boy, Chicamauga
Clemenceau, Georges	1841-1929	HOS	100	140	185		Physician, Statesman, Journalist. AManS 835
Clemens, Clarence		Music	15			20	E-Street Band saxophonist
Clemens, Orion (Bro. Samuel)		West	125		160		Sec. of Nevada Territory 1861
Clemens, S. L., as Mark Twain	1835-1910	Author	720	1445	3708	5375	ALS/Cont 19500. P/C SP 2475. AQS 2530-7500; SP/Clemens & Twain 9000
Clemens, Samuel L.	1835-1910	Author	865	1506	2870	4732	ALS/Cont 19000
Clement IX, Pope	1600-1669	Clergy		1310			Guilio Rospigliosi
Clement VIII, Pope		Clergy	550	1398			
Clement, Martin Withington		Bus	10		16		Pres. CEO Pennsylvania RR
Clementi, Muzio	1752-1832	Comp			2000		Pianist. Musical Combat/Mozart
Clervoy, Jean-Francois		Space	10			25	France
Cleveland, Carleton A.		Bus	10	35	45	45	
Cleveland, Charles		Clergy	20	25	45		
Cleveland, Frances F.	1864-1927	1st Lady	82	120	150	238	ALS As 1st Lady 250-300
Cleveland, Grover	1837-1908	Pres	234	396	557	612	ALS/Cont 1, 250-3, 500
Cleveland, Grover & Francis		Pres	418				
Cleveland, Grover (As Pres.)		Pres	261	567	834	1450	WH Card S 350, SP/1st Cabinet 1200
Cleveland, Rose Elizabeth	1846-1918	1st Lady	125		570		Cleveland's sister. WH hostess until he married
Clewes, Henry		Bus	25	45			Banker
Cliburn, Van	1934-	Music	30	85	55	149	Am. Pianist
Clifford, Clark M.	1906-1998	Cab	20	25	42	35	Sec. Defense. Advisor to Truman Thru Carter

NAME	DATES	CATEGORY	SIG	LS/DS	ALS	SP	COMMENTS
Clifford, John Henry		Gov	10	55	95		
Clifford, Nathan	1803-1881	Sup Crt	75	175	240	150	Atty Gen., Ambassador
Clifford, Rich		Space	10			30	
Clift, Montgomery	1920-1966	Ent	311	405	600	1068	4 Oscar Nominations. Reclusive Non-Conformist
Clifton, Joseph C.		Aero	15	35	60	40	
Cline, Patsy	1932-1963	Cntry Mus	540		1545	1991	
Clingan, William	d. 1790	Rev War	88	185			Delegate Cont. Cong. Early Signer Art. Conf.
Clinger, Debra		Ent	10	10	10	20	Actress
Clingman, Thomas Lanier	1812-1897	Civ War	119	295	410		CSA Gen.
Clinton, Chelsea		1st Fmly	10			25	Bill & Hillary Clinton's daughter
Clinton, De Witt	1769-1828	Statsmn	61	202	248		Promoted Erie Canal. Mayor NYC. Pres. Cand
Clinton, George	1739-1812	Rev War	180	254	768		Cntl. Congr., Gen, Gov. NY. ALS/Cont 7,000
Clinton, Henry, Sir	1730-1795	Rev War	500	1219	2350		Br. Cmdr. Am. Rev. Blamed for Loss
Clinton, Hillary Rodham		Pol	45	100	150	100	Fmr 1st Lady., Sen. NY
Clinton, James		Rev War	248	490			Gen. Revolutionary War
Clinton, James G.	1804-1849	Congr	15		35		Repr. NY
Clinton, Roger		Ent	25				Singer-Brother of Pres. Clinton
Clinton, William 'Bill'		Pres	264	610	2130	305	42nd Pres. TLS/AN 1500.
Clinton, William J. (As Pres.)		Pres	450	1790	3737	400	42nd US Pres.
Clive, Colin		Ent	319			476	
Clive, E. E.	1879-1940	Ent	30			72	Welsh actor
Clive, Edward, Baron		Royal			100		1st Earl of Powys., Eldest son of Rbt. Clive
Clive, Robert		Mil	250	600	1200		Baron Clive of Plassey
Clokey, Art		Comics	20			150	Gumby.
Cloney, Thomas	1774-1850	Mil			2500		Irish rebellion
Clontz, Marie		Author	10			12	English grammar
Clooney, George		Ent	25	92		71	Actor-Dir. Movies/TV.
Clooney, Rosemary	1928-2002	Music	20	25	35	77	Singer
Clopton, John		Congr	10				FF 35
Close, Glenn		Ent	25	35	40	50	Actress. Oscar Winner.
Clostermann, Pierre		WWII	55	85	125	108	Leading Fr. WWII ace.
Clover, Richardson		Mil	35	125			USN Adm.
Clovio, Giorgio Guilio	1498-1578	Artist	650	1400	2000		It. Miniaturist
Clowe, John Lee		Celeb	10			15	Pres. of AMA
Clune, Jackie	1967-	Celeb	10			20	Br. comedienne/caberet
Clunes, Alec	1912-1970	Ent	10	20		30	Br. Stage, Film Actor. Dir. -Prod.
Clunes, Martin		Ent	10			20	Actor
Cluseret, Gustave Paul	1823-1900	Civ War	50	91	160		Union Gen.
Clyburn, James E. C		Congr	10				Member US Congress
Clyde, Andy	1892-1967	Ent	65			255	Vintage Comedian
Clyde, June	1909-1987	Ent	10	15	15	30	Actress
Clymer, George	1739-1813	Rev War	150	483	991		Statesman. Signer Dec of Ind FF 900
Coase, Ronald		Econ	20	35		25	Nobel Economics
Coates, Albert	1882-1953	Comp	35	55	85	110	Anglo-Russian cond. & comp.
Coates, Phyllis		Ent	30			90	Lois Lane
Coats, Bob		WWII	10	22	38	35	ACE, WWII; 9. 33 Kills
Coats, Michael L.		Space	10			20	
Cobain, Kurt	1967-1994	Music	125			625	Rock; Lead singer Nirvana
Cobb, Calvin H.		Mil	15	40	75		
Cobb, Howell	1815-1868	Civ War	86	217	490		Spkr., Sec Treas., CSA Gen., Gov. GA
Cobb, Howell (WD)		Civ War	225	395	575	950	CSA Gen.
Cobb, Irvin S.	1876-1944	Author	30	47	87	95	Journalist-Humorist-Plays
Cobb, Jerrie	1931-	Aero	15	25	35	35	1st Woman to Pass NASA Astronaut Training
Cobb, Joe Frank	1916-2002	Ent	45			86	The original fat kid in the Little Rascals

NAME	DATES	CATEGORY	SIG	LS/DS	ALS	SP	COMMENTS
Cobb, Lee J.	1911-1976	Ent	35	72	85	220	Fine Char. Actor of Films & Stage
Cobb, Sylvanus	1823-1887	Author	12		130	40	
Cobb, Thos. Reade R.	1823-1862	Civ War	628	1950	2495		CSA Gen. KIA '62
Cobb, Thos. Reade R. (WD)		Civ War	1250		2098		CSA Gen. KIA '62
Cobham, Alan J., Sir	1894-1973	Aero	40	110	220	62	Br. Aviation Pioneer. Pioneered Aerial Photog.
Cobham, Gov. Gen. NZ		HOS	10	15	15	20	New Zealand
Coble, Howard C		Congr	10				Member US Congress
Cobo, Albert E.		Celeb	10	15	45	25	Detroit's Cobo Hall
Coburn, Charles	1877-1961	Ent	45	65	155	144	AA Winner. Monacle-wearing Char. Actor
Coburn, James	1928-2002	Ent	20	25	40	160	Actor. 'Our Man Flint'. AA '99
Coca, Imogene	1908-2001	Ent	24	60	75	59	Comedienne & TV Pioneer
Cochran, Eddie	1938-1960	Music	368	962	1800	1000	Star of Early Rock.
Cochran, Jacqueline	1910-1980	Aero	55	150		145	Speed record holder
Cochran, John L	1937-2005	Law	25	60	75	35	O. J. Simpson Trial Lawyer
Cochran, Robert L.		Gov	12	20	30	15	Governor NE
Cochran, Steve		Ent	15	15	30	28	
Cochran, Thad		Congr	10				US Senate (R-MS)
Cochrane, Basil, Sir		Mil	15	25	30		
Cochrane, John	1813-1898	Civ War	50	75	114		Union Gen. ALS '62 345
Cochrane, Ralph		Mil	10	15	25	25	
Cochrane, Rory		Ent	17			50	
Cockburn, George, Sir		Mil	50	100	140		Br. Adm. War 1812
Cockburn, Henry T. Lord	1779-1854	Jurist			110		Scottish Judge
Cockcroft, John D., Sir		Sci	60	110	245	75	Nobel Physics
Cocke, Philip St. George	1809-1861	Civ War	475	416			CSA Gen.
Cocke, Philip St. George (WD)		Civ War			5500		CSA Gen. Suicide '61
Cocker, Joe		Music	20	40		62	Rock Star; S Album 60-120
Cockerell, Christopher, Sir	1910-1999	Invent	35		90		Inventor of Hovercraft
Cockrell, Francis Marion	1834-1915	Civ War	78	160	227		CSA Gen., US Sen. MO
Cockrell, Ken		Space	10			20	
Coco, James	1928-1987	Ent	15	20	40	48	Nom. Letter For Oscar From Academy 225
Cocteau, Jean	1889-1963	Author	413	495	556	735	Novels, Plays. Orig. Sketch S 1200
Coda, Eraldo		Opera	10			25	Opera
Cody, Iron Eyes	1904-1999	Ent	30	70	25	105	Actor. Born Espera De Corti. Played Native Ams.
Cody, John P., Card.		Clergy	25	35	50	45	
Cody, Lew	1884-1934	Ent	20	20	25	62	
Cody, Louisa		Celeb		425			Wife of Wm. F. (Buffalo Bill) Cody
Cody, William F.	1846-1917	Celeb	689	2340	1717	1781	CW Scout, Pony Expr., Showman, CMH
Cody, William F. (Buffalo Bill)		Celeb	1060	1511	2440	3118	Signed both Ways. ALS/Cont 9300
Coffee, Gerald		Celeb	10			15	Keynote Spkr. POW in N. Vietnam, 7 years
Coffin, Charles Carleton	1823-1896	Jrnalist	92	150			Only Journalist to Cvr. Entire Civil War
Coffin, Henry Sloane		Clergy	25	35	40	50	
Coffin, Howard C.		Bus	30	45			Pioneer Auto Manufacturer
Coffin, Isaac, Sir	1759-1839	Mil	40		75		Boston Born Br. Naval Off.
Coffin, John	1756-1838	Rev War	200	500			Loyalist Gen.
Coffin, Tris		Ent	20			65	Vintage actor
Coffin, William Sloane	1924-2006	Clergy	10	18	35	25	Pol. Activist. Tried w/Dr. Spock
Coffyn, Frank		Aero	40	65		95	
Coggan, Donald, Arch.		Clergy	35	45	50	50	
Coghlan, Frank, Jr.	1916-	Ent	15			30	Child silent film star
Coghlan, Joseph B.		Mil	25	65		80	Adm USN-Spanish Am. War
Cogswell, William	1838-1895	Civ War	15	35	75		Repr. MA
Cohan, George M.	1878-1942	Comp	175	180	301	292	Actor/Plays/Dir./Singer. SP/Fam. 895, Sheet music 800
Cohen, Leonard		Music	50			235	Popular singer; SB 140-475

NAME	DATES	CATEGORY	SIG	LS/DS	ALS	SP	COMMENTS
Cohen, Octavus Roy		Author	15	30	45	25	Novels, Screenplays, Radio
Cohen, Ronald M.		Celeb	10			15	Film industry
Cohen, Stanley, Dr.		Sci	20	35		25	Nobel Med.
Cohen, Wilbur J.		Cab	10	14	22	10	Sec. HEW
Cohen, William S.		Cab	10		25	35	Sen. ME, MOC ME, Sec. Defense
Cohn, Harry		Bus	35	85	165	75	Co-Fndr. Columbia Pictures
Cohn, Jack		Bus	25	70	140	75	Co-Fndr. Columbia Pictures
Cohn, Roy	1927-1986	Law	95	240	240	140	Legal Aide Sen. McCarthy
Coit, James Brolles		Civ War	50		125		Union Gen.
Coke, Edward, Sir	1552-1634	Law		2162	3500		Eminent Eng. Jurist. Lord Chief Justice
Coke, Richard	1829-1897	Civ War	60		160		CSA Off. Gov. TX, Sen.
Coke, Thomas, Bish.		Clergy	250	350	750		
Coker, Jack		Ent	10	10	15	20	Actor
Colbert, Claudette	1903-1994	Ent	40	121		209	Chic Fr. -Am. Leading lady
Colbert, Jean-Baptiste	1619-1683	Pol			328		Fr. Min. of Finance, 1665-83 under King Louis XIV
Colby, Bainbridge	1869-1950	Cab	10	30	42		Sec. State Under Wilson
Colby, Leonard		Mil	40	90			Gen. Indian Fighter
Colden, Cadwallader		Rev War	125	240			Am. Colonialist
Cole, Cornelius		Congr	15	25	40		MOC CA 1863, Sen. CA
Cole, Cozy		Music	60			158	Blues-Jazz
Cole, Edward N.		Bus	10	12	30	20	Pres. Gen. Motors
Cole, Gary		Ent	15			45	
Cole, Graham	1952-	Ent	10			25	Br. Actor
Cole, Jack		Ent				250	Am. dancer
Cole, Michael	1945-	Ent	10	10	10	25	Actor 'Mod Squad'
Cole, Nat King	1919-1965	Music	162	282		363	Am. Jazz Pianist, Singer
Cole, Natalie		Music	15	20		42	Singer
Cole, Stephanie	1941-	Ent	15			30	Br. Actress
Cole, Sterling		Congr	10	10			Congressman NY
Cole, Thomas	1801-1848	Artist			800		Painter; Fndr. of the Hudson River School
Cole, Timothy		Artist	35		135		Wood Engraver.
Cole, Tom C		Congr	10				Member US Congress
Coleman, Booth		Ent	10			40	Planet of the Apes
Coleman, Cy		Comp	25			30	Arranger
Coleman, Dabney		Ent	15	20	25	40	Actor
Coleman, Gary		Ent	10	15	20	30	Diminutive actor
Coleman, George		Music	10			40	Jazz Sax
Coleman, Jack		Ent	15			45	
Coleman, Nancy	1912-2000	Ent	10	15	15	40	
Coleman, Norm		Congr	10			20	Senate (R-MN)
Colenso, John W., Bish.		Clergy	20	25	35		
Coleridge, John Duke	1820-1894	Law	20	30	35		Br. Lawyer, judge & Liberal Pol.
Coleridge, Samuel Taylor	1772-1834	Author	271	507	967		Br. Lyrical Poet, Literary Critic. AManS 7, 500
Coleridge-Taylor, Samuel	1875-1912	Comp	20	40	160	100	Choral, Musical Theatre, Songs. AMusQS 300
Coles, Charles 'Honi'	1911-1992	Ent	60			95	Legendary Tap Dancer-Choreographer. Tony Award
Colette, Sidonie-Gabrielle	1873-1954	Author	55	258	292	805	Fr. Novels, Journalist, Critic. 15 Pg. DS 750
Colfax, Schuyler	1823-1885	VP	62	95	201	268	Spkr. of House, Grant VP; FF 75
Colgate. James C.		Bus	10	25	50	40	Colgate University. Donor
Colgrass, Michael		Comp	20	35	85		Pulitzer, AMusQS 100
Collamer, Jacob		Cab	25	55	80		Taylor P. M. Gen.
Collette, Toni		Ent	20			40	Actress
Collier, Bo		Author	10			20	Novels
Collier, Constance	1878-1955	Ent	50		95	100	Vintage Br. Actress & famous acting coach
Collier, James W.		Congr	10	15		10	MOC MS

NAME	DATES	CATEGORY	SIG	LS/DS	ALS	SP	COMMENTS
Collier, John Allen		Congr	10		35		FF 35
Collier, Peter F.		Bus	14	35	70		
Collinge, Patricia	1892-1974	Ent	15	25	35	55	Academy Award-nominated Irish actress.
Collingwood, Charles	1917-1985	Jrnalist	20	35	62	35	News Analyst, War Corr., TV Moderator
Collins Jr., Clifton		Ent	15			45	
Collins, Cardiss	1932-	Congr	10	15		12	Longtime Dem. MOC MO
Collins, Eileen	1956-	Space	20	35	50	65	1st Female Cmdr. of the Space Shuttle
Collins, J. Lawton		Mil	30	50	80	80	Gen. WWII
Collins, Jackie		Author	15	25	60	35	Novels. Her Novel S/Dust Jacket 25
Collins, Jessica		Ent	15			45	
Collins, Joan		Ent	25	30	45	60	Actress
Collins, Judy		Ent	15	25	35	35	Singer, songwriter
Collins, LeRoy		Gov	10	10		14	Governor FL
Collins, Lottie	1865-1910	Ent	45	65	95	125	Actress, singer, dancer of the Br. theater
Collins, Mac C		Congr	10				Member US Congress
Collins, Michael	1930-	Space	208	325	1305	500	Piloted Comm. Module 1st Moon Landing. Apollo XI
Collins, Michelle	1963-	Ent	10			25	Br. Actress
Collins, Phil		Music	25	65	85	63	Singer, songwriter; S Album 125
Collins, Ray		Ent	40	50	125	103	
Collins, Reid		Celeb	10			20	News correspondent
Collins, Susan		Congr	10			15	US Senate (R-ME)
Collins, Wilkie	1824-1889	Author	100	310	560	1380	Br. Novels. 1st Br. Det. Story Writer
Collis, Charles		Civ War	42		60		Union Gen., CMH
Collishaw, Raymond		Aero	75	175	375	225	Brit. ACE, WWI
Collyer Clayton 'Bud'	1908-1969	Ent	25			82	Actor. Radio, Early TV. Game Show Host
Collyer, Robert, Dr.	1823-1912	Clergy	35	60	112		Unitarian. Lecturer. Author
Colman, Booth	1923-	Ent	15			25	Film, TV & stage actor.
Colman, Ronald	1891-1958	Ent	65	75	115	175	Suave, Sophis., Br. Leading. AA Winner
Colman, Samuel	1832-1920	Artist	20		95		Landscapes. Fndr, 1st Pres. Am. Watercolor Soc.
Colombo, Scipio		Opera	10			30	Opera
Colonna, Jerry	1903-1986	Ent	20	20	22	55	Buggy-Eyed Comed. Radio/Stage/Screen
Color Me Badd		Music	25			55	Rock (Entire Group)
Colquitt, Alfred H.	1824-1894	Civ War	127	245	507	275	CSA Gen., US Sen. & Gov. GA. Sig/Rank 295
Colson, Charles W. 'Chuck'		Clergy	20	50	75	30	Convicted Watergate Figure
Colston, Raleigh E.	1825-1896	Civ War	179	400			CSA Gen.
Colt, Samuel	1814-1862	Bus	650	2718	4295		Fndr. Colt Firearms
Colter, Jessie		Cntry Mus	10			22	Wife of Waylon Jennings
Coltrane, John		Music	1616	3300		4550	Great Jazz Saxophonist; Unsigned MusM 1500-6500
Coltrane, Robbie		Ent	10			44	Br. Char. Actor, Mystery Series Star
Colum, Padraic		Author	38	150	110	120	Irish Poet & Plays
Columbo, Franco		Ent	10			25	Actor-Body Builder
Columbo, Russ	1908-1934	Ent	80	100	200	239	Crooner. Crosby Rival. D Shotgun Accident
Columbus, Christopher		Celeb	15			30	Film industry
Colvin, Shawn		Music	25				Rock; S Album 35
Combest, Larry C		Congr	10				Member US Congress
Combs, Holly Marie	1973-	Ent	15			33	Actress.
Combs, Sean 'Puff Daddy'		Music	20			55	Rock
Comden, Betty	1917-2006	Ent	20			45	Musical duo w/Adolph Green
Comden, Betty & Green, A.		Comp	45	55		150	Collaborators. Broadway Musicals
Comingdore, Dorothy	1913-1971	Ent				215	Blacklisted actress; 'Citizen Kane'
Comiskey, Charles A.	1859-1931	Bus	412				Fndr., Owner Pres. Chicago White Sox
Commager, Henry Steele		Civ War	50	60	125		Union Gen.
Commodores		Music	50			132	Musical group; S Album 200
Como, Perry	1912-2002	Ent	25	30	40	89	Singer. Radio; Recording, TV 1948-1963

NAME	DATES	CATEGORY	SIG	LS/DS	ALS	SP	COMMENTS
Compson, Betty	1897-1974	Ent	20	30	60	90	Actress. Films-1915-1948
Compton, Ann	1947-	Celeb	10			20	News reporter
Compton, Arthur H.	1892-1962	Sci	90	205	275	150	Nobel Physics. Atomic Bomb
Compton, Fay	1894-1978	Ent	30			45	Br. Actress. Starred in Barrie Plays, 'Peter Pan'
Compton, Joyce	1907-1997	Ent	15	20	30	45	B-movie actress
Compton, Karl T.	1887-1954	Sci	90	200		110	Physicist, Pres. M. I. T.
Compton-Burnett, Ivy		Author	40	85	175		Brilliant Original Comic Novels on Family Life
Comstock, Cyrus B.	1830-1910	Mil	75		195		US Cmdr.
Conant, A. Roger		WWII	12	25	40	32	ACE, WWII, Marine Ace; 6 kills
Conant, James Bryant		Diplo	10	15	30	20	Educator, US Ambassador
Conati, Lorenzo		Opera	20			65	Opera
Conchita, Maria	1957-	Ent	15			25	Grammy-nom. Cuban-born Venezuelan singer/actress.
Condé, Louis II	1621-1686	Mil		750			One of France's Most Celebrated Generals.
Condon, Bill		Ent	14			43	
Condon, Eddie	1905-1973	Comp	50			75	Guitarist; Bandleader; jazz
Condon, Richard		Author	10	15	35	10	
Cone, Fairfax M.		Bus	10	35	45	20	Foote, Cone & Belding, Adv.
Cone, Hutchinson		Mil	25	35		55	Adm. WWI
Confalonieri, Carlo, Card.		Clergy	50	75	90	65	
Conforti, Gino	1932-	Ent	10	15	15	20	
Conger, Darva		Celeb	10			20	
Congreve, William	1670-1729	Author	190	575	1050		Br. Drama. Restoration Comedy
Congreve, William, Sir		Sci	45	125	235		Artillerist, Invented Rocket
Coningham, Sir Arthur		Aero	35	60			Cmdr. RAF 1st Tactical
Conklin, Chester	1888-1971	Ent	81	115	170	157	Silent Film Comed. W/Chaplin & W. C. Fields
Conkling, Roscoe		Congr	20	25		42	MOC, Senate NY Pol. Boss
Conlee, John	1946-	Cntry Mus	10			20	CW singer
Conley, Brian	1961-	Celeb	10			20	Br. Comed. actor
Conley, Eugene		Opera	20	30		50	Opera
Conley, Joe	1928-	Ent	10	15	15	25	"Ike Godsey" in 'The Waltons'
Connally, John B.	1917-1993	Cab	30	73	82	85	Gov. TX, Sec. Treasury
Connally, Tom	1877-1963	Congr	20	25		70	Sen. TX. Gov. TX
Connellan, Thomas		Author	10			15	Keynote Spkr.
Connelly, Billy	1942-	Celeb	15			25	Scottish Comedian
Connelly, Jennifer		Ent	20	25		47	Actress; Winner Acadamy Award
Connelly, Marc	1890-1980	Author	20	75	75	50	Am. Dramatist. Pulitzer
Connelly, Matthew J.		WH Staff	10	25	35	15	Pres. Truman Aide
Conner, Isabel		Ent	13			40	
Conner, James	1829-1883	Civ War	116	274	329		CSA Gen. 1st Bull Run, Seven Pines
Conner, Nadine		Opera	15			35	Am. Opera, Radio, Records
Conner, Patrick E.	- 1891	Bus	25	40	80		Utah mining. Stockton, UT namesake. CW Col.
Connery, Sean		Ent	45	60	68	111	Best Known for James Bond
Conness, John	1821-1909	Congr	45	85			Civil War Sen. CA
Connick, Harry, Jr.		Band	20	30		45	Big Band Leader-Singer-Pianist-Actor
Conniff, Ray	1916-2002	Comp	25	35	68	50	Comp., Conductor
Connolly, Billy		Ent	15			45	
Connolly, Kevin		Ent	20			40	Entourage
Connolly, Walter		Ent	75		90	82	
Connor, Harry P.		Aero	15	30	45	50	
Connor, John T.		Cab	10	20	35	20	Sec. Commerce
Connor, Patrick Edward	1820-1891	Civ War	50	95	130		Union Gen.
Connor, Selden	1877-1947	Artist			92		Am. Artist
Connors, Chuck	1921-1992	Ent	40	130	95	150	TV's 'The Rifleman'; SP/Johnny Crawford 400
Connors, Jessie		Ent	10			30	

NAME	DATES	CATEGORY	SIG	LS/DS	ALS	SP	COMMENTS
Connors, Mike	1925-	Ent	20			50	Actor. 'Mannix'; S script 125
Connors, Norman		Music	10			25	R&B; jazz
Connors, Patti		Ent	10	10	10	20	Married Jimmy Connors. Patty MacGuire in Playboy
Conover, Harry		Bus	10	17	25	15	Top Modeling Agency
Conquest, Ida	1876-1937	Ent	25	35	40	95	Broadway Leading lady late 1800s-early 1900s
Conrad, Charles Magill	1804-1878	Cab	45	55	190		Sec War
Conrad, Charles, Jr. 'Pete'	1930-1999	Space	60	240	195	177	3rd Moonwalker, DS cont 805
Conrad, Gerhard		Aero	10	25	45	25	
Conrad, Joseph	1857-1924	Author	412	888	1095	2212	Br. Novels. 'Lord Jim' ; SB 500-
Conrad, Kent		Congr	10				US Senate (D-ND)
Conrad, Lauren		Ent	17			50	
Conrad, Michael	1925-1983	Ent	25	30	35	75	Actor. 'Hill St. Blues'
Conrad, Robert	1935-	Ent	25	50		70	Actor. Rare 'Wild Wild West' DS 2700
Conrad, William	1920-1994	Ent	20	30		55	Actor
Conried, Hans	1917-1982	Ent	25	60	60	80	Uncle Tanoose; actor; voice-over
Conroy, Frances		Ent	15			40	Ruth Fisher, Six Feet Under
Conroy, Kevin	1955	Ent	15	20		25	Batman
Conroy, Pat		Author	15			30	Signed 1st Ed. 125-200
Consigny, Eugene A.	1841-1900	Civ War	50	85			Soldier. Witnessed Lee's surrender at Appomattox
Consort, Paul Winter		Music	50			125	Enviromental Music, Grammy
Constable, Albert		Congr	10		42		FF 42
Constable, Archibald	1774-1827	Pub	30				Encyclopaedia Britannica
Constable, John	1776-1837	Artist	360	905	2400		Br. Landscapes, Rural Life
Constantine I	1868-1923	Royal	95			425	King of Greece. Twice Abdicated; Plebicite Restored
Constantino, Florencio		Opera	75			365	Opera
Conte, John	1915-2006	Ent	15	20	25	30	
Conte, Richard		Ent	15	20	25	45	
Conti, Bill		Comp	15	85	100	50	AMusQS 65
Conti, Leonardo	d. 1945	WWII	125				Nazi Doctor
Conti, Tom	1941-	Ent	10			25	Scottish Actor
Contino, Dick		Music	10			15	Accordianist
Convy, Bert	1933-1991	Ent	25	35	40	55	Broadway, TV Star; Am. game show host
Conway, Henry Seymour	1721-1795	Mil	50	80	135		Br. Fld. Marshal. MsDs 250
Conway, Martin F.	18271882	Congr	10				Repr. KS, US Consul France
Conway, Rose A.		Cab	10	15	15	15	
Conway, Thomas		Rev War	100	135	300		Maj. Gen. Rev. War
Conway, Tim		Ent	20	25	35	47	Comedian-Actor 'McHale's Navy' SP 60
Conway, Tom	1904-1967	Ent	65			605	Vintage actor
Conwell, Russell H.	1843-1925	Clergy	35	45	40		Baptist Fndr. & 1st Pres. Temple U
Cony, Samuel		Gov	30	45	60		Civil War Gov. ME
Conyers, John	1929-	Congr	10	15		25	Congressman MI
Coogan, Jackie	1914-1984	Ent	30	40	50	100	Actor. Addams Family's Uncle Fester. SP/child 500
Coogan, Richard	1914-	Ent	20	30	40	80	Actor. Played Captain Video from 1949-1950.
Coogan, Steve	1965-	Ent	10			20	Br. comedian
Cook, Ann Turner		Model	20			30	Original Model For Gerber Baby Products
Cook, Dane		Ent	18			55	
Cook, Elisha Jr.	1902-1995	Ent	20	30	40	100	Actor. Wilmer the gunsel in 'The Maltese Falcon'
Cook, Eliza		Author			75		Poet
Cook, Everett R.		Aero	10	30		50	ACE WWI
Cook, Francis Augustus		Mil	75		55	55	Spanish Am. War
Cook, James, Capt.	1728-1779	Expl	5267	9300	27000		Br. Explr.
Cook, John	1825-1910	Civ War	50	92	140		Union Gen.
Cook, Joseph, Sir		Pol	10	20	40		Australian Statesman
Cook, Kyle		Music	15			40	Music. Lead Guitar 'Matchbox 20'

NAME	DATES	CATEGORY	SIG	LS/DS	ALS	SP	COMMENTS
Cook, Philip	1817-1894	Civ War	198	354	395		CSA Gen.
Cook, Rachel		Ent	15			45	
Cook, Rachel Leigh	1979-	Ent	15			40	Actress. Young Star
Cook, Robin		Author	15	35		25	Novels
Cook, Thomas		Bus	50	110	545		Fndr. Br. Tourist Company
Cook, Tommy	1930-	Ent	15			30	Child Actor
Cook, Walter V.		WWII	15	20	38	30	ACE, WWII; 6 kills
Cooke, Alistair, Sir	1908-2003	Author	20	95	140	75	TV Host. Masterpiece Theatre; Br. Broadcaster
Cooke, Jack Kent		Bus	15	22		20	
Cooke, Jay	1821-1905	Bus	238	804	1200	275	Banker, Financier of Union in Civil War
Cooke, John Rogers	1833-1891	Civ War	182	315			CSA Gen.
Cooke, Nicholas		Rev War		1100			Rev. War Gov. Rhode Island
Cooke, Philip St. George	1809-1895	Civ War	57	170			Union Gen. ALS/Cont 935
Cooke, Sam	1931-1964	Music	322	731		845	Rock
Cooke, Terence J., Card.		Clergy	60	75	100	95	
Cool J, LL		Ent	15			45	
Cool, Phil		Celeb	10			20	Br. Comedian
Cooley, Denton A., Dr.	1920-	Sci	20	35	90	40	Heart Transplant Surgeon
Cooley, Lyman E.		Sci	10		35		Civil Engineer
Cooley, Spade		Cntry Mus	25			65	King of Western Swing
Coolidge, Calvin	1872-1933	Pres	140	264	723	352	Autogr. Speech S 6000
Coolidge, Calvin & Cabinet		Pres	295			3500	
Coolidge, Calvin (As Pres.)		Pres	208	488	3535	576	WH Card S200-350. ALS/Cont 6450
Coolidge, Grace	1879-1957	1st Lady	65	129	136	139	FF 55-80
Coolidge, Jennifer		Ent	13			40	
Coolidge, John		Celeb	40	65			Father of Pres. Coolidge
Coolidge, Martha	1946-	Celeb	10			20	Film industry
Coolidge, Rita		Ent	15	20		30	
Coolidge, T. Jefferson		Statsmn	10	10	20		
Coolidge, William David, Dr.		Sci	45	85	165	125	Dir. Research G. E., Inventor
Coolio		Music	15			45	Rap singer
Coolio, 0		Ent	13			40	
Coombs, Patricia		Artist	10	20	35	35	
Cooper, Alfred Duff		Statsmn	10	25	60	15	1st Viscount Norwich. Author
Cooper, Alice		Music	25		40	88	Rock Alb. S 125
Cooper, Bradley		Ent	13			40	
Cooper, Chris		Ent	17			50	
Cooper, Douglas Hancock	1815-1879	Civ War	119	270	682		CSA Gen.
Cooper, Douglas Hancock (WD)		Civ War	250	650	1125		CSA gen.
Cooper, Emil		Comp	30	180	80	70	Rus. Intl. Conductor-Violinist
Cooper, Gary	1901-1961	Ent	207	316	318	811	Oscar winner., DS cont. 1552
Cooper, Gladys, Dame		Ent	40	35	65	55	Br. Stage & Film Actress
Cooper, Gordon	1927-2004	Space	50	80	125	193	Mercury 7. SP w/Schirra & Carpenter 300
Cooper, Jackie	1921-	Ent	60	85	98	137	Child-Mature Actor, Dir. 'Little Rascal'
Cooper, James	1810-1863	Civ War	75	168			Union Gen.
Cooper, James Fennimore	1789-1851	Author	95	209	1097		Am. Novels. ALS/Cont 1, 750; Chk 250
Cooper, Jeanne		Ent	10			15	Actress. Soap Star
Cooper, Jim C		Congr	10				Member US Congress
Cooper, John Sherman		Congr	10	25			Sen. KY, Statesman, Diplomat
Cooper, Joseph Alexander	1823-1910	Civ War	50	95	102		Union Gen.
Cooper, Leon N., Dr.		Sci	20	35	60	30	Nobel Physics
Cooper, Merian C.		Ent	100				King Kong, Four Feathers
Cooper, Michael 'Ibo'		Music	10			25	Music. Calvinet, Organ 'Lenny Kravitz'
Cooper, Miriam		Ent	35				

NAME	DATES	CATEGORY	SIG	LS/DS	ALS	SP	COMMENTS
Cooper, Peter	1791-1883	Indust	67	155	376	262	Inventor, 1st Steam Locomotive. ALS/Cont 2850
Cooper, Prentice		Gov	10	16			Governor TN
Cooper, Samuel	1798-1876	Civ War	114	220	322		CSA Ranking Gen.
Cooper, Samuel (WD)	1798-1876	Civ War	415	850	1860		CSA Gen. Special Cont. ALS 6325
Cooper, Thos. Sidney		Artist	10	20	35		
Coors, W. K.		Bus	20	60	95	50	Coors Brewery
Coots, J. Fred	1897-1985	Comp	35	55	142	50	Santa Claus is . 'AMusQS 150-195-1200
Coots, J. Fred & H. Gillespie		Comp	50				Santa Claus Is Coming to Town' Sht. Mus. S 495
Copas, Cowboy		Cntry Mus	82			205	D. in plane crash that killed Patsy Cline
Copeland, C. C.		Clergy	30	80	225		
Copeland, Joseph Tarr	1813-1893	Civ War	50	85	131		Union Gen.
Copeland, L. du Pont		Bus	20		50		
Copeland, Royal S., Dr.		Congr	15	70			Sen. NY. Author
Copeland, William John		Clergy	20	25	35		
Copland, Aaron	1900-1990	Comp	80	249	300	208	Major 20th C. Am. Comp. AMusQS 300-800
Copley, John Singleton	1738-1815	Artist	400	2175	3662		Outstanding Am. Portraitist
Copley, Teri	1961-	Ent	10			20	Actress
Copmpanari, Giuseppe		Opera	35			125	Opera
Coppée, Fran ois E.	1842-1908	Author	15	45	45		Fr. Poet, Novels, Dramatist
Coppens, Willy (Baron de H)		Aero	20	40	125	50	
Copperfield, David		Ent	15	30		40	Illusionist
Coppola, Francis Ford	1939-	Ent	25	80	95	50	Oscar Winning Film Dir., Screenwriter
Coquelin, Benoit-Constant	1841-1909	Ent	25	60	55	132	Fr. Actor-Manager, 'Cyrano'
Coquelin, Ernest-Alex. H. (Cadet)		Ent	15	30	50		Comedie-Francaise. Author
Corbett, Boston		Civ War	1643		2100		Shot John Wilkes Booth
Corbett, Henry Winslow		Congr	10	15	25	20	Sen. OR
Corbett, John		Ent	15			40	Sex in the City'. 'Big Fat Greek Wedding'
Corbett, Michael		Ent	10			20	Actor Young & the Restless
Corbin, Henry Clarke		Civ War	50		115		Union Gen.
Corbucci, Sergio	1927-1990	Ent	45			275	AKA Dir. of Spaghetti-Westerns
Corbusier, Le	1887-1965	Archtct	115	575	1048	575	Jeanneret, Charles Edouard. Also Painter, Writer
Corby, Ellen	1911-1999	Ent	25			56	Char. Actress. Grandma Walton
Corcoran, Kevin	1949-	Ent	20			40	Actor. 60s Disney Star, Old Yeller, Moochie
Corcoran, Michael (WD)	1827-1863	Civ War		787	1264		Union Gen. RARE
Corcoran, Noreen		Ent	20			45	Actress. 'Bachelor Father'
Corcoran, William W.		Bus	20	50			Banker, Philan.
Cord, Alex	1933-	Ent	10			25	Actor
Corden, Henry		Ent	25	55		40	Fred Flintstone (Voice)
Corea, Chick		Music	25			65	
Corelli, Franco		Opera	25	35	100	110	Opera
Corelli, Marie	1855-1924	Author	38	55	115	70	Eng. Romantic Novels. (Mary Mackay)
Corena, Fernando		Opera	20			45	Opera
Corey, Elias		Sci	20	35		30	Nobel Chemistry
Corey, Jeff	1914-2002	Ent	20			40	Am. actor; Blacklisted in the 50s
Corey, Wendell	1914-1968	Ent	35	45	80	73	Am. actor
Corgan, Billy		Music	20			65	Music. Lead Singer 'Smashing Pumpkins'
Cori, Carl F.		Sci	20	35	50	25	Nobel Med. (Insulin) Phil. Cvr. S. 150
Corio, Ann		Ent	15	15	20	35	Exotic Dancer, Stripper. Films From '40's
Corlett, Irene		Ent	10	15	15	25	Am. actress
Cormack, Allan M.		Sci	20	35	50	25	Nobel Med.
Corman, Roger	1926-	Ent	15			30	King of the B-movies
Cornbury, Edward Hyde, Lord		Colonial	135	450			1st Colonial Gov. NJ, Gov. NY
Corneliano, Mario N. di		Clergy	35	45	60	50	
Cornelius, Peter (Carl August)		Comp	55		325		Opera, Choral Works, Song Cycle

NAME	DATES	CATEGORY	SIG	LS/DS	ALS	SP	COMMENTS
Cornell, Chris		Music	15			40	Music. Lead Singer 'Soundgarden'
Cornell, Ezekiel		Mil	90	200			Brig. Gen. Am. Rev.
Cornell, Ezra		Bus	30	80	165	75	Financed Western Union Telegr.
Cornell, Joseph	1903-1972	Artist	135	400	700		Am. Surrealist Sculptor
Cornell, Katharine	1898-1974	Ent	25	35	75	128	Superb Am. Leading Stage Actress
Cornell, Lydia		Ent	15	20	20	38	
Corner, George W.		Sci	75	150		100	
Cornfeld, Bernard		Bus	10	20	55	35	
Cornforth, John W., Sir		Sci	20	35	45	40	Br. Nobel Laureate in Chemistry
Corning, Erastus	1794-1872	Bus	50	175	173		1st Pres. NY Central RR
Cornwallis, Charles E.	1738-1805	Rev War	250	500	1509		Br. Gen. Am. Revolution
Cornwell, Patricia		Author	10			15	'Southern Cross'
Cornyn, John		Congr	10				US Senate (R-TX)
Corot, J. B. Camille	1796-1875	Artist	200	440	756	3000	Barbizon School. Impressionist, Landscape Painter
Corrigan, Douglas	1907-1995	Aero	50	75	145	155	'Wrong Way' Corrigan
Corrigan, Mairead/B. William		Activist	35	70	100	50	Nobel Peace Pr. 1976
Corrigan, Michael A.		Clergy	10		30	20	Bishop
Corrigan, Ray Crash		Ent	50			150	
Corsaut, Aneta	1933-1995	Ent	25			90	Actress. Helen Crump on 'The Andy Griffith Show'
Corse, John Murray	1835-1893	Civ War	58	94	118		Union Gen.
Corse, Montgomery D.	1816-1895	Civ War	120	166	325		CSA Gen.
Corso, Gregory		Author					AMS 175
Corson, Fred P., Bish.		Clergy	20	30	50	45	
Cortelyou, George B.	1862-1940	Cab	37	100	130		Served two Pres.
Cortes, Hernando (Cortez)	1485-1574	Expl		36250			Sp. Conqueror of Mex.
Cortez, Ricardo		Ent	30			85	
Cortina, Juan N.		Mil		1500			Mexican Gen. Civil War Rio Grande Bandit
Cortot, Alfred	1877-1962	Music	78		350	225	Pianist
Corwin, Thomas		Cab	35	55	125		Fillmore Sec. Treasury
Corzine, Jon		Congr	15			20	US Senate (D-NJ)
Cosby, Bill	1937-	Ent	25	35	50	55	Comed-Actor-Prod. Authentic Sigs Rare
Cosby, George B.	1830-1909	Civ War	90	178	359		CSA Gen.
Cosby, N. Gordon		Clergy	20	30	45		
Cosell, Howard		Ent	20			70	Radio-TV Sports News
Cosgrave, William T.	1880-1965	HOS	70	150	275	225	Sinn Fein Easter Uprising.
Coslow, Sam		Comp	50	200	300	350	Academy Award 1943, author
Cosmonauts (Russian)		Space				5000	Titov, Gagarin, Tereshkova, Belyayev, Nikolayev, Popvch
Cosmovici, C. B.		Space	20			30	
Cossotto, Fioranza		Opera	10			30	Opera
Cossutta, Carlos		Opera	10			35	Opera
Costa Lo Giudice, Silvio		Opera	40				Opera
Costa, Mary		Opera	10			25	Singer. Opera-Light Opera
Costa, Michael, Sir		Comp	15	40	95	25	Br. Conductor. Opera, Ballet
Costa, Nikka		Ent	15			45	
Costa-Gavras, Constantin		Ent	20			40	Film Dir.
Costas, Bob		TV News	15			25	TV Host & Sports Commentator
Coste, Dieudonne	1898-1973	Aero	125	255	385	235	Fr. Aviator. 1st Non-Stop Flight Paris-NY 1930
Coste, Dieudonne & Bellonte, M.		Aero	210			365	
Costello, Delores (Barrymore)		Ent	28	35	65	60	
Costello, Elvis		Music	25	35	50	111	Rock Entertainer
Costello, Jerry F. C		Congr	10				Member US Congress
Costello, Lou	1906-1959	Ent	192	239		414	Radio, Film, TV Comedian
Costner, Kevin		Ent	33			50	AA Actor-Dir. -Prod.
Coswell, Henry T.		Aero	55	105	150		1st Balloon ascent 1844

C

NAME	DATES	CATEGORY	SIG	LS/DS	ALS	SP	COMMENTS
Cotrubas, Ileana		Opera	10			30	Opera
Cotsworth, Staats	1908-1979	Ent	25			50	Vintage actor
Cotten, Joseph	1905-1994	Ent	24	35	50	97	Actor. Orson Welles' Group. 'Citizen Kane' SP 40
Cottman, Joseph Stewart		Congr	10		42		FF 42
Cotton, Carolina		Cntry Mus	15			30	
Coty, Francois		Bus	100	255	475		Fr. Industrialist. Coty Perfume & Cosmetics
Couch, Darius Nash		Civ War	52	98	65		Union Gen.
Couch, Orville		Cntry Mus	15			35	Music. 50s Recording Artist
Couch, Virgil		Pol	10	20	15		Dir. National Civil Defense
Coué, Emile	1857-1926	Sci	175		500		Fr. Psychotherapist, Hypnotism
Coughlan, Marisa	1974-	Ent	10			25	Actress
Coughlin, Albert L., Sr.		Bus	10	20			Real Estate & Business Developer
Coughlin, Charles E.	1891-1979	Clergy	55	65	80		Activist Catholic Priest & Radio Evangelist
Coulouris, George	1903-1989	Ent	25			150	Br. Char. Actor specializing as a villian
Coulter, Jessie		Cntry Mus	10			25	
Coulter, Richard		Civ War	49	84	106		Union Bvt. Gen.
Courbet, Jean D. Gustave	1819-1877	Artist	225	600	1090		Leader of Realist School
Couric, Katie		Celeb	12			35	News anchor
Court, Hazel		Ent	15			38	
Courtney, Inez	1908-1975	Ent	20			50	Actress, Broadway, & 1930s film star
Courts, Ray		Ent	10			15	Show Promoter
Cousins, Norman	1915-1990	Author	20	35	50	30	Saturday Review Editor, Author
Cousins, Ralph P.	1891-1964	Aero		165		95	Army Gen-Aviation Pioneer. Developed Radio Beam.
Cousins, William E., Arch.		Clergy	20	35	45	35	
Cousteau, Jacques	1910-1997	Expl	48	201	260	143	Fr. Naval Off., Explr., ecologist, filmmaker, scientist, photog., researcher
Cousteau, Jim		Sci	25			60	Underwater Explr., Son of Jacques
Couter, John B.		Mil	15	47			
Couve de Murville, Maurice		Statsmn	10	15	25	25	Fr. Premier, Foreign Min. DeGaulle Cabinet.
Couzens, James	1872-1936	Bus	10	30			Ford Motor Co., US Senate
Covarrubias, Miguel		Artist	150	325			Mex. Book & Magazine Illustr.
Coventry, William Sir	1628-1686	Pol			225		
Covey, Richard O.		Space	15			30	
Covey, Steven Dr.		Author	10				"The Seven Habits of Highly Effective People"
Covode, John		Congr	10		37		FF 25
Cowan, Edgar		Congr	15	25	35		Civil War Sen. PA
Cowan, Jerome	1897-1972	Ent	30			180	Actor: 'The Maltese Falcon,' 'Miracle on 34th St'
Coward, Noel, Sir	1899-1973	Playwrt	122	179	267	252	Plays, Actor, Prod. AMusQS 275
Cowdin, Robert	1805-1874	Civ War	45	106	130		Union Gen.
Cowell, Simon		Ent	20			40	Prod. Am. Idol
Cowl, Jane	1883-1950	Ent	25		35	60	
Cox Family, The		Music	25				Bluegrass
Cox, Archibald		Cab	20	170	55	25	Atty Gen., 1st Watergate Spec. Prosecutor
Cox, Brian		Ent	15			45	
Cox, Christopher C		Congr	10				Member US Congress
Cox, Courtney	1964-	Ent	20			50	Actress ' Friends'
Cox, George H.		Author	10	15	30		Br. Historical Writer
Cox, Jacob D.	1828-1900	Civ War	40	85	112		Union Gen., Sec. Interior, Gov. OH
Cox, James M.		Gov	15	60	75	75	Pres. Cand., MOC, Gov. OH
Cox, Kenyon	1856-1919	Artist	30	55			Am. Mural Painter & Figural Compositions
Cox, Nikki		Ent	15			45	Actress.
Cox, Palmer	1840-1924	Artist	103	140	300	225	Author kid's Books, Illust. 'Brownies'
Cox, Ronny		Ent	10			25	Actor
Cox, Samuel S.	1824-1889	Congr	20	45	103		Civil War Repr. OH

NAME	DATES	CATEGORY	SIG	LS/DS	ALS	SP	COMMENTS
Cox, Sara	1974-	Ent	10			20	Br. TV
Cox, Wally	1924-1973	Ent	50		70	80	Actor-Comed. 'Mr. Peepers'
Cox, William R.	1832-1919	Civ War	84	133	295		CSA Gen. Sig/Rank 295, War Dte. DS 350
Coxe, Tenche		Rev War	55	100	170		Continental Congress
Coxey, Jacob S.		Reform	20	55	140	110	Led Coxey's Army to Wash. D. C
Coyote, Peter		Ent	15			45	
Coyte, Paul		Music	10			15	DJ
Crabbe, Buster	1909-1983	Ent	35	65	123	214	Actor. 'Flash Gordon'; 'Tarzan'
Crabtree, Lotta (Charlotte)	1847-1924	Ent	125	150	150	175	Am. Musical Comedy Actress
Craddock, Billy "Crash"	1939-	Cntry Mus	10	10	20	25	
Craig, Edward Gordon	1872-1966	Ent	15	40	155	190	Br. Stage Designer, Actor. AMS 650
Craig, James	1817-1888	Civ War	45	86	113		Union Gen. ALS War Dte. 175, DS 134
Craig, James	1912-1985	Ent	25			85	Actor
Craig, James Henry, Sir	1748-1812	Mil	100	185	200		Br. Gen. Wounded at Bunker Hill. Gov. Gen. Canada
Craig, Jenny		TV News	15	25		20	Talk Show Host. Diet Expert.
Craig, Larry		Congr	10			20	US Senate (R-ID)
Craig, Malin Gen.	1875-1945	Mil	45	75	125	65	Cuba, Boxer Rebellion, France WWI, WWII
Craig, Yvonne		Ent	20	25		48	Batgirl
Craigavon, James C.	1871-1940	HOS	20		35		1st P. M. Northern Ireland
Crain, Jeanne	1925-2003	Ent	20	30	40	160	Actress. Oscar Nominee 'Pinky'.
Cram, Donald J., Dr.		Sci	20	35		30	Nobel Chemistry
Cramer Jr., Robert E. (Bud) C		Congr	10				Member US Congress
Cramer, Floyd		Cntry Mus	20			33	Pianist
Cramer, Grant	1961-	Ent	10	10	15	20	Actor
Cranch, Christopher P.	1813-1892	Artist	10		25	25	
Crane Frank		Clergy	15	20	35		
Crane, Bob		Ent	135	150		242	Murdered TV Star Hogans Heroes
Crane, Charles Henry		Civ War	30	95	120		Union Gen. Surgeon
Crane, Cheryl	1943-	Celeb	30			45	Killed mom's gangster boyfriend Stompanato, 1958.
Crane, Daniel		Congr	10		25	20	MOC IL
Crane, Frank		Clergy	15	25	45		
Crane, Fred	1918-	Ent	20			90	Actor
Crane, Hart		Author	130	600	1500	350	Am. Poet, The Bridge
Crane, Henry Hitt		Clergy	25	30	50	35	
Crane, John		Mil	100	250			Gen. Revolutionary War
Crane, Philip M. C		Congr	10			20	Member US Congress IL
Crane, Richard	1918-1969	Ent	25	35		108	Actor
Crane, Roy		Comics	30			200	Wash Tubbs, B. Sawyer
Crane, Stephen	1871-1900	Author	500	1450	7720		Red Badge of Courage
Crane, Walter	1845-1915	Artist	50	140	275		Br. Painter-Illust. -Designer. ALS/Cont 600
Crane, William H.	1845-1928	Ent	30	45	90	55	Vintage Actor
Crane, William M.	1784-1846	Mil	35				War 1812 Navy
Crane, Winthrop M.		Congr	10	25		35	Crane Stationery, Gov., Sen. MA
Cranston, Alan	1917-2000	Congr	15	20		22	Sen. CA
Cranston, Bryan		Ent	15			45	
Cranston, Henry Young	1789-1864	Congr	10				Repr. RI; FF 28
Crapo, Michael		Congr	10				US Senate (R-ID)
Crass, Franz		Opera	10			25	Opera
Craven, Frank	1875-1945	Ent	22			82	Vintage Film & Stage Actor
Craven, John		Celeb	10			15	Naturalist
Craven, Wes		Ent	25			60	Dir. Sketch 125
Cravens, Jordan E.		Civ War	55		80		CSA Off., MOC AR
Crawford, Broderick	1911-1986	Ent	40	103	40	135	Char. Actor. Bad Guy Image
Crawford, Christina		Author	10	10	20	15	Daughter of Joan Crawford

NAME	DATES	CATEGORY	SIG	LS/DS	ALS	SP	COMMENTS
Crawford, Cindy		Model	20	35		122	Model-Actress.
Crawford, Francis M.	1854-1909	Author	12	15	25		Am. Novels
Crawford, Geo. W.	1798-1872	Cab		40	95		Sec. War. Gov. GA Secessionist
Crawford, J. W. 'Capt. Jack'	1847-1917	Mil	50	150	250		Indian Wars Scout. The Poet Scout; Author
Crawford, Joan	1908-1977	Ent	50	260	214	357	AA Major Star. Hurrell SP 1250
Crawford, John W.		Author	60			405	
Crawford, Johnny	1946-	Ent	40			50	Actor. 'The Rifleman'
Crawford, Michael		Ent	32	35	50	128	
Crawford, Robert		Comp	25				Air Force Song AMusQS 275
Crawford, Samuel Wylie	1829-1892	Civ War	55	85	180		Union Gen.
Crawford, William H.	1772-1834	Cab	40	155	150		Madison Sec. War. ALS/Cont 1500
Crawford-Frost, Wm. A.		Bus	15	25	70	20	
Cream		Music	620			1123	Rock. S Album Clapton, Baker, Bruce 650-1300
Creatore, Giuseppe		Band	30			120	Bandleader
Creed		Music	50			125	Music. 4 Member Rock Group
Creedence Clearwater Revival		Music	250	350		675	Rock. S Album w/John Fogerty 400. Guitar 350
Creeley, Robert	1926-	Poet	10	12		10	Am. Poet. The Charm-1st Ed. S 150
Cregar, Laird	1916-1944	Ent	162	150	250	289	300 lb. Char. Actor.
Creighton, John O.		Space	15			25	
Creighton, Johnston B. (WD)		Civ War	65	350			Union Adm.
Creighton, Mandell		Clergy	10	15	20		
Creighton, William Jr.		Congr	10				FF 30
Cremer, Peter Erich		Mil	75		120		
Crenna, Richard	1926-2003	Ent	15	20	35	48	Film-TV Actor
Crenshaw, Ander C		Congr	10				Member US Congress
Crerar, Gen. Henry D. Graham	1888-1965	Mil	24			30	WWII Canadian Gen.
Creskoff, Rebecca		Ent	13			40	
Crespin, Régine		Opera	10			60	Opera
Crestani, Lucia		Opera	30			120	Opera
Creston, Paul		Comp	10			125	
Creswell, John A. J.		Cab	20	25	40		Sen. MD, CW MOC. P. M. Gen.
Crews, John R.		Mil	10			20	Award CMH, WWII
Crews, Laura Hope	1880-1942	Ent	230	295		325	Aunt Pittypat-'Gone w/the Wind'
Crewson, Wendy	1956-	Ent	10			25	Canadian Actress. Films
Crichton, Michael		Author	14	73		50	Jurassic Park', SB 150-
Crick, Francis, Dr.		Sci	150	192	350	300	Nobel Med., Structure DNA. SP w/Watson 2500-5500
Crier, Katherine		TV News	10			15	TV Commentary, Special Analysis
Crimi, Giulio	1885-1939	Opera	40			125	Opera. Puccini Tenor Role Creator
Crimson Tide (cast)		Ent				130	
Crippen, Hawley Harvey		Crime		268	500		Murdered Wife. Executed in Eng.
Crippen, Robert L.		Space	20	35		100	Shuttle Orbiter 102 Crew
Cripps, R. Stafford, Sir	1889-1952	Statsmn	30	90	210		Br. Economist, King's Counsel
Crisp, Charles Frederick		Congr	35		50		CSA Off., ' Spkr. of House
Crisp, Charles Robert		Congr	12	20		15	MOC GA
Crisp, Donald	1879-1954	Ent	55	60	90	184	AA winner
Criss, Peter	1945-	Music	20			45	Drummer of Kiss
Crist, Brigadier-Gen. William E.	1898-1985	Mil	30			40	
Cristal, Linda		Ent	10	12	22	22	
Cristalli, Italo		Opera	60				Opera. Great Tenor. SP Pc as Faust 150 Rare
Crittenden, George Bibb	1812-1880	Civ War	85	154	260		CSA Gen.
Crittenden, John J.	1787-1863	Cab	35	60	125		Sen., MOC KY, Atty. Gen.
Crittenden, Thomas L.	1819-1893	Civ War	50	135	220	250	Union Gen. Served also in Mex. War
Crittenden, Thomas L. (WD)	1819-1893	Civ War	85		1208		Union Gen.
Crittenden, Thomas Turpin	1825-1905	Civ War	50	90	142		Union Gen.

NAME	DATES	CATEGORY	SIG	LS/DS	ALS	SP	COMMENTS
Croce, Benedetto	1866-1952	Author	25	35	80		It. Statesman, Critic, Historian
Croce, Jim	1943-1973	Music	308			445	Rock, S Album 500-800
Crocker, Charles		Bus	475	2800	3850		Am. Financier. Pres. S. P. RR
Crocker, Marcellus Monroe	1830-1865	Civ War	65	110	175		Union Gen.
Crockett, David ('Davy')	1786-1836	Mil	4890	11750	34250		Am. Frontiersman. D. at Alamo
Crockett, Samuel R.		Author	10	15	35		Scot. Abandoned Ministry
Croft, Dwayne		Opera	10			25	Opera
Croghan, George		Colonial	195	420	850		Trader, Indian Agt, Treaty Maker
Croker, Richard Boss		Pol	25	45	80		Tammany Hall Leader
Croly, George		Clergy	15	25	40		
Crompton, Richmal	1890-1969	Author	48	62	155	85	(Lamburn) Novels 'Just William' Series
Cromwell, James		Ent	10			40	SP Col./Babe 70
Cromwell, Oliver	1599-1658	HOS	2900	6543	16408		Named Lord Protector Eng.
Cromwell, Richard	1626-1712	Royal	250		1200		3rd son of Oliver Cromwell
Cromwell, Richard	1910-1960	Ent	15	20	25	65	
Cronenberg, David		Ent	10			25	Film Dir.
Cronin, Archibald J.	1896-1981	Author	15	58	109	52	Br. Physician-Novels. 'The Citadel'
Cronin, James W.		Sci	15	25	35	20	Nobel Physics
Cronkite, Walter		TV News	25	35	50	70	TV News Anchor, Commentator
Cronyn, Hume		Ent	15	35	45	87	Cronyn & Jessica Tandy SP 100-200
Crook & Chase		Ent	10			25	Lorianne & Charlie
Crook, George	1818-1890	Civ War	219	343	391	650	Union Gen. Sig/Rank 385
Crook, Mackenzie		Ent	13			40	
Crookes, William, Sir	1832-1919	Sci	98	125	240		Br. Phys., Chem., Nobel. Thallium
Crooks, Richard		Opera	20	35	45	50	Opera. Am. Tenor
Crosbie, Annette	1934-	Ent	15			25	Scottish Actress
Crosby, Bing	1901-1977	Ent	65	248	238	200	Am. Singer-Actor. Academy Award. AMusQS 75
Crosby, Bob		Band	20			35	Big Band Leader-Singer
Crosby, Cathy Lee		Ent	10	10	20	25	Actress
Crosby, David		Music	80	200		185	Rock & Roll HOF
Crosby, Gary		Ent	15	15	15	20	Actor Son of Bing
Crosby, Howard		Clergy	15	20	25		
Crosby, J. T.		WWII	15	25	40	30	ACE, WWII, Navy Ace; 5. 25 kills
Crosby, Kathryn		Ent	10	15	25	25	
Crosby, Mary		Ent	10	10	10	15	Actress wife of Bing
Crosby, Norm		Ent	10	10	15	30	Actor-Comedian
Crosby, Percy		Comics	40	90		75	Skippy' Sign Orig. Sketch 200
Crosby, Stills, Nash & Young		Music	240	368		416	Rock. S (All Four) Album 750, guitar 1625
Crosley, Powel Jr.		Bus	20	75	95	35	Crosley Radio Corp.
Crosman, Henrietta	1861-1944	Ent	25			125	40 Years on Stage. Silent Films & Talkies
Cross, Christopher		Music	15			30	Comp., Singer
Cross, David		Ent	17			50	
Cross, Marcia		Ent	15			40	Actress
Cross, Wilbur L.		Gov	10	10			Gov. CT
Crosse, Andrew	1784-1855	Sci	45		165		Br. Electrical Pioneer/Copper-Zinc Battery
Crossfield, A. Scott	1921-2006	Aero	35	45	55	202	1st US Test Pilot of X-15; SP w/Rbt. White 210
Crossman, George H.		Civ War	45		90	60	Gen.
Crothers, Rachel		Author	10	30	40	20	Am. Plays. 'Susan & God'
Crothers, Scatman	1910-1986	Ent	25	30	45	70	Char. Actor. Disney Voice
Crouse, Lindsay	1948-	Ent	15	15	30	25	Actress
Crouse, Russell		Author	10	15	45	50	Plays. 'Life w/Father'
Croves, H. (B. Traven) Torsvan	1890-1969	Author	250	800			Ger. Novels, Actor, Pacifist
Crow, Sheryl		Music	20			65	Rock; Grammy winner
Crowe, Eyre		Statsmn	10		20		Br. Circa 1923

NAME	DATES	CATEGORY	SIG	LS/DS	ALS	SP	COMMENTS
Crowe, Russell		Ent	20	35		50	Actor; AA winner
Crowe, Sara		Ent	10			20	Actress TV
Crowe, William	1925-2007	Mil	20	45		45	Adm. US Navy; Chmn. US Joint Chiefs of Staff
Crowley, Joseph C		Congr	10				Member US Congress
Crowley, Leo		Cab	10	10	12	15	Chm. FDIC. 9 Gov't Posts
Crowley, Pat	1929-	Ent	10	15	20	35	Promising Actress of 50s Films
Crowninshield, Benj. W.		Cab	35	85	185		Sec. Navy 1814
Croxton, John Thomas	1836-1874	Civ War	50	96			Union Gen.
Croy, Homer	1883-	Author	15	40			Novels, Writer, Humorist
Crozier, William		Mil	35			60	Gen. WWI, Inventor
Crudup, Billy		Ent	15			45	Actor
Cruft, Charles	1826-1883	Civ War	50	94	147		Union Gen.
Cruikshank, Eliza		Celeb			60		Mrs. George Cruicshank
Cruikshank, George	1792-1878	Artist	92	86	365	375	Illust., Caricaturist, Etcher. S drawing 213-242
Cruise, Tom		Ent	35	25	65	80	DS 'Born on the 4th of July. ' 495
Crumb, George		Comp	25		375		Pulitzer, AMusQS 200, 320
Crumb, Robert		Comics	75		655	265	Underground, Psychedelic Cartoons. Sp. Ed. S 495-805; S sketch 1000
Crume, Dillard		Music	10			20	Blues Bassist/Koko Taylor
Crummit, Frank	1889-1943	Ent	20			60	Radio/Julia Sanderson; US singer/songwriter
Cruwell, Ludwig		WWII		130			Ger. Tank Cmdr.
Cruz, Celia	1925-2003	Music				350	Salsa singer
Cruz, Penelope		Ent	35			105	Actress
Cruzen, Richard H.		Expl	20		50	75	Adm. Arctic-Antarctic/Byrd
Cruz-Romo, Gilda		Opera	10			30	Opera
Cryer, Barry	1935-	Celeb	15			25	Br. Comedian
Crystal, Billy		Ent	25	75		60	Stand-up Comedian-Actor
Csokas, Marton		Ent	17			50	
Cube, Ice		Ent	15			45	
Cuberli, Lella	1945-	Ent	10			35	Actress
Cubin, Barbara C		Congr	10				Member US Congress
Cudahy, Michael F.		Bus	25	65	135	50	Meat Packer. Refrigeration
Cuellar, Javier P.		Diplo	10			20	Sec. Gen. UN
Cugat, Xavier	1900-1990	Music	20	30	35	65	Big Band Rhumba King. Performed in Films
Cui, Cesar	1835-1918	Comp	95	200	450		Russian Mil. Engineer
Cukor, George	1899-1983	Ent	42	95		191	Stage & Screen Dir.
Culberson, John Abney C		Congr	10				Member US Congress
Culbertson, Ely	1891-1955	Author	25	80		150	Invented Culbertson Contract Bridge
Culbertson, Frank L. Jr.		Space	10			20	
Culbreth, Kennith		Author	10			20	War World II, postal rail
Culkin, Kieran		Ent	10			20	Actor. Mac's Younger Brother
Culkin, Macaulay		Ent	25			49	Child Actor
Cullen, Countee		Author	200	555	332		Am. Black Poet. 1st Ed. S 230-450
Cullom, Shelby M.	1829-1914	Congr	35	60			MOC 1865, Sen., Gov. IL
Cullum, George W.	1809-1892	Civ War	46	70	80		Union Gen
Culp, Julia		Opera	35			150	Opera
Culp, Robert		Ent	15	20	25	40	SP w/Cosby (I Spy) 130
Culshaw, Jon		Celeb	10			15	Impressionist
Culver, Molly		Ent	13			40	
Culver, Roland	1900-1984	Ent	10	15	25	50	Br. Actor
Culverhouse, Hugh		Bus	10		15		
Cumberland, Wm. Aug., Duke	1721-1765	Royal	55	205			Third Son George II. Army Cmdr. 'Butcher Cumb. '
Cumming, Alan		Ent	17			50	
Cumming, Alfred	1829-1910	Civ War	100	295	330		CSA Gen.

NAME	DATES	CATEGORY	SIG	LS/DS	ALS	SP	COMMENTS
Cummings, e. e. (Edw. Estlin)		Author	200	404	314	695	Am. Poet, Painter
Cummings, Elijah E. C		Congr	10				Member US Congress
Cummings, Homer	1870-1956	Cab	25	40	75	95	FDR Atty Gen.
Cummings, Jim		Ent	23			68	
Cummings, Robert	1908-1990	Ent	18			68	Leading Man & Light Comed. from 1935
Cunard, Samuel, Sir		Bus	90	130	210		Br. Shipowner. Cunard Line
Cunningham, Andrew B.	1883-1963	Mil	35	100	200		Br. Adm. S. Afr. & WWI
Cunningham, E. V. (Howard Fast)		Author	20			35	Suspense Novels & Sci-Fi
Cunningham, John W.		Clergy	10	15	20	20	
Cunningham, Merce	1922-	Ent	40		200	65	Dancer/Choreogr. Kennedy Award
Cunningham, R. Walter	1932-	Space	20	40	55	60	
Cunningham, Randy "Duke"		Congr	10			35	Member US Congress; naval ace
Cunningham, Winfield Scott	1900-1986	WWII		75		90	Off. in Chg. Wake Isl. During Pearl Harbor
Cuoco, Kaley		Ent	16			48	
Cuomo, Mario		Gov	15	35		50	Governor NY
Curb, Mike		Ent	10			15	Songwriter
Curie, Marie	1867-1934	Sci	1229	4036	4882	4344	Fr. Phys. -Nobel Pr. Curie Inst. DS 9500, SB 3000
Curie, Pierre	1859-1906	Sci	440	895	4575		SB 1000
Curless, Dick		Cntry Mus	10			20	
Curley, Michael J., Arch.		Clergy	45	55	65		
Curley, Pauline	1903-2000	Ent	15			40	Vintage Actress
Currie, Donald, Sir		Bus	10	20	40		Scot. Shipowner. Castle Line
Currier, Moody		Gov	10			10	Gov. NY
Currier, Nathaniel		Artist	225	800			Currier & Ives, Lithographers
Curry, Adam	1964-	Ent	10			20	Actor
Curry, Ann		Celeb	10			25	TV Personality
Curry, B.		Civ War	55	70			CSA Off.
Curry, Charles Forrest		Congr	10	15	35		MOC CA
Curry, George		Mil	30	105			1st Territorial Gov. NM
Curry, Jabez L. M.	1825-1903	Civ War	35		40		CSA Congr. Lt. Col. Cavalry
Curry, John Steuart		Artist	65		370		Orig. Ink Sketch S 750, Murals
Curry, Tim		Ent	25	35	50	71	Rocky Horror Picture Show
Curt Weldon		Congr	10				Member US Congress
Curtin, Andrew G.		Gov	46	50			Civil War Gov. PA.
Curtin, Jane		Ent	15	15	20	40	Original cast of SNL
Curtin, John (Joseph A.)	1885-1945	HOS	35			45	WWII Prime Min. New Zealand
Curtis, Alan	1940-	Ent	12	15	35	40	Br. Actor
Curtis, Benjamin R.	1809-1874	Sup Crt	50	140	235		Resigned to protest Dred Scott. Johnson Def. Atty
Curtis, Charles	1860-1936	VP	55	182	180	115	Native Am. DesC. Hoover VP
Curtis, Cyrus H. K.		Bus	35	55	140	95	Curtis Publishing Co.
Curtis, Edward Sheriff	1868-1952	Artist		500			Photographer, Native Am. s
Curtis, George Wm.	1824-1892	Author	47	67	75		Editor Harper's Weekly. Civil War
Curtis, Jamie Lee		Ent	25	25	30	58	Actress
Curtis, Ken	1916-1991	Ent	25	45		75	Festus'. Country Music. 'Son of the Pioneers'
Curtis, Newton M.	1835-1910	Civ War	50	112			Union Gen. ALS '62 155
Curtis, Robin		Ent	10	12	20	28	'Star Trek'
Curtis, Samuel Ryan	1817-1866	Civ War	50	80	222		Union Gen. Hero of Pea Ridge
Curtis, Tony	1925-	Ent	25	50	95	124	Vint. SP 300; SP/Jack Lemmon 400; SP/Janet Leigh 200
Curtis, Verna Maria		Opera	10			30	Am. Sopr.
Curtis, Wilfred A.		Aero	10	25	40	25	
Curtiss, Glenn		Aero	205	480	650	625	Am. Inventor. Pioneer Aircraft Builder
Curtiz, Michael		Ent	30	75		100	Film Dir.
Curzon, George Nathaniel	1859-1925	HOS	25		65		1st Marquis, Viceroy & Gov. India 1898-1925
Curzon, Robert (Zouche)		Expl	10		25		

NAME	DATES	CATEGORY	SIG	LS/DS	ALS	SP	COMMENTS
Cusack, Joan		Ent	15			35	Actress-Sister of John Cusack
Cusack, John		Ent	20	35		50	Actor
Cusack, Niamh	1959-	Ent	10			20	Irish Actress
Cushing, Caleb	1800-1879	Cab	40	65	68		Pierce Atty Gen., Diplomat
Cushing, Harvey, Dr.		Sci	200	550	1725		Specialist in Neurosurgery
Cushing, Peter	1913-1994	Ent	35	50	55	179	Brit. Actor., SP Star Wars 400
Cushing, Richard	1895-1970	Clergy	40	75	85	55	Rom. Cath. Cardinal
Cushing, Thomas	1725-1788	Colonial	565	642			Patriot. Prominent in Col. Congr.
Cushman, Charlotte S.	1816-1876	Ent	25	35	60	117	19th C. Stage Actress. AM. HOF
Cushman, Robert E., Jr.	1914-	Mil	25			40	Gen. US Marines. Vietnam War
Cushman, Samuel		Congr	10	20	35		MOC NH 1835
Custer, Boston	1848-1876	Mil			1220		Custer's youngest bro. Killed at Little Big Horn
Custer, Elizabeth	1842-1933	Author	250	285	521	700	Wife of George A. Custer
Custer, George A.	1839-1876	Civ War	2941	5959	8000		Union Gen. LS/Cont 15000. Killed Little Big Horn
Custer, George A. (WD)	1839-1876	Civ War	3700	7217	10350	22500	Union Gen., Indian Fighter
Custine, Adam Philippe, Count de		Rev War	100	350			Fr. Gen. Fought in Am. Revolution
Custis, George Washington Parke	1778-1859	1st Fmly	30		125		Adopted son of Pres. George Washington.
Cutcheon, Byron M.	1836-1908	Civ War	45	55	90	122	Union Gen., US V. -27th Mich. MOH.
Cuthbert, Elisha		Ent	20			60	
Cutler, Lysander	1807-1866	Civ War	67	142	215		Union Gen.
Cutler, Manasseh	1742-1823	Rev War	425	550			Am. Clergyman, Botanist, Pioneer
Cuvier, Georges, Baron	1769-1832	Sci	107	497	480		Fr. Father of Comparative Anatomy. Naturalist
Cuyler, Theodore L.		Author	10	15	35		
Cypress Hill		Music				90	Rock
Cyrus, Billy Ray		Cntry Mus	25	70		48	Singer
Cyrus, Miley		Ent	25			60	Singer; AKA Hannah Montana
Czerny, Carl		Comp	75	255	460		Master of Liszt. Etudes. Teacher
Czerny, Vincenz		Sci	110		900		Ger. Leader Abdominal Surgery
Czerwenka, Oskar		Opera	10			25	Opera
Da Ponte, Lorenzo		Author		1500			Don Giovanni, Cosi Fan Tutte, Marriage of Figaro
D'Abo, Maryan		Ent	20			68	Actress.
D'Abo, Olivia		Ent	20			55	Actress.
Dache, Lilly		Bus	55	75	130	150	Coutourier. Specialty-Hats
Daddi, Francesco		Opera	25	35	50	55	Italian tenor. Stage debut in Milan in 1891.
Dafoe, Allan Roy, Dr.	1883-1943	Sci	52	60	135	225	Delivered Dionne Quintuplets
Dafoe, Willem		Ent	18	32	40	52	Actor
Daggett, David		Congr	12				FF 48
Dagmar	1921-2001	Ent	20	50		60	The 1st major female star of TV
Dagover, Lil	1897-1980	Ent	25			93	Vintage Ger. Actress
Daguerre, Louis		Sci	200	490	1250		Fr. Inventor Daguerreotype. Photog. Pioneer
Dahl, Arlene	1924-	Ent	15		25	52	Actress.
Dahl, Perry		WWII	10	25	38	30	ACE, WWII; 9 kills
Dahl, Roald		Author	50	136	150	148	Br. Short Stories, kid's
Dahlberg, Edward		Author	20	162	35	45	Am. Writer & Critic
Dahlberg, Ken		WWII	15	30	50	40	ACE, WWII; 14 kills
Dahlgren, John A.	1809-1870	Civ War	84	312	606		Adm. Union Navy. Dahlgren Gun. Sig./Rank 220
Dahlgren, John A. (WD)		Civ War	95	400			Union Rear Adm.
Dahlgren, Ulric	1824-1864	Civ War	275	325	964	2415	Union Col. Planned Capture Jeff. Davis.
Dahmer, Jeffrey	1960-1994	Crime	235	420			Serial killer
Dailey, Dan	1914-1978	Ent	25	45	65	125	Actor-Song & Dance Man, 20th C. Musicals
Dailey, Janet		Author	10	10		10	
Dailey, Peter F.	1868-1908	Ent	25	40	55	65	Comedian
Daily, E. G.		Ent	13			40	
Dal Monte, Toti		Opera	25			95	Opera.

NAME	DATES	CATEGORY	SIG	LS/DS	ALS	SP	COMMENTS
Daladier, Edouard		HOS	30	85	150	50	Premier Fr. Arrested-Liberated
Dalai Lama XIV	1935-	HOS	85	160	225	251	Exiled Tibetan Religious Leader
D'Albert, Eugen F. C.	1864-1932	Comp	55	75	130		Ger. Opera, Piano Concertos
Daley, Cass		Ent	15	18	20	48	Comedienne. Films
Daley, John F.	1985-	Ent				20	Actor
Daley, Richard J.		Pol	20	40	85	82	Mayor Chicago. Last of Big City Bosses
Daley, Richard M.		Pol	15			25	Mayor Chicago & Son of Richard J.
Dali, Salvador	1904-1989	Artist	186	558	838	378	Sp. Surrealist Painter. AManS/Sketches S5900-7500
Dali, Tracy	1966-	Ent	10			35	Model/actress
Dallapozza, Adolf		Ent	10			25	Vienna Operettas
Dallas, Alexander J.	1759-1817	Cab	60	175	261		Madison Sec. Treasury
Dallas, George M.		VP	70	200	222		Dallas, TX Named for Him. Polk VP
Dalmores, Charles		Opera	25			85	Opera
Dalton, Abby	1935-	Ent	15	20	25	40	Actress.
Dalton, Charles	1864-1942	Ent	20	30	40	50	Respected Broadway actor, active 1896-1940
Dalton, Dorothy		Ent	20	25	65	62	
Dalton, Emmett	1871-1937	Crime	650	1511	2838	1562	Western Train Robber
Dalton, Frank		Lawman	890	3000			US Marshal-Old West
Dalton, John		Sci	135	400	750		Br. Chemist & Philosopher
Dalton, Lacy J.	1948-	Cntry Mus	10			35	Singer/songwriter
Dalton, Timothy		Ent	25	45		65	Actor; James Bond:
Dalton, Tristram	1738-1817	Pol			506		US Sen Mass
Daltrey, Roger	1944-	Music	30	50	95	108	Rock. 'Who' Lead Singer
Daluege, Kurt	1897-1946	Mil	75				Chief police Prussian Ministry
Daly, James	1918-1978	Ent	20	20	25	50	Actor. Movie-TV. Father of Tyne Daly.
Daly, John Charles	1914-1991	Ent	15			35	News Commentator. Host. 'What's My Line?'
Daly, Tim		Ent	20			40	Actor
Daly, Tyne	1947-	Ent	15	25	32	35	Actress
Dam, Henrik		Sci	70			105	Danish Biochemist. Nobel. Phil. Cvr. S 125
D'Amato, Alfonse		Congr	10			45	Sen. NY
Damian, Michael	1962-	Ent	10			20	Actor; Young & the Restless
Damita, Lili		Ent	32	80	85	82	Fr. Film Star. Mrs. Errol Flynn; S w/Flynn 200
Damon, Cathryn	1930-1987	Ent	15	20	25	45	Actress. Char.
Damon, Les	1908-1962	Ent	25	40		80	Radio Actor. 'Nick Charles' in 'Thin Man'
Damon, Matt		Ent	20	35	40	62	Actor. AA 'Good Will Hunting'
Damone, Vic	1928-	Music	15			35	Singer
Damrosch, Walter	1862-1950	Comp	32	101	115	317	Symphony Broadcast Pioneer. AMusQS 125-350
Dana, Bill	1924-	Ent	25			42	Jose Jiminez'. Early 60s Comedian-TV Writer
Dana, Charles A.	1819-1897	Pub	30	30	75	45	Owner/Ed. NY Sun. Mbr. War Dept. Civil War
Dana, James D.		Sci	25	45	65		Scientific Observer Antarctic
Dana, Napoleon J. T.	1822-1905	Civ War	50	78	111	130	Union Gen. ADS '64 300
Dana, Richard Henry	1815-1882	Author	30	55	80		Sailor, author of "2 Years Before the Mast"
Dana, Richard Henry	1787-1879	Civ War	60	200	225		Prosecutor of Jefferson Davis
Danaher, John A.		Congr	10	15		10	Sen. CT
Dance, Bill		Author	10			15	Fishing
Dandridge, Dorothy	1923-1965	Ent	75	275	135	421	Singer, Actress, Dancer
Dandridge, Ruby	1899-1987	Ent	35			275	Radio, Movies; Dorothy's Mother
Dandy, George B.	1830-1911	Civ War	50	95			Twice Brevetted Union Gen. Georgian
Dane, Karl	1886-1934	Ent	20	95		175	Danish Actor
Dane, Nathan	1752-1835	Rev War	75	95	200		Mass. Rep in Cont. Congr. from 1785-1788.
Danei, Paul Francis	1694-1775	Clergy		7500			Saint Paul of the Cross 1867
Danenhower, John Wilson		Expl	20	45	115		De Long Arctic Exped. 1879
Danes, Claire	1979-	Ent	15			42	Actress
Danforth, John C.		Congr	10			10	Sen. MO

NAME	DATES	CATEGORY	SIG	LS/DS	ALS	SP	COMMENTS
Danforth, Thomas	1622-1699	Colonial	390	470			Deputy Governor MA
D'Angelo, Beverly		Ent	15			40	Actress
Dangerfield, George		Author	10	10	25		
Dangerfield, Rodney	1921-2004	Ent	25	95	95	132	Comedian., 'No Respect'
Danges, Henry	1870-1948	Opera	35			70	Opera. Baritone. Sang in World Prem. 'Louise'
Daniel, Brittany	1976-	Ent	10			25	Actress
Daniel, John W.		Congr	15	25			Sen. VA, Disabled in CW
Daniel, Junius	1828-1864	Civ War	450				CSA gen, KIA Spotsylvania, VA
Daniel, Peter Vivian	1784-1860	Sup Crt	45	125	475		
Daniel, Price		Congr	15	40		25	Sen., Gov. TX
Daniell, Henry	1894-1963	Ent	50			150	Vintage Villainous Char. Actor
Daniels, Anthony		Ent	20			75	3CPO
Daniels, Bebe	1901-1971	Ent	25	45	75	146	Vintage Actress. Major Star 30s
Daniels, Billy		Music	20			50	Afr-Am. Vocalist. Supper Clubs & Early TV
Daniels, Charlie		Cntry Mus	15			40	
Daniels, Faith	1957-	Celeb	10			20	News anchor
Daniels, Jeff		Ent	18	35		45	Actor
Daniels, Josephus	1862-1948	Cab	25	50	160	125	Sec Navy WWI. Diplomat, Journalist, Editor
Daniels, Lisa		Ent	15			45	
Daniels, Mickey Richard Jr.	1914-1970	Ent	55			195	Orig. Cast Mbr. of 'The Little Rascals'
Daniels, Squire, Elizabeth		Author	10			20	Mystery novels, forgetful detective
Daniels, William	1927-	Ent	15			35	Actor
Daniloff, Nicholas		Jrnalist	10			15	Am. journalist
Danilova, Alexandra		Ballet	20	35	65	75	Rus-Am Ballerina, Teacher
Dankworth, Johnny		Band	15			25	Jazz Musician
Dannay, Frederick	1905-1982	Author	50	160	282		ELLERY QUEEN
Dannenberg, Konrad		Sci	25	50		55	Rocket Pioneer/von Braun
Danner, Blythe		Ent	15	20	20	35	Actress. & Mother of Gwineth Paltrow
Danning, Sybil	1947-	Ent	15	20	20	110	Actress.
D'Annunzio, Gabriele	1863-1938	Author	75	175	150	450	It. Writer, Pro-Fascist Soldier
Danny & the Juniors		Music		402			Rock group:
Dano, Paul		Ent	15			45	
Dano, Royal	1922-1994	Ent	10	10	20	50	Vintage Char. Actor
Danova, Cesare	1926-1992	Ent	15	20	25	55	
Danson, Ted		Ent	20			45	Actor
Dantine, Helmut		Ent	15	15		51	Austrian Actor of 40s-50s.
Danton, Georges-Jacques		Fr Rev	1080	2538			Guillotined Leader of Revolution
Danton, Ray	1931-1992	Ent	25	45		200	Actor
Danza, Tony		Ent	10	15	25	40	Actor. Ex-Boxer
Darby, Kim	1947-	Ent	20			40	Actress.
D'Arcleé, Haricleé		Opera	100				Fr. Sopr.
Darcy		Music	15			30	Music. Bass, Vocals Smashing Pumpkins
Darcy, Emery		Opera	15			40	Met. Heidentenor
Darden, Christopher		Law	15	35		20	O. J. Simpson Prosecuting Atty
Darges, Fritz		WWII		195			SS-Obersturmbannfuhrer; Hitler's Personal Adjutant
Darin, Bobby	1936-1973	Music	173		250	293	Singer-Actor. 'Mack the Knife' Topped Charts d. 37
Darion, Joe		Comp	10			30	Jazz. AMusQS 50
Darlan, Francois	1881-1942	Mil			448		Fr. Adm. Vichy. Assass.
Darling, Charles John Lord	1849-1936	Jurist			90		
Darling, J. N. 'Ding'	1876-1962	Comics	25			150	Pol. Cartoonist
Darlington, William	1782-1863	Author	25		155		Naturalist. Many Swiss & US plants named for him
Darman, Richard	1943-	Pol	10			15	
Darnell, Linda	1923-1965	Ent	55	145		285	D. Tragically in Fire
Darrah, Thomas		Mil	35	50		45	Gen. WWI

NAME	DATES	CATEGORY	SIG	LS/DS	ALS	SP	COMMENTS
Darrall, Chester B.		Congr	20	30	55		MOC LA. Union Surgeon CW
Darre, Richard-Walther	1895-1953	Mil	52			65	SS., Ger. cabinet Min.
Darrell, Johnny	1940-1997	Cntry Mus	20			45	
Darren, James		Ent	15			50	Actor-Singer
Darrieux, Danielle	1917-	Ent	15			35	Fr. Actress. Film & Stage
Darro, Frankie		Ent	50			150	Child Actor. Disney Voice
Darrow, Charles B.	1889-1967	Design	395	995			Developed Best Seller 'Monopoly'
Darrow, Clarence	1857-1938	Law	369	1688	1737	1539	Scopes 'Monkey Trial', Loeb & Leopold.
Darrow, Henry		Ent	15			45	
Dart, Justin		Bus	50	100	250	75	Drugstore Chain. Art Museum
D'Artagnan, Comte de		Mil			6500		Capt. Louis XIV Musketeers
Dartiguenave, Philippe Sudre		HOS	40	100			Pres. of Haiti 1915
Daru, Pierre Bruno	1767-1829	Pol	30		95		Min. of France
D'Arville, Camille		Ent	15			45	Actress
Darwell, Jane	1880-1967	Ent	105	110	167	230	Vintage Actress. AA Winner
Darwin, Charles	1809-1882	Sci	1236	3855	14205	16735	Theory of Evolution; ALS/Cont 15000. AMS 78000
Darwin, Francis Sir	1848-1925	Sci			150		Son af Charles Darwin
Daschle, Thomas		Congr	10			20	US Senate (D-SD)
Dash, Stacey	1966-	Ent	10			35	Actress
Dassin, Jules		Ent	20			45	Film Dir.
Daubigny, Charles Francois		Artist	95	280	425		Fr. Landscape Painter
Daudet, Alphonse	1840-1897	Author	35	80	175	63	Fr. Stories, Novels, Plays
Daugherty, Harry M.	1860-1941	Cab	30	55	125	50	Harding Atty Gen. Tried for Fraud & Acquitted
Daughtry, Chris	1979-	Music	20			40	Singer
Daumier, Honore		Artist	240	630	1470		Fr. Caricaturist & Serious Art
Dauphin, Claude		Ent	35			75	Fr. Leading Man
Dausset, Jean, Prof.		Sci	20	45		35	Nobel Med.
Dauvray, Helen	b 1859	Ent	25			125	"Little Nell"
Dave Clark Five		Music	150			798	Br. Rock Group 1960s
Dave Mathew Band		Music	75			125	Rock group; S Guitar 500
Dave Weldon		Congr	10				Member US Congress
Dave, Red River		Cntry Mus	10			25	Country Singer
Davenport, Addington	1670-1736	Rev War	150	265	500		Am. Colonial Jurist
Davenport, Fanny		Ent	25			62	Vintage Actress. 1889
Davenport, Harry		Ent	95		150	204	Veteran Char. Actor. 'GWTW' SP 595
Davenport, Homer C.		Comics	30	60	135		Pol. Cartoons, Uncle Sam, S draw. 391
David		Music	15			25	Music. Drummer 'Korn'
David, Felicien-Cesar	1810-1876	Comp	100	500			AMusMS 350-750
David, Ferdinand		Comp	45		225		Ger. Violinist
David, Hal		Comp	20	30	65	35	
David, Jacques Louis		Artist	175	738	610		Fr. Classical Painter
David, Keith		Ent	15			45	
David, Larry	1947-	Ent	20	35	50	50	Comedian; Creator of Seinfeld
David, Mack		Comp	20			40	Lyricist
Davidovich, Lolita		Ent	12			40	Actress
Davidson, Allen Turner		Civ War	25	80	125		CSA Congress. Lawyer, Banker
Davidson, Amy		Ent	14			41	
Davidson, Arthur	1881-1950	Bus	1100	3500			Harley-Davidson Motorcycle Fndr.
Davidson, Gordon		Bus	1500	1800			A Fndr. of Harley-Davidson. DS Stock Cert.
Davidson, Henry Brevard	1831-1899	Civ War	110	248	357		CSA Gen.
Davidson, Jim		Ent	10			40	Actor. 'Pacific Blue'
Davidson, Jo		Artist	35	75	126	105	Am. Sculptor
Davidson, Jo		Celeb			58		Songwriter
Davidson, John		Ent	10	15	15	25	Singer-Actor-Host

NAME	DATES	CATEGORY	SIG	LS/DS	ALS	SP	COMMENTS
Davidson, John W.	1824-1881	Civ War	50	84	126		Union Gen. ALS '62 630
Davidson, Loyal		Mil	35	60			
Davidson, Peter		Ent	10			20	Actor
Davidson, Randall T., Arch.		Clergy	25	35	45		
Davidson, Walter		Bus	1200	3300			Harley-Davidson Motorcycle Fndr. DS Stock Cert
Davidson, William B.	1888-1947	Ent	25			100	Char. Actor
Davidson, William H.		Bus	1000	1867	4300		Son of Wm. A. & Pres. Harley-Davidson 30s-40's
Davidtz, Embeth		Ent	13			40	
Davies, Ben		Opera				100	English Tenor
Davies, Gail		Music	10			20	Singer
Davies, Gilli		Celeb	10			15	Welsh Chef
Davies, Henry E.	1836-1894	Civ War	58	80			Union Gen.
Davies, Jeremy	1969-	Ent	10			25	
Davies, Marion	1897-1961	Ent	50	100	140	262	C. Bull Original SP 275
Davies, Peter Maxwell		Comp	40			110	Songs of a Mad King'. Opera
Davies, Ray		Music	34			60	The Kinks; S Guitar 450
Davies, Rhys		Author	10	20	35	20	Welch. Novels, Stories
Davies, Ronald N.		Law	25	50	60	30	Nazi War Trials Jurist
Davies, Thomas F., Bish.		Clergy	30	35	45		
Davies, William		Rev War	145	150	170		Sec. War of VA
Davis, Angela	1944-	Activist	20	30	50	40	Activist. Wanted Poster/Sig. 250
Davis, Ann		Ent	13			40	
Davis, Ann B.	1926-	Ent	15	25		40	Char. Actress. 'Brady Bunch'
Davis, Artur D		Congr	10				Member US Congress
Davis, Benjamin F.		Civ War	50		161		Union Cavalry Cmdr.
Davis, Benjamin O. Jr.	1912-2002	WWII	15	20	38	50	WWII Ace. 1st Afro-Am. Fighter Pilot & USAF Gen.
Davis, Bette	1908-1989	Ent	68	190	289	385	Actress; Multi Oscar Winner
Davis, Brad	1949-1991	Ent	60			122	Actor. 'Midnight Express'
Davis, Charles Henry	1807-1877	Civ War	50	89	128		Union Adm. ALS '63 275
Davis, Clifton	1945-	Ent	15			30	Actor TV
Davis, Cushman K.		Congr	12	25		30	Sen. MN
Davis, Danny K. D		Congr	10				Member US Congress
Davis, David	1815-1886	Sup Crt	64	157	252		Sen. IL. Pres Pro Tem. Executor Lincoln Estate
Davis, Don		Celeb	10			12	Potter
Davis, Dwight F.	1879-1945	Cab	30	68	130	65	Sec War. Donor of Davis Cup. Gov-Gen. Philippines
Davis, Ellabelle	1907-1960	Music	25			80	Singer
Davis, Evelyn Redmon		Author	10			12	Genealogy
Davis, Ewin L.		Congr	10	10			MOC TN
Davis, Fay	1872-1945	Ent	25	40	65	65	Actress. 1895 London Hit in 'Prisoner of Zenda'
Davis, Gail	1925-1997	Ent	20	25	30	20	Actress. 'Annie Oakley'
Davis, Geena		Ent	20	25	35	50	Oscar Winner
Davis, George	1820-1896	Civ War	68				Member of CSA Congress, Atty. Gen
Davis, Henry Greene		Civ War	50	85			Union Gen.
Davis, Henry Minton	1817-1865	Congr	20		50		Prevented MD from Joining CSA
Davis, Henry Winter		Congr	10				FF 37
Davis, Hope		Ent	13			40	
Davis, James J.		Cab	20	50	95	75	Sec. Labor, Fndr. of Moose
Davis, Jan		Space	10			20	
Davis, Jefferson	1808-1889	Civ War	625	1510	3045	4000	CSA Pres. ALS/Cont 15000, LS 55000; S Chk 1900
Davis, Jefferson (WD)	1808-1889	Civ War	788	4359	4758	5500	Pres. CSA. ALS/Cont 15900, LS/Cont 13500
Davis, Jefferson C.	1828-1879	Civ War	53	118	159		Union Gen. ANS '62 330, Sig/Rank 75
Davis, Jim		Comics	50	77	225	175	Garfield'. Repro Sketch S 150
Davis, Jim		Ent	40	40	70	82	Actor. 'Dallas'
Davis, Jim D		Congr	10				Member US Congress

D

NAME	DATES	CATEGORY	SIG	LS/DS	ALS	SP	COMMENTS
Davis, Jimmie		Gov	30	45		60	Singing LA Gov. 'You Are My Sunshine'. AMusQS 150
Davis, Jo Ann		Congr	10				Member US Congress
Davis, Joan		Ent	28			84	
Davis, John	1761-1847	Author	30	175	290		Historian, Comptroller US Treas
Davis, John	1787-1854	Gov	25	50	70		Gov. MA
Davis, John Wm.	1873-1955	Congr	20	45	75	40	Dem. Pres. Cand. Defended R. Oppenheimer
Davis, Johnny 'Scat'	1910-1983	Ent	25	30	35	40	
Davis, Jonathan		Music	12			48	Lead Singer 'Korn'
Davis, Joseph Robert	1825-1896	Civ War	149	210	350		CSA Gen.
Davis, Kristin		Ent	15			48	Charlotte York, Sex in the City; actress
Davis, Lincoln D		Congr	10				Member US Congress
Davis, Mack		Cntry Mus	15			25	Singer-Songwriter
Davis, Meyer		Music	15			35	Big Society Band
Davis, Miles	1926-1991	Music	432	695		942	Immortal Jazz Trumpet Player-Comp.
Davis, Nancy	1921-	Ent	50			150	
Davis, Nancy (Reagan)		1st Lady	80	125		170	
Davis, Nelson H.	1821-1890	Civ War	50	68	96		Union Gen. Chancellorsville
Davis, Noah		Congr	10	25	60		MOC NY 1869, Jurist
Davis, Ossie	1917-2005	Ent	20			45	Actor. Stage-Screen. Plays, Pol. Activis
Davis, Patti		Celeb	15			20	Daughter of Ronald Reagan; Author
Davis, Phil		Comics	30			250	MAndrake the Magician
Davis, Phyllis	1947-	Ent	10	12	18	25	Actress
Davis, Reuben	1813-1890	Civ War	68	138	270		CSA Gen.
Davis, Richard Harding		Jrnalist	15	25	40	120	Correspondent 6 Wars, Novels
Davis, Robert		Mil	20		25	45	Gen. WWI
Davis, Rufe	1908-1974	Ent	25			95	
Davis, Sammi	1964-	Ent	10			20	Br. Actress
Davis, Sammy, Jr.	1925-1990	Ent	50	155	80	259	Multi-talented singer, actor, dancer
Davis, Susan A. D		Congr	10				Member US Congress
Davis, Tom D		Congr	10				Member US Congress
Davis, Varina		1st Lady	245	354	556	524	Mrs. Jeff. Davis. ALS/Cont 1600-6000
Davis, Warwick		Ent				40	Actor; 'Harry Potter', 'Star Wars', 'Prin. Bride'
Davis, William George Mackey	1812-1898	Civ War	90	190	340		CSA Gen.
Davis, William W. H.	1820-1910	Civ War	42	71	120		Led 104th PA
Davison, Bruce	1946-	Ent	15			25	
Davison, Wild Bill		Music	30			75	Jazz Cornet-Bandleader
Davisson, Clinton Joseph		Sci	25	75			Nobel Physics. Bell Laboratories
Davitan, Ken		Ent	12			35	
Davout, Louis Nicolas, Duke		Fr Rev	45	210	248		Marshal of Napoleon
Davro, Bobby	1959-	Celeb	10			20	Br. Comedian
Davy, Humphry, Sir	1778-1829	Sci	118	322	643		Br. Chemist. ALS/Cont 3750, 8, 500, AManS 2500
Dawber, Pam		Ent	15	15	20	30	Actress.
Dawes, Charles G.		VP	40	110	175	295	Nobel Peace Pr.
Dawes, William	1745-1799	Rev War	3500				Patriot. Rode w/Paul Revere
Dawm Chong, Rae		Ent	10			20	Actress
Dawson, George		Clergy	20	35	60		
Dawson, John B.	1798-1845	Congr	10				Repr. LA, Maj. Gen. of Militia
Dawson, John L.		Congr	20		70		Governor Kansas Terr., MOC PA
Dawson, Richard	1932-	Ent	10	20		30	Hogan's Heroes Co-Star; Game Show host:
Dawson, Roger		Author	10			15	Art of Negotiating
Dawson, Rosario		Ent	16			48	
Dawson-Briggs, Roxanne		Ent	20			40	Actress. Star Trek
Dawson's Creek (cast)		Ent				150	Cast SP of 4
Day, Chon		Comics	10	35		50	Brother Sebastian

NAME	DATES	CATEGORY	SIG	LS/DS	ALS	SP	COMMENTS
Day, Dennis	1916-1988	Ent	20	30	45	98	Vocalist-Comed. Jack Benny Radio & TV Shows
Day, Doris	1924-	Ent	25	67		120	Am. singer, actress & animal welfare advocate
Day, J. Edward		Cab	10	15	15	15	P. M. Gen.
Day, Jeremiah		Clergy	15	20	35		
Day, Laraine	1920-2007	Ent	20	35		60	Actress
Day, Linda (George)	1944-	Ent	10	10	15	30	Actress Turned Dir.
Day, Simon	1962-	Celeb	10			20	Br. Comedian
Day, William R.	1849-1923	Sup Crt	40	90	135	65	Sec. State
Dayan, Moshe	1915-1981	Mil	175	167	1117	304	Israeli Gen., Pol. Masterminded 3 Wars; ALS Love Letters from Prison $6000-11000
Dayan, Yael		Author	10			25	Daughter of Moshe Dyan
Day-Lewis, Cecil	1904-1972	Author	15	50			Br. Poet-Laureate
Day-Lewis, Daniel		Ent	25	35		74	
Daymond, Gus		WWII	12	25	55	40	ACE, WWII, Eagle Squadron; 7 kills
Dayne, Taylor		Music	20			42	Rock
Dayton, Elias		Rev War	100	210	395		Gen. Continental Congress
Dayton, Jonathan	1760-1824	Rev War	200	215	252		Cont. Congr. Signer of Constitution
Dayton, Jonathan		Ent	17			50	
Dayton, Mark		Congr	10				US Senate (D-MN)
Dayton, William L.	1807-1867	Congr	25	40	110		John C. Fremont Running Mate
D'Azeglio, Massimo	1798-1866	Statsmn			120		Italian author & Statesman
De Acosta, Mercedes		Author	10	25	45		Intimate of Greta Garbo
de Almeida, Antonio		Cond	10			45	Specialist in Fr. Music
De Beauvoir, Simone		Author	35	95	200		Fr. Writer, Philosopher, Feminist
De Bono, Emilio		Mil	75	225			It. Fascist Pol. & Gen.
De Bray, Xavier B.	1818-1895	Civ War	125	174			CSA Gen. ALS/Cont 2500
De Broglie, Louis Victor	1892-1984	Sci	50	125	195	184	Nobel Pr. 1929. Wave theory of electronics
De Cadenet, Amanda		Ent	15			45	
De Corsia, Ted	1903-1973	Ent	20	25		50	Actor
De Courcey, Roger		Ent	10			18	Br. Ventriloquist. Operator of 'Nookie Bear'
de Duve, Christian R.		Sci	10			40	Nobel
De Falla, Manuel	1876-1946	Comp	425	883	1200		Sp. AMusQS 2000
De Forest, Lee, Dr.	1873-1961	Sci	101	371	694	650	Invented Vacuum Tube. ALS/Sci. Cont. 12500
De Gaulle, Charles	1890-1969	HOS	425	1047	1988	1122	Fr. WWII Gen., War dte TLS/Cont 1000-5000
de Gouvion Saint-Cyr, Laurent	1764-1830	Mil		120			Fr. Mil. Off. Fr. Revolution & Napoleonic wars
De Havilland, Geoffrey	1882-1965	Aero	85	160	205	150	De Havilland Aircraft Co.
De Havilland, Olivia	1916-	Ent	40	75	125	147	As 'Melanie' in GWTW; AA winner
De Hidalgo, Elvira		Opera	45			150	Coloratura Sopr. Teacher of Callas
De Kooning, Elaine		Artist	50			242	Willem's Wife. Artist in her own right.
De Kooning, Willem	1904-1997	Artist	150	225	825	358	Dutch Abstract Impressionist. Repro S 285-550
De Koven, Reginald	1859-1920	Comp	25	45	200	100	Versatile Am. Comp.
de la Barra, Francisco Leon		Statsmn	132	1225			Mex. Diplomat, Pol., Amb. US, Prov. Pres.
De La Beckwith, Bryan	1925-	Activist	15		70	55	Convicted Murderer of Medgar Evers
De La Cierva, Juan		Aero	90		295	350	Inventor Autogyro
De La Grange, Anna		Opera			80		Opera
De La Mare, Walter	1873-1956	Author	38	67	90	45	Br. Poet. Songs of Childhood. Novels
De La Pena, George	1955-	Ent	10	10	10	20	Actor
de la Reguera, Ana		Ent	13			40	
De La Renta, Oscar		Bus	15	22	35	40	Fashion Designer. Elegant Gowns
De la Rocha, Zack		Music	15			42	Lead Singer Rage Against the Machine
De La Rue, Warren	1815-1889	Sci			200		Br. Astron., Inventor Silver-Chlor. Battery
De Lagnel, Julius Adolph	1827-1912	Civ War	50	65			CSA Lt. Col, Ordnance Dept.
De Lancey, Stephen		Rev War	100	180	225		Loyalist. Lawyer. Imprisoned
de Lesseps, Ferdinand		Diplo		285	450		Fr. Dipl. & Chief Engr. Oversaw Suez Canal const.

NAME	DATES	CATEGORY	SIG	LS/DS	ALS	SP	COMMENTS
De Lint, Derek		Ent	10			25	Actor
De Lisle, Claude J. Rouget		Author			1200		Fr. Army Off. Author of 'La Marseillaise'
De Luca, Giuseppe		Opera	25	35	95	162	Opera
De Matteo, Drea		Opera	15			40	Adrianna La Cerva, Sopranos
de Merode, Cleo		Ballet				100	Fr. ballet star
De Mornay, Rebecca		Ent	10	15		35	Actress
De Palma, Brian		Ent	10	20	35	40	Film Dir.
De Paul, Saint Vincent		Clergy	1100	1600	4500		
De Peyster, John W. Jr.		Civ War	25	30	55		Aide to Gen. Kearny
De Quincey, Thomas		Author	110	170	250		AMS 650-2250
de Ravin, Emilie		Ent	17			50	
De Reszke, Edouard	1853-1917	Opera	68	225			Opera-Vintage. AMusQS 75
De Reszke, Jean	1850-1925	Opera	100	120	160	345	Opera-Vintage. SP/Brother Edouard 425
De Reszke, Marie		Opera			125		Opera
De Ridder. Anton		Opera	10		45	35	Opera
De Rita, Joe		Ent	35		65	66	Three Stooges SP 55, S Chk 125
De Rossetti, Curt		Bus	10	20			Restaurateur
de Rossi, Portia		Ent	17			50	
De Russy, Gustavus A. (WD)		Civ War	65	250	233		Union Gen.
De Sade, Marquis	1740-1814	Author	500	1324	1910		Fr. Social Deviant. Abnormal Behavior. 'Sadism'
de Seca, Vittorio	1901-1994	Ent				270	Academy Award– winning Italian Dir.
De Seversky, Alexander	1894-1973	Aero	75	140	205	145	TLS/Historical Cont. 1, 200
De Smet, Pierre	1801-1873	Clergy	225		800		Jesuit Missionary to Western Indians
De Toth, André		Ent	10			20	Film Dir.
De Trobriand, Philippe R. (WD)		Civ War	55	109	395		Union Gen.
De Valera, Eamon (Ire)	1882-1975	HOS	102	125	325	110	Pres. P. M. Cont; TLS 550
De Vere, Aubrey T.		Author	20	60	140		Ir. Poet, Critic, Hymns
De Vito, Danny		Ent	20			40	Actor
De Wilde, Brandon	1942-1972	Ent	318			567	Actor
De Windt, Harry	1856-1933	Expl	30	45	75	75	Br. Explr.
De Witt, Alexander		Congr	10		20		MOC MA
Deacon, Richard	1921-1984	Ent	50			132	Actor. 'Dick Van Dyke Show', 'Leave It to Beaver'
Dead End Kids		Ent	350				The Bowery Boys:
Deal, Bill	1944-2003	Music				60	Singer
Deal, Nathan D		Congr	10				Member US Congress
Dean, Billy		Cntry Mus	15			30	
Dean, Donald J.		Mil	25	45			WWI Victoria Cross
Dean, Eddie		Cntry Mus	10	10	20	25	
Dean, Gilbert	1819-1870	Congr	10				Repr. NY
Dean, James	1931-1955	Ent	2114	5257	3250	6203	Short, Spectacular Film career. S Chk 13000
Dean, Jimmy		Cntry Mus	15	25		35	Singer & Sausage Entrepreneur
Dean, John W.		Law	20	35	45	95	Special Counsel to Nixon. Watergate
Dean, Julia	1858-1972	Ent	15	25	35	65	Actress
Dean, Letitia	1967-	Ent	10			25	Br. Actress
Dean, Maureen		Author	10	35			(Mrs. John Dean)
Dean, Millvina	1912-	Titanic	75	90	105	111	Youngest Titanic survivor; Shipwreck Litho. S 250
Dean, Pricilla	1896-1987	Ent	20			70	Silent Film Star of early 20s
Dean, William F.	1899-1981	Mil	25	35	55	195	Gen. WWII. Hero of Korean War
Deane, Silas	1737-1789	Rev War	250	550	975		Diplomat. Negotiated Treaties. Cont. Congr.
DeAngelis, Jefferson		Ent	35			125	Actor early 1900's
Dearborn, Henry	1751-1829	Rev War	135	303	869		Rev. War Gen. Jefferson Sec War. Statesman
Dearborn, Henry A. S.	1783-1851	Congr	55	175	250		Collector Port Boston 1812-29
Dearden, John, Card.		Clergy	30	35	45	40	
Dearing, James	1840-1865	Civ War	240				CSA Gen.

NAME	DATES	CATEGORY	SIG	LS/DS	ALS	SP	COMMENTS
Deas, Zachariah Cantey	1819-1882	Civ War	138	294			CSA Gen.
Death on the Nile (Cast)		Ent				75	Signed by 6
Deayton, Angus	1956-	Celeb	10			20	English comic actor & TV presenter.
DeBakey, Michael, Dr.	1908-	Sci	22	38	75	45	Surgeon. 1st Coronary Artery Bypass Op.
Debar, William J.		Congr	10	15			Sen. KY
DeBeaune, Charlotte		Celeb		525			Mistress of Henry IV
DeBeck, Billy		Comics	30				Barney Google, Snuffy Smith
Debenham, Frank	1883-1965	Expl	40	100			Antarctic Explr.
Debizka, Hedwig von		Opera	40			150	Opera singer
DeBlanc, Jeff		WWII	15	28	52	38	ACE, WWII, CMH; 9 kills
Debolt, Bob & Dorothy		Celeb	10			15	Fndr. s of AASK(Adopt a Special Kid)
Deborba, Dorothy		Ent	11			33	
DeBray, Xavier B.	1818-1895	Civ War	95		690		CSA Gen.
Debre, Michael		HOS	10	20	50		
DeBroglie, Louis-C-V- Maurice		Sci	50	90			Physicist. Pioneer in X-Rays
DeBruhl, Harold		Author	10			15	Regional history
Debs, Eugene		Labor	119	279	388	450	US Socialist Leader. Organizer
Debussy, Claude	1862-1918	Comp	256	525	949		Fr. Comp. AMusQS 7, 500
DeButts, John D.		Bus	10	35	45	20	
Debye, Peter J. W.		Sci	55	110	175		Nobel Chemistry-Discovered Rayon
Decadenet, Amanda	1972-	Ent	10			20	Br. -born actress & Photographer.
Decamp, Rosemary		Ent	25			58	Am. Radio & Film Star
DeCarlo, Yvonne	1922-2007	Ent	28	25	35	62	Actress
DeCasseres. Benjamin		Author	10	15	25		Columnist, Editorials NY Mirror
Decatur, Stephen	1779-1820	Mil	332	2550	3150		Am. Naval Hero, War 1812
DeCisneros, Eleanora		Opera	40			185	Opera
DeCordova, Fred	1910-2001	Ent	10	15	15	30	Dir. Prod.
Dee, Francis	1909-2004	Ent	15	20	20	40	Actress & Wife of Joel McCrea
Dee, Jack	1962-	Celeb	10			20	English stand-up comedian
Dee, Ruby	1923-	Ent	15	20	20	45	1st Afr-Am w/Major Shakespeare Role, Am. Fest.
Dee, Sandra	1942-2005	Ent	35	50	75	90	Actress; Gidget
Deeley, Cat		Ent	15			45	
Deems, 'Cousin'		Cntry Mus	10			15	His 'Goat Herders'
Deep Purple		Music	80			215	Rock group: S Guitar 250-760
Deere, Allan Christopher		WWII	15	40	50	50	NZ's most famous Fighter Pilot. WWII Ace. 22 kills
Deere, John	1804-1886	Bus	300	2150	1450		Steel Plow; Deere Chk 800-1000
Deering, James		Bus	10	25	45	25	
Deering, Olive	1918-1986	Ent	15			50	Actress
Dees, Morris		Law	10			25	Lawyer, Pol. Activist. Tracks Hate Crimes
Dees, Rick		Ent	10	10	15	15	Singer Radio-TV Host
Def Leppard		Music	165			181	Rock group: S Album 260; S Guitar 235-400
DeFazio, Peter A. D		Congr	10				Member US Congress
Defoe, Daniel	1660-1731	Author	1500	7500			Br. Journalist, Novels
DeFord, Bailey		Cntry Mus	20			75	Early Black Opry Star
DeFore, Don		Ent	15			45	Actor.
DeFranco, Buddy		Band	12			25	Bandleader, Clarinetist
Degas, Edgar	1834-1917	Artist	350	980	2675		Fr. Impressionist. Ballet Scenes
DeGeneres, Ellen		Ent	25	30		53	Comedienne
DeGette, Diana D		Congr	10				Member US Congress
DeHart, John		Rev War	45	65	140		
DeHaven, Gloria		Ent	20	30	35	53	Glamor Actress-Singer-Dancer of MGM Musicals
DeHaven, Robert		WWII	15	20	40	40	ACE, WWII; 14 kills
Dehmelt, Hans G., Dr.		Sci	20	35		30	Nobel Physics
Dehner, John	1915-1982	Ent	10		25	40	Actor

NAME	DATES	CATEGORY	SIG	LS/DS	ALS	SP	COMMENTS
Deisenhofer, Johann		Sci	27	36		35	Nobel
DeKalb, Johann	1721-1780	Rev War			7500		Arrived/Lafayette. Ordered to Capture Charleston
DeKay, Tim		Ent	17			50	
Dekker, Albert	1905-1968	Ent	55		90	193	Actor
Dekker, Thomas		Ent	17			50	
DeKlerk, F. W.		HOS	75	150		90	Nobel Peace, Pr. Min. S. A.
Del Fuegos, The		Ent	20			50	
Del Monaco, Mario	1915-1982	Opera	50	65	150	208	Opera
Del Rio, Delores	1905-1983	Ent	30	35	55	65	Mexican actress
Del Toro, Benicio		Ent	20			53	Actor, AA
del Toro, Guillermo		Ent	20			60	
Del Tredici, David		Comp	15	35	80		Pulitzer, AMusQS 100
Delacroix, F. V. Eugene	1798-1863	Artist	175	385	643		Brilliant Colorist. Great Murals
DeLaCroix, Raven		Ent	10	10	10	20	Erotica
Delafield, Richard		Civ War	56	92	483		Union Gen. Engineer
DeLagnel, Juius A.	1827-1912	Civ War	85	126	200		CSA Gen.
Delahunt, William D. D		Congr	10				Member US Congress
Delancey, James	1703-1760	Colonial			750		Acting Colonial Gov. of the Province of NY
DeLancie, John	1948-	Ent	10			25	Actor; 'Q' on Star Trek
Deland, Margaret		Author	12	25	75	25	Am. Novels. Old ChesterTales
Delaney, Kim		Ent	15	30	50	43	Actress
Delano, Columbus		Cab	20				Sec. Interior, Grant
Delany, Bessie		Author	10			20	Co-Author of Best Selling Memoirs
Delany, Dana		Ent	12	22	25	47	Actress
Delany, Sarah		Author	10			20	Co-Wrote Best-Selling Memoirs
DeLauro, Rosa L. D		Congr	10				Member US Congress
DeLay, Tom		Congr	10			20	Ex-Member US Congress
Delbridge, Del		Ent	10			15	Radio Announcer
Delbruck, Max		Sci	70		200		Nobel in Med.
Deledda, Grazia		Author	45	105	320		Nobel Literature 1926
Delfino, Majandra		Ent	13			40	
DeLiagre, Alfred		Ent	15	25	35	65	
Delibes, Leo		Comp	85	220	342		Light Opera, Ballet
Delius, Frederick	1862-1934	Comp	300	400	770		Br. Orchestral, Concerti, Songs. AMusQS 4000
Delizia, Cara		Ent	13			40	
Dell, Gabriel	19191-1988	Ent	60	35	50	115	Bowery Boys
Dell, Myrna	1924-	Ent	10	15	20	35	Actress
Della Casa, Lisa	1919-	Opera	20			80	Swiss Sopr. Opera
Della Chiesa, Vivian		Opera	10		15	20	Sopr.
Della Joio, Norman		Comp	35	115	240	55	Pulitzer, AMusQS 50-175
Dellums, Ronald B.	1935-	Congr	10	15		25	Afro-Am. Congressman CA
Delna, Marie		Opera	25			90	Fr. Contralto. Opera
Delon, Alain	1935-	Ent	25			180	Fr. Actor/Prod./Dir. SP w/Bridget Bardot 200
DeLong, Phillip C.		WWII	15	25	40	35	ACE, WWII; 11. 17 kills
Delpy, Julie	1969-	Ent	20			55	Fr. Actress. 'Unbearable Likeness of Being'
DeLuca, Phil Dr.		Author	10				Marriage & relationships
DeLuise, Dom	1933-	Ent	10	13	25	40	Comedian
Delvaux, Paul		Artist					Fr. Artist; S print 270
DeMarco, Antonio		Ent	15	25			Prod.
DeMarco, Tony		Ent	10	25			Dancer
Demarest, William	1892-1983	Ent	25		50	93	Vaude. Star Turned Char. Actor
DeMille, Agnes		Ent	55	200		114	Dancer, Innovative Choreographer
DeMille, Cecil B.	1881-1959	Ent	60	152	215	193	Prod./Dir./Films TLS/Cont 500-2500; S Chk 125
DeMille, Katherine		Ent	15	20	25	60	

D

NAME	DATES	CATEGORY	SIG	LS/DS	ALS	SP	COMMENTS
DeMille, William C.		Ent	15	45		50	Early Dir., Plays, Prod.
Deming, W. Edwards		Bus				75	Consultant
DeMint, Jim D		Congr	10				Member US Congress
Demme, Ted	1963-2002	Ent	30			70	Actor
DeMonvel, Boutes		Artist	25	70	125		
DeMornay, Rebecca		Ent	20			60	Actress
DeMorse, Charles	1816-1887	Pol	95	395			Father of TX Journalism. Stock Comm. Under Lamar
Dempsey, John		Gov	12				Gov. CT
Dempsey, Patrick	1966-	Ent	25			55	Actor; Grey's anatomy
Dempsey, Stephen W.		Congr	10	25			Repr. NY
Demslow, W. W.		Comics	50			175	Illust. of Wizard of Oz
Demzn, Lev		Space	20	30		50	
Denby, Edwin	1870-1929	Cab	25	50	75	50	Harding Sec. Navy. 'Teapot Dome Scadal'
Dench, Judi		Ent	25	35	40	82	Actress, AA winner
Deneuve, Catherine	1943-	Ent	30	40	55	145	Actress, model
Denfeld, Louis E.		Mil	15	25	40	50	Adm. Chief Naval Operations WWII
Deng, Xiaoping		Pol				420	Chinese Premiere
DeNiro, Robert		Ent	27	38	45	82	Actor, AA Winner
Denis, Maurice	1870-1943	Artist	95		325		Fr. Religious Painter. Art Theoretician
Denison, Charles S.		Congr	10	10	15		Sen. IL
Denison, John H.		Clergy	10	15	25		
Denman, G. Tony		WWII	15	22	35	30	ACE, WWII, Navy Ace; 6 kills
Denman, Thomas, 3rd Baron		HOS	10	15	35		Gov. Gen. Australia
Dennehy, Brian		Ent	20	35	45	52	Mature Leading Man-Char. Actor Movies/TV
Denning, Richard	1914-1985	Ent	10	20	25	65	Handsome Film Leading Man; 40s early 50s
Dennis, Sandy	1937-1992	Ent	35	45		97	Oscar Winning Actress
Dennison, Jo Carroll	1923-	Ent	10	15	15	20	Actress
Dennison, William	1815-1882	Cab	40	95	210		Lincoln P. M. Gen. CW Gov. OH
Denos, John		Ent	10	10	30	20	TV actor 'The Young & the Restless'
Dent, Catherine		Ent	15			45	
Dent, Elliott		WWII	12	25	35	30	ACE, WWII; 6 kills
Dent, Frederick T.	1820-1892	Civ War	50	71	179		Union Gen.
Dent, S. Hubert		Congr	10	15		15	MOC AL
Denton, James		Ent	13			40	
Denton, Jeremiah A., Jr.	1924-	Congr	15	25	30	25	Adm. WWII, AL Sen. POW Vietnam War
Denver, Bob	1935-2005	Ent	25	35	40	47	Actor. 'Gilligan's Island'
Denver, James W.	1817-1892	Civ War	80	168	330		Denver, CO. Union Gen., Lawyer, Gov. KS Terr.
Denver, John	1943-1997	Music	65	180	95	174	Singer-Comp.
Denza, Luigi	1846-1922	Comp	35				AMusQS 50-110
D'Eon, Charles de Beaumont		Adven	100		400		Louis XV's secret agent to Russ
Depardieu, Gerard		Ent	20			45	
Depeche Mode		Music				53	Rock group: S Album 75
Depew, Chauncey M.	1834-1928	Finan	50	140	285	292	Orator, NY Centr. RR, US Sen. NY.
Depp, Johnny		Ent	25		40	70	Actor
Deprume, Cathryn		Ent	10			20	Actress
Derain, Andre	1880-1954	Artist	125	210	342		Postimpressionist Fauvist.
Derby, Edw. Henry Stanley	1826-1893	Statsmn	20		59		15th Earl of Derby. Sec. of the Colonies
Derby, Edward Stanley	1799-1869	HOS	50	60	102		14th Earl. Br. Prime Min.
Derek & Dominoes (all)		Ent	72			250	
Derek, Bo		Ent	20	20	25	50	Actress
Derek, John	1926-1998	Ent	20	28	35	61	Actor-Photographer
Derek, John & Bo Derek		Ent	20			66	Husband & Wife
Deringer, Henry	1786-1868	Bus	700		6500		Invented Derringer Pistol
Derleth, August		Author	20	75			

NAME	DATES	CATEGORY	SIG	LS/DS	ALS	SP	COMMENTS
Dern, Bruce		Ent	15	20	25	40	Actor
Dern, George H.		Cab	10	20	35		Sec. War, Mining Exec., Gov. UT
Dern, Laura		Ent	15	20	25	42	Actress, Daughter of Bruce Dern
Derr, Richard	1918-1992	Ent	12			40	Actor
D'Errico, Donna		Ent	15			39	Actress
Dershowitz, Alan M.		Law	15	20	35	30	Trial Attorney, Author
Desai, M. R.		HOS	10	15	25		Prime Min. India
Desanto, Sugar Pie		Music	15			35	James Brown Vocalist
Descartes, Rene		Phil	950	4035	10000		Mathematician. Analytic Geometry
Deschanel, Paul Eugene L.	1856-1922	HOS			100		Pres. France 1920. Resigned
Deschanel, Zooey		Ent	13			40	
Descher, Sandy	1945-	Ent	20			65	Child Actress
Désert, Alex		Ent	13			40	
Deshler, James	1833-1863	Civ War	372				CSA Gen., KIA Chickamauga, GA
DeSilva, Howard	1909-1986	Ent	15	20	25	60	Actor
Deslys, Gaby		Ent				50	Fr. Actress; Spy for the Fr. During WWI
Desmond, Johnny		Music	10	25		35	Singer
Desmond, Paul		Music	25			100	Blues-Jazz sax
Desmond, Shaw	1877-1960	Author	25	75			Irish Plays. Pioneered Paranormal
Desmond, William		Ent	80	150		120	Vintage Film Actor
Desperado (cast)		Ent				85	Banderas/ Hayek
Despretz, César		Sci	10		30		Fr. Physician. Inventor Electric Arc Furnace
Dessalines, Jean-Jacques	1750-1806	Revol		2500			Haitian Ruler
D'Estaing, V. Gistard		HOS	20	40	100	60	Pres. France
Destinn, Emmy	1878-1930	Opera	110		225	325	Czech Dramatic Sopr.
Destiny's Child		Music				120	S Album 145
D'Estrees, Gabrielle	1571-1599	Royal		15600			Mistress of Henri VI
Detaille, Edwouard	1848-1912	Artist	110		325		Fr. Mil. & Portr. Painter
Detmer, Amanda		Ent	17			50	
DeTreville, Yvonne		Ent	20			85	Opera, Light Opera
Deuce, Sid		Ent	13			40	
Deutekom, Cristina		Opera	10			35	Dutch Coloratura Sopr. Opera
Deutsch, Emery		Band	15				
Deutsch, Patti	1945-	Ent	10	15	15	25	
Deutsch, Peter D		Congr	10				Member US Congress
DeVane, William		Ent	20	25	25	45	Actor
Devens, Charles,	1820-1891	Mil	69	88	108	250	Union Gen. -Atty Gen.
Devereux, James P. S.		Mil	35	70	90	90	Gen. WWII, Congress MD
Devers, Jacob L.	1887-1979	WWII	30	45	60	60	Gen. WWII
Devicq, Paula		Ent	17			50	
Devine, Andy	1905-1977	Ent	40	45	65	164	Comic Sidekick of Roy Rogers
Devine, Loretta		Ent	13			40	
DeVito, Danny		Ent	20	35	50	50	Actor; Dir.
Devlin, J. Greg		Author	10			12	Authors
Devo		Music	120			150	Rock Band; S Album 150
DeVos, Rich		Bus	20			30	Fndr. Amway
DeVries, William, Dr.	1943-	Sci	15	25	40	25	Surgeon. 1st Successful Perm. Art. Heart Implant
Dew, William, Bish.		Clergy	20	30	45		
Dewar, James		Sci	85		375		Prof. Chemistry R. I., London. Liquified Air
DeWeese, Linda		Author	10			15	Books on abuse of women
Dewey, George	1837-1917	Mil	84	138	128	386	Captured Manila. Span. -Am. War. Adm.
Dewey, John	1859-1952	Author	60	155	250	200	Philosopher, Educator, Psychol.
Dewey, Orville		Clergy	15	20	25		
Dewey, Thomas E.	1902-1971	Gov	32	79	150	85	Twice Pres. Cand., Gov. NY

NAME	DATES	CATEGORY	SIG	LS/DS	ALS	SP	COMMENTS
Dewhurst, Colleen		Ent	15		35	52	
deWilde, Brandon	1942-1972	Ent	388			580	Actor; 'Shane'
DeWine, Mike		Congr	10				US Senate (R-OH)
DeWitt, Joyce		Ent	15	20	25	30	
DeWolf, H. G.		Mil	10	15		25	Canadian Adm. WWII
DeWolfe, Billy	1907-1974	Ent	25	40	45	57	Actor. 'Prissy' Stage-Film Comic
Dexter, Al		Cntry Mus	20			45	1940's star. 'Piston Packin' Mama'
Dexter, J. M.		Clergy	10	15	20		
Dexter, Timothy	1747-1806	Colonial		175	275		Merchant, Speculator
Dey, Susan		Ent	15	15	20	38	Actress
DeYoung, Russell		Bus	10			10	CEO Goodyear Tire & Rubber Co.
Dharma & Greg		Ent				200	Cast SP; S script 110
di Bonaventure, Anthony		Music	50				Italian pianist
Di Stefano, Giuseppe	1921-	Opera	30		65	75	It. Tenor Opera
Diaghilev, Sergei	1872-1929	Ballet	435	975	2250		Rus. Ballet Impresario. Developed Ballet Russes
Diamond, David		Comp	25		35		AMusQS 200
Diamond, Jack "Legs"	1894-1931	Crime		1955			Gangster, bootlegger
Diamond, Neil		Music	25	120	200	125	Comp. -Singer. S Album 120
Diamond, Selma		Ent	30	40	55	75	
Diana, Princess (Eng)	1961-1997	Royal	866	1479	2580	2417	Princess of Wales. S Christmas card 1500-2400
Diane E. Watson		Congr	10				Member US Congress
Diaz, Armando Vittorio		Mil	35	100	175	120	It. Gen. WWI
Diaz, Cameron	1973-	Ent	25	120		119	Actress
Diaz, Joey		Ent	12			35	
Diaz, Porfirio	1830-1915	HOS	100	218	425	225	Dictatorial Mex Pres. Fought Fr. Occupation
Diaz-Balart, Lincoln D		Congr	10				Member US Congress
Diaz-Balart, Mario D		Congr	10				Member US Congress
Dibdin, Thomas John	1771-1841	Celeb	45		85		Prompter/Pantomime writer at Theatre Royal
Dibrell, George Gibbs	1822-1888	Civ War	175	486	448		CSA Gen., MOC TN
Dibrell, George Gibbs (WD)		Civ War	290	546			CSA Gen.
DiCaprio, Leonardo		Ent	45	72		87	Actor
Dice Clay, Andrew		Ent	10			30	Comedian
Dicillo, Tom		Celeb	10			15	Film industry
Dick, Andy		Ent	15			30	Comedian
Dick, Fred		WWII	10	22	40	30	ACE, WWII; 5 kills
Dick, Samuel	1740-1812	Rev War	50	175	225		Continental Congress NJ. Col. 1st Battalion
Dickens, Charles	1812-1870	Author	546	998	2210	11610	Christmas Carol', ALS/Cont 5000; S Chk 650
Dickens, Charles	1837-1896	Celeb			110		Eldest son of Charles Dickens
Dickens, Jimmy		Cntry Mus	10			15	
Dickens, Kim		Ent	13			40	
Dickerson, Mahlon	1770-1853	Congr	25	85	150		Jackson Sec Navy. Gov. NJ
Dickerson, Nancy		Jrnalist	10			15	Broadcast News Pioneer
Dickey, James	1923-1997	Author	35	110	135	65	Am. Poet, Novels 'Deliverance'.
Dickinson, Angie		Ent	20	25	35	65	Actress
Dickinson, Anna Eliz.	1842-1932	Author	25	70	142		Abolitionist-Lecturer
Dickinson, Clarence		Music	15			95	Legendary Organist
Dickinson, Clement C.		Congr	10			15	MOC MO
Dickinson, Daniel S.		Congr	15	25			Sen. from NY
Dickinson, Don M.		Cab	10	20			P. M. Gen. 1888
Dickinson, Emily		Author	750	2560	7250		Autographed Poem S 20000
Dickinson, Jacob M.	1851-1928	Cab	25	45	125		Taft Sec. of War
Dickinson, James S.		Civ War	56	78	75		CSA Congressman
Dickinson, John P.		Rev War	200	382			Cont. Congr. Statesman, Administrator
Dickison, J. J.		Civ War	75	155	195		CSA Cav'ry Off., Florida's Mosby

NAME	DATES	CATEGORY	SIG	LS/DS	ALS	SP	COMMENTS
Dickman, Joseph		Mil	50				Gen. WWI
Dicks, Jacob		Gov	15	25	40		Governor NY
Dicks, Norman D. D		Congr	10				Member US Congress
Diddley, Bo	1928-2008	Music	30			117	R & B Singer-Comp. -Guitarist. Rock HOF
Didier-Pouget, W.		Artist	30	65	95		
Diebenkorn, Richard		Artist		50			Abstract
Diefenbaker, John	1895-1979	HOS	35	45	110	75	Prime Min. Canada
Diem, Ngo Dinh	1901-1963	HOS	50				Pres. So. Viet Nam
Diemer, Louis		Comp	25			45	Fr. Pianist. AMusQS 100
Diemer, Walter E.		Bus	20		75	90	Inventor Dubble Bubble Gum
Dierkop, Charles		Ent	10			30	
Dies, Martin		Congr	15	50		25	MOC TX. Un-Am. Activities
Diesel, Rudolf		Sci	900		3250		Ger. Mech. Engineer. Diesel Eng
Diesel, Vin		Ent	20			42	Actor
Diesenhofer, Johann, Dr.		Sci	20	25		40	Nobel Chemistry
Dieterle, William		Ent	30			70	Film Dir.
Dietl, Col. -Gen. Eduard	1890-1944	WWII	38			242	WWII Ger. Gen.
Dietrich, Dena		Ent	10			20	Mother Nature (Commercial)
Dietrich, Josef "Sepp"	1892-1966	WWII	195	690	950		SS Cmdr.
Dietrich, Marlene	1901-1992	Ent	42	146	125	260	Actress
Dietz, Howard		Music	20			45	Popular musician; songwriter; SB 115
Digence, Richard	1949-	Celeb	10			20	Br. Comedian
Diggs, Taye		Ent	13			40	
Dilke, Charles W. 2d Baronet		Author	10	25	45		Br. Travel Books, Pol.
Dillards		Ent	25			65	Herb, Dean, Rodney, Merle
Diller, Phyllis		Ent	15	20	30	35	Comedienne.
Dillinger, John		Crime					DS-Typed Confession S 14,000. RARE
Dillingham, T. J.		Author	I0			12	Religion
Dillman, Bradford	1930-	Ent	15	20	30	50	
Dillon, C. Douglas		Cab	10	25	30	25	Ambassador, Diplomat
Dillon, Kevin	1965-	Ent	15			40	Entourage
Dillon, Matt		Ent	20	25	35	50	Actor
Dillon, R. Crawford		Clergy	15	45	60		
Dillon, Sidney		Bus	283	590	723		RR Baron-Union Pacific RR. Jay Gould Aide
Dimitrova, Ghena		Opera	10			35	Opera
D'Indy, Vincent	1851-1931	Comp	40	125	362	583	Fr. Opera, Orchestral, Vocal Music AMusQS 300
Dinesen, Isak (Karen Blixen)	1885-1962	Author	100	500		500	Danish. Out of Africa
Dingell, John D. D		Congr	10				Member US Congress
Dingley, Nelson, Jr.		Congr	10	20	35		Governor, Repr. ME
Dinkins, David	1927-	Pol	15	35		20	1st Afr. Am. Mayor NYC
Dinning Sisters (3)		Ent	35				Jean, Jayne, Ginger
Dion		Music	60			120	Popular singer
Dion & the Belmonts		Music				75	Rock group; S Album 65
Dion, Celine		Music	20	40		65	Singer. Grammy Winner
Dior, Christian		Fash	102	213		175	Mdrn. Fashion Designer
Dippel, Andreas		Opera	35			125	Ger. Tenor. Impresario. Opera
Dire Straits		Music	50			149	Rock group; S Album 100
Dirks, Rudolph	1877-1968	Comics	70		175	400	Katzenjammer Kids
Dirksen, Everett M.	1896-1969	Congr	20	58		40	Sen., MOC IL. Powerful Pol. Figure
Disney, Roy E.		Bus	25	55		50	Brother of Walt. Disney Exec.
Disney, Walter E. (Walt)	1901-1966	Bus	1073	2395	3467	4142	Animated Film Prod., S Chk 1500-2000
Disraeli, Benjamin,	1804-1881	HOS	131	151	498		Br. PM, Novels, Lord Beaconsfield
Disraeli, Isaac	1766-1848	Author	30	140	165		Br. Man of Letters. Novels
Ditka, Mike		Celeb	15			30	Radio & TV host; NFL Coach

NAME	DATES	CATEGORY	SIG	LS/DS	ALS	SP	COMMENTS
Ditmars, Raymond L.	1876-1942	Sci	72				Herpetologist, Zoo Curator, Author
Divine		Music	77			147	Rock.
Divine, M. J., Father (Geo. Baker)		Clergy	150	319	600	225	Communal Rel. Soc., Rejected Matrimony
Dix, Dorothea L.	1794-1887	Civ War	100	145	472		Union Superintendent of Nurses. Soc. Reformer
Dix, Dorothy (Eliz. Gilmer)		Author	15	30	45	25	Am. Journalist, Editor, Advice
Dix, John Adams	1798-1879	Civ War	50	98	114	300	Union Gen., Sec. Treasury
Dix, John Adams (WD)		Civ War	95	160	297		Union Gen.
Dix, Morgan		Clergy	25	35	50		Abolitionist
Dix, Richard		Ent	25	40	65	71	Vintage Movie Star
Dix, Robert	1935-	Ent	15			30	Actor
Dixey, Henry E.	1859-1943	Ent	20	45	50	80	1st Success as Adonis
Dixie Chicks		Cntry Mus	50			120	Country Western trio; S Album 125
Dixon, Dean		Cond	35			175	1st Afro-Am. To Conduct NY Philharmonic
Dixon, Donna		Ent	15	20	25	45	Actress.
Dixon, James		Congr	10		34		FF 34
Dixon, Jeane	1918-1996	Celeb	15			30	Forecasts the Future
Dixon, Julian C.		Congr	10	15		15	Dem. MOC CA
Dixon, Thomas	1864-1946	Author	15	30	75		The Clansman. Social Critic
Dixon, Willie		Music	60			168	Rock HOF; Blues
Dizengoff, Meir	1861-1936	Zionist	50	162	350		Early Jewish Settler, Palestine. Founded Tel Aviv
Dmytryk, Edward	1908-	Ent	20			65	Film Dir. Member Hollywood Ten
Doane, G. W.		Clergy		20	25	25	
Dobbin, James C.	1814-1857	Cab	45	75	150		Pierce Sec Navy
Dobbin, John F.		WWII	20	40	65	45	ACE, WWII, Marine Ace; 7.58 kills
Dobbs, Lou		Celeb	15			25	Financial expert; TV host
Dobehoff, F. L.		Aero	15	75		75	
Dobie, Charles Cald.		Author	10	10	15	15	
Dobie, J. Frank		Author	20	50	130	75	Folklorist & Western Author
Dobrinyin, Anatole		HOS	40	130	375	375	USS R. Pol. Power
Dobson, Kevin		Ent	10	20	20	30	Actor
Dockery, Thomas P.	1833-1898	Civ War	95	368	395		CSA Gen.
Dockery, Thomas P. (WD)	1833-1898	Civ War	275	490			CSA Gen.
Docking, Robert	1925-1983	Gov	10	15	22		Governor KS
Dockstader, Lew		Ent	100				Late 19th C. minstral man
Doctorow, E. L.		Author	20	35	90	90	Am. Novels. Ragtime
Doda, Carol		Ent	10			20	Actress; erotica
Dodd, Christopher J.		Congr	10	15		20	Sen., MOC CT
Dodd, Thomas J.	1907-1971	Congr	28	58	72	45	Chief of Counsel at Nuremberg; Sen. CT
Dodd, William E.		Hist	15	60	75	25	Ambassador to Nazi Ger.
Dodderidge, Philip		Clergy	25	35	45		
Dodge, Charles C.	1841-1910	Civ War	50	54	83		Union Gen.
Dodge, Grenville M.	1831-1916	Civ War	88	195	304	375	Union Gen., RR Tycoon. Stk. Cert. S 1750-2850
Dodge, Grenville M. (WD)	1831-1916	Civ War	110	275	410		Union Gen., Repr. IA. LS/Cont 1950
Dodge, Henry	1782-1867	Congr			45		Gov. Wisc. Terr., 1st Sen., Indian Fighter
Dodge, Joseph M.		Bus	10	25	50		Banker, Built Jap. Economy
Dodge, Mary Abigail	1833-1896	Author	12	20	25		Am. Novels
Dodge, Mary Mapes	1831-1905	Author	25	40	90	100	Kid's Books. 'Hans Brinker & the Silver Skates'
Dodge, Theodore A.		Author	35				
Dodge, William Earl	1805-1883	Bus	95	482	675		Phelps, Dodge & Co. YMCA Fndr.
Dodge, William G.		Civ War	25	55	85		
Dodgson, Chas. (Lewis Carroll)		Author	333	1171	2456		1832-98. 'Alice in Wonderland'
Dods, Marcus		Clergy	40	45	60		
Dodson, Jack	1931-1994	Ent	20	20	25	45	Howard Sprague on 'The Andy Griffith Show'
Doenitz, Karl	1891-1980	WWII	89	169	309	181	Ger. Adm., WWII. TLS/Cont 7500, FDC S 90

NAME	DATES	CATEGORY	SIG	LS/DS	ALS	SP	COMMENTS
Doerflinger, Joseph		Aero	10		75	45	
Doering, Arnold		WWII	15	20	35	45	Ger. fighter pilot
Doggett, Lloyd D		Congr	10				Member US Congress
Dohanos, Steven	1907-1994	Artist	10	15			
Doherty, Shannen		Ent	17			50	
Doherty, Shannon		Ent	20			44	Actress.
Dohnanyi, Erno von	1877-1960	Comp	55	135	132		Hung. Conductor. AMusQS 350
Dohrn, Bernardine		Crime					Terrorist. FBI Fingerprint Card S 150
Doi, Takao		Space	15	25		25	
Doig, Andrew Wheeler		Congr	15	20			MOC NY 1839, Banker, Mining
Doisy, Edward A.		Sci	20	45	78	50	Nobel Med. Vitamin K
Dolby, Ray		Sci	25	35	50		Inventor Dolby Sound
Dolby, Thomas		Ent	20			40	
Dole, Charles F		Clergy	10	15	20		
Dole, Elizabeth	1936-	Congr	10			25	US Senate (R-NC)
Dole, James D.		Bus	55	145	235	175	Fdr. Hawaiian Pineapple Industry
Dole, Robert	1923-	Congr	20	20	30	65	Sen. KS. Majority Ldr. Pres. Cand.
Dole, Sanford B.	1844-1926	Bus	73	173	245	175	Pres. HI. 1st Pres. Dole Pineapple. S Chk 325
Dolenz, Ami	1969-	Ent	10			25	Actress
Dolenz, Mickey		Ent	12	25	25	45	'The Monkees'
Doles, George Pierce	1830-1864	Civ War	350				CSA gen.
Dolin, Anton		Ballet	25	40	95	75	Ballet
Dollar, Robert	1844-1932	Bus	20	55	130	50	Fndr. & Pres. Dollar Steamship Line.
Dolliver, Jonathan P.		Congr	20	35		25	Sen., MOC IA 1889
Dolukanova, Zara		Opera	75			250	Great Contralto
Domenici, Pete		Congr	10				US Senate (R-NM)
Domerque, Faith	1924-1999	Ent	15			50	Actress
Domingo, Placido		Opera	20		45	73	Opera, Concert
Dominguez, Oscar	1906-1957	Artist	70		250		Sp. Surrealist Artist
Dominick, Fred H.	1918-1966	Congr	10	15		10	MOC SC 1917-33
Domino, Fats	1928-	Music	20	48	35	100	R&B Singer-Pianist-Comp. Rock HOF. AMusQS 376
Donahue, Al		Ent	15			75	Big Band Leader
Donahue, Archie		WWII	12	25	50	45	ACE, WWII, Ace in one day; 14 kills
Donahue, Elinor		Ent	15	20	25	30	Father Knows Best' Actress.
Donahue, Phil		Ent	15			30	TV host
Donahue, Troy	1936-2001	Ent	20	30	40	65	Actor. 60s Warner Bros. Star
Donaldson, Jesse M.		Cab	15	20	35	25	1st Postman Becomes P. M. Gen.
Donaldson, Sam	1934-	Jrnalist	15			25	TV News Anchor, Commentator
Donan, Stanley		Celeb	10			15	Film industry
Donat, Peter	1928-	Ent	10		15	15	Canadian Char. Actor
Donat, Robert	1905-1958	Ent	83	122	100	228	Br. From Shakespeare to AA 'Goodby Mr Chips'
Donat, Zdislawa		Opera	10			25	Opera
Donath, Ludwig	1900-1967	Ent	20			40	Played Al Jolson's Father. WWII Anti-Nazi Films
Donavan, Elisa		Ent				25	Actress; erotica
Donavon		Music	70			120	
Donelson, Daniel Smith	1801-1863	Civ War	350				CSA Gen.
Doniphan, Alexander William		Mil	120	250	475		Fought Mex., Indians, Mormons
Donitz, Karl	1891-1980	WWII	70	145	150	162	Commanded the Ger. Navy
Donizetti, Gaetano	1797-1848	Comp	500	800	1537		AMusQS 2750; AMusMS 3000; ALS/Cont 4750
Donlan, Roger		Mil	10	25	40	30	
Donleavy, James Patrick	1926-	Author		80			
Donlevy, Brian	1899-1972	Ent	25			142	Ir. Actor w/Pershing vs Pancho Villa. Pilot WWI.
Donnell, Jeff	1921-1988	Ent	20	25	40	50	Columbia Pict. Teenage Starlet. 2nd Leads
Donnelly, Ruth	1896-1982	Ent	10	15	25	52	Chorine-Stage-Films 1927 & Next 30 Years

NAME	DATES	CATEGORY	SIG	LS/DS	ALS	SP	COMMENTS
Donner, Clive		Ent	10			25	Film Dir.
Donner, Richard	1930-	Ent	15			30	
Donner, Vyvyan		Editor	10			15	Fashion
Donohoe, Amanda	1962-	Ent	15			80	Br. Actress
Donovan		Music	70			120	Rock; S Guitar 250-450
Donovan, Elisa		Ent	15			45	
Donovan, Hedley		Editor	10		15	10	Time-Life Editor
Donovan, Jason	1968-	Ent	10			20	Australian actor & singer.
Donovan, King	1919-1987	Ent	15			30	Actor. Char. -Supporting Roles
Donovan, Raymond J.		Cab	10	15	30	15	Sec. Labor
Donovan, Tate		Ent	17			51	
Donovan, Wm. J. 'Wild Bill'	1883-1959	Mil	80	217	325	125	Fighting 69th, OSS-CIA
Doobie Brothers		Music	60			146	Signed by all; S Album 150
Doohan, James 'Scotty'	1920-2005	Ent	25	45	55	77	Star Trek Actor
Dooley, Calvin M. D		Congr	10				Member US Congress
Dooley, Paul	1928-	Ent	15	20	25	40	Actor
Dooley, Thomas A., Dr.	1927-1961	Sci	125	185	400	250	Jungle Physician, SE Asia. Med. Mission
Doolittle, Hilda	1886-1961	Author	75	205	475		Imagist Poet. Ed. 'The Egoist' Rare
Doolittle, James H.	1896-1993	Aero	68	151	275	192	WWII Gen, Test Pilot. Bombed Tokyo. Hero/MOH
Doolittle, James Rood		Congr	15	25	40		Civil War Sen. WI
Doolittle, John T. D		Congr	10				Member US Congress
Doors & Jim Morrison (4)		Music	1330	1516		2420	Rock, S Album 2527
Doors, The (3)		Music	100	165		150	Rock 'Doors' Alb. 125
Doran, Ann	1914-	Ent	15	15	25	40	Am. Char. Actress. Supporting Roles
Dorati, Antal		Cond	15	25		85	Hungarian
Dore, Gustave	1832-1883	Artist					Fr. book Illust. 19th C. , S drw6650
Doré, Paul Gustave	1833-1883	Artist	60	235	508		Fantastic Imagination. Illustrated over 90 Books
Dorff, Stephen		Ent	15			50	Actor
Dorfman, Dan		Celeb	10			15	Financial expert
Dorgan, Byron		Congr	10				US Senate (D-ND)
Doria		Ent	15			45	
Dorn, Michael	1952-	Ent	15			60	Actor
Dornan, Robert K.		Congr	10			20	MOC CA.
Dornberger, Walter R.	1895-1980	Sci	40	100	120	75	Ger. Rocket Engineer. Bell Aircraft. FDC 225
Dorr, Julia C. R.	1825-1913	Author	10	10	15		Best Known for 10 Volumes of Poetry
Dorr, Thomas	1805-1854	Reform		4500	863		Polit. Formed Own Party. Led 'Dorr Rebellion'
Dors, Diana	1931-1984	Ent	105			411	Br. 'Blonde Bombshell' of 40s.
D'Orsay, Alfred, Count	1801-1852	Artist	25	65	170		Fr. Wit, Fashion Arbiter, Society Leader
D'Orsay, Fifi		Ent	15	20	35	35	Fr. Canadian Actress. Vaude. & 30s Films
Dorsey, Jimmy	1905-1956	Band	68	150		144	Big Band Leader-Sax; AMQ 350
Dorsey, Stephen	1842-1916	Bus	35		125		RR Promoter. Repub. Sen. AR. Fraud. RR Scandal
Dorsey, Tommy	1905-1956	Band	75	150		162	Big Band Leader-Trombone
Dortch, William T.		Civ War	25	40	75		CSA Sen. NC
Dos Passos, John	1896-1970	Author	20	50	75	60	Am. Novels. Prolific Writer
Dostoevsky, Fyodor	1821-1881	Author	1500	5700	13800		Rus. Novels. 'Crime & Punishment'
Doty, James	1799-1865	Expl	50		185		Polit., Land Speculator. C. W. Territorial Gov.
Doubleday, Abner	1819-1893	Civ War	539	700	1470		Union Gen. Credited for Inventing Baseball
Doubleday, Frank Nelson	1862-1934	Bus	65	185	375		Book Publisher
Douce, Francis	1757-1834	Antiquary			120		
Doucette, Jami Dr.		Bus	10			20	Mdrn. Med
Doucette, John		Ent	20	25	35	80	Excellent Supporting Actor
Doucette, Paul		Music	15			25	Drummer 'Matchbox 20'
Doug, Doug E.	1970-	Ent	10			20	Actor
Dougherty, Dennis, Card.		Clergy	35	50	65	40	Card'l & Archbishop of Philadelphia

NAME	DATES	CATEGORY	SIG	LS/DS	ALS	SP	COMMENTS
Douglas, Beverly B.		Civ War	35	50	65		CSA Off., MOC VA
Douglas, Chas. W. H.	1850-1914	Mil	25	70	195		Br. Gen.
Douglas, Christopher	1969-	Ent	10			20	Actor
Douglas, Donald W. Jr.		Bus	25	60		45	Douglas Aircraft
Douglas, Donald W. Sr.	1892-1981	Aero	150	257	450	360	Pioneer Aircraft Mfg. FDC S by Sr. & Jr. 250
Douglas, Donna	1933-	Ent	12			40	Actress. 'Ellie Mae' in TVs 'Beverly Hillbillies'
Douglas, Eric		Ent	10			18	Son of Kirk Douglas
Douglas, Helen Gahagan	1900-1980	Congr	30	55	98	55	MOC CA, Opera, Actress
Douglas, Illeana		Ent	13			40	
Douglas, Jerry		Music	10			20	Am. Dobro player
Douglas, Kirk	1916-	Ent	30	91	95	125	Versatile Actor. Lifetime Achiement Award
Douglas, Leon		Cntry Mus	10			20	
Douglas, Lloyd C.	1877-1951	Author	25	45	75	30	Retired Min. 'The Robe', 'Magnificent Obsession'
Douglas, Melvyn	1901-1981	Ent	25	30	45	76	AA & Tony-winning actor
Douglas, Michael		Ent	20	35	45	66	Actor, AA
Douglas, Mike	1925-2006	Ent	15	20	50	30	Singer. Early TV Host
Douglas, Paul	1907-1959	Ent	10	15		35	Sportscaster, News. '48, 'Born Yesterday'
Douglas, Paul H.		Congr	10	20		25	Sen. IL
Douglas, Paul P.		WWII	15	25	45	35	ACE, WWII; 7 kills
Douglas, Robert	1909-1999	Ent	10			30	Br. Actor. Leads & Supporting Parts
Douglas, Stephen A.	1813-1861	Congr	114	329	483	650	Statesman, Pres. Cand. Debated vs Lincoln
Douglas, W. Sholto	1893-1969	WWII	45			75	Br. Air Marshall. D-Day Coastal Ops.
Douglas, William O.	1898-1980	Sup Crt	56	156	230	320	SC Judge; S opinion 355
Douglas, William Taylor		Clergy	15	20	25		
Douglas-Home, Alec		HOS	45	70	150	135	Br. Prime Min.
Douglass, Frederick	1817-1895	Abolit	286	580	6776	6325	Author, Lecturer, Editor, Abolitionist
Douglass, Robyn	1953-	Ent	10	10	15	25	Actress
Doulton, Henry, Sir	1820-1897	Invent	50	115	270		Royal Doulton China, Appliances. Art Pottery
Doumer, Paul	1857-1932	HOS	75		100		Pres. France 1931-32. Assass.
Doumergue, Gaston	1863-1937	HOS	50		195		Pres. France., P. M. France
Dourdan, Gary		Ent	13			40	
Dourif, Brad		Ent	13			40	
Dove, Billie	1903-1997	Ent	20	25	30	84	30's Movie Star.
Dow, Charles H.	1851-1902	Bus		983			Dow-Jones
Dow, Neal	1804-1897	Civ War	45	75	175		Union Gen., Temperance Reformer
Dow, Tony		Ent	15	20	25	30	Actor., Wally Cleaver
Dowden, Edward	1843-1913	Author	10	15	25		Ir. Critic, Editor, Professor, Author
Dowding, Hugh C., Lord	1882-1970	Mil	95		535		Br. Air Chief Marshal, Architect Battle of Britian
Dowling, Eddie	1895-1975	Ent	20	25	55	45	Major Broadway Star. 'Harvey'. Tony Winner
Down, Lesley-Anne	1954-	Ent	46	62	50	162	Actress. Leading Lady of Br. -Am. Films
Downey Jr., Robert		Ent	15			45	
Downey, Morton	1901-1985	Band	20	20	20	45	Irish Tenor-Bandleader
Downey, Robert, Jr.	1965-	Ent	25			53	Actor
Downey, Roma		Ent	16			50	Actress. 'Touched By An Angel'
Downey, Sheridan	1884-1951	Congr	10	35		20	Dem. Sen. CA 1938-50
Downing, Big Al	1940-2005	Music	15	20	25	30	Musician, songwriter
Downing, George, Sir	1623-1684	Statsmn	317	535			2nd Harvard Grad. Developed Downing St.
Downs, Hugh	1921-	Ent	15	20	25	28	TV Co-Host 20/20. Perennial Host
Downs, Johnny	1914-1994	Ent	55			135	Actor 'Our Gang'. Broadway, Vaude., Films
Doyle, Arthur Conan, Sir	1859-1930	Author	569	903	1867	1750	Sherlock Holmes'; ALS/Holmes Cont 16800
Doyle, Dinty		Jrnalist	10	20			Columnist
Doyle, Michael F. D		Congr	10				Member US Congress
D'Oyly Carte, Rupert		Ent	25	70	125	135	Prod. Orig. Gilbert & Sullivan Operettas
D'Oyly, George		Clergy	15	20	35		

D

NAME	DATES	CATEGORY	SIG	LS/DS	ALS	SP	COMMENTS
Dozier, James		Mil	12	30	45	20	
Dozier, Lamont	1941-	Music	10			25	Am. songwriter & record prod.
Dr. Dre		Ent	15			40	
Drabble, Margaret		Author	10	20	50		Br. Novels, Editor
Dragonette, Jessica	1910-1980	Opera	15	20	25	62	Sopr. Radio, Stage Star 30s-40s
Dragoni, Maria		Opera	10			30	Opera
Drake, Alfred	1914-1992	Ent	17			35	Singer-Actor. Musical Theatre, Concert
Drake, Betsy	1923-	Ent	20			80	Actress, 'Once upon a Time' & Mrs. Carey Grant
Drake, David		Author	25			50	Mil. sci-fi & fantasy
Drake, Frances	1906-1997	Ent	15	15	15	40	Am. Leading Lady of the 30s
Drake, Francis M.		Gov	10	25			Gov. IA. RR Builder. Fndr. Drake U
Drake, Michele	1958-	Ent	10			20	
Drake, Samuel Adams	1833-1905	Civ War	28		55		Author
Drake, Stan		Comics	20			100	'Blondie'
Drake, Tom	1918-1992	Ent	10	15	15	30	Actor. The Boy Next Door in 40s Films
Draper, Eben S.		Gov	10	12			Governor MA
Draper, Rusty		Cntry Mus	10			15	Singer
Draper, Ruth	1884-1956	Ent	10	45	75	50	Am. Monologuist
Draper, William F.	1842-1910	Civ War	35	50			Union Brevet Brig. Gen.
Draper, William H.		Clergy	20	35	40		
Drayton, Gracie		Comics	20			188	Created Campbell Soup Kids
Drayton, Thomas F.	1808-1891	Civ War	95	250	290		CSA Gen. Sig./Rank 175. RR Stock S 295
Drayton, William H.	1741-1779	Pol		506			Congressman SC
Drees, Willem		HOS	20	35	100		Survivor Buchenwald
Dreier, David D		Congr	10				Member US Congress
Dreiser, Theodore	1871-1945	Author	60	140	287	300	Am. Tragedy', 'Sister Carrie'. Magazine Editor
Drescher, Fran		Ent	15			40	Actress
Dresser, Louise	1878-1965	Ent	30		60	120	Broadway Mus. Major Silent & Sound Film Star.
Dressler, Marie	1869-1934	Ent	125			337	Actress. 1930 Academy Award 'Min & Bill'.
Drew, Daniel	1797-1879	Bus	950	6800			'Great Bear of Wall Street' Fisk-Jay Gould
Drew, Ellen	1915-2003	Ent	22	35	45	140	40s Actress.
Drew, John	1853-1927	Ent	45	75	185	127	Turn of the C. Stage Star
Drexel, Anthony J.	1826-1893	Banker	45	110			Son of Francis M. Drexel; Stock Cert. S 975
Drexel, Francis M.	1792-1863	Banker	450	2500			Fndr. Drexel & Co; became Drexel Burnham Lambert
Drexel, J. A.		Aero	40	60	100	65	
Drexel, Joseph W.	1833-1888	Bus					Banker/Philan. S Stock 1750; son, Francis Drexel
Dreyfus, Alfred	1859-1935	Mil	170	485	904	1359	Framed for Treason, Sent to Devil's Island
Dreyfus, Julia		Ent	17			50	
Dreyfus, Julia Louis		Ent	20	45		50	Actress, 'Seinfeld'. Emmys
Dreyfus, Lee Sherman		Gov	10			15	Gov. of WI
Dreyfuss, Henry		Bus		14	20		Self Sketch Henry 25
Dreyfuss, Richard		Ent	20	35	40	50	Actor. AA Winner
Dribrell, George Gibbs		Civ War	95	250	300		
Drifters		Music	85	450		105	Rock group
Drinan, Robert, Father		Congr	10			15	Catholic Activist Priest
Drinkwater, John	1882-1937	Author	20	50	125	75	Poet, Plays. Fndr., Mgr. Pilgrim Players '07
Driscoll, Bobby	1937-1968	Ent	140	155	190	450	AA '49.
Driver, Minnie		Ent	20			45	Actress
Driver, Samuel Rolles		Clergy	85	100	125		
Drouet, Robert	1870-1914	Ent	25	30	60	95	Am. actor & Plays.
Dru, Joanne	1922-1996	Ent	25			65	Actress. Screen, TV, Stage.
Druckman, Jacob		Comp	20	50	95		Pulitzer, AMusQS 250
Drudge, Matt		Celeb	10			30	Internet journalist, http://drudgereport.com
Drum, Hugh A. Lt. Gen		Mil	25	55	125	50	Gen. WWI, WWII

NAME	DATES	CATEGORY	SIG	LS/DS	ALS	SP	COMMENTS
Drum, Richard C.	1825-1909	Civ War	45	58	93		Union Gen. Sig/Rank 55, War Dte. DS 100
Drummond, Henry	1851-1897	Clergy	50	60	80		Scottish Evangelical Writer-Lecturer.
Drummond, James		Clergy	25	35	50		
Drury, Allen	1919-1998	Author	10	30	65	35	Novels. Best Seller 'Advise & Consent' S 50
Drury, Frank		WWII	10	25	40	30	ACE, WWII, Marine Ace; 6 kills
Drury, James	1934-	Ent	10			51	Actor
Dryer, Fred		Ent	10		25	25	Actor TV Series 'Hunter'. Pro Football
Du Barry, Jeanne, Comtesse	1743-1793	Royal	285	960	1200		Louis XV Mistress. Banished, Arrested, Guillotined
Du Chaillu, Paul B.	1831-1903	Expl	35	80	110	75	Brought 1st Gorillas out of Afr.
Du Maurier, Daphne, Dame		Author	45	200	150	65	Br. Novels. 'Rebecca'
Du Maurier, George	1834-1896	Author	25	45	197		Artist, Novels. Illust. of 'Punch'
Du Maurier, Gerald, Sir	1873-1934	Ent	20	50		65	Actor-Manager
Du Pont, Alfred I.		Bus	20				Banking
Du Pont, Elizabeth H		Bus	20	75	110	35	
Du Pont, Henry A.	1838-1926	Bus	98	357	750	120	Civil War MOH winner., Gunpowder Mfg., RR Pres.
Du Pont, Lammot		Bus	20			50	CEO Du Pont Chemical
Du Pont, Pete	1935-	Celeb	10			15	Pol. celebrity
Du Pont, Pierre S.		Gov	15	35		50	Governor DE, Du Pont Chemical
Du Pont, Pierre-Samuel	1739-1817l	Econ	500	1500	2700		Progenitor of Du Pont Lineage
Du Pont, R.		Aero	40	110			Am Aviation Exec.
Du Pont, Samuel Francis (WD)	1803-1865	Civ War	106	445	897		Union Adm. ALS/Superb Mex. Am. War Cont. 1800
Du Vigneaud, Vincent	1901-1978	Sci	25	55	150	100	Nobel 1955. Synthesized Penicillin
Duane, James	1733-1797	Rev War	77	180	250		1st Cont. Congr. NY Atty Gen.
Dubcek, Alexander		HOS	80	130			Czech. Reformer
Duberstein, Ken		Pol	10			20	WH Chief of Staff under Reagan
DuBois, W. E. B.	1868-1963	Author	350	675		450	Black Rights, Educator-Writer
Dubose, Dudley Mciver	1834-1883	Civ War	114	267	350		CSA Gen.
Dubose, Dudley Mciver (WD)	1043-1003	Civ War	172	360			CSA Gen., MOC GA. Sig/Rank 325
DuBridge, Lee, Dr.		Sci	30	100	145	50	Pres. Cal-Tech
Dubuffet, Jean	1931-1985	Artist	150	400	831		Swiss proponent of raw art
Dubuque, Julien	1762-1810	Pioneer	600	2500			Am. Pioneer. 1st White Settler Near Dubuque
Duc d'Otrante, Joseph	1758-1820	Pol		400			Fr. Statesman, Father of Mdrn. Pol. espionage
Duchamp, Marcel	1887-1968	Artist	125	350	775	1365	Fr. Avante Garde Artist
Duchin, Eddie		Band	25	40		117	Big Band Leader, Pianist Father of Peter
Duchin, Peter		Band	10	12	15	20	Pianist, Band Leader
Duchovny, David		Ent	24			45	Actor, ' X Files'
Duckworth, John T., Sir	1748-1817	Mil	55	180			Br. Adm., Gov. Newfoundland
Ducos, Jean Francois		Fr Rev	50	100	205		
Dudamel, Gustavo		Cond				75	Venezuelan
Dudayev, Dzhokhar		HOS	15			45	Pres. Chechen Repub.
Dudenhoeffer, Matt		Music	10			25	Music. Guitars 'Gravity Kills'
Dudicoff, Michael J.	1954-	Ent	10	15		20	Actor
Dudley, Dave	1928-	Cntry Mus	10			15	Singer
Dudley, Joseph	1647-1720	Colonial	354	1736	1200		Col. Gov. MA. Philosopher, Scholar, Divine
Dudley, Paul	1675-1751	Colonial	115	310			Jurist. Religious Activist
Dudley, Thomas V., Bish.		Clergy	35	45	50	50	
Duer, William	1747-1799	Rev War					Signer of Articles of Conf. War Dte/Cont 1500
Duesenberg, Frederick S.	1877-1932	Bus	550	1350			Champ. Bicyclist. Patented Duesenberg Motor
Duff, Arthur, Sir		Mil	15	45	70		Br. Adm.
Duff, Haylie		Ent	15			45	
Duff, Hilary		Ent	20			60	
Duff, Hillary		Ent	20			50	
Duff, Howard	1917-1990	Ent	20		25	70	Actor. Film & Radio Star.
Duff, James H.		Congr	10	15		10	Governor, Sen. PA

NAME	DATES	CATEGORY	SIG	LS/DS	ALS	SP	COMMENTS
Duffer, Candy		Music	20			45	Rock; Saxaphonist
Duffie, Alfred Napoleon	1835-1880	Civ War	35	75	90		
Duffy, Brian		Space	10			25	
Duffy, Francis P.		Clergy	15	20	25		
Duffy, Julia		Ent	10	10	20	22	Actress. 'Bob Newhart Show' Co-Star
Duffy, Patrick		Ent	20			30	Actor. 'Bobby Ewing' on 'Dallas'
Dufranne, Hector		Opera	20				Opera. Fr. Baritone
Dufy, Raoul	1877-1953	Artist	198	304	677	476	Fr. Impressionist, Fauvism
Duggan, Andrew	1923-1988	Ent	15			35	Char. Actor. Tall, Stalwart Types
Duhamel, George	1884-1966	Author		100			
Duhamel, Josh		Ent	19			58	
Duigenan, Patrick	1735-1816	Royal			720		1st United Parliament. Privy Councilor, Ireland
Dukakis, Kitty		Author	10		18		
Dukakis, Michael S.		Gov	10			25	Governor MA. Pres. Cand.
Dukakis, Olympia	1931-	Ent	15	25	35	40	Actress. Stage-Films. Char. Leads
Dukas, Paul	1865-1935	Comp	55	160	355		Fr.
Duke, Basil Wilson	1838-1916	Civ War	95	175	575		CSA Gen. War Dte ALS/Cont 3900
Duke, Charles M.		Space	30	113	310	100	Moonwalker. SP of Earth 50
Duke, David		Activist	10			20	Ex KKK Grand Wizard. Pol. ly Active
Duke, Patty	1946-	Ent	20	25	30	45	Actress, AA
Duke, Vernon	1903-1969	Comp	20	50	145		AMusQS 175-400
Dukes of Hazzard		Ent	155			200	
Dulac, Edmund	1882-1953	Artist			865		Illust., Sinbad.
Dulbecco, Renato		Sci	20	35	60		Nobel Physiology-Med.
Dullea, Keir	1936-	Ent	10	12	15	80	Actor. Films-Stage.
Dulles, Allen W.	1893-1969	Diplo	30	95	165	100	State Dept., OSS, CIA. Author
Dulles, John Foster	1888-1959	Cab	35	128	155	100	Sec. State, Diplomat, UN
Dumas, Alexandre (Fils)	1824-1895	Author	75	167	200	438	Fr. Dramatist, Novels
Dumas, Alexandre (Pere)	1802-1870	Author	110	258	463	746	Fr. Novels-Plays. 'Count of Monte Cristo'
Dumbrille, Douglass	1890-1974	Ent	40			85	Char. Actor. Smooth, Suave Villain
Dummar, Melvin E.		Celeb	20	30	45		Fraudulent H. Hughes Heir
DuMont, Allen		Sci	345				Invented 1st commercial cathode ray tube
Dumont, Margaret	1882-1965	Ent	230			615	Actress; 'Duck Soup'
Duna, Steffi	1913-1992	Ent	15		15	45	Hungarian born film actress
Dunagin, Ralph		Comics	10			20	'The Middletons'
Dunaway, Faye	1941-	Ent	15	25	30	43	Actress
Dunbar, Bonnie J.		Space	10			30	
Dunbar, Charles E., Sr.	1888-1959	Law	10	25			Chm. US War Trade Board 1914-18 WWI
Dunbar, Dixie	1915-1991	Ent	12	15	20	42	Actress-Dancer-Vaud. Star of 30s Musicals
Dunbar, Paul Lawrence	1872-1906	Author	750	1725	3500		Poet, Novels Rare, SB 1225
Duncan Jr., John J. D		Congr	10				Member US Congress
Duncan, Isadora	1878-1927	Ent	367	649	1047	1406	Am. Interpretive Dancer. Eccentric
Duncan, James	1811-1849	Mil	75				Mexican War Hero
Duncan, Johnny	1938-	Cntry Mus	10			30	Guitarist-Singer. 3 Years w/Buddy Holly
Duncan, Johnson Kelly	1827-1862	Civ War	330				CSA gen., KIA Knoxville, TN
Duncan, Lee (Rin Tin Tin)		Ent	100			120	Dog Trainer & Actor
Duncan, Michael		Ent	13			38	
Duncan, Robert	1952-	Ent	10			20	Br. TV Actor
Duncan, Sandy	1946-	Ent	15			43	Actress. TV-Stage-'Peter Pan'. Disney Voice SP 25
Duncan, Thomas	1818-1887	Civ War	50	75	120		Union Gen.
Duncan, Todd		Ent	45	125		112	1st 'Porgy'. Rare
Dundas, Henry	1742-1811	Statsmn	25	40	90		Br. Sec War. Pro War w/Am. 1st Viscount
Dundas, Robert S.	1771-1851	Royal	40	125			Br. Statesman Melville Sound
Dungey, Merrin		Ent	13			40	

NAME	DATES	CATEGORY	SIG	LS/DS	ALS	SP	COMMENTS
Dunham, Sonny		Band	15			25	Bandleader, Trumpet
Dunkel, Arthur	1932-2005	Pol	10			15	
Dunlap, John	1747-1812	Pub	450	2100			1st To Print Dec of Ind & Daily News.
Dunlap, Robert P.	1794-1859	Congr	20				MOC ME, Gov. ME
Dunlop, John T.		Cab	10	10	15	15	Sec. Labor
Dunn, Artie		Music	10			20	Music. The Three Sons
Dunn, Emma	1875-1966	Ent	25		120	175	Br. Char. Actress. 'Housekeeper'
Dunn, Holly		Cntry Mus	10			25	Singer
Dunn, James	1905-1967	Ent	60		100	211	Leading Man. AA For 'A Tree Grows in Brooklyn'
Dunn, Jennifer D		Congr	10				Member US Congress
Dunn, Shawn		Ent	13			40	
Dunn, William McKee		Civ War	25	40	70		Union Gen. (Judge, Adv. Gen. '75)
Dunnagan, Macon		Author	10			15	Adventure, Kilimanjaro
Dunne, Dominick		Author		30		35	Columnist
Dunne, Irene	1901-1990	Ent	25	35	40	131	Actress-Singer.
Dunne, Phillip	1908-1992	Author	15	20	35	35	Novels, Dir. Fndr. Screenwriters Guild
Dunne, Stephen	1918-1977	Ent	20			50	
Dunning, Debbie		Ent	20			47	Actress.
Dunnock, Mildred	1904-1991	Ent	15		35	45	Actress. AA Nom. 'Death of a Salesman'
Dunovant, John	1825-1864	Civ War	220				CSA gen., KIA Vaughn Road, VA
Dunsany, Edw. J. Plunkett, Lord	1878-1957	Author	50		225	120	Traveller, Hunter, Plays
Dunst, Kirsten		Ent	20			50	Actress
Duparc, Henri	1848-1933	Music					Fr. Comp. AMusMS 2000
DuPonceau, Pierre		Mil	25	60	140		
Duportail, Louis le Begue		Rev War		496			Fr. Gen. in Continental Army
Dupré, Marcel		Comp	45			188	Celebrated Organist
Durais, C.		Artist	10	20	50		
Duran Duran		Music	53			104	Entire Band S album 120
Durand, Asher Brown	1796-1868	Artist	85	175	385		Hudson River School. Engraver, Painter
Durant, Ariel (Ida)	1898-1981	Author	25	50	115	35	Historian w/Husband Will
Durant, Thomas C.	1820-1885	Bus	350	950	1350		Pioneer Builder & Financer of RRs
Durant, William Crapo	1861-1947	Bus	250	850	1075		Durant Motor Car. GM, Chevrolet
Durant, William 'Will'	1885-1981	Author	30	35	135	45	Historian w/Wife Aerial (Ida). Pulitzer
Durante, Jimmy	1893-1980	Ent	40	87	74	154	Comed. Burlesque, Radio, TV, Films "The Schnozz"
Durbin, Deanna		Ent	26			87	Child Singing Star. Retired Early.
Durbin, Richard		Congr	10			20	US Senate (D-IL)
Durenberger, David		Congr	10			15	Sen. MN
Durer, Albrecht	1471-1578	Artist	3000	8200	21000		Foremost Ger. Renaissance Artist.
Durham, Bobby		Cntry Mus	10			20	Singer
Durkin, Martin P.		Cab	10	25			Sec. Labor, Eisenhower
Durning, Charles		Ent	10	15	15	40	Char. Actor
Duroc, Geraud C. M.	1772-1813	Mil	25	65	150		Napol. Grand Marshal-Diplomat
Durrell, Lawrence		Author	25	70	190	40	Br-Ir Poet, Plays, Traveller
Durst, Fred		Music	15			42	Frontman for Limp Bizket
Dury, Ian		Music	20				Blockheads, S Album 104
Duryea, Charles E.	1861-1938	Invent	186	562	895	1530	Built 1st Am. Gasoline Motor Car
Duryea, Dan	1907-1968	Ent	20	25	30	74	Char. Actor. Star in 40s-50's. Vintage SP 55
Duryea, Hiram B.	1834-1914	Civ War	40		65		5th NY Infantry, Manassas
Duryee, Abram	1815-1890	Civ War	52	120	195		Union Gen. Raised Volunteer Reg. 'Duryee's Zoaves'
Duryee, Abram (WD)		Civ War		150	410		Union Gen. ANS '61 310
Duse, Eleanora	1859-1924	Ent	152	270	578	666	Great Italian Stage Actress
Dushku, Eliza	1980-	Ent	15			35	
Dussault, Nancy	1936-	Ent	10		15	25	Am. actress & singer
Dussek, Jan L	1760-1812	Comp	225	1200	2500		Czeck Pianist, Comp. Marie Antoinette was Patron

NAME	DATES	CATEGORY	SIG	LS/DS	ALS	SP	COMMENTS
Dustinn, Emmy	1878-1930	Opera	30			170	Opera. Czech Sopranosalome', 'Butterfly'
Dutra, Enrico Gaspar	1855-1974	HOS	10	20	50	35	Pres. Brazil. Gen. Outlawed Communist
Duvalier, Francois	1907-1971	HOS	75	160		135	Papa Doc. Haitian Pres.
Duvall, Clea		Ent	13			40	
Duvall, Gabriel	1752-1844	Sup Crt	60	272	588		
Duvall, Robert		Ent	20	25	30	50	AA Actor. Writer-Prod.
Duvall, Shelley		Ent	10	15	15	35	Actress
Duvé, Christian de, Dr.		Sci	20	35		30	Nobel Med.
Duyckinck, Evart A.		Editor	40		150		Literary World
Duzenbury, Wyatt		Mil	25			65	Enola Gay flight engineeer
Dvorak, Ann		Ent	25	45	30	138	Actress. Vintage Leading Lady of 30s
Dvorak, Antonin	1841-1904	Comp	350	760	1925	1960	Czech. Symphonies. AMusQS 4500-6500
Dwan, Allan	1885-1981	Ent	15			35	Veteran Am Dir. -Ex Writer
Dwight, Theodore	1764-1846	Jrnalist	35	50	150		Harvard Wits, Hartford Convention
Dwight, Timothy	1752-1817	Author	20	55			Pres, Yale. Equal Ed. of Women. Harvard Wits
Dwight, William	1827-1894	Author			150		Sanskrit scholar
Dyer, Alexander Brydie	1815-1874	Civ War	50	84	134		Union Gen.
Dyer, Edward	1543-1607	Author		1000			Br. Poet & Courtier
Dyer, Eliphlet	1721-1807	Rev War	70	155	425		Continental Congress. Jurist
Dyer, George C.		Mil	15	40	60		Adm. USN
Dyer, Leonidas Carstarphen		Congr	10			10	MOC MO 1915-1933
Dyer, Nehemiah	1839-1910	Mil	25			75	Adm.
Dylan, Bob		Music	415	2001	5710	1813	Songwriter, Poet, Folksinger. Rare S Contr. 9500
Dylan, Jakob		Music				78	Rock
Dymally, Mervyn M.		Congr	10			15	Afr-Am. Congressman CA
Dysart, Richard	1929-	Ent	15	15	20	35	Actor
Dzerzhinsky, Felix E.	1877-1926	Mil		635			Bolshevik Leader, Sectry Secret police
E. R. (cast)		Ent				125	Cast of 4 males
Eadie, Betty J.		Author	10			10	Non-Fiction
Eadie, John		Clergy	10	15	25		Scot. Theologian & Scholar
Eads, James Buchanan	1820-1887	Civ War	108	301	583	350	Engineer, Shipbuilder for Union
Eagan, Susan		Ent	20			60	
Eagels, Jeanne	1894-1929	Ent	1081			1165	Actress
Eagleburger, Lawrence	1930-	Cab	15	25		30	Bush Sec of State. Dept. Career Diplomat
Eagles		Music	425	525		705	Band S album 900
Eagleston, Glenn		WWII	20	42	70	45	ACE, WWII
Eagleton, Thomas F.	1929-2007	Congr	10	50		25	Sen. MO; VP Cand.
Eaker, Ira	1896-1987	WWII	50	80	95	124	WWII Air Force Cmdr
Eakes, Bobbie	1961-	Ent	10			25	Actress
Eakins, Thomas	1844-1916	Artist	500		4417		Am. Painter-Sculptor. Master Draftsman, Anatomy
Eames, Charles	1907-1978	Archtct	75			250	Am. Architect-Designer. Best Known for Furniture
Earhart, Amelia	1898-1937	Aero	558	1581		3257	TLS/Cont 2495; SB 900-1100
Earl Jones, James		Ent	15	20		45	Actor
Earl of Salisbury	1830-1903	Royal			235		AKA Robert Arthur Talbot Gascoyne-Cecil
Earle, George H.		Gov	10	15			Governor PA
Earle, Henry	1789-1838	Sci			180		Surgeon
Earle, Merie	1889-1984	Ent	15			40	Char. Actress into her 90s. 'The Walton's'
Earle, Virginia		Ent	15	25	35	75	Stage actress 19th C.
Early, Jubal	1816-1894	Civ War	422	752	1189	1610	CSA Gen.
Early, Jubal A. (WD)	1816-1894	Civ War	797		3234		CSA Gen.
Earp, Josephine		Celeb			4950	1292	Wife of Wyatt Earp, ALS/ Cont 4950
Earp, Virgil		Lawman	650	4500	7150		US Marshal. S Auction 8, 250
Earp, Wyatt	1848-1929	Lawman	4115	17768	27500		Legendary Gambler, Gunfighter
Earth, Wind & Fire		Music	95			125	Rock group: S Guitar 205-515

NAME	DATES	CATEGORY	SIG	LS/DS	ALS	SP	COMMENTS
East, Clyde B.		Aero	25	35		45	Am. Highest Ranking Reconnaisance Ace.
East, James		Lawman	250	749			Western Cowboy
East, John		Congr	10	20	40	35	Sen. NC, Suicide
Eastlake, Charles L., Sir	1836-1906	Artist	50	150	433		Critic, Historical Painter. Sec. Royal Inst. Br.
Eastland, James O.		Congr	10	20		35	1943-78. Powerful MS Sen. Pres. Pro Tem.
Eastman, George	1854-1932	Bus	147	270	1750	606	Fndr Eastman Kodak. Rare DS 4900
Eastman, John		Artist	40		185		Am. Artist. Portraits & Genre
Eastman, Kevin		Ent	15			45	
Eastman, Max	1883-1969	Author	35	85	115		Communust & Editor-Fdr. 'The Masses'
Easton, Florence	1882-1955	Opera	45			175	Opera. Br. Sopr. 100 Roles in 4 Languages
Easton, Sheena		Ent	15	15	25	45	Singer
Eastwood, Allison	1972-	Ent	10			38	Actress.
Eastwood, Clint	1930-	Ent	34	45		80	Actor-Prod. -Dir. AA. 2'x3' Poster S 100
Easy Rider		Ent	125			420	Signed by all three principals
Eaton, Amos Beebe	1806-1877	Civ War	36	55	102		Union Gen. Seminole & Mex. War. Sig/Rank 50
Eaton, Dorman	1823-1899	Reform	10	25	55		Jurist, Nat'l Civil Service Act
Eaton, John Henry		Cab	25	55	110		Sen. TN 1818, Sec. War
Eaton, Joseph H.	1816-1896	Civ War	50	75	75		Union Gen. ALS '65 605
Eaton, Shirley	1936-	Ent	15			56	Curvy Blonde Brit. Actress. 'Goldfinger'
Eaton, William	1764-1811	Diplo	48		88		US Consul Tunis, Tripoli Action
Eban, Abba		Diplo	15	75	75	65	Israeli Diplomat, Ambass. UN
Ebb, Fred		Comp	15		45	25	AMusQS Ebb & Kander 350
Ebbets, Charles H.		Bus	150			190	Orig. Brooklyn Dodgers Field (Ebbets Field)
Eben Emael		Mil	30	85	140	60	
Eberhart, Adolph O.		Gov	10	22			Governor MN
Eberhart, Richard		Author	10	20	45	15	Major Poet 20th C., Pulitzer
Eberlein, Gustav	1847-1926	Artist	20			72	Ger. Sculp. Mythological Subj & Bismark
Eberly, Bob		Music	10	15	10	42	Band Singer, Records
Eberly, Ray		Music	10			60	Singer. Band, Records
Ebert, Roger		Ent	15			30	TV Movie Critic
Ebsen, Buddy	1908-2003	Ent	15	20	30	102	Bev. Hillbillies', WOZ Tin-Man, SP/Tin Man 380
Eccles, John C.		Sci	20	30	40	30	Nobel Med.
Echols, John	1823-1896	Civ War	126	225	751		CSA Gen.
Echols, John (WD)		Civ War	195	722	450		CSA Gen.
Echols, Joseph Hubbard	1816-1885	Civ War	40				Member of CSA Congress
Echols, Leonard Sidney		Congr	10	15			MOC WV 1919
Eckels, James H.	1858-1907	Statsmn	20	50	100		US Comptroller of Currency
Eckener, Hugo von	1868-1954	Aero	188	348	500	429	Ger. Aeronaut, Graf Zeppelin; TLS to FDR 2750
Eckert, Thomas T. (WD)	1825-	Civ War	150				Union Gen. Telegraph Giant.
Eckhart, Aaron		Ent	16			47	
Eckstine, Billy		Band	25			67	Vocalist-Trumpet-Bandleader
Eclair, Jenny	1960-	Celeb	10			15	Comedienne
Ector, Matthew Duncan	1822-1879	Civ War	207	434			CSA Gen.
Ed, Carl		Comics	10			30	'Harold Teen'
Eddington, Arthur Stanley, Sir	1882-1944	Sci	35	140	185		Br. Mathematician, Astrophysicist
Eddy, Duane		Music	50	285		125	Rock Guitarist. HOF; S Guitar 650
Eddy, Mary Baker	1821-1910	Clergy	1138	1938	4572		Am. Fndr. Christian Science Church
Eddy, Nelson	1901-1967	Ent	40	132		112	30s-40s Actor/Singer. SP w/Jeanette MacDonald 180
Edelsheim, Macmilian von		Mil	40			65	Ger. Panzer Gen.
Eden, Anthony, Sir	1897-1977	HOS	66	103	137	158	Prime Min. 1st Earl Avon
Eden, Barbara		Ent	20	30	25	111	Actress, 'Jeannie'; SP 250 as Jeannie
Ederle, Gertrude 'Trudy'		Celeb	25			250	1st woman to swim the English Channel
Edeson, Robert		Ent	20			60	Silent Star. 'Ten Commandments'
Edge, Walter E.		Congr	15	25		20	Gov. NJ 1917, Sen. PA, Ambassador

NAME	DATES	CATEGORY	SIG	LS/DS	ALS	SP	COMMENTS
Edgerton, H. K.		Celeb	15				'March Across Dixie'
Edison, Charles	1890-1969	Cab	40	72	100	76	Sec Navy. Son of Thos. A.
Edison, Thomas Alva	1847-1931	Sci	523	1020	2704	2410	Rare DS/Elec. Lights 4500; S Chk 600-750
Edmonds, Walter Dumanx	1903-1998	Author	20	45	40	50	'Drums Along the Mohawk'
Edmondson, Adrian	1957-	Ent	10			20	Br. Actor, comedian
Edmunds, Geo. Franklin	1828-1919	Congr	10	15	30		Sen. VT 1866-91
Edmundson, Henry A.		Civ War	40	55	80		CSA Off., MOC VA
Edney, Kermit		Author	10			12	Regional history, broadcasting
Edson, Merritt A.	1897-1955	Mil	45	125		75	MOH Winner. Marine Cmdr. at Guadalcanal. WWII
Edward & Wallis (See Windsor)		Royal					Duke & Duchess of Windsor
Edward III	1312-1377	Royal		1400			Reigned 1327-1377
Edward VI (Reign of. .)		Royal		1750			Land Grant 1551 1750
Edward VII (Eng) (As King)	1841-1910	Royal		588		1495	King From 1901-10
Edward VII (Eng.)	1841-1910	Royal	110	282	347	600	As Albert Edw., Q. Vict. Eldest Son
Edward VIII (As King)	1894-1972	Royal	642	1566	4000	3000	
Edward VIII, as Prince of Wales	1894-1972	Royal	129	333	868	525	TLS/Cont 1250. SP in Investiture Robes 2050
Edward, Duke of Kent	1767-1820	Royal	55	120	350		Father of Queen Victoria
Edwards, Anthony		Ent	20	50	70	45	Actor.
Edwards, Blake		Ent	15	134		38	Film Prod. -Dir. 'Pink Panther'
Edwards, Chet E		Congr	10				Member US Congress
Edwards, Clarence		Mil	35				Gen. WWI
Edwards, Cliff	1895-1971	Ent	85	90	100	134	Singer-Actor AKA 'Ukelele Ike'. 'GWTW'
Edwards, Douglas		Jrnalist	10	10	15	20	Radio-TV News
Edwards, Edward Irving		Congr	10	15			Sen., Governor NJ
Edwards, Elaine S.		Congr	10	20		10	Sen. LA, 8/1/72-11/13/72
Edwards, George		Congr	10				
Edwards, Gordon		Bus	10			10	Business Exec., US Steel
Edwards, James B.		Cab	10	15	35	10	Governor SC, Sec. Energy
Edwards, Joan		Ent	15			50	Actress
Edwards, Joe, Jr.		Space	10			20	
Edwards, John		Congr	10			40	Sen. D-NC. 2008 Dem. Primary Cand.
Edwards, John	1815-1894	Civ War	50	90	130		Union Gen.
Edwards, Jonathan	1703-1758	Clergy	110	350	380		Considered Greatest Theologian Am. Puritanism
Edwards, Oliver	1835-1904	Civ War	50	105	125		Union Gen. Sig/Rank 65
Edwards, Penny	1928-1998	Ent	15			40	Westerns Leading Lady of 40s
Edwards, Ralph		Ent	15	20	25	40	Radio-TV M. C. 'This Is Your Life' Host-Prod.
Edwards, Vince		Ent	10			40	Actor, 'Dr. Ben Casey'
Edwin, John, the Younger	1768-1805	Ent			180		
Efron, Zac		Ent	22			65	
Egan, Michael Richard		Clergy				25	Archbishop of NY
Egan, Richard	1921-1987	Ent	15	20	25	55	Leading Man. Mainly Action Drama & Westerns
Egan, Thomas Wilberforce	1834-1887	Civ War	48	112	160		Union Gen.
Egan, Will		Ent	10			25	
Egan, William A.		Gov	10	12		10	Governor AK
Egbert, H. C.		Mil	45			65	Gen. Spanish-Am. War
Eggar, Samantha	1939-	Ent	10	12	15	38	Br. Leading Lady. Intl. Films
Eggert, Nicole		Ent	10			42	Actress. 'Baywatch'
Eggerth, Marta	1912-	Opera	20			90	Opera. Reigning Star of 40s Filmed Operettas
Eggleston, Benjamin	1816-1888	Congr	12	20	25		MOC OH
Eggleston, Edward	1837-1902	Author	15		30		Am. Regional Classic Novels
Eggleston, Geo. C.	1839-1911	Author	10	25			Editor, Novels, Civil War & Boy's Books
Eglevsky, André	1917-1977	Ballet	35	55	110	75	Rus-Am Ballet Teacher-Dancer
Ehlers, Vernon J. E		Congr	10				Member US Congress
Ehrlich, Paul, Dr.	1854-1915	Sci	150	1250	1850	1380	Nobel. Diphtheria, Syphillis

NAME	DATES	CATEGORY	SIG	LS/DS	ALS	SP	COMMENTS
Ehrlichman, John	1925-1999	Pol	20			30	Adv. To Nixon. Key in Watergate Scandal
Eichelberger. Robert L.	1886-1961	Mil	40	66	75	75	Gen. WWII. Cmdr I Corps
Eichelbrenner, E. A.		Sci	45	95	225		
Eichmann, Karl Adolf	1906-1962	WWII	1000	11075	7500		Nazi Leader. ALS/Cont Offered 50,000-60,000
Eick, Alfred		WWII	26		50	75	U-Boat Cmdr.
Eiffel, Alexandre-Gustave	1832-1923	Engr	242	656	894	1450	ALS/Cont 1750
Eigen, Manfred		Sci	20	35	80	40	Nobel Chemistry
Eigenberg, David		Ent	10			35	Actor; Steve Brady, 'Sex in the City'
Eikenberry, Jill		Ent	10			30	Actress
Eilers, Sally	1908-1978	Ent	20	25	30	90	Actress. Low Key Leading Lady 30s
Eilshemius, Louis Michel	1864-1941	Artist	35	65	290		Am. Landscape Expressionist
Einem, Gottfried von		Comp					AMusQS 175
Einstein, Albert	1879-1955	Sci	1094	4964	7591	5470	Nobel-Physics. ALS/Sci. Cont. 25,000
Eisele, Donn F.	1930-1987	Space	50			260	S Chk 110
Eisenberg, Maurice		Music	10	15		20	Cellist
Eisenhower, Arthur B.		Bus	10	15		20	Brother to Ike. Banker
Eisenhower, Barbara		Celeb	10	15		10	Daughter-in Law to Ike
Eisenhower, David	1948-	Author	15	25		25	Historian & Writer
Eisenhower, Dwight D.	1890-1969	Pres	292	612	3142	496	ALS/TLS/Cont 7500-17500.
Eisenhower, Dwight D. (As Pres.)		Pres	316	721	21510	521	Pres. chk 9500
Eisenhower, Dwight D. (WWII)		Pres	365	2250	5625	768	Supr. Cmdr. Allied Forces, ALS/Cont RARE; S D-Day Order 5000-18000, ALS: Mamie 3500-8000
Eisenhower, Edgar N.		Law	10	20		15	Brother & Lawyer to Ike
Eisenhower, John S. D.		Mil	10	20	35	25	Gen. & Only Son of Ike
Eisenhower, Julie Nixon	1948-	Celeb	10	10	25	25	Daughter & Inlaw to two Pres
Eisenhower, Mamie Doud	1896-1979	1st Lady	46	99	154	75	White House Card S 65, LS 85. FDC S 65
Eisenhower, Milton	1899-1985	Educ	10	30		20	Brother to D. D. E. Pres. Penn. State U.
Eisenhower, Susan		Bus	10			15	Author, business; DDE's Granddaughter
Eisenman, Robin G.	1953-	Ent	10	10	10	25	
Eisenstaedt, Alfred		Photog	35	40	65	150	Celeb. Photog. SB 150; S Photo Work 2500-15000
Eisenstein, Sergey	1898-1948	Ent		690	1350		Rus. Stage-Film Dir. Innovative Masterpieces
Eisley, Anthony	1925-2003	Ent	15			60	Actor
Eisner, Michael O.		Bus	20	56		35	CEO Walt Disney Co.
Eisner, William J.		Bus	10	35	45	20	
Eizenstat, Stuart E.		Pol	10	10	15	10	White House
Ejiofor, Chiwetel		Ent	15			45	
Ekberg, Anita	1931-	Ent	52			109	Swedish model, actress & cult sex symbol.
Ekland, Britt	1942-	Ent	20	20	25	68	Actress
Ekwall, William A.		Congr	10	10		10	MOC OR
El Fadil, Siddig		Ent	20			50	Actor. 'Star Trek Deep Space Nine'
Elam, Jack	1920-2003	Ent	15	25	35	57	Actor; Western Char.
Elba, Idris		Ent	15			45	
Elbert, Samuel	1743-1788	Rev War		110	170		Distinguished Off. Gov. GA
Eldard, Ron		Ent	15			45	
Elder, Ruth (Camp)		Aero	100	190	310	350	Pioneer Aviatrix
Elder, Will		Comics	30			100	Best Known for 'Little Annie Fanny' in Playboy
Elders, M. Joycelyn		Cab	15	30		20	Clinton Surgeon Gen.
Eldridge, Florence	1901-1988	Ent	10			40	Vintage Stage/Film Leading Lady. Mrs Fred March
Eldridge, Louise		Reform	10	15	30		Aunt Louisa AQS 25
Eldridge, Roy		Music	30			65	Jazz Trumpet
Electra, Carmen		Ent	15			42	Actress. Model.
Electric Light Orchestra		Music	50			83	
Eleniak, Erika		Model	35			73	Actress; Playboy magazine
Elfman, Danny		Ent	13			40	

NAME	DATES	CATEGORY	SIG	LS/DS	ALS	SP	COMMENTS
Elfman, Jenna		Ent	15			48	Actress-Comedian. '99 Golden Globe
Elg, Taina		Ballet	10			30	Fin. Ballet-Actress/Gene Kelly. Intl Films
Elgar, Edward, Sir	1857-1934	Comp	406	469	908	422	Br. Comp. AMusQS 1, 500-2000
Elgart, Les		Band	30			45	Arranger for Top Vocalists. Big Band
Elgin, 7th Earl (T. Bruce)		Diplo					SEE Bruce, Thomas
Elion, Gertrude, Dr.		Sci	20	65		35	Nobel Med. Biochemist-Leukemia-Herpes-AZT
Eliopulos, Marcus		Music	10			25	Guitar 'Stabbing Westward'
Eliot, Charles W.	1834-1926	Educ	15	50	65		Pres. Harvard
Eliot, George (Pseud.)	1819-1880	Author	137	478	1530		Br. Novels. (Mary Ann Lewes [Evans])
Eliot, T(homas) S(tearns)	1888-1965	Author	173	611	1322	860	Br. Poet, Critic, Editor, Nobel. Xmas Card S 375
Eliot, Thos. Dawes	1808-1870	Congr	25		45		CW MOC MA
Elisabeth, Queen	1876-1965	Royal		208		350	Queen of Belgium. Wife of King Albert I
Elizabeth (Rus)	1709-1762	Royal	267	1314			Czarina of Russia. Daughter of Peter the Great
Elizabeth I (Eng.)	1533-1603	Royal	4750	26140			
Elizabeth II & Philip		Royal		1237		1193	Queen of England & Consort
Elizabeth, II	1926-	Royal	225	689	1188	1261	Queen of GB. ALS/Age 10 900. DS W/Philip 800
Elizabeth, Queen Mother	1900-2002	Royal	120	300	538	750	Queen of George VI. Chk S 950
Elizabeth, Shannon		Ent	15			50	
Elizondo, Hector		Ent	10			40	Actor
Elkins, Stephen B.		Cab	15	25	60	25	Sec. War, Sen. WV
Ellen, Vera		Ent	20			60	Dancer, Films.
Ellender, Allen J.		Congr	10			10	Sen. LA
Ellerbee, Linda		Jrnalist	10	35		25	TV News, Commentator
Ellers, Joseph C.		Author	10			12	Southern mountains mysteries
Ellery, William	1727-1820	Rev War	175	355	657		Signer Dec. of Indepen.
Ellet, Alfred Washington	1820-1895	Civ War	50	90	160		Union Gen.
Ellicott, Andrew	1754-1820	Rev War	60	185	320		Surveyor, Mathematician
Ellington, Buford	1907-1972	Gov	10	10	20		Governor TN
Ellington, Duke	1899-1974	Comp	148	472		398	Big Band Leader. AMusQS 1200-2100
Elliot, Sam		Ent	10			45	Actor
Elliott, "Mama" Cass		Music	235	585		442	Sweet-Voiced Singer. 'Mamas & Papas'
Elliott, David James	1960-	Ent	15			45	Actor
Elliott, Maxine		Ent	30	40	75	75	
Elliott, Missy		Music	20			40	Rock
Elliott, R. W. B., Bish.		Clergy	25	35	40	40	
Elliott, Robert B.		Congr	10	15		15	MOC SC
Elliott, Sam	1944-	Ent	20	20	35	79	Low Key Leading Man 70s to 90s
Elliott, Stephen Jr.	1830-1866	Civ War	146	190	280		CSA Gen.
Elliott, Washington L.	1825-1888	Civ War	45	95	130		Union Gen. ALS '63 200
Elliott, Wild Bill	1904-1965	Ent	50			150	Cowboy Star from 20s-Late 50s
Ellis, Augustus Van Horne	1827-1863	Civ War		368			D. Gettysburg, Union Col.
Ellis, F. H.		Aero	15	35		30	
Ellis, Havelock	1859-1939	Sci	45	115	135	275	Br. Pioneer Advocate Sex Ed.
Ellis, Mary		Opera	20			50	Opera & Operetta Star. 1st 'Rose Marie'
Ellison, James	1910-1993	Ent	15		20	60	Cowboy Star. Johnny in 'Hopalong Cassidy'
Ellison, Ralph W.	1914-1994	Author	62	175		317	Afr. -Am. Novels. 'Invisible Man'
Ellsberg, Daniel		Activist	20	35	50	30	Leaked Pentagon Papers
Ellsberg, Edward	1891-1983	Mil	25	55	75	60	Naval Engineer, Am. WWII Adm.
Ellsworth, Ephraim E.	1837-1861	Civ War	733	5417	4500		Union Zouave Col.
Ellsworth, Ephraim E. (WD)		Civ War		7188	6862	6325	Union Zouave Col. 1st CW Martyr
Ellsworth, Oliver	1745-1807	Sup Crt	90	233	431		3rd Chief Justice. Constitutional Conv.
Ellul, Jacques		Clergy	25	30	45		
Elman, Mischa	1891-1967	Music	30	198		80	Rus. -Am. Violinist
Elman, Ziggy		Music	25			75	Trumpet. Played w/Major Bands 40s-50's.

NAME	DATES	CATEGORY	SIG	LS/DS	ALS	SP	COMMENTS
Elmendorff, Karl		Cond	25			110	Ger. Conductor.
Elmore, E. C.		Civ War	55	105			Treas. CSA. ALS 3, 500
Elphick, Michael	1945-2002	Ent	15			45	Br. Actor
Elrod, Jack		Comics	10			35	'Mark Trail'
Elson, Edward L. R.	1906-1993	Clergy	15	20	25		
Elssler, Fanny	1810-1884	Ent	250				Austrian Ballerina
Elston, John A.		Congr	10	15			Congressman CA
Eltinge, Julian	1882-1941	Ent	25	20	35	60	Female Impersonator, Silent Films
Eluard, Paul (Eugene Grindel)		Author	110	225	375		1895-1952. Fr. Poet. Exponent Surrealism
Elvira		Ent	10	15	19	33	Actress
Elwes, Cary		Ent	15			50	Actor. 'Robin Hood'
Ely, Joseph Buell		Gov	15	35	70		Gov. MA
Ely, Paul Gen.		Mil	65		140	90	Fr. Cmdr. Indochina. Dienbienphu
Ely, Ron	1938-	Ent	15	20	25	80	Actor. One of Several Tarzans. SP/Tarzan 195
Ely, Smith		Congr	15				Mayor NYC, Repr. NY
Elzey, Arnold (Jones) (WD)	1816-1871	Civ War	257		1180		CSA Gen.
Emanuel, David		Celeb	10			15	Designer
Emanuel, Elizabeth		Celeb	10			15	Designer
Emanuel, Rahm E		Congr	10			20	Member US Congress IL
Emberg, Kelly		Model	10			40	
Embry, Joan		TV News	10			25	San Diego Zoo TV Representative
Emerson, Faye	1917-1983	Ent	15			54	Film Actress-Early TV Panel Show Member
Emerson, George		Ent	10			25	Actor
Emerson, Hope	1897-1960	Ent	50			267	Am. Char. Actress. Early 30s-60s
Emerson, Jo Ann E		Congr	10				Member US Congress
Emerson, Lake & Palmer		Music	35	125		125	Rock. Alb. S (3) 125
Emerson, Ralph Waldo	1803-1882	Author	222	410	844	2530	Essayist/Phil./Poet. ALS/Cont 3500; AQS 1500-5200
Emery, Ralph	1933-	Ent	10			25	TV Host
Eminem		Music	25			99	Singer (Marshall Mathers, Slim Shady)
Emma B		Music	10			15	Rock
Emma, Queen	1836-1885	Royal	350				Wife of King Kamehameha IV
Emme		Model	10				Model
Emmerich, Roland		Celeb	10			15	Film industry
Emmett, Daniel D.		Comp	415	425	600		1st Minstral Show. Dixie
Emmons, Conant H.		Author	10			15	Novels
Emmons, Ebenezer	1799-1863	Sci	25	40	70		Early Prof. of Natural History
Emory, William Hemsley	1811-1887	Civ War	50	122	167		Union Gen. Sig/Rank 90, War Dte. ALS 355
Empey, James W., Lt. Col.		WWII	15	25		35	Ace WWII
Enders, John Franklin, Dr.		Sci	25	60	110	45	Nobel Med.
Endicott, William C.	1826-1900	Cab	25	30	55	150	Sec. War
Enesco, Georges	1880-1955	Comp	125	275	550	550	AMusQS 475-850
Enevoldson, Einer		Space	10			30	
Enfield, Harry		Celeb	10			20	Br. Comedian
Engel, Eliot L. E		Congr	10				Member US Congress
Engel, Georgia		Ent	10	12	15	32	Actress. 'Mary Tyler Moore' Show
Engel, Samuel G.	1904-1984	Ent	10			15	Prod.
England, Anthony W.		Space	10			30	
England, Sue	1928-	Ent	15			45	1940's Moppet
Engle, Frederick		Civ War	45				Union Commodore
Engle, Joe Henry		Space	25			65	Engle & Truly SP 195
Engler, Irvin		Author		25	30		Poet
English, Phil E		Congr	10				Member US Congress
English, Thos. Dunn	1819-1902	Author	28	30	45		Alice Ben Bolt'. Dr., Lawyer, Poet, MOC NJ
Englund, Robert	1949-	Ent	50			91	Horror Movies. Played 'Freddy Kruger'

NAME	DATES	CATEGORY	SIG	LS/DS	ALS	SP	COMMENTS
Engvall, Bill		Ent	17			50	
Ennis, Skinnay		Band	25			65	Singer, Musician
Enola Gay	1945	WWII				982	Prices vary depending on number of signatures
Enos, Roger	1729-1808	Mil	55	175	295		Gen., Honored VT Citizen
Enright, Richard E.		Lawman	12	24			Police Commissioner
Enriques, Rene	1933-1990	Ent	35			60	'Hill Street Blues' Lt. Calletano.
Ensign, John		Congr	10				Sen. (R-NV)
Ensley, F. Gerald, Bish.		Clergy	20	35	50	25	
Ensor, James Sydney, Baron	1860-1949	Artist	75	172	385		Belg. Painter, Etcher. Bizarre Fantasies, Masks
Entwistle, John	1944-2002	Music	50			185	Bass guitar, The Who
Enzi, Michael		Congr	10				US Senate (R-WY)
Ephron, Henry	1912-1992	Ent	15			25	Screenwriter. Worked w/wife, Nora.
Ephron, Nora	1941-	Author	15	35	65	30	Novels-Screenwriter. Parents Phoebe & Henry.
Ephron, Phoebe	1914-1971	Ent	15			35	Screenwriter-Mother of Nora & Wife of Henry
Epp, Franz Xaver von	1868-1947	WWII	50	175		122	WWII Gen., Nazi Storm Troops
Epps, Omar		Ent	15			45	
Epstein, Brian	1934-1967	Ent	310	793	1055		Beatles Manager & Promoter
Epstein, Jacob, Sir	1880-1959	Artist	150	210	375		Controversial Br. -Am. Sculptor
ER (Cast)		Ent	98			275	All 6 Original. (5) 250
Erbsen, Wayne		Author	10			12	Mountain music publisher/performer
Erdrich, Louise		Author	10			10	Novels. 'The Bingo Palace'
Erhard, Ludwig	1897-1977	HOS	25	70	170	60	Chancellor W. Ger.
Erickson, Leif	1911-1986	Ent	15			83	Singer-Actor. Many 2nd Leads
Ericsdotter, Siw		Opera	25			60	Opera
Ericson, B. A.		Aero	10	25			Piloted XC-99
Ericson, Eric		Comics	15			75	Appeared 'New Yorker' Mag. 40s-50's
Ericsson, John	1803-1889	Civ War	90	185	704	1265	Designed & Built Monitor
Erlanger, Camille	1863-1967	Comp					AMusQS 65
Ermey, R.		Ent	15			45	
Ernest Augustus II	1771-1851	Royal		225	360		1st King of Hanover(1837-51)
Erni, Hans		Artist	65		225		ALS-FDC/sig'd art
Ernouf, Manuel L. J. (Baron)		Fr Rev	35	85	160		
Ernst, Max	1891-1976	Artist	235	355	775		Surrealist-Dada Movement. Orig. Sketch S 825
Errant, James S.	1948-	Bus	10			20	Restauranteur; Gore Range Brewery
Errol, Leon	1881-1951	Ent	45			135	Talented Char. Actor in Comedy Roles
Erskine, Graves B.		Mil	30	35	65	50	Led US Marines at Iwo Jima
Erskine, John	1879-1951	Author	35	83	125		Novels, Pres. Juilliard, Musician
Erté		Artist	102	187	400	195	
Ertegun, Ahmet	1923-2006	Music	15			45	Music Prod. co-Fndr. of Atlantic Records
Ervine, St. John		Author	15	50			Br. Controversial Drama Critic
Erwin, Durward		Cntry Mus	10			20	
Erwin, James		Mil	45			60	Gen. WWI
Erwin, Sam J.		Congr	20	45		25	Sen. NC. Watergate Investigator
Erwin, Stuart	1903-1967	Ent	25			110	Char. Comed. 20s-60s. Played Mr. Average
Esaki, Leo		Sci	20	35	50	45	Nobel Physics
Escalante, Jaime		Educ	10			15	
Escobedo, Mariano	1827-1902	Mil	50	225			Captured Maximillian
Eshkol, Levi	1895-1969	HOS	94	167	400	225	Israeli P. M., Fndr. Histadrut
Eshoo, Anna G. E		Congr	10				Member US Congress
Esnault-Pelterie, Robert	1881-1957	Aero	75	250			Pioneer Aviator. Invented Aileron. Early Monoplane
Esperian, Kalen		Opera	10			30	Opera
Esposito, Jennifer	1973-	Ent	10			35	Actress & dancer
Esquirol, Jean-Et. Dominique		Sci		85			
Esser, Hermann		WWII				468	Co-Fndr. of the Nazi party

NAME	DATES	CATEGORY	SIG	LS/DS	ALS	SP	COMMENTS
Essex, David	1947-	Music	10			20	Br. Actor & singer
Essman, Susie		Ent	15			40	Comedianne
Estaing, Charles Hector T. de	1729-1794	Rev War	200	590	750		Fr. Gen-Adm. Pro Am. Hero
Este, George Peabody	1829-1881	Civ War	45	80	125		Union Gen.
Este, Isabella d'	1474-1539	Royal			10000		(Mantua) Art Patron, Diplomat.
Estefan, Gloria		Ent	12			45	Dancer-Singer.
Esterhasy, Gunt. A.		HOS	20	70	175		Austria
Esterhazy, Prince Pal A.	1786-1866	Statsmn	25		70		Austro-Hung. Diplomat. Ambassador to Eng.
Estes, Billy Sol		Celeb	15	20	45	35	Grain Storage Scandal
Estevez, Emilio	1962-	Ent	15	15	35	45	Actor-Son of Martin Sheen. Leading Man
Estil, Benjamin		Congr	15	25			Congressman VA 1825
Estrada, Erik	1948-	Ent	10	15	20	28	Leading Man. Puerto Rican DesC. TV's 'Chips'
Etheridge, Bob E		Congr	10				Member US Congress
Etheridge, Melissa		Music	15	35		55	Rock
Etter, Philippe		HOS	15	50			Switzerland
Etting, Ruth	1896-1978	Music	25	108		122	Major Vint. Singing Star of 20s
Eubanks, Bob		Ent	10	15	20	25	Game Show Host
Eugene Griessman, B.		Author	10			15	Motivational books
Eugene-Francois De Savoie	1663-1736	Mil	368				Austrian Gen.
Eugenie, Empress (Nap. III)	1826-1920	Royal	200	305	350		Influenced Nap. Fashion Leader
Euler-Chelpin, Ulf Svante von	1873-1964	Sci	20	35	60	40	Nobel Med. 1929
Eurythmics		Music	52			295	Rock; S Album 115
Eustis, Abraham		Mil	65		350		War 1812. Promoted to Br. Gen.
Eustis, Henry Lawrence	1819-1885	Civ War	50	85	130		Union Gen.
Eustis, William	1753-1825	Cab	50	118	185		Madison's Sec. War, MOC MA 1801
Evans, Bill		Music	175			1460	Jazz pianist; S Album 235
Evans, Chris		Ent	17			50	
Evans, Clement A.	1833-1911	Civ War	99	175	375		CSA Gen.
Evans, Clement A. (WD)		Civ War	200	560	891		CSA Gen.
Evans, Dale	1912-2001	Ent	25	35	60	74	Band Singer. Roy Rogers Leading Lady. SP w/RR 150
Evans, Daniel J.	1925-	Sen/Gov	15	18		20	Gov., Sen., Washington
Evans, Edith Dame	1888-1976	Ent	20	30		52	Distinguished Br. Stage Actress. Few Films
Evans, Edw. Lord Mountevans		Expl	35	90		75	Adm., Arctic Expl. Lord Mountevans 1880-1957
Evans, Gene	1922-1998	Ent	15	20	30	62	Actor. 'My Friend Flicka'
Evans, George	1797-1867	Congr	10				ME; FF 37
Evans, George De Lacy	1787-1870	Mil	150	220			Br. Col. Who Burned White House
Evans, Geraint, Sir		Opera	10			35	Opera
Evans, Joan	1934-	Ent	15	20	25	53	Teenage Roles in Early 50s. Now in Education
Evans, John V.		Gov	10	15			Governor ID
Evans, Lane E		Congr	10				Member US Congress
Evans, Lee	1964-	Ent	10			30	Br. Actor
Evans, Linda	1942-	Ent	42	65	65	59	Leading Lady. Successful TV Series 'Dynasty'
Evans, Lt. Col. D. M		Civ War	20	25	40		
Evans, Madge	1909-1981	Ent	25	30	35	113	Film Debut at 5. Film Star Until 1943. Retired
Evans, Marian (See George Eliot)		Author	137	478	1530		Br. Novels. (Mary Ann Lewes [Evans])
Evans, Maurice	1909-1989	Ent	42	73	85	72	Shakespearean Actor, Prod.
Evans, Michelle		Celeb	10			20	Miss GB-celebrity model
Evans, Nathan G. 'Shanks'	1824-1868	Civ War	189	340	709		CSA Gen.
Evans, Nathan Geo. Shanks (WD)		Civ War	265	800	1600		CSA Gen.
Evans, Nicholas		Author		40			Novels. 'The Horse Whisperer'
Evans, Oliver	1755-1819	Invent		1500			Built Am. 1st Self-Propelled Land Vehicle 1787
Evans, Ray		Comp	15	35	45	40	Am. Songwriter. 'Buttons & Bows', 'Que Sera Sera'
Evans, Robley D.	1846-1912	Mil	35	65	125	175	Adm. 'Fighting Bob Evans'
Evans, Ronald E.	1933-1990	Space	40			112	Command module pilot seat for Apollo 17

NAME	DATES	CATEGORY	SIG	LS/DS	ALS	SP	COMMENTS
Evans, Rupert		Ent	17			50	
Evans, Walker	1903-1975	Photog	75		270		Am. Photog. Documented Everyday Life
Evarts, William M.	1818-1901	Cab	40	65	95	150	Atty Gen., Sec. State, Sen NY
Everclear		Music	50			117	Rock group; S Guitar 230
Everest. F. K. 'Pete'		Aero	15	30	45	82	SP w/Crossfield 180
Everett Koop, C.		Pol	20			25	Surgeon Gen.
Everett, Chad	1937-	Ent	15	20	25	52	Actor 'Med. Center' & More
Everett, Edward	1794-1865	Pol	62	109	125	250	Fillmore Sec State, Sen. MA. Statesman, Scholar
Everett, Rupert		Ent	20			47	Actor
Everett, Terry E		Congr	10				Member US Congress
Everhart, Angie	1969-	Ent	10			35	Actress
Everly Brothers		Music	75			158	Don & Phil. 1st R & R Duo. Influence Later Artists
Everly, Don		Music	20			45	Everly Brothers
Everly, Phil		Music	20			48	Singer-Songwriter-Guitarist. 'Everly Brothers'
Evers, Charles		Activist	10	20	40	53	Succeeded Brother Medgar as Sec NAACP '63
Evers, Medgar	1925-1963	Activist		2800			AM. Civ. Rights Leader
Everybody Loves Raymond		Ent				219	TV Sitcom; S script 350
Evigan, Greg	1953-	Ent	10	15	15	25	Am. actor
Ewell, Rich'd Stoddert	1817-1872	Civ War	325	575	850		CSA Gen.
Ewell, Rich'd Stoddert (WD)		Civ War	756	1294	1450		CSA Gen.
Ewell, Tom		Ent	20	34	38	49	Actor. 'Seven Year Itch'
Ewing, Charles	1835-1883	Civ War	50	110	160		Union Gen.
Ewing, Hugh Boyle	1826-1905	Civ War	50	85	110		Union Gen.
Ewing, James	1736-1806	Rev War	100	190	320		Am. Brig. Gen.
Ewing, Thomas	1789-1871	Cab	30	65	95		Sen. OH, Sec. Treas. & Interior
Ewing, Thomas Jr	1829-1896	Civ War	48	75	120		Union Gen.
Exelmans, Remy J. I.	1775-1852	Fr Rev	65	140	230		Marshal of France
Exile (4)		Music	20			50	Rock
Exon, J. James		Sen/Gov	10	10		10	Sen., Governor NE
Eyre, Edward John	1815-1901	Expl	55		150		Gov. Australia. Eyre Rock
Eythe, William	1918-1957	Ent	15	15	20	70	Am. Actor of film, radio, TV & stage
Eytinge, Rose	1838-1911	Ent	25		65	65	19th C. Actress/Laura Keene, Booth
Fabares, Shelley	1942-	Ent	10	30	30	35	Actress. 'Coach'
Faber, John Eberhard	1822-1879	Bus	140	500	725		Eberhard Faber Pencil Co. 1st Pencil Mfg. In Am.
Fabian (See Forte, Fabian)		Ent	25			56	
Fabian, John M.		Space	10			28	
Fabio		Model	15			38	Male Model
Fabray, Nanette	1920-	Ent	10	10	15	35	Comedy Actress-Singer. 'Our Gang' as Child
Facinelli, Peter		Ent	15			45	
Factor, Max		Bus	30	125	175	83	Cosmetic Mfg.
Factor, Max Jr.		Bus	10	30	55	45	Cosmetic Mfg.
Fagan, James Fleming	1828-1893	Civ War	110	274			CSA Gen. & US Marshal For Indian Terr.
Fagerbakke, Bill		Ent	10			35	Actor 'Coach'
Fagoaga, Isidodo		Opera	15			50	Opera
Fahey, Jeff		Ent	10			35	Actor. Leading Man. 'The Marshal', 'Psycho III'
Fahnestock, Harris	1852-1914	Bus			115		
Fair, James, G.	1831-1894	Bus	30	110	180		Mining, Financier, CA Developer
Fairbairn, Sir William	1789-1874	Engr			180		
Fairbank, Calvin		Abolit	40	85	150		Freed Fugitive Slaves
Fairbanks, Charles W.	1852-1918	VP	55	110	324	200	T. Roosevelt VP. US Sen. IN
Fairbanks, Douglas, Jr.	1909-2000	Ent	41	45	102	132	Actor-Son of the Famous Father. SP w/Father 515
Fairbanks, Douglas, Sr.	1883-1939	Ent	85	135	210	236	Swashbuckling Silent Film Mega Star. UA
Fairbanks, Erastus	1792-1864	Gov	35		80		CW Gov. VT. Mfg. Platform Scales
Fairchild, Charles S.		Cab	20	35	55	40	Sec. Treasury 1887

NAME	DATES	CATEGORY	SIG	LS/DS	ALS	SP	COMMENTS
Fairchild, David G.	1869-1954	Sci	10	10	20	15	Am. Botanist. Books on Plants
Fairchild, Lucius	1831-1896	Civ War	45	50	80		Union Gen., Gov. WI, Statesman. Sig/Rank 55
Fairchild, Morgan	1950-	Ent	10	15	20	40	Actress
Fairchild, Sherman		Bus	25	60	115	40	Fairchild Camera & Equipment Co
Faircloth, Henry P.	1880-1956	Author	10	35			Noted US Social Scientist & Writer
Fairfax, George Wm.	1787-	Rev War	75	210	395		Companion of Geo. Washington
Fairfax, Thomas Lord	1691-1782	Colonial	220	550			Hist. Important Family. Settled in North-VA
Fairfield, Charles	1842-1924	Cab	25		40		Sec. Treas. under Cleveland
Fairfield, John	1797-1847	Congr	15	20	30		Sen., Gov. ME
Fairholt, Frederick	1814-1866	Artist	15		50		Engraver & Antiquarian
Fairless, Benjamin F.	1890-1962	Bus	20	45	60	60	CEO US Steel
Faisal, King	1906-1975	Royal	50	85	118	269	Saudi Arabia; Assass.
Faison, Donald		Ent	15			45	
Faith, Adam	1940-2003	Music	50			100	Early Br. Rock Star; S w/The Roulettes 240
Faith, Percy		Comp	20			110	Conductor-Arranger For Top Artists
Faithfull, Emily		Reform	25	45	55		Br. Printer-Publisher Q. Victoria
Falck, Wolfgang		Aero	20	45	60	80	
Falco, Edie		Ent	20			45	Actress; Emmy; Carmela, Sopranos
Falconer, William	1732-1769	Author	60	350			Br. Poet. Shipwrecked, Universal Marine Dict'y
Faleomavaega, Eni F.H.		Congr	10				Member US Congress. Samoa
Falk, Peter	1927-	Ent	15	20	30	149	SP As 'Columbo' 240
Falkenburg, Jinx	1919-2003	Ent	15	20	25	45	Spanish-born model & actress
Falkenhorst, Col-Gen Nikolaus von	1885-1968	WWII	35		155		WWII Ger. Gen.
Fall, Albert B.	1861-1944	Cab	40	68	95	110	Sec Interior. Teapot Dome Scandal
Fall, Leo	1873-1925	Comp				105	Austrian Operetta Comp.
Falla, Brigadier Norris S.	1883-1945	WWII	30			35	WWII New Zealand Gen.
Falla, Manuel de	1876-1946	Comp	162	360	600	900	Span. AMusQS 875, 1,000-1200
Fallieres, Clement Armand	1841-1931	Statsmn		65			Fr. Statesman., 8th Pres. of France
Fallon, Jimmy		Ent	15			45	Actor
Fallon, Walter A.		Bus	10			10	CEO Eastman Kodak Co.
Falstaff, John, Sir		Mil		8000			Model for Shakespeare's Play
Falwell, Jerry	1933-2007	Clergy	15	20	25	45	
Fancourt, Darell		Ent	15			65	D'Oyly Carte Gilbert & Sullivan Baritone Star
Faneuil, Peter		Rev War	150	275	555		Faneuil Hall, Boston
Fantin-Latour, Henri	1836-1904	Artist	40	90	170		Fr. Illust., Lithographer
Far, Frances		Comp	10	15	30	10	
Faraday, Michael	1791-1867	Sci	141	349	617	950	Br. Physicist, Chemist. ALS/Cont 1800
Farentino, James	1938-	Ent	15			45	Actor. Leading Man. Mostly TV
Fargo, Donna	1945-	Cntry Mus	10	15		25	Singer-Songwriter
Fargo, James C.		Bus	203	535	470		Wells, Fargo & Co. Am. Express
Fargo, William G.	1818-1881	Bus	328	727	1250		Wells-Fargo, Am. Express
Farias, Valentin Gomes	1781-1858	HOS	205	490			Pres. of Mexico until Defeated by Santa Ana
Farina, Dennis		Ent	10	35		44	Actor
Farinelli, Patricia		Model	10			20	
Farjeon, Eleanor	1881-1965	Author			325		
Farley, Chris	1964-1997	Ent	60			136	Comedian
Farley, James A.	1888-1976	Cab	15	50	63	30	FDR P. M. Gen. CEO Coca Cola. Pol.
Farley, John Cardinal	1842-1918	Clergy	28			65	Relig. Leader & Archbishop of New York
Farman, Henri	1874-1958	Aero	60	110	175	165	Pioneer Aviator. Plane Mfg. 1st Flight over 1 Km
Farman, Maurice		Aero	75		190		Pioneer Aviator. License #6. Brother of Henri
Farmer, Art	1928-1999	Music	10			40	Jazz Fluegelhorn-Trumpet
Farmer, Bill		Ent	17			50	
Farmer, Fannie Merritt	1857-1915	Author	190			250	Cookery Expert. 'Boston Cooking School Cook Book'
Farmer, Frances	1914-1970	Ent	141	177	160	824	Actress

NAME	DATES	CATEGORY	SIG	LS/DS	ALS	SP	COMMENTS
Farmer, James L. Jr.	1920-1999	Activist	20			60	Fndr. CORE ('42). Led Freedom Riders 60s
Farnham, Ralph	1756-1861	Mil	150				Rev. War Soldier. Fought at Bunker Hill
Farnol, J. Jeffrey		Author	10	25			Br.
Farnsworth, Charles		Mil	25			65	Gen. WWI
Farnsworth, Daniel W.		Bus		15	30		Fndr. Woolen Mills
Farnsworth, Elon John	1837-1863	Civ War	128				Union Gen., KIA Gettysburg
Farnsworth, John F.	1820-1897	Civ War	50	110	155	450	Union Gen. Sig/Rank 50
Farnsworth, Philo T.	1906-1971	Invent	315				Invented 1st TV Camera.
Farnsworth, Richard	1919-	Ent	15	22	30	55	Char. Actor. AA winner
Farnum, Dustin	1874-1929	Ent	50	75	90	130	Silent Star. 'The Squaw Man', 'The Virginian'
Farnum, William	1876-1953	Ent	38			158	Leading Man in Silent Films. 'The Spoilers'
Farouk I	1920-1965	Royal	298				King of Egypt.
Farquhar, John Hanson		Congr	10	20	30		MOC IN, Capt. Union Army
Farr, Hugh		Music	12			35	Singer-Guitarist, Sons of the Pioneers
Farr, Jamie		Ent	10	15	20	30	M*A*S*H' cast, Klinger
Farr, Karl		Music	12			35	Singer-Violinist. Member 'Sons of the Pioneers'
Farr, Sam F		Congr	10				Member US Congress
Farragut, David G.	1801-1870	Civ War	181	458	632	912	Union Adm. LS/Cont 1300. LS '64 2500
Farrakhan, Louis		Activist	70			150	Leads Nation of Islam
Farrar, Frederick W.		Clergy	25	35	50	50	
Farrar, Geraldine	1882-1967	Opera	50	80	80	132	Opera, Concert. Met. Legendary Star
Farrell, Charles	1901-1990	Ent	40	50	50	47	Top Star of Silents. Leading Man 30s-40's
Farrell, Colin		Ent	20			50	Actor
Farrell, Eileen		Opera	10			95	Opera, Concert
Farrell, Glenda	1904-1971	Ent	25	30		76	Leading Lady-Wisecracking Comedienne 30s
Farrell, Mike	1939-	Ent	10	20	25	38	Actor
Farrell, Terry		Ent	25			38	
Farrimond, Richard		Space	10			25	
Farrington, James		Congr	10		42		FF 42
Farrow, Mia	1945-	Ent	20	30	85	49	Actress
Farwell, Chas. B.	1823-1903	Congr	15		20		Sen.
Fassbaender, Brigitte		Opera	10			25	Ger. Mezzo Sopr., Opera
Fassbinder, Ranier		Ent	315			390	Ger. film Dir.
Fast, Howard	1914-	Author	15	70		25	Historical Novels, Screenplays. 'Spartacus'
Faster Pussy Cat		Music	25			55	Rock
Fat Boy		WWII				500	Nagasaki; S by Crew
Father Knows Best		Celeb	118			269	Cast SP
Fatone, Joey		Music	15			40	Popular singer
Fattah, Chaka F		Congr	10				Member US Congress
Faubus, Orval E.	1910-1994	Gov	35		70	50	Gov. AR, Blocked Integration
Faulkner, Charles J., Jr.		Congr	15	25			Sen. WV. Battle of New Market
Faulkner, Chas. J.	1806-1884	Congr		40	150		Rep. WV. Authored Fugitive Slave Act
Faulkner, Lisa	1973-	Ent	10			25	Br. Actress
Faulkner, William	1897-1962	Author	234	1103	2500	3600	Nobel Lit. '49, Pulitzer Fict. '54, 62, SB 850-2600
Fauquier, Francis		Colonial	200	575			Colonial Administrator
Faure, Felix	1841-1899	HOS	30		125		Pres. France 1895-99
Faure, Gabriel	1845-1924	Comp	120	105	344	550	Fr. 100's Songs, Chamber Music. Organist
Faure, Jean-Baptiste	1830-1914	Opera	35	110			Opera. Bass-Baritone. 'Faust', 'Don Carlos'
Faust, Chad		Ent	13			40	
Faustino, David		Ent	15			45	
Fausto, Cleva		Opera	30			65	Opera
Faversham, William	1868-1940	Ent	30			65	Created Role 'Jim Carson' in 'Squaw Man'
Fawcett, Edgar	1847-1904	Author	45	110	225	150	Verse, Novels & Plays Satirizing NY High Society
Fawcett, Farrah	1947-	Ent	20	30	40	51	Actress

NAME	DATES	CATEGORY	SIG	LS/DS	ALS	SP	COMMENTS
Fawcett, Millicent, Dame	1847-1929	Reform	30	50	162		Br. Women's Suffrage Leader
Fay, Frank	1894-1961	Ent	15	25	45	55	Broadway Leads. Few Films. Husb. Barbara Stanwyck
Fay, Joseph	1753-1803	Rev War		600	1050		
Faye, Alice	1912-1998	Ent	25	35	50	133	Actress. 20th C. Fox Musical Star from Late 30s
Faye, Julia	1893-1966	Ent	20	30	40	60	Ex Max Sennett Bathing Beauty. Early DeMille Films
Faylen, Frank	1907-1985	Ent	30			82	Am. Char. Actor from '36. Gangsters, Cops
Fayon, James Fleming	1823-1893	Civ War	80				CSA gen.
Fazenda, Louise	1895-1962	Ent	25			62	Max Sennett Silent Film Star. Top Comedienne
Fearn, Thomas	1789-1863	Civ War	117	189			Member of CSA Congress
Featherston, Winfield Scott	1820-1891	Civ War	102	255	305		CSA Gen. Sig/Rank 205
Feeney, Tom F		Congr	10				Member US Congress
Fegelein, Hermann	1906-1945	WWII	310	427			Nazi SS Leader
Fehr, Oded	1970-	Ent	20			40	Israeli film & TV actor
Feiffer, Jules	1929-	Comics	20			58	Mag. Cartoonist
Feingold, Russell		Congr	10			20	US Senate (D-WI)
Feinhals, Fritz		Opera	30			50	Ger. Baritone, Opera
Feinstein, Diane		Congr	15	20	25	25	Sen. CA
Feld, Fritz	1900-1993	Ent	15	20		50	Char. -Comedian. Mad or Eccentric Chars.
Feldman, Charles K.	1904-1968	Bus	10	20	40	25	Fndr. Famous Artists Corp. Prod., Lawyer, Agent
Feldman, Corey		Ent	15			40	Actor.
Feldman, Marty	1933-1983	Ent	62	113	95	204	Actor-Comedian. Pop-eyed Brit. Comedian
Feldon, Barbara	1939-	Ent	10	15	15	35	Actress. Leading Lady. 'Get Smart'
Feldshuh, Tovah	1952-	Ent	10	15	15	30	Actress.
Feliciano, Jose		Music	15	25		45	Guitar-Vocalist.
Felix, Maria	1914-2002	Ent	15			55	Major Star of Many Mex-Intl. Films 40s-60's
Fellini, Frederico	1920-1993	Ent	41	98		86	AA Film Dir. -Prod.
Fellows, Edith	1923-	Ent	15			40	Actress; Our Gang
Fels, Joseph		Bus	95	210	490		Fels Naptha Soap
Felt, Harry, Adm.		Mil	10	30	50	25	
Felton, Cornelius C.	1807-1882	Educ	25	45	135		Pres. Harvard 1860-62.
Felton, Happy		Band	15			35	Big Band
Felton, Rebecca L.	1835-1930	Congr	25	45	150		Sen. GA For 1 Day 11/21-11/22. 1st Woman Sen.
Fenn, Sherilyn	1964-	Ent	10			37	Actress.
Fenneman, George		Ent	12			40	Vet. Radio Personality. TV's 'You Bet Your Life'
Fenstermacher, Carol		Author	10			18	Glamour SP 42
Fenton, Ruben E.		Gov	30	50	80		Civil War Gov. NY
Fenwick, B. J., Bish.		Clergy	20	25	30		
Fenwick, Maj. -Gen. Charles P.	1891-1954	Mil	24			30	WWII Canadian Gen.
Fenwick, Millicent	1910-1992	Congr	18	28		50	MOC NJ. Lampooned in 'Doonsbury'. Pipe Smoker
Feoktistov, Konstantin		Space	25			75	Pioneer Russian Cosmonaut
Feola, Robert	1940-	Music	10	10		20	Recording artist for RCA Victor
Ferber, Edna	1887-1968	Author	85	169	287		Novels, Screenplays, Pulitzer '24. 'So Big', 'Giant'
Ferdin, Pamelyn		Ent	15			45	
Ferdinand I	1865-1927	Royal	70			580	King of Roumania, Prince of Hohenzollern
Ferdinand I	1503-1564	Royal	425	1495			Holy Roman Emperor
Ferdinand I	1793-1875	Royal	70	245			Emperor of Austria
Ferdinand II	1578-1637	Royal	100	450			Holy Roman Emperor from 1619
Ferdinand II & Isabella I		Royal		6012			
Ferdinand V	1452-1516	Royal		3038			King, Spain. Columbus Patron. DS w/Isabella 6000
Ferdinand VII (Sp)	1784-1833	Royal	125	475			His Reign Disastrous to Spain.
Ferebee, Thomas	1919-2000	WWII	30	50	120	75	Maj. Bombadier Enola Gay, S drawing 300
Ferenczi, Sandor	1873-1933	Sci	60	180	350		Hung. Psychoanalyst. Freud Friend
Fergie		Music	17			50	
Ferguson, Frank	1899-1978	Ent	25			210	Movie & TV actor

NAME	DATES	CATEGORY	SIG	LS/DS	ALS	SP	COMMENTS
Ferguson, Homer		Congr	10	15		10	Sen. MI. Ambass. Philippines
Ferguson, Maynard		Ent	20			60	Trumpet Player. Bandleader
Ferguson, Mike F		Congr	10				Member US Congress
Ferguson, Miriam A. 'Ma'	1875-1961	Gov	60	150			Governor TX. Replaced Impeached Husband
Ferguson, Samuel W.	1834-1917	Civ War	220	316	642		CSA Gen.
Ferguson, Samuel W. (WD)	1834-1917	Civ War	238	631	839		CSA Gen.
Ferguson, Sarah		Royal	25	35	50	88	Duchess of York
Ferguson, Stacy		Ent	17			50	
Ferguson, William J.		Ent	175	225	425		Actor 'Our Am. Cousin'
Ferkauf, Eugene		Bus	10	10	15	15	
Ferlinghetti, Lawrence		Author	20	75	90	75	Am. Poet, Publisher. Beat Movement
Ferlito, Vanessa		Ent	15			45	
Fermi, Enrico	1901-1954	Sci	853	1651	3094		Nobel Phys. 1st Controlled Nuclear Chain Reaction
Fernandel	1903-1971	Ent	25			125	Actor-Comed. 'Around the World in 80 Days'
Ferrara, America		Ent	25			75	
Ferrara, Franco		Cond	45			250	Conductor
Ferrara, Jeremy		Ent	20			35	Entourage
Ferrara, Jerry		Ent	16			48	
Ferrare, Cristina		Ent	10	10	15	20	Model. TV Host
Ferrari, Enzo	1898-1988	Bus	350	1207	516	1760	Luxury Sports Car Auto Mfg. & Race Car Driver
Ferraro, Geraldine		Congr	15	45	55	40	Congresswoman NY., V. P. Cand.
Ferrell, Will		Ent	32			95	
Ferrer, Jose	1912-1992	Ent	20	25	40	60	AA Actor. 'Cyrano'
Ferrer, Mel	1917-	Ent	10			25	Actor. Former Radio Prod. -Writer.
Ferrer, Miguel	1955-	Ent	10			15	Actor son of Jose
Ferrero, Edward	1831-1899	Civ War	52	108	150		Union Gen.
Ferrero, Edward (WD)	1831-1899	Civ War	69	188		300	Union Gen. Commanded Colored Div. 1863
Ferrier, Kathleen	1912-1953	Opera	55			195	Opera. Br. Contralto. 'Carmen'
Ferrigno, Lou	1952-	Ent	15		20	32	Actor. 'The Hulk'. Former Mr. Universe
Ferris, Charles Goadsby		Congr	10		38		FF 38
Ferris, Scott		Congr	12	15		15	MOC OK
Ferris, Valerie		Ent	17			50	
Ferry, Orris S. (WD)		Civ War	65	140	210	300	Union Gen., US Sen. NY
Ferry, Orris Sanford	1823-1875	Civ War	50	80	125		Union Gen.
Ferry, Thomas White	1827-1896	Congr	70	95			Sen. MI, Pres. Pro Tem Senate
Fersen, Hans-Axel, Count de	1755-1810	Rev War		1250			With Rochambeau at Yorktown. Murdered
Fesch, Joseph, Card.	1763-1839	Clergy		220	305		Married Napoleon to Josephine.
Fess, Simeon Davison	1861-1936	Congr	10	27	45	40	MOC, Sen. OH. Chmn. Nat. Rep. Comm.
Fessenden, Francis	1839-1906	Civ War	63	90	150		Union Gen.
Fessenden, Francis (WD)		Civ War	73	152	210		Union Gen. Lost Leg at Monett's Bluff
Fessenden, James D.	1833-1882	Civ War	50	70	110		Union Gen.
Fessenden, William P.	1806-1869	Cab	45	75	142		Lincoln Sec. Treasury; Senate; FF 35
Fetchit, Stepin	1892-1985	Ent	58		125	215	Actor-Comedian. Aka Lincoln Perry
Fetterman, William J.	1833-1866	Mil		5900			Indian Fighter. Ambushed & Killed w/80 men
Feuerstein, Mark		Ent	16			49	
Feuillere, Edwige	1907-	Ent	25			38	Fr. Actress. Leading Mbr. 'Comedie Francaise'
Few, William		Rev War	200	714	750		Cont. Congr. 1st GA Sen
Feynman, Richard P.		Sci	25	40	85	30	Nobel Physics.
Fibich-Hanusova, Betty		Opera			250		Opera. Great Czech Alto
Fichtner, William		Ent	13			40	
Fiderkiewicz, Alfred J., Dr.		Statsmn	40	75			Polish Statesman
Fidler, Jimmy	1900-1988	Ent	20	25	30	45	Hollywood Gossip Columnist
Fiedler, Arthur	1894-1979	Cond	34	95		76	Conductor Boston Pops
Fiedler, John	1925-	Ent	15	20	25	65	Mild, Spectacled, Char. Actor. '12 Angry Men'

NAME	DATES	CATEGORY	SIG	LS/DS	ALS	SP	COMMENTS
Field, Charles E.		Clergy	20	35	45	25	
Field, Charles William	1828-1892	Civ War	125	210	340		CSA gen.
Field, Cyrus W.	1819-1892	Bus	75	210	260		Atl. Telegr. Cable, Financier. S stock cert. 8800
Field, Davis Dudley	1805-1894	Law	25		31		Counsel: J. Gould, J. Fiske. Law Codification.
Field, Eugene	1850-1895	Author	118	250	437	350	Kid's Poet, Journalist. AManS 900-1700
Field, Henry Martyn	1822-1907	Clergy	15		35		Presb. Younger Bro. Cyrus, Davis, Stephen Field
Field, Kate		Author	10	15			
Field, Marshall, III	1893-1956	Bus	55	110	160		Communications Empire. Major Publisher
Field, Marshall, IV.	1916-1965	Bus	30	70	110	75	Pres., CEO Field Enterprises. Publisher, Editor
Field, Marshall, Sr.	1834-1906	Bus	265	525	900	650	Marshall Field & Co.
Field, Mary French		Author	10	15	20	15	
Field, Rachel	1894-1942	Author	20	85			Am. Novels, 'All This & Heaven Too'. Kid's Books
Field, Sally	1946-	Ent	15	25	32	50	AA Winning Actress
Field, Stephen J.	1816-1899	Sup Crt	75	150	300	225	US Supreme Court Justice Under Lincoln
Field, Todd		Ent	17			50	
Field, Virginia	1917-1992	Ent	15	20	25	45	Br. Actress. Interesting 2nd Leads
Fielder, James F.		Gov	10	15	25	15	Governor NJ
Fields, Benny	1894-1959	Ent				75	Minstrel & Vaude. actor
Fields, Debbi	1956-	Bus	10			25	Mrs. Field's Cookies
Fields, Gracie, Dame	1898-1979	Ent	25	35	55	80	Br. Singer & Comed. Knighted for War Effort
Fields, James T.	1817-1881	Author	10	20	45		Publisher
Fields, Lew M.	1879-1946	Ent	50				SEE Weber & Fields
Fields, Shep		Band	20			60	Big Band Leader-Songwriter-Singer 30s-40's
Fields, Stanley	1884-1941	Ent	15	15	30	60	Char. Actor. Former Boxer, Vaude.
Fields, Totie	1930-1978	Ent	15			55	Comedianne
Fields, W. C.	1879-1946	Ent	432	722	1192	1210	Comed. -Actor Stage & Screen. S Chk 300-400
Fieldy		Music	15			30	Bass Guitar 'Korn'
Fiennes, Joseph		Ent	17			50	
Fiennes, Joseph (Finnes)		Ent	20			65	Br. Actor. 'Shakespeare In Love'
Fiennes, Ralph		Ent	15			54	Br. Actor. 'English Patient'
Fiennes, Ranulph		Expl	10			30	
Fieseler, Gerhard		Aero	25	55	85	85	
Fifteen (15)		Music	30	40	50	60	Rock
Figgis, Mike		Celeb	10			15	Film industry
Figner, Medea		Ent					SEE: Mei-Figner
Figueres, Jose		HOS	15	45	110	20	
Filacuridi, Nicola		Opera	15			45	Opera
Filippeschi, Mario		Opera	25			85	Opera
Fillion, Nathan		Ent	15			45	
Fillmore, Caroline	?-1881	1st Lady	400	625	800		2nd Wife
Fillmore, M. & Daniel W.		Pres		2062			Pres. & Sectry of State
Fillmore, Millard	1800-1874	Pres	265	658	820	12000	FF 375-400-475. Historic ALS 3750
Fillmore, Millard (As Pres.)		Pres	409	1242	2869		FF 400-475. ALS/Cont 27, 500
Filner, Bob F		Congr	10				Member US Congress
Finch, Peter	1916-1977	Ent	74	120	110	179	Br. Actor. AA. Protégé of L. Olivier
Findlay, William	1768-1846	Gov	45	60	115		Gov. PA 1817, Sen. 1821
Fine, Larry	1911-1974	Ent	291	364	473	404	Member (1928) Of Three Stooges
Fine, Vivian		Comp					Am. Comp. AMusQS 75
Finegan, Bill (William J.)		Band	20			40	Big Band Leader. (Arranger/Sauter)
Finegan, Joseph	1814-1885	Civ War	123				CSA Gen.
Finkel, Fyvush		Ent	10			30	Char. Actor. 'Picket Fences' Emmy
Finlay, Frank	1926-	Ent	10	12	15	30	Br. Stage & Film Actor. Screen From '62. TV '84
Finletter, Thomas	1894-1980	Cab	10	15	30	20	Korean War Sec Air Force. Amb.
Finley, Cameron	1987-	Ent	10			25	Actor

NAME	DATES	CATEGORY	SIG	LS/DS	ALS	SP	COMMENTS
Finley, Jesse J.	1812-1904	Civ War	96	152	297		CSA Gen. US Sen.
Finley, Jesse J. (WD)	1812-1904	Civ War		6600			CSA Gen., AManS 6600
Finn, John	1909-	WWII	20			30	1st Medal of Honor awarded for WWII.
Finney, Albert	1936-	Ent	10	15	20	45	Br. Actor. 'The Entertainer', 'Tom Jones'
Finney, Charles G.	1792-1875	Clergy	50	75	110		Presb. Revivalist-Evang. Withdrew-Pres. Oberlin
Finnie, Linda		Opera	10			30	Opera
Finston, Nat W.		Comp	10			20	Conductor-Violinist, author
Finucane, Brendan 'Paddy'	1920-1942	WWII	150			500	Irish; Spitfire ace; 32 kills
Fiorella, Pascal A.		Mil	60	80	125		Fr. Gen. Cousin to Napoleon
Fiorentino, Linda		Ent	18			60	Actress
Fiorina, Carleton 'Carly'		Bus		20	25	30	Prior CEO of Hewlett-Packard
Fio-Rito, Ted		Band	15			35	Big Band Leader
Firestone, Harvey S.	1868-1938	Bus	346	825	1550	607	Fndr. Firestone Tire., S stock cert. 22000
Firestone, Jr., Harvey S.	1898-1973	Bus	25	50	85	35	Pres. CEO Firestone Tire
Firestone, Leonard K.		Bus	15	40	70	30	
Firley, Douglas		Music	10			25	Music. Keyboards 'Gravity Kills'
First Ladies		1st Lady	750				(Kennedy thru Bush) Six
First Ladies (4 Repub.)		1st Lady	250			900	Nixon, Ford, Reagan, Bush
Firth, Colin	1960-	Ent	10			232	Br. Actor
Fischer, Annie	1914-1995	Music				250	Hungarian classical pianist
Fischer, Bobby	1943-2008	Celeb	120	279	492	605	Champion Am. Chess Player; Chk 675
Fischer, Edmond H., Dr.		Sci	20	45		30	Nobel Med.
Fischer, Emil	1838-1914	Opera	40		75		Opera. Ger. Bass-Baritone. Excelled as 'Sachs'
Fischer, Harold E.		Aero	10	25	45	35	ACE, Korea, Double Ace
Fischer, Ivan		Cond				65	Hungarian
Fischer, Jenna		Ent	15			45	
Fischer, Siegfried		Aero	10	15	25	15	
Fischer-Dieskau, Dietrich		Opera	30			90	Opera
Fish, Hamilton	1808-1893	Cab	30	66	90	305	Gov., Sen., US Grant & Hayes Sec State
Fish, Nicholas		Rev War	55	118	245		Aide-de-Camp Gen. Scott
Fish, Stuyvesant		Bus	300	850			RR Baron, Financier
Fishburne, Laurence	1961-	Ent	12			50	Actor
Fishel, Danielle	1981-	Ent				30	Actress
Fisher, Amy		Crime	20		35		Shot alleged lover's wife.
Fisher, Anna L.	1949-	Space	10			35	
Fisher, Bud (Harry C.)	1885-1954	Comics	75	95		300	Mutt & Jeff'. 1st Reg. Cartoon Strip, S draw 350
Fisher, Carrie		Ent	10	36	40	41	Actress, 'Star Wars' Authentic SP 60
Fisher, Dorothy Canfield	1879-1958	Author	30	65	95		Am. Novels, Essayist.
Fisher, Eddie	1928-	Ent	15	25	20	40	Singer
Fisher, Fred J.		Bus	90				Mfg. Auto Body. GM's. Body By Fisher
Fisher, Freddie		Ent	10			35	'Schnickelfritz'
Fisher, Geoffrey F.	1887-1972	Clergy	35			50	Archbishop Canterbury
Fisher, Ham		Comics	100		225	250	Joe Palooka', S drwng 240
Fisher, Harrison		Artist	120				Orig. Art as Illust. S 700
Fisher, John S.		Gov	10	15	35		Governor PA
Fisher, John, Lord	1841-1920	Mil	15	25			Brit. Adm. of Fleet 1905. Prepared Navy For WW
Fisher, Lawrence P.		Bus	90	150	410		Co-Fndr. Fisher Body (GM)
Fisher, William F.		Space	10			25	
Fisk, Clinton B.	1828-1890	Civ War	42	85	110		Union Gen. Founded Fisk U
Fisk, James, Jr.	1834-1872	Bus	2500	11500	18000		Rarest Robber Baron. Stock Cert. S 25,000-42000
Fisk, Minnie Maddern	1866-1932	Ent	15			50	Am. Stage Actress. Made 2 Silent Films
Fiske, Bradley	1854-1942	Mil	25		45		Adm, WWI. Held 60 Patents for Navy
Fiske, John	1842-1901	Phil	30				Am. philosopher & historian
Fitch, Graham Newell		Congr	10				FF 31

NAME	DATES	CATEGORY	SIG	LS/DS	ALS	SP	COMMENTS
Fitch, Val L., Dr.		Sci	20	35		30	Nobel Physics
Fitz, Reginald H.	1843-1913	Sci	75		310		Physician. Identified Cause of Appendicitis
Fitzgerald, Barry	1888-1961	Ent	122	135	195	311	Char. Actor. AA; 'Going My Way'
FitzGerald, Edward	1809-1833	Author	90	250	760		Poet. Translator 'Rubaiyat. '
Fitzgerald, Ella	1918-1998	Music	90	153	128	323	Am. 1st Lady of Jazz DS (Conract) 350
Fitzgerald, F. Scott	1896-1940	Author	381	1545	4971	2500	Novels, Screenwriter. ALS/Gatsby Cont. $43000. Inscr. 'Tender is the Night' $13145
Fitzgerald, Garret		Statsmn	10	30			Irish Statesman
Fitzgerald, Geraldine	1912-1992	Ent	15	22	30	57	Ir. Actress. 'Wuthering Heights'
Fitzgerald, John		Rev War	35	90	190		
Fitzgerald, John F. (Honey Fitz)		Pol	40	55	95	260	Mayor Boston. JFK Grandfather
Fitzgerald, Peter		Congr	10				US Senate (R-IL)
Fitzgerald, Richard		Photog	10			15	Photographer
Fitzgerald, Tara	1967-	Ent	10			25	Br. Actress
Fitzmaurice, James Major		Aero	75				1st westward trans-Atlantic flight 1928
Fitzsimmons, Thomas	1741-1811	Rev War	244	278	376		Constitution Signer, ALS 6500
FitzSimons, Frank L.		Author	10			12	Regional history
Fitzwater, Marlin		WH Staff	10			20	
Five Satins		Music	150	405			Rock group:
Fix, Paul	1901-1983	Ent	125			310	Good Gen. Purpose Actor. 100's of Roles
Fixx, Jim	1932-1984	Author	15	35		35	Fitness; runner
Flack, Roberta		Music	15			40	Rock
Flagg, Fannie		Ent	10	10	20	20	Author, Plays
Flagg, James Montgomery	1877-1960	Artist	66	222	330	348	Painter, Illust. Self Caricature S 950; Sket 500
Flagler, D. W.		Mil	15	20	25	20	
Flagler, Henry M.	1830-1913	Bus	750	2250	6500	1800	Stand. Oil Pioneer. Fndr. So. FL
Flagstad, Kirsten	1895-1962	Ent	102		188	318	Nor. Sopr.
Flahaut, A. C. J., Count	1785-1870	Fr Rcv	25		60		Exploits in Gallantry. Gen., Diplomat, Lover
Flahiff, George B., Card.		Clergy	35	40	60	40	
Flake, Floyd H.	1945-	Congr	10	10			Congressman NY
Flake, Jeff F		Congr	10				Member US Congress
Flakus, Walter		Music	10			25	Music. Keyboards 'Stabbing Westward'
Flammarion, Nicolas-Camille	1842-1925	Sci	40	61	120		Fr. Astronomer
Flamsteed, John	1646-1719	Sci	750	2100			Br. 1st Astronomer Royal
Flanagan, Edward, Fr.	1886-1948	Clergy	90	125		170	Boy's Town Fndr.
Flanders, Ed	1934-1995	Ent				40	Actor; 'St. Elsewhere'
Flannery, Sean		Ent	17			50	
Flannery, Sean Patrick	1965-	Ent	15			44	Actor. The Young 'Indiana Jones'
Flash Gordon		Ent				200	SP w/Buster Crabbe & Jean Rogers
Flatt, Lester & Earl Scruggs		Cntry Mus	50			138	Bluegrass Pioneers
Flaubert, Gustave	1821-1880	Author	175	635	1300		Fr. Novels. Realist School
Flavin, Dick		Celeb	10			15	Sportswriter & commentator
Flavin, James	1906-1976	Ent	15	20	25	60	Ir. -Am. Supporting Actor. Usually Bewildered Cop
Flavin, Jennifer	1968-	Model	10			20	Model
Flaxman, John	1755-1826	Artist	55		200		Br. Sculptor/Illust. Designed for Wedgewood
Fleetwood Mac		Music	214			402	S album, all 5 500
Fleetwood, Mick		Music	30			55	Member Fleetwood Mac
Fleischer, Charles		Ent	10			35	Voice of Roger Rabbitt
Fleischer, Leon		Music				85	Pianist
Fleischer, Leonore		Author	15		40	30	'Shadowlands'
Fleischer, Max	1883-1972	Comics	150	312		237	Animator. Creator of 'Betty Boop'
Fleischer, Richard	1916-	Ent	15			25	Film Dir. '46's-'87
Fleischmann, Charles L.		Bus	110	450			Fleischmann's Yeast
Fleiss, Heidi		Bus	10		30	45	Hollywood Madame

NAME	DATES	CATEGORY	SIG	LS/DS	ALS	SP	COMMENTS
Fleming, Alexander, Sir	1881-1955	Sci	262	1561	2190	924	Scot Bacteriologist. Nobel for disc. Penicillin
Fleming, Ambrose	1849-1945	Sci	175		397		Br. Elec. Engineer. Invented 1st Electron Tube
Fleming, Eric	1924-1966	Ent	172	250		350	Actor. Original 'Rawhide'-TV
Fleming, Francis		WWII	10	22	40	30	ACE, WWII; 7.5 kills
Fleming, Ian	1888-1969	Author	721	2040	1880	1400	James Bond' Novels. 1st Ed. S 5,000-
Fleming, John Ambrose, Sir	1849-1945	Sci	30	65	150		Br. Electrical Engineer. Many Contributions
Fleming, Renee		Opera				62	Sopr.
Fleming, Rhonda	1923-	Ent	10	18	25	49	Actress.
Fleming, Victor	1883-1949	Ent	547	835		725	AA Dir. GWTW, WOZ. Vintage SP 8640
Fleming-Sandes, Alfred		Mil	18	50			WWI Victoria Cross
Fleta, Miguel	1897-1938	Opera	45			250	Opera. Span. Tenor
Fletcher, Bramwell	1904-1988	Ent	48			60	Br. Actor. Light Leading Man of 30s
Fletcher, Ernie F		Congr	10				Member US Congress
Fletcher, Frank Jack		Mil	25	60	120	60	
Fletcher, Harvey	1884-1981	Sci	225				Stereo Sound 1934
Fletcher, Isaac		Congr	10		45		FF 45
Fletcher, James		Space	10	20	35		Whistle Blower
Fletcher, James Cooley		Clergy	10		25		Missionary
Fletcher, John Gould	1886-1950	Author	18	35	100		Pulitzer Poet. Identified/Imagist Grp., Fugitives
Fletcher, Louise	1936-	Ent	10	10	15	56	Actress, AA; SP 160 as Nurse Ratched
Flexner, Simon	1891-1946	Med	15				Famous Pathologist
Flindt, Flemming		Ballet	25			70	Royal Danish Ballet Star
Flint, Austin	1812-1886	Med	70	215	400		Eminent Physician-Teacher
Flint, Keith		Music	10			45	Music. Lead Singer 'Prodigy'
Flint, Lawrence		Aero	10	16	35	25	
Flint, Sir William Russell	1880-1969	Artist			90		
Flippen, Jay C.	1898-1971	Ent	25			130	Actor. Vaude. Cop, Western films
Flockhart, Calista		Ent	20			45	T. V. 's 'Ally McBeal'. Broad Stage Background
Floege, Ernest		Mil		45		70	Commandant Paul. Fr. Resistance
Floren, Myron		Music	10			15	Accordian. Lawrence Welk
Florence, Thomas B.		Congr	10				FF 32
Florence, William J., Mrs.		Ent	10		25	75	Actress-Malvina Pray. Stage. Appeared w/Husb.
Florence, William Jermyn	1831-1891	Ent	15	25	40	75	Actor, Songwriter, Plays. Appeared w/Wife
Florentino, Linda		Ent	10			25	Actress
Florenz, Juan Diego		Opera				65	Bel canto tenor
Flores, Juan Jose	1800-1864	HOS		775			1st Pres. of Equador
Florey, Howard Walter		Sci	25	40	75	35	Nobel Med., Penicillin
Florey, Paul J., Dr.	1898-1968	Sci	25	35	70	45	Nobel Med./Fleming. Penicillin
Florey, Robert	1900-1979	Ent	15			45	Fr. screenwriter, dir. short films, & actor
Flotow, Frederich von	1812-1883	Comp	75	220	450		Ger. Opera, Ballet, Concertos
Flourens, Marie-Jean P.	1794-1867	Sci		50	225		Fr. Physiologist
Flower, R. P		Gov	10	15			Governor NY
Flowers, Bess	1900-1984	Ent	15	25	35	95	Over 1,000 films. 'Queen of Hollywood Extras'
Flowers, Jennifer		Celeb	10			20	Alleged affair w/Wm Clinton
Flowers, Wayland		Ent	15	15		36	Clever Marionette-Puppet Comedian
Floyd, John Buchanan	1806-1863	Civ War	162	298	403		Gov. VA. Sec. War, CSA Gen.
Floyd, John Buchanan (WD)		Civ War	242	450	1250		CSA Gen. (Buchanan's Sec War 1857-60)
Floyd, William	1734-1821	Rev War	350	1016	1370		Signer Dec of Ind ; Maj. Gen. NY Militia
Fluckey, Gene		Mil	45		75	90	Top US Submarine Cmdr.
Fluster, Lafayette		Congr	40				Pres. Pro Tem of Senate
Flynn, Edward J.		Pol	10	15	25	15	Democratic Boss NY. 'Boss Flynn'
Flynn, Errol	1909-1959	Ent	263	737	1179	634	Actor, Chk 275-400
Flynn, Joe	1925-1974	Ent	54	60	110	252	Am. Char. -Comed. TV 'McHale's Navy'
Flynt, Larry		Pub	15	30	35	28	'Hustler' Magazine Publisher

NAME	DATES	CATEGORY	SIG	LS/DS	ALS	SP	COMMENTS
Foale, Mike	1957-	Space	10			20	Br.
Foch, Ferdinand	1851-1929	Mil	100	150	285	962	Fr. Gen. WWI, Marshal. Active in Major Battles
Foch, Nina	1924-	Ent	10	10	15	40	Dutch-Born Am. Leading Lady. Assoc. Dir.
Foer, Jonathan Safran		Author	20			30	Author, Illust.
Fogelberg, Dan	1951-2007	Music	20	45		50	Singer; songwriter
Fogerty, John		Music	25	50		80	Rock, CCR
Fogler, Dan	1976-	Ent	15			45	
Fohstrom, Alma	1856-1936	Opera	125			600	Legendary Coloratura Sopr. St. Petersburg
Fokker, Anthony H.	1890-1939	Aero	200	295	525	500	Am. Aircraft Designer-Builder
Foley, Dave		Ent	15			45	
Foley, David	1963-	Ent	10			30	Canadian born actor
Foley, Mark F	1954-	Congr	10			25	FL. Resigned after allegations of solicitation
Foley, Red	1910-1968	Cntry Mus	65			85	Top Country Star
Foley, Robert	1941-	Mil	25	25		40	Gen. & Vietnam Medal of Honor Recipient
Foley, Scott		Ent	17			50	
Folger, Charles J.		Cab	10	15	35		Sec Treasury Under Arthur
Folger, William M.	1844-1928	Mil	45	115			Adm. USN. Comm. Phillipine Squadron 189-1905
Follett, Ken		Author	15	20		25	Br. Mystery Novels
Folsom, Marion B.		Cab	15	25		20	Sec. HEW. Drafter Soc. Sec. Adm.
Folsom, Nathaniel		Rev War	125		450		Am. Gen., Continental Congress
Foltz, Frederick		Mil			45	100	Gen. WWI
Fonck, Paul-René	1894-1953	Aero	1000	1900			ACE, Fr. WWI. Top Allied Ace
Fonda, Bridget		Ent	20			46	Actress.
Fonda, Henry	1905-1982	Ent	48	85		229	AA Actor. Lifetime Achievement Award
Fonda, Jane	1937-	Ent	25	52	60	121	AA Winner
Fonda, Jelles		Rev War	50	155	225		Colonial Leader, Rev. War Off.
Fonda, Peter	1939-	Ent	12	22	25	50	Actor., SP 'Easy Rider 250-585
Fonda, Ten Eyck H.		Clv War	50		95		Mil. Telegrapher Hero
Fondren, Debra Jo		Model	10			25	Playboy' '78 Centerfold of the Year.
Fong, Benson	1916-1987	Ent	25			52	
Fong, Hiram L.		Congr	10	10		15	Sen. HI
Fonseca, Roberto A.		HOS	10	16	40	20	
Fontaine, Joan	1917-	Ent	12	15	40	93	Oscar winning Actress.
Fontanne, Lynn	1887-1983	Ent	25			120	Actress. Wife/Partner Alfred Lunt; SP w/AL 275
Fonteyn, Margot	1919-1991	Ballet	40	60	135	139	Premier Ballerina. Fonteyn & Nureyev SP 350
Foo Fighters		Music		140		75	Rock group; S Guitar 315; S Album 125
Foot, Solomon		Congr	15	30	45		Repr. VT 1843, CSA Congress
Foote, Andrew Hull	1806-1863	Civ War	71	98	208		Union Adm. ALS '63 3500. Mortally Wounded 1863
Foote, Arthur Wm.	1853-1937	Comp	30	85	195		Organist. Church Music, Songs, Cantatas
Foote, H. R. B.		Mil	20	20		50	Br. Maj. Gen. Victoria Cross WWII
Foote, Henry S.		Civ War	25	40	70		US Sen., CSA Congress
Foote, Horton		Author	10		20	20	Plays, Scriptwriter
Foote, Shelby	1916-2005	Author	15	35	50	40	
Foraker, Joseph B.	1846-1917	Sen/Gov	10	32		20	Gov., OH Sen. Secretly On Std. Oil Payroll
Foran, Dick	1910-1979	Ent	15	20	35	50	Singer-Actor-Cowboy. 40 Year Career
Foray, June		Ent	10			25	Voiced Several 'Rocky & Bullwinkle' Chars.
Forbes, Bertie Chas.	1880-1954	Bus	45	80	120	90	Fndr. 'Forbes' Magazine
Forbes, George Wm.	1869-1947	HOS	25	65			NZ Prime Min.
Forbes, J. Randy F		Congr	10				Member US Congress
Forbes, M. Steve		Pub	15			30	Twice Pres. Cand.
Forbes, Malcolm S.	1919-1990	Bus	25	45	70	64	Publisher, Motorcyclist, Balloonist, Collector
Forbes, Ralph	1902-1951	Ent	15	20	30	92	Br. Stage as Child. Movies From 1921
Forbes-Robertson, John, Sir	1853-1937	Ent	25		98	58	Br. Stage, Films. SPc/Gertrude Elliott 125
Force, Manning Ferguson	1824-1899	Civ War	55	110	170		Union Gen., Medal of Honor

NAME	DATES	CATEGORY	SIG	LS/DS	ALS	SP	COMMENTS
Ford Coppola, Francis		Celeb	15	35	50	50	Film Dir.
Ford Jr., Harold E. F		Congr	10			20	Member US Congress
Ford, Benson		Bus	10	15	30	15	Ford Motor Car
Ford, Betty	1918-2007	1st Lady	50	75	95	92	
Ford, Edsel	1893-1943	Bus	171	402		500	Pres. Ford Motor Co.
Ford, Edsel B. II		Bus	10	10	20	20	Ford Motor Co.
Ford, Eileen		Bus	10	30		20	Ford Modeling Agency
Ford, Elaine		Bus	20			30	
Ford, Faith		Ent	10			43	Actress. 'Murphy Brown'
Ford, Gerald & Ford, Betty		Pres	65			175	FDC S. 250
Ford, Gerald R.	1913-2006	Pres	64	233	976	94	Signed Warren Attest. 200. Full S Pardon 1200
Ford, Gerald R. (As Pres.)	1913-2006	Pres	120	718	4160	155	TLS/Cont 1000-2500, S WHC 200; Handwritten Oath of Office 7200
Ford, Glenn	1916-1995	Ent	37	50		87	Actor
Ford, Harold	1945-	Congr	10	20		20	Longtime Afr. -Am. Dem. MOC TN
Ford, Harrison		Ent	43	50	65	104	Actor, 'Star Wars' SP 150-350
Ford, Henry	1863-1947	Bus	813	1744	4667	1665	Auto Mfg. Imp. DS 28500; SP/Orville Wright 5000
Ford, Henry II	1917-1987	Bus	10	45	55	55	Grandson, Pres. & CEO Ford Motor Co.
Ford, John	1895-1973	Ent	150	792		707	Classic Western Film Dir.
Ford, John Anson		Bus	10	10	20	10	
Ford, John S. 'Rip' (WD)		Civ War			3585		CSA Col., Cmdr. of TX Expeditionary Forces
Ford, John Thompson	1829-1894	Bus	330	481	612		Ford's Theater, Wash. D. C.
Ford, Lita	1958-	Music	15			45	Br. rock musician
Ford, Michael		Ent	10			25	Br. Actor
Ford, Paul	1901-1976	Ent	20			140	Am. Char. Actor. Stage, TV, Films. OZ Voices
Ford, Samuel Howard	1819-1905	Civ War	64	68	117		Member of CSA Congress
Ford, Sewell	1868-1946	Author		15	35		Short Story Writer
Ford, Tennessee Ernie	1919-1991	Cntry Mus	18			43	Sixteen Tons', 'Mule Train'
Ford, Wallace	1898-1966	Ent	20			75	London Born. Played Strong Chars. For 30 Years
Fordney, Joseph W.		Congr	15		30		MOC MI. Lumber, Banking
Forepaugh, Adam	1831-1890	Bus	50		75		Early Circus Owner
Forester, Cecil Scott	1899-1966	Author	65	125	210	175	Known for 'Horatio Hornblower'
Forgy, Howell M.	1908-1972	Mil	20			35	Pass the Ammunition' SB 395. Chaplain.
Forlani, Claire	1972-	Ent	15			35	English film & TV actress.
Forman, Milos	1932-	Ent	20			60	AA Dir. 'One Flew Over the Cuckoo's Nest'
Forman, Thomas M.		Rev War	45	100			
Forman, Thomas March	1809-1875	Civ War	94				Member of CSA Congress
Formes, Karl	1841-1939	Ent	15	20	25	55	
Formica, Fern		Ent	15	25		30	Munchkin, 'WOZ'
Fornay, John	1817-1881	Editor	20		48		Prominent Editor & Dem. Pol. Figure
Forney, John Horace	1829-1902	Civ War	125	155	234		CSA Gen. Sig/Rank 275, ALS '62 975
Forney, John W.	1817-1881	Jrnalist	10		25		Author
Forney, William H.	1823-1894	Civ War	96	180	388		CSA Gen., Wounded & Captured Twice. MOC AL
Forrest, Edwin	1806-1872	Ent	120	140	160	150	Early Great Am. Actor. ALS/Cont 400
Forrest, Frederick	1936-	Ent	15			55	Actor. Leading Man of 70s-80's
Forrest, French	1796-1866	Civ War	136	145	195		CSA Naval Cmdr.
Forrest, French (WD)		Civ War	225	660			CSA Naval Cmdr.
Forrest, Hal		Comics	25			125	'Tailspin Tommy'
Forrest, Helen	1917-1999	Music	10			45	Jazz vocalist
Forrest, Nathan Bedford	1821-1877	Civ War	1250	1642	6500		CSA Gen.
Forrest, Nathan Bedford (WD)		Civ War	1600		14500		CSA Gen., LS/Cont 22,500
Forrest, Sally	1928-	Ent	15			55	Ingenue-Dancer-Leading Lady in Early 50s
Forrest, Steve	1924-	Ent	15			35	Actor. Brother of Dana Andrews. Leads-2nd Leads
Forrestal, James	1892-1949	Cab	35	69		60	Sec. Navy. 1st Sec. Defense.

NAME	DATES	CATEGORY	SIG	LS/DS	ALS	SP	COMMENTS
Forrester, Pat		Space	10			25	
Forslund, Constance	1950-	Ent	10	10	15	30	
Forster, Edw. Morgan	1879-1970	Author	67	187	314		Br. Novels. 'Howard's End', 'Passage to India'
Forster, John	1812-1876	Author	18	35	85		Br. Historian, Biographer of Dickens, Swift
Forster, Robert	1941-	Ent	10			35	Actor
Forster-Nietzsche, Elisabeth	1846-1935	Celeb				240	Sister of Friedrich Nietzsche. Created Nietzsche Archive in 1894. NAZI
Forsyth, Bruce	1928-	Celeb	10			35	Br. Comedian
Forsyth, Frederick		Author	10	25	40	20	Br., Master of Spy Novels
Forsyth, James	1842-1915	Civ War	46	86	60		Adm. Served/Farragut. Also Span. -Am. War
Forsyth, James Wm.	1835-1906	Civ War	53	108	163		Union Gen. Wounded Knee. ALS/Cont 250.
Forsyth, John	1780-1841	Cab	25	55	150		Sec. of State (Jackson & Van Buren)Sen.
Forsythe, John	1918-	Ent	15	15	20	35	Leading Man. Smooth, Appealing. 'Dynasty'
Forsythe, William		Ent	17			50	
Fort, George F.		Gov	15	35	50		Governor NJ 1850
Fort, John Franklin		Gov	10	15			New Jersey
Fort, Luigi		Opera	20			50	Opera
Fortas, Abe	1910-1982	Sup Crt	50	120	200	125	Resigned from Court
Forté, Fabian (Fabian)	1942-	Ent	25	30	40	56	Rock Singer. Teenage Idol
Forti, Carmen Fiorella		Opera	25			60	Opera
Fortner, Wolfgang		Comp	50				Ger. Comp.
Forward, Walter	1786-1852	Cab	15	42	72		Sec. Treasury 1841
Fosdick, Harry Emerson	1878-1969	Clergy	35	60	90	50	Baptist Min., Author
Foss, Joe	1915-2003	WWII	32	75	85	70	ACE, WWII, Medal of Honor
Foss, Sam Walter	1858-1911	Author	10	10	20	15	Editor, Humorist. 'House By The Side of The Road'
Fosse, Bob	1927-1987	Ent	40	60	90	112	AA. Choreographer-Film Dir.
Fossella, Vito F		Congr	10				Member US Congress
Fossett, Steve	1944-2007	Celeb	25			150	Balloonist; Adventurer
Foster, Abiel	1735-1806	Congr	120	345			Cont. Congress. 1st MOC NH '89
Foster, Ben		Ent	15			45	
Foster, Charles	1828-1904	Cab	35	55	100		Gov. OH, Sec. Treas.
Foster, Dianne	1928-	Ent	15			40	Canadian Actress
Foster, Ephraim Hubbard		Congr	10				FF 36
Foster, Hal	1892-1982	Comics	100			550	Tarzan', 'Prince Valiant'
Foster, Jodie	1962-	Ent	30	110		197	Actress, Dir., AA Winner
Foster, John Gray	1823-1874	Civ War	50	65	106		Union Gen.
Foster, John Gray (WD)	1823-1874	Civ War	65	105	275		Union Gen.
Foster, John W.	1836-1917	Cab	25		58	165	Sec. State 1892, Diplomat, CW Union Off.
Foster, Lafayette S.	1806-1880	Congr	25	62	98		Civil War Sen. CT. ALS As Acting VP 800
Foster, Lafayette Sabine	1806-1880	Law			32	35	Yale law professor
Foster, Lawrence	1941-	Music	10	15	25	25	Am. conductor
Foster, Meg	1948-	Ent	10			40	Actress
Foster, Myles B.		Artist	17	40	70		
Foster, Norman	1900-1976	Ent	15	20	35	45	Actor-Dir. Stage & Films from 30s
Foster, Preston	1901-1970	Ent	28	85		132	Actor. Handsome Leading Man. Over 100 Films
Foster, Robert Sanford	1834-1903	Civ War	50				Union Gen.
Foster, Sara		Ent	15			45	
Foster, Stephen	1826-1864	Comp	1500	5500	10000		Pop Songs of Day. 'My Old Kentucky Home'
Foster, Susanna	1924-	Ent	15	30		71	Singer-Actress. 'Phantom of Opera'
Foucauld, Charles E.	1858-1916	Expl	300		875		Fr. Priest & Explr.
Foucault, Leon	1819-1868	Sci	150		715		Fr. Physicist. Speed of Light. Rotation of Earth
Fouché, Jos. Duc d'Otrante	1759-1820	Fr Rev	125	210	680		Pol., Advisor Nap.
Foulois, Benj. D.	1880-1967	Aero	50			150	Gen. Pioneer Aviator
Fountain, Pete		Music	10	15	25	45	Top Jazz-Dixieland Clarinetist

NAME	DATES	CATEGORY	SIG	LS/DS	ALS	SP	COMMENTS
Four Seasons, The		Music	90	188		345	60's Rock Group
Four Tops		Music	140			223	Motown Singing Group; Group S album 225
Fournet, Jean		Cond	25			70	Conductor
Fournier, G.		Mil	55	85			
Fowldes, Derek		Ent	10			30	Br. Actor
Fowler, Gene	1890-1960	Author	20	60		30	Journalist, Biographer, Novels
Fowler, Henry H.		Cab	10	20	35	35	Sec. Treas.
Fowler, Jim		Ent	10			15	Animal handler. Seen on 'The Tonight Show'
Fowler, William, Dr.		Sci	20	30	45	30	Nobel Physics
Fowles, John		Author	30	50	85	75	Br. Novels. Fr. Lieut's Woman
Fowley, Douglas	1911-1998	Ent	20			85	Vet. Stage-Film Char. Actor. Over 200 Films
Fox, Bernard		Ent	15			40	Actor. 'Hogan's Heroes', 'Bewitched', 'Titanic'
Fox, Charles	1749-1806	Statsmn	40	65	134		Br. Reformer, Orator, Libel Bill
Fox, Edward	1937-	Ent	10			25	Br. Actor. Blonde-Brother of James.
Fox, Fontaine T.		Comics	35	50		200	'Toonerville Trolley'
Fox, Fred S.	1910-2005	Ent	10		45	35	Actor 'Mayberry'
Fox, Gustavus V.	1821-83	Civ War	35		50		Asst Sec of Navy
Fox, James	1939-	Ent	10			35	Br. Actor. Leading Man
Fox, Jorja	1968-	Ent	15			35	ER
Fox, Kerry	1966-	Ent	10			30	Actress
Fox, Matthew		Ent	10			42	Actor
Fox, Michael J.	1961-	Ent	50	72	80	102	Actor. 'Back to the Future'
Fox, Samantha		Ent	12			49	
Fox, Samuel		Clergy	15	20	25	35	
Fox, Vivica		Ent	15			45	
Fox, Vivica A.	1964-	Ent	20			40	Actress
Fox, William	1879-1952	Bus	185	550		375	Fndr. Fox Film Corp.
Foxworth, P. E.		Celeb	10	15	35		Special FBI agent
Foxworth, Robert	1941-	Ent	10	15	15	20	Actor.
Foxworthy, Jeff		Ent	15			35	Comedian
Foxx, Jamie	1967-	Ent	25			80	AA winning actor
Foxx, Redd	1922-1991	Ent	28	95		62	Comedian. Stand-up & Sit-Com. 'Sanford & Son'
Foy, Eddie, Jr.	1905-1983	Ent	20	35	40	60	Am. Vaude. Entertainer. Few 50s-60s Films
Foy, Eddie, Sr.	1854-1928	Ent	25			60	Am. Vaude. Comedian. Few Films
Foy, Maximilian S., Count	1775-1825	Fr Rev	75	140	225		Fr. Statesman, Gen. Waterloo
Fradona, Ramon		Comics	15			50	'Brenda Starr'
Frakes, Jonathan		Ent	10	15	19	43	'Star Trek-Next Generation'
Frampton, George, Sir	1860-1928	Artist	20		48		Brit. Sculp. Edith Cavell Mem. ' Peter Pan'
Frampton, Peter		Music	20	40		50	Rock
France, Anatole (Thibault J.)	1844-1924	Author	50	130	119	225	Fr. Novels, Poetry, Critic. Nobel 1921
France, Hector		Author	30			60	Adventurer, author
Francescatti, Zino		Music	30			150	Violinist.
Franchetti, Alberto, Baron	1860-1942	Comp	35		130	90	Wrote 9 Operas, Chamber Music, Symphony
Franchi, Sergio	1933-1990	Music	15			60	Singer
Franciosa, Anthony	1928-2006	Ent	15	25	30	47	Broadway & Film 'Hatful of Rain'. AA Nomination
Francis Berry, Mary		Celeb	10			20	Afr-Am lawyer, administrator, activist & author
Francis I	1777-1830	Royal	100	300			King Two Sicilies
Francis I Fr.	1494-1547	Royal	410	750			France. Special DS 2, 750
Francis II	1768-1835	Royal	125	400	650		Last Holy Roman Emperor(Aus)
Francis V	1819-1875	Royal	990	1275			Duke of Modena
Francis, Anne	1930-	Ent	18	25	30	77	Film Leading Lady. Radio Children. Soaps
Francis, Arlene	1907-2001	Ent	15	20	25	70	Gained Popularity as Radio-TV Hostess & Panelist
Francis, Connie	1938-	Music	15	25	35	55	Singer. Top Vocalist late 50s-early 60s
Francis, David R.		Cab	15	30	50	75	Sec. Interior 1896

NAME	DATES	CATEGORY	SIG	LS/DS	ALS	SP	COMMENTS
Francis, Dick		Author	25	72	80	42	Br. Jockey Turned Mystery Writer
Francis, Genie		Ent	15	25	30	40	Actress. 'Gen. Hospital'
Francis, Jan	1951-	Ent	10			30	Br. Actress
Francis, Kay	1903-1968	Ent	25	30	70	149	One of the Highest Paid Glamour Stars-30's
Franciscus, James	1934-1991	Ent	15	20	30	48	Actor
Franck, Cesar	1822-1920	Comp	300	460	658		AMusMS 5000
Francks, Cree		Ent	10			15	Actress/Voice Artist
Franco, Francisco	1892-1975	HOS	75	260	1300	189	Sp. Gen. & Dictator
Franco, James	1978-	Ent	10			35	Actor
Frank, August		Mil	10	30	45		
Frank, Barney F		Congr	10			20	Member US Congress
Frank, Diana	1965-	Ent	10			25	
Frank, Hans		WWII	208	724	2100	330	Nazi Administrator of Poland
Frank, Marshall		Author	10			15	Mystery Novels, Pol. commentary
Frank, Otto	1889-1980	WWII	200	927			ANS, Handpainted Card 2500. Ann Frank TLS-ALS/Cont 2500-5000
Franken, Rose		Author	10	25	40		Plays
Frankenheimer, John	1930-2002	Ent	15		30	50	Film Dir.
Frankfurter, Felix	1882-1965	Sup Crt	146	640	765	631	Fndr. ACLU. Special TLS 2900
Franklin, Aretha		Music	45			154	Soul singer; Rock; S Album 140; S Guitar 240
Franklin, Benjamin	1706-1790	Rev War	5917	12075	31496		Rev. War Dte. DS 25,000; Sci. ALS 96,000
Franklin, Bonnie		Ent	10	15	20	35	Actress. 'One Day at a Time'
Franklin, Herbert H.	1867-1956	Bus	35	125			Pioneer Auto Manufacturer
Franklin, Jane	1792-1875	Author	65		220		Wife of John Franklin, Traveller, Explr.
Franklin, John, Sir	1786-1847	Expl	125	292	610		Proved NW Passage
Franklin, William	1731-1813	Colonial	150	375	722		Brit. Gov. NJ, Illegitimate Son of Benjamin
Franklin, Wm. Buell	1823-1903	Civ War	57	123	167	350	Union Gen.
Franklin, Wm. Buell (WD)		Civ War	95	180	310	450	Union Gen. AES/3 Gens 825
Franks, Trent F		Congr	10				Member US Congress
Frann, Mary	1943-1998	Ent	10	15	15	35	Actress. 'Newhart'
Frantz, Charton C.		Bus	10	35	45	20	
Frantz, Christian		Opera				50	Tenor
Franz Ferdinand	1863-1914	Royal				1380	Archduke Austria. Assass.
Franz Josef II, Crown Prince		Royal	40	75	140	50	Liechtenstein
Franz Joseph I,	1830-1916	Royal	155	648	875		Emperor of Austria
Franz, Arthur	1920-	Ent	10			40	Leading Man & Char. Actor; Radio, Stage, TV
Franz, Dennis		Ent	15			45	Actor. 'NYPD Blue' DS 95. Emmy
Franzisket, Ludwig		WWII				72	Luftwaffe ace
Fraser, Brendan		Ent	15			42	Actor
Fraser, Douglas A.		Labor	10	15		15	Union Pres.
Fraser, James Earle	1876-1953	Artist	425	650			Sculptor of Buffalo Nickel, Lincoln, St. Gaudens
Fraser, Malcolm		HOS	10			30	P. M. Australia
Fraser, Peter		HOS	10	25		20	P. M. New Zealand
Frasier (cast)		Ent	102			250	Entire ensemble
Frawley, William	1887-1966	Ent	203	400		512	Actor; 'Fred Mertz' on I Love Lucy
Frazer, James George	1854-1941	Sci	120		650		Scot Anthropologist-Classicist. 'Golden Bough'
Frazer, John Wesley	1827-1906	Civ War	198	255	805		CSA Gen. w/no shot fired, surrendered!
Frazer, Joseph W.		Bus	275	600			Kaiser-Frazer Auto Mfg.
Frazetta, Frank		Comics	50			375	'Johnny Comet'
Freddy & The Dreamers (All)		Music	105				
Frederic, Harold		Author	10	35	70		Am. Novels, Correspondent
Frederick Augustus I,	1750-1827	Royal	55	275			The Just, Saxony
Frederick Augustus II	1797-1854	Royal		250			King Saxony
Frederick I (Wurttemburg)	1754-1816	Royal	100	230			Duke of Wurttemburg

NAME	DATES	CATEGORY	SIG	LS/DS	ALS	SP	COMMENTS
Frederick II (The Great)	1712-1786	Royal	367	1038	2700		Prussia
Frederick III	1831-1888	Royal	120	260	650	500	Queen Victoria's Son-in-Law. Ger. Emp. 99 Days
Frederick IV	1671-1730	Royal		320	700		Denmark
Frederick IX	1899-1972	Royal	50	160	350		Denmark
Frederick Louis	1707-1751	Royal		103	100		Prince of Wales
Frederick V	1723-1766	Royal	90	270	500		Denmark
Frederick VI	1768-1839	Royal	85	348			Denmark
Frederick VII	1808-1863	Royal	90	220			Denmark
Frederick Wm. I	1688-1740	Royal	135	334			Prussia
Frederick Wm. II	1744-1797	Royal		142	490		Prussia. Succeded by Frederick II, The Great
Frederick Wm. III	1770-1840	Royal	80	207	475		Prussia
Frederick Wm. IV	1795-1861	Royal	100	255	750		Prussia. Insane
Frederick, Pauline	1883-1938	Ent	20	35		53	Chorus Girl at 19. Silent Cinema Star from 1915
Frederick, Pauline		Jrnalist	10		25	25	Pioneer TV Reporter. Debut 1949
Frederick, Prince of Wales	1707-1751	Royal		110			Son of Geo. II. Father of Geo. III
Fredericks, Fred		Comics	18		85	50	Mandrake The Magician
Fredericks, R. N.		Banker	12				
Freed, Alan	1921-1965	Music	430	615	3125		Am. disc jockey & promoter
Freed, Arthur	1894-1973	Ent				345	Prod., songwriter & author
Freed, Bert	1919-1994	Ent	10	15	20	45	Am. Char. Actor
Freedman, Larry		Law	10		10	20	Lawyer, Die-hard Cub fan
Freeland, Paul van		HOS	10	16	40	20	Prime Min.
Freeling, Sir Francis	1764-1836	Pol		120			1st Baronet
Freeman, Alan	1927-2006	Music	10			25	Br. DJ
Freeman, Jennifer		Ent	13			40	
Freeman, Kathleen	1919-2001	Ent	10	15		42	Long Time Char. Actress. Films-TV
Freeman, Martin		Ent	15			45	
Freeman, Mona	1926-	Ent	15	20	30	56	Ingenue-Leading Lady.
Freeman, Morgan	1937-	Ent	20		50	70	Actor. Acadamy Award
Freeman, Orville		Cab	10	20	25	20	Sec. Agriculture. Gov. MN
Freeman, Samuel		Rev War	40	45	100		Rev. War Patriot
Freeman, Ted		Space	10			48	
Freeman, Thomas W.	1824-1865	Civ War	100				Member of CSA Congress
Frehley, Ace	1951-	Music	35			60	Lead Guitarist, Kiss
Freire, Nelson		Music				150	Brazilian Pianist
Freleng, Friz	1906-1995	Comics	101	145		193	Animator Bugs Bunny, S drawing 250-500
Frelinghuysen, Frederick T.	1817-1885	Cab	20	60	105	125	Sec. State, Sen. NJ
Frelinghuysen, Joseph S		Congr	10	15			Sen. NJ
Frelinghuysen, Rodney P. F		Congr	10				Member US Congress
Fremont, Jessie Benton	1824-1902	Author	35	80	270		Far West Sketches', Wife of John C. Fremont
Fremont, John C.	1813-1890	Civ War	241	415	569	800	Union Gen. ALS/Cont 6, 500., S stock cert. 1450
Fremont, John C. (WD)		Civ War	276	485	606		Union Gen. Explr. & Statesman
Fremstad, Olive	1871-1951	Opera	95			375	Swe-Am. Sopr. Opera. Europe & Met 1903-1917
French, Daniel Chester	1850-1931	Artist	70	140	200	175	Sculptor, Lincoln Memorial
French, Dawn	1957-	Celeb	10			25	Br. Comedienne
French, John	1852-1925	Mil	50		145		1st Earl Ypres. Field-marshal
French, Michael	1962-	Ent	10			25	Br. Actor
French, Richard		Congr	10		38		FF 38
French, Samuel Gibbs	1818-1910	Civ War	120	292	527		CSA Gen.
French, Victor		Ent	15			42	
French, William H.	1815-1881	Civ War	50	110	175		Union Gen.
Freni, Mirella	1935-	Opera	10			45	It Sopr. Opera. 'Violetta', 'Mimi', 'Butterfly'
Freron, Louis M. S.	1754-1802	Fr Rev	25	45	90		Fr. Rev. Pol. Conspiracy vs Robespierre
Fresnay, Pierre	1897-1975	Ent	10			45	Fr. Actor/Dir. Important Film Personality in 30s

NAME	DATES	CATEGORY	SIG	LS/DS	ALS	SP	COMMENTS
Freud, Anna	1895-1982	Sci		240	350	395	Daughter of Sigmund Freud
Freud, Emma		Music	10			15	DJ
Freud, Lucian	1922-	Artist			1610		Ger.-born Br. artist
Freud, Sigmund	1856-1939	Sci	1324	2502	4612	6745	Psychoanalysis. ALS/Cont 7, 500-22, 500
Frey, Richard		Aero	25	50	100	65	
Friant, Louis, Count		Fr Rev	30	75	150		
Frick, Henry Clay	1849-1919	Bus	250	410	650		Carnegie Steel; S stock cert. 3800
Frick, Stephen	1964-	Space	15			30	NASA
Frick, Wilhelm	1877-1946	Mil	200	388		368	Reich's Min. of the Interior
Fricke, Janie		Cntry Mus	10			30	
Fricke, Richard I.		Bus	10	35	45	20	
Fricker, Brenda	1944-	Ent	20	35	35	61	Ir. Char. Actress. AA for 'My Left Foot'
Frid, Jonathan	1924-	Ent	65			83	Dark Shadows
Friedan, Bette	1921-2006	Fem	20	25	50	50	Am. feminist, activist & writer
Friedgen, A. E.		Bus	10	35	45	20	
Friedkin, William	1939-	Ent	10	20		25	Dir. AA for 'The Fr. Connection' 1971
Friedman, Herbert		Sci	15	35	55	20	
Friedman, Jerome I.		Sci	20	35		30	Nobel Physics
Friedman, Milton		Econ	20	35		48	Nobel Econ. SB 215; S manuscript 235-590
Friedman, Thomas	1953-	Jrnalist	10	30	50	30	Pol. journalist
Friedman, Tuviah		Celeb	25	75			Nazi hunter
Friedrich III	1831-1888	Royal				1750	Ger. Emperor & King of Prussia
Friel, Anna	1976-	Ent	10			25	Br. Actress
Friends (cast)		Ent	93			231	Cast of 6 (Authentic)
Friganza, Trixie	1870-1955	Ent	25	35	40	120	Actress. Early Films
Friml, Rudolf	1879-1972	Comp	100	275	325	212	Operettas. Major Stage-Film Hits. AMusS 750
Frisch, Karl von		Sci	15	30	40	25	Nobel Med.
Frist, William(Bill) Dr.		Congr	10			25	Sen. (R TN); Sen. Majority Leader
Fritchie, Barbara (Frietschie)		Civ War	12500				Patriotic Heroine of Civil War Incident.
Frith, William P.	1819-1909	Artist	25	45	80		Crowded Scenes of Contemporary Life. 'Derby Day'
Fritsch, Werner von		Mil	55	150	210	248	
Fritzsche, Hans		WWII	540				Radio propaganda chief Nazi Ger.
Frizzell, Lefty	1928-1975	Cntry Mus	30			80	Singer-Songwriter-Guitarist
Frobe, Gert		Ent	30			94	Ger. Char. Actor
Frohman, Daniel	1851-1940	Ent	25		84	75	Dean of Am. Theatrical Prod. s
Frohnmeyer, John		Celeb	10			15	Chmn Nat. Endowment for the Arts, 1989-1992
Froman, Jane	1907-1980	Ent	15	15	25	84	Major Singing Star. Crippled in Air Crash.
Fromm, Erich	1900-1980	Sci	42	115		75	Am. Ger. Born. Psychoanalist-Social Phil.
Fromme, Lynette 'Squeaky'		Crime	50	120	210	60	Chas. Manson Follower. Attempted Ford Assass.
Frondizi, Arturo		HOS	15	35	75	55	Pres. Argentina
Frontenac, Louis, Comte	1620-1698	Statsmn			5400		Gov. La Nouvelle France(Canada)
Frontiersmen, The		Cntry Mus	25			55	Populart Singing Group. Films-Records
Froos, Sylvia		Ent				60	Actress
Frost, Arthur B.	1851-1928	Artist	50	140		188	Illust., Uncle Remus Books
Frost, Daniel Marsh	1823-1900	Civ War	203	296	483		CSA Gen. Surrounded, Saw 1st Blood, Surrendered.
Frost, David	1939-	Ent	10			30	Br. Interviewer
Frost, Edwin B.		Sci	10	25	45		Am. Astronomer
Frost, Martin F		Congr	10				Member US Congress
Frost, Nick		Ent	18			53	
Frost, Robert	1874-1963	Author	152	380	1472	1510	Poet. Pulitzer 1924, '31, '37, '43
Frost, Sadie		Ent	10			42	Br. Actress. 'Bram Stoker's Dracula'
Frost, Stephen	1955-	Celeb	10			25	Br. Comedian
Frost, Terry	1906-1993	Ent	15			60	Vintage cowboy actor
Frothingham, Octavius B.	1822-1895	Clergy	25	35	50		Am. Unitarian. Disciple of Theodore Parker

NAME	DATES	CATEGORY	SIG	LS/DS	ALS	SP	COMMENTS
Frunze, Mikhail V	1885-1925	Mil		460			Russian revolutionary Gen.
Fry, Birkett Davenport	1822-1891	Civ War	120	280			CSA Gen., war date DS 2530
Fry, Christopher		Author	30	160	180		Br. Dramatist
Fry, Elizabeth	1780-1845	Clergy	40	125	180		Br. Quaker Philan.
Fry, Franklin C.	1900-1968	Clergy	20	25	35		Pres. Lutheran Church, World Relief, World Fed.
Fry, James Barnet	1827-1894	Civ War	40	80	135		Union Gen. Shiloh, 1st Bull Run.
Fry, Roger	1866-1934	Artist	35		225		Br. Art Critic & Artist. Lecturer
Fry, Speed Smith	1817-1892	Civ War	45		69		Union Gen.
Frye, Dwight	1899-1943	Ent	1874		1950	2000	Character actor, horror films.
Frye, Jordan		Ent	13			40	
Frye, Soleil Moon	1976-	Ent				40	Punky Brewster
Frye, Wm. P. (Actg V. P.)		VP	15				
F-Troop		Ent				95	Cast SP
Fuad I, King-Sultan	1868-1936	Royal	95	300			King-Sultan of Egypt. Gen. Fndr. Egypt. U
Fuchida, Mitsuo	1902-1976	Mil	286	579	608	320	Led Attack on Pearl Harbor. S Prl Hbr Confession 3000
Fuchs, Rutger		Mil	40	125	195	95	
Fuchs, Vivian E. Sir	1908-	Expl	27	75	158		Br. Antarctic Explr. -Geologist
Fuentes, Daisy		Ent	12			43	
Fugard, Athol	1932-	Ent	10			25	Actor, thesbian
Fujimori, Alberto		Pol				25	Pres. of Peru
Fuka-Tu'itupou, Rev. Lynette		Author	10			12	Kingdom of Tonga religious history
Fukuda, Takeo		HOS	15		50	30	Japan PM
Fukui, Kenichi		Sci	20	30	45	25	Nobel Chemistry
Fulbright, James W.	1905-1995	Congr	20	40	100	55	Sen. AR, Fulbright Scholarship
Fulford, Millie Hughes	1945-	Space	25			120	
Fulgham, Robert		Author	10			15	
Fulkerson, Abraham	1834-1902	Congr	20	35			CSA Col. MOC TN
Fuller, Alfred C.	1885-1973	Bus	125		195	175	Fndr. Fuller Brush Co. 1st Door to Door Sales.
Fuller, Alvan T.		Gov	15	25		20	Governor, MOC MA
Fuller, Buckminster R.	1895-1983	Sci	42	85	140	139	Br-Am. Architectural Engr., Geodesic Dome
Fuller, Charles E.	1887-1968	Clergy	10			30	Am. Christian Radio Evangelist
Fuller, Delores		Ent	20	65		43	Actress/Ed Wood
Fuller, Eduard		Author	10	20	40		
Fuller, John G.	1937-	Poet	10	16		20	Poet, Novels, critic
Fuller, John Wallace	1827-1891	Civ War	53	106	157		Union Gen.
Fuller, Loie	1862-1928	Ent	50	124	200	350	Am. Dancer
Fuller, Margaret	1810-1850	Reform	140	250	450		Feminist, Author. ALS/Cont, 2, 500
Fuller, Melville W.	1833-1910	Sup Crt	62	132	200	175	
Fuller, Robert	1934-	Ent	10	15	20	41	Am. Leading Man. Mostly TV. Many Westerns
Fuller, Sam	1912-1997	Ent	35			58	Film Writer-Dir.
Fuller, W. Kent		Bus	10			20	Fuller Hyland Advisors; Mayflower Descendent
Fullerton, Fiona		Ent	10			40	Actress
Fullerton, Gordon		Space	10			40	
Fulton, Fitz	1952-	Space	10		15	22	NASA research pilot
Fulton, Robert	1765-1815	Invent	511	2576	2829		Submarine, Steamboat. ALS/Cont 6500
Fulton, William S.	1795-1844	Congr	16		45		Sen. AR, Gov. AR
Funicello, Annette		Ent	62	65	88	106	Actress of 'Mickey Mouse Club'.
Funk, Casimer		Sci	25	65		30	Biochemist Discovered Thiamin
Funk, Isaac K.	1839-1912	Pub	35	80	135		Funk & Wagnalls Dictionary
Funk, Larry		Band	10			30	
Funk, Walther	1890-1960	Mil	127	276			Hitler's personal advisor
Funsten, David	1819-1866	Civ War	117	254			Member of CSA Congress
Funston, Frederick	1865-1917	Mil	75	195	300		Cuba, Span. -Am. War, MOH. Captured Aguinaldo
Funt, Alan	1914-1999	Celeb	15			35	Candid Camera

NAME	DATES	CATEGORY	SIG	LS/DS	ALS	SP	COMMENTS
Fuqua, James O.		Civ War			242		Louisiana capt.
Furcolo, Foster		Gov	10	25			Governor MA
Furnas, Robert W.		Gov	10	10			Governor NE
Furness, Betty	1916-1994	Ent	15	20	30	52	Actress. Early TV Hostess. Consumer Advocate
Furness, William H.		Clergy	10	15	20		
Furniss, Harry	1854-1925	Artist	40	120	250		Br. Illust. -Caricaturist. Pol. & Soc.
Furrer, Reinhard		Space	15			95	Ger.
Furstenberg, Betsy von		Ent	10	20		25	Fashion Designer
Furtado, Nelly		Music				40	Singer
Furtwangler, Wilhelm	1886-1954	Ent	488	360	762	1232	Controversial Ger. Cond. WWII. SPpc 840
Fuseli, Henry	1741-1825	Artist	250	500			Br. -Swiss Romantic Painter, Author
Futrell, J. M.		Gov	10	12		10	Governor AR
Fyfe, John		WWII	15			30	WWII Hero. Submarine Ace
Gabet, Sharon	1952-	Ent	10	15	20	25	Am. soap opera actress
Gabin, Jean	1904-1976	Ent	35			313	Fr. Romantic Leading Actor
Gable, Clark	1901-1960	Ent	249	484	850	1465	Actor, S Chk 350
Gable, Kay		Ent	10		15	20	Clark Gable's wife
Gabor, Eva	1920-1995	Ent	20	25	30	51	
Gabor, Zsa Zsa	1917-	Ent	30	40	45	47	
Gabreski, Frances J. 'Gabby'		WWII	35	95	125	110	US ACE, WWII, 5th Leading Fighter Ace.
Gabriel, John Peter	1746-1807	Rev War		3500			Gen., Pol., Clergy. MsDS to Ben Franklin 3500
Gabriel, Peter		Music	15			50	Rock
Gabrielle, Monique		Ent	15			25	
Gabrilowitsch, Ossip	1878-1936	Music	60	122	150	495	Rus. -Am. Pianist, Cond. AMusQS 275
Gacy, John Wayne	1942-1994	Crime	30	105	153	134	Convicted Serial Killer. Orig. Paintings 400-600
Gadsden, James		Diplo	110	350	350		Gadsden Purchase
Gadski-Tauscher, Johanna	1872-1932	Opera	40		85	128	Ger. -Born Wagnerian Sopr.
Gaffney, Drew		Space	10			20	
Gagarin, Yuri	1934-1968	Space	268	420		572	1st Man in Space, TLS/Cont 1250
Gage, Lyman J.		Cab	15	25	50	45	Sec. Treasury 1897
Gage, Nicholas		Author	10	25		15	
Gage, Thomas		Rev War	250	602	817		Br. Gen. Cmdr.-in-Chief
Gagnon, Ren, A.	1925-1979	WWII	125	162	295	250	Iwo Jima Flag Raising FDC 225
Gail, Max	1943-	Ent	10	12	15	35	Am. actor
Gaines, John P.	1795-1857	Congr	20		35		MOC OR, Soldier, Gov. OR
Gaines, Rosie		Music	10			25	Performing musical artist
Gaines, William		Celeb	67	475			Fndr. Mad Magazine
Gainey, M. C.		Ent	15			45	
Gainsborough, Thomas	1727-1788	Artist	300	603	1506		Br. Portraitist 'The Blue Boy'. Landscapes
Gaither, Burgess Sidney	1807-1892	Civ War	64	117			Member of CSA Congress
Gajdusek, D. Carleton, Dr.		Sci	20	35		35	Nobel Med.
Galanos, James	1925-	Bus	12	30	50	25	Am. fashion designer
Galard, Genevieve de	1925-	Med	40			50	Nurse, Fr. Indochina War. "Angel of Dien Bien Phu"
Galbraith, John Kenneth		Econ	15	35	65	30	Author Books Economics
Gale, Zona	1874-1938	Author	10	55	75	60	Am. Novels Short Story Writer
Galella, Ron		Photog	10	12		10	Celebrity Photographer
Galen, Clemens A. Graf von		Clergy		1010			Ger. Count, Bishop of Munster, Cardinal; Nazi opp.
Galer, Robert E., Jr.		WWII				50	Gen WWII. MOH. Air Ace
Galileo	1564-1642	Sci					Extremely rare; no known price available
Gallagher, David	1985-	Ent	10			30	
Gallagher, Megan		Ent	10			35	Actress
Gallagher, Peter		Ent	10			40	Actor
Galland, Adolf	1912-1996	WWII	48	68	188	149	ACE, Ger. WWII, Luftwaffe Head
Gallatin, Albert	1761-1849	Cab	88	345	448		Jefferson & Madison Sec Treas. ALS/cont 2415

NAME	DATES	CATEGORY	SIG	LS/DS	ALS	SP	COMMENTS
Gallatin, Albert E.	1881-1952	Artist					Pencil Sketch 250
Gallaudet, Thomas T.	1787-1851	Educ	50	125	178		Fndr. of the 1st Am. school for the deaf
Galle, Emile	1846-1904	Artist	100	325	645		Fr. Artist in Glass & Furniture Mfg.
Gallegly, Elton G		Congr	10				Member US Congress
Gallian, Ketti	1934-	Ent	15	20	25	78	
Galliano, John		Celeb	10			15	Designer
Gallico, Paul W.		Author	15	57		35	Am. Novels. 'Poseidon Adventure'
Galli-Curci, Amelita	1889-1963	Opera	56	157	210	250	Opera
Galligan, Zach	1964-	Ent	10			30	Actor. 'Gremlins'
Galli-Marie, Celestine		Opera		475			
Gallinger, Jacob Harold	1837-1918	Congr	10	20	35	20	MOC., Sen. NH 1891-1919
Gallo, Ernest & Julio		Bus	40	145		65	Award Winning Gallo Winery, Sonoma, CA
Gallo, Gustavo		Ent	20			50	Opera
Gallo, Joey	1929-1972	Crime		550			Gangster
Gallo, Robert, Dr.		Sci	20	35		40	Research. Co-discoverer HIV Virus
Galloway, Joseph	1731-1803	Rev War		3250			Continental Congr. & Army. Tory Loyalist
Galloway, Marie S., 1st Lt. ANC		Med	20		95		Nurse. Visited Hawaiian Leper Colony. 40s
Gallup, Benadam		Mil	40	150			Col. Fr. -Indian War. Groton, CT Selectman
Gallup, George, Jr.	1930-	Pollster	10	48		35	Gallup Poll. TLS/Orig. Poll re '76 Pres. 295
Galsworthy, John	1867-1933	Author	48	85	199	175	Br. Novels, Plays
Galvan, Elias G., Bish.		Clergy	20	25	35	35	
Galvin, Robert	1922-	Bus	12	17	25	20	Motorola
Galway, James		Music	10			40	Irish Flutist. AMusQS 50
Gam, Rita	1928-	Ent	10	15	15	40	Actress
Gambee, Charles R.		Civ War	20	55			Col. 53rd Ohio Vol. KIA Resecca
Gambier, James, 1st Baron	1756-1833	Mil	35	130			Br. Naval Cmdr. Adm. of the Fleet.
Gambino, Carlo	1902-1976	Crime		322			Mafia boss; Chk 350-500
Gamble, Hamilton R.	1798-1864	Civ War	35		195		CW Gov. MO. Cmmdr. -in-Chief MO Militia
Gamble, William	1818-1866	Civ War	53	123	140		Union Gen.
Gammon, James	1940-	Ent	10			35	Actor
Gance, Abel	1889-1981	Ent		295	500		Fr. Actor, Writer. One of Greatest Dir. s.
Gandhi, Indira	1917-1984	HOS	108	312	475	268	Assass. P. M. India. TLS/Cont 600, FDC S 175
Gandhi, Mohandas K.	1869-1948	Pol	1079	1800	7135	3825	Spiritual Leader India
Gandhi, Rajiv		HOS	40		85	150	P.M. of India, Assassinated
Gandhi, Sonia		Pol				30	India Pol.
Gandier, D. M., Rev.		Clergy	10	20	35		Temperance Advocate
Gandolfini, James		Ent	20			144	Actor; Tony Soprano
Gann, Ernest K.		Author	10	20	35		
Gannett, Frank E.		Bus	20	55	140	35	Newspaper, TV, Radio Empire
Gano, Richard Montgomery	1830-1913	Civ War	130				CSA Gen., physician
Gantt, Harvey	1943-	Pol	10			20	1st Afr. -Am. Mayor in Charlotte
Ganz, Rudolph		Cond	25			60	Swiss/Am. Pianist/Conductor
Garanca, Elina		Opera				55	Latvian Mezzo
Garant, Ben		Ent	15			45	
Garat, Pierre (Fils)		Opera	45		120		Tenor Son
Garat, Pierre (Pere)	1762-1823	Opera	125		300		1st Great Fr. Tenor
Garber, Jan		Band	15			35	Big Band Leader
Garbiras, Nina		Ent	13			40	
Garbo, Greta	1905-1991	Ent	1274	2573	6742	9583	Major Intl Film Star. ALS/Cont 16500
Garcelon, Alonzo		Gov	10	12			Governor ME
Garcia Menocal, Mario	1866-1941	HOS	75	160		300	Pres. Cuba 1913-21
Garcia, Andy		Ent	15	20		52	Actor
Garcia, Jerry	1942-1995	Music	200	325	525	850	Rock. S Album 500
Garcia, Joanna		Ent	13			40	

NAME	DATES	CATEGORY	SIG	LS/DS	ALS	SP	COMMENTS
Garcia, Jorge		Ent	17			50	
Garcia, Manuel	1805-1906	Ent	20		75		Musician. Invented Laryngoscope
Garcia-Robles, Alfonso, Dr.		Diplo	35		130	60	Nobel Peace Pr., Disarmament
Gardanne, Gaspard A.		Fr Rev	40	115	250		
Garde, Betty	1905-1989	Ent	10			45	Actress
Garden, Mary	1874-1967	Opera	36	45	68	100	Opera. Scottish Born, Am. Sopr.
Gardenia, Vincent	1922-1992	Ent	15			45	Actor
Gardiner, Reginald	1903-1980	Ent	15			80	Br. Actor
Gardner, Alexander		Civ War	225	1470		6900	Photographer, Chk 2340
Gardner, Ava	1922-1990	Ent	52	78	110	219	Actress.
Gardner, Dale A.		Space	10			25	
Gardner, Erle Stanley	1889-1970	Author	85	204	275	175	Lawyer & Detective Novels
Gardner, Franklin	1823-1873	Civ War	225	414	788		CSA Gen.
Gardner, Franklin (WD)	1823-1873	Civ War	375	500	1510		CSA Gen.
Gardner, Guy S.		Space	10			20	
Gardner, John L.	1793-1869	Civ War	50		105		Union Brevet Brig. Gen.
Gardner, John W.		Cab	10	30	35	15	Sec. HEW. Fndr. 'Common Cause'
Gardner, O. Max		Gov	15	20	35	20	Gov. NC. Lawyer, Industrialist
Gardner, William Montgomery	1824-1901	Civ War	120	221	327		CSA Gen.
Garfield, Allen	1939-	Ent	10			30	Am. film & TV actor.
Garfield, James A.	1831-1881	Pres	240	602	837	1615	Union Gen., DS/War Dte 3500; FF395
Garfield, James A. (As Pres.)	1831-1881	Pres	4300	12869	39667		Assass. July 1881; ALS/init. 15000. WH card 13045
Garfield, James A. (WD)	1831-1881	Civ War	550	1992	2750	1800	Union Gen., Pres. of the US
Garfield, James R.	1865-1950	Cab	20	35	70	70	Sec Interior 1907
Garfield, John	1913-1952	Ent	120	231		394	Warner Bros. Star. Born Julius Garfinkle
Garfield, Lucretia R.	1832-1918	1st Lady	95	140	180		
Garfunkel, Art		Music	25			42	Singer-Songwriter, w/Paul Simon. S Solo Album 50
Gargan, Jack		Pol				15	Chrm of thr Reform Party
Gargan, William	1905-1979	Ent	15	15	30	78	Vintage Leading Man. Films-Broadway.
Garibaldi, Giuseppe	1807-1882	HOS	176	318	362	650	It. Nationalist Leader, Soldier, Patriot
Garity, Troy		Ent	13			40	
Garland, Augustus H.	1832-1899	Cab	40	85	120		Atty Gen. & CSA Congress, Gov.
Garland, Beverly	1926-	Ent	10	20		47	Actress
Garland, Hamlin	1860-1940	Author	30	40	173	85	Pulitzer 1921. Novels, Essayist
Garland, Judy	1922-1969	Ent	468	1202		948	Actress-Singer. WOZ Spec. DS 950. S Chk 550; SP at 15 2880; S Chk 475
Garland, Samuel Jr.	1830-1862	Civ War	950				CSA Gen., KIA South Mt., MD
Garlin, Jeff		Ent	15			45	Actor; comedian
Garn, Jake	1932-	Space	15	40		50	Sen. UT
Garneau, Marc		Space	15			35	One of the six original Canadian Astronauts
Garner, Erroll		Music	68			175	Jazz Pianist
Garner, Francoise		Opera	10			35	Opera
Garner, James	1928-	Ent	10	20	28	50	Actor
Garner, Jennifer		Ent	15			45	Actress, Alias
Garner, John Nance	1867-1967	VP	50	138	182	150	VP & Spkr. FDR VP
Garner, Max Sr.		Author	10			12	Books for children
Garner, Peggy Ann		Ent	30			76	
Garnett, Francis H.		Author	20	60	125		
Garnett, Muscoe Russell H.		Congr	10				FF 20
Garnett, Richard Brooke	1817-1863	Civ War	1600	3200	5000		CSA Gen., ALS 1861 6600, KIA Gettysburg
Garnett, Robert Seldon	1819-1861	Civ War	1735		3450		CSA Gen.
Garnett, Tay		Ent	10	25			Dir. -Prod.
Garnier, Charles	1825-1898	Archtct	30		225		Designer Paris Opera House
Garofalo, Janeane		Ent	10			40	Comedianne

NAME	DATES	CATEGORY	SIG	LS/DS	ALS	SP	COMMENTS
Garr, Terri		Ent	10	15	25	35	Actress
Garrard, Kenner	1827-1879	Civ War	50	75	160		Union Gen. War Date ALS 575
Garrard, Theophilus Toulmin	1812-1902	Civ War	43	84	110		Union Gen.
Garrett, Betty		Ent	10			40	Film & Stage Comedienne
Garrett, Brad		Ent	20			42	Actor, Emmy winner
Garrett, Finis J.		Congr	10	15	25	20	MOC TN 1905
Garrett, John W.	1872-1942	Pol			155		US foreign Min.
Garrett, Leif		Celeb	10			40	Actor
Garrett, Patrick R. (Pat)	1850-1908	West	1222	2453	2732		Killed Billy the Kid. Became Sheriff. Assass.
Garrett, Scott G		Congr	10				Member US Congress
Garrett, Thomas		Abolit	100	250	395		Chief Engineer Underground RR
Garriott, Owen I.		Space	15			90	
Garrison, Jim		Law	55			150	Dist. Atty. Investigated Kennedy Assass.
Garrison, Lindley M.	1864-1932	Cab	30	65	80	75	Sec. War 1913
Garrison, Mabel		Music				60	Early 20th C. Am. coloratura Sopr.
Garrison, Vermont		WWII	12	25	45	35	ACE, WWII & Korea; 7. 33 kills
Garrison, Wm. Lloyd	1805-1879	Abolit	82	153	315	350	Reformer. Abolitionist. ALS/Cont 1200
Garros, Roland		Aero	362			425	Fr. Ace. 1st to fly Med. Invented forward-firing mach. gun
Garrott, Isham Warren	1816-1863	Civ War	407	567			CSA Gen., KIA Vicksburg, Miss.
Garroway, Dave	1913-1982	Ent	10			35	Vintage TV host
Garson, Greer	1908-1996	Ent	25	103	160	192	Actress. Oscar Winner. DS 650 for 'Mrs. Miniver'
Garson, Willie		Ent				30	Stanford Blatch, Sex in the City
Garth, Jennie		Ent	10			42	Actress. Beverly Hills 90210
Gartrell, Lucius J.	1821-1891	Civ War	95	285	317		CSA Gen.
Garvey, Marcus	1887-1940	Afr-Am Ldr		3000		2500	Back to Africa Movement. Black Nationalism
Gary, Elbert Henry	1846-1927	Bus	142	423	575	525	CEO US Steel, Gary, Ind., TLS/ALS cont 1500-2000
Gary, James Albert		Cab	15	25	40		P. M. Gen. Owned Cotton Mills 1897
Gary, John		Ent	15			35	Actor-Singer. Juvenile-Films. TV Personality
Gary, Martin Witherspoon	1831-1881	Civ War	125	267			CSA Gen.
Gascoigne, Jill	1937-	Ent	10			25	Br. Actress
Gasdia, Cecilie	1960	Music	10	15	35	40	Italian Sopr.
Gasser, Heber S.		Sci	20	35	60	50	Nobel Med.
Gassman, Vittorio		Music	25			60	Violinist
Gately, George		Comics	10			20	Heathcliff
Gates, Bill		Bus	80	95	110	233	Microsoft CEO; Philan.
Gates, Daryl		Lawman	15			30	Chief Police of L. A.
Gates, Horatio	1728-1806	Rev War	217	588	983		Gen., Cont. Army TLS/ALS cont 2000-4000
Gates, John W.	1855-1911	Bus	500	1750			Bet a Million Gates'. Steel Wire Baron
Gates, Robert		Pol	10			25	Head of CIA
Gates, Seth	1800-1877	Congr	25	40	80		Anti-Slavery Repr. from NY
Gates, Thomas	1906-1983	Cab	10	35		35	Sec. Defense under Eisenhower & Sec. Navy
Gatlin, Larry & Brothers		Ent	25			50	C & W
Gatlin, Richard Caswell	1809-1896	Civ War	150	248			CSA Gen.
Gatling, Richard J.	1818-1903	Bus	444	1047	1438		Gatling Gun. ALS/Ltrhd 9500. S stock Cert 33000
Gatti-Casazza, Giulio		Opera	50	150	250		It. Impresario. Opera Dir.
Gatty, Harold		Aero	90	240	350	350	Australian. Wiley Post Nav. SP w/Post 800
Gauguin, Paul	1848-1903	Artist	1000	3550	14795		Fr. Post-Impressionist. Important ALS 17, 500
Gaultier, Jean-Paul		Celeb	10			15	Designer
Gaumont, Leon	1864-1946	Ent	55	330	240		Fr. Film Pioneer, Exec., Inventor Sound System
Gautier, Richard "Dick"	1931-	Ent	10			35	Actor, Comedian, Comp., singer
Gavarni, Paul		Artist	85		300		
Gavassi, Allesandro, Father		Clergy	75	100	150		
Gavaudan, Pierre	1772-1840	Opera			135		Opera. Tenor
Gavin, James M.	1907-1993	Mil	47	141	185	114	Gen. WWII, 82nd Airborne, TLS/Cont 495

NAME	DATES	CATEGORY	SIG	LS/DS	ALS	SP	COMMENTS
Gavin, John	1931-	Ent	10			50	Actor, Bus., Dipl. Reagan's 1st Amb. To Mex.
Gavin, Leon		Congr	10	10		10	MOC PA 1943
Gaxton, William	1893-1963	Ent	10	15	25	60	Star of Vaude., film, & theatre
Gay Harden, Marsha		Ent				52	Actress
Gay, Enola		Aero	200			1000	Tibbets, Van Kirk, Ferebee, Caron et al. SP/Various name combos 350-1500
Gay, George A.		Civ War	15	25	45		Nat'l Cmdr. GAR 1934
Gay, George H. Jr.	1917-1994	Mil	50	85		100	Sole survivor of the Battle of Midway
Gay, Sydney Howard		Author	10	10	20		
Gaye, Marvin	1939-1984	Music	248	386		670	Soul Singer & songwriter;, Chk 400-650
Gayheart, Rebecca		Ent	13			52	Actress.
Gayle, Crystal		Cntry Mus	10			30	Singer
Gayle, John		Gov	10	35			Statesman, Jurist
Gayle, Michelle	1971-	Music	10			25	English actress & singer
Gayler, Paul		Celeb	10			15	Chef
Gaylord, Mitch		Celeb	10			20	Motivation Spkr., gymnast
Gaynor, Adam		Music	10			30	Music. Rhythm Guitar 'Matchbox 20'
Gaynor, Gloria	1949-	Music	10			30	Performing musical artist; "I Will Survive"
Gaynor, Janet	1906-1984	Ent	22	35	50	125	Actress. 1st Oscar Winner. Vintage SP 140
Gaynor, Mitzi	1930-	Ent	10			45	Actress
Gaynor, William J.		Pol	20	55	115	30	Mayor of NY; Powerful Pol. leader; Tammany Hall
Gazen, Waldemar von		Mil	40			125	Ger. Panzer Gen.
Gazzara, Ben	1930-	Ent	10			45	
Gear, John Henry	1825-1900	Congr	10	20	25		Sen. IA 1887
Geary, Anthony 'Tony'	1947-	Ent	10	15	20	35	Luke on Gen. Hospital
Geary, John W.	1819-1873	Civ War	50	108	207	300	Un. Gen., 1st Mayor San Francisco
Gebel-Williams, Gunther		Ent	12			44	Circus animal trainer. Showman/Circus Performer
Gebhardt, Karl Dr.	d. 1948	Mil	138				Nazi "doctor"
Gedda, Nicolai	1925-	Opera	15		35	40	Swe. Tenor, Opera
Geddes, Anne		Photog				92	
Geddes, James	1763-1838	Engr		567	850		Erie Canal Advocate, Chief Engineer & Surveyor
Gedrick, Jason	1965-	Ent	10			40	Am. actor
Gee, Edwin A., Dr,		Bus	10	10		10	CEO Intl. Paper Co.
Geer, Ellen	1941-	Ent	10			35	Actress
Geer, Will	1902-1978	Ent	25			130	Actor, Folk Singer. On Stage & Films from 1930-
Geezinslaw, Sam & Dewayne		Cntry Mus	15			30	
Geffrard, Nicholas Fabre		HOS	35	125			Pres. Haiti
Gehlen, Reinhard	1902-1979	Mil	40	95	140	200	Ger. WWII Gen.
Geiger, Johannes H.	1882-1945	Sci	125	350	750		Ger. Physicist. Geiger Counter
Geisel, Ernesto		HOS	12	20	25	15	
Geisel, Theodore		Author					SEE Dr. Seuss
Gell, William, Dr.		Sci	25	40			Br. Archaeologist
Gellar, Sarah Michelle		Ent	12			72	Actress. 'Buffy . '.
Gellhorn, Martha		Jrnalist			450		War correspondent
Gelston, David		Rev War	85	170			
Gemar, Charles 'Sam'		Space	10			20	
Gemini 5 (3 Sigs)		Space				116	Cooper, Conrad
Gemini 7		Space				700	Borman & Lovell
Gencer, Leyla		Opera				85	Turkish Sopr.
Geneen, Harold S.		Bus	10	10	25	10	
Genesis		Music	100			330	Rock Group; S Album 325
Genet, Edmond Citizen	1763-1834	Fr Rev	55	150	525		1st Fr. Min. to US
Genet, Jean	1910-1986	Author		950	1575		Fr. Black Prince of Letters
Genét, Jean	1910-1986	Author	175	295	450		Fr. LS/Cont 1, 275

NAME	DATES	CATEGORY	SIG	LS/DS	ALS	SP	COMMENTS
Genn, Leo	1905-1978	Ent	10	15	25	45	Br. stage actor
Genscher, Hans-Dietrich		Pol	10			20	Chairman of the West Ger. Free Democratic Party
Genthe, Arnold		Photog			350		Ger. -born Am. Photographer
Gentilini, Amerigo		Opera	15			45	Opera
Gentry, Bobbie		Cntry Mus	10			30	Comp. 'Ode to Billy Joe' Sheet Mus. S 95
Gentry, Jerauld R.	1936-2003	Space	10	25		20	Piloted experimental airplanes; AF Col.
George (Prince Denmark)	1653-1708	Royal		157			Consort of Queen Anne
George I (Eng)	1660-1727	Royal	400	793	2321		Created Cabinet System of Gov.
George I (Gr)	1845-1913	Royal	45	85	103		Assass. Greek King
George II (Eng)	1683-1760	Royal	253	611	1755		Last English Monarch to Lead His Troops in Battle
George II (Greece)		Royal	70	80	185	288	Succeeded his Brother, Constantine to Throne
George III (Eng)	1738-1820	Royal	238	653	1180		Last King of US Colonies
George IV (Eng)	1762-1830	Royal	146	377	566		13 pp. Warrant 1815 3, 500
George V & Queen Mary	1865-1936	Royal	250			866	
George V (Eng)	1865-1936	Royal	110	353	604	750	King of England
George VI & Queen Elizabeth		Royal	422	690		1750	
George VI (Eng)	1895-1952	Royal	100	356	376	500	WWII King of England. ALS as Duke York 275
George, Chief Dan		Ent	20			45	
George, Christopher	1929-1983	Ent	20	25	65	72	Am. Actor
George, David		Author	10			12	Regional history, senior citizens
George, Duke of Cambridge	1819-1904	Mil	40				Br. Cmdr. Crimean War
George, Duke of Kent	1902-1942	Royal		110			Son of George V.
George, Gladys	1900-1954	Ent	20	30	40	82	Am. Actress
George, Grace	1879-1961	Ent	25			60	Actress
George, Harold L.		Mil	35	90	170	170	
George, Henry		Econ	30	105	200	200	Author, Reformer, Editor
George, James Z. (WD)	1826-1897	Civ War		250			Conf. Brig. Gen.
George, Melissa		Ent	15			45	
George, Phyllis		Ent	10	15	20	30	Miss America
George, Susan		Ent	25	25	30	45	
George, Walter F.	1878-1957	Congr	10	30		30	Sen. GA 1922-57
Gephardt, Richard A. G		Congr	10			20	Member US Congress
Gerard, Francis R.		WWII	10	22	38	28	ACE, WWII; 8 kills
Gerard, Gil		Ent	10	10	20	35	
Gerard, James W.		Diplo	12				Ambassador
Gerard, Richard		Comp	50	95	165		AMusQS 235
Gerardy, Jean		Music	125			190	Belg. Violin-Cellist
Gere, Ashlyn	1959-	Ent				25	Actress
Gere, Richard		Ent	30	45	55	87	Actor.
Gerhardt, Elena		Opera	30			100	Opera
Gerhardt, Mike		Space	10			18	
Géricault, Theodore	1791-1824	Artist			3000		Broke Classical Tradition.
Gerlach, Jim G		Congr	10				Member US Congress
Gerlache de Gomery, Adrien		Expl	85	180	300		Belg. Naval Off'r., Antarctic
Gerland, Alfred		Aero	15	35	55	40	
German, Edward, Sir	1862-1936	Comp	35	60	64	75	Operettas. AMusQS 200
Germond, Jack		Jrnalist	10			15	Am. journalist, author, & pundit
Gernreich, Rudi		Bus	10	15	40	25	Fashion Designer
Geronimo		Am Ind	5881			11294	
Gerry, Elbridge (VP)	1744-1814	Rev War	232	569	1454		Signer Dec of Ind V. P., Gov. MA. FF 600-750
Gerry, James	1796-1873	Congr	10				Repr. PA, Physician
Gerry, Peter G.	1879-1957	Congr	10	15		20	MOC, Sen. RI 1913
Gershon, Gina		Ent	10			45	Actress
Gershwin, George	1898-1937	Comp	440	2017	4287	4508	Rhapsody in Blue', 'Porgy & Bess', S Chk 900-1045

NAME	DATES	CATEGORY	SIG	LS/DS	ALS	SP	COMMENTS
Gershwin, George & Ira		Comp	1125	3317			
Gershwin, Ira	1896-1983	Comp	80	178	283	220	Lyricist. FDC S 95, AQS 880, Contract 2950
Gertz, Jami		Ent	10			42	Actress
Gervais, John L.	1753-1798	Rev War			100		Continental Congress
Gerville-Reache, Jeanne		Opera				275	Opera. Tragic Fr. Mezzo
Gessendorf, Mechthild		Opera	10			25	Opera
Getaneh, Anna		Model	10			25	Ethiopian Intl. model
Getty, Balthazar		Ent	14			42	
Getty, Estelle	1923-2008	Ent	10	15	20	40	Actress; 'Golden Girls'
Getty, George F.		Bus		50			Fndr. Getty Oil Company
Getty, George W.	1819-1901	Civ War	44	95	140		Union Gen. ALS/Cont 740
Getty, George Wash. (WD)	1819-1901	Civ War	70	210			Union Gen. Div. Cmdr.
Getty, J. Paul	1892-1976	Bus	84	342	760	275	Oil Billionaire. S Stk. Cert. 2400, Chk 60-120
Getz, J. Laurence		Congr	10	200	20		MOC PA 1867. Publisher
Getz, Stan	1927-1991	Music	90	170		230	Am. Jazz Saxophonist
Ghali, Boutros Boutros		HOS	10			30	Pres. U. N.
Ghiaurov, Nicolai		Opera	10			25	Opera
Gholson, Samuel J.	1808-1883	Civ War	106	292	575		CSA Gen.
Ghostley, Alice	1926-2007	Ent	10		25	55	Comedienne; actress
Giamatti, Paul	1967-	Ent	15			50	Actor; 'John Adams'; Emmy
Giannini, A. P.		Bus	150	290	500		Bank of Am. Fndr.
Gibb, Andy	1958-1988	Music	89	235		163	
Gibb, Cynthia	1963-	Ent	10	15	15	25	Am. actress
Gibb, Maurice	1950-2003	Music	90			225	BeeGees
Gibbon, Edward	1737-1794	Author	300	885	1800		Br. Decline & Fall Roman Empire
Gibbon, John	1827-1896	Civ War	60	263	378		Union Gen. ALS/Cont 1760, Indian fighter
Gibbon, John (WD)		Civ War	215	360	870	950	Union Gen.
Gibbons, Barry		Bus	10			20	Fndr. Burger King
Gibbons, Billy		Ent	17			50	
Gibbons, Cedric		Ent	95	226	450		Hollywood Art Dir. 11 Awards
Gibbons, Donna		Ent	15			35	Actress
Gibbons, Floyd	1887-1939	Jrnalist	56	132	205	130	Pioneer Aviator, Adventurer. Radio News, awarded Croix de Guerre w/Palm
Gibbons, Herbert Adams		Author	10	20	45		
Gibbons, James, Card.	1834-1921	Clergy	40	98	130	150	Established Washington U, DC. Religious Leader
Gibbons, Jim G		Congr	10				Member US Congress
Gibbons, Leeza		Ent	10			25	TV host
Gibbons, Thomas	1757-1826	Bus	950	1750			Early Steamboat Tycoon; 'Gibbons vs. Ogden'
Gibbons, William	1794-1852	Bus	675	1175			Gibbons v. Ogden'; Ass. w/Cornelius Vanderbilt
Gibbs, Addison C.		Gov	10	40			Governor OR
Gibbs, Alfred	1823-1868	Civ War	50	110	160		Union Gen. ALS '64 655
Gibbs, George C.		Civ War	250				CSA prison Cmdr.
Gibbs, Georgia		Music	15			35	Big Band Vocalist
Gibbs, Marla	1931-	Ent	10	15	15	30	Actress
Gibran, Kahlil	1883-1931	Author	150	571	975	650	Lebanese-Am. author, Novels, Essayist
Gibson, Charles		Ent	10			25	TV News anchor
Gibson, Charles Dana	1867-1944	Artist	60	212	285	240	Illust. -Gibson Girl, S archive 1265
Gibson, Charles H.		Congr	10		15		Repr., Sen. MD 1885
Gibson, Debbie		Ent	10			57	
Gibson, Edmund	1669-1748	Clergy		110			Bishop of London
Gibson, Edward G.		Space	10			80	
Gibson, George	1775-1861	Civ War	50	90			Oldest Gen. in the Civil War
Gibson, Henry	1935-	Ent	10			30	
Gibson, Hoot	1892-1962	Ent	131	195		307	Vintage Film Cowboy Star

NAME	DATES	CATEGORY	SIG	LS/DS	ALS	SP	COMMENTS
Gibson, Horatio G.	1828-1924	Civ War	42				Union Brevet Brig. Gen.
Gibson, James		Mil	75	230	425		Off. War 1812. Wounded, D.
Gibson, Mel		Ent	58			146	Actor
Gibson, Randall Lee	1832-1892	Civ War	134	360	322		CSA Gen., US Sen. LA
Gibson, Randall Lee (WD)		Civ War	425	4500	2688		CSA Gen.
Gibson, Robert L.		Space	10			25	'Hoot'
Gibson, Thomas	1962-	Ent	10			30	
Gibson, Tyrese		Ent	13			40	
Gibson, William		Author	20		170		Plays. The Miracle Worker
Giddings, De Witt C.		Congr	15	25	40		MOC TX. Served in CSA Army
Giddings, Joshua R.	1795-1864	Congr	12				Repr. OH
Gide, André	1869-1951	Author	150	270	329	350	Fr. Nobel Laureate Lit., Moralist, Philosopher
Gielgud, John, Sir	1904-2000	Ent	25	55	112	87	Noted Br. Actor
Gies, Jan		WWII	125				Helped shelter the Frank family during WWII
Gies, Miep		WWII	67	112	250		Befriended & hid Anne Frank's family; SB 100
Gieseking, Walter	1895-1956	Ent	44			118	Fr. -born Concert Pianist
Giesler, Jerry		Law	10	20	40	15	Brilliant Trial Lawyer
Gifford, Francis		Ent	20	25	35	159	
Gifford, Kathie Lee		Ent	10			35	TV Personality-Singer.
Gifford, Walter S.	1885-1966	Bus	10	15	25	10	Pres. AT&T 1925-48, Chm. -'50
Gigli, Beniamino	1890-1957	Opera	110	160	250	325	Opera, Concert. SPc 225-295
Gil, Brendan		Author	16				Writer New Yorker Mag.
Gilbert, Alfred C.	1884-1961	Bus	60	95	175		Inventor Erector Set.
Gilbert, Billy		Ent	53	60	65	118	
Gilbert, Cass		Archtct	20	60			Woolworth Bldg., Supr. Court.
Gilbert, Charles Champion	1822-1903	Civ War	50	92	140		Union Gen.
Gilbert, James Isham	1823-1884	Civ War	45	110	160		Union Gen.
Gilbert, John	1899-1936	Ent	98	148	325	230	Mega Star of Silent Movies. Romantic Hero
Gilbert, John Sir	1817-1897	Artist			45		
Gilbert, L. Wolfe		Comp	20	50	95	60	
Gilbert, Lynn		Ent	10			45	Actress 1930's
Gilbert, Melissa		Ent	10	20		40	Actress
Gilbert, Sara	1975-	Ent	10			30	Actress Rosanne
Gilbert, William. S., Sir	1836-1911	Comp	165	365	592	675	Gilbert & Sullivan Operettas. Pen Drawing S 3500
Gilbreth, Lillian		Engr	30		100		1st Woman Engineer
Gilchrest, Wayne T. G		Congr	10				Member US Congress
Gilder, Richard Watson	1844-1909	Author	25		70		Editor C. Magazine
Giles, Sandra	1932-	Ent	10			25	
Giles, William Branch		Congr	30	80	115		Early, influential VA Sen. 1801
Gilford, Jack	1907-1990	Ent	15		30	65	Char. Actor. Film, Stage, TV. Blacklisted 1950's
Gill, Eric		Artist	20	66	150		Br. Sculptor, Engraver
Gill, Vince		Cntry Mus	10			45	
Gillars, Mildred		WWII	250				"Axis Sally"
Gillem, Alvan Cullem	1830-1875	Civ War	50	94	140		Union Gen.
Gillespie, Dizzy	1917-1993	Music	50	65		180	Jazz. Trumpet
Gillett, Frederick H.	1851-1935	Congr	15	35	95		MOC, Sen. MA; Spkr. of the House
Gillette, Anita	1936-	Ent	10	15	35	30	Actress. Broadway Leads. TV Series. Films
Gillette, Francis		Congr	20	60			Free-Soiler Sen. CT
Gillette, King Camp	1855-1932	Bus	358	950	3500	1250	Gillette Co. Invented Safety Razor
Gillette, William	1855-1937	Ent	60	130	182	165	Portrayed Sherlock Holmes. Actor, Plays
Gilley, Mickey		Cntry Mus	10			30	C/W Singer
Gilliam, Terry		Ent	15			250	Clever 'Monty Python' Animator & Dir.
Gilligan's Island		Ent	511			558	Signd group photo, all 7
Gillmor, Paul E. G		Congr	10				Member US Congress

NAME	DATES	CATEGORY	SIG	LS/DS	ALS	SP	COMMENTS
Gillmore, Joseph A.		Gov	35	90			Civil War Gov. NY
Gillmore, Quincy A.	1825-1888	Civ War	38	121	157		Union Gen.
Gillmore, Quincy A. (WD)		Civ War	60	145	235		Union Gen. LS '63 7975
Gilman, John T.	1753-1828	Rev War		100	140		Cont. Congr. Gov. NH
Gilman, Nicholas		Rev War	110	285	575		Continental Congress
Gilmer, Jeremy F.	1818-1883	Civ War	130	100	412		CSA Gen.
Gilmer, John H.		Civ War	25		100		CSA Congress from NC
Gilmer, Thomas W.		Cab		95	145		Tyler Sec. Navy
Gilmore, Gary	1940-1977	Crime	25	40	120		
Gilmore, James R.	1822-1903	Author	20	60	195		Merchant, Abolitionist, Novels, Songwriter
Gilmore, Joseph A.	1811-1867	Gov	35	135			Gov. NH
Gilmore, Patrick Sarfield	1829-1892.	Comp	55	102	218		'When Johnny Comes Marching Home Again', AMusQS 150-275
Gilmore, Virginia		Ent	10	15	30	25	Actress. Wife of Yul Brynner
Gilpin, Henry D.	1801-1860	Cab	25	50	75		Van Buren Atty Gen. 1840, Historian, Author
Gilpin, Peri		Ent	13			40	
Gilruth, Robert R.		Space	10			35	
Gilsig, Jessalyn		Ent	13			40	
Gimbel Brothers (6)		Bus	475				Gimbel Department Stores
Gimbel, Bernard F.	1885-1966	Bus	75	175	375	175	Gimbel Bros. Dept. Stores
Gimbel, Ellis A.	1865-1950	Bus	90	180			Last of Original Gimbel Bros.
Gimbel, Isaac		Bus				242	Fndr. of Gimbel's
Giminez, Eduardo		Opera	10			30	Opera
Ginastera, Alberto		Comp		95	175	100	Opera, Ballet
Gingold, Hermione	1897-1987	Ent	10			50	Br. Comedienne. 'Gigi'
Gingrey, Phil G		Congr	10				Member US Congress
Gingrich, Candace	1966-	Activist	10			20	
Gingrich, Newt		Congr	15	25	30	30	MOC GA Since 1973. Spkr. of House. Resigned
Ginsberg, Ruth Bader		Sup Crt	40	110		85	Clinton Appt. S Trans. Re: Bush 2000 175; S Chk 120
Ginsburg, Allen	1926-1998	Author	50	202	287	125	Beat Poet. Social Activist. TMsS 575, FDC S 50
Giordani, Marcello		Opera				50	Tenor
Giordano, Umberto	1867-1948	Comp	225	400	525	725	Opera Comp. AMusQS 450-750
Girard, Stephen	1750-1831	Rev War	125	350	325		Philan., Merchant, Banker
Girardey, Victor J. Baptiste	1837-1864	Civ War	450	576			CSA Gen.
Gisborne, Thomas		Author	30				
Gish, Dorothy		Ent	58			126	Actress. Silent Film Star
Gish, Lillian	1896-1993	Ent	40	132	75	73	Silent Star. 'Birth of a Nation'
Gissing, George Robert	1857-1903	Author	50	175	345		Br. Novels.
Gist, Mordecai	1742-1792	Rev War			631		Led Maryland regiment against the Br. forces
Gist, States Rights	1831-1864	Civ War	975	1875	4200		CSA Gen., RARE
Giuliani, Rudolph 'Rudy'		Pol	25	50	50	95	Mayor of NYC; Pres. Cand. 2008
Giulmant, Felix-Alexandre	1787-1874	Music				140	Fr. organist
Given, Robin		Ent	10			35	Actress.
Givenchy, Hubert de		Bus	35	70	95	200	Fr. Fashion Designer
Givens, Edward G. Jr.		Space	10			30	
Givot, George		Ent	10			20	Comic. 'Greek Ambassador Good Will'
Glad, Gladys	1903-1947	Ent	10	20		60	Actress. Vintage
Gladden, Adley H.	1810-1862	Civ War	534	1178			CSA Gen. ALS '61 6325. Wounded & D. 1862
Gladden, Washington		Clergy	30	40	55		
Gladstone, William E.	1809-1898	HOS	70	120	247	300	Br. Prime Min.
Glaser, Donald A.		Sci	20	35	75	35	Nobel Phys. Invented Bubble Chamber
Glaser, Lillian		Ent	10			20	Mrs. DeWolf Hopper
Glaser, Paul Michael		Ent	10			35	Actor
Glaser, Tompall		Cntry Mus	15			30	Glaser Bros. & His Outlaw Band'. Harmony Group

NAME	DATES	CATEGORY	SIG	LS/DS	ALS	SP	COMMENTS
Glasgow, Ellen		Author	40	115			Novels. Pulitzer. VA Life
Glashow, Sheldon Lee, Dr.		Sci	20	35		30	Nobel Physics
Glaspell, Susan		Author	25	65	110		Am. Plays. Pulitzer
Glass, Carter	1858-1946	Cab	15	45	60	30	Sec. Treas., Sen. VA 1902
Glass, Philip	1937-	Comp	30	50		190	Am. Orchestral, Opera, Film, Stage
Glass, Ron	1945-	Ent	10		25	30	Actor. 'Barney Miller'
Glassman, Alan		Opera	10			25	Opera
Glau, Summer		Ent	15			45	
Glazunov, Alexander	1865-1936	Comp	150	225	450	650	Rus. AMusQS 1,000-2, 750
Gleason, Jackie	1916-1987	Ent	93	100	130	342	Am. Comedian-Actor TV-Movies. 'Honeymooners'
Gleason, James	1882-1959	Ent	42	50	75	100	Grumpy Char. Actor of 30s to 50s
Gledhill, Arthur		Bus	10			10	Stanley Works
Glenn, John	1921-	Congr	30	148	225	161	Ohio Sen. -Astronaut; S Cvr. 125
Glenn, Scott	1942-	Ent	10	15	32	40	Actor. 'Silence of the Lambs', 'Nashville'
Glennon, John, Card.		Clergy	40	50	65	45	
Gless, Sharon		Ent	10	12	19	30	Actress. Long Running TV Series 'Cagney & Lacey'
Gliere, Reinhold	1875-1956	Comp	55		350		Rus. Symphony & Ballet
Globus, Yoram		Ent	10			20	Prod.
Glossop, Peter		Ent	10			30	Opera
Gloucester, Henry Wm., Duke		Royal	10	20	50	35	Son of Geo. V., Gov-Gen. Australia
Glover, Danny	1947-	Ent	10	25	30	45	Actor
Glover, John	1732-1797	Rev War	250	610	1125		Gen. Continental Army. 27th Reg. (14th)
Glover, Julian	1935-	Ent	10			35	Br. Actor
Glubb, John, Sir Pasha	1897-1986	Mil	22	45	60	100	Br. Gen. Formed, Commanded, Trained Arab Legion
Gluck, Alma		Opera	20	35	45	115	Opera, Concert, Recording
Glueck, Nelson		Archaeol	10	25	50	20	Uncovered 1500 Ancient Artifacts
Glyn, Elinor	1864-1948	Author	20	70	165	125	Br. Novels, Film Scenarios
Gneisenau, August N. Von	1760-1831	Mil			625		Prussian Gen. who served in the Napoleonic Wars
Gnys, Wladek		Aero	40			128	Shot Down 1st Plane in WWII
Goard, Nona		Aero	10	15	25	15	
Gobbi, Tito	1913-1984	Opera	20			80	It. Baritone, Opera
Gobel, George	1918-1991	Ent	10			45	Early TV
Godard, Benjamin Louis	1849-1895	Comp	75	125	238	150	Fr. Opera 'Jocelyn'. Familiar 'Berceuse'
Godard, Jean Luc	1930-	Ent	215	430		632	Fr. Film Dir., Writer.
Godard, Louis	1829-1885	Aero	300	1200	1200		Balloonist, ALS/Cont 6, 500
Godard, Magdalena		Music	15			75	Violinist
Goddard, Calvin	1768-1842	Pol	15		55		Federalist Congress 1801-05
Goddard, Paulette	1911-1990	Ent	55	55	80	188	Actress
Goddard, Robert H.	1882-1945	Sci	445	950	1869	2495	Am. Physicist. Rocket Pioneer. TLS/Cont 3500
Godden, Rumer	1907-	Author	15		65		Brit. Novels. 'Black Narcissus', 'The River'
Goderich, Fred. J. Robinson		HOS	15	40	95		Viscount Goderich. Br. P. M.
Godey, Louis A.	1804-1878	Pub	40	95	175		Godey's Ladies Book
Godfrey, A. Earl		Aero	30	60	110	75	
Godfrey, Arthur	1903-1983	Ent	15	50	55	45	Radio & Early TV Ukelele Playing-Singing Host
Godfrey, Capt. John Trevor	d. 1958	Aero	50			80	Ace/29 Victories; 16. 33 kills
Godin, Nesse		Celeb	10			15	Survivor: Shauliai, Lithuania Ghetto; Spkr.
Godolphin, Sidney, 1st Earl	1644-1712	HOS	96	240			P. M. Eng. Lord High Treas. to Queen Anne
Godoy, Manuel de	1767-1851	HOS	295				Sp. Pol., Prime Min.
Godt, Eberhard		Mil	15		70		
Godunov, Alexander	1949-1995	Ballet	33			68	Ballet. Russian Star Defected
Godwin, Archibald Campbell	1831-1864	Civ War	500	1811	3479		CSA Gen.
Godwin, Linda		Space	10			30	
Goebbels, Joseph	1897-1945	WWII	350	1012	1500	892	Nazi Min. of Propaganda
Goebel, Arthur		Aero	40			110	Pioneer Aviator

NAME	DATES	CATEGORY	SIG	LS/DS	ALS	SP	COMMENTS
Goering, Hermann W.	1893-1946	WWII	350	1062	1635	1138	Cmdr. of Lufwaffe; Marshal of the Reich. Suicide
Goethals, Angela		Ent	13			40	
Goethals, George W.	1858-1928	Engr	116	286	338	242	Chief Engr. Panama Canal. TLS/Cont 1750
Goethe, Johann W. von	1749-1832	Author	1250	2358	5525		Ger. writer, scientist, & philosopher
Goettheim, F.		Bus	10	20	45		
Goff Jr., Nathan	1834-1903	Civ War	45	60	85	150	Union Brevet Brig. Gen.
Goggin, James Monroe	1820-1889	Civ War	144				CSA Gen.
Goggins, Walt		Ent	16			47	
Gogol, Nicholai	1809-1852	Author	625	3350	6500		Father of Rus. Realistic Lit.
Going, Joanna	1960-	Ent	10			55	Actress
Golan, Menahem		Ent	10	15	15	20	Film Prod.
Gold, Missy	1970-	Ent	10			25	Actress
Gold, Thomas Ruggles		Congr	10		46		FF 46
Gold, Tracy	1969-	Ent	10			25	Actress
Goldberg, Adam		Ent	20			40	Actor
Goldberg, Arthur J.	1908-1990	Sup Crt	60	153		108	Resigned From Suprme Ct. To Become Ambass. UN
Goldberg, Bill		Ent	12			35	
Goldberg, Lucianne		Celeb	10			20	Internet journalist
Goldberg, Reiner		Opera	10			30	Opera
Goldberg, Rube	1883-1970	Comics	50	100		250	Ike & Mike', 'Boob McNutt'. Pulitzer'48; Sket 250-460
Goldberg, Stan		Comics	22			80	Archie'. Sketch 120-400
Goldberg, Whoopi	1935-	Ent	15	25	30	55	Oscar Winning Actress & Comedian
Goldblum, Jeff		Ent	10	12	15	40	Actor
Golden Eye (cast)		Ent	80			150	Brosnan, Scorupco, Janssen
Golden Girls, The (cast)		Ent	125			218	All Four
Golden, Charles, Bish.		Clergy	15	25	30	30	
Goldenson, Leonard H.		Bus	10	20	30	20	TV Broadcasting Exec.
Goldenthal, Elliot		Celeb	10			15	Film industry
Golding, Louis		Author	50	85	125	60	Br. Verse, Stories, Novels
Golding, William	1911-1994	Author	64	272	208	195	Nobel Lit., 'Lord of the Flies'
Goldman, Edwin Franco		Comp	25	50	75		Bandmaster
Goldman, Emma		Revol	75	247	435	250	Deported. Author-Editor TLS/cont 1800
Goldman, Michael		Author	10	10	15	10	
Goldman, Nahum		Zionist	15		50		Pres. World Zionist Org.
Goldman, William		Author			125		Soldier in the Rain', 'Princess Bride'
Goldmark, Peter C.		Sci	25		40		Inventor. LP Records
Goldowsky, Boris		Cond	10			35	Opera Coach. Dir. of own Opera Theatre
Goldsboro, Bobby		Cntry Mus	10			30	Singer
Goldsborough, Louis M.	1805-1907	Civ War	65	135	200		Rear Adm. USN Sig/Rank 95
Goldschmidt, Berthold	1903-	Comp				175	Ger. Works Banned by Nazis WWII
Goldschmidt, Neil E.		Cab	10	10	25	15	Sec. Transportation
Goldschmidt, Richard, Dr.	1890-1958	Sci		20	40		World Famous Geneticist
Goldsmith, Jerry	1929-2004	Comp	15			30	
Goldwater, Barry	1909-1998	Congr	25	73		55	Sen. AZ. Pres. Cand.
Goldwin, Tony		Ent	10			40	Am. actor
Goldwyn, Sam		Bus	60	182	255	195	Goldwyn Studios
Goldwyn, Sam, Jr.		Ent	10			15	Prod.
Golino, Valerie	1966-	Ent	75			121	Actress
Gollob, Gordon		WWII		165		200	WWII Ger. Air Ace. RK
Golonka, Arlene	1939-	Ent	10	15	15	30	Am. actress; Andy Griffith Show
Gombell, Minna	1892-1973	Ent	25	30	55	85	
Gomes, Carlos	1836-1896	Comp	25		175		Brazilian. Opera
Gomes, Francisco		HOS	15	55	135	75	
Gomez Martinez, Miguel A.		Cond				60	Spanish

NAME	DATES	CATEGORY	SIG	LS/DS	ALS	SP	COMMENTS
Gomez, Aurea		Opera	10			20	Opera, Brazilian Sopr.
Gomez, Maximo		Revol		415			
Gomez, Thomas		Ent	20			178	
Gomme, George L. Sir		Sci			60		
Gompers, Samuel	1850-1924	Labor	101	223	290	300	Fndr. & 1st Pres. A. F. of L.
Gonzalez, Charles A. G		Congr	10				Member US Congress
Gonzalez, Rick		Ent	13			40	
Good Will Hunting (cast)		Ent				80	Damon/ Affleck
Good, James W.		Cab	25	50			Hoover Sec. of War
Good, Meagan		Ent	13			39	
Goodall, Caroline	1959-	Ent	10			30	Actress
Goodall, Jane		Celeb	15	30		55	Animal activist
Goode Jr., Virgil H. G		Congr	10				Member US Congress
Goode, Patrick Gaines		Congr	10	27			FF 27
Goodfellas (cast)		Ent				292	Cast of 4
Gooding, Cuba		Ent	12			42	Actor.
Goodlatte, Bob G		Congr	10				Member US Congress
Goodman, Al		Band				45	
Goodman, Benny	1909-1986	Music	48	157		149	Big Band Leader-Clarinetist; Chk 150
Goodman, Dody	1915-	Ent	10			40	Am. Actress
Goodman, E. Urner		Celeb					Fndr., Order of Arrow, Boy Scouts; S OA Sash 225
Goodman, John		Ent	15			45	Actor
Goodman, Steve	1948-1984	Music	25	75		150	Songwriter; Cub fan; "City of New Orleans",
Goodpaster, Andrew	1915-2005	Mil	30	55	55	50	Highly Decorated Gen. WWII. NATO Supreme Cmdr.
Goodridge, Robin		Music	10			30	Music. Drummer 'Bush'
Goodson, Mark	1915-1992	Ent	10			40	Prod. TV
Goodway, Beverly		Celeb	10			15	Photographer
Goodwin, Ginnifer		Ent	15			45	
Goodwin, Hugh H.		Mil	25	65	126	126	
Goodwin, Nat C.	1857-	Ent	20			120	Vintage Actor
Goodwin, Nathaniel		Rev War		900			Am. Brig. Gen.
Goodyear, Charles	1800-1860	Invent	350	961	4400		Developed Rubber Vulcanization; Chk 600
Goodyear, Charles Jr.		Bus	20	60	150	30	Goodyear Tire & Rubber Co.
Goodyear, Julie	1942-	Ent	10			30	Br. Actress
Goosens, Eugene, Sir		Comp	20	45	90	85	Br. Conductor. Opera/Orchestral Works
Goossens, Eugene		Ent	15			45	
Gorbachev, Mikhail		HOS	93	250	750	185	Perestroika, Glasnost. Nobel '90 FDC 175, SB 400
Gorbachev, Raisa		1st Lady	50			125	
Gorbato, Victor	1934-	Space		45			Russian cosmonaut
Gorcey, Leo	1915-1969	Ent	115	138		274	The Bowery Boys
Gordon, Alex., 4th Duke		Rev War	20		35		
Gordon, B. Frank		Civ War		280			CSA gen.
Gordon, Bart G		Congr	10				Member US Congress
Gordon, C. Henry	1883-1940	Ent	30			190	Actor
Gordon, Charles G.	1823-1886	Mil	160	550	822	950	'Chinese Gordon', Gordon Pasha. Killed, Khartoum. ALS/Cont 13500
Gordon, Charles W.		Clergy	20	25	30		
Gordon, Dexter		Music	215	240			Blues-Jazz
Gordon, Gale	1905-1995	Ent	25	20		68	Versatile Radio, TV/LUCY, Film Actor
Gordon, Gavin	1901-1983	Ent	40			80	Vintage actor
Gordon, George H.		Civ War	40	85	135		Union Gen.
Gordon, George W.	1836-1911	Civ War	196	422	480		CSA Gen.
Gordon, Gray		Band	20			50	Big Band leader
Gordon, Huntley	1897-1956	Ent	20	25		65	Silent Film Star. In over 50 films 1918-40

NAME	DATES	CATEGORY	SIG	LS/DS	ALS	SP	COMMENTS
Gordon, Jacques		Music				175	Russian Am. fiddler
Gordon, James Byron	1822-1864	Civ War	338				CSA Gen., KIA Yellow Tavern, VA
Gordon, John Brown	1832-1904	Civ War	154	287	429		CSA Gen., Gov. & US Sen. GA
Gordon, John Brown (WD)		Civ War	350	900	2250		CSA Gen.
Gordon, Judah Leib	1830-1892	Jrnalist	175		1150		Russ. Born Writer For Jewish Haskalah
Gordon, Mack		Comp	30	60	130	40	Lyricist
Gordon, Richard		Ent	18			55	
Gordon, Richard F. Jr.		Space	22	75		50	
Gordon, Ruth	1896-1985	Ent	20	35	40	167	AA ' Harold & Maude ', Actress, Writer, Dir.
Gordone, Charles	1927-1995	Author	25			40	Afr-Am Pulitzer Pr. Winning Plays
Gore, Albert A., Jr.	1948-	VP	40	60	85	100	Vice Pres. Nobel Pr. winner
Gore, Albert A., Sr.	1907-1998	Congr	15	60			Repr-Sen. TN 1939-44, 53-71. Father of Gore Jr
Gore, Christopher		Congr	85	205	350		Gov. MA, Sen. MA 1813
Gore, Howard W.		Cab	10	30			Sec. Agriculture
Gore, Leslie		Music	10			30	Recording artist
Gore, Tipper		2nd Lady	10	20		35	
Gorgas, Josiah	1813-1883	Civ War	206	314	475		CSA Gen.
Gorgas, Josiah (WD)		Civ War	250	700	1025		CSA Gen.
Gorgas, William C., Dr.		Sci	125	412	450		Eradicated Yellow Fever
Gorham, George H.		Congr	10	20	35		
Gorham, Nathaniel	1738-1796	Rev War	375	396	1507		Pres. Continental Congress
Gorie, Dominic	1957-	Space	10			25	
Goritz, Otto	1873-1929	Opera	30			65	Operatic Baritone
Gorki, Maxim	1868-1936	Author	333	788	2225	1397	Rus. Writer. Novels; AQS 450-700
Gorman, Arthur P.	1839-1906	Congr	10	15	22		Sen. MD 1881-99
Gorman, Margaret		Ent	40			75	1st Miss Am. 1921
Gorman, R. C.		Artist	25	222			Am. Indian Artist, S repro 75-200
Gorman, Willis Arnold	1816-1876	Civ War	50	90	162		Union Gen.
Gorney, Karen Lynn		Ent	10			30	Saturday Night Fever
Gorshin, Frank	1933-2005	Ent	10	15	20	50	Actor, Impressionist.
Gosfield, Maurice	1913-1964	Ent				125	Actor; 'Duane Doberman' on Phil Silvers Show
Gosling, Ryan		Ent	20			59	
Goss, Porter J. G		Congr	10			20	Member US Congress; CIA
Gossard, Stone		Ent	10			30	Music. Vocalist 'Pearl Jam'
Gosse, Aristid V.		Sci	30		80		
Gosse, Edmund, Sir	1849-1928	Author	20	35	50	35	Br. Poet, Man of Letters
Gosselaar, Mark		Ent	32			95	
Gossellaar, Mark Paul		Ent	10			45	Actor
Gossett, Louis, Jr.		Ent	15	35		55	Actor
Gottfrederson, Floyd		Comics	100			500	Mickey Mouse Strip Art
Gotti, John	1940-2002	Crime	50		1241	150	Mafia Boss, S Chk 600
Gottschalk, Louis Moreau	1829-1869	Comp	350	750	975	2250	Pianist, AMusQS 1800-3250-4500
Goudal, Jetta	1891-1985	Ent	10	10	20	85	Vintage Hollywood star
Goudsmit, Samuel A.		Sci	20	25	40	55	Dutch Born Atomic Physicist
Gough, John B.	1817-1886	Clergy	25	60	55	125	Temperance Advocate, Reformer
Gould, Charles L.		Bus	10	35	45	45	
Gould, Chester	1900-1985	Comics	65	80	128	179	Dick Tracy. Large Tracy Sketch S 300-500
Gould, Edwin	1866-1956	Bus	50	250	350	150	Son of Jay
Gould, Elliott		Ent	10	20	25	40	Actor
Gould, George	1864-1923	Bus	95	225	350	175	Son of Jay. Lost Inherit. TLS on RR Ltrhd 1900
Gould, Glenn	1932-1982	Music	648	1153	1805	3895	Eccentric, Legendary Pianist. Comp. RARE
Gould, Gordon		Invent	15	40			Commercial Laser Inventor
Gould, Harold		Ent	10	15	15	35	Actor
Gould, Jay	1836-1892	Finan.	375	1950	6000	2700	ALS/Cont $13700; MKT Stk Cert $500, Most Stk certs

NAME	DATES	CATEGORY	SIG	LS/DS	ALS	SP	COMMENTS
							ex rare; RR Docs rare
Gould, John	1804-1881	Sci	110		700		Br. Ornithologist
Gould, Morton	1913-1996	Comp	20	45	70	275	AMusQS 200
Gould, Robert Simonton		Civ War	45	65	90		CSA Cmdr. Gould's Battalion
Gould, Samuel B.	1910-1997	Educ	15	20	25	35	
Gould, Sandra		Ent	15			60	Actress, Mrs. Kravitz 'Bewitched'
Goulding, Edmund	1891-1959	Ent		55		260	Director/Singer/Actor/Comp./Screenwriter/Novels
Goulding, Ray	1922-1990	Ent	10	15	15	45	Actor
Goulet, Robert	1933-2007	Music	10			55	Singer
Gounod, Charles	1818-1893	Comp	93	231	275	362	AMusQS 650-2, 500. Score 'Sapho' S 985
Gouraud, Henri-Joseph E.	1897-1946	Mil	50	70		100	Fr. Gen. WWI
Govan, Daniel C.	1829-1911	Civ War	90		540		CSA Gen.
Gowdy, John		Clergy	15	15	25		
Goya, Francisco		Artist	2200	7900	18750		Sp. Painter, Etcher, Lithographer
Goz, Harry	1932-2003	Ent	10	15	15	30	Broadway Musical Actor & Cartoon Voice Actor
Grabe, Ronald J.		Space	10			25	
Grable, Betty	1916-1973	Ent	57	80	150	475	GI's WWII #1 Pin-up girl; SP as WWII pin-up 700
Grace de Monaco	1928-1982	Royal	133	249	406	290	As Princess (Grace Kelly)
Grace de Monaco & Rainier		Royal	162	265	350	400	Monaco (Grace Kelly & Prince Rainier)
Grace, Eugene G.		Indust	25	65	140	40	Pres., Chmn. Bethlehem Steel
Grace, Topher		Ent	17			50	
Grace, William R.		Bus	15	30	45	30	Mayor NYC. W. R. Grace & Co.
Gracen, Elizabeth Ward		Ent	10			25	Miss Am. '82
Gracie, Archibald Jr.	1832-1864	Civ War	450	1500			CSA Gen., KIA Petersburg, VA
Gracis, Ettore		Cond				65	
Grade, Lew, Lord	1906-1998	Ent	22			35	Br. Impresario of Enter. TV-Film Prod.
Grady, Don	1944-	Ent	10			30	My Three Sons
Graf, David	1950-2001	Ent	10			40	Actor; Police Academy
Graf, Herman		WWII	35			192	Ger. ACE. #9 Worldwide; 214 kills
Graffin, Greg		Ent	17			50	
Graham, Billy	1918-	Clergy	133	145	195	250	World-Wide Evangelist
Graham, Bob		Congr	10			20	US Senate (D-FL)
Graham, C. J.		Ent	10			55	Jason
Graham, Charles Kinnaird	1824-1889	Civ War	50	90	150		Union Gen.
Graham, Donald		Bus	10	25	40	15	
Graham, Elizabeth Candler		Author	10		10	15	Books about Coca-Cola
Graham, George	1772-1830	Cab	20	50	75		Monroe Sec. War (ad int) Soldier, Statesman
Graham, Heather		Ent	10			42	Actress.
Graham, Jim 'the Commish'		Author	10			12	NC Sec of Agriculture, cookbook
Graham, John	1774-1820	Diplo	65	215	430		Aided Jefferson, Madison, Monroe
Graham, Katherine	1917-2001	Pub	15	25	60	40	Chm. CEO Washington Post
Graham, Lauren		Ent				40	Actress
Graham, Lawrence Pike	1815-1905	Civ War	45	85	140		Union Gen.
Graham, Lindsey		Congr	10			20	US Senate (R-SC)
Graham, M. Gordon		WWII	25				ACE WWII; 7 kills
Graham, Martha	1895-1986	Ent	67	194	260	325	Dancer, Teacher, Choreographer; SB 120
Graham, Robert		Artist	10			10	Sculptor
Graham, Sheila		Author	25		40	35	Journalist, Gossip Columnist
Graham, Sylvester		Invent			100		The Graham Cracker
Graham, Thomas	1805-1869	Sci			105		Scottish Chemist
Graham, Virginia	1912-1998	Ent	20			35	TV Hostess, Commentator, Panelist. Radio Actress
Graham, William A.	1804-1875	Cab	25	40	65		Fillmore Sec. Navy 1850
Grahame, Gloria	1924-1981	Ent	67	80		247	Academy Award
Grahame, Kenneth	1859-1932	Author	75	110	195		Br. Writer Wind in the Willows

NAME	DATES	CATEGORY	SIG	LS/DS	ALS	SP	COMMENTS
Grahame-White, Claude	1879-1959	Aero	60	100	250	125	1st Br. School of Aviation. Pioneer Aviator-Mfg.
Grainger, Percy	1882-1961	Comp	40	95	165	195	Austral. Pianist-Comp. SPc 150; S Sheet Mus. 350
Grajales, Antonio Maceo y	1846-1896	Mil		360	1343		Liberator of Cuba
Gramegna, Anna		Opera	45			95	Opera
Gramm, Phil		Congr	10			20	Sen. TX
Grammer, Kelsey		Ent	10	25		52	TV Series-Frasier
Gran, Tryggve	1889-1980	Aero	12	30		40	Norwegian aviator, Explr. & author
Granados, Enrique	1867-1916	Comp			975		Sp. Pianist. Piano Works, Opera AMusQS 1250
Granbury, Hiram Bronson (WD)	1831-1864	Civ War	450	6900			CSA Gen.
Grand Funk Railroad		Music	300				Rock group
Grandi, Dino, Count	1895-1988	Diplo	25	45	90	40	Mussolini Cabinet
Grandval, Marie F. C.		Comp	10		95		Fr. Woman Comp.
Grandy, Fred	1948-	Ent	10	20		30	Congressman IA-Love Boat
Grange, E. R.		Aero	10	25	45	35	
Granger, Dorothy	1912-1995	Ent				130	Actress
Granger, Farley		Ent	10	15	20	52	
Granger, Francis	1792-1868	Cab	30	60	72		Wm. H. Harrison P. M. Gen. FF 44
Granger, Gideon	1767-1822	Cab	85	200	202		P. M. Gen. 1801
Granger, Gordon	1822-1876	Civ War	49	110	163	520	Union Gen. War Date CDV 520
Granger, Kay G		Congr	10				Member US Congress
Granger, Robert S.	1816-1894	Civ War	52	100	140		Union Gen. Captured 1861
Granger, Stewart		Ent	20			55	Handsome, Swashbuckling Brit. Film Star
Granit, Ragnar		Sci	25	50	120	100	Nobel Med.
Granlund, Nils T. (NTG)		Ent	20			40	Prod. Radio, TV, Night Club
Grant III, Ulysses	1881-1968	Mil	30	55	75	75	
Grant, Abraham Phineas		Congr	15		50		FF 50
Grant, Amy		Music	10	15	15	40	Singer
Grant, Cary	1904-1986	Ent	202	382		954	Actor, Oscar Winner
Grant, Duncan	1885-1978	Artist	100		300		Scot. Impressionist. Bloomsbury Grp.
Grant, Frederick Dent	1850-1912	Mil	30	55	80		Son of US Grant
Grant, Gogi	1924-	Music	10			25	Singer
Grant, Heber J.	1856-1945	Relig	35	150	450	250	Pres. of the Mormon Church
Grant, Hugh		Ent	20			55	Br. Actor
Grant, Jesse R.		Pol	44				US Grant's son, author
Grant, Julia Dent	1826-1902	1st Lady	250	325	444		
Grant, Kathryn		Ent	10			30	Actress-Widow of Bing Crosby
Grant, Kirby	1911-1935	Ent	15		25	102	Sky King
Grant, Lee		Ent	10	30		35	Oscar winner
Grant, Lewis Addison	1828-1918	Civ War	58	85	219	200	Union Gen., Medal of Honor
Grant, Richard E.	1957-	Ent	10			30	Br. Actor
Grant, Russell		Celeb	10			15	Astrologer
Grant, Ulysses S.	1822-1885	Pres	555	1519	1844	2513	
Grant, Ulysses S. (as Pres.)	1822-1885	Pres	654	1457	2632	3500	18th Pres. of USA
Grant, Ulysses S. (WD)	1822-1885	Pres	760	2622	5478	4325	ALS/Spec. Cont. 15000-17500, S cdv 2500-5000
Grant, William T.	1876-1972	Bus	42	122	315	275	1, 176 W. T. Grant Stores in 40 States
Grantham, Leslie	1947-	Ent	10			25	Br. Actor
Granville, Bonita	1923-1988	Ent	15	45	20	102	Actress
Grapelli, Stephane		Music	20			85	Unique Jazz Violinist. SPc 60
Grapewin, Charles	1869-1956	Ent	762			1505	Am. Actor; 'Uncle Henry' in 'Wizard of Oz'
Grass Roots, The		Music		120		250	60's Group (5)
Grass, Gunter		Author	40	135	260	140	Ger. Novels. Nazi Era
Grasse, Fran. -Jos., Comte de		Rev War					Kept Aid From Cornwallis. No prices known.
Grasser, Anton		Mil				92	Infantry Gen. & Cmdr., 25th Panzergrenadier Div.
Grasser, Hartmann		Aero	14	25	50	30	

NAME	DATES	CATEGORY	SIG	LS/DS	ALS	SP	COMMENTS
Grassi, Rinaldo		Opera	35	95		85	Opera
Grassle, Karen	1944-	Ent	10	15	15	25	Actress. 'Little House on the Prairie'
Grassley, Chuck		Congr	10				US Senate (R-IA)
Grasso, Ella		Gov	10	35		20	1st Woman Governor CT
Grateful Dead (All six)		Music	930	3400		1513	Rock HOF; S Album 1500-2500
Gratiot, Charles	1788-1855	Mil	150	205			War 1812. Gen. 1828
Gratz, Barnard		Rev War	75	212	400		
Gratz, Rebecca	1781-1869	Philan			2750		Noted Am. Jewish Philan.
Graue, Dave		Comics	10			65	Alley Oop
Grauman, Sid		Ent	30	45	90	75	Owner of Opulent Theaters
Gravatt, Andrea M. D.		Author	10			12	Child safety
Gravatte, Marianne		Model	10			25	Playboy Playmate
Gravel, Maurice Mike		Congr	10			20	Sen. Alaska
Graveline, Duane E. M. D.		Space	10			25	
Graves, Peter	1925-	Ent	15	10	25	40	Actor. 'Mission Impossible', 'Airplane'
Graves, Robert	1895-1985	Author	65	175	310	110	Br. Poet, Novels, Critic
Graves, Sam G		Congr	10				Member US Congress
Graves, William		Mil	50				Gen. WWI
Gravity Kills		Music	30			65	Music. 4 Member Rock Group
Gray, Alexander	1902-1975	Ent	15			35	Actor-Singer. Broadway Musical Star. Radio-Films
Gray, Asa	1810-1888	Sci	35	60	95		Am. Botanist. Darwin Supporter
Gray, Billy		Ent	10			30	Actor
Gray, Bowman		Bus	10	15	35	15	
Gray, Colin		WWII	35		90		Top New Zealand ACE
Gray, Colleen	1922-	Ent	15	25	45	50	
Gray, Delores	1924-2002	Ent	40			65	Am. Singer, Dancer
Gray, Elisha	1835-1901	Bus	182	1800	1734		Fndr. Western Electric. Tel. Pioneer, Inventor.
Gray, Erin	1952-	Ent	10	10	20	25	Actress-Model
Gray, George	1840-1925	Congr	10		35	30	Sen. DE. Jurist. Diplomat
Gray, Gilda	1901-1959	Ent	40			132	Popularized the Shimmy
Gray, Glen	1900-1936	Band	15			47	Big Band Leader of Casa Loma Orch.
Gray, Harold	1894-1968	Comics	100			450	Little Orphan Annie; S sketch 675
Gray, Harry Jack		Bus	10	10	20	10	CEO United Technologies
Gray, Henry	1816-1892	Civ War	130	166			CSA Gen.
Gray, Horace	1828-1902	Sup Crt	60	120	180	250	1882
Gray, Isaac P.		Gov	10	15			Governor IN
Gray, Jack Stearns		Aero	150				TLS/Cont 950. Aviator
Gray, Linda		Ent	10	20	20	40	Actress
Gray, Macy		Ent	17			50	
Gray, Oscar L.		Congr	10	15		10	MOC AL 1915
Gray, Peter W.	1819-1874	Civ War	38	122			Mbr., Confederate Congress
Gray, Spalding	1942-2004	Ent	10			40	Actor; writer
Gray, Thomas	1716-1771	Author	950	1888	5100		Br. Poet. 'Elegy Written in a Country Churchyard'
Gray, William	1750-1825	Rev War	40		100		Merchant, Patriot, Privateer
Gray, William H., III	1941-	Congr	10			20	Afr-Am MOC PA. Pres. United Negro College Fund
Gray-Cabey, Noah		Ent	15			45	
Grayco, Helen	1924-	Ent	10	15	15	35	Vocalist & Wife Spike Jones
Grayson, Cary T.	1878-1938	Med	95				White House Physician to 3 Pres
Grayson, John Breckinridge	1806-1861	Civ War	152	436			CSA Gen.
Grayson, Kathryn	1922-	Ent	10	34	25	48	Singer-Actress. Starred in Lavish MGM Musicals
Great Expectations (cast)		Ent				85	DeNiro/ Hawke
Grechaninov, Aleksandr	1864-1956	Comp			45		Russian born, Am. Comp.
Greco, Jose	1918-2000	Ent	18	25		68	Dance
Greco, Juliette	1927-	Ent				65	Franch born actress

NAME	DATES	CATEGORY	SIG	LS/DS	ALS	SP	COMMENTS
Greeley, Andrew, Rev.		Clergy	10	15		10	
Greeley, Horace	1811-1872	Jrnalist	72	130	243	825	Go West, Young Man', S gun club stock cert. 9500
Greely, Adolphus W.	1844-1935	Expl	62	121	177	250	Arctic Explr., Gen.
Green, Adolph	1914-2002	Comp	10	15		40	Collaborated/Betty Comden
Green, Al		Music	10			40	Singer
Green, Anna Katherine	1846-1935	Author	50	85	125		Pioneer Am. Detective Fiction
Green, Brian		Ent	23			70	
Green, Brian Austin		Ent	10			40	Actor; Beverly Hills 90210
Green, Charles	1785-1870	Aero	40	100	250		Br. Balloonist
Green, Dorothy	1929-	Ent	10	15	15	35	Actress
Green, Dwight H.		Gov	10	15			Governor IL
Green, Fitzhugh	1888-1947	Mil	50	225			USN Cmdr. Polar Explr., Co-Author 'We'/Lindbergh
Green, Gene G		Congr	10				Member US Congress
Green, Henrietta (Hetty) H.	1834-1916	Finan	2000	9500			Wall St. Speculator. LS re Stocks 18, 800
Green, Herschel		WWII	12	28	48	35	ACE, WWII, Triple Ace; 18 kills
Green, Jeff		Celeb	10			25	Br. Comedian
Green, Johnny	1908-1989	Comp	40	80	120	122	AManS 250, 150, 350
Green, Kerri	1967-	Ent	10			35	Actress
Green, Mark G		Congr	10				Member US Congress
Green, Martin Edwin	1815-1863	Civ War	400		1455		CSA Gen., KIA Vicksburg
Green, Mitzi	1920-1969	Ent	10	15	25	45	Actress. Musicals-Stage & Film; "Little Mitzi"
Green, Paul		Author		45			Plays, Lost Colony. Pulitzer
Green, Seth		Ent	15			42	Actor. 'Buffy' Co-Star
Green, Theodore	1867-1966	Congr	10		20	15	Gov., Sen. RI
Green, Thomas	1814-1864	Civ War	147	295	450		CSA Gen. KIA Mansfield, LA
Green, Thomas (WD)		Civ War	175	725	3250		CSA Gen. KIA. DS/Rare NM CSA '62 6500
Green, Tom		Celeb	10			35	Comedian
Green, William F.	1873-1952	Labor	30	102	85	100	Pres. A. F. of L.
Greenacres		Ent				133	Cast of TV Show
Greenaway, Kate	1846-1901	Artist	504	650	578		Br. Creator kid's Books. Sketch S 450-1, 200+
Greenbaum, Everett	1919-	Ent	15			25	TV/Film Writer. 'Andy Griffith', 'M A S H'
Greenday		Music				215	Rock group; S Album 200
Greene, Carl Franklin	1887-	Aero	65	150			USAAC Col. Collier Award. 1st Pressure-Cabin Plane
Greene, Frank L.		Congr	10		20	15	MOC, Sen. VT
Greene, George S.	1801-1899	Civ War	40	85			Union Gen.
Greene, Graham	1904-1991	Author	75	160	320	245	Br. Novels, Dramatist, Critic
Greene, Lorne	1915-1987	Ent	37	115	120	123	Actor; 'Bonanza'
Greene, Michele	1962-	Ent	10	10	25	25	Actress & singer/songwriter of Latin & folk music
Greene, Nathaniel	1742-1786	Rev War	817	2518	4188		Am. Rev. War Gen. ALS/Cont 4800
Greene, Richard		Ent	15			73	Vint. Brit. Actor. Robinhood
Greene, Sarah Pratt Mc.	1856-1935	Author	20				
Greene, Shecky	1926-	Ent	10	15	15	40	Comedian
Greene, William		Author		142			
Greenfield, Terry D.		Author	10			12	Cookbooks
Greengrass, Paul		Ent	15			45	
Greenhouse, Kate		Ent	10			35	Actress
Greenleaf, John		Clergy	30	50	85		
Greenspan, Alan		Econ	15	30		35	Chairman Fed. Reserve Bd.
Greenstreet, Sidney	1879-1954	Ent	239		450	475	Casablanca, Maltese Falcon
Greenwood, Bruce		Ent	15			45	
Greenwood, Charlotte	1893-1978	Ent	25			78	
Greenwood, Edward D.		Sci	10	15	35		
Greenwood, Grace	1823-1904	Author	30	45	75	75	
Greenwood, James C. G		Congr	10				Member US Congress

NAME	DATES	CATEGORY	SIG	LS/DS	ALS	SP	COMMENTS
Greenwood, Joan	1921-1987	Ent				60	Br. Actress
Greenwood, Lee		Cntry Mus	10			35	CW Singer
Greer, Dabbs (Bill)	1917-2007	Ent	10			40	Actor
Greer, Elkanah Brackin	1825-1877	Civ War	140				CSA Gen.
Greer, Germaine		Author				100	Australian born writer & feminist
Greer, Jane	1924-2001	Ent	10	15	15	55	Actress
Greer, Pam	1950-	Ent	10			35	Actress. 'Jackie Brown'
Greg K		Music	10			25	Music. Bass Guitar 'Offspring'
Gregg, Andrew	1755-1835	Congr	30	60			Sen., MOC PA ALS/Cont 475
Gregg, David M.	1833-1916	Civ War	40	75	182	175	Union Gen. Distinguished at Gettysburg
Gregg, David M. (WD)	1833-1916	Civ War	105	188	428		Union Gen.
Gregg, John	1828-1864	Civ War	350				CSA Gen.
Gregg, John R.		Bus	65	85	150	90	Inventor Gregg Shorthand System
Gregg, Judd		Congr	10				US Senate (R-NH)
Gregg, Maxey	1814-1862	Civ War	410	600			CSA Gen. KIA Fredericksburg, VA
Gregg, Maxey (WD)		Civ War	565	4000			CSA Gen. KIA
Gregg, Virginia	1916-1986	Ent	10	12	20	42	Actress
Gregg-Thomas, Delores J.		Author	10			20	Afr. -Am. poetry
Gregory, Bettina		Celeb	10			25	Award winning Correspondent
Gregory, Bill		Space	10			25	
Gregory, Dick	1932-	Ent	20	75	88	65	Comedian-Writer-Social Activist
Gregory, F. H.		Civ War	64	100	102		Union Naval Capt.
Gregory, F. H. (WD)		Civ War	60	95	115		Union Naval Captain
Gregory, Frederick D.		Space	10	15		25	
Gregory, James	1911-2002	Ent	10	15	15	51	Actor
Gregory, Thomas W.	1861-1933	Cab	20			45	US Atty Gen. Woodrow Wilson
Greim, Robert Ritter von		WWII		340		160	Gen. Field Marshal,
Grell, Mike		Comics	10			75	Tarzan
Grenfell, Wilfred T.	1865-1940	Med	35	55	75	125	Med. Missionary, Author
Grenier, Adrian		Ent	20			40	Entourage
Grenville, George	1712-1770	HOS	250	750			Br. P. M., Author of Stamp Act Vs Am. Colonies
Grenville, Peter	1913-	Ent	10		30	40	Br. Dir. Stage & sometime Films.
Grenville, Wm. 1st Baron.	1759-1834	HOS	85	285	650		Br. Prime Min. Pro Rom. Cath. Emancipation
Gresham, Walter Quintin	1832-1895	Civ War	45	75	100		Union Gen.
Gretchaninoff, Alexander T.		Comp	65	180	395	3500	AManS 350
Gretsch, Joel		Ent	17			50	
Grévy, Jules	1807-1891	HOS	40				Pres. France 1879-87
Grew, Joseph C.	1880-1965	Diplo	20	25		35	Ambassador Japan 1931-41
Grey, Benjamin Edwards		Congr	10		26		FF 26
Grey, Chas. 2nd Earl of	1764-1845	HOS	85	98	160		Prime Min.
Grey, George Sir	1799-1882	Diplo	10	25	55		Br. Statesman
Grey, Jennifer		Ent	10			40	Actress
Grey, Joel		Ent	15	20	25	45	
Grey, Nan	1918-1993	Ent	10	15	15	30	
Grey, Virginia	1917-2004	Ent	10	15	18	40	Actress 30s to early 40s
Grey, Zane	1875-1939	Author	80	147	504	192	Dentist Turned Western Writer
Gridley, Chas. Vernon	1844-1898	Mil	250	410	895		Cmdr. of Adm. Dewey Flagship
Gridley, Richard	1711-1796	Rev War	170	450	790		Gen. Continental Army, Artillery
Grieco, Richard	1965-	Ent	10			35	
Grieg, Edvard	1843-1907	Comp	236	600	1304	2350	19th C. Norge. AMusQS 1, 800-3500
Grier, David Alan		Ent	10	40		40	Actor
Grier, Pam	1949-	Ent	35			73	Actress
Grier, Robert C.	1794-1870	Sup Crt	1000				
Grierson, Benjamin H.	1826-1911	Civ War	80		235		Union Gen.

NAME	DATES	CATEGORY	SIG	LS/DS	ALS	SP	COMMENTS
Grierson, Benjamin H. (WD)		Civ War	165	235	545		Union Gen.
Griesbach, Franz	1826-1911	Mil	25				Ger. Infantry Gen.
Griffes, Charles T.	1884-1920	Comp	175	515			Outstanding Am. Comp. ALS/Cont 3,000
Griffeth, Bill		Celeb	10			25	Business commentator
Griffin, Angela	1976-	Ent	10			25	Br. Actress
Griffin, Charles	1826-1867	Civ War	60	150			Union Gen., Indian Fighter
Griffin, Chris		Music	10			25	Jazz Trumpet
Griffin, Cyrus	1749-1810	Rev War	360	765			Continental Congress
Griffin, Gerry		Space				50	Flight Dir.
Griffin, Kathy		Ent	13			40	
Griffin, Merv	1925-2007	Ent	10			50	Enter mogul
Griffin, S. Marvin		Gov	10		30		Governor GA
Griffin, Simon Goodell	1824-1902	Civ War	40	80	120		Union Gen.
Griffin, W. E. B.		Author	10			20	Fiction
Griffith, Andy		Ent	15	45	48	66	Actor
Griffith, Corinne	1895-1979	Ent	35	58	90	103	Actress
Griffith, D(avid) W(ark)	1874-1948	Ent	232	612	875	2588	Pioneer Film Prod. -Dir.
Griffith, Hugh	1912-1980	Ent	155	275		327	Br. Actor
Griffith, Joe		Celeb	10			15	Filmography
Griffith, Melanie		Ent	25	30	55	53	Actress
Griffith, Richard	1814-1862	Civ War	325				CSA Gen.
Griffiths, Rachel		Ent	10			40	Brenda Chenowith, Six Feet Under, Emmy winner
Griggs, John W.		Cab	12	45	110		Pol. -Jurist, Gov. NJ
Griggs, S. David	1939-1989	Space	60	150		115	
Grijalva, Ra·l M. G		Congr	10				Member US Congress
Grimaldi, Joesph	1779-1837	Ent			775		
Grimaud, Helene		Music				75	Pianist
Grimblat, Pierre		Celeb	10			15	Film industry
Grimes, Bryan	1828-1880	Civ War	245	417	2013		CSA Gen.
Grimes, Karolyn	1940-	Ent	15	60		40	Actress; ZuZu in 'It's a Wonderful Life"
Grimes, Tammy		Ent	10			30	
Grimm, Jacob		Author	442	1840	3080		Grimm's Fairy Tales
Grimm, Wilhelm		Author	500	1425	2775		Grimm's Fairy Tales
Grinnell, Henry	1799-1874	Finan	45	160			Financed Arctic Exped. s
Grinnell, Josiah	1821-1891	Congr	40				Repr. IA, Fndr. Grinnell, IA & University; FF 31
Grinnell, Moses H.		Bus	25	60	120		MOC NY. Merchant Prince NY
Grint, Rupert		Ent				146	'Harry Potter'
Gris, Juan	1887-1927	Artist	175		1500		Sp Cubist Painter
Grisham, John		Author	20	70		45	The Firm, The Pelican Brief
Grisi, Giulia	1811-1869	Opera	100		202	190	It. Sopr. Great Diva. Sig w/Mario 675
Grismer, Joseph R.	1848-1922	Ent	10	25		60	Film Writer
Grissom, Virgil I. 'Gus'	1926-1967	Space	336	795		1037	Merc. 7. S Chk 450-650
Griswald, O. W.		Mil	15	35			
Griswold, John A.		Congr	10		25		MOC NY 1869
Griswold, Lawrence		Author	10			20	Real life 'Indiana Jones'
Griswold, Matthew		Congr	12	115	160		MOC PA 1891
Griswold, Putnam		Opera	20			50	Opera
Grizzard, George	1928-2007	Ent	10	15	15	40	Actor
Grizzard, Lewis		Author	20				Southern humorist
Groban, Josh		Music	15	25		45	
Grodin, Charles	1935-	Ent	10	15	25	48	Actor
Groener, Harry		Ent	10			20	Dear John
Groening, Matt		Comics	45			240	The Simpsons'. S orig art 250-625
Grofé, Ferde		Comp	100	225	272	130	AMusMS 1,850, AMusQS 360

NAME	DATES	CATEGORY	SIG	LS/DS	ALS	SP	COMMENTS
Grohl, Dave		Music	15			48	Music. Drums, Vocals Nirvana & Foo Fighters
Gromyko, Andrei A.		Statsmn	92	160	295	170	Rus. Diplomat. Ambass. to US
Gronau, Wolfgang von		Aero	75	135	235	155	Early around the world flight
Groom, Victor		Aero	20	45	75	55	
Groom, Winston		Author	20				Forrest Gump
Gropius, Walter	1883-1969	Archtct	125	200	600	425	Co-Fndr. of the Bauhaus Movement
Gropper, William	1897-1977	Artist	30	85	200	350	Am. Social Protest Artist. Radical Cartoonist
Grose, William	1812-1900	Civ War	45	90	130		Union Gen.
Gross, Chaim		Artist	35	75	165	50	Signed Lithograph 350
Gross, Clayton K.		WWII	10	16	28	22	ACE, WWII; 6 kills
Gross, Courtlandt		Bus	10	10	15	10	
Gross, Mary		Ent	10			35	Actress
Gross, Milt		Comics	20			125	Nize Baby
Gross, Samuel D.	1805-1884	Med			1100		Leading Am. Surgeon of His Time (Rare)
Grosser, Heinz		Sci	15			45	Rocket Pioneer/von Braun
Grossinger, Jennie		Bus	23	115	135	35	Grossinger's Hotel, Catskill Mts
Grossmith, George	1874-1935	Ent	10			25	Br Musical Comedy, Films, Revues
Grosvenor, Charles H.		Civ War	40	75	110		Union Gen., MOC OH
Grosvenor, Gilbert H.	1875-1966	Bus	60	100	195	195	Pres. National Geographic. Editor
Grosz, George	1893-1959	Artist	65	190	275		Expressionist Who Expressed Hatred of Bourgeoisie
Grotius, Hugo	1583-1645	Sci		130			
Grouchy, Marquis E. de		Napol	100	250			Marshal of Napoleon. Exiled
Grover, Cuvier		Civ War	50	67	90		Union Gen.
Groves, Leslie R.	1896-1970	Mil	65	145	220	163	Gen. WWII. Manhattan Project
Grow, Galusha A.	1822-1907	Congr	25	55	75	125	Repr. PA, Spkr. of the House
Growing Pains		Ent	42			125	Cast signatures
Grubbs, Gary	1949-	Ent	10			35	Will & Grace
Gruberova, Edita		Opera	15			40	Opera.
Gruelle, Johnny		Comics	35			250	Raggedy Ann & Andy
Gruen, George John		Bus	30	80	150	55	Chm. Gruen Watch Co.
Gruenther, Alfred M.	1899-1983	Mil	45	45	65	72	Gen. WWII, Pres. Am. Red Cr. Cmdr. NATO
Gruffudd, Ioan		Ent	17			50	
Grumman, Leroy R.		Bus	50	145			Grumman Aircraft
Grunberg, Greg		Ent	13			40	
Grunsfeld, John		Space	10			30	
Guardia, R. A. C.		HOS	15	50		25	Costa Rica
Guardino, Harry	1925-1995	Ent	10	15		50	Actor
Guden, Hilde		Opera	25		75	50	Opera
Guderian, Heinz	1888-1954	Mil	100	220	350	550	Ger. Panzer Gen. WWII
Gudger, V. Lamar		Congr	10	30		15	MOC NC
Gudin de la Sablonniere		Fr Rev	120	235			
Gudin, Theodore	1802-1880	Artist			130		
Gudunov, Alexander		Ballet	15		40	40	Rus. Ballet
Guelfi, Piero		Opera	10			25	Opera
Guerard, Benjamin		Pol		85			Govenor of SC
Guérin, Jules	1866-1946	Artist	10		35		Murals at Lincoln Mem'l, Penn. RR Station
Guerra, Vida		Ent	17			50	
Guest, Christopher		Ent	10	20		45	Actor
Guest, Edgar A.	1881-1959	Author	25	45	70	95	Am. Journalist-Poet of the People. SB 120
Guest, Lance	1960-	Ent	10	10	15	30	Actor
Guest, Val	1911-2006	Celeb	15			60	Film industry
Guevaro, Ernesto Che		Revol	300	2179	9500		Aide to Fidel Castro in Cuba
Guffey, Joseph F.		Congr	10	10		10	Sen. PA
Guggenheim, Daniel	1856-1930	Bus	20	50	85	60	Guggenheim Foundation

NAME	DATES	CATEGORY	SIG	LS/DS	ALS	SP	COMMENTS
Guggenheim, Harry F.		Aero		75			Pres. Guggenheim Fund (Aeronautics)
Guggenheim, Peggy		Bus	25	25	70	65	Patron of Arts. Collector
Guggenheim, William		Bus	55	125			Industrialist, Philan.
Gugino, Carla		Ent	21			63	
Guilbert, Yvette	1865-1944	Ent	40	65	252	130	Music-hall singer & actress.
Guild, Curtis Jr.		Gov	12	15			Governor MA
Guild, Nancy	1925-1999	Ent	10	15	20	45	Actress
Guildford, Henry, Sir	1489-1532	Royal	110	430			Henry VIII. Master of Horse & Comptroller of House
Guilfoyle, Paul	1949-	Ent	10	15	35	30	Actor
Guilini, Carlo Maria		Cond				175	Italian
Guillaume, Robert		Ent	10	15	20	45	Actor
Guillemin, Roger C. L.		Sci	20	35	50	60	Nobel Med.
Guillotin, Joseph-Ignace		Sci	275	1407	2170		Fr. Doctor Supported Guillotin
Guinan, Texas (Mary Louise)		Ent	25	70	90	40	Actress, Hostess of Speakeasies
Guiney, Louise Imogene		Author	50		300		Poet-Essayist
Guingand, Francis		Mil	15	35	50		Fr. Gen.
Guinier, Lani		Law	10	20		15	Afr-Am Law Professer-Writer
Guinness, Alec, Sir	1914-2000	Ent	78	85	95	152	Br. Screen Actor. AA. Obi-Wan-Kenobi
Guinness, Benjamin L.	1798-1868	Bus	30	50	110	65	Guinness Brewing Co.
Guinness, Edward C.	1847-1927	Bus	15	25	45	60	Guinness Brewing Co.
Guion, David W.	1892-1981	Comp	100				Home On The Range'. ANS 295
Guisewite, Cathy		Comics	25			85	Cathy
Guiteau, Charles	1842-1882	Assass	426	625	2144	1302	Shot Pres. Garfield
Guizot, Francois	1787-1874	Pol			55		Fr. statesman
Gulager, Clu	1928-	Ent	15		15	40	Broadway actor-vaudevillian
Gulda, Friedrich		Music				150	Pianist
Gullette, J. Carl		Author	10			12	Fort Sumter
Gumbel, Bryant		Ent	10			30	News anchor
Gumbel, Greg		Celeb	10			30	News anchor; Sports
Gummow, Bradley L.		Author	10			12	Author financial
Gunn, Anna		Ent	15			45	
Guns 'N Roses (all)		Music	102			135	
Gunsche, Otto	1917-2003	WWII	50		85	85	Hitler's last adjutant
Gunther, John	1901-1970	Author	20		75		Best Seller 'Inside Europe'
Gunton, Bob		Ent	13			40	
Gur, Mordechai	1900-1979	Mil	20	75			Israeli Gen. 6 Day War. Spec. AirMail Cov. 69.
Gurie, Sigrid		Ent	20	25	60	65	
Gurnett, Jane	1959-	Ent	10			30	Br. Actress
Gurrag-gchaa, Jugderdemidij		Space	15	50			Mongolian Astro.
Gursel, Cemal	1895-1966	HOS	20	65	90	75	Turkey
Gusmeroli, Giovanni		Opera	10			15	Opera
Gustavus II Adolph (Swe)	1594-1632	Mil	350	1378	2355		Saved Protestantism in Germ. Great Gen.
Gustavus III (Swe)	1746-1792	Royal	175	403	985		King of Sweden from 1771
Gustavus IV Adolph (Swe)	1778-1837	Royal	150				
Gustavus V (Swe)	1858-1950	Royal	75	150			
Guston, Philip	1913-1980	Artist			175		Canadian-born Am. Painter
Guthrie, Arlo		Cntry Mus	15	35	45	70	Folk Singer; S Album 160
Guthrie, James	1792-1869	Congr	22	45	80		Pierce Sec. Treas. Sen. KY
Guthrie, Thomas		Clergy	15	20	25		
Guthrie, Tyrone		Playwrt			350		
Guthrie, Woody	1912-1967	Music	300	1915	4090		Folksinger, Poet, Songwriter
Gutierrez, Luis V. G		Congr	10				Member US Congress IL
Gutierrez, Sid		Space	10			25	
Gutknecht, Gil G		Congr	10				Member US Congress

NAME	DATES	CATEGORY	SIG	LS/DS	ALS	SP	COMMENTS
Guttenberg, Steve		Ent	10		30	40	Actor
Guy, Jasmine	1964-	Ent	10			30	Actress
Guy, Thomas	1644-1724	Celeb	25	40	105		Fndr. of Guy's Hospital
Guynemer, Georges	1894-1917	Aero	225	400	650	911	ACE, WWI. A Fr. Legend
Guyot, Arnold	1807-1884	Sci	25	45	195		Geographer, Mapmaker, Educator
Guyot, Pierre		Fr Rev	25	55	125		
Guyton-Morveau, L. B. Baron	1737-?	Sci	20	50	95		Fr. Chemist
Gwenn, Edmund	1875-1959	Ent	71	90	122	170	SP 'Miracle 34th St. ' 1, 650., Sp. SP 2500
Gwin, William M.	1805-1885	Congr	20	45	60		MOC MS, Sen. CA; FF 35
Gwinnett, Button	1735-1777	Rev War	150000	320000			Rare Signer Dec. Independence
Gwynne, Anne	1918-2003	Ent	10	15	15	45	
Gwynne, Fred	1926-1993	Ent	238			392	Actor
Gye, Albani	147-1930	Opera	10			25	Canadian Sopr.
Gyllenhaal, Jake		Ent	15			45	Actor
Gyllenhaal, Maggie		Ent	10			40	Actress
Haab, Robert		HOS	25	70			Switzerland
Haag, Carl	1820-1915	Artist		30	80		Ger. -Born Br. Court Painter to Victoria
Haakon VII & Maud		Royal	200			450	King & Queen of Norway
Haakon VII (Nor)	1872-1957	Royal	120	205			1st King Independent of Sweden
Haas, Dolly	1910-1994	Ent				45	Ger. actress
Haas, Lucas		Ent	15			45	
Haas, Lukas		Ent	10			20	Actor
Haass, Richard	1951-	Pol	10			15	Pres. of the Council on Foreign Relations
Habberton, John		Author	10	15	25		
Habersham, John	1754-1799	Rev War	40	115			Cont. Congr. Maj. 1st GA Cont. Reg. A Fndr. UofG
Habersham, Joseph	1751-1815	Rev War	95	260	540		Continental Army, Cont. Congress
Hack, Shelley		Ent	10			30	Actress
Hackett, Bobby		Ent	20				Cornet/Benny Goodman
Hackett, Buddy	1924-2003	Ent	10	10	20	45	Comedian
Hackett, James K.	1869-1926	Ent	15			75	Am. stage actor
Hackett, Joan		Ent	10	15	25	58	Talented Actress.
Hackett, Raymond	1902-1958	Ent				60	Actor
Hackleman, Pleasant Adam	1814-1862	Civ War	140	195			Union Gen.
Hackman, Gene		Ent	20		35	50	SP/Denzel Washington 130
Hadary, Jonathan	1948-	Ent	10			25	Stage actor
Hadfield, Chris		Space	10			25	
Hadley, Jerry		Opera	10			24	Concert, Opera
Hadley, Reed	1911-1974	Ent	20			120	Actor
Hadley, Tony	1960-	Music	10			25	Br. Pop singer; lead-singer of Spandau Ballet
Haenschen, Gus		Music	15		25	30	Big Band
Hagar, Sammy		Music	40			59	Rock Singer-Guitarist
Hagegard, Hakan		Opera				30	Opera
Hagel, Chuck		Congr	10			20	US Senate (R-NE)
Hagen, Jean	1923-1977	Ent	20			130	Actress
Hagen, Johannes	1847-1930	Sci	15	40	100		Austr. Astron. Hagen's Clouds
Hagen, Uta	1919-2004	Ent	10	12	20	40	Ger. actress
Hagenson, Michael Eugene	1979-	Law	10			20	
Haggard, Henry Rider	1856-1925	Author	82	145	198	270	King Solomon's Mines'; AQS 470
Haggard, Merle	1937-	Cntry Mus	15			68	Singer
Haggerty, Dan	1914-1988	Ent	15		15	50	Grizzly Adams
Haggin, James Ben Ali		Bus	75	275			Am Financier, Anaconda Copper. Hearst Partner
Haggis, Paul		Ent	15			45	
Haglund, Dean		Ent	15			45	
Hagman, Larry	1931-	Ent	10	10	15	41	Actor. 'I Dream of Jeannie', 'Dallas'

NAME	DATES	CATEGORY	SIG	LS/DS	ALS	SP	COMMENTS
Hagood, Johnson	1829-1898	Civ War	159	326	408		CSA Gen. War Date S 200
Hague, Arnold	1840-1917	Expl			500		Explr. geologist; Helped develop Yellowstone
Hague, Frank		Pol	10	25	40	20	Headed Major Dem. Machine
Hahn, Hillary		Music				75	Fiddler
Hahn, Jessica		Model	10			25	Playboy
Hahn, Otto	1879-1968	Sci	98	458	275	575	Ger. Nobel Chem. Nuclear Fission. ALS/Cont 2000
Hahn, Reynaldo	1874-1947	Comp	70	160			Venezuelan. Critic, Dir. Paris Opera. AMusQS 285
Haider, Michael		Bus	15			40	Pres. Standard Oil NJ
Haig, Alexander M.		Mil	20	63	50	40	Gen. WWII, Sec. State
Haig, Dorothy, Lady		Celeb	10		25		Wife of Sir Douglas Haig
Haig, Douglas. 1st Earl	1861-1928	Mil	35	112	333	175	Br. Gen., Boer War, India, WWI
Haig, Sid		Ent	15			45	
Haight, Edward	1817-1885	Congr	10				Repr. NY, Fndr. NY Bank
Haight, Henry H.		Gov	25				San Francisco's Haight-Asbury Distr.
Haile, William	1797-1837	Congr	15				Repr. MS
Hailey, Arthur		Author	25	40	65	40	Am. Novels. Hotel, Airport
Haim, Corey		Ent	10			40	Actor
Haines, Connie	1922-	Ent	20			50	Big Band Vocalist
Haines, Daniel	1801-1877	Gov	30	45	90		Governor NJ
Haines, William	1900-1973	Ent	15	15	35	40	
Hairston, Jester	1901-2000	Comp	10			30	Am. Comp., songwriter, arranger
Haise, Fred W. Jr.	1933-	Space	25	70	120	112	Apollo 13
Haitink, Bernard		Cond				60	English Dutch
Halaby, Najeeb	1915-2003	Celeb	10	30		20	US businessman Father of Queen Noor of Jordan.
Halban, H. H., Dr.		Sci	30	65			Fr. Pioneer of Uranium Fission
Haldane, John B. S.	1892-1964	Sci		125	195		Br. Geneticist & Author
Haldeman, George W.		Aero	30	55	105	75	
Haldeman, H. R.		Pol	10	20	62	30	Nixon Watergate
Halder, Franz		Mil	55	95	160	140	Ger. Gen. Opposed Hitler
Hale, Alan Jr.	1918-1990	Ent	117	130	150	314	Actor. 'Gilligans Island'
Hale, Alan Sr.	1892-1950	Ent	52	55	95	195	Actor
Hale, Barbara	1921-	Ent	10	15	22	30	Actress. Della Street On 'Perry Mason'
Hale, Edward Everett	1822-1909	Clergy	33	102	184	240	Author 'Man Without a Country'
Hale, Eugene	1836-1918	Congr	10	15	30		MOC 1869-75, Sen. ME
Hale, George E.		Sci	20	100			Invented Spectroheliograph
Hale, John Parker	1806-1873	Congr	15	45	100		Abolitionist., Sen. NH
Hale, Lucretia Peabody	1820-1900	Author	25				
Hale, Monte	1921-	Ent	10	10	25	35	Big Time Cowboy Star
Hale, Nathan		Rev War		15000			RARE, 'I have but one life to give for my country'
Hale, Richard	1892-1981	Ent	10	15	15	35	Actor
Hale, Robert		Opera	10			30	Opera
Hale, Sarah Josepha B.	1788-1879	Author	65	170	238		Editor. 'Mary Had A Little Lamb'
Hale, Tony		Ent	15			45	
Halevy, Fromental		Comp	30		125		La Juive
Halevy, Jacques	1799-1862	Comp	45	80	135		Opera. Taught Gounod, Bizet
Halevy, Ludovic		Author	25	70	120		Novels, Libretti For Operas
Haley, Alex	1921-1992	Author	45	105	160	150	Roots', 'Malcom X'. ALS/Cont 2900; SB 250
Haley, Bill	1925-1981	Music	190	500		444	The Comets. S Alb. Pg/5 Orig. Members 375
Haley, Bill & the Comets		Ent				450	
Haley, Jack	1899-1979	Ent	135	161	188	182	Song & Dance. WOZ SP/Tin Man 350-500; S Chk 100
Haley, William J., Sir	1901-1987	Bus	15		35	40	Dir. Gen BBC & Editor of the 'Times'
Halifax, Edw. Frederick L.	1881-1958	Statsmn	20	60			1st Earl of. Viceroy of India, US Ambassador
Hall & Oates		Ent	50			90	
Hall, Abraham Oakey	1826-1898	Pol	25	35	84	125	NY Mayor, Tweed Ring, Tammany Hall

NAME	DATES	CATEGORY	SIG	LS/DS	ALS	SP	COMMENTS
Hall, Anthony		Ent	16			47	
Hall, Arsenio		Ent	10			38	Comedian; actor
Hall, Bridget	1977-	Model	10			30	Am. Supermodel
Hall, Charles M.		Clergy	10	15	20		
Hall, Christopher		Music	10			32	Music. Lead Singer 'Stabbing Westward'
Hall, David		Gov	10			15	Governor OK
Hall, David G.		Bus	10			20	
Hall, Deidre		Ent	10			35	Soaps
Hall, Edward Marshall, Sir	1858-1927	Law			60		Br. Lawyer
Hall, Ella	1976-1981	Ent	20			65	Actress. Universal Silent Star 1910-1920's
Hall, Fawn	1959-	Celeb	10	15	40	25	Sec to Oliver North during Iran-Contra affair
Hall, Gus		Pol	30	90	75	50	US Communist Party Leader
Hall, Huntz	1919-1999	Ent	58	65	75	92	Actor. Bowery Boys
Hall, Irma P.	1935-	Ent	10			35	Actress
Hall, Jerry		Ent	10			35	Model; actress
Hall, Jon	1913-1979	Ent	32	45	85	62	Bare-chested Hero of Many 40s Films
Hall, Josephine		Ent	15			60	Vintage actress
Hall, Joyce C.		Bus	80	173		155	Hallmark Greeting Cards
Hall, Juanita	1901-1968	Ent	65			94	'Bloody Mary' in 'South Pacific'
Hall, Lyman	1724-1790	Rev War	1649	2766	4875		Signer Dec. of Indepen.
Hall, Michael		Ent	17			50	
Hall, Michael C.		Ent	15			45	David Fisher, Six Feet Under
Hall, Monty		Ent	10		20	30	Game Show Host-TV
Hall, Nathan		Cab	25	40	115		Fillmore P. M. Gen.
Hall, Pauline	1860-1919	Ent	20			85	Vintage Actress
Hall, Radclyffe		Author		45	135		'Well of Loneliness'
Hall, Ralph M. H		Congr	10				Member US Congress
Hall, Regina		Ent	13			40	
Hall, Rich		Celeb	10			30	Comedian
Hall, Robert, Sir	1761-1831	Clergy	30	80	125	35	Br. Baptist Min. Great Pulpit Orator
Hall, Thurston	1882-1958	Ent				138	Actor; 'Topper'
Hall, Tom T.		Cntry Mus	10			25	Singer
Hall, William	1775-1856	Mil	40		100		Gen., War of 1812
Hallam, Henry	1777-1859	Author	35	115	180		Br. Historian
Halle, Wilma		Music			85		Violin virtuoso
Halleck, Fitz-Greene	1790-1867	Poet	30	80	105		Member of Knickerbocker Group
Halleck, Henry Wager	1815-1872	Civ War	96	213	584	700	Union Gen.
Halleck, Henry Wager (WD)	1815-1872	Civ War	182	500	1173	875	Union Gen. ALS/Cont 4, 500
Hallett, Mal		Band	20			35	Big Band Leader
Halliburton, Lloyd		Author	10			12	Civil War
Halliburton, Richard	1900-1939	Author	42	92	295	75	World Traveller, Lecturer
Halliwell, Geri	1972-	Music	15			50	Spice Girls
Halmi Sr., Robert	1924-	Ent	10			25	Prod.
Halop, Billy	1920-1976	Ent	90	95	120	134	One of Orig. Dead End Kids
Halpern, Seymour		Congr	10			15	MOC NY
Halpine, Charles G.	1829-1868	Civ War	50	75	90		Irish-Born Writer & Gen.
Halsell, James, Jr.		Space	10			25	
Halsey, Jeremiah		Colonial		480	175		New London, CT Shipbuilder, Owner. Just. of Peace
Halsey, Wm. F. 'Bull'	1882-1959	Mil	110	290	376	654	Adm. WWII. Top Adm. After Nimitz.
Halstead, Murat		Editor	10	20	35		Journalist
Halston		Bus	15	20	40	30	Designer
Halstrom, Holly		TV News	10			20	'Price is Right' Model
Hamblen, Stewart		Cntry Mus	15			30	Singer-Songwriter
Hamblin, Joseph Eldridge	1828-1870	Civ War	48	86	130		Union Gen.

NAME	DATES	CATEGORY	SIG	LS/DS	ALS	SP	COMMENTS
Hamel, Veronica		Ent	10	18	20	35	Actress
Hamer, Frank	1884-1955	Lawman	110	465			Tracked down & killed Bonnie & Clyde
Hamer, Rusty	1947-1990	Ent	63		55	75	Child Actor on 'Danny Thomas Show'
Hamill, Mark		Ent	10	20	20	62	Actor Luke Skywalker 'Star Wars'.
Hamilton, Alex. Jr.	1786-1875	Mil	20	40	135		Off. War 1812, Lawyer
Hamilton, Alexander	1757-1804	Pol	1085	4135	7434		1st Sec. Treas. FF 1200-1600. ALS/Cont 7500-20000
Hamilton, Andrew Jackson	1815-1875	Civ War	45	80	130		Union Gen.
Hamilton, Charles Smith	1822-1891	Civ War	35	80	147		Union Gen. ALS/Cont 575
Hamilton, Donald		Author	10	15	25	10	
Hamilton, Emma, Lady	1765-1815	Celeb	225	528	1062		Mistress of Lord Nelson Wife of Sir Wm. Hamilton
Hamilton, Gail		Author					See Dodge, Mary A.
Hamilton, George	1939-	Ent	10			40	Actor
Hamilton, George A, Sir		Diplo	75	540			Archaeologist, Husband Emma H.
Hamilton, Ian, Sir	1853-1947	Mil	15				Brit. Gen. Led Gallipoli Exp.
Hamilton, James		Colonial	65	160			Colonial Gov. PA
Hamilton, James Alex.	1788-1878	Mil	45	140			Off. War 1812
Hamilton, John	1887-1958	Ent	385				Daily Planet Editor Perry White on 'Superman'
Hamilton, Lee		Congr	10	20		10	Congressman IN
Hamilton, Linda		Ent	15			42	Actress
Hamilton, Lisa		Ent	13			40	
Hamilton, Margaret	1902-1985	Ent	221	245	283	768	Actress; Wicked Witch of the West in WOZ
Hamilton, Neil	1899-1984	Ent	50	55	65	103	'Commissioner Gordon' in Batman
Hamilton, Schuyler	1822-1903	Civ War	40	80	128		Union Gen.
Hamlin, Cyrus	1839-1867	Civ War	50	85	130		Union Gen., Hannibal Hamlin's son
Hamlin, Hannibal	1809-1891	VP	86	156	218		Lincoln VP, US Sen., Gov. ME., MOC. FF150-350
Hamlin, Harry		Ent	10	15	28	35	Actor
Hamlin, V. T.		Comics	50			325	Alley Oop
Hamlisch, Marvin	1944-	Comp	15	82	55	55	Conductor. AMusQS 100
Hammarskjold, Dag	1905-1961	HOS	120	565	725		Swedish Sec. Gen. United Nations. Nobel 1961
Hammer, Armand		Bus	55	290	305	185	Occidental Petroleum. Physician in Soviet Union
Hammer, M. C.		Music	25			45	Rap
Hammerstein II, Oscar	1895-1960	Comp	159	284	640	427	Lyricist-Librettist. 'Oklahoma', 'Show Boat'
Hammerstein, O., II & Kern, J.		Comp		1200			
Hammett, Dashiell	1894-1961	Author	485	1564	1725	2023	Hard-Boiled Detective Fiction. 'Maltese Falcon'
Hammond, James B.		Invent	20	100			Typewriter
Hammond, James H.	1807-1864	Congr		45	115		US Sen., Gov. SC. Cotton is King
Hammond, Jay S.		Gov	10	15			Governor AK
Hammond, L. Blaine		Space	10			20	
Hammond, William A.		Civ War	50	120	400		Union Gen./Surgeon Gen. Author
Hamnett, Katharine		Celeb	10			15	Designer
Hampden, Renn D.		Clergy	10	25	30		
Hampden, Walter	1879-1955	Ent	20		45	80	One of the great Am. stage actors
Hampson, Thomas	1955-	Opera	10			37	Opera; Am. baritone
Hampton, Hope		Ent	40			65	
Hampton, Lionel	1913-2002	Band	28			130	Big Band Leader-Vibes. Jazz Legend
Hampton, Wade	1818-1902	Civ War	280	578	816		CSA Gen., Gov., US Sen. SC
Hampton, Wade (WD)	1818-1902	Civ War	350	1250	1800		CSA Gen.
Hamsun, Knut (Pedersen)	1859-1952	Author	40	85	135	187	Nor. Nobel Lit. Neo-Romantic Novels. AManS 1850
Hanami, Kohei		Mil	80	250			
Hancock, Clarence E.	1885-1948	Congr	10	25			Repr. NY
Hancock, Herbie		Comp	10	25	45	40	
Hancock, John	1737-1793	Rev War	2322	6535	12086		1st Signer. ALS/Cont 12500, 15000. FF 2500-3000
Hancock, Winfield S.	1824-1886	Civ War	191	403	708	738	Union Gen. ALS/Cont 3300. Pres. Cand.
Hancock, Winfield S. (WD)	1824-1886	Civ War	270		1212	1319	Union Gen.

NAME	DATES	CATEGORY	SIG	LS/DS	ALS	SP	COMMENTS
Hand, Edward	1744-1802	Rev War	185	475	1000		Gen. Cont. Army. Repr. PA 1784
Hand, Learned	1872-1961	Jurist	88	305	483	700	Tenth Justice'. Distinguished Among Am. Jurists
Handel, George Frederick		Comp	1000	5800	22000		
Handelman, Stanley M.	1925-2007	Ent	10		25	35	
Handler, Ruth	d. 2002	Bus	40	75		40	Fndr. Mattel Toys
Handy, W. C.	1873-1958	Comp	198	410	250	426	AMusQS500-2200, Sheet Music S 795
Hanks, Tom		Ent	22	148	45	145	Actor. 'Forrest Gump', Oscar winner
Hanly, Thomas Burton	1812-1880	Civ War	39	100			Member of CSA Congress
Hanna & Barbera		Comics	120	145		172	Animators. Signatures/Chars. Surrounding 85
Hanna, Bill	1910-2001	Comics	30			85	'Flintstones', S drwg 125-350
Hanna, Jack	1947-	Celeb	10			20	Zookeeper
Hanna, Marcus A.	1837-1904	Indust	25	55	75	100	Sen. OH. Pol. Power Broker
Hannah, Daryl		Ent	15	38	45	46	Actress
Hannah, John A.		Educ	10				Pres. Michigan State U
Hannay, James Owen	1865-1950	Author		100			Pseudonym George A. Birmingham
Hannigan, Alyson		Ent	10			41	Actress. 'Buffy' Co-Star
Hanover, Donna		Celeb				20	Actress, Former wife of NYC Mayor Rudy Giuliani
Hansbrough, Henry C.	1848-1933	Congr	10	15	30		MOC, Sen. ND
Hansen, Gunner		Ent				58	TX Chainsaw Massacre
Hansen, Juanita	1895-1961	Ent				310	Am. Actrress
Hansen, Mark Victor		Author	10			15	Chicken Soup books
Hansen, Max		WWII				95	SS Col.
Hansen, Patti	1956-	Model				40	Supermodel
Hansen, William	1911-1975	Ent	10	15	15	45	
Hanson Brothers		Ent				65	Actors
Hanson, Beck		Music	10			48	Music. Lead Singer 'Beck'
Hanson, Gary		Celeb	10			20	Famed Framer
Hanson, Howard		Comp	15	35	80	120	Pulitzer. Dir. Eastman Sch. Music
Hanson, John	1721-1783	Rev War	3025	8500			1st Pres. Continental Congress
Hanson, Roger Weightman	1827-1863	Civ War	375	518			CSA Gen.
Haqq, Khadijah		Ent	18		55		
Haqq, Malika		Ent	18		55		
Haralson, Hugh A.	1805-1854	Congr	10				Repr. GA, Maj. Gen State Militia
Harbach, Otto	1873-1963	Ent	60	100	150		Plays, Lyricist, Music Publ
Harbaugh, Gregory J.		Space	10			25	
Harbison, John		Comp	20		75		Pulitzer, AMusQS 150
Harbord, James G.		Mil	50	92	135	150	Chief of Staff AEF WWI, RCA
Harburg, E. Y. 'Yip'		Comp	158	462	398		Over the Rainbow; S Lyrics 750-1500; Sig w/Arlen 750
Harcourt, Edward Venables		Clergy	25	30	40		
Hardee, William J.	1815-1873	Civ War	328	663	1097	1100	CSA Gen.
Hardeen, Theo	d. 1946	Ent	175	240			Magician; Houdini's brother
Hardeman, William P. 'Gotch'	1816-1898	Civ War	135				CSA Gen.
Hardenberg, K. A. von Furst		Statsmn	15	60	125		Prussian Pol.
Hardie, J. Keir	1856-1915	Pol	75			200	Scottish, Fndr. of the Labour Party
Hardie, James Allen	1823-1876	Civ War	58	196	222		Union Gen.
Hardie, James Allen (WD)		Civ War	80	248	295		Union Gen.
Hardie, Russell		Ent	10	15	25	40	
Hardin, Benjamin		Congr	12		47		FF 47
Hardin, Clifford M.		Cab	10	10	18	15	Sec. Agriculture
Hardin, Gus	1945-1996	Cntry Mus	10			50	CW Female singer
Hardin, John Wesley	1853-1895	Crime	2592	5893	12640		Notorious Gunslinger. Bullet Shot Card S 11, 750
Hardin, Martin Davis	1837-1923	Civ War	51	85	130		Union Gen.
Hardin, Ty	1930-	Ent	40			88	Bronco
Harding, Aaron	1805-1867	Congr	35	50			MOC KY. Contacts & Recommendations to Lincoln

NAME	DATES	CATEGORY	SIG	LS/DS	ALS	SP	COMMENTS
Harding, Abner Clark	1807-1874	Civ War	50	75	120		Union Gen.
Harding, Ann		Ent	15	25	35	95	Actress
Harding, Benjamin Franklin		Congr	10				FF 32
Harding, David		Cond				60	English
Harding, Florence Kling		1st Lady	75	170	190	260	White House Card S 125; S Chk 75
Harding, Mike		Celeb	10			15	Comedian
Harding, Warren G.	1865-1923	Pres	217	378	946	507	Pre-Nomination Pol. TLS/Cont 3500
Harding, Warren G. (As Pres.)	1865-1923	Pres	323	683	9572	644	ALS/Cont 15000. TLS/cont 2500. WH Cd S 500-600
Hardinge, Chas., 1st Baron		Diplo	10	25	35	35	Br. Viceroy India, Ambass. Russia
Hardinge, Henry, Sir	1785-1856	Mil			585		Br. Field Marshal
Hardwicke, Cedric, Sir		Ent	35	65	90	90	
Hardy, Oliver	1892-1957	Ent	287	902	680	823	1/2 of Popular Comedy Team
Hardy, Robert	1925-	Ent	10			40	Br. Actor
Hardy, Thomas	1840-1928	Author	229	587	830	1330	Br. Novels, Poet, Dramatist
Hardy, Thomas Masterman, Sir		Mil	75	310	215		1769-1839 Br. Adm./Nelson. MsLS re War 1812 750
Hare, John, Sir		Ent	20	30		50	
Hare, WIlllam Hobart		Clergy	35	50	65	50	
Harewood, Dorian	1950-	Ent	10			35	Actor
Haring, Keith	1958-1990	Artist	104	175	397	467	Pop Artist-Cartoonist., S drwg 500-2000
Harjo, Suzan Shown		Celeb	10			15	Pres. & Dir. of The Morning Star Foundation
Harker, Charles Garrison	1835-1864	Civ War	125		338		Union Gen.
Harkin, Tom		Congr	10			20	US Senate (D-IA)
Harkness, Georgia		Clergy	35	50	95	65	
Harlan, Andrew Jackson		Congr	10				FF 32
Harlan, James	1820-1899	Cab	22	51	125		Andrew Johnson Sec. Interior 1865; Senate; FF 31
Harlan, John Marshall	1899-1971	Sup Crt	40	85	125	150	
Harlan, John Marshall	1833-1911	Sup Crt	68	112	190	160	
Harland, Edward	1832-1915	Civ War	40	54			Union Gen.
Harland, Marion		Author	10	15	20		
Harley, William S.		Bus	1500	3533			Co-Fndr. Harley-Davidson Motorcycles
Harlow, Jean	1911-1937	Ent	1517	1400	3000	3840	30's Sex Symbol. D. at 28. Mother S Most SP
Harlow, Jean (Mama)		Ent	25	30		45	
Harman, Fred		Comics	25			250	Red Ryder
Harman, Jane H		Congr	10			20	Member US Congress
Harmon, Angie		Ent	15			48	Actress
Harmon, Judson		Cab	10	25	40	40	US Atty Gen., Gov. OH
Harmon, Mark		Ent	10	15	20	40	Actor
Harmonica Rascals		Ent	10			25	Borah Minovitch & the Harmonica Rascals
Harned, Virginia	1868-1946	Ent	15			65	Vintage Stage Actress, Mrs. Sothern
Harney, William S. (WD)		Civ War	50		330		Union Gen.
Harney, William Selby	1800-1889	Civ War	50	84			Union Gen.
Haro, Daniel	1955-	Celeb	10			25	Actor
Harold Wilson, Lord		Pol	20	30	45	55	PM of England
Harold, Gale		Ent	17			50	
Harper, Joseph W.		Pub	10	30	80		Harper' Magazine
Harper, Robert G.		Rev War	65		150		Gen. Rev. War, Statesman
Harper, Tess		Ent	10	10	20	25	Actress
Harper, Valerie		Ent	10	15	15	35	Actress
Harper, William	1790-1847	Pol	25		95		SC Nullification Leader & Slavery Advocate
Harrel, Scotty		Ent	10				C & W
Harrell, Costen J., Bish.		Clergy	20	25	40	35	
Harrelson, Woody		Ent	15			42	Actor
Harrer, Heinrich	1912-	Author	250				Seven Years In Tibet'. Tutor of Dalai Lama
Harridge, Will	1883-1971	Bus	50	125			Pres. Org. AKA Am. League

NAME	DATES	CATEGORY	SIG	LS/DS	ALS	SP	COMMENTS
Harries, George		Mil	20	35	80		Gen. WWI
Harriman, Edw. Henry	1848-1909	Bus	250	900			US RR Magnate. S RR Bonds 575+
Harriman, Edward Roland		Bus	20	55	120	35	CEO Union Pacific RR. Banker
Harriman, W. Averell	1891-1986	Gov	20	56	100	50	Gov. NY, Statesman, Diplomat, Ambassador
Harring, Laura		Ent	13			40	
Harrington, Pat		Ent	10	15	15	35	Actor; comedian
Harris		Comics	10			18	The Better Half
Harris, Arthur T., Sir 'Bomber'	1892-1984	Mil	99	125	165	150	Cmdr.-in-Chief RAF WW 99II. Head of Bomber Comm.
Harris, Barbara		Ent	10			35	Actress. Stage-Films
Harris, Barbara C.		Clergy	10			20	
Harris, Bernard A., Jr.		Space	10			30	Astronaut
Harris, Cecil		WWII	20	25	50	40	ACE, WWII; 24 kills
Harris, Charles K.	1867-1930	Music		250			Am. songwriter of popular music
Harris, Ed		Ent	15	20	20	46	Actor
Harris, Emmy Lou		Cntry Mus	10			35	Country Singer
Harris, Fred R.		Congr	10	10			Sen. OK
Harris, George E.		Congr	25	30			CSA Off. MOC NC
Harris, Isham	1818-1897	Civ War	50	68	82		Civil War Gov. TN. ALS '64 450. US Sen.
Harris, Jared	1961-	Ent	10			20	Br. Actor
Harris, Jean		Crime	35	70	375		Murdered Dr. Herman Tarnower. ALS/Cont 375
Harris, Jed		Ent	10	20			Prod. Theatre
Harris, Joel Chandler	1848-1908	Author	219	398	700		Popular Books on Black Folklore. 'Uncle Remus'
Harris, John	1726-1791	Pol	125	265	775		Fndr. Harrisburg, PA
Harris, John A.		Congr	10		15		
Harris, Jonathan		Ent	15			60	Actor. 'Lost in Space'
Harris, Julie	1925-	Ent	15	20	25	102	Actress. Broadway 'Tony' Winner. Films, TV
Harris, Katherine H		Congr	10			20	Member US Congress
Harris, Louis		Pollster	20	35		25	
Harris, Mel		Ent	10			35	Actress. '30 Something'
Harris, Nathaniel Harrison	1834-1900	Civ War	120	198			CSA Gen.
Harris, Neil Patrick		Ent	10			40	Actor
Harris, Patricia Roberts	1924-1985	Cab	25	30	40	75	1st Afr-Am Woman To Serve in Cabinet.
Harris, Paul Percy		Bus	25	45		30	Fndr. & Pres. -Emeritus. Rotary
Harris, Phil		Ent	22			45	Bandleader-Actor-Singer & Disney Voice-Over
Harris, Richard	1930-2002	Ent	20	25	45	91	Irish-Br. Actor, Harry Potter SP 100
Harris, Robert		Author	10	50			'Enigma'
Harris, Robert H.	1911-1981	Ent	10	15	20	45	Actor
Harris, Sam H.		Ent	10	25			Prod. -Manager
Harris, Thomas		Author	20	55			'Silence of the Lambs'
Harris, Thomas Maley	1817-1906	Civ War	43	70			Union Gen.
Harris, Thomas S.		WWII	15	45		30	ACE WWII, Test Pilot; 9 kills
Harris, Will		Ent	15			45	
Harris, William A.	1841-1909	Congr	30		45		Repr. & Sen. KS, CW Adj. Gen
Harris, William L., Bish.		Clergy	15	25	35		
Harrison, Albertis S. Jr.		Gov	10	20			Governor VA
Harrison, Anna Symmes	1775-1864	1st Lady	650	1118	1844		Free Frank 975; wife of WH Harrison
Harrison, Benj. & Caroline		Pres	600				Both S
Harrison, Benj. & Roosevelt, T.		Pres		2250			Civ. Serv. Commission S 2250
Harrison, Benjamin	1833-1901	Pres	210	452	752	1618	TLS/Cont 1600-2500. DS-Pres Warr. 1450; Chk 275
Harrison, Benjamin	1726-1791	Rev War	575	1005	2034		Signer Dec. of Indepen., Gov. Virginia
Harrison, Benjamin (As Pres.)		Pres	342	911	1850		Exec. Mansion Card S. 450, ALS/cont 10, 755
Harrison, Burton, Mrs.		Celeb	10			35	1890's Socialite
Harrison, Byron Patton 'Pat'		Congr	10	15		10	MOC, Sen. MS
Harrison, Caroline Scott	1832-1892	1st Lady	192	272	866	625	Wife of 1st Pres. to die in WH. ALS/1st Lady 2000

NAME	DATES	CATEGORY	SIG	LS/DS	ALS	SP	COMMENTS
Harrison, Carter H.		Mayor	20	35	40		Mayor Chicago 1897
Harrison, George		Music	953	2457	7234	1954	Beatle. S Chk $1800; DS/Settlement $237500; S Album $2385; ALS to Sutcliffe $48600
Harrison, George P., Jr.	1841-1922	Civ War	95	188	283		CSA Gen.
Harrison, George P., Jr. (WD)		Civ War	150	225			CSA Gen.
Harrison, Gregory		Ent	10	15	20	30	Actor
Harrison, Helen		Aero	40	125			Am Aviatrix
Harrison, Henry B.		Gov	12		20		Governor CT 1885
Harrison, James Edward	1815-1875	Civ War	125	212			CSA Gen.
Harrison, Jenilee		Ent	10			25	Actress 'Three's Company'
Harrison, Linda		Ent	10			35	Actress. 'Planet of the Apes'
Harrison, Mary Lord	1858-1948	1st Lady	81	129	193	200	Niece of 1st Lady Caroline Scott & Second Wife
Harrison, Noel		Ent	10			20	Br. Actor-Son of Rex Harrison
Harrison, Rex, Sir	1908-1990	Ent	36	50	130	89	Br. Actor. ' My Fair Lady' SP 150. Oscar Winner
Harrison, Richard B.	1865-1935	Ent	25	85		150	Am. Vintage Black Actor. 'The Green Pastures'
Harrison, Robert Hanson		Rev War	210	400	2502		Sec. to G. Washington
Harrison, Thomas	1823-1891	Civ War	130	190	246		CSA Gen.
Harrison, William H.	1773-1841	Pres	750	1562	4499		ADS 1790's 1400. ALS/Cont 6500-15000
Harrison, William H. (as Pres)		Pres		93750	194750		D. after 1 month. Man. LS (2 known) 167300
Harrold, Kathryn		Ent	10	12	14	35	Actress
Harrow, William	1822-1872	Civ War	50	98	208		Union Gen.
Harry, Debbie		Music	25	60		66	Rock Singer-Actress. 'Blondie'
Harry, Jackee	1956-	Ent	10			40	Image Award winning Afr.-Am. actress
Harryhausen, Ray		Ent	10			35	Film Dir.
Harshaw, Margaret		Opera	10	12	40	65	Opera. US Sopr.
Hart, Corey		Ent	10		15	35	
Hart, Dolores	1938-	Ent	10	15	25	120	Actress
Hart, Dorothy	1922-2004	Ent	15		25	40	Model; actress
Hart, Eva		Celeb	60	170	75	90	Titanic survivor
Hart, Gary W.		Congr	10	18		25	Sen. CO. One Time Pres. Hopeful
Hart, John	1711-1779	Rev War	373	457	1300		Signer Dec of Ind; Imp. DS 3490. S Cont. Curr. 430
Hart, John		Ent	10			55	The Lone Ranger
Hart, Johnny		Comics	20			175	B. C. ' & 'Wizard of Id'
Hart, Lorenz	1895-1943	Comp	641	7500			Talented Lyricist for Richard Rodgers. D. Young
Hart, Mary		Ent	10	15	15	30	'Enter Tonight' Host.
Hart, Melissa		Ent	15			45	
Hart, Melissa A. H		Congr	10				Member US Congress
Hart, Melissa Joan		Ent	12			45	Actress. 'Sabrina The Teenage Witch'
Hart, Moss	1904-1961	Author	30	55	120	318	Plays & Musical Librettist
Hart, Roxanne	1952-	Ent	10			30	Actress
Hart, T. J.		Ent	13			40	
Hart, Terry J.		Space	10	15		30	
Hart, Thomas C.		Mil	40			65	Adm. WWII
Hart, Veronica	1956-	Ent	10	15	30	35	Porn star; actress
Hart, William S.	1870-1946	Ent	122	178	234	387	1st Western Movie Star. Silent Films
Harte, Francis Brett	1836-1902	Author	82	185	237		Diplomat. Author of Frontier Life, AManS 25,000
Hartford, George L.		Bus	40	170	280		Great Atlantic & Pacific Tea Co. Huge Groc. Chain
Hartford, Huntington		Bus	20	30	50	25	Arts Patron. Playboy. Huntington Hartford Theatre
Hartford, John		Comp	10	45	70		AMusQS 95
Hartle, Russell	1889-1961	Mil	20			50	Gen. Cmdr. US Forces in Britain early WWII
Hartley, David	1729-1813	Colonial			950		Br. Min. Anti War/Colonies. S Peace Treaty
Hartley, Fred A.		Congr	20		50		Congressman NJ
Hartley, Mariette		Ent	10	15	15	30	Actress.
Hartley, Nina		Ent	15			62	Pornographic actress

NAME	DATES	CATEGORY	SIG	LS/DS	ALS	SP	COMMENTS
Hartley, Roland H.		Gov	10	12		10	Governor WA
Hartley, Thomas	1748-1800	Rev War	105		350		Lt. Col. War Cont. ALS 6500
Hartline, Haldan K.		Sci	25	80	140	75	Nobel Med.
Hartman, David		Ent	10	12	15	30	Early TV Host 'Good Morning America'
Hartman, Don		Ent	10			30	Prod.
Hartman, Lisa (Black)		Ent	10	15	25	35	
Hartman, Phil	1948-1998	Ent	71	225		150	Comedian-Actor
Hartmann, Erich	1922-1996	Aero	85	118	208	275	Ger. Ace WWII. #1 Worldwide/Most Kills
Hartmann, Franz	1796-1853	Med			240		Pioneered homeopathy
Hartnett, Josh		Ent	18			55	
Hartranft, John F.	1830-1889	Civ War	55	98	122		Union Gen. Statesman. Gov. PA. ALS/Cont 1045
Harts, William	1867-1961	Mil	10		45		Span. -Am. War. Gen. WWI. Extensive Career
Hartsfield, Henry W. Jr		Space	10	40		25	
Hartsuff, George L.	1830-1874	Civ War	43	75	132		Union Gen. S/Rank 75-95
Hartwell, Alfred S.	1836-1912	Civ War	43	73	92		Union Gen.
Harvey, George B. M.		Pub	20	70		80	Fostered Woodrow Wilson Nomination; Diplomat
Harvey, Jan	1947-	Ent	10			25	Br. Actress
Harvey, Jonathan		Congr	12		45		FF 45
Harvey, Lawrence	1928-1973	Ent	90			223	Br. Actor.
Harvey, Lilian	1906-1968	Ent	15	20	25	65	Actress
Harvey, Marilyn	1929-1993	Ent	10			60	Star of 'The Astounding She Monster'
Harvey, Paul	1918-	Jrnalist	10	25		25	Popular Syndicated Columnist-TV Commentator
Harvey, William	1578-1657	Sci	750	3750	11000		1st Theory Blood Circulation. (RARE in any form)
Harvick, Kevin		Ent	20			60	
Hasbrouck, Robert W.		WWII	50	165		75	Am. Gen. WWII
Hascall, Milo Smith	1829-1904	Civ War	45	82	130		Union Gen.
Hasen, Irwin		Comics	10			20	'Dondi'
Hashimoto, Maj. -Gen. Gun	1886-1963	WWII	25			35	WWII Jap. Gen.
Haskell, Peter	1934-	Ent	10			25	Actor
Haskil, Clara		Music	195				Legendary Classical Pianist.
Haskin, Joseph Abel	1818-1874	Civ War	50	51	105		Union Gen. Sig./Rank 65
Hassam, Childe	1859-1935	Artist	150	350	654		Foremost in Am. Impressionism. Etcher
Hassam, Crown Prince		Royal	20	45	80	75	Morocco
Hassan, al Bakr, Ahmad		HOS	10	35	90	90	
Hassan, Crown Prince		Royal	10	15	50	50	
Hasselhoff, David		Ent	15	20	25	43	'Baywatch'
Hasso, Signe	1910-2002	Ent	10			65	Actress
Hastert, J. Dennis		Pol		15	20	25	Spkr. of the House
Hastings, Alcee	1936-	Congr	10				Member US Congress
Hastings, Daniel H.		Gov	10	25			Governor PA
Hastings, Doc H		Congr	10				Member US Congress
Hastings, Warren	1732-1818	HOS	60	237	335		1st Gov-Gen. India. Colonial Adm.
Haswell, Charles H.	1809-	Civ War	46	77	109		Union Naval Architect War Dte DS 155-200
Hata, Field Mar. Shunroku	1879-1962	Mil	27			35	WWII Jap. Gen.
Hatch, Edward	1832-1889	Civ War	45	85	125		Union Gen.
Hatch, John Porter	1822-1901	Civ War	44	78	125	250	Union Gen. CMH. ADS(Gen. Orders '62)4180
Hatch, Orrin		Congr	10			20	US Senate (R-UT)
Hatch, Richard		Celeb	10			20	'Survivor' winner
Hatcher, Richard G.	1933-	Pol	10	10		25	Mayor, Gary IN
Hatcher, Teri		Ent	15			60	Actress.
Hatfield, Hurd		Ent	15	22	30	60	Actor. 'Portrait of Dorian Grey'
Hatfield, Lansing		Opera	15			95	Opera, Concert, Recital Artist
Hatfield, Mark O.	1922-	Congr	10	22		20	Sen. OR, Governor Oregon. Long Time 'Dove'
Hatfield, Willis		Celeb	115				Started the Hatfield/McCoy feud

H

NAME	DATES	CATEGORY	SIG	LS/DS	ALS	SP	COMMENTS
Hathaway, Henry		Ent	40			95	Film Dir.
Hatlo, Jimmy	1898-1963	Comics	10	45		80	'Little Iodine'
Hatosy, Shawn		Ent	13			40	
Hatten, Raymond	1887-1971	Ent				146	Actor
Hatton, Christopher, Sir	1540-1591	Statsmn		1138			Elizabeth Ist, Lord Chancellor
Hatton, Frank		Cab	50	70			Chester A. Arthur PMG
Hatton, John Liptrott		Comp			125		English Comp.
Hatton, Raymond		Ent	50			134	Vintage Actor
Hatton, Robert	1826-1862	Civ War	350	473	720		Killed at Fair Oaks 6/1/1862
Hatton, Rondo	1894-1946	Ent	765			1200	Acromegalic actor, The Creeper
Hauck, Frederick H.		Space	10			25	
Hauer, Rutger		Ent	10			42	Actor. 'Lady Hawke'
Haught, Helmut		Aero	10	15	30	20	
Haupt, Herman	1817-1905	Civ War	45	57	84		Union Gen. ALS '62 440
Hauptman, Herbert A., Dr.		Sci	20	35		30	Nobel Chemistry
Hauptmann, Anna		Celeb			315		Wife of Bruno Richard
Hauptmann, Bruno R.		Crime	1420	1840		3400	Convicted Killer Lindbergh Baby
Hauptmann, Gerhart		Author	75	248	488	365	Nobel Pr. Literature 1912
Hauser, Dr. Gayelord		Med	10			25	Healthfood Advocate. Garbo Companion
Hausner, Jerry	1909-1993	Ent	10			20	
Havel, Vaclav		HOS	20			45	Czech. Poet. Pres.
Havemeyer, William F.		Bus	125		305		Am. Sugar Refining Dynasty. Mayor NYC
Haven, Annette	1954-	Ent	10	10	20	25	
Havens, Beckwith		Aero	18	40	55	50	
Havens, Richie		Music	20			60	Guitarist; Woodstock; S Guitar 200-560
Haver, June	1926-2005	Ent	10	15	20	74	40's-50's Blonde 20th C. Fox Star
Havoc, June	1913-	Ent	10	15	20	55	Am. actress, dancer, writer, & theater Dir.
Hawes, Elizabeth		Artist	10	20	35		
Hawes, James Morrison	1824-1889	Civ War	110				CSA Gen.
Hawk, AJ		Ent	22			65	
Hawke, Ethan		Ent	18			46	Actor
Hawke, Robert	1929-	HOS	20	40	130	30	Prime Min. Australia
Hawker, Harry	1886-1921	Aero	185				Pioneer Australian Pilot & Airplane Builder. Rare
Hawkins, Anthony H., Sir	1863-1933	Author	65	145	85	95	Br. Novels. 'Prisoner of Zenda'
Hawkins, Coleman		Music	130	150		230	Jazz Tenor Sax. Band Leader
Hawkins, Dale	1936-	Music	100				Am. Rock singer, songwriter, & rhythm guitarist
Hawkins, Erskine	1914-1992	Music				193	Jazz trumpeter
Hawkins, Gordon		Opera	10			25	Am. Baritone
Hawkins, Hawkshaw	1921-1963	Music	90	130			AKA Harold Franklin Hawkins; CW singer
Hawkins, Jack		Ent	45	90		125	Br. Leading Man & Char. Actor.
Hawkins, Jimmy	1941-	Ent				50	Actor
Hawkins, John Parker	1830-1914	Civ War	42		140		Union Gen.
Hawkins, Paula		Congr	10	10		15	Sen. FL
Hawkins, Rush C.		Civ War	63	112			Union Gen.
Hawkins, Rush C. (WD)	1831-1920	Civ War		245			Union Gen.
Hawkins, Screamin Jay	1929-2000	Music				175	Singer
Hawkins, William	1770-1819	Gov	35	85			Governor NC. War 1812
Hawks, Frank Monroe	1897-1938	Aero	85	130	325	216	Pioneer Am. Aviator
Hawks, Howard		Ent	108	314		200	Diector-Prod. -Studio Head
Hawley, Joseph R.	1826-1905	Civ War	36	98	120		Union Gen., Gov. CT, Sen CT. Hero. Anti Slavery
Hawley, Steven A.		Space	10			25	
Hawn, Goldie		Ent	15	48	30	56	Actress-Comedianne
Haworth, Jill	1945-	Ent	10			25	Br. Actress
Hawthorn, Alex. Travis	1825-1899	Civ War	212	372	628		CSA Gen.

NAME	DATES	CATEGORY	SIG	LS/DS	ALS	SP	COMMENTS
Hawthorne, Julian	1846-1934	Author	40		225	60	Son of Nathaniel Hawthorne
Hawthorne, Nathaniel	1804-1865	Author	549	766	1860		Novels, Short Stories, US Consul
Hawthorne, Nigel	1929-2001	Ent	10			40	Actor
Hay, Bill (Announcer)		Ent	10	15	20	20	Radio
Hay, John H.		Mil	10		15		
Hay, John Milton	1838-1905	Cab	59	132	228	250	Lincoln Private Sec. ALS/Cont 950 War Dte
Hay, William Henry		Mil	10	15	30		
Hayakawa, Sessue	1889-1993	Ent	108			267	Jap. born actor; Bridge Over River Kwai
Hayashi, Lt. -Gen. Senjuro	1876-1942	Mil	25			50	WWII Jap. Gen.
Hayashi, Shizuya		WWII				45	MOH winner for heroism in Italy
Haydee, Marcia		Ent	10			35	Prima Ballerina in 'The Turning Point'
Hayden, Carl		Congr	10	25		20	MOC, Sen. AZ. 42 Years
Hayden, Charles	1870-1937	Banker	20	45		40	Philan. Hayden Planetarium
Hayden, Mellisa	1969-	Ent	10			25	Actress
Hayden, Nora		Ent	10			25	Actress. 'The Angry Red Planet'
Hayden, Russell		Ent	25			92	Actor. Cowboy Star
Hayden, Sterling	1916-1986	Ent	25	320		125	Reclusive Actor
Hayden, Tom		Congr	10	15		20	MOC CA. Ex-Husband of Jane Fonda
Haydn, Franz Joseph	1732-1809	Comp	2850	15500	24000		Working Draft 4 String Quartets 1. 04 Mil.
Haydon, Benj. R.	1786-1846	Artist		115	232		Br. Historical Painter, Author, Teacher
Hayek, Salma		Ent	15	25		54	Actress-'Desperado', 'Frida', Dir.
Hayes, Allison	1930-1977	Ent	235				Actress; Cult movies
Hayes, Frank K.		Aero	35	55	95	65	ACE, WWI
Hayes, George 'Gabby'	1889-1965	Ent	145	220		637	Western Star. Grizzly 'Sidekick'
Hayes, Helen	1900-1993	Ent	20	40	45	83	Was 1st Lady of Am. Theatre
Hayes, Ira H., Corporal	1923-1955	WWII	615	750		800	Iwo Jima Flag Raising FDC 550
Hayes, Isaac	1942-2008	Music	15			45	Comp. -Singer-Musician Recording Artist
Hayes, Isaac Israel	1832-1881	Expl	72	143	169		Arctic Expl. ALS/Cont 1, 500. War Dte. DS 375
Hayes, Joseph	1835-1912	Civ War	60	157	170	195	Union Gen.
Hayes, Lucy Webb	1831-1889	1st Lady	140		400	752	Mrs. Rutherford B. Hayes; Teetotaller
Hayes, Margaret	1916-1977	Ent	10	20		55	Actress
Hayes, Patrick, Card.	1867-1938	Clergy	35	45	75	50	Founded Catholic Charities
Hayes, Peter Lind	1915-1998	Ent	20			32	Comedian, Actor, Singer/Wife Mary Healy
Hayes, Robin H		Congr	10				Member US Congress
Hayes, Roland	1887-1977	Opera	80	72	175	250	Am. Tenor, Spingarn Medal '25
Hayes, Rutherford B.	1822-1893	Pres	192	471	596	1686	Union Gen. Post Pres. -Pro Education ALS 3500
Hayes, Rutherford B. (As Pres.)		Pres	310	650	1025	3100	ALS/Cont 7, 500, WH Cd. 350-475
Hayes, Rutherford B. (WD)	1822-1893	Civ War	250	775	1356		Union Gen., US Pres.
Hayes, Sean		Ent	10			45	Will & Grace
Hayne, Paul Hamilton	1830-1886	Author	80		562		ALS/Literary Cont. 2, 500. 'Laureate of South'
Hayne, Robert Young	1791-1839	Congr	75		180		Sen. SC, Gov. SC
Haynes, Dick	1911-1980	Ent				40	Actor
Haynes, Linda	1947-	Ent	10			25	Actress
Haynie, Isham Nicholas	1824-1868	Civ War	45		110		Union Gen.
Hays, Alexander	1819-1864	Civ War	192		1380		Union Gen.
Hays, Harry T.	1820-1876	Civ War	198	450			CSA Gen.
Hays, Harry T. (WD)	1820-1876	Civ War	312	1205			CSA Gen.
Hays, Robert		Ent	10			25	Singer-Actor
Hays, Wayne L.		Congr	10	20		15	MOC OH
Hays, Will H.	1879-1954	Cab	50	109		202	Film Czar. Hays Code.
Hays, William	1819-1875	Civ War	50	90	165		Union Gen. ALS '64 385, Sig/Rank 85
Haysbert, Dennis		Ent	15			45	
Hayton, Lennie	1908-1971	Music	20			75	Pianist, Comp., Musical Dir. MGM 1940-53
Hayward, George		Sci	10	20	35	15	

NAME	DATES	CATEGORY	SIG	LS/DS	ALS	SP	COMMENTS
Hayward, Louis	1909-1985	Ent	10	15	25	55	Br. Leading Man. Many Historical Films.
Hayward, Susan	1917-1975	Ent	168	195	380	466	Oscar Winning Actress. Early Death
Hayworth, J. D. H		Congr	10				Member US Congress
Hayworth, Rita	1918-1987	Ent	204	277	343	727	Glamour Star of the 40s
Hazelwood, John	1726-1800	Rev War	100	190	370		Commodore Continental Navy
Hazelwood, Joseph		Captain	10			35	Capt. Exxon Valdez-Oil Spill
Hazen, Wm. Babcock	1830-1887	Civ War	34	55	98		Union Gen. War Dte. DS 150
Head		Music	10			30	Music. Guitars, Vocals 'Korn'
Head, Edith		Ent	82			134	8 Academy Awards. Costume Design.
Headey, Lena		Ent	15			45	
Headle, Marshall		Aero	25	70		85	Lockheed Chief Test Pilot
Headley, Lynne		Ent	13			40	
Headly, Glenne	1955-	Ent	10			25	Actress
Healey, Robert C.		Author	10	15	25		
Healy, George Peter	1813-1894	Artist	105	164	838		Eminent 19th C. Portraitist
Healy, Ted	1896-1937	Ent	132	1188	162	482	Vaude. Song & Dance Man.
Heard, John		Ent	10			35	Actor
Hearn, Lafcadio	1850-1904	Author	300		1200		Irish-Greek-Am. Writer on Jap. Culture
Hearnes, Warren E.	1923-	Gov	10	10		15	Governor MO
Hearst, George	1820-1891	Bus	285		1175		Sen., Father, Wm. Randolph Hearst. S Stk. Cert. 18000-32000
Hearst, Patricia		Celeb	60	172		100	Kidnapped daughter of Hearst, Jr.
Hearst, Phoebe A. (Mrs. Geo.)		Bus	20	40	90		Philanthropies
Hearst, Wm. Randolph	1863-1951	Bus	158	313	553	731	MOC. NY. Powerful Publisher. Pres. Cand. DS 1450
Hearst, Wm. Randolph, Jr.		Bus	10	30	45	20	Son of Hearst, Sr. Newspaper Publisher
Heart		Music	65			110	Rock group; S Guitar 250-470; S Album 150
Heath, Edward	1916-	HOS	30	90	110	50	Br. Prime Min.
Heath, William	1737-1814	Rev War	233	566	1267		Gen. Cont'l Army. DS War Dte. 1275, 1400
Heatherton, Joey		Ent	10	15	20	40	Actress-Dancer-Singer
Heatherton, Ray		Band	20			70	Big Band leader
Heaton, Patricia		Ent	15			40	Everybody Loves Raymond
Heber, Reginald	1783-1826	Clergy	85	100	200		Br. Prelate, Hymn Writer. 'Holy, Holy, Holy'
Hebert, Louis	1820-1901	Civ War	112	258	685		CSA Gen.
Hebert, Louis (WD)		Civ War	202	1115			CSA Gen.
Hebert, Paul O.	1818-1880	Civ War	117	375	437		CSA Gen. Sig/Rank 200
Heche, Anne		Ent	10			40	Actress
Hecht, Ben	1894-1964	Author	25	85		50	AA. Plays, Novels, Newsman
Heckart, Eileen	1919-	Ent	10	10	15	40	Noted Char. Actress of Stage, Film, TV
Heckerling, Amy	1954-	Ent	10			35	Actress
Heckman, Charles A.	1822-1896	Civ War	38	105			Union Gen. ALS (Autobiog.)550, Sig/Rank 50+
Heder, John		Ent	20			60	
Hedin, Sven	1865-1952	Expl	102	170	203	125	Swe. Asian Explr., Geographer
Hedison, David	1927-	Ent	20	65		45	Actor. 'Voyage to Bottom of the Sea'
Hedl, Walter		Comp	15	55	90		AMusQS 175
Hedlund, Garrett		Ent	15			45	
Hedman, Robert Duke		WWII	25	45	75	50	ACE, WWII, Flying Tigers; 6 kills
Hedouville, G. M. T. J, Count		Fr Rev	70	125			Fr. Gen. Marshal
Hedren, Tippi	1930-	Ent	15		25	62	Actress. 'The Birds'
Hedrick, Roger		WWII	15	25	40	35	ACE, WWII; 12 kills
Hefley, Joel H		Congr	10				Member US Congress
Heflin, Howell		Congr	10	15	15	10	Sen. AL
Heflin, James Thomas		Congr	10	20		15	MOC, Sen. AL
Heflin, Van	1910-1971	Ent	32	75	95	212	Actor-Oscar Winner. Versatile. Leads to Westerns
Hefner, Christie		Bus	10	20	30	25	Publisher Playboy Magazine

NAME	DATES	CATEGORY	SIG	LS/DS	ALS	SP	COMMENTS
Hefner, Hugh		Bus	25	285		75	Playboy'TLS/Cont 500; SP w/Bettie Page 600
Heft, Bob		Design	20		25		Designed US 50 Star Flag
Hefti, Neal		Comp	15	35	50	40	AMusQS 195. 'Odd Couple' Theme AMusQS 45
Hegel, Geo. Wilhelm F.	1770-1831	Phil	750	1500	2950		Ger. Idealist Philosopher/Kant
Heggie, Jake		Comp				65	
Heggie, Oliver P.	1879-1936	Ent	608		1150	1940	Char. Actor
Heidegger, Martin	1889-1976	Phil			884		Ger. Existential Phenomonologist
Heidt, Horace 'Musical Knights'		Band	20			40	Big Band Leader. Sigs 12 Members 45
Heifetz, Jascha	1901-1987	Music	175	248		531	Violin Virtuoso., AMusQS 700
Heigl, Katherine		Ent	20			50	Actress
Heimlich, Henry Jay, Dr.		Sci	20	25	45	45	Created Heimlich Maneuver
Heindorff, Hans		WWII		120			Ground attack pilot. 250+ missions. Knight's Cross Recip
Heine, Heinrich	1797-1856	Author	570	4000	6500		Ger. Poet, Critic, Essayist
Heinlein, Robert A.		Author	55	165	350		Sci-Fi Fiction
Heinrich, Albert H.		Aero	35		120		
Heintzelman, Samuel P.	1805-1880	Civ War	36	95	144		Union Gen.
Heintzelman, Samuel P. (WD)		Civ War	45	145	220		Union Gen.
Heinz, Henry John	1844-1919	Bus	110		800	385	Fndr./Bro./Cousin J. Heinz Co.
Heinz, Henry John II		Bus	35				Food Manufacturer
Heinz, Henry John III	1938-1991	Congr	15	30		25	Sen. PA. Air Crash Victim. Heir to Heinz Fortune
Heinze, F. Aug.		Bus	500	2450			Montana Mining Mogul
Heinze, Karl G.		Author	10			15	
Heir, Doug		Celeb	10			20	Wheelchair athlete; Spkr.
Heisenberg, Werner, Dr.	1901-1976	Sci	102	418	675	850	Nobel Physics, ALS/Cont 950
Heiskell, Joesph Brown	1823-1913	Civ War	42		100		Member of CSA Congress
Helbig, Joachim		Aero	10	20	35	25	
Held, Anna	1865-1918	Ent	52	80	135	72	Mrs. Florenz Ziegfield. Star Yiddish Musical
Held, John, Jr.	1889-1958	Comics	165			385	Illust. Created The 'Flapper'
Heldmann, Aloys		Aero		70			Ger. WWI Ace
Heldy, Fanny		Opera	40			110	Opera
Helena, Princess		Royal	15	52	150	65	3rd Daughter Queen Victoria. Fndr. Nursing Home
Helgenberger, Marg		Ent	15			40	Actress
Heller, John R., Dr.		Sci	12	20		20	
Heller, Joseph	1923-1999	Author	15	72	60	40	'Catch 22'
Heller, Walter E.		Bus	10	15		15	Fndr., Chm. Walter E. Heller
Heller, Walter W.		Cab	10	15	30	15	
Helletsgruber, Luise		Opera	25			75	Opera
Hellinger, Mark		Author	35	105	225	40	Columnist, Plays
Hellman, Lillian	1905-1984	Author	60	150		225	Am. Dramatist, 'Little Foxes'
Hellyer, Paul T.	1923-	Celeb	10	20			Canadian Pol. & commentator
Helm, Ben Hardin	1830-1883	Civ War	235	363			CSA Gen. Killed 9/20/63 Battle of Chicamauga
Helm, Briditte	1906-1996	Ent	25			104	Ger. Actress. 1926 Cult Film 'Metropolis'
Helm, Fay	1909-2003	Ent	15			65	Actress
Helmholtz, Hermann L. von	1821-1894	Sci	180		367	500	Ger. Physician/Physicist. Invented Opthalmoscope
Helmick, Robert		Celeb	10			15	Pres. of the US Olympic Committee
Helmond, Katherine	1928-	Ent	10	10	20	35	Actress. Comedy & Straight Leads. TV-Films
Helms, Bobbie		Cntry Mus	85				CW Singer
Helms, Jesse	1921-2008	Congr	10	40		20	US Sen. NC
Helms, Richard		Pol	10	15	45	50	Former head of the CIA
Helms, Susan		Space	10			25	
Helmsley, Leona	1920-2007	Bus	10	25		35	Hotel Magnate
Helper, Hinton R.	1829-1909	Author			270	368	Am. Writer
Helps, Arthur, Sir	1817-1875	Author	10	15	40		Historian
Helton, Percy	1894-1971	Ent	20			265	

NAME	DATES	CATEGORY	SIG	LS/DS	ALS	SP	COMMENTS
Hemingway, Ernest	1899-1961	Author	974	2488	4601	3935	Nobel Lit. Pulitzer., ALS/TLS/Cont 27500; SB 2000-15000
Hemingway, Margaux	1955-1996	Ent	75			266	Actress-Daughter E. Hemingway
Hemingway, Mariel		Ent	15			46	Actress-Daughter E. Hemingway; Important ALS 215
Hemingway, Mary		Author	20	45	85		Mrs. Ernest Hemingway
Hemingway, Wayne		Celeb	10			15	Designer
Hempel, Frieda		Opera	20	35		70	Ger. Sopr., Opera
Hemphill, John	1803-1862	Civ War	117				Member of CSA Congr., Us & CSA Sen.
Hemsley, Sherman	1938-	Ent	10	15	20	35	Actor. 'The Jeffersons'.
Hench, Philip S.	1896-1965	Sci	40	75	150	150	Nobel Med. & Physiology. Cortisone, Hormones
Henderson, Archibald	1783-1859	Mil	65	195	655		Marine Gen. War 1812
Henderson, Don	1932-1997	Ent	10			25	Br. Actor
Henderson, Fletcher		Ent	15			35	Bandleader
Henderson, Florence		Ent	10	15	20	30	Brady Bunch' Mom. Singer-Actress-TV Announcer
Henderson, J. Pinckney	1808-1858	Statsmn	390	422			Gen. TX Army, Gov. TX
Henderson, John Brooks	1826-1913	Congr	25	65			Sen. From MO 1862-69. Frequent Contact/Lincoln
Henderson, Josh		Ent	13			40	
Henderson, Marcia	1929-1987	Ent	10			25	
Henderson, Ray	1896-1970	Music	65				Songwriter; AMusQS 400
Henderson, Shirley		Ent				70	Actress; 'Harry Potter'
Henderson, Skitch		Comp	16			35	Conductor, Bandleader
Hendon, Bill		Congr	10				Congressman NC
Hendricks, Barbara		Opera	10			35	Opera
Hendricks, Thos. A.	1819-1885	VP	60	130	200	350	Cleveland VP, US Sen. IN
Hendricks, William		Congr	10		43		FF 43
Hendrix, Jimi	1942-1970	Music	2378	4006	12800	5456	Leading 'Acid Rock' 60s Singer. S Album 5000
Hendrix, Jimi Experience		Music	3360				Rock Group; S Album 2500-3500
Hendrix, Wanda		Ent	60			140	Actress.
Hendry, Gloria	1949-	Ent	10			25	Actress
Heney, Hugh		Expl	325	750			Scout & Interpretor for Lewis & Clark
Henie, Sonja	1912-1969	Ent	60	82	100	210	Gold in Olympic Figure Skating
Henize, Karl G.	1926-1993	Space	10	15		65	
Henley, Don		Music	25	140		85	Comp., Singer. Eagles
Henley, Thos. Jeff.	1810-1865	Congr	10		30		MOC IN, San Francisco Postmaster
Henley, William Ernest	1849-1903	Poet			120		
Henn, Mark		Comics	10			35	Disney Animator. Little Mermain, Beauty & Beast
Henner, Marilu		Ent	10		20	35	Actress. 'Taxi'
Henreid, Paul	1908-1992	Ent	32	90	60	144	Film Leading Man/Dir. 'Casablanca'
Henri, Robert		Artist	80	175	215		Portr. Painter, Ashcan School
Henricks, Terence T.		Space	10			20	
Henrietta Maria	1609-1669	Royal		3375			Queen Mother of Charles I
Henriksen, Lance	1940-	Ent	10			25	Actor
Henry II (Fr)	1519-1559	Royal	325	854	2250		France
Henry III (Fr)	1551-1589	Royal	250	618	1500		France
Henry IV (Fr)	1553-1610	Royal	212	643	1275		Navarre. Assass.
Henry IV (Sp)	1425-1474	Royal		1675			King of Castile 'The Impotent'
Henry V (Fr)		Royal	40	65	150		Pretender to Throne
Henry VI (Eng)	1421-1471	Royal	850	3500	7250		England
Henry VII (Eng)	1457-1509	Royal	825	6250	9250		
Henry VIII (Eng)	1491-1547	Royal	5500	18000	26000		England. Father of Queen Mary & Elizabeth I
Henry, Bill		WWII	10	25	40	30	ACE, WWII, Navy Ace; 9. 5 kills
Henry, Buck		Ent	10	15	25	30	Actor. Films., writer
Henry, Gloria	1923-	Ent	10			30	Actress
Henry, Gustavous Adolphus		Civ War	52	117			Member of CSA Congress
Henry, John	1750-1798	Rev War	50	135	220		Continental Congress. Sen. MD

NAME	DATES	CATEGORY	SIG	LS/DS	ALS	SP	COMMENTS
Henry, Joseph	1797-1878	Sci	75	160	295		1st Electric Motor. 1st Dir. Smithsonian
Henry, Mike	1964-	Ent	10			35	Am. writer, Prod., voice actor & comedian
Henry, O. (Pseud.) W. S. Porter		Author					SEE William Porter
Henry, Patrick	1736-1799	Rev War	1333	2431	7143		Rev. War Leader, Statesman, ALS/cont 18, 400
Hensarling, Jeb H		Congr	10				Member US Congress
Henschel, George, Sir	1850-1934	Comp	70			150	Br. -Ger. Conductor, Singer
Henshaw, David	1791-1852	Cab	25	55	112		Tyler Sec. Navy. MA Leader Dem. Party 30 Yrs.
Hensley, Dean		Author	10			15	NASCAR, sportswriter
Hensley, John		Ent	15			44	
Henslow, John Stevens		Sci					Botanist. AMS 180
Henson, Jim	1936-1990	Ent	120	325	175	284	Created the Muppets. DS re 'Muppets' 275
Henson, John	1967-	Ent	10			25	Actor
Henson, Matthew A.	1866-1955	Expl	193	350		2500	Arctic Expl. Historical Statement 5000
Henstridge, Natasha		Ent	12			45	Actress
Henze, Hans Werner		Comp	45			165	Ger. Opera, Theater Works
Hepburn, Audrey	1929-1993	Ent	124	274	530	895	AA Winner. Belg. Born Actress-Humanitarian
Hepburn, Katherine	1907-	Ent	192	237	358	932	AA 4 Times. 3x5 SP 650; TLS/Cont 300-500
Hepworth, Barbara, Dame		Artist	70	190		125	Br. Sculptor. Reclining Figure
Herb, Ritts	1952-2002	Photog	15	25		65	Famous Hollywood Photographer
Herbeck, Ray		Band	10			20	Big Band Leader-Sax
Herbert, Caleb Claiborne	1814-1867	Civ War	72	168			Member of CSA Congress
Herbert, F. Hugh		Author	12	20	30	20	Am. Plays, Prod.
Herbert, Frank		Author	15	20	35	20	Am. Sci-Fi. 'Dune Trilogy'
Herbert, Geo. E. (Carnarvon)	1866-1923	Archaeol	32	45	148		With Carter, King Tut Tomb. 5th Earl
Herbert, Hillary	1834-1919	Cab	15	35		30	Sec. Navy Cleveland. Civil War CSA Col.
Herbert, Hugh	1887-1952	Ent	30	45	70	118	Actor. Vaude. -Stage Star. Over 100 Films
Herbert, Victor	1859-1924	Comp	50	148	278	342	'Babes in Toyland'. AMusQS 250-475, Spec SP 1840
Herford, Oliver		Comics	10	25			
Herger, Wally H		Congr	10				Member US Congress
Hergesheimer, Joseph		Author	25	65	145	30	Am. Psychological Novels
Herget, Wilhelm		Aero	20		50		
Hering, Constantine		Sci	15	25	50		1st Homeopathic School
Herkimer, Nicholas		Rev War		3700			Gen. of Militia.
Herkomer, Hubert von, Sir		Artist	25	92	140		Br. Portrait Painter
Herman, Alexis	1947-	Cab	10	20		15	Sec. Labor Clinton
Herman, Jerry		Comp	15	40	65	30	AMusQS 85 'Hello Dolly'
Herman, Pee Wee		Ent	15	15		40	
Herman, Woody	1913-1987	Band	20	35		90	Big Band Leader-Clarinetist
Hermann, Bernard	1911-1975	Comp		547			Music for Movies, Radio. Conductor CBS
Hermann, Hajo		WWII	25	50		58	Ger. Luftwaffe; SB 130
Herman's Hermits		Music	195			275	Popular Brit. Rock Group (5)
Hermine, Schonaich-Carolath		Royal		125		250	Princess. Married Emp. Wilhelm II after 1918 abdication
Herndon, William H.	1818-1891	Law	140	419	525		Law Partner of Abraham Lincoln
Herne, James A.	1839-1901	Ent	15	15	30	50	Actor-Manager
Heron, William	1742-1819	Rev War		1250			Double Agent for Am. s & Br.
Herres, Bob		Space	10			20	
Herrick, Myron T.	1854-1929	Diplo	25	35		45	Ambassador, Gov. OH, Banker. Lindbergh Friend
Herriman, George		Comics	50			525	'Krazy Kat'
Herring, Clyde L.	1879-1945	Congr	10			20	Sen. IA
Herring, John F.	1795-1865	Artist	60		275		Br. Race Horses & Sporting Events
Herring, Thomas	1693-1757	Clergy		125	140		Archbishop York & Canterbury
Herrington, John		Space	10			20	
Herriot, Edouard	1872-1957	HOS	25	65	175		Premier of Fr., Nazi Prisoner
Herriot, James (Wight)		Author	20	40	75	30	'All Creatures Great & Small'

NAME	DATES	CATEGORY	SIG	LS/DS	ALS	SP	COMMENTS
Herrmann, Adelaide		Ent				475	AKA The Queen of Magic; dancer
Herrmann, Adelaide & Alexander		Ent	125			550	Magicians
Herrmann, Bernard	1911-1975	Comp		875			Film Comp.
Herron, Francis J.	1837-1902	Civ War	42	110	160		Union Gen. Wounded, Captured, Exchanged
Herschbach, Dudley, Dr.		Sci	25	35		40	Nobel Chemistry
Herschel, John Fred. Wm., Sir	1792-1871	Sci	81	170	238	1265	Br. Astronomer, Mathematician; son of Sir William
Herschel, William, Sir	1738-1822	Sci	150	475	857		Ger. -Born Br. Astronomer, Discovered Uranus
Hersey, John	1914-1993	Author	20	40	70	60	Bell for Adano'. Pulitzer
Hershey, Alfred D., Dr.		Sci	20	30	45	30	Nobel Med.
Hershey, Barbara	1948-	Ent	15			35	Actress
Hershey, Lewis B.	1893-1977	Mil	15			25	Gen., Selective Service Adm.
Hersholt, Jean	1886-1956	Ent	20		95	98	Char. Actor. Major Star & Humanitarian
Herter, Christian	1895-1966	Cab	15	25		45	Sec. State. Gov. MA. Congressman
Hertz, Alfred		Ent	25			120	Conductor
Hertz, Gustav	1857-1894	Sci	350				Ger. Physicist. Nobel 1925.
Hertz, Heinrich	1857-1894	Sci			1610		
Hervey, Irene	1910-1998	Ent	15			80	Vintage Leading Lady. Films.
Herzberg, Gerhard, Dr.		Sci	25	65		35	Nobel Chemistry
Herzl, Theodor	1860-1904	Zionist	250	1166	2683	2065	Writer-Journalist. Imp. DS 6500-8,000; Imp. ALS 5000-6000
Herzner, Hans-Albrecht	1907-1942	Mil	700				1st Ger. Engaged in Combat WWII
Herzog, Chaim	1918-1997	HOS	35	122	175	75	Pres. Israel. Fndr & Head Mil. Intell. U. N.
Herzog, Otto		WWII		235			Ger. Gen. killed 1945
Herzog, Roman	1934-	HOS	20			60	Pres. of Ger.
Hesburgh, Theodore M., Rev.		Clergy	20	30	75	25	Longtime Pres. Notre Dame
Hess, Myra, Dame	1890-1965	Music	60	95	130	375	Br. Pianist
Hess, Rudolf	1894-1987	WWII	200	617	808	725	Nazi WWII. Second to Hitler. Suicide in Spandau
Hess, Victor F.		Sci	20	30	55	25	Nobel Physics
Hess, Walter R.		Sci	20	30	50	25	Nobel Med.
Hesse, Hermann	1877-1962	Author	195	230	430	419	Ger. Author, Artist, Poet. Nobel Pr.
Hesseman, Howard		Ent	10			35	Actor. 'WKRP-Cincinnati'
Hessen, Philipp Priz von		WWII		85			Pres. Province of Hessn-Nassau; SA Ger. Gen.
Hesse-Nassau, Adolph von		Royal	100	300			1st Duke of Luxembourg
Heston, Charlton	1924-2008	Ent	20			172	Actor; AA
Heth, Henry	1825-1899	Civ War	158	475	812		CSA Gen.
Heth, Henry (WD)		Civ War	300	1172	3820		CSA Gen. Battle of Gettysburg. LS 3000
Heuss, Theodor	1884-1963	HOS	45			95	1st Pres. of Ger. Fed. Repub. 1949-59
Hewes, Joseph	1730-1780	Rev War	2198	3714	8500		Signer Dec. of Indepen.
Hewes, Joseph & John Penn		Rev War		25000			Signers Dec. of Indepen.
Hewish, Anthony		Sci	20	40	85	30	Nobel Physics. Pulsars
Hewitt, Abram S.	1822-1903	Bus	30	60	82		Iron Manufacturer, 1st Open Hearth Furnace
Hewitt, H. K.	1887-1972	WWII	20	50	85		Am. Adm. WWII. Landings at N. Afr., Sicily, S. Fr
Hewitt, Jennifer		Ent	18			53	
Hewitt, Jennifer Love		Ent	20			48	Actress
Hewlett, William R.		Bus	25	70	145	75	SP of Hewlett & Packard 150
Hexum, Jon-Erik	1957-1984	Ent	180	230		339	Actor. Accid. killed himself on TV Series Set
Heydrich, Reinhard	1904-1942	WWII	325	1512	2025	1000	Specialist in Nazi Terror. Assass.
Heydt, Louis Jean	1905-1960	Ent	35			80	Actor
Heyerdahl, Thor	1914-2002	Expl	38	62	110	90	Norw. Ethnologist, Adventurer. 'Kon Tiki'
Heyman, Edward	1907-1981	Music	10			45	Am. musician & lyricist
Heyman, Edward		Author	10	10	25	15	
Heyrovsky, Jaroslav	1890-1967	Sci				300	Czech. Nobel Chemistry 1959
Heyse, Paul	1830-1914	Author	45	135	300		Ger. Poet, Novels, Nobel Literature
Heyward, Dorothy		Author	55	325			Co-writer of 'Porgy'. S Porgy contract 4500

NAME	DATES	CATEGORY	SIG	LS/DS	ALS	SP	COMMENTS
Heyward, DuBose	1885-1940	Author	120	262			Porgy & Bess'. LS/Cont 2, 250
Heyward, Thomas Jr.	1746-1809	Rev War	300	652	1200		Signer Dec. of Indepen.
Heywood, Anne		Ent	10			20	Br. Actress
Heywood, Eddie		Band	35			100	Big Band Leader-Piano
Hiaasen, Carl		Author	10			15	Sick Puppy
Hichens, Robert S.		Author	15	40	150		Br. Novels. 'Garden of Allah'
Hickel, Walter J.	1919-	Cab	10	15	30	15	Governor Alaska, Sec. Interior
Hickenlooper, Andrew		Civ War	30	55	80		Union Gen., Mil. Engineer
Hickenlooper, Bourke B.	1896-1971	Congr	10			20	Governor, Sen. IA
Hickman, Darryl	1931-	Ent	10			45	Actor. Child-Juvenile-Adult
Hickman, Dwayne	1934-	Ent	10			40	Actor. Dobie Gillis
Hickman, Ron		Invent	20	50			Black & Decker. Workmate
Hickok, James B. (Wild Bill)	1837-1876	West			150000		Rare
Hickox, Anthony	1964-	Celeb	10			15	Film industry
Hicks, Catherine	1951-	Ent	10		20	40	Actress
Hicks, Frank		Author	10			12	World II naval history
Hicks, Frederick Cocks		Congr	10	15			MOC NY
Hickson, Joan	1906-1998	Ent				61	English actress of theatre, film & TV
Hidalgo, Miguel y Costilla		Clergy	1525				Mexican Revolutionary & Priest
Hieb, Richard		Space	10			20	
Higginbotham, J. C.		Music	60				Blues-Jazz
Higgins, Andrew Jackson		Bus	25		50		Inventor & Bldr. WWII Higgins Landing Boat
Higgins, Charles		Sci	15	35			
Higgins, Edward	1821-1875	Civ War	125	212	281		CSA Gen.
Higgins, John Michael	1963-	Ent	15			40	Actor
Higginson, Henry L.		Bus	10	20	35		
Higginson, Thos. W.	1823-1911	Author	52	71	120	150	Author/abolitionist/soldier, Col. in Civil War
High Eagle		West				1650	Sioux Indian. Survived Battle of Little Big Horn
Highsmith, Patricia		Author				120	Thrillers
Highwaymen		Ent	335			260	Nelson, Jennings, Jennings, Cash, Kristofferson
Hildebrand, Samuel		Civ War		2750			Quantrill Raider-Murderer. The Missouri Bushwacker
Hildegarde	1906-2005	Ent	10			25	Caberet Singer, Pianist, Entertainer
Hill, Ambrose P. (WD)	1825-1865	Civ War	3500	8500	12488		CSA Gen. KIA 1865
Hill, Ambrose Powell	1825-1865	Civ War	2500	5945			CSA Gen. KIA
Hill, Archibald V.		Sci	25	45		35	Nobel Med. 1922
Hill, Arthur	1922-2006	Ent	10			40	Actor
Hill, Baron P. H		Congr	10				Member US Congress
Hill, Benjamin H.	1823-1882	Civ War	48	90	140	250	S CSA Constitution & GA Secession, Sen. From GA
Hill, Benjamin J.	1825-1880	Civ War	115	1096	352		CSA Gen. Sig/Rank 175
Hill, Benny	1924-1992	Ent	85			114	Br. Comedian
Hill, Dana	1964-	Ent	10			25	Actress
Hill, Daniel H.	1821-1889	Civ War	359	545	655		CSA Gen.
Hill, Daniel H. (WD)	1821-1889	Civ War	600		1996		CSA Gen.
Hill, David B.		Congr	10	15			Governor NY, Sen.
Hill, David Lee Tex		WWII	15	30	45	35	ACE, WWII, Flying Tigers
Hill, Dule		Ent	10			35	Actor; The West Wing
Hill, Edwin C.		Radio	10	15		20	Vintage Radio News-Commentator
Hill, Faith		Cntry Mus	10			66	C & W Singer; S Album 50
Hill, Frank		Comics	10			50	
Hill, George Roy		Ent	10	25	40	50	AA Dir.
Hill, George Washington		Bus	80	220			Am. Tobacco Co., Pres.
Hill, Grace Livingston		Author	25	40	75		Am. Novels
Hill, Isaac	1789-1851	Congr	20	35	65		Governor, Sen. NY
Hill, James J.	1838-1916	Bus	650	2500	3000	950	RR Exec., Financier. Created Great Norther RR

NAME	DATES	CATEGORY	SIG	LS/DS	ALS	SP	COMMENTS
Hill, John F.		Gov	10	15			Governor ME
Hill, Jonah		Ent				40	Actor
Hill, Jonathan A.	1831-1905	Civ War	25	35			Union Gen.
Hill, Lauryn		Music	10			38	Singer. Grammy Winner
Hill, Napoleon		Author	75	300			Think & Grow Rich'. How to Succeed Books
Hill, Octavia		Celeb			100		Philantropist
Hill, Rowland	1744-1833	Clergy	50	75	175		Eng. Evangelist. Ordained. Denied Priestly Orders
Hill, Rowland, 1st Viscount	1772-1842	Mil	35	80	129		Cmdr. in Chief. England. Gen.
Hill, Rowland, Sir	1795-1879	Invent	170	340	692		GB Penny Postage Stamp. Teacher, Soc. Reformer
Hill, Sam		Bus		175	250		Storekeeper. 1st Postmaster New Salem.
Hill, Teresa	1969-	Ent	10			35	Actress;.
Hill, Thomas	1818-1891	Educ	15	20	50		Pres. Harvard, Antioch, clergy
Hill, Walter		Ent	10			20	Film Dir.
Hill, William		Ent	10			25	Actor
Hill, Wm. J. Billy		Comp	30				Last Roundup', ' Wagon Wheels'. AMusQS 175
Hillary, Edmund, Sir	1919-	Adven	104	180	390	298	1st To Climb Mount. Everest
Hillegas, Michael	1729-1804	Rev War	225	645			1st US Treas. 1777. Sugar Refiner, Iron Mfg.
Hillegess, C. K. Cliff		Author	10			25	'Cliff's Notes' Study Helps
Hiller & Diller		Ent				95	Cast SP
Hiller, Arthur		Ent	10			20	Film Dir.
Hiller, Ferdinand	1811-1885	Comp	40	85	125		Ger. Conductor, Pianist, Comp. Operas
Hiller, Frank, Jr.		Aero	75	150	330	160	
Hiller, Wendy, Dame	1912-	Ent	20		35	104	Br. Actress. AA
Hillerich, W. A.		Bus		80			Baseball Bats
Hillerman, John	1932-	Ent	10	15	20	35	Actor
Hilles, Charles D.		Pol	10	25			Chairman G. O. P. 1924
Hillhouse, William	1728-1816	Pol			92		
Hilliard, Harriet		Ent	20			73	Band Singer, Harriet Nelson; S Sheet Mus 60
Hilliard, Henry W.	1808-1892	Civ War	39	80	110		CSA Commissioner to TN
Hilliard, Robert		Ent	20			40	Actor; Won Primetime Emmy
Hillig, Otto		Aero	40	85	150	115	
Hillis, Marjorie		Author	10	10	15		
Hillman, Chris		Music	20			45	Byrds' Co-Fndr.
Hills, Carla	1934-	Cab	10			20	3rd US Woman to hold Cabinet Position.
Hilmers, David C.		Space	10			25	
Hilton, Barron		Ent	10			20	Actor
Hilton, Conrad	1887-1979	Bus	45	96	190	82	Fndr. Hilton Hotel Dynasty
Hilton, James, Sir		Author	35	75	150	125	Lost Horizon', SB 150-450
Hilton, Nicky		Ent	16			48	
Hilton, Paris		Ent	15			46	
Himmler, Heinrich	1900-1945	Mil	333	1489	1650	712	Nazi Head of the Gestapo
Hinchey, Maurice D. H		Congr	10				Member US Congress
Hinckley, Gordon B.	1910-	Relig	35	75	250	75	Pres. of the Mormon Church
Hinckley, John, Jr.		Assass	95	150	207		Attempt on Pres. Reagan's Life
Hincks, Edward W.	1830-1894	Civ War	72	262			Union Gen.
Hindemith, Paul	1895-1963	Comp	110	295	388	475	Ger. Violinist/Teacher/Critic. SP 350. AMusQS 1200
Hindenburg, Paul von	1847-1934	HOS	167	488	950	575	2nd Pres. Weimar Rep. of Ger. Field Marshal
Hindman, Thomas C.	1828-1868	Civ War	338		548		CSA Gen.
Hindman, Thomas C. (WD)	1828-1868	Civ War	425	1028	1025		CSA Gen.
Hines, Cheryl		Ent	10	15	20	45	
Hines, Duncan	1880-1959	Bus	65	300		160	Food Critic. Duncan Hines Cake-Cookie Mix
Hines, Earl K. 'Fatha'		Music	72	142		209	Pianist, Comp., Bandleader
Hines, Frazer		Ent	10			20	Actor
Hines, Gregory	1946-2003	Ent	20	25	25	60	Dancer-Actor. Stage, TV, Films

NAME	DATES	CATEGORY	SIG	LS/DS	ALS	SP	COMMENTS
Hines, Herm		Music	10			25	Jazz Sax
Hines, Jerome		Opera	18			30	Opera, Concert. Basso
Hines, John E.		Clergy	10	15	15		
Hines, Mimi	1933-	Ent	20			30	Singer, Comedienne
Hingle, Pat	1924-	Ent	10			30	Actor. Char.
Hinkley, John		Crime			300		Attempted assassination of Ronald Reagan
Hinks, Edward W.		Civ War	53		75		CSA Gen.
Hinojosa, Rubén H		Congr	10				Member US Congress
Hinshelwood, Cyril N., Sir	1897-1967	Sci	20	45		35	Nobel Chemistry 1956
Hinton, Walter		Aero	35	65	103	80	Pilot of NC-4. MOH
Hippel, Hans Joachim von		Aero	10			35	WWI & II Fighter Pilot. Stunt Flyer
Hirohito		Royal	1500	5100	6200	8108	Japan
Hirsch, Judd		Ent	10	15	20	40	Actor-Comedian.
Hirschfeld, Al		Artist	50		142	250	Artist
Hirshfield, Harry		Comics	15			125	Abie The Agent
Hirshhorn, Joseph H.	1899-1981	Finan		150	225		Art Collector. Donated 4000 works of art
Hirt, Al		Music	10	30		60	Jazz Trumpet. Sextet S 110
Hiss, Alger	1904-1996	Diplo	40	65	238		Figure in Sensational US Spy Case
Hitchcock, Alfred	1899-1980	Ent	304	513	625	802	Self-Caricature S 750-875-1250, Chk 795
Hitchcock, Ethan Allen	1798-1870	Civ War	54	105	148		Union Gen.
Hitchcock, Ethan Allen (WD)	1798-1870	Civ War	68	150	200		Union Gen., Also Author
Hitchcock, Frank H.		Cab	15	30	35	30	Sec. Interior 1898
Hitchcock, Gilbert M.	1859-1934	Congr	10	20		15	Governor NE
Hitchcock, Michael	1958-	Ent	10			30	
Hitchcock, Patricia		Ent				95	Daughter of Alfred
Hitchcock, Raymond	1922-1992	Ent	10			30	Writer
Hitchcock, Thomas	1900-1944	Aero	120			200	Lafayette Escadrille. Greatest US Polo Player
Hitchings, George, Dr.		Sci	20	30	70	35	Nobel Med.
Hite, Les		Music	75			275	Saxophone. 'Hold Tight'
Hitler, A. & Goering, H.		WWII		3200			
Hitler, Adolf	1889-1945	HOS	1212	3482	17000	3744	Spec. DS 9500-18500, DS/Relieving Rommel 35000
Hitler, Adolph & Hess, Rudolf		WWII			1495		
Hittorff, Jacques	1792-1867	Archtct	10	25	40		Fr. St. Vincent de Paul Church.
Hitzfeld, Otto Maximilian		Mil	20			140	Ger. Infantry Gen.
Hix, John		Comics	15	50		60	Author 'Strange As It Seems'
Ho Chi Minh		HOS	810	1782	2000	1667	Vietnam; SB 3570
Ho, Don	1930-2007	Music	10			40	Singer
Hoag, R. C., Major		Space	10			25	
Hoagland, Everett		Music	20			55	Jazz Clarinetist. Bandleader
Hoar, Ebenezer R.	1816-1895	Cab	25		35		US Atty Gen 1869, Grant
Hoar, George F.	1826-1904	Congr	18	20	30		MOC, Sen. MA 1877
Hoban, James	1762-1831	Rev War	255	675			Architect White House, Wash. D. C
Hobart, David	1722-	Rev War		300			Am. Revolutionary War Off.
Hobart, Garret A.	1844-1899	VP	60	152	210	200	VP under McKinley. Banker, Lawyer. D. in Office
Hobart, John Sloss	1738-1805	Congr	25	40	70		Delegate & Sen. NY
Hobart, Rose		Ent	10			45	Actress
Hobbes, Halliwell	1877-1962	Ent	25			203	Vint. Brit. Char. Actor
Hobby, Oveta Culp	1905-1995	Cab	15	25	40	30	1st Sec. HEW
Hobson, David L. H		Congr	10				Member US Congress
Hobson, Edward Henry	1825-1901	Civ War	43	100			Union Gen.
Hobson, Richmond P.		Mil	66	120	160	200	Adm. CMH. Blew up USS Merrimac
Hobson, Valerie		Ent	25			71	Br. Vintage Film Star
Hoche, Louis-Lazare	1768-1797	Fr Rev	205	515			Rose From Corporal to Gen.
Hock, Robt C.		Space	10			20	Skylab

NAME	DATES	CATEGORY	SIG	LS/DS	ALS	SP	COMMENTS
Hockney, David	1937-	Artist	58	65	185	90	S Chk 125
Hodes, Art		Band	10			25	Pianist-Bandleader
Hodge, Al		Ent	25			200	Captain Video
Hodge, Charles		Clergy			300		Exponent & defender of Calvinism in Am.
Hodge, George Baird	1828-1892	Civ War	110	495			CSA Gen.
Hodge, John		Space				100	Control mission
Hodge, Patricia	1946-	Ent	10			30	Br. Actress
Hodgen, Isaac	1779-1832	Clergy		300			Pioneer Baptist preacher; Kentucky pioneer
Hodges, Courtney	1887-1966	Mil	39	70		82	Gen. WWII. Cmmdr. 10th, 3rd, & 1st Armies
Hodges, George H.		Gov	12		15		Kansas 1913-15
Hodges, Johnny		Music	180			250	Blues-Jazz
Hodgkin, Dorothy C.		Sci	25		35		Nobel Chemistry
Hodgson, John		Clergy	20	25	35		
Hodgson, Studholme	1708-1798	Mil		750			Br. Field Marsh. Corres. of Wm. Wildman Barrington
Hodiak, John	1914-1955	Ent	20	25	45	87	Radio Actor until WWII. Leading Roles
Hoe, Richard M.	1812-1886	Indust	90	310	532		Invented Rotary Press
Hoe, Robert	1839-1909	Bus	30	55	95		Improved Hoe Rotary & Art Press
Hoechlin, Tyler		Ent	18			55	
Hoeffel, Joseph M. H		Congr	10				Member US Congress
Hoegh, Leo A.		Gov	10			12	Governor IA
Hoekstra, Peter H		Congr	10				Member US Congress
Hoest, Bill		Comics	10		35	40	'The Lockhorns'
Hoey, Clyde R.		Pol	10	20		15	MOC, Sen., Governor NC
Hoey, Dennis	1893-1960	Ent	75		160	200	Br. Actor. Char. Roles in Br. Films
Hofer, Andreas		Mil		3000			Tyrolean Patriot, executed
Hoff, Philip H.	1924-	Gov	10	15			Governor VT
Hoffa, James R.		Labor	174	350		301	Teamsters Union (disappeared)
Hoffa, Portland	1905-1990	Ent	20			45	Comedienne, Mrs. Fred Allen. Major Radio Star
Hoffer, Eric	1902-1983	Author	25	75	150	190	Am. social writer
Hoffgen, Marga		Ent	10			35	
Hoffman, Abbie	1942-1994	Activist	90	175		125	Chicago 7
Hoffman, Dustin		Ent	30	120	75	70	Actor; AA; Rainman contract S 1150
Hoffman, Harold Giles		Gov	12	30			Governor NJ
Hoffman, Jeffrey A.		Space	10			30	
Hoffman, John Thompson		Gov	10	20	35		Governor NY 1868
Hoffman, Julius		Jurist	38	35	50	210	Controversial. Presided over 'Chicago 7'
Hoffman, Kurt-Caesar		WWII	25			120	Ger. Vice Adm. Cmdr. Of Battleship Scharnhorst
Hoffman, Paul G.	1891-1974	Bus	10	20	35	20	Mfg.:Studebaker Cars. WWII Dir. Marshal Plan
Hoffman, Phillip Seymour		Ent	20			90	Actor; AA
Hoffman, Waldau von	d. 1943	WWII				200	Ger. Cmdr. in North Africa; KIA
Hoffmann, Oswald C. J.		Clergy	10	20	25		
Hoffmann, Peter		Opera	15			55	Opera
Hoffmann, Roald, Dr.		Sci	20	30	45	25	Nobel Chemistry
Hofmann, Albert	1906-	Sci	75	515		475	Swiss Chemist. Identified Psychedelic LSD Effects
Hofmann, Josef	1876-1957	Music	60	212	175	254	Pianist, Comp. AMusQS 300
Hofmannstahl, Hugo von	1874-1929	Author		350			Austrian writer
Hofstadter, Robert		Sci	20	30	45	25	Nobel Physics
Hogan, Brooke		Ent	17			52	
Hogan, Hulk		Ent	15			35	Wrestler
Hogan, Paul		Ent	10	15	25	40	Australian Actor. 'Dundee'
Hogan's Heroes		Ent				750	Signed cast picture
Hogarth, Burne		Comics	25			175	Tarzan-2nd Artist
Hogarth, Wm.	1697-1764	Artist	995	1665	3500		Br. Painter-Engraver. 'The Rakes Progress'
Hogeback, Hermann		WWII	10			40	Ger. Bomber Pilot. RK

NAME	DATES	CATEGORY	SIG	LS/DS	ALS	SP	COMMENTS
Hogendorp, Katharine Harris van		Author	10			12	Red Cross, India
Hogg, Joseph Lewis	1806-1862	Civ War	300	481			CSA Gen.
Hoiris, Holger		Aero	40	85	155	95	
Hoke, Robert Frederick	1837-1912	Civ War	105		350		CSA Gen. ALS '62 625, Sig/Rank 180
Hokinson, Helen		Comics	20			100	Mag. Cartoonist-'The Ladies'
Holbrook, Hal		Ent	10	15	20	40	Actor. Very Versatile Film-TV Roles. 'Mark Twain'
Holbrooke, Richard C.		Pol				20	Diplomat. 1995 Dayton Agreement(Bosnia)
Holcombe, David		Author	10			12	Regional & eductional
Holden, Fay		Ent	20			60	Actress. Many 'Mother' Roles. 'Andy Hardy' Series
Holden, Gloria	1908-1991	Ent				225	Actress
Holden, Joyce		Ent	10			25	Singer-Dancer/Donald O'Connor
Holden, Ronald		Music	15			50	R&B singer; S Album 105
Holden, Tim H		Congr	10				Member US Congress
Holden, William	1918-1981	Ent	120	220		280	Actor. Oscar Winner for 'Stalag 17'
Holiday, Billie	1915-1959	Music	472	1579		1635	Legendary Jazz-Blues Singer
Holladay, Ben	1819-1887	Bus	135	350	925		Indian Trade, Army Contracts, RR, Financier
Holland, Dexter		Music	10			30	Music. Lead Singer 'Offspring'
Holland, Edmund M.		Ent	15			45	Vintage Stage Actor
Holland, John Philip		Invent	70	160	345		1st Sub/Internal Combustion Eng
Holland, Josiah Gilbert	1819-1881	Author	15	30	40		AKA Timothy Titcomb. Co-Fndr. Scribner's
Holland, Spessard L.	1892-1971	Congr	10	20			Governor, Sen. FL
Hollen, Andrea Lee		Mil	10	20	35	20	1st woman graduate, US Mil. Academy West Point
Hollen, Chris Van H		Congr	10				Member US Congress
Holley, Marietta	1836-1926	Author	10	15	35		Am. Humorist
Holley, Robert, Dr.		Sci	15	20	35	20	Nobel Chemistry
Holliday, Frederick W. M.	1828-1899	Civ War	45	85	70		CSA Off., Congress, Gov. VA Sig/Rank 75
Holliday, Judy	1922-1965	Ent	160			301	Academy Award Winning Actress 'Born Yesterday'
Holliday, Polly		Ent	10	12	15	30	Actress. Wise-Cracking 'Flo' in 'Alice'
Holliman, Earl		Ent	10			30	Actor. Supporting Player & Co-Star From 50s
Holliman, John		Jrnalist	10			15	TV News Commentator
Hollings, Ernest 'Fritz'		Congr	10			20	Sen. SC
Hollins, Geo. Nichols	1799-1878	Civ War	275	465			Commodore CSA Navy. Sig/Rank 375. War Dte DS 600
Holloman, Laurel		Ent	15			45	
Holloway, Stanley	1890-1982	Ent	78			85	Br. Char. Actor. Oscar Nominee 'My Fair Lady'
Holloway, Sterling	1905-1992	Ent	25	48		63	Played Country Bumkins, Dim Wits. Disney Voices.
Hollowell, George		WWII	12	25	38	35	ACE, WWII, Marine Ace; 8 kills
Holly, Buddy	1936-1959	Music	879	971	2946	2520	Rock Singer-Songwriter. SP w/Crickets 3500
Holly, Lauren		Ent	12			42	Actress
Hollywood Wives (cast)		Ent				65	Signed by 6
Holm, Celeste		Ent	10	50		50	Broadway Singer-Dancer. Film Actress. AA Winner
Holm, Eleanor	1913-2004	Ent	10			45	Olympic swimmer; appeared in 1 Hollywood film
Holman, Bill		Comics		45			'Smokey Stover'
Holman, Libby		Music	10	35		82	Vintage Torch Singer. TLS/Cont 150
Holman, William Steele		Congr	12	20	30		MOC IN 1859
Holmes, Augusta	1847-1903	Comp	10		85		Ir./Fr. Conventional Fr. Romantic Music
Holmes, Brent		Author	10			12	'The Road Less Gravelled'
Holmes, Burton	1870-1958	Author	15	20	45	30	In 1894 Originated Travelogues
Holmes, Christopher		Space	15	25		25	
Holmes, D. Brainerd		Celeb	10			25	Space Planner
Holmes, Herbie		Band	12			20	
Holmes, John	1944-1988	Ent				260	Porn star
Holmes, John Haynes		Clergy	15	20	30		
Holmes, Katie		Ent	15			65	Actress.
Holmes, Oliver W., Jr.	1841-1935	Sup Crt	169	311	469	882	Thirty Year Supreme Court Veteran

NAME	DATES	CATEGORY	SIG	LS/DS	ALS	SP	COMMENTS
Holmes, Oliver W., Sr.	1809-1894	Author	109	155	316	412	Poet. HOF, ALS/Cont 1, 800. AQS 475
Holmes, Phillips	1907-1942	Ent				140	Actor, Member Canadian Royal AF
Holmes, Robert D.		Gov	10	15		10	Governor OR
Holmes, Theophilus H.	1804-1880	Civ War	190	285			CSA Gen. ALS '62 1100, Sig/Rank 215
Holmquest, Donald L.		Space	10	15		20	
Holshouser, James E.		Gov	10		20	15	Governor NC
Holst, Gustav	1874-1934	Comp	45	175	300		AMusQS 275-1035
Holstrom, E. W. 'Brick'		Mil	15	35	70	25	
Holt, Jack		Ent	40	60	100	82	Actor. Tight-Lipped Hero of Silents & Talkies
Holt, Jennifer		Ent	10			40	Actress. Leading Lady To Several Western Heroes
Holt, Joseph	1807-1894	Cab	53	180	194		Lincoln Judge Adv.
Holt, Joseph (WD)		Civ War	85	265	405		Union Gen. Lincoln's Judge Advocate
Holt, Orrin		Congr	10		34		FF 34
Holt, Rush D.	1905-1955	Congr	10				Member US Congress
Holt, Tim	1918-1973	Ent	45			323	Child-Juvenile-Mature. 'Magnificent Ambersons'
Holt, Victoria		Author	10		15	12	
Holten, Samuel	1738-1816	Rev War	85	195			Patriot, Statesman, Activist. Cont'l Congr.
Holton, Linwood		Gov	10			15	Governor VA
Holtzclaw, James Thadeus	1833-1893	Civ War	130	232			CSA Gen.
Holyoake, Keith, Sir		HOS	45	95	125	50	NZ Prime Min., Gov. Gen. NZ
Holzer, Helmut		Sci	20			40	Ger. Rocket Pioneer/von Braun
Homer, Louise		Opera	35			225	Opera. Am Mezzo.
Homer, Winslow	1836-1910	Artist	330	480	1340		Remarkable Seascapes, Landscapes
Homesteaders, The		Cntry Mus	25			50	
Homma, Masaharu		WWII	75	205	340	180	Jap. Gen. Invasion of Philippines
Homolka, Oscar	1898-1978	Ent	25	30	50	50	Imposing Char. Actor. Ideal Heavy; AA Nomination
Honda, Michael M. H		Congr	10				Member US Congress
Honegger, Arthur	1892-1955	Comp	45	202	381	150	Eminent & Prolific. 'Les Six', AMusQS 575-675
Honeymooners, cast		Ent	388			633	Signed by all 4
Honeywood, Phillip		Mil			368		18th C. Br. Ragoons
Hood, Alexander Sir	1758-1798	Mil	55	135	245		Accompanied Capt. Cook
Hood, Arthur Wm.	1824-1901	Mil	20		105		Adm., 1st Baron Hood of Avalon
Hood, Darla	1931-1979	Ent	134	240		304	Child Actress'Our Gang' Series; Little Rascals
Hood, John Bell	1831-1879	Civ War	332	1700	2402	3000	CSA Gen. ALS '62 18, 150, Sig/Rank400-500
Hood, Samuel, Sir	1762-1814	Mil	35	85	135		Br. Adm. w/Lord Nelson
Hood, Thomas (Elder)	1799-1845	Author	40	140	275		Br. Humorist, Poet
Hood, Thomas, 'Tom'		Author	15	30	70		
Hooft, W. A. Visser't	1900-1985	Clergy	15	20	25	20	
Hook, James Clarke		Artist	25	40	85		Brit. Royal Academy
Hooker, John Lee		Music	92			168	Jazz Musician. Blues Legend. Guitar S 2000
Hooker, Joseph	1814-1879	Civ War	173	379	435		Union Gen. ALS/Cont 4, 500
Hooker, Joseph (WD)		Civ War	240	482	679	1500	Union Gen. ALS 4500
Hooker, Richard		Author	35			60	Creator of M*A*S*H
Hooks, Benjamin L.	1925-	Civ Rts	10	15	25	20	NAACP Exec. Dir. Civ. Rights Leader
Hooks, Kevin	1958-	Ent	10			30	Actor
Hooley, Darlene H		Congr	10				Member US Congress
Hooper, William	1742-1790	Rev War	862	4947	8750		Signer Dec. of Indepen. ADS 3,000
Hooper, William Henry		Congr	10	20	35	35	MOC UT 1859
Hoosier Hot Shots		Ent	40			65	G Ward, Hezzie, K Trietsle, F Kettering. C & W
Hooten, Ernest A.		Sci	25	65	140		Am. Anthropologist. Harvard Prof
Hootie & the Blowfish		Music	50			75	Rock group; S Guitar 300-565; S Album 90
Hoover, Herbert	1874-1964	Pres	92	268	1570	392	Cont. TLS 1300-4950, 2, 500. WH Card S 400
Hoover, Herbert & Cabinet		Pres	250				
Hoover, Herbert (As Pres)		Pres	184	600	33095	501	Historic TLS/Cont 7, 500, Unique DS 4100

NAME	DATES	CATEGORY	SIG	LS/DS	ALS	SP	COMMENTS
Hoover, J. Edgar	1895-1972	Pol	36	90	158	112	Dir. of F. B. I. for 48 Years
Hoover, Lou Henry		1st Lady	72	119	150	162	WH Card S 95-125-150
Hope, Bob	1903-2003	Ent	35	218	50	234	Comedian-Actor-Singer. Stage, Radio, TV, Films
Hope, Leslie		Ent	13			40	
Hopekirk, Helen		Author	15		25		
Hopf, Hans		Opera	25			65	Opera
Hopkins, Anthony		Ent	46	120		91	Br. Oscar Winner. 'Silence of the Lambs'
Hopkins, Antony	1921-	Comp	20		32	42	English Comp. & Broadcaster
Hopkins, Bo	1942-	Ent	10		10	30	Actor
Hopkins, Claude		Band	30			60	Pianist-Bandleader-Comp.
Hopkins, Esek	1718-1802	Mil	180	1200			1st Cmdr-in-Chief Continental Navy
Hopkins, Frederick G., Sir		Sci	45	120	200		Nobel Med. 1929
Hopkins, Harry L.	1890-1946	Cab	26	88		40	Sec. Commerce. Important Advisor-Aide to FDR
Hopkins, James H.	1832-1904	Congr	10		22		MOC. PA. Banker
Hopkins, Johns	1795-1873	Bus	175	371	3575		Financier, Philan. ALS/Cont 3575
Hopkins, Joseph A.	1915-1980	Mil		125	200	750	Mt. Suribachi Flag-ALS 1500
Hopkins, Juliet	1818-1890	Mil		305			CSA nurse
Hopkins, Mark	1813-1878	Bus		18500			Rarest of CA RR 'Big 4'. S Stk. S 35000-65000
Hopkins, Mark	1802-1887	Educ	50	195	275		Inspired Teacher, Lecturer
Hopkins, Miriam	1902-1972	Ent	32	40	70	235	Leading Lady. Ballet to Chorus Girl to Star
Hopkins, Samuel	1721-1803	Rev War	90	280	375		Off. Cont'l Army. Theologian
Hopkins, Stephen	1707-1785	Rev War	213	667	1350		Signer. Gov. RI. Important ALS 6500
Hopkins, Telma		Ent	13			40	
Hopkinson, Francis	1737-1791	Rev War	302	646	2324		Signer, Author, Comp. Designer Am. Flag
Hopkinson, Joseph	1770-1842	Jurist	78	175	200		Consti. Lawyer, MOC PA. 'Hail Columbia'. Son of Francis Hopkinson
Hopper, Dennis	1936-	Ent	15			60	Actor
Hopper, DeWolfe	1858-1935	Ent	20	40	55	75	Actor. Recitations. ALS/Casey at the Bat quote 395
Hopper, Edward		Artist	338	1283	1820		Am. artist
Hopper, Grace		Mil				60	Cmdr. USNR
Hopper, Hedda	1890-1966	Ent	20	35	45	113	Actress. Gossip Columnist. Famous for her Hats
Horch, August	1868-1951	Bus		1595			Ger. engineer & automobile pioneer; Fndr. Audi
Hordern, Michael, Sir	1911-	Ent	10	20	20	30	Br. Char. Actor
Horenstein, Jascha		Cond	60			375	Conductor
Horina, Louise		Opera	15			45	Opera
Hormel, Jay C.		Bus	45	95		75	George A. Hormel & Co. Meat Packing. New Ambass.
Horn, Alfred A. 'Trader'		Expl	70	200			Br. Expl. Ivory Coast. Afr. Rubber Trader
Hornberger, H. Richard		Author	20	30	45	25	
Horne, L. Donald		Bus	10			10	CEO Mennen Co.
Horne, Lena	1917-	Ent	15	25		58	Film Actress & Recording Star
Horne, Marilyn		Opera	15			35	Opera, Concert
Horner, H. Mansfield		Bus	10			10	Aircraft Exec.
Horner, Henry		Gov	10			20	Governor IL
Hornung, Ernest Wm.	1866-1921	Author	50		175		Brother-in-law A. Conan Doyle. Created 'Raffles'
Horowitz, David	1939-	Author	10			20	Am. neoconservative writer & activist
Horowitz, Scott		Space	10			25	
Horowitz, Vladimir	1903-1989	Music	139	235		350	Rus-born Am. Piano Virtuoso
Horrocks, Gen. Sir Brian		Mil	20	25	50	40	Cmdr. XIII Corps WWII
Horrocks, Jane	1964-	Ent	10			30	Actress
Horsford, Eben N.	1818-1874	Sci	15	25	70		Am. Analytical Chemist
Horsley, John Calcott		Artist	40		65		Brit. Royal Academy
Horsley, Lee		Ent	10			25	Actor. 'Matt Houston'
Horthy, Miklos, Adm.	1868-1957	HOS	76	190	485	250	Hungarian Adm. & Pol.
Horton, Edw. Everett	1886-1970	Ent	65	70	70	158	Actor. Delightful Comedy & Char. Leads

NAME	DATES	CATEGORY	SIG	LS/DS	ALS	SP	COMMENTS
Horton, Edward A.		Clergy	15	20	25		
Horton, Johnny		Cntry Mus				190	CW Singer
Horton, Peter		Ent	15			40	
Horton, Robert		Ent	10			60	Actor
Horton, Walter "Shakey"		Music				100	Harmonica player; blues
Hoskins, Allen "Farina"		Ent				368	Our Gang
Hoskins, Bob		Ent	10			40	Actor
Hosmer, Titus	1736-1780	Rev War	40	95	192		Continental Congress. Judge
Hostettler, John N. H		Congr	10				Member US Congress
Hotchkiss, Benjamin J.		Invent	100	295	995		Union Arms Supplier
Hotchkiss, Charles T.	1832-1914	Civ War			85		Union Gen. Atlanta Campaign
Hoth, Col. -Gen. Hermann	1885-1971	Mil	35			178	WWII Ger. Gen.
Houdini, Beatrice	1875-1943	Celeb			300		Wife of Harry
Houdini, Harry (E. Weiss)	1874-1926	Ent	931	2576	3250	3841	Am. Magician, Escape Artist
Hough, Lynn Harold		Clergy	15	20	35		
Houghton, Amo H		Congr	10				Member US Congress
Houghton, Katharine		Ent	30			45	Actress. 'Guess Who's Coming to Dinner?'
Hounsfield, Godfrey		Sci	20	30	45	25	Nobel Med.
Hounsou, Djimon	1964-	Ent	10			45	Actor; born in West Africa
House, Edw. M. 'Col. '		Diplo	35	100	310	45	Confidant of Pres. Wilson
Houseman, John		Ent	20	30		50	Actor/Dir. Stage & Film Writer.
Housman, Alfred Edward	1859-1936	Author	65	225	430		Br. Poet, Classical Scholar
Houssay, Bernando A., Dr.		Sci	65	135	250	100	Nobel Med. 1947. Activist
Houston, David	1938-1993	Cntry Mus	10			35	CW Singer
Houston, George		Congr	35	85			Civil War Sen. AL
Houston, Sam	1793-1863	Tex	631	1142	2396		Pres. Repub. TX. ALS/Cont 6500-9700,. FF 850
Houston, Temple	1860-1905	Lawyer	375		1667	750	Son of Sam Houston; Brilliant lawyer.
Houston, V. S. K.		Congr	10	25	40		MOC HI 1927
Houston, Whitney	1963-	Music	25			60	Singer-Actress
Houston, William C.	1746-1788	Rev War	55		145		Continental Congress.
Hovey, Alvin P.	1821-1891	Civ War	45	90	125		Union Gen., Gov. IN Sig/Rank 95. War Dte. DS 135
Hovey, Charles Edward	1827-1897	Civ War	45	85	120		Union Gen.
Hovhaness, Alan		Comp	70		375		Noted for Orchestral Works
Hovis, Larry	1936-2003	Ent	15			40	Actor. 'Hogan's Heroes'
How, William W., Bish.		Clergy	15	20	25		
Howard, Benjamin		Congr	10				FF 35
Howard, Bryce		Ent	15			45	
Howard, Clint		Ent	17			50	
Howard, Curly (Jerome)	1906-1952	Ent	963			1250	Rarest of the 'Three Stooges'
Howard, Edward, Card.		Clergy	35	50	75		
Howard, Jacob Merritt	1805-1871	Congr	15	30			Civil War MOC & Sen. MI; FF 28
Howard, James H.		WWII	20	30	55	45	ACE, WWII, CMH; Flying Tiger; 6 kills
Howard, John	1913-	Ent	10	20	50	60	Actor. 'Bulldog Drummond'. Navy Hero WWII
Howard, Ken		Ent	10			35	Actor
Howard, Leslie	1890-1943	Ent	239	295	290	375	GWTW. Br. Secret Serv. WWII. SP Pc 200
Howard, Milford W.	1862-1937	Congr	10			10	MOC AL
Howard, Moe	1895-1975	Ent	310	413	419	450	Three Stooges Leader; S Chk 225.
Howard, Oliver Otis	1830-1909	Civ War	61	140	211	600	Union Gen. MOH
Howard, Oliver Otis (WD)	1830-1909	Civ War	145	204	391	1102	Union Gen.
Howard, Robert, Sir	1626-1698	Author	85	325	475		Br. Restoration Dramatist/Dryden
Howard, Ron		Ent	20	40	55	72	Child, Juvenile, Mature Actor & AA Dir.
Howard, Shemp	1891-1955	Ent	414	1532		750	Three Stooges; S Chk 500-650
Howard, Sidney	1891-1939	Author	50	175	338	75	Am. Plays. Pulitzer. Screenwriter from 1929
Howard, Terrance		Ent	15			90	Actor

NAME	DATES	CATEGORY	SIG	LS/DS	ALS	SP	COMMENTS
Howard, Traylor		Ent	14			43	
Howard, Trevor		Ent	27			103	Brit. Actor. Stage, Films. AA Nominated
Howard, Wiley C.		Author	10			12	Civil War history
Howard, Willie	1886-1949	Ent	20			118	
Howe, Albion P. (WD)		Civ War	50	125	510		Union Gen.
Howe, Elias	1819-1867	Sci	200	400	3000		Invented Sewing Machine
Howe, James Wong	1888-1976	Ent	40			65	AA Winning Cinematographer. 'Hud', 'Rose Tattoo'
Howe, Julia Ward	1819-1910	Author	87	187	314	746	Battle Hymn of the Republic'. AQS w/"Mine eyes..." 2500; ALS w/BHR ref. 7000
Howe, Louis McHenry		Pol	10	20			Secretary to FDR
Howe, Richard, Earl	1726-1799	Rev War	175	420	440		Br. Adm. Rev. War. LS/Cont 1500
Howe, Robert		Rev War			2415		Continental Cmdr.
Howe, Samuel Gridley	1801-1876	Med	18	38	95		Philan./MD/Clergy/Reformer. Husb., Julia Ward Howe
Howe, Timothy O.	1816-1883	Cab	15		30		PMG(Arthur). US Sen. WI. Recommended to Lincoln
Howe, William, Sir	1729-1814	Rev War	200	550	900		Cmdr-in-Chief Br. Forces in Am. Colonies
Howell, C. Thomas	1966-	Ent	10		25	45	
Howell, Joshua Blackwood	1806-1864	Civ War	60	250			Union Gen.
Howells, William Dean	1837-1920	Author	35	75	146	391	Novels, Critic, Editor
Howes, Barbara		Author	10	10	20	10	
Howey, Steve		Ent	16			48	
Howland, Beth		Ent	10			25	Actress. TV-'Beth on 'Alice'
Howley, William	1766-1848	Clergy	25	35	40		Archbishop Canterbury
Howlin, Olin	1886-1959	Ent	45			70	Actor. 'GWTW' Collectible
Hoxie, Al	1901-1982	Ent	45			101	Actor. Westerns. Silents & Few Talkies
Hoxie, Jack	1885-1965	Ent	150				Actor-Cowboy Star in Silents & Early Talkies
Hoyer, Steny H. H		Congr	10				Member US Congress
Hoyle, Edmond	1671-1769	Author	145	675	785		Card Games. Established Rules
Hoyt, John W.		Gov	50	85			Gov. WY Terr., 1st Pres. U. WY
Hruska, Roman		Congr	10	15		10	MOC, Sen. NE
Hu, Kelly		Ent	13			40	
Hubbard, Chester D.	1814-1891	Congr	10	15	30		MOC WW
Hubbard, Elbert	1856-1915	Author	50	195	275	127	Roycrofters. 'Message to Garcia'
Hubbard, Gardiner G.	1822-1897	Celeb	30	55	170		Fndr. & 1st Pres. Nat'l Geographic Society
Hubbard, L. Ron	1911-1986	Author	57	101			Religious Activist. Scientology, Dianetics
Hubbard, Richard B.		Gov		150			Gov. TX 1876-79
Hubbard, Richard Dudley		Congr	10				FF 38
Hubbard, Thomas H.	1838-1915	Civ War	35	50			Union Gen. 30th ME
Hubble, Edwin P.	1889-1953	Sci	20	80		65	Am. Astronomer. 'Hubble Telescope' Named For Him
Hubel, David H., Dr.		Sci	20	30	45	25	Nobel Med.
Huber, Oscar, Fr.		Celeb	20		30		
Huberman, Bronislaw		Music	75				Violinist
Hubley, Adam		Rev War	75	300			Off. Cont. Army. Pol.
Hubner, Herbert		Opera	25			75	Vintage Ger. opera star
Huddleston, George		Congr	10	15		15	MOC AL 1915-1937
Hudson, Charles	1795-1881	Congr	10				MOC MA, Author Religious Textbooks
Hudson, George	1800-1871	Finan	20	50	175		Controlled 1,000 Miles Railrd. 'Railway King'
Hudson, Jennifer		Ent	22			65	Actress; AA
Hudson, Kate		Ent	15	113		50	
Hudson, Rochelle	1914-1972	Ent	25	30	50	55	Actress. Versatile Leading Lady of 30s Films.
Hudson, Rock	1925-1985	Ent	93	259	118	228	Actor
Hudson, W. H.	1841-1922	Author		135	495		Green Mansions'; Naturalist.
Hudson, William Henry		Celeb		120			Educator
Huemer, Dick		Comics	15			100	Disney Artist
Huerta, Victoriano	1854-1916	Revol	75	250	625	250	Mex. Gen., Pol. Provincial Pres. Exiled

NAME	DATES	CATEGORY	SIG	LS/DS	ALS	SP	COMMENTS
Huffington, Arianna		Celeb	10			25	Huffington Post
Huffman, Felicity		Ent	10			50	Actress. AA
Hufstedler, Shirley		Cab	10	10	15	15	Sec. Education
Huger, Benjamin	1805-1877	Civ War	100	302	399		CSA Gen.
Huger, Benjamin (WD)		Civ War	190	750			CSA Gen.
Huger, Isaac	1743-1797	Rev War	110	240	712		Gen. Continental Army
Huggins, Charles, Dr.		Sci	25			35	Nobel Med.
Huggins, Roy	1914-1996	Ent	20			30	TV Prod. -Writer. 'Fugitive'
Huggins, William, Sir	1824-1910	Sci	35	100	225	150	Br. Astron. Stellar Spectroscope
Hughes, Carol	1910-1995	Ent	12			40	Actress
Hughes, Charles E.	1862-1948	Sup Crt	42	129		239	Chief Justice, Sec. of State. TLS/Cont 750
Hughes, Coe D.		Author	10			12	Regional history
Hughes, Edwin H., Bish.		Clergy	20	25	40	35	
Hughes, Harold E.	1922-	Congr	10			20	Sen. IA
Hughes, Holly		Ent	10			20	Actress
Hughes, Howard	1905-1976	Bus	1101	2283	4553	2593	Aircraft, Oil Tools. RKO Films. Flight Cov S. 2900
Hughes, Hugh Price		Clergy	15	20	25	20	
Hughes, John	1797-1864	Clergy	25		248		1st Archbishop NY. Laid Cornerstone St. Pat's
Hughes, Langston	1902-1967	Author	166	330	815	575	Poet, Short Story Writer
Hughes, Mary Beth	1919-1995	Ent	15			100	Actress. Supporting Parts & Leads. 40s to 70s
Hughes, Nerys		Ent	10			20	Actress
Hughes, Richard	1909-1992	Rev War	50	95			Br. Adm. during Rev. War
Hughes, Richard J.		Gov	10	15			Governor NJ
Hughes, Rupert		Author	20	50	95		Poet, Author, Historian
Hughes, Sarah T.		Law	60	70	75	75	Fed. Judge Swore In L. B. Johnson 1963
Hughes, Thomas	1822-1896	Author	42		164		Tom Brown's School Days'. Social Reformer
Hug-Messner, Regula		Aero	15	30	50	35	
Hugo, Victor	1802-1885	Author	226	372	1518	1100	Novels/Pol./Poet; S poem 1700; AQS 1500; ALS w/Les Mis reference 8100
Huidekoper, Henry		Civ War	60				Union Col., 'Bucktails'
Hulbertson, Josh		Ent	15			45	
Hull, Cordell	1871-1955	Pol	65	135		96	Nobel Peace, Sec. State., Fed. Inc. Tax, FDR Cab.
Hull, Henry	1890-1977	Ent	55	55		84	Actor
Hull, Isaac	1773-1843	Mil	168	340	618		Cmdr. USS Constitution 1812. Naval Hero 1812
Hull, J. E.		Mil	25				Gen.
Hull, Josphine	1884-1957	Ent	150		205	533	Celebrated Stage Char. Actress. AA 'Harvey'
Hull, Warren	1903-1974	Ent	25			50	Singer-Actor. Comic-strip Heroes. Radio & TV MC
Hull, William		Mil	145	370	770		Revolutionary War Gen.
Hulse, Tom		Ent	10	15	20	40	Actor. 'Amadeus'
Hulshof, Kenny C. H		Congr	10				Member US Congress
Humbard, Rex		Clergy	10	15	15	15	
Humboldt, Alex., Baron von	1769-1859	Sci	84	125	267		Ger. Naturalist & Traveller
Hume, Benita	1906-1967	Ent	15			45	Br. Actress. Stage & Films. Wife of Ronald Colman
Hume, Brit		Celeb	10			20	Media/TV personality
Hume, John	1937-	Pol				50	Fndr. Soc Dem & Labour Party; 1998 Nobel Peace
Hume, Joseph	1777-1855	Pol	20	32	80		Br. Physician. Radical Pol.
Hume, Mary-Margaret		Ent	10			20	
Humes, William Young C.	1830-1882	Civ War	168	235	557		CSA Gen. Sig/Rank 165, War Dte. DS 415
Hummel, Johann Nepomuk	1778-1837	Comp	150	190	725		Hung. -Born Child Prodigy. Piano Virtuoso
Humperdinck, Engelbert		Music	10	10	20	40	Contemporary Vocalist
Humperdinck, Engelbert	1854-1921	Comp	115	225	247	242	AMusQS 450-675-950
Humphrey, George M.		Cab	10	20			Sec. Treasury
Humphrey, Hubert H.	1911-1978	VP	35	74	110	67	V. P. & '68 Pres. Cand., MN Sen.
Humphrey, Muriel	1912-1998	Congr	10	20		20	Sen. MN. Replaced Husband, Hubert as Sen.

NAME	DATES	CATEGORY	SIG	LS/DS	ALS	SP	COMMENTS
Humphreys, Andrews A.	1810-1883	Civ War	44	160	253		Union Gen Sig/Rank 100
Humphreys, Benjamin G.	1808-1882	Civ War	70				CSA Gen.
Humphreys, David		Rev War	55	150	200		ADC Washington. Poet, Diplomat
Hungerford, Cy		Comics	10			30	
Hungerford, Orville	1790-1851	Congr	15	45			MOC NY, W & R RR Pres.
Hunnicutt, Arthur	1911-1979	Ent	15			45	Stage Actor. Film Char. Parts From Early 40s
Hunt, Bonnie		Ent	10			40	Actress
Hunt, E. Howard		Official	15	25	90	25	21 Yr. Vet./CIA. Watergate
Hunt, Earl, Bish.		Clergy	20	25	35	25	
Hunt, George W. P.		Gov	15	35			Governor AZ
Hunt, H. L.	1889-1974	Bus	57	147	254	162	TX Oil King. Arch Conservative
Hunt, Helen		Ent	25			71	Actress, AA
Hunt, Henry Jackson	1819-1889	Civ War	60	80	140		Union Gen. Gettysburg.
Hunt, Henry Jackson (WD)	1819-1889	Civ War	90	186	1056		Union Gen.
Hunt, James B. Jr.		Gov	10	10			Governor NC
Hunt, James Bunker		Bus	10	15	35	15	Son of Oil Magnate H. L. Hunt
Hunt, John, Lord	1910-1998	Pol	25	40	75		Leader 1st Successful Everest Exped. 1953
Hunt, Leigh	1784-1859	Author	30		40		Br. Essayist, Poet
Hunt, Lewis Cass	1824-1886	Civ War	58	80	120		Union Gen.
Hunt, Linda	1945-	Ent	20			75	AA Winning Char. Actress.
Hunt, Marsha	1917-	Ent	10	12	20	47	Powers Model. Actress Since mid-30's
Hunt, Nelson Bunker		Bus	10	20	40	15	Son of Oil Magnate H. L. Hunt
Hunt, Pee Wee		Music	15			45	Trombone-Vocalist
Hunt, Ward		Sup Crt	65	80	175		1872
Hunt, Washington		Gov	35		60		MOC 1842, Governor NY 1850
Hunt, William H.		Cab	15	30	60	25	Sec. Navy 1881
Hunt, William Holman	1827-1910	Artist	55	165	247		Br. Pre-Raphaelite Painter
Hunt, William Morris	1824-1879	Artist	50	215	500		Am. Portraitist
Hunt, Willie P.		Gov	40			100	1st Governor of Arizona
Hunter, C. Bruce		Author	10			12	Masonic history/ritual
Hunter, David		Civ War	85	154	172	257	Union Gen.
Hunter, David (WD)	1802-1886	Civ War	102	656	385		Union Gen.
Hunter, Duncan H		Congr	10				Member US Congress
Hunter, Holly		Ent	20			50	AA Actress. 'The Piano' SP 75
Hunter, Howard W.	1907-1995	Relig	100	250	1000	150	Pres. of the Mormon Church; SB 300
Hunter, Ian		Music				55	Mott the Hoople
Hunter, Jeff	1925-1969	Ent	80	90	100	240	Actor. 'Star Trek' Capt. For Short Time
Hunter, Kim		Ent	10	35		43	AA. 'Stella', 'Planet of the Apes'
Hunter, Rachel		Model	17			50	Model
Hunter, Robert		Rev War	220	508	1035		Br. Gen. Colonial Gov. VA, NY
Hunter, Robert M. T.	1809-1887	Civ War	110	175	192		CSA Sec. State. US Sen. ALS '63 360; FF 33
Hunter, Ross	1921-1995	Ent	25			35	Actor turned Prod. 'Pillow Talk' etc
Hunter, Tab	1931-	Ent	60			106	Actor
Hunter, William	1774-1849	Diplo	55	80	125		Statesman, Sen. RI
Huntington, Agnes		Opera	25			150	Am. & Brit. Productions
Huntington, Benjamin	1736-1800	Rev War	60	175	275		Continental Congress
Huntington, Collis P.	1821-1900	Bus	120	603	950	950	Am. RR Pioneer., S RR Pass 9500, ALS/Cont 4500
Huntington, Daniel		Artist		155	250		Portrait Painter
Huntington, Ebenezer		Rev War	110	250	380		Statesman, Army Gen.
Huntington, Henry E.		Bus	98	119	200		RR Magnate. Huntington Library, San Marino,
Huntington, Jabez	1719-1786	Rev War	150	326			Maj. Gen. Militia. Merchant. Yale. Legislature
Huntington, Jabez W.		Congr	20	30	45		MOC 1829, Sen. CT 1840
Huntington, Jedediah	1743-1818	Mil	75	149	407		Gen. Am. Cont. Army. Collector of Customs
Huntington, Samuel	1731-1796	Rev War	268	1042	1169		Signer Dec of Ind Pres. Cont. Congr. AL/Cont 8625

NAME	DATES	CATEGORY	SIG	LS/DS	ALS	SP	COMMENTS
Huntington, Theo. Hastings	1650-1701	Royal	75		185		7th Earl. Lord Lt. Leicester & Derby. Treason
Huntley, Chet	1911-1974	Jrnalist	30			100	Longtime TV News Anchorman/David Brinkley
Hunton, Eppa	1822-1908	Civ War	116	270	298		CSA Gen. Sig/Rank 195
Huppert, Isabelle	1955-	Ent	10			42	Actress
Hurd, Peter		Artist	85	225	362		Painter. His LBJ Portrait Rejected by LBJ
Hurd-Wood, Rachel		Ent	32			95	
Hurlbut, Stephen A. (WD)	1815-1882	Civ War	70	135	504		Union Gen., ALS/Cont 2200
Hurlbut, Stephen Augustus	1815-1882	Civ War	40	90	130		Union Gen.
Hurley, Charles F.		Gov	12	25			Governor MA
Hurley, Elizabeth		Ent	15			50	Actress-Model
Hurley, Patrick J.	1883-1963	Cab	15	45	60	25	Sec. War, Hoover
Hurrell, George		Photog	15	50			Hollywood. 16x20 Ltd. Ed. Dietrich 1200
Hurst, Fannie	1889-1968	Author	25	35	60	50	Popular, Sentimental Novels
Hurst, Lee	1962-	Celeb	10			20	Br. Comedian
Hurston, Zora Neale	1901-1960	Author	145		750		Am. Writer, Folklorist. Black Culture
Hurt, John		Ent	14	20	25	77	Br. Actor. Offbeat Chars. 'Harry Potter'
Hurt, Mary Beth	1948-	Ent	10			33	Actress
Hurt, Mississippi John		Music	440				Legendary blues player
Hurt, William		Ent	20	25	50	62	Actor. AA 'Kiss of the Spider Woman'
Hurwitz, Hank, Dr.		Sci	20			35	Atomic Scientist
Husa, Karel		Comp	15	40	65		Pulitzer, AMusQS 150
Husak, Gustav		HOS	30			100	Pres. Czechoslovakia. Communist Hard Liner
Husband, Rick		Space	120	150		235	Perished on Space Shuttle Columbia re-entry 2003
Huskisson, William		Celeb			75		Statesman
Husky, Ferlin		Cntry Mus	10			20	Singer-Comedian. AKA Terry Preston, Simon Crum
Hussein I, King	1935-1999	Royal	92	165	385	337	King of Jordan. Hussein I & Queen Noor SP 675
Hussein, Saddam		Pol	125	267		200	Iraqi leader
Hussey, Olivia		Ent	10			35	Actress. 'Romeo & Juliet. Br. & Intl. Film
Hussey, Ruth	1911-2005	Ent	15			40	Actress. 'Philadelphia Story'. Leading Lady: 40's
Huston, Anjelica		Ent	10	40		42	AA Winning Actress. Daughter of John Huston
Huston, Danny		Ent	22			65	
Huston, John	1906-1987	Ent	40	50	50	110	AA Film Dir. -Actor
Huston, Walter	1884-1950	Ent	65	75	130	127	AA Winning Actor. 'Treasure of the Sierra Madre'
Hutchence, Michael	1960-1997	Music	25	95		136	Lead singer of the Band INXS
Hutcherson, Josh		Ent	15			45	
Hutchins, John		Congr	10				FF 41
Hutchins, Robert E.	1925-1945	Ent	495			2300	Wheezer in the Little Rascals
Hutchins, Will	1932-	Ent	10	15		45	Actor. 'Sugarfoot'
Hutchinson, Frederick Sharpe		Civ War	35		130		Union Gen.
Hutchinson, John W.		Comp	15		50		
Hutchinson, Josephine	1904-1998	Ent	10	15	25	85	Actress. Child/Mary Pickford. Films from '34
Hutchinson, Thomas	1711-1780	Colonial	168	695	320		Am. Colonial Administrator. Royal Gov. MA. Exiled
Hutchison, Kay		Congr	10			20	US Senate (R-TX)
Hutton, Betty	1921-2007	Ent	22			164	Actress-Singer of 40s Genre
Hutton, Gunilla	1944	Ent	10			25	Actress
Hutton, Ina Ray		Band	20			90	All-Girl Big Band Leader
Hutton, Jim	1933-1979	Ent	40	70	110	100	Actor, Leading Man. Timothy's Father
Hutton, Lauren		Ent	10			45	Model/actress
Hutton, Marion	1919-1987	Ent				60	Singer; older sister to Betty
Hutton, Robert		Ent	20	40	110	65	Actor
Hutton, Timothy		Ent	18	20		42	AA Winner
Huxley, Aldous	1894-1963	Author	75	258	438	350	Br. Novels. 'Brave New World'. TLS/Cont 1, 200
Huxley, Julian Sorell	1887-1975	Author	30	70	142		1st Dir., UNESCO; founding mbr. World Wildlife Fund. Knighted 1958.

Sanders Autograph Price Guide

NAME	DATES	CATEGORY	SIG	LS/DS	ALS	SP	COMMENTS
Huxley, Leonard	1860-1933	Author	20		75		Biographer, Poet. Son of Julian Huxley
Huxley, Thomas Henry	1825-1895	Sci	52	150	209		Br. Biologist
Hyacinthe, Pere	1827-1912	Clergy	50	1130	650	200	(Charles Loyson) Controversial Catholic Priest
Hyams, Leila	1905-1977	Ent	40	45	50	235	Leading Lady of 20s-30's
Hyatt, Missy		Ent	17			50	
Hyde, Arthur W.		Cab	10	15	30	15	Sec. Agriculture 1929
Hyde, Douglas		Pol		90			Fisrt Pres. of Ireland
Hyde, Edgar R.		Clergy	10	10	15		
Hyde, Henry J. H	1924-2007	Congr	10			20	Member US Congress
Hyde, Herbert L.		Author	10			12	N. C. State Sen./author
Hyde, Jonathan	1974-	Ent	10			25	Actor
Hyder, Scott		Author	10			12	Mountain poetry
Hyde-White, Wilfrid	1903-1991	Ent	20	25	35	73	Brit. Char. Actor
Hyer, Martha	1924-	Ent	15			103	Actress. Oscar Winner
Hylton, Jack	1892-1965	Band	20			70	Major Br. Bandleader
Hylton, Lord		Pol	10	15	25		Chief Whip Unionist Party
Hyman, Earle	1926-	Ent	10			30	Actor
Hynde, Chrissie		Music	25			40	Rock. 'The Pretenders'
Hyndman, Henry Mayers	1842-1921	Pol	75		350		Br Marxist-Socialist. Interesting Pol. Career
I Remember Mama (cast 5)		Ent	125			395	50's Popular TV Program
Iacocca, Lee A.		Bus	15	50		35	CEO Ford, Chrysler Motors
Ian, Janis		Ent	10	50	85	45	Singer-Actress
I'Anson, Lisa		Music	10			20	DJ
Ibert, Jacques-Francois		Comp	75		325	160	AMusQS 450-500
Ibsen, Henrik	1828-1906	Author	350	562	1231	2089	Nor. Poet/Dramatist. 'Peer Gynt', 'Doll's House'
Icart, Louis	1888-1950	Artist	115		875		Fr. Art Deco Painter-Illusrator
Ice Cube		Music	15			45	Rapper, actor, writer
Ice T		Music	20			35	Rock. Rapper
Ickes, Harold L.	1874-1952	Cab	20	35	65	30	Roosevelt Sec. Interior
Idle, Eric		Ent	10			45	Actor; SB 60
Idol, Billy		Music	10			65	Rock Star; S Album 65
Ifans, Rhys		Ent	17			50	
Iglesias, Enrique		Ent	20			55	
Iglesias, Julio		Music	15			45	Singer
Iha, James		Music	10			30	Music. Guitar 'Smashing Pumpkins'
Ihlefedl, Herbert		Aero	25	55		60	
Ikeda, Hayato		HOS	15		65		Japan
Iler, Robert		Ent				35	Anthony Sopr. Jr.
Iman		Model	15			50	Model
Imboden, John Dan'l	1823-1895	Civ War	175	288	435		CSA Gen.
Imboden, John Dan'l (WD)		Civ War	375	810	2415		CSA Gen. Spec'l ALS 4500
Imbruglia, Natalie		Music	18			48	Rock
Immelmann, Max		WWII	200	425	700	500	ACE, WWII, 1st Ger. Ace
Impellitteri, Vincent	1900-1987	Pol	10			20	Mayor of NYC
Imperioli, Michael		Ent	15			45	Actor; Christopher Moltisanti, Sopranos
Impressions		Music	50	80		100	Rock group:
Imus, Don		Ent	10			30	Talk show host
Ince, Thomas H.		Ent	40			125	Film Dir. Civil War Epics
Indecent Proposal (cast)		Ent				110	Douglas/ Moore
Indelicato, Mark		Ent	13			40	
Indiana, Robert		Artist	45	95	170	118	Colorful Contemporary Artist.
Ingalls, John James	1833-1900	Congr	30	60	85		Sen. KS
Ingalls, Laura		Aero		295			Pioneer. 1st Non-Stop Transcontinental Flight
Ingalls, Rufus	1818-1893	Civ War	34	105	211		Union Gen., Explr.

NAME	DATES	CATEGORY	SIG	LS/DS	ALS	SP	COMMENTS
Ingalls, Rufus (WD)	1818-1893	Civ War	60		525		Union Gen., Explr.
Inge, Samuel Williams		Congr	10				FF 25
Inge, William R.		Clergy	50	100	105		Br. Prelate. Gloomy Dean St. Paul's Cath., Writer
Ingels, Marty		Ent	10			35	
Ingersoll, Charles J.	1782-1862	Congr	20	25	50		MOC PA 1813
Ingersoll, Charles R.		Gov	10	15	25		Governor CT
Ingersoll, Jared	1749-1822	Rev War	75	194	325		Continental Congr., Constitution Signer
Ingersoll, Ralph Isaacs		Congr	10		38		FF 38
Ingersoll, Robert Green		Celeb	30	65	58	110	Agnostic Lecturer, Orator
Ingersoll, Robert H.		Bus	80	175	300	225	Ingersoll 1 Watch
Ingersoll, Royal E.		Mil	80	135		175	Adm. & Cmdr. of Atlantic Fleet WWII
Ingham, Samuel D.	1779-1860	Cab	35	120	96		Sec. Treasury 1829; FF 47
Ingle, Red	1906-1965	Music	25			80	Am. musician, singer & writer
Ingle, Robert P.		Bus	10	15	25	20	Ingles Grocery Chain
Inglis, James		Bus	10	20			Mfg.
Ingraham, Duncan N.		Civ War		127	215		CSA
Ingraham, Duncan N. (WD)		Civ War	172		1100		Capt. CSA Navy
Ingraham, Porter	1810-1893	Civ War	40				Member of CSA Congress
Ingram, Rex	1895-1969	Ent	60	120	90	255	Vintage Actor
Ingres, Jean-Aug. -Dom.		Artist	205		750		Fr. Leader Among Classicists
Ingrid, Victoria, Queen		Royal	20	40			Queen of Frederick IX (Denmark)
Inhofe, James		Congr	10				US Senate (R-OK)
Ink Spots, The (4)		Music	157			208	Vintage Singing Group. (All Four Sigs.)
Inman, Henry	1801-1846	Artist	110	305	650		Am. Portraitist. ALS/Cont 1250
Inman, Jerry		Cntry Mus	10			20	
Innes, Roy	1934-	Activist	15	15		25	Afr. -Am. Activist. Civ. Rights. Pres. CORE
Inness, George	1824-1894	Artist	75	225	690		Am. Landscape Painter. ALS/Cont 950
Inouye, Daniel		Congr	10			20	US Senate (D-HI)
Inskeep, Jonathan		Rev War	80	175			
Inslee, Jay I		Congr	10				Member US Congress
Insull, Samuel	1859-1938	Finan	132	975	1300		Pvt. Sec. Edison. Utilities Baron. TLS/Cont 685
International, Dana	1972-	Music	10			20	Israeli, pop singer
INXS		Music	70			251	Rock group; S Album 125
Ionesco, Eugene	1912-1994	Author	40	145	225	55	Romanian-Fr. Dramatist. Theatre of Absurd. AQS 700
Ireland, Jill	1936-1990	Ent	25			65	Actress
Ireland, John	1879-1962	Comp			500		English Comp.
Ireland, John	1914-1992	Ent	10			80	Actor
Ireland, John M. F		Gov	40	150			Gov. TX 1883-87
Ireland, Kathy		Model	20			50	Super model
Irish, James M.		Mil	10	30	50		
Irons, Jack		Music	10			30	Music. Drummer 'Pearl Jam'
Irons, Jeremy		Ent	10		25	40	Br. Actor
Ironside, Michael	1950-	Ent	10			35	Actor
Irvin, James	1800-1862	Congr	18		35		Repr. PA, Merchant, Miller, Miner
Irvine, James	1735-1819	Rev War	55	265	250		Gen. Militia. Cmdr. Fort Pitt
Irvine, William	1741-1804	Rev War	125	275	425		Gen., Continental Congress
Irving, Amy	1953-	Ent	10			35	Actress
Irving, Clifford		Author	13	30	50	40	
Irving, Edward	1792-1834	Clergy	100		375		Fndr. 'Catholic Apostolic Church'
Irving, Henry, Sir	1838-1905	Ent	48	82	137	139	Vintage Actor-Manager. LS by Bram Stoker 225
Irving, John		Author	13	15	30	68	Am. 'The World According to Garp'
Irving, Washington	1783-1859	Author	220	362	766		Am. Essayist. 'Rip Van Winkle'
Irwin, Bill	1950-	Ent	10			30	Tony award winner
Irwin, James B. 'Jim'	1930-1991	Space	54	111	190	269	Moonwalker; Chk 100; SP in WSS 1125

NAME	DATES	CATEGORY	SIG	LS/DS	ALS	SP	COMMENTS
Irwin, May	1862-1938	Ent	25		35	60	Vintage Stage Actress. 1st Film Kiss
Irwin, Noble E.	1869-1937	Mil	55	150			USN Adm. 1st Dir. Naval Aviat., Trans-Atl. Flight
Irwin, Will	1873-1948	Jrnalist			40		War Correspondent, Author
Isaacs, Jason		Ent	10			30	
Isaak, Chris		Music	30			50	Rock; S Album 60
Isabella I, Of Castile	1451-1504	Royal	850	2764	6500		Queen Spain. Columbus' Patron; DS w/FerdiMand 6625
Isabella II	1830-1904	Royal	175	268	730		Spain. Strife, Intrigue. Abdicated
Isabey, Jean-Baptiste	1767-1855	Artist		115	350		Court Painter to Napoleon & Bourbons
Isakson, Johnny I		Congr	10				Member US Congress
Ish Kabibble (Merwyn Bogue)		Ent	15			30	Novelty Singer, Kay Kyser Band
Isherwood, Christopher	1904-1986	Author	40	70	95	140	Br. -Am. Novels, Plays
Ishiguro, Kazuo		Author	15			40	'Remains of the Day'
Isken, Edward		WWII	15			35	Ger. Air Ace w/56 Victories
Isley Brothers		Music	60	80		100	Rock group:
Ismay, Hastings Lionel		WWII	25	35	60	45	Churchill Chief-of-Staff WWII
Israel, Steve I		Congr	10				Member US Congress
Israels, Jozef	1824-1911	Artist	55	180	350	225	Dutch. Hague School Genre Art. Landscapes
Issa, Darrell E. I		Congr	10				Member US Congress
Istomin, Eugene		Music	35			125	Pianist-Classical
Istook Jr., Ernest J. I		Congr	10				Member US Congress
Ito, Hirobumi (Prince)	1841-1909	Statsmn	55	140			Japan. Prime Min. 1886
Ito, Lance, Judge		Law	20			30	O. J. Simpson Trial Judge
Ito, Marquis		Statsmn	25				Jap. Statesman
Ito, Robert	1931-	Ent	10			30	Actor
Iturbi, Jose		Music	20	40		50	Classical Pianist. Jose & Amparo Iturbi S 30-95
Iturbide, Augustin de	1783-1824	Revol		875			Self Proclaimed Emperor of Mex.
Ivan IV, The Terrible		Royal	35000				
Iverson, Alfred, Jr.	1829-1911	Civ War	191	300	475		CSA Gen. Sig/Rank 240-290
Ives, Burl		Ent	30	35		77	Folk-Singer Turned Oscar Winning Actor
Ives, Charles E.	1874-1954	Comp	792	1750	2000	1200	Tonal Experiments. Pulitzer. Mysterious & Elusive
Ivey, Judith	1951-	Ent	10			35	Actress
Iveys		Music	250				Rock group preceeded Badfinger
Ivins, Marsha S.		Space	10			25	
Ivins, Molly	1944-2007	Author	10			15	Best selling author; Pol. commentor
Ivogun, Maria		Opera	45			175	Opera
Ivory Wayans, Keenan		Ent	10			35	Actor
Iwo Jima		WWII				2500	Iconic Rosenthal Photo S by Hayes, Bradley, Gagnon
Izak, Edouard		WWII	20	45		35	WWII CMH
Izzard, Eddie	1962-	Ent	10			20	Br. Comedian
Ja Rule		Music	15			45	Rap
Jabotinsky, Vladimir		Zionist	75	740	670	150	Zionist Leader WWI
Jabs, Hans-Joachim		WWII	60	150			Famed Nazi Pilot.
Jace, Michael		Ent	15			45	
Jack, Thomas M.	1831-1880	Civ War	60				CSA Col. A. D. C. to A. S. Johnston
Jackman, Hugh		Ent	22			65	
Jacks, L. P.		Clergy	15	20	45		
Jackson Five		Music	312	565		405	Rock group:
Jackson, Aaron	1973-	Ent	10			20	Actor
Jackson, Alan		Cntry Mus	18			52	C & W
Jackson, Alfred E.	1807-1889	Civ War	140		950		CSA Gen. Sig/Rank 220, War Dte. ALS 1200
Jackson, And. & Van Buren, Mar.		Pres		3450			
Jackson, Andrew	1767-1845	Pres	513	1928	2748		War of 1812 LS 3500 & up
Jackson, Andrew (As Pres.)	1767-1845	Pres	700	2428	4746		Except. ALS 26000; Land Grants 650-1000; Chk 1700
Jackson, Anne	1926-	Ent	10			35	Actress. Broadway, Radio, TV, Films

NAME	DATES	CATEGORY	SIG	LS/DS	ALS	SP	COMMENTS
Jackson, Charles T.	1805-1880	Sci	200				Co-discoverer of Ether
Jackson, Clairborne F.	1807-1862	Civ War		175	220		Civil War Gov. MO
Jackson, Conrad Feger	1813-1862	Civ War	90				Union Gen.
Jackson, Eugene Pineapple		Ent	15			80	'Our Gang' Comedies
Jackson, Glenda	1937-	Ent	15	20	30	45	Br. Oscar winner, Member of Brit. Parliament
Jackson, Gordon	d. 1996	Ent	15		50	55	Scot. 'Hudson' in 'Upstairs, Downstairs'
Jackson, Helen Hunt		Author	15	35	50	35	Am. Novels, Poet. 'Ramona'
Jackson, Henry M. 'Scoop'		Congr	10	15		20	MOC, Sen. WA
Jackson, Henry Rootes	1820-1898	Civ War	95	195	350		CSA Gen.
Jackson, Howell E.		Sup Crt	88	200		300	US Sen. 1881, Supr. Ct. 1893
Jackson, James S.	1823-1862	Civ War	170		650		Union Gen. KIA 1862. ALS/Cont 1375
Jackson, James S. (WD)		Civ War	465		1018		Union Gen. KIA 1862
Jackson, James, Dr.	1777-1867	Sci	110	220	500		1st Am. to Perform Vaccinations
Jackson, Janet		Music	25	90		59	Rock
Jackson, Jesse	1941-	Clergy	20	35	45	40	Reverend Jesse Jackson.
Jackson, Jesse, Jr.	1965-	Congr	10	15		20	Dem. MOC IL. Civ. Rights, Operation PUSH
Jackson, Joe	1954-	Music	10			35	Singer
Jackson, John King	1828-1866	Civ War	260		920		CSA Gen.
Jackson, Joshua	1978-	Ent	10			35	Young Actor
Jackson, Kate		Ent	10	15	32	35	One of 'Charlie's Angels'
Jackson, LaToya		Music	20		38	44	Singer
Jackson, Lee		Ent	15			45	
Jackson, Mahalia	1911-1972	Music	89	370		378	Gospel Singer. Queen of Gospel Music.
Jackson, Mary Anna	d. 1915	Civ War			788		Wife to Stonewall Jackson
Jackson, Maynard		Music	10	10	20	25	Big Band Trumpet
Jackson, Michael		Music	59	240		130	Legendary Pop Music Mega Star
Jackson, Nathaniel James	1818-1892	Civ War	40	85	110		Union Gen.
Jackson, Peter		Ent	15	35		55	Prod., Dir. Lord of the Rings; AA
Jackson, Rachel		1st Lady	575				Mrs. Andrew Jackson
Jackson, Randy	1956-	Music	15			40	Am. Idol
Jackson, Richard Henry	1830-1892	Civ War	45	70	120		Union Gen.
Jackson, Robert H.		Sup Crt	50	295		125	Chief Prosecutor at Nuremberg
Jackson, Samuel L.		Ent	18			68	Actor
Jackson, Samuel M.	1833-1907	Civ War	40	80	130		Union Gen. Wilderness. ALS/Cont 600
Jackson, T. J. Stonewall	1824-1863	Civ War	4835	8439	12408		CSA Gen.
Jackson, T. J. Stonewall (WD)	1824-1863	Civ War	5925	13000	19244		CSA Gen. ALS/cont 47, 375
Jackson, Thomas		Clergy	25		40		
Jackson, Victoria		Ent	10	15		35	Actress-Comedian
Jackson, Wanda		Cntry Mus	10			20	C & W Singer
Jackson, William	1759-1828	Rev War	120	350	750		Gen. Washington Aide. Diplomat
Jackson, William Henry	1843-1942	Photog	40	110			Photoed Indians on Union Pac. RR Route
Jackson, William L. 'Mudwall'	1825-1890	Civ War	140	218	417		CSA Gen.
Jackson, Wm. Hicks 'Red'	1835-1903	Civ War	110	237	250		CSA Gen. War Dte. DS 600
Jackson-Lee, Sheila	1950-	Congr	10			20	MOC TX
Jacob, Francois		Sci	20	30	55	30	Nobel Med. 1965
Jacob, Irene	1966-	Ent	10			25	Swiss actress
Jacob, John J.		Gov	12	20			Governor WV
Jacobi, Derek		Ent	10			40	
Jacobi, Lou		Ent	10			40	Actor
Jacobs, Andy		Congr	10	15			Indiana
Jacobs, Benjamin		Rev War		200			
Jacobs, Josef		Aero	30	45	80	55	
Jacobs, Lee		Author	10			12	Civil War history
Jacobs, Lou		Ent	50	100		100	Circus Clown

NAME	DATES	CATEGORY	SIG	LS/DS	ALS	SP	COMMENTS
Jacobs, William Wymark	1863-1943	Author	250		285		Br. Monkey's Paw
Jacobsen, David		Celeb	10			20	Singer songwriter
Jacobsen, Fritz		Aero	10	20	35	45	Ace WWI
Jacobson, Peter	1954-	Ent	17			50	Actor
Jacquemart, Nelie		Artist			92		
Jacquet, Illinois Jean		Music	30			70	Jazz Sax, Bandleader
Jacquot, Benoit		Ent	10			25	Fr. Film Dir.
Jacquot, Richard James, Jr.		Author	10			12	Southern mountains geology
Jadlowker, Hermann		Opera	95			245	Opera
Jaeckel, Richard	1926-1997	Ent	15			56	Familiar Char. Actor. Westerns-Tough Guys
Jaeger, James A.		Aero	10		30		
Jaehnert, Erhard		Aero	10	10	25	25	
Jaffe, Sam	1893-1984	Ent	25			41	Actor. Stage 1915. Films 30s. 'Gunga Din'. TV 50s
Jagger, Bianca		Ent	10			30	
Jagger, Dean	1903-1991	Ent	15	25	30	71	AA Winner
Jagger, Jade		Celeb	10			15	Designer
Jagger, Mick	1943-	Music	52	280		165	Lead singer of The Rolling Stones
Jahn, Sigmund		Space	15			35	
Jakes, John		Author	15	50	70	50	'Holiday for Havoc'
James I & VI (Eng)	1566-1625	Royal	750	2034	5250		King of Scotland from 1567--Eng. From 1603
James II (Eng)	1633-1701	Royal	530	1378	3167		King Eng. 1685-88
James, Daniel, Jr.		Mil	20	35	85	45	AF Gen. 1st Black 4 Star Gen.
James, Dennis	1917-1997	Ent	20			35	1938 TV Pioneer. 1st Game Show Host. Emcee
James, Etta		Music	20			40	Rock
James, Frank	1844-1915	Crime	1410	2108	3505		Quantrill Raider. Rode w/Him Throughout War
James, Harry	1916-1983	Band	20	25	40	61	Big Band Leader-Trumpet
James, Henry	1843-1916	Author	129	525	748		Am. Novels, Essayist. ALS/Cont 2500-5, 500
James, Henry	1811-1882	Author	50		120		Theological & Social Scholar
James, Kevin		Ent				40	Actor
James, Manley		Mil	10		45		WWI Victoria Cross
James, Merlin		Artist	10			15	
James, P. D.		Author	20	65	105		Notable Br. Mystery Writer
James, Sonny		Cntry Mus	10			40	Singer. The Country Gentleman. Hits from 50s on
James, Susan Saint	1946-	Ent	10			32	Actress
James, Thomas L.		Cab	15	25	45		Postmaster Gen. 1881
James, Will	1842-1942	Author	75	250	410	750	Illustrated own Western Novels
James, William	1842-1910	Sci	225	350	440	300	Psychologist, Pragmatist, Philosopher
Jameson, (Margaret) Storm		Author		40			
Jameson, Charles Davis	1827-1862	Civ War	80	128	175		Union Gen.
Jan & Dean		Music	60			75	Rock; S Album 250-400
Janacek, Leos	1854-1928	Comp	140				Czech Comp. AMusQS 2000
Jane, Thomas		Ent	20			61	
Janeway, Eliot		Author	16				
Janis, Conrad		Ent	10			25	Actor. 'Mork & Mindy'
Janis, Elsie		Ent	25		50	58	Stage, Screen Comedienne. WWI Entertainer
Janklow, William J. J		Congr	10				Member US Congress
Janney, Allison		Ent	10			45	Emmy winner
Janney, Leon		Ent	35			75	Member Original 'Our Gang' Comedies
Janney, William	1908-1992	Ent				50	Actor
Jannings, Emil		Ent	150			275	1st Academy Award Winner
Janowitz, Gundula		Opera	10			65	Opera
Jansen, Janine		Music				65	Dutch Violinist
Jansen, Marie		Opera	15			40	Opera
Jansons, Mariss		Cond	10			45	Latvian Conductor

NAME	DATES	CATEGORY	SIG	LS/DS	ALS	SP	COMMENTS
Janssen, David	1930-1980	Ent	68	125		176	Actor 'The Fugitive' Orig. TV Series; Chk 135
Janssen, Famke		Ent	10			40	Actress
Janssen, Werner		Cond	25			45	Conductor of Many US Leading Orchestras
January, Lois	1912-2006	Ent	100	125	152	135	Munchkin WOZ
Janus, Samantha	1972-	Ent	10			20	Br. Actress; singer
Jaray, Hans		Ent	10			20	Classical-Semi Classical Singer. Concert-Films
Jardine, Al		Music	20			65	Beach Boys
Jardine, William		Cab	10	15	55	20	Sec. Agriculture 1925
Jardine, William, Sir	1800-1874	Author	55		200		Writer, Editor, Naturalist
Jarman, Claude, Jr.		Ent	15			61	Oscar winner. 'The Yearling'
Jarman, Maxie		Bus	15			55	Jarman Shoes
Jarmusch, Jim	1953-	Ent	10			15	Dir., writer, actor
Jaroff, Serge		Ballet	15	20	25	35	Jaroff Ballet & Don Cossack Chorus
Jarre, Maurice		Comp	20		135		AA; Fr. Comp.
Jarreau, Al		Music	20			40	Singer
Jarrett, Art		Band	15			30	Big Band
Jarriel, Tom	1934-	Jrnalist	10			20	TV News
Jarvik, Robert, Dr.		Sci	15	35	60	40	Inventor Artificial Heart
Jarvis, Anna M.	1864-1948	Celeb	65	175			Created Mother's Day 1907
Jarvis, Gregory B.		Space	150	350		400	Killed in Challanger Disaster; S FDC 250-500
Jarvis, Howard		Reform	10			15	Sponsor Proposition 13. CA Property Tax
Jasiak, Charles 'Chuck'		Bus	10				Am. Entrepreneur
Jasmer, Brent	1965-	Ent	10			25	Actor
Jason, David	1940-	Ent	10			30	Br. Actor
Jason, Rick	1923-2000	Ent	20			148	Actor; 'Combat'
Jason, Sybil	1929-	Ent	10			75	Actress
Jassin, Lloyd		Author	10	11	25	15	Copyright author/attorney, rights expert
Javits, Jacob J.		Congr	10	20		25	MOC 1947, Sen. NY 1957
Jawlensky, Aleksey von	1864-1941	Artist			600		Russ. Painter
Jaworski, Leon		Law	15	20	45	35	Dir. Watergate Prosecution Force
Jay & the Americans		Music	40			60	Rock group; S Album 60
Jay, James, Sir	1732-1815	Sci	90	275	400		Phys. to G. Washington; Inventor
Jay, John	1745-1829	Sup Crt	451	1914	2973		Pres. Continental Congr. ALS/cont 6, 600
Jay, John (Grandson)	1817-1894	Diplo	30	65	95		Active Opposition to Slavery
Jay, Tony		Ent	32			95	
Jay-Z		Music	25			45	Rap
Jean, Gloria		Ent	10		20	35	Child Singer-Actress 30s-40's5
Jean, Norma		Cntry Mus	10			20	
Jean, Shirley		Ent				49	Little Rascals
Jean, Wyclef		Music	20			40	Rock
Jean-Baptiste, Marianne		Ent	13			40	
Jeans, James, Sir		Sci	12	30	56	20	Br. Physicist, Astron., Author
Jedlichka, Ernest		Music	45			200	Rus-Pol Pianist
Jeffers, Robinson	1887-1962	Author	65	350	450	95	Prize Winning Poet, Dramatist
Jeffers, William M.		Bus	25	70	135	50	Pres. Union Pacific RR
Jefferson Airplane (All)		Music	150			492	Rock-The San Francisco Sound
Jefferson, Blind Lemon	1897-1930	Music	1250	2500	2500		Blues-Jazz
Jefferson, Charles E.		Clergy	20	25	40		
Jefferson, Joe	1829-1905	Ent	45	70	107	80	Important Am. 19th C. Actor
Jefferson, Martha Wayles		1st Lady					Rare. Only 2 Known. No Current Price
Jefferson, T. & Madison, J.		Pres	3038	6776			Special Doc. S 30,000, MLS 25,000
Jefferson, Thomas	1743-1826	Pres	2852	8590	15864		ALS/Cont 29500-200000. FF 3200-4200; ALS in 3rd person 6000; Imp. DS 40000
Jefferson, Thomas (As Pres.)	1743-1826	Pres	3812	8800	26172		Free Frank 5,000-5950, ALS Cont. 50,000 & up

NAME	DATES	CATEGORY	SIG	LS/DS	ALS	SP	COMMENTS
Jefferson, Thomas	1859-1932	Ent	20			125	Actor. Stage & Silent Films/D. W. Griffith
Jefferson, William J. J.		Congr	10			20	Member US Congress
Jeffords, James		Congr	10				US Senate (I-VT)
Jeffrey, Francis, Lord	1773-1850	Jurist			110		Scottish Judge & critic
Jeffreys, Anne	1923-	Ent	10	14	22	32	Actress. 'Topper'
Jeffries, Fran		Ent	15			45	
Jellicoe, John R.	1859-1935	Mil	35	70	125	167	Br. Adm. WWI, P. M. New Zealand
Jenckes, Joseph	1656-1740	Colonial	90	250	520		Colonial Governor RI
Jenifer, Daniel of St. Thomas	1723-1790	Rev War		345			Signer of Constitution
Jenkins, Albert Gallatin	1830-1864	Civ War	250	316			CSA Gen.
Jenkins, Allen	1900-1974	Ent	25			81	Cigar-Chewing Char. Actor
Jenkins, Butch		Ent	10			68	Freckle-Faced Child Actor
Jenkins, Micah	1835-1864	Civ War	360				CSA Gen.
Jenkins, Richard		Ent				40	Nathaniel Fisher, Six Feet Under
Jenkins, Thornton Alex.	1811-	Civ War	35	95	160		Chief-of Staff Adm. Farragut Squad. Sig/Rank 65
Jenkins, William L. J		Congr	10				Member US Congress
Jenkinson, Charles		Rev War		120			1st Earl of Liverpool & 1st Baron Hawkesbury; Br. Sec. War, Rev War.
Jenkinson, Robert Banks	1770-1828	HOS	72	178	200		PM, 2nd Earl of Liverpool
Jenks, George Augustus		Congr	10				FF 38
Jenner, Bruce		Celeb	10			25	Olympic champion, motivation Spkr.
Jenner, Edward, Dr.	1749-1823	Sci	448	1098	6475		1st to Use. Smallpox Vaccination
Jenner, William E.	1908-1985	Congr	10	20			Sen. IN
Jenner, William, Sir	1815-1898	Sci	35	85	182		Identified Typhus-Typhoid. Queen Victoria's MD
Jennings, Al	1863-1961	Ent	250		850	480	Outlaw turned Hollywood actor
Jennings, Claudia	1949-1979	Model	240			1000	Actress; Playmate (murdered)
Jennings, Peter	1938-2005	Jrnalist	15	25	35	52	Iconic Broadcast Journalist
Jennings, Waylon	1937-2002	Cntry Mus	22	55		61	Country Singer
Jennison, Ralph D.		Bus	10	35	45	20	
Jenrette, John W. Jr.		Congr	10	20		15	MOC. SC
Jenrette, Rita		Ent	10			20	
Jensen, Ashley		Ent	15			45	
Jensen, Maren	1956-	Ent	10			60	Actress
Jenson, May		Celeb	10			15	Pol. celebrity
Jepson, Helen		Opera	15			45	Opera, Concert
Jeremy, Ron		Ent	10			30	Actor
Jergens, Adele	1917-	Ent	10			69	Actress-Model. Over 50 Mostly B-Films.
Jergens, Diane	1935-	Ent				60	Actress
Jeritza, Maria	1887-1984	Opera	50			95	Opera, Operetta, Films. 1st Met. 'Turandot'
Jernigan, Tamara E.		Space	10			25	
Jernstedt, Ken		WWII	10	25	40	35	ACE, WWII, Flying Tigers
Jerome, Addison G		Finan	300	975			Stock Market Legend in 1850's
Jerome, Jerome K.	1859-1927	Author	50	70	108		Humorist, Plays. 'Three Men in a Boat'
Jerome, Wm. Travers, III		Educ	20	40		35	Pres. Bowling Green U
Jerusalem, Siegfried		Opera	15			45	Opera. Current Leading Wagnerian Tenor. SP 4x6 25
Jesse, Edward	1780-1868	Author			65		Natural history
Jessel, George	1888-1972	Ent	28	60		91	Noted Emcee, Comic, Toastmaster
Jessup, Thomas S.	1788-1860	Mil	57	138	183		War 1812, Seminole. Gen. LS/Cont 950-1750
Jesup, William H.		Mil	10	15	25		
Jeter, Michael		Ent	10			25	'Evening Shade'
Jethro Tull		Music	150			680	Rock; 'Aqualung'
Jethro, Homer and		Cntry Mus	35			130	Henry Haynes (Guitar), Ken Burns (Mandolin)
Jett, Joan		Music	20	45		104	Rock. (& the 'Blackhearts'); S Album 100
Jewel		Music	15	150		56	Singer

NAME	DATES	CATEGORY	SIG	LS/DS	ALS	SP	COMMENTS
Jewell, Isabel		Ent	50			154	Longtime Vintage Actress. 'Emmy Slattery' GWTW
Jewell, Marshall	1825-1883	Gov	40	75	298		Gov. CT 1869-70, 71-73; Min. to Rus. 1873-74; Postmaster Gen. 1874-76.
Jewett, Sarah Orne	1849-1909	Author	45	200	433		New England Life & Folklore
Jewison, Norman		Ent	10			30	Film Dir.
Jewsbury, Geraldine Endsor	1812-1880	Author			70		
Jillian, Ann		Ent	10		15	30	Actress.
Jimenez, Enrique A.		HOS	10	15	25	15	Panama
Jimenez, Marcos P.		HOS	10	25	50	20	Venezuela
Joachim, Joseph	1831-1907	Comp	95	150	256	245	Hung. Violinist. AMusQS 250-575
Joad, Cyril Edwin M.	1891-1953	Author		30	35		Writer & teacher
Jodl, Alfred	1892-1946	WWII	256	407	550	530	Nazi Chief-of-Staff To Keitel WWII
Joel, Billy		Comp	20			64	Singer, Songwriter; S Album 125
Joel, Manuel	1826-1890	Clergy	45	125			Rabbi, Scholar. Defended Moderation vs Radicalism
Joffe, Julian Marc M. D.		Author	10			20	Renown orthopedic surgeon; Author
Joffre, Joseph Jac. Ces.		Mil	58	101	250	160	Marshal of France WWI
Johann, Zita	1904-1993	Ent	20		130	82	Actor. 'The Mummy'
Johannson, Paul		Ent	10			25	Actor. 'Beverly Hills 90210'
Johansson, Scarlett		Ent	25			75	Actress
John II, (King Castile)	1406-1454	Royal	4700	5133			Patron of Literature & Arts. Father: Q. Isabella
John III (Port.)		Royal	200	1400			King Portugal 1521-1557. Introduced Inquisition
John of Austria (Don John)		Royal	150				1629-1679
John VI	1769-1826	Clergy		230			King of Portugal
John, 1st Duke Marlborough		Mil			3000		Br. Gen. & pre-eminent statesman under Queen Anne
John, Augustus E.	1878-1916	Artist	50	135	278		Welch. Portraits, Landscapes
John, Christopher J		Congr	10				Member US Congress
John, Elton		Music	45	354	412	148	Br. Singer-Songwriter
John, Little Wille		Music		310		425	Rock, Early R&B slnger
Johns, Glynis		Ent	15	15	30	42	Br. Actress. Leading Lady. Later, Char. Roles
Johns, Jasper		Artist	100	130		167	Am. Pop Artist. FDC/Leroy Neiman 150
Johns, Patrick		Author	10			12	Authors
Johns, William Earl	1893-1968	Author			100		Creator of 'Biggles'
Johnson, Adam R. 'Stovepipe'	1834-1922	Civ War	352				CSA Gen., rare DS 3335
Johnson, Amy (Mollison)	1903-1941	Aero	60	90	135	288	Br. Aviation Pioneer
Johnson, Amy Jo		Ent	10			47	Actress.
Johnson, Andrew	1808-1875	Civ War	475	1260			Union Gen., Mil. Gov. TN, US Pres.
Johnson, Andrew	1808-75	Pres	386	990	4120	3000	ALS/Cont 19, 500. FF 675-775-1, 400
Johnson, Andrew (as Pres.)		Pres	487	1582	5806	3500	Impeached,. FF 775-1500
Johnson, Art		WWII	10	25	40	30	ACE, WWII, USAAF Ace
Johnson, Ben	1918-1996	Ent	35	70		101	Oscar winner. Popular Western Star
Johnson, Betty	1929-	Music	10			20	Caberet singer
Johnson, Bradley T.	1829-1903	Civ War	103	160	202		CSA Gen., ALS/Cont 4, 500
Johnson, Bradley T. (WD)	1829-1903	Civ War	150	280	550		CSA Gen.
Johnson, Brian		Music	10			35	Music. Lead Singer 'AC/DC'
Johnson, Bunk		Music	200			911	Jazz Trumpet
Johnson, Bushrod Rust	1817-1880	Civ War	145	300	365		CSA Gen. Mexican War
Johnson, Cave	1793-1866	Cab	50	110	195		P. M. Gen. 1st US Postage Stamps
Johnson, Chic		Ent	30			55	1/2 of Zany Comedy Team (Olsen & Johnson)
Johnson, Crockett		Comics	50			500	'Barnaby'
Johnson, David Earle		Author	10			15	Islamic history/influences
Johnson, Don		Ent	15			40	Actor
Johnson, Eastman	1824-1906	Artist	40	60	185	300	Am. Portrait & Genre Artist
Johnson, Eddie Bernice	1955-	Congr	10			20	Afr-Am Dem MOC TX
Johnson, Edward		Opera	25			75	Distinguished Canadian Tenor

NAME	DATES	CATEGORY	SIG	LS/DS	ALS	SP	COMMENTS
Johnson, Edward 'Old Alleghany'	1816-1873	Civ War	118	310			CSA Gen.
Johnson, Eliza M.		1st Lady	750	1500			
Johnson, Frank		Comics	10			40	
Johnson, Fred		Comics	10			45	'Moon Mullins'
Johnson, Gerald		WWII	45	60	75	95	WWII ace w/22 kills
Johnson, Harold K.		WWII	15	35	50	35	WWII. Prisoner. 4 Star Gen.
Johnson, Henry A.		Bus	10			15	CEO Spiegel Inc.
Johnson, Herschel	1812-1880	Civ War	40	115			Gov. GA, CSA Sen., Member of CSA Congress
Johnson, Hiram W.	1866-1945	Congr	22	60		70	Powerful Sen. CA
Johnson, Howard B.		Bus	80			95	Howard Johnson Inns
Johnson, Howard S.		Bus	12	30		25	
Johnson, Hugh S.		Cab	15	90	125	35	Gen., Dir. NRA During Depression. FDR
Johnson, Hugh S.	1916-1997	WWII	45	75	135	110	ACE, WWII, Br. RAF Top Ace
Johnson, James "Johnnie"	1916-1997	WWII	50	75	135	88	Ace, WWII, Br. RAF Top Ace
Johnson, James K.		Aero	10	25	40	35	ACE, Korea, Double Ace
Johnson, James Weldon		Author	35	100	225		NAACP, 1st Ed. 'Black Manhattan' S 695-795
Johnson, Jesse G.		WWII	35	85	170	90	Adm. WWII
Johnson, John H.	1918-2005	Pub		50		65	Publisher 'Ebony', 'Jet'
Johnson, Jonathan Eastman		Artist	35	150			Am. Portrait, Genre Painter
Johnson, Keen		Gov	10	15		10	Governor KY
Johnson, Kenny		Ent	17			50	
Johnson, L. B. & Lady Bird		Pres				600	
Johnson, Lady Bird	1912-2007	1st Lady	51	92	138	111	Vintage FDC 'Beautification of America' S 80
Johnson, LeRoy		Congr	10			10	
Johnson, Louis A.	1891-1966	Cab	15	40	60	35	Sec. Defense 1949 Truman
Johnson, Lyndon B.	1908-1973	Pres	190	343	1500	346	ALS As VP 4500. Rare ANS 950
Johnson, Lyndon B. (ss Pres.)		Pres	227	983	3129	442	TLS as Pres. 1, 250-4, 200/Cont; Rare ALS on WHS
Johnson, Lynn		Comics	27			65	'For Better Or Worst'
Johnson, Lynn-Holly	1958-	Ent	10			20	Actress
Johnson, Martin	1884-1937	Expl	15	40		55	With Osa, Wild Animal Films. Afr. Explr. s
Johnson, Michelle		Ent	15			45	
Johnson, Nancy L. J		Congr	10				Member US Congress
Johnson, Nunnally	1897-1977	Author	20	65		40	Am. Plays, Screenwriter
Johnson, Oliver	1944-2002	Music	10			30	Free Jazz
Johnson, Osa	1894-1953	Expl	15	20	35	45	With Martin, Wild Animal Films, Adventurer, Author
Johnson, Philip		Archtct	22			108	Early Skyscrapers
Johnson, Reverdy	1796-1876	Cab	25	95	105		Statesman, Atty Gen., US Sen. MD
Johnson, Richard L.		Aero	15	20	35	25	
Johnson, Richard M.	1780-1850	VP	56	152	190	400	Van Buren Vice Pres.
Johnson, Richard W	1827-1897	Civ War	40	110	140		Union Gen.
Johnson, Robert S.		WWII	20	25	45	80	ACE, WWII, #5 US
Johnson, Robert W.		Bus	55	190			Fndr. Johnson & Johnson. Important DS 750
Johnson, Robert Ward	1814-1879	Civ War	42	64	117		Member of CSA Congress
Johnson, Russell		Ent	15			60	Actor, Gilligan's Island
Johnson, Sabrina		Ent	13			40	
Johnson, Sam J		Congr	10				Member US Congress
Johnson, Samuel	1822-1882	Clergy			150		Transcendentalism
Johnson, Samuel C.		Bus	10			20	Pres. Johnson's Wax
Johnson, Samuel, Dr.		Author	1740	4080			Lexicographer, Critic
Johnson, Thomas	1812-1906	Civ War		84			Member of CSA Congress
Johnson, Tim		Congr	10				US Senate (D-SD)
Johnson, Van		Ent	15			55	MGM Leading Man in Straight Leads & Musicals
Johnson, Waldo Porter	1817-1885	Civ War		117			Member of CSA Congress
Johnson, William	1715-1774	Colonial		2250			Br. Fur Trader. Superintendent Indian Affairs

NAME	DATES	CATEGORY	SIG	LS/DS	ALS	SP	COMMENTS
Johnson, William		Mil	30		125	50	Maj. Gen USA 91st Div. AEF. WWI
Johnson, William B.		Bus	10			15	CEO Railway Express
Johnson, William Cost		Congr	10	20	35		MOC MD 1833; FF 26
Johnson, William Sam'l	1727-1819	Rev War	130	299	675		Signer US Constitution. Cont. Congr.
Johnson, Willis, Dr.	1869-1951	Educ	10			20	
Johnson-Jerald, Penny		Ent	13			40	
Johnston, Albert Sidney	1803-1862	Civ War	410	2400	3990	3500	CSA Gen., TX Sec. War., DS 9500-21127, Sig/Rank 650
Johnston, Frances	1864-1952	Photog	10	25		35	1st Famous Female Photographer
Johnston, George D.	1832-1910	Civ War	95	360	382		CSA Gen.
Johnston, J. Lawson		Bus	15	35	60		
Johnston, Joseph E.	1807-1891	Civ War	248	432	844	2210	CSA ALS/Cont 3, 500-12,000. FF 500
Johnston, Joseph E. (WD)		Civ War	350	750	1468	2271	CSA Gen. ALS 12/1861/Cont 10,000
Johnston, Kristen	1967-	Ent	10			35	Actress
Johnston, Lynn		Comics	20			75	'For Better or Worse'
Johnston, Mary		Space	10			25	
Johnston, Olin D.		Congr	10	15			US Sen. SC 1945
Johnston, Richard M.		Author	10	10	20		
Johnston, Robert	1818-1885	Civ War	42				Member of CSA Congress
Johnston, Robert Daniel	1837-1919	Civ War	110	193			CSA Gen.
Jolie, Angelina		Ent	20			95	Actress
Joliot, Fred. & Irene Curie		Sci	200				Scientific Nobel Winning Team
Joliot-Curie, Irene	1897-1956	Sci	45		205		
Joliot-Curie, Jean Frederic	1900-1958	Sci		350	500		Fr. Physicist. Nobel '35. Son-in-law Pierre/Marie
Jolley, I. Stanford	1900-1978	Ent	20			180	
Jolson, Al	1886-1950	Ent	130	287		745	Starred in 1st Talkie. SP in Blackface500
Jones, Allan	1907-1982	Ent	15	20	35	50	Film & Concert Singer. Many Popular 40s Musicals
Jones, Anne		Cntry Mus	10			20	Singer
Jones, Annisa		Ent	322			502	TV Sitcom 'Family Affair'
Jones, Anson	1798-1858	Tex	350	795	1500		Pres. TX Repub.
Jones, Anthony Armstrong		Cntry Mus	10			20	Singer
Jones, B. J.		Author	10			12	Books for children
Jones, Bob		Clergy	15	25	60	40	'Bob Jones University'
Jones, Brian	1942-1969	Music	300			950	Rolling Stones
Jones, Buck	1889-1942	Ent	139	230	300	646	Vintage Film Cowboy. Major Star
Jones, Carolyn	1929-1983	Ent	85	127	120	151	Actress. 'Morticia' on TV's 'Addams Family'
Jones, Casey		Aero	32	82	175	117	
Jones, Catherine Zeta		Ent	20			194	Actress. AA Winner
Jones, Chuck	1912-2002	Comics	25			212	Animator; S cel or sketch 200-2000
Jones, Claude A.		Mil	40	65			
Jones, Daniel	1912-1993	Comp					Welsh Comp. AMusQS 80
Jones, David (Davy)		Ent	15			40	'The Monkees'
Jones, David C., Gen.	1879-1958	Mil	10			42	Chairman/Chiefs of Staff
Jones, David R. "Neighbor"	1825-1863	Civ War	305	800			CSA Gen. Served/Beauregard & Longstreet
Jones, David R. "Neighbor" (WD)	1825-1863	Civ War	472	2895	5175		CSA Gen. D. Richmond, VA 1/15/63. Coronary
Jones, Dean	1933-	Ent	10	15	25	40	Actor. Numerous Disney Films
Jones, Dick	1927-	Ent	15			70	Actor
Jones, Doug		Ent	17			50	
Jones, E. Stanley		Clergy	35	50	75	50	
Jones, Edward F.	1828-1913	Civ War	30	55	80	150	Union Gen. War Dte. DS. 210. Sig/Rank 80
Jones, Ernest	1879-1958	Sci	20		75		Br. Psychoanalyst, Biographer of Freud
Jones, George		Cntry Mus	10			35	C & W Singer
Jones, George Washington		Civ War	57	162			Member of CSA Congress
Jones, Grace		Ent	18	20	30	52	Actress
Jones, Grandpa		Cntry Mus					(See Louis Jones) Country Music Entertainer

NAME	DATES	CATEGORY	SIG	LS/DS	ALS	SP	COMMENTS
Jones, Gwyneth		Opera	15			40	Opera
Jones, Henry	1912-1999	Ent	10			60	Actor. Char.
Jones, Henry Cox	1821-1913	Civ War	57		162		Member of CSA Congress
Jones, Howard	1955-	Music	10			25	Br. Pop singer
Jones, Inigo	1573-1652	Archtct		2500			1st sig. Br. Architect. Brought Renaissance arch. To Eng.
Jones, Isham		Band	15			40	Vintage Big Bandleader-Comp.
Jones, J. Carey		Mil	28	45		40	Adm. WWII
Jones, Jack		Music	10			25	Pop Singer Son of Alan Jones
Jones, James		Author	50	190		60	'From Here To Eternity'
Jones, James		Ent	23			69	
Jones, James Earl	1931-	Ent	10	40		52	Broadway-Films-TV Actor. Darth Vader Voice
Jones, Janet		Music	10			30	Singer.
Jones, January		Ent	16			47	
Jones, Jeffrey	1946-	Ent	10			25	Actor
Jones, Jennifer		Ent	135	198		366	AA Actress.
Jones, Jenny		Ent	10			20	TV Talk Show Host
Jones, Jesse H.		Cab	10	15	15	15	Sec. Commerce 1940
Jones, Jill		Ent	13			40	
Jones, Jim		Clergy	250	605	650	850	
Jones, JJ		Ent	15			45	
Jones, John Marshall	1820-1864	Civ War	238	704			CSA Gen. Sig/Rank 1050, War Dte DS 2850
Jones, John Paul	1946-	Music	50			175	Bassist, keyboardist, Led Zeppelin mandolinist
Jones, John Paul	1747-1792	Rev War	5750				Naval Hero. 'I have not yet begun to fight!'
Jones, John Percival		Congr	10		25		US Sen. NV 1873
Jones, John Robert	1827-1901	Civ War	120	191	587		CSA Gen.
Jones, L. Q.	1927-	Ent	10			30	Actor
Jones, Le Roi		Author					(See Baraka) Afr-Am Plays, Poet, Novels, Essayist
Jones, Lisa		Author	10			15	Romantic books
Jones, Lois Mailou	1905-1998	Artist	20		35		Noted Afr-Am Artist
Jones, Louis 'Grandpa'	1913-1998	Ent	20			35	Grandpa Jones. Country Singer, 'Hee Haw'
Jones, Louis R.		Mil	10	30			
Jones, Luther 'Casey'		Celeb	100				Legendary RR engineer
Jones, Maj. Gen. David M.		Space	10			25	
Jones, Marcia Mae	1924-2007	Ent	10			40	Child & Juvenile Actress
Jones, Mary H. 'Mother'	1830-1930	Labor	60	195	430		Agitator, Spkr., Organizer NYC Garment Workers
Jones, Norah		Music	10			45	Grammy award winner
Jones, Patrick Henry	1830-1900	Civ War	45	80	130		Union Gen.
Jones, Paula		Celeb	10			25	
Jones, Quincy		Comp	15	81	35	55	S Album 125
Jones, Randy		Ent	15			45	
Jones, Reginald V. R. V.	1911-1997	WWII			75	90	Invaluable Br. WWII Mil. Intel. Expert
Jones, Rickie Lee		Ent	15			40	
Jones, Robert McDonald	1808-1872	Civ War	54				Member of CSA Congress
Jones, Samuel	1819-1887	Civ War	110	400			CSA Gen.
Jones, Samuel (WD)		Civ War	202	615	700		CSA Gen.
Jones, Samuel Porter		Clergy	15	25	110		
Jones, Shirley		Ent	12	33		45	Actress. AA Award Winner. 'Partridge Family'
Jones, Simon		Music	10			25	Music. Bass Guitar 'The Verve'
Jones, Spike	1911-1965	Band	35			187	Big Band Leader. S Album 100
Jones, Star		Ent	10			30	TV personality; lawyer
Jones, Stephanie Tubbs J		Congr	10				Member US Congress
Jones, Tamala		Ent	15			45	
Jones, Terry		Ent	10	95		65	Actor
Jones, Thad		Music	50			120	Blues-Jazz

NAME	DATES	CATEGORY	SIG	LS/DS	ALS	SP	COMMENTS
Jones, Thomas		Space	15			20	
Jones, Thomas McKissick	1816-1892	Civ War		100			Member of CSA Congress
Jones, Thomas V.		Bus	15	30		25	
Jones, Tom		Music	12	15	25	79	Singer
Jones, Tommy		Ent	17			50	
Jones, Tommy Lee		Ent	20			60	Film DS 650
Jones, Vinnie	1965-	Ent	10			20	Br. Actor
Jones, Walter B. J		Congr	10				Member US Congress
Jones, William E.	1824-1864	Civ War	152	212	525		CSA Gen. 'Grumble'., KIA Piedmont, VA
Jones, William E. (WD)	1824-1864	Civ War	275	750	1250		CSA Brig. Gen. 'Grumble'., KIA Piedmont, Virginia
Jong, Erica		Author	10	14	25	25	Best Selling Bawdy Autobiography
Jongkind, Johan	1819-1891	Artist	200	450	860		Dutch. Master of Rendering Light
Jonson, Ben	1572-1637	Author	2850				Br. Plays. Poet. 'Volpone', 'The Alchemist'
Jope, Bernhard		Aero	10	25	40	30	
Joplin, Janis	1943-1970	Music	1225	1704	3438	2585	Blues & Rock Singer. D. of Heroin Overdose at 27
Joplin, Scott	1868-1917	Comp	700	1090	2000		Rag Time Comp.
Jordan, Barbara	1936-1996	Congr	15	60		30	Highly Respected Afr-Am. Congresswoman TX
Jordan, Dorothea	1761-1816	Ent		400			Stars of Regency stage; Mistress, King Wm. IV
Jordan, Dorothy	1906-1988	Ent	15	20	35	86	Actress
Jordan, Hamilton		Official	10	15	25	20	Chief of Staff Carter Admin.
Jordan, Jim		Ent	15	20	35	30	Top Radio Comedy Team 'Fibber McGee & Molly'
Jordan, John Alfred		Author	15			30	Afr. adventure
Jordan, June		Pol	10			15	Afr-Am Pol. activist, writer, poet, & teacher.
Jordan, Louis		Band	25			65	Big Band Leader
Jordan, Neil		Ent	10			20	Dir.
Jordan, Thomas	1819-1895	Civ War	73	252	349		CSA Gen. Mexican War
Jordan, Thomas (WD)		Civ War	140	335	663	1910	CSA Gen. Mexican War. ALS/Cont 1195
Jordan, Vernon	1935-	Pol	20	16		90	Powerful D. C. Fixer. Clinton Friend & Advisor
Jordanaires, The (4)		Music	35			95	Gospel Quartet
Jorgensen, Christine	1926-1989	Celeb	28	40	65	75	1st transsexual surgery patient
Jorn, Carl		Opera	30			85	Opera
Jory, Victor	1902-1982	Ent	52	40		144	Longtime Popular Char. Actor. GWTW
Joseph I	1678-1711	Royal		562			Holy Roman Emp., King Hungary, King of Romans
Joseph II	1741-1790	Royal	125	359	875		King Ger. & Holy Roman Empire
Joseph, Lesley	1946-	Ent	10			25	Br. Actress
Josephine, Empress	1783-1814	Royal	912	1600	2857		Fr. (First) Wife of Napoleon
Joslyn, Allyn	1901-1981	Ent	17			75	Actor. Comedic Char. Roles
Jossefy, Raphael	1853-1915	Music	25			125	Pianist, Pupil of Liszt, Teacher. AMusQS 100
Jostyn, Jennifer		Ent	10			25	Actress
Joswig, Wilhelm		Aero	10			30	
Jouett, James		Civ War	25	55	125		Union Naval Off./Farragut
Jouhaux, Benjamin	1879-1954	Reform	25	60	140	50	Nobel Peace Pr. 1951
Jourdan, Jean B., Count		Napol	55	260	305		Marshal of Napoleon
Jourdan, Louis	1919-1993	Ent	18	25	30	47	Handsome Fr. Leading Man. 'Gigi'
Journey		Music	48			118	Entire Band S; S Album 100
Jovovich, Milla		Ent	15			78	
Jowett, Benjamin	1817-1893	Educ	10	25	35		Br. Master of Balliol College Plato & Socrates Translator
Jowett, Charles		Clergy	15	20	25		
Joy, James F.	1810-1896	Bus	75	450	750		RR Baron, S stock cert. 1275
Joy, Jimmie		Band	10			20	
Joy, Leatrice	1899-1985	Ent	25			60	Silent Film Star. 'Ten Commandments'
Joyce, Alice	1890-1955	Ent	15	25		60	Silent Star actress
Joyce, Brenda	1912-	Ent	15			40	Actress. 'Jane' in 5 Tarzan Films.
Joyce, Elaine	1945-	Ent	10			30	Actress

NAME	DATES	CATEGORY	SIG	LS/DS	ALS	SP	COMMENTS
Joyce, James	1882-1941	Author	608	1768	5793	6300	Ir. Novels, Poet, Plays; SB 2850
Joyce, Richard		Mil	40	100	175		
Juan Carlos, de Borbon		Royal	55	120	245	150	King of Spain. So Designated by Franco in 1975
Juarez, Benito	1806-1872	HOS	425	749	1258	1500	Twice Pres. Mexico. Revolutionary
Judah, Henry Moses	1821-1866	Civ War	55	80	120		Union Gen.
Judah, Theodore D.		Bus		18000			Started Central Pac. RR. Rare DS 18,000
Judd, Ashley		Ent	15			50	Actress.
Judd, Chris		Ent	12			35	
Judd, Naomi & Wynona		Cntry Mus	25			65	Mother-Daughter Team
Judd, Norman B.	1815-1878	Congr	50		85		MOC. IL. Nominated A. Lincoln. Min. to Berlin
Judd, Walter H.	1898-1994	Congr	10	15		20	Congressman MN
Judd, Wyonna		Music	20			40	Rock; Country
Judge, Arline		Ent	10	15	35	26	Actress
Judge, Mike		Comics	18			55	Printed repro. S 450; actor
Julia, Raul	1940-1994	Ent	28			77	Actor. 'Addams Family'-'Gomez'
Julian, George W.	1817-1899	Congr	15	30	75		Co-Fndr. Free Soil Party, MOC. IN
Juliana, Queen		Royal	100	250	710	350	Netherlands
Jumangi (cast)		Ent				200	Williams, Hunt, Durst, Pierce
Jump, Gordon		Ent	10			40	Actor
Jung, Carl Gustav	1875-1961	Sci	450	1555	2632	2320	Swiss Psychiatrist-Psychologist
Junkers, Hugo		Sci	50		355		Ger. Airplane Engineer-Designer
Junot, Andoche		Mil	70	235			Fr. Gen., Sec. to Napoleon. Duc d'Abrante's
Jurgens, Curt	1915-1982	Ent	15			60	Scandanavian Actor
Jurgens, Dick		Band	20			45	Big Band Leader
Jusserand, Jean Jules	1855-1932	Author		22	48		Pulitzer Pr. Fr. Diplomat, Author, Scholar
Justice, Bill		Comics	25			58	The Chipmunks'. Full Size Color S 250
Juttner, Arthur		Mil	10			45	Ger. RK Winner
Juutilainen, Eino		WWII	40	40		90	Finnish ace w/93 kills
Juxon, William	1582-1663	Clergy	125	400			Archbshp. Canterbury. Attended Chas. I on Scaffold
K. C. & the Sunshine Band		Music		65		75	Rock group
Kaczmarek, Jane		Ent	15			45	
Kadar, Janos	1912-1989	HOS	50	130			Hungarian Prime Min.
Kaelin, Kato		Celeb	10	10		20	Houseguest O. J. Simpson
Kafka, Franz	1883-1924	Author	850	2655	2250		Ger. Novels. Visionary Tales. Special ALS 16500
Kaganovich, Lazar	1893-1991	Mil		211			Stalin's mass murderer
Kagen, Steve Dr.	1949-	Congr	10			20	Member of Congress WI; Allergist.
Kagesa, Lt. -Gen. Sadaaki	1893-1948	WWII	225				WWII Jap. Gen.
Kahn, Gus	1886-1941	Music		50		40	Songwriter
Kahn, Julius	1861-1924	Congr	10	15			Rep. CA 1899
Kahn, Madeline		Ent	10			46	Actress
Kahn, Otto H.	1867-1934	Bus	50	75	135	125	Banker, Philan., Arts Patron
Kahn, Yahya		HOS	30			50	Pakistan
Kahoutek, Lubos		Sci	10	15	30	15	Am. Astronomer
Kaine, Jeff		Celeb	10			15	Photographer
Kaiser, Henry J.	1882-1967	Indust	125	225		312	S. F. Bay Bridge. Grand Coulee Dam
Kai-Shek, Chiang	1887-1975	HOS	148	260	450	1050	Repub. of China
Kai-Shek, Chiang & Mme.		HOS				375	
Kai-Shek, Chiang Madame		Pol				770	Wife of Chiang kai-Shek,
Kai-Shek, Mayling S. Chiang		Author	50	275		120	Madame Chiang
Kalakaua, David	1836-1891	Royal	271	425	775	1600	King of Hawaii. Opposition To His Reform = Revolution
Kalb, Johann Baron de Kalb	1721-1780	Rev War		33400			Major Gen. KIA at Battle of Camden
Kallen, Kitty		Music		20		25	Big Band Vocalist
Kalmanoff, Martin		Comp	10		25		Numerous Works for Musical Theatre, Opera.
Kaltenborn, H. V.	1878-1965	Radio	10	15	30	15	Radio Commentator

NAME	DATES	CATEGORY	SIG	LS/DS	ALS	SP	COMMENTS
Kaltenbrunner, Ernst	1903-1946	WWII	208	1052		400	Perpetrator of Nazi Atrocities
Kalugin, Oleg		Pol	10			25	Former KGB spy
Kamburg, Arthur, Dr		Sci	10	20			Nobel
Kamehameha II, Liholiho	1797-1824	Royal	960		3850		King Hawaii
Kamehameha III, Kauikeaouli		Royal	750	1585			King Hawaii
Kamehameha IV	1824-1863	Royal		2500			King of Hawaii
Kamel, Stanley	1932-2008	Ent	10			40	Actor
Kamenev, Lev	1883-1936	Mil		347			Bolshevik leader
Kamin, Daniel	1947-	Ent	10			25	Actor
Kaminsky, Max		Band	10			30	Dixieland Jazz Bandleader
Kamio, Mitsuomi		Mil	110		225		
Kamionsky, Oscar		Opera				350	Baritone
Kammhuber, Josef		WWII	20	30	65	35	Ger. Air Defense Gen. WWII. RK
Kampelman, Max		Diplo	10			20	
Kanaly, Steve	1946-	Ent	10			30	Ray Krebs on Dallas
Kander, John		Comp	10	45	95	25	Composed w/Fred Ebb. 'Cabaret'
Kandinski, Vasili	1866-1944	Artist	200	795			Rus. Painter. Cont. TLS 1, 500
Kandor, John		Comp					See Ebb, Fred
Kane, Bob	1916-1999	Comics	72		430	268	Batman Illustr. Drawing 230-795, Comic Bk. S 100
Kane, Carol		Ent	10			47	
Kane, Elisha Kent	1820-1857	Expl	95	215	450		Grinnell Arctic Exped.
Kane, Helen	1904-1966	Ent	25			168	Boop-Boop-a-Doop Girl. Singer of the 20s
Kane, Richard		Mil	20			90	
Kane, Thomas L.	1822-1883	Civ War	48	105	160		Union Gen. ALS '63 990
Kane, Tom		Ent	18			55	
Kangaroo, Captain	1927-2004	Ent	15	25	40	83	Aka Robert James Keeshan
Kanin, Garson		Author	10	20	50	45	Plays, Dir., Screen.
Kanjorski, Paul E. K		Congr	10				Member US Congress
Kansas		Music	50	120		135	S Album 125
Kant, Immanuel	1724-1804	Author	1005	3950	7375		Ger. Philosopher, Professor
Kantner, China	1971-	Ent	10			20	Actress; daughter of Paul Kantner
Kantner, Paul		Music	15			45	Jefferson Airplane
Kantor, MacKinlay	1904-1977	Author	15	45	75	30	Am. Novels. 'Andersonville', Pulitzer 1956
Kantor, Mickey	1939-	Pol	10			20	Sec Commerce under Clinton; lawyer
Kantrowitz, Adrian, Dr.		Sci	25	70	145	145	
Kaper, Bronislaw		Comp	10	30	55	55	
Kapitza, Peter	1894-1984	Sci		375	550		Nobel Pr. Physics '78
Kaplan, Gabe		Ent	10			58	Actor
Kaplan, Gilbert		Cond				50	Mahler Specialist
Kapliolani	1834-1899	Royal	250			1500	Queen Hawaii
Kappel, Frederick R.		Bus	10			10	
Kappel, Gertrude		Opera	20			95	Wagnerian Sopr.
Kaptur, Marcy K		Congr	10				Member US Congress
Kapture, Mitzi	1964-	Ent	10			48	Actress.
Karajan, Herbert von	1908-1989	Cond	58		325	631	Austrian Classical Conductor
Karas, Anton		Comp	25	40	85	100	Third Man Theme AMusQS 350
Karloff, Boris	1887-1969	Ent	301	431	500	3043	Actor; 'Frankenstein'
Karmakar, Romuald		Ent	10			25	Ger. filmaker
Karman, Theodore von		Indust	38	78	142	80	Automobile Designer. Karman-Ghia VW
Karn, Richard	1956-	Ent	10			30	Actor; game show host
Karnes, Jay		Ent	13			40	
Karns, Roscoe	1891-1970	Ent	30			62	Actor
Karns, Todd	1921-2000	Ent				50	Harry Bailey in "It's a Wonderful Life"
Karpis, Alvin Creepy	1908-1979	Crime	142	176	300	300	30's Pub. Enemy #1

NAME	DATES	CATEGORY	SIG	LS/DS	ALS	SP	COMMENTS
Karras, Alex		Ent	10			25	
Karsavina, Tamara		Ent	50			362	Rus. -Br. Dancer
Karsh, Yousuf		Photog	30	110	238	108	Portraits, Royalty, World Famous
Karslake, Lt. -Gen. Sir Henry	1879-1942	WWII	225				WWII Br. Gen.
Kasanoff, Larry	1959-	Ent	10			20	Prod.
Kasavubu, Joseph		HOS	20	75	185	40	1st Pres. Dem. Repub. of Congo
Kaschmann, Giuseppe		Opera	60			325	Intl. Important Baritone Star
Kasdan, Sara		Author	10			15	Jewish life, humor, cooking
Kasem, Casey		Ent	10	15		62	Disc Jockey
Kasem, Jean	1954-	Ent	10			30	Actress
Kasha, Al		Comp	15			45	
Kashfi, Anna	1934-	Ent	10		30	35	Actress; former wife of Marlon Brando
Kassebaum, Nancy Landon	1932-	Congr	10	15		15	Sen. KS
Kassell, Art		Band	10			65	
Kassovitz, Mathieu	1967-	Ent	10			25	Actor; Dir.
Kastler, Alfred, Dr.	1902-1984	Sci	35	60		75	Nobel Physics '66. Orig'l Holograph Ms 850-975
Katchinsky, Victorin		Aero	20			45	
Katt, Nicky	1970-	Ent	10			30	
Katz, Bernard, Sir		Sci	15	30	45	35	Nobel Med. 1970
Katzenbach, Nicholas		Cab	10	20		15	Atty Gen. 1965
Katzenberg, Jeffrey		Bus	15	25		25	Disney CEO
Katzir, Ephraim		HOS	10			45	Pres. Israel '70's
Kaufman, Andy	1949-1984	Ent	152	225	340	245	Comedian-Actor. 'Taxi'.
Kaufman, George S.	1889-1961	Author	50	175	378	75	Dramatist, Critic, Dir. Pulitzer. TLS/Cont 275
Kaufmann, Christine	1945-	Ent	10			30	Germ. Actress. Pretty 2nd Wife of Tony Curtis
Kaunda, Kenneth		HOS	40	150	350	122	1st Pres. Zambia
Kautz, August Valentine	1828-1895	Civ War	50	80	135		Union Gen.
Kavelin, Al		Band	10			20	Big Band Leader
Kawasaki, Guy		Author	10			15	
Kawato, Masajiro Mike		WWII	60	100		250	Jap. Ace WWII, Downed Boyington; Spec SP 1000
Kay, Beatrice	1907-1986	Ent	10	20		35	Talented-Raucous Singer-Actress. Occasional Film
Kay, Dianne	1954-	Ent	10			20	
Kay, Herbie		Band	10			20	
Kay, Mary (Ash)		Bus	10	15	30	25	Cosmetics Empire
Kay, Mary Ellen	1929-	Ent				35	
Kaye, Danny	1913-1987	Ent	71	130		186	
Kaye, Darwood	1929-2002	Ent	45			70	Waldo in Little Rascals
Kaye, Sammy	1910-1987	Band	15	60		53	Big Band Leader
Kaye, Stubby	1918-1997	Ent	20	40		100	
Kazamia, Andrew	1953-	Ent	10			25	Actor
Kazan, Elia	1909-2003	Ent	25	130		67	Dir., Prod., Author
Kazan, Lainie		Ent	10			30	Actress
Keach, Stacy		Ent	10			37	Actor. 'Mike Hammer'
Kean, Charles		Ent			125		Irish actor; son of Edmund Kean
Kean, Jane	1924-	Ent	10			30	
Kean, Katja		Ent	13			40	
Kean, Thomas H.		Gov	10			15	
Keane		Music				92	Music group
Keane, Bil	1922-	Comics	20	40		60	The Family Circus'. Art 800; Sketch 200-300
Keane, Edward		Ent	10			25	
Kearny, Philip	1815-1862	Civ War	256	330	558		Union Gen.
Kearny, Philip (WD)		Civ War	409	650	1041		Union Gen. KIA
Kearny, Stephen	1794-1848	Mil	85	195	380		1st Gov. of CA; Captured CA in Mex. -Am. War.
Keating, Kenneth B.		Congr	10	15		40	Gen. WWII, MOC Sen. 1947-65

NAME	DATES	CATEGORY	SIG	LS/DS	ALS	SP	COMMENTS
Keating, Ronan	1977-	Music	10			25	Irish pop singer
Keaton, Buster	1895-1966	Ent	203	295	375	854	Great Film Comedian
Keaton, Diane		Ent	25	118		52	AA Winning Actress.
Keaton, Michael		Ent	15	45		53	Actor
Kebbel, Arielle		Ent	14			43	
Keble, John	1792-1866	Clergy	75	125	232	295	Fndr. of Oxford Movement
Kedrova, Lila		Ent	10		25	61	
Keeble, John		Author	10	30	75		
Keegan, Andrew	1979-	Ent	10			20	Actor
Keel, Howard	1919-2004	Ent	15			82	Actor; Singer
Keeler, Ruby	1909-1993	Ent	25			70	Once Busby Berkley Dancer. Wife of Al Jolson
Keena, Monica	1979-	Ent				30	Actress
Keene, Carolyn		Author	10	15	30	10	Publisher Pseud. (5 Authors)
Keene, Charles S.		Ent	10			25	
Keene, Laura	1826-1873	Ent	350	700	925		Actress. In 'Our Am. Cousin' at Ford Theater when Lincoln was shot
Keene, Tom	1896-1963	Ent	35			218	Actor
Keener, Catherine		Ent	15			45	
Keenleyside, Simon		Opera				60	English baritone
Kefauver, Estes		Congr	15	40		35	Sen. TN
Keibler, Stacy		Ent	17			50	
Keifer, Joseph W.		Civ War	25	45	60		Union Gen. & Spkr.
Keiffer, J. Warren (WD)		Civ War			1898		Union Gen.
Keillor, Garrison		Author	15	25	35	40	Humorist
Keim, Betty Lou	1938-	Ent	10			50	Actress
Keim, George May	1805-1861	Congr	15				Repr. PA, Mayor Reading, PA
Keim, William High	1813-1862	Civ War	167	487			Union Gen.
Keirstead, Wilfred C.		Clergy	10	15	20	15	
Keisha		Model	10			25	
Keitel, Harvey		Ent	15			65	Actor
Keitel, Wilhelm	1882-1946	WWII	280	484	850	548	Ger. Fld. Marshal WWII
Keith, Arthur, Sir		Author	10		35		Anthropologist, Origins of Man
Keith, Brian	1921-1997	Ent	15			77	Actor
Keith, David	1954-	Ent	10			35	Actor
Keith, George Keith E.	1746-1823	Mil	50	280	175		Br. Adm. 1746-1823. Viscount
Keith, Ian		Ent	15			60	Vintage Actor
Keith, Penelope	1940-	Ent	10			30	Br. Actress
Keith, Rosalind		Ent	10			25	
Keith, William,	1680-1749	Rev War	135	552	700		Colonial Lt. Governor PA & DE
Kekkonen, Urho		HOS	15	45			Finland
Kelcey, Herbert	1855-1917	Ent	20			75	Vintage Br. Stage Actor
Kelland, Clarence B.		Author	20	55	150	30	Am. Novels, Short Stories
Kellar, Harry		Ent	190		290	300	Magician
Kellard, Ralph	1882-1955	Ent	20			80	Actor
Kellaway, Cecil		Ent	25			78	
Kelleghan, Fiona		Author	10			12	Bibliographies
Keller, Helen	1880-1968	Author	201	765	1696	626	Blind, Deaf, Mute. TLS/Cont 1450; S Freq w/Template
Keller, Helen & A. Sullivan		Author	535		1443		
Keller, Ric K		Congr	10				Member US Congress
Kellerman, Annette		Ent	45		165	140	Aussie Dancer & Swimming Star
Kellerman, F. C., Duke Valmy		Mil	75	175	405		7 Years' War. Marshal of Nap.
Kellerman, Jonathan		Author	10			15	Author of 'Billy Straight'
Kellerman, Sally		Ent	10			55	Actress; 'Mash'
Kelley, Benjamin Franklin	1807-1891	Civ War	43		110		Union Gen.

NAME	DATES	CATEGORY	SIG	LS/DS	ALS	SP	COMMENTS
Kelley, Clarence	1911-1997	Cab	20	35	35	45	Dir. FBI
Kelley, David E.		Ent	10			35	Film industry
Kelley, Deforest		Ent	10	15	25	53	Star Trek
Kelley, Kitty		Author	12			20	Celebrity Biography
Kelley, Mikey		Ent	13			40	
Kelley, Patrick Henry		Congr	10	10			MOC MI 1913
Kelley, Virginia Clinton	1923-1994	1st Fmly	15	65			Mother of Bill Clinton
Kelley, William Darrah		Congr	10				FF 26
Kellogg, Charlotte		Philan	10	20			Mrs. Vernon Kellogg
Kellogg, Frank B.	1856-1937	Cab	26	70	95	84	Nobel Peace Pr. 1929
Kellogg, John Harvey, Dr.		Bus	45	264	150	500	Am. Phys. Health Reformer. Breakfast Cereal
Kellogg, Ray	1919-1981	Ent	10			20	Actor; Special effects
Kellogg, W. K.		Bus	110	150	325	200	Fndr. W. K. Kellogg Co.
Kellogg, William P.	1831-1918	Congr	50	100			US Sen. 1868, Gov. LA 1873-77
Kells, Maj.-Gen. Clarence H.	1892-1954	Mil	40			55	WWII US Gen.
Kelly, Daniel Hugh	1952-	Ent	10			25	Actor
Kelly, Edward J.		Pol	10	40		45	Mayor Chicago
Kelly, Emmett, Sr.	1898-1979	Ent	52	150		215	Circus Clown ' Weary Willie' Circus FDC S 125
Kelly, Gene	1912-1996	Ent	33	210		221	AA Dancer, Actor, Choreographer, Dir.
Kelly, Grace	1928-1982	Ent	230	510	1184	1445	Actress; AA
Kelly, Howard A., Dr.		Sci	20	35	60	40	Orig. Faculty Johns Hopkins U.
Kelly, Jack		Ent	15			60	
Kelly, Jean		Ent	13			40	
Kelly, Jill		Ent	24			73	
Kelly, John H.	1840-1864	Civ War	462	975			CSA Gen., Youngest Killed
Kelly, Minka		Ent	17			50	
Kelly, Moira		Ent	20			50	
Kelly, Nancy		Ent	10	20		60	
Kelly, Patsy	1910-1981	Ent	26	30	65	87	Comedienne-Actress. Wisecracking Hal Roach Star
Kelly, Paul		Ent	25			62	
Kelly, Paula	1919-1992	Music	15			25	Big Band singer
Kelly, Scott		Space	10			25	
Kelly, Sue W. K		Congr	10				Member US Congress
Kelly, Thomas W.		Mil	10	20		25	Gen. Desert Storm
Kelly, Tommy		Ent				175	Child actor
Kelly, Walt		Comics	50	200		425	Pogo
Kelsey, Fred	1884-1961	Ent	25			75	Char. Actor
Kelsey, Linda	1946-	Ent	10			25	Actress
Keltie, Sir John Scott	1840-1927	Sci			100		Geographer
Kelton, Pert	1907-1968	Ent	25		45	148	Comedienne. Original 'Alice' in The Honeymooners
Kelvin, William T., Lord	1824-1907	Sci	85	195	252	175	Kelvin Scale, Atlantic Cable
Kemble, Charles	1775-1854	Ent			70		Br. Actor
Kemble, Edward W.	1861-1933	Artist	25		42		Am. Illust. Huck Finn., ALS/sketch 175
Kemble, Frances A. 'Fanny'		Ent	35	75	110		Vintage Br. Actress-Diarist
Kemble, Priscilla	1775-1845	Ent			70		Wife of John Philip Kemble
Kemp, Hal		Band	15			40	Big Band Leader
Kemp, Jack		Cab	15			25	Sec. HUD, Pres. Cand.
Kemp, Ross		Ent	10			20	Actor
Kemp, Will		Ent	17			50	
Kempe, Rudolf		Cond				115	Ger.
Kempenfelt, Richard	1720-1782	Mil	120		410		Br. Adm. Introduced Fr. Tactics & Signal System
Kemper, Jackson, Dr.	1789-1870	Clergy	20		95		Educator
Kemper, James L.	1823-1895	Civ War	168	295	420		CSA Gen.
Kemper, James L. (WD)		Civ War	375				CSA Gen. AES 1150 '64. Wounded, Captured, Exchng.

NAME	DATES	CATEGORY	SIG	LS/DS	ALS	SP	COMMENTS
Kempf, Werner		WWII				65	Panzer Cmdr.
Kempff, Wilhelm	1895-1991	Music				280	Ger. Pianist; AQS 70
Kempka, Erich		WWII				160	Chauffeur of Hitler & his wife
Kendal, Felicity	1946-	Ent	10			25	Br. Actress
Kendal, Madge, Dame	1848-1935	Ent	12		20	35	Shakespearean Actress
Kendall, Amos	1789-1869	Cab	48	116	260		Jackson P. M. Gen, Journalist. Partner SFB Morse
Kendall, Cy		Ent	25			65	Vintage Char. Actor
Kendall, David		Law	10	15		20	Clinton Attorney
Kendall, Edward C., Dr.		Sci	30	55	100	75	Nobel Med. 1950
Kendall, Henry W.		Sci	20	35		30	Nobel Physics 1990
Kendall, Kay	1926-1959	Ent	50	120		182	Brit. Actress-Comedienne.
Kendren, John C.		Sci	15	20	30	20	
Keneally, Thomas		Author	10	20	32400	25	'Schindler's List'
Kenellopoulos, Panayotis		HOS	15	35	90		Greece
Kenly, John Reese	1818-1891	Civ War	40	80			Union Gen.
Kennan, George F.		Author	15	55			Am. Diplomat, Historian. Pulitzer
Kennedy, Anthony M.		Sup Crt	30			50	
Kennedy, Arthur		Ent	30	40	95	142	
Kennedy, Caroline		Author	20	30	40	35	Daughter of JFK, SB 25
Kennedy, Carolyn Bessette	1966-1999	Celeb	127				Wife of John Kennedy Jr.
Kennedy, Douglas	1915-1973	Ent	10			30	AKA Keith Douglas
Kennedy, Edgar		Ent	90			185	
Kennedy, Edward M. 'Ted'		Congr	15	52	75	35	Sen. MA 1962
Kennedy, Ethel		Celeb	15	50	75	35	Mrs. Robert Kennedy
Kennedy, G. A. Studdert		Clergy	20				Br. Poet, Author. Woodbine Willie
Kennedy, George	1925-	Ent	15	30		45	AA Actor
Kennedy, George C.		Aero	45			250	
Kennedy, Gerald, Bish.		Clergy	25	40	50	40	
Kennedy, Jack & Jacqueline		Pres		4200		4540	S Engr. WH Vignette 5000; 1963 S Xmas Card 15000; S wedding Photo 12000
Kennedy, Jacq. (As 1st Lady)		1st Lady	600	1234	2355	1375	
Kennedy, Jacqueline	1929-1994	1st Lady	429	799	1718	1165	SB 1200
Kennedy, Jamie		Ent	15			45	
Kennedy, Jayne	1951-	Ent	10			25	
Kennedy, John Doby	1840-1896	Civ War	125				CSA Gen.
Kennedy, John F.	1917-1963	Pres	1362	2092	3936	2236	Young ALS 5750, ALS(WWII war dated) 6500-8500
Kennedy, John F. (As Pres.)		Pres	1453	3670	11182	4344	TLS/Cont As Pres. 19500-74750. ALS S Jack 5400; S Chk 12650
Kennedy, John F., Jr.	1960-1999	Bus	168	308	483	175	Magazine Publisher 'George'; son of JFK
Kennedy, John P.		Cab	35	50	95		Fillmore Sec. Navy 1852
Kennedy, Joseph P.	1888-1969	Bus	113	299	248	300	Boston Financier, Father of JFK
Kennedy, Joseph Patrick II		Congr	15	30			Rep. MA 1987
Kennedy, Madge	1891-1997	Ent	10			40	Actress
Kennedy, Mark R. K.		Congr	10				Member US Congress
Kennedy, Martin John		Congr	10	15			MOC NY 1930-45
Kennedy, Nigel		Music	10			95	Performing musical artist
Kennedy, Patrick J. K		Congr	10				Member US Congress
Kennedy, Robert F.	1925-1968	Pol	396	484	2054	738	Atty Gen. Brother of JFK; WH Cd. 975
Kennedy, Robert F., Jr.		Author	15			25	SB 112
Kennedy, Rose Fitzgerald	1890-1995	Celeb	86	117	240	175	Kennedy Family Matriarch; Mom of JFK
Kennedy, Tom		Ent	50			122	Actor
Kenney, Bill		Music				67	Ink Spots
Kenney, George		WWII	25	60	110	70	USAAF Gen. WWII
Kenney, Kerri		Ent	15			45	

NAME	DATES	CATEGORY	SIG	LS/DS	ALS	SP	COMMENTS
Kenny G.		Music	20			42	Saxophonist
Kenny, Elizabeth, Sister	1886-1952	Sci	175			275	Pioneer Polio Treatment. Australian Nurse
Kenny, Nick		Music		20			Singer/Ink Spots
Kenny, Tom		Comics				60	Sponge Bob'; sketch 120
Kensit, Patsy		Ent	10			43	Actress
Kent, A. Atwater		Invent	20	195	90	90	Radio Mfg., Philan.
Kent, Dorthea	1916-1990	Ent				40	Actress; 'dumb blonde' roles
Kent, Edw. Augustus, Duke	1767-1820	Royal	45	150			Son of Geo. III. Father of Queen Victoria
Kent, J. Ford		Mil	90	195			Gen., Took San Juan Hill
Kent, Jack		Comics	10			35	King Aroo
Kent, James	1763-1847	Rev War	85	200	250		Legal Reporting System
Kent, Rockwell	1882-1971	Artist	42	180	244	225	Am. Landscape, Figure Painting, Illust.
Kent, Walter		Comp	40	105		75	AMusQS 125-950 (I'll Be Home for Xmas)
Kent, William	1684-1748	Artist	175	920			Sculptor, Architect, Landscape Gardener. RARE
Kent, William	1864-1928	Congr	10	15			Rep. CA 1911
Kenton, Simon	1755-1836	Pioneer	420	1783			Hunter, Trader, Spy, Gen.
Kenton, Stan	1912-1979	Band	35			99	Big Band Leader-Pianist
Kenyatta, Jomo		HOS	125	220	525	150	Prime Min. Kenya
Kenyon, Doris	1897-1979	Ent	15	25	45	65	
Kenyon, William S.		Congr	10	15	35		MOC NY 1859
Kenzle, Leila	1960-	Ent	10			25	Actress
Keogh, Myles W.	1842-1876	Mil			2700		Captn. In the 7th Cavalry; D. at Little Big Horn
Kepford, Ira		WWII	15	30	48	42	ACE, WWII; 16 kills
Kephart, Horace		Author	20			50	Southern mountain culture/history
Kepner, Wm. E.		Mil	15	35	60	60	
Keppel, Augustus		Rev War		375	750		Br. Adm. Who Influenced Br. Naval Strategy
Keppel, Francis	1916-1990	Educ	10	15	20	20	
Keppler, Joseph	1838-1894	Pub	15		45		Fndr. Puck Magazine
Kerbs, Edwin G., Dr.		Sci	20	30	55	35	Nobel Med. Krebs Cycle
Kercheval, Ken	1935-	Ent	10			30	Cliff Barnes on "Dallas"
Kerensky, Alexander	1881-1970	HOS	150	325	525	475	Rus. Leader 1917 Revolution. Prime Min. Fled
Kern, Jerome	1885-1945	Comp	202	388	725	1428	AMusQS 685-5175
Kern, Joey		Ent	18			55	
Kern, Paul B., Bish.		Clergy	20	25	35	25	
Kernan, Francis		Congr	10		35		MOC 1863, Sen. NY 1875
Kerns, Joanna	1953-	Ent	10			25	Actress
Kerns, Kurt		Music	10			25	Music. Bass & Drums 'Gravity Kills'
Kerouac, Jack	1922-1969	Author	939	2193	2260	5500	Beat Generation; S Chk 750-1250
Kerr, Deborah	1921-2007	Ent	15	45	30	134	Nominated 6 Times for Oscar
Kerr, Frederick		Ent	1450		1650		Old Baron Frankenstein
Kerr, John		Ent	10	30	25	40	Actor 'Tea & Sympathy', 'South Pacific'
Kerr, Robert S.		Congr	10	15		10	Sen., Gov. OK
Kerr, Ruth		Bus	25	35	40	50	Owner of Kerr Glass Co. Queen of Home Canning
Kerrigan, J. M.	1884-1964	Ent	568				Vintage Char. Actor. 'Johnny Gallegher' GWTW
Kerrl, Hans		Mil		65			WWII Ger. Reich Min.
Kerry, John		Congr	10			35	Sen. (D-MA); Dem. Pres Cand. 2004
Kerry, Margaret		Ent				40	Voice of Tinkerbell
Kerry, Robert		Congr	10			20	Sen.
Kersee, Jackie Joyner		Celeb	10			30	Motivation Spkr., Olympic champion
Kershaw, Joseph B.	1822-1894	Civ War	180	900	1625		CSA Gen. LS '61 3500, War Dte. Sig 350
Kerwin, Joseph P.		Space	10	35		95	
Kesey, Ken	1935-2001	Author	66	235	165	75	'One Flew Over the Cuckoo's Nest'; AMS 3600
Kesselring, Albrecht	1885-1960	WWII	148	497	293	360	Ger. Field Marshal WWII
Kestnbaum, Meyer		Bus	15	30		25	Pres. Hart, Schaffner & Marx

NAME	DATES	CATEGORY	SIG	LS/DS	ALS	SP	COMMENTS
Ketcham, Hank		Comics	30	75	60	108	Dennis the Menace'. FDC S 50., sketch 150-500
Ketcham, John H.	1832-1906	Civ War	40	75	180		Union Gen. War Dte. S 150, DS 275
Ketcham, John H. (WD)		Civ War	75	160	260		Union Gen.
Ketchum, William Scott	1813-1871	Civ War	40		100		Union Gen.
Ketelby, Albert W.		Comp	15		75		'In a Persian Market'. 'In a Monastery Garden'
Kettering, Charles F.		Invent	100	160	325	125	Engineer. Sloan-Kettering Inst. Kettering Engine
Kevorkian, Jack, Dr.		Sci	55		70	75	Euthanasia. 'Dr. Death'. 2nd Degree Murder
Key, David M.	1824-1900	Cab	30	45	90		P. M. Gen. CSA Off.
Key, Francis Scott	1779-1843	Author	506	1204	1534		Special ADS 2, 500; lawyer; poet.
Key, Philip Barton	1857-1915	Congr	10	30	40		MOC MD 1807
Key, Ted		Comics	10			75	Hazel', S drawing 85
Keyes, Erasmus D.	1818-1895	Civ War	45	90	140	300	Union Gen. ALS/Cont 1500
Keyes, Erasmus, D. (WD)		Civ War	75	160	580	750	Union Gen.
Keyes, Evelyn	1916-2008	Ent	25		40	115	Actress. SP in GWTW Costume 40-100
Keyes, Irwin	1952-	Ent	10			20	Actor
Keyes, Roger J. B. 1st Baron	1872-1945	Mil	35	30	65	75	Br. Adm. Fleet. Boxer Rebellion
Keynes, John Maynard	1883-1946	Econ	98	317	1155	250	Br. Econ. Member'Bloomsbury Group'. TLS/Cont 1600
Keys, Alicia		Music	20			60	Rock
Keys, Ancel		Sci	10	15	30	10	
Keys, Henry W.		Gov	10	20	35		Governor NH
Keyser, Ralph S.		Mil	30	50			
Keyserling, Hermann Graf	1880-1946	Phil	15	35	65	50	Ger. Social Philosopher (Spiritual Regeneration)
Khachaturian, Aram		Comp			775		Armenian Comp.
Khalid, King	1913-1982	Royal	45	65	175	250	Saudi Arabia
Khama, Seretse, Sir		HOS	65			250	1st Prime Min. of Botswana
Khambatta, Persis		Ent	22		45	90	Star Trek
Khan, Aga III	1877-1957	Relig			290		48th Imam of the Shia Ismaili Muslims
Khan, Chaka		Music	60			80	
Khan, Mohammad Ayub		HOS	30	95		70	Pres. of Pakistan 1958-1969
Khan, Yasmin, Princess		Royal	10			25	Daughter of Rita Hayworth
Khanh, Nguyen, Gen.		HOS	20	60	175	45	
Khanieff, Nikhandr S.	1922-1954	Opera				650	Leading Heroic Tenor at Bolshoi
Khatami, Mohammed		Pol				135	Pres. of Iran
Khatchaturian, Aram	1903-1978	Comp	110	180	350	316	AMusQS 300, 575, 625, 1275 ALS/cont 3000
Khomeini, Ruhollah, Ayatollah		Relig	374			1560	Iranian Moslem Leader
Khorana, Har G., Dr.		Sci	15	25	45	25	Nobel Med. 1968
Khrennikov, Tykhon		Comp		46			Russian Comp.
Khrunov, Yevgeni		Space				30	Russian cosmonaut
Khruschchev, Nikita S.	1894-1971	HOS	258	634	550	900	Premier Soviet Union
Kiam, Victor		Bus	10	25		20	Remington Electric Razor Co.
Kibbee, Guy	1882-1956	Ent	20			165	Rotund, Ruddy Faced Comed. Char. Actor 30s
Kidd, Jemma		Model	10			25	Celebrity model
Kidder, Margot		Ent	10			94	Actress.
Kiddoo, Jos. Barr		Civ War	50		90		Union Gen.
Kidman, Nicole		Ent	58			98	Actress, AA winner
Kido, Koichi	1889-1977	WWII				240	Close advisor to Hirohito
Kidron, Beeban	1961-	Celeb	10			20	Film industry Dir.
Kiel, Richard		Ent	10			58	Actor
Kielmansegg, Graf J. A.		Mil	20			35	Gen. Ger. Army
Kienzl, Wilhelm	1857-1941	Comp	15		55		Opera
Kiepura, Jan	1902-1966	Opera	42			125	Opera, Concert. Vintage, Trimmed SPc 40-50
Kier, Udo	1944-	Ent	10			25	Actor
Kiernan, James Lawlor	1837-1869	Civ War	45		120		Union Gen.
Kikuchi, Rinko		Ent	20			60	

NAME	DATES	CATEGORY	SIG	LS/DS	ALS	SP	COMMENTS
Kilban, B.		Comics	10	25		100	Cat Cartoons, The New Yorker
Kilbourne, Charles E.		Mil	15			75	Am. WWI Soldier. 3d Brig. 2d Div.
Kilbride, Percy	1888-1964	Ent	116			174	Wimpy Char. Actor. 'Ma & Pa Kettle' Films
Kilby, J. S. Jack		Sci	20	35	70	35	Inventor of Micro Chip
Kildee, Dale E. K		Congr	10				Member US Congress
Kiley, Richard	1922- 1999	Ent	15		25	80	Actor
Kilgore, Harley, M.		Congr	10	15		15	Sen. WV 1941
Kilgore, Merle		Cntry Mus	10			20	
Kilham, Hannah		Clergy	50	75	100		
Kilian, Victor	1891-1979	Ent	10		20	35	Char. Actor. Many Dark, Brooding Parts
Killinger, John W.		Congr	10	15	30		MOC PA 1859
Kilmer, Joyce	1886-1918	Author	325	562	1352		Poet. 'Trees'. AManS 3000
Kilmer, Val		Ent	28	35		79	Actor
Kilpatrick, Carolyn C. K		Congr	10				Member US Congress
Kilpatrick, Hugh J.	1836-1881	Civ War	87	185	260	415	Union Gen. Cavalry. '63 LS 1295
Kilpatrick, Hugh J. (WD)	1836-1881	Civ War	95	345	500	550	Union Gen.
Kilpatrick, James	1920-	Celeb	10			20	Pol. celebrity Conservative writer
Kimball, Dan		Cab	20	35	40	25	Sec. Navy. Aerojet Gen.
Kimball, Heber C.	1801-1868	Relig	750	1375	15000		Mormon Apostle, Opened 1st Foreign Mission in 1837
Kimball, J. Golden	1855-1938	Relig	250	500	1250	1000	Mormon leader; colorful Spkr.
Kimball, John W.		Civ War	40		80		Union Gen.
Kimball, Nathan	1822-1898	Civ War	40	75	120		Union Gen.
Kimball, Spencer W.	1895-1958	Relig	50	100	350	75	Pres. of the Mormon Church
Kimball, Ward		Comics	25			75	Musician-Discny Cartoonist. 'Firehouse 5 Plus 2'
Kimberly, John W., 1st Earl		Statsmn	20	30	110		Br. Colon'l Sec. Kimberly S. A.
Kimberly, R. Lewis	1836-1913	Civ War	30	45	75		Union Gen.
Kimbrough, Charles	1936-	Ent	10			30	Actor
Kimbrough, Emily	1898-1989	Author	10	20	42	20	'Our Hearts Were Young & Gay' writer; actress
Kimmel, Husband E.	1882-1968	WWII	312	688	760	550	US Adm. Cmdr. At Pearl Harbor; SB 425
Kimmel, Jimmy		Ent	15			40	Latenight TV host
Kind, Richard		Ent	10			40	Actor
Kind, Ron K		Congr	10				Member US Congress
Kindelberger, James H. Dutch		Bus	45			75	Pres. No. Am. Aviation. Test Pilot
Kindermann, K. B.		Aero	10	10	15	15	
Kindler, Hans		Cond	25			100	Conductor Wash., DC Nat'l Symphony
King Kalakaua		Royal				1825	King of Hawaii, 1874–91.
King, Alan	1927-2004	Ent	20	20	40	70	Stage, Film, TV, Comedian
King, Andrea	1919-2003	Ent	15			55	Actress. 2nd Leads, Other Woman 40s-50's
King, B. B.		Music	100			154	Grammy R&B Singer, Guitarist. S Album 160; S Guitar w/Clapton 835
King, Ben E.	1938-	Comp	12			40	The Drifters. 'Stand by Me' AMusQS 240; DS 240
King, Cammie	1934-	Ent	25		35	65	Bonnie "Blue" Butler in GWTW
King, Carole		Music	55			77	Rock, songwriter
King, Charles		Civ War	50		175		Soldier-Civil War Author
King, Charles	1895-1957	Ent	20			60	Actor
King, Claire	1963-	Ent	10			30	Br. Actress
King, Coretta Scott	1927-2006	Civ Rts	42	89	110	100	Mrs. Martin Luther King, Jr. Civ. Rights Activist
King, Daniel Putnam		Congr	10		38		FF 38
King, Edward J., Bish.		Clergy	25	35	50		
King, Ernest J.	1878-1956	WWII	40	158		168	Fleet Adm. Cmmdr. Chief US Fleet WWII
King, Frank		Comics	35			165	'Gasoline Alley'
King, Henry		Ent	30			75	Film Dir.
King, Horatio	1811-1897	Cab	45	175	275		P. M. Gen. 1861
King, Jack	1903-1943	Comp	10			20	Pop Songwriter AMusQS 35

NAME	DATES	CATEGORY	SIG	LS/DS	ALS	SP	COMMENTS
King, James	1791-1853	Bus	20		65		Financier, RR Pres. Son of VP Rufus King
King, James		Ent	15			45	
King, John Alsop		Gov	10		35		Gov. NY, a Fndr. Repub. Party
King, John 'Dusty'	1909-1987	Ent	20	30	45	55	
King, John Haskell	1820-1888	Civ War	42	75	110		Union Gen.
King, Larry		Ent	10	20	35	40	Talk Show Host
King, Martin Luther, III		Activist	10			30	Civ. Rights
King, Martin Luther, Jr.	1929-1968	Civ Rts	1805	6971	7500	6275	Advoc. Peaceful Nonviolence. Assass. SB 2500-4000
King, Martin Luther. Sr.		Clergy	35	45	60	65	
King, Pee Wee		Band	10			20	Country Music Bandleader-Comp.
King, Perry	1948-	Ent	10			30	
King, Peter T. K		Congr	10				Member US Congress
King, Preston	1806-1865	Congr	15	45	100		Repr. 1843, Senate NY. Suicide 1865; FF 35
King, Rufus	1755-1827	Rev War	170	475	425		Cont'l Congr. Historical ALS 2500
King, Rufus	1814-1876	Civ War	88	100	293		Union Gen.
King, Rufus (WD)		Civ War	75	425	1249		Union Gen. ALS/Cont '62 3200
King, Stephen		Author	40	210	310	208	Master of Horror & Suspense; SB 200-750
King, Steve K		Congr	10				Member US Congress
King, Thomas Starr	1824-1864	Clergy	25	35	95	40	
King, Walter Woolf		Music	15		25	48	Broadway Singing Star. 'Vagabond King' in 30s
King, Wayne		Band	15			25	Big Band Leader.
King, William R.	1786-1853	VP	181	340			Pierce VP. D. after 45 days
King, Wm. L. Mackenzie	1874-1950	HOS	40	262		55	P. M. Canada
King, Yolanda	1955-2007	Celeb	10			25	Daughter of MLK
King, Yvonne	1920-	Ent				60	Actress
Kingman, Dong		Artist	25	50	100		
Kingsford-Smith, Charles		Aero	52	125		187	FDC Trans-Tasman Fl. 225
Kingsley, Ben	1943-	Ent	20	60	40	50	AA Winning Actor 'Gandhi'
Kingsley, Charles	1819-1875	Author	45	95	145		Br. Novels, Clergyman
Kingston Trio		Music	60			215	Folk Group of 59's
Kingston, Evelyn P., 2nd Duke of		Royal			190		
Kingston, Jack K		Congr	10				Member US Congress
Kingston, William H.		Author	25		100		Br. Boy's Adventure Books
Kinison, Sam	1953-1992	Ent	110	268		242	Comedian
Kinks (5 Current Members)		Music	285			355	Rock. S Album 350
Kinman, Seth	1815-1885	Hunter				368	Famous mountain-man, trapper
Kinmont, Kathleen		Ent	10			40	Actress
Kinnear, Greg		Ent	10			40	Actor
Kinney, John	d. 1919	West				635	Leader of the John Kinney Gang (NM rustlers)
Kinney, Kathy		Ent	13			40	
Kinney, Sean		Music	10			25	Music. Drummer 'Alice in Chains'
Kinsey, Alfred, Dr.	1894-1956	Sci	70	139	210	158	Am. Sexologist Researcher; SB 550
Kinskey, Leonid	1903-1995	Ent	20			40	Russian-Born Char. Actor. 'Casablanca'
Kinski, Klaus		Ent	35		40	160	Actor-Dir.
Kinski, Natassja		Ent	15	25	45	148	Actress,
Kinsley, Michael	1951-	Jrnalist	10			20	Pol. journalist
Kinstler, E. R.		Comics	10			100	Illust.
Kintner, Robert	1909-1980	Bus	10	20	30	20	TV executive
Kip, William I., Bish.		Clergy	50	85	125		
Kipling, Rudyard	1865-1936	Author	206	331	871	900	Nobel Lit., Novels, Poet; Poem 4300
Kiplinger, Austin		Bus	10	20	45	15	Kiplinger Washington Newsletter
Kipnis, Alexander		Opera	35	75		122	Opera. Russ. Bass
Kiraly, Karch		Ent	17			50	
Kirby, Bruno	1949-2006	Ent	25			65	Actor

NAME	DATES	CATEGORY	SIG	LS/DS	ALS	SP	COMMENTS
Kirby, Edmund	1840-1863	Civ War	325				Union Gen.
Kirby, Fred. M.		Bus		2450			Founded Dime Store Chain. Woolworth Partner
Kirby, George	1923-1995	Ent	20			50	Comedian
Kirby, Jack		Comics	25			170	'Captain America'
Kirby, Rollin		Comics	20			90	
Kirchner, Ernst Ludwig	1880-1938	Artist			2380		Ger. expressionist painter
Kirk, Andy		Band	15			65	
Kirk, Claude Jr.		Gov	10	15			Governor FL
Kirk, Eddie		Cntry Mus	10			20	Country Singer-Recording Artist
Kirk, Edward Needles	1828-1863	Civ War	225				Union Gen.
Kirk, Florence		Opera	10			30	Opera
Kirk, George		WWII	12	22	40	35	ACE, WWII; 7 kills
Kirk, Grayson	1903-1997	Educ	20			40	Columbia University Pres. for Many Years
Kirk, Mark Steven K		Congr	10			20	Member US Congress IL
Kirk, Norman T.	1888-1960	Mil	30	50		55	US Gen. WWII
Kirk, Phyllis		Ent	20		95	52	Rising Star in 50s. Cvr. Life Mag. Illness Struck
Kirk, Roland		Music				308	Jazz saxophone soloist
Kirk, Tommy		Ent	10			40	Juvenile Star
Kirkby-Lunn, Louise		Opera	30			95	Opera
Kirkconnell, Clare	1953-	Ent	10			25	Actress
Kirkham, Ralph W.	1821-1893	Civ War	40	55	80		Union Gen.
Kirkland, Lane		Labor	10	15	30	15	Labor Leader. AFL-CIO
Kirkland, Sally	1941-	Ent	10			35	
Kirkland, Samuel	1741-1808	Clergy		2025	2150		Oneida Indian Missionary. Active during Rev. War
Kirkland, William Whedbee	1833-1915	Civ War	110				CSA Gen.
Kirkpatrick, Jean J.		Cab	20		35	25	Ambassador U. N. Signature on Special Piece 115
Kirkwood, Joe, Jr.		Ent	38	75	110	70	Radio, Movies & Golfer
Kirkwood, Samuel J.	1813-1894	Cab	15	25	55	45	Sec. Intertior, Gov, Sen. IA
Kirman Sr., Richard.		Gov	10			30	Governor NV
Kirov, Sergey Mironovich	1886-1934	Pol			632		Communist leader
Kirschlager, Angelika		Opera	10			30	Opera. Vienna's New Rising Star
Kirsebom, Vendela		Ent	15			50	Model-Actress 'Batman & Robin'
Kirshner, Mia		Ent				35	
Kirsten, Dorothy	1919-1992	Opera	20			48	Am. Lyric Sopr., Opera. Record 30 Yrs. At Met.
Kirwen, Dervla	1971-	Ent	10			25	Irish Actress
Kiser, Terry	1939-	Ent	10			30	Actor
Kisling, Moise	1891-1953	Artist			340		Polish Painter
Kiss (Entire Group)		Music	55			183	Rock. Alb. S 145-225
Kissin, Evgeny		Music				68	Pianist
Kissinger, Henry A.		Cab	28	70	100	57	Sec. State, Stateman, Diplomat, Prolific Author
Kistiakowsky, G. B., Dr.		Sci	40	135		70	Nobel Chemistry
Kitchener, Horatio H.	1850-1916	Mil	85	205	278	210	Ir. -born Br. Field Marshal. 1st Earl, Statesman
Kitsch, Taylor		Ent	13			39	
Kitt, Eartha	1928-	Ent	20	60		43	Actress-Singer.
Kittinger, Joe		Aero	25	45			
Kittredge, Walter		Comp	30		45		Tenting Tonight'. AMusQS 300-1, 150
Kitzhaber, John		Gov	10			12	Oregon Gov.
Kleber, Jean-Baptiste		Fr Rev	145	410	855		One of France's Greatest Generals
Kleczka, Gerald D. K		Congr	10				Member US Congress
Klee, Paul	1879-1940	Artist	900	615	1555	950	Swiss Surrealist Painter
Kleiber, Carlos		Cond				475	
Kleiman, Jon		Music	10			25	Music. Drummer 'Monster Magnet'
Klein, Calvin		Bus	15	25	35	38	Fashion-Accessory Designer
Klein, Chris		Ent	18			55	

NAME	DATES	CATEGORY	SIG	LS/DS	ALS	SP	COMMENTS
Klein, Felix	1849-1925	Sci	85		450		Ger. Mathematician: Non-Euclidean Geometry
Klein, Robert		Ent	15			42	Actor, Comedian
Kleist, Field Marshal Ewald von	1881-1954	WWII	50	175			WWII Ger. Gen.
Kleist, Paul von		WWII	50	85		100	Ger. WWII Tank Cmdr.
Klemperer, Otto		Cond	73	161	310	387	Ger. Conductor
Klemperer, Werner	1920-2000	Ent	15	40		150	Actor. 'Col. Klink' on 'Hogan's Heroes'
Kleppe, Thomas S.		Cab	10	15	30	10	MOC ND, Sec. Interior
Klimt, Gustav	1862-1918	Artist	170	575	1112		Austrian. Allegorical Murals
Kline, Franz		Artist				2000	Abstract Expressionist Artist
Kline, John K		Congr	10				Member US Congress
Kline, Kevin		Ent	15	12	45	50	Actor; AA Winner
Klingenberg, Fritz	1912-1945	Mil				150	SS Off.
Klose, Margarete	1902-1968	Opera	15			65	Opera. Ger. Mezzo-Sopr.
Kluge, Hans Gunther von	1882-1944	WWII	75		250		Ger. Gen WWII, Suicide
Klugman, Jack	1922-	Ent	10			45	Actor. 1/2 'Odd Couple'; SP w/Tony Randall 200
Klutznick, Philip M.		Cab	10	12		15	Sec. Commerce
Kmentt, Waldemar		Opera	10			65	Opera. Eminent Tenor
Knepper, Robert		Ent	13			40	
Knern, H. H.		Comics	25		95		Katzenjammer Kids
Knibb, William		Clergy	45	60	75		
Knievel, Evel	1938-2007	Celeb	10	15	35	55	Daredevil Motorcycle Rider
Knight, Austin		Ent	10			20	Br. Comedian
Knight, Christopher		Ent	18			55	
Knight, Evelyn		Music	10				With the Star Dusters
Knight, Fuzzy		Ent	90			135	
Knight, Gladys		Music	15	20	35	45	Rock. DS by Knight & 6 Pips 125
Knight, Goodwin J.	1896-1970	Gov	10	15		15	Governor CA
Knight, John S.		Bus	10	35	45	20	Publisher
Knight, John T.		Mil	25	75		35	Am. WWI Gen.
Knight, Jordan	1970-	Music	10			35	Lead singer of "New Kids on the Block"
Knight, June	1913-1987	Ent	10			40	Actress
Knight, Laura, Dame	1877-1970	Artist	60	100	175		Ranked Alongside Britain's Greatest
Knight, Pete		Aero				60	Test pilot
Knight, Phil		Bus	22	35	45	45	Nike Athletic Shoes
Knight, Shirley	1936-	Ent	10			35	
Knight, T. R.		Ent	15			45	
Knight, Ted	1923-1986	Ent	60	35	35	70	Actor. Best Remembered in 'Mary Tyler Moore Show'
Knight, Wayne		Ent	15			45	Actor, "Newman"
Knightley, Keira		Ent	27			82	
Knightly, Keira		Ent	15			55	Actress
Knipe, Joseph Farmer	1823-1901	Civ War	45		120		Union Gen.
Knollenberg, Joe K		Congr	10				Member US Congress
Knopf, Alfred A.		Bus	10	20	35		Knopf Publishing
Knote, Heinrich		Opera	20				Opera
Knott, Walter		Bus	35	70		150	Co-Fndr. Knott's Berry Farm
Knott, Walter & Cordelia		Bus	150			475	Co-Fndr. s Knott's Berry Farm
Knotts, Don	1924-2006	Ent	20	40		129	Self Sketch S 35
Knowland, William F.		Congr	10	20		25	Sen. CA, Publisher
Knowles, Beyonce		Music	20			80	Singer
Knowles, James S.	1784-1862	Author	10	25	60		
Knowles, John		Author	35			100	Br. Author
Knowles, Patric		Ent	10			70	
Knox, Alexander	1907-1995	Ent	10	15	30	40	
Knox, Buddy		Music				100	Singer Party Dolls

NAME	DATES	CATEGORY	SIG	LS/DS	ALS	SP	COMMENTS
Knox, Elyse		Ent	10	20	35	49	Actress
Knox, Frank	1874-1944	Cab	50	60	95	95	Sec. Navy. TLS/Cont 275
Knox, Henry	1750-1806	Rev War	192	506	710		Maj. Gen. Rev. War Dte. ALS 4, 500
Knox, James, Card.		Clergy	30	30	35	35	
Knox, Philander C.	1853-1921	Cab	12	25	107	70	Atty Gen., Sen. PA
Knoxville, Johnny		Ent	15			40	Actor; 'Jackass'
Knudsen, Erik		Ent	13			40	
Knudsen, William S.		Bus	20	35	85	45	Pres. GM. WWII War Prod. Dir.
Knutson, Harold		Congr	10	10		10	MOC MN
Kobayashi, Takeji		Author	25		60	60	Proletarian Literary Movement
Koch, Edward I.		Pol	10	20	35	30	Mayor NYC
Koch, Edward W.		Ent	20			35	Prod-Dir. 'Manchurian Cand. ', 'Odd Couple'
Koch, Heinrich H. Robert	1843-1910	Sci	940	1267	1813	2300	Nobel Bacteriology-Med. '05, Koch's Postulates
Koch, Howard W.	1902-1995	Ent	175			200	Prod./Dir. Film/TV Hits. AA for 'Casablanca'
Koch, Karl		WWII		585			Cmdr. of the Buchenwald concentration camp
Koch, Marvin		Author	10			12	Genealogy
Kodaly, Zoltan	1882-1967	Comp	135	300	1092	472	Hung. Comp. Cont. ALS 1750. AMusQS 1150
Koehl, Herman		Aero	75			250	1st East-West Crossing Atlantic
Koehler, Armin		Aero	10	20	35	25	
Koenig, Walter		Ent	20		45	50	Actor. 'Chkov' on Star Trek
Kogan, Claude	1919-1959	Celeb			150		Adventurer
Kohl, Hannelove		Celeb	10			15	Mrs. Helmut Kohl
Kohl, Helmut		HOS	15	30	65	65	Chancellor Ger.
Kohl, Herb		Congr	10				US Senate (D-WI)
Kohler, Walter J.		Bus	10	30		25	Fndr. Kohler Corp. Plumbing
Kohner, Susan	1936-	Ent	10			25	Actress. 'Imitation of Life'
Kokoschka, Oskar	1886-1980	Artist	129	172	450	148	Austrian. PC Repro Painting S 180
Kolbe, Jim K		Congr	10				Member US Congress
Kolff, Willem J., Dr.		Sci	15	55		40	Created Artificial Kidney
Kolker, Henry	1874-1947	Ent	15		65	50	Actor-Dir-Writer, Noted Stage, Film Char. Actor
Kolleck, Teddy	1912-2007	Pol	25	80	100	85	Mayor of Jerusalem
Kollo, Rene		Opera	10		35	25	Opera
Kollontay, Alexandra	1872-1952	Pol		328			Russian revolutionary
Kollwitz, Kathe	1867-1945	Artist			506		Ger. Sculptor, Graphic Artist
Komano, Stacy		Ent				40	'Baywatch'
Komarov, Vladimir M.	1927-1967	Space	125			289	Rus. Cosmonaut. 1st To Die During Space Flight
Kondracke, Morton	1939-	Jrnalist	10			15	Am. Pol. commentator & journalist
Konetzni, Anny		Opera	25			65	Opera
Konstantin, Leopoldine	1886-1965	Ent				470	Actress
Konya, Sandor		Opera				40	Hung. Tenor
Kook, Abraham Isaac		Clergy	45	145			Palestinian Rabbi
Koontz, Dean	1945-	Author	20	62		65	Novels. Horror. SBs 75-150
Koop, C. Everett, Dr.		Mil	10	20	50	28	Adm., US Surgeon Gen.
Kopell, Bernie		Ent	10			30	Actor. 'Get Smart', 'Love Boat'
Koppel, Ted		TV News	10	15	30	30	News
Korda, Alexander	1893-1956	Ent	40	45	90	170	Hungarian-born film Dir. & Prod.
Koren, Edward		Comics	10			75	New Yorker Cartoonist
Korfes, Maj. -Gen. Otto	1889-1964	Mil	225				WWII Ger. Gen.
Korman, Harvey	1927-2008	Ent	10			60	Comedian; actor
Korn		Music	50			125	Music. 5 Member Rock Group; S Album 80
Kornberg, Arthur		Sci	20	30	45	35	Nobel Med.
Kornby, Arthur		Sci	15		20		
Korner, Alexis	1928-1984	Music				90	English Blues Singer
Korngold, Erich Wolfgang	1897-1957	Comp	75	200	350	250	Opera/Orch./Film. Spec. S Score 985; Man. 2340

K

NAME	DATES	CATEGORY	SIG	LS/DS	ALS	SP	COMMENTS
Kornman, Mary	1915-1973	Ent	50			95	Mary in the Little Rascals
Korolev, Sergei	1906-1966	Mil		242		494	Russian missle designer, Sputnik
Korvin, Charles	1907-1998	Ent	10			60	Actor; Blacklisted in the 50s
Koscina, Sylva	1933-1994	Ent				110	Croatian born actress
Kosciusko, Thaddeus		Rev War	325	775	3148		Polish Patriot.
Kosinski, Jerzy	1933-1991	Author	50	130			Being There; The Painted Bird; SB 90
Kosleck, Martin	1904-1994	Ent	15			70	Ger. actor
Koslovsky, Ivan		Music		46			Opera singer
Kossuth, Lajos	1802-184	HOS	120	230	375	300	Hungarian Patriot, Journalist
Kostabi, Mark	1960-	Artist					Painting 750; SB 120
Kostal, Irwin		Comp	10	10	20	10	
Kostelanetz, Andre	1901-1980	Cond	15	25	45	25	Conductor
Koster, Henry		Ent	15	35		40	Film Dir.
Kostow, Robert		Bus	10			20	Financial analyst
Kostunica, Vojislav		Pol				45	Pres. of Serbia
Kosygin, Aleksei		HOS	158	406	625	268	Premier of Soviet Union
Koussevitzky, Serge	1874-1951	Cond	65		170		Russ. Conductor. Pioneered Introducing Russ. Opera
Kovack, Nancy (Mehta)	1935-	Ent	10			45	Actress
Kovacs, Ernie	1919-1962	Ent	180	252		526	1st Outrageous TV Comedian
Kovalevskaya, Sophia	1850-1891	Sci			850		Rus. Mathematician, Novels
Kovansky, Anatol		Artist	15		40	25	
Kove, Martin	1947-	Ent	10			30	Actor
Kovic, Ron		Activist	20	35	65	45	Anti Viet Nam Autobio. 'Born on the 4th of July'
Kowarski, L.		Sci	10	25	60		
Kozhedub, Ivan		WWII	75				Russian Ace WWII
Kozky, Alex		Comics	10			20	Apt. 3-G
Kozlovsky, Ivan	1900-1993	Opera					Ukrainian Tenor. No known prices
Krabbe, Jeroen		Ent	10			50	Actor
Kraft, Chris		Space	15			132	Mission control
Kraft, James L.		Bus	30	95	175	50	Fndr. Kraft Foods Co.
Kragen, Ken		Bus	10	10	20	20	Enter Business Mgr.
Kraigher, Sergej		HOS				45	Pres. Yugoslavia
Krakowski, Jane		Ent	15			45	Actress. 'Ally McBeal' Co-Star
Kral, Roy	1921-2002	Music	10	25		35	Jazz singer
Krall, Diana		Music	20			45	Rock, popular
Kramer, Billy J.		Music	60			160	Singer; SP w/the Dakotas 160
Kramer, Clare	1974-	Ent				40	Actress
Kramer, Dolly	1904-1995	Ent				60	Munchkin in WOZ
Kramer, Joseph		WWII			2800		Commandant of Auschwitz & Bergen-Belsen
Kramer, Stanley		Ent	15	122	150	45	Film Prod., Dir.
Kramer, Stephanie	1956-	Ent	10			25	Actress
Krantz, Gene	1933-	Space				380	NASA flight Dir.
Krantz, Judith		Author	25		40	35	Novels
Krasinski, John		Ent	16			48	
Krasner, Milton		Ent	20			45	Film Dir. AA
Kraus, Alfredo		Opera	15			35	Opera.
Kraus, Clemens		Cond	65			220	Austrian Conductor
Kraus, Robert		Artist	10	25	50	50	
Krause, Peter		Ent	15			48	Actor. 'Sports Night'. Nate Fisher, '6 Ft. Under'
Krauss, Clemens	1893-1954	Cond				127	Austrian
Krauss, Werner		Ent	328				
Kravitz, Lenny		Music	20	130		50	Music. S Guitar 630
Krebs, Hans Adolf, Sir	1900-1981	Sci	45	45	60	70	Ger.-born Br. Biochemist. Nobel Med., Kreb's Cycle
Krebs, Nita	1904-1992	Ent	15	20		50	Actress-Dancer 'Wizard of Oz'. Munchkin

K

NAME	DATES	CATEGORY	SIG	LS/DS	ALS	SP	COMMENTS
Kregal, Kevin		Space	10			25	
Kreisler, Fritz	1875-1962	Comp	60	110	298	194	Violinist, AMusQS 275
Kremer, Andrea	1959-	Ent	10			20	ESPN News
Kremer, Gidon		Music				65	Violinist
Krenek, Ernst	1900-1991	Comp	22	35	141	55	Austrian-Am. AMusQS 95-150-225
Krenn, Fritz		Opera	15			35	Opera
Kreps, Juanita M.		Cab	10	10	15	15	Sec. Commerce
Kresge, Sebastian S.	1867-1966	Bus	100	210	260	225	S. S. Kresge Stores
Kretschmer, Otto		WWII	78	140		148	Highest Scoring U Boat Cmdr.
Kreutzer, Conradin		Comp	125	300	650		Ger. Comp./Conductor
Krige, Alice		Ent	10	50		40	
Krips, Josef		Cond				250	Austrian
Kristel, Sylvia		Ent	55			86	
Kristofferson, Kris		Music	15		35	58	Singer; S Guitar 240
Kristyon, Eldgorn		HOS	20	35			Pres. of Iceland
Kroc, Mrs. Ray (Joan)		Bus	10	15	35	15	McDonalds
Kroc, Ray A.		Bus	30	90	150	142	McDonalds
Krock, Arthur		Cab	10	20	40	15	Bureau Chief, Columnist NY Times
Krofft, Marty		Ent	40	125		50	Puppeteer
Kroft, Steve		Ent	10			25	60 Minutes
Krol, John, Card.	1910-1996	Clergy	30	40	75	50	Archbishop of Philadelphia 1961-88 & Cardinal '67
Kroll, Gustov		Sci	10			35	Rocket Pioneer/von Braun
Kroll, Nick		Ent	13			40	
Kropotkin, Pyotr A.	1842-1921	Pol	75	175	350		Russian anarchist
Krueger, Walter	1881-1967	Mil	45	100		95	Sp. -Am., WWI & Full Gen. WWII
Krug, J. A.		Cab	10	20	30	15	Sec. Interior
Kruger, Kurt	1917-2006	Ent	10			40	Swiss-Ger. Actor
Kruger, Otto	1885-1974	Ent	30			67	Distinguished Leading & Char. Actor
Kruger, Stephanus J. P.	1825-1904	HOS	125	375		660	Krugerrand Named For Him
Krulwich, Robert		Jrnalist	10			20	PBS
Krupa, Gene	1909-1973	Music	108	130	160	157	Big Band Leader-Drums
Krupinski, Walter		WWII	15	30	45	52	Ger. Ace. WWII. RK
Krupp, Alfred	1812-1902	Bus	180	320	500		Fndr. Krupp Works
Krupp, Friedrich Alfred	1854-1902	Bus	125	270	212		Arms Manufacturer
Krylov, Ivan A.		Author	15	40	75	75	Russion Fabulist. Fables
Krzyanowski, Wladimir	1824-1887	Civ War	50	95	140		Union Gen.
Kschessinska, Joseph	1868-1942	Ent	75		250		Actor-Brother of Prima Ballerina Matilda K.
Kschessinska, Matilda M.	1872-1971	Ballet	110		580	535	Prima Ballerina Assoluta Imperial Theatre
Kuatosov, Mikhail	1745-1813	Mil		1750			Rus. Mil. Leader against Turks
Kubelik, Jan	1880-1940	Comp	40	92	250	191	Czech Violinist, AMusQS 200-575
Kubelik, Rafael		Cond	15	50		60	
Kubiszewski, Andrew		Music	10			25	Music. Drummer, Vocals 'Stabbing Westward'
Kubitschek, Juscelino		HOS	10	35	50	40	Brazil
Kubrick, Stanley	1928-1999	Ent	35	330		632	Film Dir.
Kuchel, Thomas	1910-1994	Congr	10	25			Sen. CA
Kuchler, Georg Von		Mil				306	Ger. Gen.
Kuchta, Gladys		Opera	10			30	Opera
Kucinich, Dennis J. K.		Congr	10			20	Member US Congr. Dem. Pres. Cand. 2008
Kudrow, Lisa		Ent	20			62	Actress. 'Friends'
Kuebler, Ludwig		WWII		88			Ger. Gen.
Kuharski, Kelly		Ent	12			35	
Kuhlman, Katherine		Clergy	35		50		Radio Evengelist
Kuhn, Joseph E.		Mil	30		125		Am. WWI Gen.
Kuhn, Maggie	1905-1995	Pol	20			35	Pol. & Social Activist. Fndr of Grey Panthers

NAME	DATES	CATEGORY	SIG	LS/DS	ALS	SP	COMMENTS
Kuken, William	1810-1882	Comp			85		Ger. Comp.
Kullman, Charles		Opera	20			50	Popular Operatic Tenor/Met. 20 Yrs. Some Films
Kulp, Nancy	1921-1991	Ent	80			110	Comed. -Actress; Ms. Hathaway, 'Bev. Hillbillies'
Kumalo, Dumisani		Pol	10			20	Perm. Rep. to UN for South Africa
Kuncewiczowa, Maria		Author	145		345		Escaped Nazi Ger.
Kung, Hans		Clergy	35	50	75	60	
Kunis, Mila	1983-	Ent				40	
Kunstler, William	1919-1995	Law	25	35	75	40	Defense of Radicals. Attny for Martin Luther King
Kupka, Frantisek	1871-1957	Artist	110	225	387		Czech. Abstract Art, Illust.
Kuralt, Charles		TV News	10	20	35	35	Commentator
Kuribayashi, Tadamichi	1891-1945	WWII			500		Japenese Gen. who defended Iwo Jima
Kurtz, Efrem		Cond				100	Russian conductor
Kurtz, Swoosie	1944-	Ent	10			30	Actress. Sisters
Kusch, Polykarp, Dr.		Sci	20	50		25	Nobel Physics
Kutcher, Ashton		Ent	20			45	Actor
Kutosov, Mikhail	1745-1813	Mil		1550			Rus. Mil. Leader against Turks
Kutuzov, Mikhail Illar.		Mil		1840			Soviet Field Marshall
Kuykendall, Andrew J.	1815-1891	Congr	25				Repr. IL, Union Off.
Kwan, Nancy	1939-	Ent	20	60		78	Actress
Ky, Nguyen Cao		HOS	30	100	250	75	
Kyl, Jon		Congr	10			15	US Senate (R-AZ)
Kyne, Peter B.		Author	10	15	30	10	Homsey Family Novels
Kyser, Kay		Band	15			30	Big Band Leader
L A Guns		Music	40			60	Rock; original members formed Guns & Roses
L A Law (cast)		Ent				275	10 Sigs.
L. Ken		Ent	15			45	
L. L. Cool J.		Music	20			50	Rap; rock
La Belle, Patti		Music	15			35	Singer
La Cava, Gregory		Ent	20			45	Film Dir.
La Farge, John	1835-1910	Artist	38	95	279		Am. Landscape & Figure Painter. Author
La Forge, Frank		Comp	15			45	
La Marr, Barbara		Ent	300			700	
La Motta, Vikki		Ent	10			25	Model-Actress. Wife of Jake La Motta.
La Mure, Pierre	1909-1976	Author		150	250		Fr. author best known for writing Moulin Rouge
La Paglia, Anthony	1959-	Ent	10			40	Actor
La Plante, Lynda	1946-	Ent	10			25	Br. Writer, Prod., actress
La Revelliere-Lepaux, L.		Fr Rev	25	70	145		Pol.
La Rocque, Rod	1898-1969	Ent	20		45	55	Actor
La Rue, Jack	1903-1984	Ent	10			50	Actor. Gangster Roles & Heavies
La Salle, Eriq		Ent	10			38	Actor
La Verne. Lucille	1872-1945	Ent	75			150	Vintage actress
LaBeauf, Sabrina		Ent				20	Actress. Bill Cosby Show
LaBeouf, Shia		Ent	18			54	
Labouisse, Eve Curie		Sci	15	60	90	90	Celebrity Daughter of Marie & Pierre Curie
Lacepede, Bernhard de		Sci	30	75	145		Fr. Naturalist & Pol.
LaCerva, Victor M. D.		Author	10			12	Motivation, world peace
Lacey, Ingrid		Ent	10			25	Actress
Lachaise, Gaston	1882-1935	Artist		125	188		Fr.-Am. Sculptor
Laciura, Anthony		Opera	10			25	Opera
Ladd, Alan	1913-1964	Ent	80	108	260	182	Actor. Popular Leading Man of 40s-50's
Ladd, Cheryl		Ent	10			30	TV Star. 'Charley's Angels'.
Ladd, David		Ent	10			25	Prod.
Ladd, Diane		Ent	15			45	Actress
Ladd, Kenneth	d. 1944	WWII	250			750	WWII Ace (rare); 12 kills; 8FG Windy City Ruthie

NAME	DATES	CATEGORY	SIG	LS/DS	ALS	SP	COMMENTS
Ladd, Sue Carol	1906-1982	Ent	10			35	Actress
LaDelle, Jack		Music	10			35	Recording artist
Laemmle, Carl	1867-1939	Ent	96	264	525	830	Film Pioneer, Fndr. Universal
Laennec, Reneé T. H.	1781-1826	Sci	2250	3100	4284		Fr. Phys., Invented Stethoscope
Lafayette, Marquis de	1757-1834	Rev War	450	893	2588		Gilbert Motier. Fr. Statesman. ALS/Cont 4900-9600, Great ALS 39000
LaFollette, Philip	1897-1965	Gov	15	35		50	Governor WI
LaFollette, Robert Jr.	1895-1953	Congr	10	25			Sen. WI
LaFollette, Robert M.	1855-1925	Congr	35	95			Sen. WI
LaFontaine, Henri Marie	1854-1943	Law	10	20	30		Nobel Peace Pr. Belgian Sen.
Laforgue, Jules	1860-1887	Author	150				Fr. Symbolist Poet. D. at 27. ALS/Cont 5500
Lagasse, Emeril		Celeb	10	20	30	30	Famous chef
Lagerkvist, P.		Author	30	70	175	100	Nobel Literature 1951
Lagerlof, Selma	1858-1940	Author	95	175		250	Nobel Literature 1909
Lagge, James		Clergy	20	25	35		
LaGuardia, Fiorello	1882-1947	Congr	60	89	110	150	Great Reform Mayor NYC. MOC NY. Colorful Char.
Lahm, Frank		Aero	35	75	140	90	
LaHood, Ray L		Congr	10				Member US Congress
Lahr, Bert	1895-1967	Ent	388	706		1470	Cowardly Lion' of OZ, SP as Lion 8000-11000
Lahti, Christine		Ent	10			30	Actress
Laidlie, D. A.		Clergy	15	20	25		
Laine, Frankie	1913-2007	Music	15	25		45	Singer. Recording artist of Top Hits
Laine, J. L. J., Viscount		Fr Rev	30	85	175		
Laingen, Bruce		Diplo	10			15	Iran Hostage
Laird, Melvin		Cab	10	20	25	25	Sect'y Defense
Laithwaite, Eric R.		Invent	25	95			Electromagnetic Propulsion & Air Cushion Suspensio
Lake, Alexander		Author	10			12	Afr. adventure
Lake, Arthur	1905-1986	Ent	40	55	100	123	Dagwood Bumstead of 'Blondie'
Lake, Ricki		Ent	10			25	TV Host
Lake, Simon	1866-1945	Invent	38	66	310	303	Inv. Even-Keel Sub. Sci. Drawing 3750, Chk 25
Lake, Veronica	1919-1973	Ent	358	460		639	Actress
Laker, Freddie, Sir		Bus	10			20	Airline Pres.
Lakes, Gary		Opera	10			30	Opera
LaLanne, Jack		Ent	10	15	30	20	TV Body Builder
Lalique, Rene	1860-1929	Artist	150		600		Fr. Jeweler & Decorative Glass Artisan
Lamar, Joseph R.		Sup Crt	60	95	225		
Lamar, Lucius Q. C.	1825-1893	Sup Crt	78		235		CSA Off., US Sen.
Lamar, Mirabeau B.	1789-1859	Tex	123	1946	2530		Pres., V. P. & Sec. State Repub. of TX
LaMarck, Jean Baptiste de		Sci	400	950	690		Forerunner of Darwin
Lamarr, Hedy	1913-2000	Ent	40	70	100	209	40's Beautiful Glamour Girl & Inventor
LaMartine, Alphonse de	1790-1869	Author	90	130	190		Fr. Romantic Poet-Statesman
Lamas, Fernando	1925-1982	Ent	20	25	45	77	Actor
Lamas, Lorenzo	1958-	Ent	10			30	
Lamb, Caroline, Lady	1785-1828	Celeb			1395		
Lamb, Charles	1775-1834	Author	139	350	1025		Br. Essayist, Critic. Popularly AKA 'Elia'
Lamb, Gil	1904-1995	Ent	10			30	Stage-Film Dancer, Comic
Lamb, John	1735-1800	Rev War		100			Leader of the Sons of Liberty
Lambert, Christopher		Ent	10			44	Actor
Lambert, Constant		Comp			250		Eng. Comp. & conductor
Lambert, William C.		Aero	75	135	175	150	ACE, WWI, 2nd Leading Ace
Lamm, Richard D.		Gov	10	20			CO Gov.
Lammers, Hans		WWII	95	262		360	Nazi Official. Hitler Legal Advisor
Lamond, Frederic		Comp	25		82	120	Scot. Pianist & Comp.
Lamont, Corliss		Activist	10		25		Author. Indicted for Contempt of Congress

NAME	DATES	CATEGORY	SIG	LS/DS	ALS	SP	COMMENTS
Lamont, Daniel S.		Cab	15	25	40		Sec. War, Journalist, Pol.
Lamont, Forrest		Opera	25			65	Opera
Lamont, Robert P.		Cab	25	60	95		Sec. Commerce
Lamont, Thomas		WH Staff	15	30	45		Cleveland's Pvt. Sec.
Lamont, Thomas S.		Bus	10	25	40	40	Banker. Morgan Guaranty
Lamour, Dorothy	1914-1996	Ent	25	125	140	99	Actress; SP w/Crosby & Hope 250; Sig w/Crosby & Hope 150
L'Amour, Louis	1908-1988	Author	75	675	260	150	Novels re: The Old West; SB 150
Lampson, Nick L		Congr	10				Member US Congress
Lampton, Mike		Space	10			25	
Lamson, C. M.		Clergy	10	10	20		
Lancashire, Sarah	1964-	Ent	10			25	Br. Actress
Lancaster, Burt	1910-1994	Ent	98	250		270	Rugged Leading Film Leading Man. Oscar Winner
Lance, Bert		Bus	10			15	Banker
Lanchester, Elsa	1902-1986	Ent	125	90		249	Eccentric English Actres Wife of Chas. Laughton
Land, Edwin H.	1909-1992	Invent	186	212	448	629	Polaroid Camera Inventor, rare in SP's
Land, Emory Scott		WWII	25	65			Adm. Maritime Comm. WWII
Landau, Lev	1908-1968	Sci		180			Russ. Physicist; '62 Nobel. TMsS 650
Landau, Martin		Ent	20			60	AA. Actor
Lander, Frederick West (WD)	1821-1862	Civ War	180	225	1317		Union Gen.
Landers, Ann	1918-2002	Clmnst	10	45	60	40	Advice Column
Landers, Audrey		Ent	10			45	
Landers, Judy		Ent	20			46	Actress
Landesburg, Steve		Ent	10			35	Actor
Landi, Bruno		Opera	15			60	Opera
Landi, Elissa	1904-1948	Ent	30	45	60	90	Vintage
Landis, Carole	1919-1948	Ent	80	185		274	Suicide at 29; Important DS 3100
Landis, Jessie Royce		Ent	25			95	
Landis, John		Ent	15	50		30	Film Dir. 'Blues Brothers', 'Am Werewolf
Landis, Kenesaw Mountain		Jurist	307	351		690	1st Baseball Commissioner. HOF
Landon, Alfred M.	1887-1987	Gov	27	45	75	75	Rep. Pres. Cand. vs FDR. Gov. KS
Landon, Melville D.		Jrnalist	20				(aka Eli Perkins) Columnist
Landon, Michael		Ent	95	165		151	Actor-Writer-Dir. 'Little House', 'Bonanza'
Landowska, Wanda	1879-1959	Comp	155	165	350	295	Pol-Fr Harpsichordist-Comp.
Landrieu, Mary		Congr	10				US Senate (D-LA)
Landrieu, Moon		Cab	10		15	15	Sec. HUD
Landry, Ali		Ent	15			45	
Landry, Audrey		Ent	12			35	
Landry, Robert B.		Mil	15			25	Gen. Air Aide to Pres. Truman
Landseer, Charles		Artist	30		75		R. A. & Keeper of Royal Academy
Landseer, Edwin H., Sir	1802-1873	Artist	35	65	260		Extraordinary Landscape-Animal Painter
Landseer, John		Artist	25		125		Father of Edwin H.
Landseer, Thomas		Artist	25	40	75		Brother of E. H. Landseer
Landsteiner, Karl, Dr		Sci	50	90	210		Nobel Med.
Lane, Abbe		Ent	15			46	Vocalist. Mrs. Xavier Cugat.
Lane, Allan Rocky		Ent	65			250	Cowboy-Actor
Lane, Burton		Music	25			40	Songwriter; AMusQS 60
Lane, Charles	1905-2007	Ent	15			55	Actor
Lane, Christy		Music	10			15	Gospel Singer
Lane, Diane		Ent	10			45	Actress
Lane, Evelyn		Ent	10			35	Brit. Actress. Vintage
Lane, Franklin K.		Cab	20	40		25	Sec. Interior
Lane, Harriet	1830-1903	1st Lady	210	372	938		Actg. 1st Lady, Buchanan's neice. RARE
Lane, Henry S.	1811-1881	Pol		52			

NAME	DATES	CATEGORY	SIG	LS/DS	ALS	SP	COMMENTS
Lane, James H.	1814-1866	Civ War	50	95	140	2990	Sen. KS, Union Gen., Suicide
Lane, James H. (WD)		Civ War	70	290	525		Special DS 7500
Lane, James Henry	1833-1907	Civ War	95	145	335	1970	CSA Gen.
Lane, Joseph		Gov	40	75	130		Gov. OR Terr. & 1st US Sen.
Lane, Nathan		Ent	15			55	Stage, Screen Actor-Comedian. Tony Award
Lane, Priscilla	1915-1995	Ent	15		25	48	
Lane, Rosemary		Ent	15	20	35	60	
Lane, Walter Page	1817-1892	Civ War	120				CSA Gen.
Lang Lang		Music				85	Chinese Pianist
Lang, Anton		Ent	25	30	45	45	Play Christ in the Passion Play; sketch 60
Lang, Belinda	1955-	Ent	10			25	Br. Actress
Lang, Cosmo Gordon		Clergy	25	35	45	35	
Lang, Fritz	1890-1976	Ent	144	336		440	Ger. Innovative Film Dir.
Lang, Johnny		Music				45	Singer; S Guitar 250
Lang, June	1917-2005	Ent	15			78	Actress
Lang, K D		Cntry Mus	20	20		68	
Lang, Walter	1896-1972	Ent	20			45	Film Dir.
Langan, Glenn		Ent	10	15	35	40	
Langdon, Harry	1884-1944	Ent	88	180		340	Actor of silent films & talkies
Langdon, John		Rev War	625	1000	1575		Continental Congr., Gov. NH, Signer Const'n
Langdon, Loomis		Civ War				345	Union Off.
Langdon, Sue Ane		Ent				120	Actress
Lange, David		HOS	10	15	30	15	New Zealand
Lange, Heinz	1917-2006	WWII				40	Ger. WWII Luftwaffe 70-victory flying ace
Lange, Hope		Ent	10			65	Actress
Lange, Jessica		Ent	14	95		78	AA Actress. King Kong
Lange, Ted	1948-	Ent	10			30	Actor; 'Loveboat'
Langella, Frank		Ent	15	20		51	Actor. Films-Stage
Langer, Will		Congr	10	35			Sen. ND
Langevin, James R. L		Congr	10				Member US Congress
Langford, Frances	1913-2005	Music	10	40		50	Big Band Vocalist-Films
Langley, Noel		Ent	95				Screenwriter, WOZ
Langley, Samuel P.	1834-1906	Aero	148	388	475	450	1890's Aeronautical Pioneer, Astronomer
Langlie, Arthur		Gov	12	20		15	Governor Washington
Langmuir, Irving		Sci	30	75	145		Nobel Chemistry 1932
Langtry, Lillie	1852-1929	Ent	299	450	361	430	Actress & Mistress of Edw. VII. 'Jersey Lilly'
Lanier, Sidney	1842-1881	Author	300	590	625		Most Important So. Poet of Time. ALS/Cont 2400
Lannes, Jean		Fr Rev	675	1750			Marshal of France
Lanphier, Thomas G., Jr.		WWII	165	180	182	246	ACE, WWII, Yamamoto Mission
Lansbury, Angela	1925-	Ent	15			45	Br. Star of Stage-Screen-TV
Lansing, Robert		Cab	40	125			Sec. State
Lansky, Meyer	1902-1983	Crime	167	809	1200		Mob Boss, Chk 600-900
Lantieri, Rita		Opera	10			20	Opera
Lantos, Tom L		Congr	10				Member US Congress
Lantz, Walter	1900-1994	Comics	75	132	143	141	AA, 'Woody Woodpecker' S draw 150-375
Lanza, Mario	1921-1959	Ent	166			597	Tragic Teno-Cinema Star. Early Death
LaPaglia, Anthony		Ent	17			50	
LaPlace, P. M., Marquis de	1749-1827	Sci	535				Fr. Astronomer, Mathematician
Lapoype, J. F. C., Baron		Fr Rev	20		125		
Larch, John	1914-2005	Ent	10			35	Actor
Larcom, Lucy		Author	15	25	45		
Lardner, Dionysius	1793-1859	Author	45	85	162		Irish writer on Sci. & Math.
Lardner, James L.	1802-1891	Civ War	40	95	145		Union Naval Commodore. Sig/Rank 60, DS 170
Lardner, Ring	1885-1933	Author	87	155	310	250	Am. Humorist, Social Satirist

NAME	DATES	CATEGORY	SIG	LS/DS	ALS	SP	COMMENTS
Lardner, Ring Jr.	1915-	Author	10	20	35	15	Screenwriter 'M*A*S*H'. One of 'Hollywood Ten'.
Laredo, Ruth		Music	15	20	30	35	Classical Pianist
Largent, Steve		Congr	10			20	Oklahoma. Star Football Player. MOC OK
Larionov, Mikhail	1881-1964	Artist		4600	4600		Avant-garde Russian painter
Larmouth, Kathy	1953-2007	Model	10			35	Playboy
LaRocca, D. J. Nick		Comp	50				AMusQS 250
Laroche, Loretta		Author	10			15	Motivational books
LaRosa, Julias		Music	10			25	Singer Arthur Godfey Show
LaRouche, Lyndon, Jr.	1922-	Pol	20		35	35	Perennial Cand. for Pres. of the US
Larrey, Dominick, Baron		Fr Rev	45	155	310		
Larroquette, John		Ent	10			45	Actor
Larsen, Rick L		Congr	10				Member US Congress
Larsen-Todsen, Nanny		Opera	20			65	Opera
Larson, Gary		Comics	20			100	Far Side; SB 80
Larson, John B. L		Congr	10				Member US Congress
Larter, Ali		Ent	14			43	
LaRue, Lash		Ent	10		15	30	Western actor
Lasky, Jesse L.		Bus	40	68	150	173	Pioneer Film Prod.
Lasser, Louise		Ent	10	20		30	Char. Actress-Comedian
Lasseter, John	1957-	Ent	10			20	Film Prod.
Lassiter, William		Mil	20	45	75	75	Gen. WWI Under Pershing. TLS/Cont 250
Laswell, Fred		Comics	25			150	B. Google & Snuffy Smith
Latas, Omar Pasha	1806-1871	Mil			420		Ottoman Gen. of Serb origin
Latham Loenig, Jan		Cond				50	Ger.
Latham, Hubert		Aero	160		250	225	
Latham, Louise		Ent	10			35	Char. Actress
Latham, Tom L		Congr	10				Member US Congress
Lathrop, George P.	1851-1898	Author	20	30	40	65	Am. Journalist, Writer
Latifah, Queen		Ent	18			53	
Latourette, Kenneth Scott		Clergy	20	30	45	30	
LaTourette, Steven C. L		Congr	10				Member US Congress
Latour-Maubourg, M. V. N. F.		Mil	20		75		Cavalry Gen. Napoleonic Wars
Latrobe, Benjamin H.	1764-1820	Artist	85	462	798		Am. Arch. of the White House
Latrobe, Osman		Civ War			575		CSA Off.
Lattimore, Richard		Author	10	15	25	25	
Lattler, Herman		West	70		165		Pioneer & Am. Indian Photographer
Laubach, Frank C.		Clergy	35	50	90	60	
Lauck, Chester	1902-1980	Ent	10			30	Radio. Lum & Abner
Lauder, Estee	1908-2004	Bus	10	45	65	50	Cosmetics
Lauder, Harry, Sir	1870-1950	Ent	60	80	145	82	Vintage Scottish Comedian-Singer; sketch 160
Lauer, Matt		Ent	10			30	Host of Today Show
Laughlin, Billy	1932-1948	Ent	295			1500	Froggy in the Little Rascals
Laughton, Charles	1899-1962	Ent	95	163	140	374	Brit. Actor. Versatile & Fine. Oscar Winner
Lauman, Jacob Gartner	1813-1867	Civ War	50	90	130		Union Gen.
Lauper, Cyndi		Music	25	50	85	48	Rock
Laurants, Arthur		Author	10			20	Plays
Laurel, Stan	1890-1965	Ent	152	276	402	504	Br. -Am Stage-Screen Comic Actor
Laurel, Stan & Hardy, Oliver		Ent	632			1447	Comedy team
Lauren, Dyanna	1965-	Ent				55	Am. erotic dancer, pornographic actress, & Dir.
Lauren, Ralph		Bus	10	15	40	35	Fashion Designer.
Laurencin, Marie	1885-1956	Artist	125		450		Fr. Painter & Printmaker
Laurens, Henry	1724-1792	Rev War	925	2129	2242		Pres. Continental Congress. SC Merchant
Laurie, Hugh		Ent	10			50	Br. Actor; 'House"; GG winner
Laurie, Piper	1932-	Ent	15			67	Actress

NAME	DATES	CATEGORY	SIG	LS/DS	ALS	SP	COMMENTS
Lausche, Frank J.		Gov	12	20		15	Governor OH
Lautenberg, Frank		Congr	10				US Senate (D-NJ)
Lauter, Ed		Ent				40	Actor
Lauter, Harry	1914-1990	Ent	10			40	Actor
Lauterbach, Johann C.		Music		95	195		Ger. Violinist
Lautner, Taylor		Ent	14			43	
LaVelle, Miriam		Ent				160	Actress 40s
Laverne & Shirley		Ent				122	Signed script 280-355
Lavi, Daliah		Ent	10			65	Actress
Lavigne, Avril		Music	20			60	Rock
Lavin, Linda		Ent	10			38	
Lavoisier, Antoine L. de	1743-1794	Sci	400	3625			Fr. Fndr. Mdrn. Chemistry
Law, Andrew Bonar		HOS	30	80	135		Br. Prime Min.
Law, Evander McIvor	1836-1920	Civ War	100	250	568		CSA Gen.
Law, George H.		Clergy	10		15	20	
Law, John	1671-1729	Reform	150				Scot. Economist. LS/Cont 5000
Law, John Phillip	1937-	Ent	10			40	Actor
Law, Jude		Ent	20			77	Actor
Law, Ruth		Aero	30			100	
Lawes, Lewis E.		Lawman	20	40	65	50	Prison Warden. Sing Sing
Lawford, Betty	1910-1960	Ent	15	25		45	Brit. Actress. '25 Film Debut. 'Sherlock Holmes'
Lawford, Peter	1923-1984	Ent	373	395		411	Br. Actor; 'Rat Pack' member
Lawler, Michael K.	1814-1882	Civ War	40	95			Union Gen. ALS '61 360
Lawless, Lucy		Ent	15			45	Actress; Xena, Warrior Princess.
Lawrence, 1st Baron		HOS	10	30	75		India
Lawrence, Abbott	1792-1855	Congr	25				MA. Financier. Lawrence MA
Lawrence, Barbara	1930-	Ent	25			105	Actress
Lawrence, Carol		Ent	10			30	Actress
Lawrence, Carolyn		Ent	20			60	
Lawrence, D(avid) H(erbert)	1885-1930	Author	470	718	3012		Novels. 'Lady Chatterley's Lover'; SB 650-4500
Lawrence, David L.		Gov	17	20			Governor PA
Lawrence, Elliot		Band	20			40	Big Band Leader. Multiple Emmys
Lawrence, Ernest O.	1901-1958	Sci	100	170	240	200	Nobel Physics 1939. Invented Cyclotron.
Lawrence, Gertrude	1902-1952	Ent	70	92		139	Major Br. Actress. 1st Star of 'King & I'(Stage)
Lawrence, Herbert A., Sir		Mil	10	30	50	25	
Lawrence, Jacob	1917-	Artist	15	62		30	Painter, Educator. Print S 100
Lawrence, Jerome	1915-2004	Ent	10			30	Writer
Lawrence, Joey		Ent	10			30	Actor
Lawrence, John		Colonial	35	90	175		CT Statesman, Rev. War Leader
Lawrence, Marc	1910-2005	Ent	10	15	25	45	Stage Actor. Films-'33. Swarthy Villain
Lawrence, Marjorie		Opera	15			90	Australian Opera, Concert Sopr.
Lawrence, Martin		Ent	15			45	
Lawrence, Rosina	1914-1998	Ent	20			55	Late Silent & Early Sound Film Star. 'Our Gang'
Lawrence, Scott		Ent	17			50	
Lawrence, Sharon		Ent	10			30	NYPD Blue
Lawrence, Steve		Ent	10		20	35	Singer; SP w/Eydie Gorme 60
Lawrence, Thomas, Sir	1769-1830	Artist	100	160	225		Br. Portr. Painter. Pres. Royal Academy
Lawrence, Thos. E.	1888-1935	Author	650	2405	5382	2917	Lawrence of Arabia
Lawrence, Tracy		Cntry Mus	10			25	Singer
Lawrence, Vicki		Ent	10			30	
Lawrence, Wendy		Space	10			25	
Lawrence, William	1819-1899	Congr	20				Repr. OH, Union Col.
Lawson, James M.		Clergy	20	25	35	25	
Lawson, Ken		Ent	15			45	

NAME	DATES	CATEGORY	SIG	LS/DS	ALS	SP	COMMENTS
Lawson, Maggie		Ent	13			40	
Lawson, Ted		Aero	15	30		40	
Lawton, Alexander R.	1818-1896	Civ War	110	250	360		CSA Gen.
Lawton, Alexander R. (WD)	1818-1896	Civ War	195	652	900		CSA Gen.
Laxalt, Paul	1922-	Congr	10			15	Governor, Sen. NV
Lay, Herman W.		Bus	10	25	50	30	Lay's Potato Chips
Layard, Austen Henry, Sir	1817-1894	Archaeol	75	160	410		Br. Diplomat. Excavator of Niveveh
Layat, Marcel		Invent			1000		Fr. inventor of early Helicopter prototype
Lazarev, Alexander		Cond				65	Former Bolshoi Maestro
Lazarus, Emma	1849-1887	Author		2300			The New Colossus
Lazarus, Mel		Comics	10			20	Miss Peach, Momma
Lazenby, George		Ent	15		30	79	
Lazzari, Virgillo		Opera	15			100	Italian bass
Le Boutillier, O. C. "Boots"		Mil		75		75	Yank in RAF. Last aerial witness: Red Baron's death
Le Corbusier		Artist		600			Fr. Architect, painter, writer
Le Vier, Tony		Aero				70	Early aviator racer
Lea, Homer		Mil	55	175			Predicted US-Jap. War
Leach, James A. L		Congr	10				Member US Congress
Leach, Robin	1941-	Ent	10			30	Lifestyles of the Rich & Famous
Leachman, Cloris		Ent	10	15	20	40	AA
Leadbetter, Danville	1811-1866	Civ War	150	475			CSA Gen.
Leahy, Patrick		Congr	10			20	US Senate (D-VT)
Leahy, William Daniel		Mil	35	145	105	195	Chief of Staff-FDR & Truman
Leake, Joseph Bloomfield	1828-1913	Civ War	30	55	75		Union Brevet Brig. Gen.
Leakey, Louis B.		Sci	45	80	120	125	Anthropologist, Archaeologist
Leakey, Mary D.		Sci	15	25	70	30	Anthropologist, Archaeologist
Leakey, Meave, Dr.		Sci	20	60			
Leakey, Richard, Dr.		Sci	125				Br. Anthropologist
Lean, David, Sir	1908-1991	Ent	120	145		195	Film Dir.
Leander, Zarah		Opera	35			112	Opera
Lear, Edward	1812-1888	Artist	140		907		Br. Painter & Nonsense Poet
Lear, Norman		Bus	10	15	45	35	TV Film Prod.
Lear, Tobias		Rev War	75	195	325		Pvt. Secretary to G. Washington
Lear, William P. Sr.		Bus	35	125	195	160	Lear Jet Aircraft Fndr.
Learned, Michael		Ent	10			40	Actress; 'Waltons'
Leary, Dennis		Ent	10			40	Actor
Leary, Timothy, Dr.	1920-1996	Activist	50	80	130	60	Drug Cult Ldr., Psych. Acid Print S 225; TQS 125
Lease, Mary Elizabth		Reform	15	20	40		Orator, Writer Woman Suffrage
Leavelle, James R.		Lawman	20	120		249	Detective handcuffed to Oswald when Shot
Leavenworth, Henry		Mil	250		750		Frontier Soldier, Gen.
LeBlanc, Matt		Ent	20			51	Actor. 'Friends'
LeBrock, Kelly		Ent	10	40		63	
Lebrun, Albert	1871-1950	HOS	30	50	125	75	Last Pres. 3rd Fr. Repub.
Lebrun, Chas. F. Duc de	1739-1824	Napol	35	100	150		3rd Consul/Bonaparte
LeCarre, John		Author	20	45	75	30	(David Cornwell) Br. Realistic Spy Novels
Lecuona, Ernesto	1896-1963	Comp	150			635	AMusQS 400-600
Led Zeppelin (all-org.)		Music	2100	9000		8500	'Led Zeppelin I' S Album by all 4 orig. 8200
Ledbetter, Huddy Leadbelly	1888-1949	Music			5750		Premier Am. folksingers; Jazz-Blues
Lederer, Francis		Ent	10			76	Ger. actor:
Lederman, Leon M., Dr.		Sci	15	25	50		Nobel Phyics
Ledger, Heath	1979-2008	Ent	35			300	Actor
Ledlie, James Hewett	1832-1882	Civ War	45	90	120		Union Gen.
Ledoux, Harold		Comics	10			25	Judge Parker
Ledyard, John	1770-1771	Colonial		70			Merchant, Justice of Peace. Progenitor of Line

NAME	DATES	CATEGORY	SIG	LS/DS	ALS	SP	COMMENTS
Ledyard, John	1751-1789	Expl		475			Accompanied Capt. Cook. Wrote Adventures.
Lee, Agnes	1869-1939	Author			299		Poet
Lee, Albert Lindley	1834-1907	Civ War	45	90	120		Union Gen.
Lee, Alfred		Clergy	10	15	35		
Lee, Amy		Ent	18			55	
Lee, Ang	1954-	Ent	15	20	30	40	Film Dir. AA
Lee, Anna	1913-2004	Ent	15			52	Actress; 'Gen. Hospital'
Lee, Barbara L		Congr	10				Member US Congress
Lee, Bernard	1908-1981	Ent	15			45	Actor; 'M' in the James Bond films
Lee, Brandon	1964-1993	Ent	252	424		466	Son of Bruce Lee.
Lee, Brenda		Music	20			70	Singer
Lee, Bruce	1940-1973	Ent	1230	5458	7898	4200	Legendary Cult Actor; S Chk 2000-2500
Lee, Canada	1731-1982	Ent	60			193	Actor. McCarthy Era Victim
Lee, Charles	1758-1815	Cab	110	250	550		Washington's Atty Gen.
Lee, Charles	1731-1782	Rev War			3012		Turncoat Gen. Rev. War
Lee, Christopher		Ent	20	60		98	Actor
Lee, Dixie (Mrs Bing Crosby)		Ent	10	15	25	40	
Lee, Dr. Tsung-Dao		Sci	20	30	45	25	Nobel Physics
Lee, E. Hamilton		Aero	10	25	50	35	
Lee, Edwin G.	1836-1870	Civ War	165	290	410		CSA Gen.
Lee, Fitzhugh	1835-1905	Civ War	115	198	243	374	CSA Gen. AQS 595, TLS/Cont 575
Lee, Fitzhugh (WD)		Civ War	240		1388		CSA Gen.
Lee, Francis Lightfoot		Rev War	1388	4587	5875		Signer Dec. of Indepen.
Lee, Geo. Wash. Custis	1832-1913	Civ War	183	338	386	750	CSA Gen.
Lee, Geo. Wash. Custis (WD)	1832-1913	Civ War	270		1300		CSA Gen.
Lee, Gordon 'Porky'	1933-2005	Ent	35	65		74	Little Rascals
Lee, Gypsy Rose	1913-1970	Ent	66	142		214	Burlesque Queen & Movie Star
Lee, Harold B.	1899-1973	Relig	75	200	625	100	Pres. of the Mormon Church
Lee, Harper	1926-	Author	110	604		295	To Kill a Mocking Bird' Pulitzer; SB 600-1750; S 1st Ed. TKAM 22705
Lee, Henry	1756-1818	Rev War	357	772	1184		Light-Horse Harry. Gen Rev War ALS/Imp. Cont 33563
Lee, Henry, Sir	1533-1611	Knight	125		500		Model Knight to Queen Elizabeth I
Lee, James		Ent	13			40	
Lee, Jason		Ent	18			54	
Lee, Jason Scott		Ent	10			40	Actor
Lee, Lila	1901-1973	Ent	20			65	Actress
Lee, Mark C.		Space	10			25	
Lee, Martin	1938-	Pol	10			25	Democratic Party of Hong Kong
Lee, Mary Custis		Civ War	112		587	640	Mrs. Robert E. Lee
Lee, Michele		Ent	10			30	
Lee, Mildred	1846-1905	Civ War	65	300	155		Daughter of Robert E. Lee
Lee, Peggy	1920-2002	Music	20	30	40	94	Am. jazz & traditional pop singer
Lee, Pinkie	1916-1993	Ent	15			40	Vaude. & Early TV Comedian, Kid Shows
Lee, Rex		Ent	20			40	Actor; Entourage
Lee, Richard Henry	1732-1794	Rev War	380	2800	4835		Signer Dec. of Indepen.
Lee, Robert E.	1807-1870	Mil	2366	5089	8485	5668	CSA Cmmdg. Gen. Mex. City 1848 ALS/Cont 25000
Lee, Robert E. (WD)		Civ War	3423	12513	20617	7770	ALS cont. 25,000+; Terms of Surrender 537,750
Lee, Robert E. Jr.	1843-1914	Civ War	325				Son of Robert E. Lee
Lee, Ruta	1936-	Ent	10			35	Actress
Lee, Samuel P.	1812-1897	Civ War	60	210	275	265	Union Adm.
Lee, Sheryl		Ent	13			40	
Lee, Spike		Ent	10	60		42	Film Dir.
Lee, Stan		Artist	45	140		122	Spiderman, S drawing 250-1250
Lee, Stephen Dill	1833-1908	Civ War	120	195	325		CSA Gen.

NAME	DATES	CATEGORY	SIG	LS/DS	ALS	SP	COMMENTS
Lee, Stephen Dill (WD)		Civ War	190	848	955		CSA Gen.
Lee, Tenghui		HOS	25			55	Pres. Repub. of China (Taiwan)
Lee, Tommy		Music	20			42	Rock
Lee, William H. F. 'Rooney'	1837-1891	Civ War	185		630		CSA Gen., ALS War Date/Cont 6050
Lee, William Raymond	1804-1891	Civ War	15	45	70		Union Gen.
Lee, Yuan T., Dr.		Sci	20	35	45	30	Nobel Chemistry
Leeb, Wilhelm Joseph Franz Von		WWII				306	Nazi Gen.
Leeb, Wilhelm R. Von		Mil	45		135	210	
Leech, John	1817-1864	Artist	70	125	138		Br. Caricaturist-Illust. Orig. Piece S 875
Leech, Richard		Opera	15			30	Opera
Leeds, Andrea	1914-1984	Ent	15			60	Actress
Leeds, Peter	1917-1996	Ent	10	20		35	Actor. Appeared in over 8,000 TV shows
Leese, Oliver, Sir		WWII	20	50		35	Br. Gen. WWII/Montgomery. 8th Army
Leestma, David C.		Space	10			25	
Leeves, Jane	1961-	Ent	10			48	Br. Actress
Lefebvre, F. J., Duke		Fr Rev	160	675			Marshal of Napoleon
Lefevre, Edwin		Pol	10		15		Panamanian Ambass. To Spain; Financial writer
Leftwich, John W.		Congr	10	15	30		MOC TN 1866
LeGallienne, Eva	1899-1991	Ent	15	25	50	85	Actress, Prod., & Dir.
LeGallienne, Richard		Author	35	50	162		Brit. Man of Letters
LeGarde, Tom & Ted		Cntry Mus	10			20	
Leger, Fernand		Artist	80	199	462		Fr. Abstract Painter. AManS 2750
Leggett, Mortimer Dormer	1821-1896	Civ War	45	75	120		Union Gen.
Legrand, Michel		Comp	10	15	25	25	
Leguizamo, John		Ent	15			45	Actor
LeHand, M. A. (Missy)	1898-1944	WH Staff	28	72	140	40	FDR Personal Sec. 20 Years
Lehar, Franz	1870-1948	Comp	100	165	236	227	The Merry Widow. AMusQS 225
Lehman, Herbert H.	1882-1963	Gov	10	25		25	Gov. NY, Sen. NY
Lehmann, Ernst August	1886-1937	Aero	85		365		Ger. Aeronautical Engineer
Lehmann, Lilli	1848-1929	Opera	75		100	212	Ger. Sopr. 170 Operatic Roles
Lehmann, Lotte	1888-1976	Opera	50	75	158	195	Ger. Opera. Magnificent Sopr. SPc 80-135
Lehmann, Marie		Ent	50			175	Ger. Prima Donna. Mother Lilli
Lehr, Lew	1895-1950	Ent	15	15	35	30	Writer; actor
Lehrer, Jim		Celeb	10			20	News
Leibman, Ron	1937-	Ent	10			40	Actor; writer
Leibowitz, Annie		Photog				65	
Leick, Hudson	1969-	Ent				53	Actress
Leider, Frida		Opera	35			140	Opera. Great Brunhilde
Leiferkus, Sergei		Opera	10			25	Opera
Leigh, Barbara		Ent	10			64	
Leigh, Janet	1927-2004	Ent	20	30		118	Actress; 'Psycho'
Leigh, Jennifer		Ent	13			40	
Leigh, Jennifer Jason		Ent	15			50	
Leigh, Mandy	1975-	Ent	20			80	Actress; Erotica
Leigh, Richard		Comp	15	18			
Leigh, Vivien	1913-1967	Ent	289	439	576	736	Brit. Actress. Oscar Winner.
Leigh, Vivien		Ent				4056	(As Scarlett O'Hara) Actress
Leigh, Vivien & Laurence Olivier		Ent	312	712		787	
Leighton, Frederic, Baron	1830-1896	Artist	25	90	150		Pres. Br. Royal Academy. Painter, Sculptor
Leighton, Laura		Ent	12			60	Actress. Melrose Place
Leighton, Margaret	1922-1976	Ent	15			60	Br. actress
Leik, Hudson		Ent	10			30	Actor. 'Xena'
Leinsdorf, Erich		Cond	15			120	Austro-Amer Conductor
Leisure, David	1950-	Ent	10			35	Actor; 'Joe Isuzu'

NAME	DATES	CATEGORY	SIG	LS/DS	ALS	SP	COMMENTS
Lejeune, John Archer	1867-1942	Mil	50	170	250	285	Cmdnt. Marine Corps; Greatest of All Leathernecks
Leland, Henry M.	1843-1932	Bus	875	1270			Contract Creating Lincoln Motor Co. S 14000
Leland, W. C.		Bus	20	140	140	80	
Leloir, Luis Frederico		Sci	20	40	45	25	Nobel Chemistry
Lelong, Lucien		Design	25				Fashion, Cosmetics
Lelouch, Claude	1937-	Ent	10			30	Fr. Film Dir.
LeMaire, Charles		Ent	15			25	Dir.
Lemass, Sean		HOS	10	25	60	30	Prime Min. Ireland
LeMat, Paul		Ent	17			51	
LeMay, Curtis E.	1906-1990	Mil	32	115	150	142	AF Gen. WWII. 200th Air Force, SAC
Lembeck, Harvey	1923-1982	Ent	30			75	Actor
Lembeck, Michael	1948-	Ent	10			20	Dir. Primetime Emmy
Lemeshev, Sergei		Opera				500	Opera. Russ. Tenor of Soviet Era.
Lemmon, Chris	1954-	Ent	10			25	Actor; son of Jack
Lemmon, Jack	1925-2001	Ent	25	50	62	87	AA; SP w/Tony Curtis 325; w/Walter Matthau 285
Lemnitz, Tiana		Opera	40			125	Opera
Lemnitzer, Lyman L.	1899-1988	WWII	30	40	90	142	Supreme Allied Commd'r WWII. 7th Inf. Korea
Lemon, Mark	1809-1870	Author	15		35		Br. Plays, Humorist, Co-Fndr. Punch
L'Enfant, Pierre Charles	1754-1825	Archtct	400	1062	1500		Designed New Federal City (Washington, DC)
Lengies, Vanessa		Ent	13			40	
Lenin, Vladimir Ilyich (N. Lenin)		HOS					ALS/Cont 29,000; Rare:
Lennix, Henry		Ent	15			45	
Lennon Sisters, The (4)		Ent	105	137		150	
Lennon, John	1940-1980	Music	1617	3131	18302	3762	Beatle, Author, Artist. S Album 5207
Lennon, Julian		Music	20			40	Son of John Lennon
Lennon, Thomas		Ent	13			40	
Lennox, Annie		Music				55	Singer; handwritten lyrics 300
Lennox, Harry		Ent	15			45	
Lennox, Vera	1904-1984	Ent	12			35	Br. Actress
Lenny Kravitz		Music	35			90	Music. Rock Group
Leno, Jay		Ent	25	60		56	Self Caricature S 75
Lenoir, William B.		Space	10			25	
Lenormand, René	1846-1932	Comp	30			175	Songs, String & Piano Music
Lenya, Lotte		Ent	20	125		145	Cabaret Singer, Char. Actr.
Lenz, Nicole		Ent	18			55	
Leo XIII	1810-1878	Clergy	218	264			Pope
Leonard, Ada		Band	20			70	Big Band leader
Leonard, Elmore		Author	15			25	Author of 'Get Shorty, ' many other novels
Leonard, George		Jurist	40	100			Colonial Am. Jurist
Leonard, Gloria	1940-	Ent	10			25	
Leonard, Jack		Music				25	Singer/Tommy Dorsey Orch.
Leonard, Jack E.		Ent	15			68	Comedian
Leonard, Joshua		Ent	15			45	
Leonard, Sheldon		Ent	30			58	
Leonard, Tom		Author	10			15	Scottish writer
Leoncavallo, Ruggiero	1858-1919	Comp	150	382	511	1049	AMusQS 750-1200
Leone, Sergio	1921-1989	Ent	320			797	Master of Spaghetti Western. 'Fistful of Dollars'
Leonetti, Tommy		Ent				40	Actor
Leoni, Tea		Ent	10			45	Actress
Leonov, Aleksei	1934-	Space	75	112		403	Rus. Cosmonaut, 1st Space Walker
Leontif, Wassily, Dr.		Econ	20	35		40	Nobel Economics
Leontovich, Eugenie	1900-1993	Ent	15		30	45	Actress
Leopardi, Giacomo		Author	80	350	475		Italian Poet
Leopold (Prince)		Royal				512	Duke of Albany. Q. Victoria's 4th Son.

NAME	DATES	CATEGORY	SIG	LS/DS	ALS	SP	COMMENTS
Leopold I	1640-1705	Royal		1388			King of Hungary & Bohemia, Holy Roman Emperor
Leopold II	1835-1909	Royal	120	268	540	425	Belgium
Leopold III	1901-1983	Royal	80		175		King Belgium. Queen Astrid Tragic Death
Leopold IV of Lippe	1871-1949	Royal				380	Last Prince of Lippe
Leopold V	1586-1633	Royal		250			Archduke of Austria 1619-33. Papal Bishopric 1625
Leopold, Nathan F.	1905-1971	Crime	125	280	575	250	Am. Criminal Convicted of Murder. Loeb & Leopold
Leppard, Raymond		Cond				65	English
Lermontov, Mikhail	1814-1841	Author	540	2300	4625		Novels, Poet. Killed in Duel
Lerner, Alan Jay	1918-1996	Comp	65	120	175	209	Am. Lyricist, Librettist/Loewe
Lerner, Max	1902-1992	Jrnalist	10	30	40	25	
Lerner, Michael		Ent	10			25	Actor
LeRoy, Hal	1914-1985	Ent	12			20	Tap Dancer. Dir.
LeRoy, Mervyn		Ent	50	130		458	Top Hollywod Film Dir. -Prod. 'Wizard of Oz'
Leslie, Frank	1821-1880	Pub	95				Fndr. Illustrated Newspaper
Leslie, Frank, Mrs.		Pub	20		75	75	Leslie's Magazine
Leslie, Joan		Ent	15			59	
Leslie, Preston H.		Gov	10	15			Governor KY
Leslie, Thomas J.	1796-1874	Civ War	20		35		Union Gen. Paymaster's Dept. 50 Years
Lesseps, Ferdinand, de	1805-1894	Engr	123	235	375	700	Engineer& Diplomat. Promoted Suez Canal
Lester, Buddy	1917-2002	Ent	10			30	Actor
Lesters, The (5)		Music	10			25	Gospel Singers
Letcher, John	1813-1884	Civ War	49	191	592		CW Gov. VA, ALS/Cont 2, 500
Letcher, John (WD)	1813-1884	Civ War			800		Conf. Gov. of VA
Leto, Jared	1971-	Ent	10			35	Am. actor & musician
Letterman, David		Ent	20	65		47	Comedian. TV Late Show CBS
Letterman, Jonathan	1824-1872	Civ War	95	175			Med. Services for CW Union Army
Leutze, Emanuel		Artist	75		320		Washington Crossing Delaware
Levant, Oscar		Ent	120	475		202	Pianist, Caustic Humorlst, Actor, Author
Levene, Sam		Ent	10			43	
Levenson, Sam	1911-1980	Ent	10	35		35	Radio, TV Comic
Leventhrope, Collett	1815-1889	Civ War	90	165	325		CSA Gen.
Lever, Asbury		Congr	10				MOC SC
Lever, Lord (Wm. Hesketh)		Bus	30	100	190	60	Br. Soap Mfg. Lever Brothers
Leverett, John	1662-1724	Colonial	50	130	275		Pres. of Harvard, Judge
Levi, Edward H.		Cab	10	25	45	45	Atty Gen.
Levi, Zachary		Ent	15			45	
Levi-Civita, Tullio	1873-1941	Sci	50		250		Italian. Math. Helped Found Differential Calculus
LeVier, Anthony 'Tony'	1913-1998	Aero	10		35		Air racer & test pilot for Lockheed, 1940s-70s.
Levi-Montalcini, Rita, Dr.		Sci	20	65			Nobel Med.
Levin, Carl		Congr	10			20	US Senate (D-MI)
Levin, Ira		Author	25	35		30	Rosemary's Baby
Levin, Sander M. L		Congr	10				Member US Congress
Levine, David		Comics	15			100	Caricaturist
Levine, Irving R.	1922-	TV News	10	10		20	Commentator
Levine, Jack		Artist	10	15	35		Color Print Repro 100
Levine, James		Cond	10	10	35	57	
Levinson, Barry		Ent	10			25	Dir.
Levi-Strauss, Claude	1908-	Sci	25				Belg. -Fr. Anthropologist. Legion d'Honneur 1991
Levy, David H.		Sci	15				Discovered Metor Crater
Levy, Eugene		Ent	10			40	Actor; comedian
Levy, Steven		Author	10				Computer journalist, historian
Lewinsky, Monica		WH Staff	34			54	Monica's' Story BS Monica 75-150
Lewis, (Percy) Wyndham	1882-1957	Artist	60		356		Br. Painter & Writer
Lewis, Aaron		Ent	17			50	

L

NAME	DATES	CATEGORY	SIG	LS/DS	ALS	SP	COMMENTS
Lewis, Al	1923-2006	Ent	10			45	Actor; 'Grandpa' on the TV series The Munsters
Lewis, C(live) S(taples)	1898-1963	Author	450	825	1520		Br. Medievalist, Philosopher, Scholar
Lewis, David 'Duffy'		Aero	15	30	55	40	
Lewis, Drew		Cab	10		20	15	Sec. of Transportation
Lewis, Edwin		Clergy	15	20	30		
Lewis, Emmanuele		Ent	10			30	Actor; 'Webster'
Lewis, Francis	1713-1803	Rev War	480	1600	2500		Signer Dec. of Indepen.
Lewis, Gary & the Playboys		Music				350	Music group
Lewis, Geoffrey	1935-	Ent	10			30	Actor
Lewis, Gwilym H.		Aero	20	45	80	55	
Lewis, Huey (And the News)		Music	12			120	Rock. 'Sports' Alb. S by Lewis 55
Lewis, J. C.		Music	12			25	Blues Drummer
Lewis, Jarma	1931-1985	Ent	10			45	Actress
Lewis, Jenifer	1957-	Ent	10			30	Actress
Lewis, Jerry	1926-	Ent	25	138	120	96	Comedian-Actor; SP w/Dean Martin 425-650
Lewis, Jerry L		Congr	10				Member US Congress
Lewis, Jerry Lee		Cntry Mus	38	200		90	Rock Legend
Lewis, Jimmy		Ent	13			40	
Lewis, Joe E.		Ent	20	30	45	45	Nightclub Comedian
Lewis, John	1940-	Activist	10	15			Civ. Rights Leader. Sit-Ins-Freedom Rider.
Lewis, John L		Congr	10				Member US Congress
Lewis, John L.	1880-1969	Labor	38	68	110	86	AFL-CIO Labor Leader. TLS/Cont 275
Lewis, Joseph Horace	1824-1904	Civ War	95	114	172		CSA Gen.
Lewis, Juliette	1973-	Ent	20			52	Actress
Lewis, Mel		Music				120	Blues-Jazz
Lewis, Meriwether	1774-1809	Expl	3180	5500	9500		Lewis & Clark Exped.
Lewis, Monica	1925-	Ent	10			40	Singer-Actress. Big Band Singer. Records
Lewis, Morgan		Rev War	50	400	250		Gen. Gates Chief of Staff. Gov.
Lewis, Ramsey	1935-	Ent	20			35	Pianist-Comp.
Lewis, Richard		Ent	10			40	Comedian; Actor
Lewis, Robert A.		Mil	25			50	Enola Gay pilot
Lewis, Robert Q.	1921-1992	Ent	10			45	Radio-TV Star. Game Show Host. Actor
Lewis, Ron L		Congr	10				Member US Congress
Lewis, Shari	1933-1998	Ent	65	65		63	Comedian-Pupeteer.
Lewis, Sheldon	1868-1958	Ent	30			55	Actor. Title Role 'Dr. Jekyll & Mr. Hyde', 1916
Lewis, Sinclair	1885-1951	Author	120	199	400	549	1st Am. Awarded Nobel for Lit.
Lewis, Ted		Ent	20	25		71	Bandleader-Entertainer. 'Me & My Shadow'
Lewis, Thyme	1966-	Ent	10			25	Actor
Lewis, Vera	1873-1956	Ent	50			95	Char. Actress
Lewis, William Arthur, Sir		Sci	20	25	40	25	Nobel Economics
Lewis, William Gaston	1835-1901	Civ War	110		118		CSA Gen.
Lewis, William H.		WWII	10	22	40	28	ACE, WWII; 7 kills
Lewishon, Ludwig		Author	20		25		Ger. -Born Author of 31 Books
Lewisohn, Adolph		Bus	20	45	65	50	Mining, Investment
Lewitt, Sal		Artist	25			100	
Lewitz, Charlie	1978-	Ent	10			25	Revenge of the Nerds IV
Ley, Bob		TV News	10			20	ESPN News
Ley, Robert Dr.	1890-1945	WWII	200	292	800		Nazi leader of Labour Front
Ley, Willy		Sci	25	55	85	75	Rocker Expert, Sci-Fi Writer
Leyshon, Paul		Ent	10			20	Actor
Lhermitte, Thierry	1952-	Ent	10			35	Fr. Actor
Li, Gong	1965-	Ent	30			69	Chinese-born actress
Li, Yundi		Music				60	Chinese pianist
Libby, Willard F.		Sci	20	35	55	55	Nobel Chemistry

NAME	DATES	CATEGORY	SIG	LS/DS	ALS	SP	COMMENTS
Liberace	1919-1987	Ent	126	128		154	Sig/Piano Sketch 75-95-125
Liberace, George		Music	10	15		15	Violinist Brother of Lee Liberace
Lichfield, Lord		Celeb	10			15	Photographer
Lichtenberg, Byron, Dr.		Space	10			20	
Lichtenstein, Roy	1923-1998	Artist	105	125	172	223	
Lichty, George	1905-1983	Comics	10		25		'Grin & Bear It'
Licitra, Salvatore		Opera				50	Tenor
Liddell, Henry George		Clergy	20	35	40	45	
Liddell, St John Richardson	1815-1870	Civ War	110	180			CSA Gen.
Liddy, G. Gordon	1930-	Official	10	20	50	30	Lawyer, Watergate, Convicted
Lie, Jonas		Author	15	40	60		Nor. Novels, Dramatist
Lie, Trygve	1896-1968	HOS	37	75	130	140	Norwegian 1st Sec. Gen U. N. His Bible S 475
Liebenow, William F.		WWII	50			295	PT Boat Cmdr. Who Rescued JFK
Lieber & Stoller		Music				159	Songwriters; S sheet music 120-225
Lieber, Fritz		Ent	35			100	
Lieberman, Joseph		Pol	20	25		35	Sen. from Conn., VP Cand. 2000
Liebermann, Max	1847-1935	Artist	75		250		Ger. Impressionist Painter. Orig. Pen Sketch 650
Liebig, Justus von,	1803-1873	Sci	185		812	506	Ger. Chem. Discovered Chloroform. ALS/Cont 1750
Lienart, Archille, Card.		Clergy	30	40	50	40	
Lifar, Serge		Opera	15			80	Opera
Liggett, Hunter		Mil	75	125	60	85	Am. Gen. WWI
Liggett, Louis Kroh		Bus	85	170	350		Liggett's Drug Store Chain
Light, Enoch		Band				25	Big Bandleader-Violinist
Light, Judith		Ent	12			30	
Lightburn, Joseph A. J.	1824-1901	Civ War	40	78	110		Union Gen.
Lightner, Candy		Celeb	12	30		20	1st Pres. MADD
Lightner, Winnie	1899-1971	Ent	19	25	45	60	Actress
Ligi, Josella		Opera	10			25	Opera
Ligonier, John	1678-1770	Mil	25				Br. Field Marshall of Queen Anne
Lil Bow Wow		Music	20			35	Rap; Rock
Liles, Brooks		WWII	10	20	38	22	ACE, WWII, USAAF Ace
Lilienthal, David E.		Bus	15	30		20	Co-Fndr. I. J. Fox, Furriers
Lilienthal, Otto	1848-1896	Invent	150		525		Aeronautical Eng'r, Author
Lillard, Mathew	1970-	Celeb	10			40	
Lillard, Matthew		Ent	17			50	
Lilley, Robert Doak	1836-1886	Civ War	110	154	389		CSA Gen.
Lillie, Beatrice	1894-1989	Ent	25	75	70	65	Br. Comedienne. WWII Entertainer; sketch 120
Lillie, Gordon W. (Pawnee Bill)	1860-1942	Ent	138	207	279	210	Buffalo Bill Partner. DS/Cody 3500
Lilly, Eli	1839-1898	Bus			1500		Pioneer Am. Manufacturer. Fndr. Eli Lilly & Co.
Liluokalini	1838-1917	Royal	250	450	800	1000	Queen Hawaii. Last Monarch of Hawaii. Deposed
Liman, Arthur	1932-1997	Law	10			20	
Liman, Doug		Ent	15			45	
Limbaugh, Rush		Radio	10	15	20	22	Radio/TV Commentator
Limp Bizket		Music	50			138	Rock Group
Lin, Y. S. Maya		Artist	25	100			Designed Viet Nam Wall
Lincke, Paul		Comp	70	185	325		AMusQS 675, Glow Worm
Lincoln, Abraham	1809-1865	Pres	3400	7449	11005		ALS/Cont 35000-101500, ADS/Cont 25875
Lincoln, Abraham (As Pres.)		Pres	3840	9220	22369	59102	ALS/Cont 50000-3100000
Lincoln, Benjamin	1733-1810	Rev War	60	184	425		Father of Gen. Lincoln; Major Gen. in Rev War
Lincoln, Blanche		Congr	10				US Senate (D-AR)
Lincoln, Elmo		Ent	287			871	
Lincoln, Evelyn		Official	15	20			JFK Pres. Sec.
Lincoln, Joseph		Author	13	20	30		Writer of Cape Cod Stories
Lincoln, Levi	1749-1820	Cab	35	112	120		Memb. Continental Congr. Early Atty Gen.

Sanders Autograph Price Guide

NAME	DATES	CATEGORY	SIG	LS/DS	ALS	SP	COMMENTS
Lincoln, Mary Todd	1818-1882	1st Lady	1320	2660	6318	7500	FF on Mourning Env. 3700-4600; FF 2500
Lincoln, Robert Todd	1843-1926	Cab	145	351	409		Capt. CW. Sec War. Min. to Eng. LS/Cont 750-950
Lincoln, Rufus		Rev War		1650			Present at Burgoyne Surrender
Lind, Don L.		Space	10			25	
Lind, Jenny (Goldschmidt)	1820-1887	Opera	190	210	197	750	Concert, Opera. Called 'Swedish Nightingale'
Lindberg, Charles W.		WWII	25	40		98	One of 6 Iwo Jima Flag Raiser
Lindbergh, Anne Morrow		Author	40	70	150	175	Am. Writer-Poet.
Lindbergh, Charles A.	1902-1974	Aero	457	1290	3409	2714	S 1st Fl. Cvr. 975-2750, SB 750-1500; ALS/LS/Cont 5000+
Linden, Eric		Ent	25			198	GWTW
Linden, Hal		Ent	10	20		35	
Linder, John L		Congr	10				Member US Congress
Linderman, H. R.		Civ War	10		25		Civil War Dir. of US Mint.
Lindfors, Viveca		Ent	12			65	
Lindgren, Astrid		Author				60	Pippi Longstocking
Lindholm, Berit		Opera	10			25	Opera
Lindley, Audra	1918-1997	Ent	15			35	Actress
Lindo, Delroy	1952-	Ent	10			25	Br. Actor
Lindsay, E. Lin		WWII	10	22	38	30	ACE, WWII, USAAF Ace; 8 kills
Lindsay, Howard	1889-1968	Ent	10	15	25	25	Theatrical Prod.
Lindsay, John		Pol	15	25		25	Lawyer, Author, Mayor NYC
Lindsay, Margaret		Ent	15	25	45	65	Leading Lady. 30s-40's
Lindsay, Vachel	1879-1931	Author	50	120	260	250	Poet, Artist, Prairie Troubador
Lindsey, Ben B.		Law	15				Jurist
Lindsey, George	1935-	Ent	10			40	Goober on the Andy Griffith Show
Lindstrom, Pia		Ent	10			25	Actress. TV News. Daughter Ingrid Bergman
Linenger, J. M.		Space	10			25	
Liney, John		Comics					Henry; Sketch 175; Comic strip 135
Ling, Bai		Ent				47	Chinese actress
Linkletter, Art	1912-	Ent	10	25		25	Radio-TV MC. Master of the Interview
Linn, Archibald L.	1802-1857	Congr	10				Repr. NY, County Judge
Linnaeus, Carolus von	1707-1778	Sci	925	7500			Carl von Linne. Swe. Botanist.
Linn-Baker, Mark	1954-	Ent	10			35	Actor
Linnehan, Richard		Space	10			20	
Linney, Laura		Ent	16			56	Actress; 'Abigail Adams'; Emmy
Linville, Larry		Ent	20			55	Mash
Liotta, Ray		Ent	20			48	Actor
Lipchitz, Jacques		Artist	130	210	225		Pol. -Fr. -Am. Cubist Sculptor
Lipfert, Helmut		WWII	35			70	#15 World Highest ACE. Ger.
Lipinski, William O. L		Congr	10				Member US Congress
Lipkovska, Lydia		Opera	75			325	Rus. Sopr.
Lipman, Clara	1869-1952	Ent	15			75	Stage Actress
Lipman, Maureen	1946-	Ent	10			25	Br. Actress
Lipmann, Fritz A.		Sci	25	45	70	30	Nobel Med. 1953
Lipnicki, Jonathan	1990-	Ent	10			25	Actor; 'Jerry Maguire'
Lipovsek, Marjana		Opera	10			30	Opera
Lippe-Weissenfeld, E. Priz zur		WWII		380			Luftwaffe ace
Lippman, Walter		Author	25	75		30	Journalist, Editor, Pulitzer
Lipscomb, William N., Dr.		Sci	20	35		30	Nobel Chemistry
Lipsner, B. B.		Aero	30	65		90	Pioneer Air Mail Pilot
Lipton, Peggy		Ent	10			50	Actress; 'Mod Squad'
Lipton, Thomas, Sir	1850-1940	Bus	70	118	425	215	Br. Tea Merchant-Yachtsman
Lisa, Manuel	1772-1820	Celeb	763				Am. Fur Trader
List, Emanuel	1888-1967	Opera	35			70	Austrian-born Am. bass

NAME	DATES	CATEGORY	SIG	LS/DS	ALS	SP	COMMENTS
List, Eugene	1918-1995	Ent	20			75	Actor
List, Wilhelm	1880-1971	WWII				360	Ger. Field Marshall
Lister, Joseph, Lord	1827-1912	Sci	181	363	706		Pioneer of Antiseptic Surgery. 1st Baron
Liston, Robert	1794-1847	Sci	15	30	50		Skilled Scottish Surgeon
Listowell, Earl of		Phil	20				Viscount Wm. Francis Hare
Liszt, Franz	1811-1886	Comp	350	543	1566	2575	Hung.-Born. Pianist. AMusQS 3, 800, AManS 16, 750
Litchfield, Grace D.	1849-1944	Author	10		25		
Litel, John	1892-1964	Ent	15	15	35	68	
Lithgow, John	1945-	Ent	15			40	Actor
Litjens, Stefan		Aero	10	15	25	20	
Little Anthony & the Imperials		Music	55			145	Rock group
Little Richard (Penniman)		Music	100	240		167	Rock. DS re Lease of Master Recordings 150
Little River Band		Music	25			75	S Guitar 345-630
Little, Cleavon	1939-1992	Ent	45			125	Actor; Bart in 'Blazing Saddles'
Little, Lewis Henry	1817-1862	Civ War	280				CSA Gen.
Little, Little Jack		Band	15				Big Band Leader
Little, Rich		Ent	10			40	
Little, Royal		Bus	22		55		
Littlefield, Warren		Ent	10			20	Prod.
Littlejohn, Abram N.		Clergy	10	20	35		
Littlejohn, Dewitt C.	1818-1892	Civ War	30	65	95		Union Gen.
Litvak, Anatole		Ent	40			145	Film Dir.
Litvinov, Maksim M.		Diplo	50		125	125	Soviet Foreign Min.
Liu, Lucy		Ent	10			40	Actress
Liu-Li Pei		Opera	10			35	Chinese Opera Star
Lively, Blake		Ent	15			45	
Livermore, Daniel P.		Clergy	15	20	45		
Livermore, Mary A.	1820-1905	Reform	24	64	150	230	Woman Suffrage, Temperance; AQS 60
Livingston, Alan		Comp	15	55			
Livingston, Bob (Robert)	1904-1988	Ent	20			67	Known for 30s-40's Western Roles
Livingston, Edward P.	1764-1836	Cab	25	69	175		Jackson's Sec. of State 1831
Livingston, Henry B.	1757-1823	Sup Crt	100	310	465		
Livingston, Jay		Comp	15	45	60	160	AMusQS 35-100-300-375 ('Silver Bells')
Livingston, John H.		Aero	105			145	Premier Racing Pilot entering 139. 79 1st, 43 2nd
Livingston, Margaret	1900-1984	Ent	10			45	
Livingston, Peter Van Brugh		Rev War		275			Patriot, Merchant
Livingston, Philip	1716-1778	Rev War	290	778	1500		Signer Dec. of Independ; NY Merchant
Livingston, Robert	1742-1794	Rev War	170	350	400		Dir. Bank of the US (1792)
Livingston, Robert R.	1746-1813	Rev War	195	440	1250		Cont. Congr. Administered Pres. Oath To Washington
Livingston, Robert R., Sr.	1718-1775	Law		500			Atty, Judge. Opposed Stamp Act.
Livingston, William	1723-1790	Rev War	300	888	1750		Continental Congr. Gov. NJ
Livingstone, David	1813-1873	Expl	533	910	2424		Missionary, Explr. of Africa. Author; AMS 5400
Livingstone, Ken		Pol				20	Mayor of London
Livingstone, Mary		Ent	30	35	45	40	Actress; married to Jack Benny
Liwei, Yng		Space				160	1st Chinese astronaut
LL Cool J		Ent	15			40	Actor, rapper
Llewellyn, Anthony	1933-	Space	10			30	
Llewelyn-Bowen, Lawrence		Celeb	10				Designer
Lloyd, Christopher		Ent	10	15	28	45	
Lloyd, Emily		Ent	10			40	
Lloyd, Frank A		Ent	20	50			Film Dir. AA
Lloyd, Harold	1894-1971	Ent	170	225		273	Film Comedian-Actor. Silent Into 30s
Lloyd, James	1769-1831	Congr	30	65	90		Sen. MA 1808
Lloyd, Kevin	1949-1998	Ent	10			40	Br. Actor

NAME	DATES	CATEGORY	SIG	LS/DS	ALS	SP	COMMENTS
Lloyd, Norman	1914-	Ent	15			157	
Lloyd, Sue	1939-	Ent	10			25	Br. Actress
Lloyd-George, David,	1863-1945	HOS	63	372	425	308	Br. Prime Min. WWI, 1st Earl
Lo Giudici, Franco		Opera	40			150	Opera
Loan, Nguyen Ngoc		Mil	150			375	Gen. Viet Nam
LoBianco, Tony	1936-	Ent	10			35	Actor
LoBiondo, Frank A. L		Congr	10				Member US Congress
Locane, Amy		Ent	15			35	Actress. Melrose Place
Locke, D. R.		Jrnalist					SEE Nasby, Petroleum
Locke, John	1632-1704	Author	700	1950	5000		Br. Phil. LS/Cont 12500; Medival Man. Page 13000
Locke, Samuel	1813-1890	Pol			81		
Locke, Sandra		Ent	10			40	
Locke, William John		Author	20	35	75	30	Br. Novels
Lockhart, Gene		Ent	20			112	Film Char. Actor. 30s, 40s
Lockhart, June		Ent	15			30	Actress. 'Lassie', 'Lost in Space'
Lockheed, Alan		Aero	80	150	300	150	Pioneer Aviator, Plane Designer
Locklear, Heather		Ent	20	20	30	64	Actress.
Locklin, Hank		Cntry Mus	10			55	Country Star
Lockwood, Belva A.	1830-1917	Fem	186	330	733		1st Woman to Pract. Before Supr. Ct. AQS 290-360
Lockwood, Chas. W, Capt		Civ War	100				1st MN to Enlist, Last Survivor
Lockwood, Gary		Ent	10			40	Actor '2001'
Lockwood, Henry Hayes	1814-1899	Civ War	40	75	120		Union Gen.
Lockwood, Margaret	1916-1990	Ent	12	20	55	105	Br. Film Actress
Lockyer, Herbert		Clergy	25	35	45		
Lodge, Henry Cabot	1850-1924	Congr	30	92	114	130	MOC 1887, Sen. MA 1893. TLS/cont 368
Lodge, Henry Cabot, Jr.	1902-1985	Congr	20	42	65	50	Ambassador UN, Diplomat, VP Cand.
Lodge, Oliver J., Sir	1851-1940	Sci	50	80	125	175	Br. Physicist, Spiritualist
Loeb, William		Bus	10	25	55	35	
Loebe, Paul	1875-1967	WWII	80	150			Pres. of the Ger. Reichstag 1920-24, 1925-32.
Loesser, Frank	1910-1969	Comp	340		440		Comp. of Top Broadway Hits. Movie Hits
Loew, Marcus		Bus	30	40	65	35	
Loewe, Frederick	1901-1988	Comp	163	75	145	55	AMusQS 300-1100. 'My Fair Lady', 'Camelot', Sigs of Lerner & Loewe 200
Loewy, Raymond		Bus	35	90	140	240	Designer
Lofgren, Zoe L		Congr	10				Member US Congress
Lofting, Hugh	1886-1947	Author	95				Illust. Dr. Dolittle Books. S Illustr. 195
Loftus, Cissie (Cecilia)	1876-1943	Ent	35	65		175	Br. Actress. Vaude., Stage, Musical & Film Star
Logan, Benjamin	1752-1802	Mil	350	560	675		Pioneer Hero, Indian Fighter
Logan, Ella		Music	10	15	20	25	Pop Singer. Band Vocalist. 'A Tiskit A Taskit . '
Logan, John A.	1826-1886	Civ War	52	118	177		Union Gen., Father Memorial Day. Fndr. G. A. R.
Logan, John A. (WD)		Civ War	65	210	525	750	Union Gen.
Logan, Josh(ua)	1908-1988	Ent	20	40		45	Film & Stage Prod., Writer, Dir.
Logan, Olive		Author	25	35			
Logan, Thomas M.	1840-1914	Civ War	95	225	422		CSA Gen.
Logerot, Gaston		Music		65			Fr. Double bass player
Loggia, Robert	1930-	Ent	10			45	
Loggins & Messina		Music	25		50	100	S Album 100; S Guitar 250
Loggins, Kenny		Music	20	55		52	
Logue, Donal		Ent	15			45	
Lohan, Lindsay		Ent	20			60	Actress
Loisy, Alfred		Clergy	20	25	35		
Loizerolles, Francois Aved de	1772-1845	Pol			175		A major historical figure in the Fr. Revolution
Loken, Kristanna		Ent	16			48	
Lollobrigida, Gina		Ent	20	30	30	113	Actress

NAME	DATES	CATEGORY	SIG	LS/DS	ALS	SP	COMMENTS
Lom, Herbert		Ent	22			93	Char. Actor
Lomax, Lunsford Lindsey	1835-1913	Civ War	100	275	352		CSA Gen.
Lomb, Henry	1828-1908	Bus		2600			Ger. Born Am. Optician. Co-Fndr. Bausch & Lomb
Lombard, Carole	1908-1942	Ent	240	375	468	1058	Actress
Lombard, Louise	1970-	Ent	10			20	Br. Actress
Lombardo, Guy	1902-1977	Band	20	130	65	47	Big Band Leader. Royal Canadians
Loncaine, Richard	1946-	Ent	10			20	Dir.
London, Charmian		Celeb	40			155	2nd Wife of Jack London
London, George		Opera	35			70	Opera, Concert, Met.
London, Jack	1876-1916	Author	312	938	2005	900	Am. Novels, Advent. Suicide, 40. S Chk 250-300
London, Jason	1972-	Ent	10			30	Actor
London, Jeremy		Ent	28			85	
London, Julie		Music	20			90	Vocalist-Actress. Recording Artist
London, Tom	1889-1963	Ent	50			100	
Long, Armistead L.	1825-1891	Civ War	85	100	370		CSA Gen.
Long, Dr. Loretta	1940-	Ent	10			25	Actress; Susan on Sesame St.
Long, Earl K.		Gov	20	30		25	Governor LA,
Long, Eli	1837-1903	Civ War	40				Union Gen.
Long, Huey P.		Congr	227	241		275	Sen., Gov. LA. Assass., TLS cont 2415
Long, John D.		Cab	12	30	40	20	Sec. Navy, Governor MA
Long, Johnny		Band	25			50	Big Bandleader. Violinist
Long, Justin		Ent	15			45	
Long, Lotus		Ent	10			30	Actress-Oriental Dancer
Long, Nia		Ent	13			40	
Long, Pierse	1739-1789	Rev War	30	75	180		Continental Congress
Long, Richard	1927-1974	Ent	42	50		105	Actor
Long, Russell	1918-	Congr	10	20		15	Sen. LA. Son of Huey Long
Long, Shelley		Ent	12	30	25	40	Actress 'Cheers'.
Longacre, James B.	1794-1869	Artist	140	400	950		Chief Engraver of the US Mint
Longet, Claudine		Ent	15	15	50	65	
Longfellow, Henry W.	1807-1882	Author	191	268	666	921	Poet, Harvard Prof. AManS 2295, AQS 500
Longfellow, Samuel		Clergy	40	50	75	55	
Longfellow, Stephen	1775-1849	Congr	20	50	145		MOC ME 1823
Longley, Charles T.	1794-1868	Clergy	25				Archbishop Canterbury
Longley, James B.		Gov	10	15			Governor ME
Longoria, Eva	1975-	Ent				100	Actress
Longstreet, James	1821-1904	Civ War	469	900	1439	1500	CSA Gen., Important ALS/cont 7500
Longstreet, James (WD)	1821-1904	Civ War	625		4587	2600	CSA Gen.
Longworth, Alice Roosevelt	1884-1980	1st Fmly	42	45	138	150	Born of TR's 1st wife, Alice Hathaway Lee
Longworth, Nicholas		Congr	15	58	85		Spkr. of the House, Son-in-law of T. Roosevelt
Loo, Richard		Ent	48			150	
Loomis, Dwight		Congr	10		41		FF 41
Loomis, Gustavus	1789-1872	Civ War	45	65	105		Union Gen.
Loos, Anita		Author	17	55	75	30	Am. Novels, Film Scripts
Loos, Walter		Aero	10	20	35	25	
Loper, Don		Bus	10	15	35	15	Fashion Designer
Lopes, Lisa "Left Eye"	1971-2002	Music	25			100	Singer
Lopez, George		Ent	13			39	
Lopez, Jennifer		Ent	20			144	Actress, singer
Lopez, Vincent	1895-1975	Band	20			55	Big Band Leader-Pianist
Lopez-Alegria, Michael		Space	10			20	
Loraine, Robert		Aero	15	55			
Lorca, Frederico Garcia		Author	4650				Sp. Poet, Dramatist
Lord, Daniel, Rev.		Clergy	10			35	

L

NAME	DATES	CATEGORY	SIG	LS/DS	ALS	SP	COMMENTS
Lord, E. J.		Congr	10		30		Sen. CA
Lord, Herbert M.		Mil	10	25			
Lord, Jack		Ent	42	110	140	159	Actor, Hawaii 5-0
Lord, John Wesley, Bish.		Clergy	20	35	45	45	
Lord, Marjorie	1918-	Ent	20	25		45	Actress; 'Danny Thomas Show'
Lord, Phillips H.		Ent	20		35		Writer-Prod. Radio
Lord, Walter		Author	10			15	
Lords, Traci		Ent	10	15	30	68	Actrress
Loren, Sophia		Ent	20	30		156	SP from 'Two Women' 315. AA
Lorengar, Pilar		Opera	25			40	Opera
Lorentz, Hendrik A.	1853-1928	Sci			1500		Dutch physicist. Nobel Pr. winner 1902
Lorenz, Konrad	1903-1989	Sci	62	275			Austrian Biologist
Lorillard, Peter		Bus	125	260	475		Tobacco Industry
Lorimar, George C.		Clergy	20				Author
Loring, Charles G.		Pol	35				
Loring, Gloria	1946-	Ent	10			35	Actress; Singer
Loring, Israel		Clergy	25	75	125		
Loring, Lisa		Ent	15	40		45	Actress; ' Addam's Family'
Loring, William Wing	1818-1886	Civ War	120	277	315	425	CSA Gen.
Loring, William Wing (WD)	1818-1886	Civ War	180		745		CSA Gen.
Lorne, Marion	1883-1968	Ent	80			130	Actress. Stage/TV/Films; Aunt Clara, 'Bewitched'
Lorre, Peter	1904-1964	Ent	142	225		444	Hungarian Char. Actor., 'Maltese Falcon'
Losch, Tilly		Ent	10			60	
Losey, Joseph		Ent	35			320	Film Dir.
Losigkeit, Fritz		Aero	12	15	30	20	
Lossing, Benson		Author	15	41	50		Am. Historian, Engraver
Lost in Space		Ent				400	Cast S
Lott, Felicity		Opera	15			30	Opera
Lott, Trent		Congr	12			25	Repub. an Majority Leader. Sen. MS
Loubet, Emile Francois	1838-1929	HOS			125		Pres. France 1899-1906
Louge, Mike		Space	10			26	
Loughlin, Lori		Ent	40			60	Actress
Louis II (Bavaria)	1845-1886	Royal		525			King from 1864
Louis II (Monaco)	1870-1949	Royal	50	150	210	200	Prince of Monaco
Louis Philippe (Fr)	1838-1894	Royal	75	238	260		Citizen King. Duc D'Orleans
Louis XI (Fr)	1423-1483	Royal		3500			Earliest Collectible King of France 1461-1483
Louis XII (Fr)	1462-1515	Royal	800	1750	4200		King of France
Louis XIII (Fr)	1601-1643	Royal	750	760	4000		King of France
Louis XIV (Fr)	1638-1715	Royal	450	962	3750		The Sun King
Louis XV (Fr)	1710-1774	Royal	698	750	5500		King of France
Louis XVI (Fr)	1754-1793	Royal	375	850			King of France. Guillotined
Louis XVIII (Fr)	1755-1824	Royal	191	200	1680		Louis Stanislas Xavier
Louis, Justin		Ent	18			55	
Louise Caroline Alberta,		Royal	25		65	175	Princess. 4th Daughter of Queen Victoria
Louise Vict. (Alex. Dagmar)	1867-1931	Royal	20		83	170	Princess. Royal. Daughter Edw. VII
Louise, Anita	1915-1970	Ent	15			60	Frail Leading Lady. Films 40s-50's
Louise, Tina		Ent	15	20	20	54	'Gilligans Island'
Lounge, John M.		Space	10			20	
Lousma, Jack F.		Space	10	40	60	60	
L'Ouverture, Toussant		Mil		807			Led a slave revolt against the Fr. in 1791
Love, Bessie	1898-1986	Ent	35		55	75	Vintage Actress
Love, Courtney		Ent	15			50	Actress.
Love, John A.	1916-2002	Gov	10	12		10	Governor CO
Love, Montagu		Ent	20		140	50	Vintage Char. Actor

NAME	DATES	CATEGORY	SIG	LS/DS	ALS	SP	COMMENTS
Lovecraft, H. P.		Author	220	300	738	550	Reclusive Horror Story Writer
Love-Hewitt, Jennifer		Ent	15			50	Actress.
Lovejoy, Frank	1912-1962	Ent	25			172	Successful Radio Actor to Leading Roles in Films
Lovejoy, Owen		Congr	15	30	45		MOC IL 1857-64
Lovelace, Linda	1949-2002	Ent	218			322	Activist; former porn star
Loveless, Patty		Ent	15			35	Singer
Lovell, Bernard Dr.		Sci	15	25	40	20	
Lovell, James	1737-1814	Rev War	50	195	500		Continental Congress, Pol., Patriot
Lovell, James A. Jr.	1928-	Space	35	234		196	Cmmdr. of Aborted Apollo 13; S Cvr. 140
Lovell, Mansfield	1822-1884	Civ War	142	338	386		CSA Gen.
Lovell, Mansfield (WD)		Civ War	185	560	850		CSA Gen.
Loverboy		Music	25			50	Singer
Lovett, John	1761-1818	Congr	40		135		War 1812. ALS/Cont 300
Lovett, Lyle		Cntry Mus	20			58	Popular Country Music Singer
Lovett, Robert		Cab	10			15	Sec. Defense
Lovin' Spoonful		Music	35			50	Rock group; S Album 65
Lovitz, Jon		Ent	10			40	Actor
Lovkay, John		Bus	10			10	CEO Hamilton Standard
Lovrenich, Rodger T.		Bus	10			20	Inventor of electronic ignition
Low, Abiel Abbot	1811-1893	Bus	50	110	175	195	Packet & Clipper Ships; Merch./Civ. War/Trader/Philan.
Low, David, Sir		Comics	15	45	110	140	NZ-Br Pol. 'Col. Blimp'
Low, Frederick F.		Gov	45		175		Gov, MOC CA 1860, Diplomat
Low, G. David		Space	10			20	
Low, Nicholas		Rev War	105	245	450		Prominent NY, Backed Revolution. Merchant
Low, Seth	1819-1916	Mayor	10	35	45		Merchant, Pres. Columbia U
Lowe, Ed		Invent	20			30	Kitty Litter
Lowe, Edmund	1890-1971	Ent	25	30	60	103	Handsome Leading-Man 30s-40's Films
Lowe, Hudson, Sir	1769-1844	Mil		310	500		Last custodian of Napoleon, Gov. St. Helena
Lowe, Rob		Ent	17	35		40	Actor, The West Wing
Lowe, Thaddeus S. C.	1832-1913	Civ War	210	412	717		Aeronaut, Inventor, CW Balloonist
Lowell, Amy	1874-1925	Author	35	125	250		Am. Poet, Critic., Imagist School
Lowell, Carey	1961-	Ent	10			30	Actress
Lowell, Charles Russell	1835-1864	Civ War	100				Union Gen.
Lowell, James Russell	1819-1891	Author	108	115	188	375	Poet, Hall of Fame, Educator, Editor, Diplomat
Lowell, John H.		WWII	15	25	40	35	ACE, WWII; 7. 5 kills
Lowell, Joshua A.	1801-1874	Congr	10		45		MOC ME, Dem. Presidenial Elector
Lowell, Percival	1855-1916	Sci	15	40	65		Am. Astronomer, Author. Brother of A. L. & Amy
Lowell, Robert	1917-1977	Author	42	90	185		Am. Poet. (2) Pulitzers 'Lord Weary's Castle'
Lowenstein, Allard		Congr	75			175	Dump Johnson Movement. Assass.
Lowenstein, Shoshana		Celeb				40	
Lowery, John		Congr	10	15		15	
Lowery, Joseph, Rev.		Celeb	10				Civ. Rights Leader
Lowery, Robert	1913-1971	Ent	75	125		125	Actor. 'Batman' Serial
Lowey, Nita M. L		Congr	10				Member US Congress
Lowman, Seymour	1868-1940	Cab	10	10			Ass't Sec. Treas., Lt. Gov. NY
Lown, Bert		Band	10			20	Bandleader. Bye Bye Blues
Lowrey, Mark Perrin	1828-1885	Civ War	110	225			CSA Gen.
Lowry, Robert		Gov	10	25			Governor MS
Lowry, Robert	1830-1910	Civ War	90	200			CSA Gen.
Loy, Myrna	1905-1993	Ent	24	40	50	271	Actress; Specail SP 4200
Lubbers, Bob		Comics	10			70	Tarzan
Lubbock, Francis R.	1815-1905	Civ War	150	348	398	273	CSA Governor TX. Aide-de-camp Jeff. Davis
Lubbock, Sir John	1834-1913	Author	10	22	42		Br. Banker. Author Science-Fiction Books
Lubin, Arthur		Ent	25			65	Film Dir.

NAME	DATES	CATEGORY	SIG	LS/DS	ALS	SP	COMMENTS
Lubin, Germaine		Opera	200			275	Opera. Legendary Fr. Sopr.
Lubitsch, Ernst	1892-1947	Ent	115		275	720	Ger. -Am. Vintage Film Dir.
Lubke, Heinrich	1885-1972	HOS	10		30	50	Pres. Ger. Fed. Repub.
Lucan, George C. Bingham, Earl of		Mil			75		Field Marshal
Lucas, Clyde		Band	15			25	Bandleader
Lucas, Edward		Congr	10		37		FF 37
Lucas, Frank D. L		Congr	10				Member US Congress
Lucas, George		Ent	48	700	122	100	Film Dir. 'Star Wars'; SP w/Spielberg 250
Lucas, John P.		WWII	70	150		350	Gen. Cmdr. 4th Army WWII
Lucas, Josh		Ent	18		55		
Lucas, Ken L		Congr	10				Member US Congress
Lucas, Thomas John	1826-1908	Civ War	45	80	120		Union Gen.
Lucca, Pauline		Opera	30	70	238		Opera
Lucci, Susan		Ent	20	25	40	62	Actress; Soap Star
Luccock, Halford E.		Clergy	20	35	50	40	
Luce, Clare Boothe	1903-1987	Author	30	60	70	105	Ambassador, Plays, Congresswoman
Luce, Cyrus G.		Gov	10	15	25		Governor MI
Luce, Henry R.	1898-1967	Pub	30	50	75	55	Time, Life, Fortune, Sports Illustrated
Luce, Stephen Bleecker	1827-1917	Mil	15	35	95	40	Adm. !st Pres. Naval War College
Lucid, Shannon W.		Space	10			50	Set New Space Record
Luckinbill, Laurence		Ent	22		40	50	Actor. Active in Star Trek Films
Luckner, Felix, von	1881-1966	Mil	62	80	108	108	The Sea Devil' WWII. Sank 14 Allied Ships 195
Luckner, Nicholas		Fr Rev	225	675			Marshal of Fr. Guillotined
Lucon, L. J., Card.		Clergy	45	55	75	60	
Ludden, Allan	1918-1981	Ent	25			45	TV Gameshow Host
Ludde-Neurath, Walter		Mil	15	45		45	Aide-de-camp to Donitz
Ludendorff, Erich von	1865-1937	Mil	98	232	358	389	Ger. Gen. WWI, Pol.
Ludin, Hanns		WWII	130	350			Ger. Gen. -Storm Trooper WWII
Ludington, Marshall I.	1839-1919	Civ War	30	55	80		Union Gen.
Ludlum, Robert		Author	10	25	35	20	Super Spy novels; SB 120
Ludwig I	1786-1868	Royal	65	278	1012		King of Bavaria
Ludwig II	1845-1886	Royal	55	634	1020		King of Bavaria
Ludwig, Emil		Author	40	125	200		
Lufbery, Raoul		Aero	125	350	590	400	ACE, WWI, Lafayette Escadrille
Luft, Lorna		Ent	12			35	Singer Sister of Liza Minelli. Daughter of Judy
Lugar, Richard G.		Congr	10	25		20	Sen. IN
Lugosi, Bela	1882-1956	Ent	437	1148	700	1216	Hungarian Born, 'Dracula'
Luhan, Mabel Dodge		Author			388		
Lujan, Albert		Artist	20		45		
Lukas, Foss		Comp	20			75	Versatile Ger./Am./Comp./Conductor
Lukas, Paul	1895-1971	Ent	37			158	AA; 'Watch on the Rhine'
Luke, Derek		Ent	17			50	
Luke, Frank		Mil	150	400	600	500	ACE, WWI, MOH, #3 US Ace
Luke, Keye	1904-1991	Ent	40	40		53	Chinese actor; #1 Son in Charlie Chan Films
Luks, George Benjamin	1867-1933	Artist	20	55	200		Member Ashcan School., S drw 270
Lulu Belle (& Scotty)		Cntry Mus	10			25	C & W Music. Popular Duo. 40s-50's
Lum & Abner		Ent	40			95	Top Radio Comedy Pr-30's. Chester Lauk-Norris Goff
Lumbly, Carl		Ent	15		45		
Lumet, Sidney		Ent	15		45		TV Dir. -Dramatist
Lumholtz, Carl	1851-1922	Author	15		45		
Lumiere, Louis	1862-1954	Invent	175	260	501	375	Cinematographe Projector
Lumley, Joanna	1946-	Ent	10			45	Actress
Luna, Barbara		Ent	10			25	Actress; Zorro
Lunacharsky, Anatoly		Author		368			Marxist writer

L

NAME	DATES	CATEGORY	SIG	LS/DS	ALS	SP	COMMENTS
Lunceford, Jimmie		Band	35			178	Big Band Leader-Arranger
Lund, John	1913-1992	Ent	15			60	Warner Bros. 40s-50's Leading Man
Lunden, Joan		Ent	10			30	TV Host
Lundgren, Dolph	1957-	Ent	15			42	Swedish Actor
Lundigan, William		Ent	15			40	Actor; Handsome Leading Man 40s-50's
Lundy, Jessica	1966-	Ent	10			30	Actress
Luner, Jamie		Ent	13			40	
Lunn, George R.	1873-1948	Congr	10	15			MOC. NY
Lunney, Glynn		Space	10			90	Mission Control. SP w/ Kraft, Griffin 600
Lunt, Alfred & Fontanne, Lynne		Ent	40	175		84	Popular Stage Couple30's-. DS Idiot's Delight 650
Lupino, Ida	1918-1995	Ent	22	70	75	227	Br-Am Actress, Dir.
Lupino, Stanley	1893-1942	Ent	15			35	Br. Comedian. Father of Ida
Lupone, Patti		Ent	10			40	Actress
Lupton, John	1928-1993	Ent	10			40	
Lupus, Peter		Ent				35	Actor; 'Mission Impossible'
Luria, Salvador F.		Sci	20	35	55	25	Nobel Med.
Lurie, Bob		Bus	10	25	45	15	
Luse, Harley		Cntry Mus	10			20	
Lusha, Masiela		Ent	17			50	
Luther, Hans		HOS	35	55	85	55	Chancellor Ger., Ambass. US
Luther, Martin		Clergy	12500	30000	46688		LS/Extremely Rare 49500
Lutoslawski, Witold	1913-1994	Comp		110			AMusQS 350
Lutyens, Edw. Landseer, Sir	1869-1944	Archtct		70			Br. Designed Cenotaph in London. Br. Embassy US
Lutzi, Gertrude		Opera	15			30	Opera
Lutzow, Freiherr von		WWII				240	Ger. Field Marshall
Lutzow, Gunther		Aero	175	285	445	450	
Luv, Bunny		Ent	13			40	
Lvov, Alexis F.	1798-1870	Comp	100		200		Rus. Commissioned by Czar. Russ. Nat'l Anthem
Lyautey, Louis	1854-1934	Mil	20	40	105	40	Marshal of Fr., Statesman
Lyell, Charles, Sir	1797-1875	Sci	95		425		Br. Fndr. of Mdrn. Geology
Lyle, The Great		Ent	25			50	Vintage Br. Magician
Lyman, Abe		Band	15			45	Big Band
Lyman, Charles Edwin		Clergy	15	25	50	30	
Lymon, Frankie		Music	352			595	Rock
Lymon, Frankie & Teenagers		Music	455			1278	Rock group
Lynch, David		Ent	20			80	Movie-TV Dir. ' Twin Peaks'
Lynch, Jane	1960-	Ent	15			25	Actor
Lynch, John R.		Congr		250			Former Slave. MOC MS 1873-77, '82-'83
Lynch, Kelly		Ent	10			40	Actress
Lynch, Peter		Bus	10			20	Financial expert
Lynch, Richard	1940-	Ent	10			35	Actor
Lynch, Stephen F. L		Congr	10				Member US Congress
Lynch, Thomas Jr.	1749-1779	Rev War	16912	44000			Rare Signer Declaration of Independence
Lynde, Paul	1926-1982	Ent	20	25	40	102	Comedian; actor
Lyndhurst, Nicholas	1961-	Ent	10			25	Br. Actor
Lyndon, Josias		Pol			391		Rhode Island's last Colonial governor
Lynen, Feodor		Sci	20	40		25	Nobel Med.
Lynley, Carol	1942-	Ent	10	18	35	53	Actress.
Lynn, Diana	1926-1971	Ent	20	25	35	95	Actress. Talented Pianist. 'Bedtime for Bonzo'
Lynn, Ginger		Ent	10			40	Actress; Erotica
Lynn, Jeffrey		Ent	15			60	40's Warner Bros. Leading Man
Lynn, Loretta		Cntry Mus	20			73	Country Music; S Album 60; S Guitar 300
Lynn, Porsche		Ent	25			40	Actress erotica
Lynn, Vera, Dame		Music	30			88	Br. WWII Singing Star

NAME	DATES	CATEGORY	SIG	LS/DS	ALS	SP	COMMENTS
Lynyrd Skynyrd		Music	2385	3655		4600	Legendary Rock Band; original members
Lyon, Ben	1901-1979	Ent	25			60	Actor. Star Silents-Early Talkies. w/RAF WWII
Lyon, Hylan Benton	1836-1907	Civ War	110				CSA Gen.
Lyon, Lucius	1800-1851	Congr	15		35		Sen. & MOC. MI
Lyon, Mary Mason	1797-1849	Educ	55	165	340		Provided Women's Advanced Edu. Mt. Holyoke Coll.
Lyon, Nathaniel	1818-1861	Civ War	245	262	1500		Union Gen. KIA. RARE, War date/rare 3950
Lyon, Sue		Ent	10	15	22	70	
Lyonne, Natasha		Ent	10			40	Actress
Lyons, Edmund, Lord	1790-1858	Mil	50		252		Br, Adm.
Lyons, Judson W.	1860-1940	Pol	30	125			1st Afr-Am Register of Treasury 1898-1906
Lyons, Rich'd B. P., 1st Earl	1817-1887	Diplo	35		114		Br. Min. to US in Civil War.
Lyons, William		Bus	40	80	175		
Lytell, Bert		Ent	30	45	90	65	Vintage Actor. Stage. Migrated to Films
Lytle, William Haynes	1826-1863	Civ War	100				Union Gen.
Lytton, E. George Bulwer	1803-1873	Author	25	95	208		Novels, Poet, Colonial Sec. 1st Baron
Ma, Yo Yo		Music	35			78	Cellist Superstar
Maas, Melvin G.	1898-1964	WWII	25	45	60	125	Marine Corps Gen. WWII. Wounded, Blinded. MOC MN
Mabius, Eric		Ent	13			40	
Mabley, Jackie Moms		Ent	75			130	
Mabrey, Sunny		Ent	13			40	
Mac, Bernie		Ent	15			35	Comedian
MacArthur, Arthur	1845-1912	Mil	45	268	155	150	CW Off'r, Sp. -Am. War. Gen. Father to Douglas
MacArthur, Charles		Author	15	30	55	25	Plays Husband Helen Hayes
MacArthur, Douglas	1880-1964	Mil	192	629	875	748	5 Star Gen. WWII, TLS/cont 1000-5000
MacArthur, Douglas II	1909-1997	Diplo	15	20	25	30	Ambassador to Japan. Nephew of the Gen.
MacArthur, James		Ent	12			35	Actor Son of Helen Hayes. 'Hawaii 5-0'
MacArthur, Jean		Mil	15	20	30	20	Mrs. Douglas MacArthur
MacArthur, John D.	1897-1978	Bus				35	Am. businessman & philanthropist
Macartney, Clarence E.		Clergy	15	20	25	20	
Macartney, George		HOS	10	35	85		
Macaulay, (Emilie) Rose, Dame		Author	10	20	68		Br. Novels, Critic, Verse
Macaulay, Thos. B., Lord	1800-1859	Author	45	65	102		Historian & Poet. Pol.
Macbeth, Florence		Opera	20			50	Am. Sopr.
MacChesney, Nathan Wm.		Law	10	20	50		
Macchio, Ralph		Ent	15			30	Young Actor. 'Karate Kid'
MacCormick, John	1884-1945	Opera		180			Irish tenor
MacCracken, Henry M.		Clergy	20	35	45	30	
MacDonald John D.		Author	65			195	Creator of Travis McGee
MacDonald, Charles Henry		WWII	175				WWII ace w/27 kills
MacDonald, Cordelia H.		Ent	40	75	120		1st Eva in Uncle Tom's Cabin
MacDonald, George	1875-1961	Bus	35				Pub. Utilities
MacDonald, George		Clergy	20	30	45		
MacDonald, J. Farrell		Ent	25			272	Char. Actor.
MacDonald, J. Ramsey	1866-1937	HOS	50	130	175	172	Twice Br. Prime Min.
Macdonald, Jacques E. J. A	1765-1840.	Fr Rev	75	110	250		Marshal of Napoleon
MacDonald, Jeanette	1901-1965	Ent	40	65	90	127	Teamed w/Nelson Eddy in Top Movie Hits
MacDonald, John Alexander		HOS	35	90			Premier 1857, 1st P. M. Canada
MacDonald, Ross		Author	45	145	250		Mystery Writer
MacDonald, Torbet		Congr	10				MA. JFK Roommate & Lifelong Friend
Macdonogh, P. M. W.		Mil	10	17	22		
MacDonough, Thomas	1783-1825	Mil	95	290	700		Am. Naval Off'r. Tripoli, 1812
MacDougall, Clinton	1839-1914	Civ War	40	55	80		Union Gen.
MacDowell, Andie		Ent	15			40	Actress
MacDowell, Edward	1861-1908	Comp	130	190	562	400	Songs, Concertos, Piano Pieces

NAME	DATES	CATEGORY	SIG	LS/DS	ALS	SP	COMMENTS
MacDowell, Melbourne	1856-1941	Ent	15			75	Vintage Actor
Macfadden, Bernarr	1868-1955	Bus	15	45	96	60	Physical Culturist, Publisher
Macfadyen, Dugald		Clergy	45	45	50	50	
MacFarlane, Seth		Ent	15			45	
Macfayden, Angus	1963-	Ent	10			25	Scottish actor
MacGibbon, Harriet E.	1905-1987	Ent	90			145	Actress; Mrs. Drysdale on Beverly Hillbillies
MacGraw, Ali		Ent	30	12		40	Actress.
MacGregor, Ewan		Ent	10			40	Actor, Star Wars
MacGregor, John 'Rob Roy'	1825-1892	Philan	12		50		Traveller
Machado, Anesia Pinheiro		Aero	35	55	80	65	
Machiavelli, Niccolo	1469-1527	Author	2500	9000	12500		
Macht, Gabriel		Ent	15			45	
MacInnes, Helen		Author	10	15	20		Am Best Selling Novels
Mack, Connie III		Congr	10	10		15	Sen. FL
Mack, Helen		Ent	10			35	
Mack, Lee	1968-	Celeb	10			25	Br. Comedian
Mack, Marion		Ent	10			40	
Mack, Ted	1904-1976	Ent	12			35	'Amateur Hour'
Mackaill, Dorothy		Ent	20	30	70	62	Vintage Film Actress
MacKall, William W.	1917-1991	Civ War	110	305			CSA Gen.
MacKall, William W. (WD)	1817-1891	Civ War	250		1250		CSA Gen.
MacKay, Charles		Clergy	20	25	35		
Mackay, John William		Bus	40	100	215		Fndr. Postal Telegraph Co.
MacKaye, Percy	1875-1956	Author	40	90	150		Am. Poet, Dramatist
Mackensen, August von		Mil	12	25	40	40	Ger. Gen. Fld. Marshal WWI. RK
Mackenzie, Edwina Troutt	1884-1984	Titanic	25		100		Survivor
MacKenzie, Gisele		Ent	10			25	
Mackenzie, Morell, Sir	1837-1892	Med	60	165	350		Larygologist.
Mackenzie, Ranald Slidell	1840-1889	Civ War	40	75	110		Union Gen.
Mackie, Bob		Bus	10	10	25	20	Fashion Designer
MacLachlan, Kyle		Ent	10			40	Picket Fences. Trey MacDougal, Sex in the City
MacLagan, William D., Bish.		Clergy	15	25	35		
MacLaine, Shirley		Ent	15	40	35	86	Actress
Maclane, Barton		Ent	50			158	Vint. Tough Guy. Maltese Falcon
MacLaren, Donald M.		Mil	25	40	95	95	
MacLean, Steve		Space	10	15		20	
MacLeay, Lachlan		Space	10			20	
MacLeish, Archibald	1892-1982	Author	30	55	120	75	Am. Poet, Lawyer. 3 Pulitzers
MacLeod, Gavin		Ent	10			35	
Macleod, George F.		Clergy	20	25	30		
MacMahon, Aline	1899-1991	Ent	20			165	Actress
MacMahon, Marie E. P.		HOS	35	110	225		Fr. Soldier, Pol., Marshal
MacMillan, Donald B.	1874-1970	Expl	40	60	95	118	Am. w/Peary at North Pole
MacMillan, Harold	1894-1987	HOS	30	128	250	160	Br. P. M. Lord Stockton
MacMurray, Fred	1908-1991	Ent	20	30	40	82	Film-TV Star
MacNee, Patrick	1922-	Ent	15			68	Brit. Actor. John Steed in 'The Avengers'
Macneil, Robert	1931-	Jrnalist	10			20	TV News anchor
MacNelly, Jeff		Comics	30			200	Shoe
MacNider, Hanford	1889-1968	Mil	10			35	US diplomat & US Army Gen.
Macomb, Alexander	1748-1832	Bus		98	115		Fur & Shipping Merchant. Associated/John J. Aster
Macon, Nathaniel	1758-1837	Congr	50	125	175		Sen. NC, Spkr. of House, Rev. War Soldier
MacPherson, Elle		Model	17			50	
MacRae, Gordon		Ent	15			98	Actor
MacRae, Meredith		Ent	10			30	Actress

NAME	DATES	CATEGORY	SIG	LS/DS	ALS	SP	COMMENTS
MacRae, Sheila		Ent	10			30	Actress
MacReady, George		Ent	20			40	
Macready, William C.	1793-1873	Ent	30		168		Foremost Br. Shakespearean Actor
MacVeagh, Franklin		Cab	10	25	60	20	Sec. Treasury
MacVeagh, Wayne	1833-1917	Cab	65		98		Atty Gen., Diplomat, CW Soldier
Macy, Bill	1922-	Ent	10			43	Actor
Macy, William J.	1950-	Ent	10			45	Actor. 'Pleasantville'
Madden, Charles Edw.	1919-	Mil	45	120	215	215	Brit. Adm.
Madden, John		Ent	10			20	Motion Picture Dir.
Maddox, Lester	1915-2003	Gov	20	130		65	Georgia Anti-Civ. Rights Gov.
Madeira, Jean		Opera	18			52	Am. Contralto
Madero, Francisco I.		HOS		3000			Revolutionary Pres. Mex. 1911-13
Madigan, Amy		Ent	10			35	
Madison, Dolley Payne	1768-1849	1st Lady	761	1096	2360		Free Frank 750-850-1, 200
Madison, Guy		Ent	65			79	Actor; "Wild Bill Hickcock"
Madison, J. & Monroe, J.		Pres	550	2377			Unusual DS 4500
Madison, James	1751-1836	Pres	369	1522	2874		FF 695-775-925, ALS/Cont 7500-9500
Madison, James (as Pres)	1751-1836	Pres	450	2012	4675		FF 460-600, ALS/cont 15,000-80, 500
Madonna		Music	175	830	1105	356	(Louise Veronica Cicone) Singer, actress, SB 275
Madriguera, Enric		Band	15			30	Big Band Leader
Madsen, Chris	1851-1944	West		1136			Outlaw & Indian Fighter
Madsen, Michael		Ent	10			40	Actor
Madsen, Virginia		Ent	10			40	Actress
Mae, Vanessa	1978-	Music	10			25	Violinist
Maeterlinck, Maurice, Ct.	1862-1949	Author	35	115	200	425	Nobel Literature. 'Pelleas & Melisand'
Maffett, Debbie Sue		Ent	10			30	Actress
Maffia, Roma		Ent	13			40	
Magee, John A.		Congr	10		35		MOC NY 1827. Banker, RR
Magee, Patrick	1922-1982	Ent	10			60	Actor
Magee, Walter W.	1861-1927	Congr	12	25			Repr. NY
Magg, Alois		Aero	10			15	
Magilton, Jerry		Space	10			20	
Magnani, Anna	1908-1973	Ent	120			364	Italian actress; AA
Magnus, Kurt		Sci				50	Rocket Pioneer. Peenemuende Team/USSR
Magnus, Sandra		Space	10			25	
Magrath, Andrew G.	1813-1893	Civ War	35	60	80		CSA Gov. SC. ALS '61 150
Magritte, René Francois	1898-1967	Artist	217	653	1023		Belg. Surrealist Painter. AManS 2000
Magruder, John B.	1807-1871	Civ War	285	391	535		CSA Gen. Sig/Rank 450
Magsaysay, Ramon	1907-1957	HOS	30	65	120	75	Pres. Philippines
Maguire, Tobey		Ent	20	130		68	Actor.
Maguire, W. A. Cpt.		Mil	25	50	75	75	
Mahan, Alfred Thayer		Mil	50	75	100		US Navy Off'r-Historian. CW
Maharis, George		Ent	10	30	25	40	Star of TV's 'Route 66' & Films
Mahen, Robert A.		Bus	15	30	70	70	
Mahendra Bir Bikram		Royal	35	50	135	50	King, Leader Nepal
Maher, Bill		Ent	15			35	Comedian
Mahler, Alma		Author	20		120		Author & Wife Gustav Mahler
Mahler, Gustav	1860-1911	Comp	550	1930	3080	6452	Austrian Comp. S etching 9000
Mahone, William	1826-1895	Civ War	106	250	285		CSA Gen., US Sen. VA
Mahone, William (WD)		Civ War			3680		CSA Gen.
Mahoney, Jock	1919-1989	Ent	20	35	55	49	Actor
Mahoney, John		Ent	17			50	
Mahurin, Walker M. Bud		WWII	15	35	55	60	ACE, WWII, Legendary Ace; 20. 75 kills
Maikl, George		Opera	10			20	Opera

NAME	DATES	CATEGORY	SIG	LS/DS	ALS	SP	COMMENTS
Mailer, Norman	1923-2007	Author	25	48	75	58	Naked & the Dead'; SB 200
Maillol, Aristide	1861-1944	Artist	200	460	796		Fr. Sculptor, Painter. Large Graceful Statues
Main, Majorie	1890-1975	Ent	71			228	Actress
Maintenon, Francoise, Marq. de		Royal			975		2nd Wife Louis XIV
Maisenberg, Oleg		Music				50	Austrain pianist
Maison, Nicholas J.	1771-1840	Fr Rev	35	150	175		Gen. under Napoleon
Maison, René		Opera	25			52	Opera
Maitland, Lester J.		Aero	20		40		
Majeski, Amanda	1984-	Opera	10			20	Lyric Sopr.
Majette, Denise L. M		Congr	10				Member US Congress
Major, James Patrick	1836-1877	Civ War	64	261			CSA Gen.
Major, John		HOS	15			30	Br. Prime Min.
Majorana, Gaetano (Caffarelli)		Opera			3200		Legendary Male Sopr. (castrato)
Majors, Lee		Ent	10			35	
Makarios III, Mikhail	1913-1977	HOS	50	62	140	82	Archbishop & Pres. Cyprus
Makarova, Natalia		Ballet	10			15	Ballet
Makarova, Nina		Comp			775		Armenian
Mako	1933-2006	Ent	15			46	Jap. Actor
Malakar, Sanjaya		Ent	15			45	
Malamud, Bernard	1914-1986	Author	25	40	75	75	Am. Novels, Pulitzer; SB 120
Malco, Romany		Ent	13			40	
Malcolm X	1925-1965	Civ Rts	810	3223	7000		TLS/Cont 10000-15000; S transcript 3000
Malcomson, Paula		Ent	13			40	
Malden, Karl		Ent	10	35		52	Actor. Important DS 250
Malenkov, Georgi M.	1902-1988	HOS	160	408	800	250	Union Sov. Russia. Premier
Malet, C. Francois de		Fr Rev	120	240			Gen. Court-martialed, Shot
Malher, J. P. F.		Fr Rev	25	80			
Malibran, Maria	1808-1836	Opera			1312		Fr. Mezzo-Sopr.
Malick, Wendie		Ent	20			60	
Malik, Charles Dr.	1906-1987	HOS	10	15	35	35	
Malik, Terrence		Ent	12			40	Movie Dir. 'Thin Red Line'
Malina, Joshua		Ent	10			35	The West Wing
Malipiero, Gian-Francesco		Comp					Important 20th C. Comp. AMusQS 150-225
Malis, David		Opera	10			25	Opera
Malko, Nicolai	1833-1961	Cond	75		45	197	Rus. Conductor
Malkovich, John		Ent	20	35		73	Actor
Mallarmé, Stephane	1842-1898	Author	150	750	1100		Fr. Poet. Symbolist Movement
Malle, Louis	1932-1996	Ent	35		45	55	Fr. Film Dir. 'My Dinner w/Andre'
Mallet, Tania		Ent				59	Actress; 'Goldfinger'
Mallick, Don		Space	10			20	
Mallory, Charles M.		WWII	10	22	38	30	ACE, WWII; 11 kills
Mallory, Francis	1807-1860	Congr	10				Repr. VA, Physician, RR Pres.
Mallory, Stephen R.		Civ War	125	383	360		CSA Sec. of Navy.
Malmesbury, Ist Earl	1746-1820	Pol	15	30	45		James Harris. Min., Ambass. Br. Diplomat
Malo, Gina	1908-1963	Ent	15			55	Actress
Malodva, Milada	1918-	Ent	15			45	Actress
Malone, Dorothy	1925-	Ent	40	75		130	Actress
Malone, Dumas		Author	10	30	75	40	
Maloney, Carolyn B. M		Congr	10				Member US Congress
Maloney, Francis T.	1894-1945	Congr	10	20	40		Sen., MOC CT 1933-45
Maloney, Michael	1957-	Ent	10			25	Br. Actor
Maltby, Jasper Adalmorn	1826-1867	Civ War	40	85	110		Union Gen.
Malten, Leonard	1950-	Ent	10	25		20	Film Critic, Writer, TV Personality
Malten, Therese		Opera	35			150	Opera

NAME	DATES	CATEGORY	SIG	LS/DS	ALS	SP	COMMENTS
Malthus, Thomas Robert	1766-1834	Econ	310	1100	1915		Educator, Author
Maltzen, Gunther von	d. 1953	WWII				175	Luftwaffe ace w/68 victories & Oakleaves recipient
Mamas & the Papas		Music	350	900		650	Popular 60s singing group; S Album 450
Mamas & the Papas new		Music	10			20	(Four)
Mamet, David		Ent	10			60	Film Dir. SB 65
Mamoulian, Rouben		Ent	15	45		140	Top Film & Stage Dir.
Man Ray		Artist					SEE Ray, Man
Mana-Zucca		Ent	20			100	(Zuckerman, Augusta) Singer, Comp., Pianist
Manchester, Melissa		Music	10	15		40	Singer. Concert & Recording Artist
Manchester, William		Author	10	10	20	20	
Mancini, Henry	1924-1994	Comp	25	30		62	Conductor-Pianist. AMusQS 85-250
Mandel, Howie		Ent	15			40	
Mandel, John		Ent	10			20	Prod. writer
Mandel, Marvin		Gov	10	15		22	Governor MD
Mandela, Nelson	1918-	HOS	68	170		513	Leader Afr. Nat'l Congress; SB 1200-2000
Mandela, Winnie		Pol	20	60			Ex-wife of Nelson; activist
Manderson, Charles	1837-1911	Civ War	30	55	70		Union Gen., US Sen. NE
Mandoki, Luis		Ent	10			22	Movie Dir.
Mandrell, Barbara		Cntry Mus	10			30	CW singer
Mane, Taylor	1966-	Ent				30	Canadian Actress
Mane, Tyler		Ent	16			49	
Manesh, Marshall		Ent	10			25	Will & Grace
Manet, Edouard	1832-1883	Artist	1035	1308	1746	3175	Impressionist School Creator
Maney, George E.	1826-1901	Civ War	145				CSA Gen. ALS '62 760
Manfrini, Luigi		Opera	40			125	Opera
Mangano, Silvana		Ent	60	35	60	90	Actress
Mangione, Chuck		Ent	10			25	
Mangold, James	1963-	Ent	10			25	Film Dir.
Mangum, William Person		Congr	10				FF 26
Manhattan Transfer		Ent	35			80	
Manheim, Camryn		Ent	17			50	
Manigault, Arthur M.	1824-1886	Civ War	105	288			CSA Gen. ALS '61 1650
Manilow, Barry		Music	15	45		62	Comp., Vocalist, Pianist; S Guitar 250
Manke, John		Space	10			15	
Mankiewicz, Joseph L.		Ent	20	75	55	78	AA Film Dir.
Mankiller, Wilma Chief	1945-	Am Ind	10			35	1st mod. Female leader of major Native Am. Tribe.
Manley, N. W.		HOS	12		25	20	Prime Min. Jamaica
Mann, Aimee		Music				45	Rock
Mann, Barry		Comp	25	120			Songwriter
Mann, Daniel	1912-1991	Ent	10			35	Film Dir.
Mann, Delbert		Ent	20			45	Film Dir. AA
Mann, Hank		Ent	100				Keystone Kop. Caricature S 250
Mann, Heinrich		Author	35	145	275		Ger. Novels. Exiled, Interned
Mann, Herbie		Music				200	Jazz fluist
Mann, Horace	1796-1859	Educ	35	122	173		Education Reformer, Abolitionist
Mann, Johnny		Band	15			25	
Mann, Leslie		Ent	13			40	
Mann, Manfred (All)		Music	390				Rock group
Mann, Michael		Ent	22			65	
Mann, Orrin L.	1833-1908	Civ War	20	35	60		Union Gen.
Mann, Thomas	1875-1955	Author	211	730	950	2088	Ger. Novels, Nobel Pr. 'Death in Venice'
Mann, Thomas	d. 1967	WWII	12	25	48	48	ACE, WWII, Double Ace
Manne, Shelly		Band				45	Drummer
Mannerheim, Gustave, Baron		HOS	45	290	850	505	Pres. Finland. Soldier, Patriot

NAME	DATES	CATEGORY	SIG	LS/DS	ALS	SP	COMMENTS
Mannering, Mary		Ent	15			25	Vintage Stage Actress
Manners, David	1900-1998	Ent	10		158	85	Actor
Manners-Sutton, Charles		Clergy	25	35	40		
Manning, Anne	1807-1879	Author			80		
Manning, Daniel		Cab	18	35	65		Sec. Treasury
Manning, Henry E., Card.		Clergy	40	60	95	50	
Manning, Irene	1912-2004	Ent	15	60		52	Actress
Manning, Stephen H.		Civ War	30	55	110		Union Gen.
Manning, Taryn		Ent	15			45	
Manning, Timothy J., Card.		Clergy	35	40	50	45	
Manning, William T., Bish.	1856-1947	Clergy	20	32	60	30	Episcopal Bishop of New York. 1924-46
Manoff, Dinah	1958-	Ent	10			25	Actress
Manone, Wingy		Music	10			50	Jazz Trumpet-Vocalist
Mansfield, Jayne	1933-1967	Ent	223	430	1417	824	Actress
Mansfield, Joseph K. F.	1803-1862	Civ War	164	452	650		Union Gen.
Mansfield, Joseph K. F.	1803-1862	Civ War	60				Union Gen.
Mansfield, Joseph K. F. (WD)		Civ War	225		850		Union Gen. KIA 1862, ALS/cont 3150
Mansfield, Katherine		Author		290			
Mansfield, Mike		Congr	10	25	40	15	MOC, Sen. MT
Mansfield, Richard		Ent	40		175		Vintage Stage Actor, Manager, Prod.
Manship, Paul Howard	1885-1955	Artist	40	275	412		Am. Sculptor of Prometheus Fountain
Manson, Charles		Crime	125	208	241	143	Murderer, Cult Figure
Manson, Mahlon Dickerson	1820-1895	Civ War	45	65	110		Union Gen.
Manson, Marilyn		Music				45	Singer
Manson, Shirley		Music	10			75	Music. Lead Singer 'Garbage'
Manstein, Erich von, Gen.	1887-1973	WWII	45	130	140	172	Planned Assault vs France WWII
Mantegna, Joe		Ent	10			40	Actor
Mantell, Gideon A	1790-1852.	Sci	10	25	40		Paleontologist. 4 Dinosaurs
Mantell, Robert B.		Ent	12			25	Vintage Shakespearean Actor
Mantelli, Eugenia		Opera	25			60	Opera
Manteuffel, Edwin F. von	1809-1885	Mil	75	240	420		Prussian Fld. Marshal WWI
Manteuffel, Hasso von	1897-1978	WWII	45	147	190	237	WWII Ger. Tank Cmdr. -Panzer Divisions
Mantle, Clive	1957-	Ent	10			25	Br. Actor
Mantovani		Cond	10	12		25	Conductor-Arranger
Manuel II	1889-1932	Royal	58	350			King of Portugal at 18. Father Assass.
Manzano, Sonia	1950-	Ent	10			25	Actress; writer
Manzarek, Ray		Music	15	25		35	The Doors, bassist
Manzullo, Donald A. M		Congr	10				Member US Congress
Mao Tse Tung	1893-1976	HOS	5330				Chinese Communist Leader
Maphis, Joe & Rose Lee		Cntry Mus	10			20	
Maples, Marla		Ent	10			25	Actress
Mapleson, James H.		Opera	75				Opera
Mapplethorpe, Robert	1946-1989	Artist	133	385	414		Am. Photographer
Mara, Adele		Ent	10			40	Actress
Mara, Kate		Ent	15			45	
Maragliano, Luisa	1931-	Opera	10			15	Italian Sopr.
Marais, Jean	1913-1998	Ent	10		30	48	Fr. Actor. Stage & Film
Marat, Jean-Paul	1743-1793	Fr Rev		1600	3100		Pol. -Doctor-Author. Murdered
Marbot, J. B. A. M., Marquis	1782-1854	Fr Rev	25	70	125		Napoleonic Gen.
Marceau, Marcel	1923-2007	Ent	30	70	357	71	World Renown Mime
Marceau, Sophie		Ent	12			108	Actress. James Bond films
Marcellino, Muzzy		Music	10	15	25	25	Big Band. Trumpet
March, Barbara		Ent	10			30	Star Trek
March, Fredric	1897-1975	Ent	57	65	95	127	Long Respected Stage-Film Actor. AA 'Jekyll-Hyde'

NAME	DATES	CATEGORY	SIG	LS/DS	ALS	SP	COMMENTS
March, Hal	1920-1970	Ent	10			20	Actor-TV Game Show Host
March, Jane		Ent	10			92	Actress.
March, Peyton C.	1864-1955	Mil	50	125			Am. WWI Four Star Gen.
Marchand, Nancy	1928-2000	Ent				65	Livia Soprano
Marchesi, Mathilde	1821-1913	Ent	50		160	175	Ger. Mezzo-Sopr. From Famous Family of Singers
Marcinkus, Paul C., Arch.		Clergy	45	65	100	50	
Marcks, Gerhard	1889-1981	Artist	45		345		Ger. Sculptor & Designer
Marco, James		Law	10			20	Renown lawyer
Marconi, Guglielmo	1874-1937	Sci	295	935	1295	977	It. Physicist-Inventor. Nobel. Father of Radio
Marcos, Ferdinand E.		HOS	40	118		87	Pres. Philippines
Marcos, Imelda		HOS	15	35		40	Phillipines
Marcoux, Vanni	1877-1962	Opera	20			75	Opera, Buenos Aires. Fr. Bass-Baritone
Marcovicci, Andrea	1948-	Ent	10			30	Actress
Marcus, Jerry		Comics	10			35	'Fatkat'
Marcus, Rudolph A., Dr.		Sci	20	35		30	Nobel Chemistry
Marcus, Stanley		Bus	30	75	160	60	Merchant. Nieman-Marcus
Marcy, Randolph B.	1812-1887	Civ War	35		180		Union Gen.
Marcy, Randolph B. (WD)		Civ War	50	175	460		Union Gen. ALS/Cont 750
Marcy, William L.	1786-1857	Cab	40	110	135		Sec. War, State. Sen. NY
Maren, Jerry		Ent	15			66	Actor. 'Wizard of Oz'. Lollipop Kid
Marescot, Armand S.		Fr Rev	30	80	170		
Maressyev, Alexei		WWII	135				Rus. ACE & Soviet Hero
Maret, Hugues B., Duke	1763-1839	Fr Rev	82	131	375		Napoleon Confidential Advisor., LS/cont 2500
Marey, Etienne		Sci	50		700		Fr. Physiologist. Sphygmograph
Marey, Jules	1830-1904	Sci			575		Pioneer of early cinema
Margaret of Austria	1522-1586	Royal	110	285	775		Duchess of Parma. Regent of Netherlands
Margaret, Princess	1930-2002	Royal	30	75	125	250	SP w/Eliz II 1500
Margie		Comics	20			250	Little Lulu
Margo	1917-1986	Ent	20	20	35	88	Mex. Born Actr./Dancer 'Lost Horizon'; Mrs Eddie Albert
Margolis, Cindy		Ent	17			50	
Margolis, Jeremy		Law	10	10	10	26	Inspector Gen. State of Illinois
Marguerite De Valois	1553-1615	Royal		1910			Queen of Fr., 1st Wife of Henry of Navarre
Margulies, Julianna		Ent				45	Actress
Maria (Castile)		Royal		2500			Queen of Alfonso V of Aragon
Maria Federovna		Royal		213	230		Empress of Russia
Maria Theresa	1717-1780	Royal	185	466	980		Archduchess, Qn Hung. -Bohemia
Marie	1875-1938	Royal	80	115	240	350	Queen of Romania. Wife of Ferdinand I of Roumania
Marie Amelie de Bourbon (Fr.)	1782-1866	Royal	100	240	322		Queen of Louis Phillippe I
Marie Antoinette (Fr)	1755-1793	Royal	1628	8932			Queen of Louis XVI France
Marie Louise	1791-1847	Royal	200	450	576		Empress of Fr. 2nd Wife of Napoleon I
Marie of Naples		Royal	60	110	250		Queen of King Louis-Phillipe I
Marie, Constance		Ent	19			56	
Marie, Lisa		Ent	13			40	
Marie, Rose		Ent	10	20		52	'Dick VanDyke Show', Actress-Singer-Comedienne
Marin, Cheech		Ent	10			40	Actor-Comed. (Cheech & Chong)
Marin, John		Artist	60	225	550		Am. Watercolorist, Etching
Marinaro, Ed		Ent	10			25	
Marinetti, Filippo Tommaso	1876-1944	Poet			350		Italian poet
Marini, Marino		Artist		65			
Marinuzzi, Gino		Cond				150	Italian
Marion, Francis	1732-1795	Rev War		6500	8500		The Swamp Fox
Mariscal, Don Ignacio		Statsmn	20	35	55		V. P. Mexico
Maritain, Jacques		Clergy	40	45	95	75	
Maritza, Sari	1910-1987	Ent	15			65	

NAME	DATES	CATEGORY	SIG	LS/DS	ALS	SP	COMMENTS
Markevitch, Igor		Cond	30			145	Conductor
Markey, Edward J. M		Congr	10				Member US Congress
Markham, Albert H., Sir	1831-1887	Expl	10	20	45		
Markham, Beryl	1902-1986	Aero	215	250			1st solo flight across Atlantic from GB to N. Am.
Markham, Clements, Sir	1830-1916	Author	15	25	125		Historian, Pres. Royal Geo. Soc., Geographer
Markham, Edwin	1852-1940	Author	30	108	142	120	The Man w/The Hoe
Markham, William		Colonial	200	2500			Colonial Gov. PA
Markova, Alicia		Ballet	20			50	Ballet
Markowitz, Harry M., Dr.		Econ	20	35	45		Nobel Economics
Marks, Johnny	1906-1985	Comp	35	95	125	120	AMusQS 175, TsS 'Rudolph' 850.
Marks, William, Jr.	1778-1858	Congr	35	140			PA Sen., ALS/Cont 400
Marlborough, Consuelo	1876-1964	Royal	35	185		350	Vanderbilt Heiress. 9th Duchess
Marlborough, James L.	1550-1629	Jurist	85	325			
Marley, Bob	1945-1981	Music	1273	1380		2166	Rock HOF, Reggae King. S Album 3000-4500
Marley, Ziggy	1968-	Music	15			50	Son of Bob Marley; Reggae
Marlin, Mahlon F.		Bus	40	115	225		Pres-Treas. Marlin Firearms Co.
Marlow, Lucy	1932-	Ent	10			25	Actress
Marlowe, Hugh	1911-1982	Ent	25			50	Actor
Marlowe, Jo Ann	1935-1991	Ent				60	Actress
Marlowe, Julia	1866-1950	Ent	20	35	70	137	Major Stage Star/E. H. Sothern
Marlowe, June	1903-1984	Ent	35			287	Miss Crabtree in the Little Rascals
Marlowe, Marion	1929-	Ent				40	Actress
Marly, Florence	1919-1978	Ent	15			60	Actress
Marmaduke, John S.	1833-1887	Civ War	95	300			CSA Gen.
Marmaduke, John S. (WD)	1833-1887	Civ War	167		2400		CSA Gen.
Marmont, A. F. L. V., Duke		Fr Rev	45	90			Marshal of Fr., Napoleon A-D-C
Marney, Carlyle		Clergy	20	25	35	35	
Marquand, John P.		Author	40	125	165	100	Am. Novels. Pulitzer
Marques, Antonio		Opera	35			85	Opera
Marquez, Gabriel		Author	70			245	Nobel. One Hundred Years of Solitude
Marquis, Rosalind	1915-2006	Ent				40	Actress
Marriott, J.		Bus	20	35	70	70	Marriott Hotel Chain
Marryat, Frederick	1792-1848	Mil	30	100	175		Br. Naval Cmmdr. Novels
Marsala, Joe		Music	20			65	Clarinet, Sax, Comp.
Marsalis, Branford		Music	10			35	Conductor, Sax
Marsalis, Wynton		Music	15			35	Trumpet Virtuoso. Classic-Jazz
Marsden, James		Ent	16			49	
Marsden, Jason	1975-	Ent	10			25	Actor
Marsh, Jean		Ent	10			40	
Marsh, Joan		Ent	15	20	40	65	
Marsh, Mae	1894-1968	Ent	30	40	75	145	Actress; 'Birth of a Nation'
Marsh, Marian	1913-2006	Ent				70	Actress; Svengali
Marsh, Ngaio, Dame		Author	20	35	50	40	New Zealand Mystery Writer
Marshall, Amanda		Music	15			35	Singer
Marshall, Brenda	1915-1992	Ent				158	Actress
Marshall, Brian		Music	10			25	Music. Bass Guitar 'Creed'
Marshall, Catherine	1914-	Author	65	75	150	125	A Man Called Peter', 'Christy'
Marshall, Christopher		Rev War	100				Am. Patriot & Diarist
Marshall, Drew	1886-1986	Titanic			385		Titanic survivor
Marshall, E. G.	1914-1998	Ent	10			40	Actor
Marshall, Frank		Ent	15			45	
Marshall, Frank J.	1877-1944	Celeb	125				Famous Chess Pro. US Chess Champ 1909-1936
Marshall, Gary		Ent	10			40	Film industry
Marshall, George		Ent	25	127			Impressionist

NAME	DATES	CATEGORY	SIG	LS/DS	ALS	SP	COMMENTS
Marshall, George C.	1880-1959	WWII	154	348	575	423	WWII Chief Staff. Nobel Peace Pr. Statesman
Marshall, George E.		Ent	35				Film Dir. 400+ Films
Marshall, Herbert	1890-1966	Ent	10	75		68	Sophisticated Br. Actor
Marshall, Humphrey	1812-1872	Civ War	90	195			CSA Gen.
Marshall, Humphrey (WD)		Civ War	270	512			CSA Gen. ALS/Cont 1825
Marshall, James		West	3000				1st to disCvr. gold in CA
Marshall, Jim M		Congr	10				Member US Congress
Marshall, John	1755-1835	Sup Crt	830	3005	5343		Chief Justice, sensational ALS 43, 125
Marshall, John, Sir		HOS	10	20	35	20	Prime Min. New Zealand
Marshall, Margaret		Opera	10			25	Opera
Marshall, Paula		Ent	15			45	
Marshall, Penny		Ent	10	15		40	Actress & Film Dir.
Marshall, Peter		Clergy	75	95	100	125	Senate Chaplain
Marshall, Samuel Scott		Congr	10				FF 26
Marshall, Thomas R.	1854-1925	VP	50	140	275	200	Wilson VP
Marshall, Thurgood	1908-1993	Sup Crt	132	172	260	250	1st Afro-Am. Justice; S typescript 400
Marshall, Trudy	1922-2004	Ent				40	Actress
Marshall, Tully		Ent	20			50	
Marshall, William	1885-1943	Ent	15			60	Cinematographer; 'The Shiek'
Marshall, William	1825-1896	Civ War	25	40	75		Union Gen., Gov. MN
Marshall, William	1924-2003	Ent	10			35	Blackula
Marshall, William, Sir	1865-1939	Mil	35			85	Brit. WWI Gen. France, Gallipoli, Salonika
Marston, Gilman	1811-1890	Civ War	38	80	55		Union Gen. Legislator. Sen. NH
Marterie, Ralph		Band	10			20	Big Band Leader
Martha Reeves & Vandellas		Music				215	Motown group
Martin, Benny	1928-2001	Cntry Mus	10			25	Western Recording Artist
Martin, Charles H.		Gov	10	25			Governor OR
Martin, Chris-Pin	1893-1953	Ent	50			245	Actor
Martin, Clarence D.		Gov	10	15		10	Governor WA
Martin, Dean	1917-1995	Ent	85	182	75	290	Actor-Singer-Comedian. Member Sinatra 'Rat Pack'
Martin, Dean & Lewis, Jerry		Ent	325	470		418	Comedy Team
Martin, Dean Paul	1951-1987	Music	25			100	Singer; singer
Martin, Dewey		Ent	10			25	Leading Man
Martin, Dick		Ent	15			38	Comedian-Actor. 1/2 Rowan & Martin Team
Martin, Frank	1890-1974	Comp	38		90	110	Prolific Swiss Comp. AMusQS 125
Martin, Freddie		Band	35			65	Big Band Leader-Pianist
Martin, George		Music	95	150	225	176	Beatles Prod.
Martin, Glenn L.	1886-1955	Aero	75	175	275	165	Aeronaut. Pioneer. Fndr. Plane Mfg. Co./Wrights
Martin, Hugh		Comp					AMusQS 45
Martin, James Green	1819-1878	Civ War	95	295	186		CSA Gen.
Martin, James Green (WD)	1819-1878	Civ War	182	663			CSA Gen.
Martin, John A.		Gov	12		30		Governor KS
Martin, John C.		Congr	10	10			MOC IL
Martin, Joseph W. Jr.	1884-1968	Congr	25	35		25	Spkr. of the House
Martin, Kellie		Ent	10			50	Actress
Martin, Lori	1947-	Ent	10			35	Actress
Martin, Luther	1748-1826	Rev War	70	162	360		Continental Congress
Martin, Mary	1913-1990	Ent	40	45		78	
Martin, Pamela		Ent	13			40	
Martin, Pamela Sue		Ent	10			35	Actress
Martin, Ricardo		Opera	15			45	Opera
Martin, Ricky		Music				106	Singer
Martin, Ross	1920-1981	Ent	10	20	40	108	Actor; S Chk 65
Martin, Steve		Ent	15	25		54	Comedian-Actor.

NAME	DATES	CATEGORY	SIG	LS/DS	ALS	SP	COMMENTS
Martin, Strother		Ent	35	50		80	Char. Actor
Martin, Theodore, Sir		Author	10	15	25	10	
Martin, Thomas S.	1847-1919	Congr	12	25			Sen. VA 1893. CSA Army
Martin, Tony	1912-	Music	13	22		47	Singer-Actor. 35 Top Hits
Martin, Victoria Woodhull	1838-1927	Pol	125	250	409		1st woman to run for US Presidency
Martin, William C., Bish.		Clergy	15	25	30	35	
Martin, William T.	1823-1910	Civ War	112	295	400		CSA Gen.
Martin, William T. (WD)		Civ War	170	440	488		CSA Gen.
Martindale, John Henry	1815-1881	Civ War	40	80	125		Union Gen.
Martindale, Wink		Ent	10			25	TV game show host
Martine, James E.		Congr	10	15		10	Sen. NJ
Martineau, Harriet	1802-1870	Author	50		75		Brit. Miscellaneous Writer
Martinelli, Elsa		Ent				60	Actress
Martinelli, Giovanni	1885-1969	Opera	35	60		238	It. -Am. Great Operatic Dramatic Tenor
Martinez, Benito		Ent	15			45	
Martinez, Edgar		Ent	15			45	
Martinez, Luis, Card.		Clergy	30	45	55	50	
Martinez, Olivier		Ent	15			45	
Martini, Nino		Opera	15			45	Opera, Films, Tenor
Martini, Steve		Author	10	10		10	Novels
Martino, Al		Ent	10			35	
Martino, Donald		Comp	20	35	90		Pulitzer, AMusQS 180
Martinson, Leslie		Ent	15			25	Dir. TV & Films 'Bat Man', 'PT 109'
Martinu, Bronislaw	1890-1959	Comp	240				Czech. Comp. AMusQS 900-1500
Martiny, Philip		Artist	25	40	80	30	
Marton, Eva		Opera	20			50	Opera
Marvel, Ik		Author	10		30		Pseud. Donald G. Mitchell
Marvelettes		Music	150	385		200	Rock group:
Marvin, Lee	1924-1987	Ent	117	138		278	Actor; Academy Award
Marwood, William		Official	75		350		Br. Lord High Executioner
Marx Brothers (3)		Ent	919			2107	Three Full Names
Marx Brothers (4)		Ent	1245	2612		3104	4 Full Names Rare
Marx, Arthur		Author	10	15		15	
Marx, Chico	1886-1961	Ent	159	151	325	244	
Marx, Groucho	1890-1977	Ent	209	793	675	384	Comedian. Marx Bros. Leader. S Chk 425
Marx, Harpo	1888-1964	Ent	316	835		733	
Marx, Joseph	1882-1964	Comp				175	Austrian
Marx, Karl	1818-1883	Author	3232	8000	22500	14750	Ger. Pol. Philosopher
Marx, Richard		Music	20			40	Singer
Marx, Zeppo	1901-1979	Ent	65	120		172	
Mary (of Modena)	1658-1718	Royal	140		750		Queen of James II
Mary (of Teck)	1867-1953	Royal	100	180	243	330	Queen of George V (Eng.)Mother of Two Kings
Mary Adalaide		Royal	35	70	150		(Dchs. Teck)
Mary I (Eng)	1516-1558	Royal	900	3000	7500		Queen England, Bloody Mary
Mary II (Eng)	1662-1694	Royal	370	1240	3100		Queen William II (NRPA)
Mary, Queen of Scots	1542-1587	Royal	4000	15000	18000		Executed by Elizabeth I
Masaryk, Jan	1886-1948	HOS	95	155	275	275	Pres. Czechoslavakia
Masaryk, Thomas G.	1850-1937	HOS	100	250	717	425	Czech. Philosopher, 1st Pres.
Mascagni, Pietro	1863-1945	Comp	242	375	774	350	Cavalleria Rusticana'. AMusQS 650-1, 250. SPc 225
Mascherini, Enzo		Opera	15			50	Opera
Masefield, John	1878-1967	Author	35	121	215	110	Br. Poet Laureate
Mash (Show-cast)		Ent				440	Eight Main Chars.
Masini, Angelo		Opera				500	Opera. 19th C. Intl. Star
Maskelyne, Nevil	1732-1811	Sci	85	250	390		Br. Astronomer Royal. Inventor

NAME	DATES	CATEGORY	SIG	LS/DS	ALS	SP	COMMENTS
Maslen, Scott	1971-	Ent	10			25	Br. Actor
Mason, Alfred Edw. W.	1865-1948	Author	10	30	45	20	Br. Novels
Mason, George	1725-1792	Rev War	2638	8775			Am. Planter & Rev. Statesman
Mason, Jackie		Ent	15			40	Comedian
Mason, James	1909-1984	Ent	40	62	80	144	Br. Actor-Film Dir.
Mason, James Murray	1798-1871	Civ War	49	115	200		Sen. VA, CSA Dipl./Trent Affair. ALS 700; FF 37
Mason, John Sanford	1824-1897	Civ War	40	75	110		Union Gen.
Mason, John Young		Congr			35		
Mason, Jonathan	1756-1831	Congr	40		75		Federalist US Sen. MA. Exec. Council. Investor
Mason, LeRoy	1903-1974	Ent	50			150	Actor. D. Heart Attack, 'California Firebrand' set
Mason, Marsha	1942-	Ent	10			35	Actress. Stage-Films '66+. AA Nom. 'Goodbye Girl'
Mason, Nick	1944-	Music	35			65	Drummer for Pink Floyd; S drumhead 120
Mason, Sully	1906-1970	Ent	15			60	Actor
Mason, Walt		Author	10			20	Poet
Mason, William E.	1850-1921	Congr	12	20		15	MOC, Sen. IL
Massen, Osa	1915-2006	Ent	30			65	Dan-Am Actress. Hollywood Films From Late 30s
Massena, Andre, Duke	1758-1817	Fr Rev	100	375	450		Fr. Marshal. Greatest of Napoleon's Gens
Massenet, Jules	1842-1912	Comp	75	201	148	465	Manon', 'Thais'. AMusQS 375-650-2750-3500; SB 600
Massey, Daniel	1933-1998	Ent	10			40	Br. Actor
Massey, Edith	1818-1884	Ent				40	Actress; singer
Massey, Eyre	1719-1804	Rev War	300	1250			Br. Gen Serving in N. Am. During Am. Rev.
Massey, Gerald	1828-1907	Author	25	70	95		Br. Poet, Journalist, Editor
Massey, Illona		Ent	25		30	122	
Massey, Louise	1902-1983	Cntry Mus				50	Singer
Massey, Louise & Curt		Cntry Mus	25			45	Country Western
Massey, Raymond		Ent	47	20	46	68	Fine Vintage Canadian Actor. Stage & Screen
Massie, Paul	1958-	Ent	10			30	Sounds dept.
Massie, Robert		Author		65			The Romanovs
Massine, Leonide		Ballet	20			105	Ballet Dancer, Choreographer.
Masson, Andre		Artist	40	55	95		
Mastantonio, Mary Elizabeth	1958-	Ent	10			40	Actress
Masters & Johnson		Med	20			45	Wm. H. & Virginia; Sex Researchers
Masters, Edgar Lee	1869-1950	Author	30	45	65	65	Poet, Novels, Biographer. AManS 600
Masters, Frankie		Band	10			25	Big Band Leader
Masterson, Christopher		Ent	17			50	
Masterson, Danny		Ent	17			50	
Masterson, Mary		Ent	15			45	
Masterson, Mary Stuart		Ent	10			58	Actress
Masterson, Wm. B. Bat	1853-1921	Lawman	3915	11500	12500		Scout, Sheriff, Gambler
Mastracchio, Richard		Space	10			25	
Mastroianni, Marcello	1924-1996	Ent	45			260	Fr. Actor
Mata Hari (M. G. Zelle)	1876-1917	Spy	350	930	4299	5300	Executed Secret Agent WWI
Matalin, Mary		Celeb	10			20	Pol. celebrity
Matchbox 20		Music	30	70		105	Music. 5 Member Rock Group; S drumhead 120
Maté, Rudy		Ent	15			55	Top Cinematographer
Materna, Amalie		Opera	30		120		Greatest Wagnerian Sopr. of them all'
Mather, Cotton	1663-1728	Rev War	850	1950	4200		Author, Pub. 382 Books; Unsigned Man. 4075
Mathers, Jerry		Ent	15			64	'Beaver'
Matheson, Jim M		Congr	10				Member US Congress
Matheson, Tim		Ent	10			35	Actor
Mathews, Brander	1852-1929	Author	10		35		Novels, Essayist, Drama Critic for NY Times
Mathews, Catharine VanCortlandt		Author	12				History of surveying
Mathews, George	1739-1812	Rev War	85	190			Statesman, Gen.
Mathias, Bob		Congr	10	15		25	MOC CA, Olymp. Decathlon Champ. Brief Actor

NAME	DATES	CATEGORY	SIG	LS/DS	ALS	SP	COMMENTS
Mathis, Johnny		Music	10			55	Singer; S Guitar 200
Mathis, Samantha		Ent				55	Actress ' Broken Arrow'
Matisse, Henri	1869-1954	Artist	523	745	1442	2242	Fr. Painter, Sculptor, Fauvist. SP (Pc)1550
Matlack, Timothy	1730-1829	Rev War	85	275	450		Cont. Congr. Am. Patriot. Franklin Aide
Matlin, Marlee		Ent	10		45	40	AA
Matoni, Walter		WWII	10			35	Ger. Ace WWII. RK
Matsui, Gen. Iwane	1878-1948	WWII	100			425	WWII Jap. Gen. Ordered the "Rape of Nanking"
Matsui, Robert T. M		Congr	10				Member US Congress
Matsushita, Konosuke		Bus	25	65	145	40	Jap. Electronic Giant
Mattea, Kathy		Cntry Mus	10			20	
Mattern, Jimmie		Aero	15	25	60	35	
Matthau, Walter	1920-2000	Ent	25	55		85	Actor; AA
Matthews, Christopher		Ent	10			25	TV news; 'Hardball'
Matthews, Dave		Music	20			78	Rock; S Guitar 300-1500
Matthews, DeLane		Ent	10			36	Actress Dave's World
Matthews, Frank Arnold		Clergy	20	25	35	25	
Matthews, Jessie	1907-1981	Ent	15			45	Br. Vintage Film Actress
Matthews, Stanley		Sup Crt	45	150	275		
Matthies, Charles (Karl) Leopold	1824-1868	Civ War	45	80	120		Union Gen.
Mattingly, Thos. Ken		Space	75		550	220	Apollo 13
Mattson, Conrad		WWII	10	15	28	22	ACE, WWII
Mature, Victor		Ent	70			141	
Matzenauer, Margaret		Opera	25			85	Wagnerian Sopr.
Matzky, Gerhard	1894-1983	WWII	40	85			Nazi WWII Gen.
Mauborgne, Joseph O.	1881-1971	Mil	45	150			USA Gen. Air-to-Ground Transmission. Broke Codes
Mauch, Billy	1921-2006	Ent	10	15	25	60	Actor
Mauch, Bobby		Ent	30			65	Actor, Billy's twin brother
Maugham, W. Somerset	1874-1965	Author	59	166	322	242	Br. Novels & Plays; SB 350
Mauldin, Bill		Comics	25			185	Willie & Joe
Maupassant, Guy de		Author	275	572	674		Fr. Master of Short Story
Maura, Antonio		HOS	110	165			Sp. P. M. Provoked Rif War
Maurel, Victor		Opera				85	
Maurey, Pierre		Clergy	10	15	30	25	Pres. Reform Church France
Mauro, Ermanno		Opera	15			40	Opera
Maurois, Andre (Emile Herzog)		Author	22	75	120		Fr. Biographer, Novels
Maury, Dabney H.	1822-1900	Civ War	72	230	257		CSA Gen.
Maury, Dabney H. (WD)	1822-1900	Civ War	142	280	750	1022	CSA Gen.
Maury, Matthew F.	1806-1873	Civ War	79	225	455	1550	CSA Naval Cmdr., Hydrographer
Mauser, Paul von	1838-1914	Mil	285				Ger. Weapon Mfg. Bro. Wilhelm; Mauser pistol
Mawson, Douglas, Sir		Expl	50	160	375		Australian Polar Explr.
Max Muller, Friedrich	1823-1900	Celeb			100		Orientalist & philologist
Max, Peter		Artist	170	191	210	150	Am. Contemporary Art., S Drwg 550
Maxey, Samuel Bell	1825-1895	Civ War	128	225	360		CSA Gen., US Sen. TX
Maxey, Samuel Bell (WD)		Civ War	245		775		CSA Gen.
Maxey, Virginia	1923-	Ent	10			30	Actress
Maxim, Hiram Percy	1896-1936	Sci	40	125	210		Radio amateur pioneer, W1AW
Maxim, Hiram Stevens	1840-1916	Sci	120	150	315	300	Inventor Maxim Machine Gun. Engineer
Maxim, Hudson	1853-1927	Sci	45	103	140	175	Inv. Smokeless Powder, Other Explosives, gun silencer
Maximilian	1832-1867	Royal	350	633	1250		Emperor of Mexico
Maximilian II	1811-1864	Royal	110	267	770		"King of Bravaria"
Maxon, R.		Comics	20			100	Tarzan
Maxwell, Elizabeth		Author	10			12	Regional history
Maxwell, Elsa		Clmnst	10	25	35	15	Hostess & Professional Party
Maxwell, Lois		Ent	10			45	

M

NAME	DATES	CATEGORY	SIG	LS/DS	ALS	SP	COMMENTS
Maxwell, Marilyn	1921-1972	Ent	20	40		100	Actress
Maxwell, Robert		WWII	12	25	28	28	ACE, WWII; 7 kills
Maxwell, Robert		Pub	45				D. Mysteriously
Maxwell, William		Pub	25	110	180		(Ld. Beaverbrook) Newspaper Proprietor, Statesman
May, Billy		Band	10			20	Arranger
May, Brian		Music				120	Guitarist 'Queen'; S Guitar 300
May, Edna	1878-1948	Ent	25		30	160	Vintage Stage & Film. Darling of Brit. Music Hall
May, Jodhi	1975-	Ent	10			30	Br. Actress
Mayakovski, Vladimir V.	1893-1930	Author	300	795	2200		Russian Poet & Dramatist
Mayall, John		Music	25			90	Rock
Mayall, Rik	1958-	Ent	10			25	Br. Actor & comedian
Maybank, Burnet R.		Gov	10	18		15	Governor, Sen. SC
Maye, Carolyn		Ent	10			25	
Mayer, John		Music	20			60	Popular singer
Mayer, Louis B.	1885-1957	Bus	92	168	220	355	MGM Film Studio, DS/TLS cont 750-900
Mayer, Maria, Dr.		Sci	30	85		50	Nobel Physics
Mayfair, Mitzi	1914-1976	Ent	10			50	Actress
Mayhew, Peter		Ent	17			50	Actor; 'Chewbacca'
Maynard, Bill	1928-	Ent	10			25	Br. Actor
Maynard, Ken	1895-1973	Ent	98		145	148	Western Film Hero
Maynor, Dorothy	1910-1996	Ent	25			275	30's-50's Concert & Recording Career.
Mayo Brothers		Med				742	Fndr. s of the Mayo Clinic
Mayo, 6th Earl (Rich. Bourke)		HOS	10		30		Br. Pol. Viceroy of India
Mayo, Archie		Ent				220	Dir.
Mayo, Charles H., Dr.	1865-1939	Med	140	562	380	307	Co-Fndr. Mayo Foundation
Mayo, Charles W., Dr.	1898-1968	Med	65	140	235	85	Surgeon Mayo Clinic. Prof. Surg.
Mayo, Frank	1886-1953	Ent	12			45	Actor
Mayo, Henry Thomas		Mil	30	45	125	45	Adm. Cmdr. Atlantic Fl. WWI
Mayo, Virginia		Ent	25	180		126	Longtime Warner Bros. Actress.
Mayo, William J., Dr.	1861-1939	Med	105	338	380	462	Co-Fndr. Mayo Foundation
Mayron, Anie	1952-	Ent	10			20	Actress
Mayron, Melanie		Ent	10			25	Actress; '30 Something'
Maytag, Frederick L.		Bus	95	210	375	250	Maytag Electric Appliances
Mazar, Debi		Ent	13			40	
Mazarin, Jules, Card.	1602-1661	Clergy		835			Succeeded Richelieu as Chief Min. Louis XIII
Mazurki, Mike	1907-1990	Ent	15			55	Actor
Mazurski, Paul		Ent	10			20	Film Dir.
Mazzini, Giuseppe	1805-1872	Revol	75	155	737		Italian Patriot. Unpublished ALS 2325
Mazzoleni, Ester		Opera	50			195	Opera. Dalmatian-Ital. Diva
Mbeki, Thabo		Pol				35	Pres. of South Africa
McAdam, John		Invent		850			McAdamized Roads
McAdams, Rachel	1976-	Ent				50	Actress
McAdoo, John D.		Civ War			425		CSA Gen.
McAdoo, William G.	1863-1941	Cab	25	55	95	75	Wilson Sec. Treasury & Son-In-Law. RR Czar
McAfee, John P.		Author	10			12	The 'Catch-22' of Vietnam
Mcaffee, Johnny		Music	10			20	Songwriter
McAllister, Lon		Ent	15			30	Actor
McAndrew, James W.		Mil	35			50	Am. WWI Gen. Gen Staff, Chief of Staff A. E. F.
McAndrew, Nell	1973-	Model	10			20	Celebrity model; Playboy
McArdle, Andrea		Music	10			20	Singer
McArthur, John	1826-1906	Civ War	50				Union Gen.
McArthur, Kim		Model	15			25	Playboy
McArthur, William		Space	10			20	
McAuliffe, Anthony C.	1898-1975	WWII	162	404	638	448	WWII Gen. 'Nuts', ALS Cont 5750, DS/"Nuts" 1855-2100

NAME	DATES	CATEGORY	SIG	LS/DS	ALS	SP	COMMENTS
McAuliffe, Christa	1948-1986	Space	571	1172	2940	1650	D. in Challenger Disaster
McAvoy, May	1899-1984	Ent	25			132	Vintage Film Actress; 'The Jazz Singer'
McBain, Diane	1941-	Ent	10			25	Actress; "Gen. Hospital'
McBain, Ed		Author	10	20	30	30	Novels
McBride, Chi		Ent	17			50	
McBride, Clifford	1901-1951	Comics		82			Launched the daily strip Napoleon in 1934
McBride, George W.	1854-1911	Congr	10	15			Sen. OR
McBride, John	1800-	Mil	30	75			Brit. Adm. 1793
McBride, Jon A.		Space	10	15		30	
McBride, Martina		Cntry Mus				45	CW Singer
McBride, Mary Margaret	1899-1976	Ent	10		25	25	Radio Talk Show Host. 30s-40's. Household Name
McBurney, Simon		Ent	13			40	
McCabe, Nick		Music	10			25	Music. Lead Guitar 'The Verve'
McCaffrey, Anne		Author	10			10	Novels
McCain, John S. III		Congr	20	30	45	75	Sen. AZ, Vietnam war POW; Rep Pres. Candiate 2008
McCain, John S. Jr.	1911-1981	Mil	15	35			Adm.
McCain, John Sr.	1884-1945	WWII	25	80	125		Vice Adm. WWII
McCall, Davina	1967-	Ent	10			20	Br. Actress & TV presenter
Mccall, George Archibald	1802-1868	Civ War	40	75	120		Union Gen.
McCall, Robert		Artist	25	50			Sketch 120-600
McCall, Tom	1913-1983	Gov	10	10		15	Governor OR
McCalla, Irish	1928-2002	Ent	35		25	48	Actress; 'Sheena of the Jungle'
McCallister, Lon	1923-2005	Ent	10			35	Actor
McCallum, David		Ent	15			45	
McCambridge, Mercedes	1916-2004	Ent	40		55	102	
McCampbell, David S.		WWII	25	125	95	100	ACE, WWII, Top Navy Ace, MOH; 34 kills
McCandless, Bruce II		Space	10		90	65	
McCandless, William (WD)	1835-1884	Civ War		230			Col. Of 3rd. Div, 1st Brigade at Little Round Top
McCann, Chuck	1934-	Ent	20			85	Actor
McCarey, Leo		Ent	85			125	Academy Award Dir., Prod.
McCarthy, Andrew	1962-	Ent	10			40	Actor; 'Weekend at Bernie's'
McCarthy, Carolyn M		Congr	10				Member US Congress
McCarthy, Eugene J.		Congr	20	35	50	65	Sen. MN. Pres. Cand. '68 'Peace' Cand.
McCarthy, Jenny		Ent	15			40	Actress.
McCarthy, Joseph	1908-1957	Congr	40	175	750	117	Sen. WI. McCarthyism. Notorious Red-Baiter
McCarthy, Karen M		Congr	10				Member US Congress
McCarthy, Kevin		Ent	10			40	Actor.
McCarthy, Mary		Author	45	135		50	Novels
McCartney, Paul		Music	525	1605	1386	877	Beatle; S Guitar 10,000
McCarty, Jim		Music			385		Yardbirds drummer from 1963-68.
McCaulay, Rose, Dame		Author	20			45	
McCausland, John	1836-1927	Civ War	120				CSA Gen.
McCay, Peggy		Ent	10			35	Actress. Mayberry
McCay, Winsor		Comics	100			600	Little Nemo
McClain, Gerald		Bus	10	20			Pioneer in Assisted Living Development
McClanahan, Rue		Ent	10			40	Actress
McClaran, John W.	1887-1948	Mil	35	125			USN Adm. Round-the-World Bases For 1st Flight
McClellan, George B.	1826-1885	Civ War	197	294	382	863	Union Gen. ALS/Cont '66 2200. Pres. Cand.
McClellan, George B. (WD)	1826-1885	Civ War	263	335	1279	1926	Union Gen.
McClellan, John L.	1896-1977	Congr	10	20		25	Repr., Sen. AR
McClernand, John A.	1812-1900	Civ War	45	110	140	175	
McClernand, John A. (WD)		Civ War	70	192	217		Union Gen.
McClintic, James V.		Congr	10			10	MOC OK
McClintock, Eddie		Ent	18			55	

NAME	DATES	CATEGORY	SIG	LS/DS	ALS	SP	COMMENTS
McClintock, Francis L.	1819-1907	Expl	61	115	127		Br. Adm., Arctic Navigator. Search for Franklin
McClintock, John		Space	10	15		20	
McClinton, Delbert		Cntry Mus	10			25	Singer-Musician. TX Blues Man
McCloskey, John, Card.		Clergy	95	125	250	100	
McClosky, Pete		Congr	10	10	10		
McClung, J. T. M.		Congr	10	15	10		
McClure, Doug		Ent	15			65	Actor
McClure, Samuel S.	1887-1949	Editor	12				Publisher
McClurg, Alexander C.	1832-1901	Civ War	30	55			Union Gen.
McCollum, Betty M		Congr	10				Member US Congress
McColpin, Carroll W.		WWII	25	45	75	75	ACE WWII, Maj. Gen. 8 Kills
McComas, Kendall	1916-1981	Ent			890	340	Breezy Brisbane in Our Gang Comedies
McComb, Henry S., Col.		Bus	250	875			RR Fndr. Esposed Oakes Ames
McComb, William	1828-1918	Civ War	95	235	350		CSA Gen.
McConaughey, Matthew	1969-	Ent	15			51	Actor.
McConnell, Calvin D., Bish.		Clergy	20	25	30	30	
McConnell, Francis J., Bish.		Clergy	20	25	50	30	
McConnell, James, Bish.		Clergy	20	25	35	30	
McConnell, Joseph, Jr.		Aero	75	140	175	150	ACE, Korea, Top Korea Ace
McConnell, Mitch		Congr	10			20	US Senate (R-KY)
McCoo, Marilyn		Music	10			30	Singer
McCook, Alex. M	1831-1903	Civ War	38	70	88		Union Gen.
McCook, Alex. M. (WD)	1831-1903	Civ War	45		195		Union Gen.
McCook, Anson	1835-1917	Civ War	30	55	40		Union Gen., MOC
McCook, Daniel Jr	1834-1864	Civ War	95				Union Gen.
McCook, Edward Moody	1833-1909	Civ War	45	75	120		Union Gen.
McCook, Henry C.		Clergy	10	10	15		
McCook, Robert Latimer	1827-1862	Civ War	110	190	270		Union Gen.
McCool, William	1961-2003	Space	50	125	150	150	Perished on Space Shulltle Columbia re-entry
McCord, Catherine		Ent	17			50	
McCormack, Eric		Ent	10			45	Will & Grace
McCormack, John	1884-1945	Opera	60	105	220	170	Famed Irish Tenor. Opera & Popular Ballads
McCormack, John W.	1891-1980	Congr	18	47	58	52	Spkr. of the House; S JFK Eulogy 250
McCormack, Patty	1945-	Ent	25			75	Actress
McCormic, Mary		Opera	20				Opera
McCormick, Anne O'Hare		Author	30	45	60	50	1st Pulitzer Woman Journalist
McCormick, Catherine	1972-	Ent	10			25	Br. Actress
McCormick, Cyrus H.	1809-1884	Invent	164	694	919		Invented, Mfg. the Reaper. ALS/Cont 4200
McCormick, Maureen	1946-	Ent	10			47	Actress
McCormick, Myron	1908-1962	Ent	15	25	45	55	Actor
McCormick, Nettie Fowler		Bus	25		90		Mrs. Cyrus McCormick
McCormick, Robert R., Col.		Bus	35	140	165	60	Editor Chicago Tribune
McCorvey, Norma		Celeb		150			A. K. A. Jane Roe (Roe vs Wade)
McCotter, Thaddeus G. M		Congr	10				Member US Congress
McCown, John Porter	1815-1879	Civ War	110	362			CSA Gen.
McCown, John Porter (WD)		Civ War	245	1095			CSA Gen.
McCoy, Charles B.		Bus	25		85	40	Pres. DuPont Co.
McCoy, Clyde	1903-1990	Music	15			45	Trumpet player; 'Sugar Blues'
McCoy, Frank		Mil		25	50		Am. WWI Gen.
McCoy, Sandra		Ent	13			40	
McCoy, Sylvester	1943-	Ent	10			25	Scottish Actor
McCoy, Tim		Ent	90	115		113	Col'. Am. Cowboy Star. Innumerable Westerns
McCoy, Wilson		Comics	15			75	Phantom
McCrea, Joel	1905-1990	Ent	20	40		71	Actor

NAME	DATES	CATEGORY	SIG	LS/DS	ALS	SP	COMMENTS
McCready, Jack		Author	10			12	Hunting & game preparation
McCready, Mike		Music	10			25	Music. Guitarist 'Pearl Jam'
McCreery, Richard L., Sir		WWII	30	75		40	Br. Gen. WWII/Montgomery. 8th Army
McCrery, Jim M		Congr	10				Member US Congress
McCudden, James T. B.		Aero	135	225	350	300	ACE, WWI, RAF
McCullers, Carson	1917-1967	Author	60	230	265	125	Am. Novels. 'Heart is a Lonely Hunter'
McCulley, Michael J.		Space	10			25	
McCulloch, Ben	1811-1862	Civ War	155	470	1202		CSA Gen. Morman War LS 2300
McCulloch, Henry E.	1816-1895	Civ War	145	350			CSA Gen.
McCulloch, Hugh	1808-1895	Cab	45	95	135		Lincoln, Johnson, Arthur Sec. Treas.
McCullough, Colleen		Author	35	45	60	60	Austr. Novels. Thorn Birds
McCullough, John	1832-1885	Ent	10			35	Vintage Stage Actor
McCullough, Julie		Model	15			27	Playboy Playmate
McCutcheon, George Barr	1866-1928	Author	10				
McCutcheon, John T.	1870-1949	Comics		80			Pulitzer. Pol. Cartoonist. Chicago Tribune
McCutcheon, Martine		Ent	10			20	Actress
McDaniel, Hattie	1895-1952	Ent	407	958	2100	1406	AA 'Gone w/the Wind'.
McDermont, Galt		Comp	10			25	Hair'. 'Good Morning Sunshine' AMusQS 95
McDermott, Dylan		Ent	20			46	Actor.
McDermott, Jim M		Congr	10				Member US Congress
McDevitt, Ruth	1895-1976	Ent	10			45	Actress; 'The Birds'
McDivitt, James A.		Space	30	96		92	Gemini 4 & Apollo 9 Astro.
McDonad, Michael		Music	15			45	Singer. Lead Singer for Doobie Bros.
McDonald, A. J. (Al)		Space	20				NASA Whistleblower
McDonald, Christopher	1955-	Ent	10			25	Actor
McDonald, Kevin		Ent	15			45	
McDonald, M. Nick		Celeb	20	88		120	Police Off. who captured Lee Harvey Oswald
McDonald, Marie		Ent	35	120	90	125	Actress
McDonald, Michael		Ent	15			45	
McDonald, Richard J.		Bus	92	260	450	225	MacDonald's, TLS/cont 1000-1500
McDonald, Skeets		Cntry Mus	10			20	
McDonald, Wallace		Ent				120	Silent film actor
McDonnell, James S.		Bus	20	45	95	35	Fndr., McDonnell Aircraft; S Chk 620
McDonnell, Mary		Ent	20			70	Actress; 'Dances w/Wolves'
McDonough, John		Ent	10			25	Actor
McDonough, Neil		Ent	17			50	
McDormand, Frances		Ent	10			40	Actress; AA
McDougall, Alexander		Rev War	90	200	415		Gen. Cont. Army, Cont. Congress
McDowell, Andie		Ent	10			40	Actress
McDowell, Edward	1860-1908	Comp			430		Am. Comp. & pianist from the Romantic period
McDowell, Irvin	1818-1885	Civ War	62	382	337	977	Union Gen. Mexican War
McDowell, Irvin (WD)		Civ War	120	235	525	1250	Union Gen. Special DS 400
McDowell, Malcolm		Ent	20			134	Br. Actor. US & Eng. Remember 'Clockwork Orange'
McDowell, Roddy	1928-1998	Ent	22		40	100	Talented Child Actor, Mid Life Actor & Photographer
McDuffie, George	1790-1851	Congr	15				Sen. & Repr. SC
McElmurry, Thomas		Space	10			20	
McElroy, Neil H.		Cab	15	35		25	Sec. Defense. Pres. P & G
McEnery, S. D.	1837-1910	Congr	12	25			Governor LA & Sen.
McEntire, Reba		Cntry Mus	20			60	CW Singer; S Album 65
McEntyre, Joe (New Kids)		Ent	10			30	
McEwen, Mark		Ent	10			20	Writer; actor
McFadden, Bernard	1868-1955	Pub	20	50		60	Pub. 'Physical Culture', 'True Story'. Physician.
McFadden, Gates	1949-	Ent	10			30	Star Trek
McFadden, Obadiah B.		Congr	15	30	40		MOC WA 1873

NAME	DATES	CATEGORY	SIG	LS/DS	ALS	SP	COMMENTS
McFaddon, Steve	1959-	Ent	10			25	Br. Actor
McFarland, Spanky		Ent	40	58		127	Little Rascals
McFarlane, Seth		Ent	10			22	'Family Guy' Creator/Voice
McFerrin, Bobby	1950-	Music	10			27	Singer 'Don't Worry, Be Happy'. 4 Grammys
McG		Ent	17			50	
McGann, Paul	1959-	Ent	10			25	Br. Actor
McGaryrt, William D.		WWII	15	30	45	40	ACE, WWII, Flying Tigers; 5 kills
McGaughey, Edward Wilson		Congr	10				FF 26
McGavin, Darren		Ent	30			60	
McGee, Don		WWII	25				WWII Am. Ace; 6 kills
McGee, Gale	1915-1992	Congr	10	15		10	Sen. WY
McGill, Bruce		Ent	15			45	
McGill, John		Clergy	90		450		CW Bishop of Richmond
McGillis, Kelly		Ent	10		20	45	
McGinley, Phyllis		Author	10	30	45	45	Am Poet. Pulitzer
McGinnis, George Francis	1826-1910	Civ War	40	75	125		Union Gen.
McGoohan, Patrick		Ent	95			110	Actor; "Star Trek"
McGovern, Elizabeth	1961-	Ent	10			40	Actress
McGovern, George		Congr	10	75		50	Sen. SD, Pres. Hopeful; TLS/Cont 260
McGovern, James P. M		Congr	10				Member US Congress
McGovern, John		Author	25	40			
McGowan, Alistair		Celeb	10			20	Impressionist
McGowan, Rose		Ent	20			40	Actress.
McGowan, Samuel	1819-1897	Clv War	I 10		225		CSA Gen.
McGranery, James P.		Cab	10	15	25		Atty Gen.
McGrath, J. Howard		Cab	10	20	35	35	Atty Gen.
McGrath, Kathleen Capt.		Mil				25	1st US woman to Command a warship
McGrath, Mark		Ent	15			45	
McGraw, Ali		Ent	15			145	Actress
McGraw, Charles	1914-1980	Ent				215	Actor
McGraw, Phil Dr.		Ent	10	35	50	40	"Dr. Phil"
McGraw, Tim		Cntry Mus	25			70	Singer; S guiter 425
McGregor, Ewan		Ent	15			55	Actor
McGuffy, William H.		Educ	95	475			McGuffy's Reader
McGugin, Harold C.	1893-1946	Congr	10	25			Repr. KS
McGuigan, James, Card.		Clergy	10	10	15	15	
McGuinn, Roger		Music	50			85	Byrds' Co-Fndr. S Guitar 420
McGuire Sisters		Music	60			100	Singing Group
McGuire, Barry		Music	50			60	Singer; 'Eve of Destruction'
McGuire, Dorothy		Ent	30			78	
McGuire, John	1910-1980	Ent				60	Actor
McGuire, Phyllis		Ent	10	15		25	McGuire Sisters
McGuire, Sean	1976-	Ent	10			30	Br. Actor
McGuire, Thomas B.		WWII	300	400	650	800	ACE, WWII, #2 US Ace; 38 kills; KIA 1944
McHale's Navy		Ent				475	Cast photo
McHenry, James	1753-1816	Rev War	202	329	629		Signer Constitution, Sec. War. Sr. Surgeon
McHugh, Frank	1898-1991	Ent	20	25	65	56	
McHugh, Jimmy	1894-1969	Comp	25	75			
McHugh, John M.		Congr	10				Member US Congress
McHugh, Joseph		Artist	10			15	
McIlvaine, Abraham R.	1804-1863	Congr	10				Repr. PA, Whig Pres. Elector
McInnis, Scott M		Congr	10				Member US Congress
McIntire, John		Ent	20			60	
McIntire, Rufus		Congr	10		38		FF 38

M

NAME	DATES	CATEGORY	SIG	LS/DS	ALS	SP	COMMENTS
McIntosh, James McQueen	1828-1862	Civ War	275				CSA Gen.
McIntosh, John Baillie	1829-1888	Civ War	40	75	110		Union Gen.
McIntosh, Lachlan	1725-1806	Rev War	607	861	1635		Killed Button Gwinnett in Duel
McIntyre, Frank		Mil	75	140			Am. WWI Gen.
McIntyre, James F., Arch.		Clergy	40	65	75	75	
McIntyre, Marvin H.		Cab	10	10	15		Sec. to FDR
McIntyre, Mike M		Congr	10				Member US Congress
McIntyre, O. O.		Author	15	25	40	20	Journalist, Synd. Columnist
McKay, David O.	1873-1970	Relig	75	150	625	100	Pres. of the Mormon Church
McKay, Douglas	1893-1959	Cab	15	25		20	Governor OR, Sec. Interior
McKay, Gardner	1932-2001	Ent	10			40	Am. actor; writer
McKay, Jim		Celeb	10			25	Media/TV; sports personality
McKay, Kelli		Ent	15			30	Miss USA 1991
McKean, Micheal		Ent	15			40	Actor
McKean, Thomas	1734-1817	Rev War	225	491	1550		Signer. ADS 1778 2250
McKean, Thomas Jefferson	1810-1870	Civ War	40	70	120		Union Gen.
McKee, Thomas H.		Congr	10	20			
McKeen, Charles 'Chuck'		Author	10			15	Sports autographs
McKeever, Chauncey (WD)	1829-1901	Civ War	45		175		Union Gen.
McKeldin, Theodore R.	1900-1974	Gov	10			10	Governor MD
McKellan, Ian		Ent	25			75	
McKellar, Kenneth D.	1869-1957	Congr	10	30			Sen. TN
McKellen, Ian		Ent	20			84	Actor
McKenna, Joseph		Sup Crt	35	50	80	40	Atty Gen.
McKenna, Siobhan	1923-1986	Ent	15			35	Irish actress
McKenzie, Benjamin		Ent	17			50	
McKenzie, Fay	1918-	Ent	10			35	Actress
McKenzie, Jacqueline	1967-	Ent	10			40	Australian actress
McKeon, Howard P. "Buck"		Congr	10				Member US Congress
McKeon, Nancy		Ent	10			40	
McKeon, Phillip	1964-	Ent	10			25	Actor
McKern, Leo		Ent	15			40	Rumpole
McKevitt, Anne		Celeb	10				Designer
McKinley, Ida S.		1st Lady	325	625	1345	850	FF 425; WHC S 900-1800
McKinley, Ray		Band	20				Bandleader, Drummer
McKinley, William	1843-1901	Pres	229	639	832	662	Assass. by Anarchist
McKinley, William (As Pres.)	1846-1901	Pres	352	737	2448	1012	White House Card 500-750; ALS on WHC 1000
McKinley, William (CW)	1843-1901	Pres		3000			CW Capt. War-dte LS 3000; S CDV w/CW Rank 1250
McKinly, John		Rev War	65	180			1st Gov. DE, Captured by Br.
McKinstry, Justus	1814-1897	Civ War	56	75	105		Union Gen.
McKnight, Kauffer E.	1890-1954	Artist	60		425		Br. Known For Book Illustrations, Poster Designs
McKone, John R.		Mil	10	20	40	40	
McKuen, Rod		Author	20	25	35	40	Poet
McLachlan, Sarah		Music	15			45	Singer; S Album 65
McLaglin, Andrew V.		Ent	10		25	25	Dir.
McLaglin, Victor	1886-1959	Ent	165			335	AA 'The Informer'
McLain, Raymond S.	1890-1954	WWII	30			45	Gen. WWII
McLains, The		Cntry Mus	20			45	
McLane, Louis	1786-1857	Bus	40	85	120		Jackson Sec. Treasury
McLane, Robert		Gov	35	80	135		Gov. MD, US Min. to Japan
McLaughlin, E. A.		Bus	10	35	45	20	
McLaughlin, James C.		Congr	10	15		15	MOC MI
McLaughlin, John	1942	Music	15			45	Singer; S Album 60
McLaughlin, Kyle		Ent	20			40	Actor

NAME	DATES	CATEGORY	SIG	LS/DS	ALS	SP	COMMENTS
McLaws, Lafayette	1821-1897	Civ War	165	347	637		CSA Gen. Sig/Rank 290
McLean, Don		Music	25			127	Rock, 'Am. Pie'; S Guitar 525
McLean, George P.		Congr	10	15	25		Gov., Sen. CT
McLean, John	1785-1861	Sup Crt	55	462	285		Dissented Dred Scott Opinion
McLean, Nathaniel C.	1815-1905	Civ War	45	70	120		Union Gen.
McLendon-Covey, Wendi		Ent	13			40	
McLeod, Archibald Norman	1812-1872	Clergy		2500			Hudson Bay Co. vs NW Co. Fur Trader, Author.
McLeod, Catherine	1921-1997	Ent	10			45	Actress. Films from 40s
McLintock, Francis Sir		Celeb	10	30	75		
McLuhan, Marshall		Author	25	225			SB 50
McMahon, Brien	1903-1952	Congr	10	40		15	Sen. CT
McMahon, Ed		Ent	10			40	
McMahon, Horace	1906-1971	Ent	20			50	Actor
McMahon, Julian		Ent	15			45	
McMahon, Martin T.	1838-1906	Civ War	50		175		Union Gen.
McManus, George		Comics	50			247	Bringing Up Father', Panel 1, 500
McMichael, Morton		Jrnalist	45	95			1st Editor Saturday Eve'g Post
McMillan, Edwin M.		Sci	20	35	69	30	Nobel Chemistry 1952
McMillan, James	1838-1902	Congr	12	20	35		Sen. MI 1889
McMillan, James Winning	1825-1903	Civ War	40	75	110		Union Gen.
McMillan, Kenneth	1932-1989	Ent	10			45	Actor
McMillan, Terry		Author	10	25		25	
McMillen, William L.		Civ War			65		US Cmdr.
McMonagle, Donald		Space	10			25	
McMorris, Charles H. Adm.		WWII	10			40	WWII Naval Cmdr.
McMullen, Clements	1892-	Mil	50	150			WWI Aviator, WWII Gen.
McMullen, Richard C.		Gov	10				Governor DE
McNab, Mercedes		Ent	15			45	
McNair, Evander	1820-1902	Civ War	115				CSA Gen.
McNair, Leslie J.		Mil	35	95	165	165	WWI, Gen., WWII KIA
McNair, Robert	1923-	Gov	10			10	Governor SC
McNair, Ronald E.	1950-1986	Space	98	125		215	D. in Challenger Crash
McNally, Kevin		Ent	15			45	
McNally, Stephen	1913-1994	Ent	10			25	Actor
McNamara, Maggie	1928-1958	Ent	150				Actress
McNamara, Robert S.		Cab	15	35		55	Sec. Defense, Pres. World Bank
McNamara, William		Ent	10			50	
McNamee, Graham		Ent	20				Legendary Sports Announcer
McNarney, Joseph T.		WWII	20	50		40	Gen. WWII
McNary, Charles L.	1874-1944	Congr	15	35			Sen. OR. McNary Dam
McNaughton, Kenneth	1903-	Mil	10			40	US Gen.
McNear, Howard	1905- 1969	Ent	770				Floyd the Barber on 'Andy Griffith Show' RARE
McNee, Patrick	1922-	Ent	10			40	Br. Actor
McNeil, Claudia	1917-1993	Ent	10			45	Actress
McNeil, John	1813-1891	Civ War	35	70	110		Union Gen., TLS/cont 668
McNeill, Don	1907-1996	Ent	15	15	25	30	Radio-TV. Hosted 'Don McNeill's Breakfast Club'
McNichol, Kristy		Ent	10	50		60	Actress
McNulty, Michael R. M		Congr	10				Member US Congress
McNutt, Paul V.		Gov	15	30			Governor IN
McPartland, Jimmy		Music	30	55		85	Jazz Trumpet
McPate, Randolph R.		Mil	30			95	Commandant of US Marine Corps
McPhatter, Clyde		Music	283		460	340	Classic Rocker
McPherson, Aimee Semple		Clergy	191	392	495	418	Religious zealot
McPherson, Craig		Artist	15		25	35	Am. painter & muralist

NAME	DATES	CATEGORY	SIG	LS/DS	ALS	SP	COMMENTS
McPherson, Elle		Ent	22			60	Model/actress
McPherson, Isaac V.		Congr	10	15			MOC MO
McPherson, James B. (WD)		Civ War	425	935	2810	2000	Union Gen. KIA 1864
McPherson, James Birdseye	1828-1864	Civ War	309	610		1955	Union Gen. KIA 1864
McPherson, John R.	1833-1897	Congr	12	20	30		Sen. NJ
McPherson, William		Author	15		70		Critic & Author. Pulitzer !977 for Journalism
McQuade, James	1829-1885	Civ War	40	70	178		Union Gen.
McQuade, James (WD)		Civ War	55	85			Union Gen.
McQueen, Butterfly	1911-1995	Ent	55	88		92	Actress, Prissy GWTW; S Chk 260
McQueen, Steve	1930-1980	Ent	1243	1310	2070	3336	Actor
McRae, Carmen	1920-1994	Music	25			125	Am. jazz singer, Comp., pianist, & actress
McRae, Dandridge	1829-1899	Civ War	100	210			CSA Gen.
McRae, William	1834-1882	Civ War	120	188			CSA Gen.
McRaney, Gerald	1947-	Ent	10			40	Actor
McReynolds, James C.	1862-1946	Sup Crt	35	125	145	100	Wilson Atty Gen. Justice 1914-41
McShane, Ian	1942-	Ent	10			40	Br. Actor; GG
McShann, Jay		Music	50			125	Jazz Pianist, Vocalist, Bandlead
McWethy, John	1947-2008	Ent	10			25	ABC News correspondent
McWhorter, Hamilton		WWII	12	25	45	35	ACE, WWII; 12 kills
McWilliams, Caroline	1945-	Ent	10			40	Actress
Mead, Margaret	1901-1978	Sci	55	110	170	116	Anthropologist, Lecturer, Author; SB 100
Meade, Carl J.		Space	10			22	
Meade, George G.	1815-1872	Civ War	250	422	598	1207	Union Gen. Special ALS Re. Off. 's Service 1900
Meade, George G. (WD)	1815-1872	Civ War	415	625	1250	2500	Union Gen. DS 1750
Meadows, Audrey	1922-1996	Ent	20	40		60	Actress; Honeymooners; SP w/Gleason 235
Meadows, Jayne	1920-	Ent	10			40	Married to Steve Allen; SP w/Allen 55
Meadows, Tim		Ent	15			45	
Meagher, Thomas F.	1823-1867	Civ War	65	180	325		Union Gen.
Meagher, Thomas F. (WD)		Civ War	240	500	685		Union Gen.
Meaney, Colm		Ent	15			40	Star Trek; Actor
Means, Abigail		1st Lady	125		1250		Aunt Abby'. Surrogate 1st Lady for Pierce
Means, Russell	1939-	Ent	10			40	Native Am. actor
Meany, George		Labor	25	120		65	Pres. AFL-CIO
Meara, Anne		Ent	10			40	Actress; comedianne; married to Jerry Stiller
Mears, Otto	d. 1931	West		92			Pathfinder of the San Juan
Meat Loaf		Music	20		25	45	Rock; S Album 240
Meatloaf		Music	35			75	Rock; S Guitar 240; S Album 125
Mecham, Edwin L.		Congr	10			12	Governor, Sen. NM
Medawar, Peter B., Sir		Sci	20	30	60	60	Nobel Med. 1960
Meddick, Jim		Comics	10			35	Illust. of 'Robotman'
Medeiros, Humberto, Card.		Clergy	35	50	60	50	
Medici, Catherine de	1519-1589	Royal		8240			Queen consort to Henry II
Medici, Cosimo I, de	1519-1574	Royal	375	1320			The Great. Duke of Florence
Medici, Ferdinand de	1663-1713	Royal			285		The Grand Prince of Tuscany
Medici, Fernando de	1549-1609	Royal	370	1250	3125		Son of Cosimo I. Gr. Duke
Medici, Giovanni Gastone de	1671-1737	Royal		375	525		Grand Duke of Tuscany
Medici, Leopoldo de, Card.	1652-1725	Clergy	300	385	405		Cardinal. Son of Cosimo II
Medici, Lorenzo de	1449-1492	Pol			1760		It. Statsmn. Renaissance ruler, Florentine Repub.
Medici, Marie de	1573-1642	Royal	350	430	2500		Fr. Queen Consort & Q. Regent. Queen of Henry IV
Medicis, Catherine de		Royal		650			
Medill, Joseph	1823-1899	Jrnalist	125		275		A Fndr. Repub. Party
Medill, William	1802-1865	Congr	12				Repr. OH, Gov. OH
Medina, Harold R.		Jurist	10	25		15	
Medina, Patricia	1920-	Ent	15			72	Brit. Actress

NAME	DATES	CATEGORY	SIG	LS/DS	ALS	SP	COMMENTS
Medjugorje (Jugo) Children of		Relig	300				2 Who Saw Vision Virgin Mary
Medley, Bill		Cntry Mus	10			20	
Meehan, Martin T. M		Congr	10				Member US Congress
Meek, Kendrick B. M		Congr	10				Member US Congress
Meek, Larissa		Ent	14			41	
Meeker, Nathan		Jrnalist			45		Indian agent, White River Res. Killed by Utes, 1879
Meeker, Ralph		Ent	25			40	
Meeks, Gregory W. M		Congr	10				Member US Congress
Meese, Edwin III	1931-	Cab	10	35	35	32	Atty Gen. Reagan. Resigned abruptly
Meganck, Glenn		Author	10			12	Juvenile adventures
Mehta, Zubin		Cond	12			80	Intl. Conductor
Meier, Waltraud		Opera	15			35	Opera
Mei-Figner, Medea	1859-1952	Opera				1200	Opera. It. -Russian Mezzo-Sopr.
Meighan, James		Ent				20	Radio Actor. The Falcon
Meighan, Tom		Ent	35			80	
Meigs, Montgomery C.	1816-1892	Civ War	47	85	142	350	Union Quartermaster Gen.
Meigs, Montgomery C. (WD)	1816-1892	Civ War	60	175	328		Union Gen., ALS/cont 2500
Meigs, Return J., Jr.	1764-1824	Cab	80	205	360		Monroe P. M. Gen. Mil.
Meiklejohn, G. D.		Cab	15	40			Ass't Sec. War
Meinl, Tanaka		Opera	30			75	Opera
Meir, Golda	1898-1979	HOS	131	341	600	190	TLS/Cont 1, 500-2, 500. FDC S 125
Meissonier, Ernst	1815-1891	Ent			50		Ger. film Prod.
Meitner, Lise	1878-1968	Sci	140			160	Austrian Phys. Uranium Fission. Fermi Award '66
Melachrino, George		Band	14				Arranger
Melba, Nellie, Dame	1859-1931	Opera	68	135	200	273	Australian Operatic Sopr.
Melbourne, Wm. Lamb, Lord	1779-1848	HOS	70	85	138		Q. Victoria's 1st Prime Min.
Melchior, Lauritz	1890-1973	Opera	59	100		161	Opera Danish Tenor. Wagnerian Roles at Met.
Melis, Carmen		Opera	35				Opera, Teacher
Mellencamp, John Cougar		Music	25			55	Originally John Cougar; S album 130
Mellish, David Batcheller		Congr	10				FF 28
Mellnik, Steve		WWII	10	25	35	40	US Brig. Gen.
Mellon, Andrew W.	1855-1937	Bus	125	260	450	295	Pitts. Millionaire Tycoon. Sec. Treas. Financier
Mellor, Will	1976-	Ent	10			25	Br. Actor
Melman, Yossi		Jrnalist	10			20	Israeli writer & journalist
Melnick, Bruce E.		Space	10			25	
Melnick, Natasha		Ent	13			40	
Melton, James		Opera	10			55	Am. Concert, Radio & Opera Tenor
Melvey, Justin	1969-	Ent	10			25	Australian actor
Melvill, Thomas	1751-1832	Rev War	88	262	550		Memb. Boston Tea Party
Melville, George W.	1814-1912	Mil	40	105	170		Adm., Arctic Explr.
Melville, Herman	1819-1891	Author	3605	5000	14298		ALS's/Cont 20,000-95,000
Melvin L. Watt		Congr	10				Member US Congress
Melvin, Allan	1923-2008	Ent	10			60	Actor; Phil Silvers Show
Memminger, Chris. G. (WD)	1803-1888	Civ War	178	456	817		CSA Sec. of Treasury
Memphis Belle		WWII				1000	Entire crew S picture; S picture by 8 members 600
Men at Work		Music				75	Rock group
Mencken, Henry L.	1880-1956	Author	102	198	360	700	Satirist, Editor, Essayist, Critic, Journalist
Mendel, Gregor Johann	1822-1884	Sci	400	850	2000		Laws of Biological Inheiritance
Mendeleyev, Dmitry	1834-1907	Sci			1650		Rus. Chem. Developed Periodic Table
Mendelssohn-Bartholdy, Felix	1809-1847	Comp	500	1014	2960		Ger. ALS/Cont 6, 500
Mendes, Abraham Caulle		Author	15	35	100		Fr. Poet. Plays, Verses, Libretti
Mendes, Eva		Ent				50	Actress
Mendez, Arnaldo Tamayo		Space	10			25	
Menedez, Kitty & Jose		Celeb		110			Celebrity murder victims; S Chk 205

NAME	DATES	CATEGORY	SIG	LS/DS	ALS	SP	COMMENTS
Menendez, Eric		Crime			175		
Menendez, Lyle		Crime	50	175			Convicted Murderer of Parents. S Chk 150
Menendez, Robert M		Congr	10				Member US Congress
Mengelberg, Willem	1871-1951	Ent	75			210	Dutch Conductor. AMusQS 250
Mengele, Josef	1911-?	WWII	1755				Auschwitz Dr. Experimented on Inmates. WWII
Menjou, Adolphe	1890-1963	Ent	60	45		98	Dapper, Well Dressed Film Actor.
Menk, Louis W.		Bus	10			15	CEO Intl. Harvester
Menken, Alan	1949-	Comp	20			50	Am. Comp., pianist; AA
Menken, Helen	1901-1966	Ent	22	25	30	45	Stage Star & Occasional Films. Bogart's 1st Wife
Menkes, Sara		Opera	20			55	Opera
Mennin, Peter		Comp	10		65		AMusQS 75
Menninger, Karl Dr.	1893-1990	Sci	35	66	120	109	Menninger Clinic & Foundation
Menninger, Roy		Sci	10	25	55	30	
Menninger, William C., Dr.		Sci	15	45	82	35	Psychiatrist, Pres. Foundation
Menon, V. Krisna		Diplo	20		25		Ambassador GBain
Menonous, Maria		Ent	17			50	
Menotti, Gian Carlo	1911-	Comp	80	160	210	372	It. -Am. Comp.
Mensah, Peter		Ent	15			45	
Menuhin, Yehudi	1916-1999	Music	40	78		198	Concert Violinist, Conductor, Child Prodigy
Menville, Scott		Ent	13			40	
Menzies, Robert, Sir	1894-1978	HOS	25	55	80	50	Australian Prime Min.
Meo, Sean		Celeb	10			20	Br. Comedian
Merbold, Ulf		Space	10	25		25	
Mercadante, Saverio	1795-1870	Comp	138		282		Dir. Royal Conservatory, Naples
Mercer, Archibald		Rev War			750		Patriot
Mercer, Frances	1915-2000	Ent	10			30	
Mercer, Hugh W.	1808-1877	Civ War	90	112			CSA Gen. War Date Sig. 195
Mercer, Ian	1962-	Ent	10			25	Br. Actor
Mercer, Jack		Ent				85	Voice of Popeye; animator & voice actor
Mercer, John Francis	1759-1821	Rev War	70		125		Aide-de-Camp Gen Lee
Mercer, Johnny	1909-1976	Comp	70	262		350	Vocalist, Pianist
Mercer, Mabel		Music	25			65	Jazz Singer; S sheet music 250
Mercer, Marian	1935-	Ent	10			40	Actress
Merchant, Natalie		Music	15			58	Music
Mercier, D. Joseph, Card.		Clergy	35	45	75		
Mercouri, Melina	1920-1994	Ent	25	30	45	56	Actress
Mercury (4 Astronauts)		Space					Schirra, Glenn, Slayton, Shepard S Phil. Cvr. 1050
Mercury (6 Astronauts)		Space		1300		948	No Virgil Grissom. FDC 900
Mercury (7 Astronauts)		Space				5168	All 7 Sigs
Mercury, Freddie	1946-1991	Music	550			850	Lead singer Queen
Meredith, Burgess		Ent	20	65		98	Stage Actor before Films.
Meredith, Edwin T.		Cab	10	20	30	15	Sec. Agriculture 1920
Meredith, James H.		Activist	35	120	185	60	Activist. 1st Black to enroll in U. Miss., 1962
Meredith, Lee	1947-	Ent				65	Actress
Meredith, Samuel	1740-1817	Cab	90	300	370		Rev. War Gen., 1st US Treas. Financier, Patriot
Meredith, Solomon	1810-1875	Civ War	161		450		Union Gen. Iron Brig. of West
Meredith, Sullivan Amory	1816-1874	Civ War	45	75	110		Union Gen.
Merel, Ronald H.	1948-	Law	10			20	Criminal Law
Meriam, Ebenezer		Sci			225		Meteorologist
Merivale, Philip	1886-1946	Ent	15		25	65	Vintage Br. Actor
Meriwether, Lee		Ent	10	10	12	35	
Merkel, Una	1903-1986	Ent	20			89	Actress
Merli, Francesco		Ent	25			75	Opera. Dramatic Tenor
Merli, Gino J.		WWII	15	25		35	WWII Hero CMH

NAME	DATES	CATEGORY	SIG	LS/DS	ALS	SP	COMMENTS
Merlin, Jan	1925-	Ent	15			45	Movie bad guy 50s & 60s; actor
Merlin, Philippe-Antoine	1754-1838	Fr Rev	60	140	250		Revolutionary. Min. of Justice
Merman, Ethel	1908-1984	Ent	30	82		147	Broadway Musical Star Before Movies; SB 120
Mero Irion, Yolanda		Music				100	Hungarian born Am. pianist
Merriam, Frank F.		Gov	10	15			Governor CA
Merrick, David		Ent	20	30	70	70	Theatrical Prod.
Merrick, Samuel Vaughan		Bus	40	175			Financier
Merrick, William Matthew		Congr			35		FF 35
Merrill, Aaron, Adm.		WWII	10			38	WWII Solomon Islands
Merrill, Dina	1925-	Ent	15			75	Actress
Merrill, Frank D.	1903-1955	WWII	150	250	325		Gen. WWII. Merrill's Marauders
Merrill, Gary	1914-1990	Ent	15	20	45	65	Actor
Merrill, Henry T.		Aero	30	45	100	100	
Merrill, Lewis	1834-1896	Civ War	40	65			Union Gen.
Merrill, Richard 'Dick'	1894-1982	Aero	30	55	105	105	Aviation pioneer
Merrill, Robert	1919-	Opera	22			45	Metropolitan Opera Co. Baritone
Merrill, Stuart		Author	30		125		Am. Poet. Wrote in Fr.
Merriman, Nan	1920-	Opera	20			75	Opera. US Mezzo-Sop.
Merrimon, Augustus S.	1830-1892	Congr	22	35			Sen. NC
Merritt, Chris		Opera	10				Opera
Merritt, Wesley	1834-1910	Civ War	145	165			Union Gen.
Merton, Paul	1957-	Ent	10			25	Br. actor
Merton, Thomas	1915-1968	Clergy	250	568			Priest-Writer, Poet
Mesmer, Franz Anton, Dr.	1734-1815	Sci	115	285	535		Ger. Dr., ' Mesmerise', DS/cont 3750
Messerschmitt, Wilhelm	1898-1978	Aero	139	258		383	Ger. Aircraft Designer-Mfg. 'Messerschmitt'
Messiaen, Olivier	1908-1990	Comp	70	200		450	Fr. Organist. AMusQS 475-1350
Messick, Dale		Comics	25				Brenda Starr, S drawing 145
Messick, Don	1921-1997	Ent	15		30	62	Cartoon Voice: 'Scoobie Doo', 'Boo Boo Bear'
Messing, Debra		Ent	10			45	Actress, Will & Grace
Messmer, Otto		Comics	55			400	Felix The Cat
Messner, Tammy Faye (Baker)	1942-2007	Celeb	15			40	Evangelist
Mesta, Perle		Bus	25	30	70	35	Washington Hostess
Metallica (4)		Music				120	S Guitar 250-500; S Drumhd 175; S Album 315
Metcalf, Laurie		Ent	15			40	Actress. Roseanne
Metcalf, Victor H.	1853-1936	Cab	20	55	95		Sec. Navy, Commerce, Labor
Metcalfe, Ralph H.		Congr	10	15		25	MOC IL
Metchnikoff, Elie	1845-1916	Sci	60	150		250	Nobel Physiology 1908
Metternich, Clemens von, Pr.		HOS	150	1200	240		Austrian Statesman
Metternich. Graff Wolff	1853-1934	Pol			120		Prussian & Ger. ambassador
Metzenbaum, Howard		Congr	10			20	Sen. OH
Metzer, Joe		Artist	10				Illust. Original Sm. Sketch 45
Meusel, Lucille		Opera	10			25	Sopr.
Mewes, Jason		Ent	15			45	
Mewman, Larry		Aero	25			75	
Meyer, Albert G., Card.		Clergy	35	40	50	50	
Meyer, Breckin		Ent	15			45	
Meyer, Dina		Ent	17			50	
Meyer, E. C.		Mil	10		30	30	US Army Chief of Staff, June 1979-June 1983
Meyer, George von L.		Cab	15	20	35	35	P. M. Gen. 1907
Meyer, John C.		WWII	35			195	Fighter Ace of WWII; 24 kills
Meyer, Joseph	1894-1987	Comp	75		225	125	CA Here I Come', 'If You Knew Susie,
Meyer, Steve		Author	10			12	Civil War history
Meyerbeer, Giacomo	1791-1864	Comp	170	255	379	300	Ger. Comp. of Fr. Operas, AMusQ 750
Meyerhold, Vsevolod	1874-1940	Celeb		483			Communist stage Dir.

NAME	DATES	CATEGORY	SIG	LS/DS	ALS	SP	COMMENTS
Meyers, John		Ent	15			45	
Meyers, Josh		Ent	15			45	
Meynell, Alice Christiana	1847-1922	Author					Poet, essayist, journalist. Autogr. Poem 160
Mfume, Kweisi		Congr	10			40	Head of NAACP
Miano, Robert	1942-	Ent	10			30	Actor
Miaskovsky, Nikolai	1881-1950	Comp	125				27 Symphonies
Mica, John L. M		Congr	10				Member US Congress
Michael, George		Ent	20	30	95	80	
Michaels, Barbara		Author	10		25	15	
Michaels, Bret	1963-	Music	10	20	50	45	Lead vocalist 'Poison'
Michaels, Dolores	1933-2001	Ent	10			25	Actress
Michaels, Lee		Music				65	Singer
Michaels, Lorne		Ent	15			50	Saturday Night Live
Michaels, Lorraine		Model	10			35	Playboy
Michaels, Marilyn	1944-	Ent	10			30	Actress
Michael-Vincent, Jan		Ent	10			35	Actor
Michalka, AJ	1991-	Music	15			45	
Michalka, Aly	1989-	Music	16			48	
Michaud, Michael H. M		Congr	10				Member US Congress
Michel, Frank Curtis		Space	10			25	
Michele, Denise	1953-	Ent	10			25	Former playmate, actress
Michelet, Jules	1798-1874	Author	30		77		Great Historian of Romantic School
Michelson, Albert A.	1852-1931	Sci	120		450		Nobel Physics 1907
Michelson, Charles		Pol	12	15			Speech Writer New Deal
Michener, James A.	1907-1998	Author	60	80	160	175	Am. Novels. Pulitzer; SB 150
Middleton, Arthur	1742-1787	Rev War	7180	10000	17500		Signer Dec. of Indepen.
Middleton, Charles		Ent	292			250	Actor; Ming the Merciless 'Flash Gordon' serials
Middleton, Henry	1717-1784	Rev War	3000	4500			Pres. of Congress. Special DS 9500
Middleton, Robert	1911-1977	Ent	50			132	Actor
Middleton, Thomas F.		Clergy	30	50	80		
Middleton, Troy H.	1889-1976	WWII	40	125		75	Am. WWII Gen.
Middleton, Velma		Music	30			70	Jazz Vocalist
Middleton, Walter T.		Author	10			15	WWII/ Cherokee history
Midler, Bette		Ent	20	30		64	Singer-Actress
Midnight Cowboy (cast)		Ent				75	Hoffman & Voight
Midori		Ent	15			80	
Mielziner, Jo		Ent	15		40	35	Film Dir.
Mifflin, Thomas	1744-1800	Rev War	118	265	483		Rev. War Gen. Pres. Continental Congr.
Mifune, Toshiro	1920-1997	Ent	25	35	75	133	Popular Jap. Star
Migenes, Julia		Opera	15			35	Opera
Mihalovivi, Marcel		Comp	20			150	Rumanian
Miklas, Wilhelm	1872-1956	HOS	25				Pres. Austria
Miko, Isabella	1981-	Ent				45	Actress
Mikoyan, Anastasy I.	1895-1970	HOS	100	390		125	Pres. Presidium Supr. Soviet. DS w/Molotov 625
Mikulski, Barbara		Congr	10				US Senate (D-MD)
Milam, Benjamin	1788-1835	Tex		7595			TX Independence
Milano, Alyssa		Ent	20	40		52	Actress
Milanov, Zinka		Opera	20		60	124	Metropolitan Opera
Milburn, William H.	1823-1903	Clergy	35				Blind Circuit Rider Min.
Milch, Erhard	1892-1972	WWII	100	160	250	250	Nazi Gen., Aviator
Miles, Josephine		Author	10	15	25	10	
Miles, Nelson A.	1839-1925	Civ War	120	122	262	240	Union Gen, MOH; only Off. in all: CW/Indian/Sp. Am. Wars
Miles, Sarah		Ent	15			80	Actress
Miles, Sylvia	1923-	Ent	10	20	35	40	Actress

NAME	DATES	CATEGORY	SIG	LS/DS	ALS	SP	COMMENTS
Miles, Vera	1930-	Ent	15			49	Actress
Milestone, Lewis		Ent	135			310	Film Dir.
Milhaud, Darius	1892-1974	Comp	100	187	240	368	Fr. Comp. AMusQS 475-500
Mill, James	1773-1836	Author	65	250	515		Scot. Philosopher, Historian, Econ
Mill, John Stuart	1806-1873	Author	230	325	2882		Br. Economist, Philosopher, Reformer
Mill, William Hodge		Clergy	20	25	30		
Millais, John Everett, Sir	1829-1896	Artist	45	90	218		Pre-Raphaelite Painter
Milland, Ray		Ent	30	50		117	
Millay, Edna St. Vincent	1892-1950	Author	100	225	550	685	Am. Poet, Dramatist. Pulitzer; SB 400
Millender-McDonald, Juanita		Congr	10				Member US Congress
Miller, Alice Duer		Author	15	25	45		Novels, Poet
Miller, Ann	1923-2004	Ent	15	55		188	Actress
Miller, Arthur	1915-2005	Author	65	148	205	147	Plays. Pulitzer. TMsS & AManS $3900; love letter to M. Monroe $6500; SB $350-1000
Miller, Bennett		Ent	12			35	
Miller, Brad M		Congr	10				Member US Congress
Miller, Candice S. M		Congr	10				Member US Congress
Miller, Caroline		Author	10	20			Pulitzer
Miller, Charles Henry	1842-1922	Artist	25			100	Landscape Painter
Miller, Dennis		Ent	10	30		35	Comedian-Actor-Writer.
Miller, Denny	1935-	Ent	10			57	Char. actor
Miller, Eddie		Music	20			45	Big Band Tenor Saxophonist
Miller, Frederick C.		Bus	12	32	64	25	Miller Beer
Miller, G. William		Cab	10	15	25	12	Sec. Treasury
Miller, Gary G. M		Congr	10				Member US Congress
Miller, George Funston		Congr	12		39		FF 39
Miller, George M		Congr	10				Member US Congress
Miller, Glenn	1904-1944	Band	150	278	400	491	Big Band Leader-Trombonist. WWII Casualty
Miller, H. G.		Bus	10			15	
Miller, Henry	1891-1980	Artist				385	Mdrn. artist
Miller, Henry John	1869-1926	Ent	35	88	75	70	Br. -Am. Leading Man. Henry Miller Theatre
Miller, Henry Jr.	1889-1927	Ent	35	112		95	Vintage Actor
Miller, Henry V.	1891-1980	Author	63	102	340	150	Candid Autobiogr. Novels. 'Tropic of Cancer'
Miller, Jacob W.	1800-1862	Congr	12				Sen. NJ
Miller, Jeff M		Congr	10				Member US Congress
Miller, Jesse		Congr	12		44		FF 44
Miller, Joaquin	1839-1913	Author	62		108		Am. Poet, Journalist. Spec. TLS 3500
Miller, John F.	1831-1886	Civ War	45	51	60		Union Gen., US Sen. CA
Miller, Ken		Ent	10			25	Child Actor
Miller, Larry		Ent	15			45	
Miller, Leslie A.		Gov	10	20			Governor WY
Miller, Marilyn		Ent	72		168	178	Ziegfield Follies Dancing Star
Miller, Marvin	1917-	Law	15	25	40	45	Baseball lawyer; TLS/Cont 560
Miller, Marvin		Ent		95		55	Actor; 'Millionaire'
Miller, Mitch	1911-	Cond	10			35	Conductor, Arranger
Miller, Nathan L.		Gov	15				Governor NY
Miller, Oskar von	1855-1934	Sci	115		325		Ger. Co-Fndr. of Ger. Edison Co.
Miller, Patsy Ruth	1904-1995	Ent	25	35	55	78	Actress
Miller, Penelope Ann	1964-	Ent	20			40	Actress
Miller, Rebecca	1962-	Ent	10			25	Actress
Miller, Roger		Cntry Mus	25		145	60	Comp.
Miller, Samuel F.	1816-1890	Sup Crt	95	160	392		Appointed by Lincoln
Miller, Shannon		Ent	12			35	
Miller, Sienna	1962-	Ent	15			45	Actress

NAME	DATES	CATEGORY	SIG	LS/DS	ALS	SP	COMMENTS
Miller, Stanley		Sci	15	35	65	20	
Miller, Stephen	1816-1881	Civ War	40	80	125		Union Gen.
Miller, Taylor	1954-	Ent	10			25	Actress; 'All My Children'
Miller, Warner	1838-1918	Congr	10	20	35		Repr., Sen. NY
Miller, Wentworth		Ent	13			40	
Miller, William	1820-1909	Civ War	95	178			CSA Gen.
Miller, William H. H.		Cab	10	30	50	20	Atty Gen. 1889
Miller, Zell		Congr	10				US Senate (D-GA)
Millerande, Alexandre	1859-1943	HOS	40	45	60	75	Socialist Pres. France 1920-24
Milles, Carl		Artist	30	55	90		Am. Sculptor
Millet, Aimé	1819-1891	Artist		30	75		Fr. Sculptor/Painter Works Adorn Paris Pub. Bldgs
Millet, Francis Davis	1846-1912	Artist	25	45	340		Am. Medal Winning Art. Journalist
Millet, Frank		Titanic		100			Lost on Titanic
Millet, Jean Fran ois	1814-1875	Artist	200	425	1084		Fr. Religious, Classical, Peasant
Millikan, John		Mil	10	30	50	20	
Millikan, Robert A., Dr.	1868-1953	Sci	123	169	425	200	Nobel Physics, Educator, Author; SB 130
Milliken, William G.		Gov	10	15		10	Governor MI
Millinder, Lucky		Band	40			125	Bandleader
Millman, William	1927-	Mil	14			25	Israeli Ind. Hero. Am. Vol. Sailor on Exodus
Millo, Aprile		Opera	10			35	Opera
Mills Brothers (4)		Ent	107			138	
Mills, Billy		Celeb	10			15	Olympic gold medal winner; Spkr.
Mills, Darius Ogden	1825-1910	Bus	238	875	2750		Merchant, Calif. Banking Giant. Philan. RR DS 1550
Mills, Donna		Ent	15			56	Actress
Mills, Earle W.		Mil	12	30			
Mills, Elijah Hunt	1776-1829	Congr	20		50		MOC & Sen. MA.
Mills, Hayley	1946-	Ent	15	15	25	71	Br. Actress; 'Parent Trap'
Mills, Heather		Activist	10			30	Ex-wife of Sir Paul McCartney
Mills, John, Sir	1908-	Ent	20			70	Brit. Oscar Winner.
Mills, Juliette	1941-	Ent	10			25	Br. Actress
Mills, Madison	1811-1896	Civ War	35				Union Gen. Med. Off'r. War Dte. ALS 275
Mills, Ogden L.	1884-1937	Cab	10	23	45	25	Sec. Treasury 1932. MOC NY
Mills, Roger Q.	1832-1911	Civ War	25	35	50		CSA Col., MOC TX
Mills, Wilbur	1909-	Congr	25			35	Sen. AR
Milne, A. A.	1882-1956	Author	192	905	908	1025	Winnie-the-Pooh'. AMS 5950; SB 500
Milner, Martin	1931-	Ent	10			40	Actor
Milnes, Rich. M.		Celeb	10	10	25	15	Baron of Houghton. Man of Letters. Oxford Movement
Milnes, Sherrill		Opera	10			25	Opera. Am. Basso
Milosevic, Slobodan		Pol	50			150	Fmr. Pres. of Yugoslavia
Milosz, Czeslaw, Dr.		Author	30	60		75	Nobel Literature
Milroy, Robert H.	1816-1890	Civ War	40	80	120		Union Gen. LS '61 220
Milsap, Ronnie	1944-	Cntry Mus	15		30	45	Singer. DS re 'Grammy Awards' 75
Milstein, Nathan	1904-1992	Music	45			175	Rus. Violinist
Miltonberger, Butler		Mil	35	60		40	US Gen.
Mimieux, Yvette	1942-	Ent	15	50		65	Actress
Mincus, Leon		Comp	55			375	Austro-Rus. Many Ballets
Mindil, George W.		Civ War	35		210		Union Gen. MOH
Mindszenty, Jozef, Card.		Clergy	50	75	135	95	
Minelli, Liza	1946-	Ent	15	25	50	100	Actress-Singer
Minelli, Vincente	1910-	Ent	30			82	AA Film Dir. Father of Liza Minelli
Mineo, Sal	1939-1976	Ent	106	205		468	Actor; 2 Oscar Nominations
Miner, Charles		Congr	12		48		FF 48
Miner, Jan	1917-2004	Ent	10			30	
Mingus, Charlie	1922-1979	Music	457	945		3675	Jazz Musician, S Album 865

NAME	DATES	CATEGORY	SIG	LS/DS	ALS	SP	COMMENTS
Minh, Duong Van Gen.		Mil	15	40	75	75	
Minich, Peter		Opera	10			20	Opera, Light Opera
Mink, Patsy T.		Congr	10	15		10	MOH HI
Minor, Michael		Author	10			12	Autographs, western history
Minor, Ruediger, Bish.		Clergy	25	40	45	50	
Minow, Newton N.		Law	12			15	Chairman FCC
Minter, Mary Miles	1902-1984	Ent	120	135	230	350	Vintage actress
Minton, Sherman	1890-1965	Sup Crt	40	95	150	125	
Minton, Yvonne		Opera	10			25	Opera
Mintz, Eli	1904-1988	Ent	10	15	25	25	Yiddish Theatre Veteran Char. Actor
Mintzer, Richard Dr.		Med	10			20	Renown radiologist
Mintz-Plasse, Christopher		Ent				40	Actor
Miollis, S. A. F.	1759-1828	Fr Rev	100	215			Gen. of Napoleon
Mirabeau, Honore G.	1749-1791.	Fr Rev	120	350	575		Statesman, Diplomat, Pol.
Mirabehin (M. Slade)		Celeb	25		45		Companion-Follower of Gandhi
Miramon, Miguel (Mex)		Mil	20	85	134		Cmdr. Army vs Juarez.
Miranda, Carmen	1913-1955	Ent	99	125		292	Brazilian-Portuguese Singer-Movie Star. 40s
Miranda, Isa		Ent	35			75	It. Actress
Mirisch, Walter		Ent	10			20	Motion Picture Prod.
Miro, Joan	1893-1983	Artist	126	350	706	230	Spanish Surrealist Painter; S print 250-600
Miroslava	1926-1955	Ent	25	30	70	150	Mexican actress
Mirren, Helen		Ent	20	35		122	Br. Actress; AA
Mischakoff, Mischa		Music	25		85		Legendary Violinist. 'Toscanini's Concertmaster'
Mishima, Yukio	1925-1970	Author	805	610	1837		Dichotomy Bet. Mind & Body. Suicide 1970; SB 650
Mission Impossible (Cast)		Ent				195	4 Leads incl. Tom Cruise
Mister, Mister		Ent	15			55	
Mistinguett, Madamoiselle		Ent	90			229	Moulon Rouge Dancer-Actress
Mistral, Frederic	1830-1914	Author	40	110	175	200	Nobel Literature 1904
Mistral, Gabriela		Author	20	160	350	200	Nobel Lit. '43(Godoy Alcayaga)
Mitchel, Ormsby M.		Civ War	40	127	156		Union Gen.
Mitchel, Ormsby M. (WD)	1809-1862	Civ War	125		475		Union Gen., Astronomy Prof.
Mitchell, Andrea		Celeb	10			25	Poliical news
Mitchell, Cameron	1918-1994	Ent	20			60	Actor. Leading Roles in Rugged Parts
Mitchell, Charles E.		Bus	20	35	65	25	Chmn. National City Bank
Mitchell, Edgar D.	1930-	Space	28	142	275	98	Moonwalker. Apollo 14; S beta-cloth Apollo 14 1700; Ins. Cvr. 145
Mitchell, Grant	1874-1957	Ent	35			142	Actor
Mitchell, James P.		Cab	15	25	30		Sec. Labor
Mitchell, John Cameron		Ent	20			40	Actor, writer, Dir.
Mitchell, John Grant	1838-1894	Civ War	45	80	140		Union Gen.
Mitchell, John Inscho	1838-1907	Civ War	20	45			US Sen. PA
Mitchell, John N.	1913-1988	Cab	25			60	Atty Gen., TLS/Cont 200
Mitchell, John W.		WWII	12	25	42	45	ACE, WWII; 11 kills
Mitchell, Joni		Ent	20			78	Singer songwriter; S Album 100
Mitchell, Maggie	1832-1918	Ent	50			125	Entertained 1st CSA Gov't & Troops
Mitchell, Margaret	1900-1949	Author	575	2313	2362		Pulitzer. TLS/Cont 15,000; SB 4000-5000
Mitchell, Maria	1818-1889	Sci	90	185	375		Considered 1st Woman Astronomer. Mathematician
Mitchell, Martha		Celeb	25	30		30	Wife Atty Gen. -Watergate
Mitchell, Ormsby M. (WD)		Civ War			957		Union Gen. D. 1862 RARE
Mitchell, Radha		Ent	13			40	
Mitchell, Robert Byington	1823-1882	Civ War	45	75	110		Union Gen.
Mitchell, Silas Weir		Civ War	25	95	155		Civil War Surgeon
Mitchell, Stephen Mix	1743-1835	Rev War	65	295			Cont'l Congr. Federalist Sen. PA
Mitchell, Thomas	1892-1962	Ent	186	196	239	471	Actor; GWTW; AA

NAME	DATES	CATEGORY	SIG	LS/DS	ALS	SP	COMMENTS
Mitchell, Warren	1926-	Ent	10			30	Br. Actor
Mitchell, William (Billy)	1879-1936	Aero	202	312	460	1345	Gen. WWI. Aerial Bombing. Courtmartialed. S Chk 280
Mitchell, William D.		Cab	10	25	30	20	Atty Gen.
Mitchelson, Marvin		Law	13	25		20	Trial Atty. Specialty Divorce
Mitchum, Robert	1917-1997	Ent	27	180	135	141	Actor. Versatile Leading Man
Mitford, Jessica		Author	15	25	25	20	
Mitford, Mary Russell	1787-1855	Author			128		Novels & Dramatist.
Mitra, Rhona		Ent	13			40	
Mitre, Bartolome	1821-1906	Pol				150	Pres. of Argentina 1862-1868
Mitropoulous, Dimitri	1896-1960	Comp	45	50	95	192	Greek Conductor
Mitscher, Marc A.		WWII	232			412	Adm. WWII
Mitterand, Francois		HOS	15	25	40	30	Pres. France
Mittford, Mary Russell		Author	15	20	40		Br. Poet. Historical Drama
Mix, Tom	1880-1940	Ent	157		250	470	Cowboy Star of Hollywood Silent & Early Talkies
Mizell, Jason		Music				60	Rap pioneer
Mizell, Wilmer D.		Congr	10	15			MOC KS, Prof. Baseball Pitcher
Mizrahi, Isaac	1961-	Bus	10			20	Am. fashion designer
Moakler, Shanna		Ent	16			48	
Mobley, Mary Ann		Ent	15			50	Miss America
Model, Walter	1891-1945	WWII	125	220	310	350	WWII Ger. Gen.
Modesti, Giuseppe		Opera	15			35	Opera
Modigliani, Amedeo	1884-1920	Artist	1200		4500		Italian Painter & Sculptor, Cont. ALS 35,000
Modine, Matthew		Ent	10			40	Actor
Modjeska, Helena	1840-1909	Ent	35			120	Poland's greatest actress of all time
Moelders, Werner		WWII	80				Ger. top ace of the Condor region
Moessbauer, Rudolf, Dr.		Sci	20			55	Nobel
Moeur, Benjamin B.		Gov	12	15	25		Governor Arizona
Moffat, Robert		Clergy	50	90	100		
Moffett, William A., Admiral	1869-1933	Mil	15		50	50	MOH. w/Adm. Dewey. FDC 90
Moffo, Anna	1932-2006	Opera				50	Am. Sopr.
Mohammed, Seti		Pol				35	Ruler of Morocco
Mohnke, Wllhelm		WWII	35				Ger. Gen. SS
Moholy-Nagy, Laszlo	1895-1946	Artist	80	160			Painter, Designer, Photographer
Mohr, Gerald	1914-1968	Ent	35			120	Actor
Mohr, Jay		Ent	17			50	
Mohri, Momoru		Space	12	25		25	
Mojica, Jose		Opera	60				Opera
Mol, Gretchen		Ent	20			65	Vanity Fair' Cvr. S 75
Molders, Werner		WWII	155	275	300	175	Ger. ACE, WWII, !st to 100 Kills
Molina, Alfred		Ent	10			51	Actor; 'Spiderman'
Molinari, Bernadino		Cond		125			Italian conductor
Molinari, Susan	1958-	Pol	10			20	Pol., journalist, & lobbyist from New York; MOC
Molitor, Gabriel J. J.	1770-1849	Fr Rev	75	175	250		Napoleon Gen., Marshal of Fr.
Moll, Kurt		Opera	15			35	Opera
Moll, Richard	1943-	Ent	10			30	Actor
Mollet, Guy		HOS	20	40	65		Socialist Premier France
Mollohan, Alan B. M		Congr	10				Member US Congress
Molnar, Ferenc	1878-1952	Author	72	140	275		Plays, Novels, Journalist
Moloney, Janel		Ent	10			40	Actress; 'The West Wing'
Molony, Richard Sheppard		Congr	10		41		FF 41
Molotov, Vyacheslav M.	1890-1986	Pol	95	219	318	175	Russian revolutionary, "Molotov cocktail"
Moltke, Helmuth G. von, Ct.	1800-1891	Mil	106	133	335	400	Prussian Field Marshal
Moltmann, Jurgen		Clergy	50	75	100	80	
Momaday, N. Scott		Author	10	15	25	15	

NAME	DATES	CATEGORY	SIG	LS/DS	ALS	SP	COMMENTS
Momo, Giuseppe		Opera	10			35	Opera
Mompou, Frederico		Comp					Reclusive Spanish Comp. AMusQS 495
Monaghan, Dominic	1976-	Ent	10			45	Actor; 'Lord of the Rings'
Monaghan, Tom		Bus	10				Domino's Pizza
Moncada, Fernando Rivera y		Mil		4500			Spanish Gov of California 1774-77
Moncey, Bon-Adrien J. de		Fr Rev	45	135	160		Marshal of France
Monck, George	1608-1670	Mil	95	430			1st Duke Albermarle. Restored Monarchy
Mondale, Walter		VP	25	32	45	35	
Mondell, Franklin W.		Congr	10	15		15	MOC WY
Mondrian, Piet	1872-1944	Artist	342	675	1708		Dutch. Traditional-Cubism
Monet, Claude	1840-1926	Artist	425	950	2666	1500	Fr. Impressionist Painter
Money, Hernando De Soto		Congr	10	25	45		MOC, Sen. MS. CSA Army
Money, Ken		Space	10	15		20	
Monk, Thelonious	1917-1982	Music	500	1093		2958	Jazz Musician & Comp. S Album 3500; Chk 800
Monkees, The (4)		Music	100			258	Jones, Nesmith, Dolenz, Tork S Album 380
Monroe, Bill	1911-1996	Music	45		150	110	Father of Blue Grass Music; S sheet music 125
Monroe, J. & Adams, J. Q.		Pres		3012			Pres. & Sec of State
Monroe, James	1758-1831	Pres	356	1606	3262		Free Frank 525, ALS/cont 5000-
Monroe, James (as Pres)		Pres	500	1866	4383		5th Pres. of USA, ALS/cont 14, 340-
Monroe, Marilyn	1926-1962	Ent			15000		(Norman Jean) Signed Norma Jean, Contract $9500
Monroe, Marilyn	1926-1962	Ent	2074	3132	7500	15426	ALS/Cont 15,000, S Chk 1250-2000
Monroe, Meredith		Ent	13			40	
Monroe, Vaughn	1911-1973	Music	15	25		30	Big Band era singer
Monster Magnet		Music	32			80	Music. 5 Member Rock Group
Montag, Heidi		Ent	17			50	
Montagu, Charles	1661-1715	Pol		210			Lord Halifax. Wit, Author. Created Bank of England
Montagu, Edwin Samuel	1879-1924	Pol	15	50	80	35	Br. Statesman
Montagu, John		Celeb	65	205	350		(4th Earl of Sandwich) Sandwich Named For Him
Montague, Andrew J.		Congr	10				Repr., Sen. VA
Montalban, Ricardo	1920-	Ent	10	30	25	48	Actor
Montalivet, J. P. B. Count		Fr Rev	35	100	225		
Montana, Ashley	1965-	Model				40	
Montana, Bob		Comics	40			175	Creator of Archie comics; comic strip 400
Montana, Bull	1887-1950	Ent	25			50	Actor
Montana, Lenny		Ent				420	Actor; prior professional wrestler; 'Luca Brasi'
Montana, Monte		Ent	15			45	Actor; cowboy; SB 65
Montana, Patsy		Cntry Mus	15			35	
Montand, Yves	1921-1991	Ent	25			145	Fr. Actor
Montbarey, Alex-Marie	1732-1796	Statsmn	125		633		Fr. Stateman, Min. of war 1777-80
Montcalm, Louis J. Marq. de		Mil	575	1765	3077		Cmdr. Fr. Troops in North Am.
Montefiore, Moses, Sir	1784-1885	Philan	75	160	275		Br. Jewish Philan. Sherrif of London
Montell, Lisa	1933-	Ent				25	Retired Actress-Heiress
Montemezzi, Italo		Comp		475			AMusQ 475
Montenegro, Conchita	1912-2007	Ent	20			88	Spanish. Actress
Montessori, Maria	1870-1952	Educ	258		1050	2025	1st Italian Woman Doctor, Montessori schools
Monteux, Pierre	1875-1964	Ent	35	50	365	90	Conductor
Montevecchi, Liliane	1932-	Ent	10			50	Actress
Monteverde, Alfred de		Aero	25	50	85	55	
Monteverde, George de		Aero	25	50	85	55	
Montez, Lola	1818-1861	Adven	300	2340	950		Seductress of Louis I of Bavaria.
Montez, Maria		Ent	62	55		368	Actress
Montgolfier, Jacques-Et.	1745-1799	Aero		400	585		With Joseph, 1st hot air Balloon
Montgolfier, Joseph-Michel	1740-1810	Aero		160			Special Cont. ALS 63,000
Montgomery, Anthony		Ent	17			50	

NAME	DATES	CATEGORY	SIG	LS/DS	ALS	SP	COMMENTS
Montgomery, Bernard L., Sir	1887-1976	WWII	132	196	361	320	1887-1976. of Alamein. War-dte ASL/LS/DS 500-2500
Montgomery, Douglass		Ent	10	15	25	25	
Montgomery, Elizabeth	1933-1995	Ent	35	90		140	Actress; Star of TV's 'Bewitched'; Chk 60-135
Montgomery, George		Ent	10	15	25	40	Western Actor
Montgomery, James	1771-1854	Comp	25		195		Scot. Poet-Hymnwriter
Montgomery, James Shera		Clergy	50	65	75		Chaplin US Congress
Montgomery, M., Lady		Celeb	10	10	20		Mother of Bernard L. Montgomery
Montgomery, Melba		Cntry Mus	10			20	
Montgomery, Robert	1904-1981	Ent	15	30	60	73	Actor
Montgomery, Wes	1925-1968	Music	3040				Voted best jazz guitarist in 1968
Montgomery, William R.	1801-1871	Civ War	45	75	110		Union Gen.
Monti, Carlotta		Ent	15		75	50	W. C. Fields Paramour
Monti, Nicola		Opera	35			85	Opera
Montmorency, Anne H. von		Mil		525			16th C. Fr. Field Gen.
Montoya, Carlos		Music	30	15	25	85	Classical Guitarist
Monty, Harry		Ent				68	Flying Monkey in WOZ
Moody Blues (All 5)		Music	165			355	60's Rock Group; S Album 500; S Guitar 700
Moody, Dwight L.	1837-1899	Clergy	100	287	391	300	Evangelist, LS/Cont 500
Moody, William H.	1853-1917	Sup Crt	45	125	175	150	Sec. Navy, Atty Gen, MOC
Moody, William V.		Author	30	85	125		Poet, Plays
Moody, Young Marshall	1822-1866	Civ War	120				CSA Gen.
Moog, Bob		Sci	50	70	110	65	Inventor. Synthesizer
Moon, Keith		Music	225	315		477	Rock drummer; 'The Who'; Chk 900
Moon, Sun Myung		Clergy				350	Rev. Unification Church
Mooney, Art		Band	10			20	Big Band Leader
Mooney, Debra		Ent	13			40	
Mooney, Edward, Card.		Clergy	30	40	55	40	
Mooney, Tom	1883-1942	Labor	25	60	180	275	Bombed Parade. TLS/Cont 550; labor activist
Moonlighting		Ent				100	Cast SP
Moonwalkers		Space				12500	All 12 S on one Photo
Moore, Alfred	1755-1810	Sup Crt	3000				Rev. War Soldier, NC Planter, Pol. --RARE--
Moore, Andrew B.	1806-1873	Civ War	45	115	145		CSA Gov. AL. ALS '61 1485
Moore, Arch A. Jr.		Congr	10	15			Governor, MOC WV
Moore, Arthur J., Bish.		Clergy	20	25	40	40	
Moore, Barbara, Dr.		Celeb	10		20		Br. Marathon Walker
Moore, Clayton		Ent	30			102	Longtime 'The Lone Ranger'; SP w/Silverheels 750
Moore, Clement C.	1779-1863	Author	230	350	1845		Twas the Night Before. ' Am. Educator & Poet
Moore, Colleen	1900-1988	Ent	20		52	135	Silent Screen Major Star/Travelling Doll House
Moore, Constance	1920-2005	Ent	15	60		40	Actress-Singer
Moore, Dan K.		Gov	10				Governor NC
Moore, Demi	1962-	Ent	40	162		89	Actress
Moore, Dennis M		Congr	10				Member US Congress
Moore, Dick		Ent	10			25	Dickey Moore'. Child Actor
Moore, Douglas		Comp	20	185			Am. Comp.
Moore, Dudley	1935- 2002	Ent	25			74	Actor-Pianist. Light Comedy Parts
Moore, Edward C.		Clergy	10	20	30		
Moore, Foster		Comics	15			50	'Napoleon'
Moore, Francis D., Dr.		Sci	10	30	55	20	
Moore, Gary		Ent	15			35	TV Host-Comedian. Early TV
Moore, George	1852-1933	Author	45	115	125		Irish Novels
Moore, Grace	1901-1947	Opera	70	95	350	139	Met. Opera Star-Films. D. in Plane Crash. SPc 200
Moore, Henry	1898-1986	Artist	50	122	400	126	Br. Sculptor. 'The Thinker', S print 500
Moore, Ida	1882-1964	Ent	25			75	Char. actress 30s-50's
Moore, Jeremy, Sir	1923-2007	Mil	10	15	25	25	Br. Gen. Cmdr. Land Forces, 1982 Falklands War

NAME	DATES	CATEGORY	SIG	LS/DS	ALS	SP	COMMENTS
Moore, Joanna	1934-1997	Ent	15			45	Actress
Moore, John Bassett		Law	65		250		Intl. Law. Permanent Court Intl. Justice; Jurist.
Moore, John Creed	1824-1910	Civ War	100	188			CSA Gen.
Moore, John, Sir	1761-1809	Mil	60	225	350		Br. Gen. vs Am. 'til 1783. KIA 1809
Moore, Julianne		Ent	20			120	Actress
Moore, Mandy		Ent	15			50	Singer; actress
Moore, Marianne C.	1887-1972	Author	60	111		75	Am. Poet. Pulitzer
Moore, Mary Tyler		Ent	15	65		54	Actress,
Moore, Mary Tyler (cast)		Ent	135			388	Six Main Chars.
Moore, Michael		Celeb	15			45	Film industry, Dir. AA
Moore, Patrick Theodore	1821-1883	Civ War	110				CSA Gen.
Moore, Ray		Comics	25			175	'Phantom'
Moore, Richard Channing		Clergy			160		Episcopal Bishop 1814-41
Moore, Roger		Ent	18	160		68	Followed Connery as 'James Bond'. SP as 007 65
Moore, Roy D.		Bus	10	25		20	Fndr. Newspaper-Radio Chain
Moore, Samuel P.		Civ War	484	522	800		Surgeon Gen. CSA
Moore, Sara Jane		Crime	30	80	200		Attempted Assassination Pres. Ford
Moore, Shemar		Ent	13			40	
Moore, Sydenham	1817-1862	Civ War	40	55	90		MOC AL. CSA Off.
Moore, Terry		Ent	15	50		49	Actress
Moore, Thomas	1779-1852	Author	50	105	311		Irish Poet. 'Tis The Last Rose of Summer'
Moore, Thomas O.	1804-1876	Civ War	40	75	184		Civil War Gov. of Louisiana
Moore, Victor	1876-1962	Ent	25	45		60	Vaude. Headliner. Film Wimpy Comedian
Moore, William		Colonial	90	225			Colonial Am. Statseman-Jurist
Moorehead, Agnes	1900-1974	Ent	45	177		150	Fine Radio-Film Char. Actress. 'Bewitched'
Moorer, Thomas		Mil	20	45	70	40	Adm. Survivor-Twice
Moores, Dick		Comics	10			30	Gasoline Alley'; S sketch 75-115
Morales, Esai		Ent	18			55	
Morales, Ramon V.		HOS	15	35			Ecuador
Moran, Dolores	1924-1982	Ent				88	Actress
Moran, Erin		Ent		25		35	Actress. 'Happy Days' Cast
Moran, George 'Bugs'	1891-1957	Crime		2340			Chicago Prohibition-era gangster
Moran, James P. M		Congr	10				Member US Congress
Moran, Jerry M		Congr	10				Member US Congress
Moran, Lois	1909-1990	Ent	10			40	Actress
Moran, Peggy	1918-2002	Ent				62	Actress
Moran, Polly	1883-1952	Ent				85	Actress
Moran, Thomas	1837-1926	Artist	130	225	350		Specialized in Am. West
Moranis, Rick		Ent	10			42	
Moranville, H. Blake		WWII	15	25	40	35	ACE, WWII, Navy Ace; 6 kills
Mordecai, Alfred		Mil	15		95		West Point Instructor. Gen.
More, Thomas, Sir	1478-1535	Author	19750				English lawyer, author, & statesman
Moreau, Gustave	1826-1898	Artist	35		192		Important Teacher of Matisse, Rouault
Moreau, Jeanne	1928-	Ent	10			145	Actress
Moreau, Jean-Victor		Fr Rev	90	275	300		Fr. Gen. under Napoleon
Morehead, James B.		WWII	10	22	38	28	ACE, WWII, USAAF Ace; 8 kills
Morehead, James Turner		Congr	10				FF 31
Morehead, John M.		Gov	10	25			Governor NC
Morehouse, A. P.		Gov	10	20		25	Governor MO
Moreland, Mantan	1902-1973	Ent	100	125		180	Afr. Am. comic; actor
Morell, George W.	1815-1883	Civ War	40		80		Union Gen.
Morell, George W. (WD)		Civ War	45	95	300		Union Gen.
Morello, Tom		Music	10			25	Music. Guitar 'Rage Against the Machine'
Moreno, Antonio	1887-1967	Ent				98	Actor

NAME	DATES	CATEGORY	SIG	LS/DS	ALS	SP	COMMENTS
Moreno, Bertha		Opera	20			95	Opera
Moreno, Buddy		Band				45	
Moreno, Rita		Ent	10			42	AA. 'West Side Story' Script S 50
Moreno, Tony		Lawman	10			20	Most decorated mbrs of LAPD CRASH anti-gang elite
Moretz, Chloe		Ent	13			40	
Morgan, Barbara		Space	10	35			
Morgan, Charles Hale	1834-1875	Civ War	40	70	110		Union Gen.
Morgan, Charles L.	1894-1958	Author	25	70	80		Br. Novels, Dramatist, Critic
Morgan, Dennis		Ent	10		15	48	Actor-Singer
Morgan, Edwin Barber	1806-1881	Bus	40	75	160		NY, 1st Pres. Am. Express ALS 485-985
Morgan, Edwin Denison, Jr.	1811-1883	Civ War	40	72	98		Union Gen., CW Gov., NY. ALS '62 200, US Sen.
Morgan, F. Crossley		Clergy	10	15	15	15	
Morgan, Frank	1890-1949	Ent	357	632		795	Actor; SP as WOZ 9184
Morgan, G. Campbell		Clergy	20	30	45		
Morgan, George	1743-1810	Rev War	125	425	675		Indian Agent, Speculator
Morgan, George		Cntry Mus	15			35	
Morgan, George W.	1820-1893	Civ War	40	80	120		Union Gen, War Date ALS/Cont 1650
Morgan, Harry		Ent	15			60	Actor; Vintage SP 420
Morgan, Helen	1900-1941	Ent	43	175	85	131	1st Julie in 'Show Boat'. Noted Blues singer
Morgan, James Dada	1810-1896	Civ War	40	75	100		Union Gen.
Morgan, John Hunt	1825-1864	Civ War	1448	5462	8000		CSA Gen. War dte DS/cont 12, 500; S Chk 1655
Morgan, John Pierpont, Jr.	1867-1943	Bus	149	1247	1280	250	Banker; Financier
Morgan, John Pierpont, Sr.	1837-1913	Bus	351	1633	2500	1025	Banker, Financier, Philan. Legal DS 2400
Morgan, John Tyler	1825-1907	Civ War	61	198	293	350	CSA Gen., US Sen. AL. TLS/Cont 1250
Morgan, John Tyler (WD)		Civ War	190	650	1600		CSA Gen.
Morgan, Marion	1881-1971	Ent	15			30	Writer; 'Klondike Annie'
Morgan, Michele	1920-	Ent	10			40	Fr. Actress
Morgan, Ralph	1883-1956	Ent	35			65	
Morgan, Robert		WWII				108	Co-pilot Memphis Belle
Morgan, Russ		Band	20			65	Big Bandleader. Arranger
Morgan, Sydney, Lady		Author	15	35	60		Ir. Author. The Wild Irish Girl
Morgan, Thomas H.		Med	95	200	425	125	Nobel Med. 1933
Morgan, Thos. Jeff.	1839-1902	Civ War	40	55	75		Union Gen.
Morgan, Tracy		Ent	13			40	
Morgan, Wm. H.	1825-1878	Civ War	40	55	75		
Morganna		Ent	15			58	Baseball's 'Kissing Bandit'
Morgenthau, Henry Jr.	1891-1967	Cab	35	65	145	60	FDR Sec. Treasury
Mori, Yoshiro		Pol				35	PM of Japan
Moriarty, Cathy		Ent	10			45	Actress
Moriarty, Michael		Ent	10			35	Actor
Morini, Erica		Music	20			50	Austrian-born Violinist
Morison, Patricia	1915-	Ent	15	15	30	30	Actress
Morison, Samuel E.	1887-1976	Author	35	55	155		Am. Historian. Pulitzer Pr. Twice
Morissette, Alanis		Music	20			55	Rock; S Album 75
Morita, Pat	1932-2005	Ent	10		25	40	Actor; 'Karate Kid"
Morley, Christopher	1890-1957	Author	25	45	168	350	Am. Writer, Editor, Novels
Morley, Karen	1909-2003	Ent				110	Actress
Morley, Ken	1943-	Ent	10			25	Br. Actor
Morley, Margaret W.		Author	10			25	Education, Southern mountains
Morley, Robert	1908-1992	Ent	32	75		66	Noted Br. Actor
Morphis, Joseph L.	1831-1913	Congr	10				Repr. MS, US Marshal
Morrill, Justin Smith	1810-1898	Congr	45	60	110		Repr., US Senate VT 1855-98
Morrill, Lot M.		Cab	15	30	60		Sect'y Treas., Gov., Sen. ME
Morris, Anita	1943-1994	Ent	10			45	Actress

NAME	DATES	CATEGORY	SIG	LS/DS	ALS	SP	COMMENTS
Morris, B. Wistar		Clergy	10		20		
Morris, Cavalry		Congr	12		44		FF 44
Morris, Charles		Mil	20	60			Commodore USN
Morris, Chester	1901-1970	Ent	25	37		96	Silent Child Star to Adult '29 Oscar Nominee.
Morris, Clara	1848-1925	Ent	15			65	Vintage Actress
Morris, Edmund		Author				15	Pulitzer-prize winning author., Dutch
Morris, Edward Joy	1815-1881	Congr	10				Repr. PA, Min. Turkey
Morris, Eugene 'Mercury'		Celeb	10			20	Keynote Spkr. ex-NFL great
Morris, Felix J.		Ent	15			45	Vintage Stage Actor
Morris, Gouverneur	1752-1816	Rev War	183	450	1146		Continental Congr., Diplomat
Morris, Greg	1934-1996	Ent	15			35	Actor. 'Mission Impossible' Original TV Series
Morris, Harrison Smith		Pub	30	55			Magazine Editor
Morris, Howard	1919-2005	Ent	15			65	Comedian-Actor; SP w/Don Knotts 225
Morris, James		Opera	10			25	Opera
Morris, Kathryn		Ent	13			40	
Morris, Lewis	1726-1798	Rev War	675	965	1503		Signer Dec. of Indepen. DS/Fran. Lewis 3500
Morris, Lewis, Sir		Author	10		20		
Morris, Robert	1734-1806	Rev War	420	1185	1775		Signer. Important DS 13500-22,000. Financier
Morris, Robert & J. Nicholson		Rev War		1475			Cont. DS 45,000, Cont. DS 29, 500
Morris, Robert Page W.		Congr	10				MOC MN
Morris, Samuel Wells		Congr	15		52		FF 52
Morris, Thomas A. (WD)	1811-1904	Civ War			3520		Union Gen.
Morris, Wayne	1914-1959	Ent	25		45	125	Actor; B-Western star
Morris, William	1834-1896	Artist	125	275	675		Br. Poet, Artist, Designer, Printer, Social Reform
Morris, William Hopkins	1827-1900	Civ War	40	75	105		Union Gen.
Morris, William Walton	1801-1865	Civ War	36	70	80		Union Gen. ALS '62 160
Morrison, Ernest	1912-1989	Ent	50			93	'Sunshine Sammy' in the Little Rascals
Morrison, Harold		Cntry Mus	10				
Morrison, Henry Clay		Clergy	25	35	50	50	
Morrison, Herb		Aero	40	85	160	100	Announcer of Hindenburg Crash
Morrison, Jennifer		Ent	15			45	
Morrison, Jim	1943-1971	Music	744	7895	15000	3500	The Doors. S Chk 1285-2100; S Album 14400 only knn
Morrison, Robert	1782-1834	Clergy		125	240		English Divine. 1st Missionary to China
Morrison, Samuel E.		Author	12	20			Historian
Morrison, Shelley	1936-	Ent	10			25	Actress; 'Gen. Hospital'
Morrison, Toni		Author	35	45	70	50	Nobel Literature
Morrison, Van	1945-	Music	25	290		112	Singer; S Album 300; S Guitar 350
Morrison, William Ralls		Civ War	25		80		Union Off., MOC IL
Morrissey, John	1831-1878	Pol	367	465			NY State Sen/Rep. backed by Tammany Hall, Gangster
Morrissey, Neil	1962-	Ent	10			25	Br. Actor
Morrow, Buddy		Band	20			45	
Morrow, Dwight W.		Diplo	10	35			Lawyer, Banker, Amb. to Mex.
Morrow, Jeff	1907-1993	Ent	10			55	Actor
Morrow, Rob		Ent	15			35	Actor
Morrow, Vic	1932-1982	Ent	93	108		122	Actor
Morse, Carleton E.		Radio	20	25		30	One Man's Family Vint. Radio
Morse, David		Ent	10			35	Actor
Morse, Jedediah	1761-1826	Sci		75	125		Father of Am. Geography
Morse, Samuel F. B.	1791-1872	Sci	380	1181	2375	2853	Telegraph, Pioneer Photog, artist. ALS/Cont 11168
Morse, Wayne	1900-1974	Congr	10	25		55	Sen. OR
Mortensen, Viggio		Ent				112	Actor; 'Lord of the Rings'
Mortier, Edouard A. C. J.		Fr Rev	35	115	230		Marshal of Fr., Statesman
Mortimer, Charles		Bus	10			20	CEO Gen. Foods
Morton, J. Sterling		Cab	25	50	175	145	Father Arbor Day, Sec. Agri.

M

NAME	DATES	CATEGORY	SIG	LS/DS	ALS	SP	COMMENTS
Morton, James St Clair	1829-1864	Civ War	120	250			Union Gen., KIA Petersburg
Morton, Jelly Roll	1885-1941	Music	500	750			Blues-Jazz
Morton, John	1724-1777	Rev War	443	1175	1505		Signer Dec. of Indepen., Continental Congr.
Morton, Levi P.	1824-1920	VP	50	110	160	300	Gov. NY. VP. MOC, Min. to Fr.
Morton, Oliver P.		Congr	10				Governor, Sen. IN
Morton, Peter A.		Bus	10	15			Fndr. 'Hard Rock Cafe' Chain
Morton, Samantha		Ent	14			43	
Morton, Wm. Thos. Green		Sci	170	450	825		1st To Us Ether as Anesthetic
Mosby, John S.	1833-1916	Civ War	522	1864	2532	2500	CSA Off., 'Gray Ghost'. Cont. ALS 12, 500
Mosby, John S. (WD)		Civ War		8500	9600	7625	Gray Ghost, Mosby's Rangers
Moscona, Nicola		Opera	25			45	Opera
Moscone, George R.	d. 1978	Pol	80		95	65	Mayor of SF; Murdered in office
Mosel, Tad		Author	16	20	30	30	Am. Dramatist
Moseley, Corliss Champion	1894-	Aero	65	150			1st Pulitzer Aviation Speed Pr. Winner-1920. ETC
Moseley, George Van Horn		Mil	30	110			MacArthur's Dep. Chief of Staff
Moseley-Braun, Carol		Congr	10			20	Sen. IL
Moser, Edda		Opera	10			25	Opera
Moses, Anna (Grandma)		Artist	158	323	1575	548	1860-1961. ALS/Cont 1, 500, S repro 425
Moses, George H.		Congr	10	15	35		Sen. NH. Diplomat
Moses, Mark		Ent	17			50	
Moses, Robert	1888-1981	Pol	15	40	65		Dominated NY Pol. Father of Interstate Hwy Sys
Mosher, Terry		Comics	10		10		
Mosley, Oswald, Sir	1896-1980	Pol	30	75	210	140	Fndr. Br. Union of Fascists
Mosley, Zack		Comics	25			105	Smilin' Jack; sketch 120
Moss Kanter, Rosabeth		Author	10			15	Motivational books
Moss, Kate		Model	10			80	
Moss, Ralph W.		Congr	10	15	25		MOC IN 1909
Mossadegh, Muhammad		HOS	40	75	165		Premier Iran. Nationalized Oil
Mossbauer, Rudolf L.		Sci	25	55	90	45	Nobel Physics
Mossdorf, Martin		WWII				25	Ger. RK Winner. Stuka Pilot
Mostel, Zero	1915-1977	Ent	58	67		251	Stage, Film Comedy Star; 'Fiddler'
Moszkowski, Moritz	1854-1924	Comp	50		200		Ger. Pianist. AMusQS
Motherwell, Robert	1915-1991	Artist	60	190	325	150	Am. Abstract Expressionist. Pc Repro S175; SB 120
Motion, Andrew		Author			30	40	England's poet laureate
Motley Crue (4)		Music	45			201	Rock group; S Guitar 815
Motley, John Lothrop	1814-1877	Author	30	50	118		Am. Historian, Diplomat, Hall of Fame
Mott the Hoople		Music				85	Rock group; S Album 75
Mott, Charles S.		Bus	25				Pioneer Auto. Exec. A Fndr. Gen Motors
Mott, Frank L.		Jrnalist	10		35	20	Educator, Pulitzer
Mott, Gershom	1822-1884	Civ War	40	80	95		Union Gen.
Mott, Gershom (WD)		Civ War	65	150			Union Gen.
Mott, John R.		Clergy	30	45	75	285	Nobel Peace Pr.
Mott, Lucretia	1793-1880	Fem	105	200	300	368	Reformer, Abolitionist, Suffrage
Mott, Neville F. Dr.		Sci	20	35	50	25	Nobel Physics
Moulton, Louise Chandler	1835-1908	Author	25	70	125		Bed Time Stories
Moulton, Samuel W.	1821-1905	Congr	10				Repr. IL
Moulton, William		Rev War	40	145			
Moultrie, William	1730-1805	Rev War	246	617			Rev. War Gen. Fort Moultrie Namesake; Gov SC 1785-87, 1795-97; author.
Mount, Anson		Ent	17			50	
Mount, James A.		Gov	30	100			Gov. IN
Mountbatten, Edwina, Lady		Celeb	10	35			Wife of Louis Mountbatten
Mountbatten, Louis, Lord	1900-1979	WWII	96	155	215	260	Of Burma. Adm. of Fleet WWII. 1st Earl
Mountevens, Baron		Mil	20	45		335	(E Evans) Br. WWI Naval Hero

NAME	DATES	CATEGORY	SIG	LS/DS	ALS	SP	COMMENTS
Moured, David		Celeb	10	20			Computer Guru
Mouton, Alexander		Congr	12				FF 41
Mouton, Alfred		Civ War		3220			CSA Gen.
Mouton, Jean Jacq. Alf. Alex.	1829-1864	Civ War	140				CSA Gen.
Moutrie, Alexander		Rev War	50		200		
Mowbray, Alan	1896-1969	Ent	45			100	Br. Actor
Mowbray, H. Siddons		Artist	25	40	70		Murals. J. P. Morgan Library etc
Mower, Joseph A.		Civ War	40	90	115		Union Gen.
Mowry, Tamera	1978-	Ent	10			30	Actress
Mowry, Tia	1978-	Ent	10			30	Actress
Moyers, Bill		Jrnalist	10	15	45	20	
Moynihan, Daniel Patrick	d. 2003	Congr	10	20		45	Sen. NY
Mozart, Wolfgang A.	1756-1791	Comp	26000	35000	55000		
Mr. T		Ent	10			43	Actor
Mubarak, M. Hosni		HOS	75	110	275	125	Pres. Egypt
Mucha, Alphonse	1860-1939	Artist	175	245	481	470	Czech-Born Fr. Painter-Illust. Art Nouveau; Sketch 1285
Muck, Karl, Dr.		Cond	10			50	
Mudd, Roger	1928-	Ent	10			30	Radio-TV News
Mudd, Samuel Dr.		Civ War			3500		Attended J.W. Booth after Lincoln assassination
Mudder, Sophie		Music				85	Violinist
Mueller, Frederick H.	1893-1976	Pol	10	15	30		US Administrator; Sec. of Commerce
Mueller, Reuben H., Bish.		Clergy	20	25	35	25	
Muellerleile, Marianne		Ent	13			40	
Mueller-Stahl, Armin	1920-	Music	10			30	Violinist; Actor
Muench, Aloisius J., Card.		Clergy	35	50	65	50	
Mugabe, Robert G.		HOS	20	50	145	60	Zimbabwe dictator.
Muggeridge, Malcolm		Clergy	30	40	50	35	
Muhammed, Elijah	1897-1975	Clergy	210	237		425	Leader, 'Nation of Islam'; Chk 190-230
Muhlenberg, Frederick A.	1750-1801	Rev War	125	235	395		Member of Cont. Congress
Muhlenberg, John P. G.	1746-1807	Rev War	150	302	532		Gen. Cont. Army, ALS/Cont 2400
Muhlenberg, W. Augustus		Clergy	25	40	60		
Muir, Esther	1903-1995	Ent	15			68	Actress
Muir, Jean	1911-1996	Ent	15			70	Actress
Muir, John	1838-1914	Sci	226	725	1200	1000	Scot. -Am. Naturalist, Explr. S quote 1465
Mukai, Chiaki		Space	10	25		35	
Muldaur, Diana	1938-	Ent	10			30	Actress
Muldaur, Maria	1943-	Music	10			30	Biggest hit 'Midnight at the Oasis' in 1974.
Muldoon, Robert		HOS	10	20	30	20	Prime Min. New Zealand
Mulgrew, Kate		Ent	10		15	49	Actress; 'Star Trek'
Mulhare, Edward	1923-1997	Ent	15			130	Actor
Mulheen, R. J.		Bus	10			15	CEO Boston & Maine RR Corp.
Mull, Martin		Ent	10			30	Actor; comedian
Mullally, Megan		Ent	10			45	Will & Grace
Mullane, Richard M.		Space	10			25	
Muller, Herman J.		Sci	20	35	75	60	Nobel Med. 1946
Muller, Hermann	1876-1931	Statsmn	45		200		Ger. Foreign Min. Chancellor
Mullican, Moon		Cntry Mus	10			20	
Mulligan, Gerry	1927-1996	Music	25			120	Baritone Sax. Arranger-Comp.
Mulligan, James A.	1830-1864	Civ War	227	500	690		Union Col. KIA; Irish Brig. War Dte. LS 550-850
Mulligan, Richard		Ent	10			35	Actor
Mulligan, Robert	1925-	Ent	10			20	Film Dir.
Mulliken, Robert S., Dr.		Sci	38	118	65	60	Nobel Chemistry 1966
Mullin, Willard		Comics	10			30	Sports Cartoonist
Mullowney, Deborah	1959-	Ent	10			30	Actress

NAME	DATES	CATEGORY	SIG	LS/DS	ALS	SP	COMMENTS
Mulroney, Dermot		Ent	21			63	
Mumpower, Carl		Author	10			12	Vietnam & how-to books
Mumy, Bill	1954-	Ent	10			25	Child Actor
Munch, Charles		Cond	45		335		Ger. Conductor
Munch, Edvard	1863-1944	Artist	65	350	1118	775	Nor. Painter-Printmaker
Muncheberg, Joachim		WWII				290	Luftwaffe ace & Knights Cross recipient; KIA 1943
Mundel, Ed		Music	10			25	Music. Lead Guitar 'Monster Magnet'
Mundelein, Geo. Wm., Card.		Clergy	65	110	225	90	
Mundt, Karl E.	1900-1974	Congr	10	20		35	MOC, Sen. SD, Educator
Munford, Thomas T.	1831-1918	Civ War	110		220		CSA Gen. Sig/Rank 310
Muni, Paul	1895-1965	Ent	70	72	120	181	Academy Award 'Story of Louis Pasteur' 1936
Muniz, Frankie		Ent	17			50	
Munky		Music	10			25	Music. Guitar 'Korn'
Munro, Caroline		Ent	10			38	'Bond' girl; Actress
Munro, Janet		Ent	125			410	Br. Actress. Disney Charmer
Munro, Leslie K., Sir		Diplo	10	15		25	Pres. UN Assembly
Munro, Maj. -Gen. Archibald	1886-1961	WWII	225				WWII Br. Gen.
Munro, Peter Jay	1767-1833	Jurist	30	65	155		Nephew of John Jay.
Munsel, Patrice		Opera	10	20	50	50	Met. Debut at 18
Munsey, Frank A.		Editor	15		35		Muncey's Magazine
Munson, Ona	1903-1955	Ent	160			340	Became Classic as 'Belle Watling' in GWTW
Munster, Earl of		Mil	10	25	40		
Munsterberg, Hugo	1863-1916	Sci		70		95	Ger.-Born Am. Psychologist
Munsters The		Ent	240			725	Signed entire cast
Munteanu, Petre		Opera	35	110	165		Opera
Muntz, Earl 'Madman'		Bus	13	18	25	20	Pioneer TV Advertiser-Owner
Mura, Corinna	1909-1965	Ent				560	Actress; "La Marseillaise" in the film Casablanca
Murat, Joachim	1767-1815	Fr Rev	118	325	548		Napoleon Marshal, Gov. Paris, King Naples
Murchison, Clint		Bus	10	15	25	25	TX Oil Entrepreneur Millionaire
Murchison, Clint, Jr.		Bus	10	10	20	20	
Murciano, Enrique		Ent	13			40	
Murdoch, Rupert		Bus	10	35	55	30	Intl. Newspaper Publ.
Murkowski, Lisa		Congr	10				US Senate (R-AK)
Murphy Brown (cast)		Ent				192	Seven Main Chars.; S script 130
Murphy, Audie	1924-1971	Mil	252	410	325	516	Western Film Star & WWII MOH Winner
Murphy, Ben	1942-	Ent	10			30	Actor
Murphy, Brittany		Ent				64	Actress, Provocative SP 470
Murphy, Eddie		Ent	25			76	Actor; comedian
Murphy, Edward, Jr.	1836-1911	Congr	10				Sen. NY
Murphy, Erin		Ent	10			25	Actress. Tabitha
Murphy, Frank	1890-1949	Sup Crt	40	80	120	150	
Murphy, Franklin		Gov	10			10	Governor NJ
Murphy, George L.	1902-1992	Ent	20	25	35	49	US Sen. from CA., Film Song & Dance Man
Murphy, Heidi Grant		Opera				50	Met Sopr.
Murphy, John Cullen		Comics	10			45	Big Ben Bolt & Prince Valiant
Murphy, Richard		Author	15		25		Screenwriter
Murphy, Tim M		Congr	10				Member US Congress
Murphy, Turk		Band	20	40		50	Bandleader, Comp., Trombone
Murphy, William P., Dr.		Sci	30	75	120	80	Nobel Med. 1934
Murray Abraham, F.		Ent	10			45	Actor
Murray, Al		Celeb	10			15	Comedian. The Pub Landlord
Murray, Anne		Music	10	35		30	Singer
Murray, Arthur	1895-1991	Bus	10	15	30	60	Ballroom Dance Studios
Murray, Bill		Ent	60	75		63	Comedian, actor

N

NAME	DATES	CATEGORY	SIG	LS/DS	ALS	SP	COMMENTS
Murray, Bob		WWII	12	24	42	30	ACE, WWII; 10. 33 kills
Murray, Don	1929-	Ent	10			60	
Murray, Eli	1844-1896	Civ War	30	65			Union Gen., Gov. UT Territory
Murray, George, Bish.		Clergy	25	40	50		
Murray, James A. H.	1837-1915	Educ			225		Oxford English Dictionary
Murray, Jan	1916-2006	Ent	12			35	Actor; Comedian
Murray, Jim		Jrnalist	10			20	Sports Writer, L. A. Times
Murray, John C., S. J.		Clergy	10	15	35	20	
Murray, Joseph E., Dr.		Sci	20	30		25	Nobel Med.
Murray, Ken	1903-1988	Ent	15	20	25	50	Wisecracking-Cigar Smoking Comedian. Radio-TV-Film
Murray, Mae	1889-1965	Ent	40	40	90	190	Major Silent Star
Murray, Patty		Congr	10				US Senate (D-WA)
Murray, Philip		Labor	35	45	70	50	Pres. CIO, United Steel Workers
Murray, Stuart S.		Mil	25	75		45	
Murray, William Vans		Rev War	25	40	90		Diplomat, Lawyer, MOC MD
Murrow, Edward R.	1908-1965	Jrnalist	53	124		227	'See It Now' Live WWII Reports From London
Murtha, John P. M		Congr	10			20	Member US Congress
Musante, Tony	1936-	Ent	10			30	
Muscarello, Carl		WWII				98	Sailor kissed Edith Shain at Times Square VE day
Muscarello, Carl & Shain, Edith		WWII				348	Couple who kissed at Times Square VE Day 1945
Musgrave, Marilyn N. M		Congr	10				Member US Congress
Musgrave, Story, Dr.		Space	10			65	
Musharraf, Pervez		Pol	50			220	PM of Pakistan
Muskie, Edmund	1914-1996	Cab	10	25	40	40	Sec. State. VP Cand./Humphrcy. Prcs. Cand.
Mussolini, Benito	1883-1945	HOS	140	243	1684	697	Fascist Italian Dictator. DS/Emanuelle III 125
Mussolino, Arnaldo	1893-1960	Pol				110	Youngest brother of Benito
Muybridge, Eadweard		Photog	150		400		Br.-Am Pioneer Motion Pictures
Muzio, Claudia		Opera	200			525	It. Sopr.
Mya, Mya		Ent	15			45	
Myers, Carmel		Ent	10			50	Silent Screen Vamp
Myers, Dee Dee		Celeb	10			20	Pol. celebrity
Myers, Mike		Ent	15	25		48	Actor. 'Austin Powers'
Myers, Mike & Dana Carvey		Ent				58	Wayne's World
Myers, Russell		Comics	10		25	70	Broom Hilda
Myerson, Bess	1924-	Celeb	10	20		45	Miss Am. NYC Official
Myles, Sophia		Ent	15			45	
Myrick, Daniel		Ent				20	Writer w/E. Sanchez: 'The Blair Witch Project'
Myrick, Sue Wilkins M		Congr	10				Member US Congress
Myrt & Marge		Ent	20				Vintage Radio Series
Nabokov, Vladimir	1899-1977	Author	325	2665	1750	1250	Novels, Critic, Researched Butterflies. 'Lolita'
Nabors, Jim		Ent	15	20	30	55	Actor-Comedian-Singer. 'Gomer Pyle'
Nache, Maria Luise		Opera	20			45	Opera
Nadar (F. Tournachon)	1820-1910	Artist	85	175	423		Fr. Caricaturist, Photographer, Balloonist
Nader Khan, Muhammad	1880-1933	Royal	65			140	King Afghanistan, Assass.
Nader, George		Ent	15		45	65	Actor. Fine Performer. Victim of Studio Pol.
Nader, Ralph		Pol	70			182	Pol., activist
Nadler, Jerrold N		Congr	10				Member US Congress
Nagaoka, Guishi, Gen.	1858-1933	Mil	150			975	Father of Jap. Aviation
Nagel, Anne	1912-1966	Ent	25			50	Leading Lady 30s-40's
Nagel, Conrad		Ent	20	48	45	101	Stage-Film Leading Man to Char. Actor
Nagel, Steven R.		Space	10			25	
Nagle, James	1822-1866	Civ War	45	70	95		Union Gen.
Naglee, Henry M.	1815-1886	Civ War	38	80			Union Gen. War Dte. DS 375
Nagy, Imre	1896-1958	HOS	90	188			Communist Premier Hungary. Executed

NAME	DATES	CATEGORY	SIG	LS/DS	ALS	SP	COMMENTS
Nail, Jimmy	1954-	Ent	10			25	Br. Actor
Naish, J. Carrol	1896-1973	Ent	40			134	Familiar Char. Actor
Nakasone, Y.		HOS	25	35	85	35	Japan. FDC S 35
Naldi, Nita	1897-1961	Ent	40			231	Silent Movie Actress
Nansen, Fridtjof	1861-1930	Expl	125	230	375	450	Nor. Zoologist, Statesman, Arctic Explr., Nobel
Napavilova, Zofie		Opera	25			65	Opera
Napier, Alan	1903-1988	Ent	90			148	Sometimes Menacing Char. Actor; 'Batman'
Napier, Charles	1936-	Ent	10			25	
Napier, Chas. James, Sir		Mil	25	60	150		Br. Gen. vs US War 1812
Napier, Maj. -Gen. Charles S.	1899-1946	WWII	225				WWII Br. Gen.
Napier, McVey	1776-1847	Law	10	15	30		Editor 4-7th Encyclo. Britannica
Napier, Robert C., Sir	1810-1890	Mil	45	80	80		Field Marshal, Gov. Gen. India
Napier, Sir Wm. F. P.		Mil	20	40	70		Br. Gen.
Napoleon I	1769-1821	Royal	568	1353	4167		Imp. LS 7360, DS 6500-10350, Short ANS1897-5500
Napoleon II (Duke Reichstadt)	1811-1832	HOS	260	1400	1850		Francois-Charles-Jos. Bonaparte
Napoleon III Louis	1808-1873	Royal	100	245	525	120	Louis Napoleon, Nephew of Napoleon
Napoleon, Eugene L. J. J.	1856-1879	Mil			570	575	Son of Nap. III. KIA at 23
Napolitano, Grace F. N		Congr	10				Member US Congress
Napolitano, Janet	1957-	Gov	10			20	Governor AZ
Napravnik, Eduard.	1839-1916	Comp			400		Czeck-born conductor & Comp.
Nasby, Petroleum (D. Locke)		Author	50	75	160		Humorist
Nash, Charles W.		Indust		500			Am. Mfg. Nash Motors. Leading Independent Auto
Nash, Clarence		Comics	93		235		Donald Duck'; sketch 150
Nash, Graham		Music	20	45		75	Rock; CSN & Y; S lyrics 500
Nash, John Jr.		Celeb	20			145	'A Beautiful Mind'
Nash, Kevin		Ent	37			110	
Nash, Ogden	1902-1971	Author	42	102	108	75	Poet-Humorous, Unorthodox; AQS 215
Nash, Walter		HOS	15	40	85	20	Prime Min. New Zealand
Nasir-edun Shah Qajar		Royal	750		3500		King (Shah) Persia
Nasmyth, James	1808-1890	Invent	100		185		Machinist, Engineer. Inv. Steam Hammer
Nasser, Gamal Abdel	1918-1970	HOS	100	173	350	290	Pres. Egypt
Nast, Conde	1873-1942	Bus	10	60			Traveler's guides, magazine owner
Nast, Thomas	1840-1902	Comics	135	250	145	1442	Pol. Cartoonist. Sketch 575
Nat, Yves		Music					Legendary Pianist. AMusQS 65
Nathan, George Jean		Author	10	15	35	20	Powerful Drama Critic, Editor
Nathans, Daniel, Dr.		Sci	25	35	45	30	Nobel Med.
Nation, Carry	1846-1911	Reform	235	252	712	2300	Temperance Agitator.
Natividad, Kitten		Model				40	Model
Natta, Giulio		Sci	25	35	80		Nobel Chemistry 1963
Natwick, Grim		Comics			132		Creator of Betty Boop; Sketch 125
Natwick, Mildred	1905-1994	Ent	10			60	Actress
Naumann, Johannes		WWII				40	Ger. Ace
Nava, Gregory	1949-	Ent	10			20	Dir.
Navarro, Ramon	1899-1968	Ent	35		125	205	Latin Silent Star.
Navatril, Michel		Titanic	195				Survivor
Navon, Yitzhak		HOS	20			50	Israel
Nazimova, Alla	1879-1945	Ent	65			123	Russian Stage & Screen Star
Neagle, Anna, Dame	1904-1986	Ent	20	34		107	Beautiful Br. Leading Lady. Stage-Films-Musicals
Neal, Patricia	1926-	Ent	15	25		77	Academy Award
Neal, Richard E. N		Congr	10				Member US Congress
Neal, Tom	1914-1972	Ent	25			120	Actor
Neale, Robert Hawthorne		WWII	22			70	Flying Tiger Ace. WWII; 13 kills
Nealon, Kevin		Ent	15			45	
Nebel, Rudolf		Sci	40	125		85	

NAME	DATES	CATEGORY	SIG	LS/DS	ALS	SP	COMMENTS
Neblett, Carol		Opera	10			35	Opera. US Sopr.
Necker, Jacques	1732-1804	Fr Rev	125	245			Fr. Financier & Statesman
Needham, Hal		Ent	10			20	Film Dir. -Stuntman
Neel, Louis Eugene Felix		Sci	20	30	40	25	Nobel Physics
Neely, Thomas B., Bish.		Clergy	15	25	35		
Neeson, Liam		Ent	32			65	Actor. AA
Neff, Francine I.		Cab	10	10	25	10	
Neff, Hildegarde		Ent	20			40	Ger. 40s-50's Leading Lady & Author
Neff, Pat Morris		Gov	10	15		15	Governor TX, Pres. of Baylor U.
Negley, James S.	1826-1901	Civ War	60	65	95		Union Gen., MOC. War Dte. ALS 105
Negri, Pola	1894-1987	Ent	50	118		101	Ger. Import to Am. Silent Films
Neher, Fred		Comics	18			73	
Nehring, Walter	1892-1983	WWII	40	75		65	Ger. Gen. WWII
Nehru, B. K.		Diplo	10	15		20	Ambassador
Nehru, Jawaharlal	1889-1964	HOS	90	468	600	247	Assass. 1st Prime Min. India
Neidlinger, George		Invent			500		Singer sewing machine
Neidlinger, Gustav		Opera	15			40	Opera
Neil, Stephen, Bish.		Clergy	10	15	35	20	
Neil, Vince	1961-	Music	20			50	Lead Singer, Motley Crue
Neill, James	1847-1920	Ent	15			65	Vintage Stage Actor
Neill, Noel		Ent	15			40	Actress 'Lois Lane'-Superman
Neill, Sam		Ent	15			85	Aussie Leading Man
Neill, Thomas Hewson	1826-1885	Civ War	40	70	110		Union Gen.
Neilson, Adelaide	1850 1880	Ent	40				Vintage English Actress
Neiman, LeRoy		Artist	45	110	160	135	Signed poster 250
Neitzel, Tyler Max	1991-	Ent				35	Actor
Nell, Stephen, Bish.		Clergy	10	15	35		
Nelligan, Kate	1950-	Ent	10			30	Actress
Nelly		Music	20			50	Rap
Nelly, Nelly		Ent	17			50	
Nelson, Allison	1822-1862	Civ War	352				CSA Gen.
Nelson, Ben		Congr	10				US Senate (D-NE)
Nelson, Bill		Congr	10				US Senate (D-FL)
Nelson, Craig T.		Ent	10			40	Actor
Nelson, David		Ent	15			45	Early Family Sitcom. 'Ozzie & Harriett'
Nelson, Ed	1928-	Ent	10			30	Actor
Nelson, Gaylord		Congr	10	25	40		Gov., Sen. WI
Nelson, Gene	1920-1996	Ent	15			48	Dancer-Actor. Films & Stage
Nelson, George D.		Space	10			25	
Nelson, Harriet Hilliard	1909-1994	Ent	25			58	Band Singer-Actress. 'Ozzie & Harriet'
Nelson, Horatio, Lord	1758-1805	Mil	3108	4869	8017		Br. Adm. Trafalgar Hero.
Nelson, John		Cab	20	50	95		Tyler Atty Gen.
Nelson, John C.		Author	10			12	WWII, naval
Nelson, Judd		Ent	10			40	Actor
Nelson, Knute	1843-1923	Congr	10	15		10	Sen. MN
Nelson, Lori	1933-	Ent	10			60	Actress
Nelson, Ozzie	1906-1975	Ent	35	50		85	Big Band Leader, Actor
Nelson, Ozzie & Harriet		Ent		250		234	Contract S By Both
Nelson, Richard H.		WWII	25			50	Enola Gay radio operator
Nelson, Rick		Ent	158	240	410	300	Teen TV, Rock Idol. S Album 350
Nelson, Samuel A.	1792-1873	Sup Crt	50	175	572		Appointed by Tyler
Nelson, Thomas Jr.	1738-1789	Rev War	2500	17550			Signer D of I
Nelson, Tracy		Ent	10			25	Actress-Daughter of Ricky Nelson
Nelson, William 'Bull'	1824-1862	Civ War	368		1380		Union Gen.

NAME	DATES	CATEGORY	SIG	LS/DS	ALS	SP	COMMENTS
Nelson, William L.		Congr	10	15			MOC MO
Nelson, Willie		Cntry Mus	25			125	Singer-Comp. Alb. S 100; S suitar 300
Nelson, Wm. Rockhill	1841-1915	Author	10				Journalist
Nemerov, Howard		Author	10		35	25	3rd Poet Laureate US, Teacher
Németh, Maria		Opera	20			60	Opera
Nero, Peter	1934-	Cond	10			50	Jazz Pianist
Neruda, Pablo	1904-1973	Author	435	1100	1188	625	Latin Am. Poet-Nobel Pr. Winner
Nesbit, Evelyn	1884-1967	Ent	50			525	Girl in the Red Velvet Swing
Nesbit, Wilbur		Author		20	30		
Nesbitt, Cathleen	1888-1982	Ent	15			35	Actress
Neshling, John		Cond				50	Brazilian
Nesmith, Michael		Music	20			50	Rock, Monkees; songwriter
Ness, Eliot		Lawman	345	1220			Chk 1500
Nesselrode, Carl von		HOS	75		462		Rus. Count von . Foreign Min., Chancellor
Netanyahu, Benjamin		Pol	25			60	Israel PM
Nethercutt Jr., George R. N		Congr	10				Member US Congress
Nethersole, Olga		Ent	15	40		45	Vintage Stage Actress
Netrebko, Anna		Opera				90	Russian Sopr.
Nettles, John	1943-	Ent	10			25	Br. Actor
Nettleton, Lois	1927-2008	Ent	10			30	Actress
Neubert, Frank		Aero	25	75			Scored 1st Air Victory 9/1/39
Neumann, Dorothy	1914-1994	Ent				55	Actress
Neumann, Eduard		WWII				45	Ger. ace w/13 kills
Neumann, Theresa	1898-1962	Relig	65	175	395	250	Ger. Stigmatic
Neurath, Konstantin von	1873-1956	Diplo	75	80	150	150	Ger. Imprisoned For War Crimes
Nevelson, Louise	1900-1988	Artist	50	85	155	200	Russ-Am. Sculptor. Large Abstract Wood Pieces
Neville, Aaron	1941-	Music	15			35	Singer Neville Brothers
Nevin, Ethelbert	1862-1901	Comp	75	140	320	250	Short Piano Pieces & Songs
Nevins, Allan		Author	12	30			Am. Historian, Editor, Professor
New Kids on the Block		Music	50			90	S Album 80
New, Harry S.	1858-1937	Cab	15	30	50	20	PMG 1923. US Senn, IN
Newberry, Truman H.		Cab	15	20	35		Sec. Navy 1908
Newcomb, Simon	1835-1909	Sci	65	195	228		Am. Astronomer, Mathematician
Newcome, Jack		Author	10			12	Sports history
Newell, Frederick B., Bish.		Clergy	20	25	50	30	
Newell, Richard		Bus	10	20			Am. Entrepreneur
Newhart Show		Ent				350	Entire cast S
Newhart, Bob		Ent	15	20	25	50	Comedian. 3 Successful TV Series
Newhouse, Samuel		Bus	15	25	60	25	Newspaper-Radio-TV Empire
Newley, Anthony	1931-1999	Comp	25			52	Talented Comp. -Actor-Singer
Newman, Barry	1938-	Ent	10			30	Actor
Newman, Edwin		Celeb	10			20	News Broadcaster
Newman, James		Space	10			20	
Newman, John Henry, Card.	1801-1890	Clergy	112	275	572	388	Leader Oxford Movement. ALS/Cont 1600-1800
Newman, Laraine		Ent	10			30	Comedianne, SNL
Newman, Nanette	1934-	Ent	10			25	Br. Actress
Newman, Paul	1925-2008	Ent	202	305		568	Actor/Philan. Real Sigs. RARE. SP w/Woodward 200
Newman, Phyllis	1933-	Ent	10			25	Actress
Newman, Randy		Music	10	65		90	AA songwriter; S Guitar 190
Newmar, Julie		Ent	15	10	45	56	Actress; 'Batman'
Newsom, Tommy	1929-2007	Band	10			25	Bandleader
Newton, Becky		Ent	15			45	
Newton, Helmut		Photog	235			167	Photographer
Newton, Huey P.		Activist	100			667	Activist

NAME	DATES	CATEGORY	SIG	LS/DS	ALS	SP	COMMENTS
Newton, Isaac, Sir	1642-1727	Sci	5008	10425	12520		LS/cont 16500
Newton, John	1822-1895	Civ War	40	85	140		Union Gen., War Date ALS 325
Newton, Juice		Music	10			25	Singer
Newton, Robert	1905-1956	Ent	50	65	95	109	Br. actor
Newton, Robert		Clergy	35	45	45	45	
Newton, Thandie	1972-	Ent				40	Actress
Newton, Wayne		Music	15	145		51	Singer
Newton-John, Olivia		Ent	20	118		107	Singer-Actress
Ney, Michel, Duc d'	1769-1815	Fr Mil	125	310	718		Marshal of France
Ney, Richard	1916-2004	Ent	15			35	Actor
Ney, Robert W. N		Congr	10				Member US Congress
Ngo Dinn Diem	1901-1963	HOS	100				Pres. South Vietnam
Ngor, Haing S., Dr.	d. 1996	Ent	60	60	50	112	Actor; AA winner
Nianick, Jack	1924-	WWII	10	10	15	30	WWII P-51 Flight instructor
Niarchos, Stavro		Bus	45	110	190	75	Gr. Millionaire Shipping Magnate
Niblack, Albert P.		Mil	50		145		Am. WWI Adm.
Nichol, Phil		Ent	10			20	Actor
Nicholas I	1796-1855	Royal	175	589			Emperor of Russia (Iron Czar)
Nicholas I	1841-1921	Royal	50	110	225		King of Montenegro
Nicholas II	1868-1918	Royal		1816	5698	8850	Last Czar of Russia. Executed
Nicholas, Denise	1944-	Ent	10			25	Actress
Nicholas, Grand Duke of Rus.	1856-1929	Royal				1200	Grandson of Czar Nicholas I
Nicholas, Harold & Fayard		Ent	50				Tap Dncrs. Book 'Brotherhood in Rhythm' 100+ films
Nicholas, Thomas Ian	1980-	Ent	10			25	Actor
Nicholls, Francis R. T.	1834-1912	Civ War	110	160	240		CSA Gen., Gov LA
Nichols, (John) Beverley	1893-1983	Author		125	175		
Nichols, Barbara	1929-1976	Ent	45			80	Actress
Nichols, Ebenezer B.		Bus	35	195			Major Early TX Entrepreneur. Banker
Nichols, John Anthony		Congr	10		15		MOC NC
Nichols, Mike	1931-	Ent	52	75		85	Film Dir.
Nichols, Nichelle	1932-	Ent	15			45	Actress. 'Star Trek'
Nichols, Rachel		Ent	13			40	
Nichols, Red		Music	35			60	Jazz Instrumentalist
Nichols, Ruth Roland	1901-1960	Aero	125	180			Holder of Flying Records
Nichols, William A.	1818-1869	Civ War	40	80			Gen.
Nicholson, Dana Wheeler	1960-	Ent	10			30	Actress
Nicholson, Jack		Ent	53	100		186	Actor; Academy Award Winner
Nicholson, John	1783-1846	Mil	30	75	190		Commodore US Navy
Nicholson, Julianne		Ent	13			40	
Nicholson, Meredith	1866-1947	Author	20	80	125	60	
Nickerson, Francis Stillman	1826-1917	Civ War	40	75	115		Union Gen.
Nickles, Don		Congr	10				US Senate (R-OK)
Nicks, Stevie		Music	30			147	Fleetwood Mac; S Album 260
Nicol, Alex	1916-2001	Ent	10			35	Actor; Dir.
Nicola, Nassira		Ent	10			25	Actress
Nicolai, Elena		Opera	30			85	Opera
Nicolai, Otto		Comp		85			Ger. Comp. of Te Deum & Merry Wives of Windsor
Nicolay, John G.	1832-1901	Civ War	52	143	325		Lincoln Personal Sec. Author
Nicolayev, Andrei		Space				60	
Nicollet, Joseph N.		Expl	105	225	345		1st Exped. Headwaters Miss.
Nicollier, Claude		Space	10			30	
Nicolson, Harold Sir		Diplo		100			English diplomat, writer, biographer, critic
Niebuhr, H. Richard	1892-1971	Clergy	35	60	95	95	
Niebuhr, Reinhold		Clergy	58	257	135	135	Am. Major Theologian

NAME	DATES	CATEGORY	SIG	LS/DS	ALS	SP	COMMENTS
Nielsen, Alice	1876-1943	Opera	35			150	Opera-Operetta
Nielsen, Asta		Opera	20			54	Opera
Nielsen, Brigitte		Ent	12			54	Actress; Model
Nielsen, Carl	1865-1931	Comp	180	450	686		Danish Comp., Conductor
Nielson, Leslie		Ent	10	50		40	Actor
Nielson, Carl		Comp			875		Danish Comp.
Niemack, Horst		WWII	40		125		Ger. WWII Major Gen.
Niemoller, Martin	1892-1984	Clergy	72	246	410	410	In Concentration Camp WWII
Niesen, Gertrude		Ent	10			30	
Nietzel, Tyler		Ent	13			40	
Nietzsche, Friedrich	1844-1900	Author	750	3500	6882		Ger. Poet, Philosopher, Philology
Nigh, William	1881-1955	Ent	10			35	Actor-Dir.
Nightingale, Florence	1820-1910	Sci	510	937	1703		Br. Nurse, Hospital Reformer, Humanitarian
Nighy, Bill		Ent	22			65	
Nijinsky, Vaslav	1890-1950	Ballet	1358			7025	Ballet
Nikisch, Artur		Cond	25	65	85	375	Hung. Conductor. AMusQS 100
Nikolayev, Andryan G.		Space	48			65	Russian Cosmonaut
Niles, Jack	1892-1980	Music	350				Comp. singer
Nillson, Christine	1843-1921	Opera	60		125		Swedish Opera Singer
Nilsson, Anna Q.	1888-1974	Ent	15	20		106	Actress
Nilsson, Birgit	1918-19??	Opera	15			50	Swe. Sopr., Opera
Nilsson, Christine	1843-1921	Opera				450	Swedish operatic Sopr.
Nilsson, Harry	1941-1994	Ent	65	285			Singer; Comp.
Ni'matullah, Hajji		Author	4200		7200		Mystic Scholar. Clergy
Nimersheim, Jack		Author	10		20	20	Campbell Award nominee
Nimitz, Chester W.	1885-1966	WWII	115	242	379	371	Fleet Adm. WWII., SP Surrender USS MO 1500-2300
Nimoy, Leonard		Ent	35	122	75	119	Star Trek'. SP w/Shatner 250-400
Nin, Anais	1903-1977	Author	45	125	250	150	Fr. Born Am. Author. Cont. ALS 395
Nine Inch Nails		Music				60	Rock group; S Album 50
Nirenberg, Marshall W.		Sci	15	25	45	20	Nobel Med. 1968
Nirvana (3)		Music	510	1210		942	Rock
Nisbit, Eugenius Aristides		Congr	20	80	150		MOC GA 1839
Nissen, Greta	1906-1988	Ent	10			35	Actress
Nissen, Hans Hermann		Opera	25			80	Opera
Niven, David	1909-1983	Ent	45	114	130	171	Br. Actor; AA
Nivernais, Louis M., Duc de		Mil			725		Fr. Soldier-Diplomat
Nixon, Cynthia		Ent				42	Miranda Hobbes, Sex in the City
Nixon, John	1733-1808	Rev War	125	320			Proclaimed Dec. Ind. 1st Time
Nixon, Marion	1904-1983	Ent	15			60	Actress
Nixon, Marni		Ent	10			20	Sang for Audrey Hepburn, Susan Hayward
Nixon, Patricia	1912-1992	1st Lady	44	93	232	125	S WH Card 75-130
Nixon, Richard & Pat		Pres	246	400		345	Xmas Card S by both 400; WH card S by both 275
Nixon, Richard M.	1913-1994	Pres	178	366	1653	280	TLS/cont 1500-2500
Nixon, Richard M. (as Pres.)		Pres	220	736	28680	418	TLS/Cont 2000-7475. DS/Cont 4900, Spec. SP 1035; Mock S Resig. 750
Nizer, Louis		Law	25	40	65	50	Noted Trial Attorney; SB 120
Nkomo, Joshua		HOS	55	125	275	85	Afr. Nationalist, Zimbabwe
No Doubt		Music				74	Rock group; S Album 130; S Guitar 750
Nobel, Alfred	1833-1896	Sci	250	750	2415	1000	ALS/Cont 3500
Nobile, Umberto	1885-1978	Aero	52	276	335	168	It. Aeronautical Arctic Pioneer Engineer
Noble, Chelsea	1964-	Ent				48	Actress
Noble, Edward J.	1881-	Bus	95		395		Candy Mfg. Popularized 'Lifesavers'
Noble, Emma		Model	10			20	
Noble, James		Ent	10		15	15	

NAME	DATES	CATEGORY	SIG	LS/DS	ALS	SP	COMMENTS
Noble, John W.	1831-1912	Civ War	35	50	75	150	Union Gen. CW. Sec. Interior
Noble, Ray		Band	25			50	Br.
Noble, Robert	1861-1939	Mil	20		50	35	Gen. Campaigns from Geronimo to WWI
Noboa, Gustavo		Pol				25	Pres. of Ecuador
Noel, Baptist W.	1798-1873	Clergy	20	35	38		Br. Evangelical Min.
Noel-Baker, Philip	1889-1982	Statsmn	30	40	75	75	Nobel Peace Pr.
Noguchi, Isamu		Artist	25		65		Am. Sculptor, Designer
Noguchi, Thomas T.		Celeb	10	30		18	Coroner, Los Angeles
Nolan, Jeanette		Ent	10			48	
Nolan, Kathleen	1933-	Ent	10			30	Actress
Nolan, Lloyd	1902-1985	Ent	10	35		68	Actor. Fine Versatile Film Actor
Nolan, Mae E.		Congr	10	18			Repr. CA 1923
Nolde, Emil		Artist		550			Ger. painter
Nolin, Gena Lee	1971-	Ent	20			45	Actress. 'Baywatch'
Nolte, Nick		Ent	10	25		40	
Nomura, Kichisaburo		Diplo	275				Jap. Ambassador 12/7/41
Nono, Luigi	1924-1990	Comp	115				Opera. Conductor
Noodles		Music	10			25	Music. Guitar 'Offspring'
Noonan, Fred J.	1893-1937	Aero		368			Guam-San Francisco Flight Cvr. S 995
Noonan, Peggy		WH Staff	10	20			Reagan Speech Writer
Noone, Peter		Music	20			45	Herman's Hermits
Noor, Queen		HOS	25	40	125	140	Queen of Hussein (Jordan); SP w/ Hussein 320
Norblad, Albin W.		Congr	15	30		20	Repr. OR. Intelligence Off'r WWII
Norblin, Emile		Music	85			350	Celebrated Cellist
Nordau, Simon Max	1849-1923	Sci	65	95	175	150	Hung. Phys. -Writer, AManS 1750, ALS/cont 1208
Nordenskjold, Nils Adolf E.		Expl	200				Navigated North-East Passage
Nordenskjold, Nils Otto		Expl	215				Led Antarctic Exped'n, Rescued
Nordhoff, Charles		Author	20	35	37		Collaborator of Mutiny on the Bounty
Nordhoff, Heinz, Dr.		Bus	25			50	Auto Mfg. -VW
Nordica, Lillian	1859-1914	Opera	60			350	Am. Sopr.
Nordsieck, Kenneth		Space	10			20	
Norgay, Tenzing		Celeb	68	277	255	556	Sherpa Guide. Mt. Everest
Noriega, Carlos		Space	10			20	
Noriega, Manuel A.		HOS	60	75	120	77	Gen., Notorious Pres. Panama
Norman, Jessye	1945-	Opera	20			45	Opera. US Sopr.
Norman, Lucille	1921-1998	Ent	10			40	Film Actress from 1942
Normand, Mabel		Ent	135			606	Silent Screen Comedienne. Talented-Popular
Norris, Chuck		Ent	10			45	
Norris, Frank	1870-1902	Author	125	275	525		Novels, War Correspondent
Norris, George W.		Congr	15	30		40	MOC, Sen. NE. Fathered TVA
Norris, J. Frank Dr.		Clergy	10	15	25	10	Fundamentalist Baptist Pastor
Norris, Kathleen		Author	20	40	65	25	Prolific Am. Novels
Norris, Roy		Crime		80			Serial killer
Norstad, Lauris	1907-1988	WWII	40	60		75	US Gen. WWII
North, Brownlow		Clergy	15	25	40		
North, Frederick, Lord	1732-1792	HOS	102	420	595		Br. PM During Am. Rev., 2nd Earl Guilford
North, Jay		Ent	10			42	Child actor, 'Dennis the Menace'
North, John Jr.		Author	10			12	Gangland history
North, John Ringling		Bus	40	82	135	85	Ringling Brothers Circus
North, Luther		Celeb	28	83	225		Nebraska pioneer
North, Nolan		Ent	12			35	
North, Oliver L.		Mil	20	40	75	56	Iran-Contra Affair
North, Sheree	1932-2005	Ent	15			58	Actress
North, William	1755-1836	Mil	75	185	488		Gen. Cont. Army. US Sen. NY

NAME	DATES	CATEGORY	SIG	LS/DS	ALS	SP	COMMENTS
Northam, Jeremy	1961-	Ent	10			20	Br. Actor
Northrop, John K.	1895-1981	Indust	45	125	275	110	Engineer-Designer. Fndr. Northrop Aircraft etc
Northrop, Lucius Bellinger	1811-1894	Civ War	175	278			CSA Gen.
Northrop, Patricia		Ent				60	Actress
Northrup, John H.	1893-1987	Sci	45	150		100	Nobel Chemistry 1946
Northup, Anne M. N		Congr	10				Member US Congress
Norton, Daniel Sheldon		Congr	10	10	25		Sen. MN 1865
Norton, Edward		Ent	10			55	Actor.
Norton, Eleanor Holmes N		Congr	10				Member US Congress
Norton, Gerald		Mil	20			45	Brit. WWII Hero. Victoria Cross
Norton, Ken		Ent	18			55	
Norton, Mary Teresa		Congr	10	25		15	MOC NJ 1925-51
Norton-Taylor, Judy	1958-	Ent	10			25	Actress
Norville, Deborah	1958-	Jrnalist	10			20	TV News Anchor
Norvo, Red		Band	15			40	Bandleader, Vibes, Xylophone
Norwood, Charlie N		Congr	10				Member US Congress
Norworth, Jack	1879-1956	Comp	130	380	372	295	'Take Me Out to the Ball Game'
Noseworthy, Jack	1958-	Ent	10			25	Actor
Noth, Chris		Ent	10			40	Mr. Big, Sex in the City
Notkin, Boris		Celeb	10			15	Russian TV host
Nott, Eliphalet	1773-1866	Invent	20	80			Pres. Union College 62 Years, Invented 1st anthracite coal base-burner stove
Nouira, Hedi		HOS	10		15		Tunisia
Nouri, Michael	1945-	Ent	10			35	Actor
Nourse, Amos, Dr.		Congr	35	50			Sen. ME 1/16-3/3/1857
Nourse, Carl C.		Bus	10	20			Noted Ohio Businessman
Nourse, Joseph	1754-1841	Mil	100	260			DS/Cont 2000
Novaes, Guiomar		Music	30			155	Great Classical Pianist of 20th C.
Novak, Kim		Ent	20	30	80	172	Actress
Novak, Michael		Clergy	15	20	35		
Novak, Robert		Jrnalist	10				Pol. celebrity
Novak, Vitezslav		Comp	40			150	Czech. Comp.
Novarro, Ramon	1899-1968	Ent	55		195	140	Mexican Silent Movie Star. Murdered 1968
Novatna, Jarmila		Opera	15	45		35	Czech. Sopr.
Novello, Ivor		Ent	25		80	72	Br. Actor, Comp., Film Star
Novoselic, Krist		Music	10			38	Music. Bass Guitar, Vocals. 'Nirvana'
Novotna, Jarmilia	1907-1994	Opera				55	Czech Sopr.
Nowak, Max		Sci	15			45	Rocket Pioneer/von Braun
Noyce, Philip	1950-	Ent	10			25	Dir.
Noyes, Alfred	1880-1958	Author	25	60	75	40	Br. Poet, Poetic Plays, Stories; AQS 115
Noyes, Edward F.		Gov	10	20		15	Governor OH
N'Sync (5)		Music	55	95		155	Rock Group (5); Album S 125
Nucci, Danny	1968-	Ent	10			30	Actor
Nugent, Elliott	1896-1980	Ent	10			40	Dir. Actor
Nugent, Ted		Music	12	100	35	95	Guitarist 'Amboy Dukes'; S Guitar 425
Nugent, Thomas	1700?-1772	Author			120		
Nunes, Devin N		Congr	10				Member US Congress
Nungesser, Charles	1892-1927	Aero	135	233	548	300	France's third leading WWI ace w/45 victories
Nunn, Sam		Congr	15			40	Sen. GA
Nureyev, Rudolf	1938-1993	Ent	80	112	192	240	Kirov Ballet Dancer-Choreographer
Nurmella, Kari		Opera	15			35	Opera
Nussle, Jim N		Congr	10				Member US Congress
Nutt, Clifford C.	1896-	Mil	55	150			USA Gen. -Command Pilot. Decorated; Mackay Trophy
Nutter, Mayf	1941-	Ent	10			30	Actor

NAME	DATES	CATEGORY	SIG	LS/DS	ALS	SP	COMMENTS
Nuyen, France		Ent	10			43	Actress. Interesting, Short-lived Career
Nye, Bill (Edgar Wilson)		Author	18		85		Humorist
Nye, Gerald P.		Congr	10			15	Sen. ND
Nye, James W.	1815-1876	Congr	75	140	175		Gov. Nevada Terr. 1861. Sen. NE '64
Nyerere, Julius		HOS	30	50	85	150	Prime Min., Pres. Tanzania.
Nygaard, Jeff		Ent	13			40	
Nykvist, Sven	1922-2006	Ent	10			30	Cinematographer; AA
O' Hurley, John		Ent	10			35	Actor; Mr. Peterman on 'Seinfeld'
O' Meara, Barry		Med			120		Ir. physician in Br. Navy. Attended Napoleon
Oak Ridge Boys, The (4)		Cntry Mus	35			75	Country Western singing group
Oakes, Randi	1951-	Ent	10			48	Actress
Oakie, Jack		Ent	20	95		87	
Oakley, Annie	1860-1926	West	1860	4811	7463	4639	Am. Markswoman/Buffalo Bill, S chk 3795-6158
Oakley, Violet	1874-1961	Artist	35	95			Am. Golden Age Muralist,
Oasis		Music	50			130	Rock group; S Guitar 350-665; S Album 120
Oates, Joyce Carol		Author	18	30	60	60	Am. Novels, Critic, Poet, Teacher
Oates, Lawrence E. G.	1880-1912	Expl	100		575		Antarctic Explr.
Oates, Warren	1928-1982	Ent	25			120	Actor
Oates, William C.	1833-1910	Civ War		397			Col. CSA, Little Round Top
Obama, Barack		Pol	50	95	150	200	Sen. IL; 2008 Pres. Cand. SB 200
Obasanjo, Olusegun		Pol				50	Pres. of Nigeria
Ober, W. O. 'Willy'		Aero	25		55		
Oberhardt, William		Artist	30	65	135		Pres. Portraits
Oberon, Merle	1911-1979	Ent	50			195	Actress
Oberstar, James L. O		Congr	10				Member US Congress
Oberth, Hermann, Dr.	1894-1989	Sci	68	225	60	154	Hung. Early Rocket Pioneer. TLS/Cont 4250
Obey, David R. O		Congr	10				Member US Congress
Oboler, Arch		Ent	12		35	25	Writer-Prod. of Radio Dramas
Obratszova, Elena		Opera	10			50	Opera. Glamourous Rus. Mezzo
O'Brien- Moore, Erin	1902-1997	Ent				75	Actress
O'Brien, Conan		Ent	15			40	Late Night TV Host
O'Brien, Cubby		Ent	15			30	Mickey Mouse Club
O'Brien, Edmond		Ent	20	40		65	AA
O'Brien, Frederick		Author	10			12	South Seas true adventure
O'Brien, George	1899-1985	Ent	20			105	Actor
O'Brien, Hugh		Ent	10			65	Actor; TV Wyatt Earp
O'Brien, James		Bus	10	10	35		
O'Brien, John F. (WD)		Civ War				1015	CSA Major
O'Brien, Lawrence F.	1917-1990	Cab	10	20	40	40	JFK Adviser-Strategist. P. M. Gen.
O'Brien, Margaret	1937-	Ent	15	35		75	Actress
O'Brien, Pat	1899-1963	Ent	45	65		118	Actor. Knute Rockne
O'Brien, Virginia	1919-2001	Ent	10			40	Singer-Actress
Obukhova, Nadezhda	1886-1961	Opera	75		400		Opera. Greatest Russ. Contralto of C.
O'Callaghan, Mike		Gov	10			10	Governor NV
Ocasek, Ric		Music	25			55	Rock; 'Cars'
O'Casey, Sean	1880-1964	Author	112	197	407	470	Ir. Plays. Abbey Theatre. 'Plough & the Stars'
Ochles, Wubbo		Space	10	25		25	
Ochoa, Ellen		Space	15			30	
Ochoa, Severo, Dr.		Sci	22	35	85	30	Nobel Physiology & Med.
Ochs, Adolph S.	1858-1935	Bus	75	110		125	Publisher-Fndr. NY Times
Ochsner, Albert John	1858-1925	Med	15			35	Am. physician & surgeon
O'Connell, Arthur	1908-1981	Ent	30			75	Actor
O'Connell, Charles		Bus	10	15	30	15	
O'Connell, Daniel	1775-1847	Statsmn	75	250	720		Irish Nationalist Leader

NAME	DATES	CATEGORY	SIG	LS/DS	ALS	SP	COMMENTS
O'Connell, Helen		Ent	15			45	
O'Connell, Jerry		Ent	10			38	Actor. 'Scream'
O'Connell, William H., Card.		Clergy	50	65	75	65	
O'Conner, Flannery		Author	300	4500			Am. Author. D. At Age 39
O'Connor, Basil		Law	15	25		45	1st Pres. March of Dimes; FDR Law Partner
O'Connor, Bryan D.		Space	10			20	
O'Connor, Carroll		Ent	15	45		75	Archie Bunker', actor
O'Connor, Donald	1925-2003	Ent	20			72	Singer-Dancer-Actor. 'Singin' in the Rain'
O'Connor, Glynnis	1956-	Ent	10			25	Actress
O'Connor, Sandra Day		Sup Crt	35	70	110	60	GHW Bush Appointee
O'Connor, Thos. P.	1848-1929	Author	65	194	170		Irish Journalist & Nationalist. (Tay Pay) AManS 325
O'Connor, Una		Ent	40			148	Char. Actress
O'Conor, Charles	1804-1884	Pol	60	75	175		1st Catholic Pres. Cand.
O'Conor, Herbert R.		Gov	10				Gov. MD
O'Daniel, W. Lee 'Pappy'		Congr	15	50		45	Governor, Sen. TX
O'Day, Anita		Band	20			40	Big Band-Jazz Vocalist
Oddie, Bill		Celeb	10			15	Naturalist
Odell, Benjamin Baker, Jr.		Congr	10	30	40		MOC 1895, Governor NY 1900
O'Dell, Doye	1912-2001	Cntry Mus	10			30	C & W Singer-Actor
Odell, George C. D.		Author	10	15	30		Educator, Theatre Arts
Odell, Moses F.	1818-1866	Congr	10	20	30		Rep. NY 1861
Odets, Clifford	1906-1963	Author	50	84	124	210	Plays. Golden Boy.
O'Diear, James		Author	10			12	WWII Novels/historian
O'Donald, Emmett		Aero	15	30	50	35	
O'Donnell, Chris		Ent	10			45	Actor
O'Donnell, Chris & Val Kilmer		Ent				125	'Batman'
O'Donnell, Rosie		Ent	10			40	Comedienne
O'Driscoll, Martha	1922-1989	Ent	20			65	Actress; 40s Film Leading Lady
Oe, Kenzburo	1935-	Author	90				Jap. Writer. One of Rarest Living Nobel Winners
Oersted, Hans Christian	1777-1851	Sci	2500	4750			Discovered Electromagnatism
Oesau, Walter 'Gullé		Aero	130		415	275	
Offenbach, Jacques	1819-1880	Comp	530	610	637	500	Fr. Comp. Many Operettas. ALS/Cont 1, 400
Offenhauser, Fred		Engr	130	395			Automobile, Racing Engine Mfg.
Offspring		Music	28			75	Music. 4 Member Rock Group
O'Flaherty, Liam		Author	90	254			Ir. Novels. The Informer
Ogden, Aaron		Congr	35	110	225		Am. Rev. War Soldier, Gov. NJ
Ogden, Francis B.	1783-1857	Mil	25	68	95		Inventor. Steam Eng. Pioneer
Ogden, Thomas L.	1773-1844	Law	25		45		Law Partner Alex. Hamilton
Ogden, William B.		Pol	150	950	925		1st Mayor of Chicago 1837.
Ogle, Samuel	d. 1751	Colonial	180	550			Colonial Gov. MD
Oglesby, Richard J.	1824-1899	Civ War	33	78	105	150	Union Gen., Gov. IL, US Sen. IL
Oglethorpe, James Edward	1696-1785	Colonial		5500	6325		One of the Rarest of Colonial Autographs
O'Grady, Gail	1963-	Ent	10			40	Actress
Oh, Soon-Teck	1943-	Ent	10			30	Actor
O'Hair, Madalyn Murray	1919-1995	Celeb	40	275	160		Atheist, Activist, Mysteriously Disappeared '55
O'Hanlon, Ardal	1965-	Ent	10			20	Irish Actor
O'Hanlon, George	1912-1989	Ent	15			45	Actor-Comedian
O'Hara, Catherine	1954-	Ent	10			40	Actress; 'Best in Show'
O'Hara, Geoffrey	1882-1967	Comp	20	45			AMusQS 65
O'Hara, John		Author	160	500	660		Am. Novels, Short Stories
O'Hara, John F., Card.		Clergy	50	85	100	75	
O'Hara, Mary (Alsop)		Author	20	50	75		Am. Novels. My Friend Flicka
O'Hara, Maureen	1920-	Ent	20			108	Irish-Am. Actress.
O'Hare, Edward "Butch"		WWII	350	1350			WW Naval II Ace, KIA Nov. 1943

NAME	DATES	CATEGORY	SIG	LS/DS	ALS	SP	COMMENTS
O'Herlihy, Dan	1919-2005	Ent	10			35	Actor
O'Higgins, Bernardo	1778-1842	HOS	450	1250			Chile. Soldier, Statesmn, Dictator
O'Higgins, Harvey		Author	10	20	75	15	Am. Journalist, Novels
Ohms, Elizabeth		Opera	35			150	Opera
Oi, Narimoto		Mil	40	125	195		
Oistrakh, David	1908-1974	Music			275	150	Soviet Violinist, Conductor
Oka, Masi		Ent	16			47	
O'Keefe, Dennis	1908-1968	Ent	10			55	
O'Keefe, Georgia	1887-1986	Artist	320	375	1230	596	Scenes S. W. Desert. TLS/Cont 3500
O'Keefe, Jodi		Ent	13			40	
O'Keefe, Jodi Lyn	1978-	Celeb				30	Actress
O'Keefe, Kathleen Marie		Celeb	10			21	Historian
Oland, Warner	1880-1938	Ent	150			208	Most Famous Charlie Chan
Olav V	1903-1991	Royal	45	125			King of Norway
Olbermann, Keith		Ent	10			25	News Anchor CNBC
Olcott, Chauncey	1860-1932	Comp	44	90	150	150	My Wild Irish Rose Noted Tenor
Oldenburg, Claes Thure	1929-	Artist	40	90	120	75	Swe. Sculptor. Soft Scuptures. Pc Repro S 125
Older, Charles H.		WWII	12	30	45	32	ACE, WWII, Flying Tigers; 8. 5 kills
Older, Charles S.		Civ War	25	40	55		CW Gov. NJ
Oldman, Gary		Ent	10			40	Talented, Versatile Actor. 'Dracula'
Olds, Ransom E.	1864-1950	Bus	238	950			REO & Oldsmobile Motor Cars. Stock Cert. S 240
Olds, Robin		WWII	15	30	45	50	ACE, WWII, Korea, Viet Nam; 13 kills
O'Leary, Brian		Space	10			20	
Oleynik, Larisa	1981-	Ent	10			25	Actress
Olin, John M.		Bus	10	12	20	20	Olin Industries
Olin, Ken		Ent	10			30	Actor
Olin, Lena	1955-	Ent	20			45	
Oliphant, Laurence		Author	10	25	60		Br. Writer. Cape Town, S. A.
Oliphant, Pat		Comics	10			30	
Olitzka, Rosa		Ent	35			125	Pol./Ger. Mezzo
Oliver, Andrew		Rev War	65	185	240		Am. Colonial Pol.
Oliver, Edna May		Ent	45			187	
Oliver, George	1873-1961	Author		70			
Oliver, Gordon		Ent				40	Am. Actor
Oliver, Henry W., Jr.	1840-1904	Bus	45	60			Iron & Steel Tycoon
Oliver, Jane		Ent	10			25	Actress
Oliver, John Morrison	1828-1872	Civ War	45	65	110		Union Gen.
Oliver, Paul A.	1830-1912	Civ War	25	50	75		Credit For Inventing Dynamite
Oliver, Sy		Music	30			75	Trumpet, Comp., Arranger
Olivero, Magda	1912-	Opera	20			88	Opera; Italian Sopr.
Olivetti, Adriano		Indust		200		150	Owner Olivetti Typewriter & Business Machines
Olivier, Laurence, Sir	1907-1989	Ent	50	94	175	201	Special DS 2,000. AA. FDC S 95
Olmos, Edward James		Ent	10	20	15	35	Actor
Olmstead, Frederick Law	1822-1903	Archtct	102	175	412		Landscape Arch, NY Central Park. US Capitol
Olney, Richard	1835-1917	Cab	15	25	45	75	Atty Gen., Sec. State
Olney, Thomas		Clergy	85	125	250		
O'Loughlin Gerald S.		Ent	10			20	Actor
Olsen & Johnson		Ent	35			75	Hellzapoppin'. 30s Comedy Team
Olsen, Ashley		Ent	10			35	Actress 'Full House'
Olsen, George		Band	25				Big Band leader
Olsen, Mary Kate		Ent	10			35	Actress 'Full House'
Olsen, Mary Kate & Ashley		Ent	15			60	Twin Sister Stars of 'Full House'
Olsen, Merlin		Ent	10			25	Actor; ex-football player
Olsen, Ole		Ent	25			115	

NAME	DATES	CATEGORY	SIG	LS/DS	ALS	SP	COMMENTS
Olson, Nancy	1928-	Ent	10			40	Actress
Olver, John W.		Congr	10				Member US Congress
Olyphant, Timothy		Ent	18			55	
O'Mahoney, Joseph	1884-1962	Congr	10	20			Sen. WY
O'Malley, J. Pat	1904-1985	Ent	25			50	Actor
Onassis, Aristotle		Bus	175	575		482	Grk. Shipping Magnate
Ondricek, Frantisek		Comp				950	Czech Violinist & Comp.
O'Neal, Alexander		Music	10			15	Performing musical artist
O'Neal, Edward Asbury	1818-1890	Civ War	95				CSA Gen.
O'Neal, Frederick	1905-1992	Ent	15			40	Actor
O'Neal, Ralph A.		Mil	22	40	85	70	
O'Neal, Ryan		Ent	10			35	
O'Neal, Tatum		Ent	15			50	AA
O'Neil, Barbara	1909-1980	Ent	250			595	Scarlett O'Hara's Mother in GWTW
O'Neil, Chris		Ent	13			40	
O'Neill, Charles	1821-1893	Congr	10		40		Rep. PA 1863
O'Neill, Eugene	1888-1953	Author	135	403	706	1400	Plays. Nobel & 3 Pulitzers; SB 400
O'Neill, Henry	1891-1964	Ent	15			75	Major Vint. Char. Actor
O'Neill, James	1863-1938	Ent	20	25	45	125	Vintage Actor
O'Neill, Jennifer		Ent	10			40	
ONeill, Rose	1874-1944	Celeb			800		Creator of the Kewpie Doll
O'Neill, Thomas 'Tip'	1912-1994	Congr	20	35		48	Spkr. of the House. MA MOC
Onizuka, Ellison S.	1946-1986	Space	125			189	Challenger
Ono, Yoko		Ent	40	745	100	91	Artist. John Lennon's widow. DS w/Lennon $5900; SP w/Lennon $3000
Ontkean, Michael	1946-	Ent	10			35	Canadian Actor
Opatoshu, David	1918-1996	Ent	20	35		35	Actor
Opdycke, Emerson	1830-1884	Civ War	45	70	100		Union Gen.
Opdyke, George	1805-1880	Civ War	20	45			CW Mayor of NY. Chk S '62 900
Opp, Julie		Opera	12			25	Opera
Oppenheimer, J. Robert, Dr.	1904-1967	Sci	574	985	4500	1322	Dir. Manhattan Proj. Father, Atom Bomb; SB 1060
Opper, Frederick Burr	1857-1937	Comics	25		100	75	Happy Hooligan, S drwg 750
Orbach, Jerry	1935-2004	Ent	20			65	Actor
Orbison, Roy	1936-1988	Cntry Mus	194	200		237	Blind Singer-Pianist; S Album 300
Orczy, Emmuska, Baroness	1865-1947	Author	40	125	160	150	Br. Novels, Plays. 'Scarlet Pimpernel'
Ord, Edward O. C.	1818-1883	Civ War	41	145	375	375	Union Gen-Indian Fighter
Ord, Edward O. C. (WD)	1818-1883	Civ War		750			Union Major Gen.
Ordzhonikidze, Grigory	1886-1937	Pol		242			Russian Communist leader
Orenstein, Leo		Comp				100	Russ. -US Pianist-Comp.
Orff, Carl	1895-1982	Comp	50	200		139	Ger. Opera. 'Carmina Burana'
Orfila, Matthieu		Sci			65		Fndr. of Toxicology
Orgonotzova, Ludmilla		Opera	10			25	Opera
Orient, John H., Bish.		Clergy	10	10	15		
Orita, Zenji		WWII	50	160	255	100	Leading Jap. submarine captain
Orlando, Vittorio E.	1860-1952	HOS	65	135	275		It. Prime Min., Pres. One of Big Four
Orman, Suzie		Bus	15	25		30	
Ormandy, Eugene		Cond	40	65	100	108	Hung. -Am. Conductor Philadelphia Symph. Orch.
Orme, William Ward	1832-1866	Civ War	45	70	120		Union Gen.
Ormond, Julia	1965-	Ent	25			60	Br. Actress
Orne, Azor	1731-1796	Rev War	100	450			Maj. Gen. Am. Forces
Ornish, Dean		Celeb	10			18	Med. expert, author
Ornstein, Leo		Comp		375			Comp., pianist
O'Rorke, Patrick Henry	1837-1863	Civ War			1236		Union, KIA Little Round Top 1863
Orpen, William, Sir	1878-1931	Artist	45	120	390	390	Portrait, Genre, War Painter

Sanders Autograph Price Guide

O

NAME	DATES	CATEGORY	SIG	LS/DS	ALS	SP	COMMENTS
Orr, Marjorie		Celeb	10			15	Astrologer
Orr, Robert L.		Civ War	45	110			MOH Major 61st Pennsylvania Inf.
Orr, William T.		Ent	25				Film Dir. -Prod.
Orth, Godlove Stein	1817-1882	Congr	20		45		MOC IN. CW Off. Min. to Austr-Hung; FF 31
Ortiz, Ana		Ent	14			42	
Ortiz, Solomon P. O		Congr	10				Member US Congress
Ortiz, Tito		Ent	15			45	
Orton, Arthur	1834-1898	Crime			180		The Roger Charles Tichborne Claimant
Orvis, Charles F.		Bus		322	633		Fndr. Orvis
Orwell, George	1903-1950	Author		1538			Pen-name of Eric Blair. Rare if S Pen-name
Ory, Edward Kid		Band	100			200	Dixieland Bandleader
Osborn, Super Dave		Ent	12			20	Comic Daredevil; Albert Brooks's brother
Osborn, Thomas Ogden	1832-1904	Civ War	50	70	125		Union Gen.
Osborne, Baby Marie	1911-	Ent	10			40	Actress
Osborne, Henry Z.		Congr	10	20		15	MOC CA 1917
Osborne, Joan		Music	10			20	Singer
Osborne, John	1929-1994	Author	10	20	65	60	Br. Plays, Screenwriter
Osborne, Sidney P.		Gov	10	15		10	Governor AZ
Osborne, Thomas A.		Gov	10	15		10	Governor KS
Osborne, Tom O		Congr	10				Member US Congress
Osborne, Will	1906-1981	Band	20			35	1st Crooner. Bandleader 1924 to Late 50s
Osbourne, Jack		Ent	10			25	Osbourne's
Osbourne, Kelly		Ent	10			25	Osbourne's
Osbourne, Ozzy		Music	25	35		75	
Osbourne, Sharon		Ent	10			30	Osbourne's
Oscar I	1799-1859	Royal	100	280	550		King Sweden & Norway
Oscar II	1829-1907	Royal	50	190	300		King Sweden & Norway
Ose, Doug O		Congr	10				Member US Congress
Osgood, Charles		Ent	10			20	TV News, Host
Osgood, Samuel		Rev War	125	385	535		Cont'l Congress, 1st P. M. Gen.
O'Shea, Danny		Ent				40	Appeared in Mack Sennett comedies.
O'Shea, Michael	1906-1973	Ent	10	35		40	Actor-Films from 30s. Career Ended as Detective
Osler, William, Dr.	1849-1919	Med	252	1092	1820		Can. Phys., Important Med. Historian
Oslin, K. T.		Music	10			45	Singer
Osmena, Sergio		HOS	65	200			Pres. Philippines 1944-46
Osment, Haley Joel		Ent	10			40	
Osmond Brothers (3)		Ent	115			174	
Osmond, Donny		Ent	10		15	35	
Osmond, Ken		Ent	10			35	Actor; Eddie Haskell on 'Leave it to Beaver'
Osmond, Marie		Ent	10			35	
Osten, Hans Georg von der		Aero				60	Ger. Ace WWI/Richthofen
Ostenso, Martha		Author	25	45	70		Am. Novels, Poet
Osterhaus, Peter J.	1823-1917	Civ War	45	79	116		Union Gen.
Osterkamp, Theo		Aero	35	60	130	70	
Osterman, Kathryn	1883-1956	Ent	20			50	Silent Films
Ostermann, Max		WWII				325	Luftwaffe ace w/102 kills; KIA 1942
Osterwald, Bibi		Ent				85	Actress
O'Sullivan, Gilbert	1946-	Music	25	75			Irish singer-songwriter; unsigned lyrics 575
O'Sullivan, Maureen	1911-1998	Ent	15	25	35	75	Ir. Actress. Jane to 'Tarzan'. Mia Farrow's Mother
Osvoth, Julia		Opera	20			45	Opera
Oswald, Lee Harvey	1939-1963	Assass	2081	8250	13257		Assassin of John F. Kennedy
Oswald, Marguerite		Celeb			690		Mother to Lee Harvey Oswald
Oswald, Marina (Porter)		Celeb	183	168	180	150	Mrs. Lee Harvey Oswald
Oswald, Mark		Opera	10				Opera

NAME	DATES	CATEGORY	SIG	LS/DS	ALS	SP	COMMENTS
Oswald, Steve		Space	10			20	
Oteri, Cheri		Ent	13			40	
Otis, Carre		Model	10			40	Nude SP 160
Otis, Elita Proctor	1851-1927	Ent	15			85	Silent Films
Otis, Elwell S.		Civ War	45	66	65		Union Gen.
Otis, Harrison Gray	1837-1917	Bus	75	125	250		Gen., Publisher. L. A. Times
Otis, Harrison Gray	1765-1848	Congr	25	68	75		Repr. 1797, Sen. MA 1817 MA
Otis, James	1725-1783	Rev War	180	436	750		Statesman, Eloquent Lawyer
Otis, Johnny		Ent	25	130		50	R & R Prod., Dir. HOF
Otis, Samuel A.	1740-1814	Rev War	242	340	2990		Continental Congr.
O'Toole, Annette	1952-	Ent	10			90	Actress
O'Toole, Peter		Ent	15			80	Actor. AA winner
Otter, C. L. "Butch" O		Congr	10				Member US Congress
Otto I (Otho I)	1815-1867	Royal	105	248	375		King of Greece
Oudinot, Charles N. Duc de		Napol	70	162			Marshal of Napoleon
Ouida (Marie Louise de la Ramee)	1839-1905	Author	25	60	118		Br. Novels. 'A Dog of Flanders'
Ould, Robert	1820-1882	Civ War	60	142	168		CSA Col. POW Exch. ALS '65 690
Ouspenskaya, Maria	1876-1949	Ent	226	295		449	Wolf Man's mother
Outcault, Richard		Comics	75			450	Yellow Kid, Buster Brown
Outlaw, Edward C.		WWII	12	25	40	32	ACE, WWII, Ace in a Day; 6 kills
Over There, Over		Ent	32			95	
Overall, Park	1957-	Ent	10			30	Actress
Overman, Lynn	1887-1943	Ent	15			60	30's-40's Film Char. Actor
Overmyer, Robert	1936-1996	Space	15			65	2nd Space Shuttle Flight
Ovington, Earle	1879-1936	Aero	45	105	100	245	Pilot 1st Air Mail Plane
Owanneco, Chief	1645-1710	Am Ind		50000			Last of the Mohicans
Owen, Clive		Ent	18			53	
Owen, David, Sir		Econ	10	25	40	15	Intl. Planned Parenthood
Owen, John		Clergy	10	10	15	20	
Owen, Joshua T.	1821-1887	Civ War	40				Union Gen.
Owen, Joshua T. (WD)		Civ War	70		225		Union Gen.
Owen, Reginald	1887-1972	Ent	75			95	Actor; 'Mary Poppins'
Owen, Richard, Sir	1804-1892	Sci	95	130	175		Anatomist, Zoologist. Inventor of Name 'Dinosaur'
Owen, Robert	1771-1858	Pol		149	250		Br. Utopian Socialist
Owen, Robert Dale	1801-1877	Congr	20		98		Scottish Born. Repr. IN. Reformer, clergy; FF 43
Owen, Ruth Bryan (Rohde)		Diplo	20	30		30	1st US Woman Diplomat-MOC FL
Owens, Buck		WWII	12	28	45	45	ACE, WWII, Marine; 7 kills
Owens, Buck	1929-2006	Cntry Mus	20			65	CW Singer
Owens, Charlie		Artist					LA Times. Art work S 950
Owens, Major R. O		Congr	10				Member US Congress
Owens, Tex		Cntry Mus	10			20	Wrote 'Cattle Call'
Oxenberg, Catherine		Ent	15			40	
Oxley, Michael G. O		Congr	10				Member US Congress
Oxnam, G. Bromley, Bish.		Clergy	35	50	95	45	
Oxnam, Robert		Author	10			15	
Oy, Jenna von		Ent	10			65	Actress
Oz, Frank		Ent	10	20		95	Yoda'; Muppets; SP/ w Henson 225
Ozawa, Seiji		Cond				65	Jap.
Paar, Jack	1918-2004	Ent	15	25	35	70	Original late night TV host
Pabst, Fred		Bus	125	233		322	Pabst Brewing Co.
Pabst, Gustav	1866-1943	Bus		300			Am. brewer, son of Frederick
Paca, William	1740-1799	Rev War	750	977	2455		Signer. LS (WD)2750
Pacca, Bartolomeo, Card.		Clergy	45	300			Sec. of State to Pope Pius VII
Pace, Lee		Ent	15			45	

NAME	DATES	CATEGORY	SIG	LS/DS	ALS	SP	COMMENTS
Pacetti, Iva		Opera	25			108	Opera
Pache, Jean Nicholas		Fr Rev	20	65	145		
Pacheco, Asis		Opera				150	Brasilian tenor
Pacino, Al		Ent	30	865		211	Actor
Pack, Denis, Sir		Mil	25	80	125		
Packard Dave & Bill Hewlett		Bus				152	
Packard, David		Bus	20	45	90	75	Co-Fndr. Hewlett-Packard. SP w/Hewlett 150
Packard, James Ward	1863-1928	Bus		5800			Fndr. of Packard Automobile
Packard, Kelly		Ent				50	Actress
Packard, Vance		Author	10	20	45	15	Am. Nonfiction Writer
Packer, Mason R.		Celeb			950		Gold Rush speculator
Packham, Chris		Author	10			15	Naturalist
Packwood, Bob		Congr	10	25		35	Sen. OR
Pacula, Joanna	1957-	Ent	10	10		60	Actress
Padalecki, Jared		Ent	17			50	
Paderewski, Ignace J.	1860-1941	Comp	152	310	450	514	Pianist, AMusQS $350-850. Briefly headed Poland
Padgett, Lemuel P.		Congr	10	15		20	MOC TN 1901-22
Paduca, Duke of		Cntry Mus	20			40	
Paer, Ferdinando		Comp	40	110	250		Italian Opera Buffo
Paganini, Nicolo	1782-1840	Comp	4075		4339		Revolutionized Violin Technique. Violin Virtuoso
Page, Anita	1910-	Ent	20			212	Actress
Page, Bettie	1923-	Model	20			420	The 'Gibson Girl' Model; Common in nude SP's
Page, Carroll S.		Congr	10	25		20	Governor 1890, Sen. VT 1908
Page, Diamond		Ent	15			45	
Page, Ellen		Ent	18			55	
Page, Geraldine		Ent	30			93	AA actress
Page, Jimmy		Music	25			100	Music. 'Led Zeppelin' lead guitarist
Page, Joanna	1978-	Ent	10			30	Actress
Page, John	1743-1808	Rev War		380			Patriot, Activist, Gov. VA
Page, Kimberly		Ent	13			40	
Page, Patti	1927-	Music	15	40		55	Singer
Page, Richard Lucian	1807-1901	Civ War	100	190	542		CSA Gen. Sig/Rank 150
Page, Thomas Nelson	1853-1922	Author	15	35	150		Am. Novels, Diplomat, Lawyer
Page, William	1811-1885	Artist	150		410		Am. Portr. Painter. ALS/Cont 1150
Page, William Tyler		Congr	20				
Paget, Charles, Sir	1778-1839	Mil	25				Brit. Adm. Napoleonic Wars
Paget, Debra		Ent	10			80	Actress
Paget, James, Sir	1814-1899	Med	50	75	200		English Physician. Pathology. Paget's Disease
Pagliughi, Lina		Opera	35			140	Opera
Pahlavi, Mohammed Riza	1919-1980	HOS	150	412	310	342	SP Shah of Iran & Farah Diba Pahlavi 475
Paige, Janis	1922-	Ent	15		15	75	Actress. Warner Bros. Musicals & Light Comedy
Paige, Mabel	1880-1954	Ent	15			75	Vintage Radio Comedienne-Actress
Paine, Charles Jackson	1833-1916	Civ War	60	95	130		Union Gen.
Paine, Eleazar Arthur	1815-1882	Civ War	40	75	110		Union Gen.
Paine, Halbert Eleazer	1826-1905	Civ War	35	75	120	400	Union Gen. & lawyer
Paine, John Knowles		Comp	15	40	50		Paine Hall at Harvard
Paine, Robert Treat	1731-1814	Rev War	240	454	912		Signer Dec. of Indepen., Cont. Congr.
Paine, Thomas	1737-1809	Rev War	6500	12500	22500		Am. Philosopher-Author
Paine, William A.		Bus		875			Fndr. Paine-Webber Brokerage House
Pakula, Alan J.	1928-1998	Ent	10	10		25	Prod. -Dir.
Pal, George	1908-1980	Ent	50			125	Prod. -Dir. Special Effects Expert. Puppets
Palacio, Ernesto		Opera	10			30	Opera
Palade, George E., Dr.		Sci	20	35		25	Nobel Med. 1974
Palance, Jack	1919-2006	Ent	20	35		127	AA Actor

NAME	DATES	CATEGORY	SIG	LS/DS	ALS	SP	COMMENTS
Palet, Jose		Opera				220	Opera. Fonotipia Tenor
Paley, Petronia		Ent	10			25	Actress; 'Annie Hall'; 'The Guiding Light'
Paley, William S.		Bus	20	30	70	30	Founded CBS in 1928
Palfrey, Francis Winthrop		Civ War	40		75		Union Gen.
Palfrey, John G.	1796-1881	Abolit	32	50	68		
Palillo, Ron		Ent				35	Actor; Arnold Horshack on ' Welcome Back Kotter'
Palin, Michael	1943-	Ent	15			45	Comedian. Monty Python. 'Full Circle' Book S. 65
Palin, Sarah		Pol	25	35	50	100	Gov. AL; Repub. an VP Cand. 2008
Pall, Gloria (Voluptua)		Ent	15	40		100	Actress
Pallette, Eugene		Ent	55			186	Rotund, Gravel Voiced Char. actor
Pallone Jr., Frank P		Congr	10				Member US Congress
Palma, Tomas Estrada	1835-1908	HOS	75	153	250		1st Pres. Cuba
Palme, Olaf	1927-1986	HOS	45	410	145	135	Premier Sweden. Assass. '86
Palmer, A. Mitchell		Cab	10	25	40	30	MOC PA. Atty Gen.
Palmer, Alice Freeman	1855-1902	Educ	20	35	50		Pres. Wellesley. Member HOF
Palmer, Betsy	1926-	Ent	10			25	Actress. Stage-Films. Active Early TV Panelist
Palmer, Geoffrey	1927-	Ent	10			35	Br. Actor
Palmer, Gregg		Ent	10			40	Actor. Supporting Roles, 2nd Leads Since Early 50s
Palmer, Innis N.	1824-1900	Civ War	55	65			Union Gen. Led Only Cavalry at Bull Run
Palmer, Jimmy		Band	15			40	Bandleader
Palmer, John McCauley	1817-1900	Civ War	55	110	176		Union Gen. & Pol. Figure. US Sen. -Gov. IL
Palmer, Joseph Benjamin	1825-1890	Civ War	110	977			CSA Gen.
Palmer, Lilli	1912-1986	Ent	20	35		88	Ger. Actress. Charming, Elegant Leading Lady
Palmer, Patsy	1972-	Ent	10			20	Br. Actress
Palmer, Potter		Bus	275	975	1650	475	Palmer House Hotel, Chicago. Stock S 1450
Palmer, Robert		Music	20			45	Singer
Palmerston, Henry J. T., Lord	1784-1865	HOS	48	166	147		Prime Min. Eng. Ended Crimean War
Palminteri, Chaz		Ent	10			65	Actor
Palminteri, Chazz		Ent	15			45	
Paltrow, Bruce	d. 2002	Ent	25			40	Prod.
Paltrow, Gwyneth		Ent	20	35		100	Actress. 'Shakespeare in Love'. AA
Paluzzi, Luciana		Ent	15			82	Actress; 'Bond' girl
Pan, Hermes		Ent	30		50	65	Choreographer. Dance Dir. 1933-73. AA
Panabaker, Danielle		Ent	17			50	
Pancake, James		Bus	10	20			Ohio Businessman & Race Driver
Panerai, Rolando		Opera	10			25	Opera
Panetta, Leon		Congr	15			30	NY. White House Chief of Staff
Panettiere, Hayden		Ent	17			52	
Pangborn, Clyde		Aero	75	140	250	220	Aviation Pioneer
Pangborn, Franklin	1894-1958	Ent	60	60		194	Comedic Char. Actor
Pankhurst, Christabel D.	1880-1958	Fem	25	65	160		Br. Woman Suffrage Advocate
Pankhurst, E. Sylvia	1882-1960	Fem	55	118	250	660	Br. Woman Suffrage Advocate. Newspaper Editor
Pankhurst, Emmeline	1858-1928	Fem	40	125	240	500	Br. Leader of Women's Suffrage
Pannenberg, Wolfhart A.		Clergy	35	85	100	75	
Panova, Valery Panov-Galina		Ballet				250	Legendary English prima ballerina
Pantaleoni, Romilda		Opera			200		Opera. 1st Desdemona
Pantas, Lee		Author	10			12	Southern mountains guide books
Pantoliano, Joe		Ent	10			45	Ralphie Cifaretto, Sopranos
Paola Vega, Yenny		Ent	13			40	
Papanin, Ivan Dmitrijewicz	1894-1986	Expl	30	52	125		Russian Polar Explr.
Papen, Franz von	1879-1969	WWII	79	196	350	405	Served under Adolph Hitler
Papp, Joseph		Ent	30	40		55	Major Theatrical Prod.
Pappano, Antonio		Cond				75	Am.
Pappas, Ike	1933-	Ent	10			25	Actor

NAME	DATES	CATEGORY	SIG	LS/DS	ALS	SP	COMMENTS
Paquin, Anna		Ent	20			60	New Zealand Child Actress. 'The Piano', AA
Paradis, Vanessa	1972-	Ent	10			60	Fr. Singer-Actress
Paradise		Ent				50	Western TV drama series; S by all seven actors
Parazynski, Scott		Space	10			20	
Paris, Joel B., III		WWII	15	25	40	35	ACE, WWII; 9 kills
Parish, Hunter		Ent	15			45	
Park, Charles E.		Clergy	15	20	25		
Park, Chung Hee	1917-1979	HOS	65			92	Pres. Korea. Assass.
Park, Frank		Congr	10	15	25		MOC GA 1913
Park, Ray		Ent				40	Darth Maul, Star Wars I
Park, Roy H.		Bus	10	25	55	20	Owner 'Duncan Hines' & Broadcast Stations
Parke, John Grubb	1827-1900	Civ War	40	95	150		Union Gen. Sig/Rank 55, DS 115
Parker, Alton B.	1852-1926	Jurist	20	35	101	100	Judge, Pres. Cand. 1904
Parker, Amasa Junius		Congr	10		42		FF 42
Parker, Amelia, Mrs.		Celeb	10	15	25		Alton B. Parker Wife
Parker, Andrea		Ent	15			45	
Parker, Cecilia	1905-1993	Ent	15			90	Actress. 'Andy Hardy's' Sister
Parker, Charlie	1920-1955	Music	852	3077		4455	Alto Sax Jazz Musician. 'The Bird'.
Parker, David		Mil	15	35	60		
Parker, Dorothy		Author	425				Critic, Poet, Humorist; SB 450
Parker, Edward P.		Bus	65	150			Parker Bros. Pen Co.
Parker, Eleanor	1922-	Ent	10			38	Actress
Parker, Ely Samuel	1828-1895	Civ War	80	195			Seneca Indian Chief, Union Gen.
Parker, Fess	1925-	Ent	15	65	65	71	Actor. Remembered Lovingly as 'Davy Crockett'
Parker, Frank		Ent	10			20	Jack Benny's 1st Vocalist
Parker, Frank		Mil	50	75			Am. WWI Gen.
Parker, Gilbert	1861-1921	Author	12		50		
Parker, Graham		Music	20			35	S Album 30
Parker, Isaac	1768-1830	Law	35	125	140		Founded Harvard Law School
Parker, Isaac C.	1838-1896	Law	451	675	1725		"The Hanging Judge"
Parker, James	1776-1868	Congr	15				Repr. NJ (Grandfather of Rich'd W. Parker)
Parker, James	1768-1837	Congr	15				Repr. MA
Parker, Jameson	1947-	Ent	10			30	Actor
Parker, Jean	1915-2005	Ent	15		30	90	Actress
Parker, Joel	1816-1888	Gov	15	30	75		Civil War Gov. NJ
Parker, Mary		Ent	15			45	
Parker, Mary Louise		Ent	12			45	Actress
Parker, Molly		Ent	16			48	
Parker, Moses		Rev War					POW ALS 625
Parker, Robert A.		Space	10			20	
Parker, Roy, Jr.	1954-	Comp	10		15	25	
Parker, Sarah		Ent	17			50	
Parker, Sarah Jessica		Ent	20	25		65	Actress; 'Carrie Bradshaw', Sex in the City
Parker, Suzy	1932-2003	Ent	10			60	Actress
Parker, Theodore	1810-1860	Clergy	50	70	175		Abolitionist, Social Reformer
Parker, Thomas		Rev War	55	90	145		Cont. Army. Gen.
Parker, Tom, Col.	1909-1997	Ent	25	200		148	Elvis Presley's Manager-Agent
Parker, Trey		Comics					South Park; sketch 225-260
Parker, Willard	1912-1996	Ent	10			30	Actor-Husband Virginia Field
Parker, William, Sir	1781-1866	Mil	145		300		Br. Adm. Captured Ports thus Ending 'Opium War'
Parkhurst, Charles H.	1842-1933	Clergy	36	30	60	50	Reformer. Anti Tammany Hall
Parkins, Barbara	1942-	Ent	10			30	Actress; 'Peyton Place'
Parkinson, Dian		Model	10			30	'The Price is Right' model
Parkman, Francis	1823-1893	Author	25	70	150		Historian. The Oregon Trail

NAME	DATES	CATEGORY	SIG	LS/DS	ALS	SP	COMMENTS
Parks, Bert	1914-1992	Ent	10			40	'Miss America' host
Parks, Gordon	1912-	Author	20	50	75	40	Learning Tree. Photojournalist-Prod. -Dir.
Parks, Larry	1914-1975	Ent	40			120	Actor; 'The Al Jolson Story'
Parks, Rosa L.	1913-2005	Activist	100	145		200	Civ. Rights Activist, Bus Boycott; S Litho 150-300;
							S Chk 250; SB 300
Parkyakarkus	1904-1958	Ent	15			60	Comed; Super Dave Osborne & Albert Brooks' Dad
Parnell, Charles Stewart	1846-1891	Statsmn	55	145	356		Ir. Nationalist Leader; Fought forHome Rule.
Parr, Ralph		Aero	12	28	42	32	ACE, Korea, Double Ace
Parran, Thomas		Congr	10				MOC MD
Parrilla, Lana		Ent	15			45	
Parrish, Anne	1888-1957	Author	15	20	30		Am. Novels
Parrish, Helen	1923-1959	Ent	15			80	Actress
Parrish, Julie	1940-2003	Ent	10			60	
Parrish, Maxfield	1870-1966	Artist	200	348	769	750	S Repro 600. TLS/Cont 950, ALS/Cont 1840, S Chk 200
Parry, Charles Hubert H., Sir		Comp	10	25	50		Historian, Dir. Royal Coll. Music
Parry, William E., Sir	1790-1855	Expl	75	95	225		Br. Adm. Arctic Explr.
Parseval, August von		Aero	80				Ger. Aeronautical Engineer
Parsons, Albert Ross		Comp	10			20	
Parsons, Dave		Music	10			25	Music. Bass Guitar 'Bush'
Parsons, Estelle	1927-	Ent	10	10		35	Actress
Parsons, Lewis Baldwin	1818-1907	Civ War	40	70	100		Union Gen.
Parsons, Louella O.	1882-1972	Ent	60	118	125	132	Very Powerful Hearst Enter Journalist
Parsons, Mosby M.	1822-1865	Civ War	170				CSA Gen. ALS '65 1650, Sig/Rank 250
Parsons, Samuel Holden	1737-1789	Rev War		400	475		Cont'l. Gen. MsLs/Cont 1500
Parsons, Squire		Music	10			25	Award-winning gospel songwriter/singer
Part of Five (cast)		Ent				175	Cast of 7
Parton, Dolly		Cntry Mus	15	30		75	S Guitar 425
Parton, James	1822-1891	Author	15				
Parton, Stella		Cntry Mus	10			20	
Partridge, Bernard, Sir		Artist			45		Brit. Punch Cartoonist
Partridge, Wm. Ordway		Artist	10	20	50	30	Am. Sculptor. Portrait Busts
Parvis, Taurino		Opera	40			110	Opera
Pasch, Moritz		Sci	60		95		Ger. Mathemat'n. Pasch's Axiom
Pascrell Jr., Bill P		Congr	10				Member US Congress
Pasero, Tancredi		Opera	30			75	Opera
Paskalis, Kostas		Opera	15			45	Opera
Pasquarella, Gus		Photog	55			·	Photo Hindenburg Burning 1500
Passman, Otto E.		Congr	10			10	MOC LA
Pasternak, Boris	1890-1960	Author	358	732	1551		Rus. Poet, Novels. 'Dr. Zhivago'. Nobel Pr. 1958
Pasternak, Joe		Ent	30	65	100	70	Film Dir.
Pasteur, Louis	1822-1895	Sci	645	948	2158	3118	Fr. Biolog. Pasteurization, Vaccines. AManS 15000
Pastor, Ed P.		Congr	10				Member US Congress
Pastor, Tony		Band	10			35	Big Bandleader
Pastore, John A.		Gov	10	10			Governor RI
Pastore, Vincent		Ent				40	Big Pussy Bompensiero, Sopranos
Patat, Frederic		Space	12	25		25	
Patch, Alexander M.	1889-1945	WWII	60	175	260	250	Am. Gen. WWII
Pate, Michael	1920-	Ent	10			40	Australian actor
Paterson, Caroline	1965-	Ent	10			30	Actress
Paterson, Jodi Ann		Model				75	Playboy
Paterson, John	1744-1808	Rev War	70	200	325		Berkshire Minute-Men. Gen.
Patey, Janet		Ent	20		80		Actress
Patinkin, Mandy		Ent	20			40	Actor-Singer. Chicago Hope
Patman, J. Wm. Wright		Congr	10			10	MOC TX 1929

NAME	DATES	CATEGORY	SIG	LS/DS	ALS	SP	COMMENTS
Paton, Alan	1902-1989	Author	40	248	318		S. Afr. Pol. Activist; 'Cry, the Beloved Country'
Patric, Jason		Ent	10			50	Actor
Patrick, Butch		Ent	10		25	38	Eddie Munster
Patrick, Dan		TV News	10			30	Sports Anchorman
Patrick, Dennis	1918-202	Ent	10			40	Actor
Patrick, Gail	1911-1980	Ent	15			82	
Patrick, John		Author	10	15			
Patrick, Marsena R.	1811-1888	Civ War	35	50	122		Union Gen.
Patrick, Marsena R. (WD)	1811-1888	Civ War	45	85	118		Union Gen.
Patrick, Robert		Ent	16			48	
Patrick, Tera		Ent	17			50	
Patten, Gilbert		Author	30	70	160	50	(Burt Standish) Fictional Hero Frank Merriwell
Patten, Luana	1938-1996	Ent	15			60	One of 1st 2 Walt Disney Contract Players
Patterson, Annie W.		Comp					Signed Bars of Music 50
Patterson, Basil	1926-	Pol	10	20		30	Vice-Chm. Dem. National Committee
Patterson, Daniel Tod	1786-1839	Mil	45	145	225		Navy Commandant vs Jean Lafitte
Patterson, Francis Engle	1821-1862	Civ War	110				Union Gen.
Patterson, James Willis		Congr	10				FF 25
Patterson, John		Gov	12	25			Governor AL
Patterson, Melody	1949-	Ent	10			40	Actress. 'Wrangler Jane' on 'F Troop'
Patterson, Paul L.		Gov	10	10		10	Governor OR
Patterson, Richard North		Author	10			10	Fiction
Patterson, Robert	1792-1881.	Civ War	45	70	100		Oldest Commissioned CW Maj. Gen. SB 320
Patterson, Robert P.		Cab	20	35	45	25	Sect'y War
Patterson, Scott		Ent	15			45	
Patti, Adelina (Niccolini)	1843-1919	Opera	100	121	287	262	Great Operatic Coloratura. (Baroness Ledenbrun)
Patti, Amalia		Opera	40		135	150	Opera
Pattison, Robert T.		Gov	10	25		15	Governor PA
Patton, Francis L.		Clergy	15	20	25	25	
Patton, George S.	1833-1864	Civ War	280		3750		(Grandfather) KIA in Civil War. ALS 6/26/63 7500
Patton, George S., III		Mil	10	20	45	45	Son of WWII Gen.
Patton, George S., Jr.	1885-1945	Mil	822	1675	1926	3817	Cmdr. 3rd Army WWII, TLS/ALS Cont 5000-15000
Paul I & Frederica		Royal	200				King & Queen of Greece
Paul I (Rus)	1754-1801	Royal	180	621	1400		Czar Russ. Son of Cath. Great. Assass.
Paul, Adrian	1959-	Ent	10			60	Br. Actor. 'Highlander'
Paul, Alexandra	1963-	Ent	10			35	Actress
Paul, Arthur		Invent	10		20	32	
Paul, Gabriel Rene	1813-1886	Civ War	70	160			Union Gen.
Paul, Les		Ent	25	35		90	Manufacturer of Guitars; S Guitar 250-600
Paul, Ron P		Congr	10			25	Member US Congress; Pres. Candiate 2008
Paul, Wolfgang	1913-	Sci		30		30	Nobel Physics 1989
Paulding, Hiram	1797-1878	Civ War	28	50	170		Adm. Commanded Navy Yard NY During Civil War
Paulding, James Kirke	1778-1860	Cab	35	125	165		Van Buren Sec. Navy, War
Pauley, Ed		Bus	10	45		25	Powerful CA Oil Tycoon. Treas. Dem. Party
Pauley, Jane		Celeb	10			25	TV news anchor
Paulham, Louis		Aero	40	75	135	80	
Pauling, Linus	1901-1994	Sci	58	172	410	99	Nobel in Chemistry, Nobel Peace. SP(Pc) 125
Paulsen, Valademar		Sci	40	120			
Paulson, Pat	1927-1997	Ent	10			35	Comedian
Paulson, Sarah		Ent	12			35	
Paulucci, Jeno F.		Bus	15	25	35	20	
Paulus, Friedrich von	1890-1957	WWII	200	750			Ger. Field Marshal. Stalingrad
Pauly, Rose		Opera	20			60	Opera. Unequaled as Elektra
Pavarotti, Luciano	1935-2007	Opera	25	55	85	115	Opera, Concert; Italian tenor

NAME	DATES	CATEGORY	SIG	LS/DS	ALS	SP	COMMENTS
Pavie, Auguste-Jean-Marie		Diplo	40	145	230		Fr. Explr. Laos, Mekong
Pavlov, Ivan	1849-1936	Sci	585	4300	2488	3900	Rus. Physiologist.
Pavlova, Anna	1885-1931	Ballet	228	625	450	496	Russian Premiere Ballerina. SP Pc 450
Pavon, Jose Maria M. y	1765-1815	Clergy		3250			Revolutionary Mex. Priest. Leader of Rebel Forces
Pawnee Bill (Lillie, G. A.)		Ent					SEE Lillie, G. A.
Paxinou, Katina	1900-1973	Ent	100	250	270	206	1943 AA, Supp. Actress, 'For Whom the Bell Tolls'
Paxton, Bill		Ent	10			47	Twister/Helen Hunt SP 130
Paxton, Elisha F. 'Bull' (WD)	1828-1863	Civ War	638	2700			CSA Gen., Stonewall Brigade
Paxton, Elisha Franklin 'Bull'	1828-1863	Civ War	341	1064			CSA Gen.
Paycheck, Johnny	d. 2002	Cntry Mus	10			35	
Payer, Julius von	1842-1915	Expl	90	225		285	Austr-Hung. No. Polar Exped., Painter
Paymer, David		Ent	18			55	
Payne, Alexander		Ent	17			50	
Payne, Donald M. P		Congr	10				Member US Congress
Payne, Eugene B.	1835-1910	Civ War	25	45	65		Union Gen.
Payne, Freda		Music	10			30	'Band of Gold' Singer
Payne, Frederick	1903-1978	Pol	10		25		Mayor, Governor, US Sen. from Maine
Payne, Henry C.		Cab	15	20	35		P. M. Gen. 1902
Payne, John	1912-1989	Ent	15	30	55	93	Actor
Payne, John Barton		Cab	10		15		
Payne, John Howard	1791-1852	Comp	62	180	320		Actor, Author. Home Sweet Home
Payne, T. H.		Cab	10	25			
Payne, William H.		Civ War	85		356		CSA Gen.
Payne, William H. (WD)	1830-1904	Civ War	170	390			CSA Gen.
Payne, William W.	1807-1874	Congr	10				Repr. AL, Lawyer, Planter
Pays, Amanda	1959-	Ent	10			40	Brit. Actress'Max Headroom', 'The Flash' etc
Payton, Gary	1948-	Space	10	20		40	
Payton, Khary		Ent	15			45	
Payton-Noble, Jo Marie	1950-	Ent	10			35	Actress
Peabody, Andrew Preston	1781-1883	Clergy	15	20	35	30	Unitarian Theologian, Author
Peabody, Charles, Dr.		Sci	10	20	25		
Peabody, Eddie	1902-1970	Ent	15	15	35	60	Actor
Peabody, Endicott		Clergy	35	45	60		Fnder. of Groton School.
Peabody, Endicott 'Chub'	1920-1997	Pol	10	28	35		Gov. MA. Coll. Football Hall of Fame at Harvard
Peabody, Francis Dr.		Med	10	25	85		
Peabody, George	1795-1869	Bus	54	135	349		Merchant, Financier
Peabody, George F.	1852-1938	Banker	35	90	385	150	Merchant, Financier, Philanthropy
Peabody, Nathaniel	1741-1823	Rev War	40	125	180		New Hampshire patriot
Peale, Chas. Wilson	1741-1827	Artist	268	525	920		Off. Portrait Painter, Engr.
Peale, Norman Vincent	1898-1993	Clergy	23	59	112	120	Bestselling Author; Marble Collegiate Church
Peale, Rembrandt	1778-1860	Artist	245	550	1392		Am. Portrait & Historical. Artist AManS 1800
Peale, Titian	1799-1885	Artist		225	562		ALS/Cont 975
Pearce, Alice		Ent	70			245	The original Gladys Kravitz on Bewitched
Pearce, Dave		Music	10			20	DJ
Pearce, Dutee Jerauld		Congr	12		46		FF 46
Pearce, Guy		Ent				40	
Pearce, James Alfred		Congr	10	30	35		MOC, Sen. MD 1835
Pearce, Nayan		Ent				80	Actress
Pearce, Richard	1943-	Ent	10			25	Film Dir.
Pearce, Stevan P		Congr	10				Member US Congress
Pearl Jam (Entire Group)		Music	75			193	Rock, Alb. S 235; S Guitar 250-500
Pearl, Minnie	1912-1996	Cntry Mus	20			120	Grand Ole Opry Star
Pears, Peter	1910-1986	Opera		120		120	Tenor
Pearson, Lester B.	1897-1972	HOS	35	65	90	75	P. M. Canada, Nobel Peace Pr.

NAME	DATES	CATEGORY	SIG	LS/DS	ALS	SP	COMMENTS
Pearson, Neil	1959-	Ent	10			35	Br. Actor
Pearson, Virginia	1886-1958	Ent				120	Actress; Silent films
Peary, Harold	1908-1985	Ent	20			120	Actor
Peary, Robert E.	1856-1920	Expl	100	206	444	575	Am. Adm. Arctic Explr. 1st To Reach North Pole
Pease, Charles E.		Civ War	25				Carried Surrender Letter. ALS 1862 225
Pease, Elisha M.		Gov		395			Comptroller Repub. TX. Gov. TX
Peck, Gregory	1916-2003	Ent	45	355		381	AA Actor
Peck, John James	1821-1878	Civ War	40		110		Union Gen.
Peck, Robert Newton		Author	10	15	25		Am. Novels
Peck, William Raine	1818-1871	Civ War	100	162			CSA Gen.
Peckham, Rufus W.	1838-1909	Sup Crt	50	120	195	150	
Peckinpah, Sam	1925-1984	Ent	235	535		460	Dir.
Pederson, Monte		Opera	10			30	Opera
Pederzini, Gianna	1900-1988	Opera	25			100	Opera. Mezzo-Sopr.
Pedro II	1825-1891	Royal	72	266	305		Emperor Brazil 1831-89
Peek, Kim	1951-	Celeb	10			15	Inspired autistic Raymond Babbitt in 'Rainman'
Peel, John	1939-2004	Music	20			40	Legendary Br. DJ
Peel, Robert, Sir	1788-1850	HOS	45	75	124		Prime Min. Eng. 'Bobbies' Named for Him
Peeples, Nia	1961-	Ent	15			48	Actress
Peerce, Jan	1904-1984	Opera	28	40		83	Great Operatic Tenor. Long Career w/Met.
Peet, Amanda		Ent	15			45	
Pegg, Simon		Ent	18			55	
Pegler, Westbrook		Author	20	20	35	20	Am. Journalist, Columnist
Pegram, John	1832-1865	Civ War	650	838	1800		CSA Gen.
Pegram, John (WD)		Civ War	895	1795	7062		CSA Gen.
Pei, I. M.		Archtct	35	75	140		Intl. Recognized
Peirce, Benjamin	1809-1880	Sci	20	30	80		Mathematician, Astronomer
Peldon, Courtney		Ent	13			40	
Pelham, Henry	1696-1754	HOS	60	150	265		Prime Min.
Pelham-Holles, Thomas		HOS	50	105	170		Brother of Henry. Prime Min.
Pell, John		Hist	10	25			Museum Dir.
Pell, Stephen H. P.		Hist	10	25			Curator
Pellegrini, Margaret	1923-	Ent	15	20		60	Munchkin, Wizard of Oz
Pellegrino, Francis		WWII				112	Pilot 509th Bomb Gp. (Atomic Bomb)
Pelletier, St. Marie Euphraise	1796-1868	Clergy			2500		Saint Canonized 1940
Pelosi, Nancy P		Congr	10			45	Member US Congress; Spkr. of the House
Pelouze, Louis H.	1831-1878	Civ War	35	65	110		Union Gen. War Dte. DS 350
Pemberton, John C.	1814-1881	Civ War	120	220	360	550	CSA Gen. Originated COCA COLA
Pemberton, John C. (WD)	1814-1881	Civ War	210	714	812	1250	CSA Gen. Originator COCA COLA
Pemsel, Max		WWII				60	Nazi Gen. Chief of Gen. Staff of the 7th Army
Pena, Elizabeth	1961-	Ent	10			35	Actress
Pence, Mike P		Congr	10				Member US Congress
Pender, William Dorsey	1834-1863	Civ War	475	1265			CSA Gen. War Dte. ALS 3, 250
Penderecki, Krzysztof		Comp	20		90		Pol. Opera, Religious Music
Pendergast, Thomas J.		Pol	17	50	105	35	KS Democratic Pol. Boss
Pendleton, Alex 'Sandie'	1840-1864	Civ War	175	350	475		CSA Staff Off. -T. J. Jackson
Pendleton, Edmund	1721-1803	Rev War	350	680	660		Continental Congress
Pendleton, George Hunt	1825-1889	Congr	20	35	75		Pres. Cand. Sen. OH
Pendleton, Nat	1895-1967	Ent	30	45	60	40	Actor
Pendleton, Nathanael G.	1793-1861	Congr	20				Repr. OH, Father of G. H. Pendleton
Pendleton, Nathaniel	1756-1821	Rev War			195		Burr-Hamilton duel
Pendleton, William Nelson	1809-1883	Civ War	196		560	485	CSA Gen., Pre War Clergyman
Penn & Teller		Ent	10			40	
Penn, Arthur	1922-	Ent	10			40	Dir.

NAME	DATES	CATEGORY	SIG	LS/DS	ALS	SP	COMMENTS
Penn, Chris	1965-2006	Ent	10			40	Actor; Sean Penn's brother
Penn, John	1740-1788	Rev War	1525	5008	7500		Signer Dec of Ind SB 7500; War-dte LS 8500-10500
Penn, John	1729-1795	Colonial		244	375		Lt. Governor of Pennsylvania
Penn, Kal		Ent	17			51	
Penn, Sean	1962-	Ent	25	149	40	87	Actor-Dir. -Writer; DS w/Madonna 1500
Penn, Thomas	1702-1775	Colonial		150			Son of William. Proprietor of PA
Penn, William	1644-1718	Relig	1650	5631	7500		Eng. Quaker Fndr. PA. AManS 9,000.
Pennell, Joseph	1857-1926	Artist	55	160	320		Am. Artist, Printmaker
Penner, Joe	1904-1941	Ent	20	25	45	50	Actor
Penney, J. C.	1875-1971	Bus	48	158	210	184	Fndr. of J. C. Penney. Informative TLS 1500
Pennington, Ann	1893-1971	Ent	25	30	70	110	Ziegfield Star
Pennington, William	1796-1862	Congr	48	70			Gov. PA. Spkr. of House
Pennoyer, Sylvester		Gov	10	15			Governor OR
Penny, Joe	1956-	Ent	10			20	Br. Actor
Penny, Little Joe		Cntry Mus	10			15	Music. 50s Western Recording Artist
Pennypacker, Galusha	1844-1916	Civ War	200	260	375		Union. Boy Gen.
Pennypacker, Samuel W.		Gov	15	25		30	Jurist, Author, Gov. PA
Penrose, Boies	1860-1921	Congr	12	15			Sen. PA. Pres. Pro Tempore
Penrose, William Henry	1832-1903	Civ War	45	80	115		Union Gen.
Penske, Thomas H.		Bus	10	30		20	
Penzias, Arno, Dr.		Sci	15	35	65	25	Nobel Physics
Pepin, Jacques		Celeb	10			15	Famous chef
Peppard, George	1928-1994	Ent	15			103	Actor
Pepper, Art		Band	30			75	Bandleader
Pepper, Barry		Ent	17			50	
Pepper, Claude	1900-1989	Congr	22	38		25	Sen. FL
Pepper, George Wharton		Congr	10	15			Sen. PA 1922
Pepperell, William, Sir	1696-1759	Mil	175	360	550		Merchant. Gen. in Fr-Indian War
Pepys, Samuel	1633-1703	Author	570	1880			Br. Sec. of the Navy. Revealing Diarist.
Pequet, Henri		Aero	16		37		
Perahia, Murray		Music				175	Pianist
Perceval, Spencer	1762-1812	HOS	120	250			Only Br. P. M. Assass.
Percival, John 'Mad Jack'		Mil	30	95	145		Am. Navy. War 1812 Exploits
Percy, Charles		Congr	10	15		25	Sen. IL
Percy, Hugh	1742-1817	Mil	50	145	250		Br. Gen.
Percy, Walker	1916-1990	Author	30	55	75	60	Am. Novels
Peregrym, Missy		Ent	16			48	
Pereira, William L.		Archtct	10	35	75	20	Intl. Recognized
Perelman, S. J.		Author	45		160		Humorist, Film Scripts
Peres, Shimon		HOS	35	110		79	Israeli Prime Min. Nobel Peace Pr. SB 215
Perez De Cuellar, Javier	1920-	Pol	10	25		25	Secretary-Gen. of the United Nations
Perez, Charles	1964-	TV News	10			15	TV reporter
Perez, Mariano		HOS	15	25	85	20	Pres. Colombia
Perez, Rosie	1964-	Ent	10			40	Actress
Perez, Vincent	1962-	Ent	25			70	The Crow Star
Perham, Josiah		Bus		75			1st Pres. of Northern Pacific RR
Perier, Jean		Opera	25			75	Fr. Baritone. 45 Year Career
Perignon, D. C. Marquis de	1754-1818	Mil	65	180	375		Marshal of Napoleon
Perkins, Anthony	1932-1992	Ent	58	130	60	158	'Psycho' SP 200
Perkins, Carl	1932-1998	Cntry Mus	15		50	103	Singer-Songwriter. Rock 'n Roll HOF.
Perkins, Elizabeth		Ent	10			35	Actress
Perkins, Frances		Cab	25	70	145	60	1st Woman Cabinet Member. Sec. Labor
Perkins, George C.	1839-1923	Congr	14	20			Governor, Sen. CA 1893
Perkins, Marlin	1905-1986	TV News	15			25	Zoologist

NAME	DATES	CATEGORY	SIG	LS/DS	ALS	SP	COMMENTS
Perkins, Millie	1938-	Ent	10			75	Actress
Perkins, Osgood	1892-1937	Ent	35			80	Actor; Father to Anthony
Perkins, Pine Top		Music				115	Pianist
Perkins, Thomas H.		Bus	20	45	90		
Perlman, Itzhak		Music	30			46	Am. Violinist
Perlman, Rhea		Ent	10			40	Actress; 'Cheers'
Perlman, Ron		Ent	10			50	Actor
Peron, Eva (Evita)	1919-1952	HOS	250	400	363	680	Argentina. Statesman
Peron, Juan & Eva		HOS		615			
Peron, Juan Domingo	1895-1974	HOS	125	180	238	348	Pres. & Dictator of Argentina
Perot, H. Ross		Bus	15	35		30	Pres. Cand.
Perpich, Rudolph G.		Gov	10	15		15	Governor MN
Perrault, Charles	1628-1703	Author		1250	2600		Fr. Poet. Fairy Tales.
Perret, Gene		Ent	10			20	Writer
Perrin, Abner Monroe	1827-1864	Civ War	280				CSA Gen., KIA Spottsylvannia 1864
Perrin, Claude	1784-1841	Mil		160			Marshal of France
Perrin, Jean	1870-1942	Sci	75	385		235	Nobel Pr. '26 Physics. TMsS 1,000
Perrine, Valerie	1943-	Ent	10			35	Actress
Perrineau, Harold		Ent	15			45	
Perris, Adriana		Opera	10			30	Opera
Perry, Alexander J.	1829-1913	Civ War	25	45			Union Brvt. Gen., Nephew Commodore Perrry
Perry, Antoinette		Ent		200			Tony Award
Perry, Edward Aylesworth	1831-1889	Civ War	110	200			CSA Gen.
Perry, Lila	1959-	Ent	10			25	Child Star. TV Shows of Mid 60s
Perry, Madison S.		Gov	15	45			Governor FL
Perry, Matthew		Ent	10			53	Friends Actor
Perry, Matthew C.	1794-1858	Mil	217	1513	950		Father of the Steam Navy
Perry, Nora		Author	10	10	20		Novels
Perry, Oliver H.	1785-1819	Mil	550	850	1875		
Perry, Ralph Barton		Author	10	20	35		Philosopher, Pulitzer Pr.
Perry, William Flank	1823-1901	Civ War	110	168			CSA Gen.
Perryman, Lloyd		Cntry Mus	10			20	
Perse, Saint-John		Poet	60				Fr. Poet & Dipl. Awarded Nobel Pr. Lit., 1960
Pershing, John J.	1860-1948	Mil	81	241	455	673	Cmdr in Chief AEF WWI. Imp. ALS 895; SP w/Foch 1500
Persichetti, Vincent		Comp	10	25	60	25	
Persoff, Nehemiah	1919-	Ent	10			40	Israeli born actor
Persons, Wilton B.		Official	10	15	25	10	Gen. Chief Ass't to Pres. DDE
Pertile, Aureliano	1855-1952	Opera	40			106	Opera. Favorite of Toscanini at La Scala
Perulli, Franco		Opera	20			50	Opera
Perutz, Max		Sci	20	40	75	50	Nobel Chemistry 1962
Pesci, Joe	1943-	Ent	25	35		60	AA; Actor; SP w/DeNiro 390
Petain, Henri-Phillippe.	1856-1951	HOS	60	125	172	223	Hero WWI. Treason WWII
Peter & Gordon		Music	75			125	Singing Duo; S Guitar 240
Peter I	1844-1921	Royal	90	225	400		King of Serbia
Peter I, The Great	1672-1725	Royal	1250	4859	15500		Czar of Russia
Peter, Paul & Mary		Music	35			95	Folk singing group
Peterman, Melissa		Ent	13			40	
Peters, Absalom		Clergy	15	20	35		
Peters, Bernadette		Ent	10			59	Actress
Peters, Brock	1927-2005	Ent	15			70	Actor
Peters, Jean	1926-2000	Ent	30	45	50	150	Actress; wife of Howard Hughes
Peters, John Andrew		Congr	10				FF 20
Peters, Mike		Comics	10			45	Mother Grimm
Peters, Richard Jr.	1744-1828	Rev War	40	95	150		Soldier, Jurist, Continental Cong

NAME	DATES	CATEGORY	SIG	LS/DS	ALS	SP	COMMENTS
Peters, Roberta		Opera	10			25	Opera, Concert
Peters, Susan	1921-1951	Ent	75	85	95	100	Actress
Peters, Tom		Author	10			15	Motivational books
Petersen, Paul	1945-	Ent	10			30	Child actor; 'Donna Reed Show'
Peterson, Bruce A.		Space	10			20	
Peterson, Chesley		WWII	15	30	55	40	ACE, WWII, Eagle Squadron; 6 kills
Peterson, Collin C. P		Congr	10				Member US Congress
Peterson, Donald H.		Space	10			20	
Peterson, John E. P		Congr	10				Member US Congress
Peterson, Oscar	1925-2007	Music	25	65		65	Jazz Pianist
Peterson, Roger Tory		Author	20	35		25	
Petiet, Claude		Fr Rev	125	265			
Petion, Alexandre	1770-1818	HOS	225	292			Haitian Gen., Pres. Southern Haiti
Petraeus, David Gen.		Mil	10			25	Gen. Cmdr. in Iraq
Petrella, Clara		Opera	20			50	Opera
Petri, Thomas E. P		Congr	10				Member US Congress
Petrie, Wm. M. Flinders, Sir		Archaeol	125	166			Pyramids At Giza. Paved the Way For Carter et al
Petrillo, James C.		Labor	20	55			Czar of Musician's Union
Petrocelli, Daniel		Law	15			20	Prosecuted O. J. Simpson in Civil Suit for Goldman
Petroff, Paul		Ballet	30				Am. Ballet Dancer-Teacher
Petrone, Rocco		Space				100	Dir. of launch operations
Petrova, Olga		Ent	35			75	Silent Films
Petrovna, Elizabeth		Royal		1500			Russian; Tsarina, daughter of Peter the Great
Pettet, Joanna	1942-	Ent	10			25	Br. Actress
Pettigrew, James J.	1828-1863	Civ War	222	608			CSA Gen.
Pettigrew, James, J. (WD)	1828-1863	Civ War	375	5750			CSA Gen. AES '61 13, 200
Pettit, Charles		Rev War	70	185	315		Continental Congress
Pettit, Don		Space				20	
Pettus, Edmund W.	1821-1907	Civ War	123	213	559		CSA Gen. ALS War Dte 3500
Pettus, John J.	1813-1867	Civ War	30	55	70		Mississippi War Gov.
Petty, Lori		Ent	13			40	
Petty, Tom		Ent	35	255		130	Heartbreakers; S Guitar 300-500; S Album 150
Peugeot, Eugene		Bus	50	130	315		Fndr. Peugeot Automobile Co.
Pfeiffer, Dedee		Ent	26			78	
Pfeiffer, Michelle		Ent	20	25	30	85	Actress
Pflug, Jo Ann	1944-	Ent	10			30	
Phelan, James D.	1864-1930	Congr	10	25	40		Sen. CA 1915
Phelps, Austin		Clergy	20	30	40		
Phelps, John Smith	1814-1886	Civ War	35	65	100		Union Gen., Gov. MO
Phelps, John Wolcott	1813-1885	Civ War	35	135	200		Raised 1st Negro Troops
Phelps, Noah	1740-1809	Mil	100	275			Soldier, Patriot, Spy
Phelps, William Walter	1839-1894	Congr	10		25		Repr. NJ
Phifer, Mekhi		Ent	15			45	
Philbin, Mary	1903-1993	Ent	25			80	Silent Film Star & Beauty Queen
Philbin, Regis		Ent	20	30	35	45	TV Host
Philbrick, Herbert A.	1915-1993	Celeb	15	30	60	25	I Led Three Lives Agent
Philip (Duke Edinburgh)	1921-	Royal	110	208	325	268	Prince Consort Elizabeth II
Philip II (Sp)	1527-1598	Royal	295	2542			King of Spain 1556-1598. Husband of Mary Tudor
Philip III (Sp)	1578-1621	Royal	250	463			Ruled Portugal, as Philip II
Philip IV (Sp)	1605-1665	Royal	150	347	1250		Ruled Portugal, as Philip III
Philip V (Sp)	1683-1746	Royal	138	255			Fndr. Bourbon Dynasty
Philipp, Isadore		Music	20		65		Pianist
Philippe II (Duc d'Orleans)		Royal		500			Regent of Fr. for Louis XV
Philippi, Alfred		WWII				75	Ger. Gen. WWII. RK

Sanders Autograph Price Guide

P

NAME	DATES	CATEGORY	SIG	LS/DS	ALS	SP	COMMENTS
Philipps, Busy		Ent	15			45	
Phillip II (Spain)		Royal		470			
Phillip, Jack W.		Mil	27	80			Captain USN
Phillippe, Ryan		Ent	15			55	Actor
Phillips, Bijou		Ent	18			55	
Phillips, Bill		Cntry Mus	10			20	
Phillips, Chynna		Ent				30	Singer-Actress
Phillips, Irna	1901-1973	Ent	10			20	Writer
Phillips, J. B.		Clergy	35	50	95	95	
Phillips, Jack		Titanic			680		Chief radio operator
Phillips, John	1935-2001	Music	25			100	Fndr. Mamas & the Papas
Phillips, John		Space	10			20	
Phillips, Julia		Celeb	10			15	Film industry
Phillips, Julianne	1960-	Ent	10			30	Actress
Phillips, Lou Diamond		Ent	10			45	Actor
Phillips, Mackenzie		Ent	10			35	
Phillips, Michelle		Ent	10	60		40	
Phillips, Phil		Comp	15			35	Singer-Songwriter
Phillips, Robert		Space	10			20	
Phillips, Sam	1923-2003	Music		388			Am. record Prod. S Guitar 515
Phillips, Scott		Music	10			25	Music. Drummer 'Creed'
Phillips, Wendell	1811-1884	Reform	27	74	125	125	Abolitionist, Orator, Civ. Rights; AQS 145
Phillips, William		Rev War	225	633	825		Br. Major Gen.
Phillips, Wm.		Cab	10	15	20		
Phillpotts, Eden		Author	10	35	55		(Harrington Hext) Novels/Plays/Poems/Mystery
Phillpotts, Henry		Clergy	25	35	40		Under Sec.
Phipps, Spencer	1685-1757	Colonial	125	375			Br. Colonial Gov. MA
Phish		Music	50			125	S Album 125; S Guitar 460
Phoenix, Joaquin		Ent	10			55	Actor
Phoenix, River	1971-1993	Ent	172	510		402	Actor
Physick, Philip Syng	1768-1837	Med	225	908	690		Father of Am. Surgery
Piaf, Edith	1915-1963	Ent	260	385	995	476	Legendary Intl. Chanteuse
Piaget, Jean	1896-1980	Sci		268			Swiss Psychologist
Pianchettini, Pio	1799-1851	Comp					Pianist. ANS Framed/Portrait 3500
Piatigorsky, Gregor	1903-1976	Music	75	135	220	400	Rus./Am. Cellist. AMusQS 100
Piatt, Abram Sanders	1821-1908	Civ War	40		95		Union Gen.
Piazza, Marguerite		Opera	10			25	Am. Met Sopr.
Piazzi, Giuseppe	1746-1826	Sci			6500		Italian monk, mathematician, & astronomer
Picabia, Francis	1879-1953	Artist			225		Fr. Painter. A Leader of Dadaist Movement
Picard, Charles-Emile	1856-1941	Sci	70	240	430		Fr. Mathematician
Picardo, Robert		Ent				40	Actor. Star Trek Voyager.
Picasso, Pablo	1881-1973	Artist	703	1213	2107	1718	Signed sketch 7500-15500
Picasso, Paloma		Artist	25		95		Artist-Designer. Daughter
Piccaluga, Nino		Opera	30			80	Opera
Piccard & Jones		Aero				44	Balloonists
Piccard, Auguste	1884-1963	Sci	45	115	195	115	Sw. Physicist. Bathyscaphe
Piccard, Jacques		Sci	15	40	75	20	
Piccard, Jean-Felix		Sci	65	195		125	Chemist, Aeronautical Eng.
Piccaver, Alfred		Opera	75			225	Br. Tenor, Opera
Piccolomini, Marietta		Opera	100	275		275	It. Sopr.
Pichegru, Charles		Fr Rev	35	115	195		Fr. Gen. Strangled In Prison
Pick, Lewis A.	1890-	WWII	35	125		40	Gen. WWII
Pickens, Francis W.		Civ War	68	618	867		CSA Gov SC
Pickens, Jane		Ent	25			50	(Pickens Sisters) & Actress/Singer

357

NAME	DATES	CATEGORY	SIG	LS/DS	ALS	SP	COMMENTS
Pickens, Slim		Ent	100	135		127	
Pickens, T. Boone		Bus	20	55		30	Oilman
Pickering, Charles W. "Chip"		Congr	10				Member US Congress
Pickering, John	1737-1805	Rev War	167	215			Impeached & Convicted by Congr.
Pickering, Thomas		Diplo	10			20	Ambassador to Russia
Pickering, Timothy	1745-1829	Rev War	175	313	780		Sec. War & State, TLS/Cont 2300, ALS/Cont 2500
Pickering, William, Dr.		Sci	15	35	60	25	Astronomer. Lowell Observatory
Pickett, Bobby Boris		Ent				40	Actor; musician; S Guitar 260
Pickett, Cindy		Ent	10			30	Actress
Pickett, George Edward	1825-1875	Civ War	2662	3612	6794		Rare war-date ALS 15,000
Pickett, LaSalle C.		Celeb					Wife of Gen. George Pickett; SB 360
Pickett, Wilson		Music	40			80	Singer
Pickford, Jack		Ent	50			150	
Pickford, Mary	1893-1979	Ent	55	120	135	455	Fndr. Un. Artists. Silent Star. AA; SP w/Fairbanks 1010
Pickford, Mary & Buddy Rogers		Ent	95			275	
Picon, Molly	1898-1992	Ent	35	30		55	Stage & Film Star of Yiddish & Am. Theatre
Picquart, Georges	1854-1914	Mil		150			Fr. Gen. Dreyfus affair
Pidgeon, Walter	1897-1984	Ent	20	40		87	Am. Film Actor
Pied Pipers, The (3)		Music	20			45	Big Band Singing Group
Pierce, Benjamin	1809-1880	Sci	20		62		Am. Math. & Astronomy. Harvard Prof.
Pierce, Benjamin	1757-1839	Rev War	60	135	200		Father of Pres., Gov. NH
Pierce, Byron Root	1829-1924	Civ War	64	85	114		Union Gen.
Pierce, David Hyde		Ent	10			45	'Niles' in Frasier
Pierce, Fr. & Davis, Jeff.		Pres		3814			Pres. & Sectry of War
Pierce, Franklin	1804-1869	Pres	542	786	1054		FF 300-595
Pierce, Franklin (as Pres)		Pres	562	1524	1981		14th Pres. of USA
Pierce, Guy	1970-	Ent	10			62	Actor
Pierce, James	1900-1983	Ent	25	115		80	Actor; Vintage Tarzan
Pierce, Jane M.	1806-1863	1st Lady	215	500	895		Wife of Franklin Pierce
Pierce, Mark Robert	1950-	Music	10	10	15	25	Created music for special needs children
Pierce, Samuel, Jr.	1922-	Cab	25		40	70	Afr-Am Sec. HUD Under Reagan. Key in HUD Scandal
Pierce, Web		Cntry Mus	10			10	
Pierné, H. C. Gabriel	1863-1937	Comp	15	50	135	375	Conductor. AMusQS 250
Pierre White, Marco		Celeb	10			15	Chef
Pierrepont, Edwards	1817-1892	Cab	45	55	92		Grant Atty Gen. 1875. Prosecution of Surratt
Pierson, Roland		Aero	10	25	35	30	
Pietz, Amy		Ent	15			45	
Pigni, Renzo		Opera	15			35	Opera
Pike, Albert	1809-1891	Civ War	148	375	390		CSA Gen. Sig/Rank 180
Pike, Christopher		Author	10		15	10	Novels
Pike, James A., Bish.	1913-1969	Clergy	70	120	262	90	Episcopal Bishop.
Pike, Rosamund		Ent	13			40	
Pike, Zebulon	1751-1834	Rev War	45	85	135		Off. Revolutionary Army
Pike, Zebulon M.	1779-1813	Mil	245	700	1250		Gen. Discovered Pike's Peak
Pilatre De Rozier, Jean F.		Aero	125		500		Pioneer Balloonist
Pilcher, Rufus		Aero	10		35		Early Aviator; Cmdr. 379th Bombardment Group
Pile, William Anderson	1829-1889	Civ War	50		150		Union Gen.
Pileggi, Mitch	1952-	Ent	10			30	Actor
Pilgram, Janet	1934-	Model				75	POM 7/55, Playboy
Pillow, Gideon J.	1806-1878	Civ War	135		473		CSA Gen.
Pillow, Gideon J. (WD)	1806-1878	Civ War	168	440	750		CSA Gen. ALS/Cont 3, 750
Pillsbury, Charles		Bus			550		Fndr. of Pillsbury Flour Co.
Pillsbury, George A.		Bus		1759	2400		Fndr. of Pillsbury Flour. ALS on Lttrhd. 3850
Pillsbury, John S.		Bus	85	553			Governor MN, Pillsbury Flour

NAME	DATES	CATEGORY	SIG	LS/DS	ALS	SP	COMMENTS
Pillsbury, Parker		Reform	15	25	60		
Pilsudski, Joseph Klemens		Mil	115	320	550	550	Pol. Gen., Statesman, Dictator
Pinay, Antoine (Fr)		HOS	15	35	50		Fr.
Pinchback, Pinckney		Congr	125	350	495		Sen.
Pinchot, Bronson	1959-	Ent	10			30	Actor
Pinchot, Gifford	1865-1946	Gov	35	120	125		Governor PA, Forester
Pinckney, Charles	1757-1824	Rev War	375		1500		Continental Congress, MOC, Sen. SC
Pinckney, Charles C.	1746-1825	Rev War	175	413	1231		Gen., Diplomat, XYZ Affair
Pinckney, Henry Laurens		Congr			55		
Pinckney, Pauline		Author	10	10	20		
Pinckney, Thomas	1750-1828	Rev War	200	516			Continental Army, Gov. SC
Pincus, Harry		Artist	10	30	60		
Pine, Courtney		Music	10			15	Singer
Pine, Phillip	1920-2006	Ent	10			30	Actor
Pine, Virginia	1912-1984	Ent				60	Actress
Pinero, Arthur Wing, Sir	1855-1934	Author	20	35	65	60	Br. Dramatist, Actor
Pingel, Rolf		Aero	10	15	30	25	
Pingree, Hazen S.		Gov	10	15			Governor MI
Pink		Music				50	Singer
Pink Floyd		Music	891	1625		1950	S Album 350-3175; S Guitar 6935
Pinkerton, Allan	1819-1884	Civ War	300	749	1365	1150	Dir. Union Secret Service Bureau During Civil War
Pinkerton, Robert A.		Bus	35	105	220	220	CEO Pinkerton's Inc. Detectives
Pinkerton, William A.	1846-1923	Bus		163		585	Son of Fndr. of Pinkerton Nat. Detective Agency
Pinkett, Jada		Ent	10			40	Actress
Pinkney, William	1764-1822	Cab	90	225	275		MOC, Sen. MD. Atty Gen. 1811
Pinochet, Augusto		HOS	30	115	245	112	Chilean Mil. Leader
Pinter, Harold		Author	20			77	Br. Plays. Small (4x5) SP 50
Pinza, Ezio	1892-1957	Opera	60	140		103	It.-Am. Basso, Opera, Films
Piper, William Thomasr.		Aero	175	380	207		Fndr. Piper Aircraft Corp.
Pirandello, Luigi	1867-1936	Author	70	162	425	390	Nobel Lit. ALS/Cont 2, 400
Pirchoff, Nelly		Opera	10			30	Opera
Pire, Dominique George		Clergy	55		90	65	
Piscopo, Joe		Ent	10			35	Comedian
Pissarro, Camille	1830-1903	Artist	200	695	1334		Fr. Impressionist-Pointillist
Piston, Walter	1894-1976	Comp	60	95	125	150	Pulitzer Music 1947 & 1960; S score 225
Pitcher, Thomas Gamble	1824-1895	Civ War	45	75			Union Gen.
Pitkin, William	1729-1789	Colonial	30	102			Jurist, Army Major., Mfg. Gunpowder. Chf. Just. CT
Pitkin, William	1694-1769	Colonial	65	475			Soldier, Colonial Judge & Gov. CT
Pitney, Gene	1940-2006	Music	25	255		130	Singer
Pitney, Mahlon	1858-1924	Sup Crt	60	85	160	150	MOC NJ 1895
Pitt, Brad		Ent	25	428	35	101	Actor
Pitt, Ingrid	1937-	Ent	15			60	Polish-born actress
Pitt, John, Sir	1756-1835	Mil	45		80		Gen. Cmdr. Failed Walcheren Exp.
Pitt, William (Elder)	1708-1778	HOS	302	1600	1020		The Great Commoner
Pitt, William (Younger)	1759-1815	HOS	115	261	361		England's Youngest Prime Min.
Pittenger, William	1840-	Clergy	15		25		Mil. (Civil War)
Pittner, William		Clergy	15				
Pitts, Joseph R.		Congr	10				Member US Congress
Pitts, Zazu	1894-1963	Ent	40	45		170	Silent movie actor, then talkies
Piven, Jeremy		Ent	20			45	Emmy winner; actor
Plainsmen, The		Cntry Mus	25			50	
Plana, Tony		Ent	12			35	
Planck, Max	1858-1947	Sci	400	850	922	1030	Nobel Physics 1918. ANS Pc 500
Plancon, Pol	1854-1914	Opera	125		210	85	Opera

NAME	DATES	CATEGORY	SIG	LS/DS	ALS	SP	COMMENTS
Planer, Nigel	1953-	Ent	10			25	Br. Actor
Plant & Page (Both)		Music				175	Rock, Led Zeppelin
Plant, Robert		Music	35			74	S Album 125
Plasson, Michel		Cond				60	Fr.
Plath, Sylvia		Author		5000			Am. author; TLS/Cont 15,000
Plato, Dana	1964-1999	Ent	20			78	Actress; 'Diff'rent Strokes'
Platt, Ed	1916-1974	Ent	75			138	Actor; 'Chief' on 'Get Smart'
Platt, James Henry		Congr	10				FF 27
Platt, Marc		Ent	10			35	Dancer-Choreographer
Platt, Orville H.	1827-1905	Congr	10	15			Sen. CT
Platt, Thomas C	1833-1910	Congr	15		33	40	Sen. NY
Platters, The (5)		Music				285	Singing Group
Platts, Todd Russell P		Congr	10				Member US Congress
Playfair, Lyon, 1st Baron		Sci	10	25	40		Br. Chem. Mdrn. Sanitation
Pleasant, Mary E. ('Mammy')	1813-1904	Celeb	400	535			Former Slave
Pleasence, Donald	1919-1995	Ent	15			58	Actor
Pleasonton, Alfred	1824-1897	Civ War	58	120	200		Union Gen. ALS War Dte 1, 200
Pleasonton, Alfred (WD)		Civ War	90	185	425		Union Gen. Sherman's Chief Cavalry
Pleshette, Suzanne	1937-2008	Ent	10			50	Actress
Plimpton, George	1927-2003	Author	15	35	40	30	SB 90; TLS re: Bobby Kennedy 230
Plimpton, Martha	1970-	Ent				30	Actress
Plishka, Paul		Opera	10			25	Opera
Plitsetskaya, Maya		Ballet	15			40	Ballet
Plowright, Joan	1929-	Ent	10			40	Br. Actress
Plummer, Amanda		Ent	16			25	Actress
Plummer, Christopher	1929-	Ent	15			61	Actor
Plummer, Joseph Bennett	1816-1862	Civ War	120				Union Gen.
Plunkett, Charles P.	1864-1930	Mil	45	135			USN Adm. Transatlantic Flight Operations 1919
Poco		Music	75			125	Rock group; S Guitar 260-350; S Album 120-360
Podesta, Rossana	1934-	Ent	10			60	Intl. Films. Beautiful Italian Actress.
Podgorney, Nikolay V.	1903-1983	Pol		140			Soviet Communist leader
Podmore, Thomas		Clergy	10	10	15	15	
Poe, Edgar Allan	1809-1849	Author	8419		30490		AMS 35000
Poe, Orlando Metcalfe	1832-1895	Civ War	40	70	105		Union Gen.
Poehler, Amy		Ent	15			45	
Pogany, Willy	1882-1955	Artist	70	190			Illust., Muralist, Designer
Poggi, Gianni		Opera	10			25	Opera
Pogue, William R.		Space	15			35	
Poincaré, Raymond	1860-1934	HOS	40	60	100	105	3 Times Prime Min. France
Poindexter, John		Mil	20			40	US Adm. Iran-Contra
Poindexter, Joseph B.		Gov	10	15			Governor Hawii, Federal Judge
Poindexter, Miles		Congr	10	15			Repr., Sen. WA 1909
Poinsett, Joel R.	1779-1851	Cab	82	205	280		Sec. War. Poinsettia Flower
Pointer Sisters		Ent	30	120		87	
Poiret, Paul	1879-1944	Design	125	525			Fr. Dress Designer
Poitier, Sidney	1924-	Ent	20	65		164	1st Afr-Am AA Winning Actor
Poland, John S.		Mil		120			Civil War; Indian Wars
Poland, Luke P.		Congr	10	15	30		MOC, Sen. VT 1865
Polando, John		Aero	30	60	110	75	
Polanski, Roman		Ent	35	60		102	Fugitive Dir., AA winner
Polansky, Mark		Space	10			25	
Polaski, Deborah		Opera	10			25	Opera
Poli, Afro		Opera	10			45	Opera
Police, The		Music	215			265	S Album 300; S Guitar 500-1150

P

NAME	DATES	CATEGORY	SIG	LS/DS	ALS	SP	COMMENTS
Polignac, Camille J.	1832-1913	Civ War	110				CSA Gen.
Poling, Daniel A.		Clergy	20	30	60	35	
Polizzi, Harry		Celeb	10	20			Book Dealer
Polk, J. & Buchanan, J.		Pres	1150	3006			
Polk, James K.	1795-1849	Pres	513	1392	2271		FF 975. Pol. ALS 5250
Polk, James K. (As Pres.)		Pres	558	1609	2973		FF 975-1200
Polk, Leonidas	1806-1864	Civ War	382	958	2121		CSA Gen. KIA. Episcopal Bishp. Fndr. U of South
Polk, Leonidas (WD)	1806-1864	Civ War	500	1750	3035		CSA Gen.
Polk, Lucius Eugene	1833-1892	Civ War	100				CSA Gen.
Polk, Sarah Childress		1st Lady	357	583	855	1250	Banned Dancing & Drinking in WH
Pollack, Sidney	1934-2008	Ent	15	30	30	50	AA Dir. -Actor
Pollack, Sir George	1786-1876	Mil			260		
Pollack, Sydney		Ent	25			75	
Pollak, Kevin		Ent	15			45	
Pollan, Tracy		Ent	10			30	Actress; married to Michael J. Fox
Pollard, Michael		Ent	15			45	
Pollard, Michael J.	1939-	Ent	10	40		45	Actor; 'Bonnie & Clyde', 'Dobie Gillis'
Pollard, Snub	1889-1962	Ent	50			200	Keystone Cop
Pollard, Sue	1949-	Ent	10			25	Br. Actress
Pollock, Channing	1880-1946	Author	30	55	80	75	Am. Plays, Essayist
Polo, Teri		Ent	13			40	
Pombo, Richard W. P		Congr	10				Member US Congress
Pomeroy, Earl P		Congr	10				Member US Congress
Pomeroy, Samuel Clarke	1816-1891	Congr	35	50	25		Civil War Sen. KS 1861. 2X Cleared of Bribery
Pometti, Vincenzo		Ent	10			25	Actor
Pompadour, Mme. J. A.,	1721-1764	Royal	250	525	1130		Duchess. Louis XV Mistress
Pompidou, Georges		HOS	35	65		355	Premier, Pres. France
Pomus, Jerome Doc		Music	45		125		Rock; HOF
Ponchielli, Amilcare		Comp	175		1002		It. Opera. La Gioconda. Ballets; AMusQS 700
Pond, Enoch		Clergy	15	25	30		
Pond, Julian		Sci	50		325		
Ponder, James		Gov	12	20			Governor DE
Poniatowski, Jozef A.	1763-1813	Mil	470	1570	2150		Prince. Rarest Napoleon Marsh'l
Pons, Juan		Opera	10			25	Opera
Pons, Lily	1904-1976	Opera	40	75	125	82	Fr. -Born Am. Coloratura Sopr. Met. Star.
Ponselle, Carmela		Opera	25				Mezzo Sister of Rosa
Ponselle, Rosa	1897-1981	Ent	62	100	150	195	Acclaimed for 'Norma'. SP in Opera Debut Role 475
Pontchartrain, Louis de	1643-1727	Diplo	250		1250		Fr. Statesman
Ponti, Carlo	1912-2007	Ent	15	20		45	It. Film Prod.
Ponting, Herbert George	1870-1935	Photog	25	60	165		
Ponty, Jean-Luc	1942-	Music	15	40		65	Virtuoso Fr. violinist & jazz Comp.
Pool, Tilaman E.		WWII	10	22	38	28	ACE, WWII, Navy Ace; 6 kills
Poor, Enoch		Rev War	175	550	875		Gen. Patriot, Hero
Poore, Benjamin A.	1866-1940	Mil		75		40	Am. WWI Gen.
Pop, Iggy		Music	30	150		65	
Pope Gregory XVI	1765-1846	Clergy		1042			Roman Catholic Pope 1831-46
Pope John Paul I	1912-1978	Clergy		682			Pope From August-September 1978. 33 Days.
Pope John Paul II	1920-2005	Clergy	800	625		1550	Karol Wojtyla. Polish. Pope since 1978
Pope John XXIII	1881-1963	Clergy	645	1790	1265	2254	Angelo Giuseppe Roncalli
Pope Paul III	1468-1549	Clergy		1850			
Pope Paul VI	1897-1978	Clergy		460		602	SP Pope Paul VI & Cardinal Jozef Mindszenty 925
Pope Pius IX	1792-1878	Clergy	337	650	400		Giovanni M. M. Ferretti
Pope Pius VII	1740-1823	Clergy	300	820			Barnaba Chiaramonti
Pope Pius X	1835-1914	Clergy		1010	633	1750	Giuseppe Melchiorre Sarto

NAME	DATES	CATEGORY	SIG	LS/DS	ALS	SP	COMMENTS
Pope Pius XI	1857-1939	Clergy	275	632	3200	848	Achille Ambrogio Damiano Ratti
Pope Pius XII	1876-1958	Clergy		1059		940	Eugenio Pacelli
Pope, A. J.		WWII	20	35			WWII Am. Ace; 7. 25 kills
Pope, Alexander	1849-1924	Artist	150	370	600		Am. NY Auction Still Life Sold 475,000 '82
Pope, Alexander	1688-1744	Author	558	1232	1942		Br. Poet, Satirist, Critic
Pope, Generoso Jr.		Bus	10	40	50	25	It.-Born Publ. Il Progresso
Pope, James Pinckney	1884-1966	Congr	10	15		20	Sen. ID. Dir. TVA
Pope, John	1822-1892	Civ War	58	132	210	310	Union Genl. Cmdr. 2nd Bull Run
Pope, John (WD)		Civ War	68	160	558		Union Gen.
Popescu, Petru	1944-	Ent	10			25	Writer
Popeye		Ent	50			150	Cast signing
Popham, William	1752-1847	Rev War			375		Aide-de-Camp to Gen. Clinton
Popkin, John S.	1771-1850	Clergy		40	75		Greek Scholar & Harvard Prof. of Greek
Popovic, Cojetko		Assass	40		270		1 of 7 assassins of Franz Ferdinand in Sarajevo
Popovich, Pavel		Space	35			68	Rus. Cosmonaut
Popp, Lucia		Opera	15			50	Opera
Porizkova, Paulina		Ent	20			44	Model-Actress.
Porsche, Ferdinand Ferry	1909-1998	Bus	250	498		304	Creator of Sportscar
Porsche, Ferdinand, Dr.	1875-1951	Bus	350	475		650	Designed Volkswagon Beetle
Port, Whitney		Ent	15			45	
Portal, Charles		Aero	20	40	80	50	
Porter, Andrew	1820-1872	Civ War	50		75		Union Gen.
Porter, Cole	1891-1964	Comp	196	367	1212	600	AMusQS 1250, S Chk 1050
Porter, David	1780-1843	Mil	56	110	189		Am. Naval Off. Fought 3 Wars
Porter, David Dixon	1813-1891	Civ War	80	155	300	370	Union Adm., Mex. War, Civil War
Porter, Don	1912-1997	Ent	15			60	Actor
Porter, Fitz-John	1822-1901	Civ War	44	107	208	997	Union Gen. Special ALS 825-900
Porter, Gene Stratton		Author	50	110	175	125	Am. Novels. Freckles
Porter, George, Sir		Sci	15	35	60	25	Nobel Chemistry 1967
Porter, Horace	1837-1921	Civ War	45	75	98		Union Gen. -MOH. LS/Cont 1750
Porter, James D.		Gov	10	20	35		Governor TN
Porter, James M.	1793-1844	Cab	20	77	120		Sec. War 1843, Jurist, RR Pres.
Porter, Jane	1776-1850	Author	100		325		Br. Romance Novels
Porter, John		Congr	10				Member US Congress IL
Porter, Katherine Anne	1890-1980	Author	40	95	160	150	Am. 'Ship of Fools', Pulitzer
Porter, Noah	1811-1892	Clergy	30	65	100		Editor. Pres. of Yale
Porter, Peter		Cab	65	145	180		Sec. War J. Q. Adams
Porter, Quincy		Comp	17	45			Dean & Dir. New Eng. Conservatory
Porter, Scott		Ent	13			40	
Porter, William Sidney	1862-1910	Author	442	725	1347	835	(O. Henry) Am. Short-Story Writer
Portes-Gil, Emilio		HOS	35		85		Pres. Mexico
Portman, Eric	1901-1969	Ent	20			40	
Portman, Natalie		Ent	15			76	Actress, 'Star Wars'
Portman, Rob P		Congr	10				Member US Congress
Portsmouth, Duchess (Chas II)		Royal	65	465	625		Louise-Renee' de Keroualle. 1649-1734
Posey, Carnot	1818-1863	Civ War	275				CSA Gen.
Posey, Parker	1968-	Ent	20			47	Actress; 'Best in Show'
Possart, Ernst		Music	15		55	50	Classical Musician
Post, Augustus		Aero	25	45	55	50	Pioneer Aviator, Balloonist
Post, Emily	1873-1960	Author	90	105	80	95	US Etiquette Authority of Her Time
Post, Marjorie Merriweather		Bus	15	35	70	25	Philan., Postum Cereal
Post, Markie	1950-	Ent	10			77	Actress
Post, Wiley	1900-1935	Aero	212	310	700	879	1st Solo Around the World Flight. FFC '31 595
Post, Wiley & Gatty, Harold		Aero	425	442		760	SB 300

NAME	DATES	CATEGORY	SIG	LS/DS	ALS	SP	COMMENTS
Postlethwaite, Pete	1946-	Ent	10			40	Br. Actor
Poston, Tom	1921-2007	Ent	10			40	Actor
Potter, (Helen) Beatrix	1866-1943	Author	250	600	1461	750	Illustr. Own kid's Books. 'Peter Rabbit', SB 1550
Potter, Alonzo	1800-1865	Clergy			40		Am. Episcopal Bishop
Potter, Edward E.	1823-1889	Civ War	40	75	110		Union Gen. 1st North Carolina
Potter, Harry		Ent					S poster, Daniel Radcliffe, Emma Watson, Rupert Grint & Chris Rankin 570-760
Potter, Joseph Haydn	1822-1892	Civ War	40		95		Union Gen.
Potter, Robert Brown	1829-1887	Civ War	50	95			Union Gen.
Potts, Annie	1952-	Ent	10			55	Actress
Potts, Benjamin Franklin	1836-1887	Civ War	40	60	95		Union Gen.
Poulenc, Francis-Jean	1899-1963	Comp	135	337	484		Member Group of Six. Pianist
Poulson, Norris		Mayor	10	10			Mayor L. A.
Poulter, Thomas C.		Expl	20	40			2nd Arctic Exped.
Pound, Ezra	1885-1972	Author	205	1321	1134	1052	Poet, Editor, Critic, Translator; SB 515
Pounder, CCH		Ent	13			40	
Poundstone, Paula		Ent	10			32	Standup Comedienne
Povey, Len		Aero	10	15	25	20	
Povich, Maury		TV News	10			25	TV Host
Powderly, Terence V.	1849-1924	Labor	45	95		50	Am. Labor Leader
Powell, Adam Clayton	1908-1972	Congr	40	40	55	70	Contoversial Min., MOC NY. Barred, Reelected
Powell, Bud	1924-1966	Music	1170				Jazz pianist. 1 of most infl. in jazz history.
Powell, Colin L.	1937-	Mil	35	94		77	Gen. Secretary of State
Powell, Dick	1904-1963	Ent	40	45	60	164	Actor
Powell, Eleanor	1910-1982	Ent	15	25	35	121	Popular 40s Film Tap Dancer Musical Star
Powell, Jane		Ent	15			52	Actress
Powell, Jeremiah		Rev War	75		245		Pres. of Mass. Bay Colony Rev. Times
Powell, John Wesley		Expl	250	391			Geologist. Pioneer Expl. West US
Powell, Lewis F., Jr.	1907-1998	Sup Crt	60	95		125	Supreme Court Justice
Powell, Maud		Music	20			90	Violinist
Powell, Max		Cntry Mus	10			20	
Powell, Robert	1944-	Ent	10			30	Br. Actor
Powell, Ross E.		Mil	10	15	30		
Powell, Talmage		Author	10	20	45	15	Am. Novels Mysteries
Powell, Teddy		Band	20			70	Big Band leader
Powell, William	1892-1985	Ent	60	310		607	Actor; SP w/Myrna Loy 260
Powell, William Henry	1825-1904	Civ War	45	75	138		Union Gen.
Power, Paul	1902-1968	Ent				45	Char. Actor
Power, Tyrone	1913-1958	Ent	80	123		232	Actor
Powers, Bert		Celeb	10			10	White House Aide
Powers, Francis Gary		Aero	110	148		125	U2 Downed Pilot Over USSR LS/Cont 795
Powers, Hiram	1805-1873	Artist	60	160	325	350	19th C. Major Sculptor
Powers, John Robert		Bus	10	20	25	25	Fndr. One of 1st Modelling Agy.
Powers, John 'Shorty'	1923-1980	Space	30	40			NASA Spokesman. A-OK
Powers, Mala	1931-2007	Ent	10			40	
Powers, Preston		Artist	25	65	165		
Powers, Richard		Ent					SEE Tom Keene
Powers, Ridgely C.		Gov	10	15	30		Governor MS
Powers, Stefanie		Ent	27			80	
Powers, Stephanie	1942-	Ent	10			80	Actress; SP w/Rbt. Wagner 60
Pownall, Thomas	1722-1805	Colonial	150	311	630		Lt. Gov. NJ, Gov. MA Bay, SC
Powter, Susan		Author	10				Non-Fiction
Powys, John C.	1872-1963	Author	28	60			Novels, Poet, Critic, Philosopher
Powys, Llewelyn		Author	30	45	50	60	Essayist, Novels

NAME	DATES	CATEGORY	SIG	LS/DS	ALS	SP	COMMENTS
Powys, Theodore Francis	1875-1953	Author	80		350		Br. Allegorical Novels. AManS 1980
Poynter, Edward John, Sir		Artist	10	35	75		Pres. Royal Academy
Pozzo di Borgo, Carlo A.	1764-1842	Diplo	100		260		Opponent of Napoleon
Prado, Perez		Band	25				
Praed, Michael	1960-	Ent	10			25	Br. Actor
Praed, Winthrop M.	1802-1839	Author	50		230		Poet
Pran, Dith		Photog	10	20	45	20	Cambodian Photographer
Pratt, Calvin Edward	1828-1896	Civ War	40		105		Union Gen.
Pratt, Chris		Ent	17			50	
Pratt, Elmer 'Geronimo'	1947-	Activist	10			15	AKA Geronimo Ji-Jaga; ranking mbr: Black Panthers
Pratt, Francis & Whitney, Amos		Invent		465			Pratt & Whitney Engine
Pratt, Kyla		Ent	13			40	
Pratt, Orson	1811-1881	Relig	750	1500		5000	Mormon Apostle; Theologian; Brother to Parley
Pratt, Parley P.	1807-1857	Relig	5000	15000	25000		Mormon Apostle
Pratt, Ruth	1877-1965	Congr	10	30			Repr. NY 1929-33
Pratt, Thomas G.		Congr	10	20	25		Gov. 1845, Sen. MD 1849
Pratt, Victoria		Ent	16			48	
Preble, George H.		Civ War	20	60	85		Adm. USN. DS/Cont 250
Precourt, Charlie		Space	10			20	
Preddy. George E.		Aero	10	30	45	30	
Preger, Kurt		Opera	10			20	Opera
Prelog, Vladimir		Sci	20	30	45	45	Nobel Chemistry 1975
Premice, Josephine	1926-2001	Ent	20			40	Actress
Preminger, Otto	1906-1986	Ent	50	120		83	Important Film Dir.
Prentice, John		Comics	10			40	Rip Kirby
Prentiss, Benjamin M.	1819-1901	Civ War	45	85	125		Union Major Gen.
Prentiss, Benjamin M. (WD)		Civ War	75	160	275		Shiloh
Prentiss, Paula	1938-	Ent	12			35	Actress
Prepon, Laura	1980-	Ent	10			60	Actress
Pres. OATH		Pres		4417			5 PRES. Printed Transcript, S by 5. S by 6 6500
Pres. S (4)		Pres	1250			1546	4 PRESIDENTS (Reagan-Ford-Carter-Nixon)
Pres. S (5)		Pres	1412			3712	Ford, Nixon, Bush, Reagan, Carter. WH Engr. S 3700
Prescott, Oliver	1731-1804	Rev War	125	276	525		Suppression of Shay's Rebellion
Prescott, Wm. Hickling		Author	30	60			
Presley, Elvis	1935-1977	Ent	1534	2794	12206	2711	ALS/Cont 20000-30000
Presley, Lisa Marie		Celeb	20			35	Singer, Daughter of Elvis Presley; S CD 65-220
Presley, Priscilla	1945-	Ent	20		40	142	Legal DS 500., SP w/Elvis 3000; SB 175
Presley, Vernon		Celeb	15			60	Father of Elvis Presley
Presnell, Lowell		Author	10			12	History of mining
Presser, Jackie	1926-1988	Labor	10	25		25	Am. labor leader. Pres. of the Teamsters
Preston, J. A.		Ent	10			25	Actor
Preston, John Smith	1809-1881	Civ War	95				CSA Gen.
Preston, Kelly	1962-	Ent	10			40	Actress
Preston, Robert	1918-1987	Ent	25			80	Actor-Singer 'Music Man'
Preston, William	1816-1887	Civ War	125	423	540		CSA Gen.
Preston, William (WD)		Civ War	157	590	735		CSA Gen.
Preston, William Ballard	1805-1862	Cab	25	50	110		CSA Sen., Wardte SP 3,000
Preston, Wm. C.	1794-1860	Congr	15	35			Sen. SC
Pretenders		Music	75			250	S Album 80; S Guitar 350
Pretorius, Major P. J.		Author	15			40	Afr. adventure
Pretty Things, The		Music	40			80	Br. Rock Group (All 5)
Preuss, Georg		Mil	20		40		
Previn, Andre		Music	20	60	80	85	Conductor, Comp., & pianist; SB 50
Previn, Dorey		Comp	10			20	

NAME	DATES	CATEGORY	SIG	LS/DS	ALS	SP	COMMENTS
Prevost, Eugene-Marcel		Author	10	25	55		Fr. Moralist, Feminist Fiction
Prey, Hermann		Opera	10			30	Opera
Price, Bruce D		Author	10			12	Genealogy
Price, Channing	1843-1863	Civ War	75		1668		CSA Adjuvant Gen.
Price, David E. P		Congr	10				Member US Congress
Price, James H.		Gov	10	15			Governor VA
Price, Leontyne	1927-	Opera	25		45	118	Am. Sopr., Opera
Price, Lindsay	1976-	Celeb				20	
Price, Margaret		Opera	15			45	Opera
Price, Ray		Cntry Mus	10			20	C & W
Price, Sterling	1809-1867	Civ War	218	370	394		CSA Gen. Gov. MO
Price, Sterling (WD)		Civ War	380		4500		CSA Gen. AES 575
Price, Vincent	1911-1993	Ent	45	65	80	120	Self Sketch S 130-200
Pride, Charley	1938-	Cntry Mus	10			45	1st Afr-Am Major Country Music Star
Prien, Guenther	1908-1941	WWII	300			360	Ger. WWII U-Boat Cmdr. Important SP 2000
Priest, Ivy Baker		Cab	10	15	30	20	US Treas.
Priest, Pat	1936-	Ent	15			55	Actress;. 'Munsters'. 'Marilyn Munster'
Priest, Royce W.		WWII	10	22	35	30	ACE, WWII, USAAF Ace; 5 kills
Priestley, Jason		Ent	20			60	Actor
Priestley, John Boynton	1894-1984	Author	20	35	60	50	Plays, Novels, Plays
Priestley, Joseph	1783-1804	Sci	347	1064	1536		Br. Clergyman, Chemist.
Priestley, William O., Sir		Med	50	120	200		Obstetric Physician
Prieur-Duvernois, Claude-A.		Fr Rev	35	125			Count, Fr. Revolutionary
Prigogine, Ilya		Sci	20	30	45	25	Nobel Chemistry 1977
Prima, Louis		Band	20			112	Big Band Leader-Trumpeter; SP w/Keely Smith 210
Primrose, Archibald P.	1847-1929	HOS	30	70	145		Br. Prime Min.
Primrose, William		Music	75			250	Great Violinist
Prince		Ent	110	528		200	
Prince Andrew	1845-1913	Royal				1105	Prince Andreas son of George I
Prince Charles		Royal	175	507	1130	550	Eldest son, Queen Elizabeth II. Prince of Wales
Prince, Henry	1811-1892	Civ War	40	65	85		Union Gen. Pre War ALS 650
Prince, John Dyneley		Educ	10	25		15	Dean Graduate School NYU
Princess Alice of Battenberg		Royal				570	Mother, Prince Philip; 'Righteous Among the Nations' at Yad Vashem
Princess Anne		Royal	85	250		120	Daughter of Elizabeth II; Royal Photo 1970
Princess Augusta Sophia		Royal		315			Princess, GB & Ir. (1768–1840). Daughter, Geo. III
Princess Caroline		Royal	30			250	(Monaco). Daughter of Grace & Rainier
Princess Elizabeth	1770-1840	Royal			260		Daughter of George III
Princess Haya	1974-	Royal				242	Daughter of the King of Jordan
Princess Stephanie		Royal	45			83	Princess of Monaco
Principal, Victoria	1950-	Ent	10	60	25	55	Actress
Pringle, Aileen	1895-1989	Ent	15	15	35	60	Actress
Prinz, Dianne		Space	10			20	
Prinz, Rosemary	1930-	Ent	10			25	Actress
Prinze, Freddie	1954-1977	Ent	130	195		225	Comedian
Prinze, Freddie, Jr.	1976-	Ent	10			40	Actor
Prior, Matthew	1664-1721	Pol		500			English Poet & Diplomat.
Pritchard, Jeter C.	1857-1921	Congr	10	15			Sen. NC 1895
Pritchard, John, Sir		Cond				45	Opera & Mozart Specialist
Probst, Jeff		Ent	15			45	
Procol Harum		Music	85			380	S Album 350
Procter, Emily		Ent	13			40	
Proctor, Edna Dean	1838-	Author	35		80		Am. Poet, Magazine Writer
Proctor, Redfield	1831-1908	Cab	12	25	50	30	Gov, Sen. VT, Sec. War

NAME	DATES	CATEGORY	SIG	LS/DS	ALS	SP	COMMENTS
Proctor, Richard Anthony		Sci	10	15	35		Br. Astonomer, Science Writer
Proffit, George		Congr	10				FF 25
Profumo, John		Pol	40	148		100	Br. Traitor. Member of Parliament
Profumo, Valerie (Hobson)		Ent	10		25	25	Br. Film Star
Prokofieff, Serge	1891-1953	Comp	425	1250	1888	2500	Russ. AMusQS 2500-5000
Proops, Greg	1959-	Ent	10			30	Comedian; actor
Prosky, Robert	1930-	Ent	10			35	Actor
Protti, Aldo		Opera	10			20	Opera
Proust, Marcel	1871-1922	Author	500	875	1550	6000	ALS/Cont 3300
Prout, William	1785-1850	Sci		245	175		English Chemist & Physician
Prouty, Jed	1879-1956	Ent	30			45	Actor
Proval, David		Ent				65	Richie Aprile, Sopranos
Provine, Dorothy	1937-	Ent	15			65	Actress
Provost, David		Pol		390			Mayor of New York 1699-1700
Provost, Jon	1950-	Ent	18			60	Young Actor. 'Timmy' from 'Lassie' TV Series
Prowse, David		Ent	42			114	Actor; ' Darth Vadar'; 'Star Wars'
Prowse, Juliet		Ent	10	12	15	47	Actress, dancer
Proxmire, William		Congr	10	10		20	Sen. WI
Prudent, Emile		Music				85	Fr. Pianist
Prudhomme, Paul		Celeb	10			15	Famous chef
Prudhomme, Rene Fran. A. Sully		Author			175		Fr. Poet & Philosopher
Prutzmann, Hans-Adolf	d. 1945	WWII	125				Nazi SS leader. "Werewolf" Bands
Pryce, Deborah P		Congr	10				Member US Congress
Pryce, Jonathan		Ent	10			40	Br. Actor
Pryor, David		Gov	10	15			Governor AR
Pryor, Mark		Congr	10				US Senate (D-AR)
Pryor, Richard	1940-2005	Ent	50	158		265	Actor; Comedian
Pryor, Roger	1901-1974	Ent	15	20		55	Actor
Pryor, Roger A.	1828-1919	Civ War	127	260	244		CSA Gen. US MOC. 1859-61
Pryor, Roger A. (WD)		Civ War	175		650		CSA Gen.
Public Enemy		Music	100			120	Rock
Pucci, Emilio		Bus	10	25	40	15	It. Fashion Designer
Puccini, Giacomo	1858-1924	Comp	512	562	706	1423	AMusQS 850-4,000; S score 3500
Puck, Wolfgang		Bus	10	10		20	Successful Chef & Owner of 'Spago'
Pudovkin, Vsesolod	1893-1953	Ent	75		322	368	Russian film Dir.
Puelo, Johnny	1907-1983	Music	10			50	Johnny Puleo & His Harmonica Gang
Puente, Tito		Band	10			55	Big Band Leader.
Puett, Clay		Bus	25	60		35	
Pulitzer, Joseph	1847-1911	Bus	90	622	745		Pulitzer Pr. Editor-Publisher. Rare ALS 4500
Pulitzer, Joseph, Jr.		Bus	20	25		30	Editor-Publisher
Pulitzer, Ralph	1879-1939	Bus	54		250		Journalist, Pres. Press Publishing NY World
Pulitzer, Roxanne	1951-	Author	10			25	Writer, actress
Pullenberg, Albert		Sci	20			60	Rocket Pioneer/von Braun
Pullman, Bill		Ent	12			45	Actor
Pullman, George M.	1831-1897	Bus	280	753	900	1000	Pullman RR Car. ALS on Lttrhd. 9600
Pullman, Hattie Sanger		Philan	15	25	30		Mrs. George M. Pullman
Pulp Fiction (cast)		Ent	265			286	Travolta/ Jackson; Cast S poster 625-1025
Pulsford, Nigel		Music	10			25	Guitar 'Bush'
Puma, Salvatore		Opera	10			20	Opera
Punshon, W. Morley		Clergy	25	40	50		
Pupin, Michael, Dr.	1858-1935	Sci	59	150	210	250	Physicist-Inventor-Author; SB 40
Purcell, Dominic		Ent	15			45	
Purcell, Edward M., Dr.		Sci	20	30	45	45	Nobel Physics 1952
Purcell, Irene	1901-1972	Ent				120	Actress

NAME	DATES	CATEGORY	SIG	LS/DS	ALS	SP	COMMENTS
Purcell, Lee	1947-	Ent	10			35	
Purcell, Sarah	1948-	Ent	10			30	
Purdy, James		Author	15	50			
Purl, Linda	1955-	Ent	15			62	Actress
Purvis, Melvin	1903-1960	Lawman	90	170	406	250	FBI Agent. Hunted Most Wanted. S Chk 200-500
Purvis, Robert		Abolit	25	40	85		Underground RR
Pusey, Edward B.	1800-1882	Clergy	45	55	110	150	Anglican High Church Leader of Oxford Movement
Pusey, Nathan M.	1907-	Educ	15	30	75	50	Pres. Harvard
Pusey, Pennock		Pol	10	15			Gov. Official
Pushkin, Alexander	1799-1837	Author	2200	5250	16200		Rus. Poet, Dramatist, Novels
Pusser, Buford		Lawman	50	150		145	Walking Tall Tenn. Sheriff; SB 315; S Chk 350
Putin, Vladimir V.		Pol	100	220		450	Former Pres. of Russia
Putman, Frederick Ward	1839-1915	Sci		30	55		Anthropologist-Naturalist. Curator of Top Museums
Putnam, Adam H. P		Congr	10				Member US Congress
Putnam, George Haven	1844-1930	Bus	30	80			Publishing House. Putnam & Sons
Putnam, George Palmer	1814-1872	Bus	40	75	110		Book Publisher, Author
Putnam, Israel	1718-1790	Rev War	250	725	1250		Don't Fire Till. War Dte. MsLS 3500
Putnam, Rufus		Rev War	175	405	592		Gen. Ohio Pioneer
Puzo, Mario	1921-1999	Author	120	260	300	89	Am. Novels. The Godfather; SB 635-1210
Py, Gilbert		Opera	10			25	Opera
Pyfrom, Shawn		Ent	15			45	
Pyle, Artimus		Music	20			65	Lynyrd Skynyrd Drummer. S Drumhd 150, S Sket 120
Pyle, Denver	1920-1997	Ent	10			35	Actor; 'Dukes of Hazzard'
Pyle, Ernie	1900-1945	Author	283	391	485	350	Correspondent WWII, Pulitzer, KIA; SB 375
Pyle, Howard	1853-1911	Artist	175	375	750		Am. Art Nouveau Illust.-Author
Pynchon, John	1626-1703	Colonial			3750		Statesman, Soldier.
Qaddafi, Muammar el-(Alg)		HOS	65	150	350	218	Chairman Libyan-Arab Repub.
Quackenbush, Stephen (WD)	1823-1890	Civ War	35		165		Union Naval Off.
Quaid, Dennis		Ent	20			45	Actor
Quaid, Randy		Ent	10			40	Actor
Qualen, John	1899-1987	Ent	10			60	Actor
Qualls, D. J.		Ent	12			35	
Quang, Thich Tri		HOS	20	45	125	30	
Quant, Mary		Bus	10	10	20	10	Br. Fashion Designer.
Quantrill, William C.	1837-1865	Civ War	2750	6500	12000		CSA Army Guerilla Leader
Quarles, William A.	1825-1893	Civ War	97	308			CSA Gen. Sig. War Dte. 150
Quarry, Robert	1925-	Ent	10			65	Actor
Quasimodo, Salvatore		Author	25	40	55	30	Nobel Literature 1959
Quast, Wilbur 'Bill'		WWII	15			50	WWII hero
Quay, Matthew Stanley	1833-1904	Civ War	40	75	120		Union Col., MOH
Quayle, Anthony	1913-1989	Ent	20	25	55	60	Br. Actor
Quayle, Dan	1947-	VP	35	52		62	Sen. IN, Bush VP. S WH Crd 50; SP w/GHW Bush 260
Quayle, Marilyn		2nd Lady	20			35	
Queen		Music	1024	1970		1725	Rock, S Album 1500
Queen Latifa		Celeb	20			45	Actress, singer
Queen Mary of England		Royal				642	Consort of George V
Queen, Ellery		Author					SEE Dannay
Quentin, Caroline	1961-	Ent	10			25	Br. Actress
Quesada, Elwood R.		Mil	25	30	45	180	Gen. ASAF
Quesada, Vincente Fox		Pol	15			45	Former Pres. of Mexico
Questel, Mae		Ent	50				Original Voice of Betty Boop
Quie, Albert Harold		Congr	10			10	MOC MN
Quigg, Lemuel Ely		Congr	10	10			MOC NY 1894
Quillan, Eddie	1907-1990	Ent	20			45	Actor

NAME	DATES	CATEGORY	SIG	LS/DS	ALS	SP	COMMENTS
Quilter, Roger		Comp			150		English Comp.
Quinby, Isaac Ferdinand	1821-1891	Civ War	35	65	80		Union Gen.
Quincy, Josiah	1772-1864	Congr	40	60	95		Repr. MA. Pres. Harvard
Quine, Richard		Ent	10			40	Actor turned Dir.
Quinlan, Kathleen		Ent	10			50	Actress
Quinn, Aidan		Ent	10			45	Actor
Quinn, Anthony	1915-2001	Ent	20	38		80	AA Winning Mex. -Irish Actor. 'Zorba'
Quinn, Carmel		Ent	10			20	
Quinn, Jack Q		Congr	10				Member US Congress
Quinn, Martha		Ent	10			15	MTV
Quinn, Robert E.		Gov	10	15			Governor RI
Quinn, William F.		Gov	10	10		15	Governor HI
Quinones, John		TV News	10			20	Reporter
Quintard, Charles Todd		Clergy	75	95	160		Served CSA Army as Phys.
Quinto, Zachary		Ent	16			48	
Quirk, Michael J.		WWII	12	25	40	30	ACE, WWII; 11 kills
Quirke, Pauline	1959-	Ent	10			25	Br. Actress
Quiros, Jean B.		HOS	45	70			
Quisling, Vidkun	1877-1955	WWII	115	220	382	475	Executed Nazi Collaborator
Quitman, John A.	1799-1858	Pol	25				Acting Gov. Miss., 1835-36. Brig. Gen. Mexican War
Quivers, Robin	1952-	Ent	10			20	Media/TV personality; 'Howard Stern Show'
R. E. M.		Music				192	Rock; S Guitar 260; S Album 250
R. Kelly		Music	20			45	Rap
Ra, Sun		Music	150			350	Blues-Jazz
Raab, Julius		HOS	10	15	35	15	Chancellor Austria
Raabe, Meinhardt		Ent	25		60	45	Munchkin WOZ
Rabaud, Henri	1873-1949	Comp	35			200	Fr. Comp. -Conductor. Opera. AMusQS 120
Rabl, Isador I.	1898-1988	Sci	42	60	80	40	Nobel Physics 1944. Delopment of Radar, A Bomb
Rabin, Yitzhak	1922-1996	HOS	116	359	525	250	PM Israel, Nobel. Assass. '96; TLS/Cont 900-
Rabinowitz, Solomon		Author					SEE Aleichem, S. (Pen Name)
Raboy, Mac		Comics	20			95	Flash Gordon
Rachin, Alan		Ent	10			40	Actor
Rachmaninoff, Sergei	1873-1943	Comp	358	868	1383	1553	AMusQS 2000-4500
Racine, Jean	1639-1699	Author	4500				Fr. Dramatist.
Rackham, Arthur	1867-1939	Artist	60	175	325		Br. Illust. kid's Books. Water Color
Radanovich, George R		Congr	10				Member US Congress
Radcliffe, Daniel		Ent				263	Actor; 'Harry Potter'
Radford, Michael	1946-	Ent	10			25	Film Dir.
Radford, William	1808-1890	Civ War	40	125	170		Union Commodore
Radford, William	1814-1870	Congr	10	15	30		Repr. NY
Radhakrishnan, Sarvepalli	1888-1975	HOS	75	167	380	178	Pres. India, Philosopher, Educator, Author
Radner, Gilda	1946-1989	Ent	68	262		182	Am. Comedienne
Radziwill, Lee		Celeb	20	35		30	Sister to Jackie Kennedy
Rae, Alexa		Ent	13			40	
Rae, Cassidy	1976-	Ent	10			40	Actress
Rae, Charlotte	1926-	Ent	10			35	Actress
Rae, Corrine Bailey		Music	20			50	Singer; S Guitar 180
Raeder, Erick	1876-1960	Mil	100	266	330	250	Ger. Navy Cmdr., Convicted of War Crimes WWII
Raff, Joseph Joachim		Comp	25		150		Ger. Wide Variety of Music
Rafferty, Frances	1922-2004	Ent	10			35	Actress
Raffin, Deborah		Ent	10			53	
Rafko, Kaye Lani		Ent	10			25	Miss Am. 1988
Raft, George	1895-1980	Ent	45	120		184	Actor
Rage Against the Machine		Music	32			90	Music. Rock Group

NAME	DATES	CATEGORY	SIG	LS/DS	ALS	SP	COMMENTS
Raglan, Fitzroy Somerset, Lord		Mil	40	115	105		Crimean War. Raglan Sleeve
Ragsland, Rags	1905-1946	Ent	40			90	Comedian
Rahall II, Nick J. R		Congr	10				Member US Congress
Rahman, Abdul		HOS	10	35	80	15	Malaysia. 1st Ambass. US
Raimi, Sam		Ent	13			40	
Raimondi, Ruggero		Opera	20			50	Opera
Rainer, Luise	1910-	Ent	15	35	40	96	Austrian Two Time Oscar Winner. Back to Back
Raines, Ella	1920-1988	Ent	15			51	Actress
Rainey, Ford	1908-2005	Ent	10			40	Actor
Rainey, Gertrude 'Ma'		Music		990	1100		'Mother of the Blues'
Rainey, Henry Thomas		Congr	10	15			MOC IL 1903-21, Spkr.
Rainger, Ralph		Comp	20			40	AMusQS 95
Rainier III, Prince		Royal	70	95	205	95	Monaco; SP w/Gacr Kelly 240-900
Rain-in-the-Face		Am Ind	5750			8260	
Rains, Claude	1899-1967	Ent	219	252		330	Brit. Char. Actor. 'Casablanca'
Rains, Gabriel James	1803-1881	Civ War	110	417			CSA Gen.
Rains, James E. (WD)	1833-1862	Civ War		4850			CSA Gen. KIA
Rainwater, Leo James		Sci	20	30	45	25	Nobel Physics 1975
Rainwater, Marvin		Cntry Mus	15			30	
Raisa, Rosa	1893-1963	Opera	30	45		60	Opera. Created Title Role in Turandot
Raitano, Natalie		Ent	13			40	
Raitt, Bonnie		Music	10			113	Rock; S Album 140
Raitt, John	1917-2005	Ent	40			70	Actor; Father to Bonnie
Rakosi, Matyas	1892-1971	Pol		120			Stalinist Prime Min. of Hungary
Raksin, David	1912-2004	Comp					Am. Comp. AMusQS 75
Raleigh, Walter, Sir	1552-1618	Expl	5750	23000			Renaissaince Explr., poet
Rall, Guenther	1918-	WWII	40	82	172	87	#3 ACE, WWII, Ger./275 Kills.
Rall, Johann Gottlieb		Rev War		8400			Hessian Rev. War Col. D. Battle of Trenton 1776.
Ralston, Esther	1902-1994	Ent	10	15	45	68	Am. Leading Lady 20s-30's
Ralston, Jobyna	1899-1967	Ent	25	35	65	65	Actress
Ralston, Vera Hruba	1921-2003	Ent	10			40	
Ralston, William		Bus	55	90	150		Fndr. Bank of California; S Chk 115
Rama VI	1881-1925	Royal	135				King Siam (Thailand)
Ramamurthy, Sendhil		Ent	15			45	
Rambeau, Marjorie	1889-1970	Ent	20	25	45	80	Actress
Rambo, Dirk	1941-1967	Ent	20			125	Actor
Ramey, Samuel	1942-	Opera	10			40	Opera; Am. bass
Ramirez, Carlos		Opera	10				Baritone
Ramirez, Edgar		Ent	15			45	
Ramirez, Efren		Ent	15			45	
Ramon, Ilan		Space	75			250	Israeli; D. Space Shuttle Columbia re-entry 2003
Ramone, Johnny	1948-2004	Music	25			95	Romones Rock Group
Ramones		Music	185			316	Rock group; S Album 550; S Guitar 900
Ramos, Mel		Artist				83	Pop artist
Ramos, Ramon		Band	10			35	1930's Big Band Leader
Ramos, Sarah		Ent	13			40	
Rampling, Charlotte		Ent	15			73	Brit. Actress-Model.
Ramsay, George Douglas	1802-1882	Civ War	40	75	100		Union Gen.
Ramsay, William, Sir	1852-1916	Sci	150	410	750		Nobel Chemistry 1904
Ramseur, Stephen D. (WD)	1837-1864	Civ War		13000			CSA Gen. RARE
Ramseur, Stephen Dodson	1837-1864	Civ War	354	775			CSA Gen.
Ramsey, Alexander		Cab	20	45	90		CW Gov. MN, Hayes Sec. War
Ramsey, Dewitt Clinton		WWII	15	45		45	US Naval Adm.
Ramsey, Michael, Arch.		Clergy	35	45	50	45	

NAME	DATES	CATEGORY	SIG	LS/DS	ALS	SP	COMMENTS
Ramsey, Norman F., Dr.		Sci	15	25		20	Nobel Physics 1989
Ramstad, Jim R		Congr	10				Member US Congress
Rand, Ayn	1905-1982	Author	600	1906		1500	Objectivist Novels, AManS 2128
Rand, Sally	1903-1979	Ent	25	85		147	Fan Dancer 20s-30's
Randall, James R.	1839-1908	Comp	100		760		Maryland, My.
Randall, Samuel J.		Congr	10	20			MOC PA 1863-90
Randall, Tony	1920-2004	Ent	10	15	20	50	Actor; SP w/Klugman 200
Randolph, A. Philip	1889-1979	Labor	65	75			US Black Labor Leader 1925. Train Porter's Strike
Randolph, Beverly	1755-1797	Rev War	100	325			Early Gov. Virginia 1788
Randolph, Boots		Music	10			20	Country Rockabilly Saxophonist
Randolph, Charles D.		Author	75	210	315		Buckskin Bill Assoc./Wm. Cody. Novels/West. Poetry
Randolph, Edmund J.	1753-1813	Rev War	165	491	634		Sec. State, Washington Aide de. ADS/Cont 1600
Randolph, Geo. Wythe	1818-1867	Civ War	268	410	565		CSA Gen. ALS '62 825
Randolph, John	1733-1883	Rev War	80	265	485		(of Roanoke) MOC, Sen. VA
Randolph, Joyce	1925-	Ent	10	10		45	Actress. 'Trixie' on 'The Honeymooners'
Randolph, Lillian	1898-1980	Ent	100			250	
Randolph, Peyton	1721-1775	Rev War	425	1783			1st Pres. Continental Congress
Randolph, Thos. Mann, Jr.	1768-1828	Congr	75	275			Repr. & Gov. VA. Special ALS 2800
Randy & the Rainbows (3)		Music	20				Rock
Rangel, Charles B.	1930-	Congr	10			20	Afr.-Am MOC NY. Imp. Advocate for Disadvantaged
Ranier, Luise	1910-	Ent				80	Two-time Academy Award-winning Ger. film actress
Rank, J. Arthur, 1st Baron		Ent	25		75	55	Br. Industrialist, Film Magnate
Rank, Otto	1884-1939	Sci	200		425		Austrian Psychoanalyst
Rankin, Jeannette	1880-1973	Congr	80	200			Voted against both World Wars
Rankin, Nell		Opera	10	20		25	Am. Contralto-Mezzo
Rankin, Robert J.		WWII	12	25	42	35	ACE, WWII, Ace in a Day; 10 kills
Ransier, Alonzo Jacob		Congr	75				MOC SC
Ransom, John Crowe		Author	35	85	200		Am. Poet, Critic, Professor
Ransom, Matthew W.	1826-1904	Civ War	110	186	245		CSA Gen.
Ransom, Robert Jr	1828-1892	Civ War	100				CSA Gen.
Ransom, Robert, Jr. (WD)	1828-1892	Civ War	220	1250	2850		CSA Gen. (1828-92)
Ransom, Thomas E. G.	1834-1864	Civ War	120		288		Union Gen.
Rapaport, Lester		Artist	10	15	30	15	
Rapaport, Michael		Ent	17			50	
Rapee, Erno		Cond	15			45	Hung. -Am. Radio City Music Hall
Raphael	1483-1520	Artist		30000			Raphael Sanzio D'urbino
Raphael, Sally Jessy		Ent	10			25	TV Talk Show Hostess
Rapper, Irving	1898-	Ent	15			35	40's Film Dir. 'Now Voyager'
Rappold, Marie		Opera	30			95	Opera, Concert
Rash, Steve		Ent	10			20	Dir.
Rashad, Phylicia		Ent	10			35	Actress
Raskob, John J.		Bus	10	20		15	CEO Gen. Motors
Rasmussen, Knud J. V.	1879-1933	Expl	200		325	350	Danish Arctic Explr., Author
Raspberry, William		Jrnalist	10			15	Pulitzer Pr. columnist
Rasputin, Gregori E.	1872-1916	Clergy	2500	5130	7250		Rus. Mystic. Influenced Royal Family. Assass.
Rasuk, Victor		Ent	32			95	
Rathbone, Basil	1892-1967	Ent	198	240	388	419	Menacing, Leading Man & Sophisticated 'Villain'
Rathbone, Henry Reed	1837-1911	Civ War	565	1380	1500		Union Col., Accompanied Lincoln to Ford's theater
Rathbone, Monroe J.		Bus	10			15	Exxon. Important Oil Innovations
Rather, Dan		TV News	10			30	News anchor
Ratner, Payne		Gov	10	15			Governor KS
Ratoff, Gregory	1897-1960	Ent	30	65		208	Actor
Ratzenberger, John		Ent	10			35	Actor; Comedian; 'Cheers'
Rau, Johannes		Pol				20	Pres. of Ger.

NAME	DATES	CATEGORY	SIG	LS/DS	ALS	SP	COMMENTS
Raum, Green B.	1829-1909	Civ War	28	65		127	Union Gen., MOC IL
Rauschenberg, Bob		Artist	50	85		350	Color Pc Repro. S 165; collages
Raveau, Alice		Opera			175		Fr. contralto
Ravel, Maurice	1875-1937	Comp	358	828	1193	2500	AMusQS 1, 675-3, 800-4, 800
Rawdon-Hastings, Francis, Lord	1754-1826	Rev War	100	220	310		Br. Off'r. Bunker Hill
Rawlings, Edward V.		Mil	10	20			
Rawlings, Marjorie Kinnan		Author	45	150			Am. Pulitzer. The Yearling
Rawlins, John A.	1831-1869	Civ War	60	75	184		Union Gen., Sec. War 1869
Rawlinson, Herbert	1886-1953	Ent	15	20	45	65	Br. Actor. Starred in dozens of B Westerns,
Rawls, Lou	1933-2006	Music	15	25		50	Singer
Rawson, Edward	1615-1693	Colonial	125	350	685		Colonial Sec. ADS 1500
Ray, Aldo	1926-1991	Ent	15	30		40	Actor
Ray, Dixie Lee		Gov	15			40	Governor WA
Ray, James Earl	1928-1976	Assass	125	134	149		Assass. Martin Luther King, Jr.
Ray, Johnnie	1927-1990	Music				155	Singer-Actor
Ray, Leah	1915-1999	Ent	10			45	Actress
Ray, Man (Rudnitsky)	1890-1976	Artist	258	385			Surrealist Painter, Photographer. ANS 285
Ray, Nicholas		Ent				670	Dir.
Ray, Rachael		Ent	10			40	TV chef
Ray, Robert D.		Gov	10			10	Governor IA
Ray, Susan		Cntry Mus	10			10	
Rayburn, Gene	1917-1999	Celeb	15			35	TV Gameshow host
Rayburn, Sam	1882-1961	Congr	40	81		68	Spkr. of the House, TX. Was Spkr. Longest
Raye, Collin		Cntry Mus	10			30	Singer
Raye, Martha	1916-1994	Ent	20	58		51	Comedianne
Rayleigh, John W. S.	1842-1919	Sci			402		Nobel Physics. 3rd Baron
Raymond, Alex		Comics	60		95	95	Flash Gordon. Spec. Ltrhd. TLS 225
Raymond, Gene	1908-1998	Ent	10	15	25	50	Actor
Raymond, Henry J.		Bus	30	75	150		Fndr. New York Times, MOC NY
Raymond, Jim		Comics	15			75	Blondie
Raymond, John T.	1836-1887	Ent	20			95	Vintage Actor
Raymond, Paula	1924-2003	Ent	20			100	Actress
Razaf, Andy		Comp	45		225		Lyricist Ain't Misbehavin'
Rea, Stephen	1946-	Ent	10			30	Irish actor
Read, Albert Cushing		Aero	40	85	180	115	Adm. Record Flight, WWI & WWII
Read, Dolly	1944-	Ent	10			25	Br. Actress
Read, George	1733-1798	Rev War	388	565	1695		Signer Dec. of Indepen.
Read, Jacob	1752-1816	Rev War	75	180	240		Rev War Col. Pol.
Read, James	1953-	Ent	10			25	Actor
Read, T. Buchanan	1822-1872	Artist	17	30	40		Poet. 'Sheridan's Ride'
Readdy, William F.		Space	10			20	
Reade, Charles		Author	30	70	135		Br. Novels, Dramatist
Reagan, John H.	1818-1905	Civ War	113	303	408		CSA Postmaster Gen., DS cont 1610
Reagan, Maureen	1941-2001	Celeb	10	15	30	25	Pol. Daughter of Pres. Reagan; actress
Reagan, Nancy		1st Lady	50	78	141	102	
Reagan, Ron, Jr.		Ent	10			30	Dancer
Reagan, Ronald	1911-2004	Pres	318	600	1429	423	Personal Paternal ALS 18,000
Reagan, Ronald (As Pres.)		Pres	444	1909	6154	557	SP w/Nancy 380-500. SP of Reagan Lib. 1500-2000
Real, Pierre F., Count		Fr Rev	15	35	80		
Reale, Antenore		Opera	20			55	Opera
Ream, Vinnie		Artist			450		Am. Sculptor
Reaser, Elizabeth		Ent	13			40	
Reason, Rex	1928-	Ent	10			41	Ger. actor
Reasoner, Harry	1923-1991	TV News	15			20	60 Minutes

NAME	DATES	CATEGORY	SIG	LS/DS	ALS	SP	COMMENTS
Reckell, Peter	1955-	Ent	10			25	Actor
Rector, George		Bus	20			35	World Famous Chef-Rector's NY
Rector, Henry M.	1816-1901	Gov	75	180			CSA Gov. AR. War Dte. DS 875
Red Hot Chili Peppers (4)		Music	75			312	S Guitar 430-900; S Album 215
Redding, Otis	1941-1967	Music	605			3075	Rock
Reddy, Helen		Music	10		20	30	Singer
Redenbacker, Orville	1907-1995	Bus	10	30	35	35	Popcorn King. Agricultural Expert, Gourmet Popcorn
Redfield, Billy	1927-1976	Ent	15			65	Actor
Redfield, William C.	1889-1932	Cab	10	30	45	45	Sec. Commerce 1913
Redford, Robert		Ent	55	189		181	Actor-Prod., Dir., Writer.
Redgrave, Lynn	1943-	Ent	10			40	Actress; SB 35.
Redgrave, Michael, Sir	1908-1985	Ent	24	60	55	65	Actor. Stage-Films from 30s
Redgrave, Vanessa	1937-	Ent	20	35		75	Br. Leading Lady. Numerous AA Nominations
Redman, Don		Music	20			45	Jazz Musician
Redmond, John E.	1856-1918	Pol	10	15	40	50	Irish Leader of Home Rule
Redon, Odilon	1840-1916	Artist	70		435		Flowers-Phantoms. Lithographer & Engraver
Redouté, Pierre Joseph	1759-1840	Artist	200	625	1392		Belg-Fr. Painter, Lithographer. Known for Flowers
Reed, Alan	1907-1977	Ent	48			50	Char. Actor, Original 'Fred Flintstone' Voice
Reed, Barry		Author	10			15	Creator of 'Dan Sheridan',
Reed, Carol, Sir	1906-1976	Ent	45	100		150	Influential Br. Film Dir.
Reed, David H. C.		Clergy	20	25	35	30	
Reed, Donna	1921-1986	Ent	87	150		192	AA Winner. 'It's A Wonderful Life'.
Reed, Erik		Ent	10			20	Actor
Reed, Isaac		Congr	10				FF 32
Reed, Jack		Congr	10				US Senate (D-RI)
Reed, James Alexander		Congr	10	15		10	Sen. MO 1910
Reed, Jerry		Ent	10			25	Singer-Actor
Reed, John	1887-1920	Author	188	1130	1050	1250	Radical Am. Journalist & Revolutionist
Reed, Joseph	1741-1785	Rev War	84	505	275		PA Statesman, Continental Cong.
Reed, Lou		Music	20			58	Singer, S Guitar 120
Reed, Nikki		Ent	15			45	
Reed, Oliver	1938-	Ent	15			80	Br. Actor. Br., Am. & Intl. Films. Leading Man
Reed, Phillip	1908-1996	Ent	10	20	35	60	Actor
Reed, Rex	1938-	Ent	10			30	Showbiz Interviewer & Gossip Columnist
Reed, Robert	1932-1992	Ent	40	70		75	Actor. 'The Brady Bunch'
Reed, Roland	1894-1972	Ent	15			35	Prod.
Reed, Shanna	1956-	Ent				130	Actress & dancer
Reed, Stanley	1884-1980	Sup Crt	48	350	175	125	TDS 1500 (Opinion) F. D. R. Court
Reed, Thomas Brackett	1839-1902	Congr	15	35	45		Spkr. of the House. ME
Reed, Walter	1851-1902	Sci	400	925	2040	1250	Am. Army Surgeon. Proved Mosquito=Yellow Fever
Reed, Walter	1916-2001	Ent	10			35	Actor
Reedy, George		Cab	10			10	
Rees, Roger	1944-	Ent	10			35	Actor
Rees, Thomas		Bus	10	25	45	25	
Reese, Della		Ent	15	45		40	Actress-Singer 'Touched By An Angel'
Reese, Jim		Band	10			20	Am. Ragtime & early jazz bandleader
Reeve, Christopher	1952-2004	Ent	143	235	150	230	Actor. 'Superman'
Reeves, Chuck		Celeb	10			15	Keynote Spkr. ex-NFL great
Reeves, George	1914-1959	Ent	684	1100	1350	2742	Orig. TV 'Superman'. GWTW, ALS/ DS/cont 6000
Reeves, Jim	1923-1964	Cntry Mus	213	273		279	Country Singer. S Album 210
Reeves, Keanu	1965-	Ent	20	63		61	Actor
Reeves, Martha		Comp	10			25	Comp. -Entertainer
Reeves, Perrey		Ent	13			40	
Reeves, Ronna		Music	10			20	Singer

NAME	DATES	CATEGORY	SIG	LS/DS	ALS	SP	COMMENTS
Reeves, Steve	1926-2000	Ent	18			140	Actor, Mr. America, World & Universe
Reeves-Smith, Olive	1894-1972	Ent	10			50	Actress
Refice, Licinio	1855-1954	Comp	20			55	Mostly Church Music. 2 Operas. AMusQS 85, clergy
Regan, Donald		Cab	10	15		30	Sec. Treasury
Regan, Phil	1906-1996	Ent	10			65	Actor-Singer. Films From 1930's
Reger, Max	1873-1916	Comp	75	250	750		Ger. Comp.
Regnault de Saint-Jean	1761-1819	Fr Rev	35		105		Fr. Pol. Aided Napoleon. Exiled
Regula, Ralph R		Congr	10				Member US Congress
Rehan, Ada		Ent	20			40	Fine Vintage Shakespearean Actress
Rehberg, Dennis R. R		Congr	10				Member US Congress
Rehm, Dan		WWII	12	25	45	30	ACE, WWII; 9 kills
Rehnquist, William H.	1924-2005	Sup Crt	65	122	182	138	Chief Justice. S Conf. Ballot 3900; S transcript re: Bush 2000 415-1940
Reich, Wilhelm	1897-1957	Sci	120	325	650		Austr. Psychoanalyst. Author.
Reichenau, Field Mar. Walter von	1884-1942	WWII	40			108	WWII Ger. Gen.
Reicher, Frank		Ent				260	Ger. -born actor
Reichers, Lou		Aero	30	45	60	65	
Reid, Albert T.		Comics	20			112	Pol. Cartoonist. FDR Genre
Reid, Christian		Author	10			12	19th cen. 'The Land of the Sky'
Reid, Frances	1914-	Ent	10	12		25	
Reid, George	1733-1815	Rev War	65				Am. Revolutionary War Gen.
Reid, Harry		Congr	10			20	US Senate (D-NV); Spkr. of the House
Reid, Hugh Thompson	1811-1874	Civ War	40	70	110		Union Gen.
Reid, Samuel C.	1783-1861	Mil	70	195			Naval Cmdr. War 1812. Designed US Flag
Reid, Tara		Ent				45	Actress
Reid, Tim	1944-	Ent	10			30	Actor
Reid, Wallace	1891-1923	Ent	162			364	Actor-Dir-Screenwriter.
Reid, Whitelaw	1837-1912	Jrnalist	30	45		130	Correspondent, Ambassador
Reif, Keith		Music	88				'Yardbirds'
Reifel, Benjamin		Congr	10			10	MOC SD
Reightler, Ken		Space	10			25	
Reik, Theodor	1888-1969	Sci	90	218	360		Austrian Psychoanalyst
Reilly, Charles Nelson	1931-2007	Ent	10			35	Actor
Reilly, James William	1828-1905	Civ War	35	65	90		Union Gen.
Reilly, John C.	1965-	Ent	15			45	Actor
Reinburg, J. Hunter		WWII	15	35	50	40	ACE. WWII, Marine Ace; 7 kills
Reinecke, Karl		Comp	55	145	225	250	Ger. Pianist, Conductor, Teacher
Reiner, Carl	1922-	Ent	15	60	30	45	Movie-TV Actor-Writer-Dir.
Reiner, Fritz		Cond	50	150		131	Hung. Conductor
Reiner, Rob	1947-	Ent	17	25		50	Like Father, Carl, Writer-Dir. -Actor
Reinert, Ernst Wilhelm		WWII	20			62	Ger. Ace. RK
Reinhardt, Django		Music	825	895		2325	Legendary blues & jazz guitarist
Reinhardt, George-Hans		WWII				175	Ger. Gen.
Reinhardt, Max	1873-1943	Ent	115	148	410	284	Austrian Innovative Theatre Dir.
Reinhold, Judge		Ent	10			40	Actor. 'Beverly Hills Cop'
Reinking, Ann	1949-	Ent	10			40	Dancer-Choreographer. Tony. 'All That Jazz'
Reisch, Walter	1900-1983	Ent	10	60		35	Screenwriter. Shared AA for 'Titanic' Script
Reischauer, Edwin O.	1910-1990	Educ	10			25	Fndr. Japan Institute; US Ambassador to Japan
Reiser, Paul		Ent	20			48	Actor-Comedian. 'Mad About You'. Emmy
Reiserer, Russell		WWII	15		40	40	ACE WWII; 9 kills
Reitsch, Hanna	1912-1979	Aero	162	165	270	146	Flew 1st Practical Helicopter
Reitz, Francis W.		HOS	50	135			South Africa
Reizen, Mark		Opera				750	Opera
Rejane, Gabrielle-Charlotte		Ent	35		80	85	Vintage Fr. Tragedienne

NAME	DATES	CATEGORY	SIG	LS/DS	ALS	SP	COMMENTS
Réjane, Gabrielle-Charlotte Réju		Ent	15	70	105		
Remarque, Erich Maria	1898-1970	Author	98	360	375	175	'All Quiet on the Western Front'
Remer, Otto		WWII	40			88	SS Gen. WWII. RK
Remick, Lee	1935-1991	Ent	30			100	Actress
Remington, Eliphalet	1793-1861	Bus	350	392	425		E. Remington & Sons. Bond S 6500; S Chk 120-240
Remington, Frederic	1861-1909	Artist	486	805	1220	1850	Sculptor, Writer, War Correspond. SB 1885
Remington, Samuel		Bus			1450		Gun Manufacturer. ALS on Lttrhd. 1450; S Chk 240
Renaldo, Duncan	1904-1980	Ent	25		93	126	Actor, 4th 'Cisco Kid'; SB 145
Renaud, Maurice		Opera	35			175	Opera. Important Fr. Baritone
Renaud, Paul		HOS	50			100	Premier France
Renault, Louis	1877-1944	Jurist	35	95	125		Fndr. Renault Freres. Autos. Nobel Peace Pr. 1907
Renay, Liz		Ent	20				Actress/Model. Mafia Connection: Mickey Cohen
Renner, Karl, Dr.	1870-1950	HOS	25	50	105	80	Fndr., Pres. Austrian Repub.
Rennie, George	1791-1866	Sci			80		Civil engineer
Rennie, John	1761-1821	Engr			625		Br. Civ. Eng. Built Waterloo Bridge
Rennie, Michael	1909-1971	Ent	120			180	Actor, 'The Day the Earth Stood Still"
Reno, Janet		Pol	10			20	Atty Gen.
Reno, Jean		Ent	10			40	Actor
Reno, Jesse Lee	1823-1862	Civ War	776				Union Gen., KIA 1862 South Mountain
Reno, Kelly	1966-	Ent	10	35		25	Actor
Reno, Marcus A.	1835-1889	Mil	805	2507	11500		Battle of Little Big Horn., ALS cont. 16, 500
Renoir, Jean	1894-1979	Ent	165	290	340	362	Fr. Inovative Film Maker-Son of Impressionist
Renoir, Pierre-Auguste	1841-1909	Artist	275	788	2119	3655	Repro Artwork S 3,000-5,000
Rent, cast		Ent	75			120	Tony Award Winning Broadway Musical. 20-25 Sigs.
Renwick, Edward Sabine	1823-1912	Invent	25	55	195		Inventor Breech-Loader & Mdrn. Poultry Indust
Renwick, James		Archtct			2000		Am. architect
Renzi, Rick R		Congr	10				Member US Congress
REO Speedwagon		Music	65			215	Rock (Signed by All); S Album 65
Repplier, Agnes	1855-1950	Author	10	15	35	50	Am. Dean of Essayists. Biographer
Requesens, Luis de Zuniga	1528-1576	Mil	750				Sp. Soldier. Succeeded Duke of Alba as Gov. RARE
Resnick, Laura		Author	10			12	Novels
Resnick, Mike		Author	12	20	40	15	Hugo & Nebula SF award winner
Resnick, Regina		Opera	15			60	Opera
Resnik, Judith A.	1946-1986	Space	108	300		342	Postal Cvr. 125-175, Challenger
Respighi, Ottorino	1879-1936	Comp	75	200	550		It. Opera, Orchestral, Choral. AMusQS 550
Reston, John 'Scotty'		Author	15	20	35	25	Journalist, Synd. Columnist
Rethberg, Elisabeth	1894-1976	Opera	40			142	Ger-Am Sopr. Opera. Admired by Toscanini-Strauss
Rethers, Harry F.		Mil	40				Am. WWI Qtrmaster Gen.
Rethy, Ester		Opera	10	15	35	30	Opera, Operetta
Rettig, Tommy	1941-1996	Ent	45			65	Juvenile Actor. 'Jeff' on 'Lassie'
Reubens, Paul	1952-	Ent	10			35	AKA Pee Wee Herman
Reuhl, Mercedes	1954-	Ent	25			50	Actress-Stage-Films. AA 'The Fisher King'
Reuter, Edzard		Bus	40	60	250	150	
Reuter, Erich		WWII				75	Ger. Major-Gen.
Reuterdahl, Henry	1871-1925	Artist	20			75	Painted Navy warships & recruiting posters, WWI
Reuther, Walter P.	1907-1970	Labor	25	35	65	50	Pres. UAW-CIO. Gained Many Benefits for Union
Revelle, Hamilton	1872-1958	Ent	20			75	Actor
Revell-Smith, Maj. -Gen. Wm.	1894-1956	WWII	225				WWII Br. Gen.
Revels, Hiram Rhoades	1822-1901	Congr	300				1st Elected Black Sen., MS. 1st Pres. Alcorn State
Revere, Anne	1903-1990	Ent	25		45	180	Stage-Screen Char. Actress. AA 'National Velvet'
Revere, Joseph Warren	1812-1880	Civ War	50	92	130		Union Gen.
Revere, Paul	1735-1818	Rev War	5038	12067	19125		ALS 26000, DS/Cont 75000/ DS w/J Hancock 95,000
Revere, Paul & the Raiders		Music	375				Rock Group
Rex, Simon		Ent	15			45	

NAME	DATES	CATEGORY	SIG	LS/DS	ALS	SP	COMMENTS
Rexroth, Kenneth	1905-1982	Author	10	35	65	20	Am. Columnist, Poet, Avant-Garde
Rey, Alejandro	1930-1987	Ent	25			45	Actor; Argentine-Born
Rey, Alvino		Band	20			75	Big Band Leader
Rey, H. A.	1898-1977	Author	50		470		Curious George
Rey, Margret	1906-1996	Author	50		200		Curious George
Reybold, Lt. -Gen. Eugene	1884-1961	WWII	30	35	55		WWII US Gen.
Reyes, Silvestre R		Congr	10				Member US Congress
Reymann, Hellmuth		Aero	30		75		
Reynolds, Albert		HOS	20			30	P. M. Ireland
Reynolds, Alexander W.	1816-1876	Civ War	116	175	486		CSA Gen. Captured-Exchanged. Sig/Rank 195
Reynolds, Burt	1936-	Ent	16	57		45	Actor; 'Smokey & The Bandits', 'Boogie Nights'
Reynolds, Craig	1907-1949	Ent	10			40	Actor
Reynolds, Daniel H.	1832-1902	Civ War	92		385		CSA Gen. Sig/Rank 125-160
Reynolds, Debbie	1932-	Ent	15	75		46	Actress; SP w/Gene Kelly 175; w/Eddie Fisher 60
Reynolds, Donn		Cntry Mus	10			20	Aust. 50s Yodeling Cowboy
Reynolds, Frank	1923-1983	Jrnalist	10			25	Broadcasting News Pioneer
Reynolds, Gene	1925-	Ent	10			40	Juvenile Actor. Mature Dir.
Reynolds, John Fulton	1820-1863	Civ War	515	1428			Union Gen. KIA Gettysburg. Sig/Rank 1375
Reynolds, John Hazard		Congr	10				FF 25
Reynolds, Joseph Jones	1822-1899	Civ War	35	110	132		Union Gen., Indian Fighter. Sig/Rank 75
Reynolds, Joshua, Sir	1723-1792	Artist	350	1300	1690		Br. Portraitist, 1st Pres. Royal Academy
Reynolds, Marjorie	1917-1997	Ent	20	30	40	47	Actress. 'Holiday Inn', 'GWTW' Collectible
Reynolds, R. J.		Bus	225	750			Fndr. Tobacco Empire
Reynolds, Richard Samuel		Bus	45	110	240	125	Reynolds Metal Co., Aluminum
Reynolds, Thomas M. R		Congr	10				Member US Congress
Reynolds, William	1931-	Ent	15			60	Actor
Reynolds, William H.	1910-	Ent	15			25	Film Editor. AA 'The Sting'. Three AA Nominations
Rezner, Trent		Music	10			45	Music. Lead Singer 'Nine Inch Nails'
Rhames, Ving		Ent	10			35	Actor
Rhea, Caroline		Ent	10			35	Actress
Rhee, Syngman	1875-1965	HOS	125	180	280	1243	1st Pres. So. Korea
Rhett, Alicia	1915-	Ent	300		510		SP N/A. GWTW Collectible.
Rhett, Robert Barnwell	1800-1876	Civ War	152	285	440		ALS/Cont 2, 500. The Father of Secession
Rhodes, Billie	1894-1988	Ent	15			50	Actress. Star of Al Christie Comedies from 1911
Rhodes, Cecil John	1853-1902	HOS	112	230	392	1175	S. Afr. Fndr. Rhodesia. Rhodes Scholarship Fund
Rhodes, Erik	1906-1990	Ent	20			50	Am. Comic Actor From Musical Comedy Stage. Films
Rhodes, John J.		Congr	10			10	MOC AZ 1953-83
Rhodes, Zandra		Celeb	10			15	Designer
Rhymes, Busta		Music	20			45	Rap
Rhys-Davies, John		Ent	15			45	Br. Actor. 'Indiana Jones' Films
Ribbentrop, Joachim von	1893-1946	WWII	165	479	622	525	Hitler Foreign Affairs Advisor. Convicted & Hung
Ribbentrop, Rudolf von		Mil	65	95	150		
Ribicoff, Abraham	1910-	Cab	10	15	35	20	Gov., Sen. CT. Sec. HEW
Ribisi, Giovanni		Ent	17			50	
Ricardo, David	1772-1823	Econ	425				Fndr. Classical School of Pol. Economy
Ricci, Christina		Ent	20			52	Actress.
Ricci, Frederico		Comp			150		Neopolitan Comp.
Ricci, Ruggero		Music				100	Violinist
Ricciarelli, Katia		Opera	10			25	Opera
Rice, Alexander H.	1818-1895	Congr	10	15	20		Sen. & Gov. MA
Rice, Alice C.	1870-1942	Author	70		220		Kid's Books. 'Mrs. Wiggs of Cabbage Patch'
Rice, Americus Vespucius	1835-1904	Civ War	40	75	110		Union Gen.
Rice, Anne		Author	25			50	Novels
Rice, Dan (Dan'l McLaren)	1823-1900	Bus	38	100	341		Circus Clown & Owner

NAME	DATES	CATEGORY	SIG	LS/DS	ALS	SP	COMMENTS
Rice, Donna	1958-	Celeb	15			20	Scandal w/Gary Hart
Rice, Elliott Warren	1835-1887	Civ War	45		95		Union Gen.
Rice, Elmer	1882-1967	Author	80	138	162	130	Pulitzer Pr. Plays
Rice, Florence	1907-1974	Ent	15			60	Actress
Rice, Grantland	1881-1954	Jrnalist	160	188		310	Sportswriter-Sportscaster. One Reel Sports Films
Rice, Henry M.		Congr	10		15		Sen. MN 1858-63
Rice, James Clay	1829-1864	Civ War	110	379	488		Union Gen.
Rice, Merton S.		Clergy	20	30	40		
Rice, Samuel Allen	1828-1864	Civ War	110		468		Union Gen.
Rice, Tim	1944-	Comp	25	30	65	45	Comp. Disney Films
Rice-Davies, Mandy		Celeb	10			20	Involved In Br. Scandal
Rich, Adam	1968-	Ent	10			25	Actor
Rich, Buddy	1917-1987	Band	47	130		292	Big Bandleader-Drummer
Rich, Charlie	1932-1995	Music	15			55	Rockabilly 50-60s. Country Superstar. S Album 80
Rich, Christopher		Ent	17			50	
Rich, Irene	1891-1988	Ent	25			95	Silent Film Star. Few Talkies. Radio Star
Richard, Robert		Ent	14			43	
Richards, Adriana		Ent	10			30	Juvenile Actress in 'Jurassic Park'
Richards, Ann	1933-2006	Gov	10			25	Governor TX
Richards, Cliff		Music	15			70	Rock
Richards, Denise		Ent	10			44	
Richards, Dickinson W.	1895-1973	Sci	25	35	70	50	Nobel Med. 1956. Perfected Heart Catherization
Richards, J.		Ent	15			45	
Richards, Jeff	1922-1989	Ent	25			110	Actor
Richards, Keith		Music	25			175	Rock. 'Rolling Stones' Guitarist; S Guitar 935
Richards, Kelly		Music				60	Singer
Richards, Lloyd	1923-	Ent	10			20	Afr-Am Stage Dir.
Richards, Michael		Ent	20			60	'Kramer' on Seinfeld
Richards, Richard N.		Space	10			35	
Richards, William		Congr	15		50		Rep. NY 1871
Richardson, Dorothy	1872-9857	Author	32	115	187		Br. Introduced Stream of Consciousness Technique
Richardson, Elliot		Cab	10	25	45	20	Atty Gen. Watergate Period
Richardson, Friend W.		Gov	10		15		Gov. CA 1923-27
Richardson, Ian	1934-2007	Ent	10			45	Actor
Richardson, Israel Bush	1815-1862	Civ War	150	292			Union Gen., KIA Antietam
Richardson, Joely	1965-	Ent	10			30	Br. Actress
Richardson, John P.		Gov	15	25	86		Governor SC 1840
Richardson, John, Sir	1787-1865	Expl	20	60	118		Surgeon-Naturalist. Franklin Exped.
Richardson, Kevin		Ent	17			50	
Richardson, Miranda	1958-	Ent	22			50	Br. Actress. 'Enchanted April', 'The Crying Game'
Richardson, Natasha		Ent	15			50	Br. Actress-Daughter of Vanessa Redgrave
Richardson, Ralph, Sir	1902-1983	Ent	20	25	50	65	Distinguished Br. Stage-Film Actor. AA Nominations
Richardson, Robert Vinkler	1820-1870	Civ War	260	525			CSA Gen.
Richardson, Tony	1928-1991	Ent	20			30	Br. Stage & Film Dir. AA 'Tom Jones'. Aids
Richardson, William A.	1821-1896	Cab	18	48	95		Sec. Treas. 1873
Richardson, William Alex.	1811-1875	Congr	10		20		Sen. IL
Richelieu, Armand E. du	1766-1822	HOS	105	240	350		Fr. Statesman & Cardinal
Richelieu, Armand-Jean, Card.	1585-1642	HOS	275	1177	2150		1585-1642. Statesman & Card'l. Special DS 3, 450
Richens, Gabrielle		Model	10			15	Celebrity model
Richey, Helen		Aero	25	50	55		
Richey, Lawrence		Cab	10	10			
Richie, Lionel		Comp	10	52		38	Comp. -Singer-Arranger
Richie, Nicole		Ent	10			50	Actress
Richman, Charles	1865-1940	Ent	10	15	30	65	Actor

R

NAME	DATES	CATEGORY	SIG	LS/DS	ALS	SP	COMMENTS
Richman, Harry	1895-1972	Ent	15	50	35	45	Flew 'Lady Peace' 1st R/T Atlantic Crosssing
Richter, Andy		Ent	17			50	
Richter, Burton, Dr.		Sci	20	45	70	35	Nobel Physics 1976
Richter, Charles, Dr.	1900-1985	Sci	120	175		145	Devised Richter Scale. Earthquake Measure
Richter, Gerhard		Artist					Pop artist; SB 120
Richter, Hans (Janos)	1843-1916	Cond	150		475	225	Ger. Conductor. AMusQS 240-350
Richter, Jason James	1980-	Ent	10			30	Actor
Richter, Svyatoslav		Music	235			62	Renowned Russian classical pianist
Richters, Christine	1966-	Model	10			20	Playboy
Richthofen, Manfred von	1892-1918	Aero	7000			8471	ACE, WWI, 'The Red Baron'
Rickard, George L. Tex		Bus	350	525		675	Boxing Promoter & Entreprenuer. DS 2,000
Rickenbacker, Edw V.	1890-1973	Aero	76	125	225	388	ACE, WWI, Auto Race, Exec. TLS/Cont 1500; SB 200
Ricketts, Charles	1866-1931	Artist	40	60	136		Artist, designer
Ricketts, James Brewerton	1817-1887	Civ War	45	70	110		Union Gen.
Rickles, Don	1926-	Ent	15			55	Comedian.
Rickman, Alan	1946-	Ent	10			70	Actor; 'Harry Potter'
Rickover, Hyman G.	1900-1986	Mil	75	178	434	350	Rus-Born Am. Adm. Father of Atomic Sub.
Riddle, Georgie		Cntry Mus	10			35	50's Western Recording Artist
Riddle, Nelson		Music		120			Orchestra leader
Ride, Sally K.		Space	15	36	63	105	1st US Woman in Space
Riders in the Sky (3)		Music	10			40	CW singing group
Ridgway, Joseph		Congr	15		53		FF 53
Ridgway, Matthew B.	1895-1993	WWII	44	141	146	96	Supr. Allied Cmdr. WWII/KW, TLS/ALS Cont 500-1500
Riefenstahl, Leni	1902-	Photog	26	42	80	180	Ger. -actress Hitler's Favorite
Rieger, Vince		WWII	12	25	40	30	ACE, WWII, Navy Ace; 5 kills
Riegger, Wallingford	1885-1961	Comp	20	65	125	80	Am. Orchestral, Choral, 12 Tone
Rifkin, Adam	1966-	Ent	10			25	Actor; writer
Rifkin, Ron	1939-	Ent	10			35	Actor
Rigal, Delia		Opera	15			45	Opera
Rigg, Diana	1938-	Ent	20	35	45	110	Br. Leading Lady. Prominence in 'The Avengers'
Riggs, Clinton E.		Invent	24			40	Created Highway Yield Sign
Riggs, Tommy	1908-1967	Ent	10			40	Ventriloquist; (& Betty Lou); actor
Righteous Brothers		Music	65	320		161	Bill Medley & Bobby Hatfield
Riis, Jacob A.	1849-1914	Author	18	50	85		Dan. -Am. Journalist. ALS/Cont 350
Rikhter, Syvatoolav		Music		120			Russian virtuoso pianist.
Riley, James Whitcomb	1849-1916	Author	95	175	260	475	The Hoosier Poet. 'Little Orphant Annie'. SB 180
Riley, Jeannie C.	1945-	Cntry Mus	10			30	Singer. Intl. Star w/'Harper Valley PTA'
Riley, Larry	1953-1992	Ent	15			55	Actor
Riley, Lisa	1976-	Ent	10			30	Actress
Riley, Richard		Pol	10			15	US Sect'ry Education
Rilke, Rainer Maria	1875-1926	Author	145	445	1849		Czech. Lyric Poet-Translator. Highly Influential
Rimes, Leann		Music	15	60		50	Singer. Country-Pop
Rimsky-Korsakov		Comp			1285	4715	Russian Comp. AMusQS 800; SB 2300
Rinehart, Mary Roberts	1876-1958	Author	20	45	75	75	Am. Novels, Plays. Mysteries-Romances
Ring, Blanche	1877-1961	Ent	15			65	Vintage Silent Star Actress
Ringel, Julius		WWII	30			118	Ger. Gen. WWII
Ringgold, George H.	1814-1864	Civ War	20	40	55		Union Paymaster War Dte DS 80
Ringling, Albert C.	1852-1916	Bus	132	425			Ringling Bros. & Barnum & Bailey; S Chk 240
Ringling, Charles	1863-1926	Bus	120	453			Ringling Bros. & Barnum & Bailey; S Chk 130-240
Ringling, Henry		Bus	112	328		125	Special DS 1, 250; S Chk 130
Ringling, John	1866-1936	Bus	145	406	500	700	Ringling Bros(Owner-Performer)& Barnum & Bailey
Ringling, Otto	1858-1911	Bus	230	650			Ringling Bros. & Barnum & Bailey
Ringling, William		Bus	70	130		150	2nd Generation Owner
Ringo, John		Crime	2000	6500			Early West. Cowboy Gunslinger

NAME	DATES	CATEGORY	SIG	LS/DS	ALS	SP	COMMENTS
Ringwald, Molly		Ent	10	20	40	50	Actress
Rinna, Lisa		Ent	10			35	Actress
Rio Rita		Ent	15			55	Her All-Girl NBC Orchestra. 1930's
Riorden, Shane		Author	10			12	Reading for children
Ripley, Eleazar W.	1782-1839	Mil	68		250		Gen. War 1812
Ripley, George	1802-1880	Reformer	140	350	780		Critic, Editor, Unitarian Clergy
Ripley, J. R.		Author	10				Mystery Novelss
Ripley, James Wolfe	1794-1870	Civ War	50	65	95		Union Gen.
Ripley, Robert	1893-1949	Comics	161	180	225	196	Believe It Or Not'; SB 160-510
Ripley, Roswell S.	1823-1887	Civ War	122	220	425		CSA Gen. Nephew of Union Gen.
Ripley, Roswell S. (WD)	1823-1887	Civ War	290	450	1025		CSA Gen.
Risner, James R.		Mil	10	25	35	20	
Ritchard, Cyril	1896-1977	Ent	20			53	Br. Dancer & Comedian.
Ritchie, Adele	1874-1930	Ent	20		50	45	Vintage Musical Theater Star
Ritchie, Albert C.		Gov	10		35		Gov. MD
Ritchie, Gen. Sir Neil Methuen	1897-1985	WWII	225				WWII Br. Gen.
Ritchie, Neil, Sir		Mil	15	35	60	30	Gen.
Ritchie, Steve	1942-	Aero	15	35	45	35	US Gen. Only USAF Ace of Vietnam War
Ritt, Martin	1919-1990	Ent	30			65	Film-Stage-Tv Dir. Taught at Actor's Studio
Rittenberg, Sidney	1921-	Celeb	10			15	Interpreter & Chinese scholar
Rittenhouse, David	1732-1796	Sci	850	1150	4500		Am Astronomer, 1st US Telescope
Ritter, Burwell Clark		Congr	10		38		FF 38
Ritter, John	1948-2003	Ent	48	10	15	118	Light Romantic-Comedy Roles. Son of Tex Ritter
Ritter, Tex	1907-1974	Cntry Mus	85			154	Major Singing Cowboy Star, S Album 92
Ritter, Thelma	1905-1969	Ent	87	60		277	Am Char. Actress & Comedienne.
Ritterscheim, Karl		Opera	10			25	Opera
Ritz Brothers, The (3)		Ent	80			208	Jimmy, Al, Harry. Zany Nightclub Act. A Few Films
Ritz, Jimmy	1903-1985	Music	15			40	The Middle Ritz Brother
Rivera, Chita	1933-	Ent	10			35	Actress
Rivera, Diego	1886-1957	Artist	227	740	970	1375	Mex. Pol. -Soc. Muralist, S repro 425-1265; SB 460
Rivera, Geraldo		Ent	20	42		35	TV Host
Rivers, Joan	1933-	Ent	10			35	Comedienne.
Rivers, Johnny		Music	15	55		40	Singer
Rivers, Larry	1923-2002	Artist	40	75	250		Forerunner Pop Art Movement
Rivers, Melissa		Ent	15			45	
Rives, Amelie	1863-1945	Author	12	60	85		
Rivington, James	1724-1802	Rev War	100	225			Journalist-Publisher-Spy
Rizzo, Frank L.		Pol	10	20		25	Mayor Phila. Fmr. Chief of Police
Roach, Hal, Jr.		Ent	10			15	
Roach, Hal, Sr.	1892-1992	Ent	80	143		125	AA Film Pioneer. Our Gang Comedy. Silent-Sound
Ro'Al, Zhang	1713-1746	Artist		700			Chinese Painter
Roane, John Selden	1817-1867	Civ War	110				CSA Gen.
Roarke, Hayden		Ent	52			65	Actor. 'Jeannie' 'Dr, Bellows'
Roarke, John	1952-	Ent	10			35	Actor
Robards, Jason, Jr.	1920-2000	Ent	15	22		65	Am. Stage-Film Actor. AA 'Julia'
Robb, AnnaSophia		Ent	13			40	
Robb, Robert G.		Civ War		178			CSA Navy Cmdr.
Robbins, Asher		Congr	12				FF 38
Robbins, Brian		Ent	12			35	
Robbins, Frederick C., Dr.		Sci	20	30	45	25	Nobel Med. 1954
Robbins, Gale	1922-1980	Ent	15			45	Singer-Leading Lady; Actress
Robbins, Harold	1916-	Author	20	40	75	60	Am. Novels. The Carpetbaggers
Robbins, Jay T.		WWII	10	25	40	45	ACE, WWII; 22 kills
Robbins, Jerome	1918-1998	Ballet	40	75	110	85	Ballet Dancer, Choreographer. AA 'The King & I'

NAME	DATES	CATEGORY	SIG	LS/DS	ALS	SP	COMMENTS
Robbins, John	1808-1880	Congr	12		25		Repr. PA, Steel Mfg.
Robbins, Marty	1925-1982	Cntry Mus	65			90	Country & Pop Singer-Songwriter
Robbins, Reg. L.		Aero	25			60	Pioneer Aviator
Robbins, Tim	1958-	Ent	23			45	Actor-Singer-Songwriter-Screenwriter-Dir.
Robert Wexler		Congr	10				Member US Congress
Roberti, Margherita		Opera	15			30	Am. Sopr.
Roberts, Barbara		Gov	10			20	Governor Or
Roberts, Benjamin Stone	1810-1875	Civ War	35	65	90		Union Gen.
Roberts, Beverly	1914-	Ent	10			45	Actress
Roberts, Cokie		Jrnalist	10			20	TV-Radio Journalist
Roberts, David	1896-1964	Artist	40	90	162		Scottish Painter
Roberts, Doris		Ent	10	15	15	42	Char. -Comedienne. 'Everybody Loves Raymond'
Roberts, Eric	1956-	Ent	10			45	Leading Man, 70s. AA Nom. 'Runaway Train'
Roberts, Frederick Sleigh Fld Mar	1832-1914	Mil	40	82	125	260	1st Earl. Field Marshal, Kandahar
Roberts, Jack		Cntry Mus	10			20	
Roberts, John	1955-	Jurist	20			100	Chief Justice of theUS Supreme Court.
Roberts, Jonathan	1771-1854	Congr	30		75		Introduced Important Legislation
Roberts, Julia	1967-	Ent	40	60	120	139	Actress, AA Winner
Roberts, Kenneth	1885-1957	Author	25	80	150		Am. Historical Novels. 'Northwest Passage
Roberts, Lee S.		Comp	30	65	150		AMusQS 285
Roberts, Leonard		Ent	12			35	
Roberts, Oral	1918-	Clergy	18	60	50	60	Am. Evangelist. Oral Roberts U
Roberts, Oran M.		Gov	15		30		Gov. TX 1879-83
Roberts, Owen J.	1875-1955	Sup Crt	60	135	220	100	Justice 1930-45. Dean U. of Penn. Law School
Roberts, Pat		Congr	10				US Senate (R-KS)
Roberts, Pat Hutchison		Author	10			10	Cookbook author, editor
Roberts, Pernell	1928-	Ent	60	78		205	Actor. Original 'Bonanza' Brother. 'Trapper John'
Roberts, Robin		TV News	10			20	News Anchor
Roberts, Roy	1900-1975	Ent	15			125	Actor
Roberts, Tanya		Ent	10			54	Actress.
Roberts, Tony	1939-	Ent	10			30	Actor
Roberts, William Paul	1841-1910	Civ War	85	180	320		CSA Gen. Youngest In CSA Service. Sig/Rank 150
Roberts, Xavier		Bus	15	20	35	25	Cabbage patch dolls
Robertson, Alice Mary		Congr	10		20	25	MOC OK, Self-Taught Creek Indian
Robertson, Archibald		Artist		250			Scottish Artist
Robertson, Beverly H.	1827-1910	Civ War	113	158	320		CSA Gen. Sig/Rank 185
Robertson, Cliff	1925-	Ent	20	25		47	Am. Leading Man. Stage-Films. AA 'Charley'
Robertson, Dale	1923-	Ent	10			53	Am. Actor. Western Star
Robertson, Felix H.	1839-1928	Civ War	85		262		CSA Gen. Sig/Rank 150
Robertson, James	1720-1788	Rev War			975		Br. Gen. Fought in Rev. War
Robertson, Jerome B. 'Polly'	1815-1891	Civ War	125	368			CSA Gen.
Robertson, Kathleen		Ent	15			45	
Robertson, Morgan		Author	15		60		Sea Stories
Robertson, Pat, Rev.	1930-	Clergy	20	25	50	30	Rt. Wing Evangelical, Pres. Hopeful
Robertson, Robbie		Music	15			50	Singer; S Guitar 240-425
Robertson, Willard	1886-1948	Ent	15			35	Am. Char. Actor. Lawyers & Wardens
Robeson, George M.	1834-1896	Cab	15	62	92		Sec. Navy 1869-1877
Robeson, Paul	1898-1976	Ent	97	165	280	334	Am. Singer, Actor, Athlete, Activist
Robespierre, Maximilien	1758-1794	Fr Rev	1200	1958	12500		Revolutionist Leader. 'Reign of Terror'. Sp. DS 4275
Robilio, Victor		Author	10			12	Fine wines, wineries
Robin, Mado		Opera	40			225	Opera. Coloratura.
Robinson Peete, Holly		Ent	15			45	
Robinson, Bill 'Bojangles'	1878-1949	Ent	100	235	450	501	Afro-Am. Tap-Dancer, Entertainer. 30s Films
Robinson, Dwight P.		Bus	10	15	25	15	

NAME	DATES	CATEGORY	SIG	LS/DS	ALS	SP	COMMENTS
Robinson, Edward	1794-1863	Archaeol		185	395		Biblical Scholar. Explored Palestine-Syria.
Robinson, Edward A.	1869-1935	Author	55	125	215		Am. Poet, 3 Pulitzers
Robinson, Edward G.	1893-1973	Ent	108	122	140	252	Actor Famous for Gangster Roles & Art Collection
Robinson, Gary Edward	1951-	Bus	10			20	World renown investor
Robinson, George D.	1834-1896	Gov	10			35	Repr. & Gov. MA
Robinson, James F.	1800-1882	Gov		200			Gov KY. During the Civil War
Robinson, James Sidney	1827-1892	Civ War	40	75	110		Union Gen.
Robinson, John	1761-1828	Rev War	60	175	340		Soldier, Merchant
Robinson, John C.	1817-1897	Civ War	52	192	220		Union Gen., MOH Gettysburg. Sig/Rank 100
Robinson, Joseph T.	1872-1937	Congr	20		25		Sen. Arkansas
Robinson, Lucius		Gov	10	20	40		Governor NY 1876
Robinson, Patrick	1963-	Ent	10			25	Br. Actor
Robinson, Rachel		Celeb	10			20	Wife of Jackie Robinson; Philantropist
Robinson, Smokey		Music	50			140	Motown artist; S Album 125
Robinson, Tony	1946-	Ent	10			35	Br. Actor
Robson, Flora, Dame	1902-1984	Ent	28	25	40	75	Distinguished Br. Stage & Film Actress. 30s-80s
Robson, Linda	1958-	Ent	10			25	Br. Actress
Robson, May	1858-1942	Ent	40			69	Australian-Am. Stage Actress. Films 1915-1942
Robson, Stuart	d 1946	Ent	20	25	45	65	Vintage Actor, Actor/Father w/same name 1836-1903
Rochambeau, Count de	1725-1807	Rev War	350	578	989		Fr. Gen. in Am. Revolution, DS/cont 1725
Roche, James M.	1906-	Bus	10	15	30	20	Pres. Ford Motor Co., CEO Gen. Motors
Rochefort, Henri, Marquis de	1830-1913	Author	18	30	50		Fr. Journalist. Anti Napoleon III
Rochester, Laurence Hyde, Earl		Pol		180			
Rochford, Leonard		Aero	20	40			Br. Ace WWI
Rochon, Debbie	1968-	Ent	10			35	Canadian-Actress
Rock, Blossom (Blake, Marie)	1896-1978	Ent	125			225	Sister-Jeanette MacDonald. 'Addams Family''Granny'
Rock, Chris		Ent				40	Comedian
Rock, John	1890-	Sci	25	80			Developed 1st Birth Control Pill
Rockefeller, Abby A.		Bus	15	30	52	25	Socialite-Wife of John D., Jr.
Rockefeller, David		Bus	15	38	55	25	Banker
Rockefeller, Happy		Bus	10	15	25	10	Wife of Nelson Rockefeller
Rockefeller, John		Congr	10				US Senate (D-WV)
Rockefeller, John D.	1839-1937	Bus	380	1188	1983	1412	DS/Oil Contrct 9450; S Stock Cert w/Flagler 1500-2500
Rockefeller, John D., Jr.	1874-1960	Bus	35	80	150	125	Rockefeller Ctr. Philan. Son of John D.
Rockefeller, Laurance		Bus	10	15	25	10	Philan.
Rockefeller, Nelson A.	1908-1979	VP	28	58	75	60	Governor NY. Ford's VP. TLS as VP 325
Rockefeller, Winthrop	1912-1973	Gov	10	20		15	Governor AR
Rockerfeller, John (Jay) D., IV		Gov	10	15		10	Governor WV. Confidential Pol. ALS 450
Rockwell, George Lincoln		Activist	35	100	115	80	Am. Nazi Party; Chk 120
Rockwell, John Arnold		Congr	10		29		FF 29
Rockwell, Norman	1894-1978	Artist	108	233	400	307	Am. Illust. -Artist. FDC S 125. Print S 500-
Rockwell, Orrin Porter	1813-1878	Frontier		17500			Bodyguard to Mormon leaders; S w/an "X"
Rockwell, Robert	1920-2003	Ent	10			50	Actor. Leads & Supporting Actor. 'Our Miss Brooks'
Rockwell, Sam		Ent	15			45	
Roddenberry, Gene	1931-1991	Ent	119	425		280	Creator of 'Star Trek'
Roddey, Philip D.	1826-1897	Civ War	105	375	415		CSA Gen.
Roddey, Philip D. (WD)	1826-1897	Civ War	200	878	2498		CSA Gen.
Rodenburg, Carl	1894-1992	WWII	40			75	Ger. Gen. Stalingrad. WWII.
Roderick, Brande		Ent	17			50	
Roderick, Milton David		Bus	10			10	CEO US Steel
Rodes, Robert Emmett	1829-1864	Civ War	425		1675		CSA Gen. KIA RARE
Rodes, Robert Emmett (WD)		Civ War	750		8425		CSA Gen. RARE
Rodgers, Anton	1933-2007	Ent	10			45	Br. Actor
Rodgers, Geo. Washington	1822-1863	Civ War	75	130	260		Union Navy. KIA Fort Wagner

NAME	DATES	CATEGORY	SIG	LS/DS	ALS	SP	COMMENTS
Rodgers, Jimmie	1897-1933	Cntry Mus	225	760		1830	Legendary Country Music Singer-Comp.
Rodgers, John	1812-1882	Civ War	60	160	178		Un. Naval Commodore, -Explr.
Rodgers, John	1771-1838	Mil	50	75	100		Distinguished US Naval Off.
Rodgers, John		Aero	65	125	240	135	
Rodgers, R. & Hammerstein, O.		Comp	310			1463	Oscar Hammerstein III
Rodgers, Richard	1902-1979	Comp	58	364		128	Pulitzer. AMusQS 460. DS w/Hart 1000
Rodgers, Richard & Hart, Lorenz		Comp	675	1180			Comp. s
Rodin, Auguste	1840-1917	Artist	360	391	899	1386	Fr., SP of Sculpture 1250-1700
Rodman, Hugh		Mil	55				Adm. USN, Am. WWI
Rodman, Isaac Peace	1822-1862	Civ War	110				Union Gen.
Rodney, Caesar	1728-1784	Rev War	515	1023	1775		Signer Dec. of Indepen.
Rodriguez, Ciro D. R		Congr	10				Member US Congress
Rodriguez, Freddy		Ent	15			45	
Rodriguez, Michelle		Ent	14			42	
Rodriguez, Paul		Ent	15			45	
Rodriguez, Robert		Ent	14			43	
Rodriguez, Valente		Ent	15			45	
Rodriquez, Freddy		Ent				40	Actor; 'Fererico Diaz', Six Feet Under
Rodzinski, Artur	1892-1958	Cond	30	75		75	Pol. -Am. Conductor.
Roe, Edward Payson	1838-1888	Author	15	25	35		Novels, Clergy
Roe, Tommy		Music	30			40	Singer
Roebling, John A.	1806-1869	Engr	85	175	325		Designed the Brooklyn Bridge
Roebling, Washington A.	1837-1926	Engr	92	225	360		Built the Brooklyn Bridge
Roebuck, Alva Curtis		Bus	235	1039		375	Co-Fndr. Sears & Roebuck. Stock Cert. S 1900
Roederer, Pierre C., Count		Fr Rev	20	50	95		
Roeg, Nicolas	1928-	Ent	10			20	Br. Dirctor
Roell, Werner		WWII	10			30	Ger. RK Winning Stuka Pilot
Roemer, Sarah		Ent	13			40	
Roentgen, Julis		Comp				120	Ger. Comp.
Roentgen, Wilhelm	1845-1923	Sci	604	942	2610		1st Nobel in Physics. Discovered X Rays
Roethke, Theodore		Author	35	60	125	75	Am. Poet. Pulitzer
Rogallo, Francis M.		Invent	27		45		Invented Hang Glider.
Rogatchewsky, Joseph		Opera	20			85	Ukranian. Lyric/Dramatic Tenor
Rogen, Seth		Ent				40	Actor
Roger, Gustav		Opera	40		160		Opera. Creator of Important Tenor Roles
Rogers, Andrew Jackson	1828-1900	Congr	10				MOC NJ, Teacher, Lawyer
Rogers, Bernard W.		Mil	10	25	50	40	
Rogers, Carroll P.		Bus	10	15	35	15	
Rogers, Charles 'Buddy'	1904-1999	Ent	20	20	35	65	Actor, 20s-30s. SP w/Pickford 130
Rogers, Fred	1928-2003	Ent	22	35		88	Mr. Rogers'
Rogers, Ginger	1911-1995	Ent	45	110		236	Actress, Dancer. AA. SP/Astaire 675-900
Rogers, Harold R		Congr	10				Member US Congress
Rogers, Jean	1916-1991	Ent	25			80	40's Adventure Serial Queen. 'B' Movie Leads
Rogers, John	1829-1904	Artist	150	350	305		Sculptor of the Rogers Groups
Rogers, Joseph W.		Aero	15	30	60	35	
Rogers, Kenny		Music	20	50		38	Singer-Actor-Prod.
Rogers, Kenny & the 1st Edition		Music	210				Singing group
Rogers, Marianne & Kenny		Cntry Mus	10			35	
Rogers, Mike R		Congr	10				Member US Congress
Rogers, Mimi	1956-	Ent	15			58	Actress. Leading Lady Film & TV
Rogers, Randolph	1825-1892	Artist	18		30		Sculptor
Rogers, Richard		Space	10			20	
Rogers, Robert	1731-1795	Rev War	335	1195	3300		Frontier Soldier. 'Rogers Rangers'. Fled to Eng.
Rogers, Roy	1912-1998	Ent	45	140		192	King of Cowboys. SP w/Dale 135-195; DS/Dale 145

NAME	DATES	CATEGORY	SIG	LS/DS	ALS	SP	COMMENTS
Rogers, Samuel	1763-1855	Author	15	30	59		Br. Poet. Patron of The Arts
Rogers, T. S.		Mil	75				Am. WWI Rear Adm. US N., USS Utah
Rogers, Wayne		Ent	15			35	Actor. 'Mash'
Rogers, Will	1879-1935	Ent	190	340	1030	454	America's Favorite Humorist. Plane Crash/Wiley Post
Rogers, Will Jr.		Congr	10			25	Congressman CA, Actor
Rogers, William F.	1820-1899	Civ War	35	40	55		Union Gen.
Rogers, William Findlay		Congr	10		10		MOC NY, Soldier CW
Rogers, William P.		Cab	12	20	35	25	Sec. State
Roget, Peter M., Dr.	1779-1869	Med	75	85	220		Br. Physician & Savant. Roget's Thesaurus
Rohan, Louis Prince de	1734-1803	Clergy		225			Cardinal & Grand Aumonier of France
Rohm, Ernst	1887-1934	WWII	300	1033	3595		Nazi Cmdr. of SA (stormtroopers)
Rohmer, Eric	1920-	Ent	40	218			Fr. Dir. Literate, Articulate Searching. 60s
Rohmer, Sax (A. S. Ward)	1886-1959	Author	80	240	338	182	Br. Mystery Novels. 'Fu Manchu'; AQS 235
Rohrabacher, Dana R		Congr	10				Member US Congress
Rohrer, Henreich	1933-	Sci	20		45		Nobel Physics 1981
Rojo, Gustavo	1923-	Ent	10			45	Actor
Roker, Al		Ent	10	15		25	TV Weatherman
Rokossovsky, Konstantin K.		WWII	125	391			Soviet WWII Gen.
Roland de La Platiere, Jean	1734-1793	Fr Rev	40	95	185		Fr. Statesman. Leader of Gerondists. Suicide
Roland, Gilbert	1905-1994	Ent	20	30		94	Latin Romantic Leading Man Silent & Sound Films
Roland, Ruth	1893-1937	Ent	22	55		120	Silent Serials & One Time Child Star. 'Baby Ruth'
Roldan, Salv. C.		HOS	10	20	50	15	Columbia
Rolfe, William James		Author	10			15	
Rolland, Romain	1866-1944	Author	35	85	130	105	Nobel Lit. 1915, AMans 2,000
Rolle, Esther	1920-1998	Ent	15			42	Actress
Rolling Stones (5)		Music	1073	2500	1500		Rock Group (5); S Album 2000;
Rollins, Ed		Celeb	10			15	Pol. celebrity
Rollins, Edward Henry		Congr	15	22	35		NH RR Tycoon & Bank Executive
Rollins, Henry		Ent	17			50	
Rollins, Sonny		Music	30			55	Jazz Tenor Sax
Rolls, Charles S.	1877-1910	Bus	933	1100	1250		Roll-Royce Motors. Aviator. Flying Record.
Rolph, James		Gov	10		35	20	Governor CA
Roman, Ruth	1922-1999	Ent	60			80	Leading Lady Films from 40s
Romano, Ray		Ent	15			40	Everybody Loves Raymond
Romanoff, Michael, 'Prince'	1890-1972	Bus	30	65	145	55	Romanoff's Restaurant. Hollywood. (H. Gurgason)
Romanov, Stephanie		Ent	10			40	Actress. Models, Inc.
Rombauer, Irma S.		Author	10			10	'The Joy of Cooking'
Romberg, Sigmund	1887-1951	Comp	105	353	350	241	Hung. -Am. Composed 'Hit' Operettas. AMusQS 650
Rome, Harold		Comp	15	50	100	30	AMusQS 125. Many Pop Hits
Rome, Sydney		Ent	10			35	Actress
Romero, Cesar	1907-1993	Ent	30	38		111	Actor. Handsome Film Star from '30's. 'Batman'
Romero, George		Ent	15			45	
Romijn, Rebecca		Ent	18			53	
Rominger, Kent		Space	10			20	
Romjin, Rebecca		Ent	10			46	Actress
Romjue, Milton Andrew		Congr	10	12		10	Rep. MO 1917
Rommel, Erwin	1891-1944	Mil	428	657	2728	2069	Ger. Field Marshal WWII, D-Day cont LS 20,000
Romney, George	1734-1802	Artist	150	475	600		Signed Original Sketch 1, 500
Romney, George W.	1907-1995	Gov	20	30	55	22	Pres. Am. Motors. Gov. MI., Pres. Cand.
Romney, Mitt		Gov	15	20	25	25	Former Gov. MA
Romulo, Carlos P.	1899-1985	HOS	48	60	95	75	Philippines. Pres. UN, Pulitzer. Gen. WWII
Ronan, Saoirse		Ent	17			50	
Ronettes		Music	150	445		200	Rock Group
Ronne, Edith M.		Expl	20	30			Antarctic Land Named Edith Ronne Land

NAME	DATES	CATEGORY	SIG	LS/DS	ALS	SP	COMMENTS
Ronne, Finn	1899-1980	Expl	25		70		Proved Antarctic a Continent. 'Ronne Ice Shelf'
Ronstadt, Linda		Music	20	38	40	102	Singer: Pop-Standards-Country; S Chk 50
Rooker, Michael	1955-	Ent	10			30	Actor
Rooney, Andy	1919-	TV News	10			25	News Commentor
Rooney, Mickey	1920-	Ent	25	55		112	Actor
Roosa, Stuart R.		Space	125			232	
Roosevelt, Edith Kermit	1861-1948	1st Lady	60	110	130	375	FF 70
Roosevelt, Eleanor	1884-1962	1st Lady	84	193	270	385	Own Persona as UN Delegate & Social Worker
Roosevelt, Eleanor (As-1st Lady)		1st Lady	142	277	730	515	WH card S175, TLS/Cont1500-4025, ALS/cont3950
Roosevelt, F. & Churchill, W.		Pres		20350			DS 'Sail on, O Ship of State' 96,000
Roosevelt, Franklin & Eleanor		Pres		200		1466	
Roosevelt, Franklin D.	1882-1945	Pres	265	1200	2049	714	TLS/Cont 1500-5000, ALS/Cont 9500; S Stamp Auction Bidsheet 6600
Roosevelt, Franklin D. (As Pres.)		Pres	349	1650	19757	931	WHC 600-1375; TLS/cont 5000-25000; Chk 800+
Roosevelt, Franklin Jr.		Congr	10			20	MOC NY. Businessman-Farmer
Roosevelt, James		Congr	10	25	45	20	MOC CA. Marine Corps Gen.
Roosevelt, John A.		1st Fmly	20	35			FDR Son
Roosevelt, Nicholas J.		Rev War	25	60	135		Inventor
Roosevelt, Quentin	1897-1918	Mil	50	120	200	200	Shot Down in France. WWI, TR's son
Roosevelt, Sarah D.	1854-1941	Pres	75	118	152	150	FDR Mother
Roosevelt, Theodore	1858-1919	Pres	258	822	1578	1310	ALS/TLS/Cont 8000-20000, ALS/TLS War-dte 5000-20000
Roosevelt, Theodore (As Pres.)		Pres	462	1069	3280	1850	ALS/TLS/Cont 12,000, WH Cd. 600-750
Roosevelt, Theodore, Jr.	1887-1944	Mil	40	160	212	85	TR's son. KIA Normandy; MOH
Root, Elihu	1845-1937	Cab	50	60	120	135	Sec. War, Sec. State, Nobel Peace Pr.
Root, George F. (G. Wurzel)	1820-1895	Comp	50	150	135		Many Popular & Civil War Songs. AMusQS 895-1, 195
Root, Jesse		Rev War	25	75	125		Continental Congress
Root, Joseph Moseley		Congr	10		20		FF 20
Root, Stephen		Ent	18			55	
Rootes, Thomas Read		Civ War	215	360	475	1765	CSA Naval Cmdr., War Date LS 975
Roper, Daniel	1867-1943	Cab	10	30	50	50	Sec. Commerce 1933
Rops, Felicien	1833-1898	Artist	65	165	477		Belg. Licentious Subjects. Graphic Artist
Rorem, Ned		Comp	20	45	278		Pulitzer1976, AMusQS 175
Rorke, Hayden	1910-1987	Ent	75			179	Actor; Dr. Bellows in 'I Dream of Jeannie'
Rorschach, Hermann	1884-1922	Sci	200	3700			Swiss Psychiatrist Developed Ink Blot Test
Rosas, Juan M. de		HOS	10	25	40		Argentina
Rose, Axl		Music	25			78	Rock (Guns N' Roses)
Rose, Billy	1899-1966	Ent	25	85	100	85	Entrepreneur, Prod. Husband of Fanny Brice
Rose, Charlie		Celeb	10			20	Media/TV personality
Rose, David		Comp	10	20	35	30	Musical Dir. MGM. 'Holiday for Strings'. AMusQS 60
Rose, Fred	1897-1954	Cntry Mus	30			60	Country Music HOF. Fndr. Acuff-Rose Pub. Co.
Rose, Juanita		Cntry Mus	10			20	
Rosecrans, William S.	1819-1902	Civ War	72	187	243		Union Gen.
Rosecrans, William S. (WD)	1819-1902	Civ War	144		1348		Union Gen.
Rosellini, Albert D.		Gov	10			10	Governor WA
Rosenbaum, Michael	1972-	Ent	13			40	Actor
Rosenberg, Alfred	1893-1946	WWII	182	861		515	Nazi Head of Foreign Policy. War Criminal, hanged
Rosenbloom, 'Slapsie Maxi'		Ent	55			120	Heavyweight Boxer-Actor
Rosendahl, Charles E.		Aero	75	170	225	200	Am. Adm. Premiere US Dirigible Capt.
Rosenman, Samuel I.		Jurist	10	20	55	15	Confidant-Advisor to FDR
Rosenquist, James		Artist	20	55	150		Am. Pop Art. Huge Canvases. Pc Repro. S 85
Rosenthal, Joe	1911-2006	Photog	70	258	290	813	Iwo Jima
Rosenthal, Laurence		Comp	10	10	20	10	
Rosenthal, Moriz		Ent	75		105		Pol. Pianist

NAME	DATES	CATEGORY	SIG	LS/DS	ALS	SP	COMMENTS
Rosenwald, Julius	1862-1932	Bus	283	848			Bought out Roebuck (of Sears)DS/Sears Sig. 12500
Rosing, Bodil	1878-1942	Ent	10			45	Actress
Ros-Lehtinen, Ileana R		Congr	10				Member US Congress
Ross, Charlotte	1968-	Ent	10			30	Actress
Ross, Craig		Music	10			25	Music. Guitar 'Lenny Kravitz'
Ross, David	1755-1800	Rev War			385		Cont'l Army & MOC MD.
Ross, Dianna	1944-	Music	35	70	130	118	Singer-Actress. 'Supremes'; S Album 70
Ross, Gary		Ent	20			60	
Ross, George	1730-1779	Rev War	300	691	1340		Signer Dec of Ind Cont. Congr., LS/cont1900
Ross, Herbert		Ent	10			20	Dir.
Ross, Jerry L.		Space	10			25	
Ross, Joe E.		Ent	100			335	Comedian. Frazzled Char.
Ross, John	1790-1866	Am Ind	312	700	910		Chief Cherokee Nation. Coowescoowe
Ross, John, Sir	1777-1856	Expl	70	180	275		Arctic Exped. s. Author
Ross, Katharine	1942-	Ent	15	30		72	Leading Lady. AA Nom. 'The Graduate'.
Ross, Lanny	1906-1988	Opera	15		25	35	Vintage Radio Tenor of 30s & 40s
Ross, Lawrence Sullivan	1838-1898	Civ War	165	310	475		CSA Gen., TX Governor. In Over 100 Battles
Ross, Leonard Fulton	1823-1901	Civ War	40	75			Union Gen.
Ross, Lewis W.		Congr	10	15	30		MOC NY 1863
Ross, Marion		Ent	15	25		30	Actress. 'Happy Days'
Ross, Mike R		Congr	10				Member US Congress
Ross, Nellie Tayloe	1876-1977	Gov	35	75	145		1st Woman Governor in US, WY
Ross, Robert		Author	10			10	Mystery Writer. Poe Award
Ross, Ronald, Sir	1857-1932	Sci		125	275		Br. Phys. Nobel 1902 for Studies in Malaria
Ross, Samuel	1822-1880	Civ War	40	55	70		Union Gen. 20th Conn.
Ross, Sobieski		Congr	10	15	25		MOC PA 1873
Ross, Tracee		Ent	15			45	
Ross, Vernon 'Gené		Author	10			12	Agriculture
Rossdale, Gavin		Music	12			55	Lead Singer 'Bush'
Rosselini, Isabella	1952-	Ent	15	60		48	Leading Lady Daughter of Ingrid Bergman
Rossellini, Renzo		Comp		475			AmusQ 475
Rosser, Thomas L.	1836-1910	Civ War	125	302	550	775	CSA Gen. Sig/Rank 175
Rossetti, Christina	1830-1894	Author	45	125	250		Br. Poet. Sister of Dante
Rossetti, Dante Gabriel	1828-1882	Artist	130	235	630		Br. Poet & Painter
Rossetti, Wm. M.	1829-1919	Author	75		408		Pre-Raphaelite Art Critic. AQS 300
Rossi, Dick		WWII	10	25	45	35	ACE, WWII, Flying Tigers; 6 kills
Rossini, Gioacchino	1792-1868	Comp	500	893	1489	2566	AMusQS 3900; S sheet music 1550
Rossmann, Edmund		WWII	20			50	Ger. Ace WWII. RK
Rostand, Edmond	1868-1918	Author	70	200	450	860	Fr. Plays. 'Cyrano de Bergerac'.
Rostenkowski, Dan		Congr	15	25		30	Powerful Rep. IL
Rostropovich, Mstislav		Cond	25	75	130	121	Cello Virtuoso, Conductor.
Roth, David Lee		Music	30	75		59	Ex Van Halen Group
Roth, Eli		Ent	15			45	
Roth, Lillian	1910-1980	Ent	35	52	85	110	Vocal Star; Actress
Roth, Philip	1933-	Author	35	78	90	45	Portnoy's Complaint', 'Goodbye Columbus'; SB 75
Roth, Tim	1961-	Ent	20			42	'Pulp Fiction'
Rothafell, S. L. 'Roxy'		Ent	15	25	40	45	NY Entrepreneur, Theatre Owner
Rothenstein, William, Sir	1872-1945	Artist	20	55	88		Off'l Artist WWI & II
Rothes, John Leslie, 1st Duke	1630-1681	Royal		180			
Rothier, Leon		Music			75		Fr. Bass
Rothman, Steven R. R		Congr	10				Member US Congress
Rothrock, Cynthia		Ent	10			40	Actress
Rothschild, Alfred	1842-1918	Banker	35	90	150		Grandson of Nathan Mayer
Rothschild, Alix de		Banker	70	190	375		

NAME	DATES	CATEGORY	SIG	LS/DS	ALS	SP	COMMENTS
Rothschild, Amschel Mayer	1773-1855	Banker		1000			Eldest Son of Mayer Amschel
Rothschild, Guy de Baron		Banker	15	350	80	85	
Rothschild, Jakob	1792-1868	Banker	125	588			Founded Paris Branch
Rothschild, Karl	1788-1855	Banker	200	575			Fndr. of Naples Branch
Rothschild, Leopold de	1845-1917	Banker	35	75	150		Grandson of Nathan Mayer
Rothschild, Lionel Nathan	1808-1879	Banker	25	90	128		Son of Nathan Mayer
Rothschild, Mayer Amschel	1743-1812	Banker	145	400	550		Fndr. House of Rothschild
Rothschild, Nathan, 1st Baron	1840-1915	Banker	50	150			Eldest son of Lionel
Rothschild, Nathan Meyer	1777-1836	Banker	260	527			Fndr. London Bank Branch. Banking Empire
Rotten, Johnny		Music	18	40		80	S Album 60
Rouault, Georges	1871-1958	Artist	200	475	645	490	Landscapes, Religious, Clowns
Rouget de Lisle, Claude-Joseph	1760-1836	Comp	118	295	912		Composed 'La Marseillaise'. Fr. National Anthem
Roundtree, Richard	1942-	Ent	10			40	Actor
Rourke, Mickey	1950-	Ent	20			54	Actor
Rous, F. Peyton, Dr,	1879-1970	Med	20	100	195	25	Am. Pathologist. Nobel Med. 1966. Tumor Viruses
Roush, Clara		Author	10	15		15	
Rousseau, Jean-Jacques	1712-1778	Author	398	905	2950		Fr. Philosopher, Pol.
Rousseau, Lovell H.	1818-1869	Civ War	45	85			Union Gen. Congress
Rousseau, Theodore	1812-1867	Artist	75	175	475		Fr. Leader of Barbizon School
Roussel, Albert-Charles	1869-1937	Comp			610		Leading Fr. Comp. after WWI; AMusQS 140
Routh, Brandon		Ent				120	Actor; 'Superman'
Routledge, Patricia	1929-	Ent	10			30	Br. Actress
Roux, Albert		Celeb	10			15	Chef
Roux, Pierre Paul Emile	1853-1933	Sci	20	45	90	40	Fr. Bacteriologist w/Pasteur. Dir. Pasteur Inst
Rovero, Ornella		Opera	15			45	Opera
Rowan, Andrew S.		Mil	35	95	165	95	Delivered Message to Garcia
Rowan, Carl	1925-	Jrnalist	15	35		45	1st Afr-Am Ambass to Finland. Head US Info. Agy.
Rowan, Dan	1922-1987	Ent	35	35		50	Comed. w/Dick Martin. 'Laugh-In'; DS w/Martin 120
Rowan, John	1773-1853	Congr	30	75			Rep. 1807, Sen. KY 1825
Rowan, Stephen C.	1808-1890	Civ War	40	75	155		Union Naval Commodore
Rowcroft, Maj. -Gen. Sir Eric B.	1891-1963	WWII	225				WWII Br. Gen.
Rowe, Brad		Ent	18			55	
Rowe, Leo S.		Cab	10	20	35	10	Ass't Sec.
Rowe, Misty	1952-	Ent	10			50	Actress
Rowland, Adele	1883-1971	Ent	10			45	Silent Film Actress
Rowland, David		Colonial	45	150			Member Stamp Act Congress
Rowlands, Gena	1934-	Ent	10	20	25	60	Actress. Multi AA Nominations
Rowlandson, Thomas	1756-1827	Artist	250	625	900		Br. Portrait Painter-Caricaturist, Illust.
Rowley, Thomas Algeo	1808-1892	Civ War	40		110		Union Gen.
Rowling, J. K.		Author	50	150	238	100	Harry Potter; SB 600-3000; S true 1st Ed. of 1st Harry Potter. 33460
Rowling, William E.		HOS	10	15	20	35	Prime Min. New Zealand
Roxas y Acuna, Manuel	1892-1948	HOS	35	90	230	110	1st Pres. Philippines Repub.
Roy, Deep		Ent	15			45	
Roy, Maurice, Card.		Clergy	30	30	40	35	
Royale, Candida		Ent				40	Actress
Roybal-Allard, Lucille R		Congr	10				Member US Congress
Royce, Edward R. R		Congr	10				Member US Congress
Royce, F. Henry, Sir	1863-1933	Bus	350	700	900		Co-Fndr. Rolls-Royce, Ltd.
Roylance, Pamela	1952-	Ent	10			25	Actress; 'Days of Our Lives'
Roze, Marie		Opera	40			145	Opera
Rozema, David Lee		Clergy	10	15	25	15	
Rozsa, Miklos	1907-	Comp		400	500		Hung. Known Best for Film Music. AA(3).
Rubattel, Rudolph		HOS	30	55			Switzerland

NAME	DATES	CATEGORY	SIG	LS/DS	ALS	SP	COMMENTS
Rubens, Alma	1899-1931	Ent	65	85	165	146	Actress. Major Film Star Early 20th C.
Rubens, Paul A.		Comp	15		60		Br. Musical Comedy. AMusQS 75
Rubens, Peter Paul	1577-1640	Artist	2000	9250	21750		Flem. Baroque Landscapes, Portraits
Rubenstein, Zelda		Ent				70	Actress
Rubik, Erno		Sci	35	65	85	45	Hung., Mathematician; Rubik's Cube
Rubin, Jerry	1938-1994	Activist	15	25	50	55	Chicago 7
Rubin, Robert		Pol	10			20	Prior Sect'y of the Treasury
Rubini, Jan	1904-1989	Ent	20			65	Actor
Rubinoff, David	1897-1986	Music	18	40		45	Rubinoff & His Violin. Eddie Cantor Show Regular
Rubinstein, Anton	1829-1894	Comp	108	240	518	445	Pianist. AMusQS 850-1800, AManS 4750
Rubinstein, Artur	1887-1983	Music	50	125	205	334	Pol./Am. Pianist, AMusQS 425
Rubinstein, Helena	1870-1965	Bus	72	150	225	281	Beautician Who Invented the Cosmetics Industry
Rubinstein, Ida		Ballet	125			500	Rus. Ballerina/Nijinsky
Rubinstein, John	1946-	Ent	10			18	Actor-Dir. -Comp. Son of Artur
Rubio, P. Ortiz		HOS	35			50	Pres. Mex. 1930-32
Ruby, Harry	1895-1974	Comp	30	133	155	110	AMusQS 265; S Album 70
Ruby, Jack	1911-1967	Assass	125	306	1018		Killed Lee Harvey Oswald. AManS 1300, Chk 250-475
Rucker, Daniel H.	1812-1910	Civ War	30	65	90	150	Union Col., Bvt. Gen.
Ruckman, John W.		Mil	75				Am. Gen.
Rudd, Paul		Ent	15			45	
Rudel, Hans-Ulrich	1916-1982	WWII	118	208	197	217	Most Highly Decorated Ger. Ace
Rudman, Warren B.		Congr	10			20	Sen. NY
Rudner, Rita		Ent	10			30	Actress-Standup Comedienne
Rudnick, Paul	1957-	Ent	10			20	Writer
Rudolf, Archduke (Aus)	1858-1889	Royal			750	985	Dual Suicide at Mayerling/Baroness Marie Vetsera
Rudorffer, Erich		WWII	40			75	Ger. World's 7th Highest Ace
Rue, Sara		Ent	13			39	
Ruehl, Mercedes		Ent	13			40	
Ruff, Charles F.	1817-1885	Civ War	40	55	85		Union Gen.
Ruffalo, Mark		Ent	15			46	
Ruffin, David	1941-1991	Music	45	210		510	Lead singer of the Temptations; Chk 250
Ruffo, Titta	1887-1953	Opera	100		765	410	It. Operatic Baritone
Ruge, Friedrich		Mil	68			102	Ger. Vice Adm.
Ruger, Thomas H.	1833-1907	Civ War	30	50	85		Union Gen.
Ruggles, Charles 'Charlie'	1886-1970	Ent	40			69	Char. Comedian. 100s Films 1928-66
Ruggles, Daniel	1810-1897	Civ War	120	249	608		CSA Gen. ALS/Cont 4900
Ruggles, Daniel (WD)		Civ War	162	637	756		CSA Gen., ALS/cont 2295, TLS/cont 1980
Ruggles, Wesley	1889-1972	Ent	20	25	45	195	Film Dir. Original Keystone Cop. Dir. 1922-46
Ruick, Barbara	1932-1974	Ent	10		15	55	Actress-Daughter of Lorene Tuttle Radio Star
Rukeyser, Louis	1933-2006	Bus	10	15	20	20	Economic commentor
Rumble Fish		Music				125	S Album 260
Rumpler, Edward		Aero	20	40	75	50	
Rumsfeld, Donald		Cab	10	20	45	25	Sec. Defense
Runcie, Robert A. K., Arch.		Clergy	30	40	50	40	
Runco, Mario		Space	10			20	
Run-D. M. C.		Music	20			40	Rock; Rap
Rundgren, Todd		Music	25			65	Singer; S Album 75; S Guitar 235
Rundstedt, Karl R. Gerd von	1875-1953	WWII	125	218	228	350	Ger. Fld. Marshal. Cmdr. Armies in Pol., Fr., USSR
Runger, Gertrud		Opera	15			50	Opera
Running Horse, Chief		Am Ind	10		30		
Running Water, Chief		Am Ind	75		275		Model For US Indian Head Nickel
Runyon, Damon	1884-1946	Author	113	301	425	188	Short Stories & Sports Writer; SB 270
Ruppersberger, C. A. Dutch R		Congr	10				Member US Congress
Ruppert, Jacob	1867-1939	Bus	100	202	415	225	Fndr. Ruppert Brewing Co.

NAME	DATES	CATEGORY	SIG	LS/DS	ALS	SP	COMMENTS
Rush, Barbara	1927-	Ent	10			45	Actress; GG winner
Rush, Benjamin	1745-1813	Rev War	812	1069	2559		Signer Dec. of Indepen. Prominent Physician
Rush, Bobby L. R		Congr	10			20	Member US Congress
Rush, Geoffrey		Ent	15			55	Autralian Oscar Winning Actor.
Rush, Isadore		Ent	10			30	Stage
Rush, Richard	1780-1859	Cab	76	121	260		Atty Gen., Sec. Treas, Sec. State., TLS/cont 800
Rusher, William	1923-	Pub	10			15	Publisher of the National Review
Rusk, Dean	1909-1994	Cab	20	71		47	Sec. State Under JFK
Rusk, Jeremiah M.	1830-1893	Civ War	40	55	75		Union Brevet Brig. Gen., cabinet member
Rusk, Johnny		Cntry Mus	10			20	
Rusk, Thos. Jefferson	1803-1857	Mil	185	280	310		TX Provisional Gov. & Sec. War. US Sen. TX
Ruskin, John	1819-1900	Artist	60	208	358		Br. Painter, Art Critic, Author, Social Reformer
Rusling, James F.	1834-1918	Civ War	30	30	45		Union Gen. Bvt.
Russ, William		Ent	15			45	
Russell, Anna	1911-2006	Ent	10		25	150	Br. Vintage Stage
Russell, Bertrand	1872-1970	Author	68	215	528	374	Philosophy, Math., Nobel Pr. Lit.
Russell, Bruce		Comics	25			50	Pol. Cartoonist, Pulitzer
Russell, Charles		Gov	10	15			Governor NV
Russell, Charles M.	1864-1926	Artist	525	1400	4300		Known For Cowboy-West Art; SB 2300
Russell, David Abel		Congr	10	25	35		Repr. NY 1835
Russell, David Allen	1820-1864	Civ War	175	922			Union Gen., KIA Winchester
Russell, Harold	1914-2002	Ent	10	15	25	52	Mil. Hero, AA 'Best Years of Our Lives'
Russell, Henry	1874-1936	Ent	10	20			Theatrical Mgr. & Singer
Russell, Jane	1921-	Ent	12	40	60	169	Actress Famous for 'The Outlaw'.
Russell, John	1921-1991	Ent	20			72	Actor. Western Star in 'The Lawman'
Russell, John, Lord	1792-1878	HOS	38	80	125		Br. Prime Min., 1st Earl
Russell, Johnny		Music	10			20	Singer-Songwriter
Russell, Jonathan	1771-1832	Diplo	390	800			Treaty of Ghent
Russell, Keri		Ent	15			45	TV/'Felicity'.
Russell, Kurt	1947-	Ent	20			68	Actor
Russell, Leon		Music	15			65	Legendary Rocker; S Album 90
Russell, Lillian	1861-1922	Opera	70	145	194	320	Vintage Musical, Operetta Star
Russell, Mark		Ent	10			25	
Russell, Richard B., Jr.	1897-1971	Congr	20	35	35		Gov., Sen. GA. Cont. TLS 300
Russell, Richard M.		Congr	10	10			Rep. MA
Russell, Rosalind	1911-1976	Ent	48	56	80	196	Actress. Sophisticated Comedy. AA Nom. (4)
Russell, Samuel Lyon		Congr	10				FF 29
Russell, Sol Smith		Ent	20			40	Vintage Comedian
Russell, Theresa	1957-	Ent	10			35	Actress
Russell, William H.	1802-1873	Pol	50		167		Pvt sectry to Henry Clay
Russell. George W.	1867-1935	Author	40	145		55	Leader Irish Literary Renaissance
Russell-McCloud, Patricia		Celeb	10			15	Orator
Russert, Tim	1950-2008	Celeb	10	20		35	Pol. commentator
Russo, René	1954-	Ent	25			43	Actress-Model. 'Ransom'
Rust, Albert	1818-1870	Civ War	90	200	256		CSA Gen. AES '155
Rustin, Bayard		Activist	15	35	70	25	Civ. Rights Activist
Rutan, Dick		Aero	15	30		30	
Rutan, Dick & Jeana Yeager		Aero	120	175		229	Non-Stop Trans-World w/o Refueling
Rutgers, Henry	1745-1830	Rev War	95	210	298		Benfactor Rutgers University
Rutherford, Ann	1920-	Ent	18	30		43	Actress; GWTW
Rutherford, Ernest	1871-1937	Sci	510	582	750	950	NZ Born Physicist. Nobel Chem. 1908
Rutherford, Kelly	1968-	Ent	15			40	Actress
Rutherford, Margaret, Dame	1892-1972	Ent	90	145	160	271	Brit. Actress. Oscar Winner. 'Miss Marple'SPc 330
Rutledge, Edward	1739-1800	Rev War	300	497	1847		Signer of D of I

NAME	DATES	CATEGORY	SIG	LS/DS	ALS	SP	COMMENTS
Rutledge, John	1739-1800	Sup Crt	425	600	2432		Cont. Congr. Chief Just. Brother to Edward
Rutledge, Wiley B.	1894-1949	Sup Crt	46	115	265	50	
Ruttan, Susan		Ent	10			30	Actress
Ryan, Amy		Ent	13			40	
Ryan, Blanchard	1964-	Ent	25			75	Actress
Ryan, George		Pol				15	Gov IL
Ryan, Irene	1903-1973	Ent	120			178	Comedienne/PartnerTim
Ryan, James W.	1858-1907	Congr	12				Repr. PA
Ryan, Jeri		Ent	14			45	Actress. 'Star Trek'
Ryan, Meg	1961-	Ent	35			120	Actress
Ryan, Michelle		Ent	20			60	Actress
Ryan, Mitch	1928-	Ent	10			40	Actor
Ryan, Paul R		Congr	10				Member US Congress
Ryan, Peggy	1924-2004	Ent	10	15	35	52	Actress
Ryan, Robert	1913-1973	Ent	65	80		230	Actor
Ryan, Sheila	1921-1975	Ent	20			98	Actress
Ryan, T. Claude		Aero	85	300		225	Ryan Aircraft Mfg. -Designer
Ryan, Timothy J. R		Congr	10				Member US Congress
Rydell, Bobby		Music	25			95	50's singer; S Album 85
Ryder, Albert P.	1847-1917	Artist	90	250	560		Am. Landscapes, Marine, Portraits
Ryder, Mitch & Detroit Wheels		Music		110		125	Singer
Ryder, Winona		Ent	20			54	Actress
Ryle, Martin, Sir		Sci	35	110	190	45	Nobel Physics 1974
Rysanek, Leonie		Opera				85	
Ryun, Jim R	1947-	Congr	10				Member US Congress
Saarinen, G. Eliel		Archtct	20	65	150	40	Am. Foremost Arch. of His Day
Sabatier, Paul		Sci	60		180		Fr. Chem. Nobel 1912
Sabatini, Rafael	1875-1950	Author	40	55	105		It. Historical Romance Novels, Dramatist.
Sabato, Antonio Jr.		Ent	10			58	Model
Sabin, Albert Bruce, Dr.	1906-1993	Med	60	137	175	142	Physician-Virologist; Oral Polio Vaccine
Sabin, Dwight May		Congr	10	10		10	Rep. MN 1883
Sabin, Florence R., Dr.	1871-1953	Sci	25		145	120	1st Woman Elected to Nat'l Acad. of Sciences
Sabine, Edward, Sir	1788-1883	Mil	45		190		Br. Gen. w/Ross & Parry on Arctic Exped.
Sablon, Jean	1906-1994	Music	20	25	45	45	Vintage Fr. Romantic Singer
Sabo, Martin Olav S		Congr	10				Member US Congress
Sabu (Dastagir)	1924-1963	Ent	55			129	Overnight Star in 'Elephant Boy'
Sacco, Nicola	1891-1927	Crime			3700		With Vanzetti Convicted of Murder
Sacher-Masoch, Leopold von	1836-1895	Author	155	338	840		Word Masochism Attributed to Abnormality
Sachkoff, Katee		Ent	15			45	
Sachs, Nelly		Poet				85	Poet & Plays.
Sackett, Frederic	1868-1941	Congr	10	25			Sen. KY. Business. Ambass. Ger.
Sackler, Howard		Author	10	15	25	10	
Sacks, Oliver, Dr.		Med	15	45		30	Awakenings'. Neurologist
Sackville-West, Lionel, Sir		Diplo	10	25	40		2nd Baron
Sackville-West, Victoria Mary	1892-1962	Author	100	301	425		Br. Poet & Novels
Sadat, Anwar	1918-1981	HOS	115	247	325	451	Assass. Pres. of Egypt
Sade		Music	20			60	Vocalist
Sade, D. A. F., Marquis de	1740-1814	Author	351	1110	1751		Sadist, Sadistic Attributed. Prison Confinement.
Safer, Morley		Jrnalist	10			25	'60 Minutes' Regular
Saffro, Yale L.	1918-1990	Artist	10	15	20	50	80th Fghter Sq. WWII., Artist., S Art 500-5000
Safire, William		Author	10			20	Journalist. Newspaper Columnist. TV Guest
Sagal, Katey		Ent	15			45	
Sagan, Carl, Dr.		Sci	20	120	155	120	Am. Astronomer, Author. Pulitzer; SB 120
Sagan, Francoise	1935-2004	Author				260	Fr. writer

NAME	DATES	CATEGORY	SIG	LS/DS	ALS	SP	COMMENTS
Sage, Russell	1816-1906	Bus	100	208	1100	550	Financier, Speculator/J. Gould. Invented 'Options'
Sagendorf, Bud	1915-1994	Comics	45			250	Popeye'-after Segar; Sketch 150-325
Sager, Carole Bayer		Comp	10			25	
Saget, Bob		TV News	10			45	TV Host & Actor. 'Full House'
Sahl, Mort	1927-	Ent	15	25	30	45	Comedian
Said, Nuri		HOS	10	15	35	10	Pr. Min. Iraq
Sailing, John	1847-1959	Civ War	100		395		Last Surviving Certifiable CSA C. W. Soldier
Saint Hilaire, L. V. Jos.		Fr Rev	30	75	155		
Saint Laurent, Yves		Bus	25	40	70	40	Fashion Designer; SB 235
Saint Paul of the Cross		Relig			2030		
Saint Phalle, Niki de	1930-	Artist	80				Fr. Artist.
Saint, Edward		Celeb				115	Medium who attempted to contact Houdini
Saint, Eva Marie	1924-	Ent	10			43	Leading Lady. AA For 'On the Waterfront'
Saint, The		Ent	285				Signed by Roger Moore & Leslie Charteries
Saint-Cyr, Gouvion		Mil	50	175	190		Fr. Marshal, Min. of War
Saint-Elme, Ida		Author			60		Fr.
Saint-Exupery, Antoine de	1900-1944	Aero	145	192	225	135	Fr. Aviator. auth. kid's Books, S bk 920
Saint-Gaudens, Augustus	1848-1907	Artist	225	335	738	1150	Known For Monumental Sculptured Projects
Saint-Just, Louis A. L. de	1767-1794	Fr Rev	375	1368			Guillotined. Fr. Revolutionary
Saint-Saens, Camille	1835-1921	Comp	120	284	395	501	Organist, Opera, AMusQS 450-865
Saito, Hiroshi	d. 1939	Pol	10	15	35	50	Jap. Ambassador to US
Saito, Makoto, Baron		HOS	90	205	167		Prime Min. Japan
Sakai, Saburo	1916-2000	WWII	58			221	3rd Highest Jap. Ace
Sakall, S. Z. 'Cuddles'	1884-1955	Ent	150	72		173	Szakall. Hungarian Char. Actor from 1916
Sakharov, Andrei & Elena Bonner		Sci	425				Nobel Phys., Pol. Activists
Sakharov, Vladimir		Celeb	20			40	Communist agent
Salalm, Abdus		Sci	20	30	55	25	Nobel Physics 1979
Salan, Raoul		Mil	20	45	95	50	
Salazar, Jose, Card.		Clergy	30	30	35		
Sale, Charles 'Chic'	1885-1937	Ent	28	40	65	72	Comedian-Actor
Salenger, Meredith	1970-	Ent	10			40	Actress
Sales, Soupy	1926-	Ent	15	20	25	65	Comed. Early Entry to kid's Programming
Saleza, Albert		Opera	40			70	Opera. Tenor
Salinger, J [erome] D [avid]		Author	1272	5399	6500		Novels 'Catcher in the Rye'.
Salinger, Pierre	1925-2004	Jrnalist	15	30	42	38	Press Sec. Pres. JFK; Author; Sb 35
Salisbury, Frank O.	1874-1962	Artist	25	75	125		Pres. portrait painter; S Sketch 710
Salisbury, Harrison		Author	15				Pulitzer Journalist, Editor
Salisbury, Peter		Music	10			25	Music. Drummer 'The Verve'
Salk, Jonas, Dr.	1914-1995	Sci	96	190	598	194	Polio Vaccine Booklet S 200; Parenteral vaccine
Salmi, Albert	1928-1990	Ent	60			348	Actor
Salminen, Sally		Author	15	40	75		
Salomon, Friedrich	1826-1897	Civ War	44	75	110		(Frederick) Union Gen.
Salt, Jennifer	1944-	Ent	10			35	Actress
Salt, Titus, Sir	1803-1876	Bus	10	20	40		Pioneer Wool Industry. Inventor
Salten, Felix	1870-1946	Author	95	100	240		Austrian Author of Bambi
Salt-N-Pepper		Music	20			45	Rock
Saltonstall, Leverett	1892-1979	Congr	12	20		15	Sen. MA
Salvini, Tomaso		Ent	45			175	Tragedian w/Booth; AQS 45
Salzedo, Carlos	1885-1961	Music	25			96	Classical harpist
Sam & Dave		Music	100			300	Soul
Sam the Sham & Pharoahs		Music	35			85	Rock
Samaroff-Stokowski, Olga		Ent	20			88	Acclaimed Pianist, Teacher, Critic
Samberg, Andy		Ent	13			40	
Sambora, Richie		Music	10			40	Rock

NAME	DATES	CATEGORY	SIG	LS/DS	ALS	SP	COMMENTS
Samms, Emma	1960-	Ent	10			49	Br. Actress
Sammt, Albert		Aero	30			65	
Sample, Samuel Caldwell		Congr	10				FF 32
Samples, Candy		Ent	25			75	Erotic star
Sampson, Will		Ent	55	65	85	168	Actor
Sampson, William T.	1840-1902	Mil	40	110	160	135	Am. Adm. Cmdr-in-Chief, Sp. -Am. War
Samuel, Herbert	1870-1963	Diplo	43	125	165		Br. 1st High Comm. (Governor) of Palestine
Samuelson, Paul A., Dr.		Econ	25	40		35	Nobel Economics
San Giacomo, Laura		Ent	15			60	Actress. TV Series 'Don't Shoot Me'
San Juan, Olga	1927-	Ent	15			60	Singer-Dancer-Actress
San Martin, Jose de	1778-1850	HOS	500	585	2650		Soldier Hero of Argentina
Sanborn, Franklin B.	1831-	Author	10	15	15		Journalist, Editor, Biographer
Sanborn, John Benjamin	1826-1904	Civ War	35	65	90		Union Gen.
Sanborn, Katherine A.		Author	10	20	35		
Sanchez, Eduardo		Author				20	Writer of The Blair Witch Project (with Myrick)
Sanchez, Kiele		Ent	15			45	
Sanchez, Loretta S		Congr	10				Member US Congress
Sanchez, Oscar	1941-	Pol	10			25	Pres. of Costa Rica
Sanchez, Roselyn		Ent	13			40	
Sanchez, Sonia		Author	10			15	
Sanchez-Gijon, Aitana	1968-	Ent	10			40	It. Actress
Sand, George	1804-1876	Author	82	200	404		Fr. Non-Conformist. ALS/Cont 3500. (A. A. Dupin)
Sand, Shauna	1971-	Celeb	10			25	Model/actress
Sandburg, Carl	1878-1967	Poet	89	225	250	258	Biographer, Journalist. S Orig. Pencil Portr. 750; SB 175. AQS 2670
Sanders, Bernard S		Congr	10				Member US Congress
Sanders, George	1906-1972	Ent	84		92	368	Actor. AA Award
Sanders, George R.	1926-1998	Author	10			25	'Autograph Price Guide'
Sanders, Gregg		Ent	10			30	Actor; 'CSI'
Sanders, Harland 'Col. '		Bus	100	260	270	288	KFC Col. Sanders
Sanders, Horace T.	1820-1865	Civ War	32	75	180		Union Gen. Sig/Rank 50. Wounded-Bled to Death
Sanders, John C. Calhoun	1840-1864	Civ War	650				CSA Gen.
Sanders, William Price	1833-1863	Civ War	234				Union Gen.
Sanderson, Julia	1888-1975	Ent	10	20	30	45	Vintage Radio Team w/Frank Crummit
Sandler, Adam		Ent	30	55		65	Actor. Comedian.
Sandlin, Max S		Congr	10				Member US Congress
Sandoz, Mari	1896-1966	Author	25	50	95	75	Western Writer
Sands, Comfort	1748-1834	Rev War			400		Served on the Committee of Safety
Sands, Tommy	1937-	Ent	10	45		45	Actor
Sandstrom, Beatrice		Titanic	50	55	60	220	Titanic survivor
Sanford & Son		Ent	148			175	TV Show; dual signatures
Sanford, Edw. Terry		Sup Crt	75	195			
Sanford, Isabel	1917-2004	Ent	15			120	Actress
Sanger, Frederick		Sci	20	35	60	45	Nobel Chemistry 1958
Sanger, Margaret	1883-1966	Reform	75	462	350	345	Birth Control Advocate
Sangster, Margaret E.		Author	30	55	175		Journalist, Poet, Editor
Sangster, William E.		Clergy	25	40	55		Br. Meth. Min. -Author
Sankey, Ira D.		Clergy	120	127	259	100	Singing Evangelist. Associated/Dwight Moody
Sankford, Henry		Clergy	35	50	60		
Sano, Roy L., Bish.		Clergy	20	25	35	25	
Sansom, Art		Comics	10			20	The Born Loser
Santa Anna, Antonio L. de	1794-1876	HOS	375	2159	3192	2500	Gen., Revolutionary, Pres. Mex.
Santa Cruz, Andres	1792-1865	HOS	95	245			Gen. Pres. Bolivia. Exiled
Santa Rosa, Annibale S.		Mil	25	70	150		Count. It. Piedmontese Insurgent

NAME	DATES	CATEGORY	SIG	LS/DS	ALS	SP	COMMENTS
Santana		Music	295			350	Rock group; S Album 250-1100
Santana, Carlos		Music	40			116	Singer; S Guitar 425
Santander, Francisco de Paula	1792-1837	HOS			450		Pres. Columbia.
Santayana, George		Author	65	175	288	150	Poet, Philosopher, Critic
Santelmann, William H.		Ent		25			Marine Corps Bandmaster
Santerre, Antoine J.	1752-1809	Sci		175			Proved theory of Mdrn. combustion
Santiago, Tessie	1975-	Celeb				35	Actress
Santley, Charles, Sir	1834-1922	Opera	40				Baritone. Debut 1857. Retired 1911
Santo, Al		Ent	13			40	
Santoro, Rodrigo		Ent	15			45	
Santorum, Rick		Congr	10				US Senate (R-PA)
Santos, Joe		Ent	10			40	Actor
Santos-Dumont, Alberto	1873-1932	Aero	206	345	580	610	Brazil. Aeronaut. PioneerAirman
Santunione, Orianna		Opera	10			20	Opera
Saperstein, Abe M.		Bus	50	120		150	Owner-Coach-Fndr. Harlem Globetrotters
Sara, Mia	1967-	Ent	15			45	Actress; ' Ferris Bueller's Day Off"
Sarandon, Chris	1942-	Ent	10			40	Actor; 'Princess bride'
Sarandon, Susan		Ent	12	40	40	47	AA, Actress.
Sarasate, Pablo de	1844-1908	Comp	113	172	250		Violin Virtuoso, AMusQS 275-460
Sarbanes, Paul		Congr	10				US Senate (D-MD)
Sardi, Vincent	1915-	Bus	10			15	Fndr. Sardi's Restaurant NYC
Sardou, Victorien	1831-1908	Playwrt	20	45	125	150	Fr. Librettist, Bourgeois Drama
Sarett, Lew		Author	75	100			
Sarfatti, Margherita		Author	10	30	50		
Sarg, Tony	1882-1942	Artist	15	350		75	Illust. -Marionette Maker
Sargent, Dick	1930-1994	Ent	35		60	113	Darren', Bewitched
Sargent, John G.		Cab	15	30	60	25	Atty Gen. 1925
Sargent, John Osborne	1811-	Law	10		65		Lawyer, Author. Pol. Activist
Sargent, John Singer	1856-1925	Artist	95	238	342	775	Am. World Famous Portraitist
Sargent, Kenny		Music	20			45	Big Band Singer
Sargent, Sir Malcolm	1895-1967	Comp				100	Orchestral Comp.
Sargent, Winthrop		Rev War	160	180	240		Cont'l Army, 1st Gov. MS Terr.
Sarnoff, David	1891-1971	Bus	80	465	650	166	Broadcasting Pioneer. TLS on RCA Lttrhd. 1450
Sarocco, Suzanne		Opera	10			25	Opera
Saroyan, William	1908-1981	Author	60	158	210	150	Plays. Pulitzer 'The Time of Your Life'; SB 200
Sarsgaard, Peter		Ent	10			40	Actor
Sartain, John	1808-1897	Artist	25	85	100		Sartain's Union Magazine
Sarton, May		Author	10	15	40		
Sartre, Jean-Paul	1905-1980	Author	225	598	678		Leader Existentialist Movement. ALS/Cont 1350
Sasso, Will		Ent	17			50	
Sassoon, Siegfried	1886-1967	Author	50	225	420		Br. Poet. Anti-War Verses
Sassoon, Vidal		Bus	15	20	25	20	Hair Design & Products
Satie, Erik	1866-1925	Comp	200	825	1668		Eccentric, Avant Garde Music
Sato, Eisaku		HOS	20	55	150	150	Premier Japan. Nobel Peace
Sauckel, Fritz	1894-1946	WWII	260	285			Nazi War Criminal. Hanged
Sauer, Emil von		Music	15	15	75	30	Pianist
Sauguet, Henri		Comp	65		275		Fr. Opera, Ballet AMusQS 250
Sauken, Dietrich von		WWII	25			75	Panzer Gen.
Saulsbury, Grove		Gov	10			15	Governor DE
Saumarez, James, Sir,	1757-1836	Mil	90	265	600		Br. Adm., Battle of the Nile
Saunders, Alvin		Congr	15	35	80		Sen. KY, CW Gov. Nebr. Territory
Saunders, Edward Watts		Congr	10	20			Rep. VA 1906
Saunders, Jennifer	1968-	Ent	10			35	Br. actress
Saunders, John Monk		Ent	10	25			ANS 35, writer/Dir.

NAME	DATES	CATEGORY	SIG	LS/DS	ALS	SP	COMMENTS
Saunders, Lori	1941-	Ent	10			35	Actress
Saunders, Stuart T.	1909-	Bus	10				CEO Penn-Central RR
Sautet, Claude	1924-2000	Ent	10			20	Film writer
Savage, Ann	1921-	Ent	15			80	Actress
Savage, Fred		Ent	10			40	Actor; 'Wonder Years', 'Princess Bride'
Savage, Jeannie		Celeb	10			15	Photographer
Savage, John		Ent				50	Actor; 'Deerhunter'
Savage, M. J.		Clergy	15	30	45		
Saval, Dany	1945-	Ent	10		25	35	Fr. Actress
Savalas, George		Ent	165			190	
Savalas, Telly	1924-1994	Ent	15	43		138	Actor. TV's 'Kojak'. Oscar Nominee
Saving Private Ryan (cast)		Ent				110	Hanks/ Damon., Hanks & Sizemore 85
Savitch, Jessica	1947-1983	Jrnalist	35	140		159	TV-News.
Savitt, Jan		Band	15			45	
Savles, Thomas F, Bish.		Clergy	30	40			
Savoia, Attilio		Artist	15	40	75		
Sawhala, Julia	1968-*	Ent	10			30	Br. Actress
Sawyer, Charles		Cab	10	25	30	25	Sec. Commerce 1948
Sawyer, Diane		Jrnalist	10	20		35	TV Broadcast Journalist
Sawyer, Forest		Celeb	10			20	Media/TV personality
Sawyer, Joe	1906-1982	Ent	75			120	
Sax, Adolphe		Invent	80	180	375		Invented Saxophone & Others
Saxbe, William B.		Cab	10		20	15	Atty Gen. 1974
Saxe, John G.		Author	10	30	55	55	
Saxon, John	1935-	Ent	10			52	Actor; GG winner
Saxton, Jim S		Congr	10				Member US Congress
Saxton, Rufus	1824-1908	Civ War	45	68	116		Union Gen.
Say, Jean-Baptiste	1767-1832	Econ			1200		Fr. Pol. economist.
Sayao, Bidu	1902-1999	Opera	15			40	Opera Sopr.
Sayer, Leo		Music	15			45	Performing musical artist
Sayers, Dorothy	1893-1957	Author	183	467	565	350	Br. Mystery Novels. Lord Peter Wimsey. AQS 210
Sayle, Alexei		Ent	10			35	Br. Actor
Sayles, John	1950-	Ent	10			40	Actor
Saylor, Sid	1895-1962	Ent				285	Actor
Sayn-Wittgenstein, Heinrich	KIA 1944;	WWII				645	Knight's Cross w/Swords recipient
Scacchi, Greta	1960-	Ent	10			76	It. Actress
Scaggs, Boz		Music	15			40	Rock
Scagliarini, Eleanora		Opera	10			40	Opera
Scales, Alfred Moore	1827-1892	Civ War	124				CSA Gen.
Scales, Alfred Moore (WD)		Civ War	165		342		CSA Gen.
Scales, Prunella	1932-	Ent	10			25	Br. Actress
Scalia, Antonin		Sup Crt	30	45		75	TLS/Cont 575; SB 175-240
Scalia, Jack		Ent	10			40	Actor
Scammell, Alexander	1746-1781	Rev War	350		1500		Off. Wounded D. 1781
Scammon, Eliakim Parker	1816-1894	Civ War	45	70	110		Union Gen.
Scancarelli, Jim		Comics	10				Gasoline Alley; comic strip 125
Scantlin, Wes		Ent	15			45	
Scarborough, John		Clergy	10	15	20		
Scarlatti, Alessandro	1660-1725	Comp	725	4150	12000		115 Operas, Over 600 Cantatas
Scarwid, Diana	1955-	Ent	10			35	Actress
Schaal, Richard	1928-	Ent	10			35	Actor
Schaal, Wendy	1954-	Ent	10			40	Actress
Schacht, Hjalmar	1877-1970	WWII	51	158	300	275	Nazi. Pres. of Reichsbank
Schaech, Johnathon	1969-	Ent	10			40	Actor; 'That Thing You Do'

NAME	DATES	CATEGORY	SIG	LS/DS	ALS	SP	COMMENTS
Schafer, Natalie		Ent	20			85	Actress, 'Gilligan's Island', SP w/Jim Backus 138
Schaff, Phillip		Clergy	40	55	75	50	
Schaffner, Franklin J.	1920-1989	Ent	30			75	Dir. AA
Schaffner, Hans		HOS	10			20	Pres. Austria
Schakowsky, Janice D. S		Congr	10				Member US Congress
Schall, Thomas D.		Congr	10	15			Rep., Sen. MN 1915
Schallert, William	1922-	Ent	10			40	Actor
Schally, Andrew V., Dr.		Sci	22	30	45	30	Nobel Med. 1977
Schanberg, Sydney, H.		Author	10	30	75	15	
Scharwenka, Franz Xavier		Comp	25		75	150	Pianist. Fndr. of Conservatory
Schary, Dore		Ent	15		25	30	Prod., Dir., Writer
Schary, Emanuel		Artist	10	25	35		
Schaub, Julius	1898-1967	WWII	86			175	SS Gen. Hitler's Adjutant
Schawlow, Arthur L., Dr.		Sci	22	30	35	25	Nobel Physics 1981
Scheel, Jeff		Music	10			40	Music. Lead Singer 'Gravity Kills'
Scheer, Reinhard	1863-1928	Mil	35	45	100	55	Ger. Adm. Battle of Jutland.
Scheff, Fritzi	1882-1954	Opera	20	15	30	25	Austr-Am. Sopr. Musical Theatre & Silent Films
Scheidemann, Philippe		HOS	10	20	50	40	1st Chancellor of Repub. 1919
Scheider, Roy	1932-2008	Ent	15	60		75	Actor; 'Jaws'
Schell, Augustus	1812-1884	Bus	275	850			Financier & C. Vanderbilt Attorney
Schell, Maria	1926-2005	Ent	15			75	Intl. Austrian Film Star 50s
Schell, Maximillian	1930-	Ent	45	90		68	Actor; AA
Schell, Richard	1810-1879	Bus		975			Commodore Vanderbilt's Aide During 'Erie War'
Schelling, Frederich W. J. von		Phil			505		Ger. idealist philosopher of the Romantic period
Schenk, Robert C.		Civ War	33	60	61		Union Gen., Rep OH, Ambassador
Scherchen, Hermann		Cond	20	242		125	
Scherer, Paul		Clergy	20	25	40	30	
Schick, Bela, Dr.		Med	60	135	225	125	Hung. -Am Pediatrician. Schick Test for TB
Schiele, Egon	1890-1918	Artist	2000	2798		3675	Austrian Expressionist Painter
Schiff, Adam B. S		Congr	10				Member US Congress
Schiff, Jacob H.	1847-1920	Bus	75	140	265		Banker, Philan. Wall Street Brokerage
Schiff, Richard		Ent	10			40	Actor; 'The West Wing'
Schiffer, Claudia	1972-	Model	18			57	Ger. Model
Schifrin, Lalo		Comp	10	20	25	30	Argentine Comp. Film Themes. AMusQS 40-150
Schildkraut, Joseph	1896-1964	Ent	68	101		177	AA winner
Schiller, Hans von		Aero	20		45		
Schilling, David		WWII	18	38	60	45	ACE, WWII; 22. 5 kills
Schimmel, Robert		Ent	15			25	Comedian
Schimmelfennig, Alexander	1824-1865	Civ War	45	80			Union Gen.
Schimmelfennig, Alexander (WD)	1824-1865	Civ War	1600				Union Brig. Gen. at Chancellorsville & Gettysburg
Schindler, Oskar		WWII	5600				"Righteous Gentile"
Schine, G. David		Bus	20			25	Hotel Chain Owner
Schiotz, Fredrik A.		Clergy	20	25	35	30	
Schipa, Tito	1889-1965	Opera	55			140	Opera. Important Tenor
Schippers, Thomas		Cond				150	Am.
Schirach, Balder von	1907-1974	WWII	132	311	375	250	Ger. Nat'l Dir. Hitler Youth Movement; SB 200
Schirra, Walter M.	1923-2007	Space	40	85	158	170	Mercury 7. SP w/Cooper 230; SP w/Stafford 280
Schirripa, Steven R.		Ent	10			40	Bobby ' Bacala' Baccalieri, Sopranos
Schlafly, Phyllis	1924-	Pol	10	20	35	35	Activist, Feminist
Schleicher, Kurt von	1882-1934	WWII	195	500			Last Chancellor of the Weimar Repub.
Schlesinger, Arthur Jr.	1917-2007	Author	10	40	50	20	Historian. JFK Spec. Asst. Pulitzer 1946; SB 60
Schlesinger, James R.		Cab	10	10	25	25	Sec. Defense 1973
Schlesinger, John	1926-2003	Ent	10			45	Film Dir. AA
Schlesinger, Leon	1884-1949	Ent		415			Film Prod. 'Merrie Melodie'

NAME	DATES	CATEGORY	SIG	LS/DS	ALS	SP	COMMENTS
Schlessinger, Laura Dr.		Celeb	10			25	Dr. Laura'
Schley, Winfield Scott	1839-1909	Mil	87	128	183	150	Am. Naval Off. Arctic rescue of Greely
Schliemann, Heinrich	1833-1890	Archaeol	570	750	1716		Discovered Ancient Troy. ALS re Mycenae 5,000
Schmalz, Wilhelm		Mil	15	40	75	75	
Schmidt, August		WWII				60	Gen. Major & Cmdr. of the 20th Infantry
Schmidt, Friedrich		Space	30				
Schmidt, Harvey		Comp	20				Am. Comp. AMusQS 400; 'Try to Remember'
Schmidt, Helmut		HOS	15	25	40	25	Ger. Pol. Leader, Chanc.
Schmidt, Joseph		Opera				352	
Schmidt, Maarten, Dr.		Sci	10	25	30	20	
Schmidt, Walter		WWII				310	WWII Ger. Co. 3rd, BN, SS-Panzer Gren
Schmidtmer, Christiane	1939-2003	Ent	10			60	Ger. Actress
Schmied, Francois-louis	1873-1941	Artist	90		375		Fr. Art Deco Painter-Illust.
Schmitt, Harrison H.		Space	48	76	130	179	Apollo 17 Moonwalker, TLS/cont 632
Schmitt-Walter, Karl		Opera	10			35	Opera. Baritone. Wide Repertoire
Schnabel, Artur	1881-1951	Music	108	155	220	105	Austrian Pianist
Schnaut, Gabriella		Opera	10			25	Opera
Schneider, Erich		WWII				60	Knight's Cross
Schneider, John		Ent	10			35	Singer-Actor
Schneider, Rob		Ent	10			40	Comedian
Schneider, Romy	1938-1982	Ent	75			142	Fr. Actress
Schneider, Wm. C.		Space	10				SKYLAB
Schnittke, Alfred	1934-1998	Music	20		170		Comp.
Schnitzer, George C. Jr.		Author	10			12	Author/publisher
Schnitzler, Arthur	1862-1931	Author	40	125			Austrian playwrite
Schochet, Bob		Comics	10				
Schoenberg, Arnold	1874-1951	Comp	262	812	690	675	Austrian-Born. AMusQS 1450-2000
Schoenebeck, Carl Aug. von		WWII	115			175	Ger. Gen. WWI ace who flew w/von Richtofen
Schoenert, Rudolf		WWII	10			50	Ger. ace
Schoepf, Albin Francisco	1822-1886	Civ War	45		90		Union Gen.
Schoepfel, Gerhard	1912-	WWII	10			50	Ger. Ace w/45 kills
Schofield, John McAllister	1831-1906	Civ War	50	140	150		Union Gen. MOH At Wilson's Creek
Schofield, John McAllister (WD)	1831-1906	Civ War	125	155	340		Union Gen., Sec. War 1868
Schofield, Philip	1962-	Ent	10			25	Br. Actor
Scholtz, Klaus		WWII				100	Knights Cross w/Oakleaves. Capt. U-Boat U-108
Scholtz-Klink, Gertrude		WWII		120			Powerful woman in the Nazi party
Schopenhauer, Arthur	1788-1860	Author	700	2250	4375		Ger. Philosopher
Schorner, Ferdinand	1892-1973	WWII	40		120		Ger. Gen.
Schorr, Daniel		Jrnalist	10			45	CBS Correspondent Till '76. Nat'l Pub. Radio Now
Schorr, Friedrich		Opera				150	Wagnerian bass-baritone
Schrader, Paul	1946-	Ent	10	15		20	Film Dir.
Schramm, Margit		Ent	10			20	Opera, Operetta
Schreiber, Avery		Ent	10			30	
Schreiber, Helmut		WWII				45	S. S. Major & Knight's Cross recipient.
Schreiber, Liev		Ent				35	Actor
Schreiner, William Philip	1857-1919	Pol			120		PM of South Africa during the Boer War
Schricker, Henry F.		Gov	10			10	Governor IN
Schrieffer, John R.		Sci	10	20	35	15	Nobel Physics 1972
Schriver, Edmund	1812-1899	Civ War	30	55	70		Union Gen.
Schrock, Edward L. S		Congr	10				Member US Congress
Schroder, Rick		Ent	18			55	
Schroder-Devrient, Wilhelmine		Opera			675		
Schroeder, Barbet	1941-	Ent	10			20	Prod. Dir.
Schroeder, Christa		WWII				75	Hitler's personal secretary.

NAME	DATES	CATEGORY	SIG	LS/DS	ALS	SP	COMMENTS
Schroeder, Patricia	1940-	Congr	10	10		20	Rep. CO
Schroeder, Patrick A.		Author	10				Civil War
Schroeder, Rick		Ent	10			45	Actor
Schroeder-Feinen, Ursula		Opera	10			30	Opera
Schroer, Werner		WWII				155	Ger. Ace WWII. RK
Schroeteler, Heinrich		WWII				75	Ger. Capt. U-667, U1023. RK
Schubert, Franz	1797-1828	Comp	2200	4567	10000		
Schuk, Walter		WWII	25	45		85	Ger. 12th Highest ACE
Schulberg, Budd		Author	30	55		50	Novels, Screenwriter. 'On The Waterfront'
Schuller, Gunther		Music	35			55	Pulitzer'94 in Music. AMusQS 250
Schuller, Robert	1926-	Clergy	15	20		25	
Schultz, Theodore William		Sci	10	15	25		Nobel Economics
Schulz, Charles	1922-2000	Comics	126	369	490	329	S Snoopy Sket 750-2000. S 'Peanuts' Orig. Strip 20000-71000
Schulze, William		Sci	15			60	Rocket Pioneer/von Braun
Schumann, Clara	1819-1896	Comp	70	221	581	925	Ger. Pianist-Comp. ALS/Cont 3,000, AMusQS 635
Schumann, Conrad	1942-1998	Celeb				135	1st Ger. Volksarmeesoldat fugitive to jump barbed wire into W. Ger.
Schumann, Elizabeth		Opera	45			140	Opera
Schumann, Heinz		WWII				90	Luftwaffe ace
Schumann, Robert	1810-1856	Comp	800	1100	4590		AMusQS 15,000 (3rd Symph). 22,000(Die Nonne)
Schumann-Heink, Ernestine		Opera	45		100	126	Austrian; Concert. Contralto
Schumer, Charles		Congr	10			20	US Senate (D-NY)
Schuricht, Carl		Cond				70	Ger. conductor
Schurz, Carl	1829-1906	Civ War	45	107	220		Union Gen., US Sen. MO. Advisor to 5 Pres. FF 53
Schuschnigg, Kurt von	1897-1977	HOS	50	85	225	1125	Austrian Chancellor. Deposed & Imprisoned by Nazis
Schuyler, Philip J.	1733-1804	Rev War	275	529	889		Soldier, Statesman. Rev. War Gen. Cont'l Congr
Schwab, Charles M.	1862-1939	Indust	102	247	1150	221	Pres. Carnegie, US & Bethlehem Steel/Mil. Salary
Schwab, Frank X.		Pol	10	20			Mayor Buffalo, NY
Schwantner, Joseph		Comp	10		55	40	Pulitzer, AMusQS 95
Schwartz, Arthur		Comp					Dancing in the Dark'; AMusQS 410
Schwartz, Melvin, Dr	1932-	Sci	24			30	Nobel Physics 1988
Schwartz, Scott		Ent	10			25	Actor. 'Xmas Story' SP 30
Schwartz, Scotty		Ent	13			40	
Schwartz, Sherwood		Ent				35	Writer 'Brady Bunch'
Schwartz, Stephen		Comp	55	200			'Godspell'
Schwarz, Gerard		Cond				75	
Schwarzenegger, Arnold		Ent	38	50	70	92	Actor-Prod. Governor of CA
Schwarzkopf, Elizabeth		Opera	15			63	Opera
Schwarzkopf, Norman		Mil	25	92		100	Gen. Desert Storm
Schwatka, Frederick	1849-1892	Mil	150	350	625		Indian Fighter
Schwedtman, Ferd. D.		Sci	10	15		10	
Schweickart, Russell L.		Space	25	125		88	
Schweiker, Richard S.		Congr	10	10		10	Rep., Sen. PA 1961
Schweitzer, Albert, Dr.	1874-1965	Sci	195	371	694	899	Nobel. Clergy. 3x4 SP 350-650. AMusQS 650
Schwellenback, Lewis B.		Cab	10	35	70	45	Sec. Labor 1945
Schwimmer, David		Ent	15			50	Actor. Friends
Schwinger, Julian, Dr.		Sci	20	30	55	55	Nobel Physics 1965
Schwitters, Kurt	1887-1948	Artist	250	775			Ger. Best Know For His Collages
Sciorra, Annabella		Ent	10			40	Actress
Scitar, Ted 'TVT'	1951-	Music	10			20	Guitar/sax/keyboards/drums/vocals. The VooDoos.
Scobee, Dick	1939-1989	Space	100	250	345	288	Challenger; FDC 120
Scofield, Glenni W.		Congr	10	15	25		Rep. PA 1863
Scofield, Paul	1922-2008	Ent	50		128	70	Brit. AA Winner. 'Man for All Seasons'

NAME	DATES	CATEGORY	SIG	LS/DS	ALS	SP	COMMENTS
Scoggins, Tracy		Ent	10			45	Actress
Scopes, John T.	1900-1970	Educ	200	1200		750	Defendant In Monkey Trial
Scorsese, Martin		Ent	15	228		68	Film Dir. AA
Scorupco, Izabella		Ent	10			60	Actress; 'Golden Eye '
Scotchie, Joseph		Author	10			12	Conservative Pol., literary critism
Scott, April		Ent	15			45	
Scott, Ashley		Ent	13			40	
Scott, Blanch Stuart	1891-1970	Aero	90		225	250	1st Fem. Pilot to Solo
Scott, Charles	1739-1813	Rev War	125	275	525		Gen., Indian Fighter, Gov. KY
Scott, Charles Wm. A.		Aero	25	50	80	50	Br. Won Harmon Trophy
Scott, Cyril Meir		Comp	15	30	55	75	Br. Orchestral, Piano, Chamber
Scott, David R.	1932-	Space	58	175		172	Cmdr. of the Apollo 15 mission; moonwalker
Scott, David S		Congr	10				Member US Congress
Scott, Debra Lee	1953-2005	Ent				40	Actress
Scott, E. Irwin		Bus		965	1475		One of Fndr. s of Scott Paper Co.
Scott, Earl		Cntry Mus	10			35	Music. 50s Western Recording Artist
Scott, Fred	1902-1991	Ent	18			46	Vintage Cowboy Actor
Scott, George C.	1927-1999	Ent	20	65		220	Actor; AA; ' Patton'
Scott, Gordon		Ent	15			54	Actor; 'Tarzan'
Scott, Gustavus		Rev War	35	90	140		Lawyer, Patriot (MD)
Scott, Hazel		Music	35	45		115	Piano-Organ
Scott, Hugh		Congr	10	15		25	Sen. PA
Scott, Hugh L.		Mil	30	95	250		Am. WWI Gen. 7 Chief of Staff
Scott, Jack		Music	10	60		60	Rock
Scott, Jerry		Comics	10		140	45	Nancy; Sketch 60
Scott, John		Congr	10				FF 34
Scott, John Morin		Rev War	35	169	150		Gen., Patriot, Rep. NY
Scott, Klea		Ent	13			40	
Scott, Lizabeth	1922-	Ent	40			60	Actress
Scott, Martha	1912-2003	Ent	15			50	Actress
Scott, Pippa	1935-	Ent	10			35	Actress
Scott, Randolph	1903-1987	Ent	40	55		143	Actor; Western Hero
Scott, Raymond		Comp	25	40	65	50	Big Band Leader, Arranger
Scott, Robert C. S		Congr	10				Member US Congress
Scott, Robert Falcon	1868-1912	Expl	150	295	1050		Br. Arctic Expedition
Scott, Robert Kingston	1826-1900	Civ War	45		90		Union Gen., Gov. SC
Scott, Robert Lee, Jr.		WWII	25	35	60	47	ACE, WWII, 'God Is My Co-Pilot'; 10 kills
Scott, Thomas		Ent	10			40	Actor; 'That Thing You Do"
Scott, Thomas		Clergy	40	50	75		
Scott, Thomas A.	1824-1881	Bus	238	762	1125		Pennsylvania RR Baron
Scott, Thomas Moore	1829-1876	Civ War	50				CSA Gen.
Scott, Tony	1944-	Ent	10			20	Br. Prod.
Scott, W. Kerr		Congr	10			25	Gov. NC 1949, Sen. NC 1954
Scott, Walter, Sir	1771-1832	Author	115	431	546		Poet, Novels, Historian
Scott, Willard		Ent	10			20	TV weatherman
Scott, Winfield	1786-1866	Civ War	125	296	339	386	Union Gen. rare AManS 1840 2500
Scott, Winfield (WD)		Civ War	130	375	1000		Union Gen.
Scott, Zachary	1914-1965	Ent	40			119	Actor
Scotti, Antonio		Opera	40		100	185	It. Baritone, Opera
Scotto, Renata		Opera	15			50	Opera
Scowcroft, Brent		Mil	10	30		20	Gen., Statesman, Pres. Advisor
Scranton, Bill		Gov	10	15		15	Gov. PA. Pres. Cand.
Scriabin, Alexander	1872-1915	Comp	750	3500	5000	2717	Rus. Symphonies.AMusQS 3500-6000
Scribe, Eugene	1791-1861	Author	10	35	130		Fr. Librettist. Meyerbeer, Halevy

NAME	DATES	CATEGORY	SIG	LS/DS	ALS	SP	COMMENTS
Scribner, Charles	1821-1871	Pub	110	138	350		Publishing Giant. Stk. Cert. S 1750
Scrimm, Angus	1926-	Ent	15			35	Actor
Scripps, William E.		Aero	15	90		40	
Scruggs, Jan		Celeb	10			20	Fndr. of the Vietnam Veterans Memorial
Scudder, Horace E.	1838-1902	Author	10	30	55		Ed. Atlantic Mnthly, Biographer
Scuderi, Sara		Opera	35			85	Opera
Scullin, James H.	1876-1953	HOS	40			70	P. M. Australia
Scully-Power, Paul		Space	25			65	STS-41G mission
Scurry, William Read	1821-1864	Civ War	488		4255		CSA Gen.
Seaborg, Glenn T.	1912-1999	Sci	53	130	150	62	Chm. AEC. Nobel Chem. '51. Pluto.-A Bomb; AMan. 820
Seacrest, Ryan		Ent	18			55	
Seal		Music	20			40	Rock
Seale, Bobby	1936-	Activist	25			55	Pol. Activist. Co-Fndr. Black Panthers, Chicago 8
Seals & Crofts		Music				45	Music group
Seals, Dan		Cntry Mus	10			15	
Searle, Ronald		Comics	20	45	80		Painter, Author. 'St. Trinians School Girls'
Sears, Claudius Wistar	1817-1891	Civ War	105				CSA Gen.
Sears, Edmund		Clergy	20	25	35		
Sears, Richard Warren		Bus		6500			Sears Fndr. DS Sears Contract 12, 500
Seaton, George	1911-1979	Ent	35			70	Writer; Dir. AA
Seawell, Molly Elliot		Author	10	15	35	10	
Sebastian, John		Music	15			45	Singer-Songwriter. The Lovin' Spoonful
Sebastini, H. F. B.	1772-1851	Fr Mil		80	150		Gen. under Napoleon, Marshal of Fr.
Seberg, Jean	1938-1979	Ent	66	110	390	372	Fr. Actress
Sebold, Alice		Author	10			20	Best selling Author
Sechelles, Marie-Jean Her. de		Fr Rev			895		Atty to Louis XVI
Sedaka, Neil		Music	15			40	Entertainer; Comp. AMusQS 35; S Album 40
Seddon, James A.		Civ War	150	450	493		CSA Sec. War
Seddon, James A. (WD)		Civ War	210	905	1912		CSA Sec. War Dte.
Seddon, Margaret R.		Space	10			25	
Sedgwick, Catherine M.	1789-1867	Author	10	20	45		Am. Early Novels. Moral Tales
Sedgwick, Charles Baldwin		Congr	10				FF 32
Sedgwick, John	1813-1864	Civ War	192	497	632		Union Gen. (Uncle John). KIA Spotsylvania
Sedgwick, Kyra		Ent	15			41	Actress
See, Elliot M. Jr.	1927-1966	Space	225			325	D. w/Chas A. Bassett in T-38 training flight
Seeburg, Justus Percival		Bus	40	120	195		
Seeger, Pete	1919-	Comp	35	60	95	48	Folk Singer; S Guitar 250
Seeley, Blossom	1891-1974	Ent	20			75	Actress
Seeley, Jeannie		Cntry Mus	10			20	
Seelye, Julius Hawtry		Clergy	15	20	25		College Pres., Rep. MA
Segal, Erich		Author	20	30			Love Story
Segal, George		Artist	65		80	150	Sculptor
Segal, George		Ent	15			60	Actor
Segal, Steven		Ent	25			52	Actor
Segal, Vivienne	1897-1992	Ent				65	Actress
Segar, Elzie C.		Comics	125			575	Popeye
Segar, Joseph E.		Congr	10	20			Rep. VA 1862
Seger, Bob		Music	20			55	Rock; S Guitar 340
Seger, Bob & Silver Bullet Band		Music				200	Rock group; S Album 160
Seger, C. B.		Bus	15	45	85	40	
Segonzac, Andre Dunoyer de	1884-1974	Artist				130	Painter & engraver
Segovia, Andres	1894-1987	Music	71	300	475	343	Classical Guitar Virtuoso
Segre, Emilio, Dr.		Sci	20	35	50	30	Nobel Physics 1959
Segura, Wiltz P.		WWII	15	25	40	30	ACE, WWII, USAAF Ace. Flew/Chennault; 6 kills

NAME	DATES	CATEGORY	SIG	LS/DS	ALS	SP	COMMENTS
Segurola, Andres de		Opera	45			150	Sp. Bass
Seidel, Toscha		Music	20			75	Noted Rus. -Am. Violinist
Seidelman, Susan	1952-	Ent	10	10		20	Film Dir.
Seidl, Anton		Cond		250			Austro-Hungarian conductor
Seignolle, Claude		Author	120	175	220		
Seinfeld (Cast)		Ent	150			360	Four Main Chars.; S script 1000
Seinfeld, Jerry		Ent	30	225		130	Comed., Hndwrtn. Script 8230; S. Script 350-500
Seipel, Ignas Dr.		HOS	10	30	80	40	Austrian Prelate & Chancellor
Seka		Ent	20			110	Legendary adult film star
Selassie, Haile	1892-1975	HOS	266	569	730	1661	(Tafari Makonnen) Emperor of Ethiopia
Seldes, Gilbert		Author	25	126			Am. playwrite, screenwriter
Selena	1971-1995	Music	225			460	Queen of Tejano music'; S Album 300
Selfridge, Harry G.	1858-1947	Bus	15	65	110	75	Fndr. Selfridge's, London Dept. Store
Selfridge, Thos. O.	1836-1924	Civ War	40	85	120		Union Naval Cmdr.
Sellecca, Connie		Ent	10			40	Actress
Selleck, Tom		Ent	10	60	30	65	Magnum P. I. ' TV Star. SP 75
Sellers, David Foote		Mil	20	55	95	95	
Sellers, Jim		Music	10			25	Music. Bass Guitar 'Stabbing Westward'
Sellers, Peter	1925-1980	Ent	228	254	292	326	Br. comic actor
Sellers, Winfield S.		Mil	15	40	75	75	
Selman, John Henry	1839-1896	West	1200	1448			Killed John Wesley Hardin
Selous, Frederick Courteney		Author	20			40	Afr. adventure
Selznick, David O.	1902-1965	Bus	89	286	370	780	Film Prod. (GWTW). S Chk 350
Selznick, Irene		Ent	10	15		20	Film Executive
Sembrich, Marcella	1858-1935	Opera	85		300	350	Opera, Concert. Polish Sopr.
Semenov, Mikhail		Sci	10	20			Russian/Am. Physicist
Semenov, Nikolai		Sci		55			Rus. Chem., Physicist. Nobel 1956
Semmelweis, Ignaz	1818-1865	Med	500	1200	3200		Hung. Obstetrician. Antisepsis
Semmes, Paul J.	1815-1863	Civ War	831	1365	1875		CSA Gen. Sig/Rank 1450
Semmes, Raphael	1809-1877	Civ War	352	685	2640	1750	CSA Adm. Sig/Rank 475
Semple, James	1798-1866	Congr	15				Sen. IL, Elsa, IL Fndr.
Sendak, Maurice		Author	20	65		60	Writer/Illust., kid's books; S Sket $400-760; SB $175
Senechal, Michel		Opera	10			25	Opera
Senn, Nicholas		Sci	35		80		Physician. Spanish Am. War
Sennett, Mack	1880-1960	Ent	220	443		871	Historic DS 4500; SB 250
Sensenbrenner Jr., F. James S		Congr	10				Member US Congress
Sergeant, John	1779-1852	Congr	65	85	135		Rep. PA. ALS/Cont 1600
Sergeant, John	1944-	Jrnalist	10	20	35	20	Broadcaster
Sergievsky, Boris		Aero	75			150	
Serkin, Rudolf	1903-1991	Music	40	130	155	115	Austr. -Born Piano Virtuoso, AMusQS 50-175
Serkis, Andy		Ent				68	Actor; 'Lord of the Rings'
Serling, Rod	1924-1975	Author	124	346	375	398	Creator 'Twilight Zone'
Serpico, Frank		Lawman	10	20	45	20	UnderCvr. Detective-Hero
Serra, Junipero Fr.		Clergy		372000			Fndr. of Mission San Juan Capistrano
Serrano, José E. S		Congr	10				Member US Congress
Serurier, Jean M. P., Count		Fr Rev	50	145	215		Marshal of Napoleon
Service, Robert W.	1874-1958	Author	75		235	235	Canadian Poet, Author, Versifier
Sessions, Jeff		Congr	10				US Senate (R-AL)
Sessions, Pete S		Congr	10				Member US Congress
Sessions, Roger		Comp	25	45	203		Pulitzer, AMusQS 250
Sessions, William L.		Pol	25	75		30	Dir. FBI
Seton-Thompson, Ernest	1860-1946	Author	75	115	216	180	Co-Fndr. Boy Scouts. Wildlife Stories. Illustr.
Setzer, Brian		Music	10	60		40	Singer. Brian Setzer Orchestra.
Seuss, Dr. (Theodore Geisel)	1904-1992	Author	140	412	702	500	Sket 500-3000., S Print 300, S FDC 540; SB 500-750

NAME	DATES	CATEGORY	SIG	LS/DS	ALS	SP	COMMENTS
Severance, Joan	1958-	Ent	15			82	Actress
Severeid, Eric	1912-1992	Jrnalist	15			40	TV-Radio Anchor & Sr. Commentator/Cronkite
Severeid, Susanne		Model	10			35	Actress
Severinson, Doc	1927-	Music	10		25	30	Trumpet, Big Band
Sevier, John	1745-1815	Rev War	525	1350	2100		Hero of Battle of King's Mt. Historical DS 3750
Sevigny, Chloe		Ent	10			40	Actress
Sevitzky, Fabien		Cond				75	Russian
Sewall, David		Rev War	20	50	110		Jurist, Patriot, Justice Peace
Sewall, Samuel	1757-1814	Congr	25		60		Rep. MA 1796. MA Chief Justice
Sewall, Samuel	1652-1730	Colonial	275	909	1300		Salem Witchcraft Trials
Sewall, Stephen	1652-1730	Colonial		2157			Jurist; Clerk of Court, 1692 Salem Witch Trials. Bro. of Samuel Sewall
Seward, Frederick Wm.	1830-1915	Cab	30	48	80		Ass't Sec. State
Seward, William H.	1801-1872	Cab	58	271	217	745	Lincoln's Sec. State. LS/Re Assassination 1750
Sewell, William J.	1835-1901	Civ War	40	65	90		Union Gen., US Sen. NJ
Sex Pistols		Music		435		250	Rock
Sexton, Anne	1928-1974	Author	65	420			Am. Poet. 1967 Pulitzer.
Sexton, Dr. Ralph Jr.		Clergy	10			12	TV evangelist
Sexton, Dr. Ralph Sr.		Clergy	10			12	Author, longtime evangelist
Sexton, Walton R.		WWII	10	30	45	30	Adm. US Navy. WWII
Seyfried, Amanda		Ent	15			45	
Seymour, Anne	1909-1988	Ent	10			40	
Seymour, George F., Bish.		Clergy	25	25	40		
Seymour, Horatio	1810-1886	Gov	30	60	80		Civil War Gov. NY. Pres. Cand.
Seymour, Jane	1951-	Ent	15			61	Br. Actress
Seymour, Stephanie		Ent	20			66	Model/actress
Seymour, Truman	1824-1891	Civ War	64	115	292		Union Gen. At Ft. Sumter When Surrendered
Seyss-Inquart, Artur von	1892-1946	WWII	310			380	Nazi, War Criminal. Austian Chancellor: Anschluss
Shabazz, Attallah	1958-	Celeb	10				Daughter of Malcolm X
Shackelford, James Murrell	1827-1909	Civ War	45	84			Union Gen.
Shackelford, Ted	1946-	Ent	10			35	Actor
Shackleton, Ernest H., Sir	1874-1922	Expl	456	1068	3918	5360	Br. Antarctic Explr. S Chk 500-2500
Shadegg, John B. S		Congr	10				Member US Congress
Shadix, Glenn		Ent	15			45	
Shaffer, Paul	1949-	Ent	10			35	Band leader 'Letterman Show'
Shaffer, Peter L.		Author	10	20	35	15	
Shafter, William R.	1835-1906	Civ War	30	65	104	150	Union Gen. MOH. Indian Fighter
Shaftesbury, A.A.C. 7th Earl	1801-1885	Reform	25	80	160		Pol., M. P., Statesman, Social Reformer
Shah, Zahir		Royal	50				King Afghanistan
Shahn, Ben		Artist	55	150	240	145	Am. Painter-Graphic Artist; SB 120
Shain, Edith		Celeb				125	Nurse in Famous VJ Day photo, w/Muscarello 350
Shakira		Music	10			44	Singer
Shakur, Tupac	1971-1996	Music	210	345		325	Assass. rapper/actor
Shalamar		Ent	12	15	60	50	
Shaler, Alexander	1827-1911	Civ War	42	55	78		Union Gen. MOH
Shalikashvili, John	1936-	Mil	10	25		20	Chm. Joint Chiefs of Staff
Shamir, Yitzhak		HOS	25	95	105	81	7th Prime Min. Israel
Shamroy, Leon	1901-1974	Ent	20			50	Dir., Cinematographer. AA
Shandling, Garry	1949-	Ent	15			50	Comedian. TV Emmy Winner
Shannon, Del	1934-1990	Music	55			234	Singer
Shannon, Wilson		Gov	25	65	100		Kansas Peacemaker 1870
Shapiro, Donald A.	1950-	Law	10			20	Distinguished trial lawyer; BFF
Shapiro, Harry		Artist	10	25	45		
Shapiro, Karl		Author	10	30	70	20	

NAME	DATES	CATEGORY	SIG	LS/DS	ALS	SP	COMMENTS
Shapiro, Robert		Law		15		20	O. J. Simpson Trial Attorney
Shapley, Alan		Mil	10	35	50		
Shapley, Harlow	1885-1972	Sci	35	90	150		Astronomer. Dir. Harvard Observ.
Shapp, Milton J.		Gov	10	20			Governor PA
Sharan, Shri Chakradhar		HOS	15	35		75	Pres. India
Sharett, Moshe (Shertok)	1894-1965	HOS	50	165	325		Israeli Prime Min.
Sharif, Omar		Ent	15	25	60	74	Egyptian Actor-Champion Tournament Bridge
Sharkey, Ray	1952-1993	Ent	10	22		50	Actor
Sharman, Helen		Space		55		45	1st Br. Astronaut in Space Aboard Apollo-Soyuz
Sharnova, Sonia		Opera	10			25	Am. Contralto
Sharon, Ariel		Mil	25	65	125	235	Israeli Gen., PM
Sharon, William		Congr	45	110	200		Sen. NV, Banker & Financier
Sharp, Jacob Hunter	1833-1907	Civ War	110				CSA Gen.
Sharp, U. S. Grant		Mil	10	25	35	35	
Sharp, William		Artist	15	40	105		
Sharpe, George H.	1828-1900	Civ War	30	45			Union Gen., 120th New York
Sharpe, Karen	1934-	Ent	10			30	Actress
Sharpe, William, Dr.		Econ	22	30			Nobel Enconomics 1990
Sharpton, Al, Rev.		Clergy	15			25	
Shatner, William		Ent	30	428		232	Actor. StarTrek DS 5700; SP w/Nimoy 250-400
Shaud, Grant	1961-	Ent	10			30	Actor; 'Murphy Brown'
Shaunessy, Charles	1955-	Ent	10			30	Br. Actor
Shavelson, Melville	1917-2007	Ent	10			25	Writer
Shaver, Helen	1951-	Ent	10			30	Actress
Shavers, Charlie	1920-1971	Music	120		135		Jazz era Trumpeter
Shavers, China		Ent	13			40	
Shaw, Andrew J.		Celeb	10	20			Explr. & Musician
Shaw, Anna Howard	1847-1919	Fem	35	80	175		Physician, Suffragist, Clergy
Shaw, Artie	1910-2004	Band	25	90	210	262	Big Band Leader-Clarinetist
Shaw, Bernard		Jrnalist	10			20	TV Broadcast Journalist
Shaw, Brewster H.		Space	10			25	
Shaw, Clay	1913-1974	Bus	119	316			Only person tried for conspiracy, JFK assass.
Shaw, Eugene Clay, Jr.		Congr	10				Member US Congress
Shaw, George Bernard	1856-1950	Author	225	830	850	3060	Ir. Plays, Critic. Nobel Pr. FDC 500
Shaw, Irwin	1913-1984	Author	20	40	65	50	Am. Novels, Short Story Writer
Shaw, Lemuel	1781-1861	Rev War	45	85	105		Chf. Justice MA Supreme Court
Shaw, Leslie M.	1848-1932	Cab	30	35	50		Sec. Treasury 1902
Shaw, Robert	1927-1978	Ent	110	487		165	Actor
Shaw, Robert Gould	1837-1863	Civ War	1900				Union Col. in Cmd. of all-Black 54th Mass Reg.
Shaw, Suzanne		Celeb	10			15	Media/TV personality
Shawn, Dick		Ent	40			78	
Shawn, Ted	1891-1972	Ent	45			120	Am. Dancer-Choreographer
Shay, John		Ent	10			40	Actor
Shayne, Robert	1900-1992	Ent	35	60		172	Inspector Henderson 'Superman'
Shays, Christopher S		Congr	10				Member US Congress
Shays, Daniel	1747-1825	Rev War	295	747			Led Shay's rebellion
Shazar, Zalman		HOS	20			60	Israel
Shea, George Beverly		Clergy	15	20	25	30	Singing Evangelist
Shea, John	1949-	Ent	10			35	Actor
Shea, William A.		Bus	10	20	40	10	
Shear, Rhonda	1954-	Ent	10			30	Actress
Shearer, Harry		Ent	15			40	Actor
Shearer, Moira		Ballet	68		70	72	Ballet. 'The Red Shoes'
Shearer, Norma	1902-1983	Ent	70	181	550	242	AA. actress

NAME	DATES	CATEGORY	SIG	LS/DS	ALS	SP	COMMENTS
Shearing, George		Music	20	120		65	Jazz Pianist
Sheedy, Ally		Ent	10	15		40	Actress
Sheehan, John	1885-1952	Ent	10			60	Char. Actor
Sheen, Charlie		Ent	10	15		46	Actor
Sheen, Fulton J.	1895-1979	Clergy	40	60	95	58	Archbishop Rochester, NY. TV Personality
Sheen, Martin		Ent	15	75		52	AA, The West Wing
Sheffer, Craig		Ent	10			40	Actor
Sheffield, Johnny	1931-	Ent	20	275		125	As Child Played Tarzan's Son
Shehan, Lawrence J., Card.		Clergy	35	45	50	60	
Shekoni, Judith	1978-	Ent	10			35	Br. Actress
Shelby, Carrol		Bus				60	Car design
Shelby, Isaac	1750-1826	Rev War	300	339	550		Off. VA Militia. 1st Gov. KY
Shelby, Joseph O.	1830-1897	Civ War	385	828	1250	2200	CSA Gen. S Chk 120
Shelby, Joseph O. (WD)	1830-1897	Civ War	450				CSA Gen.
Shelby, Richard		Congr	10				US Senate (R-AL)
Sheldon, Charles M.	1857-1946	Clergy	20	35	50	50	
Sheldon, Sidney		Author	10	15	25	15	Am. Novels
Shelley, Charles Miller	1833-1907	Civ War	125	977			CSA Gen.
Shelley, Mary Wollstonecraft	1797-1851	Author	1130	2500	9618		Frankenstein
Shelley, Percy Bysshe		Author	1060	2182	4375		ALS/Cont 14,000; S Chk 1500
Shelley, Rachael		Ent	15			45	
Shelly, Adrienne	1966-2006	Ent	15			50	Actress; Dir.
Shelton, Deborah		Ent	10			40	Miss USA
Shelton, Marley		Ent	16			47	
Shelton, Marly		Model				48	Fashion Model
Shepard, Alan B.	1923-1998	Space	56	246		492	1st Am. In Space, Mercury 7. Moonwalker. S Cvr. 150-320; SP w/JFK 325
Shepard, Dax		Ent	15			45	
Shepard, Ernest Howard		Artist	45	184			Illust. for" Winnie the Pooh", S drwg 1840
Shepard, Isaac Fitzgerald	1816-1889	Civ War	35	60	90		Union Gen.
Shepard, William	1737-1817	Rev War		360			Revolutionary War Off.
Shepherd, Ben		Music	10			25	Music. Bass, Vocals 'Soundgarden'
Shepherd, Cybill		Ent	10	25		45	Actress
Shepherd, William M.		Space	10			15	
Shepis, Tiffany	1979-	Ent	10			25	Actress.
Shepley, George Foster	1819-1878	Civ War	52	70	110		Union Gen.
Sheppard, Dick		Clergy	25	35	50	30	
Sheppard, Morris		Congr	10	20		15	Rep., Sen. TX. Author 18th Amend.
Sheppard, Sam		Celeb					Acquitted murder suspect AQS 1035
Shera, Mark	1949-	Ent	10			20	Actor
Sheridan, Ann	1915-1967	Ent	35			172	Actress
Sheridan, Dinah	1920-	Ent				40	Br. Actress
Sheridan, Jim	1949-	Ent	10			20	Film Prod.
Sheridan, Nicollette		Ent	15			63	Actress
Sheridan, Philip H.	1831-1888	Civ War	240	276	525		Cavalry
Sheridan, Philip H. (WD)	1831-1888	Civ War	281	1050	1975	1892	Union Gen.
Sheridan, Richard Brinsley	1751-1816	Author	65	260	370		Ir. Dramatist, Pol. 1751-1816
Sheridan, Tony	1940-	Music		278			Singer/songwriter/guitarist. Beatles collaborator
Sherlock, Nancy		Space	10			20	
Sherman, Allan	1924-1973	Music				120	Folksinger; 'Hello Mudda, Hello Fadda'
Sherman, Bobby	1943-	Music				55	Singer; actor
Sherman, Brad S		Congr	10				Member US Congress
Sherman, Ellen		Civ War			120		Wife of William T. Sherman
Sherman, Forrest P.		WWII	20	50	95	95	Adm. WWII. Ch. Naval Operationsl

NAME	DATES	CATEGORY	SIG	LS/DS	ALS	SP	COMMENTS
Sherman, Francis Trowbridge	1825-1905	Civ War	45	75	100		Union Gen.
Sherman, Frederick C.		Mil	35	45	70	50	Adm. Cmdr Carrier Lexington
Sherman, George		Ent	10			25	Actor
Sherman, James S.	1855-1912	VP	60	140	210	200	Taft VP. MOC; FF 27
Sherman, John	1823-1900	Congr	62	140	176	150	Sherman Act, TLS/Cont 600. RR ALS 1450; FF 63
Sherman, Richard & Robert		Comp	40	100	100		AMusQS 150
Sherman, Roger	1721-1793	Rev War	302	677	1312		Signed All 4 Major Fed. Papers
Sherman, Thomas West		Civ War	30	55	85		Union Gen.
Sherman, William T.	1820-1891	Civ War	302	472	694	3074	Union Gen. ALS/CW Cont 7500-17500; S Chk 275-500
Sherman, William T. (WD)	1820-1891	Civ War	375	2050	4250	3013	Cont. ALS's go up to & incl. 50,000+
Sherriff, Robert C.	1896-1975	Author	45		140	80	Plays, Novels, Screenwriter
Sherrill, Carolyn		Author	10			12	Children
Sherwood, (Mary) Martha	1775-1851	Author	10	15	35		Br. Author Juvenile Tales
Sherwood, Bobby	1914-1981	Ent	10			45	Actor
Sherwood, Don S		Congr	10				Member US Congress
Sherwood, Isaac R.		Congr	10	15		20	Rep. OH 1873
Sherwood, Percy		Comp	25			60	Ger. Pianist. AMusQS 75
Sherwood, Robert E.	1896-1955	Author	30	128	140	75	Am. Plays, Speeches FDR, Pulitzers
Sherwood, Samuel	1779-1862	Congr	20	35	50		Rep. NY 1813
Shicoff, Neil		Opera				75	Am. tenor
Shields, Arthur	1896-1970	Ent	10			35	Actor-Brother Barry Fitzgerald
Shields, Brooke	1965-	Ent	10	12	140	94	Actress; S Chk 60; SB 70
Shields, James	1806-1879	Civ War	42	65	80		Challenged Lincoln to a Duel
Shigeta, James	1933-	Ent	10			40	Actor
Shillaber, Benjamin P.	1814-1890	Author		50	110		Humorist-Editor
Shimada, Shigetaro	1883-1976	WWII				250	Japenese Adm.
Shimkus, John S		Congr	10				Member US Congress
Shimmerman, Armin		Ent	15			40	Star Trek
Shinn, Conrad S.		Aero		35		75	Landed 1st Plane at So. Pole
Shipman, Nina		Ent	10			30	Hawaiian actress
Shipp, John Wesley		Ent				105	Actor; 'Flash'
Shippen, Edward		Rev War	45	95	165		Ch. Justice PA, Statesman
Shipstad, Henrik	1881-1960	Congr	10	20		25	Sen. MN 1922
Shiras, George, Jr.		Sup Crt	90	250	375		
Shire, David	1937-	Comp	15			30	Oscar winner
Shire, Talia		Ent	15	208		42	
Shirelles		Music	70	215		160	Singing group
Shirer, William L.		Author	15	40		25	News Commentator. 'Berlin Diary' S 50
Shirley, Anne	1918-1993	Ent	15	15	35	79	Actress
Shirley, William	1693-1771	Colonial	165	350	885		Cmdr. -in-Chief, Explr., Colonial Gov. MA
Shivers, Allan		Gov	12			30	Governor TX
Shlotz-Klink, Gertrud	1902-1999	WWII	125	375			Leader of all Nazi women's organizations
Shockley, William, Dr.		Sci	35	144	165	98	Nobel Physics 1956. Transistor, sketch 70-250
Shoemaker, Eugene & Carolyn		Sci	45			75	Discovered Meteor Crater
Shoemaker, Lazarus D.		Congr	10	20			Rep. PA 1871
Shoemaker, Vaughn		Comics	10			75	Pulitzer Pr. Editorial Cartoonist. John Q. Pub.
Shoemaker, William L.		Author	10		15		
Shoen, Sam		Bus	10	15	35	25	
Shomo, William Arthur		WWII	15	32	50	40	ACE, WWII, CMH; 8 kills
Shoop, Pamela Susan		Ent	10			25	Actress
Shor, Bernard Toots		Bus	30	45	75	35	NY Restaurateur. Celebrity Host
Shore, Dinah	1917-1994	Ent	15	31	40	64	Singer-Actress-TV Host. Golf Sponsor; S Chk 100
Shore, Pauley		Ent	10			30	Actor
Shore, Roberta	1943-	Ent	10			30	Actress. Movies-TV Disney Star. 'The Virginian'

NAME	DATES	CATEGORY	SIG	LS/DS	ALS	SP	COMMENTS
Short, Bobby	1924-2005	Music	10			35	Nightclub Pianist-Vocalist
Short, Martin		Ent	15			45	
Shortridge, Samuel	1861-1952	Congr	10	20			Sen. CA 1920
Shostakovich, Dmitri	1906-1975	Comp	275	578	1125	1425	ALS/Cont 3, 200, 4000, AMusQS 750-2500
Shoumatoff, Elizabeth		Artist	35	45	75		Painting FDR At Time of Death. Repro S 295
Shoup, David M.	1904-1983	WWII	30	40	80	122	MOH Winning Cmdr. 2nd Marines. Commandant
Shoup, Francis, A.	1834-1896	Civ War	115		506		CSA Gen.
Shoup, George L.	1836-1904	Congr	12	20	35		1st Gov. ID, Sen. ID 1890
Show, Grant	1962-	Ent	10			40	Actor
Showalter, Max	1917-2000	Ent	10			35	Actor
Shower, Kathy		Ent				90	Actress-Model
Shrimpton, Jean	1942-	Ent	40			65	Br. Actress
Shriner, Herb	1918-1970	Ent	15			55	Actor
Shriner, Wil	1953-	Ent	10			20	Dir. actor
Shriver, Eunice Kennedy		Celeb	15	25	40	50	Sister JFK, Wife Sargent Shriver
Shriver, Loren J.		Space	10			28	
Shriver, Maria		Jrnalist	10			40	Broadcast Journalist
Shriver, Sargent		WH Staff	10	20	25	30	Created Job Corps
Shroyer, Sonny	1935-	Ent	10			35	Actor
Shrum, Cal	1910-1996	Ent	10			45	Cowboy Actor
Shubert, Lee	1873-1953	Bus	20	70	85	40	Theatrical Mgr. -Prod.
Shubrick, William B.		Mil	40				Cmdr. Frigate Constitution, War 1812
Shue, Andrew		Ent	10			47	Actor
Shue, Elisabeth	1963-	Ent	10			54	Actress
Shugart, Alan		Invent	10	20		20	Computer Disk Drive
Shulman, Ellen L.		Space	10			25	
Shulman, Max	1919-1988	Author	25			80	Creator Dobie Gillis
Shultz, George P.		Cab	15	25	40	35	Sec. State, Labor, Treasury
Shulze, Matt		Ent	17			50	
Shum, Mina		Ent	10			20	Dir.
Shuman, Eleanor		Titanic	50	202	70	75	Titanic survivor Deceased 3/98
Shumard, Bob		WWII	25			50	Enola Gay asst flight engineer
Shuster, Bill S		Congr	10				Member US Congress
Shuster, W. Morgan		Bus	10	15	35	15	Chm. Appleton-C. -Crofts
Shwarzkopf, Elisabeth		Opera				250	
Sibelius, Jan	1865-1957	Comp	315	644	1170	1108	Fin. Symph. AMusQS 1600-1850-3500, SPc 1115
Sibley, Henry Hastings	1811-1891	Civ War	45				Union Gen. Indian fighter. 1st Gov. of Minn.
Sibley, Henry Hopkins	1816-1886	Civ War	102	316	474		CSA Gen., Indian Fighter, Invented Sibley tent
Sicard, L'Abbe		Educ			1200		Fr. Teacher of the deaf
Sickles, Daniel E.	1819-1914	Civ War	80	198	279	437	Union Gen., MOH winner; S Chk 130
Sickles, Noel		Comics	20			175	Scorchy
Siddons, F. Scott, Mrs.		Ent	25			50	Vintage Actress
Siddons, Sarah Kemble	1755-1831	Ent	175		577		18th-19th C. Br. Tragedienne
Sidey, Hugh	1927-2005	Jrnalist	10			15	Life, Time magazine
Sidgwick, Henry	1838-1900	Phil			125		
Sidney, George	1916-2002	Ent	15			60	Film Dir. GG
Sidney, Robert, Sir	1563-1626	Mil	150	920			Poet Brother of Sir Philip. Earl of Essex
Sidney, Sylvia	1910-1999	Ent	15		25	102	Vintage Actress
Siegbahn, Kai Manne		Sci	30	55	100	90	Nobel Physics 1981
Siegel & Shuster		Comics	200				Superman
Siegel, Bugsy		Crime					Signed Passport 14, 280
Siegel, Don	1912-1991	Ent	175	250			Film Dir.
Siegel, Hans		WWII				60	Major C. O. Hitlerjugend Division
Siegel, Jerry	1915-1996	Ent	40	250		150	One of Creators. Superman

NAME	DATES	CATEGORY	SIG	LS/DS	ALS	SP	COMMENTS
Siegel, Joel	1943-2007	Jrnalist	10			20	TV Film Reviewer
Siegfried & Roy		Ent	25			85	Animal Trainers; LV Showmen
Siegmeister, Elie		Comp	25	40	80	60	
Siems, Margarethe		Opera	45			110	Opera
Sienkiewicz, Henryk	1846-1916	Author			350		Polish Writer. Nobel. Quo Vadis
Siepi, Cesare		Ent	15			65	Opera. Self-Taught Bass
Sievers, Wolfram		WWII	46				Asst. to Himmler
Sigall, Joseph		Artist	100	190	385		Pres. Portraits & Eur. Royalty
Sigel, Franz	1824-1902	Civ War	43	109	174		Union Gen.
Sigel, Franz (WD)	1822-1899	Civ War		260			Union Brig. Gen.
Sighele, Mietta		Opera	10			30	Opera
Sigler, Jamie		Ent	15			44	
Sigler, Jamie Lynn		Opera				40	Meadow Sopr.
Sigler, Kim		Gov	10	15		10	Governor MI
Signac, Paul	1863-1935	Artist	144	179	464		Fr. Watercolor Land & Seascapes. Neo-Impressionist
Signoret, Simone	1921-1985	Ent	110			149	Oscar winner
Sigourney, Lydia Howard H.	1791-1865	Author	70	110	200		Most Famous Lady Writer in Am 1830's.
Sigsbee, Charles D.		Mil	35	105	165	165	Capt. USN The Maine
Sihanouk, Norodom, Prince	1922-	HOS	50	95	155	125	Cambodia
Sikes, Cynthia	1954-	Ent	10			35	Actress
Sikking, James		Ent	17			50	
Sikking, James B.		Ent	10			35	Actor
Sikorsky, Igor I.	1889-1972	Aero	62	130	180	210	Designed & Built 1st Helicopter. Aviation HOF
Silhouette, Etienne de	1709-1767	Cab		950			Fr. Contr. Gen., Financier, Silhouette so Named
Silja, Anja		Opera	15			35	Opera
Sill, Joshua Woodrow	1831-1862	Civ War	125	440			Union Gen., KIA Stone River TN
Sill, Susan		Space	10			25	
Silla, Felix	1937-	Ent	10			30	Actor. 'Addams Family'
Silliman, Benjamin	1816-1885	Sci	30	52	125		Am. Chemist. Editor. Professor
Silliman, Gold Selleck	1732-1790	Rev War	85	160			Col. & Brig. Gen.
Sills, Beverly	1929-2007	Opera	15		25	74	Am. Sopr.
Sills, Milton	1882-1930	Ent	30	40	75	67	Leading Man of Silent Films
Siloti, Alexander		Comp	50		225	75	Pianist, Conductor
Silva, Henry		Ent	10			60	Actor
Silva-Herzog, Jesus		Pol	10			15	Mexican Min. of Finance
Silver, Abba Hillel		Zionist	15	50			Zionist Leader
Silver, Joe	1922-1989	Ent	10			35	Actor
Silver, Ron		Ent	15			40	Actor-Dir.
Silverberg, D. M. 'Dave'		Sci	10			15	Fndr. of Aestiva, creator of webcentric HTML/OS
Silverheels, Jay		Ent	145	272		599	'Tonto' in Lone Ranger
Silverman, Jonathan		Ent	10			40	Actor
Silverman, Robert		Music	10	15		45	Contemporary Pianist
Silvers, Phil	1912-1985	Ent	60	120	150	156	Am. Comedian-Actor. 'Sgt Bilko'; S Chk 60
Silverstone, Alicia	1976-	Ent	10	35		60	Actress.
Silvestri, Constantin		Cond				100	Russian
Sim, Alastair	1900-1976	Ent	90	115		162	Br. Actor
Simenon, Georges	1903-1989	Author	50	100	275	125	Fr-Belg. Creator Inspector Maigret
Simeon II		Royal	80				King of Bulgaria 1937
Simeon, Charles		Clergy	45	75			
Simmons, E. H. H.		Bus	25	40			Pres. NY Stock Exchange
Simmons, Gene		Music	20			65	Kiss
Simmons, Jaason	1970-	Ent	10			35	Australian actor
Simmons, Jean	1929-	Ent	10	15	22	63	Brit. Actress.
Simmons, Richard	1948-	Ent	10			30	Diet & Aerobics

Sanders Autograph Price Guide

NAME	DATES	CATEGORY	SIG	LS/DS	ALS	SP	COMMENTS
Simmons, Richard	1913-2003	Ent	15			40	Actor
Simmons, Rob S		Congr	10				Member US Congress
Simmons, Russell	1957-	Ent	15			45	Prod. actor
Simms, Ginny		Music				22	Band Vocalist
Simms, James Phillip	1837-1887	Civ War	95	150			CSA Gen.
Simms, William G.		Author	35	100	250		Lawyer, Pro-Slavery Editor
Simms. John Gill	1818-1898	Civ War	40	63	95		Member Conf. Congress
Simon & Garfunkel		Music	189	450		252	S Album 500-1200
Simon, Carly		Music	20			58	Singer/Comp. S Guitar 350; S Lyrics 265; S Album 60
Simon, Claude		Author	150				Nobel Literature 1985
Simon, Herbert A.		Sci	20	35	50	50	Nobel Economics
Simon, Jules	1814-1896	HOS		45	110		French Premier. Orator. Prof. Phil., Sorbonne
Simon, Neil		Author	45	70	123	65	Plays, Screenwriter; SB 60
Simon, Norton		Indust	15	35	65	25	Norton Simon, Inc., Philanthropy
Simon, Paul		Comp	20	198		76	Entertainer, songwriter SB 420; S Album 200
Simon, Paul Martin		Congr	10			20	Repr., Sen. IL
Simon, Simone	1910-2005	Ent	20			60	Fr. Actress
Simon, William E.		Cab	10	15	25	20	Sec. Treasury
Simoneau, Leopold		Opera	10			62	Canadian tenor
Simpson, Alan		Congr	10	10		15	Sen. WY
Simpson, Ashlee		Ent	17			50	
Simpson, Carole	1940-	TV News	10			20	News
Simpson, James H.	1813-1883	Civ War	40	70			Union Gen.
Simpson, James Y., Sir		Sci	35	95	385		Scot. 1st Obstetric Ether Use
Simpson, Jessica		Ent	20			89	Actress
Simpson, Junior		Ent	10			25	Br. Comedian; actor
Simpson, Louis		Author	20			65	Am. Poet
Simpson, Matthew	1811-1884	Clergy	90				Methodist Bishop. Lincoln Eulogy
Simpson, Michael K. S		Congr	10				Member US Congress
Simpson, O. J.		Ent	15			55	Actor; criminal
Simpson, Russell	1880-1959	Ent	50			120	Actor; Grapes of Wrath, Meet John Doe
Simpson, William H.	1888-1980	WWII	40	90	140	100	Gen. WWII
Sims, William S.	1858-1936	Mil	30	80	90	75	Adm. USN WWI, Pulitzer Author
Sinatra, Frank	1915-1998	Music	498	959		1094	Actor-Singer; AA
Sinatra, Nancy		Music	10	20	20	25	Singer
Sinclair, Harry F.		Bus	140	175	350	200	Teapot Dome
Sinclair, Upton	1878-1968	Author	69	178	182	178	Am. Writer-Socialist Pol., Novels
Sinding, Christian A.		Comp	45	120	280		Symphonies, Concertos, Sonatas; Norwegian
Sinese, Gary		Ent	20			50	Lt. Dan in Forrest Gump; actor.
Singer, Bryan	1965-	Ent	10			20	Prod.
Singer, Isaac Bashevis	1904-1991	Author	40	200	338	142	Nobel Lit. '78. Polish Passport 1800, US 1000; SB 160
Singer, Isaac M.	1811-1875	Invent	575		2500		Singer Sewing Machine
Singer, Lori	1957-	Ent				85	Actress
Singer, Marc		Ent	10	12		65	Actor; 'Beastmaster'
Singlaub, John K.		Mil	35	50	75	50	Gen. WWII
Singleton, Penny	1908-2003	Ent	10	20		44	'Blondie' (Dagwood & Blondie) Popular 40s Films
Sinise, Gary		Ent	15	20	30	48	Oscar winner
Sinopoli, Giuseppe		Cond	15			70	Italian
Sioli, Franco		Ent	10			15	Opera
Siple, Paul A.		Aero	22	45			Explr., Geographer
Sirhan, Sirhan		Assass	650	786			Assass. Sen. Robt. Kennedy
Sirica, John J.	1904-1993	Jurist	20	35		50	Watergate Judge. Respected Federal Judge; AQS 120
Sirico, Tony		Ent				50	Pauly Walnuts, Sopranos
Sirk, Don		Ent	65				Film Dir.

NAME	DATES	CATEGORY	SIG	LS/DS	ALS	SP	COMMENTS
Siroky, Villiam		HOS	50				Premier Czech.
Sirola, Joe	1929-	Ent	10			30	Actor
Sirtis, Marina		Ent	10			52	Br. Actress; 'Star Trek'
Siskel, Gene	1947-1999	Ent	12			20	Film Critic. Siskel & Ebert
Sisley, Alfred	1839-1899	Artist	150	400	1232		Fr. Impressionist. Landscape Painter
Sisqo	1978-	Music	20			40	Rock; Am. R&B singer
Sissle, Noble		Band	25			258	Big Band Leader-Arranger
Sisto, Jeremy		Ent	10			40	Actor; Billy Chenowith, 'Six Feet Under'
Sitgreaves, John		Rev War	30	75	145		Off. Continental Congress
Sitting Bull (T. Iyotake)		Am Ind	5769			7475	Sioux Indian Leader
Sitwell, Edith, Dame	1887-1964	Author	50	110	118	185	Br. Poet, Critic, Novels; Autographed Poem 785
Sitwell, Francis Osbert	1892-1969	Author	25		126		
Sitwell, Osbert, Sir	1892-1969	Author	35	70	148		Plays, Novels
Sixty Minutes (all)		Ent	25			60	
Sizemore, Tom		Ent	15			45	
Sizoo, Joseph R.		Clergy	20	25	35		
Skaggs, Ricky		Cntry Mus	20	85		65	
Skala, Lilia	1896-1994	Ent	10		25	50	Actress
Skarsgard, Stellan		Ent	15			45	
Skelly, William Grove		Bus	320				Fndr. Skelly Oil, Financier
Skelton, Ike S		Congr	10				Member US Congress
Skelton, Red	1913-1997	Ent	52	113	150	136	Film-TV Comed. Sm. Original Clown Painting S 395
Skerrit, Tom		Ent	10	25		40	Actor. Emmys.
Skinner, B. F.		Author	90	95	95	125	Behavioral Psychology-Theorist
Skinner, Cornelia Otis	1901-1950	Ent	10	40	50	80	Actress, Monologuist, Author
Skinner, Cortlandt	1728-1799	Mil	40	85	155		Born NJ. Loyalist Gen.
Skinner, Frank	1957-	Celeb	10			20	Br writer; actor; comedian
Skinner, Otis	1858-1942	Ent	53	45	120	120	Vintage Stage Star
Skinner, Samuel K.		Cab	10	20			Sect'y Transportation
Skinner, Stella		Artist	25	40	75		
Skipworth, Alison	1863-1952	Ent	15	15	30	50	Br. Actress
Skorish, Michael		Celeb	10			15	Local small town hero; Maker 'Dr. Dick Pizza'
Skorzeny, Otto	1908-1975	WWII	178	265	540	500	Nazi SS Off. & Adventurer
Skouras, Spyros	1893-1971	Bus	20			175	Fndr-Pres-Chm 20th C. Fox
Skovhus, Boje		Opera	10			25	Opera
Skye, Ione		Ent	17			50	
Slack, Freddie		Band				45	
Slack, James Richard	1818-1881	Civ War	35	65			Union Gen.
Slack, William Yarnell	1816-1862	Civ War	393	442			CSA Gen.
Slade, Chris		Music	10			25	Music. Drummer 'AC/DC'
Slade, William	1786-1859	Congr	12				Repr. VT, Gov. VT
Slater, Christian	1969-	Ent	10			50	Actor
Slater, Helen		Ent	10			62	Actress
Slatin, Sir Rudolf Carl von	1857-1932	Adven				600	Austrian adventurer w/Britian & egypt
Slattery, Tony	1959-	Ent	10			25	Br. Comedian
Slaughter, Frank G.		Author	10	15	35	20	
Slaughter, James Edwin	1827-1901	Civ War	290				CSA Gen.
Slaughter, Louise McIntosh S		Congr	10				Member US Congress
Slavin, Jonathan		Ent	15			45	
Slayton, Donald K. 'Deke'	1924-1993	Space	45	75	100	122	Mercury 7 Astro; Flight DS 750
Sledd, Patsy	1944-	Cntry Mus	10			25	Singer
Slemmer, Adam Jacoby	1829-1868	Civ War	81	127			Union Gen.
Slepak, Vladimir		Celeb	10			15	Most famous of the refuseniks
Slezak, Leo	1873-1946	Opera	45	60		120	Great Austrian Tenor, Opera. SPc 75

NAME	DATES	CATEGORY	SIG	LS/DS	ALS	SP	COMMENTS
Slezak, Walter		Ent	15			142	Actor
Slick, Gracie		Music	26			58	Jefferson Airplane
Slidell, John	1793-1871	Civ War	60	130	195		Statesman, CSA Diplomat
Slingerland, John I.		Congr	10				MOC; FF 31
Sliwa, Curtis		Celeb	10			20	Fndr. of Guardians
Sliwa, Lisa		Celeb	10	15		15	NY Street Protection Group
Sliwinski, Josef		Music	20		100	75	Polish Pianist
Sloan, Alfred P. Jr.	1875-1966	Bus	85	90	145	65	Sloan-Kettering Inst. CEO GM. Philan. SB 55
Sloan, John	1871-1951	Artist	85	275	612	145	Am. Painter, Etcher, Illust. 'Ashcan School'
Sloan, John	1779-1856	Cab	20	45	95		Fillmore Treas. of US
Sloane, Eric	1905-1985	Artist	25	120			Am. Arist & writer
Sloane, Everett		Ent	30			55	
Sloane, Lindsay		Ent	13			40	
Sloat, John Drake	1780-1867	Mil	45	95	130		Took California from Mexico
Slobodskaya, Olga	1888-1970	Opera				125	Russian Sopr.
Slocum, Henry Warner	1827-1894	Civ War	51	120	196		Union Gen., Rep. NY
Slough, John P. (WD)		Civ War	160		950		Union Gen. Killed in Gunfight 1867
Slough, John Potts	1829-1867	Civ War	95	160	225		Union Gen.
Sly & the Family Stone		Music	150			300	Rock group
Small, John Humphrey		Congr	10		15		Rep. NC 1899
Smallens, Alexander		Cond	20			50	World Premiere Porgy & Bess
Smallwood, Norma		Ent	20			50	Miss Am. 1926
Smallwood, William	1732-1792	Rev War			483		Rev War Off.
Smart, Jean	1951-	Ent	10			35	Actress; '24'
Smashing Pumpkins		Music	45			112	Music. 4 Member Rock Group
Smathers, George A.		Congr	10		25	25	Rep., Sen. FL 1947
Smear, Pat		Music	20			55	Music. Lead Singer 'Foo Fighters'
Smedberg, William	1871-1942	Mil		35		40	WWI Gen. Hero of Sp. -Am. War
Smedley, Richard		Ent	10			25	Actor
Smetana, Bedrich	1824-1884	Comp	1500		7207	7150	Czech. Operas, Symphonies
Smiley, Delores		Cntry Mus	10			20	
Smilie, Carole	1961-	Ent	10			20	Br. TV presenter
Smirnoff, Dimitri		Opera	30	55	95	200	Russian Tenor
Smirnoff, Yakov		Ent	10			30	Russian comedian
Smith, Adam	1723-1790	Econ	3450				Architect of Br. Pol. Econ
Smith, Adam S		Congr	10				Member US Congress
Smith, Addison T.		Congr	10	10	15		Rep. ID 1913
Smith, Al		Comics	15			60	Mutt & Jeff; comic strip 140-280
Smith, Albert & Blackton, Stuart		Ent					SEE: Blackton
Smith, Alexis	1921-1993	Ent	15	60		111	Warner Bros. Beautiful 40'-50's Leading Lady
Smith, Alfred E.	1873-1944	Gov	35	65	75	102	Pres. Cand., Gov NY. 1st Catholic Nom.
Smith, Amber		Ent	17			50	
Smith, Andrew Jackson	1815-1897	Civ War	40	70	100		Union Gen.
Smith, Anna Nicole	1967-2007	Ent	125	315		340	Model-Actress; S Chk 680
Smith, Armistead B.		WWII	10	22	38	28	ACE, WWII, Navy Ace; 10 kills
Smith, Ashbel	1805-1886	Civ War	140		615		TX Patriot., Surgeon Gen. TX Rev Army
Smith, Bessie	1892-1937	Music	200			1650	Am. Blues Singer
Smith, Betty		Author	40	60	150		'A Tree Grows in Brooklyn'
Smith, Billie		Music				120	Alto Sax. One of greatest sax players of the 30s
Smith, Bob		Congr	10			15	MC from Oregon. Agricultural Comm. Chm.
Smith, Bubba		Ent	17			50	
Smith, C. Aubrey	1863-1948	Ent	40		60	94	Actor; 'Rebecca'
Smith, Caleb	1808-1864	Cab	45	122	365		Lincoln Attorney Gen.
Smith, Carl		Cntry Mus	10			20	

NAME	DATES	CATEGORY	SIG	LS/DS	ALS	SP	COMMENTS
Smith, Charles E.		Cab	15		25	20	P. M. Gen. 1898
Smith, Charles Ferguson	1807-1862	Civ War	95	184			Union Gen.
Smith, Charles Kingsford	d. 1935	Aero	280	1025		530	The last pilot shot down by the Red Baron
Smith, Charles M.		Gov	10	15			Governor VT
Smith, Charles M.	1953-	Ent	10			20	Dir.
Smith, Christopher H. S		Congr	10				Member US Congress
Smith, Connie		Cntry Mus	10			20	
Smith, Courtney Thorne		Ent				40	Actress
Smith, Cyrus Rowlett	1899-1990	Aero	40	75		75	Am. Airlines. Aviation Hall of Fame. Cabinet
Smith, Dean C.		Aero		50		50	Early airmail pilot
Smith, Delia		Celeb	10			15	Cookery Writer
Smith, Edmund Kirby	1824-1893	Civ War	354	668	782	1655	CSA Gen.
Smith, Edmund Kirby (WD)	1824-1893	Civ War	390	1040	1460		CSA Gen.
Smith, Edward K.	1850-1912	Titanic	625	3225	7248		Capt. of Ill-Fated 'Titanic'
Smith, Edward W.		Mil		240			Wrote last order to Custer
Smith, Elinor		Aero	45	100	160	130	
Smith, Elizabeth Oakes		Reform	90	205	385		Early Supporter Woman Suffrage
Smith, Ellison	1864-1944	Congr	10	25			Sen. SC
Smith, Elmo		Gov	10	25			Governor OR
Smith, Elton		Aero	15	30			World Helicopter Record '52
Smith, Emma	1804-1879	Relig	10000	25000	35000		Wife, Joseph Smith; Hymn writer; 'The Elect Lady'
Smith, F. E.	1872-1930	Pol	36				Br. Conservative statesman & lawyer
Smith, Francis Hopkinson	1838-	Artist	15	20	35		Am. Engineer-Artist-Illust.
Smith, Francis M. Borax		Bus	30	65	95		Fndr. US Borax Co.
Smith, Frank, Bish.		Clergy	15	20	25	25	
Smith, Frederick W.		Bus	15	30	55	20	Fndr., Chm. Federal Express
Smith, George Albert	1870-1951	Relig	100	375	900	900	Pres. of the Mormon Church
Smith, George Washington		Congr	10	15			Rep. IL 1889
Smith, Gerrit	1797-1874	Congr	45		175		Abolitionist, Reformer, Rep. NY, Philan.
Smith, Giles Alexander	1829-1876	Civ War	45	85			Union Gen.
Smith, Gipsy		Clergy	25	45	75	35	
Smith, Gordon		Congr	10			15	US Sen. from Oregon
Smith, Green Clay	1826-1895	Civ War	35	75	110		Union Gen., Congress KY
Smith, Gustavus Adolphus	1820-1885	Civ War	46	64	108		Union Gen.
Smith, Gustavus W. (WD)	1821-1896	Civ War		250			Conf. Major Gen.
Smith, H. Allen		Congr	10			10	MOC. CA 1957
Smith, Hal	1916-1994	Ent				265	Actor
Smith, Hamilton		Sci	20	30	45	25	Nobel Med. 1978
Smith, Harry		Jrnalist	10	10		15	Broadcast Journalist
Smith, Harry J.		Author	10			12	'World's 13th Greatest Cookbook
Smith, Hoke	1855-1931	Cab	10	35	70	30	Gov., Sen. GA, Sec. Int. 1911
Smith, Holland	1882-1967	WWII		372			"Howlin' Mad". Comm. Amphib. & Fleet Marine Forces
Smith, Howard	1893-1968	Ent	25			40	Active Char. Actor 40s. 'Death of a Salesman'
Smith, Howard K.		Jrnalist	15			46	TV CBS News Anchor Opposite Huntley-Brinkley
Smith, Hyrum	1800-1844	Relig	1750	5400			Mormon Patriarch; Brother to Joseph
Smith, Ian		HOS	10	20	50	30	South Africa
Smith, Ida B. Wise		Reform	30	55	95		Temperance Advocate, WCTU
Smith, J. Gregory		Gov	10	15		10	Governor VT
Smith, Jaclyn		Ent	10	15	20	51	Actress; 'Charlie's Angels'.
Smith, James	1719-1806	Rev War	250	925	3375		Signer Dec. of Indepen.
Smith, James Argyle	1831-1901	Civ War	95	267			CSA Gen.
Smith, James C., Sr.		Bus	10			20	Westinghouse, Aerospace Division
Smith, James Y.		Gov	35	60			Civil War Gov. RI
Smith, James, Jr.	1851-1927	Congr	10	15			Sen. NJ 1911

NAME	DATES	CATEGORY	SIG	LS/DS	ALS	SP	COMMENTS
Smith, Jay R.	1915-2002	Ent	50			125	Freckles in the Little Rascals
Smith, Jeff	1939-2004	Celeb	15			40	Frugal Gormet
Smith, Jessie Wilcox		Artist				365	Illust.
Smith, Joe		Ent	15			45	
Smith, John	1931-1995	Ent				153	Actor
Smith, John	1580-1631	Colonial	2200	11500	29000		
Smith, John Eugene	1816-1897	Civ War	40		85		Union Gen.
Smith, John Eugene (WD)		Civ War			295		Union Gen. who fought at Shiloh & Vicksburg
Smith, John N.	1943-	Ent	10			15	Dir.
Smith, John Pye		Clergy	20	25	35		
Smith, Joseph	1832-1914	Relig	1042	2750			Fndr. Morman Church
Smith, Joseph F.	1838-1918	Relig	100	250	600	1250	Pres. Mormon Church,. Nephew to Joseph; SB 250
Smith, Joseph Fielding	1876-1972	Relig	50	125	625	100	Pres. of the Mormon Church
Smith, Julia Holmes, Dr.		Sci	90		425		1st Pres. Women's Med. Assoc.
Smith, Kate	1907-1986	Ent	35	65	90	198	Clear, Strong-voiced. 'God Bless America'
Smith, Keely	1932-	Music	10			50	Vocalist for Louis Prima. Jazz. SP w/Prima 210
Smith, Keith & Ross		Aero		95			Won £10000: fastest flight GB-Australia (1919)
Smith, Kellita		Ent	13			40	
Smith, Kent	1907-1985	Ent	10			55	Harvard Educated Actor. Atypical Hollywood Lead.
Smith, Kevin	1970-	Ent	10			15	Writer
Smith, Kurtwood		Ent	18			55	
Smith, L. C.		Bus	50	135	240		L. C. Smith Typewriters, Business Machines
Smith, Lamar S. S		Congr	10				Member US Congress
Smith, Maggie		Ent	25	25	30	46	Br. AA 'Prime of Miss Jean Brodie', 'Harry Potter'
Smith, Margaret Chase		Congr	10	20		20	Columnist, Rep., Sen. ME
Smith, Martha	1953-	Ent	10			25	Actress
Smith, Martin Luther	1819-1866	Civ War	75	217	240		CSA Gen.
Smith, Martin Luther (WD)		Civ War	130	299	1400		CSA Gen. ALS/Cont 2750
Smith, Matthew		Rev War	40	75			
Smith, Melancton	1810-1893	Civ War	58	106	152		Un. Adm. Served Under Farragut
Smith, Melancton	1744-1798	Rev War	75	140			Continental Congress
Smith, Michael J.		Space	250	285		325	Challenger
Smith, Morgan Lewis	1821-1874	Civ War	40	70	100	335	Union Gen.
Smith, Nels H. F.		Gov	10	10		15	Governor WY
Smith, Nick S		Congr	10				Member US Congress
Smith, Patti	1946-	Music	40		80	90	Rock Singer; S Album 40
Smith, Preston	1823-1863	Civ War	312				CSA Gen., KIA Chickamauga
Smith, Queenie	1898-1978	Ent				60	Actress
Smith, Rex	1955-	Ent				40	Actor
Smith, Richard	1735-1803	Rev War	50	130	250		Continental Congress
Smith, Robert	1757-1842	Cab	55	170	290		Atty Gen., Sec. Navy, Sec. St.
Smith, Robert		Music				60	Singer; 'Cure'
Smith, Robert 'Buffalo Bob'		Ent	16	60	62	113	Howdy Doody'. Early TV Personality. SB 160
Smith, Robert H. 'Snuffy'		WWII	15	30	50	45	ACE, WWII, Flying Tigers; 5 kills
Smith, Robert T.		WWII	15	30	40	40	ACE, WWII, Flying Tigers; 8. 9 kills
Smith, Rodney 'Gipsy'	1860-1947	Clergy	40	55	75	75	
Smith, Roger		Ent	10			42	Actor
Smith, Rolland		Author	10			15	Award winner: adventure, animals wild & in zoo
Smith, Roy L., Bish.		Clergy	20	30	45	30	
Smith, Samuel F.	1752-1839	Rev War	75	175	255		Gen., Rep., Sen. MD.
Smith, Samuel Francis	1808-1895	Author	76	396	532	881	AQS 'America', 4 Stanzas, 1750. Poet, Clergy. AQS 300-3200
Smith, Shawnee	1970-	Ent	10			35	Actress
Smith, Shelley	1952-	Ent	10			30	Actress

NAME	DATES	CATEGORY	SIG	LS/DS	ALS	SP	COMMENTS
Smith, Sidney		Comics	30			150	The Gumps'; Sketch 120
Smith, Stanley	1903-1974	Ent	20			55	Stage
Smith, Steve		Space	10			20	
Smith, Stuff		Music				260	One of preeminent jazz violinists of swing era
Smith, Susan M.		Model	10			35	Playboy
Smith, Thomas A.		Mil	95	161			Fort Smith Arkansas. Gen.
Smith, Thomas Benton	1838-1923	Civ War	575				CSA Gen.
Smith, Thomas Church Haskell	1819-1897	Civ War	36	64	92		Union Gen.
Smith, Thomas Kilby	1820-1887	Civ War	54	86	168		Union Gen.
Smith, Tom E.		Bus	10			20	Pres. Food Lion Grocery Chain
Smith, Truman	1791-1884	Sen/Cab	10	25	40		Rep., Sen. CT, Sec. Interior
Smith, W. Angie, Bish.		Clergy	20	25	35	25	
Smith, W. Wallace		Clergy	40	45	60		
Smith, Walter Bedell	1895-1961	WWII	45	128	152	80	Gen. WWII, Ambass., Dir. CIA
Smith, Will		Ent	15			54	Actor
Smith, William	1797-1887	Civ War	100	357	295		CSA Gen., Congress, Gov. VA.
Smith, William (WD)		Civ War	220		3475		CSA Gen.
Smith, William Duncan	1825-1862	Civ War	280				CSA Gen.
Smith, William Farrar	1824-1903	Civ War	50	114	188	250	Union Gen., ALS/cont 795
Smith, William S.	1755-1816	Rev War	65	95	225		Rev. Off. A Fndr. & Pres. Soc. of Cincinnati
Smith, William Sidney, Sir	1764-1840	Mil	50		185		Br. Adm. Napoleonic War
Smith, William Sooy	1830-1916	Civ War	50		95		Union Gen.
Smith, Willie The Lion	1910-1967	Music	75			125	Jazz Alto-Baritone Sax, Clarinet
Smith, Yeardley		Ent	16			48	
Smithers, Jan		Ent	15			68	Actress
Smits, Jimmy		Ent	20			50	Actor. L. A. Law, NYPD Blue
Smoot, Reed	1862-1941	Congr	25	60	80	75	Sen. UT. 1st Morman Sen.
Smothers Bros. (both)		Ent	15	50		70	Tommy & Dick; S Album 60
Smucker, Paul		Bus	10			25	Smuckers Jams & Jellies
Smuts, Jan Christian	1870-1950	HOS	40	130	148	202	Fld. Marshal. Pres. Un. So. Afr
Smyth, Thomas Alfred	1832-1865	Civ War	105				Last Union Gen. Killed in War
Smythe, Reg		Comics	20	78		78	Created Andy Capp; S comic strip 160
Snell, George D., Dr.		Sci	15	30	45	45	Nobel Med. 1980
Snipes, Wesley		Ent	15			50	Actor
Snodgrass, W. D.		Author	25	75		65	
Snoop Dogg		Ent				75	Rapper; actor
Snow, Brittany	1986-	Ent	10			50	Actress
Snow, Charles Percy	1905-1980	Author	25	55	90	75	Br. Novels, Physicist
Snow, Eliza R.	1804-1887	Relig	750	5000	12500		Mormon poet; "Prophetess"; Poem 20000
Snow, Grant		Ent				40	Actor
Snow, Hank		Cntry Mus	25	80		50	RCA Country Music Star
Snow, Lorenzo	1814-1901	Relig	1000	6500	10000		Pres. of the Mormon Church; Brother to Eliza:
Snow, Tony (Robert Anthony)	1955-2008	WH Staff	10			25	White House Press Sec'y; TV Personality
Snowdon, Leigh	1929-1982	Ent	10			40	Actress
Snowdon, Lisa	1971-	Ent	10			25	Br. Actress
Snowe, Olympia	1947-	Congr	10				US Senate (R-ME)
Snyder, Howard		Mil	10	25			
Snyder, John W.		Cab	15	30		25	Sec. Treas.
Snyder, Liza		Ent	13			40	
Snyder, Simon		Gov	10	15	35		Governor PA
Snyder, Tom	1936-2007	Celeb	10			20	Media/TV personality
Snyder, Vic S		Congr	10				Member US Congress
Snyderman, Nancy Dr.		Celeb	10			20	Media/TV personality
Soarez, Elena		Ent	10			20	Writer; Prod.

NAME	DATES	CATEGORY	SIG	LS/DS	ALS	SP	COMMENTS
Sobieski, Leelee		Ent				56	Actress
Sobieski, Maria Clementina	1702-1735	Royal		260			Polish born princess
Sobinov, Leonid	1872-1934	Opera	90		360	375	Russian Tenor
Sockman, Ralph		Clergy	15	20	25		
Soddy, Frederick, Dr.	1877-1956	Sci	60	160	275	250	Nobel Chemistry 1921
Soderberg, Steven		Ent	17			50	
Soderbergh, Steven		Ent				50	Dir./Prod./Writer
Soderstrom, Elisabeth		Opera				35	Opera
Soglow, Otto		Comics	20			100	The Little King; Sketch 60
Sohn, Lee		Music	10			20	Singer
Sokoloff, Marla		Ent				40	Actress
Sokoloff, Vladimir		Ent	25				
Soles, P. J.	1950-	Ent	10			35	Ger. Born Actress
Solis, Hilda L. S		Congr	10				Member US Congress
Solomon, Charles		Crime	60	300			Prohibition-Era Bootlegger. Assass. '33
Solow, Robert M., Dr.		Econ	22	30		25	Nobel Economics 1987
Solti, Georg, Sir		Cond	28	45		193	Conductor. Winner of Multiple Grammys
Solzhenitsyn, Alex.	1918-	Author	92	273	648	185	Sov. Novels. Nobel Lit. 1970; SB 120-400
Somers, Suzanne		Ent	15			52	Actress, entrepreneur
Somerset, Lord Fitzroy		Mil	40	115	105		SEE : Raglan
Somervell, Arthur, Sir		Comp	20	55	85		Br. Oratorios. AMusQS 150
Somervell, Brehon B.	1892-1955	WWII	35	125			Gen. WWII
Somerville, Edith Anna Oenene	1858-1949	Author			225		Writer, painter, feminist
Sommer, Elke		Ent	15			65	Actress; model
Sommerfeld, Arnold		Sci			1605		Ger. Theo. Physicist. Pioneered develop. atomic & quantum physics
Sommers, Joannie	1941-	Music	10			35	Actress; singer
Sommerville, Arthur		Author	10			12	Biblical prophecy
Somoza, Anastasio		HOS	20	95			Nicaragua
Sondergaard, Gale	1899-1985	Ent	40			106	Actress; AA
Sondheim, Stephen	1930-	Comp	45	97	142	151	AMusQS 175-375
Sonny & Cher		Ent	125			249	
Sons of the Pioneers		Cntry Mus	100			395	Spencer, Brady, Nolan, K & H Farr, Perryman
Sontag, Henrietta Rossi		Opera	70		165	165	Opera
Sontag, Susan		Author	10	25	45	20	
Soo, Jack	1917-1979	Ent	65			80	Actor
Soong, T. V. (Tzu-wen)		Diplo	35	50			Chinese Financier, Negotiator
Sooter, Rudy		Cntry Mus	10			20	
Soper, Donald O.		Clergy	20	25	30	30	
Soprano's		Ent				412	Cast of 5; cast of ten 500
Sopwith, Thos. O. M., Sir		Aero	62	115	190	125	Br. Pioneer. ALS/Cont 850
Sorbo, Kevin		Ent	10			40	Actor
Sorenson, Ted		Author	10	25	35		JFK Aide
Sorkin, Arleen	1956-	Ent	10			25	Actress
Sorma, Agnes		Opera	25				Opera
Sorrel, Gilbert M. (WD)	1838-1901	Civ War	295	2175	2400		CSA Gen.
Sorrel, Gilbert Moxley	1838-1901	Civ War	248	558	710		CSA Gen.
Sorrvia, Agnes		Opera	20			45	Opera
Sorum, Matt		Ent	15			45	
Sorvino, Mira		Ent	15			45	AA 1996. Supporting Actress
Sorvino, Paul		Ent	15			45	Actor
Sossamon, Shannyn		Ent	15			45	
Sothern, Ann	1912-2001	Ent	15	30	35	93	Actress
Sothern, Edward Askew	1846-1923	Ent	30	85	120	45	Actor. 19th C. Romantic Idol

NAME	DATES	CATEGORY	SIG	LS/DS	ALS	SP	COMMENTS
Soto, Talisa		Ent	10			55	Actress
Soucek, Appolo, Lt.		Aero	15	25			World Altitude Records
Souder, Mark E. S		Congr	10				Member US Congress
Souez, Ina		Opera		50			Opera. Great Mozart Sopr.
Soul, David		Ent	10			35	Actor
Soule, Pierre		Civ War	75	170	285		Sessessionist. US Sen. LA., CSA Gen.
Soult, Nicolas Jean de Dieu		Fr Mil	105	208	388		Duke. Nap. Marshal of Fr., Min. War
Soundgarden		Ent	35	120		64	Music. 4 Member Rock Group
Sousa, John Philip	1854-1932	Comp	164	470	575	650	Bandmaster. AMusQS 600-1200
Sousley, Franklin	1925-1945	WWII	500				Iwo Jima flag raiser 1945 (rare)
Soustelle, Jacques		HOS	10	15	40	15	
Souter, David H.		Sup Crt	58			75	Jurist
South Park		Comics				145	Trey Parker & Matt Stone
Southampton, 1st Earl of	1505-1550	Royal	75	215	450		Pol. Sec. to Cromwell
Southampton, Thos. W., 4th Earl	1607-1667	Royal	35	150			Lord Treas.
Southcott, Joanna		Clergy	45	60	90		Br. Religious Fanatic
Southey, Robert	1774-1843	Author	95	280	450		Br. Poet Laureate 1813
Southworth, Edward		Celeb			1950		California Gold Rush. 49er
Sovine, Red		Cntry Mus	12				
Soyer, Moses	1899-1974	Artist			55		Russian/Am. social realist painter; Sketch 130
Soyer, Raphael	1899-1987	Artist	20	50	140	120	Signed Repro. 200-500; S sketch 700; SB 65
Soyinka, Wole (Akinwande O.)		Author	25	80			Nigerian. Nobel Literature 1986
Spaak, Paul-Henri		HOS	15	30	50	50	Belg. Fndr. EEOC, NATO
Spaatz, Carl Tooey	1891-1974	WWII	60	139	195	148	Gen. WWII, AF Cmdr. Strategic Bombing
Spacek, Sissy		Ent	10	90		52	Actress; AA
Spacey, Kevin		Ent	15			58	Actor; AA
Spade, David		Ent	18			53	
Spader, James		Ent	10			52	Actor
Spaeth, Sigmund		Comp				75	Am. Comp.
Spaight, Richard Dobbs	1758-1802	Rev War	92	293			Cont. Congr. Signer Constitution; Killed Duel
Spain, Fay	1933-1983	Ent	10			35	Actress
Spalding, Albert	1888-1953	Comp	30			138	Violinist, AMusQS 85-250
Spalding, J. Walter		Bus	25	50	90	75	
Spall, Timothy	1957-	Ent	10			45	Br. Actor; 'Harry Potter'
Spallanzani, Lazzaro	1729-1799	Sci	120	400	1021		It. Physiologist. Artificial Insem.
Spani, Hina		Ent	20			110	Magnificent spinto Sopr.
Spano, Joe	1946-	Ent	10			35	Actor
Spano, Vincent	1962-	Ent				55	Actor
Sparkman, John	1899-1985	Congr	12			25	Sen. AL. VP Cand.
Sparks, Chuncey		Gov	10	20			Governor AL
Sparks, Jared	1789-1866	Author	15	35	70		US Historian, Editor, Publisher, Harvard Pres.
Sparks, Ned	1883-1957	Ent	25	30	60	65	Actor
Sparks, William E.		Mil	15	30	50		
Sparv, Camilla	1943-	Ent	10			40	Swe. actress
Spate, Wolfgang		WWII			125		Ger. Ace WWII. Test Pilot
Spaulding, Elbridge Gerry	1809-1897	Congr	20	45			MOC NY. 'Father of the Greenback'
Spaulding, R. Z.		Bus	15	40	55	25	
Speakes, Larry		Cab	10	10	16	16	
Speaks, Oley		Comp	38	90	125		'On The Road To Mandalay'
Spear, Ellis	1834-1917	Civ War	75	150	350	550	20th Maine Gen. Gettysburg.
Spears, Aries		Ent	15			45	
Spears, Britney		Ent	25	50		125	Singer; Dancer
Spears, James Gallant	1816-1869	Civ War	40	100	140		Union Gen.
Specter, Arlen		Congr	10			20	US Senate (R-PA)

NAME	DATES	CATEGORY	SIG	LS/DS	ALS	SP	COMMENTS
Spector, Phil		Music	89	118		112	Rock HOF; S Guitar 320; S Album 240
Speed, James	1812-1887	Cab	62	80	300		Lincoln Atty Gen. ALS/Cont 995
Speed, John Gilmer		Author	10	15	25		Journalist. Biographer
Speedman, Scott		Ent	15			45	
Speer, Albert	1905-1981	WWII	63	134	268	191	Hitler Architect/Nazi Leader. FDC S 120; SB 130
Speer, Robert Elliott		Clergy	15	20	25		
Speer, Robert Milton		Congr	10	10	20		Rep. PA 1871
Speidel, Hans	1897-1987	WWII	50	90	165	150	Nazi Gen., Rommel Chief-of Staff
Speight, John J.	1885-	Congr	10	25			Lawyer & Judge at Nurnberg War Crimes Trial
Speir, Dona		Model	15			80	Playboy Ctrfold
Speke, John	1827-1864	Expl			2250		Found Lake Tanganyika/Rich. Burton
Spelling, Aaron	1923-2006	Ent	10	115		25	Film Prod., Writer
Spelling, Randy	1978-	Ent				25	Actor
Spelling, Tori		Ent	10			50	Actress
Spellman, Francis, Card.	1889-1967	Clergy	30	76	95	70	
Spelvin, Georgina		Ent	10			50	Erotica
Spence, Jerry		Law	10			20	Prominent Lawyer
Spencer Davis Group		Music	189			250	Rock; S Album 300
Spencer, George Eliphaz	1836-1893	Civ War	35	45	65		Union Gen., Sen. AL 1868
Spencer, Herbert, Sir	1820-1903	Author	43	102	158		Br. Philosopher
Spencer, Jesse		Ent	15			45	
Spencer, John	1946-2005	Ent	10			55	Actor; Emmy winner
Spencer, John C.	1788-1855	Cab	25	60	105		Tyler Sec. War
Spencer, John P. 5th Earl		Pol	10	15	35		Liberal Leader House of Lords
Spencer, Joseph	1714-1789	Rev War	200	650			Am. Maj. Gen. Defended NY.
Spencer, Ross H.		Author	12			20	Humorous mystery novels
Spender, Stephen	1909-1995	Author	40	85	120	90	Br. Poet, Critic. Protest Poetry
Spendlove, Rob	1953-	Ent	10			20	Br. Actor
Spenser, Tim		Cntry Mus	15			25	Fndr. Sons of the Pioneers
Sperrle, Hugo	1885-1953	WWII	40	110	160	125	Ger. Gen. Field Marshal & Air Force Cmdr.
Sperry, Elmer A.	1860-1930	Sci	195	375	550	450	Inventor Gyroscope. Co-Fndr. 'Sperry-Rand'
Sperry, Roger W.		Med	22	30	35	60	Nobel Med. 1981
Spheeris, Penelope	1945-	Ent	10			20	Dir.
Spice Girls		Music	50			150	Rock Group
Spielberg, David	1939-	Ent	10			25	Actor
Spielberg, Steven		Ent	71	258	295	171	AA., Prod. -Dir. SP w/George Lucas 250
Spillane, Mickey	1918-2006	Author	35	62	110	61	Am. Detective Fiction. Mike Hammer; SB 130
Spiner, Brent		Ent	15			50	Star Trek
Spinetti, Victor	1933-	Ent				145	Br. Actor
Spingarn, Arthur B.		Activist			500		Civ. Rights activist; Pres. NAACP
Spinner, Francis E.	1802-1890	Cab	35	55	76		Treas. 4 Pres. Civil War Treas. S Chk 465. FF 32
Spinners		Music		130		150	Singing group
Spinola, Francis Barretto	1821-1891	Civ War	127	150	225		Union Gen.
Spitzer, Eliot		Gov	15			20	Ex-Governor of NY
Spivak, Charlie		Music	20			60	Big Band Leader-Trumpeter
Spock, Benjamin, Dr.		Med	58	65	120	61	Am. Pediatrician-Psychiatrist.
Spofford, Harriet P.	1835-	Author	10	25	40		Am. Romantic Poet, Novels
Spohr, Louis	1784-1859	Music	85		483		Classical Violinist
Spong, Hilda	1875-1955	Ent	15			65	Stage actress
Spontini, Gaspare, Count de		Comp	95		458		It. Influenced Wagner Operas
Spooner, John C.	1843-1919	Congr	10	15		10	Sen. WI 1885
Spooner, Ken		Author	10			12	Stock cars
Spooner, William A.		Clergy	25	35	45		Br. Creator of The Spoonerism
Sprague, Charles A.		Gov	10	20		15	Governor OR

NAME	DATES	CATEGORY	SIG	LS/DS	ALS	SP	COMMENTS
Sprague, Frank Julian		Sci	55	100	165	115	Inventor Ass't To Thos. Edison
Sprague, John Wilson	1817-1893	Civ War	40	70	95		Union Gen. MOH.
Sprague, William	1830-1915	Civ War	40	55	75	150	Union Gen., CW Gov. RI, Senate
Sprague, William Buell		Clergy	38	58	110		
Spratt Jr., John M. S		Congr	10				Member US Congress
Spreckels, Claus		Bus	95	325		175	Am. Sugar Manufacturer
Sprengel, Herman Johann P.	1834-1906	Sci				180	
Spring, Gardiner		Clergy	25	35	45		
Spring, Samuel		Clergy	20	25	35		
Spring, Sherwood C.		Space	10			20	
Spring, Woody		Space	10			25	
Springer, Jerry		Ent	15			42	Host of Controversial Talk Show; SB 60
Springer, Robert C.		Space	10			26	
Springfield, Dusty	1939-1999	Ent	141			155	Br. Singer
Springfield, Rick		Music	14	40		60	Singer; Album 45
Springfield, Sherry		Ent	10			50	Actress; ' E. R. '
Springsteen, Bruce		Music	150	285		333	S Album 570-3000; S Guitar 3000; SP/E St. Band 1280
Sproul, William Henry	1867-1932	Congr	10	10			Repr. KS. Farmer. Oil & Gas Exploration
Spruance, Presley	1785-1863	Congr	12	20	40		Sen. DE 1847
Spruance, Raymond A.	1886-1969	WWII	40	80	130	100	Am. Adm. Victor at Midway WWII
Spurgeon, Charles H.	1834-1932	Clergy	90	425	521		Br. Evangelist & Baptist Min.
Spurlock, Morgan		Ent	15			45	
Spurzheim, Johann Kaspar	1776-1832	Sci			500		Ger. Physician, co-Fndr. of phrenology
Squeeze		Music				70	Rock
Squibb, Edward R.		Bus	75	360	255		Pioneer Mfg. of Pharmaceuticals; Chk 175
Squier, Emma		Author	10	10	15		
Squier, George O.		Mil	100				Gen. Inventor Radio Devices
Sßnchez, Linda T. S		Congr	10				Member US Congress
St. Clair, Arthur	1734-1818	Rev War	193	524	913		Gen., Pres. Cont. Congr. ALS in 3rd person 300.
St. Clement, Pam	1942-	Ent	10			20	Br. Actress
St. Cyr, Lili	1917-1999	Ent	20	160		86	Exotic Dancer-Actress.
St. Denis, Ruth	1878-1968	Ent	50	140	185	210	Dancer, Choreographer
St. Gaudens, Augustus		Artist	235			350	Sculptor
St. George, T. R. 'Ozzie'		Author	10			28	Post WWII: 'C/O Postmaster'
St. Jacques, Raymond	1930-1990	Ent	15			45	Actor
St. James, Susan		Ent	10			40	Actress. 'Kate & Allie', 'McMillan & Wife'
St. John, Al Fuzzy	1893-1963	Ent	200			500	Silent-film comic
St. John, Isaac M.	1827-1880	Civ War	125		740		CSA Gen. Sig/Rank 175
St. John, Jill		Ent	15	60		57	
St. Johns, Adela Rogers		Author	10	25	45	15	Star Hearst Reporter. Novels
St. Laurent, Louis		HOS	10			50	P. M. Canada
St. Leger, Frank		Cond				75	Br. -Am. Conductor
St. Patrick, Mathew		Ent				40	Actor; Keith Charles, Six Feet Under
St. Vincent, John Jervis	1735-1823	Mil	35	65	160		Br. Adm. of the Fleet. Earl of Vincent
Stabbing Westward		Music	35			85	Music. 5 Member Rock Group
Stabenow, Debbie		Congr	10				US Senate (D-MI)
Stabile, Dick		Band	20			40	Big Band Leader
Stacey, John		Aero	10	20	30	20	
Stack, Robert	1919- 2003	Ent	10	32		51	Actor; AA; 'Untouchables'
Stack, Rose Marie Bowe	1932-	Ent	10			35	Actress
Stacpoole, Henry de Vere		Author	15	45	80		Writer, Pub. ist
Stade, Frederica von		Opera	15			35	Opera
Stadlman, Anthony		Aero	10	20	30	20	
Stael, Anne-Louise, Mme. De	1766-1817	Author	65	185	675		Fr. Writer. Exiled By Napoleon

NAME	DATES	CATEGORY	SIG	LS/DS	ALS	SP	COMMENTS
Stafford, Jo		Music	15	70		50	40's-50's Top Vocalist; DS w/Frankie Laine 120
Stafford, Leroy Augustus	1822-1864	Civ War	260				CSA Gen.
Stafford, Robert T.		Gov	10	15	20		Governor VT
Stafford, Susan	1945-	Ent	10			25	Actress
Stafford, Thomas P.	1930-	Space	30	770		72	SP w/Cernan 300; DS w/Slayton 150
Stager, Anson	1825-1885	Civ War	20	40	65		Gen. Supt. Govt. Telegraphs
Stahel, Julius	1825-1912	Civ War	40	92	141	483	Union Gen.
Stahl, Gerald		Aero				233	Engineer 509th Bomb Gp. (Enola Gay)
Stahl, Leslie		Jrnalist	10	15		25	TV. 60 Minutes
Stahl, Nick		Ent				30	
Stahl, Richard	1932-2006	Ent				40	Actor
Stainback, Ingram M.		Gov				25	Gov. HI 1942-51
Stainer, John, Sir.	1840-1901	Comp	68	100			Comp. & organist; AMusQS 400
Staite, Jewel		Ent	17			50	
Staley, Layne		Music	10			40	Music. Lead Singer 'Alice in Chains'
Stalin, Joseph	1879-1953	HOS	1148	4050	6746	4000	USSR Dictator. Rare WWII DS 8900
Stalin, Svetlana		Celeb	35	80	125	75	Daughter of Stalin
Stallone, Sylvester		Ent	35	215		144	Actor.
Stamos, John		Ent	10			40	Actor
Stamp, Terence	1939-	Ent	10			45	Actor; 'Star Wars' Supreme Chancellor Valorum
Stanberry, William		Congr	10		38		MOC; FF 38
Stanbery, Henry		Cab	10	20	45		Atty Gen. 1866
Stander, Lionel		Ent	10	15	25	45	Actor
Standing, Guy, Sir		Ent	25			60	
Standing, Wyndham	1880-1963	Ent				70	Actor
Stanford, Leland	1824-1893	Congr	213	700	975	800	RR Pres, Fndr. Stanford U., Gov CA S Stk. 30000, FF 235
Stanford, R. C.		Gov	10	15		10	Governor AZ
Stang, Arnold	1925-	Ent	10			48	Comedian
Stanhope, Edward		Mil	10	20	30		
Stanhope, Hester, Lady	1776-1839	Adven	15	48	95		Adopted Eastern Ways. Prophetess
Stanhope, Phil. H., 5th Earl		Hist	10	20	25		Lord Mahon. M. P., Author
Stanhope, Phil. H., 7th Earl		Celeb	10	20	45		
Stanhope, Philip D.	1694-1773	Pol	125	420	625		4th Earl Chesterfield. Statesman, Wit
Stanislaus I Leszczynski	1677-1766	Royal	175				Stanislaw I, King of Poland
Stanislavski, Konstantin	1863-1938	Ent	275	440	519	1152	Rus. Actor, Dir., Prod. Method Acting Tech.
Stanislaw II Augustus P.	1732-1798	Royal	95	575	730		Last King of Poland
Stanley, Arthur		Bus	10			15	Pres. Stanley Works
Stanley, David Sloane		Civ War	40	65	90		Union Gen. Wardte ALS 750
Stanley, Freelan O.		Invent	325		1400		Auto. Pioneer. Stanley Steamer
Stanley, Harold	1885-1963	Bus	15	50	65		One of thte Fndr. 's of Morgan Stanley
Stanley, Henry M., Sir	1841-1904	Expl	225	452	1644	900	Found David Livingstone, ALS/cont 2070
Stanley, Henry, Capt.		Mil	10	25	40		
Stanley, Reed	1884-1980	Sup Crt	40	90			
Stanley, Wendell M.		Sci	20	25	90	30	Nobel Chemistry 1946
Stannard, George Jerrison	1820-1886	Civ War	40		80		Union Gen.
Stans, Maurice H.	1908-1998	Cab	25	40		40	Nixon Sec. Commerce. Watergate Scandal
Stansbury, Howard	1806-1863	Expl	20	55	100		Surveyor, Mil.
Stanton, Benjamin		Congr	20	45	100		Rep. OH. ALS/Cont 250
Stanton, Edwin M.	1814-1869	Cab	100	239	388	356	LS/Cont 3300; Sec. War ASL/Cont 6500; Chk 120
Stanton, Elizabeth Cady	1815-1902	Fem	161	295	457		1st Pres. Nat'l Women's Suffrage; AQS 930
Stanton, Frank L.		Author	10	15	25		Am. Journalist, Poet, Publ.
Stanton, Frank, Dr.		Bus	15	45	80	80	Pres. CBS
Stanton, Harry		Ent	15			45	
Stanton, Harry Dean		Ent	10			40	Actor

NAME	DATES	CATEGORY	SIG	LS/DS	ALS	SP	COMMENTS
Stanwyck, Barbara	1907-1990	Ent	40	68		222	Actress. Major Film & TV Star
Stapleton, Jean	1923-	Ent	45	50		50	Actress. "Edith Bunker. " SP w/O'Connor 110
Stapleton, Maureen	1925-2006	Ent	10	10		45	Actress
Stapp, John, Col.		Mil	10	15	20	20	
Stapp, Olivia		Opera	10			35	Opera
Stapp, Scott		Music	10			35	Music. Lead Singer 'Creed'
Star Trek (cast)		Ent				650	Original cast of 6
Star Wars (Cast)		Ent				2000	Full cast S picture
Stark, Benjamin	1820-1898	Congr		30	70		Sen. OR, A Fndr. of Portland
Stark, Fortney Pete S		Congr	10				Member US Congress
Stark, Harold R.	1880-1972	WWII	35	55	80	75	Adm., Cmdr. Eur. Waters WWII
Stark, John	1728-1822	Rev War	540	808	3855		War Dte LS 2500 Gen. Fr & Indian War, Bunker Hill
Stark, Pauline		Ent				55	Silent film actress.
Starke, Peter Burwell	1815-1888	Civ War	120	225			CSA Gen.
Starke, William Edwin	1814-1862	Civ War	360				CSA Gen., KIA Antietam
Starkey, Thomas A., Bish.		Clergy	20	35	40		
Starkweather, John Converse	1830-1890	Civ War	64		110		Union Gen.
Starr, Belle		Crime	2500	7625			Early West Bandit Queen
Starr, Blaze		Ent	15		566	85	Stripper; sketch 560
Starr, Dixie	1912-2002	Ent	20			50	Western Movies. Mrs. Jack Hovie
Starr, Edwin	d. 2003	Music	10			25	"War"
Starr, Kay		Music	10			60	Big Band Singer; Vocalist
Starr, Kenneth		Law	10	40		29	Special Counsel Re. Clinton Investigation
Starr, Leonard		Comics	25			160	Little Orphan Annie
Starr, Michael		Music	10			25	Music. Bass 'Alice in Chains'
Starr, Ringo		Music	102	411	595	237	Beatles Drummer. Endorsed Chk 675; S Album 495
Starr, Ryan		Ent	12			37	
Starrett, Charles Durango	1904-1988	Ent	25	35		70	Early Cowboy Film Star
Starzl, Thomas E., Dr.		Sci	15	25		20	Transplant Specialist
Stasova, Helena		Celeb			328		Famous Russian woman
Stassen, Harold E.		Gov	10	15	35	20	Governor MN
Stassevitch, Paul		Music	25		60		Influenced a Generation of Violinists
Statler, Ellsworth M.		Bus	75	205	375	150	Statler Hotel Chain
Statlers, The		Cntry Mus	25			50	Singing group; S Album 60
Staunton, Imelda		Ent	14			43	
Stead, Wm. Thomas	1849-1912	Titanic	40	75	160	225	D. On Titanic; Journalist
Stearns, Cliff S		Congr	10				Member US Congress
Stebbins, George C.		Clergy	45	70	95		
Steber, Eleanor		Opera	75			250	Opera, Concert
Stedman, Edmund C.	1833-1908	Author	55	90			Poet, NY Stock Broker, Publ.
Steedman, G. W. (WD)		Civ War		650			Conf. Col. Chief Doctor Johnson's Island Prison
Steedman, James Blair	1817-1883	Civ War	40	80			Union Gen.
Steel, Danielle		Author	10	20		25	Novels
Steele, Barbara	1937-	Ent	20			40	Br. Actress. Leads in Br., Am. & Intl. Films
Steele, Bob		Ent				82	Western actor
Steele, Bob & Twin, Bill	1904-	Ent	25	30	45	50	Silent Films at Age 14 to Western Starring Roles
Steele, Frederick	1819-1868	Civ War	60	95	185		Un. Gen. War Dte/Cont ALS 2500
Steele, Karen	1931-1988	Ent	15			45	Actress
Steele, Richard, Sir	1672-1729	Author	200	600	1320		Essays, Drama. 'The Tatler'
Steele, Tommy	1936-	Ent	15		25	25	Pop Singer-Actor. Former Merchant Seaman
Steele, William	1819-1885	Civ War	110	228			CSA Gen.
Steely Dan		Music	25			125	Rock (2); S Album 185
Steenburgen, Mary		Ent	10			40	AA Actress
Stefansson, Vilhjalmur	1879-1962	Expl	43	95	140	250	Arctic Explr., Ethnologist

NAME	DATES	CATEGORY	SIG	LS/DS	ALS	SP	COMMENTS
Stefanyshyn-Piper, Heide		Space	10			30	
Steffens, Lincoln	1866-1936	Author	40	75	125	80	Journalist. Leader Muckrakers
Steger, Will	1944-	Expl	35	95			Arctic Explr.
Stegner, Wallace		Author	20		45	60	Am. Novels. Pulitzer
Steichen, Edward J.	1879-1973	Artist	178	212	375	475	Pioneer in Photography as Art Form
Steig, William		Comics	40		1070		New Yorker Cartoonist
Steiger, Rod	1925-2002	Ent	25	35		74	AA 'In The Heat of The Night'; S Chk 60
Steimle, Edmund A.		Clergy	10	15	20		
Stein, Ben	1944-	Ent	10			40	Comedian; actor
Stein, Gertrude	1874-1946	Author	232	765	727	795	Expatriate Am. Writer. Resided Paris From 1903
Stein, Jules	1896-1981	Bus	35	84			Am. musician, physician, & business leader
Stein, Larry	1978-	Bus	10			15	Intl. Man of Mystery
Steinbeck, John	1902-1968	Author	299	1276	1868	1338	Pulitzer, Nobel Lit., DS 2, 500; SB 1000-
Steinem, Gloria		Fem	12	25	45	35	Fndr., Ed. 'Ms' Mag. Feminist Pol. Leader; SB 40
Steinhoff, J. 'Mickey'		Aero	15	25	50	30	
Steinlen, Theophile	1859-1923	Artist	35	105	250		Fr. Known For Posters, Lithography
Steinmetz, Charles P.	1865-1923	Sci	60	218	175	350	Ger.-Born Elec. Engr. Wizard of GE. C Chk 60-80
Steinway, Henry Z.		Bus	35	125		95	Steinway Piano
Steinway, Theodore		Bus		235			Piano manufacturer
Steinwehr, Adolph Wil. von	1822-1877	Civ War	45	80	120		Union Gen. Geographer, Cartographer
Steiwer, Frederick	1883-1939	Congr	10		15		Sen. OR 1926
Stekel, Wilhelm		Sci	65	275			Austrian Psychiatrist
Stella, Antonietta		Opera	25			55	Opera
Stempel, Robert		Bus	25	60		35	Pres. & CEO of Gen. Motors
Sten, Anna	1908-1993	Ent	45			45	Russ. Actress
Stendhal (Marie H. Beyle)	1783-1842	Author	350	1020	2315		19th C. Fr. Novels. Served in Napoleon's Army
Stengle, Charles I.		Congr	10	15	25		Rep. NY 1923
Stenholm, Charles W. S		Congr	10				Member US Congress
Stennis, John C.		Congr	10	15			Sen. MS 1947. Pres. Pro Tem.
Stephanopoulos, George		Pol	10	20		30	White House Aide. Author
Stephen, Adam	1730-1791	Rev War	120	210	320		Gen. Trenton, BrAndywine
Stephens, Alexander H.	1812-1883	Civ War	106	166	290	322	US MOC & Gov. GA, VP CSA. FF 190
Stephens, Alexander H. (WD)		Civ War	275	525	735		V. P. CSA
Stephens, George F.	1859-	Artist	20		65		Sculptor, Lecturer. Single Tax Advocate
Stephens, James	1882-1950	Author				190	Irish Poet & Novels.
Stephens, William D.	1859-1944	Congr	10	30			Governor CA, Sen. CA
Stephenson, George	1781-1825	Sci	275	425	695		Invented 1st Practical Steam Locomotive
Stephenson, Henry	1871-1956	Ent	35			125	Br. Char. Actor
Stephenson, Robert	1803-1859	Sci	90	245	412		Br. RR Engineer-Devloper Steam Locomotive
Stephenson, William		Mil				60	WWI fighter pilot; WWII master spy
Stepp, Hans	1914-2006	WWII	15			50	Ger. WWII Luftwaffe Stuka ace
Steppat, Ilse	1917-1969	Ent				166	Actress
Steppenwolf		Music	240	250		150	Rock Group (All); S Guitar 460
Sterling, Andrew B.		Comp	20	50	100		
Sterling, Jan	1921-2004	Ent				72	Actress
Sterling, Robert	1917-2006	Ent	15			60	Actor
Sterling, Tisha		Ent				40	Actress; 'Batman'
Stern, Daniel		Ent	10			35	Actor
Stern, Henry Aaron		Clergy	20	20	25		
Stern, Howard		Ent	20	75		55	Shock jock; SB 130-280
Stern, Isaac		Music	15	35	110	60	Violinist. AMusQS130; SB 120; S Album 60
Sternberg, Joseph von	1894-1969	Ent	113	235		434	Film Dir.
Sterne, Laurence	1713-1768	Author	95	375			Br. Whimsical, Eccentric Humor
Sterner, Jerry	1938-2001	Ent	10			30	Actor

NAME	DATES	CATEGORY	SIG	LS/DS	ALS	SP	COMMENTS
Sterrett, Cliff		Comics	35			225	'Polly & Her Pals'
Stettinius, Edward R., Jr.	1900-1949	Cab	30	70	95	75	FDR, Truman, Sec. State
Steuart, George Hume	1828-1903	Civ War	100	156	237		CSA Gen.
Steuben, Friedrich von	1730-1794	Rev War	883	1564	2830		Pruss. Off. Cont. Army ALS/Cont 9750-29500
Stevens, Albert W., Capt.	1846-1949	Aero	25	50			Balloonist. Record Holder. Aerial Photographer
Stevens, Andrew		Ent	10			40	Actor
Stevens, Brinke		Ent	10			40	Actress. Scream Queen
Stevens, Cat	1948-	Music	165	45		250	Singer; S Album 120; AKA Yusuf Islam
Stevens, Clement H. (WD)	1821-1864	Civ War	375	1750	2650		CSA Gen. D. of Wounds Rec'd Atlanta
Stevens, Connie	1938-	Ent	53	40		62	Actress-Singer.
Stevens, Craig	1918-2000	Ent	18			60	Actor
Stevens, Dave		Artist	10			15	Rocketeer Creator
Stevens, Ebenezer		Rev War	75	195			Memb. Boston Tea Party
Stevens, Fisher		Ent	17			50	
Stevens, George	1904-1975	Ent	133	150		150	Film Dir. -Major Productions. AA (2)
Stevens, Harry M.		Celeb	25	230			Introduced Hot Dogs to the Ballpark
Stevens, Inger	1934-1970	Ent	130	145		345	Actress. Burlesque-Chorus Girl-TV-Movies-Suicide
Stevens, Isaac Ingalls	1818-1862	Civ War	164	442	454		Union Gen., KIA Chantilly VA
Stevens, James F.	1892-1971	Author	125	310			Paul Bunyan Stories
Stevens, John	1748-1838	Rev War	25	50	110		Off. Engineer. Perfected Steam Engine
Stevens, John Paul, III		Sup Crt	40	85		65	Signed transcript re: Bush 2000 120
Stevens, K. T.	1919-1994	Ent	10			35	Actress
Stevens, Mark	1916-1994	Ent				85	Actor
Stevens, Onslow	1902-1977	Ent	30	62		132	Numerous Film Leads. Ran Afoul of Wm. R. Hearst
Stevens, Ray	1939-	Cntry Mus	10			25	Singer. Recording Artist
Stevens, Risé	1913-	Opera	20	25	75	39	Opera, Concert, Films; Am. mezzo-Sopr.
Stevens, Robert T.		Cab	10	25		20	Sec. Army
Stevens, Stella	1936-	Ent	15	45		51	Actress
Stevens, Tabitha	1970-	Ent	10			25	Actress; Erotica
Stevens, Ted		Congr	10				US Senate (R-AK)
Stevens, Thaddeus	1792-1868	Congr	35	90	141		MOC PA 1849-68, Abolitionist
Stevens, Wallace	1879-1955	Author	288	853		2000	20th C. Am. Poet, Pulitzer
Stevens, Walter Husted	1827-1867	Civ War	212				CSA Gen.
Stevens, Warren	1919-	Ent	15			40	Actor
Stevenson, Adlai E.	1835-1914	VP	55	108	119	193	Cleveland Vice Pres., MOC, PM Gen.
Stevenson, Adlai E.	1900-1965	Gov	40	88	105	95	Gov. IL, Twice Pres. Cand.
Stevenson, Adlai E., III		Gov	10	10		15	Gov. IL
Stevenson, Andrew	1784-1857	Congr	15	20	35		MOC VA 1821. Spkr. of House. Min. to GB. Chk 40
Stevenson, Carter L.	1817-1888	Civ War	129	399	500		CSA Gen. Vicksburg
Stevenson, Carter L. (WD)		Civ War	305	740	948		CSA Gen. Captured & Exchanged
Stevenson, Coke		Gov	10	15			Governer TX
Stevenson, John Dunlap	1821-1897	Civ War	50				Union Gen.
Stevenson, McLean		Ent	35	45		107	Actor. 'Mash'
Stevenson, Rick		Celeb	10			15	Film industry
Stevenson, Robert Hooper		Civ War	25	40	75		Union Brevet Brig. Gen.
Stevenson, Robert Louis	1850-1894	Author	585	1239	1999	17918	Novels, Poet, Essayist. 'Treasure Island' etc; AQS 2925-3370; S Chk 525-650
Stevenson, Sonia		Celeb	10			15	Chef
Stevenson, Thomas G.	1836-1864	Civ War	95	174			Union Gen.
Stevenson, Thomas G. (WD)	1836-1864	Civ War	350				Union Brig. Gen.
Stewart, Alexander P.	1821-1908	Civ War	208	295	244		CSA Gen.
Stewart, Alexander P. (WD)		Civ War	275	920	580		CSA Gen.
Stewart, Alexander T.	1803-1876	Bus	10	25	45		Am. Merchant, Founded Garden City, L. I.
Stewart, Catherine Mary	1959-	Ent	10			40	Actress

NAME	DATES	CATEGORY	SIG	LS/DS	ALS	SP	COMMENTS
Stewart, Charles	1778-1869	Mil	110	275			Cmdr. USS Constitution War 1812
Stewart, Elaine	1929-	Ent	25			100	Actress
Stewart, French		Ent	10			40	Actor
Stewart, James (Jimmy)	1908-1997	Ent	50	165	395	330	Actor; AA; S 'Harvey' Original 350-800
Stewart, James E.		WWII	15	25	40	30	ACE, WWII; 11. 5 kills
Stewart, James S.		Clergy	30	45	60	45	
Stewart, John		Ent	20			40	The Daily Show
Stewart, John A.		Bus	10	10	25		
Stewart, Jon		Ent	15			45	
Stewart, Lisa	1968-	Ent	10			25	Actress
Stewart, Martha		Author	10	25		69	Columnist. TV Hostess
Stewart, Nick	1910-2000	Ent	15			92	Actor
Stewart, Patrick		Ent	10			54	Actor
Stewart, Paul	1908-1986	Ent	15			65	Actor-TV Dir., Radio/Orson Welles Mercury Theatre
Stewart, Peggy	1923-	Ent	10			40	Swimmer-Rider-Actress. Films at 14. Westerns
Stewart, Potter	1915-1985	Sup Crt	35	107		185	
Stewart, Rex	1907-1967	Music	75	95	120	150	Jazz musician; Cornet
Stewart, Robert L.		Space	10			25	
Stewart, Rod		Music	25	122		63	Rock & ballad singer; S Album 130
Stewart, Walter	1756-1796	Rev War		225			Am. Gen. 3rd Penn. Aide de Camp to Gen. Gates
Stewart, William	1827-1909	Congr	25	45	70		Drafted US Mining Law-1872 Sen. NV
Stewart, Wynn		Cntry Mus	10			20	Singer
Steyn, Martinus T.	1857-1916	HOS	35				Last Pres. Orange Free State
Stiborik, Joe		WWII	30			50	Enola Gay Radar Operator WWII
Stickney, Dorothy	1896-1998	Ent	15			45	Actress. Stage Leading Lady. Early Films
Stieglitz, Alfred	1864-1946	Photog	265	675	795		Revolutionized Camera Technique
Stiers, David Ogden		Ent	285			110	Actor. 'Mash'. Reluctant Signer
Stigler, George J.		Econ	20	25	40	25	Nobel Economics 1982
Stiles, Julia		Ent	10			40	Actress
Stiles, Ryan		Ent	15			45	
Stiles, William H.	1808-1865	Congr	20		65		MOC GA, CSA Col.
Still, William Grant	1895-1978	Comp	120	161	385	238	1st Afro-Am. Symphony Conductor
Stiller, Ben		Ent	10			47	Actor
Stiller, Jerry		Ent	10			45	Comic Actor. 1/2 of Stiller & O'Meara; 'Seinfeld'
Stills, Stephen		Music	40	60		120	Singer; S Album 120; S Guitar 250
Stilwell, Joseph W.	1883-1946	WWII	120	205	475	425	Gen. WWII. 'Vinegar Joe'.
Stimson, Henry L.	1867-1950	Cab	40	74	95	80	Sec State 1929; In Many Cabs; SP w/G. Marshall 345
Sting		Music	42			81	Rock singer, poet; S Guitar 350; S Album 175
Stirling, Linda	1921-1997	Ent	15			40	Actress
Stirling, Wm. Alex., Lord	1726-1783	Rev War	385	950	1950		Gen. Continental Army
Stitt, Sonny		Music	85			200	Blues-Jazz; Saxophone
Stock, Frederick A.		Comp	20	35	50	75	Dir. Chicago Symphony Orch.
Stock, Harold		Bus	10	35	50	20	
Stockdale, James B.		WWII	31	30		30	Adm. WWII. Perot Running Mate for V. P.
Stockton, Frank R.	1834-1902	Author	25	50		50	Juvenile Fiction, Novels, Editor
Stockton, Richard	1730-1781	Rev War	650	1747	3500		Declaration of Independence
Stockton, Richard	1764-1828	Congr	20	35	50		MOC, Sen. NJ 1796
Stockton, Robert Field	1795-1866	Mil	125	230	325		Sen. NJ. Conquered Calif. Named Stockton, CA
Stockwell, Dean	1936-	Ent	10			60	Actor. AA Nomination 'Quantum Leap'
Stockwell, Guy		Ent	10			30	Actor-Brother to Dean
Stockwell, Harry	1902-1984	Ent	50			122	
Stoddard, Richard H.	1825-1903	Author	20	30	45		Poet, Writer, Literary Critic, Novels
Stoddart, James Henry	1825-1903	Author	45	420			Poet & critic
Stoddert, Benjamin	1751-1813	Rev War	95	270	430		1st Sec. Navy 1798

NAME	DATES	CATEGORY	SIG	LS/DS	ALS	SP	COMMENTS
Stoica, Chivu		HOS	50				Premier Romania
Stoker, Bram	1847-1912	Author	242	325	533		Ir. Business Advisor-Sec. Henry Irving. 'Dracula'
Stokes, Carl Burton	1927-1996	Pol	20	30	40	45	1st Afr-Am Mayor of Major Am. City, Cleveland
Stokes, James Hughes	1815-1890	Civ War	35		80		Union Gen.
Stokes, Louis	1925-	Congr	10	20		15	Repr. OH
Stokes, William	1814-1897	Civ War	35		70		Union Gen., MOC TN
Stokowski, Leopold	1882-1977	Cond	58	126	105	238	Br-Am. Flambouyant Conductor AMusQS 350
Stolbrand, Charles John	1821-1894	Civ War	45	57	105		Union Gen.
Stolle, Bruno	1915-	WWII	15			50	Luftwaffe ace; 35 kills
Stollery, David		Ent	10			40	Actor; Marty of 'Spin & Marty'
Stoloff, Morris	1893-1980	Music	10			30	Musical Dir. -Conductor. AA (3)
Stoltenberg, Gerhardt	1928-2001	Pol	10			15	Ger. Pol.
Stoltz, Eric		Ent	10			40	Actor
Stolz, Robert	1880-1975	Comp	20	75		40	Conductor. Composed 65 Operettas
Stolz, Teresa	1834-1902	Opera	40	75	400		Sopr.
Stone Temple Pilots (All)		Music	35			83	Rock Drumhead S 150; S Guitar 430
Stone, Charles Pomeroy	1824-1887	Civ War	55		140		Union Gen.
Stone, Cliffie	1917-1998	Cntry Mus	10			40	Singer, Songwriter, Record Exec.
Stone, Ezra		Ent	25	35		50	Vintage Radio's 'Henry Aldrich'
Stone, Fred	1873-1959	Ent	20		30	105	Vaude. Star of 1st 'The Wizard of OZ' on stage
Stone, George E.	1903-1967	Ent	20			45	Song & Dance-Vaude. -Stage-Char. Roles
Stone, Harlan Fiske	1872-1946	Sup Crt	98	127	260	270	Chief Justice
Stone, Harold J.	1911-2005	Ent	15			45	Actor
Stone, Irving	1903-1989	Author	20	60	60	50	Historical Biographical Novels & Successful Films
Stone, John Samuel		Clergy	20		85		
Stone, Lewis	1879-1953	Ent	25	40	68	115	Am. Leading Man in Silents. Later Char. Actor
Stone, Lucy (Blackwell)	1818-1893	Reform	62	180	260	1000	Suffragist, Women's Rights Pioneer.
Stone, Marcus		Artist		15	30		Illustrated for Chas. Dickens
Stone, Matt		Ent	32			95	
Stone, Milburn	1904-1980	Ent	130	148	165	257	Actor; 'Gunsmoke' 'Doc'
Stone, Oliver	1946-	Ent	90	170		49	Oscar Winning Film Dir. Writer, Prod.
Stone, Paula	1912-1997	Ent	25		30	50	Actress; Western Heroine
Stone, Peter H.		Author	20		70		Plays. AA '64, Tony '69, '81, Emmy '63
Stone, Reynolds	1909-1979	Artist			80		Designer & engraver.
Stone, Sharon		Ent	20	200	110	192	Actress; S Chk 130
Stone, Thomas	1743-1787	Rev War	625	1305	3500		Signer Dec. of Indepen.
Stoneman, George	1822-1894	Civ War	60	129	179		Union Gen., Gov. of CA. Sig/Rank 170
Stoney Mtn. Cloggers		Cntry Mus	30				
Stooges, The Three (3)		Ent	1524	1620		4525	Original Stooges; SP w/ Curly-Joe 650
Stoopnagle, Col. Lemuel Q.		Ent	15	15	30	30	Vint. Radio (Fred. C. Taylor). ' Stoopnagle & Bud'
Stoops, Herbert M.		Artist	20				Illust., S drwg 200
Stopes, Marie Charlotte	1880-1958	Reform	85		250		Birth Control Pioneer
Stoppard, Tom	1937-	Author	20	45	70	65	Czech Born. Br. Plays of Verbal Brilliance
Storch, Larry	1923-	Ent	10			40	Actor-Comedian. 'F Troop'
Storchio, Rosina	1876-1945	Opera	70			400	It. Sopr. Created Cio-Cio-San in Mme. Butterfly
Stordahl, Axel		Music	25			65	Arr. For Vocalists, Sinatra's Mus. Dir., 40s-50s
Storey, June	1918-1991	Ent	10			45	Western Leading Lady. 10 films w/Gene Autry
Storm, Gale		Ent	10			56	Star of Early TV Series "My Little Margie"
Storm, Tempest		Ent	10	18	28	61	Stripper; S Chk 65
Stormare, Peter		Ent	13			40	
Storms, Harrison A.	1916-1992	Engr	10		25		Managed design & const. of Apollo command module
Storrs Richard Salter	1821-1900	Clergy	25	35	50		Congr. Min. -Scholar-Author
Story, John P.		Mil	65	125			Am. WWI Gen.
Story, Joseph	1779-1845	Sup Crt	130	225	570		ALS/Cont 2500

NAME	DATES	CATEGORY	SIG	LS/DS	ALS	SP	COMMENTS
Stossel, John		Celeb	10			20	Media/TV personality
Stossel, Ludwig		Ent				128	Actor
Stott, John		Clergy	15	25	30		
Stoughton, Edwin Henry		Civ War	55			120	Union Gen.
Stoughton, William	1632-1701	Colonial	450	1200			Gov. MA, Stoughton Hall, Harvard
Stout, Rex	1886-1975	Author	90	125		75	Created Detective 'Nero Wolfe'
Stovall, Marcellus Augustus	1818-1895	Civ War	110	192			CSA Gen.
Stowe, Harriet Beecher	1811-1896	Author	264	382	1204	2055	Suffragist, Anti-Slavery. AManS 3, 850; SB 2000
Stowe, Madeleine		Ent	28			85	
Stowe, Madeline		Ent	22			42	Actress
Stracciari, Riccardo	1875-1955	Opera	42			262	Opera. Baritone/46 Year Career
Strachen, Michaela	1966-	Ent	10			35	Actress
Strachey, Lytton		Author	70	175	475		Br. Member of Bloomsbury Group
Strachwitz, Hyazinth Graf		WWII				165	Ger. 1st Division Tank Cmdr.
Stradlin, Izzy		Music	15			40	Guns N' Roses
Strahl, Otho French	1831-1864	Civ War	320				CSA Gen., KIA Franklin TN
Straight, Beatrice		Ent	10			40	AA
Straight, George		Cntry Mus	15			45	Singer
Strain, Julie		Ent	21			62	
Strait, Donald G.		WWII	12	25	40	35	ACE, WWII; 13. 5 kills
Strait, George		Cntry Mus	10			45	Singer
Strait, Horace Burton		Congr	10	15			Rep. MN 1873, Banker, Agri.
Strait, Steven		Ent	15			45	
Stranahan, Robert A., Jr.		Bus	10			10	CEO Champion Spark Plugs
Strand, Paul	1890-1976	Photog	30	85	420		Am. Known for Photo Documentaries
Strange, Glenn		Ent	465	500		560	Actor; Monster films
Strank, Michael	1919-1945	WWII	500				Iwo Jima flag raiser1945 (rare)
Strasberg, Lee	1901-1982	Ent	35	40	55	88	Drama Coach. Hd. Actor's Studio. Actor
Strasberg, Susan	1938-1999	Ent	15	25	35	40	Actress
Strassmann, Fritz	1902-1980	Sci	75	270			Ger. Chemist/Otto Hahn Worked on Nuclear Fission
Stratas, Teresa	1938-	Opera	25			50	Opera; Actress
Stratemeyer, George F.		WWII	30	40		50	Am. Gen. TLS cont 200
Strathairn, David		Ent	10			40	Actor
Strathmore, Earl of	1855-1921	Royal	25		50		Grandfather of Queen Elizabeth II
Stratten, Dorothy	1960-1980	Model	405	935		1219	Playboy Playmate of the year 1980; actress
Stratton, Chas. S.	1838-1883	Ent	172		475	475	AKA Barnum's Gen. Tom Thumb
Stratton, Chet	1915-1970	Ent				50	Actor
Stratton, Samuel S.		Congr	10	10		10	Rep. NY. Navy Intelligence
Stratton, William G.		Congr	10	10			Rep., Gov. IL
Stratton, Winfield	1848-1902	Bus	250	1300	1500		"Midas of the Rockies", S stock cert. 1875
Straub, Robert W.		Gov	10	15			Gov. OR
Straus, Nathan	1848-1931	Bus	60	95	140	130	Owner R. H. Macy Co. Dept Store
Straus, Oscar	1870-1954	Comp	110	175	250	280	The Chocolate Soldier. AMusQS 250
Straus, Oskar	1870-1954	Comp				215	AMusQS 150; Viennese Comp.
Strause, Charles		Comp	10	15	30	25	
Strauss, Adolf		WWII	10			40	Ger. Gen.
Strauss, Eduard II	1910-1969	Comp	125				Younger Brother of Johann. AMusQS 150.
Strauss, Franz Josef		HOS	15	30	60	50	
Strauss, Isador & Ida		Titanic		1655			Perished aboard the Titanic
Strauss, Johann	1804-1849	Comp	240	445	1775		Aus. Waltzes. Cond. Own Orchest
Strauss, Johann III	1866-1939	Comp				120	Austrian Comp. & conductor
Strauss, Johann, Jr.	1825-1899	Comp	317	1345	1355	1395	The Waltz King; AMusQS 2100-3500
Strauss, Peter		Ent	15			45	Actor
Strauss, Richard	1864-1949	Comp	257	365	646	1294	Ger. Conductor. AMusQS 525-1050

NAME	DATES	CATEGORY	SIG	LS/DS	ALS	SP	COMMENTS
Strauss, Robert	1913-1975	Ent	25			60	Actor
Strauss, Robert		Cab	10	12	20	20	
Stravinsky, Igor	1882-1971	Comp	214	614	664	1207	Russ-Am. AMusQS 975-2500, DS/cont 1600
Stravinsky, Sulima		Music	40			120	Pianist
Straw, Ezekiel A.		Gov	10	15			Governor NH
Strawbridge, James Dale		Congr	10	15			Rep. PA/. CW Brigade Surgeon
Stray Cats		Music	35			100	Rock; S Guitar 240; S Album 180
Strayhorn, Billy		Music	352				Jazz Musician
Streep, Meryl		Ent	55	85		130	AA; Actress
Street, Julian		Author	15				
Streett, St. Clair		Aero	50	165			Alaskan Air Exped.
Streib, Werner		WWII				60	Ger. Ace WWII. RK
Streich, Rita		Opera	10			25	Opera
Streicher, Julius	1885-1946	WWII	126	225			Nazi War Criminal
Streight, Abel	1828-1892	Civ War	30	55	70		Union Brevet Brig. Gen.
Streisand, Barbra		Ent	80	238	430	218	AA., songstress, Dir. Chk 175-340
Stribling, Thomas S.		Author	12	25	60		Am. Novelist. Pulitzer
Strickland, Ted S		Congr	10				Member US Congress
Strindberg, August	1849-1912	Author	240	275	1850	2500	Swe. ALS/Cont 1400-2200
Stringfield, Sherry		Ent	10			40	Actress ER
Stringham, Silas Horton	1798-1876	Civ War	35	65	90		Union Adm. Led Atlantic Blockade Fleet
Stritch, Samuel Cardinal		Clergy	40	45	75	55	
Strode, Woody	1914-1994	Ent	50			71	Actor-Athlete
Stroheim, Eric von	1885-1957	Ent	161	232	195	554	Austrian. Classic Film Dir. -Actor; Chk 120
Stromberg, Hunt		Ent	10	15		30	Film Prod., Dir.
Strong, Caleb	1745-1819	Rev War	78	188	338		1st US Sen. & Gov. MA. Constitutional Con.
Strong, Frederick	1855-1935	Mil	20		65	80	Army Gen. Indian Fighter. Span-Am War
Strong, George C.	1832-1863	Civ War	235	694			Union Gen. Mortally Wounded '63
Strong, Maj.-Gen. Sir K.W. Dobson	1900-1982	WWII	225				WWII Br. Gen., Sir Kenneth William
Strong, Tara		Ent	13			40	
Strong, William	1808-1895	Sup Crt	80	170	300		
Strong, William Kerley	1805-1867	Civ War	40	75			Union Gen.
Stroud Twins		Ent	18			40	
Stroud, Robert	1890-1963	Crime	75	251	350		Birdman of Alcatraz. Remarkable 7 pp. ALS $15000
Strouse, Charles	1928-	Comp	20	125	200	75	Broadway Comp. 'Annie' AMusQS 120
Struck, Heinz		Sci	10			35	Rocket Pioneer/von Braun/von Braun
Struthers, Sally		Ent	10			30	Actress; 'All in the Family'
Stryker (4)		Music	10			20	Gospel Singers
Stuart, Alexander H. H.	1807-1891	Cab	25	60	95		Fillmore Sec. Interior
Stuart, David	1816-1868	Civ War	44	80	110		Union Gen.
Stuart, George R.		Clergy	10	15	20		
Stuart, Gilbert	1755-1828	Artist	650	2300			Portraitist. Pres-Royalty
Stuart, Gloria	1910-	Ent	20			108	Actress
Stuart, J. E. B.	1833-1864	Civ War	3077	5550	8574		CSA Gen., Calvary.
Stuart, J. E. B. (WD)	1833-1864	Civ War	4500	7958	14973		CSA Gen. ALS/Cont 19000
Stuart, James	1688-1766	Royal		530			Claimant of the thrones of Scotland & England
Stuart, John	1898-1997	Ent	10			50	Actor
Stuart, John T.	1808-1885	Law	65	293			Lincoln's law partner
Stuart, Leslie		Comp	20				Floradora AMusQS 200
Stuart, March B.		Mil	30	75			Supt. West Point
Stuart, Marty		Cntry Mus	10			25	
Stuckart, Wilhelm		Mil	75				Drafted the Nuremberg laws
Studebaker, Clement	1831-1901	Bus	200	483	562		Auto Pioneers. Studebaker Bros.
Studebaker, Jr., Clement		Bus	40	105	195	75	Studebaker Bros. Mfg. Co.

NAME	DATES	CATEGORY	SIG	LS/DS	ALS	SP	COMMENTS
Student, Kurt	1890-1975	WWII	45	176			Ger. Gen., paratroopers
Studer, Cheryl		Opera	10			35	Opera
Stultz, Wilmer		Aero	50	135		150	Pioneer Aviator/A. Earhart; FDC w/Earhart 920
Stumbaugh, Frederick S.	1817-1897	Civ War	45	70	95		Union Gen.
Stump, Felix B.	1894-1972	Mil	40	80			Adm. Capt. Lexington WWII
Stumpff, Hans-Juergen		WWII	46				Gen. Luftwaffe
Stupak, Bart S		Congr	10				Member US Congress
Sturge, Joseph	1793-1859	Philan	15	20	95		Quaker Pacifist, Reformer, Abolitionist
Sturgeon, Daniel		Sen/Cab	25	70	125		Sen. PA 1839, US Treas. 1853
Sturges, John	1911-1992	Ent	30	60	75	150	Am Dir; 'Great Escape'
Sturges, Preston	1898-1959	Ent	270	337	350	522	Film Dir., Prod., Writer
Sturgis, Samuel D.		Civ War	60	135	142		Union Gen.
Stuyvesant, Peter	1600-1672	Pol		3000			Dutch Col./Gov. tried to resist Eng. seizure of NY
Styne, Jule		Comp	45	95	125	167	AMusQS 180, 370
Styron, William		Author	20	35	80	155	Sophie's Choice' AManS 1p 200; SB 60-120
Styx		Music	50	190		315	Rock group; S Album 145
Suarez, Ray	1957-	TV News	10			15	TV News correspondent
Suchet, David	1946-	Ent	10			65	Br. Actor. Poirot
Suchet, Louis G., Duc d'A		Napol	85	215	390		Marshal of Napoleon
Sucre, Antonio de	1795-1830	Mil	295	1517			Liberator of Venezuela, Gen. &2 Bolivar's Ass't
Sudarmono, Pratiwi		Space	12	25		25	
Suenens, Leo Joseph, Card.		Clergy	45	75	90	90	
Suharto, Gen.		HOS	15	30	75	75	Indonesia
Sukarno, Achmad	1902-1970	HOS	95				1st Pres. (Later as Dictator) of Indonesia
Sukhoi, P.		Mil		145			Designer of Russian aircraft
Sullavan, Margaret	1909-1959	Ent	60	65	120	154	Actress
Sullivan, Anne (Annie)		Educ	100		425		TLS/Cont 1000; SP w/Keller 1365; S Prog. w/Keller 1225
Sullivan, Arthur, Sir	1842-1900	Comp	175	450	645	1000	Gilbert & Sullivan., AMusQS 1, 200
Sullivan, Barry	1912-1994	Ent	10	15		50	Actor
Sullivan, Ed	1902-1974	Ent	50	78	85	198	Columnist, TV Host. 'Ed Sullivan Show'
Sullivan, Francis L.	1903-1956	Ent	10	20		50	Actor
Sullivan, James		Rev War	65	95	200		Continental Congress, Gov. MA
Sullivan, Jean	1923-2003	Ent				80	Actress
Sullivan, Jeremiah Cutler	1830-1890	Civ War	65	85			Union Gen.
Sullivan, John	1740-1795	Rev War	200	1200	1500		Continental Congress, Major Gen.
Sullivan, John S		Congr	10				Member US Congress
Sullivan, Kathryn D.	1951-	Space	15	25	45	57	1st Am. woman to walk in space
Sullivan, Maxine		Music				250	Jazz singer
Sullivan, Nicole		Ent	13			40	
Sullivan, Pat		Comics	50		280	400	Felix The Cat
Sullivan, Peter John	1830-1890	Civ War	40	60	85		Union Gen.
Sullivan, Susan	1942-	Ent	10			25	Actress
Sullivan, Tom		Author	10			15	Pulitzer-Prize nominated Novels
Sullivan, William	1774-1839	Author	20	40	95		Pol., Gen. Militia, Orato
Sully, Alfred		Civ War	57	80	110	110	Union Gen.
Sully, Thomas	1783-1872	Artist	145	270	295		Lead Portrait Painter of His Day
Sully-Prudhomme, René, F. A	1839-1907	Author	30	52	123		Swiss. Poet, 1st Nobel Literature
Sulzberger, Art Ochs, Jr.		Bus	10	25	30	15	NY Times
Sulzer, William		Congr	15	35		25	Rep., Gov. NY, Impeached 1913
Sumi, Jo		Opera	10			35	Opera. Korean Coloratura
Sumlin, Hubert		Music				100	Legendary blues man
Summer, Donna		Music	10	15		50	Singer; S Album 60
Summerall, Charles Pelot	1867-1954	Mil	10	20	35	40	Gen., Pres. Citadel 1931-53
Summerfield, Arthur E.		Cab	15	20	30	20	P. M. Genera, Modernized Systeml

NAME	DATES	CATEGORY	SIG	LS/DS	ALS	SP	COMMENTS
Summers, Hope	1896-1979	Ent				70	Actress
Summersby, Kay		WWII	95	175			D. D. Eisenhower's WWII Aide
Summerville, Slim	1892-1946	Ent	35			192	
Summey, Jason		Author	10			12	'Staying in school'
Sumner, Charles	1811-1874	Civ War	50	80	165		Abolitionist. Fndr. Rep. Party. US Sen. FF 35
Sumner, Edwin Vose	1797-1863	Civ War	84		175		Union Gen.
Sumner, Increase	1746-1799	Gov	80	170			Rev. War Jurist & Stateman
Sumner, John B.	1780-1862	Clergy	25				Archbishop Canterbury
Sumter, Thomas	1734-1832	Rev War	375	864			Soldier, Rep., Sen., SC 1789
Sun Yat-Sen	1866-1975	HOS	700	925	3025	2500	1st Pres. Chinese Repub.
Sunday, William A. 'Billy'	1862-1935	Clergy	197	260	275	379	19th C. Early Evangelist-Baseball Player; AQS 220
Sung, Kim Il		HOS	50			150	North Viet Nam
Sununu, John		Cab	12	15	25	15	Chief of Staff White House
Superman		Ent				150	TV series; S by Cain & Hatcher
Supertramp		Ent	35			130	
Supervia, Conchita	1895-1936	Opera	150			437	Spanish Opera Singer
Suplee, Ethan	1976-	Ent	10			40	Actor
Suppé, Franz von		Comp	110	225	450	395	Aus. Opera, Operetta, Choral
Supreme Court (Burger)		Sup Crt	1170			1708	Burger Court
Supreme Court (Fuller)		Sup Crt				6252	All 9
Supreme Court (Hughes)		Sup Crt	1970			2080	
Supreme Court (Rehnquist)		Sup Crt	515			1092	All 9
Supreme Court (Stone)		Sup Crt				3000	All 9 Justices. 1941-42 Roosevelt
Supreme Court (Taft)		Sup Crt				6030	Wm. H. Taft Court
Supreme Court (Vinson)		Sup Crt				2545	All 9
Supreme Court (Waite)		Sup Crt	645				Morrison R. Waite Court
Supreme Court (Warren)		Sup Crt		1400		2146	Possibly Most Influential.
Supremes, The		Music	183			500	Ross, Wilson, Birdsong S Album 760; S sheet music 400; S Guitar 570
Surratt, Mary		Crime		16275			Lincoln Conspirator; 1st woman executed by US
Susann, Jacqueline		Author	45	50	120	60	Valley of the Dolls'; SB 50-60
Susskind, David	1920-1987	Ent	15			25	Controversial TV Prod.
Sutcliffe, David		Ent	17			50	
Sutcliffe, Stuart		Music	410	450	2500		Early Beatles, S sketch 585-2070; ALS/Cont 6415
Sutherland, Donald		Ent	22			53	Actor
Sutherland, George	1862-1942	Sup Crt	50	110	225	225	Justice 1922-38. Brit. Born. Opposed FDR
Sutherland, Graham		Artist		135			English artist
Sutherland, Joan	1926-	Opera	25		40	42	Magnif. Australian Sopr. Opera, Concert; SB 45
Sutherland, Keifer		Ent	10			67	Actor; '24'
Sutherland, Kiefer		Ent	21			63	
Sutro, Adolph H. J.		Bus	90	165	200		Prussian-Born Mining magnate. Sutro Tunnel
Sutter, John A.	1803-1880	Pioneer	1548	1750	3515	3500	Sutter's Fort. ALS/Cont 15,000
Sutton, Frank	1923-1974	Ent	50			141	Actor; Sgt. Carter on 'Gomer Pyle'
Sutton, Grady		Ent	10	15		40	
Sutton, John	1908-1963	Ent	15			70	Br. Actor
Sutton, Michael	1790-	Ent	10			25	Actor
Sutton, Willy	1901-1980	Crime	130	210	290	300	Bank Robber. Multi Prison Escapes
Suvari, Mena		Ent	16			48	
Suvorov, Alexander	1729-1800	Mil			414		Russian Field Marshal
Suzman, Janet	1939-	Ent	20			35	Actress; Oscar Nominated-'Nicholas & Alexandra'
Suzuki, Teiichi		WWII				120	Masterminded Jap. wartime economy
Svanholm, Set		Opera	15			55	Opera
Svenson, Bo	1944-	Ent	10			35	Swedish actor
Swaggart, Jimmy		Clergy	10	30	35	35	Evangelist

NAME	DATES	CATEGORY	SIG	LS/DS	ALS	SP	COMMENTS
Swain, Dominique	1980-	Ent	15			78	Actress; 'Lolita'
Swan, James	1754-1830	Rev War	180	540	575		Finan'l Speculator. Scottish-Born Patriot
Swan, Paul		Music	15	60			Guitarist
Swank, Hilary		Ent	15			91	Actress; AA
Swann, Thomas		Congr	10	15			Sen., Gov, MD. Pres. B & O RR
Swanson, Claude A.	1862-1939	Cab	18	25	60	50	Sec. Navy 1933 FDR
Swanson, Gloria	1897-1983	Ent	50	160		216	Actress; SB 175
Swanson, Kristy		Ent	15	40		55	Actress (See Zane, Billy)
Swart, Charles R.	1894-	HOS	10		20	40	
Swarthout, Gladys	1900-1969	Opera	25	75		68	Opera & Film Star
Swasey, Ambrose		Bus	40	90			
Swayne, Noah H.		Sup Crt	45	144	195		
Swayne, Wager		Civ War	45	60	105		Union Gen.
Swayze, John Cameron	1906-1995	Ent	10			25	Radio, TV News & Commercials
Swayze, Patrick		Ent	20			60	Actor
Swearingen, John		Bus	10	25	40	15	CEO Continental Ill. Corp.
Sweat, Lorenzo DeMedici		Congr	10	15	25		Rep. ME 1863
Swedenborg, Emanuel	1688-1772	Sci	3000	4000			Swe. Science, Philosophy, Religion
Sweeney, Brian		Lawman	10			15	Law Enforcement No. Ireland
Sweeney, Charles W.		WWII	25	86	290	75	Cmdr., dropped Atomic bomb on Nagasaki
Sweeney, D. B.		Ent				40	Actor
Sweeney, John E. S		Congr	10				Member US Congress
Sweeney, Walter C.		Mil	10	15	25	25	Gen. Tactical Air Cmd.
Sweeny, Allison	1976-	Ent	10			40	Actress
Sweeny, Thomas William	1820-1892	Civ War	40		90		Union Gen.
Sweet, Blanche	1895-1986	Ent	40		45	167	Important Silent Film Star
Swenson, Bo		Ent	10			30	Actor. 'Walking Tall'
Swenson, Ruth Ann		Opera	10			25	Opera
Swett, James E.		WWII	15	30	50	42	ACE, WWII; 15. 5 kills
Swift, Frederick W.	1831-1916	Civ War	35	45	60		Union Gen., MOH
Swift, George B.		Pol	10	25			Mayor of Chicago
Swift, Harold Higgins		Bus	20	50	95	35	Chm. Swift & Co., Meatpackers
Swift, John W.	1750-1819	Rev War	65	180			Merchant. Soldier
Swift, Jonathan	1667-1745	Author	2500	7300	13230		Satirist, Poet, Clergy, Pol.
Swigert, John L. 'Jack'		Space	178	268		1045	Apollo 13
Swinburne, Algernon C.	1837-1909	Author	185	295	1008		Br. 19th C. Lyric Poet
Swing, DJ		Music	10			15	DJ
Swing, Philip D.	1884-1963	Congr	10	25		15	Repr. CA
Swingers		Ent				55	Movie cast S by Jon Favreau & Vince Vaughn
Swinnerton, Frank		Author	20	55	100		Br. Novels, Critic
Swinnerton, James		Comics	35			180	Little Jimmy; sketch 150
Swinton, Ernest D.	1868-1951	Mil	45	110	310		Br. Inventor of Tank
Swisten, Amanda		Ent	13			40	
Swit, Loretta		Ent	15			33	Actress; 'Mash'
Switzer, Carl 'Alfalfa'	1926-1959	Ent	552			1565	'Our Gang' Comedies; Little Rascals
Swope, Gerard		Bus	60				CEO Gen. Electric
Swope, Herbert Bayard	1882-1958	Author	10	25	45	30	Journalist, War Corresp., Pulitz
Swope, James S.		WWII	15	25	40	30	ACE, WWII; 9. 66 kills
Sydney, Sylvia	1910-1999	Ent				118	Actress
Sydow, Max von	1929-	Ent	15	30	15	90	Swe. Actor
Sykes, Geo. 'Tardy George'	1822-1880	Civ War	65	98	165		Union Gen.
Sykes, Jerome H.		Opera	15			30	Light Opera
Sykes, Wanda		Ent	10			40	Actress; comedianne
Sylva, Carmen		Author	50	75			Elizabeth, Queen of Romania

NAME	DATES	CATEGORY	SIG	LS/DS	ALS	SP	COMMENTS
Sylva, Marguerite	1876-1957	Ent	15			65	Vintage Actress
Symington, Stuart		Cab	10	15	35	25	Sen. MO, Sec. Air Force
Symmes, John Cleves		Rev War	110	375	550		Patriot. Continental Congress
Szakall, S. 'Cuddles'	1884-1955	Ent	150			325	Char. Actor
Sze, Alfred Sao-ke	1877-1958	Mil	400				Boxer rebellion Sino-Jap. war leader
Szell, George		Cond			850	125	Hung. Conductor. AMusQS 125
Szent-Gyorgyi, Albert		Sci	35	65	125	50	Nobel Med. 1937
Szeryng, Henryk		Music	60				Violinist
Szigeti, Joseph	1892-1973	Music	40	75		359	Hung. -Am. Violinist. AMusQS 125
Szilard, Leo	1898-1964	Sci	51	225		95	Nuclear/Phys. TLS/Cont 2500
Szold, Henrietta	1860-1945	Zionist	168	410	642		Fndr., Pres. Hadassah
Szyk, Arthur		Artist	40	65	90		Detailed Portaits, Manus. Miniaturist. S Chk 120
Szymanowski, Karol M.		Comp	125	235	505		AMusMS 1250
T. Rex		Music	250				Rock
Tabb, John Banister	1845-1909	Clergy	48		200		Rom. Cath. clergy, Poet. CSA
Taber, Robert	1885-1957	Ent	15			70	Actor
Taccani, Giuseppe		Opera	35			225	Opera, Noted Tenor
Taft, Charles P.		Pub	10	15	25	15	Owner-Ed. Cincinnati Times-Star
Taft, Helen Herron	1861-1943	1st Lady	78	240	420	409	ALS White House 300-1200
Taft, Helen Manning		1st Fmly	40	80	120	150	1st Daughter
Taft, Henry Wallace	1859-1945	Law	10	10	15	25	Pol., Writer Brotherof Pres. Wm. Howard Taft
Taft, Lorado	1860-1936	Artist	48	110	130	155	Influential Am. Sculptor-Author
Taft, Robert A.	1889-1953	Congr	20	35		30	S caric. 75. US Sen. OH. Taft-Hartley Amendment
Taft, Robert, Jr.	1917-	Congr	10	20		15	Rep., Sen. OH.
Taft, William Howard	1857-1930	Pres	142	330	778	422	ALS/Cont As Chief Justice 2200-4500; TLS/Cont 5500+; SP as SC Justice 1500
Taft, William Howard (as Pres.)		Pres	216	624	3141	525	White House Card S 325-375. TLS/Cont 1800
Tagliabue, Carlo		Opera	45			175	Opera
Tagliavini, Feruccio		Opera	35			95	
Taglioni, Marie	1804-1884	Ballet	175	300	935		It. Premier Ballerina; 2 page S contract 2000
Tagore, Rabindranath, Sir	1861-1941	Author	100	258	350	389	Nobel Pr. Lit., Indian Poet; SP w/Einstein 1885
Tait, A. C., Arch.		Clergy	12	35	50		
Tait, Arthur Fitzwilliam		Artist	28	55	110		Landscape Artist
Taka, Miiko		Ent	15			25	Jap. Actress
Takahira, Kogoro, Baron	1854-1926	Diplo	45				At Treaty Signing of Russo-Jap. War.
Takamoto, Iwao		Comics					Scooby-Doo', 'Flintstones'. S Sket 60-120; SB 50
Takei, George		Ent	15			60	Actor. 'Star Trek'; S sketch 70
Talbert, Melvin, Bish.		Clergy	20	25	30	35	
Talbot, Gloria	1931-2000	Ent	10			40	Actress
Talbot, Helen	1924-	Ent	10			35	Actress
Talbot, Lyle	1902-1996	Ent	10			45	Actor. B-Movie Lead then Westerns & Sci-Fi
Talbot, Nita	1930-	Ent	10			40	Actress
Talbot, Wm. Henry Fox	1800-1877	Sci	295		1250		Br. Inventor of Photogr. Process
Talbott, Harold D.		Cab	10	15		20	Sec. AF
Talcott, Joseph	1669-1741	Colonial	175	525	1200		Colonial Governor CT
Talent, James		Congr	10				US Senate (R-MO)
Talese, Gay		Author	10	20		20	Am. Novels
Taliaferro, William B.	1822-1898	Civ War	95	600	418		CSA Gen.
Taliaferro, William B. (WD)		Civ War	188	422			CSA Gen.
Talking Heads		Music	120			160	Rock group; S Album 125
Tallchief, Maria		Ballet	20	20	35	55	Ballerina
Talley, Marion		Opera	15		45	60	Am. Sopr.
Talleyrand, Charles Maurice de	1754-1838	HOS	185	322	570		Grand Chancellor of Napoleon. Important DS 5850
Talmadge, Benjamin	1754-1835	Rev War	220	475			Served Throughout War. Rep. NY

NAME	DATES	CATEGORY	SIG	LS/DS	ALS	SP	COMMENTS
Talmadge, Constance	1887-1973	Ent	45			152	Silent Star. 'Intolerance'.
Talmadge, Eugene		Gov	20	60	95	35	Governor GA
Talmadge, Herman		Congr	10	25		20	Gov., Sen. GA. Senate Watergate Committee
Talmadge, Norma	1893-1957	Ent	45	100		107	Silent Screen Star
Talmage, Thomas De Witt	1832-1902	Clergy	50	70	95		Am. Divine, Editor
Talman, William	1915-1968	Ent	80	90	150	125	Actor; 'Perry Mason'
Talvela, Marti		Opera	30			75	Opera. Finnish Basso
Tamara	1910-1943	Ent				120	Actress
Tamblyn, Amber		Ent				40	Actress
Tamblyn, Russ		Ent	10			50	Actor-Dancer
Tambor, Jeffrey		Ent	15			40	Actor
Tamhori, Lee	1950-	Ent	10			20	Dir.
Tamiroff, Akim	1899-1972	Ent	30	40	75	176	Russ. Char. Actor
Tancredo, Thomas G. T		Congr	10				Member US Congress
Tandy, Jessica	1904-1994	Ent	22	55	50	62	AA-& Tony Awards. SP w/ Hume Cronyn 120-200
Taney, Roger B.	1777-1864	Sup Crt	98	245	369		Chief Justice., Dred Scott Decis., ALS/cont 2500
Tanner, Antwon		Ent	13			40	
Tanner, Henry Ossawa		Artist	270		750		Religious Subjects, Realistic
Tanner, Joe		Space	10			20	
Tanner, John Riley		Gov	12	20			Governor IL
Tanner, John S. T		Congr	10				Member US Congress
Tanner, Richard 'Diamond Dick'	1869-1943	West	200			650	Companion to Wild Bill Hickok
Tanning, Dorothea	1910-	Artist	35		200		Am. Painter
Tansman, Alexandre		Comp	40	125		240	Comp. -Pianist. Operas, Symphonies, Films
Tanyev, Sergey		Comp			500		Russian classical Comp.
Tappan, Arthur	1786-1865	Abolit	25	65	125		Merchant, Philan.
Tappan, James C.	1825-1906	Civ War	80	135	245		CSA Gen. S/Rank 145
Tarantino, Quentin		Ent	20			50	AA Pulp Fiction Writer-Dir.
Tarbell, Ida M.	1857-1944	Author	20	45	65	65	Muckraking Journalist re Std. Oil
Tarkington, Booth	1869-1946	Author	60	148	404	240	Plays/Novels/Pulitzer. TLS/Cont 425; SB 165
Tarleton, Banastre, Sir		Rev War	135	365	742		Barbaric Br. Gen. Am. Rev.
Tarnower, Herman Dr.		Med	15	50	135	60	Murdered Diet Dr.
Tartakov, Joakim		Ent			450		Opera. Imperial Russ. Baritone Star
Tartikoff, Brandon	1949-1997	Bus	15	25	35	60	TV executive
Tashlin, Frank	1913-1972	Ent	15			25	Dir.
Tashman, Lilyan	1899-1934	Ent	30	40	75	180	Vintage Actress. Major Star in 30s
Tassigny, J. M. G. de		Mil	35	90	140		Fr. Gen.
Tate, Allen	1899-1979	Author	10	30	75		Am. Poet, Critic, Biographer
Tate, Harry	1872-1940	Ent	10			50	Brit. Music Hall Comedian. Silent Films
Tate, Henry, Sir, 1st Baronet		Bus	40	105	240		Br. Sugar Refiner Philan., Art-Tate Gallery.
Tate, Jackson R.		Mil	30		65	50	Adm. WWII.
Tate, Larenz		Ent	15			45	
Tate, Sharon	1943-1969	Ent	1520	2665		8360	Actress; Murdered By Manson Gang
Tati, Jacques	1908-1982	Ent	234			240	Fr. Actor; 'Monsieur Hulot's Holiday'
Tattersall, Richard	1724-1795	Bus	20	45	105		Rendevous For Sporting-Betting
Tattnall, Joseph		Civ War			715		CSA Naval Capt.
Tatum, Art		Music	75			495	Blues-Jazz
Tatum, Channing		Ent	15			45	
Tatum, Edward L.	1909-1975	Sci	45	70	125		Nobel 1958. Research in Molecular Genetics
Taube, Henry, Dr.		Sci	25	40		30	Nobel Chemistry 1983
Tauber, Richard	1892-1948	Opera	50			130	Opera, Austrian-Born, Br. Tenor
Taufflieb, Gen.		Mil	45	120	215	100	
Taurog, Norman		Ent	50	102		150	Film Dir. Orig artwork 1345
Tauscher, Ellen O. T		Congr	10				Member US Congress

NAME	DATES	CATEGORY	SIG	LS/DS	ALS	SP	COMMENTS
Taussig, Frank William	1859-1940	Econ	10	25			Author. Chm Tariff Bd.
Tauzin, W. J. (Billy) T		Congr	10				Member US Congress
Tavernier, Bertrand	1941-	Ent	10			20	Dir.
Tawes, J. Millard		Gov	10	15			Governor MD
Tawney, James A.		Congr	10	15	25		Rep. MN 1893
Tayback, Vic	1930-1990	Ent	20			42	Char. Actor. Films-TV 'Alice'; GG
Taylor, Bayard	1825-1878	Author	20	67	135		Journalist, Traveller, Diplomat
Taylor, Caleb Newbold	1813-1887	Congr	15		35		MOC PA. Visited Lincoln/Recommendations
Taylor, Charles H.		Congr	10			15	Congressman NC
Taylor, Christine	1971-	Ent	10			40	Actress; married to Ben Stiller
Taylor, Deems		Comp	35	80	90	50	Musicologist, Critic, Author
Taylor, Don	1920-1998	Ent	20			35	Actor turned Dir. Star of 40s-50's Films
Taylor, Dub	1907-1994	Ent	35			290	Western Char. Actor
Taylor, Elizabeth	1932-	Ent	166	570		750	AA. MGM Early Contract S 1500, DS/cont 450-750
Taylor, Estelle	1894-1958	Ent	20	25	45	120	Vintage Actress
Taylor, Gene T		Congr	10				Member US Congress
Taylor, George	1716-1781	Rev War	8000	15900	57500		Rare Signer Decl of Independence, Partial DS 6325
Taylor, George William	1808-1862	Civ War	110				Union Gen.
Taylor, Glen H.	1904-1984	Congr	10	25		25	Sen. ID, Actor, Singer
Taylor, Graham		Clergy	15	25	35		
Taylor, Henry C.		Mil	30	60	95		Adm. Spanish-Am. War
Taylor, James		Music	58	78	160	95	Singer-Guitarist; S Guitar 175-400; S Album 100
Taylor, James Willis		Congr	10	10	20		Rep. TN 1919
Taylor, Joan	1929-	Ent	10			40	Actress. Paramount Contractee. Mostly Westerns
Taylor, John	1808-1887	Relig	1000	6500	10000		3rd Pres. of the Mormon Church
Taylor, John W.	1784-1854	Congr	30	55	75		Spkr. of US House of Reps
Taylor, Joseph P.	1796-1864	Civ War	65	175			War 1812 & CW Union Gen.
Taylor, Karin	1971-	Model	10			30	Model
Taylor, Kent	1907-1987	Ent	15			45	Actor
Taylor, Laurette	1884-1946	Ent	32	40	50	175	Actress; Major Star of Am. Theatre
Taylor, Lili	1967-	Ent	10			40	Actress
Taylor, Margherita	1972-	Ent	10			35	Actres; model
Taylor, Mary		Cntry Mus	10			20	Singer
Taylor, Maxwell D.	1901-1987	Mil	30	84	125	147	Gen. WWII
Taylor, Meshach	1947-	Ent	10			25	Actor; 'Designing Women', 'Dave's World'
Taylor, Nelson	1821-1894	Civ War	40		85		Union Gen.
Taylor, Nikki		Ent	15			56	Actress-Model
Taylor, Rachel		Ent	15			45	
Taylor, Richard	1826-1879	Civ War	290	783			CSA Gen. Son of Pres. Taylor
Taylor, Richard (WD)	1826-1879	Civ War	382	1653	3500		CSA Gen. Son of Pres. Taylor
Taylor, Richard E., Dr.		Sci	20	50			Nobel Physics 1990
Taylor, Rip		Ent	22			65	
Taylor, Robert	1911-1969	Ent	43	90	125	201	Am. Actor & Leading Man
Taylor, Robert L.	1850-1912	Congr	10	15		15	Gov., Rep. & Sen. TN
Taylor, Rod		Ent	10	65		42	Actor
Taylor, Sandra	1966-	Ent	10	60		40	Actress
Taylor, Tamara		Ent	13			40	
Taylor, Thomas H.	1825-1901	Civ War	80	115	275		CSA Gen.
Taylor, Thomas H. (WD)		Civ War	125	210	468		CSA Gen.
Taylor, Vaughn	1910-1983	Ent	20			50	Actor
Taylor, W. Randy		Author	10			12	Motivation, inspiration
Taylor, Walter H.		Civ War	50	94			CSA Col. Aide-de-camp R. E. Lee
Taylor, William, Bish.		Clergy		40	50	75	
Taylor, Zachary	1784-1850	Pres	720	1910	4014		Gen. in Mexican War. ALS/Cont 8500

NAME	DATES	CATEGORY	SIG	LS/DS	ALS	SP	COMMENTS
Taylor, Zachary (As Pres.)		Pres	1150	5400	11800		3rd Rarest in Pres. S Items. FF 2500
Taylor-Young, Leigh	1945-	Ent	10			35	Actress
Tazewell, Littleton		Congr	45	135	232		MOC 1800, Sen. 1824, Gov. VA
Tchaikovsky, Modest		Opera			950		Younger brother of Piotr
Tchaikovsky, Piotr I.	1840-1893	Comp	1731	4060	5531	5441	Rus. Opera, Symphony, Ballet.
Tchelitchew, Pavel	1898-1957	Artist	75		500		Russian-born Am. Painter
Tcherepnin, Alexander	1899-1977	Comp	50	125	200		Russian Pianist. AMusQS 350
Tchernihovsky, Saul		Author	175		550		Rus-Hebrew Dr., Poet, Translator
Te Kanawa, Kiri, Dame	1944-	Opera	40	55		60	New Zealand Born. Opera, Concert
Teagarden, Charlie		Music	10			45	Jazz Trumpet
Teagarden, Jack		Band	60	100	120	164	Big Band Leader-Trombonist
Teal, Ray	1902-1976	Ent	50			240	Actor
Teale, Edwin W.	1899-1980	Photog			75	30	Photographer, Pulitzer Writer.
Tearle, Conway		Ent	25			175	Vintage Br. Actor
Tearle, Godfrey, Sir		Ent	20			50	Br. Actor. Vintage
Teasdale, Sara	1894-1933	Author	95	160		175	Poet; Suicide at 39
Teasdale, Verree	1903-1987	Ent	20	25	45	50	Vintage Actress 30s-40's. Wife of Adolf Menjou
Tebaldi, Renata		Opera	25			96	Opera. Italian Sopr.
Tedder, Arthur	1890-1967	Mil	46				Br. Chief Air Marshal
Tedrow, Irene	1907-1995	Ent	10			40	Char. Actress 40s-50's. Mother Parts
Teegarden, Aimee		Ent	13			38	
Teissedre De Fleury, Francois		Rev War			633		
Teitjens, Therese		Opera	50			190	Opera
Telfair, Edward		Rev War	50	95	150		Continental Congress from GA
Telford, Thomas	1757-1834	Engr		105	330		Br. Road & Bridge-builder
Teller, Edward, Dr.	1908-2003	Sci	65	90	210	110	Fermi Award. Father of 'H-Bomb'
Teller, Henry M.	1830-1914	Cab	30	40	50	75	Sect'y Interior 1882, Arthur
Telva, Marion		Opera	15			40	Opera. Noted Contralto
Temin, Howard M., Dr.		Med	20	35	55	25	Nobel Med. 1975
Tempest, Marie	1862-1942	Ent	25	35	50	50	Br. Actress
Temple, Frederick	1821-1902	Clergy	22		90		Archbishop Canterbury, Educator, Author
Temple, Shirley		Ent	98			476	Actress; Prices reflect childhood signatures
Temple, Shirley (Black)		Ent	24	25	40	60	Actress; SB 150
Temple, Wm.		Clergy	40	45	85	65	Archbishop Canterbury
Templeton, Alec		Music	10			50	Br. Blind Jazz Pianist
Templeton, Ben		Music	10			20	Motley Crew
Templeton, Faye		Music	25	30	60	65	Musical Career For Over 50 Year
Temptations (All Orig.)		Music	1090			1250	Motown group; S Guitar 1250
Ten Broeck, Abraham	1734-1810	Rev War	100	160	325		Gen. Judge, Banker
Tennant, Frederick R.	1866-1957	Clergy	15	20	25		English Theologian
Tennant, Veronica		Ballet	10			25	National Ballet of Canada
Tennant, Victoria		Ent	10			40	Actress
Tenniel, John, Sir	1820-1914	Artist	70	110	260		Illustr. 'Alice in Wonderland'
Tennille, Toni		Music	10			30	Singer. 'The Captain & Tennille' SP w/Captain 35
Tennyson, Alfred, Lord	1809-1892	Author	288	298	552	852	Br. Poet Laureate
Tennyson, Jean		Opera	10			20	Am. Sopr.
Teresa, Mother	1911-1997	Clergy	150	663	965	554	Nobel Peace, 1979; S prayer card $500; SB $655; S Chk $200
Tereshkova, Valentina		Space	52	95		411	1st Woman in Outer Space
Terfel, Bryn		Opera	10			35	Welsh Operatic Baritone
Terhune, Alfred Payson	1872-1942	Author	50	75	130	50	Famous Writer of Dog Stories
Terhune, Max	1891-1973	Ent	60			120	Western Sidekick in Repub. & Monogram Series
Terkel, Studs	1912-	Author	10	25	50	40	Columnist, Biographer, TV
Ternina, Milka		Opera	20		135		Opera. Croatian Sopr.

NAME	DATES	CATEGORY	SIG	LS/DS	ALS	SP	COMMENTS
Terrell, Bob		Author	10			25	Author, Newspaper Columnist
Terrill, James Barbour	1838-1864	Civ War	260	4200			CSA Gen.
Terrill, William Rufus	1834-1862	Civ War	40				Union Gen.
Terriss, Ellaline		Ent	15			48	Br. Actress. 19th C.
Terry, Alfred Howe	1827-1890	Civ War	127	425	429		Union Gen., Cmdr.
Terry, Clark		Music	50			120	Jazz Trumpet, Fluegelhorn
Terry, Ellen, Dame	1847-1928	Ent	35	70	135	188	Br. Actress Partner of Henry Irving. SP Pc 145
Terry, Fred	1864-1933	Ent	10	15	25	40	Br. Stage & Film Star
Terry, Henry D.	1812-1869	Civ War	45	65	100		Union Gen. Sig/Rank 65
Terry, Lee T		Congr	10				Member US Congress
Terry, Paul		Comics	50			198	Animator-Mighty Mouse
Terry, Phillip	1909-1993	Ent	10			40	Actor. Films from 30s. Leads-2nd Leads in B Films
Terry, Ruth	1920-	Ent	10			30	Actress-Singer. Films at 16. Numerous Westerns
Terry, William	1814-1888	Civ War	85		270		CSA Gen. Sig/Rank 120
Terry, William Richard	1827-1897	Civ War	90	195	370		CSA Gen. Sig/Rank 200, War Dte. DS 625
Tesla, Nikola, Dr.	1856-1943	Sci	535	2552	2704	2075	Physicist, Electrical Genius. Power Systems
Tetard, J.		Aero	45	60	170	100	
Tetrazzini, Luisa	1871-1940	Opera	50	100	120	145	It. Opera. SPc 300 as 'Lakme'
Tevis, Lloyd		Bus		475			Mining & Partner of Geo. Hearst & Haggin
Texada, Tia		Ent	14			43	
Teyte, Maggie		Opera	35			130	Opera
Thacher, James, Dr.	1754-1844	Rev War	85	175	338		Revolutionary War Surgeon
Thackeray, Wm. Makepeace	1811-1863	Author	99	317	517		Br. Novels 'Vanity Fair'
Thaden, Louise McP.		Aero		295			Altitude, Endurance, Speed Records
Thagard, Norman E.		Space	10			30	
Thalberg, Irving	1899-1936	Ent	161	263	388	300	MGM's Boy Genius Prod. Chk 200
Thalberg, Sigismund		Music			60		Pianist
Thant, U	1909-1974	HOS	45	70	125	125	UN Sec. Gen.
Tharp, Sister Rosetta		Music	115			165	Jazz Vocalist-Guitar
Tharp, Twyla		Ent	20	60		40	Dancer-Choreographer
Thatcher, Henry Knox	1806-1880	Civ War	55	95	155		Union Naval Cmdr. Sig/Rank 85
Thatcher, Margaret, Dame		HOS	45	140	225	147	Prime Min. Engr. P. M. SB 125-250
Thatcher, Peter		Clergy	75	100	150		
Thaves, Bob		Comics	10			20	'Frank & Ernest'
Thaw, Harry K.		Bus	75	156	325	250	Playboy. Shot Sanford White. Major Scandal
Thaw, Russell T.		Aero	20				Racing Pilot
Thaxter, Celia	1835-1894	Author	20	40	95	150	Am. Poet
Thaxter, Phyllis	1921-	Ent	10			40	Stage & Film Leading Lady
Thayer, Abbott	1849-1921	Artist	15	35	70		Am. Ideal Figures, Landscapes
Thayer, Celia		Author	10	10	15		Am. Novels, Screenwriter
Thayer, John		Titanic		340			D. on Titanic; 2nd VP of Pennsylvania RR
Thayer, John Milton	1820-1906	Civ War	45	70	95		Union Gen., Gov. WY Terr.
Thayer, Silvanus	1785-1872	Mil	80	165	380		Father of the Mil. Academy'
Thayil, Kim		Music	10			25	Music. Lead Guitar 'Soundgarden'
Thebaw		HOS	145				Burma
Thebom, Blanche		Opera	20	35		75	Am. Contralto, Opera, Concert
Theiss, Ursula		Ent	10			30	Ger. Actress. Several Hollywood Films 50s
Theissen, Tiffany Amber		Ent	15			55	Actress
Thelen, Bob		WWII	10	25	40	35	ACE, WWII, Blue Angels; 6. 5 kills
Theron, Charlize		Ent	45			108	Actress; AA
Thesiger, Ernest	1879-1961	Ent	164		190	300	Actor
Thevenot, Melchisedec	1620-1692	Author	20		95		"The Art of Swimming"
Thewlis, David	1963-	Ent	10			25	Br. Actor
Thibodeaux, Keith		Ent	20			35	Child Actor. Played 'Little Ricky' on 'I Love Lucy

NAME	DATES	CATEGORY	SIG	LS/DS	ALS	SP	COMMENTS
Thicke, Alan		Ent	10			35	Actor-Humorist. 'Growing Pains'
Thielicke, Helmut		Clergy	20	50	65	60	Germ. Evangel. Theologian
Thien, Dinh Le		Ent	10			30	Actor
Thieriot, Max		Ent	12			35	
Thiers, Louis-Adolphe	1797-1877	Fr Rev	45	85	170		1st Pres. 3rd Repub.
Thiessen, Tiffani		Ent	17			50	
Thieu, Nguyen Van		HOS	45	95	150	510	So. Viet Nam
Thinnis, Roy	1938-	Ent	10			30	Actor
Thirsk, Bob		Space	10	15		20	
Thirtysomething		Ent				140	Cast photo
Thoma, Gen. Wilhelm Knight von	1891-1948	WWII	252				WWII Ger. Gen. of Panzer Troops
Thomas, Allen	1830-1907	Civ War	95	425			CSA Gen.
Thomas, Ambroise	1811-1896	Comp	75	335	212	250	Fr. Romantic Comp. Operas.AMusQS 525
Thomas, Andrew		Space	10			20	
Thomas, B. J.		Music	20			60	Singer-Songwriter; singed tambourine 145
Thomas, Betty		Ent	10			35	Actress
Thomas, Bryan Morel	1836-1905	Civ War	110				CSA Gen.
Thomas, Charles	1840-1878	Civ War	25	45	60		Union Brevet Major Gen.
Thomas, Clarence	1948-	Sup Crt	45			53	Signed transcript re: Bush 2000 130
Thomas, Craig		Congr	10				US Senate (R-WY)
Thomas, Danny	1914-1991	Ent	20	80		60	Comedian. 'Danny Thomas Show'
Thomas, Dave		Bus	15	25		58	Fndr. Wendy's. TV Spokesman. S Sketch 120; SB 90
Thomas, Donald		Space	10			25	
Thomas, Dylan	1914-1953	Author	510	1279	4585	1500	Welsh Poet, Plays, Short Stories
Thomas, E. Donnall, Dr.		Sci	15	25		30	Nobel Med. 1990
Thomas, Eddie Kaye	1980-	Ent				35	Actor
Thomas, Edward Lloyd (WD)	1825-1898	Civ War	150	3200			CSA Gen.
Thomas, George		Celeb	50	55	60	70	Titanic survivor
Thomas, George Henry	1818-1870	Civ War	176	422	568	800	Union Gen. 'Rock of Chickamauga', LS/cont 1500
Thomas, Heather		Ent	15	40	30	43	Actress
Thomas, Heck		West		622			Special DS 2500
Thomas, Henry Goddard	1837-1897	Civ War	40	65			Union Gen.
Thomas, Isaiah	1749-1831	Colonial	135	380	1000		Publ. 1st Eng. Bible in America, printer
Thomas, James, Bish.		Clergy	20	25	35	30	
Thomas, Jay		Ent	10			45	Actor
Thomas, Jess		Opera	15			40	Opera
Thomas, John	1724-1776	Rev War	510	855	1750		Am. Physician & Gen. Cont'l Army
Thomas, John Charles	1891-1960	Opera	20	45	45	45	Multi Media Am. Baritone
Thomas, Jonathan Taylor	1981-	Ent	10			62	Child Actor, 'Home Improvement'
Thomas, Khleo		Ent	15			45	
Thomas, Kristin Scott		Ent	15			50	Actress
Thomas, Larry		Ent	10			25	Actor; 'Soup Nazi'
Thomas, Lorenzo	1804-1875	Civ War	45	65	92	356	Union Gen.
Thomas, Lorenzo (War Dte)	1804-1975	Civ War	50	110	210	500	Union Gen. Seminole, Mexican & Civil Wars
Thomas, Lowell	1892-1981	Ent	15	30	35	112	World Traveller. Top Radio Commentator 30s-40's
Thomas, Marlo		Ent	10	25		40	Actress & Daughter of Danny
Thomas, Michael Tilson		Cond	15			50	Am. Conductor
Thomas, Milton		Music				50	Violinist
Thomas, Norman	1884-1961	Pol	40	100	212	100	6 Times Pres. Cand. Socialist Leader
Thomas, Olive	1894-1920	Ent	65	70	150	215	Actress. Jack Pickford's wife
Thomas, Philip Evan		Bus	10	15	25		
Thomas, Richard		Ent	10	15	20	60	Actor
Thomas, Rob		Music	10			30	Music. Lead Singer 'Matchbox 20'
Thomas, Robert Bailey		Author	20	45	105		Publisher, Editor 'Farmer's Almanac'

NAME	DATES	CATEGORY	SIG	LS/DS	ALS	SP	COMMENTS
Thomas, Samuel	1840-1903	Civ War	35	55			Union Gen.
Thomas, Seth E.	1785-1859	Bus	125	250	415	315	Fndr. Seth Thomas Clock Co.
Thomas, Seth E., Jr.	1816-1888	Bus	65	175	350		Cont'd Seth Thomas Clock Co.
Thomas, Stephen	1809-1903	Civ War	45	65	95		Union Gen.
Thomas, Terry	1911-1990	Ent	50		100	145	Br. Comedian-Actor
Thomas, Theodore		Cond	15			30	Conductor. NY & Chic. Symph.
Thomas, William		Ent	312			2000	Little Rascals
Thomas, William M. T		Congr	10				Member US Congress
Thomason, John	1893-1944	Artist					Signed drawing 70
Thomasson, William P.	1797-1882	Congr	12	15			MOC KY, Union Off. CW
Thompson Twins		Ent	30			75	Signed by Both
Thompson, Benj. (Rumford)	1753-1814	Rev War	275	450	1138		Count von Rumford. Br. Phys., Inventor, Loyalist
Thompson, Benjamin	1798-1852	Congr	10	15	25		MOC MA 1845
Thompson, Bennie G. T		Congr	10				Member US Congress
Thompson, Brian		Ent				45	Actor; 'Star Trek'
Thompson, Denman	1833-1911	Ent	20			80	Vintage Stage Actor
Thompson, Derek	1948-	Ent	10			30	Irish Actor
Thompson, Dorothy	1894-1961	Author	35	55	110	67	Journalist, Correspondent, Columnist, Wit
Thompson, Emma	1959-	Ent	20			66	Br. Actress-Plays AA.
Thompson, Ernest Seton	1860-1946	Author			185		Wildlife author & artist; Fndr. Boy Scouts
Thompson, Fred		Celeb	15	25	40	45	Actor, Sen. TN; 2008 Pres. Cand.
Thompson, Gordon		Ent	10			30	Actor
Thompson, Hank		Cntry Mus	10			15	Singer-Songwriter
Thompson, Hunter	1937-2005	Author		250		345	Fear & Loathing in Las Vegas'; SB 300-600
Thompson, J. Walter	1847-1928	Bus	100	170		150	J. Walter Thompson Adv. Agency. Bond S 2400
Thompson, Jacob	1810-1885	Civ War	75	160	325		Sec. Interior, CSA Secret Agt., served in Cabinet
Thompson, Jim		Gov	10	10		20	Governor IL
Thompson, John P.		Bus	15	30	65	20	Pres. Southland Corp.
Thompson, John T.	1860-1940	Invent	75	262	395		USA Off., Inventor Thompson Sub-Machine Gun
Thompson, Kay	1908-1998	Author					Eloise' children's books; SB 570
Thompson, Lea		Ent	10	10		35	Actress. 'Back to Future', 'Caroline in the City'
Thompson, Linda	1950-	Ent	10			30	Actress
Thompson, M. E.		Gov	10	15			Governor GA
Thompson, Marshall	1925-1992	Ent	15		25	48	Actor. Juvenile Leads-40's. Mature Leads 50s
Thompson, Merriwether J.	1826-1876	Civ War	135	260	730		CSA Gen.
Thompson, Merriwether J. (WD)		Civ War	212		2401	850	MO Militia Gen. Noted Guerrilla Fighter
Thompson, Mike T		Congr	10				Member US Congress
Thompson, Milt		Aero				135	X-15 pilot
Thompson, Orlo & Marvis		Cntry Mus	20			45	Signed by both
Thompson, Rex	1942-	Ent				60	Actor; 'King & I'
Thompson, Richard W.		Cab	25	45	70		Sec. Navy 1809
Thompson, Robert E.		Clergy	10	10	15		
Thompson, Ruth Plumly	1891-1976	Author	280	670			Oz Books. Widow of Frank Baum
Thompson, Smith	1768-1843	Sup Crt	50	110	248		Monroe Sec Navy; Ass. Supr. Ct. Justice. S Chk 120
Thompson, Stephen W.		Mil				125	Credited w/the 1st US air victory in WWI
Thompson, Sue		Cntry Mus	10			25	Singer
Thompson, Wm. H. Big Bill	1869-1944	Mayor	125				Gangster Era Mayor. Backed by Al Capone
Thomson, Andrew		Clergy	35	65	75		
Thomson, Charles	1729-1824	Rev War	165	490	856		Wealthy Merch. LS As Sec. Cont'l Congr. 1, 750
Thomson, Elihu	1853-1937	Sci	525	1250			Electrical Engineer-Inventor. Over 700 Patents
Thomson, Fred C.	1890-1928	Ent				158	Western actor
Thomson, Geo. Paget, Sir	1892-1975	Sci	55			100	Nobel Physics 1937
Thomson, Hugh		Artist	25		100		Br. Illust.
Thomson, Joseph J., Sir	1856-1940	Sci			1046		Discovered electron

NAME	DATES	CATEGORY	SIG	LS/DS	ALS	SP	COMMENTS
Thomson, Virgil	1896-1989	Comp	40	98	112	102	Conductor & Music Critic, AMusQS 125-225
Thorborg, Kerstin		Opera	20			75	Opera
Thorburn, Grant		Colonial	40	95			Grocery, Seed Merchant. Hero
Thoreau, Henry David	1817-1862	Author	1715	6500	12500		Retired to 'Walden Pond. Unsigned Man. 5700
Thornberry, Mac T		Congr	10				Member US Congress
Thorndike, Sybil, Dame	1882-1976	Ent	25	48		42	Br. Preeminent Actress. Seven Decade Career
Thorne, Chas. Rob't	1814-1893	Ent	65	80		120	Actor
Thorne, Dyanne		Ent				50	Actress
Thorne-Smith, Courtney		Ent	10			40	Actress
Thornhill, Claude		Band	12			45	Big Band
Thornhill, F. D.		Mil	15	25	40		
Thornton, Billie Bob		Ent	15	90		52	Actor. Writer-Dir.
Thornton, Charles Tex		Bus	10	15	25	15	
Thornton, Dan		Gov	10			10	Governor CO
Thornton, Kathryn		Space	10			27	
Thornton, Matthew	1714-1803	Rev War	508	1619	3392		Signer Dec. of Indepen.
Thornton, William	1759-1828	Rev War	125	250	325		Am. Architect. Designed Capitol
Thornton, William		Space	10			20	
Thornton, William A.	1803-1866	Civ War	35				Union Gen. '62 DS 95
Thornton, William E., Dr.		Space	10			20	
Thornton, Willie Mae	1926-1984	Music	345	440	475		Am. Jazz-Gospel Singer
Thorpe, Jeremy		Pol	10	20	45	15	Br. Parliamentarian
Thorpe, Rose Hartwick		Author	10	20	35		Am. 'Curfew Must Not Ring Tonight'
Thorson, Ralph 'Papa'		Lawman	10	25	45	20	Bounty Hunter
Thorton, Matthew	1714-1803	Rev War		1700			Signed DOI; Pol. leader in the Am. Revolution
Thorvaldsen, Bertel		Artist	105	325	140		Dan. Sculptor 'Lion of Lucerne'
Three Dog Night		Music	100			200	Rock; S Album 150
Three Suns, The		Music	15			45	Pop-Jazz Musicians
Three's Company		Ent				150	Cast signatures
Throop, Enos T.		Gov	25	55			Governor NY 1829
Thruston, Charles Mynn	1798-1873	Civ War	45	85			Union Gen.
Thruston, Gates P.	1835-1920	Civ War	25	30	55		Union Gen.
Thuot, Pierre		Space	10			15	
Thurber, James	1894-1961	Author	105	442	529	305	Am. Humorist & Comic Artist
Thurman, Allen G.	1813-1895	Congr	10	30	45		Sen. OH
Thurman, Howard		Clergy	35	40	50	50	
Thurman, Uma		Ent	12	30	65	188	Actress
Thurmond, J. Strom		Congr	10	20		25	Sen., Governor SC
Thursby, Emma		Opera	30				Am. Sopr.
Thurston, Howard	1869-1936	Ent	145	275	465	635	Thurston The Magician; SB 575
Thurston, John M.	1847-1916	Congr	15		30		Sen. NE 1895
Thurston, Lorrin A.	1858-1931	Pol	35		55		Pioneer Hawaiian Pol. Leader
Tiahrt, Todd T		Congr	10				Member US Congress
Tibbatts, John W.	1802-1852	Congr	10		55		MOC KY, Off. Mexican War
Tibbett, Lawrence	1896-1960	Opera	75	75		81	Opera, Concert, Films, Radio
Tibbetts, Paul W.	1915-2007	WWII	45	95	152	102	Pilot of Enola Gay WWII. Gen.
Tibbits, William Badger	1837-1880	Civ War	40		700		Union Gen.
Tibbits, William Badger (WD)	1837-1880	Civ War			700		
Tiberi, Patrick J. T		Congr	10				Member US Congress
Tidball, John C.	1825-1906	Civ War	25	45	60		Union Brevet Major Gen.
Tiege, Karl		Artist	80		275		Czech. Surrealist Painter
Tiegs, Cheryl		Ent	15			61	Model
Tierney, Gene	1920-1991	Ent	30	48	50	185	Actress. 'Laura'.
Tierney, Harry		Comp	40	95	195		AMusQS 350

NAME	DATES	CATEGORY	SIG	LS/DS	ALS	SP	COMMENTS
Tierney, John F. T		Congr	10				Member US Congress
Tierney, Lawrence	1919-2005	Ent				45	Actor
Tietjens, Therese		Opera	40			135	Ger. Sopr. Opera
Tiffany		Music		65		85	Singer
Tiffany, Charles Lewis	1812-1902	Bus	240	450	717	1275	Fndr. Tiffany & Co. Jewelry Designer. Artist
Tiffany, Louis Comfort		Artist	225	1020			Stained glass artist. Spec. Ed. Book S 3200
Tiffin, Pamela	1942-	Ent	58			74	Actress
Tigrett, John Burton		Author	10			12	Business success
Tilden, Samuel J.	1814-1886	Gov	75	160	275		Gov. NY, Pres. Cand.
Tilghman, James		Rev War	88	182	356		Lawyer, Pol. S Chk 765
Tilghman, Lloyd	1816-1863	Civ War	140	290	502		CSA Gen. KIA
Tilghman, Lloyd (WD)	1816-1863	Civ War	235	635	1980		CSA Gen. KIA.
Tilghman, Matthew		Rev War	225		825		Cont. Congress. ALS/Cont 2750
Tilghman, William M. Bill	1755-1827	Lawman	225	1166	1654		Early Western Sheriff
Tilkin-Servais, Ernest		Opera	25			85	Opera
Tilley, Reade		Aero	10	20	35		Am. Air Ace as Member of Royal Air Force; 7 kills
Tillich, Paul		Clergy	70	125	125	136	
Tillinghast, Joseph Leonard		Congr	10		36		MOC; FF 36
Tillis, Mel		Cntry Mus	10			35	Songwriter-Singer
Tillis, Pam		Music		35		45	Singer
Tillman, Benjamin 'Pitchfork Ben'	1847-1918	Congr	25	40	55		Sen. SC 1894
Tillman, Floyd		Cntry Mus	10			25	Songwriter-Singer-Guitarist-Mandolinist
Tillotson, Johnny		Cntry Mus	22	88		50	Singer
Tillson, Davis	1830-1895	Civ War	40		70		Union Gen.
Tillstrom, Burr	1917-1985	Ent	25		65	50	Actor
Tilly, Jennifer		Ent	10		10	42	Actress
Tilly, Meg		Ent	10			45	Actress
Tilton, Charlene		Ent	25			55	Actress
Tilton, Martha		Music	12			65	Big Band Singer, Recording Artist
Tilton, Theodore	1835-1907	Jrnalist			90		Sued Henry Ward Beecher for Adultery
Tilton, Wm. Stowell		Civ War	40	50			Union Brevet Brig. Gen.
Tilzer, Albert von		Comp	40	110	200	55	Fndr. ASCAP
Timberlake, Bob		Artist	15			20	Painter, Designer. Litho S 600+
Timberlake, Justin		Music	15	60		60	Singer
Timiryazev, Kliment	1843-1920	Sci	112				Botanist, physician
Timken, Henry	1831-1909	Invent	85	140	225		Timpken Tapered Roller Bearings
Timken, William Robert		Bus	35	95	155	60	Pres. Timken Roller Bearings
Timothy, Christopher	1940-	Ent	10			25	Br. Actor
Ting, Samuel C. C., Dr.		Sci	20	35	50	25	Nobel Physics 1976
Tingey, Thomas	1750-1829	Mil	140	350	525		Continental Navy
Tingley, Clyde		Gov	12	20		15	Governor NM 1935
Tinker, Grant C.		Ent	10			20	TV Film Prod.
Tiny Tim	1932-1996	Music	25	35		78	Singer. 'Tiptoe Through The Tulips'; S Album 60
Tiny, Texas		Cntry Mus	10			20	Singer
Tiomkin, Dimitri	1894-1979	Comp	50	352	365	460	Music For Major Movie Production. AMusQS 225-675
Tippett, Michael, Sir	1905-1998	Comp	40	85		150	Br. Comp. & Conductor
Tippit, J. D.		Celeb	500				Dallas policeman killed November 22, 1963
Tisch, Laurence A.		Bus	15			45	CEO of CBS
Tisserant, Eugene, Card.		Clergy	35	45	50	40	
Tissot, James	1836-1902	Artist	68	175	202		Fr. Painter, Engraver, Enameler
Titchener, Paul		Bus	10	35	45	20	
Tito, Marshal (Josip Broz)	1892-1980	HOS	85	175	280	362	Yugoslav Statesman. Communist
Titov, Gherman		Space	45			95	DS w/Gargarin 170
TLC		Music	95			250	Rock group

NAME	DATES	CATEGORY	SIG	LS/DS	ALS	SP	COMMENTS
Tobey, Charles W.		Congr	10			10	Governor, Rep., Sen. NH
Tobey, Ken	1917-2002	Ent	10			120	Actor
Tobias, George	1901-1987	Ent	40			162	Actor. Stage, Films-1939-70's.
Tobin, Genevieve	1899-1995	Ent	15		30	45	Actress. Warner Bros. Leads-2nd Leads from 30s
Tobin, James, Dr.		Econ	22	30		25	Nobel Economics 1981
Tobin, Maurice		Cab	10	20	30	15	Sec. Labor 1948, Gov. MA
Tocqueville, Alexis de	1805-1859	Author	45	150	425		Fr. Pol., Statesman, Writer
Tod, David		Gov	10	25			Governor OH
Todd, Alexander Robertus, Sir		Sci	30	85		40	Nobel Chemistry 1957
Todd, Ann	1909-1993	Ent	20			115	Br. Actress. Intl. Film Star From 30s
Todd, Henry D., Jr.	1866-	Mil	15		35		WWI Genl
Todd, John Blair Smith	1814-1872	Civ War	45	75	120		Union Gen.
Todd, Michael	1909-1958	Ent	40			155	Prod. Sig. w/Eliz. Taylor 225
Todd, Richard	1919-	Ent	40			45	Ir. Actor. AA Nomination for 'Hasty Heart'
Todd, Robert		Aero	15	30	45	25	
Todd, Thelma	1905-1935	Ent	146	235	350	667	Actress. Mysterious Death at 30
Todt, Fritz	1891-1942	WWII	95	225			Engineer & senior Nazi figure
Todt, Raymond		Aero			50	60	Pilot in Navy's 1st flight from SF to Honolulu
Tognini, Michel		Space	15	25		35	
Togo, Heihachiro, Marquis	1846-1934	Mil	178	315	448	448	Jap. Adm. Sino-Jap. War
Togo, Shigenori		Diplo	250			400	Jap. Foreign Min. -Statesman
Tojo, Hideki	1884-1948	WWII	700	860	1500	1148	Prime Min. Jap. Adm. Pearl Harbor. Executed
Toklas, Alice B.	1877-1967	Author	45	185	807		Companion of Gertrude Stein; sig w/Stein 240-515
Tokody, Ilona		Opera	10			25	Opera
Tokyo Rose (Iva I. Toguri)	1916-2006	WWII	250	312	847	950	WWII Radio Propagandist; Pardoned by Ford
Toland, George Washington		Congr	10		36		MOC; FF 36
Toler, Sidney	1874-1947	Ent	295	340		554	2nd 'Charlie Chan' After Warner Oland
Tolkien, John R. R.	1892-1973	Author	1250	4808	8998		Br. Writer of 'Lord of the Rings'
Tolstoy, Alexandra, Countess		Author	25		80	60	
Tolstoy, Ilya	1866-1933	Jrnalist			120		Son of Leo; Manuscript 915
Tolstoy, Leo, Count	1828-1910	Author	1200	1775	2988	4613	Rus. Novels & Moral Philosopher
Tolvald, Linus		Sci	10			30	Creator of Linux
Tomagno, Francesco		Cond	40		250		Opera
Tombaugh, Clyde W.	1906-1997	Sci	25	338	432	94	Astronomer. Disc. Pluto, 1930; ALS/Pluto Cont 1790
Tombstone		Ent				225	Cast S; Kilmer, Paxton, Elliott, Russell
Tomei, Marissa		Ent	20			62	Actress; AA
Tomlin, Lily		Ent	10	10	15	48	Comedienne
Tomlin, Pinky		Band	10			35	Scat Singer
Tomlinson, David	1917-2000	Ent				60	Br. Actor; 'Mary Poppins'
Tommy James & Shondells		Music	95			200	Rock
Tompkins, Angel	1943-	Ent	10			35	Actress
Tompkins, Daniel	1774-1825	VP	68	152	140		Monroe VP, Governor NY
Tompkinson, Steven	1965-	Ent	10			30	Br. Actor
Tompson, Alexander K.		Clergy	15	25	35		
Tonderai, Mark		Music	10			15	DJ
Tone, Franchot	1905-1968	Ent	35		50	116	Am. Leading Man & Later Char. Actor
Tong, Pete		Music	10			15	DJ
Tong, Sammee	1901-1964	Ent	25			95	Peter on Bachelor Father
Tong, Shen		Celeb	10			15	Chinese dissident
Tony, Simon		Music	10			25	Music. Guitar, Keyboard 'The Verve'
Toole, John Lawrence	1832-1906	Ent			75		Br. Comic actor
Toombs, Robert A.	1810-1885	Civ War	102	210	162	1725	CSA Gen. & Sec. State. Sig/Rank 205
Toomey, Patrick J. T		Congr	10				Member US Congress
Toomey, Regis	1898-1991	Ent	15	20		50	Actor

NAME	DATES	CATEGORY	SIG	LS/DS	ALS	SP	COMMENTS
Toon, Thomas Fentress	1840-1902	Civ War	95				CSA Gen.
Toones, Fred Snowflake	1906-1962	Ent	150			300	Actor
Toorop, Jan (Dutch)	1858-1928	Artist	25	100	210	125	Posters, Tiles, Stained Glass. Leader of Luminists
Toper, Justin		Celeb	10			15	Astrologer
Topol, Chaim	1935	Ent	10			45	Israeli Actor. Stage, Films. AA Nominated(Fiddler)
Topp, Erich		WWII	35		175	62	Ger. U Boat Cmdr. WWII
Topping, Dan		Bus	10	15	30	20	Millionaire One Time Owner NY Yankees
Torbert, Alfred Thomas A.	1833-1880	Civ War	40	65	95		Union Gen.
Torisu, Kennosuke		WWII	60		175	150	Submarine Attack on Pearl Harbor
Tork, Peter		Ent	15	35		45	Singer-Actor 'The Monkees'
Torme, Mel	1925-1999	Music	20	50	125	62	Vocalist, Comp. AKA 'The Velvet Fog'; S Chk 40
Torn, Rip		Ent	15			50	Actor; Emmy
Torrance, Ernest	1878-1933	Ent	65			125	Scot. Silent Films. Ex Opera
Torrence, Ridgely	1875-1950	Author	25	30	85		Am. Poet, Editor, Dramatist
Torres, Jacques		Celeb	10			15	Famous chef
Torres, Liz		Ent	10			30	
Torres, Raquel	1908-1987	Ent	20			50	Mex. Actress. Several Early Sound Films
Torrey, R. A.		Clergy	20	35	50		
Tors, Ivan	1916-	Ent	15			35	Prod. -Dir. -Screenwriter. USAAF-OSS
Toscanini, Arturo	1867-1957	Cond	148	221	442	615	AMusQS 750-950, AMusMS 3, 750. SP Pc 625
Tosti, Paolo		Comp	25	60	122		Italian Comp.
Toto	1898-1967	Ent	65			250	It. Comedy Star. Films From 1936
Toto		Music				250	Rock group; S Guitar 470
Totten, Jos. G.	1788-1864	Civ War	33	40	85		Union Gen. Wardte DS 200-400, Sig/Rank 50
Totter, Audrey	1918-	Ent	10	15		60	Actress. Radio Dramas, TV Soaps, Films 1939
Toucey, Isaac	1792-1869	Cab	25	80	120		Polk Atty Gen. 1848, Sec. Navy '57
Toulouse-Lautrec, Henri	1864-1901	Artist	975	3450	4550		Fr. Parisian Nightlife. Over 300 Lithographs
Toumanova, Tamara		Ballet	30		150	85	Rus-Am Ballerina
Tourel, Jennie		Opera	20			50	Opera
Tourgee, Albion W.	1838-1905	Author	15	20	45		Lawyer, Judge, Diplomat
Toussaint-L'Ouverture, Pierre	1743-1803	Statsmn		2310			Haitian Gen. Led Haitian Slave Revolt 1791
Tovey, John Sir	1885-1971	WWII				150	Br. Royal Navy Adm. Sunk the Bismarck
Tower, John	1925-1991	Congr	10	15		25	Sen. TX
Tower, Zealous B.	1819-1900	Civ War	30	46	68		Union Gen.
Towers, Constance	1933-	Ent	10	20		45	Actress
Towery, Twyman L		Author	10			12	Financial/business how-to
Towl, E. Clinton		Bus	20		55		
Towle, Tom		Aero			45	50	Early aviator
Towne, Katherine		Ent	14			42	
Towne, Robert	1934-	Ent	10			30	Film writer; AA
Townes, Charles Hanson		Sci	30	80	65	40	Inventor. Nobel (Laser & Maser)
Townley, James		Clergy	35	50	75		
Towns, Edolphus T		Congr	10				Member US Congress
Townsand, Colleen (Evans)		Ent	10			35	Actress. Short Career In Films. 50s-
Townsend, Edward D.	1817-1893	Civ War	45	50	68		Union Gen., War date(Cont.) 7950
Townsend, Francis Everett	1867-1960	Sci	40			150	Social Reformer & Physician. Old Age Pension Plan
Townsend, Frederick	1825-1897	Civ War	30	55	90		Union Brevet Brig. Gen.
Townsend, George A. (Gath)		Author	15		40		War Correspondent
Townsend, Lynn		Bus	10	20	35	20	CEO-Pres. Chrysler Corp.
Townsend, M. Clifford		Gov	10	15			Governor IN
Townsend, Pete		Music	45			225	Lead Singer 'The Who'; S lyrics 305
Townsend, Peter		Mil	10	35	50	25	
Townsend, Robert		Ent	10	15		20	Film Dir.
Townsend, Stuart		Ent				40	Actor

T

NAME	DATES	CATEGORY	SIG	LS/DS	ALS	SP	COMMENTS
Townsend, Washington		Congr	10	20			Rep. PA 1969
Toy Story (cast)		Ent		178		188	Hanks, Varney, Potts, Rickles
Toynbee, Arnold	1852-1883	Author	25	62	170	80	Br. Economist, Sociologist
Toynbee, Arnold Joseph	1889-1975	Author	20	45	84	30	Br. Historian, Prof., Paris Peace Conf.
Tozzi, Giorgio		Opera	20			100	Opera
Trachte, Don		Comics	25			75	Henry'; sketch 115
Tracy, Arthur		Music	20			45	The Street Singer'.
Tracy, Benjamin F.	1830-1915	Civ War	40	55	90		Union Gen. MOH.
Tracy, Edward Dorr	1833-1863	Civ War	279	645	938		CSA Gen.
Tracy, Edward Dorr (WD)	1833-1863	Civ War	575	1040			CSA Gen. KIA 5/1/63.
Tracy, Lee	1898-1968	Ent	15			75	Actor-Broadway '24; Screen '29. Fast-Talking Roles
Tracy, Spencer	1900-1967	Ent	192	310	325	550	Actor; AA
Traffic		Music	221			350	Rock group., S Album 135
Tragically Hip		Music				75	Canadian Rock Band
Train, Arthur		Author	10	15	35		
Train, George Francis	1824-1904	Bus	36	65	116		Eccentric Financier, Author
Trapier, James H.	1815-1865	Civ War	153	299	410		CSA Gen. AES '61 575
Trapp, Maria von, Baroness	1905-1987	Celeb	68	130	250	240	Sound of Music' Fame.
Trask, Diana	1940-	Cntry Mus	10			20	Australian Pop-Country Singer
Trask, Spencer		Bus		950			Fndr. Spenser Trask & Co., Wall Street
Traubel, Helen		Opera	50			92	Opera. Am. Sopr. Concerts, Radio, Films
Trautloft, Hannes		WWII	25			50	Ger. Ace WWII RK
Travalena, Fred	1942-	Ent	10			35	Actor-Comedy
Travanti, Daniel J.		Ent	10			35	Actor; 'Hill Street Blues'
Traveling Wilburys		Music		3500			Signed by all group members
Traven, Berwick (Torsvan)	1890-1969	Author	265	800	1765		Ger. Novels, Actor, Pacifist
Travers, Henry	1874-1965	Ent	349			1460	Actor; Clarence the Angel in It's A Wonderful Life
Travers, Pamela L.		Author	25	125			'Mary Poppins' Books
Travers, Patricia		Music	10			30	Violinist.
Traverso, Giuseppe		Opera	15			45	Opera
Travis, Daniel		Ent	25			75	
Travis, David Lee		Music	10			15	BBC DJ
Travis, Kylie		Ent	10			52	Actress
Travis, Merle		Cntry Mus	20			40	Top Multi-Talented Guitarist, Singer, Songwriter.
Travis, Nancy	1961-	Ent	18			105	Actress
Travis, Randy		Cntry Mus	15	32		41	Singer. S Guitar 315
Travis, Richard	1913-	Ent	10			20	Actor; Hollywood Realtor
Travis, William Barret	1809-1836	Tex		6554	17068		Co-Cmdr. Alamo. TX Frontier. Imp. DS 172904-191200
Travolta, John		Ent	25	65		61	Actor; S Album 120
Treacher, Arthur	1894-1975	Ent	20		75	51	Lawyer-Trained. Became Perennial Br. Butler in 30s
Treadway, Allen Towner		Congr	10	15			MOC MA 1913
Treadwell, John		Rev War	25	60	95		Del. CT. Elected to Cont. Congr.
Treas, Terri	1957-	Ent	10			35	Actress
Trebek, Alex		Ent	10	15	20	35	Perennial Host of 'Jeopardy' TV Game Show
Trebor, Robert	1953-	Ent	10			35	Actor; Hercules/Xena
Tree, Herbert Beerbohm, Sir	1852-1917	Ent	30	85	145	112	Br. Actor-Mgr. Fndr. Royal Academy
Treen, Mary	1907-1989	Ent	10	15	30	65	Actress; Comedienne; 'It's A Wonderful Life'
Treilhard, Jean-Baptiste	1742-1810	Fr Rev	25	40	75		Fr. Pol. Important in Drafting Legal Codes
Trejo, Danny		Ent	13			40	
Trelawny, Edward	1792-1881	Author		445	750		Br. Author-Adventurer. Companion Shelley & Byron
Tremayne, Les	1913-2003	Ent	10			30	Br. Actor; Abundant radio work
Tremonti, Mark		Music	10			25	Music. Guitar, Vocals 'Creed'
Trench, Richard C., Arch.		Clergy	45	60	95	65	
Trenholm, George A.	1807-1876	Civ War	102	213	422		CSA Sec. Treasury

NAME	DATES	CATEGORY	SIG	LS/DS	ALS	SP	COMMENTS
Trent, William	1717-1787	Mil		600			Fndr. of Trenton, NJ
Trettner, Henrich 'Heniz'	1907-2006	WWII	20	45		50	Ger. Gen.
Trevelyan, George Otto, Sir	1838-1928	Author	15	35	75		Br. Historian, Sec. To Admiralty, Author
Treves, Frederick, Dr.	1853-1923	Sci	175		428		Dr. To Elephant Man
Trevor, Claire	1910-2000	Ent	38			75	AA Winning Actress. 'Key Largo', 'Stagecoach'
Trigg, Liz		Celeb	10			15	Food Writer
Trilling, Lionel	1905-1975	Author	10	30	50	25	Am. Lit. Critic. Professor, Essayist
Trimble, Isaac Ridgeway	1802-1888	Civ War	185	300	544		CSA Gen.
Trimble, Isaac Ridgeway (WD)		Civ War	429	1114	1850		CSA Gen.
Trimble, Lawrence	1825-1904	Congr	15		25		MOC KY
Trinh, Eugene		Space	10			20	
Tripler, Charles E.		Sci	75	185			Inventor Liquid Air
Triplett, Phillip		Congr	10				MOC; FF 27
Trippe, Juan T.	1899-1981	Aero	30			55	Fndr. Pan Am. Airways. Clipper Service
Tripplehorn, Jeanne	1963-	Ent	15			50	Actress
Trist, Nicholas P.	1800-1874	Diplo	75	225			Am. Negotiated Treaty of Guadaloupe
Tritt, Travis		Cntry Mus	15			35	Singer
Tritton, William Ashbee, Sir		Sci	25	70	125	40	Developed Mil. Tank
Trollope, Anthony	1815-1882	Author	107	145	705		Br. Novels. 50 Novels, ALS/cont 1350
Trollope, Frances	1780-1863	Author	30	55	95		Br. Novels. Mother of Anthony
Trollope, Thomas A.	1810-1892	Author		25	50		Novels, History. Tremendous Output
Trotsky, Leon	1879-1940	HOS	389	1124	1750	1225	Communist Revolution leader-Assass.
Trotter, James Monroe	1842-1892	Civ War	40	250			Former Slave. Union Soldier.
Trotter, Mark C.		Clergy	15		35		
Troubridge, Thomas, Sir		Mil	75		250		Br. Adm., Battle of the Nile
Troup, Bobby	1918-1999	Music	20			35	Pianist, Comp., Vocalist-Actor
Troup, Frank W.		WWII	15			35	WWII Air Ace; 7 kills
Trowbridge, John T.	1827-1916	Author	15		25		
Trower, Robin		Music	15			55	Singer; S Guitar 175
Troyanos, Tatiana		Opera	15			40	Opera
Troyer, Verne		Ent	20			50	
Trudeau, Gary		Comics	40	40		250	1st Cartoonist Awarded Pulitzer-Editorial Cartoons; SB 40; Sketch 120-350
Trudeau, James B. (WD)	1818-1887	Civ War			400		Conf. Brig. Gen.
Trudeau, Pierre	1919-	HOS	25	60	95	60	Prime Min. Canada
Trueblood, D. Elton		Clergy	15	30	45	35	
Truett, George W.		Clergy	15	35	50	35	
Truex, Ernest	1890-1973	Ent	20			65	Char. Actor From Silent Era into 50s-60's
Truffaut, Francois	1932-1984	Ent	83	422		518	Fr. Dir. & Critic, ALS/Cont 800
Trujillo, Rafael	1891-1961	HOS	70	95		256	Dominican Repub. Assass.
Truly, Richard H.		Space	15	25		52	
Truman, Benj. C.	1835-1916	Author	20		45		Soldier-Author
Truman, Bess W.	1885-1982	1st Lady	60	74	118	111	S WH Card 85-195
Truman, Harry S.	1884-1972	Pres	138	361	1670	302	ALS/Cont 14,000-39500
Truman, Harry S. (As Pres.)		Pres	307	634	5231	516	ALS/TLS/Cont 7500-28750, S appt 1250-5000; WHC 500
Truman, Margaret (Daniel)	1924-2008	1st Fmly	25	65	80	35	Author; Daughter of Harry S. Truman
Trumbo, Dalton	1905-1976	Author	50	200		75	Blacklisted Screenwriter. AA For 'The Brave One'
Trumbull, Annie E.	1858-1949	Author	15		25		
Trumbull, Douglas	1942-	Ent	10			15	Dir.
Trumbull, John	1756-1843	Artist	100	565	1350		ALS/Cont 8,000. Engr. by R. Riker S 750
Trumbull, John	1750-1831	Author	85	182			CT Poet & Lawyer
Trumbull, Jonathan	1710-1785	Rev War	250	450	577		Confidant of G. Washington. ADS Special 1100
Trumbull, Jonathan Jr.	1740-1809	Rev War	90	184	347		Sec. Washington's Staff
Trumbull, Lyman	1813-1896	Congr	25	80	140	200	US Sen. Abolitionist. FF 462

NAME	DATES	CATEGORY	SIG	LS/DS	ALS	SP	COMMENTS
Trump, Donald J.		Bus	15	45	75	40	Entrepreneur
Trump, Ivana		Celeb	10			25	Ex Mrs. Donald Trump
Truscott, Lucian K., Jr.	1895-1965	Mil	45	125		150	TLS/Cont 225
Truth, Sojourner	1797-1883	Abolit	3680				Relig. Missionary, RARE any form. Only 3 Known
Truxton, William Talbot		Civ War	30	55	95		Union Naval Off. Adm. 1882
Truxtun, Thomas	1755-1822	Rev War	145	522	800		Cmdr. USS Constellation
Tryggvason, Bjarni		Space	10			20	
Tryon, Tom		Ent	10	20	25	25	Actor-Author
Tryon, William	1728-1788	Rev War	145	375	770		Colon'l Gov. NC, Gov. NY
Tschernenko, Konstantin	1911-1985	HOS	75			375	Pres. Soviet Union 1984-'85
Tshombe, Moise	1919-1969	HOS	55	160	195	70	Prime Min., Zaire(Congo Rep.)TLS/Cont 795-1250
Tsiolkovsky, Konstantin	1857-1935	Sci		1439	1075		Pioneer Rus. Space Prog. ALS/Cont 6500, AMS 2300; SB 2875
Tsongas, Paul E.		Congr	15	35	25	20	Sen. MA, Pres. Hopeful 1992
Tubb, Ernest	1914-1984	Cntry Mus	25		290	123	Country Music Hall of Fame
Tubb, Justin	1935-	Cntry Mus	10			15	Singer-Son of Ernest Tubb
Tuchman, Barbara W.		Author	35	125	155	45	2 Time Pulitzer Pr., Historian
Tucker, Forrest	1919-	Ent	30	35	40	91	Actor. Husky, Blonde Bully in 40s, Hero in 50s
Tucker, John R. (WD)	1812-1883	Civ War	180	290			CSA Navy Commdr. 1812-83
Tucker, Michael		Ent	10			35	Actor
Tucker, Orrin		Band	15			25	Big Band Leader
Tucker, Richard		Opera	30	45		78	Opera
Tucker, Samuel	1747-1883	Rev War	150	325	675		Am. Naval Hero. Commodore
Tucker, Sophie	1884-1966	Ent	32	40	95	141	Burlesque, Vaude., 'Last of the Red Hot Mamas'
Tucker, Tanya	1958-	Cntry Mus	10	45		40	Country Singer
Tucker, Thomas T.	1745-1848	Rev War	55	105	175		Soldier, Statesman, Treas.
Tucker, Tilghman M.		Congr	20	35	55		Sen. 1838, Governor MS 1841
Tucker, Tommy		Band	15			50	Big Band
Tucker, William Feimster	1827-1881	Civ War	110				CSA Gen.
Tuckerman, Henry T.	1813-1871	Poet					Am. poet & essayist; AQS 120
Tudor, Anthony		Ent	35	45		100	Br. Dancer, Choreographer
Tudyk, Alan		Ent	15			45	
Tuell, Jack M., Bish.		Clergy	20	25	35	30	
Tufts, Cotton	1734-1815	Rev War	75	175	262		Highly Esteemed Physician. Patriot
Tufts, Sonny	1911-1970	Ent	20	25		60	Singer/Actor. Became mocked Alchoholic
Tukhachevsky, Mikhail N.	1893-1937	Mil		368			Russian Revolutionary, Army Marshal
Tulford, Nellie Hughes		Space	10			15	
Tully, Alice		Philan	15	30		35	Lincoln Ctre. Tully Hall
Tully, Grace G.	1900-1984	WH Staff	20	38	62	50	Sec. to FDR
Tully, Jim	1891-1947	Ent				90	Actor; writer
Tully, Susan	1967-	Ent	10			25	Br. Actress
Tully, Tom	1908-1982	Ent	25			102	Vet. of US Navy, Legit. Stage, Radio & Many Films
Tully, Tom		Cab	10	15	35	15	
Tumulty, Joseph P.	1879-1954	WH Staff	15	35	75	40	Important Aide to Pres. Wilson
Tune, Tommy		Ent	10			40	Dancer, Choreographer. 'Tony' Award Winner
Tunnell, James M.		Congr	10	30		20	Sen. DE 1940
Tunney, John V.	1934-	Congr	10			10	MOC, Sen. CA
Tupper, Martin F.	1810-1889	Invent	25		50		Brit. Author-Poet. 'Proverial Philosophy'
Turchin, John Basil	1822-1901	Civ War	40	68	130		Union Gen.
Turchin, John Basil (WD)		Civ War	75	650			Union Gen.
Tureck, Roslyn		Music				50	Violinist
Turgenev, Ivan	1818-1833	Author	295	446	778	710	Russ. Novels, Dramatist. AQS 1450
Turkel, Ann		Ent	15			55	Model
Turkel, Joseph	1927-	Ent				65	Actor

NAME	DATES	CATEGORY	SIG	LS/DS	ALS	SP	COMMENTS
Turkel, Studs		Author	10	20	35	35	Columnist. TV Commentator
Turlington, Christy		Model	15			50	Super Model
Turner, Edward	1798-1837	Sci	32		175		Scot. Chemist. Atomic Weights of Elements
Turner, Eva, Dame	1892-	Ent	40	65		75	Opera. Vocal Phenomenon
Turner, Frederick J.	1861-1932	Author	55		225		Pulitzer Pr. 1932. Historian
Turner, Ike	1931-2007	Ent	20			65	Sig w/Tina 150; Sp w/Tina 225
Turner, Janine		Ent	20			42	Actress
Turner, Jedediah		Invent		130			Inventor of the thrashing machine
Turner, Jim T		Congr	10				Member US Congress
Turner, John Wesley	1833-1899	Civ War	143	173	361		Union Gen. Sig/Rank 145
Turner, Joseph M. W.	1775-1851	Artist	225	605	930		Br. Landscape Painter
Turner, Kathleen		Ent	10	20		45	Actress
Turner, Lana	1920-1995	Ent	37	73		200	Actress
Turner, Michael R. T		Congr	10				Member US Congress
Turner, Morrie		Comics	10			20	'Wee Pals'
Turner, Philip		Rev War	70	135	250		Surgeon During War
Turner, Roscoe, Col.	1895-1970	Aero	110	125		132	Pioneer Aviator. Early Race Pilot. Speed Records
Turner, Stansfield		Mil	25			45	Adm. Dir. of the CIA.
Turner, Ted		Bus	20			35	Turner Broadcasting
Turner, Tina		Music	20	125	40	95	Singer; S Guitar 350; S Guitar w/Ike 1000
Turow, Scott		Author	10	15	20	25	Best selling author
Turpie, David		Congr	15	25	35		Sen. IN 1863
Turpin, Ben	1869-1940	Ent	140	325	450	266	Cross-Eyed Max Sennett Comic. Silents; S Chk 150
Turreau De Garambouville		Fr Rev	25		85		
Turtles		Music	200			250	Signed by All; S Album 100
Turturro, Alda		Ent				40	Janice Soprano
Turturro, John		Ent	10			42	Actor
Turturro, Nick	1962-	Ent	10			30	Actor
Tusmayan, Barsag		Opera	10			25	Opera
Tussaud, Marie	1760-1850	Artist	200	725			Swiss Modeler in Wax. 'Madame Tussaud's Exhibit
Tuttle, Horace		Sci		60			Astronomer. Co-discovered Temple-Tuttle Comet
Tuttle, James Madison	1823-1892	Civ War	35	75	120		Union Gen.
Tuttle, Lurene	1907-1986	Ent	10			45	Top Radio Dramatic Star. Supporting Roles in Films
Tuttle, Wes & Marilyn		Cntry Mus	15			30	Duet. Turned Evangelist. w/Religious Music Only
Tutu, Desmond, Bish.		Clergy	55	95	225	89	Nobel Peace Pr. SB 120
Tutwiler, Margaret D.		Cab	10	15		15	Ass'y Sec. State
Tuve, Merle Antony	1901-1982	Sci	35	80	155	50	Neutron, Ionosphere, Radar
Twain, Mark & Samuel Clemens		Author	1062	1995	5167		Both Signatures
Twain, Mark (see Clemens)		Author					
Twain, Shania		Music	12			76	Singer. Pop-Country; S Guitar 200-500
Tweed, Shannon		Ent	15	40		68	Actress-Model.
Tweed, William Marcy	1823-1878	Pol	100	191	392	750	Boss' Tweed. Corrupt Pol., S stock cert. 3600
Tweeden, Leeann		Ent	16			47	
Tweedy, Jeff		Music	20			40	Rock
Twelvetrees, Helen	1908-1958	Ent	25			167	Actress
Twichell, Ginery		Congr	10		31		MOC; FF 31
Twiggs, David E.	1790-1862	Civ War	140	685	1208		CSA Gen. Sig/Rank 205
Twiggy (Nee: Leslie Hornsby)		Ent	25			45	60's Brit. Fashion Model. Actress
Twining, Nathan F.	1897-1982	WWII	50	135	185	120	Gen. WWII. Commanded 15th Air Force
Twiss, Peter	1921-	Aero	10	15	30	20	Br. pilot, who held the World Air Speed Record
Twister		Ent				71	Movie; S by Bill Paxton & Helen Hunt
Twitty, Conway	1933-1993	Cntry Mus	30	108		95	Rocker turned Country Superstar; S Album 120
Two Guns White Calf	1872-1934	Am Ind	650		2000	886	Buffalo Nickel Model. Sketch 860
Twohy, David		Ent	12			35	

NAME	DATES	CATEGORY	SIG	LS/DS	ALS	SP	COMMENTS
Tydings, Millard E.	1890-1961	Congr	20	50		30	Rep., Sen. MD, Author
Tyler, Aisha		Ent	13			40	
Tyler, Asher	1798-1875	Congr	10		32		MOC NY, Fndr. Elmira Rolling Mill; FF 28
Tyler, Beverly	1927-2005	Ent	10			30	Actress
Tyler, Bonnie	1951-	Ent	15			35	Br. Actress
Tyler, Buffy		Ent	18			55	
Tyler, Daniel	1799-1882	Civ War	47	85	125		Union Gen.
Tyler, Edward Burnett, Sir		Sci	15	30	50		Prof. Anthropology Oxford
Tyler, Erastus Bernard	1822-1891	Civ War	45	68	95		Union Gen.
Tyler, Gerald E.		WWII	10	25	40	30	ACE, WWII; 7 kills
Tyler, John	1790-1862	Pres	326	1058	1416		As VP. ALS/Cont 7500, FF 400, Ex. Rare CW ALS 5000
Tyler, John (as Pres.)		Pres	500	1400	2208		10th US Pres. DS w/Webster 2000-2500, DS w/Calhoun 2000-2500; FF 450
Tyler, John Jr.	1819-1895	Civ War	20	50			CSA, Acting Chief Bureau of War
Tyler, Julia Gardiner	1820-1889	1st Lady	150	350		650	Special DS 1100
Tyler, Liv		Ent	18			57	Actress
Tyler, Moses Coit		Author	10	15	25		Historian. Am. Historical Assoc
Tyler, Robert	1816-1877	Civ War	40	65	150		Pres.'s Son., CSA Register of Treasury
Tyler, Robert C.	1833-1865	Civ War	220	580	850		CSA Gen. Killed April 16, 1865
Tyler, Robert Ogden	1831-1874	Civ War	58	90	147		Union Gen.
Tyler, Royall	1757-1826	Rev War	25	50	120		Jurist, Author, Plays
Tyler, Steven		Music	15			60	Lead Singer Aerosmith
Tyler, T. Texas		Cntry Mus	15			30	Singer. 'Deck 'O Cards'
Tyler, Tom	1903-1954	Ent	352			927	Actor; Mummy, Captain Marvel, & the Phantom.
Tyndale, Hector	1821-1880	Civ War	43	75	128	175	Union Gen.
Tyndale, Hector (WD)	1921-1980	Civ War	50	125	185		Union Gen.
Tyndall, John	1820-1893	Sci	44	90	142		Irish Physicist, Natural Philosopher
Tyner, James N.		Cab	10	40	75		P. M. Gen. 1876
Tyner, McCoy		Music	10	20		30	Jazz Pianist-Comp.
Tyson, Cathy	1965-	Ent	10			35	Br. Actress
Tyson, Cicely		Ent	35			55	Actress.
Tyson, Don		Bus	15			25	Pres., Fndr., CEO Tyson's Chicken
U-2 (All)		Music	185			325	Irish Rock Group
Udall, Mark U		Congr	10				Member US Congress
Udall, Morris K.		Congr	10			10	Repr. AZ
Udall, Tom U		Congr	10				Member US Congress
Udet, Ernst	1896-1941	Aero	460	475	700	567	WWI Ger. Ace. 2nd to Richthofen.
Udy, Helene	1962-	Ent	10			30	Actress
Ueberroth, Peter		Bus	10	25	40	20	
Uecker, Bob		Ent	10			30	
Ufford, Edward S.		Clergy	40	50	70		
Uggams, Leslie	1943-	Ent	10			40	Actress
Uhlenbroek PhD, Charlotte		Celeb	10			15	Naturalist
Ulbricht, Walter	1893-1973	Pol		412			Pres. of East Ger. 1960-1973
Ulene, Art Dr.		Celeb	10			15	Med. Spkr.
Ullman, Daniel	1810-1892	Civ War	35	65	90		Union Gen.
Ullman, Tracey	1959-	Ent	20			43	Actress; comedianne
Ullmann, Liv	1938-	Ent	10			45	Actress
Ulmanis, Karlis		HOS	90				1st Pres. Latvia. Fate Unknown
Ulric, Lenore	1892-1970	Ent				120	Actress
Ulrich, Skeet	1970-	Ent	10			47	Actor
Umberto I (It)	1844-1900	Royal	50	150	375	62	King Italy
Umberto II		Royal				60	
Umeki, Miyoshi	1929-2007	Ent	214			4082	Actress; Chk 325

NAME	DATES	CATEGORY	SIG	LS/DS	ALS	SP	COMMENTS
Umstead, William B.		Gov	10		20		Governor NC
Underwood, Adin Ballou	1828-1888	Civ War	40		80		Union Gen.
Underwood, Blair		Ent	15			45	
Underwood, Carrie		Cntry Mus	15			70	CW Singer; S Guitar 240
Underwood, J. T.		Invent	25	295	200		Underwood Typewriter
Underwood, Oscar W.		Congr	10			10	Rep., Sen. AL
Undset, Sigrid	1882-1949	Author	35			240	Nor. Nobel Pr. Winner
Unger, Debra		Ent	15			45	
Unger, Jim		Comics	15	20		25	Henry
Ungher, Caroline	1803-1877	Opera			150		Opera. Great Contralto
Union, Gabrielle		Ent	15			45	
Unreal, Minerva		Ent	25			60	
Unruh, Howard B.	1921-	Crime	80				Mass murderer
Untermeyer, Louis	1885-1977	Author	20	35	60	50	Am. Poet, Critic, Satirist, Biogr.
Untouchables (cast)		Ent				225	Movie cast of 4
Updike, John	1932-	Author	25	80	70	52	Am. Novels, Poet, Short Story Writer; SB 135
Upham, Charles	1908-	Mil	100	250			One of Only 3 Men to Win Victoria Cross Twice
Upham, Charles	1802-1875	Clergy	30		95		Unitarian Min., Author, Whig Congressman
Upjohn, E. Gifford, Dr.		Bus	125	450			Fndr. Upjohn Pharmaceuticals
Upshaw, Dawn		Opera	10			25	Opera
Upshaw, William D.		Congr	10			10	Rep. GA 1919, Evangelist
Upshur, Abel Parker	1790-1844	Cab	30	95	110		Tyler Sec. Navy, State
Upton, Emory	1839-1881	Civ War	32	63	135		Union Gen. Wardte DS 465
Upton, Fred U		Congr	10				Member US Congress
Urban, Karl		Ent	17			50	
Urban, Keith		Cntry Mus	25			80	CW singer; S Guitar 240
Urbanowicz, Witold A.		WWII	35	70	125	60	Pol. ACE, WWII
Ure, Mary	1933-1975	Ent	25			100	Scottish actress; AA nomination
Urey, Harold C.	1893-1981	Sci	87	252	433		Nobel in Chemistry 1934. Disc. Heavy Hydrogen
Urich, Robert	1946-2002	Ent	10	15	25	38	Actor. 'Spencer '
Urie, Michael		Ent	14			43	
Uris, Leon		Author	20	58	125	52	Am. Novels. 'Battle Cry', 'Exodus'
Uritskii, Moisei		Mil		483			Russian Revolutionary
Urso, Camilla		Music	25			40	Fr. Violinist
Ursuleac, Viorica		Music	30			85	Great Strauss Singer & WWII Heroine
Urvanowicz, Witold A.		WWII	20	45	75	50	ACE, WWII, Polish Ace
Usher		Music	20			45	Rap; Rock
Usher, John P.		Cab	40	110	195		Sec. Interior 1863-65
Ussishkin, Menachem	1863-1941	Zionist	175		625		Rus-Zionist Leader. A Fndr. Hebrew U
Ustinov, Peter	1921-2004	Ent	30	45	60	105	Plays, Author, Actor. AA
Utley, Garrick		Jrnalist	10			25	TV Reporter & Commentator
Utrillo, Maurice	1833-1955	Artist	200	396	460	281	Fr. Montmartre, Paris Scenes; S portrait 1725
Vaccaro, Brenda		Ent	10			35	Actress
Vaccaro, Tracy	1962-	Model	10			35	Playmate; Actress
Vadim, Roger	1928-2000	Ent	20	45		120	Film Dir.
Vague, Vera		Ent	25				SEE Barbara Jo Allen. Comedienne
Vai, Steve		Music	15			120	Rock; S Guitar 180-240
Valdengo, Giuseppe		Opera	15			40	Opera
Valderrama, Wilmer		Ent	16			48	
Vale, Virginia	1920-2006	Ent	15			50	Actress
Valens, Richie	1941-1959	Music	1290	1757		1685	Singer; S 45 RPM 5400
Valenti, Jack	1921-2007	Ent	10	20	35	40	Pres. Motion Picture Assoc. Special Ass't LBJ
Valentine, Karen		Ent	10			35	Actress
Valentine, Lewis		Lawman	35	105		50	Legend'y NY Police Commissioner

NAME	DATES	CATEGORY	SIG	LS/DS	ALS	SP	COMMENTS
Valentine, Steve		Ent	17			50	
Valentines		Music				120	Australian rock Band; S by all 5
Valentino, Jean Acker		Ent				225	1st wife of Rudolph Valentino.
Valentino, Natacha		Ent				735	Wife of Rudolph Valentino from 1923-26.
Valentino, Rudolph	1895-1926	Ent	977	1162	1350	2758	Top Film Star. Death Created Legend; Chk 915-2500
Valery, Paul A.	1871-1945	Author	45	105	170		Fr. Noted Poet, Philosopher
Valette, A. J. M.		Fr Rev	25		75		
Valetti, Cesare		Opera	20			50	Opera
Vallandigham, Clement L.	1820-1871	Civ War	69		130		Civil War 'Copperhead' (Peace Dem.); MOC; FF 75
Vallee, Rudy	1901-1986	Ent	20	60		84	Am. Singer (Crooner). Radio-TV Personality
Vallejo, Boris		Artist					Signed litho 230; S print 260
Vallejo, Mariano Guadalupe		Mil	140	450			Early CA Off'l & Mil. Leadr
Valli, Frankie		Music	25			75	Singer; Lead of Four Seasons
Valli, Virginia	1898-1968	Ent	15			65	Actress; Films From 1915-1931
Valli, Alida	1921-2006	Ent	38			135	Actress
Vallone, Raf	1916-2002	Ent	15			50	Italian actor
Vambery, Arminius	1832-1913	Author			270		
Van Alen, James Henry	1819-1886	Civ War	46	87			Union Gen.
Van Allan, Richard		Opera	10			25	Opera
Van Allen, James		Sci	45	70	110	68	Nobel Physics. Rocket Research. Van Allen Belt
Van Ark, Joan		Ent	10			35	Actress
Van Buren, Abigail	1918-	Jrnalist	10	18	30	30	Am. Syndicated Columnist
Van Buren, James D.		Official	15	30			Son of Pres. Van Buren
Van Buren, Martin	1782-1862	Pres	221	678	860		FF 450-475, ALS/Cont 2500-5900
Van Buren, Martin (As Pres.)		Pres	300	1110	2830		Free Frank 350-475
Van Buren, Raeburn		Comics	10			50	Abbie & Slats
Van Cleef, Lee	1925-1989	Ent	25			218	Actor; One of the great movie villains; Chk 70
Van Cleve, Horatio Phillips	1809-1891	Civ War	45	75	115		Union Gen.
Van Dam, Rip	1662-1736	Colonial	60	175	360		Merchant, Pol., Col. Gov. NY
Van Damme, Jean-Claude		Ent	20			46	Actor
Van Den Berg, Lodewik, Dr.		Space	10				
Van Der Beek, James		Ent	10			45	Actor
Van der Rohe, Ludwig Mies	1886-1969	Archtct	120	350			Ger-Am. Exponent of Glass & Steel Architecture
Van Derbur, Marilyn	1937-	Celeb	10			20	Miss Am. 1958; author
Van Derveer, Ferdinand	1823-1892	Civ War	40		85		Union Gen.
Van Devanter, Willis	1859-1941	Sup Crt	45	86	175	150	Justice 1910-37
Van Dien, Casper	1968-	Ent	10			51	Actor
Van Dine, S. S. (W.H. Wright)		Author	45	100	190	225	Created Philo Vance
Van Dongen, Kees	1877-1968	Artist	30	45	116		Fauvist Painter, Portraitist, S drwg 184
Van Doren, Carl		Author	15	45	60	20	Pulitzer in Biography
Van Doren, Mamie	1931-	Ent	15	68		78	Actress
Van Doren, Mark	1894-1973	Author	15	57	60	30	Critic, Editor, Pulitzer Poetry
Van Dorn, Earl	1820-1863	Civ War	518		1566		CSA Gen. Assass.
Van Dorn, Earl (WD)		Civ War	850		5775		CSA Gen. Assass.
Van Dresser, Marcia	1877-1937	Ent	15			75	Vintage Actress
Van Druten, John W.		Author	10	20	35	15	Plays, Novels
Van Dusen, Henry P.		Clergy	15	15	25	20	
Van Dyck, M. Ernest		Opera	15	25		40	Tenor
Van Dyke, Dick		Ent	20			85	Actor; comedian
Van Dyke, Dick (cast)		Ent	175			322	Cast SP
Van Dyke, Henry	1852-1933	Clergy	20	40	55		Min. To Netherlands-Luxem.
Van Dyke, Jerry		Ent	10			35	Actor, Dick Van Dyke's brother
Van Dyke, Leroy	1919-	Cntry Mus	10			20	Songwriter. 'The Auctioneer', 'Walk on By'
Van Dyke, Nicholas	1738-1789	Rev War	110	275	625		Statesman, Continental Congress

NAME	DATES	CATEGORY	SIG	LS/DS	ALS	SP	COMMENTS
Van Dyke, W. S.		Ent	55			100	Dir. of The Thin Man series of films
Van Fleet, James, Gen.	1892-1992	WWII	28	75	95	95	Gen. WWII. US 8th Army, Korea
Van Fleet, Jo		Ent	15	20	45	60	Actress; AA
van Gogh, Vincent	1853-1890	Artist	3500	5500	16000		Dutch Painter. Individual Style
Van Halen (original)		Music	125	661		567	S Album 650-1100; S Guitar 1000
Van Halen, Alex	1953-	Music	20	95		50	Comp.
Van Halen, Eddie		Music	50	265		158	Rock. 1982 Chk S 200; S Guitar 1010-2385
Van Heusen, James		Comp	60	90	175	100	AMusQS 250
Van Hoften, James D.		Space	10			20	
Van Horn, Burt		Congr	10	20			Rep. NY 1861, Manufacturer; MOC; FF 26
Van Horne, David		Rev War	45		75		
Van Kirk, Theodore		WWII	40	85	210	94	Enola Gay Nav. Log from Hiroshima Flight 358500
Van Leer, Darryl		Ent	10			30	Actor
Van Loon, Hendrik Willem		Author	18	30	125	40	Historian, Journalist, Lecturer, Illust.
Van Loon, William		Jrnalist	10		50		Lecturer
Van Ness, Cornelius P.		Gov	15	35	60		Jurist, Gov. VT, Min. Sp.
Van Nuys, Frederick	1874-1944	Congr	10			25	Sen. IN 1932
Van Outen, Denise		Model	10			44	Celebrity model
Van Patten, Dick		Ent	10			35	Actor
Van Patten, Joyce		Ent	10			35	
Van Peebles, Mario		Ent	15			45	Actor-Dir.
Van Rensselaer, Henry	1810-1864	Civ War	75				Rep. NY 1841, Union Gen.
Van Rensselaer, Solomon	1774-1852	Mil		350			Am. soldier & Pol. Lt. Col. In War of 1812
Van Rensselaer, Stephen	1764-1839	Mil	75	170	218		Gen War 1812. Helped estab. Rensselaer School
Van Sant, Gus	1952-	Ent	10			20	Dir. 'Good Will Hunting'
Van Schaick, Goose		Rev War			2900		Gen. Rev. War. Served Honorably Thru The War
Van Sloan, Edward	1881-1964	Ent	125		635	250	Actor
Van Stade, Frederica		Opera	15			45	Opera
Van Sweringen, Otis P.		Bus	15	40	90	35	RR Exec-Developer Shaker Height
Van Valkenburgh, Debbie	1952-	Ent	10			30	Actress
Van Vechten, Carl		Author	40	75	110	75	Am. Novels, Staff NY Times
Van Vleck, John H., Dr.		Sci	30	45	75		Nobel Physics 1977
Van Vliet, Stewart	1815-1901	Civ War	46	120	90		Union Gen. Indian Fighter
Van Vooren, Monique	1925-	Ent	10			30	Belgium actress
Van Wagoner, Murray D.		Gov	10			15	Governor MI
Van Wyck, Charles Henry	1824-1895	Civ War	48	100	140		Union Gen.
Van Zandt, Philip	1904-1958	Ent	50				Actor
Van Zandt, Ronnie	1948-1977	Music	365				Lead singer of Band Lynyrd Skynyrd
Van Zandt, Stevie		Ent				50	Silvio Dante, Sopranos. Member of E Street Band
Van Zealand, Paul, Visc.		HOS	15			35	Premier Belgium, Foreign Min.
Van, Bobby		Ent	10				Dancer
Van, Gloria	1920-2002	Ent	10			35	Actress
Van, Isabelle		Ent	10				Dancer
Van, Jackie		Ent	10			15	Dancer
VanCamp, Emily		Ent	13			40	
Vance, A. T., Capt.		Aero	20	35			Record Polar Flight
Vance, Cyrus		Cab	10	20	35	25	Sec. State, Sec. Army
Vance, Jack		Author	10	15	20	15	Hugo & Nebula winning SF writer
Vance, Louis Joseph		Author	15	35	90		Am. Novels
Vance, Robert Brank	1828-1899	Civ War	120	174	336		CSA Gen., Sig/Rank 145
Vance, Vivian	1909-1979	Ent	202	416		755	Actress. Lucy's TV Sidekick. Lucy SP 450
Vance, Zebulon Baird	1830-1894	Civ War	54	117	165		CSA Gov. & Sen. of NC, Opposed J. Davis
Vandamme, Dominique Rene		Napol	50	150	210		Battle of Waterloo
Vandenberg, Arthur H.	1884-1951	Congr	20	70		25	Sen. MI, Pres. Pro Tem.

NAME	DATES	CATEGORY	SIG	LS/DS	ALS	SP	COMMENTS
Vandenberg, Hoyt S.	1899-1954	Mil	40	62	75	65	
Vander Jagt, Guy		Pol	10			15	MI Representative
Vander Pyl, Jean		Ent	10			15	Voice Wilma-Pebbles Flintstone
Vanderbilt, Alfred Gwynn		Bus	15	35	65	65	
Vanderbilt, Amy	1908-1974	Author	10	25	40	35	Columnist, Authority on Manners
Vanderbilt, Cornelius	1794-1877	Bus	273	1232	1751	2880	Commodore', Finan. RR/Steamships. ALS cont 25000
Vanderbilt, Cornelius	1843-1899	Bus	250	825	1750	1250	Grandson of 'Commodore'. RRs, 'Breakers'
Vanderbilt, Cornelius, Jr.	1898-1974	Jrnalist	25	103	125	40	
Vanderbilt, George Wash.	1862-1914	Bus	250	750	1100	800	Grandson of 'Commodore'. 'Biltmore House'
Vanderbilt, Gloria		Bus	25	45	80	35	Fashion Designer. Artist. Litho S 125
Vanderbilt, Harold S.	1884-1970	Bus	168				Philan. -Businessman
Vanderbilt, Jacob H.	1807-1893	Bus	500	1900	2950		Brother of 'Commodore'. RRs & Steamships
Vanderbilt, William H.	1821-1885	Bus	300	778	2225	1400	Commodore' Son. Philan. Giant RR Empire
Vanderbilt, William H., Jr.		Bus	45	120	250	75	Governor RI
Vanderbilt, William K.	1849-1920	Bus	250	650	1500	800	Commodore' Gr. Son. RR Exec., Financier-Yachtsman
Vandergrift, Alexander A.	1887-1973	Mil	45	100	175	150	1st Marine Div. Gen. WWII. MOH at Guadalcanal
Vanderlyn, John	1775-1852	Artist	250	275	750		Am. Pres. Portraits, Capitol
Vanderpoel, Aaron		Congr	10		28		MOC; FF 28
Vandever, William	1817-1893	Civ War	40		85		Union Gen.
Vandross, Luther		Music	20			60	Rock
Vane, Henry The Younger	1613-1662	Statsmn		582			GB Statesman. Opp. Cromwell's Protectorate
Vane, John R., Dr.		Med	20	30	50	25	Nobel Med. 1982
Vaness, Carol		Opera	10			35	Opera
Vanili, Milli		Music	10			40	Singer
Vanilla Ice		Music	20			40	Rock; S Album 40
Vanity		Ent	10	50		70	
Vanous, Lucky	1961-	Ent	10			30	Actor
Vanzetti, Bartolomeo	1888-1927	Crime	600	1800	4186		Convicted Murderer, Electrocuted, Anarchist
Vardalos, Nia		Ent	10			40	Actress; 'My Big Fat Greek Wedding'
Varela, Leonor		Ent				40	Actress
Varese, Edgard	1883-1965	Comp	185	199	502		Fr. -Am. Music Pioneer; AMusQS 415
Vargas, Alberto		Artist	135	345	402	417	Repro Varga Girl S 325-450; SB 320
Vargas, Getuilio		HOS	50	150		75	Revolutionary Pres. Brazil.
Vargas, Jacob		Ent	17			50	
Varick, Richard	1753-1831	Rev War	65	118	180		Soldier, Washington's Sec.
Varmus, Harold E., Dr.		Sci	25	60		35	Nobel Med. 1989
Varnay, Astrid		Opera	10			61	Opera
Varney, Jim	1949-2000	Ent	58			193	Actor
Vartan, Michael		Ent	17			50	
Vasarely, Victor	1908-	Artist	45	130		90	Hungarian. Op Art Repro S 75-150-275
Vasquez, Roberta		Model	10			25	Actress; playmate
Vassar, Matthew	1792-1868	Bus	200	525			Fndr. Vassar College. ALS/Cont 3400
Vasto, Lanzo del	1901-1981	Phil			150		A western disciple of Gandhi
Vaubois, J. F. G.		Fr Rev	20	25	40		
Vaughan, Alfred J., Jr.	1830-1899	Civ War	80		400		CSA Gen. Sig/Rank 150
Vaughan, Robert		Clergy	10	15	25		
Vaughan, Sarah	1924-1990	Music	55	108	210	135	Am. Jazz Vocalist-Pianist
Vaughan, Stevie Ray	1954-1990	Music	470	2500	3400	912	Guitarist, S Album 760-850
Vaughan-Williams, Ralph, Sir	1872-1958	Comp	92	242	595	175	Established Br. Nat'l Musical Style. SP Pc 450
Vaughn, George A.		WWII	35	55	95	65	ACE, WWII
Vaughn, Herbert, Card.		Clergy	30	50	90	75	
Vaughn, John Crawford	1824-1875	Civ War	110				CSA Gen.
Vaughn, John Crawford (WD)	1830-1899	Civ War	195	325	750		CSA Gen.
Vaughn, Robert	1932-	Ent	10	10	15	44	Actor. S 'Man From Uncle' Comic Book 50

V

NAME	DATES	CATEGORY	SIG	LS/DS	ALS	SP	COMMENTS
Vaughn, Vince		Ent	15			50	Actor
Vaughn, William S.		Bus	10	10		10	Pres. Eastman Kodak
Vaux, Roberts	1786-1836	Philan	110		522		Prison Reform, Houses of Refuge
Veach, Charles L.		Space	10			15	
Veatch, James Clifford	1819-1895	Civ War	40		100		Union Gen.
Vedder, Eddie		Music	20			120	Lead Singer Pearl Jam. S Guitar 200-570; S Album 130
Vedder, Elihu		Artist	45	135	140		Drew From Dreams & Fantasy
Vedral, Joyce L.		Author	10			10	Non-Fiction
Vedrines, Jules		Aero	200	395	650	265	
Vee, Bobby		Music	15			50	Singer/14 Top 40 Hits 1960-68; S Album 70
Vega, Alexa		Ent	14			43	
Vega, Mackenzie		Ent	13			40	
Veidt, Conrad	1893-1950	Ent	68	90	130	158	
Veit, Stan		Author	10	10	20	20	Computer Shopper, PC historian
Vejvoda, Jaromir	1902-1988	Comp	70				'The Beer Barrel Polka' AMusQS 195
Velez, Lupe		Ent	85	78	175	153	Fiery Latin 20th C. Fox Musical Star.
Veloz & Yolanda		Ent	15			35	30-40's Ballroom Dance Team
Velßzquez, Nydia M.		Congr	10				Member US Congress
Velvet Underground		Music	228			350	Rock Group; S Album 380
Venable, Evelyn	1913-1993	Ent	15	20	40	45	Actress
Venable, William Webb		Congr	10	15		10	Rep. MS 1916, Judge
Vendela		Ent	20			40	Model/actress
Vendome, L. J., Duke de	1654-1712	Fr Mil	150	450			Marshal of France
Vendy, Krista		Ent	10			30	Actress
Ventimiglia, Milo		Ent	17			50	
Ventura, Charlie		Band	40				Am. Bandleader-Saxophonist
Venture, Jesse		Gov	15	135		90	Governor of Minnesota; Former Prof. wrestler
Ventures		Music				230	Instrumental group; S Guitar 240; S Album 180
Venuta, Benay	1911-1995	Ent	10			45	Actress
Verdi, Giuseppe	1813-1901	Comp	1175	1750	4908	4098	AMusQS 4750, 5,000, 5, 700, 7, 500, 12, 500
Verdin, James, Lt. Cdr.		Aero	10	25			US Navy Pilot. Record Holder
Verdon, Gwen	1925-	Ent	10		75	188	Dancer-Actress-Singer, Top Broadway Star, Films
Verdugo, Elena	1926-	Ent	15			45	Actress
Verdy, Violette		Opera	10			30	Opera
Vereen, Ben	1946-	Ent	10	20		38	Dancer, Singer, Actor
Vereshchagin, Vassili V.	1842-1904	Artist	35		150	500	Paintings of Russian Wars
Vergara, Sofia	1972-	Ent	10			40	Actress
Vergennes, Chas. G., Le Comte de	1717-1787	Statsmn	175	375	1725		Fr. Ambass. Supported Am. Rev.
Verhoeven, Paul	1938-	Ent	10			20	Film Dir.
Verlaine, Paul	1844-1896	Author	150	376	639		Fr. Symbolist Poet
Vermehren, Werner		Aero	15	35	55	58	Ger. Capt. WWI Zepps.
Verne, Jules	1828-1905	Author	185	1283	1045	4453	Fr. Sci-Fi Novels 'Around the World in 80 Days'
Verneuil, Edouard Poulletier de	1805-1873	Sci			65		Geologist & paleontologist
Vernier, Theodore, Count		Fr Rev	35	100			
Verplanck, Gulian Crommelin		Congr	12		45		MOC; FF 45
Vertes, Marcel		Artist			500		Hung. -born Fr. Artist
Verve, The		Music	40			125	Music. 5 Member Rock Group
Vessey, John W.		Mil	10			30	
Vest, George G.	1830-1904	Civ War	30	55			CSA Cong. From MO
Vetch, Samuel	1668-1732	Colonial	250	800	2250		Colonial Mil. Governor
Vetri, Victoria	1944-	Ent	25			40	Actress
Veverka, Jaroslav		Opera	20			45	Opera
Vezzani, Cesare		Opera	45			150	Opera. Corsican Dramatic Tenor
Viardot, Pauline		Music	30		231	100	Singer from Manual Garcia Musical Family

NAME	DATES	CATEGORY	SIG	LS/DS	ALS	SP	COMMENTS
Vickers, Jon		Opera	15			55	Opera. Dramatic Tenor; AMusQS 65
Vickers, Martha	1925-1971	Ent	20			212	Model-Actress.
Victor Amadeus III	1726-1796	Royal	95	295			King of Sardinia
Victor Emmanuel I	1759-1824	Royal	130	325	585		King of Sardinia
Victor Emmanuel II (It)	1820-1878	Royal	125	320	525	500	King of Italy 1861-1878
Victor Emmanuel III	1869-1947	Royal	100	123			King Italy 1900-46
Victor Emmanuel III & Mussolini		Pol		185			DS by both
Victor, Claude Perrin	1766-1841	Fr Mil	75	140	210		Marshal of Napoleon
Victor, Henry	1892-1945	Ent	65			200	Br. Actor; Silent Movies.
Victoria, Crn Prin. of Prussia		Royal			2000		Queen Victoria's eldest daughter
Victoria, Duchess of Kent	1786-1861	Royal	50		150		Mother of Queen Victoria
Victoria, Empress (Fred III, Ger)	1840-1901	Royal	85		488		Imperial Presentation Frame & SP 3700
Victoria, Guadalupe		Pol		860			1st Pres. of Mexico
Victoria, Mary Louisa		Royal	40	110	136		
Victoria, Queen	1819-1901	Royal	243	568	635	2330	Great Britain DS by Victoria & Albert 575
Victoria, Queen Eugenie of Spain		Royal			210	500	Granddaugher, Queen Victoria
Vidal, Christina		Ent	13			40	
Vidal, Gore	1925-	Author	10	72	35	30	Novels, Plays, Critic, Screenplays. SB 120
Vidocq, Francois	1775-1875	Celeb		368			Fr. agent, spy
Vidor, Florence	1895-1977	Ent	40	45	65	120	Silent Film Star. Wife of Dir. King Vidor
Vidor, King	1894-1982	Ent	30	75		85	AA Film Dir. LS/Cont 250
Viele, Egbert L.	1825-1902	Civ War	38	70	78	100	Union Gen, Eng'r. Sig/Rank 40, WarDte DS 150
Viereck, George Sylvester	1884-1962	Poet		350			Poet, writer, propagandist
Vietinghoff genannt Scheel, H. von	1887-1952	WWII	225				WWII Ger. Gen. Heinrich von
Vieuxtemps, Henri	1820-1881	Comp	150	450			
Vigneaud, Vincent du		Sci	10	25	45	45	
Vigran, Herb	1910-1986	Ent	10	15		45	Actor. Vintage Char. Actor
Vila, Bob		Ent	10			25	TV Tool Show. 'This Old House' Host
Vila, George R.		Bus	10	20	32	15	CEO Uniroyal Tire
Vilas, Jack	1881-1976	Aero	20	25		50	1st Flight Across Lake Michigan 1913
Vilas, William F.		Cab	30	30	45	35	P. M. Gen., Sec. Interior 1888. Cleveland Cabinet
Viljoenk, B. J.		Mil	35		145		
Villa, Francesco (Pancho)	1878-1923	Mil	1100	2681	5200	4000	Mexican Guerilla Leader, Revolutionary
Villa-Lobos, Heitor	1887-1959	Comp	100	262	525	333	Brazilian. AMusQS 500, AMusMS 350-1,000
Villalpando, Catalina Vasquez		Cab	15			30	US Treas.
Villechaize, Herve	1943-1993	Ent	25	60		110	Actor. 'Fantasy Island', 'Tattoo'
Villepique, John B.	1830-1862	Civ War	288	375	690		CSA Gen. Sig/Rank 350-395 Rare
Villetto, Rev. Robert		Author	10			12	Religion
Villiers, Alan J. Captain	1903-1982	Author	10		25		Australian. Maritime, Adventure, History
Villiers, Frederic		Artist	10	20	50	40	
Villon, Jacques (Psued)	1875-1963	Artist	65		210		Pseud. Gaston Duchamp. Bro. Marcel Duchamp. Sket 60
Vinay, Ramon		Opera	70			288	Opera. Sang Otello Intl.
Vincent, Gene	1935-1971	Music	133			320	Rock
Vincent, Jan-Michael	1944-	Ent	10		15	40	Actor
Vincent, June	1920-	Ent	10			35	Actress. Secondary Leads & Supporting Roles
Vincent, Romo	1908-1989	Ent	10			35	Actor. Char., Supporting Player
Vincent, Stenio Joseph	1874-1959	HOS	125				Pres. Haiti. Lawyer, Diplomat
Vincent, Strong	1837-1863	Civ War	375	3295			Union Gen., 3rd Brigade. KIA Gettysburg.
Vincent, Thomas M.	1832-1909	Civ War	41	80	128		Union Gen.
Vinson, Carl	1883-1991	Congr	20	40		70	Rep. GA 1914
Vinson, Frederick M.	1890-1953	Sup Crt	80	157	250	350	Chief Justice, Cabinet, Rep. KY
Vinson, Helen	1907-1999	Ent	15	20	40	70	Actress. Sophisticated Leading Lady of 30s-40's
Vinton, Bobby		Comp	15	25		45	Singer; AMusQS 50
Vinton, David	1803-1873	Civ War	40	55	80		Union Gen., 1st P. O. W.

NAME	DATES	CATEGORY	SIG	LS/DS	ALS	SP	COMMENTS
Vinton, Francis Laurens	1835-1879	Civ War	45	60	90		Union Gen.
Vinton, Francis Laurens (WD)	1847-1879	Civ War	300				Union Br. Gen.
Vinton, Will	1948-	Ent	10	25		20	Am. Dir. & Prod. of animated films
Virchow, Rudolf	1821-1902	Sci	233	600	935	1725	Fndr. Cellular Pathology
Virtanen, A. I.	1895-1973	Sci	30	85	145	55	Nobel Chemistry 1945
Visclosky, Peter J. V		Congr	10				Member US Congress
Vishinsky, Andrei		HOS	70	230	370	120	Rus. 1st Deputy Foreign Min.
Visitor, Nana	1957-	Ent	15			40	Actress; 'Star Trek'
Vitter, David V		Congr	10				Member US Congress
Vittor, Frank		Artist	40		165		
Vivian, Richard H. Sir		Rev War	50	125	255		
Vlaminck, Maurice de	1876-1958	Artist	100	235	368	312	Fr. Fauvist Painter
Vodges, Israel	1816-1889	Civ War	50	75	100		Union Gen.
Voelker, John D.		Author	10	10	15	15	
Vogel, Mike		Ent	15			45	
Vogl, Heinrich		Ent	75		285		Important Early Wagnerian Tenor
Voight, Deborah		Opera	10			25	Opera
Voight, Jon		Ent	12		30	48	Actor; AA; SP w/Dustin Hoffman 120
Voinovich, George		Congr	10				US Senate (R-OH)
Voisin, Gabriel	1880-1973	Aero	65	135	225	250	Fr. Airplane Mfg. & Pioneer Experimentor
Vokes, Christopher	1904-1985	WWII	40	65	80	65	WWII Canadian Gen.
Volcker, Paul A.		Cab	10		20	15	Chm. Federal Reserve
Voliva, Wilbur G.	1870-1942	Clergy	30		50		
Volk, Leonard W.	1828-1895	Artist	55	350	475		Sculptor. Famed for Lincoln Works.
Volkov, Vladislav	1935-1971	Space	100			270	Russ. Astronaut Soyuz 7. Killed in Soyuz 11
Voll, John J.		WWII	18	40	65	45	ACE, WWII; 21 kills
Volstead, Andrew J.	1860-1947	Congr	30	60	95	125	MOC MN 1903. Volstead Act
Volta, Alessandro	1745-1827	Sci	400	2500	2917		It. Volt, Electrical Unit, For Him
Voltaire, Francois M.	1694-1778	Author	500	3774	5498		Fr. Writer-Philosopher-Satirist
Volz, Nedra	1908-2003	Ent	10			30	Actress
von Bernstorff, John Heinrich		Diplo	30		100		Ger. Amb. To US. Member Ger. Reistag
Von D'niken, Erich		Author	15	30	75	30	Sci-Fi
von Papen, Baron Franz	1879-1969	WWII	80	200	550	350	Ger. Nobelman & secret agent. Chancellor, 1932.
Von Strade, Frederica	1945-	Opera				30	Am. mezzo-Sopr.
Vonnegut, Kurt, Jr.	1922-2007	Author	120	165	195	119	Am. Black-Humor Novels; SB 200-300; sketch 625
Voorhees, Daniel W.		Congr	15	40			Rep., Sen. IN 1861
Voronoff, Serge	1866-1951	Sci	35		205		Rus. Phys. Used Animal Glands for Rejuvenation
Vorster, Balthazar J		HOS	25	70	165	50	Prime Min. South Afr.
Voskhod 1		Space				225	Crew
Voss, James		Space	10			20	
Voss, Janice		Space	10			20	
Vosseller, Aurelius B.		Mil	35	95			
Voyant, Claire		Celeb	10			15	Astrologer
Voysey, Charles	1828-1912	Clergy	35	50	75		Fndr. of the Theistic Church.
Vraciu, Alex		WWII	15	25	50	35	ACE, WWII; 19 kills
Vrooman, Peter		Rev War			185		NY Col.
Vrtis, James E.		Bus	10			20	Software engineer; RTF
Vubu, Joseph Kasa	1917-1969	Pol				300	1st Pres. of the Democratic Repub. of the Congo
Vuillard, Edouard	1868-1940	Artist	120	290	324		Fr. Painter, Printmaker, Illust., Decorator
Vyshinsky, Andrei		Pol		184			Soviet Deputy Foreign Min.
Wachtel, Theodor	1823-1893	Opera	70		195		Opera. 19th C. Ger. Tenor
Wade, Benjamin Franklin	1800-1878	Congr	40	70	95		Sen. OH 1851-69
Wade, Ernestine "Sapphire"		Ent				340	Sapphire Stevens in 'Amos 'n Andy', radio & TV
Wade, Henry		Law		380			Prosecutor of Jack Ruby

NAME	DATES	CATEGORY	SIG	LS/DS	ALS	SP	COMMENTS
Wade, Keptha H.		Bus		875			Telegraph & RR Pioneer. 'Big 3 Telegraph' 1860's
Wade, Leigh		Aero	30	60	80	50	Pilot '24 Round The World
Wade, Melancthon Smith	1802-1868	Civ War	50	75	110		Union Gen.
Wade, Russell		Ent				45	Actor
Wadlow, Robert		Celeb				200	'World's tallest man'
Wadopian, Eliot		Music	10			25	Bassist. Paul Winter Consort. 'Grammy'
Wadsworth, James S.	1807-1864	Civ War	230	410	500		Union Gen. KIA Battle of the Wilderness
Wadsworth, James W., Jr.	1877-1952	Congr	12	30			Sen. NY
Wadsworth, Jeremiah	1743-1804	Rev War	150	332	384		Commissary Gen. Cont. Army. CT. Merchant
Wadsworth, Peleg		Rev War	115	315			Gen., Aide Artemas Ward
Waesche, Russell Randolph	1886-1946	Mil	30	50			US Coast Guard Commandant
Wagener, David D.	1792-1860	Congr	12		45		MOC PA, Fndr. Easton Bank
Wagner, Adolf		WWII		475		460	Nazi, Bravarian Min. of Interior
Wagner, Cosima	1837-1930	Celeb	85	150	385	400	Wife of Rich'd. Daughter of Liszt. ALS/Cont 1850
Wagner, George Day	1829-1869	Civ War	45	95	130		Union Gen.
Wagner, Jack		Ent	15			45	
Wagner, Jane		Author	10	15		20	Plays. Emmy & Peabody Awards
Wagner, Jill		Ent	15			45	
Wagner, Josef		WWII		120			Participated in the plot against Hitler
Wagner, Lindsay		Ent	10			40	Actress
Wagner, Natasha Gregson		Ent	10			45	Actress-Daughter Natalie Wood
Wagner, Richard	1813-1883	Comp	1192	3377	3972	6055	Ger. ALS/Cont 8500; AMusQS 12440-18685
Wagner, Robert		Ent	15	25	25	69	Actor
Wagner, Robert F.	1877-1953	Congr	20	30	45	40	Senate NY 1926, Wagner Act
Wagner, Siegfried	1869-1930	Music			350		Conductor, son of Richard
Wagner, Wolfgang		Ent				50	Grandson of Richard. Dir. Of Bayreuth Festival
Wagoner, Porter	1930-	Cntry Mus	10			35	Duets/Norma Jean & Dolly Parton
Wagstaff, Patty		Celeb	10			15	Aerobatic pilot
Wahl, Ken		Ent	15			45	Actor
Wahl, Lutz		Mil	30		75		Am. Gen. WWI
Wahlberg, Donnie		Ent	17			50	
Wahlberg, Mark		Ent	20			94	Actor
Waigel, Theo, Dr.		Pol	10	10		15	Ger. Gov. Official
Wainwright III, Loudon	1946-	Ent	80				Actor
Wainwright, Charles S.	1826-1905	Civ War	40	75			Union Gen.
Wainwright, James	1938-1999	Ent	10			35	Actor
Wainwright, Jonathan	1864-1945	Mil	20		32		MOC NY, Capt. NY Vols. Span-Am War
Wainwright, Jonathan M.	1883-1953	WWII	85	230	300	228	Am Gen WWII/MOH. Death March. SP/Mac. 995; SB 150
Wainwright, Maj.-Gen. Charles	1893-1961	WWII	252				WWII Br. Gen.
Waite, H. Roy	1884-1978	Aero	15	25	40		Early aviator
Waite, Morrison R.	1816-1888	Sup Crt	60	130	175	250	ALS as Chief Justice Supreme Court 435
Waite, Ralph	1928-	Ent	10	10	15	40	Actor. 'John Walton'
Waite, Terry	1939-	Humanit	25		40	35	Also Hostage Negotiator; author; SB 40
Waitley, Dennis		Author	10			15	Author, keynote Spkr.
Wakely, Jimmy	1914-	Cntry Mus	30			93	Major Country Star During 40s & Early 50s
Wakeman, Rick	1949-	Music	15			30	Br. Comp.
Waksman, Selman A.	1888-1978	Med	45	635	395	145	Nobel Med. 1952
Walburn, Raymond	1887-1969	Ent	10	15	40	80	Vintage Comedic Char. Actor
Walch, Hynden		Ent	15			45	
Walcott, Fred C.	1869-1949	Congr	10	30			Sen. CT 1929. Mfg., Banker
Walcutt, Charles C.	1838-1898	Civ War	52	70	80		Union Gen. Sig/Rank 45, War Dte DS175
Wald, George	1906-	Med	15	30	50	25	Nobel Med. 1967
Wald, Jerry		Band	10			40	Big Band
Wald, Lillian D.	1867-1940	Reform	30	90	175	50	1st City School Nurse Service

NAME	DATES	CATEGORY	SIG	LS/DS	ALS	SP	COMMENTS
Walden, Greg		Congr	10			15	MOC from Oregon
Waldheim, Kurt	1918-	HOS	30	55	75	57	P. M. Austria. Sec. Gen U. N. WWII War Criminal
Waldman, Myron		Comics					Animated cel 150-500; 'Popeye'
Waldo, Anna Lee		Author	15			20	
Waldo, Janet		Ent	10			20	Major Radio Actress. Judy Jetson Voice
Waldren & Kreitlow		Music	15				Folk music
Waldron, Henry B.		Congr	10				MOC; FF25
Waldron, Hicks B.		Bus	10			10	CEO Heublein Inc.
Walesa, Lech		HOS	35	65		113	Nobel Peace Pr., Pres. Poland. FDC S 30
Walgreen, Charles Rudolph	1873-1939	Bus	35	70	145		Pharmacist Fndr. of Walgreen Drugs
Walke, Henry	1809-1896	Civ War	35		90		Rear Adm.
Walken, Christopher		Ent	15		30	55	Actor. 'Deer Hunter'
Walker, Alice	1944-	Author	23			45	Novels. 'Color Purple' ; SB 85
Walker, Benjamin	1753-1818	Rev War	50	125			Rev. Army Off. Rep. NY
Walker, Charles		Space	10			15	
Walker, Clint		Ent	56	48	100	65	Actor-Cowboy
Walker, David M.		Space	10			30	
Walker, Francis Amasa	1840-1897	Civ War	60	116	172		Union Gen. Rose From Private. Sig/Rank 75
Walker, Frank C.		Cab	10	15		10	P. M. Gen. 1940
Walker, Fred L.		Mil	10	35	50		
Walker, Gilbert C.		Gov	15	20	25		Gov. VA 1869, Rep. VA 1875
Walker, Henry Harrison	1832-1912	Civ War	100	140	206		CSA Gen.
Walker, Hiram		Bus			90		Fndr. Walkerville, Ont. & Can. Club Whiskey.
Walker, James	1794-1874	Clergy	15	25	44		Pres. Harvard
Walker, James Alexander	1832-1901	Civ War	95				CSA Gen.
Walker, James J. 'Jimmie'	1881-1946	Pol	25	90	120	225	Flamboyant Mayor NYC. Corruption Charges
Walker, Jimmy		Ent	10			30	Actor-Comedian. 'Good Times'
Walker, John Brisben		Jrnalist	10	30			Editor 'Cosmopolitan Magazine'
Walker, John George	1822-1893	Civ War	110	229	283		CSA Gen. Sig/Rank 195
Walker, Justin		Ent	10			25	Actor
Walker, Leroy Pope	1817-1884	Civ War	117	187	220		CSA Gen.
Walker, Leroy Pope (WD)	1817-1884	Civ War	265	440	640		CSA Gen. -1st CS Sec. of War
Walker, Lucius Marshall	1829-1863	Civ War	280				CSA Gen.
Walker, Mary E.	1832-1919	Civ War	510	795	810	1500	Union Nurse & Surgeon, MOH, ALS/Cont 10,000
Walker, Meriwether L.		Mil	40		125		Am. WWI Gen. Panama Canal Zone Gov.
Walker, Mort		Comics	15			73	Beetle Bailey'; comic strip 300-600; sketch 120
Walker, Nancy	1921-1992	Ent	20			65	Comedienne-Actress. Broadway, Films
Walker, Paul	1973-	Ent	10			38	Actor. Co-Star 'Varsity Blues'
Walker, Percy	1812-1880	Congr	15	35			MOC AL, Med., Soldier
Walker, Reuben Lindsay	1827-1890	Civ War	80		285		CSA Gen. Comdr. Artillery in 64 Battles
Walker, Robert J.	1801-1869	Cab	25	55	80		Polk Sec. Treasury. Largely Created US Dept. Int.
Walker, Robert Jarvis C.		Congr	12	20			MOC PA. 1881.
Walker, Robert, Jr.		Ent	10			25	Actor son of Rob't Walker & Jennifer Jones
Walker, Robert, Sr.	1918-1951	Ent	92	190	150	363	Actor Leading-Man-Husband of Jennifer Jones
Walker, Roy		Celeb	10			15	Impressionist
Walker, T. Bone		Music	30			85	Jazz Guitar-Vocalist
Walker, Walton H.	1898-1950	Mil	30	55	102	75	Gen. Killed in Korea 1950
Walker, William S.	1822-1899	Civ War	85		305		CSA Gen. Sig/Rank 150-200
Walker, Wm Henry T.	1816-1864	Civ War	233	342	575		CSA Gen. KIA
Walker, Wm. Henry T. (WD)	1816-1864	Civ War	350	1350	1742		CSA Gen. KIA 1864
Wallace, Alfred R.	1823-1913	Sci	75	160	372		Developed Theory of Evolution Same Time As Darwin
Wallace, Beryl		Ent				160	Star of Earl Carroll's Hollywood Theater/Restaurant
Wallace, Chris		Celeb	10			20	Media/TV personality
Wallace, Dee		Ent	10	125		25	Actress. 'E. T. '

NAME	DATES	CATEGORY	SIG	LS/DS	ALS	SP	COMMENTS
Wallace, Dewitt	1889-1981	Pub	30			85	Fndr. Readers Digest
Wallace, Dillon		Author	10	15	30	10	
Wallace, Edgar	1875-1932	Author	75	270	345	442	Popular Thriller Writer
Wallace, George		Ent	13			40	
Wallace, George C.		Gov	25	70	78	53	4 Term AL Governor. Pres. Cand.
Wallace, Henry A.	1888-1965	VP	30	72	148	120	FDR V. P., Sec. Agr., Sec. Commerce
Wallace, Henry C.	1866-1924	Cab	15	25	50	20	Sec. Agriculture 1921
Wallace, Irving		Author	20	45	75	75	Am. Novels; SB 90
Wallace, Jean	1923-1990	Ent	10			55	Actress
Wallace, John		Civ War	100	300			Black Leader 1860's
Wallace, John Winfield		Congr	10				MOC; FF 27
Wallace, Lewis 'Lew'	1827-1905	Civ War	134	316	350		Union Gen. -Statesman-Author 'Ben Hur'
Wallace, Lila Acheson		Bus	10	25	35	20	
Wallace, Lurleen B.		Gov	20	30		25	Governor AL. Replaced Husband
Wallace, Marcia		Ent	10			30	Actress
Wallace, Marjorie		Ent	10			25	Miss USA, Actress
Wallace, Mike		Jrnalist	18	15	25	30	News Journalist. '60 Minutes'
Wallace, Vincent	1812-1865	Music					Comp. AMusQS 80
Wallace, William H. L.	1827-1901	Civ War	85	258			CSA Gen
Wallace, William H. L. (WD)	1827-1901	Civ War	175	425			CSA Gen.
Wallach, Eli		Ent	15	90		64	Stage-Film Char. Actor
Wallenberg, Knut	1853-1938	Finan	60	155			Swe. Enskilda Bank, Statesman
Wallenberg, Raoul	1912-?	WWII		10925			Righteous Gentile WWII, Swedish Diplomat
Wallenda, Debbie		Ent	20			40	Trapeze Artist. 'Flying Wallendas'
Wallenda, Karl	1905-1978	Ent	30			303	Trapeze Artist. Killed on High Wire; SB 120
Wallenstein, Alfred, Dr.		Cond	20			75	Am. Cellist/Conductor
Waller, Littleton		Mil	100				Marine Gen. 1880-1920
Waller, Robert James		Author	10			10	Novels
Waller, Thomas 'Fats'	1904-1943	Comp	188	417	525	792	Jazz Pianist. AMusQS 900
Waller, Thomas M.		Gov	15	25	40		Governor CT 1883
Walley, Deborah	1943-2001	Ent	10			40	Actress
Walley, John	1644-1712	Mil		250			Comm. 1st exped. Fr. & Indians in Can., 1689
Wallin, Florence		Author	10			12	Novels
Wallington, Jimmy	1907-1972	Ent	15	25		60	Radio/TV/Actor 'Burns & Allen', ' Life of Riley'
Wallis, Barnes, Sir		Aero	30	100		·	Br. Aircraft Designer. Inventor
Wallis, Hal	1898-1986	Ent	60	90		92	Major Film Prod. & Exec.
Wallis, Shani	1933-	Ent	10			25	Br. Actress
Wallmann, Jeff		Author	10	10	15	10	
Walmsley, Jon	1956-	Ent	10			25	Br. Actor
Walpole, Horace	1717-1797	Author	150	450	1160		Br. Wit, Letter Writer (2700), Novels
Walpole, Hugh Seymour, Sir	1884-1941	Author	30	105	120		Novels, Plays, Biographer
Walpole, Robert, Sir	1676-1745	HOS	96	288	575		1st Recognized Prime Min. of England
Walpole, Spencer H.	1830-1907	Celeb	15		25		English historian & civil servant.
Walsh, Blanche		Ent	15			55	Vintage Actress
Walsh, David I.	1872-1947	Congr	10	15			Governor MA 1914, Sen. 1919
Walsh, Dylan	1963-	Ent	10			35	Actor
Walsh, James T. W		Congr	10				Member US Congress
Walsh, Joe		Music	25			100	Singer, 'Eagles'; S Album 120; S Guitar 500
Walsh, John		Ent	10	20	35	30	Fox TV Host
Walsh, Kate		Ent	15			45	Actress
Walsh, Kenneth		WWII	15	25	50	50	ACE, WWII, MOH; 21 kills
Walsh, Kerri		Ent	22			65	
Walsh, M. Emmet	1935-	Ent	10			40	Actor
Walsh, Raoul	1887-1980	Ent	40			175	Film Dir. -Actor From 1912. Dir. 1914-1964

NAME	DATES	CATEGORY	SIG	LS/DS	ALS	SP	COMMENTS
Walsh, Thomas J.	1859-1933	Cab	15	40		25	Sen. MT 1912. FDR Atty Gen.
Walston, Ray	1914-2001	Ent	10	15	20	55	Actor
Walt, Lewis W.	1913-1989	Mil	20			75	Korea. Sr. Marine Gen. Vietnam
Walter, Bruno	1876-1962	Cond	62		118	452	Ger. Conductor. AMusQS 200. SP Pc 100-275
Walter, Gustav		Opera	65		160		Wagnerian Tenor, Famous Lieder Singer
Walter, Jessica	1940-	Ent	10			40	Actress
Walters, Barbara	1931-	Ent	10	25	35	50	TV Anchor
Walters, Jamie	1969-	Ent				40	Actor; '90210'
Walters, Julie		Ent	10			55	Actress; AA
Walters, Vernon A.	1917-2002	Mil	10		10	20	US Ambassador to UN. Lt. Gen.
Walthall, Edward C.	1831-1898	Civ War	133	210	449		CSA Gen.
Walthall, Edward C. (WD)		Civ War	190	1272			CSA Gen.
Walthall, Henry B.	1878-1936	Ent	40		55	85	Stage Actor. 'Birth of a Nation'
Walton, Bill		Ent	15			45	
Walton, Ernest T. S., Dr.		Sci	75				Nobel Physics 1951
Walton, George	1741-1804	Rev War	353	779	1675		Signer, Cont'l Congr, Gov. GA., ADS/Cont 2, 500
Walton, Gladys	1896-1993	Ent	10			55	Actress
Walton, Sam M.		Bus	58	145		125	Fndr. Wal-Mart.
Walton, William, Sir	1902-1983	Comp	70	90	332	150	AMusQS 230-750
Waltons		Ent				462	TV series; cast signatures; S script 515
Walz, Carl		Space	10			20	
Wambaugh, Joseph		Author	12	25	40	20	Am. Novels re Law Enforcement
Wamp, Zach W		Congr	10				Member US Congress
Wanamaker, John	1838-1922	Bus	60	75	110	138	Dept. Store Pioneer of Money Back Guarantee Fame
Wanamaker, Zoe		Ent	10			25	Actress. Stage
Wander, Charles David	1954-	Law	10			20	Renowned Br. Corporate Lawyer
Wang, Cheng-T'ing		Diplo	20	60	90		Chin. Pol. Leader, Ambass.
Wang, Taylor		Space	10			20	
Wanger, Walter	1894-1968	Ent	30	40		60	Am. Film Prod. Served Time For Shooting Agent
Wapner, Jos. A., Judge		Jurist	10			25	TV Judge
War		Music	35			70	Rock Group (All)
Warburton, Irvine 'Cotton'		Ent	30		45		AA Film Editor, Football Star
Ward, A. S.		Author					SEE: Rohmer, Sax
Ward, Aaron	1790-1867	Mil	15	35	50		Gen. & Pol.
Ward, Artemas	1834-1867	Author	20	35	60		(Pseud. of C. F. Browne) Humorist. Vanity Fair
Ward, Artemas	1727-1800	Rev War	375	785	1500		Revolutionary War Cmdr.
Ward, Burt		Ent	15			40	TV Batman's Robin; SP w/Adam West 125-175
Ward, David		Opera	10			35	Opera
Ward, Henry	1732-1797	Rev War	175	430	870		Colon'l Congr. Pro Independence
Ward, Henry A.	1834-1906	Sci	40	90	150		Scientist, Explr., museum builder
Ward, J. H. Hobart	1823-1903	Civ War	35	77	101		Union Gen. Sig/Rank 50
Ward, John Q. Adams	1830-1910	Artist	25	80	118	80	Am. Sculptor
Ward, Joseph, Sir		HOS	15	25	60		PM New Zealand
Ward, Marcus L.		Congr	15	25			MOC NJ 1873
Ward, Mary A. (Mrs. Humphrey)		Author	10	30	60		Br. Moral, Reforming Novels
Ward, Rachel		Ent	10			55	Aus. Actress.
Ward, Richard	1689-1763	Colonial	150	425			Colon'l Gov. RI
Ward, Samuel	1725-1776	Rev War		625	775		Patriot, Farmer, Merchant, Colon'l Legislator
Ward, Sela		Ent	12			40	Actress
Ward, Susan		Ent	16			47	
Ward, William Thomas	1808-1878	Civ War	40	64	85		Union Gen.
Warden, Jack	1920-2006	Ent	15			50	Actor
Wardlaw, Ralph W.		Clergy	30	35	45		
Ware, Eugene F.	1841-1911	Author	15	30			

NAME	DATES	CATEGORY	SIG	LS/DS	ALS	SP	COMMENTS
Ware, Henry	1764-1845	Clergy	15	25	55		Led Unitarian Separation
Ware, Linda	1925-1975	Music	10			95	40's Teen Singing Star in Films; actress
Warfield, David	1866-	Ent	35	40	75	75	Am. Stage Actor
Warfield, Marsha		Ent	10			30	Actress. 'Night Court'
Warfield, William	1920-2002	Ent	10	15	20	85	Afr-Am Singer-Actor. 'Ol' Man River' Baritone
Warhol, Andy	1930-1987	Artist	258	337	450	367	Pop Art. S Repros 450-4600; S Chk 1220; SB 300-1850
Waring, Fred		Music	15	42	25	65	Big Band & Chorus. Waring Blender
Waring, Richard		Ent				40	Actor
Warner, A. P.		Bus	45	145		75	(Borg-Warner) Fndr. Stewart-Warner. Speedometer
Warner, Adoniram J.	1834-1910	Civ War	35		115		Union Gen., MOC OH 1879
Warner, Charles Dudley	1829-1900	Author	20	65	115		Am. Man of Letters, Editor, Essays
Warner, Harry M.		Bus	95	245	395	300	Fndr. Warner Bros. (One of Four)
Warner, Henry B.	1876-1958	Ent	25			100	Br. Actor. Am. Films 1914. Christ 'King of Kings'
Warner, Jack L.	1891-1978	Bus	72	232	300	270	Fndr. Warner Bros. (1 of Four)DS re MGM 900
Warner, James		Aero	25		40		
Warner, James Meech	1836-1897	Civ War	45	65	108		Union Gen.
Warner, John		Congr	10			20	US Senate (R-VA)
Warner, Julie		Ent				40	Actress
Warner, Malcolm Jamal		Ent	10			35	Actor. 'Cosby Show'
Warner, Seth	1743-1784	Rev War	200	575	1200		Off. Leader/ Ethan Allen. Fndr. Green Mt. Boys
Warner, Ty		Bus	10			25	Beanie Babies
Warner, William	1826-1906	Civ War	50	60	80		Union Major Gen.
Warnow, Mark		Band	10			25	Big Band Leader
Warrant		Music	45			72	Rock Group (All)
Warren Commission		Pol				975	Photo of Entire Comm. S; Kennedy Assassination
Warren, Chas. Marquis	1912-	Author	10	15	25	30	Screenwriter, Prod, Dir, Novels. Films & TV
Warren, Earl	1891-1974	Sup Crt	70	147	200	122	Chief Justice, Governor CA
Warren, Fitz-Henry	1816-1878	Civ War	40	84	138		Union Gen.
Warren, Francis	1844-1929	Congr	40	65	80		CW MOH, Gov., Sen. WY
Warren, Gouverneur (WD)		Civ War	360	917			Union Gen.
Warren, Gouverneur K.	1830-1882	Civ War	145	241	456	1438	Union Gen., ALS/Cont 1, 250
Warren, Harry	1893-1981	Comp	30	45		60	Over 300 Songs. 3 Oscars. AMusQS 275-450
Warren, James	1726-1808	Rev War	128	200	540		Patriot, Merchant, Colon'l Assembly
Warren, Jennifer	1941-	Ent	10			35	Actress
Warren, Joseph	1741-1775	Rev War	6875	18000			Physician, Gen, Active Patriot. KIA.
Warren, Joseph, Sr.		Colonial	45	135	175		
Warren, Lavinia	1841-1919	Ent	60			295	Mrs. Tom Thumb, Chas. Stratton; Sig. w/Thumb 350
Warren, Leonard		Opera	75			150	Opera. Am. Baritone
Warren, Lesley		Ent	15			45	
Warren, Leslie Ann	1946-	Ent	10			48	Actress
Warren, Michael	1946-	Ent	10			35	Actor
Warren, Robert Penn	1905-1989	Author	35	50	75	85	Am. Poet, Novels. Pulitzers 1st US Poet Laureate
Warren, Russell	1783-1860	Archtct	25		165		RI Designer of Many Early Banks, Churches
Warren, William	1812-1888	Ent	15		25		Am. Char. Actor
Warrick, Ruth	1915-2005	Ent	15	20	30	80	40's Leading Lady. 'Citizen Kane'. Singer, Soaps
Warsitz, Erich	1906-1983	WWII	15	35	65	40	30s Ger. test pilot. Flight-Captain in Luftwaffe
Warwick, Dionne		Music	15			55	Singer
Warwick, Evelyn F.		Celeb	35	125			Countess. Mistress of Edward VII
Warwick, Robert R.	1587-1658	Pol		475			2nd Earl. Gov. Eng. Plantation Owners in America
Washburn, Bryant	1889-1963	Ent	15			52	Actor. Star of Silents. Char. Actor Till 40s
Washburn, Cadwallader C.	1818-1882	Civ War	37	60	70	150	Union Gen., Gov. WI 1855. War Dte. DS 225; Chk 60
Washburn, Israel, Jr.	1813-1883	Gov	20	40	65		Civil War Gov. ME; MOC; FF 39
Washburn, W. D.		Congr	10	15			MOC MN 1879, Sen. 1889
Washburne, Elihu B.	1816-1887	Cab	20	40	75		Sec. State 1869, Min. Fr.

NAME	DATES	CATEGORY	SIG	LS/DS	ALS	SP	COMMENTS
Washington, Booker T.	1856-1915	Author	301	359	662	1495	Built Tuskegee, AMS 1840
Washington, Bushrod	1762-1829	Sup Crt	108	350	630		S Chk 470
Washington, Denzel		Ent	20	40		100	AA; Actor
Washington, Dinah	1924-1963	Music	108			656	Extraordinary Vocalist. Late 40s to Early 60s
Washington, George	1732-1799	Pres	5916	17603	26800		Washington & Jefferson DS 25000; ALS/Cont 50000
Washington, George A.	1763-1793	Pres			900		George Washington's nephew
Washington, George C.		Congr	15	35	55		MOC MD 1827
Washington, Harold		Congr	20	25	35	25	MOC IL 1981, Mayor Chicago 1983
Washington, John A.	1821-1861	Civ War	155		788		CSA Lt. Col., G. Washington Nephew. Killed 1861
Washington, Martha	1732-1801	1st Lady	6112		20592		1st Lady
Washington, Ned		Comp	45			100	
Washington, William	1752-1810	Mil	65	165	315		Patriot. Gen.
Wassel, Corydon M., Dr.		Mil	45	85	150	50	Med. Missionary China. WWII Hero
Wasserman, Dale		Comp	15		35	30	'Man of LaMancha'
Wassermann, August von	1866-1925	Sci	430				Ger. Bacteriologist. Blood Test for Syphilis. RARE
Watanabe, Gedde		Ent	10			35	Actor
Waterhouse, Benjamin	1754-1846	Sci	300	765	2750		Pioneer in Small Pox Vaccination
Waterhouse, J. W.		Artist	12		50		
Waterhouse, Richard	1832-1876	Civ War	148	376	833		CSA Gen. War Dte. ALS 1050
Waterloo, Stanley		Author	10	20	35		
Waterman, F. D.		Bus	75	195			Waterman Pen
Waterman, Robert		Author	10			15	
Waterman, Waldo		Aero	15	30	35	45	Pioneer aviator
Waters, Ethel	1896-1977	Ent	55	177	128	174	Prominent Black Actress-Singer. Stage-Films
Waters, John		Ent				35	Dir.
Waters, Maxine W		Congr	10				Member US Congress
Waters, Muddy	1915-1983	Music	600			1118	Jazz Musician
Waters, Roger		Music				180	Pink Floyd; S Album 160; S Guitar 300-1000
Waterston, Robert Classie		Clergy	10	15	30		
Waterston, Sam	1940-	Ent	10	12	15	75	Actor; SP w/Ngor 120
Watie, Stand	1806-1871	Civ War	212	446			CSA Gen.
Watkins, Henry George		Expl	250		650		Youngest Arctic Expl. D. at 25
Watkins, Louis Douglass	1833-1868	Civ War	50		85		Union Gen.
Watkinson, William L.		Clergy	15	20	35		
Watson, Barry		Ent	10			40	Actor
Watson, Diane E. W		Congr	10				Member US Congress
Watson, Elkanah	1758-1842	Bus			90		Merchant/banker/promoter. Est. NY canals. Father of Country Fairs
Watson, Emily		Ent	10			45	Actress
Watson, Emma		Ent				220	Actress; 'Harry Potter'
Watson, Harold F.		WWII	10	30	45	35	Jimmy Doolittle raider
Watson, J. Crittenden	1842-1923	Mil	25	60	105		Union Naval Off. Adm.
Watson, James D., Dr.		Sci	125	270	450	350	Nobel Med. 1962. Genetics, DNA. SP w/Crick 5360-6845; SB 240-1050
Watson, James E.	1863-1948	Congr				40	Sen. IN. Majority Leader
Watson, John	1850-1907	Clergy	15		35		Presbyterian Min. -Author
Watson, Minor	1889-1965	Ent	10			75	Fine Stage-Film Char. Actor
Watson, R. J. Doc		WWII	10	22	38	30	ACE, WWII, USAAF Ace; 5 kills
Watson, Thomas A.	1854-1934	Sci	65	420	315	450	Ass't To A. G. Bell. Teleph. Pioneer
Watson, Thomas E.	1856-1922	Congr	15	35			US Sen. GA, 1904 Pres. 'I Cand.
Watson, Thomas J., Jr.	1914-1993	Bus	75	126	225	175	Developed IBM. Chmn. in Productive Growth Years
Watson, Thomas J., Sr.	1874-1956	Bus	80	210		250	Fndr. IBM; S stock certificate 295
Watt, James		Cab	10	10	20	20	Controversial Sec. Interior 1981
Watt, James	1736-1819	Sci	500	1095	2250		Scottish Inventor. Steam Engine

NAME	DATES	CATEGORY	SIG	LS/DS	ALS	SP	COMMENTS
Watt, James, Jr.	1769-1848	Sci	45	85	185		Marine Engineer. Son of Inventor
Watt, Melvin L. W		Congr	10				Member US Congress
Watt, Mike		Ent	13			40	
Watterson, Bill		Comics	125			165	Calvin & Hobbes'; SB 290-555
Watterson, Henry	1840-1921	Jrnalist	20	58	105	95	CSA Army. Ed., Pulitzer; Fndr. Louisville Courier-Journal
Watts, Charlie		Music	50			133	Rolling Stones drummer; S drumhead 120-240
Watts, George Frederick	1817-1904	Artist	62	150	255		Br. Painter & Sculptor
Watts, Naomi		Ent	15			45	Actress
Watts, Thomas H.	1819-1892	Civ War	60		460		CSA Atty Gen., Gov. AL. Sig/Rank 60, War DS 270
Waugh, Evelyn	1903-1966	Author	40	75	130	90	Brideshead Revisited'. ALS/Cont 1350
Waul, Thomas Neville	1813-1903	Civ War	95	168	368		CSA Gen.
Wavell, Archibald, Sir	1883-1950	Mil	50	158	175	65	Br. Field Marshal, Viceroy India
Waxman, Franz		Comp		228			Ger. born Comp.
Waxman, Henry A. W		Congr	10				Member US Congress
Wayans, Damon		Ent	10			42	Actor
Wayans, Keenen Ivory		Ent	10			42	Actor
Wayans, Marlon		Ent	25			75	
Wayans, Shawn		Ent	25			75	
Wayne, Anthony	1745-1796	Rev War	502	1590	1856		Mad Anthony. ADS 4500
Wayne, Carol		Ent		55	130	137	
Wayne, David	1914-1996	Ent	15	60		45	Broadway Since '38. Wide Variety Films Roles-40's
Wayne, Henry C.	1815-1883	Civ War	117	265	563	250	CSA Gen.
Wayne, Henry C. (WD)		Civ War	175	336			CSA Gen.
Wayne, James M.	1790-1867	Sup Crt	85	200	350		
Wayne, John	1907-1979	Ent	746	1455	850	1734	Actor, DS Wayne & John Ford 1, 500-2500
Wayne, Pat		Ent	10			30	Actor-Son of John
Weare, Meshech	1713-1786	Rev War	100	270			Pres. of New Hampshire Council DS 2500
Weatherhead, Leslie D.		Clergy	30	35	60	40	
Weathers, Carl		Ent	10			40	Actor
Weatherwax, Ken	1955-	Ent	115	160			Actor; Pugsley on 'Addams Family'
Weaver, Charlie		Ent				140	Actor; AKA 'Cliff Arquette'
Weaver, Dennis	1924-2006	Ent	55	115		50	Support Roles early 50s+. TV Star. SP/Arness 235
Weaver, Doodles	1911-1983	Ent	15			45	Actor; Eccentric Comedy Act. Films, Clubs
Weaver, Erasmus		Mil	35		125		Am. WWI Gen.
Weaver, James B.	1833-1912	Civ War	30		65		Union Gen., Pres. Cand.
Weaver, Robert C.		Cab	20	45		45	1st Afro-Am. Cabinet Member. Sec. HUD
Weaver, Sigourney		Ent	14	60		48	Actor
Weaver, Walter Reed	1885-1944	Mil	45	150			Extensive Aviation Career
Webb, Alexander S.	1835-1911	Civ War	58	104	153		Union Gen.
Webb, Alexander S. (WD)	1835-1911	Civ War	150	250			Union Br. Gen.
Webb, Beatrice Potter	1858-1943	Reform	45	130			Member Fabian Society. SP Pc/ Matthew Webb 375
Webb, Charles Henry		Author	10	15	30		
Webb, Chick	1905-1939	Music				455	Jazz Drummer
Webb, Clifton	1891-1966	Ent	58	35		224	Dancer-Actor. Silents in 20s-To Villain in 'Laura'
Webb, Del		Bus	15	50		50	Desert Inn Casino', Las Vegas
Webb, Jack	1920-1982	Ent	62	142		156	Radio-TV Actor. 'Dragnet' SP w/Alexander 315
Webb, James E.		Space	10			25	Adm.
Webb, Jimmy	1946-	Comp	20	35		95	Singer-Songwriter
Webb, Matthew	1848-1883	Celeb			250		Captain Webb'. 1st Man to Swim English Channel
Webb, Richard		Ent	15			50	Capt. Midnight'
Webb, Samuel B.		Rev War	115	432	645		Fndr. Soc. of Cincinnati
Webb, Sidney	1859-1947	Reform	40		125	150	Br Economist, Fabian Society. SP Pc/Beatrice 375
Webb, U. S.		Pol	10		25		California Official
Webb, W. R. 'Spider'		WWII	15	30	45	35	ACE, WWII, Ace in a Day

NAME	DATES	CATEGORY	SIG	LS/DS	ALS	SP	COMMENTS
Webbe, Samuel Jr.		Comp			175		
Webber, Andrew Lloyd	1948-	Comp	82	250		190	Br. Musical Theatre. 'Cats', 'Phantom of the Opera'; S Guitar 240-425
Webber, Robert	1924-1989	Ent	15	20		50	Actor. Versatile Lead, 2nd Lead & Char.
Weber (Joe) & Fields (Lew)		Ent	85			175	Pioneer Vaude. Comedians
Weber, Joe	1867-1942	Ent	25	35	45	45	Vintage Comedian/Lew Fields
Weber, Karl Maria von	1786-1826	Comp	375	872	1930		9 Operas. Leader Ger. Romantic & Nationalist Music
Weber, Kay		Music				115	Singer
Weber, Ludwig		Mil				50	WWI Ger. Pilot
Weber, Max	1824-1901	Civ War	45	56	90		Union Gen.
Weber, Steven		Ent	10			40	Actor
Weber, Walt		Author	10			12	Mountains to Sea Trail, mountain hiking
Webster, Ben		Music	255				Tenor Sax-Arranger
Webster, Daniel	1782-1852	Congr	108	362	645		LS/Cont 1750. ALS/Cont 2500-5000; FF 125-175
Webster, Harold T.	1885-1952	Comics	20	45		125	The Timid Soul'. 'Caspar Milquetoast'; comic 255
Webster, Jean	1876-1916	Author	15	45	135		Am. Novels. 'Daddy-Long-Legs'
Webster, Joseph Dana	1811-1876	Civ War	35	60	95		Union Gen.
Webster, Noah	1758-1843	Author	197	567	1838		Am. Lexicographer. Dictionary of Eng. Language
Webster, Paul Francis		Comp	20	50	70	45	
Webster, William		Cab	10			25	Dir. FBI
Wedekind, Erika		Opera	20		50		Opera. Legendary 19th C. Sopr.
Wedell, Jimmie		Aero	12	30	40	35	Air races 1930's
Wedemeyer, Gen. Albert C.	1896-1960	WWII	35	78	110	100	WWII US Gen.
Wedge, Chris		Ent	13			40	
Wedgwood, John H., Sir		Bus	15	25	40	35	Decorative Ceramics. Major World Prod.
Wedgwood, Josiah	1730-1795	Artist	450	1295	1890		Fndr. World Famous Wedgwood Pottery.
Weed, Marian		Opera	15			50	Opera
Weed, Stephen Hinsdale	1831-1863	Civ War	150				Union Brig. Gen., KIA Gettysburg.
Weed, Thurlow	1797-1882	Pol	15	30	62		Influential Pol. Leader NY, Journalist
Weede, Robert		Opera	10			35	Opera, Concert, Operetta
Weedon, George		Rev War	270	515	1900		Gen Cont'l Army. ALS/Cont 2500
Weeks, Anson		Band	15			45	Dancin' w/Anson. Big Bandleader
Weeks, John W.	1860-1926	Cab	15	35	70		Sec. War 1921. US Sen. MA
Weeks, Sinclair	1893-1972	Cab	10	15	35	20	Sec. Commerce 1953. US Sen.
Weems, Ted		Band	20	20	62	45	Big Band Leader-Trombone. Vocalist-Perry Como
Weezer		Music				140	Rock group
Weicker, Lowell Jr.		Congr	10	20		20	Repr. CT 1969, Sen. 1971. Watergate Committee
Weidler, Virginia	1927-1968	Ent	20			145	Actress
Weidman, Jerome		Author	10	10	20	10	
Weikl, Bernd		Opera	10			20	Opera
Weil, Andrew		Med	10			20	Med. expert; Hololistic approaches
Weill, Kurt	1900-1950	Comp	250	852	950	750	Ger-Am Opera/Ballet/Mus. Comedy/Films. AMusQS 2660
Weinberg, Steven, Dr.		Sci	25	35		30	Nobel Physics 1979
Weinberger, Casper		Cab	10	10	30	30	Sec. HEW, Sec. Defense, Sec. State
Weiner, Anthony D. W		Congr	10				Member US Congress
Weiner, Gerald A.		Bus	10			20	Businessman & scholar
Weingartner, Felix von	1863-1942	Comp	90	125	342	150	Austrian Conductor & Writer on Music
Weir, Bob		Music	25			85	Grateful Dead; S Guitar 240-1055
Weir, Julian Alden		Artist	40	135	250		Early Am. Impressionist
Weir, Peter		Ent	10			25	Movie Dir.
Weir, Robert Walter	1803-1889	Artist	50	135	288		Prof. Drawing At West Point. Taught R. E. Lee
Weircook, Henry		Mil	60				Only pilot to become an ace in both WWI & II
Weisbart, David		Ent	15			25	Dir. -Prod.

NAME	DATES	CATEGORY	SIG	LS/DS	ALS	SP	COMMENTS
Weiser, Jan Conradi	1696-1760	Pol	290	950	1600		Helped Form Iroquois-Eng. Alliance Against Fr.
Weisiger, David A.	1818-1899	Civ War	80	282			CSA Gen. ALS/Cont 1045, Sig/Rank 175
Weisman, Kevin		Ent	15			45	
Weiss, John	1818-1879	Clergy	10	15	28		Unitarian Author, Abolitionist
Weiss, Michael T.		Ent	12			48	Actor. 'The Pretender'
Weiss, Otto		WWII				80	Knight's Cross w/Oak Leaves recipient
Weissenberger, Theodor		WWII				335	WWII flying ace w/208 kills
Weissmuller, Johnny	1904-1979	Ent	191	223		289	Actor; Tarzan; Olympic Gold Swimmer
Weisz, Rachel		Ent	17			50	
Weitz, John	d. 2002	Author				35	
Weitz, Paul J.	1932-	Space	10			35	Astronaut; test pilot
Weitzel, Godfrey	1835-1884	Civ War	30	99	146		Union Gen.
Weitzel, Godfrey (WD)		Civ War	45	130	250		Union Gen. 1835-84
Weizman, Vera		1st Lady	25	80		35	Widow of 1st Pres. Israel
Weizmann, Chaim	1874-1952	HOS	382	1302	3348	923	1st Pres. Israel., LS/Cont 3950
Weizmann, Ezer		HOS	25	65			Israeli AF Gen. Pres. of Israel
Welby, Amelia		Author	450		2900		Poet. Appreciated by E. A. Poe
Welch, Herbert, Bish.		Clergy	15	25	30	35	
Welch, Jack		Bus	10			20	Ex-CEO of GE
Welch, Joseph N.		Celeb	60				TV duel w/Joseph McCarthy. Spec. Army Counsel
Welch, Raquel		Ent	45	145		134	Actress
Welch, Robert A.		Bus	25	40	82	35	Batchelor Oil Multi-Millionaire
Welch, Tahnee	1968-	Ent	10			30	Actress
Welchel, Lisa		Ent				40	Actress
Weld, Tuesday	1943-	Ent	15	45		100	Actress
Welden, Ben	1901-1997	Ent	10			35	Actor
Weldon, Curt W		Congr	10				Member US Congress
Weldon, Dave W		Congr	10				Member US Congress
Weldon, Felix de		Artist	60	85			Iwo Jima Memorial Statue
Welensky, Roy, Sir		HOS	20	55	115		
Welk, Lawrence	1903-1992	Band	10	20	35	40	Big Band Leader. TV Variety Show. SB 70
Weller, Jerry W		Congr	10				Member US Congress
Weller, Peter		Ent	10			40	Actor
Weller, Thomas H., Dr.		Med	25	35	50	30	Nobel Med. 1954
Welles, Gideon	1802-1878	Cab	88	194	306	675	Lincoln Sec Navy, LS/war-dte 775-850; ALS/war-dte 1845
Welles, Orson	1915-1985	Ent	161	1392	1775	678	AA. Actor-Dir. -Prod-Writer; Chk 500
Welles, Sumner	1892-1961	Diplo	25	75	150	55	State Dept., Ambassador
Wellington, 1st Duke of	1769-1852	HOS	270	544	397		Arthur Wellesley, LS/Cont 700, ALS/cont 1750
Wellington, George Louis	1852-1927	Congr	12	20			MOC 1895, Sen. MD
Wellman, Manly Wade		Author	35	100		60	North Carolina Literary Figure
Wellman, Walter	1858-1934	Expl	60	145	230	175	Aviator-Explr. Derigible Time Distance Record
Wellman, William A.	1896-1975	Ent		200			Dir. AA
Wells, B. H.		Mil	30	75			Am. WWI Gen.
Wells, Carolyn		Author	10	25	40	15	Sketches, Parodies, Detective
Wells, Carveth	1887-1957	Author	20	45	110	60	Explr., Author, Lecturer
Wells, Claudia		Ent	10			20	Actress
Wells, Dawn		Ent	10			46	Actress. Gilligan's Island
Wells, H(erbert) G(eorge)	1866-1946	Author	217	395	679	1265	Sci-Fi Novels, ALS/Cont 6000-10200. SB 415-750
Wells, Henry	1805-1878	Bus	258	963	2325		Wells-Fargo, Fndr. Am. Express
Wells, Henry & Fargo, James		Bus	850	958			Wells-Fargo, Am. Express
Wells, Henry & Fargo, William		Bus		1070			Wells-Fargo. Am. Express Stk. Cert. S 800
Wells, James M.		Gov	15	40			Governor LA 1865
Wells, Junior	1934-1998	Music	25			85	Blues harmonica player
Wells, Kitty	1918-	Cntry Mus	10			45	Onetime 'Queen of Country Music'. Country HOF

NAME	DATES	CATEGORY	SIG	LS/DS	ALS	SP	COMMENTS
Wells, Mary	1943-1992	Music	45			262	Motown singer
Wells, William	1837-1892	Civ War	50	75	140		Union Gen. MOH.
Wells, William (WD)		Civ War	158	240			Union Gen.
Wellstone, Paul	d. 2002	Pol	10			45	Sen. MN
Welsh, Thomas	1824-1863	Civ War	113	187			Union Gen.
Welstein (Wells), Harvey	1950-	Celeb	10			15	Gen. Manager of Chicago Radio Stations
Welty, Eudora		Author	65	167	612	100	Am. Short Stories, Novels.
Welty, Ron		Music	10			25	Music. Drummer 'Offspring'
Wenck, Walter	1900-1982	WWII	40	75	120	230	WWII Ger. Gen.
Wendelin, Rudolph		Comics	32			125	Smokey the Bear'. FDC 250, S drwg 150-300
Wendt, George		Ent	15	85		40	Actor. 'Cheers'
Wendt, Guenther	1924-	Space	15	25		40	Ger. -Am. Engr., US manned spaceflight program
Wenham, David		Ent	17			50	
Wenrich, Percy		Comp	55	125			AMusQS 175, 350
Wentworth, Benning	1696-1770	Colonial	140	470	850		Col. Gov. NH. Bennington, VT
Wentworth, John	1737-1820	Rev War	125	425	700		Colonial Governor of N. H.
Wentworth, Joshua	1742-1809	Rev War		320	975		Soldier, State Sen. NH, Decl. Cont. Congr. Appt.
Werfel, Franz	1890-1945	Author	100			350	Aus. '40 Days of Musa Dagh', 'Song of Bernadette'
Wermuth, Arthur W.		WWII	20	35	50	35	WWII Hero
Werner, Charles		Comics					Cartoon 440; sketch 235
Werner, Oskar	1922-1984	Ent	25	60	45	120	Smart, Sensitive Actor. AA Nom. 'Ship of Fools'
Werrenrath, Reinald	1883-	Opera	15		23	50	Am. Baritone. Met. Debut 1919
Wertz, Harold	1927-1999	Ent	50			95	Bouncey in the Little Rascals
Wesley, Charles	1707-1788	Clergy	188		1035		Methodist Divine. Authored Several Thousand Hymns
Wesley, John	1704-1791	Clergy	1345		2438		Methodist Fndr
Wesley, Samuel	1663-1735	Clergy	50				Father of John & Charles Wesley. AQS 580
Wessell, Vivian		Ent	20		40	75	Vintage actress
Wessells, Henry Walton	1809-1889	Civ War	40	56	105		Union Gen.
Wesselmann, Tom		Artist	50			120	
Wesselowsky, Alessandro		Opera	40			160	Opera
Wesson, Daniel B.	1825-1906	Invent	60		235		Inventor, Mfg., Gunsmith (Smith & Wesson)
Wesson, Edwin		Invent			150		Gunsmith, "Smith & Wesson"
West Wing		Ent	75			150	TV series; S script 145-690
West, Adam		Ent	10	25		45	Actor. 'Batman' TV Series; SP w/ Ward 175
West, Benjamin	1738-1820	Artist	200	779	1514		Am. Born Historical Painter, S drwg 2070
West, Dottie	1932-	Cntry Mus	15			62	Singer. Many Awards, a Few Movies, 400 Songs
West, Evelyn	1922-2004	Ent				100	Burlesque stripper turned Actress.
West, Francis Henry	1825-1896	Civ War	30	46	75		Union Gen. War Dte LS 250
West, Jessamyn		Author	12	30	35	20	Popular Novels
West, Joseph R.	1822-1898	Civ War	38	88			Union Gen.
West, Kanye		Ent	20			65	
West, Mae	1892-1980	Ent	73	177	300	238	Provocative Seductress. S Chk 150
West, Morris L.		Author	15	45	80	30	'Shoes of The Fisherman'
West, Rebecca, Dame	1892-1983	Author	20	110	135	50	Br. Novels, Critic, Historian
West, Richard L.		WWII	10			30	ACE WWII; 14 kills
West, Robert M.		Civ War		240			Dec. for Meritorious Cond. at Battle of 5 Forks
West, Roy O.		Cab	25	40			Sec. Interior 1928
West, Shane		Ent	14			41	
West, Timothy	1934-	Ent	10			35	Br. Actor
Westall, William		Artist	15	40	95		
Westheimer, Ruth, Dr.		Med	10	15	25	25	Sex Therapist. Radio-TV Personality
Westinghouse, George	1846-1914	Bus	125	359	788	350	Fndr. Westinghouse. Over 400 Patents; Chk 355
Westlife		Ent				75	Band of 5
Westman, Nydia	1902-1970	Ent	15	15	35	55	1st as Child Stage Actress. From '32 Comic Support

NAME	DATES	CATEGORY	SIG	LS/DS	ALS	SP	COMMENTS
Westminster, 2nd Earl		Royal	15	50			Robert Grosvenor
Westmore, Wally		Ent	15			50	Hollywood Makeup Dir.
Westmoreland, Wm. C.	1914-1993	Mil	30	112	167	74	Gen. WWII, Korean & Viet Nam War; SB 120-235
Weston, Agnes, Dame	1840-1908	Celeb	15			35	Philan. & temperance activist
Weston, Diane		Ent	10			25	Actress
Weston, Edward	1886-1958	Artist	35		600		Am. Western Photographer. ALS/Cont 600
Weston, Edward	1850-1936	Bus	40	125	315	75	Weston Electrical Instruments.
Weston, Logan Col.		Mil	10				Author, served WWII, Korea, Vietnam
Weston, Paul	1912-1996	Ent	18			200	Comp. -Arranger-Conductor-Pianist For Top Stars
Westover, Russ	1887-1966	Comics	25		45	75	Tillie The Toiler'; sketch 120
Westwood, Vivienne		Celeb	10			15	Designer
Wetherbee, James D.		Space	10			20	
Wettig, Patricia		Ent	10			40	Award Winning Actress-TV
Wexler, Robert W		Congr	10				Member US Congress
Weyer, Kurt		Mil	15			60	
Weygand, Maxime	1867-1965	Mil	40	75	110	150	Fr. Gen. Foch's Chief of Staff. WWI, WWII
Weyman, Stanley J.	1855-1928	Author	25	35	75		Brit. Novels
Whale, James	1889-1957	Ent	1970	3445	2792	3965	Br. Dir.: 'Frankenstein', 'Bride of Frankenstein', 'The Invisible Man'. Sketch $1200
Whalen, Grover	d 1962	Pol	10	30		15	Merchant-NYC Official Greeter
Whalen, Michael	1902-1974	Ent	15			60	Leading Man of Many 'B' Movies. 30s-40's
Whales of August		Ent				350	Signed by all four stars
Wharton, Edith N.	1862-1937	Author	205	335	913		Pulitzer, 'Age of Innocence', 'Ethan Frome'
Wharton, Gabriel C.	1824-1906	Civ War	80		294		CSA Gen. DS '64 470, Sig/Rank 125
Wharton, John A.	1828-1865	Civ War	181	564	1100		CSA Gen. Killed in Feud 4/6/1865.
Wharton, John A. (WD)		Civ War	700	900	2042		CSA Gen.
Wharton, Thomas Jr.	1735-1778	Rev War	143	1875	1482		Gov. PA, Patriot. Pres. PA 1777. Wealthy Merchant
Whately, Kevin	1951-	Ent	10			25	Br. Actor
Wheatley, Melvin E., Bish.		Clergy	20	25	35	30	
Wheaton, Frank	1833-1903	Civ War	50	70	104		Union Gen.
Wheaton, Nathaniel S.	1792-1862	Clergy	10		36		Fndr. Trinity College, Hartford, Washington Coll
Wheaton, Wil		Ent	18			55	
Wheaton, Will		Ent	20			45	Actor. 'Star Trek', 'Westley'
Wheatstone, Charles, Sir	1802-1875	Sci	100	320	565		Br. Physicist, Inventor
Wheeler & Woolsey		Ent				160	Comedy team
Wheeler, Bert	1895-1968	Ent	25			110	Comedy Team Wheeler & Woolsey. Vaude., Films
Wheeler, Burton K.	1882-1975	Congr	25	70		35	Sen. MT 1922. Progressive Party V. P. Cand.
Wheeler, Charles B.		Mil	35	125			Am. WWI Gen.
Wheeler, Earle G.		Mil	15			50	
Wheeler, Ellie		Ent	10	15	25	25	
Wheeler, Joseph	1836-1906	Civ War	104	235	244	950	CSA Gen. 'Fightin Joe'
Wheeler, Joseph (WD)	1836-1906	Civ War	295	972	1525		CSA Gen.
Wheeler, Ken		Ent	17			50	
Wheeler, Lyle	1905-1990	Ent	15	20	45	50	Film Art Dir. AA 'Gone w/the Wind' & 4 More
Wheeler, William A.	1819-1887	VP	67	140	200		Hayes VP
Whelan, Arleen	1916-1993	Ent	10		25	35	Actress. Redheaded Leading Lady. Late 30s-50's
Whelchel, Lisa		Ent	10			30	Actress. 'Facts of Life'
Wherry, William M.	1836-1918	Civ War	45	55			Union Gen. MOH
Whewell, William	1794-1866	Sci		90			1st to Measure Tides in S. Pac. To Learn of Forces
Whipple, Abraham	1733-1819	Rev War	250	750			Fired 1st Gun of Rev. on Water
Whipple, Amiel Weeks	1816-1863	Civ War	115	235	539		Union Major Gen.
Whipple, Edwin Percy	1819-1886	Author	15		30		Essayist, Critic, Lecturer
Whipple, Fred L.	1906-	Author	10	25		18	Astronomer. Rocket Research
Whipple, George H.	1878-1976	Sci	45	75	150		Nobel Med. 1934

NAME	DATES	CATEGORY	SIG	LS/DS	ALS	SP	COMMENTS
Whipple, Henry B.	1822-1901	Clergy	50	100	200		Episcopal Bishop. Reforms re Cruelty to Indians
Whipple, William	1730-1785	Rev War	645	1180	2093		Signer Dec of Ind
Whipple, William D.	1826-1902	Civ War	30	50	58		Union Gen. Sherman Aide-de-Camp. Sig/Rank 40
Whirry, Shannon		Ent	10			50	Actress; 'Exit'.
Whisner, William T.		WWII	20	45	75	50	ACE, WWII; 15. 5 kills
Whistler, James McNeill	1834-1903	Artist	240	525	1007	1150	Am. Painter, Etcher. Lived Abroad Never to Return
Whitaker, Forest		Ent	10			102	Actor; AA
Whitaker, Johnnie		Ent	10		30	40	Actor
Whitaker, Walter Chiles	1823-1887	Civ War	45	68	98		Union Gen.
White, Albert Smith		Congr	10		26		FF 26
White, Alice	1907-1983	Ent	30	45		150	Vintage Actress. Late Silents & Early Sound Films
White, Andrew Dickson	1832-1918	Educ	20	75	85	50	Co-Fndr. Cornell University, Diplomat
White, Anthony Walton	1750-1803	Rev War	75	165	250		Washington Aide-de-Camp. Gen.
White, Barry	1944-2003	Music				140	Am. record Prod., songwriter & singer.
White, Betty	1922-	Ent	10			55	Actress. 'Golden Girls', 'Mary Tyler Moore'. Emmys
White, Byron R.		Sup Crt	40	102	125	120	
White, E. B.		Author	30	178			'Charlotte's Web'
White, Edw. H. & McDivitt, J.		Space	230	495		1131	
White, Edward D.	1845-1921	Sup Crt	50	127	225	299	Chief Justice
White, Edward H. II	1930-1967	Space	298	1284	2433	1340	1st Am. To Walk In Space
White, George		Ent	40	58	75	100	Fndr. -Prod. 'George White's Scandals'
White, George Stuart	1835-1912	Mil	40		65		Br. Fld. Marshal. Ladysmith Seige
White, Horace	1834-1916	Jrnalist	25		75		Editor NY Evening Post. Corresponded/Lincoln
White, Horace	1865-1943	Gov	10	25			Gov. NY
White, Hugh		Gov	10	20		15	Governor MS 1936
White, I. D.	1901-1990	WWII	10			50	US Cmdr. in Europe
White, Jacqueline	1922-	Ent	10			40	Actress
White, Jaleel		Ent				40	Actor
White, Jesse	1917-1997	Ent	25	40		45	Char. Actor. TV 'Maytag' Spokesman
White, Jessica		Ent	13			40	
White, Jim		Expl	40		175		Discovered Carlsbad Caverns
White, Josh		Music	60			225	Am. Folk Singer
White, Julius	1816-1890	Civ War	40	55	85		Union Gen.
White, Lee 'Lasses'		Music	25				Minstrel
White, Paul Dudley, Dr.	1886-1973	Sci	30	60	75	80	Heart Specialist
White, Pearl	1889-1938	Ent	150		290	179	Queen of the Silent Serials
White, Robert, Maj.		Aero	10	25		30	'60 Speed & Altitude Records
White, Sanford	1853-1906	Archtct	100	393	680	450	Murdered By Harry K. Thaw. TLS/Cont 1, 600-5, 500
White, Stewart E.	1873-1946	Author	10	20	40	30	Am. Western Adventure Stories
White, Ted		Ent				60	Actor; 'Jason'
White, Theodore		Author	10	15	25	20	Detailed Pres. Campaigns
White, Vanna		Ent	10			40	TV Personality. 'Wheel of Fortune'
White, Vanna & Pat Sajak		Ent	15			45	'Wheel of Fortune'
White, Wallace H., Jr.	1877-1952	Congr	10	15			MOC ME 1917, Sen. 1930
White, William	1748-1836	Clergy	130	180	200		1st Protestant Episcopal Bishop
White, William Allen	1868-1944	Author	25	45	85	60	Pulitzer Journalist. 'Sage of Emporia'
White, Windsor T.		Bus	110		550		Pioneer Auto-Truck Mfg.
Whitehouse, James	1833-	Artist	25		75		Tiffany Designer-Engraver of Many Major Pieces
Whitelaw, Billie	1932-	Ent	15			45	Br. Actress. Stage 50s. Leading Lady TV, Films 60s
Whiteman, Paul	1890-1967	Music	53	85	120	124	King of Jazz. 'Rhaposdy in Blue'; AMusQS 325
Whitestone, Heather		Ent	15			40	Miss Am. 1995. Hearing impaired
Whitfield, Ed W.		Congr	10				Member US Congress
Whitfield, John Wilkins	1818-1879	Civ War	72	144	220		CSA Gen.
Whitfield, June	1925-	Ent	10			25	Br. Actress

NAME	DATES	CATEGORY	SIG	LS/DS	ALS	SP	COMMENTS
Whitfield, Mitchell		Ent	13			40	
Whitford, Bradley		Ent	10			40	Actor; The West Wing
Whiting, Jack	1901-1961	Ent	10			60	Actor
Whiting, John D.		Diplo	10		20		Jerusalem
Whiting, Margaret		Music	15			70	Pop Vocalist
Whiting, Richard		Comp	50		135	100	Top Pop & Standards. AMusQS 150
Whiting, William Henry	1824-1865	Civ War	155		250		CSA Gen.
Whiting, William Henry (WD)	1824-1865	Civ War	235		1923		CSA Gen.
Whitlam, Gough		HOS	10			20	Prime Min. Australia
Whitley, Ray	1901-	Cntry Mus	10			55	Singing Cowboy. Movies from '38. Major Sidekick
Whitman, Charles S.		Gov	10	25		15	Governor NY 1915
Whitman, Slim	1924-	Cntry Mus	10			30	Singer
Whitman, Stuart	1928-	Ent				40	Actor
Whitman, Walt	1819-1892	Author	874	2500	2916	2808	Am. Poet. Self-Ed. 'Leaves of Grass'; Chk 2500
Whitmore, James	1921-	Ent	15			68	Actor. Excellent Char. Actor
Whitney, Adeline D.	1824-1906	Author	20		35		AQS 60
Whitney, Asa	1797-1872	Bus	30		100		Promoter of Transcontinental RR
Whitney, C. V.		Bus	15	35	70	25	
Whitney, Casper		Pub	10	25	35		Publisher
Whitney, Courtney		WWII	15	40	75	35	Gen. WWII. MacArthur Aide
Whitney, Eli	1765-1825	Invent	762	2115	2952		Am. Inventor Cotton Gin
Whitney, Grace		Ent	15			45	
Whitney, Grace Lee		Ent	15	30	35	60	Actress. 'Star Trek'
Whitney, Josiah D.	1819-1896	Sci	65		275		CA State Geologist. Mt. Whitney in His Honor
Whitney, Richard		Bus	35	50			Pres. NY Stock Exchange
Whitney, William Collins	1841-1904	Cab	25	45	82	35	Financier, Cleveland Sec. Navy
Whitson, Peggy		Space	10			25	
Whittaker, Charles E.	1901-1973	Sup Crt	50	84	175	125	
Whittaker, James		Expl		90		60	1st Am. to reach the summit of Everest
Whittaker, Sally	1963-	Ent	10			20	Br. Actress
Whitten-Brown, Arthur, Sir		Aero	250	375			Pioneer Aviator/John Alcock
Whittier, John Greenleaf	1807-1892	Author	62	273	363	150	Quaker Poet. Abolitionist; poem 295
Whittle, Frank, Sir		Invent	40	425	520	112	Invented jet engine
Whittlesey, Elisha	1783-1863	Statsmn	30		75		Fndr. of Whig Party
Whittlesey, Frederick		Congr	12		45		MOC; FF 45
Whitty, May, Dame	1865-1948	Ent	35	45	85	308	Grand Old Brit. Char. Actress. 2x Nominated AA
Who, The (All 4)		Music	412			710	Rock. DS 2050
Whorf, Richard	1906-1966	Ent	15			60	Actor-Prod. -Dir.
Wickard, Claude		Cab	15	25			Sec. Agriculture 1940
Wicke, Lloyd C., Bish.		Clergy	15	25	35	30	
Wicker, Irene	1905-1986	Music	10			35	Vintage Radio's 'Singing Lady'
Wicker, Roger F. W		Congr	10				Member US Congress
Wickersham, George W.	1858-1936	Cab	15	45	75	45	Taft Atty Gen. 1909
Wickes, Mary	1910-1995	Ent	20			100	Char. Comedienne. Films 40s-70s
Wickham, William C.	1820-1888	Civ War	110	290			CSA Gen.
Wickham, William C. (WD)	1820-1888	Civ War	145	395			CSA Gen.
Wickliffe, Charles A.		Cab	30	60	95		P. M. Gen. 1841
Widmark, Richard	1914-2008	Ent	15	20	40	136	Actor
Widor, Charles Marie		Comp	30		222		Fr. Organist, Teacher
Wieck, Dorothea	1908-1986	Ent	15			45	Ger. Actress
Wieghorst, Olaf		Artist	60	225	350	180	Dean of Western Art
Wiemann, Ernst		Opera	10			20	Opera
Wien, Noel	1899-1977	Aero	25	55	105	65	Pioneer aviator in Alaska. Fndr. Wien Air Alaska
Wiere Brothers		Ent	15			50	Harry Wiere, Herbert Wiere & Sylvester Wiere

NAME	DATES	CATEGORY	SIG	LS/DS	ALS	SP	COMMENTS
Wiesel, Elie		Author	20	45	68	25	Nobel Peace 1986. Holocaust Auth; SB 160-235
Wiesel, Torsten S., Dr.		Sci	22	30	45	25	Nobel Med. 1981
Wiesenthal, Greta	1886-1970	Ent				160	Ger. dancer & choreographer
Wiesenthal, Simon		Activist	30	425	655	95	Famed Nazi Hunter
Wiest, Diane		Ent	20		35	42	Actress. AA Winner
Wigfall, Louis T.	1816-1874	Civ War	175	242	632	278	CSA Gen. CSA Sen. Sig/Rank 210
Wiggin, Kate Douglas	1856-1923	Author	60	85	140	125	Author of Popular kid's Books.
Wigglesworth, Edward	1804-1876	Editor	10		30		Harvard Law Grad. Mercantile Business. Charities
Wigglesworth, Frank		Comp					AMusQS 100
Wigglesworth, Richard B		Congr	10	10			MOC MA 1928, Diplomat
Wigner, Eugene P. Dr.		Sci	30	40	70	30	Nobel Physics 1963. Atomic Nuclei. Typescr. S 150
Wihan, Hanus		Music	30		120		Czech Viol-Cellist. AMusQS 85
Wilberforce, Samuel, Bish.	1805-1873	Clergy	30	45	60		Soapy' Wilberforce. Evol. Controversy/T. Huxley
Wilberforce, William	1759-1833	Abolit	50	145	300		Br. Anti-Slavery Pol., Philan.
Wilbur, Curtis D.		Cab	10	25	35	25	Sec. Navy 1924
Wilbur, Ray Lyman		Cab	15	25	55	20	Sec. Interior 1929
Wilbur, Richard		Author	15		35	10	US Poet Laureate. Pulitzer. LS/Cont 135
Wilburn Bros.		Cntry Mus	10			35	Teddy & Doyle
Wilcox, Cadmus M.	1824-1890	Civ War	108	234	320		CSA Gen.
Wilcox, Cadmus M. (WD)	1824-1890	Civ War	190	400			CSA Gen.
Wilcox, Ella Wheeler	1850-1919	Author	20	35	150	120	Journalist, Poet, Essayist, Daily Syndicated Poem
Wilcoxon, Henry	1905-1984	Ent	20		35	82	Actor. Important Roles/ DeMille. Supporting in Bs
Wilcutt, Terry		Space	10			20	
Wild Choir		Music	15			35	Rock
Wild, Edward A.	1825-1891	Civ War	88	171	236		Union Gen. Sig/Rank 95, War Dte DS 175
Wild, Jack	1952-2006	Ent	15			95	Actor. 'The Artful Dodger' in 'Oliver'
Wilde, Cornel	1915-1989	Ent	10	22	40	103	Actor
Wilde, Oscar	1856-1900	Author	968	2752	4994		Ir./Eng. Poet, Plays. AQS 2000-3200
Wilde, Percival		Author	20	55	110		Plays, Novels
Wilder, Billy	1906-2002	Ent	25	50	65	88	Multiple AA Film Dir. Prod. Cont. DS 285
Wilder, Douglas		Gov	10			15	1st elected Afro-Am. Governor in US
Wilder, Gene	1935-	Ent	18	40		97	Actor-Comedian. 'Young Frankenstein'; SB 60-90
Wilder, Laure Ingalls		Author	525		3025		Little House on the Prairie
Wilder, Marshall P.		Ent	15	20	30	35	Vintage Reciter, Imitator.
Wilder, Thornton	1897-1975	Author	68	180	286	155	Plays, Novels. 3 Pulitzers, ALS/Cont 675
Wilding, Michael	1912-1979	Ent	30			72	Br. Actor. Ex Leading-Man Husband Eliz. Taylor
Wilentz, David T.	1915-2008	Law	25	45		35	Prosecuted Bruno Hauptmann, Lindbergh kidnapping
Wiley, Alexander	1884-1967	Congr	15	40			Sen. WI 1938
Wiley, Harvey W., Dr.	1844-1930	Sci	80	195			Created FDA. Investigated Food Adulteration
Wilhelm I (Ger)	1797-1888	Royal	130	348	446		King of Prussia, Emperor Ger.
Wilhelm II (Kaiser)(Ger)	1859-1941	Royal	135	319	572	325	Official DS 8500. Last Emperor of Ger.
Wilhelm, August	1882-1951	Mil	120			135	Son of Kaiser. WWI Gen.
Wilhelmina, Queen	1880-1962	Royal	110		400		Netherlands. Abdicated in Favor of Juliana
Wilhelmj, August	1845-1908	Music	25				Ger. Violinist
Wilk, Brad		Music	10			25	Music. Drummer 'Rage Against the Machine'
Wilke, Robert J.	1914-1989	Ent	20			75	Actor
Wilkenson, Kendra		Ent	15			45	
Wilkenson, Tom		Ent				40	Actor
Wilkerson, Guy		Ent	25			65	
Wilkes, Charles	1798-1877	Civ War	60	121	152		Union Adm., Explr. Sig/Rank 70, War Dte. DS 180
Wilkes, Earle		Mil	10			50	
Wilkie, David, Sir	1785-1841	Artist	60	88	137		Br. Genre Paintings, Portraits
Wilkins, Geo. Hubert, Sir	1888-1958	Expl	60	228	210	55	Led Arctic & Antarctic Exped.
Wilkins, Roy	1901-1981	Activist	15	35	70	45	Sr. Statesman of Civ. Rights

NAME	DATES	CATEGORY	SIG	LS/DS	ALS	SP	COMMENTS
Wilkins, T. H.		Sci	15	25	40	20	
Wilkinson, Geoffrey		Sci	15	25	40	25	Nobel Chemistry 1985
Wilkinson, James	1757-1825	Rev War	125	342	477		Gen., Implicated In Aaron Burr Conspiracy
Wilkinson, June	1940-	Ent	10			56	Br. Actress
Wilkinson, Raven		Ballet	10			12	Ballerina
Wilks, Matthew		Clergy	15		25	50	
Will, George		Jrnalist	10			20	Pol. celebrity; Cub fan
Willard, Charles	1883-1977	Aero	15	25	100	75	Early aviator; #4 pilot's license issued to him
Willard, Edward S.		Ent	15		35	45	Vintage actor
Willard, Frances E.	1839-1898	Educ	50	231	259		Pres. WCTU Prof., Northwestern U. Temperance
Willard, Frank		Comics	35			182	Moon Mullins'; sketch 40-260; comic strip 335
Willard, Fred		Ent	10			48	Actor
Willard, John		Ent	10			25	Plays
Willcox, Orlando B.	1823-1907	Civ War	48	130	227		Union Gen. Sig/Rank 60
Willebrands, John, Card.		Clergy	30	45	65	40	
Willem I	1772-1848	Royal		692			Prince of Orange, King Netherlands
Willett, Marinus	1740-1830	Rev War	52	91	252		Off. Cont. Army. Mayor NYC
Willhelm II		Pol	150	350			Kaiser of Ger. from 1888 to 1918
William II of Holland		Royal		230			King
William III (Eng)	1650-1702	Royal	605	1609	2500		Wm. III & Mary II DS 2195. Jointly Ruled
William IV (Eng)	1765-1837	Royal	112	312	322		The Sailor King, DS 995, ALS/cont 1750
William V, Duke of Bravaria	1548-1626	Royal		850			
William, Warren	1894-1948	Ent	10	15	40	78	Am. Film Leading Man & Char. Actor
Williams, Alford J., Jr.		Aero	25	45	95	125	Navy's 1st Chief Test Pilot
Williams, Alpheus Starkey	1810-1878	Civ War	40	65	90		Union Gen., War date AES 184
Williams, Andy	1927-	Music	20	35		48	Singer
Williams, Barry		Ent	10			30	Actor. 'Brady Bunch'
Williams, Bart		Ent	10			30	Actor
Williams, Ben Ames	1889-1953	Author	15	25	40	25	Am. Novels
Williams, Bill	1915-1992	Ent	10	15		45	Actor; Husband of Barbara Hale
Williams, Billy Dee	1937-	Ent	10	25		48	Actor, 'Empire Strikes Back'
Williams, Bransby	1870-1961	Ent	75				Stage & Cinema Actor
Williams, Brian		Jrnalist	10			25	Broadcast News TV; News anchor
Williams, Charles Cootie		Music				352	Blues-Jazz
Williams, Cindy		Ent	10	40		40	Actress, 'Laverne & Shirley'; SP/Ron Howard 90
Williams, Cliff		Music	10			25	Music. Bass Guitar 'AC/DC'
Williams, Clifton C.	1932-1967	Space	175			750	
Williams, David Henry	1819-1891	Civ War	40		105		Union Gen.
Williams, Donald E.		Space	10			20	
Williams, Edward F.		Author	10			12	Civil War & Tennessee history
Williams, Edward M.		Bus	35	90	155		
Williams, Edy	1942-	Ent	10			45	Actress
Williams, Eleazer	1787-1858	Clergy	45	115	160		Am. Missionary; Author
Williams, Emyln		Author				35	Br. Plays, actor & writer
Williams, Esther	1923-	Ent	15	40		62	Actress-Swimmer-Part-Time Model. Major Star
Williams, G. Mennan	1911-	Pol	10	20		35	5 Times MI Gov., Ambass. Philippines. 'Soapy'
Williams, Geoffrey		Sci	10	20	35	20	
Williams, George H.		Cab	10	25	40		Atty Gen. 1872, Sen. OR
Williams, Gluyas	1888-1982	Comics	10		45	75	New Yorker Cartoonist; sketch 65
Williams, Grant	1930-1985	Ent	45			125	Actor
Williams, Griff		Band	25				Big Band
Williams, Guinn Big Boy	1899-1962	Ent	75			150	Actor. Starred in Many Westerns.
Williams, Gus		Ent	10			25	Showman
Williams, Guy	1924-1989	Ent	355	200		654	Actor. 'Lost in Space', 'Zorro'

NAME	DATES	CATEGORY	SIG	LS/DS	ALS	SP	COMMENTS
Williams, Hal	1938-	Ent	10			40	Actor
Williams, Hank	1923-1953	Cntry Mus	548	1352		1025	Major Country Singing Star
Williams, Hank Jr.		Cntry Mus	20	30		38	
Williams, Harland Col.		Ent				30	
Williams, Harrison A., Jr.	1919-	Congr	15	35		20	Rep. 1953, Sen. NJ
Williams, J. R.		Comics	18	25		85	'Way Out West'
Williams, JoBeth		Ent	10	15		55	Actress
Williams, Joe		Music	15			85	Jazz Vocalist
Williams, John		Comp	20	65	75	70	Conductor. AMusQS 200-800; Album 100
Williams, John Sharp		Congr	10	20		20	MOC MS 1893, Sen. 1910
Williams, John Stuart	1818-1898	Civ War	102	252			CSA Gen.
Williams, Jonathan		Author	10	15	25		
Williams, Kellie Shanygne	1976-	Ent	10			35	Actress
Williams, Kimberly		Ent	10			25	Actress
Williams, Lucinda		Music				80	Rock
Williams, Mary Alice		Jrnalist	10			20	TV News Journalist
Williams, Mary Lou		Music				230	Jazz singer
Williams, Mason		Music	10			35	Singer-Guitar Soloist-Comp.
Williams, Michelle		Ent	12			40	Actress.
Williams, Montel		Ent	10			25	Talk Show Host-TV
Williams, Nelson Grosvenor	1823-1897	Civ War	40	80			Union Gen.
Williams, Olivia	1968-	Ent	10			30	Br. Actress
Williams, Otho	1749-1800	Rev War	175	420	735		Off. Fought/Gates & Greene
Williams, Paul		Comp	10	20		35	Actor-Singer
Williams, Robbie		Music	70	95		120	Singer
Williams, Robin		Ent	22	90		52	Actor-Comedian. AA
Williams, Roger		Music	10		20	32	Pianist-Arranger
Williams, Russ		Music	10			15	DJ
Williams, Seth	1822-1866	Civ War	35	67	74		Union Gen. War Dte. LS 175, Sig/Rank 55
Williams, Tennessee (Thos L.)	1914-1983	Author	128	650	615	535	Pulitzer. 'Cat on a Hot Tin Roof' &'Streetcar'
Williams, Tex		Cntry Mus	10			60	Big Band-Singer-Leader
Williams, Thomas	1815-1862	Civ War	352				Union Gen. KIA Baton Rouge, LA
Williams, Thomas Wheeler		Congr	12		48		MOC; FF 48
Williams, Tony		Music				110	'Platters'
Williams, Treat		Ent	10			40	Actor
Williams, Van		Ent	255			275	TV's 'Green Hornet'
Williams, Vanessa		Ent	20	90		45	Miss America, singer, actress
Williams, Vaughan R.	1872-1958	Comp					SEE Vaughan-Williams
Williams, Warrene		Author	10			12	Financial, nonprofits
Williams, William	1731-1811	Rev War	200	367	771		Signer Dec. of Indepen. Statesman
Williams, William Carlos	1883-1963	Author	195	363	702	525	Am. Poet, Novels, Physician; Chk 150; SB 265
Williams, Willie, Chief		Lawman	10			25	Los Angeles Chief of Police
Williamson, Fred	1938-	Ent	10			35	Actor
Williamson, Hugh	1735-1819	Rev War		2000			Cont. Congr. Signer of the Constitution. RARE.
Williamson, James A.	1829-1902	Law	10		20		
Williamson, James Alexander	1829-1902	Civ War	36	57	80		Union Gen.
Williamson, Marianne		Author	10			10	Non-Fiction
Williamson, Nicol	1938-	Ent	10			40	Scottish actor
Williamson, Robert	1806-1859	Tex		858			TX Independence
Willich, August von	1810-1878	Civ War	40		100		Union Gen.
Willie Wonka (cast)		Ent				200	Cast of 5
Willie, David		Author	10			12	Poetry
Williiams, Roger Q.		Aero	15		25		'29 Record Non-Stop Flight
Willing, Foy	1915-	Cntry Mus	10			25	The Riders of the Purple Sage

NAME	DATES	CATEGORY	SIG	LS/DS	ALS	SP	COMMENTS
Willing, Thomas		Rev War	75	250			Banker, Continental Congress
Willis, Bruce		Ent	20	128		85	Actor
Willis, Nathaniel P.	1806-1867	Author	20	40	118		Major Editor Poetry Mags. Plays, Critic
Willis, Richard S.		Clergy	20	25	35		
Willkie, Wendell	1892-1944	Pol	35	45	60	50	Pres. Cand.
Wills, Bob	1905-1975	Cntry Mus	215	262		327	Bob Wills & His TX Playboys
Wills, Chill	1903-1978	Ent	55			116	Actor. Char. Actor. Many Western & Other Genre
Wills, Mark		Ent	17			50	
Willson, Meredith	1902-1984	Comp	88	365	635	200	'The Music Man'
Willys, John North		Bus	60	110	245	90	Auto Pioneer, Diplomat. (Originally 'Willys Jeep')
Wilmer, Richard Hooker, Bish.		Clergy	10	25	40		
Wilmot, David	1814-1868	Congr	40	75	90		Repr. & Sen. PA. ' Wilmot Proviso'
Wilson, August		Author	10	30	45	20	Dramatist, Dir., Pulitzer, Tony
Wilson, Bill W.		Celeb			2500	1322	Fndr. AA; SB 1200-4000
Wilson, Brian		Music	50	75		150	Singer-Songwriter-Prod. 'Beach Boys'; Chk 115
Wilson, Bridget	1976-	Ent	10			35	Actress
Wilson, Bridgette		Ent	15			45	
Wilson, Carl		Music	25			100	Beach Boys
Wilson, Carnie	1968-	Ent	10			30	Singer, TV host
Wilson, Chandra		Ent	15			45	
Wilson, Charles Edward	1886-1972	Bus	20	75			Pres. Gen. Electric
Wilson, Charles Erwin	1890-1961	Bus	20	35	70	30	Pres. GM., Sec. Defense 1953
Wilson, Claudius Charles	1831-1863	Civ War	338				CSA Gen., KIA Ringgold, GA
Wilson, Demond	1946-	Ent	10			40	Actor. 'Sanford & Son'
Wilson, Dennis	1944-1983	Ent	90			172	'Beach Boys'
Wilson, Dick	1916-2007	Ent	10			25	Actor; 'Mr. Whipple'
Wilson, Don		Ent	10			62	Jack Benny Announcer & Sidekick
Wilson, Dooley	1894-1953	Ent	422			672	Actor; 'Casablanca'; Sam the piano player
Wilson, E. Willis		Gov	12	25			Governor WV 1885
Wilson, Earl		Jrnalist	10	15	25	20	Powerful Synd. Columnist
Wilson, Edith Bolling	1872-1961	1st Lady	85	142	294	272	ALS as 1st Lady 350-805; WHC 260; SB 260
Wilson, Edmund	1895-1972	Author	25	85	143		Am. Critic. ALS/Cont 650
Wilson, Edmund Beecher	1856-1939	Author	350	450			Am. Biologist. Morphology, Cytology, Heredity
Wilson, Ellen Louise		1st Lady	338	420	795		1st Wife-Pres. Wilson; WHC 2885
Wilson, Flip	1934-1998	Ent	40	40		60	Comedian. 'Flip Wilson Show'. 'Geraldine'
Wilson, Francis	1854-1935	Ent	12		15	25	Vintage Actor
Wilson, Gahan		Comics	20		125	62	Cartoonist: Playboy/New Yorker. Sket 200-625; SB 125
Wilson, George W. Lt.		Celeb	15	35	120		
Wilson, Gretchen		Music	20			120	Singer
Wilson, Harold, Sir	1916-1995	HOS	38	65	110	70	Br. Prime Min.
Wilson, Heather W		Congr	10				Member US Congress
Wilson, Henry	1812-1875	VP	66	118	225	350	Grant VP. D. in Office. ALS rare as VP. FF 51
Wilson, Jackie	1934-1984	Music	239	598		450	Singer
Wilson, James	1742-1798	Rev War	325	892	7875		Scot-Born Signer, Jurist. ALS/Cont 4000. SB 2250
Wilson, James	1835-1920	Cab	25	50	95		Sec. Agriculture 1897
Wilson, James G.	1833-1914	Civ War	30		80		Union Gen. Led 4th US Colored Cavalry
Wilson, James H.	1837-1925	Civ War	72	100	160		Union Gen. Cavalry. Captured Jefferson Davis
Wilson, Joe W		Congr	10				Member US Congress
Wilson, John Lockwood	1850-1912	Congr	15	30	40		MOC 1889, Sen. WA 1895
Wilson, Joseph R.		Celeb	40		175		Father of Woodrow Wilson
Wilson, Julie		Ent	10			48	Actress
Wilson, Justin	1914-2001	Celeb	15			40	Cajun Cook
Wilson, Kemmons		Bus	20	60	80	70	Fndr. 'Holiday Inn' Chain Hotels-Motels
Wilson, Lois	1894-1988	Ent	15	15	35	40	Actress in Many Paramount Silents. Talkies to '49

NAME	DATES	CATEGORY	SIG	LS/DS	ALS	SP	COMMENTS
Wilson, Luke		Ent	10			40	Actor; Brother to Owen
Wilson, Marie	1916-1972	Ent	25	35	65	65	My Friend Irma' Early TV. Years Wiith Ken Murray
Wilson, Mary		Music	10			50	Rock, 'The Supremes'
Wilson, Meredith		Comp				153	"Music Man'; S sheet music 265
Wilson, Nancy		Music				55	Singer
Wilson, Owen		Ent	10			75	Actor; Brother to Luke
Wilson, Peta		Ent	25			88	Actress
Wilson, Pete	1933-	Gov	10	20		20	Governor CA
Wilson, Rainn		Ent	13			40	
Wilson, Richard	1936-	Ent	10			35	Actor
Wilson, Rita		Ent	15			45	
Wilson, Robert, Dr.		Sci	15	25	35	25	Nobel Physics 1978
Wilson, Sloan		Author	15	35	58	25	'Man in the Grey Flannel Suit'
Wilson, Stephanie		Ent	10			25	Actress
Wilson, Teddy	1912-1986	Music	120		175	505	Pianist-Arranger. Big Band; Am. jazz pianist.
Wilson, Tom		Comics	20			50	Ziggy'; sketch 100-200
Wilson, W. & Roosevelt, F. D.		Pres		3500			DS by both
Wilson, Whip	1911-1964	Ent				235	Actor; B Westerns
Wilson, William B.	1862-1934	Cab	10	25	50	40	Organized United Mine Workers. Sec. Labor 1913
Wilson, William Sydney	1816-1862	Civ War	35	85	98		Member of CSA Congress
Wilson, Woodrow	1856-1924	Pres	231	618	1058	489	AQS 2950, ALS/cont 3000-5000
Wilson, Woodrow (As Pres.)		Pres	410	723	5467	701	LS/Cont 2500-9500, DS/cont 4600-18400; WHC 625
Wiman, Dwight Deere		Bus	15	25			John Deere Farm Implements
Winans, Ross		Invent	85	250			RR Equipment
Winant, John	1889-1947	Gov	25			40	Gov. NH, WWII Ambassador to Britain.
Wincer, Simon	1943-	Ent	10			20	Australian film Dir.
Winchell, Paul	1922-2005	Ent	10	25	35	78	Ventriloquist; Invented artificial heart
Winchell, Walter	1897-1972	Jrnalist	30	38	45	75	Powerful Radio-Newspaper Columnist; Chk 120
Winchester, Oliver F.	1810-1880	Indust	338	850	1500		Winchester Repeating Arms, Inc. LS on Lttrhd 5850
Winchester, Wm. P. Sir, 1st Marq.		Statsmn	275	955			Elizabeth I. Lord Treas. Eng. 1485-1572
Wincot, Jeff	1957-	Ent	10			30	Can. Actor
Wincott, Michael		Ent	15			45	
Winder, Charles Sidney	1829-1862	Civ War	428	640			CSA Gen., KIA Cedar Mt, VA
Winder, Charles Sidney (WD)	1829-1862	Civ War	1555		6335		CSA Gen. 1829-62 KIA
Winder, John Henry	1800-1865	Civ War	112	297	392		CSA Gen.
Winder, John Henry (WD)	1800-1865	Civ War	160	506	470		CSA Gen. Commandant Libby & Andersonville
Winder, Levin		Rev War	15		55		Gov. MD 1812
Windgassen, Wolfgang		Opera	15			45	Opera
Windler, Martin		Space				85	Mission control
Windom, William		Cab	20	35	60	40	Sec. Treasury 1881; MOC; FF 25
Windsor, Barbara	1937-	Ent	10			40	Br. Actress
Windsor, Claire	1897-1972	Ent	20			65	Blonde-Blue-eyed 20s Silent Star.
Windsor, Duke & Duchess of		Royal	590	2500		1978	Edward & Wallis
Windsor, Edward Duke		Royal	120	1315		330	
Windsor, Marie	1922-	Ent	15			40	Actress. Many 2nd Leads & Westerns.
Windsor, Wallis, Duchess of		Royal	110	180	660	300	1896-1986. Cont. ALS 775, FDC S 150; SB 150
Winfield, Paul	1939-2004	Ent	10			45	Actor
Winfrey, Oprah		Ent	20	25	35	50	Actress-TV Host. Award Winner. Prod.
Wing, Toby	1915-2001	Ent	10	15	25	78	Vintage Film Actress
Wingate, Francis R., Sir	1861-1953	Mil	35	75	140	75	Gen. Succeeded Kitchener. Gov. -Gen. of Sudan
Winger, Debra		Ent	10	43	42	70	Actress
Wingert, Wally		Ent	15			45	
Winget, Larry		Author	10			15	
Winkler, Betty		Ent	10			25	Top Radio Performer-40's

NAME	DATES	CATEGORY	SIG	LS/DS	ALS	SP	COMMENTS
Winkler, Henry	1945-	Ent	15	15	20	51	The Fonz. SP w/Ron Howard 160; S Chk 40
Winkler, K. C.	1956-	Ent	10			50	Actress
Winner, Septimus	1827-1902	Comp	92	205	350		Wrote Many Pop Songs. AMusQS 495-1,000
Winninger, Charles	1884-1969	Ent	25		50	67	Much Seen Char. Actor 30s-50's. 'Cap'n Andy'
Winninger, Tom		Author	10			15	Leading Market Strategist
Winningham, Mare	1959-	Ent	10			40	Actress. AA Nominee
Winokur, Marissa	1973-	Ent	10			35	Actress
Winship, Blanton	1869-1947	Mil	40			125	Gen. Sp-Am & Phil. Insurrection. Billy Mitchell
Winship, Blanton	1809-1894	Pol	30			75	Orator, Philan.
Winslet, Kate		Ent	28			74	Br. Actress. 'Titanic'
Winslow, Edward	1714-1784	Rev War	35	50	90		Loyalist. Port Plymouth Collector
Winslow, Edward	1699-1753	Colonial	225	675			Silversmith. Gov. Official
Winslow, John	1753-1819	Rev War	40	65	110		Soldier, Hero, Patriot, Gen.
Winslow, John Ancrum	1811-1873	Civ War	141	242	355	506	Union Naval Cmmdr. Kersage. ALS/Cont 2415
Winslow, John F.		Civ War	130	162	225		Builder of the 'Monitor'
Winslow, Thyra Samter		Author				50	Writer, critic, & journalist; short stories
Winsor, Kathleen		Author	15	35	90	30	Novels 'Forever Amber'
Winstead, Mary		Ent	15			45	
Winter, William	1836-1913	Author	20	30	34		Drama Critic, Poet, Biographer
Winters, Dick		WWII	40	85	150	285	Band of Brothers
Winters, Jonathan		Ent	10			45	Comedian. Standup-TV-Films
Winters, Linda		Ent				40	Actress
Winters, Roland	1904-1989	Ent	35	45	85	166	Actor 'Charlie Chan'. 'Third & Last'. SP w/Victor Sen Young 455
Winters, Shelley	1920-2006	Ent	15	40	25	80	Actress; AA
Winthrop, John	1714-1779	Rev War	200	685			Physicist-Astron. Science Leader
Winthrop, John, The Younger	1638-1707	Colonial	800	1900	4750		Col. Gov. CT.
Winthrop, Robert C.	1809-1894	Congr	21	40	41		Served out Daniel Webster's Term. Spkr.
Winthrop, Theodore	1828-1861	Author	75		450		Soldier. Killed CW. Heroic CW Death. AMans 950
Winthrop, Thomas L.	1760-1841	Rev War	40	55	100		Merchant. Widely Esteemed
Winwood, Estelle	1883-1984	Ent	30	35		65	Br. Char. Actress. Often Eccentric Parts
Winwood, Steve		Music	35			100	Rock Singer; S Album 125
Wire		Ent				240	Entire S cast photo
Wire, Calvin C.		WWII	10	15	30	25	ACE, WWII; 7 kills
Wirt, William	1772-1834	Cab	40	100	155		Atty Gen. 1817. Author
Wirth, Don		Author	10			12	Fishing
Wirtz, Willard		Cab	10	10	20	15	Sec. Labor 1962
Wirz Commission		Civ War		1380			Signed by all eleven members of the Wirz Comm.
Wirz, Henry Hartmann		Civ War	603	3850	5400		CSA Cmdr. Andersonville. Only person executed for Civil War war crimes
Wisch, Teddy		WWII	110		165	60	Ger. Gen.
Wise, Henry A.	1806-1876	Civ War	73	160	290		CSA Gen. Gov., Sen. VA
Wise, Henry A. (WD)	1806-1876	Civ War	130	240	502		CSA Gen., DS/cont 3750
Wise, Ray		Ent	15			45	
Wise, Robert	1914-2005	Ent	15	65		50	Dir. 2 AA. 'Sound of Music', 'West Side Story"
Wise, Stephen S.	1874-1949	Clergy	32	88	110	125	Jewish Leader, TLS/cont 1100
Wiseman, Joseph		Ent	10			70	Actor
Wiseman, L. H.		Clergy	10	15	25	20	
Wiseman, Nicholas	1802-1865	Clergy	25	45	74		Br. Cardinal of Catholic Church. Author
Wiseman, Rosalind		Author	10			15	
Wisliceny, Gunther-Ehrhardt		WWII	25			55	Ger. SS-Panzer Div. RK
Wisoff. Peter		Space	10			20	
Wistar, Isaac Jones	1827-1905	Civ War	40	65	90		Union Gen.
Wister, Owen	1860-1938	Author	50	110	225	150	Am. Novels, 'The Virginian'

NAME	DATES	CATEGORY	SIG	LS/DS	ALS	SP	COMMENTS
Withers, Googie	1917-	Ent				40	Actress
Withers, Jane	1926-	Ent	10	20	45	78	Actress; Shirley Temple Sidekick
Withers, Jones Mitchell	1814-1890	Civ War	110				CSA Gen.
Withers, Robert W	1835-1896.	Civ War	32	45	75		CSA Col., US Sen. VA. War Dte. S 70, DS 105
Witherspoon, Jimmy	1921-1997	Music	14			65	Jazz Musician; blues singer; actor
Witherspoon, John	1723-1794	Rev War	712	2845	7500		Signer Dec. of Indepen., Active Clergy When S
Witherspoon, Reese		Ent	15	120		70	Actress; AA
Witt, Alicia	1975-	Ent	10			52	Actress
Witt, Katarina		Ent	15			45	
Wittber, Bill	1879-1970	Aero	20	50	75	80	Australian aviation pioneer
Witte, Serge	1849-1915	HOS	25	50	95	340	1st Constitutional Russian Prime Min. SP Rare
Wittig, Georg F. K.		Sci	25	50		40	Nobel Chemistry 1979
Wittman, Stephen J.		Aero			65	70	Early aviation racer pilot
Wixell, Ingvar	1931-	Opera	20			45	Opera
Wodehouse, P. G.	1881-1975	Author	62	165	186	335	Br. Novels, 'Jeeves'. SB 145
Wofford, William Tatum	1824-1884	Civ War	85	250			CSA Gen.
Woggon, Elmer		Comics	10			35	'Big Chief Wahoo'
Woidick, Franz		WWII	15			50	Luftwaffe ace
Wolcott, Derek		Author	15	25		25	Poet. Nobel Literature
Wolcott, Edward O.	1848-1905	Congr	10	25			Sen. CO 1889
Wolcott, Oliver	1726-1797	Rev War	259	485	2000		Signer Dec of Ind Gov. CT. FF Addr. Leaf 875,
Wolcott, Oliver, Jr.	1760-1833	Cab	50	134	200		Washington & Adams Sec. Treas. FF 350
Wolf, David		Space	10			25	
Wolf, Frank R.		Congr	10				Member US Congress
Wolf, Gary		Ent	10			15	Voice of Roger Rabbitt
Wolf, George (Wolfe)	1777-1840	Gov	35	90	185		Gov. PA 1829, Statesman
Wolf, Hugo	1860-1903	Comp	175		2500		Austrian; ALS/Cont 3500
Wolf, Scott		Ent	15			56	Actor; 'Party of Five'
Wolfe, Ian	1896-	Ent	10			40	Stage. Hollywood Films Mid-30s. Shady Chars.
Wolfe, James	1727-1759	Mil	1550		8250		Br. Gen. Fr. & Indian War
Wolfe, Thomas	1900-1938	Author	525	1386	2500		Look Homeward Angel'. S Chk 425-945; SB 1500
Wolfe, Tom		Author	15	40	70	35	Am. Novels
Wolfe-Barry, John, Sir	1836-1918	Civ Engr	15	30	45		London Electr. RR, Docks, Bridges
Wolff, Joseph		Clergy	35	40	50		
Wolff, Karl		WWII	100	198		190	Ger. Gen. SS
Wolff, Ludwigg		WWII				62	Ger. Gen.
Woll, Matthew		Labor	10	30	80		Lux. -Am. Labor Leader
Wolper, David	1928-	Ent	12	15	20	30	Film Prod., Executive
Wolseley, Garnet J., Visc.	1833-1913	Mil	25	60	105	90	Br. Field Marshal; Crimean War. Led Nile Exped.
Wolsey, Thomas	1475-1530	Statsmn		7800			Influential Cardinal, Statesman. Very Active
Womack, Lee Ann		Music				45	Singer
Wonder, George		Comics	20			95	'Terry & The Pirates'
Wonder, Stevie		Comp	214			237	Blind, Thumbprint Subs for Sig., S Album 265; S harmonica 575
Wong, Anna May	1907-1961	Ent	85	150	92	192	1st Major Chinese Film Star
Woo, John		Ent	10			52	Actor
Wood, Edward F. L.	1881-1959	Statsmn	15	35	50	25	Diplomat, Ambassador to US
Wood, Elijah		Ent	15			56	Actor
Wood, Evan		Ent	17			50	
Wood, Evelyn, Sir.		Mil	20		55		Br. Fld. Marshal (Boer War)
Wood, F. Derwent		Artist	10	25	60		
Wood, Fernando	1812-1881	Civ War	20	45	60		Civil War Mayor NYC. Tammany MOC. 'Copperhead'
Wood, Garfield 'Gar'		Sci	60		80	75	Boat Designer, Builder, Racer
Wood, Grant	1891-1942	Artist	200	585	750		Am. Gothic'

NAME	DATES	CATEGORY	SIG	LS/DS	ALS	SP	COMMENTS
Wood, Haydn	1882-1959	Comp	20	55	85	60	AMusQS 100-150
Wood, Henry J.	1869-1944	Comp	35	60		60	Br. Conductor. Fndr. of the 'Proms'
Wood, James	1750-1813	Rev War	60	82	132		House of Burgesses; Gov. VA
Wood, John Taylor	1830-1904	Civ War	86	189	322		CSA Cmdr. Navy
Wood, Lana	1946-	Ent	12	15	20	56	Actress. 'James Bond'.
Wood, Leonard, Dr.	1860-1927	Mil	45	121	132	205	Gen T. Roosevelt's Rough Riders.
Wood, Murray		Ent	20	80		85	Actor; Munchkin. ' Wizard of OZ'
Wood, Natalie	1938-1981	Ent	170	272		523	Am. Child & Top Adult Actress. SP/R. Wagner 524
Wood, Nigel		Space	10			25	
Wood, Peggy	1892-1978	Ent	20	35		50	Theatre & TV Award Winner. 'I Remember Mama'
Wood, Robert		Space	10			20	
Wood, Robert E.		Mil	20	70		25	Business (Sears), Gen. WWII
Wood, Robert W.	1868-1955	Sci	10	25		45	Physicist. Manhattan Project
Wood, Sam	1883-1949	Ent	40			90	Dir. -Prod. 'Goodby Mr. Chips', 'Night at Opera'
Wood, Sharon		Celeb	10			15	1st No. Am. Woman to summit Mt. Everest
Wood, Sterling Alexander	1823-1891	Civ War	128	334	550		CSA Gen.
Wood, Sterling Alexander (WD)		Civ War	150	534	1541		1823-91. CSA Gen. Wounded. Resigned 1863
Wood, Thomas J.	1823-1906	Civ War	45	76	95		Union Gen. Sig/Rank 60
Wood, Thomas Waterman	1823-1903	Artist	10	20	55		Pres. Am. Water-Color Society
Woodard, Alfre		Ent	10			40	Actress
Woodbury, Daniel Phineas	1812-1864	Civ War	80	134			Union Gen.
Woodbury, Levi	1789-1851	Sup Crt	35	80	130		Gov., Sen., Sec. Navy & Treas. (Busy Pol.)
Woodcock, Amos Walter, Gen.		Mil	10	20		25	War Crimes Prosecution Staff. WWII
Woodfill, Samuel		Mil	10	30	50	50	Major WWI, MOH Winner
Woodford, Stewart L.	1835-1913	Civ War	55	85	120		Union Gen., Led 103rd Colored Troops. Gov. NY
Woodhouse, Henry	1884-1970	Finan	65	265	375		Author. Major collector. Orig. name: Mario Terenzio Enrico Casalegno
Woodhull, Nathaniel	1722-1776	Rev War		688			"God save us all", Am. gen.
Woodhull, Victoria C.	1838-1927	Reform	125	240	510		1870's Feminist. Legalized Prostitution.
Woodring, Henry H.	1890-1967	Cab	21	45	70	58	FDR Sec. War. TLS/Cont 300
Woodruff, Judy		Celeb	10			20	Media/TV personality
Woodruff, Wilford	1807-1898	Relig	750	1500	3000		Pres. of the Mormon Church
Woods, Charles Robert	1827-1885	Civ War	34	60	92		Union Gen. Sig/Rank 55-75
Woods, Donald	1906-1998	Ent	15	20	30	50	Actor
Woods, Ilene		Ent	17			50	
Woods, James		Ent	15	15	30	45	Actor
Woods, Phil		Music	15			45	Jazz Alto Sax-Clarinet
Woods, Rose Mary		WH Staff	15		35	75	Nixon Sec. Watergate
Woods, William B.	1824-1887	Sup Crt	75	140	225	250	Also a Civil War Gen.
Woodward, Bob		Jrnalist	10	25	40	38	Broke Watergate w/Bernstein. SB w/Bernstein 150
Woodward, Edward		Ent	10			45	Br. Actor. Active in TV Series'
Woodward, George W.	1809-1875	Congr	15		25		MOC PA, Attorney, Judge; FF 25
Woodward, Joanne		Ent	15	20		72	Oscar Winning Actress; SP w/Paul Newman 200
Woodward, Marjorie	1919-2000	Ent	10			40	Actress; 40s Glamour Girl
Woodward, Robert Burns	1917-1979	Sci	20	40	78	35	Nobel Chemistry 1965
Woodworth, Samuel	1784-1842	Author	45	140	350		Wrote 'The Old Oaken Bucket'
Wool, John E.	1784-1869	Civ War	40	65	112		Union Gen., 1812 Vet., ALS'47 2000
Wool, John E. (WD)	1784-1869	Civ War	100	260	635		Union Gen.
Wooley, Monty	1888-1963	Ent				159	Actor
Wooley, Sheb	1921-2003	Cntry Mus	12			42	Actor-Singer; Co-Star 'Rawhide'
Woolf, Edgar Allan	d. 1943	Ent		215			Am. Screenwriter; 1 of 3 WOZ screenwriters
Woolf, Virginia	1882-1944	Author	580	2075	7702	4500	Br. Novels, Essayist; SB 1000-1500
Woollcott, Alexander		Jrnalist	30	95		150	Drama Critic, Actor, Essayist. Algonquin Round Tbl
Woolley, Mary E.	1863-1947	Educ	30	50	75		1st Woman Grad. Brown U. Pres. Mt. Holyoke

NAME	DATES	CATEGORY	SIG	LS/DS	ALS	SP	COMMENTS
Woolley, Monty	1888-1963	Ent	60	85		175	Char. Actor Star of 'Man Who Came To Dinner'
Woolrich, Cornell		Author	150	550			Am. Writer of Detective Fiction
Woolsey, Lynn C. W		Congr	10				Member US Congress
Woolsey, Theodore D.	1801-1889	Educ		38	75		Pres. Yale 186-1871
Woolson, Albert	1846-1956	Civ War	113	185	295		Last Surviving Union Soldier
Woolworth, Charles S.		Bus	250	1250			F. W. Woolworth's Bro. -Partner. Stk. Proxy S 1650
Woolworth, Frank W.	1852-1919	Bus	450	684	1550		Fndr. F. W. Woolworth Co. TLS/Cont 9500
Woorinen, Charles		Comp	10	20	40	40	Pulitzer, AMusQS 100
Wooster, David	1710-1777	Rev War	250	875	2638		Gen. Continental Army. Mortally Wounded
Wopat, Tom		Ent	10			38	Actor; 'Dukes of Hazzard'
Worden, Al M.	1932-	Space	25	175	175	79	Command Module Pilot Apollo 15
Worden, Hank	1901-1992	Ent	20			120	Actor
Worden, John L.	1818-1897	Civ War	196	246	315		Union Navy, Comdr. Monitor.
Wordsworth, Christopher		Clergy	20	30	35	35	
Wordsworth, William	1770-1850	Author	366	796	1625		Br. Romantic Poet Laureate. AQS 2500
Work, Hubert	1860-1942	Cab	15	30	45	50	Sec. Interior 1923
Worley, Jo Ann		Ent	10			30	'Laugh In' Comedienne
Worley, Michael		Comics					Sketch of Ren & Stimpy 120
Worth, Irene	1916-2002	Ent	10			35	Actress
Worth, William J.	1794-1849	Mil	30	75	125		Gen. Mexican War
Wouk, Herman		Author	30	120	115	62	Am. Novels; 'Caine Mutiny' Pulitzer; SB 150-300
Woulfe, Michael		Fash	10			30	Film
Wozniak, Steve		Invent	42	75	295	75	Co-Inventor of 1st Apple Computer, S drwg 1207
Wray, Fay	1907-1998	Ent	45			167	1st King Kong Heroine. 'King Kong'; SB 235
Wren, Christopher	1632-1723	Archtct	1500	6453			St. Paul's Cathedral, London.
Wren, Percival Christopher	1885-1941	Author			135		
Wright, Ambrose Ransom	1826-1872	Civ War	90	140			CSA Gen.
Wright, Bobby	1942-	Cntry Mus	10			30	Actor-Singer. 'McHale's Navy'
Wright, C. S.	1887-1975	Expl	15	35		45	Can. Mbr. Robert Scott Antarctic Exped. 1911-1913
Wright, Cobina Sr. & Jr.		Ent	40			30	Socialite-Actresses of the 40s
Wright, Edgar		Ent	13			40	
Wright, Edyth		Music	15			25	Band Vocalist
Wright, Frank Lloyd	1867-1959	Archtct	722	2093	3345	4588	ALS/Cont 4000-4750. S Chk 500-750; Wkg Draw 20560
Wright, George	1803-1865	Civ War	40		90		Union Gen.
Wright, Harold Bell	1872-1944	Author	10	20	35	25	Am. Novels & Min. 'Shepherd of the Hills'
Wright, Henry C.	1797-1870	Reform	10	20	35		Anti-Slavery Reformer-Lecturer
Wright, Horatio G.	1820-1899	Civ War	48	75	120	460	Union Gen. Sig/Rank 65
Wright, Jeffrey		Ent	15			45	
Wright, Jerauld	1898-1995	Mil	10	35		40	Navy Adm. Veteran of WWI & WWII
Wright, Jim (James Claude)	1922-	Congr	10	30		20	Rep. TX 1955, Spkr.
Wright, John J., Card.	1909-1979	Clergy	40	75	90	65	
Wright, Luke E.	1846-1922	Cab	15	45	90	35	Sec. War 1908, Ambass. Japan
Wright, Marcus J.	1831-1922	Civ War	88	160	255		CSA Gen. Sig/Rank 175-250
Wright, Marcus J. (WD)	1831-1922	Civ War	140	260	358		CSA Gen.
Wright, Orville	1871-1948	Aero	466	1213	2917	2276	TLS/Hist. Cont. 15000, S Chk 500-750; SP/1st flight 2500
Wright, Orville & Wilbur		Aero		8500		10945	1st Flight Pioneers
Wright, Richard	1908-1960	Author	70	225		375	Wrote of Suffering, Prejudice; SB 375-1400
Wright, Robin Penn		Ent	10			40	Actress. 'Jenny' in Forrrest Gump
Wright, Silas, Jr.	1795-1847	Congr	20		60		Gen, Statesman, Gov. & Sen. NY; FF 44
Wright, Teresa	1918-2005	Ent	30			118	AA for 'Mrs. Miniver'
Wright, Turbutt	1741-1783	Rev War	50	80	115		Continental Congress
Wright, Wilbur	1867-1912	Aero	1800	4500	12370	10882	Historic SP 12, 500, TLS 15,000, Chk 1930-2735
Wright, Will	1891-1962	Ent				165	Actor
Wright, William		Mil	25		125		Am. WWI Gen.

NAME	DATES	CATEGORY	SIG	LS/DS	ALS	SP	COMMENTS
Wrigley, Philip K.	1894-1977	Bus	90	100	200	125	Wrigley Gum; Chicago Cubs
Wrigley, William, Jr.	1861-1932	Bus	128	458	387	315	Fndr. Wrigley Gum Mfg.
Wu, David W.	1955-	Congr	10				Member US Congress, Oregon
Wu, Kristy		Ent	13		40		
Wuhl, Robert		Ent	18		55		
Wuhrer, Kari		Ent	19		56		
Wunderlich, Fritz		Opera	75		313		Opera
Wunsche, Max		WWII	50		231		Hitler's Adj. WWII
Wyant, Alexander Helwig	1836-1892	Artist	85		350		Of Hudson River School. Landscapes. ALS/Cont 750
Wyatt, Jane	1910-2006	Ent	15		48		Actress. Broadway. Film Leading Lady From 1934
Wyatt, Wendell		Congr	10	10		15	MOC OR 1964
Wyden, Ron		Congr	10				US Senate (D-OR)
Wyeth, Andrew	1917-	Artist	170	248	539	368	Eminent Am. Painter.
Wyeth, Henriette		Artist	75	225			Artist in Her Own Right. Sister of Andrew Wyeth
Wyeth, Jamie		Artist	80	108	225	219	Orig. Ink Sketch 260-750; SB 360
Wyeth, John A.		Med	65		250		Noted Surgeon; Author.
Wyeth, N. C.	1882-1945	Artist	265	470	766	875	Am. Painter-Illust. Classic kids Books; Sket 1170
Wyle, Noah		Ent	10		40		Actor
Wyler, Gretchen	1932-2007	Ent	10		45		Actress
Wyler, William	1902-1981	Ent	82		110		3 Best Picture Acad. Awards
Wylie, Elinor	1885-1928	Author	60	95	285		Am. Poet, Novels; SB 2340
Wylie, Philip	1902-1971	Author	15	30	60	50	Iconoclastic Author. 'Generation of Vipers'
Wylie, Robert	1839-1877	Artist	45	150			
Wyllys, Samuel	1739-1823	Rev War	15	35	45		Mil. Sec. State of CT
Wyman, Bill		Music	40		495	136	Rolling Stones Bass Guiitar; SB 125-200
Wyman, Jane	1917-2007	Ent	14	25	40	106	AA; Actress
Wyman, Willard G.	1898-1969	WWII	40	65	90	75	4 Star Gen. WWII
Wymore, Patrice	1926-	Ent	15			70	Actress-Model-Singer. Married Errol Flynn 1950
Wyndham, Charles, Sir	1837-1919	Ent	15	32	45	58	Br. Actor-Mgr, Physician, Civil War Surgeon
Wyndham, John	1903-1969	Author				845	Br. science fiction author
Wyndham, Mary, Lady	1861-1931	Ent	20			65	Stage Actress
Wyndorf, Dave		Music	18			35	Music. Lead Singer 'Monster Magnet'
Wynette, Tammy	1942-1998	Cntry Mus	25			95	Singer-Actress. Queen of Country. 50 Albums
Wynn, Albert Russell W		Congr	10				Member US Congress
Wynn, Ed	1886-1966	Ent	62	92	100	136	Vaude. Comic. Ziegfield Follies Spec'l DS 350
Wynn, Keenan	1916-1986	Ent	25	30		53	Actor-Son of Ed Wynn
Wynter, Dana	1931-	Ent	15			45	Br. Actress
Wynter, Sarah		Ent	15			45	
Wynyard, Diana	1906-1964	Ent	15			50	Br. Charming, Graceful Leading Lady 30s-40's
Wysong, Forrest R.	1894-1992	Aero	10	15	30	25	Early aviator
Wyszynski, Stefan, Card.	1901-1981	Clergy	50	65	100	190	Defied Communist Gov.
Wythe, George	1726-1806	Rev War	672	1614	4000		Signer. ALS/War Dte. 7500. Historic DS 7900
Xenakis, Iannis	1922-	Comp	75			175	Greek Comp.
Xenia, Alexandrova	1875-1960	HOS	75		412		Russia. Grand Duchess. Sister of Nicholas II
X-Files		Ent				100	Cast SP
Yadin, Yigael		Sci		55			War Hero. World Famous Archaelogist
Yale, Brian		Ent	10			22	Music. Bass Guitar 'Matchbox 20'
Yale, Elihu	1648-1721	Statsmn			5000		Benefactor of Yale University
Yalkovsky, Isabelle		Music				65	Pianist
Yalow, Rosalyn S.		Sci	15	35	50	35	Nobel Med. 1972
Yamamoto Mission Suvivors		WWII				364	
Yamamoto, Isoroku, Adm.		WWII	150	295	625	625	Led Pearl Harbor Attack, 12/7/1941
Yamanashi, Hanzo		Mil	95	265			
Yamasaki, Minoru	1912-1986	Archtct	10	25	60	25	Am. Architect. Designed World Trade Center

NAME	DATES	CATEGORY	SIG	LS/DS	ALS	SP	COMMENTS
Yamashiro, Katsumari		WWII	100			380	Autograph Manuscript 950; Collided w/PT-109 (JFK)
Yamashita, Tomoyuki	1883-1946	Mil	150	502	460	885	Jap. Gen. Hanged for war crimes
Yancey, William Lowndes		Congr	20				MOC; FF 85
Yang, Chen N.		Sci	15	20	35	20	Nobel Physics 1957
Yang, Y. C.		Diplo	10			20	Ambassador to Repub. of Korea
Yankovic, Frankie	1915-1998	Music	10			30	Slovenian-Am. accordionist
Yankovic, Weird Al		Ent	10			25	Comedian
Yanni		Music	25			60	Singer
Yarbrough, Cedric		Ent	15			45	
Yardbirds		Music	532			602	Rock Group. Special SP 2171; S Guitar 240-1140
Yarnell, Bruce	1935-1973	Ent				50	Actor; Baritone roles at San Francisco Opera
Yarnell, Celeste		Ent				95	Actress; 'Star Trek'
Yarnell, Harry E.	1875-1959	Mil	40	75		60	Adm. Fleet Cmdr.
Yarnell, Lorene	1948-	Ent	10			35	Shields & Yarnell; actress; dancer
Yarrow, Ernest A.		Clergy	15	20	25		
Yarwood, Mike		Celeb	10			15	Impressionist
Yasuhito, Chichibu Prince		Royal				800	
Yates, Edmund	1831-1894	Author	15	25	40		Br. Journalist-Novels, Editor
Yates, George W.	1843-1876	Mil		862			Capt'n 7th Cavalry Little Big Horn
Yates, Peter W.	1747-1826	Rev War	50	120	175		Continental Congress
Yates, Richard	1815-1873	Civ War	25	40	60		Civil War Governor IL 1861
Yaw, Ellen Beach		Opera	30			200	Am. Sopr.
Yeager, Chuck	1923-	WWII	45	50	85	270	Ace, WWII, Pioneer, Test Pilot, Broke Sound
Yeager, Jeana		Aero	15	30			
Yeager, Jeana & Dick Rutan		Aero	75	100		105	Voyager
Yearwood, Trisha		Cntry Mus	10			52	Singer
Yeates, Jasper	1745-1817	Rev War	25	45	60		Jurist
Yeats, Jack Butler		Artist	25	60	150		Brother of Wm. Butler Yeats
Yeats, Wm. Butler	1865-1939	Author	380	1439	2739	3350	Nobel Poet, Dramatist; Abbey Theatre; SB 625
Yeltsin, Boris		HOS	248	428		482	Russia
Yen, C. K.		HOS	50	175			Pres. Repub. China
Yen, Hulda		Aero		225			Chinese aviatrix
Yeoh, Michelle		Ent	10			85	Actress; SP w/ Bronson 115-180
Yerby, Frank G.	1916-1991	Author	35	60	80	70	Novels
Yerkes, Charles T.		Bus	35	100			Capitalist. TLS/Cont 450
Yes		Music	45			120	Rock DS 125. S by all 5 1984; album S 150-450
Ying, Ye		Ent	10			20	Prod.
Yoakam, Dwight		Cntry Mus				45	C W Singer
Yogananda, Paramhansa		Relig			495		Yoga
Yon, Pietro A.	1886-1943	Comp	25				Ital-Am. 'Gesu Bambino' AMusQS 195
Yorgesson, Yogi		Cntry Mus	10			20	
York, Alvin, Sgt.	1887-1964	Mil	219	399	575	522	MOH WWI; SB 310; Chk 240-400
York, Dick	1928- 1992	Ent	85			125	Darrin on Bewitched 1964-69
York, Michael		Ent	10			40	
York, Susanna	1941-	Ent	10			35	Br. Actress
York, Zebulon	1819-1900	Civ War	110				CSA Gen.
Yorty, Sam	1909-1998	Pol	15	20		15	MOC. CA, Mayor L. A. Unsuccessful Pres. Cand.
Youmans, Vincent		Comp	55	165	255	150	'Tea for Two.' AMusMS 800
Young Rascals		Music				225	Rock group; S Album 125-425
Young, Alan	1919-	Ent	10	15	20	55	Early TV Comedian. 'Mr Ed';. 'Alan Young Show'
Young, Andrew		Pol	10	20	35	25	Mayor Atlanta
Young, Angus		Music	25			130	Lead Guitarist AC/DC. S Pickgrd 260; Guitar 2380
Young, Ann Elizabeth		Celeb	125				One of Brigham Young's Plural Wives
Young, Art		Comics	20		70	125	Pol. Cartoonist

NAME	DATES	CATEGORY	SIG	LS/DS	ALS	SP	COMMENTS
Young, Brigham	1801-1877	Clergy	670	1878	4450	3738	Morman Leader. Rare DS 8500
Young, Burt		Ent	10			35	Actor
Young, Charles Augustus		Sci	35	140	225		Am. Astronomer, Author
Young, Charles Wm. (Bill)		Congr	10				Member US Congress
Young, Chic	1901-1973	Comics	35	145		100	5 Orig. Pcs. S for WWII Cartoons. 2000; Sket 460
Young, Clara Kimball	1890-1960	Ent	45			75	Vintage Stage Actress
Young, Coleman		Pol	10	15		20	Mayor of Detroit
Young, Dean		Comics	25				Dagwood'. Orig. Strip 130-275
Young, Don Y		Congr	10				Member US Congress
Young, Faron	1932-1996	Cntry Mus	10			40	Singer
Young, Gig	1913-1978	Ent	60	60	70	146	Actor; AA:
Young, Henry E.		Civ War	25	45	70		CSA Major, Judge Advocate
Young, John		Space	62	272		438	Moonwalker. Apollo 16, Shuttle Cmdr.
Young, John		Congr	15	25	45		Rep. NY 1836
Young, Leste ' Prez'		Music	250	350		2030	Blues-Jazz; tenor sax
Young, Loretta	1913-2000	Ent	80			222	Actress. AA & Emmy
Young, Lyman		Comics	10			50	Tim Tyler's Luck
Young, Malcolm		Music	10			25	Music. Rhythm Guitar 'AC/DC
Young, Neil		Music	50	65		140	SB $500; S Album $125; S Guitar $500-1000
Young, Owen D.	1874-1962	Bus	15	25	50	20	CEO GE. Financier, Law, Advisor to Pres.
Young, Pierce Manning Butler	1836-1896	Civ War	133	156	300		CSA Gen. S War Dte. 155, DS 350
Young, Richard		Photog	10			20	Photographer
Young, Robert	1907-1998	Ent	15	35	35	62	Actor. 'Father Knows Best', 'Marcus Welby'
Young, Roland	1887-1953	Ent	50			115	Br. Actor; Remembered for 'Topper'
Young, Samuel B. M.	1840-1924	Civ War	46	65	91		Union Gen. Bvt.
Young, Sean		Ent	15	20		40	Actress
Young, Thomas L.	1832-1888	Civ War	30		65		Union Brevet Brig. Gen.
Young, Trummy		Music	25			145	Jazz Musician
Young, Vince		Ent	15			44	
Young, Whitney		Activist	10	20	45	20	Am. Civ. Rights Leader. Author
Young, William Hugh	1838-1901	Civ War	90				CSA Gen.
Youngdahl, Luther		Gov	10	15		10	Governor MN 1947
Younger, Bob	1853-1889	Crime	2500				Fought/Quantrill. D. in Prison. Bro: Cole, Jim, John
Younger, Thomas C. (Cole)	1844-1946	Crime	2763	4232	11250		Bank Robber. Jesse James Gang; sig w/ Jim 3570
Youngman, Henny	1906-1998	Ent	20	25	30	55	Club & TV Comedian.
Youssapoff, Felix Prince		Royal			450		Plotted to assassinate Rasputin
Ysaye, Eugene-Auguste	1858-1931	Comp	60			178	Belg. Violin Virtuoso, Conductor. AMusQS 100-120
Yudenich, Nikolay N.		Mil	95				Rus. Gen. Russo-Jap. & WWI
Yukawa, Hideki		Sci	35	45	70		Nobel Physics 1949
Yulee, David Levy	1810-1886	Civ War	45		140		CSA Congress
Yun Phat, Chou	1955-	Ent	30			90	Actor
Yun, Isang	1917-	Comp			80	150	Korean Born. Kidnapped by S. Korean Agents
Yune, Rick		Ent				60	Actor
Yung, Victor Sen		Ent	117			150	Actor; Hop Sing on 'Bonanza'
Yunge, Traudl		WWII	35				Hitler's Pers'l Sec. End of WWII
Yurka, Blanche	1886-1974	Ent	30		40	98	Hamlet/Barrymore
Yusupov, Felix		Royal			350	600	
Yutang, Lin		Author	50	165			Chin. Novels, Philosophy, Plays
Yvon, Adolphe	1817-1893	Artist			92		Painter
Zabeleta, Nicanor		Opera	40			150	Opera
Zablocki, Clement John		Congr	10			20	Rep. WI 1949
Zabriskie, Andrew C.		Bus	35		140		Capitalist, Financier
Zadora, Pia		Ent	10			50	Actress
Zaharoff, Basil	1850-1936	Bus	75			1495	Arms trader/financier. Dir./Chmn. of Vickers, WWI

NAME	DATES	CATEGORY	SIG	LS/DS	ALS	SP	COMMENTS
Zahn, Steve		Ent	10			40	Actor
Zahn, Timothy		Author	10			35	Star Wars Trilogy
Zais, Melvin		Mil	10	20	35	35	
Zajic, Dolora		Opera	10			25	Opera
Zamboni, Maria		Opera	40			200	Opera
Zancanaro, Giorgio		Opera	10			30	Opera
Zandonai, Riccardo	1883-1944	Comp		60		195	Opera
Zane, Billy		Ent	15			40	Actor; 'Phantom' Cast of 100+. 'Titanic'
Zangwill, Israel	1864-1926	Author	40	72	78	125	Br. Plays, Novels, Poet, Journalist
Zanuck, Darryl F.	1902-1979	Ent	52	215		141	Prod. Co-Fndr. 20th C. Fox
Zanuck, Richard Darryl		Ent	10		20	25	Film Prod., Exec.
Zapata, Emiliano	1879-1919	Revol	500	1170	1625		Mex. Guerilla Leader
Zappa, Frank	1940-1993	Music	182	235		295	SP w/Mothers of Invention $260; S Album $350
Zapruder, Abraham		Celeb	40				Filmed JFK Assassination in 8mm
Zaragoza, Ignacio	d. 1862	Mil		235			Mexican Gen.
Zaslow, Jeffery		Jrnalist	10			20	Senior writer & columnist for Wall Street Journal
Zavodszky, Zoltan		Opera	30			85	Opera
Zeani, Virginia		Opera	15			45	Opera
Zeeman, Pieter	1865-1943	Sci	200		975		Nobel for Physics 1902. Dutch Physicist
Zefferelli, Franco	1923-	Ent	12			35	Film Dir.
Zelenski, Wladyslaw		Comp	50		150		Polish Music Teacher
Zell, Harry von		Ent	10	15	25	25	Radio Announcer-Comedian-Jack Benny Sidekick
Zellerbach, James D		Bus	15	40	85	35	US Ambassador, Industrialist
Zellweger, Renee		Ent	10			71	Actress; AA:
Zelnick, Bob		TV News	10			20	News corres. Prof. Nat/Intl Affairs, Boston U.
Zeman, Jacklyn	1953-	Ent	10			52	Gen. Hospital
Zemekis, Robert		Ent	10	15		25	Film Dir.
Zemke, Hubert Hub		WWII	15	35	65	40	ACE, WWII, Triple Ace; 17.75 kills
Zemlinsky, Alexander		Comp	90	265			Aus. Conductor
Zenatello, Giovanni		Opera	45		65	125	Opera
Zeppelin, Ferdinand, Graf von		Aero	200	538	841	2350	1838-1917. Inventor Dirigible Air Ship
Zerbe, Anthony	1936-	Ent	10		25	45	Actor
Zeta-Jones, Catherine		Ent	60			145	Actress; AA winner
Zetland, 2nd Earl, Thos. L.	1795-1873	Pol	60	90	120		Freemason Untd Grnd Lodge of Eng. Grand Master 1844-70
Zetterling, Mai	1925-1994	Ent	15			50	Actress
Zhukov, Georgi K.	1896-1974	Mil	225	382	492	450	Rus. Marshal. Soviet Hero WWII., DS/cont 1207
Ziegfeld, Florenz	1869-1931	Ent	150	221	458	417	Am. Vaud. Prod. Famous 'Follies', ALS/Cont 950
Ziegler, George M.	1834-1912	Civ War	35	40	60		Union Gen., Bvt.
Ziegler, Karl		Sci	45	65	70	55	Nobel Chemistry 1969
Ziegler, Ronald L.	d. 2002	WH Staff	10	20	25	20	White House Aide. Nixon Press Sec.
Ziegler, Vincent C.		Bus	10			10	CEO Gillette Safety Razor Co.
Ziering, Ian		Ent	10			40	Actor; 'Beverly Hills 90210'
Ziering, Nikki	1971-	Ent				45	Model; actress
Zilli, Aldo		Celeb	10			15	Chef
Zimbalist, Efrem, Jr.	1918-	Ent	15		40	53	Actor. Leading Man Films. Early TV Leads
Zimbalist, Efrem, Sr.		Music	45			265	Violinist, Comp.
Zimbalist, Stephanie		Ent	10			60	Actress
Zimmer, Constance		Ent	18			55	
Zimmer, Hans		Comp				58	AA
Zimmer, Norma		Ent	10			20	Early TV Vocalist for Lawrence Welk
Zimmerman, Tabea		Music				65	Ger. Violinist
Zindel, Paul		Author	10	20		25	Plays
Zinnemann, Fred	1907-1997	Ent	20		35	145	AA Film Dir.

NAME	DATES	CATEGORY	SIG	LS/DS	ALS	SP	COMMENTS
Zinoviev, Grigori E.	1883-1936	Pol			575		Soviet Communist leader, purged by Stalin
Ziolkowski, Korczak		Artist	15	35	65	40	SB 145
Zmed, Adrian		Ent	10			35	Actor
Zog I		Royal	40			750	King Albania
Zola, Emile	1840-1902	Author	138	275	462	2070	Fr. Novels & Social Reformer
Zollicoffer, Felix K.	1812-1862	Civ War	280	382	561		CSA Gen.
Zollicoffer, Felix K. (WD)	1812-1862	Civ War	575	1750			CSA Gen. KIA
Zombie, Rob		Music	10			50	White Zombie Lead Singer
Zombie, Sheri		Ent	15			45	
Zook, Samuel K. (WD)	1823-1863	Civ War			4250		Union Brig. Gen.
Zook, Samuel Kosciusko	1821-1863	Civ War	188	1859	2475		Union Gen., KIA Gettysburg
Zorina, Vera	1917-2003	Ballet	20			57	Ballerina, Films, Stage
zu Guttenberg, Enoch		Cond				50	Ger.
Zuazo, Hernan Siles		HOS	10	15	25	15	
Zucco, George	1886-1960	Ent	231			1330	Br. Actor
Zucherman, Pinchas		Music	10			65	Violinist
Zukoffsky, Louis		Author	25		80	50	Am. Poet
Zukor, Adolph	1873-1976	Ent	50	90	200	220	Fndr. Paramount. Pioneer Film Prod.
Zuloaga, Ignacio		Artist	25	75			Sp. Painter
Zumwalt, Elmo R., Jr.	1920-2000	WWII	20	30	55	60	Bud'. Adm. WWII
Zuniga, Daphne	1962-	Ent	10			40	Actress
Zweig, Arnold		Author	25	65		50	Ger. Novels, Plays
Zweig, Stefan	1881-1942	Author	30	200	600	80	Aus. Psychoanalytical Biogr.
Zweigert, Eugen, Lt.		WWII	100				Ger. ACE WWII
Zwick, Ed		Ent	18			55	
Zwicky, Fritz		Sci	20	35			Am. Astronomer. Jet Propulsion
Zworykin, Vladimir		Sci	70	250	230	195	Am. Inventor TV System. Father of Am. TV
ZZ Top		Music	75			185	Rock Band, S Album 125-250; S Guitar 425-700

Sports Autograph Prices

Prices for Baseball, Basketball, Football, Hockey and Boxing
are for independently authenticated and certified material.
Prices for Formula One, Golf, NASCAR and Tennis are for
items that may or may not be independently authenticated,
but are unquestionably genuine.

Baseball

PLAYER	HOF	DIED	SIG	LETTER	SP	SIGNED BALL	SIGNED BAT
Aaron, Hank	1982		50	175	70	90	200
Adcock, Joe		1999	12	50	25	60	100
Alexander, Grover	1938	1950	900	2,000	3,500	10,000	-
Allen, Dick			15	100	25	50	60
Allen, Mel	1978		30	100	50	125	-
Alomar, Roberto			20	75	35	40	100
Alou, Felipe			10	75	20	35	50
Alou, Moises			10	100	25	55	125
Alston, Walter	1983	1984	50	150	100	600	-
Amoros, Sandy		1992	30	150	50	125	200
Anderson, Garret			10	75	20	50	100
Anderson, Sparky	2000		10	75	20	35	80
Anson, Cap	1939	1922	2,000	2,500	-	35,000	-
Aparicio, Luis	1984		20	150	25	40	80
Appling, Luke	1964	1991	12	100	25	100	250
Ashburn, Richie	1995	1997	20	125	30	85	175
Averill, Earl	1975	1983	15	150	60	800	-
Bagwell, Jeff			20	100	30	55	125
Baines, Harold			10	50	15	35	50
Baker, Dusty			10	75	20	35	50
Baker, Frank "Home Run"	1955	1963	400	1,500	1,250	3,500	-
Bancroft, David	1971	1972	125	500	400	1,800	-
Banks, Ernie	1977		25	200	40	50	125
Barlick, Al	1989	1995	12	150	30	40	75
Barrow, Edward	1953	1953	200	150	500	3,500	-
Bauer, Hank			12	75	15	25	40
Baylor, Don			10	50	15	25	40
Beckley, Jacob "Jake"	1971	1918	5,000	10,000	-	-	-
Bell, Gus		1995	35	75	75	125	200
Bell, James "Cool Papa"	1974	1991	35	250	65	500	-
Beltran, Carlos			20	100	40	55	125
Beltre, Adrian			15	100	25	55	125
Bench, Johnny	1989		25	150	30	45	125
Bender, Chief	1953	1954	400	750	1,000	5,000	-
Berg, Moe		1972	275	1,000	800	3,500	-
Berkman, Lance			10	50	20	50	100
Berra, Lawrence "Yogi"	1972		25	150	40	55	125
Biggio, Craig			10	75	20	35	100
Blue, Vida			5	35	15	25	40
Blyleven, Bert			15	75	20	30	60
Boggs, Wade	2005		30	150	40	40	125
Bonds, Barry			75	250	125	300	500
Bonds, Bobby		2003	25	125	40	30	75
Bottomley, Jim	1974	1959	500	1,500	1,000	4,500	-
Boudreau, Lou	1970	2001	12	50	25	35	-
Bouton, Jim			8	40	15	25	40
Bowa, Larry			5	35	12	25	40
Boyer, Clete			10	35	15	25	40
Boyer, Ken		1982	65	250	300	500	800
Branca, Ralph			8	30	15	25	40
Bresnahan, Roger	1945	1944	1,000	3,000	3,500	5,000	-
Brett, George	1999		35	150	50	65	150
Brock, Lou	1985		25	250	30	45	100
Brouthers, Dan	1945	1932	4,000	-	-	-	-

Baseball

PLAYER	HOF	DIED	SIG	LETTER	SP	SIGNED BALL	SIGNED BAT
Brown, Bobby			12	30	30	25	50
Brown, Kevin			20	100	30	35	90
Brown, Mordecai "3 Finger"	1949	1948	750	1,500	1,800	4,500	-
Brown, Ray	2006	1965	5,000	-	-	-	-
Brown, Willard	2006	1996	1,000	2,000	2,500	4,000	-
Buckner, Bill			12	50	20	25	60
Buehrle, Mark			10	50	15	55	125
Bulkeley, Morgan	1937	1922	1,000	1,500	-	-	-
Bunning, Jim	1996		15	75	25	40	70
Burdette, Lew			10	40	20	25	50
Burgess, Smoky			20	100	50	100	125
Burkett, Jesse	1946	1953	1,000	4,000	3,000	15,000	-
Campanella, Roy	1969	1993	800	2,000	2,000	6,000	2,500
Campaneris, Bert			5	50	15	30	50
Canseco, Jose			15	150	35	30	100
Carew, Rod	1991		20	300	35	40	100
Carey, Max	1961	1976	25	150	75	1,300	-
Carlton, Steve	1994		20	100	35	45	100
Carter, Gary	2003		25	100	30	50	75
Carter, Joe			10	100	15	40	85
Cartwright, Alexander	1938	1892	1,200	2,000	-	-	-
Carty, Rico			10	40	20	30	50
Cash, Norm		1986	50	300	150	400	250
Cepeda, Orlando	1999		15	85	30	40	100
Chadwick, Henry	1938	1908	2,500	4,000	-	-	-
Chance, Frank	1946	1924	5,000	15,000	-	15,000	-
Chandler, Albert "Happy"	1982	1991	25	75	50	150	200
Charleston, Oscar	1976	1954	5,000	9,000	-	-	-
Chavez, Eric			10	50	25	55	125
Chesbro, Jack	1946	1931	4,000	7,500	8,000	-	-
Chylak, Nestor	1999		300	800	700	2,500	-
Cicotte, Ed		1969	375	1,000	900	2,000	-
Clark, Will			15	75	25	30	80
Clarke, Fred	1945	1960	250	500	750	2,000	-
Clarkson, John	1963	1909	5,000	-	-	-	-
Clemens, Roger			50	250	75	125	200
Clemente, Roberto	1973	1972	850	1,750	1,500	7,000	3,500
Cobb, Ty	1936	1961	800	2,000	1,750	9,000	25,000
Cochrane, Mickey	1947	1962	350	750	650	2,750	-
Colavito, "Rocky"			15	100	35	35	100
Collins, Edward	1939	1951	400	500	1,500	3,500	-
Collins, Jimmy	1945	1943	3,000	7,500	7,500	-	-
Combs, Earle	1970	1976	85	400	275	1,500	-
Comiskey, Charles	1939	1931	700	1,500	2,500	-	-
Concepcion, Dave			10	75	20	35	50
Cone, David			25	100	40	50	75
Conigaliaro, Tony		1990	80	300	200	700	500
Conlan, Jocko	1974	1989	20	75	40	175	250
Connolly, Tom	1953	1961	500	1,000	1,200	2,700	-
Connor, Roger	1976	1931	5,000	-	-	-	-
Connors, Chuck		1992	30	150	60	100	150
Cooper, Andy	2006		3,000	-	-	-	-
Coveleski, Stan	1969	1984	20	150	60	500	-
Cox, Bobby			15	75	30	35	60

Baseball

PLAYER	HOF	DIED	SIG	LETTER	SP	SIGNED BALL	SIGNED BAT
Crawford, Sam	1957	1968	250	450	750	2,500	-
Cronin, Joe	1956	1984	40	150	75	1,000	-
Crosetti, Frank		2002	15	100	30	60	150
Cummings, William "Candy"	1939	1924	5,000	-	-	-	-
Cuyler, Hazen "Ki Ki"	1968	1950	600	1,500	1,500	5,000	-
Dandridge, Ray	1987	1994	25	250	50	100	225
Davis, George	1998	1940	10,000	25,000	-	-	-
Dawson, Andre			10	75	30	35	90
Day, Leon	1995	1995	50	300	50	125	200
Dean, Dizzy	1953	1974	175	500	500	1,300	-
Delahanty, Ed	1945	1903	7,500	15,000	-	-	-
Delgado, Carlos			20	75	40	40	85
Dent, Bucky			10	40	15	25	50
Dickey, Bill	1954	1993	35	200	60	250	350
Dihigo, Martin	1977	1971	1,500	3,500	2,500	2,500	-
DiMaggio, Dom			20	100	25	40	70
DiMaggio, Joe	1955	1999	150	1,200	200	375	2,500
DiMaggio, Vince		1986	50	300	150	700	400
Doby, Larry	1998	2003	25	150	30	35	100
Doerr, Bobby	1986		8	75	20	30	70
Dryfuss, Barney	2008		-	-	-	-	-
Drysdale, Don	1984	1993	35	200	75	150	225
Duffy, Hugh	1945	1954	500	1,000	800	3,000	-
Durocher, Leo	1994	1991	30	200	50	175	250
Dykstra, Len			15	100	15	30	75
Eckersley, Dennis	2004		20	100	25	35	80
Edmonds, Jim			15	100	40	60	100
Ennis, Del		1996	15	100	30	75	75
Erskine, Carl			8	40	15	25	40
Evans, Billy	1973	1956	400	450	900	3,000	-
Evans, Darrell			8	50	20	30	60
Evans, Dwight			10	75	20	30	60
Evers, Johnny	1946	1947	900	1,500	1,750	10,000	-
Ewing, Buck	1939	1906	3,000	-	-	-	-
Faber, Red	1964	1976	100	500	175	1,500	-
Feller, Robert	1962		10	75	20	25	60
Ferrell, Rick	1984	1995	12	100	30	60	125
Fidrych, Mark			10	75	20	30	75
Fielder, Cecil			25	125	30	50	80
Fingers, Rollie	1992		15	100	30	35	75
Fisk, Carlton "Pudge"	2000		35	150	40	45	125
Flick, Elmer	1963	1971	75	300	250	2,000	-
Flood, Curt		1997	50	200	75	275	350
Ford, Whitey	1974		20	150	40	50	100
Foster, Andrew "Rube"	1981	1930	5,000	10,000	-	-	-
Foster, George			10	75	15	30	75
Foster, Willie	1996	1978	2,000	-	-	-	-
Fox, Nellie	1997	1975	200	750	400	3,000	500
Foxx, Jimmie	1951	1967	700	2,000	2,000	20,000	-
Frick, Ford	1970	1978	45	150	175	1,600	-
Frisch, Frankie	1947	1973	65	250	175	2,000	-
Furillo, Carl		1989	40	150	85	350	250
Galarraga, Andres			10	75	25	35	85
Galvin, Jim	1965	1902	4,000	-	-	-	-

PLAYER	HOF	DIED	SIG	LETTER	SP	SIGNED BALL	SIGNED BAT
Garagiola, Joe			8	50	20	30	75
Garcia, Mike		1986	30	200	125	400	500
Garciaparra, Nomar			20	150	60	75	150
Garvey, Steve			10	75	20	20	50
Gehrig, Lou	1939	1941	3,000	8,500	8,500	32,000	37,500
Gehringer, Charlie	1949	1993	20	125	25	100	300
Giambi, Jason			25	150	50	50	125
Gibson, Bob	1981		25	250	35	45	100
Gibson, Josh	1972	1947	6,000	-	15,000	33,000	-
Gibson, Kirk			10	75	20	30	75
Giles, Warren	1979	1979	45	125	250	1,200	-
Gilliam, Jim		1978	75	250	150	2,000	-
Glavine, Tom			25	125	35	40	100
Gomez, Lefty	1972	1989	25	150	75	250	250
Gonzalez, Juan			15	125	30	45	80
Gooden, Dwight			30	200	45	50	100
Gordon, Joe			60	250	225	800	800
Goslin, Goose	1968	1971	175	500	500	2,500	-
Gossage, Rich	2008		12	75	20	25	50
Grace, Mark			15	75	35	40	90
Grant, Frank	2006	1937	-	-	-	-	-
Green, Shawn			15	100	30	50	100
Greenberg, Hank	1956	1986	100	300	400	1,500	-
Griffey, Ken Jr.			35	500	50	65	225
Griffith, Clark	1946	1955	175	350	500	2,000	-
Grimes, Burleigh	1964	1985	25	200	85	275	-
Groat, Dick			8	50	20	25	50
Grove, Lefty	1947	1975	50	375	175	1,500	-
Guerrero, Vladimir			25	150	40	65	175
Guidry, Ron			12	75	20	30	50
Gwynn, Tony	2007		30	200	45	55	125
Haddix, Harvey		1994	15	75	25	60	75
Hafey, Chick	1971	1973	50	300	250	2,500	-
Haines, Jesse	1970	1978	30	275	175	1,500	-
Hamilton, Billy	1961	1940	4,000	-	-	8,000	-
Hanlon, Ned	1996	1937	4,000	-	-	-	-
Harrelson, Ken			10	50	30	35	75
Harridge, William	1972	1971	125	125	250	2,000	-
Harris, Bucky	1975	1977	70	400	150	2,500	-
Hartnett, Gabby	1955	1972	90	600	400	2,000	-
Heilmann, Harry	1952	1951	500	800	800	2,800	-
Helton, Todd			20	100	35	75	100
Henderson, Rickey			35	250	50	45	125
Henrich, Tommy			8	50	20	30	60
Herman, William	1975	1992	15	125	35	90	200
Hernandez, Orlando			25	125	40	40	75
Hershiser, Orel			10	75	25	30	50
Hill, Pete	2006		-	-	-	-	-
Hodges, Gil		1972	400	750	500	2,000	750
Hoffman, Trevor			12	75	25	35	60
Hooper, Harry	1971	1974	30	150	125	1,800	-
Hornsby, Rogers	1942	1963	450	1,000	900	4,000	-
Houk, Ralph			10	50	20	30	60
Howard, Elston		1980	100	350	300	2,000	2,500

Baseball

PLAYER	HOF	DIED	SIG	LETTER	SP	SIGNED BALL	SIGNED BAT
Howard, Frank			10	50	20	30	70
Hoyt, Waite	1969	1984	25	125	75	1,000	-
Hubbard, Cal	1976	1977	75	350	250	1,300	-
Hubbell, Carl	1947	1988	25	200	60	150	300
Hubbs, Ken		1964	250	700	400	1,000	-
Huggins, Miller	1964	1929	2,000	3,500	5,000	5,000	-
Hulbert, William	1995	1882	-	10,000	-	-	-
Hunter, James "Catfish"	1987	1999	25	200	40	75	150
Irvin, Monte	1973		10	75	25	30	75
Jackson, Bo			15	125	25	35	75
Jackson, Joe "Shoeless"		1951	5,000	-	20,000	40,000	-
Jackson, Reggie	1993		40	150	55	70	175
Jackson, Travis	1982	1987	30	200	50	275	500
Jenkins, Fergie	1991		10	100	25	30	80
Jennings, Hughie	1945	1928	2,000	4,000	5,000	8,000	-
Jensen, Jackie		1982	30	200	150	350	-
Jeter, Derek			40	400	100	150	350
John, Tommy			10	75	15	25	50
Johnson, Ban	1937	1931	500	600	2,000	-	-
Johnson, Judy	1975		30	250	45	125	250
Johnson, Randy			35	200	45	75	125
Johnson, Walter	1936	1946	850	1,500	1,500	18,000	-
Jones, Andruw			20	150	35	45	125
Jones, Chipper			20	150	35	45	150
Joss, Addie	1978	1911	-	-	-	-	-
Justice, David			20	100	30	40	80
Kaat, Jim			12	75	20	30	50
Kaline, Al	1980		15	150	35	40	125
Keefe, Tim	1964	1933	-	-	-	-	-
Keeler, Willie	1939	1923	2,000	-	-	-	-
Kell, George	1983	1984	15	150	75	400	-
Kelley, Joe	1971		2,500	5,000	5,000	3,500	-
Kelly, "King" Mike	1945		7,500	-	-	-	-
Kelly, George	1973		25	100	20	30	60
Kent, Jeff			20	150	30	45	80
Killebrew, Harmon	1984		15	150	35	45	125
Kiner, Ralph	1975		12	100	25	35	80
Kingman, Dave			15	100	20	35	75
Klein, Chuck	1980		500	1,500	900	2,500	-
Klem, Bill	1953	1951	500	1,200	900	5,000	-
Kluszewskl,Ted		1988	40	200	150	350	-
Koosman, Jerry			8	50	20	30	50
Kornerko, Paul			15	100	40	55	125
Koufax, Sandy	1972		65	500	75	300	175
Kubek, Tony			40	100	50	100	150
Kuenn, Harvey		1988	25	100	45	175	225
Kuhn, Bowie	2007		-	-	-	-	-
Lajoie, Napoleon "Larry"	1937	1959	500	2,000	1,500	6,000	-
Landis, "Judge" Kenesaw	1944	1944	450	600	700	4,000	-
Larkin, Barry			10	125	35	40	20
Larsen, Don			10	75	20	30	50
LaRussa, Tony			15	75	15	30	50
Lasorda, Tom	1997		25	200	30	40	80
Lazzeri, Tony	1991	1946	1,000	2,000	2,500	3,500	-

Baseball

PLAYER	HOF	DIED	SIG	LETTER	SP	SIGNED BALL	SIGNED BAT
Lemon, Bob	1976	2000	10	125	20	30	70
Leonard, Buck	1972	1997	20	200	40	60	150
Lindstrom, Fred	1976	1981	35	175	75	1,800	-
Lloyd, John "Pop"	1977	1965	6,000	-	-	-	-
Lombardi, Ernie	1986	1977	50	250	175	1,300	-
Lopat, Ed		1992	20	100	25	100	120
Lopez, Al	1977	2005	25	150	30	65	125
Lyle, Sparky			10	75	20	25	50
Lyons, Ted	1955	1986	20	125	60	700	-
Mack, Connie	1937	1956	275	350	800	1,800	-
Mackey, James "Biz"	2006	1965	5,000	-	-	-	-
MacPhail, Larry	1978		250	375	500	75	-
MacPhail, Lee	1998		25	100	50	100	100
Maddux, Greg			30	200	50	75	150
Maglie, Sal		1992	25	125	75	375	-
Manley, Effa	2006	1981	1,000	2,200	-	-	-
Mantle, Mickey	1974	1995	275	1,200	300	650	1,500
Manush, Heinie	1964	1971	65	250	250	2,000	-
Maranville, Rabbit	1954	1954	400	1,000	750	2,500	-
Marichal, Juan	1983		20	150	25	40	80
Maris, Roger		1985	450	1,000	750	2,000	850
Marquard, Rube	1971	1980	35	250	100	1,500	-
Martin, Billy		1989	75	250	150	400	500
Martin, "Pepper"		1965	150	500	400	1,800	-
Martinez, Dennis			15	75	20	30	60
Martinez, Edgar			25	150	40	50	80
Martinez, Pedro			30	200	50	150	150
Martinez, Tino			25	125	50	45	125
Mathews, Eddie	1978	2001	25	250	50	65	150
Mathewson, Christy	1936	1925	5,000	15,000	20,000	30,000	-
Matsui, Hideki			40	200	100	250	300
Mattingly, Don			25	150	40	50	125
Mays, Willie	1979		50	250	55	100	150
Mazeroski, Bill	2001		12	75	25	30	80
McCarthy, Joe	1957	1978	40	200	175	900	-
McCarthy, Tom	1946	1922	2,000	5,000	-	-	-
McCarver, Tim			10	75	20	30	50
McCovey, Willie	1986		25	200	35	50	100
McDougald, Gil			10	50	20	30	50
McGinnity, Joe	1946	1929	2,500	8,000	-	-	-
McGowan, Bill	1992	1954	400	800	850	4,000	-
McGraw, John	1937	1934	1,000	3,000	2,500	6,000	-
McGraw, Tug		2004	15	75	50	75	50
McGriff, Fred			15	50	30	35	100
McGwire, Mark			50	500	150	300	650
McKechnie, Bill	1962	1965	225	500	500	1,800	-
McLain, Denny			20	75	35	35	75
McNally, Dave		2002	25	125	45	75	100
McPhee, Bid	2000	1943	5,000	25,000	-	-	-
Medwick, Joseph "Ducky"	1968	1975	50	350	175	2,000	-
Mendez, Jose*	2006	1928	-	-	-	-	-
Minoso, Minnie			10	75	25	30	75
Mize, Johnny	1981	1993	15	125	25	75	250
Molitor, Paul	2004		25	125	40	50	150

Baseball

PLAYER	HOF	DIED	SIG	LETTER	SP	SIGNED BALL	SIGNED BAT
Morgan, Joe	1990		20	100	35	45	100
Munson, Thurman		1979	800	2,000	1,500	2,500	2,500
Murcer, Bobby			15	75	25	35	60
Murphy, Dale			12	75	25	30	70
Murray, Eddie	2003		40	250	40	65	100
Musial, Stan	1969		25	125	45	75	150
Mussina, Mike			25	125	30	45	80
Nettles, Graig			10	100	20	30	60
Newcombe, Don			10	50	20	30	50
Newhouser, Hal	1992	1998	15	125	25	50	85
Nichols, Kid	1949	1953	500	900	1,200	4,000	-
Niekro, Phil	1997		15	100	25	35	80
Nomo, Hideo			30	150	50	60	100
O'Doul, Lefty		1969	75	350	250	1,000	-
Oh, Sadaharu			40	100	50	60	125
Olerud, John			12	60	20	35	65
Oliva, Tony			12	75	20	30	60
Oliver, Al			10	50	15	30	60
O'Malley, Walter	2007		-	-	-	-	-
O'Neill, Paul			30	150	35	50	80
Ordonez, Magglio			15	75	30	50	100
O'Rourke, Jim	1945	1919	3,500	8,000	-	-	-
Ortiz, David			25	125	40	55	125
Ott, Mel	1951	1958	700	1,500	1,200	30,000	-
Paige, Satchel	1971	1982	175	1,000	500	1,500	-
Palmeiro, Rafael			20	125	35	40	100
Palmer, Jim	1990		20	150	30	35	90
Parker, Dave			12	75	20	30	60
Pennock, Herb	1948	1948	550	1,000	1,500	8,000	-
Perez, Tony	2000		20	150	35	35	100
Perry, Gaylord	1991		10	75	25	35	75
Perry, Jim			8	40	15	30	50
Pettitte, Andy			25	125	40	50	125
Piazza, Mike			30	150	65	75	175
Pierce, Billy			8	40	15	30	50
Piersall, Jimmy			10	40	20	30	50
Pinella, Lou			12	75	20	30	50
Pinson, Vada			40	200	75	250	350
Plank, Edward	1946	1926	7,000	10,000	-	-	-
Podres, Johnny			8	40	15	25	50
Pompez, Alex	2006	1974	1,000	2,500	-	-	-
Posey, Cumberland	2006	1946	1,000	2,500	-	-	-
Powell, Boog			8	50	20	30	50
Puckett, Kirby	2001	2006	40	250	35	55	125
Pujols, Albert			50	300	85	150	200
Radbourne, Charles	1939	1987	-	20,000	-	-	-
Raines, Tim			15	75	20	30	50
Ramirez, Manny			25	250	50	65	150
Randolph, Willie			15	150	25	30	60
Raschi, Vic		1988	25	125	50	200	250
Reese, Harold "Pee Wee"	1984	1999	35	200	50	65	175
Reynolds, Allie		1994	20	100	30	80	125
Rice, Jim			12	100	25	30	60
Rice, Sam	1963	1974	75	350	250	1,500	-

Baseball

PLAYER	HOF	DIED	SIG	LETTER	SP	SIGNED BALL	SIGNED BAT
Richard, J.R.			10	75	20	30	80
Richardson, Bobby			8	50	15	25	50
Rickey, Branch	1967	1965	350	500	700	2,500	-
Ripken Jr, Cal	2007		60	500	75	100	200
Rivera, Mariano			35	200	40	50	80
Rixey, Eppa	1963	1963	275	375	750	2,500	-
Rizzuto, Phil ,	1994	2007	20	125	35	40	90
Roberts, Robin	1976		10	100	25	30	80
Robinson, Brooks	1983		10	75	35	40	100
Robinson, Frank	1982		25	250	40	45	125
Robinson, Jackie	1962	1972	800	1,200	1,500	6,000	-
Robinson, Wilbert	1945	1934	1,200	1,500	2,000	6,000	-
Rodriguez, Alex			50	300	55	75	150
Rodriguez, Ivan			25	200	40	55	100
Roe, Preacher			10	50	20	35	80
Rogan, Bullet	1998	1967	5,000	-	-	-	-
Rolen, Scott			20	125	35	45	100
Rose, Pete			25	250	35	45	125
Rosen, Al			10	50	25	35	75
Roush, Edd	1962	1988	15	150	60	300	-
Ruffing, Red	1967	1986	40	300	100	600	-
Rusle, Amos	1977	1942	3,500	10,000	7,500	25,000	-
Ruth, George H. "Babe"	1936	1948	3,000	6,000	7,500	20,000	27,500
Ryan, Nolan	1999		35	300	60	65	150
Sain, Johnny		2006	12	50	15	25	50
Sandberg, Ryne	2005		35	150	35	55	125
Santana, Johan			20	100	40	55	125
Santo, Ron			12	50	20	30	75
Santop, Louis	2006	1942	-	-	-	-	-
Schalk, Ray	1955	1970	85	350	600	2,000	-
Schilling, Curt			20	150	35	75	100
Schmidt, Jason			15	100	40	55	125
Schmidt, Mike	1995		35	150	55	65	150
Schoendienst, Red	1989		12	75	25	35	70
Score, Herb			10	50	20	30	60
Scully, Vin			25	75	75	150	-
Seaver, Torn	1992		25	150	40	50	100
Selee, Frank	1999	1909	5,000	-	-	-	-
Sewell, Joe	1977	1990	15	75	50	150	250
Shantz, Bobby			8	35	15	25	40
Simmons, Al	1953	1956	350	600	750	2,500	-
Simmons, Ted			12	100	15	30	40
Sisler, George	1939	1973	65	500	275	2,500	-
Skowron, Bill			8	40	15	25	40
Slaughter, Enos	1985	2002	12	100	20	35	60
Smith, Hilton	2001	1983	500	2,500	1,500	3,500	-
Smith, Lee			10	100	25	35	100
Smith, Ozzie	2002		20	150	35	45	125
Smoltz, John			25	100	25	40	85
Snider, Duke	1980		20	125	35	50	125
Soriano, Alfonso			30	100	40	100	125
Sosa, Sammy			40	250	65	125	250
Southworth, Billy	2008		-	-	-	-	-
Spahn, Warren	1973	2003	20	150	35	55	125

Sanders Autograph Price Guide — Baseball

PLAYER	HOF	DIED	SIG	LETTER	SP	SIGNED BALL	SIGNED BAT
Spalding, Albert	1939	1915	2,500	4,000	2,000	-	-
Speaker, Tris	1937	1958	500	900	1,000	4,500	-
Stanky, Eddie		1999	12	50	30	60	80
Stargell, Willie	1988	2001	20	200	35	45	150
Staub, Rusty			12	75	20	30	50
Stearnes, Turkey	2000		-	-	-	-	-
Stengel, Casey	1966	1975	150	500	350	1,200	-
Strawberry, Darryl			20	100	30	35	100
Stuart, Dick		2002	30	125	35	50	100
Sutter, Bruce	2006		20	100	20	30	60
Suttles, Mule	2006	1966	-	-	-	-	-
Sutton, Don	1998		20	150	30	40	75
Suzuki, Irchiro			50	300	100	150	250
Taylor, Ben	2006	1953	-	-	-	-	-
Tejada, Miguel			20	125	30	50	100
Terry, Bill	1954	1989	20	125	75	150	-
Thomas, Frank(CWS)			20	150	35	35	100
Thome, Jim			12	100	30	50	100
Thompson, Sam	1974		5,000	-	-	-	-
Thomson, Bobby			8	75	20	35	80
Tiant, Lewis			8	50	15	30	50
Tinker, Joe	1946	1948	1,000	2,000	1,800	4,000	-
Torre, Joe			20	125	20	35	100
Torriente, Cristobal	2006	1938	-	-	-	-	-
Trammell, Alan			12	75	25	30	75
Traynor, Pie	1948	1972	175	500	375	4,000	-
Tresh, Tom			8	40	20	25	50
Valenzuela, Fernando			15	100	25	35	60
Vance, Dazzy	1955	1961	350	700	2,000	2,800	-
VanderMeer, Johnny		1997	15	100	35	60	150
Vaughn, Arky	1985	1952	500	1,800	1,000	3,500	-
Veeck, Bill	1991	1986	125	200	350	800	-
Vizquel, Omar			10	75	30	35	80
Waddell, Rube	1946	1914	-	-	-	-	-
Wagner, Honus	1936	1955	750	1,500	1,500	5,500	-
Walker, Larry			20	125	35	35	100
Wallace, Bobby	1953	1960	475	1,200	1,200	3,500	-
Walsh, Ed	1946	1959	400	1,000	1,500	4,000	-
Waner, Lloyd	1967	1982	25	250	75	750	-
Waner, Paul	1952	1965	375	800	600	4,000	-
Ward, Monte	1964	1925	4,000	7,500	-	-	-
Weaver, Earl	1996		15	150	30	40	70
Weiss, George	1971	1972	100	150	300	1,800	-
Welch, Mickey	1973	1941	4,000	-	-	20,000	-
Wells, David			35	200	60	100	125
Wells, Willie	1997	1989	350	900	800	2,200	-
Wheat, Zack	1959	1978	85	400	350	2,500	-
Whitaker, Lou			15	75	20	30	50
White, Sol	2006	1955	-	-	-	-	-
Wilhelm, Hoyt	1985	2002	15	125	25	35	70
Wilkinson, J.L.	2006	1964	-	-	-	-	-
Williams, "Smokey" Joe	1999		-	-	-	-	-
Williams, Bernie			30	200	40	50	80
Williams, Billy	1987		15	125	30	35	80

Baseball

Sanders Autograph Price Guide

PLAYER	HOF	DIED	SIG	LETTER	SP	SIGNED BALL	SIGNED BAT
Williams, Dick	2008		8	50	15	30	60
Williams, Ted	1966	2002	175	1,000	250	375	1,500
Willis, Vic	1995	1947	3,000	6,000	-	-	-
Wills, Maury			10	50	15	30	60
Wilson, Hack	1979	1948	850	2,000	1,500	4,000	-
Wilson, Jud	2006	1963	-	-	-	-	-
Winfield, Dave	2001		25	150	40	45	125
Wood, "Smokey" Joe		1985	30	150	100	350	-
Wood, Kerry			20	100	40	50	125
Woodling, Gene		2001	15	75	25	50	100
Wright, George	1937	1937	1,000	1,800	2,000	-	-
Wright, Harry	1953	1895	1,500	3,500	-	-	-
Wynn, Early	1972		30	150	30	50	125
Yastrzemski, Carl	1989		35	250	40	50	125
Yawkey, Tom	1980	1976	250	350	450	2,300	-
Young, Cy	1937	1955	750	2,500	1,500	7,000	-
Youngs, Ross	1972	1927	4,000	-	7,500	-	-
Yount, Robin	1999		30	150	40	50	150
Zimmer, Don			8	50	20	25	40
Zito, Barry			15	100	30	50	75

PLAYER	DIED	HOF	SIG	SP	SIGNED BALL	SIGNED JERSEY
Abdul-Jabbar, Kareem		1995	60	120	175	400
Allen, Ray			15	30	125	200
Anthony, Carmelo			20	35	75	150
Archibald, Nate		1991	15	20	125	175
Arizin, Paul		1977	10	25	150	200
Artest, Ron			10	25	100	150
Auerbach, Red	2006	1968	25	50	200	250
Auriemma, Gena		2006	-	-	-	-
Barkley, Charles		2006	35	45	175	300
Barlow, Thomas	1983	1980	10	15	45	100
Barry, Rick		1986	10	25	125	175
Baylor, Elgin		1976	15	30	150	200
Beckman, John	1968	1972	130	250	-	-
Bee, Clair	1983	1967	10	15	45	100
Bellamy, Walt		1993	15	35	125	175
Belov, Sergei		1992	10	15	45	100
Biasone, Danny	1992	2000	20	75	200	-
Bibby, Mike			15	30	100	150
Bing, Dave		1990	10	25	175	200
Bird, Larry		1998	50	55	250	350
Blazejowski, Carol		1994	10	15	45	100
Blood, Ernest	1955	1960	10	15	-	-
Borgmann, Bennie	1978	1961	-	-	-	
Bradley, Bill		1982	75	90	175	225
Brand, Elton			10	25	100	150
Brennan, Joseph	1989	1975				
Brown, Larry		2002	15	35	100	200
Bryant, Kobe			40	50	200	325
Calhoun, Jim		2005	10	20	75	150
Camby, Marcus			10	25	100	150
Cann, Howard C.	1992			120		
Carnesecca, Lou		1992	15	20	125	175
Carter, Vince			25	50	200	300
Cervi, Alfred		1985	15	35		
Chamberlain, Wilt	1999	1979	215	250	350	500
Chancellor, Van		2007				
Chaney, John		2001	10	25	100	
Conradt, Jody		1976	15	25	100	
Cooper, Charles	1984	1976				
Cousy, Bob		1970	10	40	380	225
Cowens, Dave		1991	20	35	125	175
Crum, Denny		1994	10	20	75	
Cunningham, Billy		1986	10	20	125	175
Daley, Chuck		1994	10	25	100	
Dantley, Adrian		2008	10	25	100	
Davidson, Bill		2008				
Davies, Bob	1990	1969	50	75	275	350
Davis, Baron			15	30	100	150
DeBernardi, Forrest	1970	1961				
DeBusschere, Dave	2003	1982	10	20	195	175
Dehnert, Henry	1979	1969				
Diaz-Miguel, Antonio	2000	1997	25	45	150	
Donovan, Anne		1995	10	25	100	
Drexler, Clyde		2004	20	45	150	250

Basketball

Sanders Autograph Price Guide

PLAYER	DIED	HOF	SIG	SP	SIGNED BALL	SIGNED JERSEY
Dumars, Joe		2006	15	30	100	150
Duncan, Tim			25	45	125	200
Embry, Wayne		1999	15	25	75	120
Endacott, Paul	1977	1971				
English, Alex		1997	10	20	100	125
Erving, Julius		1992	30	75	250	300
Ewing, Patrick		2008				
Ewing, Patrick			35	50	200	300
Ferrandiz, Pedro		2007				
Finley, Michael			15	25	100	150
Foster, Buid	1996	1964	75	150	300	
Francis, Steve			15	30	125	175
Frazier, Walt		1987	15	20	125	175
Friedman, Max	1986	1971				
Fulks, Joe	1976	1977	160	200	500	
Gaines, Clarence	2005	1982	10	25	100	
Gale, Laddie	1996	1977				
Gallatin, Harry		1991	15	30	100	
Gamba, Sandro		2006				
Garnett, Kevin			35	50	175	325
Gates, William "Pop"	1999	1989	30	75	200	
Gavitt, David		2006				
Gervin, George		1996	10	20	125	175
Ginobili, Manu			20	35	75	150
Gola, Tom		1975	10	25	150	200
Gomelsky, Alexander		1995	15	30	125	
Goodrich, Gail		1996	15	30	100	
Gottlieb, Edward	1979	1972				
Greer, Hal		1981	10	20	100	150
Groza, Alex	1995			130		
Gruenig, Robert	1958	1963				
Hagan, Cliff		1977	10	25	125	175
Hannum, Alex	2002	1998	15	35	150	
Hanson, Victor	1982	1960				
Hardaway, Anfernee			10	25	100	150
Hardaway, Tim			15	25	100	150
Harris, Lusia		1992	10	25	75	
Harshman, Marv		1985	10	25	75	
Haskins, Don		1997	15	30	125	
Havlicek, John		1983	15	25	175	225
Hawkins, Connie		1991	15	20	125	175
Hayes, Elvin		1990	15	20	100	150
Haynes, Marques		1998	10	25	100	
Hearn, Chick	2002	1991	30	75	250	
Heinsohn, Tom		1986	12	30	165	225
Hinrich, Kirk			20	35	75	150
Holman, Nat	1998	1964	25	50	200	300
Holzman, Red	1998	1985	25	40	200	300
Houbregs, Robert		1987	10	20	100	
Houston, Allan			10	25	100	150
Howard, Juwan			10	20	100	125
Howell, Bailey		1997	10	20	100	
Hyatt, Charley	1978	1959	120	150		
Iba, Henry	1993	1968	75	175	400	

490

PLAYER	DIED	HOF	SIG	SP	SIGNED BALL	SIGNED JERSEY
Irish, Edward "Ned"	1982	1964				
Issel, Dan		1992	20	40	150	175
Iverson, Allen			30	45	200	275
Jackson, Phil		2007				
Jackson, Phil			30	60	125	200
James, LeBron			65	100	200	350
Jamison, Antawn			10	25	100	150
Jeanette, Buddy	1998	1994	160	200	250	300
Johnson, Erwin "Magic"		2002	50	125	200	350
Johnson, William	1980	1976				
Johnston, Donald Neil	1978	1990				
Jones, K.C.		1988	10	20	125	175
Jones, Sam		1983	10	20	125	175
Jordan, Michael			100	300	600	1,250
Kidd, Jason			15	30	125	200
Knight, Bobby		1990	15	30	100	
Krause, Edward	1992	1975				
Krzyzewski, Mike		2001	25	50	150	
Kundla, John		1995	10	20	100	
Kurland, Robert		1961	10	30	75	
Lanier, Bob		1992	10	20	100	150
Lapchick, Joseph	1970	1966	50			
Lemon, Meadowlark		2003	25	50	150	250
Lewis, Reggie	1993		40	100	250	500
Lieberman, Nancy		1996	10	20	100	
Lovellette, Clyde		1987	10	20	100	150
Lucas, Jerry		1979	15	20	100	150
Macauley, Ed		1960	10	20	150	175
Malone, Karl			35	45	215	295
Malone, Moses		2001	15	25	100	150
Maravich, Pete	1988	1987	300	1,600	2,500	3,000
Marbury, Stephon			10	20	100	150
Marion, Shawn			20	35	100	150
Martin, Kenyon			10	25	100	175
Martin, Slater		1981	10	25	150	200
McAdoo, Bob		2000	10	25	100	150
McCracken, Emmett "Branch"	1970	1960	130			
McCracken, Jack	1958	1962	2,600			
McDermott, Robert	1963	1988				
McGrady, Tracy			15	35	150	250
McGuire, Alfred	2001	1992	30	75	225	
McGuire, Dick		1993	15	30	125	
McGuire, Frank	1994	1977		150	400	
McHale, Kevin		1999	15	30	125	175
McLendon, John	1999	1978	20	45	175	
Meanwell, Walter	1953	1959				
Meyer, Ray		1978	15	35	125	
Meyers, Ann		1993	10	25	100	
Mikan, George	2005	1959	20	160	200	250
Mikkelsen, Vern		1995				
Miles, Darius			10	25	100	150
Miller, Andre			10	20	100	150
Miller, Cheryl		1995	15	30	125	200
Miller, Reggie			15	30	125	200

Basketball

PLAYER	DIED	HOF	SIG	SP	SIGNED BALL	SIGNED JERSEY
Ming, Yao			20	40	150	250
Mokray, Bill	2001	1988				
Monroe, Earl		1989	15	20	125	175
Moore, Billie		1999	10	25	75	
Mourning, Alonzo			25	50	125	200
Mullin, Chris			20	35	125	175
Murphy, Calvin		1993	10	30	125	
Murphy, Charles	1992	1960	30	75	350	
Mutombo, Dikembe			10	25	100	150
Naismith, James	1939	1959	1,000			
Nash, Steve			25	50	125	200
Newton, Charles		2000	16	25	100	150
Nikolic, Aleksander	2000	1998	75	150	350	
Niwitzki, Dirk			15	35	150	250
Novosel, Mirko		2007				
O'Brien, John	1967	1961				
O'Brien, Larry	1990	1991		200	500	
Odom, Lamar			15	30	100	150
Olajuwon, Hakeem			30	60	200	275
O'Neal, Jermaine			10	25	100	150
O'Neal, Shaquille			50	85	250	325
Page, Harlan	1965	1962				
Parish, Robert		2003	15	30	125	200
Payton, Gary			15	30	125	200
Pettit, Bob		1970	10	15	55	150
Phillip, Andy	2001	1961		200	500	
Pierce,Paul			15	30	100	175
Pippen, Scottie			30	50	215	300
Podoloff, Maurice	1985	1974				
Pollard, Jim	1993	1978		100	300	
Ramsay, Jack		1992	15	30	125	200
Ramsey, Frank		1982	10	25	125	200
Reed, Willis		1981	15	25	150	200
Rice, Glen			10	20	100	150
Riley, Pat		2008				
Riley, Pat			15	30	100	
Risen, Arnold		1998	10	25	125	200
Robertson, Oscar		1979	50	65	175	250
Robinson, David			35	45	150	225
Robinson, Glenn			10	25	125	175
Rodman, Dennis			30	40	125	200
Roosma, John	1983	1961				
Rudolph, Marvin "Mendy"	1979	2007	50	150	350	
Rupp, Adolph	1977	1969		400	900	
Rush, Cathy		2008				
Russell, Bill		1974	235	260	375	500
Russell, John	1973	1964				
Saperstein, Abe	1966	1971	175	265		
Schayes, Dolph		1972	12	20	150	200
Schmidt, Ernest	1986	1974				
Schommer, John	1960	1959				
Sedran, Barney	1962	1964	120			
Sharman, Bill		2004	15	35	125	200
Smith, Dean		1982	25	50	125	200

Basketball

PLAYER	DIED	HOF	SIG	SP	SIGNED BALL	SIGNED JERSEY
Sprewell, Latrell			10	25	100	150
Stackhouse, Jerry			10	25	100	150
Stagg, Amos	1965	1959	120	200		
Steinmetz, Christian	1963	1961				
Stockton, John			25	45	175	250
Stojakovic, Predrag			15	30	125	200
Stokes, Maurice	1970	2004	500	1,100	3,500	
Stoudamire, Damon			20	35	100	150
Strom, Earl	1994	1995		150	350	-
Summitt, Pat		2000	15	30	100	-
Szczerbiak, Wally			10	20	100	150
Terry, Jason			10	25	100	150
Thomas, Isiah		2000	10	25	125	175
Thompson, David		1996	15	35	150	200
Thompson, John	1990	1962	-	300	400	
Thompson, John R.		1999	20	40	100	-
Trester, Arthur	1944	1961	-	-	-	-
Twyman, Jack		1983	10	25	125	175
Unseld, Wes		1987	15	30	100	150
Van Exel, Nick			10	25	100	150
Vandivier, Robert	1983	1975	-	75	300	-
Vitale, Dick		2008	-	-	-	-
Wachter, Edward	1966	1961	120	-	-	-
Wade, Dwyane			20	35	75	150
Wade, L. Margaret	1995	1985	-	100	300	-
Walker, Antoine			10	30	125	175
Wallace, Rasheed			20	45	125	200
Walsh, David	1975	1961	-	-	-	-
Walton, Bill		1993	10	25	150	200
Wanzer, Bobby		1987	10	25	100	150
Watts, Stanley	2000	1986	20	40	175	-
Webber, Chris			15	40	150	250
Wells, Clifford	1977	1972	-	-	-	-
West, Jerry		1979	20	35	150	250
Wilkens, Lenny		1988	10	15	125	175
Wilkins, Dominique		2006	15	35	125	175
Williams, Jason			10	25	100	150
Williams, Jay			10	25	100	150
Williams, Roy		2007	-	-	-	-
Wooden, John		1961	20	60	350	-
Worthy, James		2003	25	45	150	200
Yardley, George	2004	1996	15	30	125	175
Zollner, Fred	1982	1999	-	-	-	-

Boxing

PLAYER	DIED	HOF	SIG	LETTER	SP	SIGNED GLOVE
Ali, Muhammad		1990	100	350	200	350
Ali, Muhammad (Vintage)		1990	250	750	500	1,000
Ambers, Lou	1995	1992	30		80	250
Angott, Sammy	1980	1998	35		85	250
Apostoli, Fred	1973	2003				
Arcel, Ray	1994	1991	35	50	85	150
Arguello, Alexis		1992	25	35	35	110
Arizmendi, Baby	1963	2004				
Armstrong, Henry	1988	1990	75	250	350	800
Attell, Abe	1970	1990	100	275	375	850
Baer, Max	1959	1995	150	300	400	1,000
Basilio, Carmen		1990	10	25	35	125
Benitez, Wilfred		1996	15		50	150
Benvenuti, Nino		1992	15		45	175
Berg, Jackie Kid	1991	1994	25	50	65	165
Blackburn, Jack	1942	1992	150	250	350	
Braddock, James	1974	2001	400		950	
Brenner, Teddy		1993	5		15	45
Britton, Jack	1962	1990	85	150	250	
Brown, Joe	1997	1996	10		25	100
Brown, Panama Al	1951	1992	150	250	350	
Burley, Charley	1992	1992	15		35	100
Burns, Tommy	1955	1996	250	650	1,500	6,000
Canto, Miguel		1998	10		25	75
Canzoneri, Tony	1959	1990	150	250	250	1,000
Carnera, Primo	1967		150	350	450	2,250
Carpentier, Georges	1975	1991	150	250	275	1,100
Cerdan, Marcel	1949	1991	500	1,000	1,000	1,500
Cervantes, Antonio		1998	15		35	150
Charles, Ezzard	1975	1990	150	250	450	1,000
Clancy, Gil			5		15	45
Conn, Billy	1993	1990	25		150	350
Corbett, James J.	1933		250	500	800	12,000
D'Amato, Cus	1985	1995	35	100	75	
Darcey, Les	1917	1993	450	1,800	2,500	
DeJesus, Esteban			75		250	
Delaney, Jack	1948	1996	175	350	350	
Dempsey, Jack	1983	1990	75	150	250	1,000
Dempsey, Nonpareil	1895	1992	350	850	1,500	
Dixon, George	1909	1990	650	1,800	3,500	
Donovan, Arthur		1993	25	65	75	
Dundee, Angelo		1994	8		15	45
Dundee, Chris	1998	1994	10		35	125
Dundee, Johnny	1965	1991	75		150	450
Dunphy, Don		1993	15		35	50
Duran, Roberto		2007	12		40	125
Duva, Lou		1998	5		15	45
Elorde, Flash	1985	1993	65		150	250
Fitzsimmons, Bob	1917	1990	1,500	3,500	4,500	10,000
Fleischer, Nathaniel S.	1972		25	45	65	135
Flowers, Tiger	1927	1993	250	650	950	
Foreman, George		2003	25		75	225
Foster, Bob		1990	5		15	65
Frazier, Joe		1990	10		75	175

Boxing

PLAYER	DIED	HOF	SIG	LETTER	SP	SIGNED GLOVE
Fullmer, Gene		1991	5		25	80
Futch, Eddie	2001	1994	8		15	50
Galaxy, Khaosai		1999	10		25	75
Galento, Tony			35		200	400
Gans, Joe	1910	1990	250	1,800	2,500	3,000
Gavilan, Kid		1990	15		40	150
Genaro, Frankie	1966	1998	5		45	
Giardello, Joey		1993	10		25	80
Gibbons, Mike	1956	1992	100		250	
Gibbons, Tommy	1960	1993	50		150	
Goldstein, Ruby	1984	1994	10		35	
Gomez, Wilfredo		1995	10		35	100
Graham, Billy	1992	1992	15		45	100
Graziano, Rocky	1990	1991	45		150	250
Greb, Harry	1926		800	2,000	3,500	
Griffith, Emile		1990	5		15	45
Griffo, Young	1927	1991	250	350	450	
Hagler, Marvin		1993	25		65	125
Harada, Fighting		1995	10		25	75
Hart, Marvin			1,500	3,500	6,500	9,000
Herman, Pete	1973	1997	25		85	
Holmes, Larry		2008	10		35	125
Jack, Beau	2000	1991	10		35	100
Jackson, Peter	1901	1990	350	650	1,500	
Jacobs, Mike	1953	1990	15	35	45	
Jeanette, Joe	1958	1997	650	1,800	2,500	
Jeffries, James J.	1953	1990	350	750	1,500	8,000
Jofre, Eder		1992	10		25	100
Johnson, Harold		1993	5		20	75
Johnson, Jack	1946	1990	350	850	2,500	5,500
Ketchel, Stanley	1910	1990	1,500	3,500	4,500	
Kid Chocolate	1988	1994	150	250	450	
Kilbane, Johnny	1957	1995	75		250	
King, Don		1997	10		25	65
La Barba, Fidel	1981	1996	10		45	85
LaMotta, Jake		1990	10		35	125
Langford, Sam	1956	1990	650	1,500	2,500	
Leonard, Benny	1947	1990	150	250	350	1,800
Leonard, Sugar Ray		1997	15		35	125
Lewis, John Henry	1974	1994	45		175	750
Lewis, Ted "Kid"	1970	1992	45		150	
Liston, Sonny	1970	1991	550		1,200	4,000
Loughran, Tommy	1982	1991	75	125	150	400
Louis, Joe	1981	1990	150	250	475	3,000
Lynch, Benny	1946	1998	175	400	400	
Marciano, Rocky	1969	1990	400	750	800	5,000
Markson, Harry		1992	250	750	1,000	
Maxim, Joey		1994	10		25	75
McCoy, Charles"Kid	1940	1991	5		15	65
McGovern, Terry	1918	1990	150		350	
McLarnin, Jimmy	2004	1991	20	75	50	
Mercante, Arthur		1995	5		35	
Miller, Freddie	1962	1997	5		15	45
Montgomery, Bob		1995	45		150	

Boxing

PLAYER	DIED	HOF	SIG	LETTER	SP	SIGNED GLOVE
Monzon, Carlos	1995	1990	30		150	250
Moore, Archie	1998	1990	25		50	125
Muhammad, Matthe Saad		1998	15		45	100
Napoles, Jose		1990	5		20	55
Nelson, Battling	1954	1992	40		95	500
Norton, Ken		1992	15		30	85
O'Brien, Phila. Jack	1942	1994	10		35	100
Odd, Gilbert		1992	75	175	250	
Olivares, Ruben		1991	5		20	75
Ortiz, Carlos		1991	8		25	80
Ortiz, Manuel	1970	1996	5		25	80
Parnassus, George	1975	1991	25		150	
Patterson, Floyd		1991	10		50	175
Pedroza, Eusebio		1999	5		25	90
Pep, Willie		1990	15		45	125
Perez, Pascual	1977	1995	8		25	75
Pryor, Aaron		1996	15		30	125
Quarry, Jerry			10		60	200
Rickard, George "Tex"	1929	1990	150		425	1,250
Robinson, Sugar Ray	1989	1990	35		400	1,500
Rodriguez, Luis	1996	1997	15		85	250
Rosenbloom, Maxie	1979	1993	30		125	1,500
Ross, Barney	1967	1990	25		200	325
Saddler, Sandy		1990	15		75	175
Sanchez, Salvador	1982	1991	500		1,000	1,800
Schmeling, Max	2005	1992	50	150	110	225
Sharkey, Jack	1994	1994	50		175	525
Spinks, Michael		1994	15		30	125
Stevenson, Teofilio			10		75	200
Steward, Emanuel			15		35	100
Stribling, Young	1933	1966	10		25	65
Sullivan, John L.	1918	1990	450		2,000	15,000
Tiger, Dick	1971	1991	125		275	400
Torres, Jose		1997	25		75	125
Tunney, Gene	1978	1990	100	250	300	700
Villa, Pancho	1925	1994	50		125	250
Walcott, Barbados Joe	1935	1991	75		250	
Walcott, Jersey Joe	1994	1990	50	200	100	350
Walker, Mickey	1981	1990	40		140	1,000
Welsh, Freddie	1927	1997	65		250	
Wilde, Jimmy	1969	1990	10		25	400
Williams, Ike	1994	1990	15		35	125
Wills, Harry	1958	1992	10		35	3,000
Wright, Chalky	1957	1997	150		350	
Zale, Tony	1997	1991	20		40	350
Zarate, Carlos		1994	25		75	175
Zivic, Fritzie	1984	1993	35		150	600

Football

PLAYER	DIED	HOF	SIG	SP	CHECK	GLAC	LETTER	SIGNED BALL	SIGNED JERSEY
Adderley, Herb		1980	10	20	-	25	50	100	150
Aikman, Troy		2006	25	50	-	75	75	225	325
Alexander, Shawn			15	20	-	-	-	100	150
Allen, George	1990	2002	200	350	-	-	350	500	-
Allen, Marcus		2003	25	45	-	80	50	150	200
Alworth, Lance		1978	15	30	-	40	60	125	175
Alzado, Lyle	1992		75	250	-	-	300	500	600
Ameche, Alan	1988		100	400	400	-	400	1,000	-
Atkins, Doug		1982	10	20	25	25	50	100	150
Badgro, Morris "Red"	1998	1981	12	25	-	50	50	100	200
Barber, Tiki			15	30	-	-	50	100	200
Barney, Lem		1992	10	20	-	25	50	100	150
Battles, Cliff	1981	1968	75	200	-	-	150	500	-
Baugh, Sammy		1963	15	35	-	50	75	200	300
Bednarik, Chuck		1967	10	20	30	25	50	100	150
Bell, Bert	1959	1963	200	1,250	200	-	750	-	-
Bell, Bobby		1983	10	20	-	25	50	100	150
Berry, Raymond		1973	10	20	75	25	50	100	150
Bethea, Elvin		2003	10	30	-	40	50	100	150
Bettis, Jerome			15	35	-	-	-	100	150
Bidwill, Charles Sr.	1947	1967	2,000	-	-	-	2,000	-	-
Biletnikoff, Fred		1988	15	25	-	30	50	100	150
Blanda, George		1981	15	40	-	50	50	150	150
Bledsoe, Drew			10	30	-	-	50	100	275
Blount, Mel		1989	10	20	-	30	50	100	-
Bradshaw, Terry		1989	25	40	-	-	75	175	175
Brady, Tom			30	50	-	-	75	175	265
Brees, Drew			10	25	-	-	150	100	300
Brooks, Derrick			10	25	-	-	75	100	175
Brown, Bob		2004	15	40	-	50	75	125	175
Brown, Jim		1971	30	50	-	60	60	175	150
Brown, Paul	1991	1967	40	100	-	250	150	750	250
Brown, Roosevelt	2004	1975	12	40	-	25	75	125	-
Brown, Tim			15	20	-	-	50	100	150
Brown, Willie		1984	10	25	-	25	70	100	200
Bruce, Isacc			10	25	-	-	50	100	150
Bryant, P. (Bear)			125	450	-	-	60	100	150
Buchanan, Buck	1992	1990	40	200	-	125	400	600	-
Bulger, Marc			15	30	-	-	75	125	175
Buoniconti, Nick		2001	15	35	-	40	50	100	150
Butkus, Dick		1979	25	40	-	45	75	150	225
Campbell, Earl		1991	15	30	-	30	75	100	200
Canadeo, Tony	2003	1974	15	45	50	50	50	200	150
Carr, Joe	1939	1963	1,500	-	-	-	2,000	-	-
Carson, Harry		2006	20	50	-	75	100	150	175
Carter, Chris			15	35	-	-	50	125	150
Casper, Dave		2002	15	40	-	50	100	150	175
Chamberlin, Guy	1967	1965	500	800	-	-	800	2,000	-
Christiansen, Jack	1986	1970	40	200	-	-	75	750	-
Clark, Earl "Dutch"	1978	1963	75	250	-	-	200	750	-
Coles, Laverneas			10	25	-	-	60	100	200
Connor, George	2003	1975	15	30	-	35	50	150	150
Conzelman, Jimmy	1970	1964	225	500	-	-	500	1,000	-
Creekmur, "Lou"		1996	12	20	-	30	50	100	150

Football

PLAYER	DIED	HOF	SIG	SP	CHECK	GLAC	LETTER	SIGNED BALL	SIGNED JERSEY
Csonka, Larry		1987	20	35	-	40	75	125	225
Culpepper, Daunte			10	25	-	-	50	125	250
Cunningham, Randall			15	25	-	-	50	125	175
Davis, Al		1992	175	400	-	500	500	500	-
Davis, Terrell			25	50	-	-	50	225	325
Davis, Willie		1981	10	20	-	30	50	100	150
Dawson, Len		1987	15	25	-	25	50	100	200
Dean, Fred		2008	10	15	-	-	-	125	150
DeLamielleure, Joe		2003	12	25	-	25	50	100	150
Dickerson, Eric		1999	25	40	-	45	100	150	250
Dierdorf, Daniel		1996	12	25	-	30	50	100	150
Ditka, Mike		1988	20	40	-	45	75	150	200
Donovan, Art		1968	12	25	-	30	50	100	150
Dorsett, Tony		1994	25	40	-	45	60	150	225
Driscoll, John	1968	1965	250	500	-	-	600	2,000	-
Dudley, William		1966	10	20	-	35	50	100	150
Dunn, Warrick			15	25	-	-	50	100	150
Edwards, Albert "Turk"	1973	1969	200	400	-	-	600	1,000	-
Eller, Carl		2004	10	35	-	45	75	100	150
Elway, John		2004	45	50	-	125	150	250	350
Esiason, Boomer			10	25	-	-	75	100	200
Ewbank, Weeb	1998	1978	25	50	75	50	50	300	225
Faulk, Marshall			20	45	-	-	50	150	155
Favre, Brett			40	60	-	-	75	225	325
Fears, Tom	2000	1970	20	40	40	45	50	200	150
Finks, Jim	1994	1995	200	500	-	-	200	1,000	-
Flaherty, Raymond "Red"	1994	1976	25	50	-	60	60	300	-
Ford,"Len"	1972	1976	500	1,000	-	-	300	-	-
Fortmann, Danny	1995	1965	50	200	-	2,500	150	750	-
Fouts, Dan		1993	20	40	-	35	50	150	225
Friedman, Benny	1982	2005	350	600	-	-	250	1,000	350
Gannon, Rich			15	20	-	-	100	100	250
Garcia, Jeff			15	25	-	-	60	100	175
Gatski, Frank	2005	1985	10	20	-	25	50	100	150
George, Bill	1982	1974	100	400	-	-	250	1,000	-
George, Eddie			20	30	-	-	60	100	175
Gibbs, Joe		1996	25	40	-	50	50	125	225
Gifford, Frank		1977	30	50	-	50	100	150	200
Gillman, Sid	2003	1983	20	45	-	35	50	150	150
Graham, Otto	2003	1965	20	40	-	45	50	150	200
Grange, Red	1991	1963	75	200	-	250	300	500	750
Grant, Bud		1994	20	35	-	35	50	125	200
Greene, Joe		1987	20	35	-	40	75	125	200
Gregg, Forrest		1977	15	25	-	25	50	100	150
Griese, Bob		1990	20	35	-	40	75	125	200
Griese, Brian			10	25	-	-	-	100	100
Groza, Lou	2000	1974	12	30	-	35	50	125	150
Guyon, Joe	1971	1966	350	600	-	-	600	1,000	-
Halas, George	1983	1963	90	250	-	-	175	1,000	-
Ham, Jack		1988	15	35	-	40	50	125	150
Hampton, Dan		2002	20	30	-	40	50	100	-
Hannah, John		1991	10	20	-	25	50	100	250
Harrington, Joey			10	25	-	-	-	100	250
Harris, Franco		1990	25	45	-	50	60	150	175

Football

PLAYER	DIED	HOF	SIG	SP	CHECK	GLAC	LETTER	SIGNED BALL	SIGNED JERSEY
Harrison, Marvin			20	40	-	-	-	125	225
Haynes, Mike		1997	15	30	-	35	50	125	150
Healey, Ed	1978	1964	75	150	-	-	150	300	-
Hein, Mel	1992	1963	20	50	-	-	75	200	250
Hendricks, Ted		1990	12	20	-	30	50	100	150
Henry, Wilbur "Pete"	1952	1963	600	1,500	800	-	-	-	-
Herber, Arnie	1969	1966	250	800	-	-	500	-	-
Hewitt, Bill	1947	1971	1,500	-	-	-	3,000	-	-
Hickerson, Gene		2007	50	100	-	-	-	-	-
Hinkle, Clarke	1988	1964	60	150	-	-	200	600	-
Hirsch, Elroy	2004	1968	15	30	-	35	40	150	175
Holmes, Priest			10	25	-	-	50	100	175
Holmgren, Mike [coach]			15	40	-	-	100	125	(1)
Horn, Joe			10	20	-	-	-	100	150
Hornung, Paul		1986	20	30	-	40	75	125	200
Houston,"Ken"		1986	10	20	-	25	50	100	150
Hubbard, Robert "Cal"	1977	1963	60	250	150	-	250	1,500	-
Huff, Robert "Sam"		1982	15	30	-	40	60	125	200
Hunt, Lamar	2006	1972	20	40	-	45	50	200	150
Hutson, Don	1997	1963	35	75	-	150	150	400	300
Irvin, Michael		2007	25	40	-	75	60	125	200
Jackson, Bo			25	40	-	-	100	150	225
Jackson, Tom			10	25	-	-	40	100	150
James, Edgerrin			20	35	-	-	100	125	200
Johnson, Brad			12	30	-	-	50	100	200
Johnson, Jimmy		1994	10	25	-	25	50	100	150
Johnson, John		1987	10	20	-	30	75	100	150
Joiner, Charlie		1996	12	25	-	25	50	100	150
Jones, Deacon		1980	12	25	-	30	75	100	175
Jones, Stan		1991	10	20	-	25	50	100	150
Jordan, Henry	1977	1995	500	850	650	-	1,000	2,000	-
Jurgensen, Sonny		1983	15	25	-	35	50	125	175
Karras, Alex			10	25	-	-	50	100	150
Kelly, Jim		2002	25	50	-	60	50	125	200
Kelly, Leroy		1994	15	25	-	25	50	100	150
Kemp, Jack			35	50	-	-	60	200	150
Kiesling, Walt "Babe"	1962	1966	1,500	-	2,000	-	3,000	-	-
Kinard, Frank	1985	1971	100	250	-	-	250	750	-
Kinnick, Nile		1943	4,000	5,000	-	-	7,500	-	-
Krause, Paul		1998	10	20	-	30	50	100	150
Lambeau, Earle	1965	1963	900	2,000	-	-	2,500	-	-
Lambert, Jack		1990	20	35	-	40	75	150	225
Landry, Tom	2000	1990	30	45	-	75	100	250	200
Lane, Dick	2002	1974	15	30	-	30	50	125	150
Langer, Jim		1987	12	20	-	30	50	100	150
Lanier, Willie		1986	10	20	-	25	50	100	150
Largent, Steve		1995	15	30	-	35	60	125	200
Lary, Robert Jr. "Yale"		1979	10	20	30	25	50	100	150
Lavelli, Dante		1975	10	20	-	25	50	100	150
Law, Ty			10	25	-	-	50	100	150
Layne, Bobby	1986	1967	75	250	-	-	250	650	-
Leemans, Alphonse	1979	1978	225	500	-	-	450	1,000	-
Levy, Marv		2001	20	35	-	35	50	100	150
Lewis, Ray			20	35	-	-	60	125	225

PLAYER	DIED	HOF	SIG	SP	CHECK	GLAC	LETTER	SIGNED BALL	SIGNED JERSEY
Lilly, Bob		1980	10	25	-	30	50	100	175
Little, Larry		1993	10	25	-	25	50	100	150
Lofton, James		2003	15	30	-	40	50	125	150
Lombardi, Vince	1970	1971	350	1,000	450	-	1,250	5,000	-
Long, Howie		2000	25	50	-	50	50	125	150
Lott, Ronnie		2000	20	40	-	45	50	125	150
Luckman, Sid	1998	1965	25	75	-	150	50	450	225
Lyman, William	1972	1964	125	350	-	-	250	500	-
Mack, Tom		1999	10	20	-	30	50	100	150
Mackey, John		1992	15	25	-	30	50	100	150
Madden, John		2006	35	75	-	75	75	150	200
Manning, Peyton			40	75	-	-	100	150	235
Mara, Tim	1959	1963	3,000	-	-	-	-	-	-
Mara, Wellington	2005	1997	30	50	-	50	75	150	150
Marchetti, Gino		1972	10	20	-	25	50	100	150
Marino, Dan		2005	40	55	-	100	150	175	350
Marshall, George Preston	1969	1963	400	800	-	-	600	-	-
Martin, Curtis			20	25	-	-	50	100	165
Matson, Ollie		1972	15	20	-	25	50	100	150
Matthews, Bruce		2007	15	35	-	45	-	-	-
Matuszek, John	1989		60	150	-	-	250	350	450
Maynard, Don		1987	10	20	-	25	50	100	150
McAfee, George		1966	10	20	-	25	50	100	150
McAllister, Deuce			10	20	-	-	-	100	150
McCormack, Mike		1984	10	20	-	25	50	100	150
McDonald, Tommy		1998	10	20	-	25	50	100	150
McElhenny, Hugh		1970	12	25	-	30	50	100	175
McMahon, Jim			15	25	-	-	50	100	175
McNabb, Donovan			30	50	-	-	100	125	250
McNair, Steve			20	35	-	-	60	125	150
McNally, Johnny	1985	1963	400	1,000	-	-	1,000	-	-
Meredith, Don			25	50	-	-	150	150	400
Michalske, Mike	1983	1964	50	150	-	-	125	400	-
Millner, Wayne	1976	1968	125	250	-	-	250	750	-
Mitchell, Bobby		1983	10	20	-	25	50	100	150
Mix,"Ron"		1979	20	20	30	25	50	100	150
Monk, Art		2008	15	20	-	-	-	150	200
Monk, Art			10	25	-	-	50	100	150
Montana, Joe		2000	30	75	-	75	150	150	325
Moon, Warren		2006	20	35	-	50	75	125	190
Moore, Lenny		1975	10	20	30	25	50	100	150
Moss, Randy			35	50	-	-	50	125	275
Motley, Marion	1999	1968	20	45	-	45	50	175	150
Muhammad, Mushin			10	20	-	-	-	100	150
Munchak, Mike		2001	10	20	-	30	50	100	150
Munoz, Anthony		1998	12	25	-	30	50	100	150
Musso, George	2000	1982	15	35	-	35	50	150	150
Nagurski,"Bronko"	1990	1963	80	175	175	-	250	600	500
Namath, Joe		1985	40	75	-	75	300	225	300
Neale, Earl	1973	1969	150	275	-	-	400	-	-
Nevers, Ernie	1976	1963	75	200	-	-	250	1,000	-
Newsome, Ozzie		1999	10	20	-	25	50	100	150
Nitschke, Ray	1998	1978	40	75	-	75	125	250	200
Noll, Chuck		1993	15	35	-	40	75	125	150

Sanders Autograph Price Guide — **Football**

PLAYER	DIED	HOF	SIG	SP	CHECK	GLAC	LETTER	SIGNED BALL	SIGNED JERSEY
Nomellini, Leo	2000	1969	10	25	-	35	75	125	150
O'Brien, Dave			500	1,000	-	-	1,500	-	-
Olsen, Merlin		1982	15	25	-	35	75	100	200
Otto, Jim		1980	15	40	-	35	50	125	150
Owen, Stephen	1964	1966	350	700	-	-	600	-	-
Owens, Terrell			25	45	-	-	100	125	200
Page, Alan		1988	15	25	-	30	75	125	175
Palmer, Carson			15	30	-	-	60	100	200
Parcells, Bill [coach]			35	60	-	-	150	150	(1)
Parker, Clarence		1972	10	20	-	25	40	100	150
Parker, Jim	2005	1973	12	25	75	25	50	125	150
Paterno, Joe			30	75	-	-	150	200	-
Payton, Walter	1999	1993	75	175	450	125	250	400	350
Pennington, Chad			15	30	-	-	60	100	200
Peppers, Julius			15	30	-	-	50	100	175
Perry, Fletcher "Joe"		1969	15	25	-	30	50	100	150
Piccolo, Brian	1970		400	1,000	-	-	1,500	2,500	2,500
Pihos, Pete		1970	15	25	-	25	60	100	150
Plunkett, Jim			10	25	-	-	50	100	175
Pollard, Fritz	1986	2005	350	750	-	-	750	1,000	300
Portis, Clinton			15	30	-	-	50	100	175
Rashad, Ahmad			15	35	-	-	60	100	175
Ray, Hugh	1956	1966	2,500	-	-	-	-	-	-
Reeves, Dan	1971	1967	750	1,000	-	-	1,000	-	-
Renfro, Mel		1996	12	25	-	25	50	100	150
Rice, Jerry			30	60	-	-	50	150	275
Riggins, John		1992	50	85	-	100	200	150	250
Ringo, Jim	2007	1981	10	20	-	30	50	100	150
Robustelli, Andy		1971	10	20	-	30	50	100	150
Rockne, Knute	1931		1,000	2,500	-	-	2,500	-	-
Roethlisberger, Ben			25	45	-	-	100	125	-
Rooney, Art	1988	1964	50	100	-	-	200	350	-
Rooney, Dan		2000	20	40	-	45	100	150	150
Rozelle, Pete	1996	1985	75	200	250	200	150	400	-
Sanders, Barry		2004	40	75	-	75	150	175	320
Sanders, Charlie		2007	10	25	-	35	75	125	-
Sanders, Deion			25	45	-	-	100	150	225
Sapp, Warren			15	30	-	-	100	100	225
Sayers, Gale		1977	25	40	-	40	100	125	200
Schmidt, Joe		1973	10	20	-	25	50	100	150
Schramm, Tex	2003	1991	20	45	-	50	75	150	175
Scott, Jake			25	35	-	-	100	100	-
Seau, JR			25	30	-	-	50	100	175
Selmon, Lee		1995	15	25	-	-	75	125	175
Sharpe, Shannon			15	25	-	-	50	125	200
Sharpe, Sterling			20	30	-	-	75	125	175
Shaw, Billy		1999	10	20	-	25	50	100	150
Shell,"Art"		1989	15	25	-	35	75	100	175
Shula, Don		1997	25	40	-	45	75	150	200
Simms, Phil			15	30	-	-	75	125	300
Simpson,O.J.		1985	45	60	-	75	150	150	200
Singletary, Mike		1998	15	30	-	40	75	125	200
Slater, Jackie		2001	15	20	-	25	50	100	150
Smith, Bruce			20	40	-	-	50	100	190

Football

PLAYER	DIED	HOF	SIG	SP	CHECK	GLAC	LETTER	SIGNED BALL	SIGNED JERSEY
Smith, Bruce (Heisman Winner)			500	1,000	-	-	1,000	-	-
Smith, Emmitt			40	60	-	85	125	200	295
Smith, Jackie		1994	12	20	-	25	50	100	175
St. Clair, Bob		1990	15	25	-	30	50	100	175
Stabler, Ken			15	25	-	-	75	100	175
Stallworth, John		2002	15	30	-	40	75	125	150
Starr,"Bart"		1977	40	75	-	75	125	150	250
Staubach, Roger		1985	30	50	-	45	125	150	250
Stautner,"Ernie"	2006	1969	15	25	-	30	75	125	150
Stenerud, Jan		1991	10	20	-	25	50	100	150
Stephenson, Dwight		1998	10	20	-	25	50	100	150
Strahan, Michael			20	35	-	-	75	100	150
Stram, Hank	2005	2003	25	75	-	100	150	175	-
Strong,"Ken"	1979	1967	75	175	90	-	125	600	-
Stydahar, Joseph	1977	1967	75	200	-	-	150	750	-
Summerall, Pat			25	35	-	-	60	100	-
Swann, Lynn		2001	75	100	-	125	150	150	175
Tarkenton, Fran		1986	20	35	-	40	60	150	200
Taylor, Bobby			10	25	-	-	50	100	175
Taylor, Fred			15	20	-	-	50	100	150
Taylor, Jim		1976	15	25	-	30	75	125	-
Taylor, Lawrence		1999	25	45	-	45	100	125	150
Taylor,"Charles"		1984	10	20	-	25	50	100	250
Testaverde, Vinny			10	25	-	-	50	100	150
Theismann, Joe			10	25	-	-	50	100	175
Thomas, Emmitt		2008	10	20	-	-	-	125	100
Thomas, Thurman		2007	20	30	-	50	75	125	185
Thorpe, Jim	1953	1963	900	2,000	-	-	1,500	2,200	-
Tippett, Andre		2008	15	25	-	-	-	200	175
Tittle, Y.A.		1971	10	25	-	35	75	100	200
Tomlinson, LaD.			25	40	-	-	75	125	175
Trafton, George	1971	1964	150	300	150	-	250	650	-
Trippi, Charles		1968	10	20	40	25	50	125	150
Tunnell, Emlen	1975	1967	90	200	-	-	150	750	-
Turner, Clyde	1998	1966	25	40	60	75	75	300	225
Unitas,"Johnny"	2002	1979	35	75	-	125	150	350	250
Upshaw, Gene		1987	10	25	-	30	75	125	150
Urlacher, Brian			25	40	-	-	75	150	250
Van Brocklin, Norm	1983	1971	75	175	-	-	200	1,000	-
Van Buren, Steve		1965	10	20	-	25	75	125	150
Vick, Michael			15	40	-	-	150	200	250
Walker, Ewell	1998	1986	15	25	-	50	50	125	225
Walsh, Bill	2007	1993	25	75	-	85	150	200	200
Ward, Hines			10	20	-	-	-	100	150
Warfield, Paul		1983	10	20	-	30	50	100	175
Warner, Kurt			15	40	-	-	100	150	275
Waterfield, Bob	1983	1965	75	200	-	-	200	1,000	-
Webster, Mike	2002	1997	25	75	-	75	125	150	150
Wehrli, Roger		2007	10	30	-	35	75	125	150
Weinmeister,"Arnie"	2000	1984	15	50	-	45	75	175	150
White, Randy		1994	10	25	-	35	50	100	200
White, Reggie	2004	2006	50	125	-	-	200	250	235
Wilcox, Dave		2000	10	20	-	25	50	100	150
Williams, Ricky			20	30	-	-	100	125	200

Football

PLAYER	DIED	HOF	SIG	SP	CHECK	GLAC	LETTER	SIGNED BALL	SIGNED JERSEY
Williams, Roy			10	20	-	-	50	125	175
Willis,"Bill"		1977	10	30	-	25	50	100	150
Wilson,"Larry"		1978	10	20	-	25	50	100	175
Winslow, Kellen		1995	15	20	-	30	75	125	175
Wojciechowicz, Alex	1992	1968	25	75	-	1,000	100	250	300
Wood,"Willie"		1989	10	20	-	30	50	100	150
Woodson, Charles			15	30	-	-	60	100	200
Woodson, Rod			15	25	-	-	50	100	175
Yary, Ron		2001	10	20	-	30	50	100	150
Young, Steve		2005	30	50	-	100	75	150	200
Youngblood, Jack		2001	15	25	-	35	75	100	150
Zimmerman, Gary		2008	10	15	-	-	-	125	150

FORMULA ONE

PLAYER	DIED	SP	COMMENTS
Abecassis, George	1991	218	(1913-1991) GP driver 1951-52
Adamich, Andrea de		50	(1941-) GP driver 1968-73
Ahrens, Kurt		20	(1940-) GP driver 1966-69
Albers, Christijan		58	(1979-) Current Minardi F1 driver
Alboreto, Michele	2001	50	(1956-2001) Ferrari Vice-World Champ. 1985
Alesi, Jean		55	(1964-) GP driver 1989-2001 Ferrari driver 1991-95
Alliot, Philippe		50	(1953-) GP driver 1984-94
Allison, Cliff	2005	50	(1932-2005) GP driver 1958-61Ferrari driver 1959-60
Alonso, Fernando		60	(1981-) Youngest F1 World Champ. 2005-2006
Ammermüller, Michael		58	(1986-) Ger. car driver - Red Bull test driver
Amon, Chris		58	(1943-) GP driver 1963-76, Ferrari driver 1967-69
Anderson, Bob	1967	725	(1931-1967) GP driver 1963-67
Andretti, Mario		50	(1940-) World Champ. 1978 4-time Indy Champ.
Andretti, Michael		45	(1962-) McLaren/Ford GP driver 1993
Angelis, Elio de	1986	225	(1958-1986) Shadow driver 1979, Lotus 1980, Brabham 1986
Apicella, Marco		22	(1965-) GP driver 1993
Arnoux, Rene		50	(1948-) GP driver 1978-89 7-time GP winner
Arrundell, Peter		58	(1933-) GP driver 1963-66
Ascari, Alberto	1955	5100	(1918-1955) World Champ. 1952/53 & Ferrari legend
Ashmore, Gerry		15	(1936-) GP driver 1961-62
Attwood, Richard		40	Lotus & BRM GP driver 1964-1969
Badoer, Luca		45	(1971-) GP drive 1993-96, Ferrari 1993 & 99
Baghetti, Giancarlo	1995	200	(1934-1995) GP driver 1961-67
Bailey, Julian		15	(1961-) GP driver 1988-91
Baldi, Mauro		29	(1954-) GP driver 1982-85
Bandini, Lorenzo	1967	600	(1935-1967) GP driver 1961-67
Barbazza, Fabrizio		18	(1963-) GP driver 1991-93
Barber, Skip		51	
Barilla, Paola		36	GP driver
Barrichello, Rubens		60	(1972-) Prior Ferrari race car driver, now Honda
Bartels, Michael		15	(1968-) Lotus/Judd GP driver 1991
Barth, Edgar	1965	100	(1917-1965) Porsche driver; winner European Hill Climbs
Baumgartner, Zolt		60	(1981) Jordan Pilot in the season 2003
Bayol, Elie	1996	175	(1914-96) GP driver 1952-56
Beaufort, Carel de	1964	600	(1934-1964) GP 1957-64. Died in his own build Porsche F1
Bechem, Gunther		29	(1921-) GP driver 1953
Behra, Jean	1959	800	(1921-1959) GP driver 1952-59
Bellof, Stefan	1985	225	(1957-1985) GP driver 1984-85
Belmondo, Paul		22	(1963-) GP driver 1992
Belso, Tom		44	(1942-) GP driver 1973-74
Beltoise, Jean-Pierre		45	(1937-) GP driver 1966-74
Beretta, Olivier		30	(1969-) Larrousse/Ford Grand Prx driver 1994
Berger, Gerhard		45	(1959-) GP driver 1984-97, Ferrari driver 1987-1989 & 1993-1995
Berghe von Trips, Graf	1961	1400	(1928-1961) GP driver 1956-61
Bernard, Eric		22	(1964-) GP driver 1989-91
Bernoldi, Enrique		28	(1978-) Current Arrows race car driver
Bertaggia, Enrico		15	F1 race car driver
Beuttler, Mike	1988	145	(1940-1988) GP driver 1971-73
Bira, Prince	1985	580	(1914-85) Siamese Prince & successful motor racing driver
Blokdyk, Trevor		290	(1935-) GP driver 1963-65
Blundell, Marc		40	(1966-) GP driver GP driver
Bondurant, Robert		30	(1933-) Ferrari GP driver 1965-66. Raced Le Mans for Carroll Shelby
Bonnier, Joakim	1972	250	(1930-1972) GP driver 1956-71
Bouillon, Jean-Christoph		25	(1969-) GP driver 1995

PLAYER	DIED	SP	COMMENTS
Bourdais, Sebastien		85	(1979-) French F1. One of the top drivers of all time.
Boutsen, Thierry		45	(1957-) GP driver 1983-93
Brabham, David		22	(1965-) GP driver 1990
Brabham, Jack		40	(1926-) World Champ. 1959, 1960 & 1966
Brack, Bill		30	(1935-) GP driver 1968-72
Brambilla, Tino		55	(1934-) It. Formula 3 Champ. 1966; Ferrari GP starter 1969
Brambilla, Vittorio		55	(1937-2001) GP driver 1974-80
Brawn, Ross		75	Ferrari technical director
Briatore, Flavio		58	(1950-) Managing director of the Renault F1 team.
Brivio-Sforza, Antonio	1995	290	Alfa Romeo driver & driver of the first Scuderia Ferrari 1933-37.
Brooks, Tony		50	(1932-) GP driver 1956-61, Ferrari driver 1959, GP winner
Brown, Alan		70	(1919-) GP driver 1952-54
Brown, Warwick		44	(1949-) GP driver 1976
Brundle, Martin		45	(1959-) GP driver 1984-96, GP star: or McLaren, Benetton, Jordan
Bruni, Gianmaria		60	(1981-) It. Minardi driver
Bucci, Clemar		174	(1920-) So. Am. Land speed record, 4 World Champ. GP, 1954
Bucknum, Ronnie	1992	218	(1936-92) GP driver 1964-66
Buemi, Sebastien		58	(1988-) Swiss. urrently competing in Formula Three Euroseries.
Burgess, Ian		45	(1930-) GP driver 1958-63
Burti, Luciano		50	(1975-) Jaguar & Prost race car driver
Bussinello, Roberto		58	(1927-99) GP driver 1961-65. BRM & Alfa Romeo driver
Button, Jenson		60	(1980-) Youngest driver to score a world Champ. point.
Byrne, Tommy		44	(1958-) GP driver 1982
Cabianca, Giulio	1961	1175	(1923-61) GP driver 1958-60
Caffi, Alex		22	(1964-) GP driver 1986-92
Campari, Giuseppe	1933	1450	(?-1933) Alfa legend. Drove w/Ascari & Nuvolari. D. Monza 1933
Campos, Adrian		18	(1960-) GP driver 1987-88
Cantoni, Heitel	1997	653	GP driver 1952
Capelli, Ivan		22	(1963-) GP driver 1985-89
Carroll, Adam		40	(1982-) Br. driver.
Castelotti, Eugenio	1957	1500	(1930-1957) GP driver 1955-57
Caze, Robert le		73	(1917-) Cooper Climax GP driver 1958
Cecotto, Johnny		22	(1956-) GP driver 1983-84
Cevert, Francois	1973	475	(1944-73) GP driver 1970-73. D. training for the US GP 1973.
Chapman, Colin	1982	255	(1928-82) GP driver 1956 & Lotus leader
Charlton, Dave		35	(1936-) GP driver 1965-1975
Cheever, Eddie		36	(1958-) GP driver 1978-89
Clark, Jim	1968	1600	(1936-1968) World Champ. 1963 & 1965
Collins, Peter	1958	2000	(1951-58) GP driver 1952-58. D. Nürburgring 1958
Collomb, Bernard		50	(1930-) GP driver 1961-64
Constantine, George	1968	508	(1918-?) Cooper GP driver 1959
Conway, Mike		73	(1983-) Br. racing driver
Cordts, John		36	(1935-) GP driver 1969
Coulthard, David		75	(1971-) MBZ GP driver
Courage, Piers	1970	525	(1942-1970) GP driver 1966-70
Crawford, Jim		29	(1939-) GP driver 1975
Creus, Antonio		44	(1960-) GP driver 1960
Crook, Anthony		58	(1920-) GP driver 1952-53
Da Matta, Cristiano		75	(1973-) Brasilian Toyota driver 2003
Da Silva Ramos, Nano		55	(1925-) Gordini GP driver 1955-56
Daigh, Chuck		218	(1923-) GP driver 1960
Danner, Christian		36	(1958-) GP driver 1985-88
Davidson, Anthony		58	(1981-) Open Formula Nippon Champ. 1999, Minardi & Arrows
Davis, Colin		15	(1932-) GP driver 1959

FORMULA ONE
Sanders Autograph Price Guide

PLAYER	DIED	SP	COMMENTS
De Cesarias, Andrea		29	(1959-) GP driver 1980-94
de Filippis, Maria Teresa		44	(1926-) GP Driver (1958-59)
De La Rosa, Pedro		40	(1971-) New MBZ driver
de Palma, Ralph	1956	254	(1884-1956) 1st IndyCar Champ., 1911 (before called Indy)
Delétraz, Jean-Denis		18	F1 race car driver
Depailler, Patrick	1980	200	(1944-1980) GP driver 1972-80
di Grassi, Lucas		58	(1984-) Brazilian racing driver.
Diniz, Pedro		45	(1970-) GP driver 1995-2000
Donnelly, Martin		55	(1964-) GP driver 1989-90
Donohue, Mark Neary	1975	218	(1937-1975) Drove 1500+ bhp "Can-Am Killer" Porsche 917-30
Doornbos, Robert		58	(1981-) Dutch F1 driver for the Minardi team
Downing, Ken		30	(1923-) GP driver 1952
Driver, Paddy		36	(1934-) GP driver 1963-74
Dumfries, Johnny		40	(1958-) Le Mans winner in 1988
Ecclestone, Bernie		75	(1930-) F1 boss & GP driver 1958
Edwards, Guy		29	(1942-) GP driver 1974-77
Elford, Vic		25	(1916-) GP driver 1968-71
England, Paul		218	(1929-) GP driver 1957
Ertl, Harald	1982	90	(1948-1982) GP driver 1975-80
Fabi, Teo		22	(1955-) GP driver 1982-87
Fagioli, Luigi	1952	1900	(1898-1952) It. Champ. Pre-war race car driver.
Fangio, Juan Manuel	1995	290	(1911-1995) World Champ. 1951, 1954, 1955, 1956, 1957
Farina, Giuseppe	1966	3000	(1906-1966) It. 1st F1 World Champ., 1950.
Ferrari, Enzo	1988	2500	(1898-1988) It. Race Car Designer. Founded Ferrari in 1929
Filippi, Luca		73	(1985-) Competes in single seaters in Europe.
Filippis, Teresa de		58	(1926-) GP driver 1958-59
Firman, Ralph		80	(1975-) New Jordan/Ford GP driver 2003
Fisichella, Giancarlo		40	(1973-) It. on Renault team.
Fittipaldi, Christian		44	(1971-) GP driver 1992-94
Fittipaldi, Emerson		100	(1946-) World Champ. 1972.74; Won Indy 500 & 1989 Indycar
Fittipaldi, Wilson		51	GP driver 1972-75
Flinterman, Jan	1992	145	(1919-1992) GP driver 1952
Flockhart, Ron	1962	580	(1923-1962) GP driver 1954-60
Follmer, George		36	(1934-) GP driver 1973
Fontana, Norberto		22	(1975-) Sauber GP driver 1997
Frankenberg, Richard von	1973	85	Famous Porsche driver 1951-57
Frentzen, Heinz Harald		50	(1967-) GP driver 1994-
Frere, Paul	2008	55	(1917-2008) GP driver 1952-56 Ferrari driver 1955-56
Friesacher, Patrick		0	(1980-) Current Austrian Minardi driver
Gabbiani, Beppe		22	(1957-) GP driver 1978-81
Gachot, Bertrand		22	(1962-) GP driver1989-95
Galli, Nanni		44	(1940-) GP driver 1970-73 Ferrari driver 1972
Gamble, Fred		44	GP driver 1960
Ganley, Howden		35	(1941-) GP driver 1971-74
Gardner, Frank		29	(1930-) GP driver 1964-68
Gartner, Jo	1986	95	(1954-1986 Le Mans) GP driver 1984
Gaze, Tony		30	(1920-) GP driver 1952
Gendebien, Oliver	1998	220	(1924-98) GP driver 1956-61 Ferrari driver 1955-62
Gene, Marc		44	(1974-) Minardi GP driver 2000
Gerard, Bob	1990	326	(1914-1990) GP driver 1950-57
Gerini, Gerino		120	(1928-) GP driver 1956-58
Gethin, Peter		50	(1940-) Won fastest-run GP in history, Monza 1971.
Giacomelli, Bruno		15	F1 race car driver
Gibson, Dick		58	(1918-) GP driver 1957-58

PLAYER	DIED	SP	COMMENTS
Ginther, Richie	1989	220	(1930-1989) GP driver 1960-67. Ferrari driver 1960-61
Glock, Timo		75	(1982-) Scored a World Champ. point in first F1 race
Godia-Sales, Francesco	1992	290	(1921-1992) GP driver 1951-58
Goethals, Christian		73	(1928-) GP driver 1958
Gonzales, José-Froilan		85	(1922-) GP driver 1950-60. 1st Ferrari winner, Silverstone 1951
Graffenried, Emmanuel de		70	(1914-) GP driver 1950-56 1st Swiss GP winner
Grassi, Lucas di		58	(1984-) Brazilian driver.
Gregory, Masten	1985	600	(1932-1985) GP driver 1957-65
Grosjean, Romain		44	(1986-) Renault test driver & upcoming F1 star
Grouillard, Olivier		22	(1958-) GP driver 1989-92
Guerrero, Roberto		58	(1958-) GP driver driver 1982-83
Gugelmin, Mauricio		22	(1963-) GP driver 1988
Guichet, Jean		50	Ferrari driver 1964-1966 Le Mans winner in 1964.
Gurney, Dan		55	(1931-) GP driver 1959-70 Ferrari driver 1959
Hahne, Hubert		36	GP driver 1966-68
Hailwood, Mike	1981	220	(1940-81) "Mike the bike" GP driver 1963-74 Motorcycle champ
Hakkinen, Mika		110	MBZ F1 World Champ. 1998 & 1999
Halford, Bruce	2001	30	(1931-2001) GP driver 1956-60
Hall, Jim		70	(1935-) GP driver 1960-63
Hamilton, Duncan	1994	120	(1920-1994) GP driver 1951-53
Hamilton, Lewis Carl		150	(1985-) Br. Signed by McLaren at age 12
Hansgen, Walt	1966	2175	(1919-1966) GP driver 1961-64
Hanstein, Fritz Huschke von	1996	75	(1919-1996) "Renn Baron". Won Mille Miglia '40. Rennleiter '61-64
Harris, Mike		44	(1939-) GP driver 1962
Hart, Brian		28	(1936-) GP driver 1967
Hawthorn, Mike	1959	3000	(1929-1959) World Champ. 1958
Hayje, Boy		218	(1949-) GP driver 1976-77
Heidfeld, Nick		55	(1977-) Prost, Sauber, Jordan & new BMW driver
Helfrich, Theo	1978	943	(1913-1978) GP driver 1952-54
Henne, Ernst	2005	60	Set speed record for motorcycles: remains unbroken 14 years.
Henton, Brian		22	(1949-) GP driver 1975-82
Herbert, Johnny		25	(1964-) GP driver 1989-
Herrmann, Hans		35	(1938-) GP driver 1953-61
Hill, Damon		110	(1960-) Son of Graham Hill & World Champ. 1996
Hill, Graham	1975	425	(1929-1975) Only driver ever to have won the "Triple Crown".
Hill, Phil		87	(1927-) Ferrari World Champ. 1961; 3-time Le Mans winner
Hirate, Kohei		73	(1986-) Jap. F1 motorsport driver.
Hirt, Peter	1992	145	(1910-?) GP driver 1951-53
Hobbs, David		45	(1967-) GP driver 1967-74
Hoffmann, Ingo		36	(1953-) GP driver 1976-77
Hülkenberg, Nico		58	(1987-) Karting debut in 1997 at 10. Williams test driver 2008.
Hulme, Denis	1992	150	(1936-1992) World Champ. 1967
Hunt, James	1993	220	(1947-1993) World Champ. 1976
Hutchison, Gus		70	(1937-) GP driver 1970
Ickx, Jacky		58	World record six-times Le Mans winner & sports car legend
Ide, Yuji		110	(1975-) Honda driver
Ireland, Innes		0	(1930-1993) GP driver 1959-66. Lotus driver
Irvine, Eddie		65	Former Ferrari driver & now drives for Jaguar.
Irwin, Chris		580	(1942-) GP driver 1966-67
Jabouille, Jean-Pierre		55	(1942-) GP driver 1974-81
Jani, Neel		30	(1983-) Red Bull Racing Junior team test driver.
Jarier, Jean-Pierre		30	GP driver 1971-83
Johansson, Stefan		44	(1956-) GP driver 1980-92 Ferrari driver 1985-86
Jones, Alan		60	(1946-) World champ. 198.0 Took Williams to the GP front-line.

FORMULA ONE

PLAYER	DIED	SP	COMMENTS
Jordan, Eddie		44	Jordan Team chief
Karthikeyan, Narain		75	(1977-) "The Fastest Indian in the World"
Katayama, Ukyo		35	(1963-) GP driver 1992-97
Keegan, Ruppert		51	(1955-) GP driver 1977-82
Keizan, Eddie		51	(1944-) GP driver 1973-75
Kessel, Loris		15	(1950-) GP driver 1976-77
Kiesa, Nicolas		58	Current Minardi driver
Kinnunen, Leo		40	(1943-) GP driver 1974
Klerk, Peter de		35	(1936-) GP driver 1963-70
Klien, Christian		55	New Austrian Jaguar pilot
Kling, Karl	2003	80	(1910-2003) GP driver 1954-55
Kobayashi, Kamui		73	(1986-) Jap. driver
Koinigg, Helmuth		392	(1948-1974) GP driver 1974
Kovalainen, Heikki		75	Raced in the 2005 GP2 Series for Arden. Renault Star 2007
Krakau, Willi		145	GP Non Starter 1952
Kubica, Robert		75	(1984-) Won the World Series by Renault Champ. in 2005
Laffite, Jaques		0	(1943-) GP driver 1974-86
Lagorce, Franck		18	F1 race car driver
Lammers, Jan		22	(1956-) GP driver 1979-92
Lamy, Pedro		22	GP driver
Larini, Nicola		30	(1964-) GP driver 1987-97, Ferrari driver 1992 & 94
Larrauri, Oscar		22	(1954-) GP driver 1988-89
Lauda, Mathias		44	(1981-) Son of three-time world Champ. Niki Lauda
Lauda, Niki		55	(1949-) World Champ. 1975, 1977 (Ferrari) & 1984 (McLaren)
Laurent, Roger	1998	200	(1913-1998) GP driver 1952
Lavaggi, Giovanni		22	GP driver 1995-96
Lawrence, Chris		90	(1947-) Cooper/Ferrari GP driver 1966
Lederle, Neville		22	(1939-) Lotus/Climax GP driver 1962-65
Lees, Geoff		22	F1 race car driver
Lehto, J. J.		29	F1 race car driver
Leoni, Lamberto		44	(1953-) GP driver 1977-78
Leston, Les		44	(1920-) GP driver 1956-57
Lewis, Jack		51	(1936-) GP driver 1960-61
Ligier, Guy		22	(1930-) GP driver 1966-67
Liuzzi, V.		55	Upcoming F1 Star & RED BULL driver
Lombardi, Lella	1992	250	(1943-1992) GP driver 1974-75
MacDowel, Michael		22	(1932-) GP driver 1957
Macklin, Lance	2002	73	(1919-2002) HWM/Alta & Maserati GP driver 1952-1955
Magee, Damien		44	(1945-) GP driver 1975-76
Maglioli, Umberto	1999	200	(1928-99) GP driver 1953-56 Ferrari driver 1953-55
Magnussen, Jan		22	MBZ GP driver 1996
Mairesse, Willy	1969	600	(1928-1969 suicide) GP driver 1960-66 Ferrari driver 1960-63
Mansell, Nigel		55	(1953-) World Champ. 1992
Mantovani, Sergio		58	(1920-2001) GP driver 1953-55
Manzon, Robert		75	(1917-) GP driver 1950-56
Marko, Helmut		28	(1943-) GP driver 1971-72
Marques, Tarso		36	GP driver in 1996, 1997 & 2001
Marsh, Tony		22	(1931-) GP driver 1957-61
Martini, Pierluigi		25	GP driver
Marzotto, Dr. Giannino	1955	150	Deceased Ferrari race car driver 1953-55 & Mille Miglia winner
Marzotto, Paolo		110	It. Pilot. Won 1952 with his Ferrari 225 Sport Vignale
Marzotto, Vittorio E.		110	Ferrari driver 1954. Won Monaco GP 1952 (Ferrari 225MM)
Mass, Jochen		22	GP driver 1972-83
Massa, Felipe		60	(1981-) Ferrari F1 driver since 2006

PLAYER	DIED	SP	COMMENTS
Mazet, Francois		51	(1943-) GP driver 1971
McAlpine, Kenneth		90	(1920-) GP driver 1952-55
McLaren, Bruce	1970	450	(1937-1970) GP driver 1958-70. Vice world champ, 1960. Founded McLaren
McNish, Allan		70	(1969-) F1 Toyota newcomer & LeMans 1998 winner
McRae, Graham		29	(1940-) GP driver 1973
Meier, Georg	1990	350	(1910-90) 3x Auto Union race car driver 1939
Merzario, Arturo		50	(1943-) GP driver 1972-79. Ferrari driver 1972-73
Mieres, Roberto		58	GP driver 1953-55
Migault, Francois		40	(1944-) GP driver 1972-75
Miles, John		25	(1943-) GP driver 1969-70
Milhoux, Andre		40	(1928-) GP driver 1956
Mitter, Gerhard	1969	220	(1935-1969) D. during pract., Ger. GP. Won Targa Florio, 1969
Modena, Stefano		22	F1 race car driver 1987-92
Montagny, Franck		28	(1978-) Fr. Currently 3rd driver for the Toyota F1 team.
Monteiro, Tiago da Costa		50	(1976-) Current Jordan F1 GP driver
Montermini, Andrea		22	GP driver 1995-96
Montoya, Juan-Pablo		145	1998 F3000 champ., 1999 CART champ., 2000 Indy 500 winner
Morbidelli, Gianni		22	(1968-) GP driver 1990-92
Morgan, Dave		50	(1944-) GP driver 1975
Moser, Silvio	1974	850	(1941-74) Swiss Cooper, Brabham & Silvio Moser GP driver
Moss, Stirling		100	(1929-) GP driver 1951-61
Munaron, Gino		30	(1928-) Ferrari GP driver 1960
Musso, Luigi	1958	1600	(1934-58) GP driver 1953-58
Nakajima, Kazuki		73	(1985-) Son of Jap. ex-F1 driver, Satoru Nakajima.
Nakano, Shinji		55	F1 race car driver
Narain, Karthikeyan		87	(1977-) Indian Jordan F1 driver
Nazzaro, Felice	1940	4000	(1881-1940) It. Won French GP: 1907,'22; Targa Florio: 1907, '13.
Nedell, Tiff		18	(1951-) GP driver 1980
Neubauer, Alfred	1980	200	(1891-1980) Racing mgr., MBZ GP team from 1926 to 1955
Neve, Patrick		60	(1949-) GP driver 1976-77
Nicholson, John		44	(1941-) GP driver 1974-75
Noda, Hideki		44	F1 race car driver
Olivier, Jackie		60	(1942-) GP driver 1968-77. Le Mans winner in Ford GT40
Ongais, Danny		180	(1942-) GP driver 1977-78
Opel, Rikki von		35	(1947-) GP driver 1973-74
Owen, Arthur		73	(1915-) GP driver 1960
Pace, Carlos	1977	450	(1944-1977) GP driver 1972-77
Pagani, Nello		44	(1911-) GP driver 1950
Paletti, Riccardo	1982	850	(1958-1982) It. Fatally crashed on start grid in 2nd F1 start
Palm, Torsten		30	(1947-) GP driver 1975
Panis, Olivier		40	F1 race car driver
Papis, Massimiliano		36	GP driver 1994-95
Parkes, Mike	1977	450	(1931-1977) GP driver 1959-67 Ferrari driver 1966-67
Patrese, Riccardo		40	F1's longest with 256 GP starts; 6 times a winner
Pease, Al		22	(1921-) GP driver 1967-69
Penske, Roger		22	(1937-) GP driver 1967-69
Perdisa, Casare	1998	150	(1932-1998) GP driver 1955-57 Ferrari driver 1957
Perkins, Larry		15	(1950-) GP driver 1974-77
Perrot, Xavier		22	(1950-) GP driver 1969
Peters, Josef		42	(1914-2001) Veritas/BMW GP driver 1952
Peterson, Ronnie	1978	350	(1944-78) GP driver 1970-78 Ferrari driver 1970-72
Picard, Francois	1996	110	(1921-1996) GP driver 1958
Pieterse, Ernest		145	(1938-) GP driver 1962-63
Pietsch, Paul		50	(1911-) GP driver 1950-52

FORMULA ONE

PLAYER	DIED	SP	COMMENTS
Pilette, André	1993	125	(1918-1993) GP driver 1951-64 Ferrari driver 1956
Pilette, Teddy		30	(1942-) GP driver 1974-77
Piper, David		60	Ferrari race car driver 1969
Piquet, Nelson		60	(1952-) World Champ. in 1981, 1983 & 1987
Piquet Jr., Nelson A.		73	(1985-) Son of former F1 world Champ. Nelson Piquet
Pironi, Didier	1987	350	(1952-1987) GP driver 1978-82
Pirro, Emanuelle		22	GP driver
Pizzonia, Antonio		58	(1980-) New Brasilian Jaguar/Cosworth driver 2003
Poele, Eric van de		18	(1961-) GP driver 1991-92
Pollet, Jaques		145	(1932-) GP driver 1954-55
Pon, Ben		44	(1936-) GP driver 1962
Portago, Alfonso de	1957	1160	(1928-1957) Ferrari driver killed in crash: 1957 Mille Miglia.
Pozzi, Charles	2001	57	(1909-2001) GP driver 1950
Pretorious, Jackie		15	(1934-) GP driver 1965-73
Prost, Alain		90	(1955-) F1 World Champ. 1985, 1986, 1989 & 1993
Pryce, Tom		0	(1949-1977) GP driver 1974-77
Purley, David	1985	350	(1945-1985) GP driver 1973-77
Raikkonen, Kimi		90	(1979-) Sauber, MBZ & new Ferrari driver
Ramos, Nano da Silva		73	(1953-) GP driver 1955-56
Raphanel, Pierre-Henri		30	F1 race car driver
Rathmann, Jim		36	1960 Indianapolis Winner
Ratzenberger, Roland	1994	400	(1960-1994) D. during 2nd qualifying session, San Marino GP
Rebaque, Hector		80	(1956-) Mexican GP driver 1977-81
Redman, Brian		50	(1937-) Won all but the elusive Le Mans 24 hour race.
Regazzoni, Clay	2006	73	(1939-2006) GP driver 1970-82 Ferrari driver 1970-73 & 1974-76
Reutemann, Carlos		110	(1942-) 1 of 4 drivers to qualify for pole position in his first GP
Revson, Peter	1974	500	(1939-1974) D. during practice run for the 1974 South African GP
Ribeiro, Alex		22	(1948-) GP driver 1976-79
Riess, Fritz	1992	400	(1922-1992) GP driver 1952
Rindt, Jochen	1970	1300	(1942-1970) World Champ. 1970. D. 1970 training for the It. GP
Robarts, Richard		29	(1944-) GP driver 1974
Rodriguez, Pedro	1971	1000	(1940-1971) D. in race, Germany. Won Le Mans 24 hours, 1968
Rodriguez, Ricardo	1962	1500	(1942-62) GP driver 1961-62
Rolt, Tony		60	(1918-) Winner of the Le Mans 24 hours 1953, GP driver 1950-55
Rooyen, Basil van		18	(1938-) GP driver 1968-69
Rosberg, Keke		80	(1948-) Williams World Champ. 1982
Rosberg, Nico		65	Upcoming F1 Star & son of Keke Rosberg
Rosier, Louis	1956	2750	
Rosset, Ricardo		29	GP driver
Rossi, Valentino		150	(1979-) Conqueror of the 125, 250 & 500 World Champs.
Rothengatter, Huub		15	(1954-) GP driver 1984-86
Ruby, Lloyd		58	(1928-) GP driver 1961
Ruttman, Troy	1997	150	(1930-1997) GP driver 1958
Sala, Luis Perez		15	F1 race car driver 1988-89
Salazar, Eliseo		20	(1954-) GP driver 1961-62
Salo, Mika		40	(1966-) Ferrari GP driver 1999
Salvadori, Roy		40	(1922-) GP driver 1952-62. Won Le Mans for Aston Martin: 1959
Sato, Takuma		73	(1977-) Jap. Jordan & Toyota race car driver
Scarfiotti, Ludovico	1968	2000	GP driver 1963-68. Ferrari driver.
Scheckter, Ian		40	(1947-) GP driver 1974-77
Scheckter, Jody		60	(1950-) Ferrari World Champ. 1979.
Schell, Harry		1088	(1921-1960) GP driver 1950-60
Schenken, Tim		44	(1943-) GP driver 1970-74
Schetty, Dr. Peter		42	(1942-) Ferrari race car driver 1969-70

PLAYER	DIED	SP	COMMENTS
Schiatarella, Domenico		22	GP driver
Schiller, Heinz		44	(1930-) Swiss Lotus/BRM GP driver 1962
Schlesser, Jo		348	(1952-68) GP driver 1966-68
Schneider, Bernd		15	(1964-) GP driver 1988-89
Schumacher, Michael		175	(1969-) WORLD Champ. 1994, 1995, 2000, 2001, 2002, 2003,2004
Schumacher, Ralf		73	(1975-) BMW Williams F1 driver
Schwelm Cruz, Adolfo		50	(1923-) GP driver 1953
Seidel, Wolfgang	1987	350	(1926-1987) GP driver 1953-61
Senna, Ayrton	1994	1200	(1960-1994) World Champ. 1988, 90 & 91
Senna Lalli, Bruno		73	(1983-) Nephew of 3-time F1 world Champ. Ayrton Senna
Serafini, Dorino	2000	75	(1909-2000) GP driver 1950 Ferrari driver 1950-51
Serra, Chico		22	(1957-) GP driver 1981-83
Servoz-Gavin, Johnny		44	(1942-) GP driver 1967-70
Shelby, Carroll		73	(1923-) GP driver 1958-59
Siffert, Jo	1971	390	(1936-71) GP driver 1962-71
Soler-Roig, Alex		220	(1932-) GP driver 1970-72
Sospini, Vincenzo		18	GP driver
Speed, Scott		65	(1983-) US. Red Bull Racing Junior team
Spence, Mike	1968	450	(1936-1968) GP driver 1963-68
Starrabba, Prince Gaetano	1999	73	(1932-1999) Lotus/Maserati GP driver 1961
Stewart, Ian		44	
Stewart, Jackie		100	(1939-) World Champ. 1969, 71&73
Stohr, Siegfried		22	(1952-) GP driver 1981
Streiff, Philippe		58	(1955-) GP driver 1984-88
Stuck, Hans Joachim		15	(1951-) GP driver 1974-79
Sullivan, Danny		40	(1950-) GP driver 1983
Surer, Marc		50	(1951-) Formula 2 Champ. 1979, GP driver 1979-86
Surtees, John		58	(1934-) F1 World Champ. 1964 & 7x motorcycle world Champ.
Sutil, Adrian		73	(1983-) Spyker F1 racing driver
Suzuki, Aguri		22	(1960-) GP driver 1988-90
Swaters, Jacques		28	(1926-) GP driver 1951-54 Ferrari driver 1953-54
Tadini, Mario		145	1949 Ferrari race car driver - deceased 1983
Takagi, Toranosuke		50	(1974-) Tyrell & Arrows GP driver 1998-99
Tambay, Patrick		50	(1949-) GP winner for Ferrari. 2x CanAm Champ., US
Tarquini, Gabriele		22	(1962-) GP driver 1987-92
Taylor, Trevor		44	(1936-) Team-mate, Clark at Lotus. F1; 2x Br. F1 Junior Champ.
Thackwell, Mike		29	(1961-) GP driver 1980-84
Thompson, Eric		15	(1919-) GP driver 1952
Thorpe, Leslie	1993	145	(1916-93) GP driver 1954
Tingle, Sam		36	(1921-) GP driver 1963-1969
Todt, Jean		58	(1946-) CEO, Scuderia Ferrari, Ferrari's F1 constructor.
Trintignant, Maurice		73	(1917-) GP driver 1950-64
Trulli, Jarno		55	(1974-) GP driver since 1997 & current Renault driver
Tuero, Esteban		22	GP driver
Tyrrell, Ken	2001	254	(1924-2001) Br. Driver. Founded Tyrrell F1 constructor.
Ulmen, Toni		326	(1906-76) GP driver 1952
Unser, Bobby		22	(1934-) GP driver 1968
Vaccarella, Nino		58	(1933-) GP driver 1961-65. Ferrari driver 1965
van der Garde, Giedo		73	(1985-) Dutch racing driver.
Verstappen, Jos		40	F1 race car driver
Vettel, Sebastian		80	(1987-) Ger. 3rd driver for BMW Sauber F1 team.
Villeneuve, Gilles	1992	1950	(1950-1992) D. qualifying for Belgian GP. GP driver 1977-82
Villeneuve, Jacques		145	(1971-) World Champ. 1997
Villoresi, Luigi	1997	175	(1909-1997) "Gigi". Won Targa Florio: '39, '40. Mille Miglia 1952

PLAYER	DIED	SP	COMMENTS
Villota, Emilio de		29	(1946-) GP driver 1976-82
Volonterio, Ottorino		73	GP driver 1954-1957
Wacker, Fred	1998	100	(1918-1998) GP driver 1953-54
Wallace, Andy		15	
Walter, Heini		36	(1927-) GP driver 1962
Watson, John		50	(1946-) GP driver 1973-85
Webber, Mark		73	(1976-) Australian BMW, Minardi & Jaguar driver
Weidler, Volker		15	F1 race car driver
Wendlinger, Karl		35	(1968-) GP driver 1991-93
Westbury, Peter		35	(1938-) GP driver 1969-70
Widdows, Robin		29	(1942-) GP driver 1968
Wietzes, Eppie		58	(1938-) GP driver 1967 & 74
Williams, Jonathan		50	(1942-) GP driver 1967 Ferrari driver 1967
Wilson, Justin		73	New Minardi race car driver
Wilson, Max		22	GP driver 1996
Winkelhock, Manfred	1985	110	(1952-1985 North York, Canada) GP driver 1980-85
Winkelhock, Markus		73	(1980-) MF1 Racing touring car racing driver
Wisell, Reine		87	(1941-) GP driver 1970-74
Wunderink, Roelof		58	(1948-) Ensign/Ford driver 1975
Wurz, Alexander		44	GP driver
Yamamoto, Sakon		87	(1982-) Jap. F1 racing driver, currently with the Spyker team
Yoong, Alex		30	(1976-) Malaysian Minardi race card driver
Zanardi, Alessandro		50	(1966-) GP driver 1991-99
Zorzi, Renzo		57	(1946-) GP driver 1975-77
Zuber, Andreas		73	(1983-) Aus. iSport team for 2007

PLAYER	DIED	SIG	TLS	ALS	CHECK	SP	SIGNED BALL
Armour, Tommy	1968	375	600	1,250	-	1,250	-
Azinger, Paul		10	-	-	-	25	25
Ballesteros, Seve		10	-	-	-	25	30
Barber, Jerry	1994	25	50	125	-	75	225
Berg, Patty	2006	10	30	50	-	25	100
Bolt, Tommy	2006	10	50	100	-	25	75
Boros, Julius	1994	35	75	150	-	125	225
Braid, James	1950	275	500	750	-	1,000	-
Brewer, Gay	2007	20	-	-	-	40	50
Burke, Jack		10	25	75	-	50	50
Burkemo, Walter	1986	125	250	400	-	300	-
Burton, Richard	1989	150	-	-	-	-	-
Carr, Joe	2004	25	75	150	-	75	150
Colbert, Jim		10	-	-	-	20	20
Cooper, Harry	2000	25	50	125	-	100	100
Cotton, Henry	1987	150	350	500	-	450	-
Couples, Fred		20	-	-	-	40	40
Creavy, Tom	1979	300	-	-	-	-	-
Crenshaw, Ben		10	-	-	-	25	30
Daly, Fred	1990	100	225	-	-	-	-
Daly, John		10	-	-	-	25	30
Demaret, Jim	1983	300	500	750	-	750	-
Diegel, Leo	1951	125	250	400	-	400	-
Dutra, Olin	1983	125	250	400	-	400	-
Duval, David		15	-	-	-	40	45
Elkington, Steve		10	-	-	-	20	20
Els, Ernie		10	-	-	-	30	30
Evans, Chick	1979	150	250	500	-	500	-
Faldo, Nick		10	-	-	-	30	40
Farrell, Johnny	1988	75	150	300	-	250	-
Faulkner, Max	2005	50	100	200	-	100	150
Ferrier, Jim	1986	50	100	150	-	125	-
Fleck, Jack		10	30	75	-	25	30
Floyd, Ray		10	-	-	-	30	30
Ford, Doug		10	25	50	-	30	25
Garcia, Sergio		10	-	-	-	40	40
Ghezzi, Vic	1976	75	150	250	-	250	-
Guldahl, Ralph	1987	500	750	1,500	-	1,500	-
Hagen, Walter	1969	350	750	1,000	-	1,500	-
Harbert, Chick	1992	25	75	150	-	100	325
Harmon, Claude	1989	400	750	1,250	-	1,000	-
Harper, Chandler	2004	10	50	100	50	50	75
Herbert, Jay	1997	25	50	100	-	50	150
Herbert, Lionel	2000	25	75	125	-	75	175
Herd, Alexander "Sandy"	1944	400	750	1,000	-	-	-
Hogan, Ben	1997	100	200	500	150	250	400
Inkster, Julie		10	-	-	-	20	25
Janzen, Lee		10	-	-	-	25	25
Jones, Bobby (modern)	1971	750	1,250	-	-	2,500	-
Jones, Bobby (vintage)	1971	2,000	4,000	7,500	-	5,000	-
Keiser, Herman	2003	100	175	300	-	250	400
Kite, Tom		10	-	-	-	20	25
Kroll, Ted	2002	25	50	75	-	50	100
Langer, Bernhard		10	-	-	-	30	30

Golf

PLAYER	DIED	SIG	TLS	ALS	CHECK	SP	SIGNED BALL
Lehman, Tom		10	-	-	-	25	25
Leonard, Justin		10	-	-	-	25	30
Little, Lawson	1968	100	200	400	-	400	-
Locke, Bobby	1987	175	375	600	-	500	-
Lopez, Nancy		10	-	-	-	25	30
Love, Davis III		10	-	-	-	35	35
Manero, Tony	1989	50	100	175	-	125	-
Mangrum, Lloyd	1973	125	250	500	-	400	-
McLeod, Fred	1976	225	400	650	-	500	-
Mickelson, Phil		10	-	-	-	30	30
Middlecoff, Cary	1998	125	250	500	-	300	250
Montgomerie, Colin		10	-	-	-	25	25
Nagle, Kel		25	50	100	-	50	50
Nelson, Byron	2006	50	150	300	-	75	200
Nicklaus, Jack		95	-	-	-	200	225
Norman, Greg		25	-	-	-	50	75
O'Meara, Mark		10	-	-	-	30	35
Ouimet, Francis	1967	500	750	1,250	-	1,250	-
Padgham, Alfred	1966	275	-	-	-	-	-
Pak, Se Ri		10	-	-	-	30	35
Palmer, Arnold		50	-	-	-	90	100
Parks, Sam Jr.	1997	75	125	250	-	175	250
Parnevik, Jesper		10	-	-	-	20	20
Pate, Steve		10	-	-	-	20	20
Pavin, Corey		10	-	-	-	30	35
Perry, Alf	1980	225	-	-	-	-	-
Picard, Henry	1997	75	200	500	400	200	300
Player, Gary		15	-	-	-	35	45
Price, Nick		10	-	-	-	30	30
Ray, Edward	1943	500	-	-	-	-	-
Revolta, John	1991	75	150	300	-	150	-
Rodrigues, Chi Chi		10	-	-	-	25	30
Rosburg, Bob		5	25	50	-	25	25
Runyan, Paul	2002	40	75	125	-	75	125
Sarazen, Gene	1999	25	100	300	100	100	200
Shute, Denny	1974	125	250	400	-	350	-
Singh, Vijay		10	-	-	-	30	35
Smith, Horton	1963	500	750	1,250	1,500	1,500	-
Snead, Sam	2002	50	150	300	-	150	250
Sorenstam, Annika		20	-	-	-	45	55
Stadler, Craig		10	-	-	-	30	35
Stewart, Payne	1999	250	-	-	-	350	350
Stranahan, Frank		25	75	100	-	50	75
Strange, Curtis		10	-	-	-	30	35
Taylor, J.H.	1963	200	400	600	-	1,250	-
Thomson, Pete		20	50	75	-	50	50
Toski, Bob		10	25	50	-	30	30
Travers, Jerome	1951	125	250	400	250	-	-
Trevino, Lee		15	-	-	-	35	35
Turnesa, Willie	2001	25	75	150	-	100	150
Urzetta, Sam		10	30	75	-	30	50
Van Wie, Virginia	1997	25	75	150	-	100	150
Vardon, Harry	1937	750	1,500	3,000	-	-	-
Wall, Art	2001	25	50	100	-	100	100

Golf

PLAYER	DIED	SIG	TLS	ALS	CHECK	SP	SIGNED BALL
Ward, Harvie	2004	25	50	75	-	50	150
Watkins, Lanny		10	-	-	-	25	30
Watson, Tom		15	-	-	-	35	40
Wethered, Joyce	1997	100	-	-	-	-	-
Wood, Craig	1968	600	-	-	-	2,000	-
Woods, Tiger		150	-	-	-	250	550
Yates, Charlie	2005	50	100	150	-	100	125
Zoeller, Fuzzy		15	-	-	-	35	40

Hockey

PLAYER	DIED	HOF	SIG	SP	PUCK
Abel, Sid	2000	1969	10	40	50
Amonte, Tony			8	25	30
Arbour, Al		1996	6	15	20
Armstrong, George		1975	35	110	125
Bailey, Ace	1992	1975	45	150	200
Barber, Bill		1990	8	20	25
Barry, Marty	1969	1965	40	125	-
Bathgate, Andy		1978	6	15	15
Bauer, Bobby	1964	1996	10	35	45
Belfour, Ed			15	55	60
Beliveau, Jean		1972	10	25	30
Benedict, Clint	1976	1965			
Bentley, Doug	1972	1964	60	175	-
Bentley, Max	1984	1966	60	175	-
Blake, Toe	1995	1966	45	150	-
Boivin, Leo		1986	8	25	30
Bossy, Mike		1991	10	25	30
Bouchard, Butch		1966	7	20	20
Boucher, George "Buck"	1960	1960	100	300	-
Bourque, Ray		2004	15	55	75
Bower, John		1976	5	10	10
Bowman, Scotty		1991	10	30	30
Brimsek, Frank	1998	1966	30	100	90
Broadbent, Punch	1971	1962	60	175	-
Broda, Turk	1972	1967	150	500	-
Brodeur, Martin			18	65	70
Brooks, Herb	2003	2006			
Bucyk, John		1981	6	15	15
Bure, Pavel			12	35	40
Cheevers, Gerry		1985	6	15	15
Chelios, Chris			12	45	50
Cherry, Don			15	30	35
Clancy, King	1986	1958	40	125	-
Clapper, Dit	1978	1947	40	125	-
Clarke, Bobby		1987	15	45	50
Coffey, Paul		2004	20	40	75
Colville, Neil	1987	1967	40	125	-
Conacher, Charlie	1967	1961	125	400	-
Cook, Bill	1986	1952	60	190	-
Cook, Bun	1988	1995			
Costello, Murray		2005	10	25	40
Coulter, Art	2000	1974	45	150	150
Cournoyer, Yvan		1982	6	15	15
Cowley, Bill	1993	1968	45	150	-
Day, Hap	1990	1961	60	175	-
Delvecchio, Alex		1977	6	15	15
Denneny, Cy	1970	1959	60	175	-
Dionne, Marcel		1992	8	18	20
Dryden, Ken		1983	45	150	150
Duff, Dick		2006	10	25	40
Dumart, Woody	2001	1992	8	25	25
Durnan, Bill	1972	1964	100	300	-
Dutton, Red	1987	1958	30	100	-
Esposito, Phil		1984	12	30	35

PLAYER	DIED	HOF	SIG	SP	PUCK
Esposito, Tony		1988	10	25	30
Fedorov, Sergei			15	50	75
Fesitov, Viacheslav "Slava"	2001		12	35	45
Flaman, Fern		1990	6	15	20
Fletcher, Cliff		2004	10	25	40
Forsberg, Peter			12	45	60
Francis, Emile		1982	6	15	20
Francis, Ron		2007	10	25	40
Frederickson, Frank	1979	1958	45	150	-
Gadsby, Bill		1970	6	15	20
Gainey, Bob		1992	12	35	40
Gardiner, Herb	1972	1958	60	200	-
Gartner, Mike		2001	12	35	40
Geoffrion, Bernie	2006	1972	8	20	25
Giacomin, Ed		1987	8	20	25
Gilbert, Rod		1982	8	20	25
Gillies, Clark		2002	15	35	75
Goheen, Frank "Moose"	1979	1952			
Goodfellow, Ebbie	1985	1963	40	115	-
Goulet, Michel		1998	8	20	25
Gregory, Jim		2007	10	25	40
Gretzky, Wayne		1999	75	225	250
Hainesworth, George	1950	1961	125	400	-
Hall, Glenn		1975	8	20	25
Harvey, Doug	1989	1973	125	400	-
Hasek, Dominik			25	85	100
Hawerchuck, Dale		2001	8	20	20
Hextall, Bryan	1984	1969	45	150	-
Horner, Red	2005	1965	20	50	75
Horton, Tim	1974	1977	250	600	1000
Hotchkiss, Harley		2006	10	25	40
Howe, Gordie		1972	25	75	80
Howe, Syd	1976	1965	30	100	-
Howell, Harry		1979	6	15	20
Hull, Bobby		1983	15	35	50
Hull, Brett			20	65	100
Irvin, Dick	1957	1958	125	350	-
Jackson, Busher	1966	1971	60	175	-
Jagr, Jaromir			18	60	100
Johnson, Ching	1979	1958	45	150	-
Johnson, Tom		1970	6	15	20
Joliat, Aurel	1986	1947	75	250	-
Joseph, Curtis			15	40	50
Kariya, Paul			15	40	50
Keats, Duke	1972	1958	60	175	-
Kelly, Red		1969	6	15	20
Kennedy, Teeder		1966	6	15	20
Keon, Dave		1986	10	30	35
Kharlamov, Valeri	1981	2005			
Konstantinov, Vladimir			20	50	75
Kurri, Jari		2001	25	45	75
Lach, Elmer		1966	6	15	20
Lafleur, Guy		1988	10	22	25
LaFontaine, Pat		2003	10	25	50

Hockey

PLAYER	DIED	HOF	SIG	SP	PUCK
Langway, Rod		2002	8	25	40
Laperriere, Jacques		1987	6	15	20
Lapointe, Guy		1993	8	20	25
Laprade, Edgar		1993	8	20	25
Leetch, Brian			15	40	50
Lemaire, Jacques		1984	10	22	25
Lemieux, Mario		1997	45	125	150
Lindbergh, Pelle			75	300	750
Lindros, Eric			15	40	50
Lindsay, Ted		1966	6	15	20
Lumley, Harry	1998	1980	12	35	40
MacInnis, Al		2007	10	25	40
Mahovlich, Frank		1981	6	18	20
McDonald, Lanny		1992	8	20	25
Messier, Mark		2007	10	25	40
Messier, Mark			30	100	120
Mikita, Stan		1983	8	25	30
Modano, Mike			15	40	50
Moore, Dickie		1974	8	20	25
Morenz, Howie	1937	1945	500	1500	-
Mosienko, Bill	1994	1965	60	175	200
Mullen, Joe		2000	8	20	25
Murphy, Larry		2004	10	25	40
Neely, Cam		2005	20	40	75
Olmstead, Bert		1985	15	40	50
Orr, Bobby		1979	25	65	100
Parent, Bernie		1984	10	20	25
Park, Brad		1988	8	15	20
Patrick, Lester	1960	1947	175	375	-
Patrick, Lynn	1980	1980			
Perreault, Gilbert		1990	6	15	20
Pilote, Pierre		1975	6	15	20
Plante, Jacques	1986	1978	40	175	200
Potvin, Denis		1991	8	20	25
Pratt, Babe	1988	1966			
Primeau, Joe	1989	1963			
Pronovost, Marcel		1978	8	20	25
Pulford, Bob		1991	8	25	30

PLAYER	DIED	HOF	SIG	SP	PUCK
Quackenbush, Bill	1999	1976	50	150	175
Ratelle, Jean		1985	20	65	100
Rayner, Chuck	2002	1973	6	15	15
Reardon, Ken		1966	8	20	20
Richard, Henri		1979	6	18	20
Richard, Maurice	2000	1961	25	75	100
Richter, Mike			15	50	75
Robinson, Larry		1995	10	25	45
Roy, Patrick		2006	25	50	75
Sakic, Joe			10	35	40
Salming, Borje		1996	8	20	25
Savard, Denis		2000	8	20	25
Savard, Serge		1986	8	20	25
Sawchuk, Terry	1970	1971	250	500	1000
Schmidt, Milt		1961	6	15	20
Shanahan, Brendan			15	40	45
Shore, Eddie	1985	1947	100	300	-
Shutt, Steve		1993	6	15	15
Sittler, Darryl		1989	10	22	25
Smith, Billy		1993	8	20	20
Smith, Clint		1991	6	15	15
Stanley, Allan		1981	6	15	15
Stasny, Peter		1998	8	20	20
Stevens, Scott		2007	20	50	75
Storey, Red		1967	6	15	15
Taylor, Cyclone	1979	1947			
Thompson, Tiny	1981	1959	6	175	-
Thorton, Joe			8	25	30
Tretiak, Vladislav		1989	8	25	30
Trottier, Bryan		1997	8	22	25
Ullman, Norm		1982	6	15	15
Watson, Harry P.	2002	1994	6	15	15
Wilson, Phat	1970	1962	100	250	-
Worsley, Gump		1980	8	20	22
Yzerman, Steve			25	75	100

NASCAR

PLAYER	DIED	SIG	SP or CARD	1:24 SCALE DIE-CAST CAR
Allison, Bobby		10	30	50
Allison, Davey	1993	100	120	200
Allison, Donnie		20	30	100
Allmendinger, A.J.		10	20	50
Almirola, Aric		5	20	40
Andretti, John		5	20	40
Baker, Buddy		15	30	80
Barrett, Stanton		5	10	40
Benson, Johnny		10	20	50
Biffle, Greg		15	30	60
Blaney, Dave		12	15	50
Bodine, Brett		5	10	40
Bodine, Geoff		10	20	40
Bodine, Todd		10	20	40
Bonnett, Neil	1994	75	100	125
Bowyer, Clint		20	30	80
Burton, Jeff		15	30	80
Busch, Kurt		15	20	75
Busch, Kyle		20	30	100
Carpentier, Patrick		15	20	50
Childress, Richard		25	30	100
Cope, Derrick		10	10	40
Craven, Ricky		10	10	50
Earnhardt Jr., Dale		50	60	125
Earnhardt Sr., Dale	2001	100	150	200
Edwards, Carl		20	30	80
Elliot, Bill		15	30	100
Franchitti, Dario		15	30	50
Gant, Harry		15	20	80
Gibbs, J.D.		10	20	60
Gibbs, Joe		25	30	100
Gilliland, David		10	20	50
Gordon, Jeff		50	60	125
Gordon, Robby		10	20	40
Green, Jeff		5	10	40
Hamilton Sr., Bobby		20	50	100
Hamlin, Denny		15	30	80
Harvick, Kevin		20	30	75
Hendrick, Rick		20	30	80
Hendrick, Ricky	2004	50	50	100
Hornish Jr., Sam		15	30	50
Hylton, James		15	20	40
Irvan, Ernie		10	20	80
Jarrett, Dale		20	30	80
Jarrett, Jason		5	20	40
Jarrett, Ned		15	20	80
Johnson, Jimmie		25	30	100
Johnson, Junior		15	20	65
Karne, Kasey		20	30	100
Kenseth, Matt		20	30	100
Kulwicki, Alan	1993	100	120	200
Kvapil, Travis		5	20	40

PLAYER	DIED	SIG	SP or CARD	1:24 SCALE DIE-CAST CAR
Labonte, Bobby		20	30	60
Labonte, Terry		15	20	75
Lamar, Burney		5	10	40
Logano, Joey		25	30	100
Lorenzen, Fred		15	20	40
Marcis, Dave		5	10	60
Marlin, Sterling		10	20	50
Martin, Mark		20	30	80
Mast, Rick		5	20	50
Mayfield, Jeremy		10	30	50
McClure, Eric		5	10	40
McDowell, Michael		5	15	40
McMurray, Jamie		10	20	50
Mears, Casey		10	20	60
Menard, Paul		15	20	40
Montoya, Juan Pablo		20	30	80
Nemechek, Joe		10	20	40
Newman, Ryan		15	30	80
Parsons, Benny	2007	30	30	100
Pearson, David		20	20	100
Petty, Kyle		10	20	60
Petty, Lee	2000	50	60	150
Petty, Richard		25	30	100
Ragan, David		10	10	40
Raines, Tony		5	10	40
Reutimann, David		10	15	40
Richmond, Tim	1989	150	200	400
Riggs, Scott		10	20	40
Roush, Jack		20	30	80
Rudd, Ricky		10	20	80
Sadler, Elliot		15	20	60
Said, Boris		15	20	50
Sauter, Johnny		10	10	40
Schrader, Ken		10	20	40
Skinner, Mike		5	10	40
Smith, Regan		5	15	40
Sorenson, Reed		10	20	50
Stewart, Tony		30	40	100
Truex Jr., Martin		10	20	80
Vickers, Brian		10	15	50
Villeneuve, Jaques		15	20	40
Wallace, Kenny		5	20	40
Wallace, Rusty		20	30	80
Waltrip, Darrell		25	30	100
Waltrip, Michael		10	20	50
Yarborough, Cale		25	30	125
Yeley, J.J.		5	20	40

Tennis

PLAYER	DIED	SIG	SP	BALL
Agassi, Andre		15	80	95
Ashe, Arthur	1993	60	250	300
Becker, Boris		10	35	40
Bjorkman, Jonas		10	25	25
Blake, James		10	20	25
Borg, Björn		15	60	70
Brugera, Sergi		10	25	25
Capriati, Jennifer		10	35	40
Chang, Michael		10	50	60
Coetzer, Amanda		10	20	25
Connors, Jimmy		15	50	65
Courier, Jim		10	30	35
Davenport, Lindsay		10	35	40
Davydenko, Nikloay		10	20	25
Dementieva, Elena		10	20	25
Djokovic, Novak		10	20	25
Edberg, Stefan		10	30	35
Evert, Chris		15	45	60
Federer, Roger		25	100	120
Fererer, David		10	20	25
Fernandez, Mary Joe		10	20	25
Gerulaitis, Vitas	1994	35	125	150
Gonzalez, Fernando		10	20	25
Gonzalez, Pancho	1995	25	75	95
Graf, Steffi		10	40	45
Hingis, Martina		15	50	60
Ivanisevi, Goran		10	35	40
Ivanovic, Ana		10	20	25
Jankovic, Jelena		10	20	25
Kafelnikov, Yevgeny		10	20	25
King, Billie Jean		10	45	65
Korda, Petr		10	25	30
Kournikova, Anna		15	75	95
Krajicek, Richard		10	20	25
Kuznetsova, Svetlana		10	20	25
Laver, Rod		10	25	30
Lendl, Ivan		10	40	60
Martin del Potro, Juan		10	20	25
Martin, Todd		10	25	30
Martinez, Conchita		10	20	25
McEnroe, John		25	70	95
Murray, Andy		10	30	35
Muster, Thomas		10	25	30
Nadal, Rafael		10	100	120
Nalbandian, David		10	20	25
Nastase, Ilie		15	50	55
Navratilova, Martina		15	45	50
Newcombe, John		10	30	35
Novotná, Jana		10	20	25
Pierce, Mary		10	20	25
Radwanska, Agnieszka		10	20	25
Rafter, Patrick		10	20	25
Riggs, Bobby	1995	50	100	125
Roddick, Andy		10	20	25

PLAYER	DIED	SIG	SP	BALL
Sabatini, Gabriela		10	30	35
Safina, Dinara		10	20	25
Sampras, Pete		10	70	85
Sánchez Vicario, Arantxa		10	20	25
Schnyder, Patty		10	20	25
Seles, Monica		10	45	55
Shriver, Pam		10	20	25
Smith Court, Margaret		10	25	30
Stich, Michael		10	20	25
Tilden, Bill	1953	125	350	400
Wilander, Mats		10	25	30
Williams, Serena		20	75	85
Williams, Venus		20	75	85
Wills Moody, Helen	1998	10	30	35
Zvonareva, Vera		10	20	25

Sanders Guide Approved Autograph Dealer Directory

Sanders Guide Approved Autograph Dealers are dealers and auction houses that have earned a solid reputation for dealing in genuine autographs, and provide a lifetime money-back guarantee of authenticity.

The dealer and collector organizations and autograph authentication services listed are likewise ones that we consider highly reputable.

Many of the businesses and organizations in this directory have display advertisements that tell you more about what they can offer you. The page of their ad is at the end of their listing.

MULTI-CATEGORY DEALERS

Markus Brandes Autographs GmbG
Quality & rare autographs in F1 motorsports, world leaders, art, history, literature, music and science. Specialists in important letters, photos, manuscripts & documents.
Founder of www.isitreal.com and the International Autograph Society
www.autogramme.com
brandes@autogramme.com
Wiesenwinkel 1, 8593 Kesswil, Switzerland
Phone:++41 714602841

Elmers Nostalgia
Autographs in all categories. Monthly Catalogs. Owner Jon Allan was the 1998 Sanders Award Winner.
UACC RD#32, UACC Outstanding Dealer
Jon Allan, Owner. 50+ Years Collecting
www.elmers.net
jon2@elmers.net
Phone: 207.324.2166
3 Putnam Street
Sanford, ME 04073   **See Page 550**

Heritage Auction Galleries
The world's Largest Collectible Auctioneer and the third largest overall auction house. Frequent ongoing auctions in multiple categories, including music, entertainment, sports & manuscripts, all regularly featuring rare and high-profile autographs. Glossy color catalogs. Steve Ivy and Jim Halperin, co-founders.
www.HA.com; Phone: 800.872.6467.
3500 Maple Avenue
Dallas, TX 75219   **See inside front cover**

Historical Collections
"The Friendly Dealers." We've earned a reputation as honest & fair dealers for 20 years. Selling: Hollywood, presidents, music, artists, authors, politicians, scientists and more.
UACC RD #6
John & Shirley Herbert, Owners
www.historicalcollections.com
jherbert2007@att.net; Phone: 713.723.0296
Gallery: Rummell Creek Village Antiques
13190 Memorial Drive, Houston, TX 77079

MULTI-CATEGORY DEALERS

Larry's Books & Autographs
Jazz and Blues Autographs
Modern First Edition Books
PADA, UACC RD #87
Larry Rafferty, Owner
Dealer for 17 years
www.MrBebop.com
sales@MrBebop.com
Phone: 510.666.8505
1563 Solano Ave. # 379
Berkeley, CA 94707

Richard MacCallum Autographs
Dealing in all types of autographs. We sell autographs and buy collections from all areas of history. From motion pictures to world leaders. We have no website or email. Just one-on-one personalized service since 1972.
US Phone: 847.432.7942; Fax: 847.432.8685
England Phone: 0798.922.0386
866 Auburn Court
Highland Park, IL 60035   **See Page 550**

Mastro Auctions
Premier catalog auctions every other month, including sports, historical documents, coins, comics, rock 'n' roll, Hollywood, and autographs.
Bill Mastro, Chairman & CEO
www.mastroauctions.com
customerservice@mastroauctions.com
Phone: 630.472.1200
7900 S. Madison St.
Burr Ridge, IL 60527   **See Page 548**

Todd Mueller Autographs
Weekly auctions featuring autographs from historic to entertainment, music & sports. We need your autographs — we buy everything! We pay high prices and pay quickly.
Todd Mueller, President
www.toddmuellerautographs.com
mueller@toddmuellerautographs.com
Phone: 719.494.1990
P.O. Box 63750
Colorado Springs, CO 80962 **See Pages 530-1**

PJ's Collectibles
Leaders in service on authentic collectibles.
Autographs in all fields. Large selection online.
Weekly eBay seller = pjscollectiblesplus
UACC RD #244 & IADA-CC Certified
Paul J. Cross, Jr., Owner. Established in 1986
www.pjscollectibles.net
pjscollectibles@aol.com
Phone: 303.353.1727 Habla Espanol
105 Paladium Place
Taylors, SC 29687

RRAUCTION
The world's foremost monthly autograph
auction, offering outstanding items including
presidents, historical, space, art, lit, music,
entertainment, sports & more. Cash advances
and fast consignment payouts. Reliable,
remarkable results since 1980! Free catalog.
www.rrauction.com
Phone: 800.937.3880; Fax: 603.732.4288
5 Route 101A Suite 5
Amherst, NH 03031   **See Inside Back Cover**

Safka & Bareis Autographs
Est. 1985. Signed & unsigned photos, letters,
programs & documents in all categories, specializing in film, music, opera, theater & ballet. We buy single items or entire collections.
FREE PRINTED CATALOGUES
PADA & Manuscript Society
www.safka-bareis.com
safkabareis@yahoo.com
Phone & fax: 718.263.2276
P.O. Box 886, Forest Hills, NY 11375

Shafran Collectibles
We buy and sell autographs in all fields, and
specialize in presidential, sports and historical autographs. Fast and friendly service. We
need your autographs!
UACC RD #299, MS
Brad & Allison Shafran, Founders
www.shafrancollectibles.com
brad@shafrancollectibles.com
eBay Seller ID: shafrancollectibles
Phone: 516.978.0094   **See Page 553**

Signature House
The leading discount auction house. Buying
or selling, we have the expertise you need.
Free appraisals; overnight payment.
UACC, MS
Gil & Karen Griggs, Owners. Est. 1994
www.signaturehouse.net
editor@signaturehouse.net
Phone: 304.842.3386; Fax: 304.842.3001
407 Liberty Ave.
Bridgeport, WV 26330   **See Page 546**

Signatures In Time
Something for everyone. Send for a free copy
of my massive list of signed photos, books,
documents, letters & more. We need your
autographs! Fast response & fair cash offers.
Randy Thern, Owner
randy@signaturesintime.com
Phone: 715.445.3251
eBay Seller ID: Signaturesintime2
P.O. Box 180
Scandinavia, WI 54977   **See Page 554**

Drew Totten Autographs
Serving the discriminating collector since
1989. We offer signed pieces from movies,
TV, music, politics and more! We buy, sell &
trade first quality authentic memorabilia.
UACC Member #6946 – in good standing
Auctions: drewtotten.auctionhosting.com
Website: http: www.drewtotten.com
Email: dtotten@sover.net
Phone: (802) 442-2776
P.O. Box 4416, Bennington, VT 05201

uSTAR.net
Over 5,000 online celebrity photos. We em-
phasize customer service. Gift wrapping and
express delivery available.
UACC RD #279
Robert K. Miller, Owner
www.ustar.net
autographs@ustar.net
Phone: 877.774.4633
P.O. Box 22288
Sarasota, FL 34233

Abraham Lincoln Book Shop, Inc.
Lincolniana, The Civil War, U.S. Presidency — books, autographs, photographs, art & statuary. Buying & selling quality material.
PADA, ABAA, ABA, MS
Daniel R. Weinberg, Owner. Est. 1938
www.alincolnbookshop.com
lincolnian@aol.com
Phone: 312.944.3085
357 W. Chicago Ave.
Chicago, IL 60610   **See Page 540**

Alexander Autographs
One of the word's largest auctioneers of historic letters, documents, manuscripts, imprints and relics. Lifetime guarantee.
PADA, UACC RD #8
Bill Panagopulos, Owner. Since 1991
www. alexautographs.com
info@alexautographs.com
Phone: 203.276.1570; Fax: 203.504.6290
860 Canal Street,
Stamford, CT 06902   **See Page 560**

Catherine Barnes
For integrity & fair treatment. Historical autographs & documents. Buying Presidents, U.S. History, Science, Finance, Literature, Art, European History. Established 1985
PADA, ABAA, MS, UACC
www. barnesautographs.com
mail@barnesautographs.com
Phone: 215.247.9240
P.O. Box 27782-G
Philadelphia, PA 19118   **See Page 541**

David M. Beach
Wanted: Jay Gould & other big Robber Barrons & businessmen. Letters, stock certificates, documents. Also old cigar box labels & salesmen sample books. I also buy & sell antique stock certificates. I am the big buyer.
antiquestocks@cfl.rr.com
Phone: 407.688.7403
P.O. Box 471356
Lake Monroe, FL 32747   **See Page 553**

Edward N. Bomsey Autographs, Inc.
Buying & selling quality autographed letters, documents and photographs for over 35 years. All items sold are guaranteed authentic without limitation or reservation!
PADA, UACC RD #52, ABAA, MS
enbainc@cs.com
www.bomsey-autographs.com
Phone: 703.642.2040
7317 Farr Street
Annandale, VA 22003-2516   **See Page 540**

Early American History Auctions
Specialist in historic autographs and Americana, Colonial coinage and currency, Washingtonia, political, Lincoln and Civil War related material.
Dana Linett, Pres. Dealer since 1985.
www.earlyamerican.com
sales@earlyamerican.com
Phone: 858.759.3290; Fax: 858.759.1439
P.O. Box 3507
Rancho Santa Fe, CA 92067   **See Page 547**

Jim Hayes, Antiquarian
Specializing in War Between the States, Black history, presidential cabinets, American & military history. Authored 4 books.
UACC RD #72, Lifetime Member
Jim and Celie Hayes, Owners. Since 1978.
www.hayesautographs.com
jim@hayesautographs.com
Phone: 843.795.0732
P.O. Drawer 12560
James Island, SC 29422   **See Page 552**

History In Ink Historical Autographs
Buying and selling in all fields. Specializing in presidential, Supreme Court, royalty and military. Leading expert on Harry S. Truman and family. More than 20 years experience.
UACC RD #281, MS, IAS
Rick Schnake, Owner
See high resolution images online.
www.historyinink.com
rick@historyinink.com
Phone: 417.234.6845   **See Page 552**

Steven L. Hoskin Historical Autographs
American historical autographs, documents, letters & manuscripts. Specializing in U.S. Presidents and Civil War notables.
PADA, UACC, MS
Steven L. Hoskin, Owner
www.civilwarautographs.com
shoskin@civilwarautographs.com
Phone: 941.586.8396
P.O. Box 2148
Venice, FL 34284   **See Page 542**

The Inkwell Autograph Gallery
The premier source for authentic autographs, Civil War, Presidential, historical & more. We also offer in person signed books in all fields. Located in Gettysburg, PA. We buy & sell.
UACC & MS
Lenamarie Natale, Owner
www.inkwellgallery.com
info@inkwellgallery.com
Phone: 717.337.2220   **See Page 555**

Kaller Historical Documents, Inc.
Autographs, letters, manuscripts, rare books, historical documents & more. We build collections for individuals, corporations & museums.
PADA
Robin Kaller, President
www.americagallery.com
www.searchofouterspace.com
Phone: 800.860.1776; Intl.: 732.617.7120
P.O. Box 384
Marlboro, NJ 07746   **See Page 557**

Stuart Lutz Historic Documents, Inc.
Buying & selling historic letters and documents signed by Signers of the Declaration of Independence forward, in many genres.
PADA, ABAA, UACC RD #166, MS
Stuart K. Lutz, President
www.historydocs.com
historydocs@aol.com
Phone: 877.428.9362
784 Morris Turnpike, #161
Short Hills, NJ 07078   **See Page 543**

Main Street Fine Books & Manuscripts
Broad selection of letters, documents, signed photographs and signed books in most fields. Established 1990.
PADA, ABAA, UACC RD #26
William Butts & Yolanda Butts, Owners
www.wcinet.com/msfbooks
msfb@att.net
Phone: 815.777.3749
206 N. Main St.
Galena IL 61036   **See Page 542**

Pages of History
Buying & selling Presidents, VP's, first ladies, judiciary, heads of state, Rev. War, Civil War, world wars, aviation, sports & entertainment.
UACC RD #36
Jerry Docteur, Owner. Established 1983.
www.pagesofhistory.net
pagesofhistory@stny.rr.com
Phone: 607.724.4983; Fax: 607.724.0120
P.O. Box 2840
Binghamton, NY 13902   **See Page 555**

Profiles in History
Dealers of guaranteed-authentic original historical autographs, letters, documents, vintage signed photos & manuscripts. Now accepting Hollywood memorabilia auction consignments from film, TV and music.
Joseph M. Maddalena, President & CEO
www.profilesinhistory.com
Phone: 800.942.8856; Fax: 310.859.3842
26901 Agoura Road, Suite 150
Calabasas Hills, CA 91301   **See Page 545**

Scott J. Winslow Associates, Inc.
Private treaty & auction sales. Comprehensively illustrated catalogs. We are actively buying, selling & accepting consignments for upcoming auctions. PADA Member
Scott Winslow, Pres. Dealer since 1985.
www. scottwinslow.com
info@scottwinslow.com
Phone: 800.225.6233; Fax: 603.641.5583
P.O. Box 10240
Bedford, NH 03110   **See Page 538**

HISTORICAL

University Archives
America's most renowned dealer of rare and valuable documents and relics. Sanders Guide back cover advertiser for 15 years.
UACC RD #5, Lifetime Member
John Reznikoff, Founder & President
www.universityarchives.com
john@universityarchives.com
Phone: 203.454.0111; Fax: 203.454.3111
49 Richmondville Ave.
Westport, CT 06880   **See Back Cover**

Elmers Nostalgia — History and politics at affordable prices. See our listing, **Page 521**

End of History Category

CLASSICAL MUSIC

Roger Gross Ltd. Music Autographs
Classical music related autographs bought & sold. Signed photos, letters, musical quotes, documents, scores, books, ephemera, memorabilia & unsigned photos of composers, conductors, instrumentalists, opera singers and ballet. — PADA
www.rgrossmusicautograph.com
rogergross@earthlink.net
Phone: 212.759.2892; Fax: 212.838.5425
225 East 57th St., NY, NY 10022   **See Pg. 540**

La Scala Autographs
Buying, selling & appraising classical music autographs for 35 years. From Pavarotti, Caruso or Callas to the great composers.
PADA, ABAA, ILAB
James Camner, President
www.musicautographs.com
lsautog@aol.com
Phone: 800.622.2705
301 North Harrison St, Box 900
Princeton, NJ 08540   **See Page 542**

CLASSICAL MUSIC

J.B. Muns Musical Autographs
Classical musical autographs: signed letters, photographs, musical quotations, documents, manuscripts, books. Also unsigned photographs & books. Catalogs issued.
PADA, ABAA, ILAB
Joyce Muns, Owner. Established in 1964.
jbmuns@aol.com
Phone: 510.525.2420; Fax: 510.525.1126
1162 Shattuck Ave.
Berkeley, CA 94707   **See Page 543**

ROCK, POP, JAZZ & BLUES

Signed, Sealed, Delivered
The worlds first strictly music autograph dealer. We buy & sell authentic rock & pop autographs. Huge online catalog.
Roger Epperson, Owner
www.signedsealeddel.com
Authentication: www.rogerepperson.com
roger@signedsealeddel.com
Phone: 713.664.7498; Fax: 713.664.7594
6025-B Edgemoor
Houston, TX 77081   **See Page 555**

Starbrite Autographs
We buy & sell Hollywood and Rock 'n' Roll autographs: photos, memorabilia, books & more. Lifetime guarantee of authenticity.
UACC RD #194
Steven Cyrkin, Pres.
www.starbriteautographs.com
sales@starbriteautographs.com
Phone: 800.380.1777; Intl.: 714.263.3563
P.O Box 25559
Santa Ana, CA 92799

Larry's Books & Autographs — Jazz and Blues autographs. See our listing, **Page 521**

End of Rock, Pop & Jazz Category

Turn Page for More Listings

Ed Bedrick Autographs
Dealer of in person signed photos. Contemporary TV & movies. Monthly Auctions. Former U.A.C.C. Regional Director
UACC RD #49
Ed Bedrick, Owner. Dealer for 20 years.
www.edbedrickautographs.com
scorpio741@aol.com
Phone: 401.943.2578
151 Ausdale Rd.
Cranston, RI 02910

Galaxy Autographs
The finest selection of Science Fiction related material available and at an affordable price. We sell worldwide.
UACC RD #288, AFTAL Dealer #016
Willie Bath, Owner. Over 10 years exper.
www.galaxy-autographs.co.uk
info@galaxy-autographs.co.uk
Phone: +44 (0)7973 906233
112 Kings Road West
Swanage, BH19 1HS, UK

Howard Hurwitz Autographs
Vintage Hollywood and big band era autographed photos bought and sold. 500 images online. A full listing of our inventory can be sent upon request.
UACC RD #67
www.silverscreenautographs.com
howhur@verizon.net
Phone: 717.691.7776
32 Skyline Drive
Mechanicsburg, PA 17050   **See Page 552**

Profiles in History
Dealers of guaranteed-authentic original historical autographs, letters, documents, vintage signed photos & manuscripts. Now accepting Hollywood memorabilia auction consignments from film, TV and music.
Joseph M. Maddalena, President & CEO
www.profilesinhistory.com
Phone: 800.942.8856; Fax: 310.859.3842
26901 Agoura Road, Suite 150
Calabasas Hills, CA 91301   **See Page 545**

Starbrite Autographs
We buy & sell Hollywood and Rock 'n' Roll autographs: photos, memorabilia, books & more. Lifetime guarantee of authenticity.
UACC RD #194
Steven Cyrkin, Pres.
www.starbriteautographs.com
sales@starbriteautographs.com
Phone: 800.380.1777; Intl.: 714.263.3563
P.O Box 25559
Santa Ana, CA 92799

Elmers Nostalgia — Entertainment autographs from the '30s to '70s. See our listing, **Page 521**

End of Entertainment Category

FlatSigned Inc.
50,000 rare, autographed and first edition collectible books. Publishers of leather bound signed limited editions. Appraisals, authentication and book grading, auctions.
Tim Miller, President & CEO
www.flatsigned.com
timmiller@flatsigned.com
Phone: 615.331.5066; Fax: 615.331.5077
501 Metroplex Dr. Suite 208-209
Nashville, TN 37211   **See Page 549**

Kaller Historical Documents, Inc.
We build collections for individuals, corporations & museums. We are selling an original flown Vostok space capsule and a spectacular collection of important artifacts and formerly secret documents on space travel.

www.SearchOfOuterSpace.com

Phone: 732-617-7120
PO Box 384, Marlboro, NJ 07746 **See Page 559**

ORGANIZATIONS

Professional Autograph Dealers Assoc., Inc.
PADA is an international organization made up of the finest and most highly respected autograph dealers. There are 44 members in the U.S. and Europe.
www.padaweb.org
Phone: 888.338.4338
P.O. Box 1729S
Murray Hill Station
New York, NY 10016
See PADA & PADA Dealer Pages 536-543

The Manuscript Society
An international organization of persons and institutions devoted to the collection, preservation, use and enjoyment of autographs and manuscripts. Become a member today!
Ed Oetting, Executive Director
www.manuscriptsociety.org
manuscrip@cox.net
1960 East Fairmont Drive
Tempe, AZ 85282 **See Page 532**

AUTHENTICATION SERVICES

Global Authentication, Inc.
Recognized by eBay as a trusted & safe authority on authentication, our experience and expertise are the foundation of our brand. First web-based verification service for autographs! 24-hour turnaround.
Steve Sipe, Director of Autographs
www.gacard.net
Phone: 949.366.9500; Fax: 949.498.5390
232 Avenida Fabricante. Suite 109/Box 4
San Clemente, CA 92672 **See Page 551**

**Professional Authentication Services
& Standards Co. LLC (PASS-CO)**
The leading provider of authentication and grading services for a variety of historical collectibles.
Scott Winslow, Pres., PADA Member
www. Pass-co.com
info@pass-co.com
Phone: 866.727.7262
334 Route 101 West
Bedford, NH 03110 **See Pg. 539**

AUTHENTICATION SERVICES

PSA & PSA/DNA Authentication Services
PSA/DNA is the world's leading authetication and grading service for sports, historical and entertainment autographs.
A division of Collectors Universe
Joe Orlando, President
www.psadna.com
info@psadna.com
Phone: 800.325.1121; Fax: 949.833.7660
P.O. Box 6180
Newport Beach, CA 92658 **See Page 533**

End of Approved Dealer Directory

Approved Dealer Displays

We want to thank the reputable organizations, dealers, auction houses and others serving the autograph field for their sponsorship of *The Sanders Autograph Price Guide.* Sanders Guide Approved Dealers are dealers and auction houses with a solid reputation for dealing in genuine autographs and provide a lifetime money-back guarantee of authenticity. The dealer and collector organizations and autograph authentication services listed are also ones that we consider highly reputable.

University Archives

Heritage Auctions

RRAUCTION

Professional Autograph Dealers
    Association (PADA)

Todd Mueller Autographs

Kaller Historical Documents

Alexander Autographs

Profiles in History

PSA & PSA/DNA

Early American History Auctions

FlatSigned

Global Authentication

PASS-CO

Scott J. Winslow Associates, Inc.

Catherine Barnes Autographs

The Manuscript Society

Mastro Auctions

Signature House

History in Ink

Shafran Collectibles

Signed, Sealed, Delivered

Abraham Lincoln Book Shop

David M. Beach

Elmer's Nostalgia

Steven L. Hoskin Historical
    Autographs

Stuart Lutz Historical Documents

Richard MacCallum Autographs

Edward N. Bomsey Autographs

Roger Gross Ltd.

Howard Hurwitz Autographs

The Inkwell Autograph Gallery

Jim Hayes, Antiquarian

La Scala Autographs

Main Street Fine Books

J.B. Muns Musical Autographs

Pages of History

Signatures in Time

Irion Books

Become a Member Today!

The Manuscript Society

Membership Offers You

Interesting articles, manuscript price reports, book reviews, and more in the Society's quarterly journal—*Manuscripts*.

Noteworthy news from the autograph world, both national and international, in the Society's newsletter—*The Manuscript Society News*.

Congenial, stimulating events featuring important manuscript-related venues during the Society's annual meeting and locally-organized events.

Ed Oetting, Executive Director
1960 East Fairmont Drive
Tempe, AZ 85282 USA
manuscrip@cox.net

Join today at
www. ManuscriptSociety.org

An international organization of persons and institutions devoted to the collection, preservation, use and enjoyment of autographs and manuscripts

©2008 The Manuscript Society

So, You Think You Are The Sultan of Signatures?

PROVE IT!
Introducing the PSA Autograph Registry

The PSA Set Registry™ has taken the collectibles world by storm with over 37,000 registered sets on-line. After experiencing a tremendous amount of success in such a short time, we are excited to introduce our newest category—autographs.

From legendary athletes to Hollywood icons, from moonwalkers to Presidents, the themes are virtually endless. Choose from one of our existing autograph categories or create your own, and let your imagination run wild on the PSA Autograph Registry. It is a place where collectors can showcase their prized signatures

and see how their collections stack up against the best in the world.

We are confident this new category will bring the same level of excitement to autographs as it has to trading cards, tickets and the like. Be a part of a community that shares the same passion that you have for collecting—be a part of something big.

For more information about the PSA Autograph Registry or how to get your prized autographs certified and graded, please call toll free at 800-325-1121 or visit our website at www.psadna.com.

The Foundation of All Great Collections
Visit www.psadna.com or call toll free 800-325-1121

© 2008 Collectors Universe, Inc. 823003

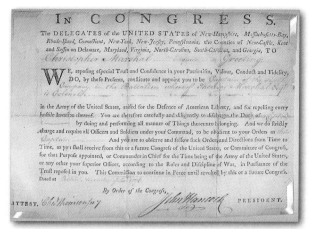

1776 Congressional military appointment signed by John Hancock as president of the Continental Congress.

1966 sketch of Robert Oppenheimer, considered the father of the atomic bomb, by the author's father, Yale Saffro. Oppenheimer signed the sketch shortly thereafter.

Ink drawing of photojournalist Joe Rosenthal's iconic photograph, "Raising the Flag on Iwo Jima." Rosenthal signed and inscribed the drawing to the artist, Yale Saffro.

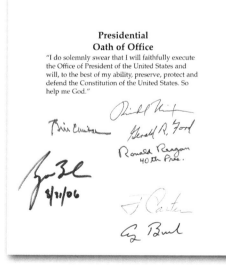

Presidential Oath of Office signed clockwise from top right by presidents Nixon, Ford, Reagan, Carter, George H.W. Bush, George W. Bush and Clinton

Marilyn Monroe photograph signed and inscribed to her hairdresser, Gladys Whitten, whom she called "Gladness." Courtesy Profiles in History.

Professional Autograph
Dealers Association, Inc.

The Professional Autograph Dealers Association

For more information on PADA or our distinguished members,
please visit our website at www.PADAweb.org

Abraham Lincoln Book Shop, Inc.
Alexander Autographs, Inc.
Adam Andrusier Autographs
Antiquariat Inlibris
Catherine Barnes
Edward N. Bomsey Autographs, Inc.
Julian Browning Autographs
Gary Combs Autographs, Inc.
Lisa Cox Music
Sophie Dupre Autographs
Bruce Gimelson
Golden Age Autographs
Thomas A. Goldwasser Rare Books
Roger Gross, Ltd. - Music Autographs
Harmonie Autographs and Music, Inc.
David J. Holmes Autographs
Steven L. Hoskin Historical Autographs
Houle Rare Books & Autographs
International Autograph Auctions, Ltd.
Seth Kaller, Inc.
Kotte Autographs
La Scala Autographs, Inc.
George H. LaBarre Galleries, Inc.
Larry's Books and Autographs

Lion Heart Autographs, Inc.
James Lowe Autographs, Ltd.
J. & J. Lubrano
    Music Antiquarians, LLC
Stuart Lutz Historic Documents, Inc.
Main Street Fine Books
    & Manuscripts, Ltd.
Nancy McGlashan, Inc.
J. B. Muns, Fine Arts
    Books & Musical Autographs
Noble Enterprises
North Shore Manuscript Co., Inc.
The Raab Collection
Max Rambod, Inc.
Kenneth W. Rendell, Inc.
Joe Rubinfine
Safka & Bareis Autographs
Seaport Autographs
Barry A. Smith, Inc.
    Historical Americana
Christophe Stickel Autographs
Gerard A. J. Stodolski, Inc.
John Wilson, Ltd.
Scott J. Winslow Assoc., Inc.

For the Only Guarantee You Will Ever Need,
Look for the PADA Logo.

Carole Lombard signed and inscribed photograph. Courtesy Profiles in History.

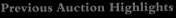

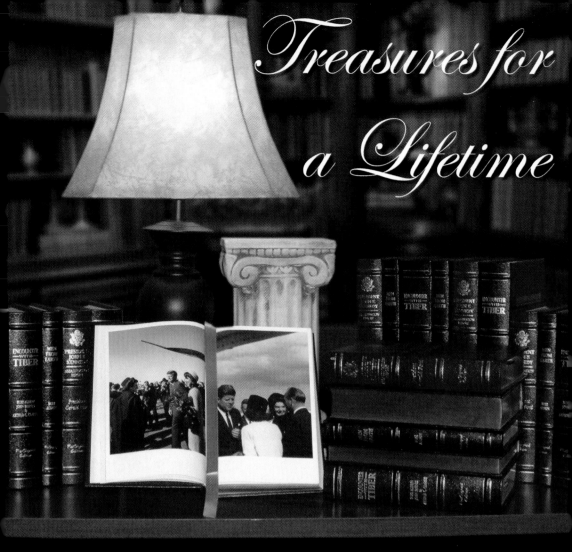

This May be the Most Important Autograph Authentication Advertisement You Read

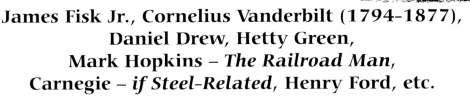

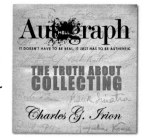

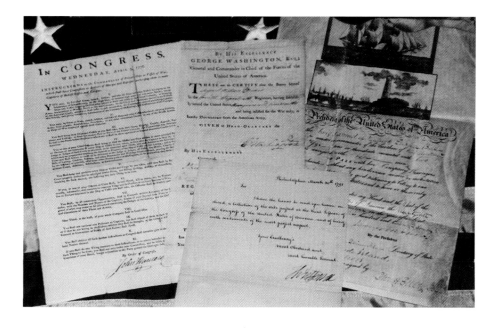

James Dean signed and inscribed photograph. Courtesy Profiles in History.

Kaller Historical Documents, Inc.

www.SearchOfOuterSpace.com

A leader in collection-building for museums,
individuals and corporations

P.O. Box 384
Marlboro, NJ 07746
Phone: 732-617-7120

VOSTOK 3KA-2 FLOWN SPACE CAPSULE

On October 4, 1957, the Soviet Union launched
its Sputnik satellite in an opening salvo of the
space race. America was galvanized, not only to
catch up, but ultimately pledging to send a man
to the moon.

On March 25, 1961 this Vostok
capsule was launched car-
rying a mannequin and
Zvezdochka the dog.
It spent 115 hours
in space, making
it the first vehicle
designed for space
travel to achieve orbit
and return to earth
in a manner safe for
human transporta-
tion. The success of this
mission led directly to the
first manned space
flight by Yuri Gagarin,
18 days later.

Ironically, early Soviet
successes and America's
response eventually led to
greater cooperation between their space programs. This Vostok capsule is perhaps the most
important space vehicle offered for sale.